OFFICIAL
JOURNAL OF THE PROCEEDINGS
OF THE
CONVENTION
FOR THE
REVISION AND AMENDMENT
OF
THE CONSTITUTION
OF THE
STATE OF LOUISIANA.

BY AUTHORITY.

NEW ORLEANS:
W. R. FISH, PRINTER TO THE CONVENTION
1864.

JOURNAL OF THE CONVENTION

FOR THE

REVISION AND AMENDMENT OF THE CONSTITUTION

OF

LOUISIANA.

WEDNESDAY, April 6th, 1864.

The Convention met in Liberty Hall, New Orleans, at 12 M., in pursuance of paragraph XI of General Orders No. 35, of Major General N. P. Banks, the commanding general of the department, as follows:

XI. The delegates duly elected to the Convention shall meet at Liberty Hall. Executive Building, in the city of New Orleans, at 12 o'clock M., on Wednesday, the 6th day of April, 1864.

At fifteen minutes past 12 o'clock, T. B. Thorpe, a member of the Convention, called it to order.

J. R. Terry nominated Alfred Shaw as temporary president. Carried unanimously.

W. R. Fish nominated Alfred C. Hills as temporary secretary. Carried unanimously.

In response to the unanimous invitation of the Convention, Rev. Dr. Newman offered prayer.

The following communications from S. Wrotnowski, secretary of state, were then read:

STATE OF LOUISIANA,
Office of the Secretary of State.

In conformity to General Orders No. 35, under date of the 11th of March last, of Maj. Gen. N. P. Banks, commanding the Department of the Gulf, and to the proclamation of his excellency, Michael Hahn, governor of this State, bearing date of the 16th of said month, for an election to be held on the 28th of the same month of March, for the choice of delegates to a Constitutional Convention to be elected for the revision and amendment of the Constitution of the State of Louisiana,

The undersigned, did, this day, examine the returns received of the votes given at the elections of the 28th of March last, and found the following named delegates obtained, in the following parishes, the greatest number of votes, so far as received up to this date, to-wit:

ORLEANS.

First Representative District—Joseph Gorlinski, R. B. Bell, Geo. F. Brott, W. T. Stocker, John Stumpf, J. B. Schroeder, E. Murphy.

Second Representative District—Terrance Cook, Joseph H. Wilson, John Henderson, Jr., J. H. Stiner, M. W. Murphy, P. K. O'Conner, Alfred C. Hills, T. B. Thorpe, J. J. Healy, Geo. A. Fosdick, W. H. Hire.

Third Representative District—John W. Thomas, James Fuller, John Sullivan, J. R. Terry, O. W. Austin, John Foley, George Howes, H. W. Waters, P. Harnan.

Fourth Representative District—Alfred Shaw, R. King Cutler, Judge E. H. Durell, E. J. Wenck, Louis Gastinel.

Fifth Representative District—Edmund Abell, John Buckley, Jr., Xavier Maurer, J. P. Montamat, A. Mendiverri.

Sixth Representative District—J. V. Bofill, F. M. Crozat, Dr. F. M. Bonzano, Adolphe Bailey.

Seventh Representative District—Judge R. K. Howell, J. G. Baum, M. D. Kavanagh, H. Millspaugh.

JOURNAL OF THE CONVENTION FOR THE REVISION

Eighth Representative District—J. A. Spellicy, O. H. Poynot, J. K. Cook.
Ninth Representative District—H. Maas, E. Goldman, Edward Hart.
Tenth Representative District—John Purcell, C. W. Stauffer, W. R. Fish, Benj. Campbell, T. Barrett, Geo. W. Geier, R. S. Abbott, James Duane, Edmund Flood, J. L. Davies.
Right Bank of Mississippi (Algiers)—J. H. Flagg, W. H. Seymour.

ASCENSION.
Robert J. Duke, Emile Collin and J. E. Richard obtained, each, 61. Election contested.

ASSUMPTION.
Joseph Dupaty, James Ennis, E. J. Pintado.

BATON ROUGE (EAST).
W. D. Mann, P. A. Kugler, H. J. Heard.

BATON ROUGE (WEST).
Sidney A. Lobdell.

CONCORDIA.
Robert W. Taliaferro.

FELICIANA (EAST).
Jansin T. Paine, Martin Schnurr.

JEFFERSON.
Robert Morris, Samuel Pursell, Christian Roselius, John Payne.

LAFOURCHE.
J. B. Bromley, E. H. Knobloch, C. H. L. Gruneberg.

MADISON.
R. V. Montague.

PLAQUEMINES.
Lewis Lombard, Thos. J. Decker. Election contested. Votes supposed to be 246. Not entirely returned.

ST. BERNARD.
Thomas Ong.

ST. JAMES.
R. Beauvais.

ST. JOHN THE BAPTIST.
Young Burke.

ST. MARY.
Charles Smith.

TERREBONNE.
R. W. Bennie, Adolphe Gaidry.

Total number of Delegates—Orleans.. 63
                      Country Parishes 27
                                          ——
                                          90

Total number of votes as far as received up to the 5th April, 1864, at 2 o'clock, P. M.................. 6184

And, therefore, the undersigned has the honor to transmit herewith to the honorable the president and members of the Convention the following statement, together with all the original returns from the parishes of this State.

Signed under his hand, at New Orleans, the 6th day of April, in the year of our Lord 1864, and of the independence of the United States of America the eighty-eighth.
[Signed]   S. WROTNOWSKI,
                              Secretary of State.

OFFICE SECRETARY OF STATE,
  STATE OF LOUISIANA,
    New Orleans, April 6th, 1864.

To the honorable president of the Constitutional Convention of Louisiana:

SIR—Permit me to send you and leave to your disposition the two herewith accompanying books:

"The Rules and Orders of the House of Representatives," and "The Legislative Guide," belonging to the State Library—and believe me, very respectfully, your obedient servant,
[Signed]   S. WROTNOWSKI.

Accompanying these communications were the manual referred to and the original election returns.

The roll was then called by the secretary, when the following delegates—eighty-two in number—answered to their names:

Joseph Gorlinski, John Stumpf, R. B. Bell, J. B. Schroeder, Geo. F. Brott, E. Murphy, W. T. Stocker, Terrance Cook, Alfred C. Hills, Joseph H. Wilson, T. B. Thorpe, John Henderson, Jr., J. J. Healy, J. H. Stiner, George A. Fosdick, M. W. Murphy, W. H. Hire, P. K. O'Conner, John W. Thomas, John Foley, James Fuller, George Howes, John Sullivan, H. W. Waters, J. R. Terry, P. Harnan, O. W. Austin, Alfred Shaw, E. J. Wenck, R. King Cutler, Louis Gastinel, E. H. Durell, Edmund Abell, J. P. Montamat, John Buckley, Jr., A. Mendiverri, Xavier Maurer, J. V. Bofill, Dr. M. F. Bonzano, F. M. Crozat, Adolphe Bailey, R. K. Howell, M. D. Kavanagh, J. G. Baum, H. Millspaugh, J. A. Spellicy, J. K. Cook, O. H. Poynot, H. Maas, Edward Hart, E. Goldman, John Purcell, Geo. W. Geier, C. W. Stauffer, W. R. Fish, James Duane, Benjamin Campbell, Edmund Flood, J. L. Davies, J. T. Barrett, J. H. Flagg, W. H. Seymour, Joseph Dupaty, James Ennis, H. J. Heard, P. A. Kugler, Martin Schnurr, Robert Morris, Samuel Pursell, Christian Roselius, John Payne, J. B. Bromley, E. H. Knobloch, C. H. L. Gruneberg, Lewis Lombard, Thomas J. Decker, Thomas Ong, R. Beauvais, Young Burke, Charles Smith, R. W. Bennie, Adolphe Gaidry.

Mr. Montamat moved to refer the communication of the secretary of state, containing a list of the delegates elect, to a committee of five. Carried.

The chair named Messrs. Thomas, Samuel Pursell, R. W. Bennie, C. H. L. Gruneberg and George F. Brott, as said committee.

AND AMENDMENT OF THE CONSTITUTION OF LOUISIANA. 5

The chair subsequently stated that in appointing the committee he had overlooked the fact that Mr. Montamat had made the motion for the appointment of the committee. If there was no objection he would add the name of Mr. Montamat as chairman of the committee. No objection being made, the name of Mr. Montamat was accordingly added.

Mr. Fish moved that a committee of three be appointed to report rules and regulations for the government of the Convention, and also to report what officers are necessary to carry on the business of the Convention. The motion was put to vote and declared lost.

A division of the House was then called for, pending which

R. K. Howell called for a division on the question, whereupon

Mr. Fish withdrew the last proposition contained in the motion.

A division was then taken on the first part of the motion, namely, to appoint a committee to report rules and regulations, when it appeared that 30 voted for and 41 against the motion, when it was declared to be lost.

Mr. Terry moved that the members of the Convention proceed to draw for seats.

Mr. Stocker moved to lay the motion on the table. Carried.

Mr. Harnan offered the following :

Resolved, That all motions and resolutions be put in writing.

On motion, the resolution was laid on the table.

On motion of Mr. Thomas, the Convention then adjourned until Thursday at 12 o'clock.

ALFRED C. HILLS,
Secretary pro tem.

THURSDAY, April 7th, 1864.

The Convention met at 12 o'clock, M., Alfred Shaw, president *pro tem.*, in the chair.

The roll was called and a quorum was found to be present.

Prayer was offered by Rev. J. W. Horton.

The minutes of the first day's proceedings were read and approved.

Mr. Montamat, from the Committee on Credentials, submitted the following report :

To the honorable the chairman and members of the Constitutional Convention :

The undersigned Committee on Credentials beg leave to submit the following report.

Having examined the returns of election from the parishes hereinafter named, your committee find that the following named gentlemen were duly elected :

ORLEANS.

First Representative District—Joseph Gorlinski, R. B. Bell, Geo. F. Brott, W. T. Stocker, John Stumpf, J. B. Schroeder, E. Murphy.

Second Representative District—Terrance Cook, Joseph H. Wilson, John Henderson, Jr., J. H. Stiner, M. W. Murphy, P. K. O'Conner, Alfred C. Hills, T. B. Thorpe, J. J. Healy, Geo. A. Fosdick, W. H. Hire.

Third Representative District—John W. Thomas, James Fuller, John Sullivan, J. R. Terry, O. W. Austin, John Foley, George Howes, H. W. Waters, P. Harnan.

Fourth Representative District—Alfred Shaw, R. King Cutler, Judge E. H. Durell, E. J. Wenck, Louis Gastinel.

Fifth Representative District—Edmund Abell, John Buckley, Jr., Xavier Maurer, J. P. Montamat, A. Mendiverri.

Sixth Representative District—J. V. Bofill, F. M. Crozat, Dr. M. F. Bonzano, Adolphe Bailey.

Seventh Representative District—Judge R. K. Howell, J. G. Baum, M. D. Kavanagh, H. Millspaugh.

Eighth Representative District—J. A. Spellicy, O. H. Poynot, J. K. Cook.

Ninth Representative District—H. Maas, E. Goldman, Edward Hart.

Tenth Representative District—John Purcell, C. W. Stauffer, W. R. Fish, Benj. Campbell, J. T. Barrett, Geo. W. Geier, R. S. Abbott, James Duane, Edmund Flood, J. L. Davies.

Right Bank of Mississippi (Algiers)—J. H. Flagg, W. H. Seymour.

ASSUMPTION.

Joseph Dupaty, James Ennis, E. J. Pintado.

AVOYELLES.

L. P. Normand, H. C. Edwards.

BATON ROUGE (EAST.)

W. D. Mann, P. A. Kugler, H. J. Heard.

BATON ROUGE (WEST.)

Sidney A. Lobdell.

CONCORDIA.

Robert W. Taliaferro.

FELICIANA (EAST.)

Jansen T. Paine, Martin Schnurr.

JEFFERSON.

Robert Morris, Samuel Pursell, Christian Roselius, John Payne.

LAFOURCHE.
J. B. Bromley, E. H. Knobloch, C. H. L. Gruneberg.

MADISON.
R. V. Montague.

RAPIDES.
M. R. Ariail, A. Cazabat, J. A. Newell, Thos. M. Wells.

ST. BERNARD.
Thos. Ong.

ST. JAMES.
R. Beauvais.

ST. JOHN THE BAPTIST.
Young Burke.

ST. MARY.
Charles Smith.

TERREBONNE.
R. W. Bennie, Adolphe Gaidry.

Your committee find that in the parish of Ascension, Robert J. Duke received the highest number of votes, and was duly elected.

That Emile Collin and J. E. Richard each received an equal number of votes, and consequently neither of them was elected.

Your committee have thought proper, under such circumstances, to recommend that another election be ordered in said parish of one delegate.

Upon investigating the returns from the parish of Plaquemines, it appears that the sheriff thereof was guilty of the following acts of negligence, which, in the opinion of your committee, renders the election in that parish null and void :

First—He did not appoint deputies, or cause the polls to be opened at all the various precincts in that parish.

Second—He did not cause any return to be made of the result of the poll at Fort Jackson.

Third—He has made no official return whatever of the election in that parish.

Your committee would recommend that another election be ordered in that parish.

All of which is respectfully submitted,
JOHN MONTAMAT. *Chairman.*

It was moved and seconded that the report be adopted, pending which motion Messrs. Lombard and Decker addressed the Convention relative to their respective claims.

Mr. Terry moved as an amendment that a committee of five be appointed to investigate the claims of the delegates from Plaquemines.

It was moved to lay the amendment on the table, which was carried on a division of the House by a vote of 49 in the affirmative and 16 in the negative.

Mr. Cazabat moved to adjourn until Monday next at 12 o'clock.

The yeas and nays were called for, when 7 voted for the motion and 76 against it, whereupon it was declared to be lost.

The question recurring on motion to adopt the report, Mr. Terry offered the following amendment :

Resolved, That the report of Committee on Credentials be adopted, with exception of that portion which refers to the disputed seats, be laid on the table, and the House proceed to business.

On motion of Mr. Stocker the amendment was laid on the table.

The report of the committee was then adopted.

Mr. Bell moved to proceed to a permanent organization of the Convention.

Mr. Thomas moved as a substitute that a committee of five be appointed to report what officers are necessary to transact the business of the Convention. Lost.

Mr. Montamat offered as a substitute a resolution that the Convention proceed to a permanent organization as to president, secretary, sergeant-at-arms, door-keeper and messenger.

Mr. Montamat's substitute was adopted.

Mr. Henderson moved to vote for president by ballot.

Mr. Montamat moved to lay the motion on the table. Carried by 65 against 24.

Mr. Abell moved to admit Messrs. Balch and Dufresne as delegates from the parish of Iberville.

Mr. Wilson moved as an amendment that the matter be referred to the Committee on Credentials. Lost.

The motion to admit the gentlemen was then adopted, and Messrs. Balch and Dufresne were declared to be members of the Convention.

The Convention then proceeded to an election for president, when the following gentlemen were nominated : R. K. Howell, E. H. Durell, M. F. Bonzano, Christian Roselius, T. B. Thorpe, J. R. Terry and Alfred Shaw.

Messrs. Shaw and Terry declined to be candidates.

The Convention then proceeded to vote

by roll-call, when R. K. Howell received 25 votes, E. H. Durell 35 votes, M. F. Bonzano 15, Christian Roselius 7, and T. B. Thorpe 1.

There being no election, the names of Messrs. Bonzano, Roselius and Thorpe were withdrawn, when the Convention proceeded to a second vote, which resulted as follows:

For E. H. Durell 43, namely:

Messrs. Gorlinski, Bell, Brott, Stumpf, Murphy E., Cook, Murphy M. W., Stiner, O'Conner, Thorpe, Healy, Hire, Thomas, Fuller, Sullivan, Terry, Waters, Shaw, Bofill, Crozat, Bailey, Howell, Maas, Goldman, Hart, John Purcell, Stauffer, Fish, Campbell, Barrett, Geier, Duane, Davies, Flagg, Seymour, Schnurr, Roselius, Payne, Knobloch, Gruneberg, Smith, Bennie, Gaidry—43.

For R. K. Howell 41, namely:

Messrs. Stocker, Schroeder, Wilson, Henderson, Fosdick, Austin, Foley, Harnan, Cutler, Durell, Gastinel, Wenok, Abell, Buckley, Maurer, Montamat, Mendiverri, Bonzano, Baum, Millspaugh, Kavanagh, Spellicy, Poynot, Cook, Flood, Dupaty, Ennis, Kugler, Heard, Morris, Samuel Pursell, Ong, Beauvais, Burke, Normand, Edwards, Cazabat, Newell, Balch, Dufresne, Hills—41.

Mr. Thorpe moved that the election of Mr. Durell be declared unanimous. Carried.

On motion, Messrs. Howell, Roselius and Bonzano were appointed a committee to escort Mr. Durell to the chair.

On taking his seat, the president addressed the Convention as follows:

Gentlemen of the Convention—I thank you heartily for the honor you have conferred upon me in making me your president; and I thank you still more heartily for this proof of your confidence in my abilities and my patriotism. When, in presiding over your deliberations, I may show weakness, I know that you will give me of your strength; and that I shall not be disappointed in my expectation of finding with you that courtesy which is the best aid to an efficient business in every legislative body.

Gentlemen—In this time of great trouble, in this supreme hour of our country's battle for its life, you have been entrusted by your fellow-citizens with duties commensurate with those of the soldier in the field; you have been called upon to finish the labor which he, necessarily, leaves incomplete.

Gentlemen—On the 26th day of January, 1861, a few ambitious and bad men assembled in Convention, and, representing a minority of the people of the State, declared "the connection between the State of Louisiana and the Federal Union dissolved;" you, gentlemen, have been chosen, the elect of the loyal people of Louisiana, to undo that work of folly and of crime; to restore the State to its former legitimate position in the Union; to replace it under the protecting folds of that flag which, everywhere, upon the land and upon the seas, has been ever hailed as the symbol of liberty and equal rights.

Gentlemen—You are all familiar with the rise and progress of the grand drama which is being enacted in these days upon this continent, and of which we also are a part. With this knowledge, you will accept the progress of ideas; you will accept the changes which great convulsions in the opinions and in the societies of men make a necessity; you will willingly exchange a dead past for a living future.

Gentlemen—The first, chief cause of the present rebellion is patent to you all; you have been called together, invested with the plenary powers which, under our institutions, belong to an organic political body, not only for the purpose of restoring the State to the Union, but also for the equal purpose of removing that fatal cause of strife and rebellion from Louisiana forever. You will, I know, perform those and the many other duties confided to your charge boldly, with decision; looking only to the prosperity and happiness of your State, and of our common country.

Mr. Bell moved to elect a secretary by ballot.

Mr. Montamat moved to lay the motion on the table. Carried.

The Convention then proceeded to the election of a secretary, when the following gentlemen were nominated: Messrs. Neelis, McClellan, Girard, White, Reynolds, Holland, Derickson and Murphy. The vote being taken by roll-call, Neelis received 44, Derickson 10, McClellan 8, Holland 6, White 6, Girard 4, Murphy 2. Mr. Neelis having a majority of the votes was declared to be duly elected.

Messrs. Henderson, Thorpe and Campbell were appointed a committee to escort Mr. Neelis to his seat.

A motion was made to ballot for sergeant-at-arms. This was laid on the table, and the following gentlemen were nominated: T. F. McGuire, C. Baumbach, Thos. K. Flanigan, M. DeCoursey. The roll was called, but there was no choice. Mr. Flanigan then withdrew, and the roll was again called, but with the same result. The secretary read the names again, and the following vote was cast: DeCoursey 41; Baumbach 36; McGuire 1. Mr. DeCoursey was accordingly declared elected sergeant-at-arms.

It was moved by Mr. Brott that the committee appointed to wait on the secretary, also wait upon the sergeant-at-arms, and inform him of his election. The motion was carried unanimously.

On motion, the Convention adjourned until Friday at 12 o'clock M.

ALFRED C. HILLS,
Secretary pro tem.

FRIDAY, April 8th, 1864.

At a quarter past 12 o'clock, the president called the Convention to order, and stated that the proceedings would be opened with prayer by the Rev. Mr. Bass.

After the prayer by the Rev. Mr. Bass, the secretary proceeded to call the roll, and it appeared that 78 members were present. The chair announced a quorum present, and that the Convention was ready to proceed to business.

Mr. Hills, the former secretary *pro tem.*, stated that he had been requested to read the minutes of yesterday's proceedings; which were accordingly read and adopted.

Mr. Harnan offered the following preamble and resolution:

Whereas, We are informed, upon what appears to be good authority, that already two members of this Convention have been assaulted, one for performing his duties as a member of this Convention; therefore

Resolved, That said persons be reported to the proper authorities for proper punishment.

In offering the resolution, Mr. Harnan stated that himself and one other member of the Convention had been violently assaulted on account of their official action in the Convention, and he thought the matter should be taken up by the Convention.

A motion was made to lay the resolution on the table, and lost.

Mr. Bell moved that a committee of three be appointed by the chair to investigate the matter complained of. Upon putting the question to a vote the president declared the motion carried.

A division was called for, and the decision of the chair sustained——48 yeas, 30 nays.

The chair appointed Messrs. Wilson, Morris and Roselius. A motion was made to add the name of Col. T. B. Thorpe. Col. Thorpe begged to be excused, and the committee stood as first appointed.

Mr. J. W. Thomas moved that the Convention proceed to take up the unfinished business of the previous day, and to complete its organization by the election of a doorkeeper and messenger.

Mr. Cazabat moved as an amendment that the officers not already elected be appointed by the chair.

Mr. Wilson offered a substitute, authorizing the sergeant-at-arms to appoint his assistants, including a door-keeper and messenger.

Mr. Montamat obtained the floor, and stated that he thought all these motions out of order, and moved that the Convention proceed to elect a door-keeper.

Another motion was made that the president appoint a door-keeper.

Nominations for door-keeper were declared in order, and the following nominations were made: Mr. Crozat nominated Mr. A. Martin, Mr. Harnan nominated Mr. Mallory, Mr. Duane nominated Mr. McCarty, Mr. Healy nominated Mr. Coyle, Mr. Purcell nominated Mr. Baumbach, Mr. Stauffer nominated Mr. Piersell, Mr. Shaw nominated Mr. Frieny, Dr. Gruneberg nominated F. X. Martin, Mr. Terry nominated Mr. Sullivan, Mr. Cook nominated Mr. Miller, Mr. Maurer nominated Mr. Ernst.

Upon calling the roll it appeared that Mr. Mallory received 3 votes, Mr. Piersell received 4 votes, Mr. McCarty 4 votes, Mr. Coyle 15, Mr. Baumbach 29, Mr. Frieny 3, Mr. Sullivan 6, Mr. Miller 1, Mr. Ernst 1.

No candidate having received a majority of all the votes cast, there was no election.

Mr. Baum moved that all except the three highest candidates on the list be withdrawn. The motion was carried. Upon the second vote Mr. Baumbach received 45 votes, Mr. A. Martin 14, and Mr. Coyle 22. Mr. Baumbach was elected.

Mr. Montamat moved that the election of Mr. Baumbach be declared unanimous. The motion was carried.

Nominations for messenger being next in

AND AMENDMENT OF THE CONSTITUTION OF LOUISIANA.

order, Mr. Maurer nominated Mr. Leclerc, Mr. Terry nominated Mr. E. G. Maguire, Mr. Duane nominated E. Murphy, jr., Mr. Gorlinski nominated Piotrowski, Mr. Thomas nominated Mr. Clark, Mr. Healy nominated Mr. Coyle.

Upon the first vote, 9 votes were cast for Mr. Leclerc, 17 for Mr. McDonald, 2 for Maguire, 3 for Murphy, none for Piotrowski, 21 for Clark, 25 for Coyle. There being no election, Mr. Stauffer moved to proceed to a second vote, and that the vote be restricted to the two candidates highest in the list in the previous vote.

The motion was carried, and on the second vote Mr. Clark received 44 votes and Mr. Coyle 36.

Mr. Clark was elected.

Mr. Wilson moved that the election of Mr. Clark be declared unanimous. Carried.

Mr. Heard moved the election of an assistant secretary. The motion was tabled.

Mr. Stauffer offered the following resolution:

Resolved, That a committee of five be appointed by the president to report rules for the government of this Convention, and the additional number and character of the officers and employés required for the transaction of business.

Mr. Heard offered the following as a substitute:

Resolved, That a committee of seven be appointed by the president to prepare rules and orders for the government of this Convention, and that until said committee reports, the proceedings be governed by Jefferson's Manual and the rules and orders of the Senate and House of Representatives of the State of Louisiana as adopted in 1856.

A motion was made, and carried, to lay the substitute on the table.

Mr. Stauffer withdrew his resolution, to permit Mr. Montamat to offer the following:

Resolved, That the governor be requested to issue his proclamation, ordering an election, as early as possible, for one delegate from the parish of Plaquemines and one from the parish of Ascension, to represent the above named parishes in this Convention.

The resolution was adopted.

Mr. Terry offered the following resolution:

Resolved, That the status of every member of this Convention be—viz : That he be a legally qualified voter of the State, who has subscribed to the oath of the president's proclamation of the 8th of December, 1863; that each and every member produce the same to the secretary by 12 M., on the 9th day of April, 1864, or be required to take the same before the president of this Convention.

A motion was made to lay the resolution on the table.

The ayes and nays were called and the motion was lost:

AYES—Messrs. Gorlinski, Brott, Stocker, Stumpf, Thomas, Fuller, Sullivan, Austin, Waters, Cutler, Abell, Bailey, Howell, Kavanagh, Spellicy, Poyñot, Hart, Flagg, Seymour, Mann, Heard, Roselius, Gaidry, Balch, Dufresne, Bonzano—26.

NAYS—Messrs. Bell, Schroeder, Murphy E., Cook T., Henderson, Wilson, Stiner, Murphy, O'Conner, Hills, Thorpe, Healy, Fosdick, Hire, Terry, Foley, Harnan, Shaw, Buckley, Maurer, Montamat, Mendiverri, Bofill, Crozat, Baum, Millspaugh, Cook J. K., Maas, Goldman, Stauffer, Fish, Campbell, Barrett, Geier, Duane, Flood, Davies, Dupaty, Ennis, Normand, Edwards, Kugler, Schnurr, Morris, Purcell, Cazabat, Payne, Bromley, Knobloch, Newell, Ong, Smith, Bennie—53.

Mr. Thomas moved, as an amendment, that the president of the Convention administer the "iron-clad" oath to each and all the members of this Convention.

A motion to lay this amendment on the table was lost.

Mr. Cazabat offered as a substitute, that each and every member of the Convention do now rise in his seat, raise his right hand, and in the presence of Almighty God and this Convention, while the president administers to them the oath prescribed by the president's proclamation of December 8th, 1863.

Mr. Cazabat's motion was lost.

A motion to lay Mr. Thomas's amendment on the table, was then made and carried.

A motion was again made to lay the original motion of Mr. Terry on the table, and lost.

Another motion to adjourn was lost.

A motion was made that the secretary take down the dates of the "iron-clad" of each member and read them to the Convention. Lost.

A motion to adjourn was lost.

The question then recurring upon the original resolution, the ayes and nays were called for, and the following vote was the result:

AYES—Messrs. Gorlinski, Bell, Stocker, Buckley, Stumpf, Schroeder, Gastinel, Murphy, Cook, Wilson, Stiner, Murphy, Abell, O'Conner, Hills, Thorpe, Healy, Fosdick, Hire, Thomas, Austin, Foley, Harnan, Shaw, Cutler, Wenck, Maurer, Terry, Montamat, Mendiverri, Bofill, Crozat, Baum, Kavanagh, Millspaugh, Poynot, Spellicy, Cook, Goldman, Hart, Purcell, Stauffer, Fish, Campbell, Barrett, Geier, Duane, Flood, Davies, Dupaty, Ennis, Norman, Edwards, Mann, Kugler, Schnurr, Morris, Pursell, Paine, Bromley, Gruneberg, Cazabat, Newell, Ong, Beauvais, Burke, Gaidry, Smith, Bennie, Dufresne. Mr. Thomas begged to be excused from voting. The chair put the question to the Convention, and Mr. Thomas withdrew his request and voted aye—70.

NAYS—Messrs. Brott, Henderson, Fuller, Sullivan, Waters, Bonzano, Bailey, Howell, Maas, Flagg—10.

Mr. Austin offered the following resolution:

Resolved, That every member of this Convention of foreign birth be required to furnish evidence of his citizenship to the president on or before Saturday, the 9th inst., at 12 o'clock M.

Mr. Hills rose to a point of order. He thought that the substance of the resolution was embodied in the resolution of Mr. Terry, already adopted.

A motion to lay on the table was carried.

Mr. Harnan thought not.

Mr. Hire asserted that it was not.

On motion, the resolution was laid on the table.

Mr. Gorlinski offered the following resolution:

Resolved, That this Convention complete its organization by the election of the following named officers, viz: A vice-president, an assistant secretary, postmaster, printer and four reporters.

On motion, the resolution was laid on the table. Mr. R. B. Bell offered the following resolution:

Resolved, That the proceedings of this Convention be published each day in the True Delta, Era and Times newspapers of this city.

On motion, this resolution was tabled.

Mr. Samuel Pursell offered the following resolution:

Resolved, That the clergy of this city and environs be invited to meet together and furnish a list of those willing to act as chaplains to this Convention, one of them in rotation each day.

A motion was then made to adjourn until 12 o'clock to-morrow. Carried.

JOHN E. NEELIS,
Secretary.

SATURDAY, April 9th, 1864.

The Convention met pursuant to adjournment at 12 o'clock M., Hon. E. H. Durell presiding.

After prayer by the Rev. Mr. Strong, the roll was called, and the following members answered to their names, viz:

Abell, Austin, Bailey, Barrett, Baum, Bell, Bennie, Bofill, Bromley, Brott, Buckley, Burke, Balch, Campbell, Cook J. K., Crozat, Davies, Dufresne, Edwards, Fish, Flagg, Flood, Foley, Fosdick, Fuller, Gastinel, Geier, Goldman, Gruneberg, Gaidry, Healy, Harnan, Hart, Heard, Henderson, Hills, Hire, Howell, Howes, Kavanagh, Kugler, Maas, Mann, Maurer, Millspaugh, Montamat, Montague, Morris, Murphy E., Murphy M. W., Newell, Normand, Ong, Payne of Jefferson, Paine of Feliciana, Poynot, Purcell J., Purcell S., Schroeder, Seymour, Shaw, Smith, Spellicy, Stocker, Sumpf, Stiner, Stauffer, Sullivan, Terry, Thorpe, Thomas, Waters, Wenck, Wilson, and Mr. President—75.

It appearing that there were but seventy-five members present, the chair directed the sergeant-at-arms to bring in a member to make a quorum.

Two members entering, the chair announced that a quorum was present.

The minutes of the previous day's proceedings were read and adopted, and the secretary proceeded to read several communications, one from the secretary of state, accompanying the returns of the election of the parish of Iberville, announcing the election of Messrs. Balch and Dufresne; one from R. S. Abbott, tendering his resignation as a member of the Convention; and one from Mr. Roselius, tendering his resignation as a member of the Convention.

Mr. Foley moved the acceptance of the resignations.

Mr. Hills moved, as an amendment, that the resignation of Mr. Abbott be accepted, and that Mr. Roselius be requested to assign reasons for his resignation.

The motion was carried on division, by ayes 44, nays 32.

Mr. Hills then moved to reconsider the motion.

Mr. Hills moved to lay the amendment on the table.

Upon putting the question to vote, the chair was unable to decide, and directed a division with the following result: ayes 44, nays 32. The amendment was tabled.

Mr. Balch called for the ayes and nays on the main resolution.

Mr. Hills moved to lay the resolution on the table. Lost.

The ayes and nays were then called on the resolution, with the following result: 47 ayes, 27 nays. The motion was adopted.

Mr. Sullivan offered the following resolution:

Resolved, That no person shall be eligible to any office or employment whatsoever in the gift of this Convention but duly qualified voters of this State and of the United States; also that they shall exhibit to the president of the Convention that they have complied with the president's proclamation of the 8th of December, 1863.

A motion was made to lay the resolution on the table.

The ayes and nays were called, and the resolution was tabled by the following vote: yeas 66, nays 13.

Mr. Thomas moved to strike out that portion referring to messengers.

A motion was made to lay the resolution on the table.

The motion was carried on a division, by a vote of 66 yeas to 13 nays.

Mr. Thomas offered the following resolution:

Resolved, That this Convention proceed to elect an officer, who shall be styled the official printer of the Convention; whose duty it shall be to print and publish the proceedings, to perform all other necessary printing for the Convention, and to be responsible for the punctual and satisfactory execution of the work.

A motion to lay on the table was lost.

The resolution was then put on its passage, and the result was as follows:

YEAS—Austin, Bailey, Barrett, Baum, Beauvais, Bell, Bennie, Edwards, Fish, Flagg, Foley, Fosdick, Fuller, Geier, Murphy E., Murphy M. W., Newell, Normand, Payne Jno., Paine J. T., Purcell Jno., Bofill, Bonzano, Bromley, Brott, Buckley, Burke, Balch, Campbell, Cazabat, Cook J. K., Cook T., Cutler, Duane, Dupaty, Dufresne, Goldman, Gruneberg, Gaidry, Hart, Heard, Henderson, Hills, Hire, Howes, Kavanagh, Knobloch, Kugler, Maurer, Millspaugh, Montague, Seymour, Shaw, Smith, Spellicy, Stocker, Stumpf, Stiner, Stauffer, Sullivan, Terry, Thorpe, Thomas, Waters, Wilson—65.

NAYS—Flood, Gastinel, Howell, Mann, Montamat, Morris, O'Conner, S. Pursell, Schroeder, Wenck—10.

The chair declared the resolution carried.

Mr. Gastinel appealed from the decision of the chair on the ground that there was not a quorum voting.

The question was put to the Convention, with the following result:

YEAS—Abell, Austin, Bailey, Barrett, Baum, Beauvais, Bell, Bennie, Bofill, Bonzano, Bromley, Brott, Buckley, Burke, Balch Campbell, Cazabat, Cook T., Cutler, Davies, Duane, Dufresne, Edwards, Fish, Flagg, Flood, Fuller, Geier, Gorlinski, Gruneberg, Gaidry, Hart, Heard, Henderson, Hills, Hire, Howes, Kavanagh, Knobloch, Kugler, Mann, Maurer, Millspaugh, Montamat, Murphy E., Murphy M. W., Newell, Normand, O'Conner, Paine J. T., Poynot, Purcell J. Pursell S., Schroeder, Schnurr, Seymour, Shaw, Spellicy, Stocker, Stumpf, Sullivan, Stiner, Stauffer, Terry, Thorpe, Thomas, Waters, Wilson—68.

NAYS—Cook J. K., Foley, Fosdick, Howell, Montague, Morris, Smith—7.

The chair announced that the decision was sustained; that if there was a quorum present, members must be considered as voting blank.

Mr. Foley moved a call of the roll to ascertain whether a quorum was present.

The chair remarked that that was the proper way to decide the question.

The roll was called, and it was ascertained that there were 75 members present.

A motion was made to adjourn until Monday. Lost.

A motion to take a recess of fifteen minutes was voted down.

Mr. Thomas then moved to dispatch the sergeant-at-arms to bring in absent members.

After waiting a short time, the roll was again called, and 81 members being found present, the resolution was again put upon its passage and carried, two more members having entered during the calling of the yeas and nays. The vote was 83.

AYES—Abell, Austin, Bailey, Barett, Baum, Beauvais, Bennie, Bofill, Bonzano, Bromley, Brott, Buckley, Burke, Balch, Campbell, Cazabat, Cook J. K., Cook T., Cutler, Davies, Duane, Dufresne, Edwards, Fish, Flagg, Foley, Fosdick, Fuller, Gastinel, Geier, Goldman, Gorlinski, Gruneberg, Gaidry, Healy, Harnan, Hart, Heard, Henderson, Hills, Hire, Howell, Howes, Kavanagh, Knobloch, Kugler, Maas, Mann, Maurer, Mendiverri, Millspaugh, Montamat, Montague, Morris, Murphy E., Murphy M. W., Newell, Normand, O'Conner, Ong, Payne Jno., Paine J. T., Poynot, Purcell Jno., Pursell Sam'l, Schroeder, Schnurr, Seymour, Shaw, Smith, Spellicy, Stocker, Stumpf, Stiner, Stauffer, Sullivan, Terry, Thorpe, Thomas, Waters, Wilson—82.

NAYS—Flood—1.

The resolution was adopted.

Nominations having been declared in order:

Mr. Thomas nominated Mr. Fish.

Mr. Maun nominated Mr. Hills.

Mr. Brott nominated Mr. May.

Mr. Gorlinski nominated Fish and Hills.

The nominations were then closed.

Mr. Campbell moved to vote by ballot.

A motion to lay on the table was seconded and carried.

The roll was called with the following result:

FOR FISH, 65—Abbott, Abell, Austin, Bailey, Barrett, Baum, Beauvais, Bell, Bennie, Bofill, Bonzano, Buckley, Burke, Campbell, Cazabat, Cook J. K., Cook T., Cutler, Davies, Duane, Edwards, Flagg, Foley, Waters, Fuller, Gastinel, Geier, Goldman, Gruneberg, Gaidry, Healy, Hart, Heard, Henderson, Hire, Howes, Kavanagh, Knobloch, Maas, Maurer, Mendiverri, Millspaugh, Montamat, Morris, Murphy E., Murphy M. W., Newell, Normand, O'Conner, Ong, Payne J., Poynot, Purcell J., Pursell S., Schroeder, Seymour, Spellicy, Stocker, Stumpf, Stiner, Stauffer, Sullivan, Terry, Thorpe, Thomas.

FOR HILLS, 12—Dupaty, Dufresne, Flood, Fosdick, Harnan, Howell, Kugler, Mann, Montague, Paine J. T., Schnurr, Smith.

FOR MAY, 5—Bromley, Brott, Balch, Hills, Wilson.

FOR FISH AND HILLS, 2—Gorlinski, Wenck.

Blank 1.

Mr. Hills moved that Mr. Fish be unanimously declared printer.

The motion was carried.

Mr. Foley asked for information if the resolutions adopted yesterday, requiring members to show evidence of having taken the oath prescribed by the president's proclamation of December 8th, 1863, had been complied with. After waiting to examine the oath, the list was read, and it was announced that all the members, except Messrs. Airial, Crozat, Ennis, Lobdell, Wenck, Wells and Pintado, had complied with the terms of the resolution.

These members were not present, several of them not having reported since the opening of the Convention.

Mr. Stauffer called up the following resolution, tabled on the 8th:

Resolved, That a committee of five be appointed to draft rules and regulations for the government of this Convention, and that they report on Monday next.

The resolution was adopted.

The chair appointed Messrs. Stauffer, Thomas, Shaw, Heard and Bennie.

Mr. Montamat offered the following resolution:

Resolved, That the governor and State officers elected on the 22d February last, and Capt. Stephen Hoyt, acting mayor of the city of New Orleans, be and are hereby invited to occupy a seat within the room, whenever the Convention may not be in secret session.

Upon putting the question to vote, the resolution was declared adopted.

Mr. Cazabat sent up a motion to reconsider the action of the Convention in regard to the resignation of Messrs. Roselius and Abbott.

The chair decided that members must offer resolutions from their seats.

Col. Thorpe moved a reconsideration of the action of the Convention in regard to the acceptance of the resignations of Messrs. Abbott and Roselius, on the ground that there was not a quorum present when the vote was taken.

Judge Howell offered the following resolutions, and moved that they be read by the secretary and made the order of the day for Monday:

Resolved, That a committee of——members be appointed by the president of this Convention, to whom shall be referred the subject of the immediate and permanent abolition of slavery in the State of Louisiana, with instructions to report, as early as practicable, an ordinance or provisions in relation thereto, to be incorporated into the constitution of this State.

2. That a committee of —— members be appointed by the president, with instructions to recommend a preamble to the constitution of this State, and report as early as possible.

3. That a committee of —— members be appointed by the president, to whom shall be referred the subject of the distribution of the powers of the government of the State of Louisiana, as set forth in the first title of the constitution of the State adopted in 1852, with instructions to recommend changes, alterations and amendments, if any they may deem proper and expedient, and report thereon as soon as possible.

4. That a committee of —— members be appointed by the president, to whom shall be referred the subject of the legislative department, as set forth in the second title of said constitution, with instructions to recommend changes, alterations and amendments, if any they may deem proper and expedient, and report thereon as soon as possible.

5. That a committee of —— members be appointed by the president, to whom shall be referred the subject of the executive department, as set forth in the third title of said constitution, with instructions to recommend changes, alterations and amendments, if any they may deem proper and expedient, and report thereon as soon as possible.

6. That a committee of —— members be appointed by the president, to whom shall be referred the subject of the judiciary department, as set forth in the fourth title of said constitution, with instructions to recommend changes, alterations and amendments, if any they may deem proper and expedient, and report thereon as soon as possible.

7. That a committee of —— members be appointed by the president, to whom shall be referred the subject of impeachments, as set forth in the fifth title of said constitution, with instructions to recommend changes, alterations and amendments, if any they may deem proper and expedient, and report thereon as soon as possible.

8. That a committee of —— members be appointed by the president, to whom shall be referred the subject of general provisions, as set forth in the sixth title of said constitution, with instructions to recommend changes, alterations and amendments, if any they may deem proper and expedient, and report thereon as soon as possible.

9. That a committee of —— members be appointed by the president, to whom shall be referred the subject of internal improvements, as set forth in the seventh title of said constitution, with instructions to recommend changes, alterations and amendments if any they may deem proper and expedient, and report thereon as soon as possible.

10. That a committee of —— members be appointed by the president, to whom shall be referred the subject of public education, as set forth in the eighth title of said constitution, with instructions to recommend changes, alterations and amendments, if any they may deem proper and expedient, and report thereon as soon as possible.

11. That a committee of —— members be appointed by the president, to whom shall be referred the subject of the mode of revising the constitution, as set forth in the ninth title of said constitution, with instructions to recommend changes, alterations and amendments, if any they may deem proper and expedient, and report thereon as soon as possible.

12. That a committee of —— members be appointed by the president, to whom shall be referred the subject of the schedule, as set forth in the tenth title of said constitution, with instructions to recommend changes, alterations and amendments, if any they may deem proper and expedient, and report thereon as soon as possible.

13. That a committee of —— members be appointed by the president, to whom shall be referred the subject of the ordinance as set forth in the eleventh title of said constitution, with instructions to recommend changes, alterations and amendments, if any they may deem proper and expedient, and report thereon as soon as possible.

Mr. Montamat moved to have 300 copies printed for the use of the members. Carried.

A motion to lay the resolution on the table was lost.

A motion to adjourn till Monday at 12 o'clock was carried.

JOHN E. NEELIS,
Secretary.

MONDAY, April 11th, 1864.

At 12 o'clock the president called the Convention to order, and the proceedings were opened with prayer by the Rev. Mr. De Ossey, of the Christian Commission.

The secretary called the roll and the following gentlemen answered to their names, viz:

Messrs. Abell, Bailey, Barrett, Beauvais, Bell, Bofill, Bonzano, Bromley, Brott. Buckley, Balch, Burke, Campbell, Crozat. Davies, Dufresne, Edwards, Flagg, Flood, Foley, Fosdick, Geier, Goldman, Gorlinski, Gruneberg, Gaidry, Healy, Harnan, Heard, Henderson, Hills, Howell, Howes, Kavanagh, Knobloch, Kugler, Maas, Mann, Maurer, Millspaugh, Montamat, Montague, Morris, Murphy E., Murphy M. W., Newell, Normand, O'Conner, Ong, Schnurr, Seymour, Shaw, Smith, Spellicy, Stocker, Stumpf, Stiner, Stauffer, Sullivan, Terry, Thomas,

Waters, Wenck, Wilson, and Mr. President—65.

No quorum being present, the chair directed the sergeant-at-arms to bring in absent members.

After a few minutes delay the roll was again called, and the following gentlemen answered to their names, viz:

Abell, Austin, Bailey, Barrett, Bell, Bofill, Bonzano, Bromley, Brott, Buckley, Burke, Balch, Campbell, Cazabat, Crozat, Davies, Duane, Dupaty, Dufresne, Edwards, Fish, Flagg, Flood, Foley, Fosdick, Fuller, Gastinel, Geier, Goldman, Gorlinski, Gruneberg, Gaidry, Healy, Harnan, Hart, Heard, Henderson, Hills, Hire, Howell, Howes, Kavanagh, Knobloch, Kugler, Maas, Mann, Maurer, Mendiverri, Millspaugh, Montamat, Montague, Morris, Murphy E., Murphy M. W., Newell, Normand, O'Conner, Ong, Poynot, Purcell J., Schroeder, Schnurr, Seymour, Shaw, Smith, Spellicy, Stocker, Stumpf, Stiner, Stauffer, Sullivan, Terry, Thorpe, Thomas, Waters, Wenck, Wilson, and Mr. President—78.

Mr. Stauffer, chairman of the Committee on Rules and Regulations for the Government of the Convention, then submitted the following report:

The committee appointed to draft Rules of Order for this Convention, beg leave to submit the following as their report:

Rules and Regulations of the Convention of the People of Louisiana.

THE DUTIES AND RIGHTS OF THE PRESIDENT.

I. He shall take the chair every day at the hour to which the Convention shall have adjourned on the preceding day, and immediately call the members to order. If a quorum should be in attendance, he shall cause the journal of the preceding day to be read.

II. He shall preserve order and decorum; may speak to points of order in preference to members, rising from his seat for that purpose; he shall decide questions of order, subject to an appeal to the Convention made by any two members, on which appeal no member shall speak more than once, unless by leave of the Convention.

III. He shall rise to put a question, but may state it while sitting.

IV. Questions shall be distinctly put in this form, to-wit: "As many of you as are of opinion that (as the question may be) say aye," and, after the affirmative voice is expressed—"As many as are of contrary opinion say no." If the president doubt, or if a division be called for, the Convention shall divide; those in the affirmative of the question shall rise from their seats, and afterwards those in the negative. The president shall then rise and state the decision of the Convention.

V. The president shall have the right to examine and correct the journal before it is read. He shall have a general direction of the hall. He shall have a right to name any member to perform the duties of the chair, but such substitution shall not extend beyond an adjournment.

VI. In all cases of election by the Convention the president shall vote; in other cases he shall not vote, unless the Convention be equally divided, or unless his vote, if given to the minority, will make the division equal; and in case of such equal division, the question shall be lost.

VII. All committees shall be appointed by the president, unless otherwise especially directed by the Convention, in which case they shall be elected by the Convention; and, if upon such vote, the number required shall not be elected by a majority of the votes given, the Convention shall proceed to a second ballot, in which a plurality shall prevail; and in case a greater number than are required to compose or complete a committee, shall have an equal number of votes, the Convention shall take another vote.

VIII. All acts, addresses, and joint resolutions shall be signed by the president; and all writs, warrants and subpœnas, issued by order of the Convention, shall be under his hand, and attested by the secretary.

IX. In case of any disturbance or disorderly conduct in the gallery or lobby, the president (or chairman) shall have power to order the same to be cleared.

RULES OF DECORUM AND DEBATE.

X. When any member is about to speak in debate or deliver any matter to the Convention, he shall rise from his seat and respectfully address himself to "Mr. President."

XI. If any member, in speaking or otherwise, transgresses the rules of the Convention, the president shall, or any member may, call to order; in which case the member so called to order shall immediately sit down, unless permitted to explain; and the Convention shall, if appealed to, decide on the case, but without debate. If the decision be in favor of the member called to order, he shall be at liberty to proceed; if the decision be against him and the case require it, he shall be liable to the censure of the Convention.

XII. When two or more members happen to rise at once, the president shall name the one who is first to speak.

XIII. No member shall speak more than twice on the same question, nor more than

AND AMENDMENT OF THE CONSTITUTION OF LOUISIANA. 15

an hour on each occasion, without leave of the Convention, nor more than once until every member choosing to speak shall have spoken. But the mover of any proposition shall have the right to open and close the debate; and in case the proposition comes from any committee, then the member making the report from the committee shall have the right to open and close the debate in like manner.

XIV. While the president is putting any question, or addressing the House, no member shall walk out of, or across, the house; nor shall any one, in such case, when a member is speaking, entertain private discourse or cross the hall between him and the speaker.

XV. No member shall vote on any question in the result of which he has a separate and distinct interest, nor in any case when he was not within the bar of the Convention when the question was put. And when any member shall ask leave to vote, the president shall propound to him the question: *Were you within the bar when the question was put?* But when the yeas and nays are taken, and any member ask leave to vote, the president shall inquire of him whether he was within the bar *when his name was called?*

XVI. Upon a division and a count of the Convention upon any question, no member without the bar shall be counted.

XVII. Every member who shall be in the Convention when a question is put, shall give his vote, unless the Convention, for reasons assigned, shall excuse him. No member shall be allowed to make any explanation of a vote he is about to give, or asked to be excused from voting, after the secretary, under order of the Convention, shall have commenced calling the yeas and nays.

XVIII. When a motion is made and seconded, it shall be stated by the president; or, being in writing, it shall be handed to the chair, and read aloud by the secretary, before debated.

XIX. Every motion should be reduced to writing, if the president or any member desire it.

XX. No person, except the commanding general of the department, the governor of any State, the heads of departments of this State, the mayor of the city, and such other persons as the Convention may see proper, shall be admitted within the bar of the Convention.

XXI. After a motion is stated by the president, or read by the secretary, it shall be deemed to be in possession of the Convention, but may be withdrawn by the mover with the consent of the member who may have seconded the proposition.

XXII. When a question is under debate, no motion shall be received but to adjourn; 2d, to lie on the table; 3d, for the previous question; 4th, to postpone to a certain day; 5th, to commit; 6th, to amend; or 7th, to postpone indefinitely—which several motions shall have precedence in the order in which they are arranged, and no motion to postpone to a day certain, to commit, or to postpone indefinitely being decided, shall be again allowed on the same day and at the same stage of the motion or proposition. A motion to strike out the enacting words of a motion shall have precedence of a motion to amend, and, if carried, shall be considered equivalent to its rejection.

XXIII. The previous question shall be put in this form: "Shall the main question now be put?" It shall only be admitted when seconded by a majority of the members present, and, when carried, its effects shall be to put an end to all debate, and to bring the Convention to a direct vote—1st, upon the pending amendment, and so on, back to the first amendment offered; 2d, upon amendments, reported upon a committee, if any; and 3d, upon the main question.

On a motion for the previous question, and prior to the seconding of the same, a call of the Convention shall be in order; but after a majority shall have seconded such motion, no call shall be in order prior to a decision of the main question. On a motion for a previous question there shall be no debate.

All incidental questions of order arising after a motion is made for the previous question, and pending such motion, shall be decided, whether on appeal or otherwise, without debate. After a call for the previous question has been sustained by the Convention, the question shall be put and determined in order as above, without debate on either amendments or the main question.

XXIV. Any member may call for a division of a question, when the same will admit of it.

XXV. No new motion or proposition on a subject different from that under consideration shall be admitted under color of amendment, or as a substitute for the motion or proposition under debate.

XXVI. When a motion has been once made and carried in the affirmative or negative, it shall be in order for any member of the majority to move for a reconsideration thereof; provided it is made on the same day or the next sitting day, before the order of the day is taken up. And a motion for immediate reconsideration shall supercede a notice that a reconsideration will be moved.

XXVII. When the reading of a paper is called for, and the same is objected to by any member, the Convention shall determine whether said paper shall be read or not.

XXVIII. If a pending question be not disposed of, owing to an adjournment of the Convention, and be revived on the succeeding day, no member, who has spoken twice on the day preceding, shall be allowed to speak again without leave.

XXIX. When motions are made for the reference of a subject to a select standing committee, and a standing committee, the question for the reference to a standing committee shall be first put.

ORDER OF BUSINESS FOR THE DAY.

XXX. As soon as the journal is read and the names of the members called, the president shall ask if there are any petitions, memorials, or resolutions to be presented. The petitions, memorials and resolutions having been presented and disposed of, reports, first from standing and then from select committees, shall be called for; after which the president shall dispose of the messages, communications, resolutions and ordinances on his table, and then proceed to call the order of the day, which shall always be taken up at 12 o'clock M.

XXXI. The unfinished business in which the Convention was engaged at the time of the last adjournment shall have the preference in the orders of the day; and no motion, or any other business, shall have the preference in the orders of the day; and no motion, or any other business, shall be received without special leave of the Convention until the former is disposed of. The order of the day shall be as follows:

1. The unfinished business in which the Convention was engaged at its last adjournment.
2. Special orders of the day.
3. Ordinances and resolutions, in the order in which they have been presented to the Convention.

XXXII. Petitions, memorials and other papers, addressed to the Convention, shall be presented by the president or by a member in his place; a brief statement of the contents thereof shall be made verbally by the member introducing the same.

XXXIII. Any ten members, after organization of the Convention, are authorized to compel the attendance of absent members.

XXXIV. Upon calls for the Convention, and in taking the yeas and nays on any question, the names of the members shall be call alphabetically.

XXXV. All questions relating to the propriety of business shall be decided without debate.

XXXVI. A motion to adjourn, and a motion to fix the day to which the Convention shall adjourn, shall always be in order, except when the yeas and nays are being called; and when the question has just previously been put and negatived, these motions, and the motion to lie on the table, shall be decided without debate.

XXXVII. No member shall absent himself from the service of the Convention unless he have leave or be unable from sickness to attend.

XXXVIII. No committee shall have the right to appoint a clerk without the consent of the Convention being first obtained, except the Committee on Enrollment.

XXXIX. It shall be in order for the Committee on Enrollment to report at any time.

XL. All officers appointed or elected by the Convention shall hold them during the pleasure of the Convention only.

XLI. All ordinances before the Convention shall be taken up and acted upon in the order in which they are numbered, and it shall be the duty of the secretary to number every ordinance in its regular order upon its first reading.

XLII. No standing rule or order of the Convention shall be rescinded or changed without one day's notice being given of the motion thereof. Nor shall any rule be suspended, except by a vote of two-thirds of the members present. Nor shall the order of business, as established by the rules of the Convention, be postponed or changed, except by a vote of at least two-thirds of the members present.

XLIII. After a resolution shall have been adopted by the Convention it shall be engrossed in a fair hand, and after examination and report by the Committee on Enrollment, shall be signed by the president and secretary.

XLIV. The proceedings of the Convention shall be entered on the journal as concisely as possible, care being taken to detail a true and accurate account of the proceedings.

XLV. Every vote of the Convention shall be entered on the journal with a concise statement of the question; and a brief statement of the contents of each petition, memorial or paper presented to the Convention, shall be also inserted on the journal.

XLVI. In case any secretary, sergeant-at-arms or doorkeeper of the Convention fail to perform his duty, the secretary shall make a report thereof to the Convention without delay.

XLVII. The secretary shall read the journal daily from the sheet on which the minutes are written; and after being so read and corrected, the said minutes shall be recorded in the journal, and copies, authenticated by the signature of the secretary, shall be prepared for delivery at his desk to the printer by 10 o'clock on the day following that on which it shall have been read.

XLVIII. The secretary shall be responsible to the Convention for the accuracy of the journals and for the fidelity and prompt execution of all work ordered by the Convention; he shall keep the bill book in his own handwriting; he shall endorse all bills, joint resolutions, and all documents proper to be endorsed; he shall keep in his charge all bills and documents in the custody of the Convention, and keep them in proper order.

XLIX. The duties of the sergeant-at-arms shall be to attend the Convention during its sittings, to have the charge of the chamber of the Convention, and the committees rooms, and offices belonging thereto, to keep the same in order, and execute the commands of the Convention from time to time, together with all such process, issued by authority thereof, as shall be directed to him by the president.

L. The secretary or assistant secretary shall rise and remain standing whilst reading any document to the Convention.

LI. The assistant secretary of the Convention shall, in the event of the absence, resignation or death of the secretary, take charge of and attend to all the duties of his office until his successor shall be elected. It shall also be his duty to write with his own hand the journal of the Convention, when not acting as secretary.

LII. The duties of the doorkeeper shall be to keep the door of the lobby, announce messages and perform such other duties as the president may require.

LIII. No less than one-fifth of the members present shall be entitled to call for the yeas and nays on any question.

LIV. A quorum shall consist of a majority of the members elected and admitted to this Convention.

LV. The officers of this Convention shall consist of a president, secretary, two assistant secretaries, and as many clerks as may be required, an official printer, four reporters, a doorkeeper, two messengers, a postmaster, and such other officers as the Convention may deem necessary from time to time.

LVI. On any question of order or parliamentary practice, when these rules are silent or inexplicit, Jefferson's Manual, or Cushing's work on Parliamentary Law, shall be considered as authority.

The following committees shall be appointed by the chair as standing committees of this Convention:

1. A Committee on Elections, to be composed of five members.
2. A Committee on Preambles and Distribution of Powers, to consist of five members.
3. A Committee on the Legislative Department, to consist of seven members.
4. A Committee on Executive Department, to consist of seven members.
5. A Committee on Judiciary Department, to consist of seven members.
6. A Committee on Impeachment, to consist of three members.
7. A Committee on General Provisions, to consist of seven members.
8. A Committee on Internal Improvements, to consist of five members.
9. A Committee on Public Education, to consist of five members.
10. A Committee on Mode of Revising the Constitution, to consist of five members.
11. A Committee on Schedule, to consist of three members.
12. A Committee on Ordinances, to consist of five members.
13. A Committee on Enrollment, to consist of five members.
14. A Committee on Printing, to consist of three members.
15. A Committee on Finance, to consist of three members.

C. W. STAUFFER,
Chairman.

Mr. Montamat moved to print 300 copies for the use of the Convention, and that the report be made the order of the day for the 12th inst., at 2 o'clock.

Mr. Stauffer moved to amend by striking out 300, and inserting 200.

The mover accepted the amendment, and the motion was put to vote and carried.

Mr. Wilson then moved that the chair appoint another member on the committee appointed to inquire into the circumstances of assaults on two members of the Convention, in accordance with a resolution offered by Mr. Harnan on the second day of the session, in place of Mr. Roselius, resigned.

The motion was carried, and the chair appointed Mr. Shaw.

The hour for taking up the resolutions of Mr. Howell, offered the previous day, having arrived, the chair announced that they would now be taken up.

Mr. Thomas stated that they were in substance embodied in the report of the Committee on Rules and Regulations, and he would therefore move to lay them on the table till the 12th inst.

Mr. Brott moved to amend by striking out " till the 12th inst." and inserting " subject to call."

The amendment was accepted by the mover.

The question was then put to vote. The chair was unable to decide the vote, and directed a division, upon which it appeared that the motion was lost—ayes 29, nays 47.

Mr. Mann moved the adoption of the resolution, but withdrew his motion to permit Judge Howell to present a motion to fill the blanks.

Mr. Abell offered a substitute, but was declared out of order.

Judge Howell's motion was then presented, to fill the blank in the first resolution with the number 5, in the second with 3, 3d with 3, 4th with 5, 5th with 7, 6th with 11, 7th with 5, 8th with 13, 9th with 3, 10th with 9, 11th with 5, 12th with 5, 13th with 5.

Mr. Abell stated that he had a substitute to offer for the entire resolutions of Mr. Howell.

The chair decided him out of order.

Mr. Harnan moved to amend the motion of Mr. Howell respecting the filling the blanks, by striking out the number 9, in regard to the 10th resolution, and inserting the words "one member from each Representative District in the Parish of Orleans, and one from each of the other parishes."

Mr. Shaw made a motion to take up the resolutions to fill the blanks one at a time in their order.

Mr. Harnan's motion was withdrawn, and Mr. Shaw's put to vote and carried.

Mr. Stauffer asked that the substitute of Mr. Abell be read to the Convention.

The chair decided that the substitute was not in order.

Mr. Abell attempted to offer his substitute, and the chair called him to order.

Mr. Stauffer appealed from the decision of the chair.

The chair stated that the motion before the Convention was to fill the blanks in the resolutions offered by Mr. Howell, and that until that motion was disposed of a substitute for the resolutions was foreign to the subject-matter of the motion before the Convention, and was therefore out of order. The question was upon sustaining the decision of the chair.

The yeas and nays were called, and the chair was sustained by the following vote:

YEAS—Messrs. Austin, Barrett, Bell, Buckley, Burke, Balch, Cazabat, Cook T., Crozat, Duane, Dupaty, Fish, Flagg, Flood, Foley, Fosdick, Fuller, Gastinel, Geier, Gorlinski, Gruneberg, Gaidry, Healy, Harnan, Henderson, Hills, Hire, Howell, Howes, Kavanagh, Knobloch, Kugler, Mann, Mendiverri, Millspaugh, Montamat, Montague, Murphy E., Murphy M. W., Newell, Normand, O'Conner, Payne of Jefferson, Poynot, Purcell J., Schnurr, Shaw, Smith, Spellicy, Stocker, Stumpf, Stiner, Sullivan, Terry, Thorpe, Waters, Wenck, Wilson—58.

NAYS—Messrs. Bailey, Baum, Beauvais, Bennie, Bonzano, Brott, Cook J. K., Davies, Dufresne, Goldman, Heard, Maas, Maurer, Morris, Ong, Pursell S., Stauffer, Thomas —18.

A motion was made to proceed to the election of an assistant secretary.

A member asked if a quorum was present.

The chair directed the secretary to call the roll, when the following members answered to their names, viz:

Messrs. Abell, Austin, Bailey, Barrett, Beauvais, Bell, Bofill, Bonzano, Bromley, Brott, Buckley, Burke, Campbell, Cazabat, Cook T., Crozat, Davies, Duane, Dupaty, Edwards, Fish, Flagg, Flood, Foley, Fosdick, Fuller, Gastinel, Geier, Goldman, Gorlinski, Gruneberg, Gaidry, Healy, Harnan, Hart, Heard, Henderson, Hills, Hire, Howell, Howes, Kavanagh, Knobloch, Kugler, Maas, Mann, Maurer, Millspaugh, Montague, Morris, Murphy E., Murphy M. W., Newell, Normand, O'Conner, Ong, Payne J., Purcell J., Pursell S., Schroeder, Schnurr, Seymour, Shaw, Smith, Stocker, Stumpf, Stiner, Stauffer, Sullivan, Terry. Thorpe, Thomas, Waters, Wenck, Wilson.

Mr. Thomas moved an adjournment until 2 o'clock to-morrow.

Upon putting the question to vote, the chair was unable to decide and directed a division, upon which it appeared that the question was carried—yeas 43, nays 32.

Minutes adopted.

JOHN E. NEELIS,
Secretary.

TUESDAY, April 12th, 1864.

At 2 o'clock the Convention was called to order and the roll called, when the following gentlemen answered to their names, viz:

Messrs. Abell, Ariail, Austin, Barrett, Baum, Bell, Bofill, Bonzano, Brott, Buckley, Burke, Campbell, Cazabat, Cook J. K., Cook T., Crozat, Davies, Duane, Dufresne, Dupaty, Fish, Flagg, Flood, Foley, Fosdick, Fuller, Gastinel, Geier, Goldman, Gorlinski, Gruneberg, Gaidry, Healy, Hart, Heard, Hills, Hire, Howell, Howes, Knobloch, Kugler, Maas, Mann, Maurer, Mendiverri, Millspaugh, Montamat, Montague, Morris, Murphy E., Murphy M. W., O'Conner, Ong,

Paine, Poynot, Purcell J., Pursell S., Schroeder, Schnurr, Seymour, Shaw, Smith, Spellicy, Stocker, Stumpf, Stiner, Stauffer, Sullivan, Terry, Thorpe, Thomas, Waters, Wenck, Wilson, and Mr. President—75.

There being no quorum, the chair dispatched the sergeant-at-arms to bring in a member, which being done—

The minutes of the previous day's proceedings were read and adopted.

The chair then announced that the first business in order was the disposition of the report of the Committee on Rules and Regulations, and directed the secretary to read the report.

A motion was made that it be read by its title. Carried.

Mr. Hills moved to amend the title "Rules and Regulations of the Convention of the People of Louisiana" by striking out the words "of the People of," and substituting "for the Amendment and Revision of the Constitution of."

The amendment was carried, and the title, as amended, adopted.

A motion was then made to take up the report section by section. Carried.

Section I was taken up and adopted.
Section II was adopted.
Section III was adopted.
Section IV was adopted.
Section V was adopted.
Section VI was adopted.
Section VII was taken up.

Mr. Foley moved to strike out the word "ballot" in the fifth line, and substitute the word "vote." Carried, and the section as amended adopted.

Section VIII was taken up.

Mr. Hills moved to strike out the words "joint resolutions" in the first line. Carried, and the section as amended adopted.

Section IX was adopted.
Section X was taken up.

Mr. Bell moved to amend by adding the words "and members."

A motion was made and carried to lay the amendment on the table, and the section was adopted.

Section XI was taken up and adopted.
Section XII was taken up and adopted.
Section XIII was taken up.

Mr. Foley moved to amend by inserting the word "half" before the words "an hour," in the 2d line. Carried, and the section as amended adopted.

Section XIV was adopted.
Section XV was adopted.
Section XVI was adopted.
Section XVII was adopted.
Section XVIII was adopted.
Section XIX was taken up.

Mr. Hills moved to strike out the word "should" and substitute "shall" in the first line.

An amendment to the amendment was moved to strike out also the word "motion" and substitute "resolution."

Mr. Hills accepted the amendment, and on putting the question it was carried.

Mr. Goldman moved to amend by adding the words, "and notice shall be given by the president when it is about to be offered."

A motion was made to lay this amendment on the table. Carried.

The section as amended was then adopted.
Section XX was adopted.
Section XXI was adopted.
Section XXII was taken up.

Mr. Thorpe moved to amend by striking out the words "*but to adjourn*" in the second line.

The amendment was tabled and the section adopted.

Section XXIII was adopted.
Section XXIV was adopted.

A motion was made to strike out the words "*when the same will admit of it.*"

A motion to lay the amendment on the table was made.

Upon putting the question to vote, the chair was unable to decide, and directed a division.

The amendment was tabled—ayes 44, nays 9.

Section XXV was taken up.

Mr. Cazabat moved to amend by inserting the word "resolution" after the word "motion," in the first line.

A motion to lay the amendment on the table was carried, and the section adopted.

Section XXVI was taken up.

Mr. Gorlinski moved to amend by striking out the words "same day," in the fourth line.

On motion, tabled.

Mr. Goldman moved to amend by striking out the words "provided it is made on the same day."

On motion, tabled.

The section was adopted.

Section XXVII was adopted.

Section XXVIII was adopted.

Section XXIX was taken up.

A motion was made to strike out the word "*standing*," the second word in the second line. Carried.

A motion was made to strike out the word "*and*" in the second line and substitute "*or*." Carried, and the section as amended was adopted.

Section XXX was taken up.

Mr. Cazabat moved to amend by striking out "12 o'clock M." and insert "1 o'clock P. M."

Mr. Goldman moved to lay the amendment on the table. Lost.

Mr. Hills moved to strike out "12 o'clock" and insert "blank o'clock." A motion to amend Mr. Hills's amendment by striking out "blank o'clock" and inserting "3 o'clock," was lost.

A motion to strike out the eighth line and the three last words of the seventh was carried, and the section as amended adopted.

Section XXXI was taken up.

A motion to amend, by striking out of the third and fourth lines the words "and no motion, or any other business, shall have the preference in the order of the day," was made.

A motion to table the amendment was lost.

The amendment was adopted, and the section as amended was adopted.

Section XXXII was adopted.

Section XXXIII was adopted.

Section XXXIV was adopted.

Section XXXV was adopted.

Section XXXVI was adopted.

Section XXXVII was adopted.

Section XXXVIII was taken up.

A motion was made to strike it out of the report. Carried.

Section XXXIX was adopted.

Section XL was taken up.

Mr. Goldman moved to amend. by striking out the word "them" in the first line and inserting "*their places.*"

A motion was made to lay the amendment on the table. Carried.

Mr. Cazabat moved to amend by striking out the word "them" in the second line, and substituting "*their offices.*"

The motion was carried, and the section, as amended, was adopted.

Section XLI was adopted.

Section XLII was adopted.

Section XLIII was adopted.

Section XLIV was adopted.

Section XLV was adopted.

Section XLVI was taken up.

Mr. Wilson moved to amend "*the secretary shall make a report thereof to*" and insert therefor "the president shall notify."

A motion to lay the amendment on the table was lost.

The amendment was adopted.

The section, as amended, was adopted.

Section XLVII was taken up.

A motion was made to amend by striking out the words "10 o'clock" in the fifth line.

A motion to lay the amendment on the table was carried, and the section was adopted.

Section XLVIII was taken up.

Mr. Cazabat moved to amend by striking out the word "*hills*" and the word "*john*" in the fourth line.

The amendment was carried, and the section, as amended, adopted.

Mr. Wilson moved a reconsideration. Lost.

Section XLIX was adopted.

Section L was adopted.

Section LI was adopted.

Section LII was adopted.

Section LIII was taken up.

Mr. Montamat moved to amend by striking out the words "no less than one-fifth" in the first line, and inserting "any two."

A motion was made to lay the amendment on the table.

Upon taking the vote, the chair was unable to decide, and directed a division.

The motion to table was carried. Ayes 39, noes 33.

Mr. Montamat moved to amend by striking out the words "*no less than one-fifth*" and substitute "*any number.*"

Mr. Shaw rose to a point of order.

AND AMENDMENT OF THE CONSTITUTION OF LOUISIANA. 21

The chair decided that the amendment was in order.

A motion was made to lay the amendment on the table. Carried.

The section was then put on its passage and adopted.

Section LIV was then taken up.

A motion was made to so amend that the section shall read: "A quorum shall consist of seventy-six members."

A motion was made to lay the amendment on the table.

The yeas and nays were called, when the following vote was read:

YEAS — Messrs. Beauvais, Bell, Brott, Burke, Cook J. K., Cook Terrance, Fish, Flagg, Fuller, Goldman, Gaidry, Heard, Henderson, Hire, Maas, Murphy M. W., O'Conner, Purcell John, Seymour, Smith, Stauffer, Terry, Wilson—23.

NAYS—Abell, Ariail, Austin, Bailey, Barrett, Baum, Bofill, Bonzano, Buckley, Campbell, Cazabat, Crozat, Davies, Duane, Dupaty, Dufresne, Flood, Foley, Fosdick, Gastinel, Geier, Gorlinski, Gruneberg, Healy, Harnan, Hart, Hills, Howell, Howes, Knobloch, Kugler, Mann, Maurer, Mendiverri, Millspaugh, Montamat, Montague, Morris, Murphy E., Newell, Ong, Payne J., Poynot, Purcell Samuel, Schroeder, Schnurr, Shaw, Spellicy, Stocker, Stumpf, Stiner, Sullivan, Thorpe, Thomas, Waters, Wenck—56.

Mr. Hills moved to amend the amendment by adding the words, "and when any member shall absent himself from the hall for three successive roll calls without presenting a reasonable excuse, his seat shall be declared vacant, and an election shall be ordered to fill the vacancy."

A motion to lay the amendment on the table was carried.

The first amendment was carried, and the section, as amended, adopted.

Section LV was taken up.

Mr. Montamat moved to strike out the words "four reporters" in the third line, and insert "one official reporter and three assistants."

Mr. Cazabat moved to amend by substituting "two" for "four," in the third line.

Mr. Shaw moved to lay the amendment on the table. Carried.

Mr. Howell moved to substitute the words "one reporter" for "four reporters." Carried, and the section, as-amended adopted.

Section LVI was taken up.

Mr. Henderson moved to amend by striking out the words "or Cushing's work on Parliamentary Law" in the second and third lines, and all subsequent to the third line.

A motion to table the amendment was lost.

The amendment was adopted.

The section as amended was adopted.

A motion was made to reconsider section LI.

The motion was carried.

A motion to amend by inserting "sergeant-at-arms" in the second line was carried, and the section, as amended, adopted.

Mr. ——— moved to reconsider section XXI. Lost.

Mr. Wilson moved the adoption of the report as amended as a whole.

The motion was carried.

Mr. Shaw moved to take up the resolutions of Mr. Howell. Made the order of the day.

The chair announced that the resolutions, having been made the order of the day, would be taken up.

Mr. Cazabat moved a recess of five minutes.

Mr. Beauvais moved to adjourn till 4 o'clock P. M. to-morrow.

A motion to amend by striking out "4," and inserting "12 o'clock" was carried, and the Convention adjourned.

Minutes adopted.

JOHN E. NEELIS,
Secretary.

WEDNESDAY, April 13, 1864.

At twenty minutes past 12 o'clock, the chair called the Convention to order, and the proceedings were opened with prayer by the Rev. J. G. Bass.

The roll was called and the following members answered to their names, viz:

Messrs. Abell, Ariail, Austin, Bailey, Barrett, Baum, Beauvais, Bell, Bonzano, Brott, Buckley, Burke, Campbell, Cazabat, Cutler, Davies, Duane, Dupaty, Edwards, Ennis, Fish, Flagg, Flood, Foley, Fosdick, Fuller, Geier, Goldman, Gorlinski, Gruneberg, Gaidry, Healy, Harnan, Hart, Heard, Henderson, Hills, Hire, Howell, Howes, Kugler, Maas, Mann, Mendiverri, Montamat, Montague, Morris, Murphy E., Newell, Normand,

O'Conner, Ong, Payne, Pintado, Purcell, Schnurr, Seymour, Shaw, Smith, Spellicy, Stocker, Stumpf, Stiner, Stauffer, Sullivan, Terry, Thorpe, Thomas, Wilson, and Mr. President—70.

The chair directed the sergeant-at-arms to bring in members.

After waiting some ten or fifteen minutes, Messrs. Murphy, Wenck, Millspaugh, Knobloch, Kavanagh, Mendiverri and Gastinel having entered the hall, a quorum was found to be present.

The minutes of the previous day's proceedings were read and adopted.

The chair announced that the first business in order was receiving of petitions.

No petition being presented, resolutions being next in order.

J. Randall Terry offered the following resolutions, viz:

Whereas, At a convention of delegates assembled in this hall on the 26th day of January, 1861, and purporting to represent the people of this State, it was ordained and declared in the words following—that is to say:

" An Ordinance to dissolve the union between the State of Louisiana and other States, united with her under the compact entitled ' The Constitution of the United States of America.'

" *We the people of the State of Louisiana, in Convention assembled, do declare and ordain, and it is hereby declared and ordained,* That the ordinance passed by us in Convention on the 22d day of November, in the year 1811, whereby the constitution of the United States of America and the amendments of the said constitution were adopted; and all laws and ordinances by which the State of Louisiana became a member of the Federal Union, be and the same are hereby repealed and abrogated; and that the Union now subsisting between Louisiana and other States, under the name of ' The United States of America,' is hereby dissolved.

" *We do further declare and ordain,* That the State of Louisiana hereby resumes all rights and powers heretofore delegated to the government of the United States of America; that her citizens are absolved from all allegiance to said government; and that she is in full possession and exercise of all those rights of sovereignty which appertain to a free and independent State.

" *We do further declare and ordain,* That all rights acquired and vested under the constitution of the United States, or any act of Congress, or treaty, or under any law of this State, and not incompatible with this ordinance, shall remain in force, and have the same effect as if this ordinance had not been passed."

Now we, the people of the State of Louisiana, loyal to the constitution of the government of the United States, do hereby announce, declare and ordain, that the said pretended ordinance of secession, so passed by disloyal traitors, without the authority of the people and in violation of the Federal constitution, together with all other ordinances, acts and proceedings of said secessionists in said Convention, and of the pretended State government instituted under the said ordinance of secession, are *utterly null* and *void.*

Resolved, That, representing the people of the State of Louisiana, this Convention hereby declares its adherence and the adherence of the people of the State of Louisiana to the constitution of the United States, and that we will by all our efforts sustain and uphold the government of the United States in its efforts to suppress the present unjust and most wicked rebellion.

Mr. Henderson moved to lay the resolution on the table. Carried. Ayes 42, nays 21.

Mr. Montamat offered the following resolution, viz:

Resolved, That the members of this Convention shall severally receive from the public treasury a compensation for their services, which shall be *eight* dollars per day, during their attendance on, going to and returning from the sessions of this Convention.

Be it further resolved, That a committee of *five* be appointed by the chair for the purpose of fixing the compensation of the several officers and employés of this Convention, and what appropriation is necessary to defray the expenses, and to report as early as possible.

Mr. Harnan moved to amend by striking out the words fixing the compensation at eight dollars a day, and making it read " members shall serve gratuitously."

A motion was made and carried to lay the amendment on the table.

Mr. Cazabat moved to lay the original motion on the table.

The motion was lost.

Mr. Montamat moved the adoption of the resolution.

The yeas and nays were called and the result was as follows:

YEAS—Messrs. Abell, Austin, Baum, Beauvais, Bell, Buckley, Burke, Cook J. K., Crozat, Duane, Flagg, Foley, Gastinel, Geier, Gruneberg, Gaidry, Healy, Hender-

AND AMENDMENT OF THE CONSTITUTION OF LOUISIANA. 23

son, Howes, Kavanagh, Knobloch, Mendiverri, Montamat, Murphy M. W., Normand, O'Conner, Pintado, Poynot, Purcell John, Pursell Samuel, Schroeder, Seymour, Smith, Spellicy, Stocker, Stiner, Sullivan, Terry—39.

NAYS—Messrs. Ariail, Barrett, Bonzano, Brott, Campbell, Cazabat, Cook T., Cutler, Dupaty, Ennis, Fosdick, Goldman, Gorlinski, Harnan, Hart, Heard, Fish, Flood, Hills, Hire, Howell, Kugler, Maas, Mann, Millspaugh, Montague, Morris, Murphy E., Newell, Ong, Payne John, Paine J. T., Schnurr, Shaw, Stumpf, Stauffer, Thorpe, Thomas, Waters, Wilson—39.

There being a tie vote, the chair gave the casting vote in the negative, and the resolution was lost.

Mr. Montamat offered the following resolution:

Resolved, That the constitution which shall be framed by this Convention shall have no effect until the same shall have been ratified by the vote of the majority of the qualified voters of Louisiana at the ballot-box, at the various election precincts of the State, under the regulations and laws in regard to the election of State officers. Those voting for the constitution shall endorse on their ticket "Ratification," and those voting against it "No Ratification." The governor shall publish a proclamation duly notifying the people of this State of the holding of said election, and ordering the sheriffs of the several parishes of this State to cause an election to be held under the existing laws. Said election to take place twenty days after the adjournment of the Convention.

On motion of Mr. Wilson the resolution was laid on the table.

Mr. Pursell, of Jefferson, offered the following resolution:

Resolved, That the clergy of this city and environs be and are hereby invited to meet together and furnish a list to the secretary of those willing to act as chaplains to this Convention—one of the number, in rotation, each day.

The resolution was tabled.

Mr. Abell offered the following preamble and resolutions:

Whereas, General Order No. 38, dated Headquarters Department of the Gulf, New Orleans, March 22, 1864, the United States, through their proper officer, Major General Banks, has assumed to levy and collect taxes of the people of this State without their consent, and appropriate the same for domestic purposes, as will appear by the following educational order, officially set forth in the words and figures following, to-wit:

EDUCATION OF FREEDMEN.

HEADQUARTERS DEPARTMENT OF THE GULF, }
New Orleans, March 22, 1864. }

General Orders No. 38.

In pursuance of the provisions of General Orders No. 23, current series, for the rudimental instruction of the freedmen of this department, placing within their reach the elements of knowledge which give intelligence and greater value to labor, and reducing the provisions necessary therefor to an economical and efficient school system;

It is ordered that a Board of Education, consisting of three persons, be hereby constituted, with the following duties and powers:

1st. To establish one or more Common Schools in each and every school district that has been or may be defined by the parish provost marshals under orders of the provost marshal general.

2d. To acquire by purchase, or otherwise, tracts of land, which shall be judged by the Board necessary and suitable for school sites, in plantation districts, to be not less than one-half acre in extent; to hold the same in trust to themselves until such schools shall have been established, when they shall transfer all the right and title thereto that may have vested in them to the superintendent of public institutions, or other competent State authority:

3d. To erect upon said plots of land such school-houses as they may judge necessary and proportioned to the wants of the population of the district, where there are no buildings available and proper for school purposes. And in this, as in all other duties, they shall exercise the strictest economy.

4th. To select and employ proper teachers for said schools, as far as practicable, from the loyal inhabitants of Louisiana, with power to require their attendance for the purpose of instruction in their duties, one week at least at a Normal School, to be conducted by the Board.

5th. To furnish and provide the necessary books, stationery and apparatus for the use of such schools, and in addition thereto to purchase and furnish an outfit of a well-selected library, &c., for each freed person in the several school districts who is above the age of attending school duty, at a cost to each, including a case to contain the same, not exceeding two and a half dollars, which sum shall be included in the general tax hereinafter provided, but shall be deducted from the laborer's wages by his employer, when such books are furnished.

6th. To regulate the course of study, discipline and hours of instruction for children on week days, and adults on Sundays; to require such conformity to their regulations and such returns and reports from their teachers as they may deem necessary to secure uniformity, thoroughness and efficiency in said schools.

7th. To have generally the same authority and perform the same duties that assessors, supervisors and trustees have in the Northern States, in the matter of establishing and conducting Common Schools.

And for the full accomplishment of these purposes and the performance of the duties enjoined upon them, the Board shall have full power and authority to assess, and levy a School Tax upon real and personal property, including crops of plantations, in each and every before mentioned School District. The said taxes so levied shall be sufficient in amount to defray the cost and expense of establishing, furnishing and conducting for the period of one year the school or schools so established in each and every of the said districts; and said taxes shall be collected from the person or persons in the occupation of the property assessed.

8th. The taxes so assessed and levied in and for each district shall be collected and paid over to the Board by the parish provost marshal, within thirty days after the tax list and schedule shall have been placed in his hands; and he shall forthwith report to the Board whether there are in the districts of this parish any buildings available and suitable for school-houses, and shall at all times, when required, assist by his authority the Board in carrying out the spirit of this order. The taxes, when collected, shall be forthwith deposited in the First National Bank of New Orleans, subject only to the order of the whole Board, which shall make a monthly exhibit of accounts and report of their doings to the commanding general.

9th. In the performance of all their duties the Board shall co-operate, as far as practicable, with the superintendent of Public Education, recently elected.

10th. The current school year shall be estimated from February 1st, 1864, to February 1st, 1865.

11th. The following officers and citizens are appointed upon this Board, and will be obeyed and respected accordingly:

Colonel H. N. Frisbie, Twenty-second Infantry, Corps d'Afrique.

Lieutenant E. M. Wheelock, Fourth Infantry, Corps d'Afrique.

Isaac G. Hubbs, New Orleans.

By command of Major General Banks:
RICHARD B. IRWIN.

Whereas, Taxes imposed without the consent of the people are unconstitutional and injurious to their rights and liberties; be it

Resolved, 1st—That the rights asserted in the order aforesaid are unconstitutional and in derogation of the sovereignty, honor and dignity of the State and the dearest rights of the people.

2d—That any legislation, or attempt to legislate or any amendment or attempt to amend the constitution of Louisiana, will be a virtual admission of the right claimed and an abandonment of the just rights of the people of Louisiana.

3d—That this Convention ought to adjourn until all the powers belonging to the people, supposed to be abridged by said order, be restored to them by their representatives.

4th—*Be it further resolved,* That the Convention do adjourn until ——, 1864, in order to correspond with General Banks and the authorities of the general government of the United States, before taking any further action, to ascertain the wish and puposes of the general government in the premises; and

Be it further resolved, That the foregoing resolutions are not intended to impair or controvert in any manner the right of the general government to require the State of Louisiana to contribute by taxes or otherwise her just proportion of the expenses of the war.

Mr. Brott moved to lay the resolution on the table.

The ayes and nays were called:

YEAS--Messrs. Ariail, Austin, Bailey, Barrett, Beauvais, Bell, Bonzano, Brott, Burke, Cazabat, Cook J. K., Cook Terrance, Crozat, Cutler, Duane, Dupaty, Edwards, Ennis, Fish, Flagg, Flood, Foley, Fosdick, Gastinel, Geier, Gorlinski, Gaidry, Harnan, Hart, Heard, Henderson, Hills, Hire, Howell, Howes, Kavanagh, Knobloch, Kugler, Mann, Maurer, Mendiverri, Millspaugh, Montague, Morris, Murphy E., Murphy M. W., Newell, Normand, O'Conner, Ong, Payne John, Paine J. T., Poynot, Purcell John, Pursell Sam., Schroeder, Schnurr, Seymour, Shaw, Smith, Spellicy, Stocker, Stumpf, Stiner, Stauffer, Sullivan, Terry, Thorpe, Thomas, Waters, Wenck, Wilson—72.

NAYS—Messrs. Abell, Baum, Buckley, Campbell, Goldman, Gruneberg, Maas, Montamat, Pintado—9.

The resolution was tabled.

The hour for taking up the special order of the day, Mr. Howell's resolutions, having arrived, they were taken up.

Mr. Hills moved that they be taken up *seriatim.*

The motion was carried.

Section I was read.

AND REVISION OF THE CONSTITUTION OF LOUISIANA. 25

Mr. Abell offered the following as a substitute:

Whereas, Slavery having existed in this country by custom from its earliest settlement by sanction of the constitution and laws of the United States, and of the constitution and laws of this State; and

Whereas, The owners of slaves have acquired property therein by virtue of said custom, constitution and laws, and under the protection and guarantee thereof; and

Whereas, All that is good and truly great in individuals or States must have its foundation in good faith and justice ; be it, therefore

Resolved, That no proposition for the "abolition of slavery" be entertained by this Convention until ways and means are first provided for a full, fair and equitable compensation to all lawful owners, either by the future labor of the slave, or out of the treasury of this State, or of the United States, and for the removal of all emancipated slaves from the State.

A motion was made to lay the substitute on the table.

The motion was carried.

Mr. Cazabat moved to amend the resolution by inserting the word "*unconditional*" after the word "*immediate*," in the second line.

A motion was made and carried to lay the amendment on the table.

A motion was made to lay the original resolution on the table.

The motion was lost.

Mr. Cutler moved to fill the blank with the number "5." Carried.

The resolution was then put on its passage and adopted.

A motion to reconsider was made and carried.

A motion to strike out "5" and insert "11." Carried.

The question on the adoption of the resolution was then put, and the resolution as amended was adopted.

Section II was taken up.

A motion was made and carried to fill the blank with the number "7," and the resolution was adopted.

Section III was taken up.

A motion to fill the blank with the number "7" was made and carried, and the resolution was adopted.

Section IV was taken up.

Mr. Baum moved to fill the blank with the number "13."

A motion was made to fill the blank with the number "5."

A motion to lay the last motion on the table was made and lost.

A motion was then made to adopt the resolution with the blank filled with the number "5."

The motion was lost.

Mr. Purcell moved to fill the blank with the number "9."

The motion was carried, and the resolution, with the blank thus filled, was adopted.

Section V was taken up.

Mr. Abell moved to fill the blank with the number "7."

The motion was carried, and the resolution adopted.

Section VI was taken up.

A motion was made to fill the blank with the number "7."

A motion to lay on the table was lost.

The motion to fill with the number "7" was carried.

The resolution was adopted.

Section VII was taken up.

Mr. Hills moved to fill the blank with the number "5."

Mr. Baum moved to fill the blank with the number "9."

Mr. Goldman moved to lay the last motion on the table.

The motion was carried.

The motion of Mr. Hills to fill the blank with "five" was carried and the resolution was adopted.

Section VIII was taken up.

A motion to fill the blank with the number "11" was carried, and the resolution was adopted.

Section IX was taken up.

A motion to fill the blank with the number "5" was carried and the resolution was adopted.

Section X was taken up.

A motion to fill the blank with the number "7" was carried and the resolution was adopted.

Section XI was taken up.

A motion to fill the blank with "5" was carried and the resolution adopted.

Section XII was taken up.

A motion to fill the blank with the number "7" was carried and the resolution was adopted.

Section XIII was taken up.

A motion to fill the blank with the number "5" was carried and the resolution was adopted.

Mr. Montamat offered the following, and moved that it be added to the resolutions of Mr. Howell, as section XIV, viz:

That the following standing committees be

appointed by the chair, to wit: One on enrollment, to consist of five members; one on finances, to consist of five members; one on contingent expenses, to consist of five members, and one on printing, to consist of three members.

The motion was carried.

Mr. Montamat moved the adoption of the resolutions as a whole.

The motion was carried and the resolutions adopted as a whole.

Mr. Howell moved a reconsideration.

A motion was made and carried to lay the motion for reconsideration on the table.

Mr. Gorlinski offered the following resolution, viz:

Resolved, That all applause in this hall, pending discussion, is out of order, and shall be disallowed.

A motion was made to lay the resolution on the table.

The motion was lost.

The question upon the adoption of the resolution was put, and the resolution was lost.

Mr. Sullivan offered the following resolution:

Whereas, It is currently reported that many members of this Convention are not citizens of the United States, but owe allegiance to foreign powers; and

Whereas, It becomes the duty of this Convention to have its members placed above suspicion; be it therefore

Resolved, That the members of this Convention of foreign birth be required to exhibit to the president of this Convention evidence of their naturalization, on or before Thursday next, the 14th instant, at 12 o'clock M

Mr. Hire moved to lay the resolution on the table.

The motion to lay on table was lost.

A motion was made to adopt.

The yeas and nays were called, with the following result:

YEAS—Messrs. Ariail, Austin, Barrett, Baum, Beauvais, Bell, Bennie, Brott, Buckley, Balch, Campbell, Cook J. K., Cook T., Cutler, Duane, Dufresne, Edwards, Flagg, Flood, Foley, Gastinel, Gorlinski, Gaidry, Healy, Harnan, Hart, Heard, Hills, Howes, Kavanagh, Knobloch, Mann, Maurer, Montamat, Montague, Murphy M. W., Normand, Newell, O'Conner, Ong, Payne J., Panie J. T., Pintado, Pursell S., Seymour, Smith, Spellicy, Sullivan, Terry, Thomas, Waters—51.

NAYS—Messrs. Bailey, Bonzano, Burke, Crozat, Dupaty, Ennis, Fish, Fosdick, Geier, Goldman, Gruneberg, Henderson, Hire, Howell, Kugler, Maas, Millspaugh, Murphy E., Purcell J., Schroeder, Shaw, Stocker, Stiner, Stauffer, Shaw, Thorpe, Wenck, Wilson—27.

The resolution was adopted.

A motion to adjourn was lost.

Mr. Bell offered the following:

Resolved, That we proceed to elect two assistant secretaries, one postmaster, one reporter, and one messenger.

The resolution was adopted.

Nominations for assistant secretary being in order, the names of Messrs. Murphy, Hamilton, Gannon, Winfree and Parkhurst were put in nomination.

Upon the first vote, no candidate having received a majority of all the votes, there was no election.

Upon the second vote Mr. Murphy received a majority of all the votes cast, and was declared elected.

Messrs. Hamilton, Winfree, Gordon and Kruse were put in nomination for second assistant secretary.

Upon the first vote neither candidate received a majority of all the votes cast, and there was no election.

On the second vote no candidate received a majority of all the votes cast, and there was no election.

On the third vote Mr. S. J. Hamilton received a majority of all the votes cast, and was declared elected.

Mr. Henderson moved that the assistant secretaries be declared unanimously elected.

The motion was carried.

Mr. Brott offered the following resolution:

Resolved, That Adjutant Gen. L. Thomas, U. S. A., be and he is hereby invited to a seat within the bar of the House.

The names of Messrs. A. P. Bennett and H. A. Gallup were put in nomination for reporter.

Upon the first vote Mr. Bennett received 50 votes and Mr. Gallup 24.

Mr. Bennett was elected.

Mr. Terry made a motion to proceed to elect a short-hand reporter.

The motion was laid on the table.

Mr. Thomas moved that the reporter be authorized to employ three assistants.

Mr. Montamat moved to amend by striking out the word "three" and inserting "two."

Mr. Cazabat moved to lay the amendment on the table.

The motion was tabled.

The motion of Mr. Thomas was adopted.

Messrs. Toomey, Davis, Miller, Gannon, Gordon, Smith and Koch were put in nomination for postmaster.

Upon the first vote, no candidate having received a majority of all the votes cast, there was no election.

Upon the second vote, Mr. Gannon received 47 votes, and Mr. Koch 30.

Mr. Gannon having received a majority of all the votes cast, was elected.

Mr. Brott moved that Charles Benedict be declared elected messenger by acclamation.

The motion was carried.

Mr. Thomas moved that the sergeant-at arms be authorized to employ two assistants.

Mr. Montamat moved to lay the motion on the table.

Lost.

The motion of Mr. Thomas was then put to vote and carried.

A motion to adjourn till Friday, the 15th inst., at 12 o'clock, was made and carried, and the Convention adjourned accordingly.

Approved.

JOHN E. NEELIS,
Secretary.

FRIDAY, April 15th, 1864.

The chair called the Convention to order at 12 o'clock, and announced that the proceedings would be opened with prayer by the Rev. Mr. Mason, of the Catholic church.

Mr. Mason offered up the prayer in the French language, and the secretary proceeded to call the roll.

The roll was called and the following members answered to their names:

Messrs. Abell, Ariail, Austin, Bailey, Barrett, Baum, Beauvais, Bell, Bonzano, Brott, Buckley, Burke, Bennie, Bofill, Bromley, Campbell, Cazabat, Cutler, Cook J. K., Cook T., Crozat, Davies, Duane, Dupaty, Edwards, Ennis, Fish, Flagg, Flood, Foley, Fosdick, Fuller, Geier, Goldman, Gorlinski, Gruneberg, Gaidry, Healy, Harnan, Hart, Heard, Henderson, Harris, Hire, Howell, Howes, Kugler, Maas, Mann, Mendiverri, Montamat, Montague, Morris, Murphy E., Newell, Normand, O'Conner, Ong, Payne, Pintado, Pursell S., Schnurr, Seymour, Shaw, Smith, Spellicy, Stocker, Stumpf, Stiner, Stauffer, Sullivan, Terry, Thorpe, Thomas, Wilson, and Mr. President—76.

Mr. Heard rose to a question of privilege. He desired to ask a leave of absence for his colleague, Mr. Kugler, on account of illness of some members of his family.

On putting the question the Convention granted the request.

Mr. Fish offered the following resolution, viz:

Resolved, That the Governor of the State be requested to issue his proclamation ordering an election, as early as possible, for one delegate from the Tenth Representative District, to fill a vacancy in the representation from said district and parish.

Mr. Henderson desired to know if there was a vacancy, and moved that the resignation of Messrs. Roselius and Abbott be accepted, and that the governor be requested to issue his writs of election to fill the vacancies.

Mr. Cazabat moved to lay the resolution on the table. Lost.

The motion of Mr. Henderson was then put and carried.

Mr. Stocker offered a resolution directing the printer of the Convention to print 300 copies of the constitutions of 1812, 1845 and 1852.

Mr. Montamat moved to amend by striking out 300 and inserting 200. Carried.

Judge Howell offered the following substitute:

Resolved, That the State librarian be requested to furnish each member with a copy of Phillips's Revised Statutes, during the sitting of this Convention.

The substitute was adopted.

Mr. Stocker offered the following resolution:

Resolved, That the rules and regulations be so amended as to require all ordinances and resolutions to lie over one day, unless referred to some committee, before being acted upon by the Convention.

It was decided that the resolution must, under the rules, lie over one day before being acted on, and Mr. Stocker gave notice that he should offer the resolution the next day.

Mr. Thomas moved that the printer be instructed to furnish 200 copies of the resolutions of Judge Howell for the use of the House.

Mr. Montamat moved to amend by adding the names of the various committees.

Mr. Hills moved to amend by instructing the printer to print the titles of the several sections in the margin.

The amendments were adopted, and the resolution, as amended, adopted.

Mr. Pursell offered the following:

Resolved, That the consideration for a just appreciation of the former services in the cause of the Union, and the great respect entertained by the loyal people of the State of Louisiana for the Hon. C. Roselius, and the fact of his election by the *spontaneous* action of the truly loyal people of the parish where he has served so long and faithfully,

28   JOURNAL OF THE CONVENTION FOR THE AMENDMENT

that he be invited to withdraw his resignation, and to resume his seat in this Convention.

Mr. Henderson moved to lay the resolution on the table.

The resolution was tabled.

Mr. M. W. Murphy offered the following resolutions :

Resolved, That the members of this Convention shall receive from the public treasury a compensation for their services, which shall be ten dollars per day during their attendance, going to and returning from the sessions of this Convention.

Be it further resolved, That a committee of five be appointed by the chair to fix the compensation of the officers and emyloyés of this Convention, and also the mileage of members from the country parishes, and to report as early as possible.

Mr. Brott moved a division of the resolutions.

Mr. Foley moved to lay the resolutions on the table, subject to call.

A motion to lay on the table was lost, and the vote being taken on the resolution, it was adopted.

The motion to divide was lost. The resolution was adopted.

Col. Thorpe offered the following resolution :

Resolved, That a committee of —— members be appointed by the president, to whom all matters shall be referred, brought before this Convention, affecting our relations with the Federal government—the committee to be called the Committee on Federal Resolutions.

Mr. Brott moved to amend by filling the blank with the number five. The amendment was accepted and the resolution adopted.

Mr. Montamat offered the following resolution :

Be it resolved, That the sum of one hundred thousand dollars be, and the same is hereby appropriated out of the general fund, for the purpose of paying the members, officers and employés of this Convention, the mileage and per diem to which they are respectively entitled ; the same to be paid by the treasurer of the State, on the warrant of the President of the Convention.

Mr. Cazabat moved to lay the resolution on the table.

The motion was lost.

A motion to adopt was made, upon which the ayes and nays were called, with the following result :

YEAS — Messrs. Abell, Austin, Baum, Beauvais, Bell, Bennie, Bofill, Buckley, Cook J. K., Cook T., Crozat, Duane, Dufresne, Foley, Gorlinski, Gaidry, Healy, Heard, Henderson, Howes, Mann, Maurer, Mendiverri, Montamat, Montague, Murphy M. W., O'Conner, Poynot, Pursell S., Schroeder, Smith, Spellicy, Stiner, Sullivan, Terry, Waters, Wilson—37.

NAYS—Messrs. Barrett, Bonzano, Bromley, Brott, Burke, Campbell, Cazabat, Davies, Dupaty, Ennis, Fish, Flagg, Flood, Fosdick, Gastinel, Geier, Goldman, Harnan, Hart, Hills, Hire, Howell, Maas, Millspaugh, Morris, Murphy E., Ong, Payne John, Pintado, Purcell John, Seymour, Shaw, Stocker, Stumpf, Stauffer, Thorpe, Thomas—37.

There being a tie, the chair voted nay.

Mr. Cazabat asked for the calling of the roll as a quorum was not voting.

The roll was called and seventy-seven members found present.

The chair directed the roll to be called again, and the vote was as follows :

YEAS—Messrs. Abell, Austin, Baum, Beauvais, Bell, Bennie, Bofill, Buckley, Burke, Cook J. K., Cook Terrance, Crozat, Davies, Duane, Dufresne, Flagg, Foley, Geier, Gorlinski, Gaidry, Healy, Heard, Henderson, Hire, Howes, Maurer, Mendiverri, Millspaugh, Montamat, Montague, Murphy M. W., O'Conner, Poynot, Purcell J., Pursell Sam., Schroeder, Seymour, Smith, Spellicy, Stiner, Sullivan, Terry, Thorpe, Waters, Wilson—45.

NAYS—Messrs. Ariail, Bailey, Barrett, Bromley, Bonzano, Brott, Campbell, Cazabat, Dupaty, Ennis, Fish, Fosdick, Gastinel, Goldman, Harnan, Hart, Hills, Howell, Maas, Mann, Morris, Murphy E., Ong, Payne J., Pintado, Shaw, Stocker, Stumpf, Stauffer, Thomas—30.

And the resolution was adopted.

The following standing committees were announced, having been appointed by the chair, in pursuance of resolutions previously adopted :

EMANCIPATION. — Bonzano, chairman ; Howell, Abell, Edwards, Goldman, Stocker, Cazabat, Bennie, Murphy E., Paine J. T., Schroeder—11.

PREAMBLE—Heard, chairman ; Montague, Sullivan, Cook T., O'Conner, Spellicy, Waters—7.

DISTRIBUTION OF POWERS—Thomas, chairman ; Kugler, Foley, Bofill, Stumpf, Ong, Bromley—7.

LEGISLATIVE DEPARTMENT — Fosdick, chairman ; Thorpe, Stauffer, Cazabat, Hire,

Knobloch, Schnurr, Taliaferro, Wells—9.

EXECUTIVE DEPARTMENT.—Fish, chairman; Austin, Gruneberg, Bromley, Crozat, Davies, Mann—7.

JUDICIARY DEPARTMENT.—Howell, chairman; Heard, Beauvais, Fuller, Henderson, Cutler, Seymour—7.

IMPEACHMENT—Wilson, chairman; Bailey, Gastinel, Morris, Paine J. T., Smith—6.

GENERAL PROVISIONS—Mann, chairman; Cook J. K., Foley, Geier, Maas, Wenck, Buckley—7.

INTERNAL IMPROVEMENTS — Gorlinski, chairman; Ariail, Campbell, Flood, Healy—5.

PUBLIC EDUCATION — Hills, chairman; Howes, Lobdell, Burke, Hart, Murphy M. W., Terry, Wells, Gaidry, Balch, Edwards, Maurer—11.

MODE OF REVISING THE CONSTITUTION.—Cutler, chairman; Knobloch, Baum, Stiner, Harnan—5.

SCHEDULE—Gruneberg, chairman; Dupaty, Shaw, Dufresne, Ennis, Flagg, Gaidry—7.

ORDINANCE—Shaw, chairman; Poynot, Kavanagh, Kugler, Mendiverri—5.

ENROLLMENT—Thorpe, chairman; Brott, Millspaugh, Pintado, Crozat—5.

FINANCE—Brott, chairman; Montamat, Normand, Schnurr, Sullivan—5.

EXPENSES—Pursell S., chairman; Bell, Duane, Newell, Payne J., of Jefferson—5.

PRINTING—Purcell J., chairman; Fuller, Barrett—3.

Mr. Stauffer submitted the following resolution, with the request that it be read and permitted to lie over till to-morrow:

Resolved, That a committee of five members be appointed by the president to wait upon the proper State officers and ascertain if any and what amount of bonds have been issued, and what amount, if any, remain outstanding, which bonds have been issued for the purpose of arming and equipping the State militia against the lawful authority of the United States, and in violation of the constitution and laws of this State.

Mr. Montamat offered the following resolution, the rules being suspended:

Resolved, That the Committee on Enrollment be, and they are hereby authorized to appoint one chief clerk and as many enrolling clerks as may be necessary.

The resolution was adopted.

Mr. Hills moved that when the Convention adjourn, it adjourn till 5 o'clock to-morrow evening.

Mr. Montamat amended till 1 o'clock, Mr. Stauffer till 12, and Mr. Harnan till 7.

On motion all the amendments were laid on the table.

The motion of Mr. Hills was then carried.

Mr. Stocker offered the following resolution:

Resolved, That a committee of five be appointed by the president to inquire into the cause of the absence of Messrs. Wells, of Rapides, and Taliaferro, of Concordia; and also to inquire into the expediency of ordering an election to fill their places.

Mr. Heard moved to amend by adding the name of Mr. Lobdell, of West Baton Rouge.

Mr. Cazabat moved to lay it on the table, which was lost.

The amendment was carried, and the resolution as amended adopted.

The chair appointed Messrs. Stocker, Montague, Ariail, Mann and Heard.

Mr. Gastinel offered the following resolution, which was adopted:

Resolved, That a committee of five members of this body be appointed by the president to wait upon the governor and inform him that the Convention is organized and prepared to receive any communication he may have to make to this body.

The chair appointed Messrs. Gastinel, Shaw, Thomas, Goldman and Bofill.

Col. Thorpe offered the following:

Resolved, That section 54 of the rules of the Convention read as follows: "A quorum shall consist of two-thirds of the members elected and admitted to this Convention."

Which was laid over.

Mr. Howell said that he had been requested by the president to ask the members to remain after the adjournment in order to perfect the organization of the committees.

The Convention then adjourned till to-morrow at 5 o'clock P. M.

Adopted.

JOHN E. NEELIS,
Secretary.

SATURDAY, April 16, 1864.

The Convention met pursuant to adjournment.

In the absence of the president the secretary took the chair and called the Convention to order.

JOURNAL OF THE CONVENTION FOR THE AMENDMENT

Mr. Hills moved that Judge Howell be appointed president pro tem., which motion being unanimously carried,

Judge Howell took the chair and introduced the Rev. Mr. Hopkins, who opened the proceedings with prayer.

On a call of the roll the following members answered to their names :

Messrs. Abell, Ariail, Austin, Bailey, Barrett, Baum, Beauvais, Bell, Bofill, Bonzano, Bromley, Brott, Buckley, Burke, Cazabat, Cook J. K., Cook T., Crozat, Cutler, Davies, Duane, Dufresne, Edwards, Ennis, Fish, Flagg, Flood, Foley, Fosdick, Fuller, Gastinel, Geier, Goldman, Gorlinski, Gaidry, Healy, Hart, Heard, Henderson, Hills, Hire, Howell, Howes, Kavanagh, Knobloch, Maas, Mann, Maurer, Mendiverri, Millspaugh, Montamat, Montague, Morris, Murphy E., Murphy M. W., Newell, Normand, O'Conner, Paine, Pintado, Poynot, Purcell J., Pursell S., Schroeder, Schnurr, Seymour, Shaw, Smith, Spellicy, Stocker, Stumpf, Stiner, Sullivan, Terry, Thorpe, Thomas, Wenck, Wilson—78.

The secretary commenced reading the minutes, when Mr. Montamat moved to dispense with the reading.

Mr. Cazabat moved to lay the motion to dispense with the reading on the table. Lost.

The vote was taken on the motion to dispense with the reading of the journal, and it was lost.

The journal was then read and adopted, without correction.

Mr. Montamat offered the following resolution :

Resolved, That the sum of $100 be paid to the assistant secretary *pro tem.*, for his services before the Convention was organized.

The resolution was unanimously adopted.

Mr. Bell offered a resolution to authorize each committee to appoint as many clerks as they may deem necessary, which was referred to the Committee on Enrollment.

Mr. S. Pursell offered the following resolution :

Be it resolved, That article ninety-six of the constitution of the State of Louisiana be so altered and amended as to read thus : "All civil officers for the State at large shall be voters of and reside in the State, and all district or parish officers shall be voters in and reside within their district or parish, and shall keep their offices in such places therein as may be required by law."

Which resolution, after a motion had been made to refer to the Committee on General Provisions, was laid on the table.

Mr. Montamat offered the following resolution :

Resolved, That Hon. A. A. Atocha, provost judge of the Department of the Gulf, be and is hereby invited to a seat within the bar of this Convention.

Mr. Goldman moved to lay it on the table.

Mr. Montamat demanded the yeas and nays, and the result was—yeas 9, nays 73, as follows :

YEAS—Messrs. Bailey, Bonzano, Bromley, Ennis, Flagg, Goldman, Hills, Maas, Millspaugh—9

NAYS—Messrs. Abell, Ariail, Austin, Barrett, Baum, Beauvias, Bell, Bofill, Brott, Buckley, Burke, Cazabat, Cook J. K., Cook T., Crozat, Cutler, Davies, Duane, Dufresne, Edwards, Fish, Flood, Foley, Fosdick, Fuller, Gastinel, Geier, Gorlinski, Gaidry, Healy, Harnan, Hart. Heard, Henderson, Hire, Howell, Howes, Kavanagh, Knobloch, Kugler, Lobdell, Mann, Maurer, Mendiverri, Montamat, Montague, Morris, Murphy E., Murphy M. W., Newell, Normand, O'Conner, Payne of Jefferson, Poynot, Purcell J., Pursell S., Schroeder, Schnurr, Seymour, Shaw, Smith, Spellicy, Stocker, Stumpf, Stiner, Stauffer, Sullivan, Terry, Thorpe, Thomas, Waters, Wenck, Wilson.

Mr. Thorpe moved to amend by inviting all the judicial officers in the city to seats within the bar.

The amendment was accepted and the resolution was then put upon its passage, upon which a division of the house was called, resulting in—ayes, 68 ; nays, 8. The resolution, as amended, was adopted.

Mr. Brott offered the following :

Resolved, That the attorney general of the State be and is hereby requested to give this Convention his legal opinion as to the right of this body to exercise legislative powers, to appropriate moneys from the public treasury.

On motion of Mr. Henderson, the resolution was laid on the table.

Mr. Gastinel offered the following resolution :

Resolved, That the journal and debates of the Convention be printed by the printer of this Convention in English and French separately, and that each member of the Convention be furnished with three copies of the journals and debates for distribution among his constituents, each member to select copies in either language.

AND REVISION OF THE CONSTITUTION OF LOUISIANA. 31

Mr. Hills moved to amend by striking out the section requiring the publication in the French language.

Mr. Healy moved to lay the amendment on the table. The ayes and nays being called for, the following gentlemen voted:

AYES—Messrs. Abell, Austin, Bailey, Baum, Beauvais, Bell, Bofill, Bonzano, Bromley, Brott, Buckley, Cazabat, Cook J. K., Cook T., Crozat, Cutler, Dufresne, Dupaty, Edwards, Ennis, Fish, Flagg, Foley. Fosdick, Fuller, Gastinel, Goldman, Gorlinski, Gruneberg, Gaidry, Healy, Hart, Heard, Hire, Howes, Maas, Mann, Maurer, Mendiverri, Millspaugh, Montamat, Murphy M. W., Newell, Normand, Pintado, Poynot, Purcell Jno., Schnurr, Seymour, Shaw, Smith, Spellicy, Stocker, Stumpf, Stiner, Sullivan, Terry, Thorpe, Thomas, Wenck—60.

NAYS—Messrs. Ariail, Barrett, Burke, Campbell, Davies, Duane, Flood, Geier, Henderson, Hills, Howell, Montague, Morris, Murphy E., O'Conner, Payne John, Pursell Sam'l, Schroeder, Stauffer, Wilson—20.

Mr. Hills's amendment was laid on the table.

Mr. Goldman then amended by adding the German, which was adopted.

Mr. Stocker offered the following substitute:

Resolved, That the official printer be, and he is hereby authorized to print for the use of the Convention 300 copies of the journal in each of the following languages: English, French, German and Spanish.

Which resolution was lost.

Mr. Terry moved to amend the substitute by adding the word Irish, which was declared by the president to be adopted, when the yeas and nays were called with the following result.

YEAS—Messrs. Campbell, Crozat, Davies, Flagg, Flood, Geier, Healy, Terry and Wenck—9.

NAYS—Messrs. Austin, Bailey, Barrett, Baum, Beauvais, Bell, Bofill, Bonzano, Bromley, Brott, Buckley, Cazabat, Cook J. K., Cook T., Cutler, Dufrense, Duane, Dupaty, Edwards, Ennis, Fish, Foley, Fosdick, Fuller, Gastinel, Gorlinski, Gaidry, Hart, Heard, Henderson, Hills, Hire, Howell, Howes, Maas, Mann, Maurer, Mendiverri, Millspaugh, Montague, Morris, Murphy E., Murphy M. W., Normand, O'Conner, Payne Jno., Poynet, Purcell Jno., Pursell S., Schroder, Schnurr, Seymour, Shaw, Smith, Spellicy, Stocker, Stumpf, Stiner, Stauffer, Sullivan, Thorpe, Thomas, Wilson—63.

Mr. Terry's motion was lost.

A motion was made to strike out all excepting the English and French languages. Mr. Cazabat moved to lay the substitute on the table. Carried.

The original resolution offered by Mr. Gastinel was then put and adopted.

By Mr. Sullivan,

Resolved, That the delegates of foreign birth, who have not produced their naturalization papers, showing to this Convention that they are citizens of the United States, agreeably to resolution passed on Wednesday last. shall produce their naturalization papers immediately, or their seats will be declared vacant in this body.

Mr. Foley moved to amend by saying, "those members who have not produced their naturalization papers, should swear that they were naturalized citizens."

Mr. Healy stated that some of them from the country could not produce their papers, and moved to table the whole, which was carried.

Mr. Bell moved that the secretary read the names of those members of foreign birth who had produced their certificates of naturalization to the president in obedience to the resolution, but after some remarks by several members, the resolution was laid on the table.

Resolution by Mr. S. Pursell:

Be it resolved, That the following be adopted as an article in the constitution of the State of Louisiana:

No profession, occupation, business or calling, requiring a license from any authority within this State, shall be exercised or carried on by any other than citizens of the United States, and those having made their legal declaration of becoming citizens.

The motion was seconded, when Mr. Cazabat moved to table it, and Mr. Thomas to refer it to the Committee on General Provisions, which were seconded.

The president stated he considered these motions out of order, but would put them, if desired. No request to do so was moved.

The following was presented:

Resolved, That the sergeant-at-arms be instructed to procure for the members and secretary of this Convention, five copies of such daily papers as may be selected by them.

The motion was seconded.

Mr. Thomas moved to insert "three" instead of "five," and was seconded. The amendment was then carried, and the original resolution adopted as amended.

Mr. Montamat moved that the Committee on Finance be authorized to appoint a warrant clerk, which motion was carried.

Mr. Seymour presented the following:

Whereas, The resolution adopted on the — instant, requiring the members of this Convention to produce evidence of having taken the oath prescribed by the president in his proclamation of December 8th, 1863, was intended and should be so construed as to apply only to such members, if any, who had not, up to that date, taken the oath of allegiance to the United States, under the previous military orders in this department; be it

Resolved, That the resignation of the Hon. Christian Roselius be set aside, and that he be invited to resume his seat as a member of this Convention.

Resolution was tabled.

Mr. Fosdick moved to adjourn until the 21st, at 12 o'clock, on account of sitting of committees.

Resolution tabled.

Mr. Healy moved to adjourn till Monday, 3 P. M. Seconded.

Mr. Cazabat amended to Monday week at 5 o'clock, which was seconded.

Mr. Sullivan moved to lay the motion and amendment on the table. Carried.

Mr. Hills moved that when the Convention adjourn, they do so until Saturday, 4 o'clock, for reasons previously stated. Lost.

Mr. Terry moved that when the Convention adjourn, it adjourns till Wednesday evening at 5 o'clock, which was carried by a vote of 46 to 26.

The president appointed as the Standing Committee on Federal Relations, Messrs. Howell, Brott, Montague and Henderson.

The chair appointed as the committee to fix the compensation of the officers and employés of the Convention, Messrs. M. W. Murphy, Terry, Mann, Fosdick and Ennis.

Mr. Stocker called up the following, offered on Friday:

Resolved, That the rules and regulations be so amended as to require all ordinances and resolutions to lie over one day (unless referred to some committee) before being acted upon by the Convention.

The resolution was adopted.

Mr. Thomas, chairman of the Committee on the Distribution of Powers, reported that the committee, after due deliberation, had come to the unanimous conclusion that the constitution of 1852 should not be changed in any respect in the title which treats upon the subject of the distribution of powers, and submitted the same to the consideration of the Convention.

Mr. Brott moved to refer the report back to the committee with instructions to incorporate the title reported on in their report.

The motion was carried.

A motion to adjourn was then made and carried, and the chair declared the Convention adjourned till Wednesday next, at 5 o'clock P. M.

Minutes adopted.

JOHN E. NEELIS,
Secretary.

WEDNESDAY, April 20th, 1864.

The Convention met pursuant to adjournment, and was called to order by the president at the hour of five P. M.

The proceedings were opened with prayer by the Rev. Mr. Andrews.

The roll was called by the secretary, and the following gentlemen answered to their names:

Messrs. Abell, Ariail, Austin, Barrett, Bell, Bofill, Bonzano, Bromley, Burke, Cazabat, Cook J. K., Cook T., Crozat, Davies, Dufresne, Duane, Dupaty, Durell, Edwards, Ennis, Foley, Fosdick, Fuller, Gastinel, Geier, Goldman, Gorlinski, Gruneberg, Gaidry, Healy, Harnan, Hart, Heard, Henderson, Hills, Hire, Howell, Howes, Kavanagh, Knobloch, Maas, Mann, Maurer, Mendiverri, Millspaugh, Montague, Morris, Murphy E., Murphy M. W., Newell, Normand, O'Conner, Ong, Payne John, Poynot, Purcell J., Pursell S., Schroeder, Schnurr, Seymour, Shaw, Smith, Spellicy, Stocker, Stumpf, Stiner, Stauffer, Sullivan, Terry, Thorpe, Thomas, Waters, Wenck, Wilson—74.

There being no quorum present, the president directed the sergeant-at-arms to procure the attendance of absent members.

The following gentlemen, Messrs. Balch, Bailey, Baum, Beauvais, Buckley, Brott, Campbell, Fish, Flood and Montamat, having entered the hall and taken their seats, the president announced that a quorum was present.

AND REVISION OF THE CONSTITUTION OF LOUISIANA. 33

The minutes of Saturday, being read and amended, were approved.

Mr. Foley moved a reconsideration of the resolution relative to the publication of the proceedings of this Convention in English and French. The president declared Mr. Foley not in order.

Resolutions now being in order, Mr. Howell offered the following:

Resolved, That hereafter this Convention shall meet at 11 o'clock A. M., and adjourn at 3 o'clock P. M., daily, (Sundays excepted) and the order of the day shall be promptly taken up at the hour of 12 M., each day.

Laid over until to-morrow.

Mr. Smith offered the following:

Resolved, That the Committee on General Provisions be instructed to embody in their report an article or articles, making it obligatory on the first Legislature to convene under the constitution to compel the several parishes, corporations, as well as private citizens, throughout the State, that have issued sight drafts, notes or *shinplasters*, payable in Confederate money, or otherwise, to provide for the redemption of the same in current funds.

Mr. Mendiverri offered the following:

Resolved, That the State auditor furnish this Convention, as soon as practicable, with a statement showing the receipts and expenditures of the State treasury under the administration of General G. F. Shepley, late military governor of the State, as far as the books and records in his possession may show, and expressing each item of receipt and expenditure in detail; also, if any balance was received from the late treasurer, and if so, the amount and the kind and description of funds.

Mr. Wilson moved to lay it on the table, which motion was lost, and the original resolution was adopted.

Mr. Stocker then called attention to his rule adopted at the last meeting, according to which every resolution was to lie over until the following day, unless referred to a special committee.

Mr. Hills offered the following resolution, to lie over until to-morrow:

Resolved, That the secretary be directed to obliterate from the records of this Convention the resolution inviting A. A. Atocha and the judicial officers of this parish to occupy a seat in this Convention.

Mr. Wilson moved to lay on the table. Decided out of order.

Mr. Sullivan offered the following:

Resolved, That a committee consisting of five members be appointed by the president of this Convention for the purpose of corresponding with and requesting the authorities in Washington City for the return, to the State of Louisiana, of Powers's grand statue of Washington, taken from the Capitol building in Baton Rouge by the United States forces, on the occupation of that place by the Federal army, and sent by them as a trophy to adorn the Central Park, New York city, where it is now placed.

The president was unable to determine upon a *viva voce* vote, and upon a rising vote the resolution was adopted by 49 yeas to 23 nays.

Mr. Wenck offered the following, which was seconded:

I move a reconsideration of the vote adopting the resolution requiring the journal and debates of this Convention to be published in the English and French languages, and furnishing each member with three copies thereof.

Mr. Montamat moved to lay it on the table. The vote was taken, resulting as follows: Ayes 42, nays 37.

The question then recurred upon the adoption of Mr. Wenck's motion to reconsider, when the ayes and nays were called. Ayes 40, nays 44, as follows:

YEAS—Messrs. Ariail, Barrett, Bonzano, Brott, Burke, Campbell, Cook J. K., Davies, Duane, Ennis, Flood, Fosdick, Geier, Goldman, Gorlinski, Harnan, Heard, Henderson, Hills, Howell, Howes, Kavanagh, Kugler, Lobdell, Maas, Mann, Montague, Morris, Ong, Payne J., Pintado, Pursell S., Schroeder, Smith, Spellicy, Stocker, Stumpf, Stiner, Stauffer, Sullivan, Wenck, Wilson—40.

NAYS—Messrs. Abell, Austin, Balch, Bailey, Baum, Beauvais, Bell, Bofill, Buckley, Cazabat, Cook T., Crozat, Cutler, Dufresne, Dupaty, Durell, Edwards, Fish, Flagg, Foley, Fuller, Gastinel, Gruneberg, Gaidry, Healy, Hart, Hire, Knobloch, Lobdell, Maurer, Mendiverri, Millspaugh, Montamat, Murphy E., Murphy M. W., Newell, Normand, O'Conner, Pintado, Poynot, Seymour, Shaw, Terry, Thorpe, Thomas—44.

Mr. Gorlinski offered the following resolutions:

Resolved, That the regular hour for the meeting of this Convention, during the remainder of its sittings, shall be 12 o'clock M., and any member not answering to his name when the roll is called, shall forfeit the sum of two dollars, to be deducted from his per diem, and any member who shall be absent from his seat an entire day, shall forfeit his per diem for each day he shall fail to attend, unless absent by permission of the Convention, or for sickness, either in his own person or family, the proof of which shall be a certificate from a regular physician.

Resolved further, That the secretary keep a record of the names of all members not answering at roll call, and the names of all members who shall be absent from their seats an entire day, and for each day so absent, unless they have leave of absence from the Convention; and to make a list of said members at the end of every week, a copy of which shall be furnished the Committee on Finance and a copy to the president of the Convention, who will strictly enforce the penalties as prescribed in the foregoing resolution.

The resolutions were seconded.

Mr. Austin moved the resolution be laid on the table, whereupon Mr. Stocker desired that his resolution of the last day's meeting should be read for the information of the Convention.

The following was then read:

Resolved, That the Rules and Regulations be so amended as to require all orders and resolutions to lie over one day, unless referred to some committee, before being acted upon by the Convention.

Mr. Sullivan's motion to lay it on the table was decided to be out of order.

Mr. Montamat notified the House that he should, at the next sitting, introduce a resolution to amend Article 52 of the Rules and Regulations.

Mr. Gaidry offered the following:

Whereas, All the constitutions ever framed in this State have decreed that all judicial and legislative proceedings should take place in the French and English languages;

And Whereas, Several members of this Convention, who are true republicans and loyal to the core, but are not very familiar with the English language, have been delegated to this convention by constituents who are also unacquainted with the said language—which right to choose delegates as they please said constituents possessed, as they are the sovereign people, and that to deny such supreme right would be tantamount to disfranchise said people;

Resolved, That all resolutions and motions to be presented in this Convention be translated into the French language, so that the members from the several parishes, who are not familiar with the English language, be fully aware of what they are voting upon.

Mr. Cazabat stated that in order to facilitate the progress of business he presented the following:

Whereas, This Convention is assembled for the purpose only of *revising and amending the constitution of Louisiana*, and for no other purpose,

Be it Resolved, That no resolution on any other subject but that above stated, shall be received or entertained by this Convention.

Mr. Wenck offered the following:

Resolved, That the resolution adopted allowing each member of this Convention a compensation of ten dollars a day, be repealed.

M. Harnan called for the reading of Judge Howell's resolution, which was as follows:

Resolved, That the resolution adopted on Friday, 15th April, 1854, in the following words, to-wit: "*Be it resolved,* That the sum of one hundred thousand dollars be and the same is hereby appropriated out of the general fund, for the purpose of paying the members, officers and employés of this Convention, the mileage and per diem to which they are respectively entitled; the same to be paid by the treasurer of the State, on the warrant of the president of the Convention," be and the same is hereby rescinded.

Resolved, first, That the resolution, adopted on Friday, 15th April, 1864, in the following words, to-wit: "*Resolved,* That the members of this Convention shall receive from the public treasury a compensation for their services, which shall be ten dollars per day during their attendance on, going to and returning from the session of this Convention," be and the same is hereby rescinded.

Resolved, second, That the compensation for the services of the members of this Convention shall be the same as allowed to the members of the General Assembly by the constitution adopted in 1852.

Mr. Goldman seconded.

Mr. Montamat remarked that this had already been voted down, and the president informed him it was to lie over till to-morrow.

Mr. Austin reiterated Mr. Montamat's statement, to which the president made the same reply as before.

Mr. Goldman offered the following:

Resolved, That the amendment to publish an official report in the German language is hereby embodied in the original motion to publish in the English and French languages.

The president decided it was out of order.

Mr. Cazabat asked to reconsider the resolution of Mr. Sullivan in relation to the statue of Washington, when that gentleman said he had no objection to the resolution lying over till to-morrow.

Mr. Brott tendered his resignation as a member of the Committee on Enrollment, which was accepted by the Convention, and the president appointed Mr. Mendiverri to supply the vacancy.

The president announced that the report of the committees would be presented in order.

Mr. Bonzano, as chairman of the Committee on Emancipation, stated that they had not yet completed their labor.

Mr. Heard, as chairman of the Committee on Preamble, submitted the following:

To the Honorable the President and Members of the Constitutional Convention :

The committee appointed by the president to prepare a preamble to the constitution which is to be framed by this Convention, beg leave to make the following report:

They have thought it best so adopt the preamble to the constitutions of eighteen hundred and forty-five and fifty-two—which reads as follows: "We, the people of the State of Louisiana, do ordain and establish this constitution," and recommend its adoption.

Respectfully submitted.
H. J. HEARD, *Chairman.*

The report was adopted.

Mr. Thomas, as chairman of the Committee on Distribution of Powers, submitted the following:

Your committee on Distribution of Powers respectfully submit the following report:

That Articles Nos. 1 and 2 of the constitution of 1852 ought not in any manner to be altered or changed, which articles read as follows:

"Art. 1. The powers of the government of the State of Louisiana shall be divided into three distinct departments, and each of them be confided to a separate body of magistracy, to-wit; those which are legislative to one, those which are executive to another, and those which are judicial to another.

"Art. 2. No one of these departments, nor any person holding office in one of them, shall exercise power properly belonging to either of the others, except in the instances hereinafter expressly directed or permitted."

All of which is respectfully submitted.
JOHN W. THOMAS, *Chairman.*

The report was adopted.

Mr. Fosdick, as chairman of the Committee on Legislative Department, reported progress, as did Mr. Fish, chairman of the Committee on Executive Department, and also Mr. Howell, chairman of the Committee on Judicial Department.

Mr. Wilson, as chairman of the Committee on Impeachment, submitted their report, which Mr. Hills moved be referred back to the committee, which motion, being seconded by Mr. Waters, was carried.

Mr. Mann, as chairman of the Committee on General Provisions, reported progress, as did Mr. Gorlinski, chairman of the Committee on Internal Improvements, and also Mr. Hills, chairman of the Committee on Public Education.

Mr. Cutler, chairman of the Committee on Mode of Revising the Constitution, reported progress, as did Mr. Gruneberg, chairman of the Committee on Schedule, and Mr. Shaw, chairman of the Committee on Ordinance.

Mr. Thorpe, chairman of the Committee on Enrollment, stated that the report was in the hands of the president.

Mr. Brott, chairman of the Committee on Finance, reported that the committee had no finances on hand, and had no occasion to draw any warrants.

Mr. S. Pursell, chairman of the Committee on Expenses, and Mr. J. Purcell, chairman of the Committee on Printing, reported progress.

Mr. Wilson moved to adjourn till Monday next, 5 P. M., that the committees might perfect their reports.

The motion was seconded, and Mr. Crozat amended to 12 o'clock, and Mr. Montamat amended to Saturday at 12 o'clock, which was lost.

On motion of Mr. Bell, the Convention then adjourned till 12 o'clock, Thursday, the 21st inst.

Minutes adopted.
JOHN E. NEELIS,
Secretary.

THURSDAY, April 21st, 1864.

The Convention met at 12 o'clock M., pursuant to adjournment, and was called to order by the president.

The proceedings were opened with prayer by the Rev. Mr. Gilbert.

The secretary called the roll, when the

following gentlemen answered to their names:

Messrs. Abell, Ariail, Austin, Balch, Bailey, Barrett, Beauvais, Bell, Bofill, Bonzano, Brott, Buckley, Burke, Campbell, Cazabat, Cook J. K., Cook T., Crozat, Davies, Dufresne, Duane, Edwards, Ennis, Fish, Flagg, Flood, Foley, Fosdick, Geier, Goldman, Gorlinski, Gruneberg, Gaidry, Healy, Harnan, Hart, Heard, Henderson, Hills, Hire, Howell, Howes, Kavanagh, Knobloch, Kugler, Maas, Mann, Maurer, Mendiverri, Millspaugh, Montamat, Montague, Murphy E., Murphy M. W., Newell, Normand, O'Conner, Poynot, Pursell S., Purcell J., Schroeder, Seymour, Shaw, Smith, Spellicy, Stumpf, Stiner, Stauffer, Sullivan, Terry, Thorpe, Thomas, Wenck, Wells, and Mr. President—76.

The president announced that a quorum was present.

The secretary then proceeded to read the minutes of the previous day's proceedings.

On motion of Mr. Stiner, the reading of the names of members was dispensed with

The minutes were adopted.

Mr. Goldman said that, according to the report, his resolution, which was

Resolved, That the amendment to publish an official report in the German language is hereby embodied in the original motion to publish in the English and French languages—

Was decided by the president to be out of order, and wished to know if the chair had a right to declare such a motion out of order when the amendment had been carried, remarking that he did not hear the decision of the chair or he should have appealed at the time, but that under the circumstances he asked permission of the Convention to appeal then.

The president decided that the appeal should have been made at the time of the decision.

Upon Mr. Thomas's statement that he desired to be excused on account of illness, Mr. Sullivan moved his request be granted, which was accordingly done.

Upon Mr. Goldman's asking the chair if his appeal was out of order, he was informed that it was so considered, and the Convention, upon the question being put, sustained the chair.

Mr. Heard presented a letter from his colleague (Mr. Schnurr) asking to be excused from the Convention on account of illness in his family, and no objection being made, that was ordered.

The chair informed the Convention that as there were no petitions or memorials, resolutions were in order and that new ones took precedence.

Mr. Gorlinski presented the following:

Whereas, On the evacuation of Baton Rouge, after the ever-memorable battle of the 5th day of August, 1862, Colonel Payne, of the Fourth Wisconsin volunteers, then commanding the post of Baton Rouge, crowned his heroic deeds of that day by an act which has secured to the use of this Convention and the State, a valuable public library, together with Thorpe's great painting of General Zachary Taylor, and other paintings, which now adorn the hall of this Convention, and also saved Hiram Powers's statue of Washington, which is said now to be in the Patent Office at the national capital—all of which would have been stolen or destroyed by fire, which demolished the State House, had not Colonel Payne caused the same to be removed to this city, when by order of General Butler they were protected as the property of the State; therefore, be it

Resolved, That the thanks of this Convention and of the people of Louisiana are due and are hereby tendered to Major General B. F. Butler and Colonel Payne for saving the above mentioned valuable State property.

Resolved further, That the governor be and is hereby requested to correspond with the authorities at Washington, and make suitable arrangements for the return and reception of the above mentioned statue of Washington and its future disposition in this State.

Mr. Campbell presented the following:

Whereas, The United States bounty paid to soldiers enlisting in the army, cannot be paid to men enlisting in the First and Second regiments of New Orleans volunteers, now being raised under Cols. Kilborn and Brown, because of their being organized for a specific purpose, that of the city defence alone, and wishing to aid in filling the same;

Resolved, That the sum of ——— dollars be and the same is hereby appropriated by the State, to pay a bounty to each man who may hereafter enlist in the First and Second regiments of New Orleans volunteers, and that the governor is hereby authorized to carry the same into effect according to his best judgment.

Mr. Stocker said he considered this a very important resolution, and, in order that all might vote upon it understandingly, moved that it be printed and laid upon the members' desks by the morrow morning.

Motion was seconded but apparently lost on viva voce vote, when a division was called, and it was declared lost—nays 36, yeas 34.

Mr. Hills presented the following:

Resolved, That No. XXXII of the Rules and Regulations of this Convention be so amended as to require members offering resolutions to read the same, or make a statement of their contents from their sents.

Mr. Stocker moved a suspension of the rules in order that the section might be adopted at once.

Motion seconded.

Mr. Stauffer thought the XXXII Rule provided the same, but was informed that it did not, and upon *viva voce* the resolution to dispense with the rules was undecided, whereupon a rising vote was taken and decided in the affirmative—yeas 54, nays 5.

The resolution was then unanimously adopted.

The chairman of the Standing Committee on Emancipation, Legislative Powers, Executive and Judiciary Departments, reported progress.

Mr. Wilson as chairman of the Committee on Impeachment, submitted the following:

To the President and Members of the Convention to " Revise and Amend the Constitution of Louisiana :"

Your committee respectfully submit the following report:

The power of impeachment shall be vested in the House of Representatives.

Impeachments of the governor, lieutenant governor, attorney general, secretary of state, state treasurer, and of the judges of the inferior courts, justices of the peace excepted, shall be held by the Senate; the chief justice of the Supreme Court, or the senior judge thereof, shall preside during the trial of such impeachment. Impeachments of the judges of the Supreme Court shall be tried by the Senate. When sitting as a Court of Impeachment, the Senators shall be upon oath or affirmation, and no person shall be convicted without the concurrence of two-thirds of the Senators present.

Judgments in cases of impeachments shall extend only to removal from office, and disqualification from holding any office of honor, trust, or profit under the State; but the convicted parties shall, nevertheless, be subject to indictment, trial, and punishment according to law.

All officers against whom articles of impeachment may be preferred, shall be suspended from the exercise of their functions during the pendency of such impeachment; the appointing power may make a provisional appointment to replace any suspended officer until the decision of the impeachment.

The Legislature shall provide by law for the trial, punishment and removal from office of all other officers of the State by indictment or otherwise.

JOS. H. WILSON, *Chairman*.
A. J. BAILEY,
CHARLES SMITH,
L. GASTINEL,
ROBT. MORRIS.

The report was unanimously adopted on motion of Mr. Stocker.

Mr. Foley's motion, to print two hundred copies of the report for the members, was lost.

Messrs. Mann, Gorlinski, Hills, Cutler, Gruneberg and Shaw, as chairmen of Committees on General Provisions, Internal Improvements, Public Education, Mode of Revising the Constitution, Schedule and Ordinance, reported progress.

Messrs. Brott, S. Pursell and J. Purcell, chairmen of Committee on Finance, Expenses and Printing, announced that they had no reports to make.

Mr. Thorpe, as chairman, said the Committee on Federal Relations would report in the morning.

Mr. Gastinel submitted the following report of the Select Committee:

On behalf of the committee appointed to wait upon his excellency the governor, and inform him that the Convention was organized, and to inquire whether he had any communication to make to this body, I beg leave to report:

That the committee waited upon his excellency, who in substance replied that he did not consider that it would be becoming, nor within his province to transmit a message, or make suggestions, or recommendations to the Convention, but that he would stand ready at any time to afford all facilities and information that may be required by this body from the Executive Department.

The committee having done their duty, beg leave to be discharged.

L. GASTINEL, *Chairman*.

Upon Mr. Foley's motion the report was adopted.

Mr. M. W. Murphy, chairman of the Special Committee on fixing the compensation of the officers and employés of the

JOURNAL OF THE CONVENTION FOR THE REVISION

Convention, presented the following report:

Mr. President—Your committee on fixing the compensation of officers and employés of the Convention, make the following report:

John E. Neelis, secretary	$14 per day.
Thomas H. Murphy, assistant secretary	10 ..
S. G. Hamilton, assistant secretary	10 ..
Michael DeCoursey, sergeant-at-arms	10 ..
Two assistant sergeants-at-arms, each	5 ..
Two messengers, each	5 ..
One postmaster	5 ..
One doorkeeper	5 ..
One reporter and three assistants, each	6 ..
One warrant clerk	6 ..
Enrolling clerks, each	6 ..

In relation to the compensation of the printer of the Convention, your committee ask for further time to report.

The mileage of all members from the country parishes, twenty cents per mile, going and coming.

All compensation to officers and employés shall commence from the day of their election or appointment.

(Signed) M. W. MURPHY, Chairman.
GEO. A. FOSDICK,
J. RANDALL TERRY,
W. D. MANN.

On motion of Messrs. Wilson and Heard, the report was referred back to the committee.

Mr. Stauffer arose to a point of order, and called for a report from the Select Committee appointed at the commencement of the session to investigate matters in regard to an assault upon some of the members of the Convention.

Mr. Wilson, as chairman of said committee, stated that a report would soon be made.

Resolutions laid over until this session were announced as next in order, which the members were requested to call for in course.

Mr. Howell's resolution was first read:

Resolved, That hereafter this Convention shall meet at 11 o'clock A. M., and adjourn at three o'clock P. M., daily, (Sundays excepted); and the order of the day shall be promptly taken up at the hour of 12 M. each day.

Mr. Stauffer moved as an amendment "at 10 o'clock," and to strike out "adjourn at 3 o'clock."

Motion seconded.

Mr. Wilson offered a substitute "to meet permanently at 5 o'clock."

Seconded but laid on the table.

After some further discussion, the resolution was amended "to 12 o'clock," and the hour of order of the day having been amended "to 1 o'clock," the resolution was adopted.

The following (Mr. Cazabat's) resolution was read and laid on the table:

Whereas, This Convention is assembled for the purpose only of *revising and amending the Constitution of Louisiana*, and for no other purpose;

Be it Resolved, That no resolution on any other subject but that above stated, shall be received or entertained by this Convention.

Mr. Sullivan's resolution:

Resolved, That a committee, consisting of five members, be appointed by the president of this Convention for the purpose of corresponding with and requesting the authorities in Washington City for the return, to the State of Louisiana, of Powers's grand statue of Washington, taken from the Capitol building in Baton Rouge by the United States forces on the occupation of that place by the Federal army, and sent by them to the Patent Office at Washington, where it is now placed.

Mr. Gorlinski offered a substitute for this resolution, but the president decided that it was not in order.

The resolution was then put to vote, a division being called for, resulting ayes 53, nays 21.

The resolution was adopted.

The president appointed on this committee Messrs. Sullivan, Stiner, Burke, Ennis and Waters.

Mr. Smith's resolution was then taken up and read, as follows:

Resolved, That the Committee on General Provisions be instructed to embody in their report an article or articles, making it obligatory on the first Legislature to convene under the constitution to compel the several parishes, corporations, as well as private citizens throughout the State, that have issued sight drafts, notes or *shinplasters*, payable in Confederate money, or otherwise, to provide for the redemption of the same in current funds.

Mr. Cazabat moved to lay the resolution on the table, which was seconded, but lost.

Mr. Cutler moved to refer the resolution to the Committee on General Provisions.

AND AMENDMENT OF THE CONSTITUTION OF LOUISIANA. 39

Before the question was put, Mr. Stocker called for the reading of the resolution a second time.

The motion to refer was lost.

The question on the adoption of the resolution was then put, and a division being called for was lost by a vote of 48 nays to 13 yeas.

Mr. Howell called for his resolutions, and the following were read:

Resolved, That the resolution adopted on Friday, 15th April, 1864, in the following words, to-wit:

"*Be it resolved,* That the sum of one hundred thousand dollars be and the same is hereby appropriated out of the general fund, for the purpose of paying the members officers, and employés of this Convention, the mileage and per diem to which they are respectively entitled; the same to be paid by the treasurer of the State, on the warrant of the president of the Convention," be and the same is hereby rescinded.

Resolved, first, That the resolution, adopted on Friday, 15th April, 1864, in the following words, to-wit: "*Resolved,* That the members of this Convention shall receive from the public treasury a compensation for their services, which shall be ten dollars per day during their attendance on, going to, and returning from the sessions of this Convention," be and the same is hereby rescinded.

Resolved second, That the compensation for the services of the members of this Convention shall be the same as allowed to the members of the General Assembly by the constitution adopted in 1852.

On motion of Mr. Sullivan, the resolution was laid on the table.

Mr. Gorlinski called for the following:

Resolved, That the regular hour for the meeting of this Convention, during the remainder of its sittings, shall be 12 o'clock M., and any member not answering to his name, when the roll is called, shall forfeit the sum of two dollars, to be deducted from his *per diem,* and any member who shall be absent from his seat an entire day, shall forfeit his *per diem* for each day he shall fail to attend, unless absent by permission of the Convention, or for sickness, either in his own person or family, the proof of which shall be a certificate from a regular physician.

Resolved, further, That the secretary keep a record of the names of all members not answering at roll-call, and the names of all members who shall be absent from their seats an entire day, and for each day so absent, unless they have leave of absence from the Convention; and to make a list of said members at the end of every week, a copy of which shall be furnished the Committee on Finance and a copy to the president of the Convention, who will strictly enforce the penalties as prescribed in the foregoing resolution.

The resolutions were laid on the table.

Mr. Cazabat called the attention of the Convention to the fact that the resolution of Mr. Mendiverri, in regard to the statement showing the receipts and expenditures of the State treasury under the administration of Gen. G. F. Shepley, late military governor of the State, was adopted against the rule requiring all orders and resolutions to lie over one day before being acted upon by the Convention.

He therefore moved a reconsideration of the vote by which that resolution was adopted.

Mr. Cazabat having stated, in answer to a question by the president, that he voted against the resolution, he was declared out of order.

The president stated that he believed the resolution was properly adopted.

On motion of Mr. Shaw, the Convention adjourned until 12 o'clock M. on Friday, the 22d inst.

Approved.

JOHN E. NEELIS,
Secretary.

FRIDAY, April 22, 1864.

At 12 o'clock M., the Convention was called to order by the president, and after prayer by the Rev. Mr. Jones, the secretary called the roll and the following gentlemen answered to their names:

Messrs. Abell, Ariail, Balch, Barrett, Baum, Bell, Bofill, Bonzano, Buckley, Burke, Campbell, Cazabat, Cook J. K., Crozat, Cutler, Davies, Dufresne, Duane, Duke, Edwards, Ennis, Fish, Flagg, Flood, Foley, Fosdick, Fuller, Geier, Goldman, Gorlinski, Gruneberg, Gaidry, Healy, Harnan, Hart, Heard, Henderson, Hills, Hire, Howell, Howes, Kavanagh, Knobloch, Kugler, Maas, Mann, Maurer, Mendiverri, Millspaugh, Montamat, Montague, Morris, Murphy E., Murphy M. W., Newell, Normand, O'Conner, Payne J., Poynot, Purcell J., Pursell S., Schroeder, Seymour, Shaw, Smith, Spellicy, Stocker, Stumpf, Stiner, Stauffer, Sullivan, Terry, Wenck, Wells, Wilson, and Mr. President—76.

A quorum being present, the minutes of

the preceding day were read, and the reading of the names of members, resolutions, the order of the day, and reports of committees, being dispensed with, the minutes were adopted.

Mr. Terry presented the following resolution to lie over:

Resolved, That no person is eligible for State or municipal office who has not the qualifications required in a voter for members of this Convention; and if there are any persons holding office under the State or municipal authorities not so qualified, they shall be promptly removed.

Mr. Gorlinski offered the following, which was also laid over:

Resolved, That the following be adopted as an additional standing rule of this Convention:

Rule 56.—It shall be in order for any member to propose, without previous notice, any amendment or substitute for an original proposition, which may be under consideration, provided the same does not conflict with Rule 25.

Mr. Abell offered the following:

Resolved, That the report of the several Committees on Amendments be printed and required to lie over at least two days.

Resolution seconded.

The rules were, upon Mr. Montamat's motion, suspended, and it was immediately adopted.

Messrs. Bonzano and Fosdick, chairmen of Committees on Emancipation and Legislative Department, reported progress.

Mr. Fish, chairman of Committee on Executive Department, announced that there was no report.

Mr. Howell, chairman of Committee on Judiciary Department, reported progress.

Mr. Foley, at the request of Mr. Mann, chairman of Committee on General Provisions, read the following:

Mr. President—Your Committee upon General Provisions begs leave to make the following report:

Article 1. Members of the General Assembly and all officers, before they enter upon the duties of their offices, shall take the following oath or affirmation:

"I (A B) do solemnly swear (or affirm) that I will support the constitution and laws of the United States and of this State, and that I will faithfully and impartially discharge and perform all the duties incumbent on me as ———, according to the best of my abilities and understanding, so help me God!"

Art. 2. Treason against the State shall consist only in levying war against it, or in adhering to its enemies, giving them aid and comfort. No person shall be convicted of treason unless on the testimony of two witnesses to the same overt act, or his own confession in open court.

Art. 3. The Legislature shall have power to declare the punishment of treason; but no attainder of treason shall work corruption of blood or forfeiture, except during the life of the person attainted.

Art. 4. Every person shall be disqualified from holding any office of trust or profit in this State, and shall be excluded from the right of suffrage, who shall have been convicted of treason, perjury, forgery, bribery, or other crimes or misdemeanors.

Art. 5. All penalties shall be proportioned to the nature of the offence.

Art. 6. The privilege of free suffrage shall be supported by laws regulating elections, and prohibiting, under adequate penalties, all undue influence thereon from power, bribery, tumult, or other improper practice.

Art. 7. No money shall be drawn from the treasury but in pursuance of specific appropriation made by law, nor shall any appropriation of money be made for a longer term than two years. A regular statement and account of the receipts and expenditures of all moneys shall be published annually, in such a manner as shall be prescribed by law.

Art. 8. It shall be the duty of the General Assembly to pass such laws as may be proper and necessary to decide differences of arbitration.

Art. 9. All civil officers for the State at large shall reside within the State, and all district or parish officers within their districts or parishes, and shall keep their offices at such places therein as may be required by law.

Art. 10. All civil officers, except the governor and judges of the Supreme and Inferior Courts, shall be removable by an address of two-thirds of the members of both Houses, except those the removal of whom has been otherwise provided for by this constitution.

Art. 11. In all elections by the people, the vote shall be taken by ballot, and in all elections by the Senate and House of Representatives, jointly or separately, the vote shall be given *viva voce*.

Art. 12. No member of Congress, nor person holding or exercising any office of trust or profit under the United States, or either of them, or any foreign power, shall be eligible as a member of the General Assembly, or hold or exercise any office of trust or profit under the State.

Art. 13. None but citizens of the United States shall be appointed to any office of trust or profit, or be employed on the *public works* in this State, providing the same be paid from the public funds, except the compensation is less than nine hundred dollars ($900) per annum.

Art. 14. The laws, public records, and the judicial and legislative written proceedings of the State, shall be promulgated, preserved and conducted in the language in which the constitution of the United States is written.

Art. 15. That no power of suspending the laws shall be exercised, unless by authority of the Legislature.

Art. 16. Prosecutions shall be by indictment or information. The accused shall have a speedy public trial, by an impartial jury of the parish in which the offence shall have been committed. He shall not be compelled to give evidence against himself; he shall have the right of being heard, by himself or counsel; he shall have the right of meeting the witnesses face to face, and shall have compulsory process for obtaining witnesses in his favor; he shall not be twice put in jeopardy for the same offence.

Art. 17. All persons shall be bailable by sufficient sureties, unless for capital offences, where the proof is evident, or the presumption great, and the privilege of the writ of *habeas corpus* shall not be suspended, unless when in cases of rebellion or invasion the public safety may require it.

Art. 18. Excessive bail shall not be required; excessive fines shall not be imposed; nor cruel and unusual punishments inflicted.

Art. 19. The right of the people to be secure in their persons, houses, papers and effects, against unreasonable searches and seizures, shall not be violated, and no warrants shall issue but upon probable cause, supported by oath or affirmation, and particularly describing the place to be searched and the persons or things to be seized.

Art. 20. No *ex post facto* law, nor any law impairing the obligations of contracts, shall be passed, nor vested rights be divested, unless for purposes of public utility, and for adequate compensation previously made.

Art. 21. That all courts shall be open, and any person, for any injury done him, in his lands, goods, person or reputation, shall have remedy by due course of law, and right and justice administered without denial or unreasonable delay.

Art. 22. The press shall be free. Every citizen may freely speak, write and publish his sentiments on all subjects, being responsible for an abuse of this liberty.

Art. 23. The Legislature shall have power to grant aid to companies or associations of individuals, formed for the exclusive purpose of making works of internal improvement, wholly or partially within the State, to the extent only of one-fifth of the capital of such companies, by subscription of stock or loan in money or public bonds; but any aid thus granted shall be paid to the company only in the same proportion as the remainder of the capital shall be actually paid in by the stockholders of the company; and, in case of loan, such adequate security shall be required as to the Legislature may seem proper. No corporation or individual association receiving the aid of the State, as herein provided, shall possess banking or discounting obligations.

Art. 24. No liability shall be contracted by the State, as above mentioned, unless the same be authorized by some law for some single object or work, to be distinctly specified therein, which shall be passed by a majority of the members elected to both Houses of the General Assembly, and the aggregate amount of debts and liabilities incurred under this and the preceding article shall never, at any one time, exceed eight millions of dollars.

Art. 25. Whenever the Legislature shall contract a debt exceeding in amount the sum of one hundred thousand dollars, unless in case of war, to repel invasion or suppress insurrection, they shall, in the law creating the debt, provide adequate ways and means for the payment of the current interest and of the principal when the same shall become due. And the said law shall be irrepealable until the principal and interest are fully paid and discharged, or unless the repealing law contains some other adequate provision for the payment of the principal and interest of the debt.

Art. 26. The Legislature shall provide by law for all change of venue in civil and criminal cases.

Art. 27. No lottery shall be authorized by this State, and the buying and selling of lottery tickets within the State is prohibited.

Art. 28. No divorce shall be granted by the Legislature.

Art 29. Every law enacted by the Legislature shall embrace but one object, and that shall be expressed in the title.

Art. 30. No law shall be revived or amended by reference to its title; but in such case the act revived, or section amended, shall be re-enacted and published at length.

Art. 31. The Legislature shall never adopt any system or code of laws by general reference to such system or code of laws, but in all cases shall specify the several provisions of the law it may enact.

Art. 32. Corporations, with discounting privileges, may be either created by special acts or framed under general laws. But no corporation or individual shall have the privilege of issuing notes or bills except those which are already chartered.

Art. 33. In case of the insolvency of any

bank or banking association, the bill holders thereof shall be entitled to preference in payment over all other creditors of such bank or association.

Art. 34. No person shall hold or exercise, at the same time, more than one civil office of trust or profit, except that of justice of the peace.

Art. 35. Taxation shall be equal and uniform throughout the State. All property on which taxes may be levied in this State, shall be taxed in proportion to its value, to be ascertained as directed by law. No one species of property shall be taxed higher than another species of property of equal value, on which taxes shall be levied. The Legislature shall have power to levy an income tax, and to tax all persons pursuing any occupation, trade or profession.

Art. 36. The citizens of the city of New Orleans shall have the right of appointing the several public officers necessary for the administration of police of the said city, pursuant to the mode of election which shall be prescribed by the Legislature; Provided, That the mayor and recorders shall be ineligible to a seat in the General Assembly, and the mayor and recorders shall be commissioned by the governor as justices of the peace, and the Legislature may vest in them such criminal jurisdiction as may be necessary for the punishment of minor crimes and offences.

Art. 37. The Legislature may provide by law in what case officers shall continue to perform the duties of their offices until their successors shall have been inducted into office.

Art. 38. The Legislature shall have power to extend this constitution and the jurisdiction of this State over any territory acquired by compact with any State, or with the United States, the same being done by consent of the United States.

Art. 39. None of the lands granted by Congress to the State of Louisiana for aiding in constructing the necessary levees and drains, to reclaim the swamp and overflowed lands in the State, shall be diverted from the purposes for which they were granted.

Art. 40. The Legislature shall pass no law excluding citizens of this State from office for not being conversant with any language except that in which the constitution of the United States is written.

Respectfully submitted,
W. D. MANN, Chairman.
ERNEST WENCK,
JOHN FOLEY,
J. K. COOK,
JOHN BUCKLEY, JR.,
GEO. GEIER,
H. MAAS.

Mr. Narnan moved the report of the committee be adopted, and made the special order of the day for Thursday next.

Motion seconded and carried, the resolution of Mr. Abell in regard to lying over being in the meantime read for the benefit of the Convention.

Mr. Hills, chairman of the Committee on Public Education, read their report.

To the president and members of the Convention for the revision and amendment of the Constitution of Louisiana:

The undersigned, members of the Committee on Public Education, have the honor to submit the following

REPORT.

Article —. There shall be elected a superintendent of Public Education, who shall hold his office for the term of two years. His duties shall be prescribed by law, and he shall receive such compensation as the Legislature may direct; Provided, That the General Assembly shall have power, by a vote of the majority of the members elected to both Houses, to abolish the said office of superintendent of Public Education whenever, in their opinion, said office shall be no longer necessary.

Art. —. The General Assembly shall establish free public schools throughout the State for all children, and shall provide for their support by general taxation on property, or otherwise; and all moneys so raised or provided, shall be distributed to each parish in proportion to the number of children between such ages as shall be fixed by the General Assembly; but all schools for colored children shall be separate and distinct from schools for white children.

Art. —. In order to promote the more extensive diffusion of knowledge, the General Assembly shall make annual appropriation for the encouragement of private schools throughout the State, but the General Assembly shall not be required to make such appropriation for private schools in the parish of Orleans that do not number two hundred pupils, and in other parishes the General Assembly shall determine what private schools are sufficiently large to deserve such appropriations.

Art. —. The English language only shall be taught in the common schools in this State.

Art. —. An university shall be established in the city of New Orleans. It shall be composed of four faculties, to-wit: one of law, one of medicine, one of the natural sciences and one of letters. The Legislature shall provide by law for its organization, but shall be under no obligation to contribute to the establishment or support of said university by appropriations.

ART. —. The proceeds of all lands heretofore granted by the United States to this State for the use or support of schools, and

AND AMENDMENT OF THE CONSTITUTION OF LOUISIANA. 43

of all lands which may hereafter be granted or bequeathed for any other purpose, which hereafter may be disposed of by the State, and the proceeds of the estates of deceased persons to which the State may become entitled by law, shall be held by the State as a loan, and shall be and remain a perpetual fund on which the State shall pay an annual interest of six per cent., which interest together with the interest of the Trust Funds, deposited with this State by the United States, under the act of Congress approved June 23, 1836, and all the rents of the unsold lands shall be appropriated to the support of such schools, and this appropriation shall remain inviolable.

Art. —. All moneys arising from the sales which have been, or may hereafter be made of any lands heretofore granted by the United States to this State for the use of a seminary of learning, and from any kind of donation that may hereafter be made for that purpose, shall be and remain a perpetual fund, the interest of which, at six per cent. per annum, shall be appropriated to the support of a seminary of learning for the promotion of literature, and the arts and sciences, and no law shall ever be made diverting said fund to any other use than to the establishment and improvement of said seminary of learning, and the General Assembly shall have power to raise funds for the organization and support of said seminary of learning in such manner as it may deem proper.

ALFRED C. HILLS, Chairman.
M. W. MURPHY,
X. MAURER,
RANDALL TERRY,
T. M. WELLS,
GEORGE HOWES.

Edward Hart signs the above, intending to offer an amendment to the third clause.

H. C. Edwards signs, dissenting entirely from third clause in said report.

I coincide with Mr. Edwards.
YOUNG BURKE.

Mr. Montamat moved it be the special order of the day for Tuesday next.

Mr. Hart, of the Committee on Education, gave notice that he should offer the following amendment:

In order to promote the more extensive diffusion of knowledge, it shall be the duty of the General Assembly to make annual appropriations for the encouragement of all private schools throughout the State, which are, or may hereafter be, incorporated by legislative enactments.

Mr. Balch stated that, though a member of the committee, he was, through indisposition, unable to attend its meeting, and moved that the consideration of the report should be postponed until Saturday, 30th inst., as he intended to discuss several provisions.

Motion seconded and carried.

Mr. Stocker said he thought he rose in time to object to the adoption of the amendment, as he understood that amendments must be offered at the same time with the report, but was informed that Mr. Hart's amendment was in fact a minority report.

Mr. Cutler, chairman of Committee on Mode of Revising the Constitution, reported progress.

No report of Committee on Schedule.

Mr. Shaw, chairman of Committee on Ordinances, reported progress. The same was stated of the Committee on Enrollment.

The Committee on Finance had no report to make, nor had the Committee on Printing.

The Committee on Expenses, through their chairman, Mr. S. Pursell, reported progress.

The Committee on Federal Relations had agreed upon no report.

Mr. Howell, as chairman of Committee on the Judiciary Department, submitted the following:

To the president and members of the Convention to revise and amend the Constitution of the State of Louisiana:

The Committee of Judiciary Department beg leave to report the following articles, and recommend their adoption as a portion of the constitution of this State on the subject of Judiciary, to-wit:

TITLE IV—JUDICIARY DEPARTMENT.

Article 1. The Judiciary power shall be vested in a Supreme Court, in such inferior courts as the Legislature may, from time to time, order and establish, and in justices of the peace.

Art. 2. The Supreme Court, except in cases hereinafter provided, shall have appellate jurisdiction only; which jurisdiction shall extend to all cases when the matter in dispute shall exceed three hundred dollars; to all cases in which the constitutionality or legality of any tax, toll or impost whatsoever, or of any fine, forfeiture or penalty imposed by a municipal corporation, shall be in contestation; and to all criminal cases on questions of law alone whenever the offence charged is punishable with death or imprisonment at hard labor, or when a fine exceeding three hundred dollars is actually imposed.

Art. 3. The Supreme Court shall be composed of one chief justice and four associate justices, a majority of whom shall constitute a quorum. The chief justice shall receive a salary of ten thousand dollars, and each of the associate justices a salary of nine thousand dollars, annually, until otherwise provided by law. The court shall appoint its own clerks.

Art. 4. The Supreme Court shall hold its sessions in New Orleans from the first Monday of the month of November to the end of the month of June inclusive. The Legislature shall have power to fix the sessions elsewhere during the rest of the year; until otherwise provided, the session shall be held as heretofore.

Art. 5. The Supreme Court and each of the judges thereof shall have power to issue writs of *habeas corpus*, at the instance of all persons in actual custody under process, in all cases in which they may have appellate jurisdiction.

Art. 6. No judgment shall be rendered by the Supreme Court without the concurrence of a majority of the judges comprising the court. Whenever the majority cannot agree, in consequence of the recusation of any member or members of the court, the judges not recused shall have power to call upon any judge or judges of the inferior courts, whose duty it shall be, when so called upon, to sit in the place of the judge or judges recused, and to aid in determining the case.

Art. 7. All judges, by virtue of their office, shall be conservators of the peace throughout the State. The style of all process shall be "the State of Louisiana." All prosecutions shall be carried on in the name and by the authority of the State of Louisiana, and conclude against the peace and dignity of the same.

Art. 8. The judges of all courts within the State shall, as often as it may be possible so to do, in every definitive judgment refer to the particular law in virtue of which such judgment may be rendered, and in all cases adduce the reasons on which their judgment is founded.

Art. 9. The judges of all courts shall be liable to impeachment; but for any reasonable cause, which shall not be sufficient ground for impeachment, the governor shall remove any of them, on the address of three-fourths of the members present of each House of the General Assembly. In every such case the cause or causes for which such removal may be required shall be stated at length in the address, and inserted in the journal of each House.

Art. 10. The judges, both of the Supreme and Inferior Courts shall, at stated times, receive a salary which shall not be diminished during their continuance in office; and they are prohibited from receiving any fees of office, or other compensation than their salaries for any civil duties performed by them.

Art. 11. The judges, both of the Supreme and Inferior Courts, shall be appointed by the governor by and with the advice and consent of the Senate, and they shall hold their offices during good behavior.

Art. 12. The clerks of the Superior Courts shall be appointed by the judges thereof, and they shall hold their offices during good behavior, subject to removal by the judges respectively, with the right of appeal in all such cases to the Supreme Court.

Art. 13. The Legislature shall have power to vest in clerks of courts authority—to grant such orders and do such acts as may be deemed necessary for the furtherance of the administration of justice, and in all cases the power thus granted shall be specified and determined.

Art. 14. The jurisdiction of justices of the peace shall not exceed, in civil cases, the sum of one hundred dollars, exclusive of interest, subject to appeal in such cases as shall be provided for by law. They shall be appointed by the governor, with the advice and consent of the Senate, and shall hold their offices during good behavior. They shall have such criminal jurisdiction as shall be provided by law.

Art. 15. There shall be an attorney general for the State, and as many district attorneys as may be hereafter found necessary. They shall be appointed by the governor, with the advice and consent of the Senate, and shall hold their offices during the term for which the governor shall have been elected. Their duties shall be determined by law.

Art. 16. A sheriff and a coroner shall be appointed in each parish, by the governor, with the advice and consent of the Senate, and they shall hold their offices for the term for which the governor shall have been elected, unless sooner removed. The Legislature shall have power to increase the number of sheriffs in any parish.

All of which is respectfully submitted.

R. K. HOWELL, Chairman.
H. J. HEARD,
R. KING CUTLER,
JOHN HENDERSON, JR.,
R. BEAUVAIS,
WM. H. SEYMOUR,
JAMES FULLER.

Mr. Harnan's motion that it be made the order of the day for Friday, the 29th, was carried.

Mr. Sullivan offered an amendment, but, not being a member of the committee, was informed that he could do so only when the matter came up for discussion.

Messrs. Montamat and Wilson, as chair-

AND AMENDMENT OF THE CONSTITUTION OF LOUISIANA. 45

men of Committees on Credentials and Assault of Members, reported progress.

Mr. Stocker, as chairman of Committee in Relation to Absent Members, stated that they had diligently tried to make a report, but had not received such information as would justify them in reporting.

Mr. M. W. Murphy, as chairman of Committee on Compensation, presented the following, viz :

Mr. President—Your committee, appointed to fix the compensation of the officers and employés of this Convention, beg leave to present the following, viz :

President of the Convention. $20 per day.
John E. Neelis, secretary.... 15 ..
S. G. Hamilton, assistant secretary.................. 10 ..
Thomas H. Murphy, assistant secretary.............. 10 ..
M. DeCoursey, sergeant-at-arms................... 15 ..
Two assistant sergeants-at-arms..................... 6 ..
Two messengers, each...... 5 ..
One postmaster............ 8 ..
One doorkeeper............ 8 ..
Chief reporter............. 12 ..
Three assistant reporters, each 10 ..
One warrant clerk......... 10 ..
Enrolling clerks, each...... 6 ..

The mileage of each member from the country parishes, twenty cents per mile, going and coming.

All compensation to officers and employés shall commence from the date of their election or appointment.

All of which is respectfully submitted.
M. W. MURPHY, Chairman.
W. D. MANN,
J. RANDALL TERRY,
JAMES ENNIS.

Mr. Fosdick presented the following minority report :

To the president and members of the Convention :

The undersigned, one of the committee appointed to fix the compensation of the officers and employés of the Convention, begs leave to submit the following report that they shall receive as follows :

Secretary................$15 per day.
Assistant secretaries, each.... 10 ..
Sergeant-at-arms............ 10 ..
Two Assistant sergeants-at-arms, each............... 6 ..
Two messengers, each....... 3 ..
One postmaster............. 5 ..
One door-keeper............ 5 ..
One reporter............... 8 ..
Three assistant reporters, each................... 8 ..
One warrant clerk.......... $6 per day.
Enrolling clerk, each........ 6 ..
Translating clerks, each...... 8 ..

The mileage of each member from the country parishes, 20 cents per mile, coming from and returning to——. All compensation to officers and employés to commence from the date of their election or appointment.

All of which is respectfully submitted.
GEORGE A. FOSDICK.

Mr. Hills moved to make it the special order of Saturday, the 23d inst. Seconded.

Mr. Bell rose to a point of order in regard to reports lying over two days, and was informed by the chair that that resolution referred only to reports of standing committees.

M. Hills's motion having been seconded was carried.

Mr. Edwards's resolution to print 200 copies of the Judiciary Report, was decided out of order.

Communications were read from the secretary of state announcing the election of new members Messrs. Duke and Collins, from Ascension.

On motion of Mr. Gastinel, the communications were referred to the Committee on Credentials.

Unfinished business was next in order.

The following (Mr. Gorlinski's resolution) was read :

Whereas, On the evacuation of Baton Rouge, after the ever-memorable battle of the 5th day of August, 1862, Colonel Payne, of the Fourth Wisconsin volunteers, then commanding the post of Baton Rouge, crowned his heroic deeds of that day by an act which has secured to the use of this Convention and the State, a valuable public library, together with Thorpe's great painting of General Zachary Taylor, and other paintings, which now adorn the hall of this Convention, and also saved Hiram Powers's statue of Washington, which is said now to be in the Patent Office at the national Capitol—all of which would have been stolen, or destroyed by fire which demolished the State House, had not Colonel Payne caused the same to be removed to this city, when, by order of General Butler, they were protected as the property of the State ; therefore, be it

Resolved, That the thanks of this Convention and of the people of Louisiana are due and are hereby tendered to Major General B. F. Butler and Colonel Payne for saving the above mentioned valuable State property.

Resolved, further, That the governor be and is hereby requested to correspond with the authorities at Washington, and make suitable arrangements for the return and reception of the above mentioned statue of Washington and its future disposition in this State.

Resolution seconded, as was Mr. Sullivan's motion to lay on the table, which prevailed.

Mr. Goldman's call for the yeas and nays was not responded to.

Mr. Campbell's resolution was ordered to be read by the chair:

Whereas, The United States bounty paid to soldiers enlisting in the army, cannot be paid to men enlisting in the First and Second regiments of New Orleans volunteers, now being raised under Cols. Killborn and Brown, because of their being organized for a specific purpose—that of the city defence alone—and wishing to aid in filling the same,

Resolved, That the sum of —— dollars be and the same is hereby appropriated by the State, to pay a bounty to each man who may hereafter enlist in the First and Second regiments of New Orleans volunteers, and that the governor is hereby authorized to carry the same into effect according to his best judgment.

Mr. Montamat moved to refer it to the next Legislature.

A motion to lay it on the table was carried.

Mr. Harnan's motion to adjourn was lost.

Mr. Schroeder offered the following, to lie over until to-morrow.

Resolved, That the resolution adopted on Friday, April 15, 1864, in the following words, to-wit:

Resolved, That the members of the Convention shall receive from the public treasury a compensation for their services, which shall be ten dollars per diem, during their attendance on, going to and returning from the sessions of this Convention, be and the same is hereby rescinded.

Resolved, That the compensation for the services of the members of this Convention shall be referred to a special committee.

Mr. Stocker remarked that a resolution to the same effect was offered and acted upon yesterday, and wished to know if this was properly presented, to which the president replied that the Convention could pass a resolution one day and rescind it the next; but that in any event, it would probably administer a proper rebuke to any member who unnecessarily delayed business.

Upon motion of Mr. Kavanagh, the Convention adjourned until 12 o'clock Saturday, the 23d inst.

Approved April 23d, 1864.

JOHN E. NEELIS,
Secretary.

SATURDAY, April 23, 1864.

The Convention met at 12 o'clock, M., pursuant to adjournment, and after prayer by the Rev. Mr. Thomas, the secretary called the roll and the following gentlemen answered to their names, :

Messrs. Abell, Ariail, Austin, Balch, Bailey, Barrett, Beauvais, Bell, Bofill, Bonzano, Buckley, Burke, Campbell, Cazabat, Collin, Cook J. K., Cook T., Davies, Duane, Dufresne, Duke, Dupaty, Edwards, Ennis, Fish, Flagg, Flood, Foley, Fosdick, Fuller, Gastinel, Geier, Goldman, Gorlinski, Gruneberg, Gaidry, Healy, Harnan, Hart, Heard, Henderson, Hills, Howes, Kavanagh, Knobloch, Kugler, Maas, Mann, Maurer, Mendiverri, Millspaugh, Montamat, Morris, Murphy E., Murphy M. W., Newell, Normand, O'Conner, Payne J., Pintado, Poynot, Purcell J., Pursell S., Schroeder, Seymour, Shaw, Smith, Spellicy, Stumpf, Stiner, Stauffer, Terry, Thomas, Thorpe, Wells, Wilson—76 members present.

A quorum being present the secretary then proceeded to the minutes of the preceding day.

Mr. Hills moved that the reading of resolutions and reports of committees in the minutes be dispensed with, unless the minutes were amended and adopted.

Mr. S. Pursell offered the following, hoping it would not be disposed of in a summary manner, but be considered on its merits:

Resolved, That the following be offered as a substitute for Art. 35 of the report of the Committee on General Provisions, and that it be made the order of the day and taken up with said report:

Art. —. Taxation shall be equal and uniform throughout the State. All property shall be taxed in proportion to its value, to be ascertained as directed by law. The General Assembly shall have power to exempt from taxation property actually used for church, school or charitable purposes. The General Assembly shall levy an income tax upon all persons pursuing any profession, occupation, trade or calling, and all such persons shall obtain a license as provided by law. All tax on income shall be *pro rata* an the amount of income or business done.

AND AMENDMENT OF THE CONSTITUTION OF LOUISIANA. 47

Declared out of order.

Mr. Austin offered the following:

Resolved, That the report of the committee appointed to fix the compensation of the officers and employés of this Convention be and is hereby amended so as to make the compensation of enrolling clerks eight dollars per day, and that the officers and employés be entitled to their compensation from the first day's sitting of this Convention.

Mr. Hills moved a suspension of the rules to adopt the following:

Resolved, That in reading the minutes of this Convention the secretary shall dispense with the reading of all roll-calls, giving simply the results, all resolutions that lie over under the rules, and all that were laid on the table, and all printed reports, unless otherwise directed by the Convention.

A motion to suspend the rules in order to adopt the resolution was carried, and the resolution adopted immediately thereafter upon Mr. Hills's motion.

Mr. Abell offered the following:

Resolved, That when a report of a standing committee is taken up it shall be considered section by section (*seriatim*) and that no section shall be finally adopted until it has undergone three readings on separate days.

Mr. Fuller presented the following:

Resolved, That one day's notice shall be given of any amendment or substitute to be proposed to the report of any of the standing committees.

Mr. Foley offered a resolution:

Resolved, That the secretary be directed to cause the various reports of the committees of the Convention to be printed in such form as will admit of amendments therein; and that the secretary be directed to cause the same to be printed without delay by the printer of this Convention.

Mr. Foley moved to suspend the rules in order to adopt the resolution immediately.

Motion carried, and resolution unanimously adopted thereupon.

Reports of standing committees were called up.

No report of Emancipation Committee.

Mr. Fosdick, as member of Committee on Legislative Department, reported progress, as did the Executive Department Committee.

Mr. Cutler, as chairman of Committee on Mode of Revising the Constitution, submitted the following:

To the president and members of the State Constitutional Convention:

Your committee, to whom was referred the "mode of revising the consitution," beg leave to submit the following report, and recommend the adoption of the following instead of article 141 of the constitution of 1852:

Art.— Any amendment or amendments to this constitution may be proposed in the Senate or House of Representatives, and if the same shall be agreed to by two-thirds of the members elected to each house, such proposed amendment or amendments shall be entered on their journals with the yeas and nays taken thereon. Such proposed amendment or amendments shall be submitted to the people at an election to be ordered by said Legislature, and held within ninety days after the adjournment of the same, and after thirty days' publications according to law; and if a majority of the voters at said election shall approve and ratify such amendment or amendments, the same shall become a part of the constitution. If more than one amendment be submitted at a time, they shall be submitted in such manner and form that the people may vote for or against each amendment separately.

Respectfully submitted.
   R. King Cutler, Chairman.
   E. A. Knobloch,
   Jos. G. Baum,
   J. H. Stiner,
   Patrick Harnan.

The motion that the report be received, 200 copies printed, and be made the order of the day for May 3, was amended by Mr. Hills to Tuesday next, and carried as amended.

Messrs. Gruneberg and Shaw, as chairmen of Committees on Schedule and Ordinance, reported progress.

No report was offered from either the Committee on Enrollment or that on Finance.

Mr. S. Pursell, charman of Committee on Expenses; reported progress, as did Mr. J. Purcell, chairman of Committee on Printing.

No report was received from the Committe on Federal Relations.

Neither the Special Committee or the Committee on Credentials made any report.

The Committee on Assault of Members reported progress.

Mr. Stocker, chairman of Committee in relation to Absent Members, stated that the committee were not then prepared to make such a report as would be satisfactory.

The secretary read a communication from the secretary of state, in relation to Mr. T. J. Decker, returned from the parish of Plaquemines.

On motion of Mr. Hills, the matter was referred to the Committee on Credentials.

Unfinished business was next in order.

Mr. Terry called for the reading of the following:

Resolved, That no person is eligible for State or municipal office who has not the qualifications required in a voter for members of this Convention; and if there are any persons holding office under the State or municipal authorities not so qualified, they shall be promptly removed.

The motion to lay upon the table was seconded, but negatived by a rising vote of 7 to 37.

The yeas and nays were then called with the following result:

YEAS—Messrs. Ariail, Austin, Cutler, Flagg, Henderson, Maas, Mann, Newell, Payne J., Seymour, Wells—11.

NAYS—Messrs. Abell, Bailey, Baum, Barrett, Beauvais, Bell, Bofill, Burke, Campbell, Cazabat, Cook J. K., Cook T., Crozat, Davies, Dufresne, Duane, Dupaty, Edwards, Flood, Foley, Fosdick, Gastinel, Geier, Gorlinski, Goldman, Gruneberg, Gaidry, Healy, Harnan, Hart, Hills, Hire, Howell, Howes, Kavanagh, Knobloch, Kugler, Maurer, Mendiverri, Millspaugh, Montamat, Montague, Morris, Murphy E., Murphy M. W., Normand, O'Conner, Ong, Pintado, Poynot, Purcell J., Pursell S., Schroeder, Shaw, Spellicy, Stocker, Stumpf, Stiner, Stauffer, Sullivan, Terry, Thorpe, Thomas, Wenck, Wilson, Collin, Duke—68.

After a lengthy discussion, in which several members participated, the question was put on the adoption of the original resolution. The yeas and nays being called for, the vote was taken, with the following result:

YEAS—Messrs. Bailey, Baum, Campbell, Flagg, Flood, Foley, Fosdick, Gastinel, Harnan, Healy, Hills, Howes, Murphy E., Murphy M. W., Sullivan, Terry, Thorpe, Wilson—18.

NAYS—Messrs. Abell, Ariail, Austin, Barrett, Balch, Beauvais, Bell, Bofill, Buckley, Burke, Cazabat, Cook J. K., Cook T., Collin, Crozat, Cutler, Davies, Dufresne, Duane, Dupaty, Duke, Edwards, Ennis, Fish, Fuller, Gaidry, Geier, Goldman, Gorlinski, Gruneberg, Hart, Heard, Henderson, Hire, Howell, Kavanagh, Knobloch, Kugler, Maas, Mann, Maurer, Mendiverri, Millspaugh, Montamat, Montague, Morris, Newell, Normand, O'Conner, Ong, Payne J., Pintado, Poynot, Purcell J., Pursell S., Schroeder, Seymour, Shaw, Smith, Spellicy, Stocker, Stumpf, Stiner, Stauffer, Thomas, Wenck, Wells—68.

Resolution was accordingly lost.

It being 1 o'clock P. M., Mr. Stocker called for the order of the day. Mr. Montamat called for the resolution of Mr. Gaidry. Mr. Stocker submitted to the president the question whether his motion should not take precedence.

The president decided that Mr. Gaidry's resolution was "unfinished business," and as such must take precedence.

Mr. Montamat called for the reading of Mr. Gaidry's resolution, which was the following:

Whereas, All the constitutions ever framed in this State have decreed that all judicial and legislative proceedings should take place in the French and English languages;

And whereas, Several members of this Convention, who are true republicans and loyal to the core, but are not very familiar with the English language, have been delegated to this Convention by constituents who are also unacquainted with the said language—which right to choose delegates as they pleased said constituents possessed, as they are the sovereign people, and that to deny such supreme right would be tantamount to disfranchise said people;

Resolved, That all resolutions and motions to be presented in this Convention be translated into the French language, so that the members from the several parishes, who are not familiar with the English language, be fully aware of what they are voting upon.

Mr. Henderson's motion to lay on the table was carried.

The special order of the day, viz: the report of the Special Committee on Compensation of Officers and Employés of the Convention, was then taken up.

Mr. Hills moved to strike out that part of the report fixing the compensation of the president, which was seconded by Mr. Goldman.

Mr. Montamat amended to fifteen dollars.

Mr. Goldman moved to table.

Mr. Terry amended, "subject to call."

Rejected, and motion carried.

Mr. Henderson moved to lay Mr. Hills's motion on the table, and that gentleman called for the yeas and nays, when the following was the result:

YEAS—Messrs. Abell, Austin, Barrett,

AND AMENDMENT OF THE CONSTITUTION OF LOUISIANA. 49

Beauvais, Bell, Burke, Campbell, Cook T., Crozat, Cutler, Ennis, Fish, Fuller, Geier, Goldman, Heard, Henderson, Kugler, Maas, Mann, Maurer, Mendiverri, Montamat, Murphy M. W., O'Conner, Payne J., Purcell J., Shaw, Stocker, Stumpf, Stiner, Sullivan, Terry, Thorpe, Thomas—36.

NAYS—Messrs. Ariail, Bailey, Baum, Balch, Bofill, Buckley, Cook J. K., Collin, Davies, Duane, Dupaty, Duke, Edwards, Flagg, Flood, Foley, Fosdick, Gaidry, Gastinel, Gorlinski, Gruneberg, Healy, Harnan, Hart, Hills, Hire, Howell, Howes, Kavanagh, Knobloch, Millspaugh, Morris, Montague, Murphy E., Newell, Normand, Ong, Pintado, Poynot, Schroeder, Seymour, Smith, Spellicy, Stauffer, Wenck, Wells—46.

Motion to lay on the table lost.

On the vote being taken to strike out, a division was called for, with the result of 39 yeas to 31 nays.

Mr. Stocker called for the yeas and nays on the roll.

They were called with the following result:

YEAS—Messrs. Ariail, Bailey, Baum, Beauvais, Bofill, Buckley, Burke, Campbell, Cook J. K., Collin, Duane, Dufresne, Duke, Flagg, Fosdick, Foley, Gastinel, Gaidry, Goldman, Gruneberg, Harnan, Hart, Hills, Howell, Howes, Kavanagh, Maas, Maurer, Mendiverri, Millspaugh, Morris E., Newell, Normand, Ong, Pintado, Poynot, Pursell S., Seymour, Smith, Stumpf, Stauffer, Sullivan, Wenck, Wells—46.

NAYS—Messrs. Abell, Austin, Barrett, Bell, Cazabat, Cook T., Crozat, Cutler, Davies, Dupaty, Edwards, Ennis, Fish, Flood, Fuller, Geier, Gorlinski, Healy, Heard, Henderson, Hire, Knobloch, Kugler, Mann, Montamat, Montague, Murphy M. W., O'Conner, Spellicy, Stocker, Stiner, Terry, Thorpe, Thomas, Wilson—34.

Motion to strike out carried.

COMPENSATION OF SECRETARY.

Mr. Montague moved to increase to twenty. Seconded.

Mr. Montamat's motion to table it was carried.

Report was adopted.

ASSISTANT SECRETARIES' COMPENSATION.

Mr. Stocker's amendment to twelve-and-a-half was lost, and the report adopted in regard to compensation of both secretaries.

REPORT ON SERGEANT-AT-ARMS.

Mr. Fosdick's amendment to ten dollars a day was, upon Mr. Henderson's motion, tabled, and the report adopted.

Assistant sergeants-at-arms' compensation was taken up.

Mr. Healy's amendment to ten dollars a day was, upon Mr. Montamat's motion, tabled, by a rising vote of 51 yeas to 26 nays.

The same disposition of Mr. Foley's amendment to eight dollars a day, upon motion of the same party, was made.

The report was then adopted.

MESSENGER'S COMPENSATION.

Mr. Fosdick's amendment to three dollars was, upon Mr. Henderson's motion, tabled, as was Mr. Healy's amendment to six dollars, upon Mr. Goldman's motion.

Report adopted.

POSTMASTER'S COMPENSATION.

Mr. Fosdick's amendment to five dollars a day was tabled and report adopted.

BOOK-KEEPER'S COMPENSATION.

Report adopted.

CHIEF REPORTER'S COMPENSATION.

Mr. Stocker's amendment to fifteen dollars a day adopted, and then the report as amended.

ASSISTANT REPORTERS' COMPENSATION.

Report adopted.

WARRANT CLERK'S COMPENSATION.

Report adopted.

The report on compensation of enrolling clerks and mileage was adopted.

M. Stocker moved that the compensation of officers commence on the 6th April. Carried.

The entire report, as amended, was then adopted.

Mr. Montamat moved that translating clerks be employed at a salary of $10 per day. Lost.

The report, as amended, reads as follows:

John E. Neelis, secretary...... $15 00 ..
Assistant secretaries........... 10 00 ..
Sergeant-at-arms............... 15 00 ..
Assistant sergeants-at-arms..... 6 00 ..
Two messengers, each......... 5 00 ..
Postmaster.................... 8 00 ..
Doorkeeper.................... 8 00 ..
Chief reporter................. 15 00 ..
Three assistant reporters, each.. 10 00 ..
Warrant clerk .... 10 00 ..
Enrolling clerks, each......... 6 00 ..

On motion of Mr. Montague, the Convention adjourned until Monday at 12 o'clock M.

Approved.

JOHN E. NEELIS,
Secretary.

MONDAY, April 25th, 1864.

The Convention met pursuant to adjournment, at 12 o'clock M., Hon. E. H. Durell presiding, and after prayer by the Rev. Mr. Hopkins, the secretary called the roll, and the following gentlemen answered to their names:

Messrs. Abell, Ariail, Austin, Bailey, Barrett, Baum, Bennie, Bofill, Bonzano, Bromley, Burke, Campbell, Cook T., Crozat, Cutler, Duke, Davies, Dufresne, Duane, Edwards, Ennis, Fish, Flagg, Flood, Foley, Fosdick, Fuller, Gastinel, Geier, Goldman, Gorlinski, Gruneberg, Gaidry, Healy, Harnan, Hart, Heard, Henderson, Hills, Hire, Howell, Howes, Kavanagh, Knobloch, Kugler, Maas, Mann, Maurer, Millspaugh, Montamat, Murphy E., Murphy M. W., Newell, Normand, O'Conner, Ong, Payne J., Pintado, Poynot, Purcell J., Pursell S., Schroeder, Seymour, Shaw, Smith, Spellicy, Stocker, Stumpf, Stiner, Stauffer, Sullivan, Terry, Thorpe, Thomas, Wells, Wilson and Mr. President—78, members present.

The secretary then proceeded to read the minutes of last day's proceedings which, after being corrected, were adopted.

Mr. Goldman rose to a question of privilege, but was ruled out of order. He then moved to adjourn till to-morrow, to go into committee of whole to wait on Admiral Farragut, to-morrow being the anniversary of the recapture of New Orleans by the Federal troops.

On motion of Mr. Montamat it was laid on the table.

There being no petitions or memorials, resolutions were declared in order.

Mr. Crozat wished to consider his vote taken on the amendment of Mr. Hills, in regard to the compensation of the president of the Convention.

Mr. Montamat seconded.

Mr. Foley amended to reconsider the vote on the whole resolution to strike out the compensation of the president. Seconded.

Mr. Goldman's motion to lay it on the table was declared lost, and a division called for, with the following result: nays 63, yeas 5.

The motion to reconsider was then put and carried.

Mr. Montamat moved the adoption of the report as presented.

Mr. Goldman moved to lay it on the table. Lost.

The motion to adopt the report was then put, and a divisoin called for.

Mr. Hills called for the yeas and nays, and the secretary read the roll with the following result:

YEAS—Messrs. Abell, Austin, Bailey, Barrett, Beauvais, Bell, Bennis, Bofill, Burke, Cazabat, Cook T., Crozat, Cutler, Davies, Duane, Dupaty, Ennis, Fish, Fuller, Gaidry, Heard, Henderson, Hire, Kugler, Maas, Mann, Maurer, Mendiverri, Montamat, Montague, Murphy M. W., O'Conner, Payne J., Pintado, Purcell J., Pursell S., Shaw, Smith, Stocker, Stiner, Terry, Thorpe, Thomas, Wilson—44.

NAYS—Messrs. Ariail, Baum, Bonzano, Bromley, Collin, Campbell, Cook J. K., Duke, Dufresne, Edwards, Flagg, Flood, Foley, Fosdick, Gastinel, Geier, Goldman, Gorlinski, Gruneberg, Healy, Harnan, Hart, Hills, Howes, Kavanagh, Knobloch, Millspaugh, Murphy E., Normand, Ong, Poynot, Schroeder, Seymour, Spellicy, Stumpf, Stauffer, Sullivan, Wells—38.

The report was adopted.

Mr. Kavanagh offered the following resolution:

Resolved, That the officers of the Police Department on duty at this hall shall receive the sum of four dollars per day for their services rendered as such.

Mr. Foley moved the rules be suspended for its adoption. Carried.

Mr. Thomas moved that they be allowed the same pay that they had received from the city.

Mr. Foley moved to lay it on the table. Carried.

Mr. Foley then moved the adoption of the original resolution, and it was carried by a vote of 46 yeas to 27 nays.

REPORTS OF STANDING COMMITTEES.

Chairman of Committee on Emancipation had no report.

Chairman of Committee on Legislative Department reported progress.

Mr. Fish, chairman of Committee on Executive Department, stated the committee had agreed to adopt the third article as it stood, without amendment.

Mr. Foley called for the reading of the article.

Mr. Goldman asked to be excused from the Convention on the ground that it was a holiday, and was requested by the chair to take his seat until the report was offered.

AND AMENDMENT OF THE CONSTITUTION OF LOUISIANA. 51

Mr. Fish then read the article in question.
Mr. J. Purcell moved the report be received.
Mr. Fosdick moved that the committee be requested to make their report in writing. Carried.
The chairman of Committee on Internal Improvement reported "progress."
The chairman of Committee on Schedule reported "progress."
The chairman of Committee on Ordinance reported "progress."
The Committee on Federal Relations submitted the following report:

To the president and members of the State Constitutional Convention:

The chairman of the committee entitled "Federal Relations," beg leave to submit the following report:
The constitution and laws of the United States shall be the supreme law of the land, anything in the constitution or laws of this State to the contrary notwithstanding.
(Signed)   T. B. THORPE, Chairman,
JOHN HENDERSON, JR.,
R. V. MONTAGUE.

REPORTS OF SPECIAL COMMITTEES.

Mr. Montamat, chairman of Committee on Credentials submitted the following report:

NEW ORLAENS, April 15, 1864.

To the honorable the president and members of the Constitutional Convention:

Gentlemen—Your Committee on Credentials, having examined the returns of the elections from the parish of Plaquemines for one delegate to represent the said parish in the Convention, respectfully beg leave to report that Mr. Thomas J. Decker was duly elected, and he being duly qualified is entitled to a seat in this Convention.
Respectfully submitted.
JOHN T. MONTAGUE, *Chairman.*

Col. T. B. Thorpe, on behalf of the Committee on Enrollment, reports as duly elected the following gentlemen:
Messrs. Felix Lambert, chief clerk; Léon Laugrin, Elzear Cambray, translators.
Mr. Wilson moved the names be added to the report of the Committee on Compensation.
Mr. Hills amended to add the names to the roll of the employés of the Convention. Carried.
Mr. Maurer moved the compensation be referred to the Finance Committee, which
Mr. Hills amended to the Committee on Compensation. Carried.
Chairman of Committee on Expenses reported rapid progress.
Chairman of Committee on Printing had no report.
Chairman of Committee on Assault of Members stated they would be able to report to-morrow.
Chairman of Committee on Absent Members said they were not yet prepared to report.
Chairman of Committee on Statue of Washington had no report.

UNFINISHED BUSINESS.

Unfinished business was then declared in order.
Mr. Thomas called for the resolution offered by Mr. Fuller on Saturday, and it was read by the secretary.
Resolved, That one day's notice shall be given of any amendment or substitute to be proposed to the report of any of the standing committees.
Mr. Foley's motion to lay it on the table was seconded and carried, when a division was called for, and the resolution laid on the table by a vote of 49 yeas to 26 nays.
Mr. Abell's resolution was read.
Resolved, That when a report of a standing committee is taken up, it shall be considered section by section (*seriatim*), and that no section shall be finally adopted until it has undergone three readings on separate days.
Mr. Montamat moved its adoption, which was seconded and carried.
On motion of Mr. Kavanagh the Convention adjourned until 12 o'clock to-morrow.
Approved.
JOHN E. NEELIS,
Secretary.

TUESDAY, April 26th, 1864.
At 12 o'clock M. the Convention was called to order by the president, and after prayer by the Rev. Dr. Newman the secretary called the roll, and the following gentlemen answered to their names:
Messrs. Abell, Ariail, Austin, Balch, Bailey, Barrett, Beauvais, Bell, Bonzano, Bromley, Brott, Buckley, Burke, Cazabat, Cook T., Collin, Crozat, Davies, Decker, Dupaty, Dufresne, Duane, Duke, Edwards, Ennis, Fish, Flagg, Flood, Foley, Fosdick, Gasti-

nel, Gaidry, Geier, Goldman, Gorlinski, Gruneberg, Harnan, Hart, Healy, Heard, Henderson, Hills, Hire, Kavanagh, Knobloch, Kugler, Maas, Maurer, Mendiverri, Millspaugh, Montamat, Montague, Murphy E., Murphy M. W., Newell, Normand, Ong, O'Conner, Payne J., Pintado, Poynot, Purcell J., Pursell S., Schroeder, Seymour, Shaw, Smith, Spellicy, Stumpf, Stiner, Stauffer. Sullivan, Thomas, Wenck, Wells, Wilson—76 members present.

The secretary proceeded to read the minutes of yesterday's proceedings, which were amended and approved.

Mr. Edwards offered the following:

Whereas, Positive information has been received by members of this Convention that all kinds of depredations are daily committed in the parish of Avoyelles and other Western portions of Louisiana, within the Federal lines, by guerrillas and other bands of disorganized men; that there is neither safety nor protection for the life and property of loyal citizens, who are driven away from their homes and families on account of their devotion to the sacred cause of the Union and liberty; that no respect is shown by those bands of guerrillas to either age, sex or condition; therefore, be it

Resolved, That the attention of the adjutant general of this State be called to the actual deplorable condition of affairs in the parish of Avoyelles, in order that proper and necessary means be put in force for the protection and safety of loyal citizens from the guerrillas' raids or attacks from the enemy.

Be it further resolved, That a committee of three be appointed by the president of this Convention to wait on the adjutant general of this State, and furnish him the necessary information in regard to this matter.

Mr. Cazabat moved a suspension of the rules, in order to put the resolution on its passage. Carried.

Mr. Hills's motion to lay the resolution on the table was carried.

Mr. Hills submitted the following:

Resolved, That the members of this Convention, not absent with leave, who do not answer to the first roll-call of the secretary, shall forfeit one-half their per diem allowance for every day of such absence.

A motion to suspend the rules for its adoption was lost, and the resolution was laid over until to-morrow.

REPORTS OF COMMITTEES.

Mr. Fish, chairman of the Committee on the Executive Department, submitted a report.

On motion of Mr. Austin, the reading of the report was dispensed with, the same having been read to the Convention on yesterday.

On motion of Mr. Sullivan the report was received, and made the order of the day for Monday, 2d day of May next.

Mr. Wilson, chairman of Special Committee on the Assault of Members, submitted their report, with the details of the evidence before them.

Mr. Duane moved the testimony of accused be stricken out. Lost.

Mr. Montamat moved to lay the report on the table. Lost.

Mr. Gastinel moved to lay the motion over to await the decision of the courts. Lost.

Mr. Hills moved that a committee of three be appointed to take the matter into consideration. Lost.

Mr. Brott moved that the report be recommitted to the original committee, which motion was amended on motion of Mr. Foley, by adding the name of Thorpe to that committee.

The motion, as amended, was carried.

THE ORDER OF THE DAY, TO-WIT:

The report of the Committee on Mode of Revising the Constitution was then taken up, and passed its first reading.

Mr. Hills moved to adopt the report.

The president decided that the motion was not in order, as the report must lay over under the rules.

Mr. Heard moved to suspend the rules, in order to a second and third reading, with a view to its adoption, upon which motion the vote was taken, and a division being called for, the vote resulted: ayes 28, nays 42, and the motion was lost.

Mr. Montamat moved to adjourn, but withdrew for the following resolution presented by Mr. Wells:

Whereas, It is right and proper that sufficient time be allowed for the calm consideration of the perplexing and important questions now before this Convention, and in order to give ample opportunity and further time for the country parishes to send their delegates, by which the State at large may be more fully represented and heard;

Be it Resolved, That this Convention adjourns on Saturday, the 30th inst., until the 1st June, 1864, at 12 o'clock M., or until such time as called by order of the president of this Convention.

Mr. Montamat's motion to adjourn was lost upon division called. Yeas 29, nays 42.

Mr. Cazabat moved to suspend the rules for the purpose of taking action on Mr. Wells's resolution. Lost.

Mr. M. W. Murphy presented the following:

Resolved, That the compensation of chief clerk of the Bureau of Enrollment be fixed at $12 per day, and two translating clerks, each $10 per day.

Mr. S. Pursell gave notice that he would offer substitutes for the first five articles of the Report of the Committee on Education, which substitutes were then read by him.

Mr. Stocker moved that the substitutes be printed for the use of the Convention. Carried.

Several motions to adjourn to stated periods were made and lost.

On motion of Mr. Hills, the Convention then adjourned to 12 o'clock to-morrow.

Minutes adopted.

JOHN E. NEELIS,
Secretary.

WEDNESDAY, April 27th, 1864.

The Convention was called to order at 12 o'clock M., and after prayer by the Rev. Mr. Deossy, of the U. S. Christian Commission, the secretary called the roll and the following gentlemen answered to their names:

Messrs. Abell, Ariail, Balch, Barrett, Bell, Bofill, Bonzano, Buckley, Burke, Campbell, Cazabat, Cook J. K., Cook T., Crozat, Collin, Davies, Dufresne, Decker, Dupaty, Edwards, Ennis, Fish, Flagg, Foley, Fosdick, Geier, Goldman, Gorlinski, Gruneberg, Gaidry, Healy, Harnan, Hart, Heard, Hills, Kavanagh, Kugler, Maas, Maurer, Millspaugh, Murphy E., Murphy M. W., Newell, Normand, O'Conner, Ong, Payne J., Pintado, Poynot, Purcell J., Seymour, Shaw, Smith, Spellicy, Stumpf, Stiner, Sullivan, Wells, and Mr. President—59.

There being no quorum present the president directed the sergeant-at-arms to procure the attendance of absent members.

Messrs. Austin, Bromley, Brott, Gastinel, Hire, Howell, Knobloch, Mendiverri, Montamat, Montague, Morris, Pursell S., Schroeder, Stocker, Stauffer, Wilson and Beauvais, having entered the hall and taken their seats, the president announced that a quorum was present.

The minutes of yesterday's proceedings were then read by the secretary, amended and adopted.

Mr. Bonzano presented a memorial from A. Vallas, Ph. D., late acting superintendent and professor of the State Seminary of Louisiana, on the subject of education.

After reading the memorial, Mr. Bonzano moved that it be referred to the Committee on Education, and that it be printed for the use of the Convention, which motion was carried.

Mr. Bonzano, as chairman of the Committee on Emancipation, then presented a report, which was accepted, and made the order of the day for Wednesday, 4th day of May next.

Mr. Abell, also of the Committee on Emancipation, submitted a minority report.

Mr. Hills moved that it be received and made the special order of the day for Monday next.

Mr. Stauffer moved to amend Mr. Hills's motion by making it the order of the day for Wednesday next, 4th May, and the motion as amended was carried.

Mr. Sullivan offered substitutes for nine articles of the report of the Judiciary Committee.

On motion of Mr. Wilson the substitutes were received and ordered to be printed.

On motion of Mr. Stocker the substitutes were made the order of the day for Friday, 29th inst.

Mr. Brott, chairman of the Committee on Finance, submitted a report, which was adopted.

The report of the Committee on Federal Relations was called up and passed its second reading.

Mr. Brott asked leave to bring in a minority report on to-morrow. Granted.

Mr. Thorpe, chairman of the Committee on Enrollment, reported as correctly enrolled the following resolutions:

Resolution allowing one hundred dollars to H. A. Gallup, for services as assistant secretary before the organization of this Convention.

Resolution requesting the state librarian

to furnish each member with a copy of the Revised Statutes.

Resolution fixing the compensation of the members of the Convention, and also appointing a committee of five to fix the salary of the officers and employés of this Convention.

Resolution inviting the governor to issue his proclamation to fill a vacancy for a delegate from the Tenth Representative District.

On motion of Mr. Montamat, the report was received and the president requested to sign the enrolled resolution referred to therein.

Mr. S. Pursell offered the following substitute to the report of the Committee on Federal Relations:

The United States of America is one government. The several States auxiliary thereto, with local powers.

Mr. Wilson moved to lay it on the table. Lost.

On motion of Mr. Shaw, the substitute was referred to Committee on Federal Relations.

Mr. Cazabat offered a substitute for the report of the Committee on Preamble.

On motion it was referred to the Committee on Preamble.

Mr. Hills then called up his resolution of the day previous, relative to the attendance of members.

Mr. Montamat moved to lay it on the table, when the yeas and nays were called for and the vote taken, with the following result:

AYES—Messrs. Austin, Balch, Baum, Beauvais, Bofill, Bromley, Buckley, Burke, Campbell, Crozat, Cutler, Davies, Dufresne, Dupaty, Decker, Edwards, Fish, Gastinel, Gruneberg, Harnan, Heard, Hire, Kavanagh, Knobloch, Kugler, Mendiverri, Montamat, Morris, Murphy M. W., Newell, Normand, O'Conner, Ong, Payne J., Pintado, Purcell J., Pursell S., Seymour, Stocker, Sullivan, Thorpe—41

NAYS—Messrs. Abell, Ariail, Barrett, Bell, Bonzano, Brott, Cazabat, Cook J. K., Cook T., Collin, Ennis, Foley, Fosdick, Goldman, Gorlinski, Gaidry, Healy, Hart, Hills, Howell, Maas, Maurer, Millspaugh, Montague, Murphy E., Poynot, Schroeder, Shaw, Smith, Spellicy, Stumpf, Stiner, Stauffer, Thomas, Wenck, Wells, Wilson—37.

The resolution was, therefore, laid on the table.

Mr. M. W. Murphy then called up his resolution relative to the compensation of enrolling clerks and translators. On motion it was referred to the Committee on Compensation.

The order of the day was then taken up, to-wit: The second reading of the report of the Committee on the Mode of Revising the Constitution.

Mr. Howell moved to amend third line of article —, by striking out the words "two-thirds," and substituting the words "three-fourths."

A motion to lay the amendment on the table was lost; yeas 17, nays 41.

A motion to reconsider the vote just taken was carried.

Mr. Thorpe then offered the following resolution:

Resolved, That the final vote upon the section providing for the revising or amending the constitution lie upon the table after all articles preceding it in order be adopted.

Messrs. S. Pursell and Cazabat moved to suspend the rules in order to the adoption of the resolution, but the chair decided that the question then in order, was upon the adoption of Mr. Howell's amendment, which was then put and the amendment was lost.

The rules were then suspended, and Mr. Thorpe's resolution was taken up and adopted.

The Convention then adjourned until tomorrow at 12 o'clock M.

Minutes adopted.

JOHN E. NEELIS,
Secretary.

THURSDAY, April 28, 1864.

Pursuant to ajournment the Convention met, a 12 o'clock M., and was called to order by the president and, after prayer by the Rev. Mr. Strong, the roll was called by the secretary and the following gentlemen answered to their names:

Messrs. Abell, Ariail, Austin, Balch, Bailey, Barrett, Baum, Beauvais, Bell, Bennie, Bofill, Bonzano, Bromley, Buckley, Brott, Burke, Cook J. K., Cook T., Crozat, Cutler, Collin, Davies Dufresne, Duane, Decker, Dupaty, Edwards, Ennis, Fish, Flagg, Flood, Foley, Fosdick, Geier, Goldman, Gorlinski, Gruneberg, Gaidry, Healy,

AND AMENDMENT OF THE CONSTITUTION OF LOUISIANA. 55

Harnan, Hart, Heard, Hills, Hire, Kavanagh, Knobloch, Kugler, Maas, Maurer, Mendiverri, Millspaugh, Montamat, Montague, Murphy M. W., Newell, Normand, O'Conner, Payne J., Pintado, Poynot, Purcell J., Pursell S., Seymour, Shaw, Smith, Spellicy, Stumpf, Stiner, Stauffer, Sullivan, Terry, Thomas and Wells—72 members present.

There being no quorum, the sergeant-at-arms was sent for absent members.

The following gentlemen entered the hall and took their seats:

Messrs. Henderson, Howell, Murphy E., Stocker—76 members present.

The president announced a quorum present, and the minutes of yesterday's proceedings were read and adopted.

Mr. Goldman offered a memorial.

The president informed him that as the memorial was signed only by himself, he being a member of the Convention, could not present it.

Mr. Goldman then offered the following resolution:

Be it Resolved, That banking corporations, under the authority of the State, are prohibited, and that those banks which are doing banking business at present, or have done so hitherto, are hereby forbidden to continue such business.

EDMUND GOLDMAN.

Laid over.

Mr. Gruneberg offered the following resolution:

Whereas, The Constitutional Convention of the State of Louisiana has been called principally to decide on the abolition of slavery in this State; *whereas,* the adoption of this measure, in whatever manner or form, will necessarily require great modifications in all parts of the organic law of the State; *whereas,* for these reasons this Convention cannot or ought not to come to a final decision on the reports of any of the standing committees on constitutional amendments, before voting on emancipation; *and, whereas,* the question of emancipation being the most important of all, requires the longest and most mature deliberation of this assembly;

Be it therefore Resolved, That this Convention will take in consideration, first, the reports of all the standing committees on constitutional amendments, with substitutes and amendments thereto, except the report of the Committee on Emancipation—but they shall not pass further than a second reading; that then the report of the Committee on Emancipation shall be taken up, and be then regularly passed to a final vote; and that afterwards the reports of all the other standing committees shall pass their third reading and to a final vote thereon;

And moreover, Resolved, That the Convention shall only adjourn from day to day until the reports of all standing committees on constitutional amendments, except that of emancipation, shall have passed a second reading.

Laid over.

REPORTS OF STANDING COMMITTEES.

Committee on Legislative Department reported progress.

Committee on Executive Department made no report.

Committee on Internal Improvements made no report.

Committee on Schedule no report.

Committee on Ordinance no report.

Committee on Enrollment reported.

Mr. Millspaugh, in behalf of Mr. Thorpe, chairman of Committee on Enrollment, reported as correctly enrolled, the following resolutions:

1. Resolution requesting the governor to issue his proclamation for and election of delegates from the parishes of Plaquemines and Ascension.

2. Resolution relative to the statue of Washington.

3. Resolution relative to the per diem of members.

4. Resolution relative to auditor of public accounts, requesting a statement regarding the administration of his excellency Geo. F. Shepley, late military governor.

On motion of Mr Bell, the report was received and the president requested to sign the resolutions reported enrolled.

Mr. Balch called for the reading of the resolution relative to the governor's proclamation.

On motion of Mr. Stiner, the reading was dispensed with.

Committee on Assault of Members reported progress.

Mr. Sullivan, chairman of Committee on Statue of Washington, reported that the committee had opened correspondence with the secretary of war upon the subject referred to them. Report received.

Mr. M. W. Murphy presented the following:

To the president and members of the Convention:

The committee appointed to fix the compensation of officers and employés of this Convention, submit the following report on unfinished business:

The compensation of the chief clerk of enrollment to be ten dollars per day; that of two translating clerks, each, ten dollars per day, to commence from the 6th April, 1864.

M. W. MURPHY, Chairman.
J. RANDALL TERRY,
JAMES ENNIS,
GEO. A. FOSDICK.

On Mr. Foley's motion the report was adopted.

Mr. Brott, chairman of Finance Committee, stated that, according to his opinion, the appropriation of $100,000 made by this Convention did not apply to other expenses than mileage and per diem of members and employés of the Convention. He desired that the Committee on Expenses should report before the Committee on Finance make any further report.

Committee on Expenses had "no report."

Mr. Stocker rose to state that according to his recollection the sum of one hundred thousand dollars had been provided to meet contingent expenses.

The resolution referred to was read.

Mr. Brott's motion: That the Committee on Expenses be instructed to make an estimate of money required and bring in a bill for the same.

Mr. Purcell, chairman of the Committee on Expenses, explained that they had merely approved bills.

Mr. Brott stated that his motion was seconded by Mr. Beauvais.

The president stated that it must lay over one day.

The special order of the day was then taken up, to-wit:

The report of the Committee on General Provisions.

The report was read, and upon motion of Mr. Cutler, the second and third readings were postponed until the reports of the preceding committees had been acted upon.

The report of the Committee on Federal Relations was then taken up and read by the secretary.

Mr. Brott presented a minority report of the committee.

Mr. Balch moved to lay the minority report upon the table.

Mr. Foley called for the yeas and nays.

Upon Mr. Bell's motion, the report was adopted; but upon Mr Hills's suggestion, that the yeas and nays had been demanded, the president directed them to be called, when the vote was taken as follows:

YEAS—Messrs. Abell, Balch, Davies, Henderson—4.

NAYS—Messrs. Ariail, Austin, Bailey, Barrett, Bell, Bofill, Bonzano, Brott, Bromley, Burke, Campbell, Cook T., Cook J. K., Crozat, Cutler, Collin, Decker, Dufresne, Duane, Dupaty, Ennis, Fish, Flagg, Flood, Foley, Fosdick, Gastinel, Gaidry, Geier, Goldman, Gorlinski, Harnan, Hart, Healy, Heard, Hills, Hire, Kavanagh, Knobloch, Kugler, Maas, Maurer, Mendiverri, Millspaugh, Montague, Murphy E., Murphy M. W., Newell, Normand, O'Conner, Payne J., Pintado, Poynot, Purcell J., Pursell S., Schroeder, Shaw, Smith, Spellicy, Seymour, Stumpf, Stine, Stauffer, Sullivan, Terry, Thorpe, Thomas, Wells, Wilson—70.

Consequently the motion of Mr. Balch was lost.

Mr. Wilson moved that the minority as well as the majority report of the Committee on Federal Relations, be made the order of the day for Tuesday, May 3d, 1864. Carried.

On motion of Mr. Austin, the minority report was ordered to be printed.

Mr. Balch moved to adjourn *sine die*.

Mr. Campbell seconded.

Motion lost.

Mr. Stauffer rose to a question of privilege, and moved that the sergeant-at-arms be instructed to remove the member from Iberville, and a vote of censure passed upon him for his conduct in this Convention.

Mr. Stocker's motion to table was declared lost, and upon the yeas and nays being called was plainly so. Yeas 25, nays 48.

The roll was called, to see if a quorum was present, when 76 members answered.

On Mr. Hills's suggestion, Mr. Stauffer stated his reasons for offering the resolution, and withdrew it.

Mr. Balch explained why he moved to adjourn *sine die*.

Mr. Purcell's substitute for the report of

AND AMENDMENT OF THE CONSTITUTION OF LOUISIANA.

Committee on Federal Relations (presented on yesterday) was read.

Mr. Hills moved that any action upon it be postponed until the minority report should be acted upon.

Motion carried.

Mr. Hills, chairman of the Committee on Education, submitted a report upon the memorial of A. Vallas.

Mr. Wilson's motion to receive and print and make the order of the same day as the reports, was carried.

On motion, the Convention adjourned to meet on Friday, the 29th instant, at 12 M.

Minutes adopted.

JOHN E. NEELIS,
Secretary.

FRIDAY, April 29, 1864.

The president called the Convention to order at 12 o'clock M., and, after prayer by the Rev. Mr. Gilbert, the secretary called the roll, and the following gentlemen answered to their names:

Messrs. Abell, Ariail, Austin, Balch, Bailey, Barrett, Baum, Beauvais, Bell, Bofill, Bonzano, Bromley, Buckley, Burke, Cazabat, Cook J. K., Cook T., Crozat, Collin, Davies, Dufresne, Decker, Dupaty, Edwards, Ennis, Fish, Flagg, Flood, Fosdick, Fuller, Geier, Goldman, Gorlinski, Gruneberg, Gaidry, Healy, Harnan, Hart, Heard, Henderson, Hills, Howell, Kavanagh, Knobloch, Kugler, Maas, Maurer, Mendiverri, Millspaugh, Montamat, Montague, Morris, Murphy E., Murphy M. W., Newell, Normand, O'Conner, Ong, Payne J., Pintado, Poynot, Purcell J., Pursell S., Schroeder, Schnurr, Seymour, Shaw, Smith, Spellicy, Stocker, Stumpf, Stiner, Stauffer, Sullivan, Terry, Thorpe, Thomas, Waters, Wenck, Wells and Wilson—81 members present.

The minutes of yesterday were read and approved.

Mr. Harnan offered a resolution relative to absent members, and providing a remedy for such absence.

Mr. Montamat moved to suspend the rules in regard to said resolution, which motion was carried.

Mr. Montamat then moved to lay the resolution on the table, upon which motion a division was called: ayes 37, nays 26. Carried.

r. Bell asked leave to present a petition. Granted.

He then presented a petition from Mr. Henry Copeland, acting sergeant-at-arms during the first six days of the Convention, relative to his compensation.

On motion of Mr. Wilson, the petition was referred to the Committee on Compensation of officers and employés.

Mr. Samuel Pursell, chairman of the Committee on Expenses, offered a resolution appropriating twenty-five thousand dollars, for contingent expenses of the Convention

The rules were suspended and the resolution adopted.

The secretary then read a communication from the secretary of state relative to the election of Benjamin H. Orr as delegate from the Tenth Representative District, and a protest against said election by T. F. McGuire.

Mr. Hills moved to refer the whole matter to the Committee on Credentials.

Mr. Goldman called up his resolution of yesterday relative to banks and banking.

A motion was made to lay the resolution on the table, upon which the yeas and nays were called with the following result:

YEAS—Messrs. Abell, Austin, Bailey, Barrett, Baum, Beauvais, Bell, Bofill, Bromley, Buckley, Burke, Cook T., Crozat, Dufresne, Edwards, Fish, Flagg, Flood, Fuller, Geier, Healy, Harnan, Henderson, Hire, Kavanagh, Maas, Mendiverri, Montamat, Murphy E., Murphy M W., Howell, Harnan, Poynot, Shaw, Stocker, Spellicy, Stumpf, Terry, Wilson—39 yeas.

NAYS—Messrs. Ariail, Bonzano, Cazabat, Cook J. K., Collin, Davies, Duane, Decker, Ennis, Foley, Fosdick, Goldman, Gorlinski, Gruneberg, Gaidry, Hart, Heard, Hills, Howell, Knobloch, Kugler, Maurer, Millspaugh, Montague, Morris, Murphy, Ong, Payne J., Pintado, Purcell J., Pursell S., Schroeder, Seymour, Smith, Stiner, Stauffer, Sullivan, Thorpe, Thomas, Waters, Wenck, Wells—42 nays.

The motion to lay on the table was lost.

Mr. Thomas moved that the resolution be referred to the Committee on General Provisions.

Mr. Stauffer moved to amend Mr. Thomas's motion by referring it to a committee of five, to be appointed by the president, to be called the Committee on Banks and Banking. Amendment lost.

Mr. Campbell moved to refer to a particular day. Lost.

Mr. Stocker moved that the resolution be made the order of the day for the first day of January, 1865.

Mr. Davies moved to lay Mr. Stocker's motion on the table, upon which motion a division was called for—ayes 55, nays 10—and Mr. Stocker's motion was laid on the table.

Mr. Hills renewed the motion to refer to the Committee on General Provisions.

The question upon referring to the Committee on General Provisions was then put and carried.

Mr. Foley moved that Mr. Howell be added to the Committee on General Provisions, in consequence of the illness of the chairman of that Committee. Laid over.

Mr. Gruneberg's resolution of yesterday, relative to the postponement of any definite action on the report of the Committee on Emancipation, until the reports of all the other standing committees shall have passed second reading. On motion of Mr. Thomas, it was ordered to be printed and made the order of the day for Monday next, 2d day of May.

The special order of the day, viz : The second reading of the report of the Committee on Judiciary, together with the amendments of Messrs. Henderson and Sullivan, were then taken up.

Mr. Cazabat moved to adjourn. Lost.

Mr. Stauffer offered a substitute for articles 11 and 12. Ordered to be printed.

Mr. Montamat offered an amendment to sections 11 and 12. Ordered to be printed.

The motion to make the report and amendments the order of the day for Friday next, May 6th, 1864, was lost.

Friday, 6th May, was then fixed for the third reading.

Mr. Cutler moved that the reports of committees be considered in regular order, according to the classification of the constitution of 1852, and offered a resolution to that effect.

On motion to reconsider the vote fixing the third reading for Friday, May 6th, prox., the motion was carried.

On motion of Mr. Henderson, the rules were suspended for the purpose of taking up the report of the committee, as also the amendments and substitutes.

Mr. Cutler said his resolution would cut off all debate, and for the purpose of discussion he would waive the resolution.

Mr. S. Pursell moved to take up and adopt Mr. Sullivan's amendments.

Mr. Shaw moved to take up the report section by section. Carried.

Mr. Wilson moved to adjourn the debate until Monday next, May 2d.

A motion to lay Mr. Wilson's motion on the table was lost. Ayes 25, nays 47.

The question then recurred on Mr. Wilson's motion to adjourn the debate to Monday next. Division—ayes 31, nays 51.

Mr. Cutler then offered the following resolution :

Resolved, That the third reading of the report of the Judiciary Committee, all substitutes and amendments thereto, be postponed for the action of this Convention thereon until after all preceding reports of the committees, according to the classification, as fixed in the constitution of 1852, be acted upon and adopted by this Convention.

Carried.

Mr. Stauffer moved the adoption of the first article of the report. Adopted.

Mr. Abell offered a substitute for the second article. Received and read.

Mr. Henderson offered a substitute for the second article. Received and read.

On motion of Mr. Sullivan, the Convention then adjourned.

Minutes adopted.

JOHN E. NEELIS,
Secretary.

SATURDAY, April 30th, 1864.

The Convention met and was called to order by the president, at 12 o'clock M., and, after prayer by the Rev Mr. Gilbert, the secretary called the roll and the following gentlemen answered to their names :

Messrs. Abell, Austin, Bailey, Barrett, Baum, Beauvais, Bell, Bofill, Brott, Buckley, Burke, Collin, Cazabat, Cook J. K., Cook T., Crozat, Davies, Decker, Dufresne, Edwards, Ennis, Fish, Flagg, Flood, Foley, Geier, Goldman, Gorlinski, Gruneberg, Gaidry, Healy, Harnan, Hart, Heard, Henderson, Hills. Hire, Kavanagh, Knobloch, Kugler, Maas, Mann, Maurer, Mendiverri, Millspaugh, Montamat Montague, Murphy E., Murphy M. W., Newell, Normand, O'Conner, Pintado, Poynot, Purcell J., Schroeder, Schnurr, Seymour, Shaw, Smith, Stumpf

AND AMENDMENT OF THE CONSTITUTION OF LOUISIANA.

Stiner, Stauffer, Sullivan, Terry, Thomas, Waters, Wilson, Wells—69 members.

There being no quorum present the sergeant-at-arms was directed to procure the attendance of absent members.

Upon Messrs. Bromley, Campbell, Cutler, Duane, Howell and Wenck, entering and taking their seats, the president announced that a quorum was present.

The minutes of yesterday were read and approved.

Mr. Thomas offered a preamble and resolutions relative to presidential electors.

The rules were suspended and the resolutions adopted.

The president appointed on the committee, raised by said resolutions, to report as to the manner in which seven electors for President and Vice-President of the United States shall be chosen in this State, for the coming presidential election, viz.: Messrs. Thomas, (chairman) Cazabat, S. Pursell, Fish, and Heard.

Mr. Campbell offered the following amendment:

Art. —. No tax, State or municipal, shall be imposed by the General Assembly upon the actual capital engaged in the following industrial arts, viz: All manufactories of cloth, leather, yarn and cotton bagging,— and those engaged in shoe manufacturing, provided twenty hands, at least, are employed. The General Assembly may, however, exempt such others as they deem advisable; this exemption to be allowed for the term of ten years from and after the date of its establishment.

Mr. Stiner offered the following:

Art. —. That no licenses be granted to gambling houses in the State.

On motion of Mr. Hills, the two foregoing propositions were referred to the Committee on General Provisions.

Mr. Gorlinski, on behalf of the Committee on Internal Improvements, stated that the committee would report on Monday.

Mr. Millspaugh, on behalf of the Committee on Enrollment, reported as correctly enrolled, the resolution appropriating twenty-five thousand dollars for the contingent expenses of the Convention.

Mr. J. Purcell, on behalf of the Committee on Printing, submitted a written report.

Mr. Gastinel moved that the report be printed, and made the special order of the day for Friday next, May 5th.

The yeas and nays were called on Mr. Gastinel's motion, resulting as follows:

YEAS—Messrs. Ariail, Austin, Bailey, Barrett, Beauvais, Bonzano, Bromley, Burke, Campbell, Cook T., Cutler, Davies, Dufresne, Edwards, Ennis, Flagg, Foley, Fosdick, Gastinel, Gaidry, Geier, Goldman, Gorlinski, Gruneberg, Harnan, Hart, Heard, Henderson, Hills, Hire, Howell, Knobloch, Kugler-Maas, Mann, Maurer, Millspaugh, Montague, Morris, Murphy E., Murphy M. W., Newell, Normand, O'Conner, Ong, Pintado, Purcell J., Pursell S., Schroeder, Schnurr, Seymour, Smith, Stumpf, Stiner, Stauffer, Sullivan, Terry, Thorpe, Waters, Wenck—60.

NAYS—Messrs. Abell, Baum, Bell, Bofill, Buckley, Collin, Cook J. K., Crozat, Decker, Duane, Flood, Montamat, Poynot, Stocker, Thomas, Wilson—16.

Consequently, the motion was carried.

Mr. Wilson, of the Committee on Assault of Members, said the committee would report on Thursday next.

The other committees reported progress.

Mr. Foley called up his resolution adding the name of Mr. Howell to the Committee on General Provisions, and the same was adopted.

On motion of Mr. Abell, the discussion on the report of the Judiciary Committee, as also upon the amendments therefor, was postponed until the reports of the committees preceding the judiciary shall have been disposed of.

The report of the Committee on Education being the special order of the day, was next taken up and read, together with the substitutes of Messrs. S. Pursell and Hart.

Messrs. Sullivan, Stauffer, Davies, Gruneberg and Bonzano offered amendments to various sections of the report, but, on motion of Mr. Heard, the report was taken up section by section, and the amendments were withdrawn for the purpose of being offered in their proper places.

Article first of the report being read, Mr. Davies offered an amendment, striking out that portion authorizing the General Assembly to abolish the office of superintendent of Public Education.

The vote was taken on a motion to lay Hr. Davies's motion on the table:

YEAS—Messrs. Ariail, Austin, Balch, Bar-

JOURNAL OF THE CONVENTION FOR THE REVISION

rett, Baum, Bell, Buckley, Campbell, Cazabat, Cook J. K., Cook T., Cutler, Decker, Duane, Dufresne, Edwards. Fosdick, Gorlinski, Harnan, Hart, Healy, Heard, Henderson, Hills, Howell, Maurer, Montamat, Montague, Murphy M. W., Newell, Normand, O'Conner, Ong, Poynot, Smith, Spellicy, Sullivan, Terry, Thorpe, Wells, Wilson—41.

NAYS—Messrs. Bailey, Beauvais, Bofill, Bonzano, Bromley, Burke, Crozat, Davies, Ennis, Fish, Flagg, Flood, Foley, Gastinel, Gaidry, Geier, Goldman, Gruneberg, Hire, Knobloch, Kugler, Maas, Mann, Mendiverri, Millspaugh, Morris, Murphy E., Purcell J., Pursell S., Schroeder, Schnurr, Seymour, Stocker, Stumpf, Stiner, Stauffer, Thomas, Waters, Wenck—39.

Mr. Pursell offered the following substitute for article 1 :

MR. S. PURSELL'S SUBSTITUTE.

Art. —. There shall be elected a superintendent of Public Education, who shall hold his office for the term of four years. His duties shall be prescribed and compensation fixed by the General Assembly.

On motion to adopt Mr. Pursell's substitute, the yeas and nays were ordered, with the following result:

YEAS — Messrs. Abell, Bailey, Barrett, Beauvais, Bell, Bromley, Burke, Campbell, Collin, Cutler, Davies, Duane, Ennis, Flagg, Foley, Gastinel, Gaidry, Geier, Goldman, Healy, Hire, Knobloch, Maas, Mann, Maurer, Mendiverri, Millspaugh, Morris, Murphy E., Normand, Ong, Pursell S., Schroeder, Shaw, Spellicy, Stocker, Stumpf, Stiner, Stauffer, Terry, Thorpe, Thomas, Wenck—43.

NAYS—Messrs. Ariail, Austin, Buckley, Cazabat, Cook J. K., Cook T., Decker, Dufresne, Dupaty, Flood, Fosdick, Gorlinski, Gruneberg, Harnan, Hart, Heard, Henderson, Hills, Howell, Kugler, Montamat, Montague, Murphy M. W., Newell, O'Conner, Pintado, Poynot, Schnurr, Sullivan, Waters, Wilson—31.

No quorum voting, a call of the House was ordered, when, it being ascertained that there was no quorum in the House, on motion the Convention adjourned until 12 o'clock on Monday next.

Minutes adopted.

JOHN E. NEELIS,
Secretary.

MONDAY, May 2, 1864.

The Convention met at 12 o'clock M., and the roll being called the following gentlemen answered to their names :

Messrs. Abell, Ariail, Austin, Barrett, Bell, Bofill, Bonzano, Bromley, Brott, Burke, Campbell, Cook J. K., Crozat, Davies, Du fresne, Duane, Duke, Edwards, Ennis, Fish, Flagg, Flood, Foley, Fosdick, Gastinel, Geier, Gorlinski, Gaidry, Healy, Harnan, Hart, Heard, Henderson, Hills, Hire, Kavanagh, Kugler, Maas, Mann, Millspaugh, Montamat, Montague, Murphy M. W., Normand, O'Conner, Ong, Payne J., Pintado, Poynot, Purcell J., Pursell S., Schroeder, Schnurr, Seymour, Smith, Spellicy, Stocker, Stumpf, Stiner. Stauffer, Sullivan, Terry, Thomas, Waters, Wells and Wilson—66 members present.

There being no quorum, the sergeant-at-arms was directed to bring in absent members.

Messrs. Cutler, Baum, Mendiverri, Buckley, Collin, Cook T., Thorpe, Beauvais, Wenck and Cazabat. having taken their seats, the president announced that a quorum was present.

The minutes of Saturday were read and approved.

Mr. Terry offered the following :

Whereas, Several persons are holding offices, State and municipal, who are not citizens of the State, or qualified, as per order of the president, December 8, 1863 therefore, be it

Resolved, That all persons holding State or municipal offices not qualified voters of the State, or who have not complied with the oath of the President's proclamation of December 8, 1863, that it is the sense of this Convention, they should be promptly removed by the governor of the State and mayor of the city, who are respectfully requested to enforce this resolution.

The rules having been suspended, a motion to lay on the table was lost.

The question then recurring on the adoption of the resolution, the yeas and nays were ordered, with the following result :

YEAS—Messrs. Baily, Bell, Bofill, Bonzano, Bromley, Campbell, Cazabat, Cook J. K., Cook T., Crozat, Collin, Duke, Davies, Duane, Durfresne, Ennis, Fish, Flagg, Flood, Foley, Geier, Gorlinski, Gaidry, Healy, Harnan. Hart, Henderson, Hills, Hire, Kavanagh, Maas, Millspaugh, Murphy E., Newell, Normand, O'Conner, Payne J., Poynot, Purcell J., Pursell S., Schroeder, Seymour, Shaw, Smith, Spellicy, Stocker, Stumpf, Stiner, Stauffer, Sullivan, Terry, Thorpe, Waters, Wenck, Wells and Wilson —56.

NAYS—Messrs. Abell, Austin, Barrett, Baum, Beauvais, Brott, Buckley, Burke, Cutler, Fuller, Gastinel, Heard, Kugler, Mann, Mendiverri, Montamat, Montague, Murphy M. W., Ong, Schnurr and Thomas—21.

AND AMENDMENT OF THE CONSTITUTION OF LOUISIANA. 61

Consequently the resolution was adopted.
Mr. Henderson moved a reconsideration of the foregoing vote, which was lost.
Mr. Bromley offered the following resolutions:
Resolved, That the future sessions of this Convention shall be of not less than four hours' duration.
Resolved, That the pay per diem of the members of this Convention shall cease on and after the fortieth day of its organization.
The rules having been suspended, on motion of Mr. Montamat the foregoing resolutions were laid on the table.
Mr. Montamat, on behalf of the Committee on Credentials, stated that Mr. J. T. Maguire requested to withdraw his protest against the election of Mr. Orr—which was granted, whereupon Mr. Montamat submitted the following report:
To the honorable president and members of the Constitutional Convention:
Gentlemen—Your Committee on Credentials, after due examination of all witnesses produced before us by Mr. T. F. McGuire, contesting the election of Mr. B. H. Orr, as a delegate from the Tenth Representative District, beg leave to report that Mr. B. H. Orr has been duly elected as a delegate to this Convention, to represent the Tenth Representative District of the city of New Orleans: that he is duly qualified, and entitled to a seat in this Convention.
All of which is respectfully sumbited.
JOHN P. MONTAMAT, *Chairman.*
The report was received and adopted, and Mr. Orr took his seat.
Mr. Henderson asked and obtained leave of absence for Mr. Montague.
The president laid before the Convention a communication from the secretary of state, enclosing the returns of the late election in the parish of Jefferson, to fill the vacancy occasioned by the resignation of Christian Roselius, Esq.
Referred to Committee on Credentials.
The following resolutions, by Mr. Gruneberg, being the special order of the day, were then taken up:
Whereas, The Constitutional Convention of the State of Louisiana has been called principally to decide on the abolition of slavery in this State; *whereas* the adoption of this measure, in whatever manner or form, will necessarily require great modification in all parts of the organic law of the State; whereas, for these reasons this Convention cannot or ought not to come to any final decision on the reports of any of the standing committees on constitutional amendments, before voting on emancipation; *and whereas*, the question of emancipation being the most important of all, requires the longest and most mature deliberation of this assembly;
Be it therefore Resolved, That this Convention will take into consideration, first, the reports of all the standing committees on constitutional amendments, with substitutes and amendments thereto, except the report of the Committee on Emancipation, but they shall not pass further than a second reading; that then the report of the Committee on Emancipation shall be taken up, and be then regularly passed to a final vote; and that afterwards, the reports of all the other standing committees shall pass to a third reading and to a final vote thereon; and moreover resolved, that this Convention shall only adjourn from day to day until the reports of all the standing committees on constitutional amendments, except that of emancipation, shall have passed a second reading.

On motion of Mr. Wilson, the resolutions were adopted.

The Convention then resumed the consideration of the unfinished business, upon which it was engaged on Saturday last, viz: the second reading of the report of the Committee on Public Education.

Mr. S. Pursell moved the adoption of the following substitute for the first article of the report:

There shall be elected a superintendent of Public Education, who shall hold his office for the term of four years. His duties shall be prescribed and compensation fixed by the General Assembly.

On this motion the yeas and nays were ordered, resulting as follows:

YEAS—Messrs. Abell, Bailey, Barrett, Beauvais, Bell, Bennie, Bonzano, Bromley, Brott, Buckley, Burke, Campbell, Collin, Crozat, Cutler, Davies, Duane, Dufresne, Duke, Ennis, Fish, Flagg, Flood, Foley, Fuller, Gastinel, Gaidry, Geier, Gruneberg, Heard, Hire, Kugler, Maas, Mann, Mendiverri, Millspaugh, Montague, Murphy E., Normand, Ong, Orr, Payne J., Pintado, Purcell J., Pursell S., Schroeder, Seymour, Shaw, Stocker, Stumpf, Stiner, Stauffer, Terry, Thomas, Wenck—55.

NAYS—Messrs. Ariail, Austin, Cazabat, Cook J. K., Cook T., Edwards, Gorlinski, Harnan, Hart, Healy, Hills, Murphy M. W., Newell, O'Conner, Poynot, Schnurr, Spellicy, Sullivan, Thorpe, Waters, Wells, Wilson—22.

Consequently the motion prevailed and the substitute was adopted.

Mr. Sullivan offered the following substitute for the second section of the report, viz:

The General Assembly shall establish free public schools throughout the State, for all free white children, by general taxation or otherwise, and all moneys shall be distributed to each parish in proportion to the number of white children between such ages as shall be fixed by the General Assembly.

A motion to lay on the table was negatived, whereupon a lengthy discussion arose, pending which the Monvention adjourned.

Minutes adopted.

JOHN E. NEELIS,
Secretary.

TUESDAY, May 3, 1864.

The Convention was called to order by the president at 12 o'clock M., and after prayer by the Rev. Mr. Horton, the roll was called and the following gentlemen answered to their names:

Messrs. Abell, Barrett, Bennie, Bofill, Bonzano, Bromley, Buckley, Burke, Collin, Cook J. K., Crozat, Davies, Decker, Duane, Dufresne, Duke, Edwards, Ennis, Foley, Fosdick, Fuller, Geier, Goldman, Healy, Heard, Henderson, Hills, Howes, Kavanagh, Maas, Mann, Hillspaugh, Murphy M. W., Newell, Normand, O'Conner, Payne J., Paine J. T., Pintado, Poynot, Pursell S., Schroeder, Schnurr, Stumpf, Terry, Thomas, Wells, Wilson and Mr. President—50.

There not being a quorum present, the sergeant-at-arms was directed to procure the attendance of absent members.

Messrs. Ariail, Balch, Baum, Beauvais, Bell, Campbell, Cook T., Dupaty, Fish, Flagg, Gastinel, Gaidry, Harnan, Hart, Hire, Kugler, Mendiverri, Montamat, Murphy E., Ong, Orr, Smith, Stiner, Stauffer, Sullivan, Thorpe and Waters having taken their seats, the president declared a quorum present.

The minutes of yesterday were read and adopted.

Mr. Sullivan offered the following resolution, which was laid over under the rules:

Resolved, That the clerks, officers and employés of this Convention be and are hereby exempt from serving, during the session of the Convention, as jurors in the several District Courts of this parish.

Mr. Montamat offered the following:

Resolved, That the resolution adopted by this House fixing the hour of 12 o'clock M. for the meeting of this Convention, be and the same is hereby repealed.

Resolved, further, That this House will hereafter meet at 11 o'clock A. M.

Mr. Fosdick moved to suspend the rules for the purpose of taking up Mr. Montamat's resolution. Lost.

Mr. Fosdick, chairman of Committee on Legislative Department, submitted a written report.

Mr. Hills moved that the report be accepted, and made the order of the day for this day week.

Mr. Stauffer moved to amend Mr. Hills's motion, so as to lay over the report, to come up in its regular order, which amendment was accepted, and the motion as amended was carried.

Mr. Montamat, chairman of the Committee on Credentials, submitted a report relative to the election of Mr. John A. Meyer, which report was received, and Mr. Meyer invited to take his seat in the Convention.

Mr. M. W. Murphy, chairman of the Committee on Compensation of officers and employés of the Convention, reported that Mr. Copeland requests leave to withdraw his petition, heretofore referred to this committee.

The report was received and Mr. Copeland's request granted.

The second reading of the report of the Committee on Education, being unfinished business of yesterday, was then taken up and discussed at great length.

Mr. Hire moved that the Convention adjourn to 6 o'clock this evening; but the motion being lost, the Convention then adjourned until 12 o'clock M. to-morrow.

Minutes adopted.

JOHN E. NEELIS,
Secretary.

WEDNESDAY, May 4, 1864.

The Convention was called to order at 12 M., and the proceedings were opened with prayer by the Rev. Mr. Andrews. The roll was called and the following gentlemen answered to their names:

Messrs. Abell, Ariail, Austin, Balch, Barrett, Bell, Bennie, Bofill, Bonzano, Bromley,

AND AMENDMENT OF THE CONSTITUTION OF LOUISIANA. 63

Buckley, Burke, Campbell, Collin, Cook J. K., Cook T., Crozat, Davies, Decker, Duane, Dufresne, Duke, Dupaty, Edwards, Ennis, Flood, Fosdick, Geier, Goldman, Gorlinski, Gruneberg, Gaidry, Healy, Hart, Heard, Henderson, Hills, Hire, Howes, Knobloch, Kugler, Maas, Mann, Maurer, Mayer, Millspaugh, Montamat, Murphy M. W., Newell, Normand, Ong, Orr, Payne J., Pintado, Poynot, Purcell J., Pursell S., Schroeder, Schnurr, Seymour, Shaw, Smith, Spellicy, Stumpf, Stiner, Stauffer, Sullivan, Terry, Thorpe, Waters, Wells, Wilson—72.

Messrs. Fish, Flagg, Foley, Montamat and Murphy E., having taken their seats, the president declared a quorum present.

The minutes of yesterday were then read and adopted.

Mr. Stauffer offered the following resolutions:

Resolved, That the following be printed and added as articles amending the report of the Committee on General Provisions.

Art.—. No person who now holds, or may hereafter hold any office, civil or military under the so-colled Confederate States, or under any authority adverse to the government of the United States, shall be eligible to any office of honor, trust or profit in this State.

Art. — No debt created by or under the so-called Confederate States, or under the sanction of any usurping power, shall be recognized and paid.

Laid over.

The reports of committees were called for.

Mr. Shaw, chairman of the Committee on Ordinance, reported progress.

Mr. Wilson, chairman of Committee on Assault of Members, gave notice that he would report to-morrow.

There being no other reports Mr. Sullivan called up his resolution of yesterday, exempting the officers and employés of the Convention from serving on juries during the sitting of the Convention. Adopted.

Mr. Bonzano moved to take up the reports of the Committee on Emancipation, which, being declared out of order,

Mr. Thorpe moved to suspend the rules in order to take up the order of the day, to-wit: the reports of the Committee on Emancipation, upon which motion the ayes and nays were ordered, resulting as follows:

YEAS — Messrs. Austin, Bell, Bennie, Bonzano, Bromley, Brott, Buckley, Burke, Collin, Cook J. K., Cook. T., Davies, Duane, Duke, Edwards, Ennis, Fish, Flagg, Flood, Foley, Fosdick, Gastinel, Geire, Goldman, Gorlinski, Gaidry, Healy, Hart, Henderson, Hills, Hire, Howes, Kugler, Maas, Mann. Millspaugh, Murphy E., Newell, Normand, Pintado, Poynot, Purcell J., Pursell S., Schroeder, Schnurr, Shaw, Smith, Spellicy, Stiner, Stauffer, Terry, Thorpe, Thomas, Wilson—54.

NAYS—Messrs. Abell, Balch, Bailey, Barrètt, Bofill, Campbell, Crozat, Decker, Dufresne, Dupaty, Gruneberg, Heard, Knobloch, Maurer, Mayer, Mendiverri, Montamat, Murphy M. W., O'Conner, Ong, Orr, Seymour, Stumpf, Sullivan, Waters, Wells— 26.

Whereupon the president declared the rules suspended, and the reports of the Committee on Emancipation were then taken up.

Mr. Abell moved to make the whole matter the order of the day for Monday next. Laid on the table.

Mr. Hills moved to dispose of the reports of the Committee on Emancipation before taking up any other business. Carried.

Mr. Bonzano called for the reading of the reports, whereupon Mr. Montamat called for the reading of the minority report as having preference, which report was then read by the secretary.

Mr. Foley moved to lay the minority report òn the table, upon which motion the yeas and nays were ordered, with the following result:

YEAS—Bell, Bennie, Bromley, Burke, Collin, Cook J. K., Davies, Duane, Dupaty, Fish, Flagg, Flood, Foley, Fosdick, Geier, Goldman, Gorlinski, Gaidry, Healy, Hills, Hire, Knobloch, Maas, Morris, Newell, Normand, Pintado, Pursell S., Schroeder, Schnurr, Shaw, Smith, Stauffer, Terry, Thorpe—35.

NAYS—Messrs. Abell, Balch, Bailey, Barrett, Beauvais, Bofill, Bonzano, Brott, Buckley, Campbell, Cazabat, Cook T., Crozat, Cutler, Decker, Dufresne, Duke, Edwards, Ennis, Gastinel, Heard, Henderson, Howes, Kugler, Maurer, Mayer, Mendiverri, Millspaugh, Montamat, Murphy E., Murphy M. W., O'Conner, Ong, Orr, Purcell J., Poynot, Seymour, Spellicy, Stocker, Stumpf, Stiner, Sullivan, Thomas, Waters, Wenck, Wells and Wilson—47.

Mr. Henderson then moved that the minority report be rejected.

Mr. Bonzano moved to adjourn the question until Monday next.

The president decided that the rules must

be suspeneded before the question could be put.

Mr. Stocker then moved to suspend the rules for that purpose. A division being called, there was not a quorum voting, when the ayes and nays were called with the following result :

YEAS—Messrs. Abell, Austin, Balch, Bailey, Barrett, Bell, Bofill, Bonzano, Buckley, Campbell, Cook T., Crozat,Decker, Dufresne, Duke, Edwards, Fosdick, Gastinel, Healy, Heard, Maurer, Mendiverri, Millspaugh, Montamat, Murphy M. W., Murphy E., Normand, O'Conner, Ong, Orr, Poynot, Schroeder, Seymour, Spellicy, Smith, Stocker, Stumpf, Stiner, Sullivan, Waters, Wenck—41.

NAYS—Messrs. Ariail, Beauvais, Bennie, Bromley, Brott, Burke, Collin, Cazabat, Cook J. K., Cutler, Davies, Duane, Ennis, Fish, Flagg, Flood, Foley, Geier, Goldman, Gorlinski, Gaidry, Hart, Henderson, Hills, Hire, Howes, Kavanagh, Knobloch, Kugler, Maas, Mann, Mayer, Morris, Newell, Pintado, Purcell J., Pursell S., Schnurr, Shaw, Staffer, Terry, Thorpe, Wells, Wilson—44.

The motion to suspend was lost.

After a lengthy discussion a motion to adjourn was made and lost.

Mr. Hills having last occupied the floor, and having been called to order by the president, the limited time having expired, it was moved and carried that he be allowed to proceed with his argument.

Mr. Hills returned thanks for the courtesy extended him, but declined further discussion to-day, when, on a motion of Mr. Austin, the Convention adjourned until to-morrow at 12 o'clock M.

Minutes adopted.

JOHN E. NEELIS,
Secretary.

THURSDAY, May 5, 1864.

At 12 o'clock M. the president called the Convention to order. The roll was called and the following gentlemen answered to their names :

Messrs. Abell, Ariail, Austin, Bailey, Barrett, Baum, Beauvais, Bell, Bofill, Bonzano, Buckley, Burke, Campbell, Cook J. K., Cook T., Crozat, Davies, Decker, Duane, Dufresne, Duke, Edwards, Ennis, Flagg, Fish, Flood, Foley, Fosdick, Gastinel, Goldman, Geier, Gorlinski, Gruneberg Gaidry, Healy, Hart, Heard, Hills, Howes, Kavanagh, Kugler, Knobloch, Maas, Mann, Maurer, Meyer, Mendiverri, Millspaugh, Montamat, Murphy M. W., Newell, Normand, O'Conner, Orr, Payne J., Pintado, Poynot, Purcell J., Pursell S., Schroeder, Schnurr, Seymour, Shaw, Smith, Spellicy, Stumpf, Stiner, Stocker, Stauffer, Sullivan, Terry, Thorpe, Waters, Wells, Wilson—77.

Minutes of yesterday read by the secretary and approved.

No reports from committees.

Mr. Terry offered the following preamble and resolution :

Whereas, Large sums of money have during the past year been remitted to this State for the purpose of aiding in the formation of a free State government in Louisiana. and it is now a fitting time that the said moneys should be applied to the patriotic purpose of the donors ; and this Convention is informed that said moneys are in the hands of the so-called "Free State General Committee," of which Thos. J. Durant is president. James Graham, secretary, and Edward Heath, treasurer ;

Resolved, That the auditor and treasurer of the State be requested to report to this body whether said funds have been paid into the treasury of the State, for the purpose of being properly devoted to the objects of the contributors ; and if not, that the said auditor and treasurer be empowered to demand of the said Thos. J. Durant, Jas. Graham and Edward Heath, and officers of said committee, the delivery of said funds, or an account of the uses to which they may have been applied ; and that the said auditor and treasurer be instructed to make such further inquiries and investigations as may be necessary, and report the result thereof to this Convention.

Resolution laid over one day.

Mr. Bell offered the following :

Resolved, That the thanks of this Convention be and are hereby tendered Captain Stephen Hoyt, U. S. army, and acting mayor of the city, and G. W. R. Bayley, city surveyor, for the able and efficient manner in which they have by their untiring energy and attention fitted up this hall for the Louisiana State Constitutional Convention.

Mr. Stauffer called up his resolution of yesterday, which, upon motion of Mr. Hills, was referred to Committee on General Provisions.

Mr. Abell offered the following resolution.

Resolved, That the sergeant-at-arms be and is hereby directed to ascertain the cause of the non-attendance at the Convention of the Hon. R. K. Howell, of the Seventh Representative District.

Amended by Mr. Hills so as to include all

AND AMENDMENT OF THE CONSTITUTION OF LOUISIANA.

members who have already taken their seats.

The rules were suspended, and the resolution carried as amended.

Mr. Campbell offered the following resolution:

Resolved, That no vote on emancipation be taken by this Convention until every member of this Convention be present.

Which resolution was laid over one day under the rules. The unfinished business was then taken up.

Mr. Brott offered an amendment to section 6th of the minority report of the Committee on Emancipation.

Mr. Sullivan moved to adjourn.

Lost.

Mr. Abell then proceeded to make the concluding argument on the adoption of the minority report of the Committee on Emancipation, but gave way to Mr. Cazabat, who desired to express his views on the subject, reserving the privilege of resuming his argument hereafter.

Mr. Cazabat having occupied the time allotted, the Convention adjourned.

Minutes adopted.

JOHN E. NEELIS,
Secretary.

FRIDAY, May 6, 1864.

The Convention met and was called to order by the president, pursuant to adjournment, and after prayer by the Rev. Mr. Strong the roll was called and the following gentlemen answered to their names:

Messrs. Abell, Balch, Bailey, Barrett, Beauvais, Bofill, Bromley, Burke, Campbell, Collin, Cook J. K., Cook T., Crozat, Decker, Dufresne, Duke, Dupaty, Edwards, Ennis, Fish, Flagg, Flood, Gaidry, Geier, Goldman, Gorlinski, Gruneberg, Hart, Healy, Heard, Henderson, Hills, Hire, Howes, Kavanagh, Kugler, Maas, Mann, Maurer, Mayer, Millspaugh, Montamat, Normand, Orr, Pintado, Poynot, Schroeder, Schnurr, Seymour, Shaw, Smith, Spellicy, Stumpf, Stiner, Stauffer, Sullivan, Taliaferro, Terry, Thorpe, Waters, Wells, Wilson, and Mr. President—63.

There being no quorum present, the sergeant-at-arms was directed to bring in absent members.

Messrs. Austin, Bell, Bonzano, Davies, Foley, Fosdick, Fuller, Harnan, Knobloch, Morris, Payne J., Paine J. T., Purcell J., Pursell S., and Stocker, having taken their seats, the president announced a quorum present.

The minutes of yesterday's proceedings were read and approved.

Mr. Thorpe, as chairman of the Committee on Enrollment, reported the following resolution:

Resolved, That the printer of this Convention be instructed to print two thousand copies of the journal, one-half of said number to be in the French language and one-half of said number to be in the English language.

Mr. Wilson moved to amend the resolution by making the number two thousand each. No action.

Mr. Montamat moved to amend by making the number three thousand.

On the question being put, Mr. Montamat's amendment was lost.

The resolution was then adopted as reported by the committee.

There were no reports from committees.

Mr. Wilson, chairman of the Committee on Assault of Members, reported that owing to a misunderstanding of Mr. Henderson's resolution, the committee could not now report.

The president then laid before the Convention the resignation of Mr. Howell, which was read by the secretary.

Mr. Henderson moved that it be accepted, and that the governor be duly informed of the vacancy in this Convention, occasioned thereby.

Upon this motion a division was called. Ayes 55, nays 22.

Mr. Campbell then called up his resolution of yesterday, prohibiting any vote on the question of emancipation until all the members of this Convention shall be present.

Mr. Foley moved to lay the resolution on the table, upon which motion a division was called. Yeas 45, nays 23.

Mr. Foley moved to reconsider the acceptance of Mr. Howell's resignation.

Mr. Henderson moved to lay Mr. Foley's motion on the table. Carried.

The unfinished business of yesterday (the reports of the Committee on Emancipation) was then taken up and the discussion resumed.

Mr. Abell having had the floor for half an

hour, was called to order by the president.

Mr. Hills rose to a point of order, and stated that Mr. Abell was entitled to the floor by a vote of the Convention of yesterday.

The president having decided in the negative on the point of order raised, Mr. Hills appealed to the Convention, upon which question the yeas and nays were ordered, resulting as follows:

YEAS—Messrs. Bell, Burke, Cazabat, Collin, Crozat, Cutler, Davies, Ennis, Fish, Flagg, Flood, Foley, Gaidry, Goldman, Gorlinski, Heard, Henderson, Hire, Mann, Morris, Newell, Payne J., Purcell J., Pursell S., Schroeder, Schnurr, Shaw, Stauffer, Thorpe, Wilson—30.

NAYS—Messrs. Abell, Bailey, Barrett, Beauvais, Bofill, Bonzano, Bromley, Buckley, Cook J. K., Cook T., Decker, Dufresne, Dupaty, Edwards, Fosdick, Fuller, Gastinel, Geier, Harnan, Hart, Healy, Hills, Kavanagh, Knobloch, Maas, Maurer, Mayer, Mendiverri, Millspaugh, Montamat, Normand, Orr, Paine J. T., Pintado, Poynot, Seymour, Smith, Spellicy, Stocker, Stumpf, Stiner, Sullivan, Taliaferro, Terry, Thomas, Wells—47.

Consequently the chair was not sustained, and Mr. Abell proceeded with his argument.

At the conclusion of Mr. Abell's argument, Mr. Hills offered the following resolution:

Resolved, That every vote on the subject of emancipation shall be taken by yeas and nays, and that members not present shall be sent for by the sergeant-at-arms and required to record their votes.

A call of the House being ordered, it was found that 76 members were present, being a quorum.

A motion to adjourn, was lost upon a division of 20 yeas to 47 nays.

Mr. Hills moved to suspend the rules to take up his resolution.

Mr. Henderson insisted on a strict adherence to the rule requiring a two-thirds vote to suspend the rules.

Upon the question to suspend the rules a division was called for, and the rules suspended by a vote of 61 ayes, 2 nays.

The question then recurred on the adoption of Mr. Hills's resolution, and a division being called for, resulted: ayes 66, nays 1; consequently the resolution was adopted.

The vote was then taken on the motion to reject the minority report of the Committee on Emancipation, resulting as follows:

YEAS—Messrs. Ariail, Austin, Bailey, Barrett, Baum, Beauvais, Bell, Bonzano, Brott, Bromley, Burke, Cazabat, Collin, Cook J. K., Cook T., Crozat, Cutler, Davies, Duane, Dupaty, Edwards, Ennis, Fish, Flagg, Flood, Foley, Fosdick, Fuller, Gaidry, Geier, Gorlinski, Goldman, Harnan, Hart, Healy, Henderson, Heard, Hills, Hire, Howes, Kavanagh, Knobloch, Kugler, Maas, Mann, Millspaugh, Morris, Murphy E., Newell, Normand, Orr, Payne J., Paine J. T., Pintado, Poynot, Purcell J., Pursell S., Schroeder, Seymour, Shaw, Smith, Spellicy, Stocker, Stiner, Stauffer, Taliaferro, Terry, Thorpe, Thomas, Wells, Wilson—71.

NAYS—Messrs. Abell, Balch, Bofill, Buckley, Campbell, Decker, Dufresne, Duke, Gastinel, Gruneberg, Maurer, Mayer, Mendiverri, Montamat, Murphy M. W., O'Conner, Stumpf, Sullivan, Waters—19.

Consequently the minority report was rejected.

On motion, the Convention adjourned.

Minutes adopted.

JOHN E. NEELIS,
Secretary.

SATURDAY, May 7th, 1864.

The Convention met at 12 o'clock M., and was called to order by the president.

The roll was called, and the following gentlemen answered to their names:

Messrs. Ariail, Austin, Abell, Balch, Bailey, Barrett, Baum, Bell, Bofill, Bonzano, Bromley, Brott, Buckley, Burke, Campbell, Collin, Cook J. K., Crozat, Davies, Decker, Duane, Dufresne, Duke, Dupaty, Edwards, Ennis, Fish, Flagg, Flood, Foley, Fosdick, Geier, Goldman, Gorlinski, Gruneberg, Healy, Harnan, Hart, Heard, Henderson, Hills, Hire, Howes, Kavanagh, Knobloch, Kugler, Maas, Mann, Maurer, Mayer, Mendiverri, Millspaugh, Murphy E., Murphy M. W., Newell, Normand, O'Conner, Orr, Payne Jno., Paine J. T., Pintado, Purcell Jno., Poynot, Pursell Sam., Schroeder, Seymour, Shaw, Smith, Spellicy, Stumpf, Stiner, Stauffer, Sullivan, Taliaferro, Terry, Thomas, Waters, Wells and Wilson—79 members present.

The minutes of yesterday were read, and, on motion of Mr. Abell, their adoption was suspended, for the purpose of allowing gentlemen who were not present yesterday to vote *nunc pro tunc* on the question of the motion to reject the minority report of the Committee on Emancipation, and accordingly the following gentlemen voted:

YEAS—Messrs. Baum, Brott, Collin, Dupaty, Gorlinski, Harnan, Murphy E., Paine J. T.—8.

AND AMENDMENT OF THE CONSTITUTION OF LOUISIANA.

NAYS—Messrs. Balch, Bofill, Campbell, Dufresne, Gruneberg, Mendiverri—6.

The minutes were then amended, on motion of Mr. Abell, by including the names of these gentlemen in the vote of yesterday, and were then adopted as amended.

On motion of Mr. Hills, the sergeant-at-arms was directed to bring in absent members who had not voted on the question of emancipation, in order to record their votes.

Mr. Henderson moved a suspension of the rules, with a view to rescinding the acceptance of the resignation of Mr. Howell.

Mr. Hills moved to amend by a motion to reconsider the vote on Mr. Howell's resignation.

The question on the motion to suspend the rules being then put, resulted as follows:

AYES—Messrs. Ariail, Bailey, Barrett, Baum, Bell, Bonzano, Bromley, Brott, Burke, Collin, Cook J. K., Cook T., Crozat, Duane, Duke, Dupaty, Ennis, Flagg, Flood, Foley, Fosdick, Gastinel, Geier, Goldman, Gorlinski, Heard, Henderson, Hills, Hire, Howes, Kavanagh, Maas, Mayer, Mendiverri, Millspaugh, Murphy E., Orr, Poynot, Seymour, Shaw, Smith, Spellicy, Stocker, Stumpf, Stiner, Stauffer, Taliaferro, Terry and Wilson—49.

NAYS—Messrs. Abell, Balch, Bofill, Buckley, Campbell, Davies, Decker, Dufresne, Gruneberg, Healy, Harnan, Hart, Knobloch, Mann, Maurer, Montamat, Murphy M. W., Normand, O'Conner, Payne Jno., Payne J. T., Pintado, Purcell Jno., Pursell Sam., Sullivan and Waters—26.

Consequently there not being two-thirds in favor of a suspension of the rules, the question was lost.

Mr. Bromley offered the following resolution, which was laid over:

Whereas, The citizens of this State, residing in the country parishes, are in a continual state of alarm, bordering on a panic, which threatens an interruption of all labor, by a simultaneous abandonment of all unprotected parishes in the country, in consequence of raids from the guerrillas; therefore be it

Resolved, That a committee of five be appointed to confer with the governor and the adjutant general of this State to devise ways and means to organize the militia, whereby we may be properly protected in life, in liberty and pursuit of happiness.

Mr. Sam'l Pursell offered the following:

ART.—. Taxation shall be equal and uniform throughout the State. All property shall be taxed in proportion to its value, to be ascertained as directed by law. The General Assembly shall have power to exempt from taxation, property actually used for church, school or charitable purposes. The General Assembly shall levy an income tax upon all persons pursuing any profession, occupation, trade or calling ; and all such persons shall obtain a license as provided by law. All tax on income shall be pro rata on the amount of income or business done.

ART.—. No profession, occupation, business or calling, requiring a license from any authority within the State, shall be carried on, exercised or followed by any other than citizens of the United States, or those having made legal declaration of becoming citizens.

ART.—. The General Assembly shall provide by law for the establishment of a Poor-House, in each parish of the State, for the care of the destitute within their respective limits, and to be conducted as shall be provided by law.

ART.—. All civil officers for the State at large shall be voters of and reside within the State ; and all district or parish officers shall be voters of and reside within their respective parish or district, and shall keep their offices at such places therein as may be required by law.

ART.—. The seat of Government shall be at the city of New Orleans. The General Assembly shall have power to dispose of the present Capitol property in Baton Rouge, and provide, by purchase or othewise, suitable lands and buildings for a State Capitol in New Orleans.

Mr. Brott offered a resolution:

Resolved, That this Convention adjourn *sine die*, at 2 o'clock, P. M. on the 25th inst.

Mr. Hire offered the following:

Resolved, That after next Monday, this Convention hold an evening session, to commence at 6 o'clock P. M., to afford an opportunity for all members to address this Convention, without prolonging our session to an unnecessary length.

Mr. Millspaugh, on behalf of the Committee on Enrollment, reported as correctly enrolled the resolution relative to the publication of two thousand copies of the journal in English and French.

Mr. Wilson, chairman of the Committee on Assault of Members, reported progress.

Mr. Campbell offered the following:

Resolved, That the Committee on Assaulted Members be now discharged.

The order of the day was then taken up, but previous to any discussion, Mr. Abell moved to adjourn until 12 o'clock on Monday, upon which question a division was called—ayes 51, nays 31; consequently the motion was carried, and the Convention adjourned.

Minutes adopted.

JOHN E. NEELIS,
Secretary.

MONDAY, May 9th, 1864.

The Convention met at 12 o'clock M., and was called to order by the president.

The roll was called, and the following gentlemen answered to their names:

Messrs. Abell, Ariail, Bell, Bonzano, Buckley, Burke, Cook J. K., Crozat, Dufresne, Duke, Edwards, Ennis, Fish, Flagg, Geier, Goldman, Gruneberg, Healy, Hart, Heard, Henderson, Hills, Howes, Maas, Mann, Mayer, Millspaugh, Murphy M. W., Newell, Normand, O'Conner, Ong, Pintado, Pursell S., Schroeder, Schnurr, Seymour Shaw, Spellicy, Stocker, Stumpf, Stiner, Terry, Thorpe, Waters, Wenck, Wells, Wilson and Mr. President—49 members present.

There being no quorum the sergeant-at-arms was directed to bring in absent members, and after some delay the following members took their seats, viz:

Messrs—Austin Bailey. Barrett, Bofill, Brott, Campbell Collin, Cook T., Davies, Dupaty, Flood, Foley, Fosdick, Fuller, Gastinel, Gorlinski, Harnan, Hire, Maurer, Mendiverri, Montamat, Murphy E., Payne J., Purcell J., Smith, Stauffer, Taliaferro and Thomas—28 members.

The president announced that a quorum was present.

The minutes of yesterday were read and approved.

RESOLUTIONS.

Mr. S. Pursell offered the following:

Whereas, The notes issued by the city of New Orleans being the only currency now in circulation in this State fully entitled to the confidence of the people, (the currency of the United States excepted); and whereas, designing and bad men, traitors to their country and false to every obligation due to that generous magnanimity that permits them to remain under the protection of a good government, are using every means to depreciate the said notes of the city of New Orleans; therefore be it

Resolved, That any institution or person refusing to receive the said city issue, either on deposit or in payment, is unworthy the confidence of the people, and deserve the attention of the authorities competent to rectify such matters.

Resolved, That this Convention urgently recommend and desire that all heads of departments, either civil or military, having power in the premises, do suppress any and all banks that may be in operation by sufferance, and failing in their duty in accordance with the exigency of the times.

Laid over under the rules, and, on motion of Mr. Stocker, ordered to be printed.

Mr. S. Pursell offered the following:

Whereas, In the fitting up of Liberty Hall for the use of this Convention, provision was made for the accommodation of an audience, and a portion of the same was specially appropriated for ladies, but which fact was not publicly made known; therefore be it

Resolved, That the ladies be and are hereby invited to attend the sessions of this Convention.

Rules suspended and resolution adopted.

Mr. Stumpf then presented the following:

Whereas, The object of this war on the part of the United States against the so-called Confederate States is first, to maintain the Union, to enforce the laws and uphold the Constitution of these United States and all acts of Congress made in pursuance thereto; and in doing this we must not be unmindful of those truly loyal citizens whose interest and whose only wealth consisted in that species of property which the war has destroyed, or rendered useless as property; be it, therefore,

Resolved, by this Convention, That all truly loyal citizens of Louisiana, who have taken the President's Amnesty Oath of Dec. 8, 1863, up to this date, be paid by the United States government a reasonable indemnity for each and every slave assessed in their name as property for the year 1861.

Laid over.

Mr. Thorpe, on behalf of the Committee on Assault of Members, submitted a written report which was received, and made the order of the day for Wednesday next, 11th inst.

Mr. Henderson called up his resolution rescinding the action of the House, in accepting Mr. Howell's resignation.

On the adoption of the resolution, a standing vote was taken resulting ayes 34, nays 40, but there being no quorum voting the yeas and nays were called for with the following result:

YEAS—Messrs. Ariail, Bailey, Barrett, Bonzano, Brott, Campbell, Cazabat, Cook J. K., Cook T, Cutler, Davies, Duane, Dufresne, Duke, Ennis, Fosdick. Fuller. Gastinel, Goldman, Gorlinski, Harnan, Heard, Henderson, Hills, Hire, Howes, Knobloch,

AND AMENDMENT OF THE CONSTITUTION OF LOUISIANA.

Maas, Mann, Mendiverri, Millspaugh, Murphy E., Normand, Ong, Payne J., Seymour, Spellicy, Stocker, Stumpf, Stiner, Taliaferro, Thorpe, Waters, Wells and Wilson—45.

NAYS—Messrs. Abell, Bell, Bofill, Buckley, Burke, Collin, Crozat, Dupaty, Edwards, Flagg, Flood, Geier, Gruneberg, Healy, Hart, Maurer, Montamat, Murphy M. W., Mayer, Newell, O'Conner, Pintado, Purcell J., Pursell S., Schroeder, Schnurr, Stauffer, Sullivan and Terry—29.

Consequently Mr. Henderson's motion prevailed, and was so announced by the president.

Mr. Montamat stated that no quorum had voted and moved to adjourn, upon which motion a division was ordered resulting as follows : ayes 34, nays 38.

No quorum voting a call of the house was ordered, when 75 members were found to be present, and there still being no quorum, Mr. Montamat again moved to adjourn, when the yeas and nays were ordered.

YAES—Messrs. Abell, Ariail, Bailey, Bofill, Brott, Buckley, Burke, Collin, Cook J. K., Dufresne, Duke, Dupaty, Flagg, Fuller, Gastinel, Geier, Gruneberg. Harnan, Hart, Heard, Henderson, Howes, Knobloch, Maas, Maurer, Mayer, Mendiverri, Montamat, Murphy M. W., O'Conner, Purcell J., Schnurr, Seymour, Spellicy, Sullivan and Waters—36.

NAYS—Messrs. Barrett, Bell, Bonzano, Cazabat, Cook T., Crozat, Cutler, Davies, Duane, Edwards, Ennis, Flood, Fosdick, Goldman, Gorlinski, Healy, Hills, Hire, Mann, Millspaugh, Murphy E., Newell, Normand, Ong, Payne J., Pintado, Pursell S., Schroeder, Shaw, Smith, Stocker, Stumpf, Stiner, Stauffer, Taliaferro, Terry, Thorpe, Wells and Wilson—39.

Consequently the Convention refused to adjourn.

The Convention then resumed its action on the majority report of the Committee on Emancipation, which having been read was taken up section by section.

Mr. Wilson moved to amend the first section by adding in the third line, the words "and that loyal owners shall be compensated."

Mr. Goldman moved to lay the amendment on the table, upon which motion the yeas and nays were called.

YEAS—Messrs. Ariail, Austin, Bailey, Bonzano, Burke, Collin, Cazabat, Cook J. K., Cutler, Davies, Duane, Dupaty, Edwards, Ennis, Fish, Flagg, Flood, Foley, Fosdick, Goldman, Gorlinski, Healy, Harnan, Hills, Hire, Howes, Maas, Mann, Millspaugh, Murphy E., Newell, Normand, Payne J., Pintado, Pursell S., Schroeder, Schnurr, Shaw, Smith, Spellicy, Stauffer, Taliaferro, Terry, Thorpe, Wells—45.

NAYS—Messrs. Abell, Barrett, Bell, Bofill, Brott, Buckley, Cook T., Crozat, Dufresne, Duke, Fuller, Gruneberg, Hart, Heard, Henderson, Knobloch, Maurer, Mayer, Mendiverri, Montamat, Murphy M. W., O'Conner, Ong, Seymour, Stocker, Stumpf, Stiner, Sullivan, Waters, Wilson—30.

Consequently, Mr. Wilson's amendment was laid on the table.

Mr. Montamat moved to adjourn, upon which the yeas and nays were ordered :

YEAS—Messrs. Abell, Bofill, Buckley, Burke, Collin, Cook J. K., Crozat, Duane, Dufresne, Duke, Dupaty, Fuller, Heard, Henderson, Knobloch, Maas, Maurer, Mayer, Mendiverri, Montamat, Muryhy M. W., O'Conner, Ong, Schnurr, Seymour, Stocker, Stumpf, Sullivan, Waters—29.

NAYS—Messrs. Ariail, Austin, Bailey, Barrett, Bell, Bonzano, Brott, Cazabat, Cook T., Cutler, Davies, Ennis, Flagg, Flood, Foley, Fosdick, Goldman, Gorlinski, Healy, Harnan, Hart, Hills, Hire, Howes, Mann, Millspaugh, Murphy E., Newell, Normand, Payne J., Pintado, Pursell S., Schroeder, Shaw, Smith, Spellicy, Stiner, Stauffer, Taliaferro, Terry, Thorpe, Wells and Wilson—43.

The Convention refused to adjourn.

There being no quorum the doors were ordered to be closed, and the sergeant-at-arms was dispatched for absent members.

After some delay a call of the house was ordered, and 78 members found to be present. The president announced a quorum present.

Mr. Stauffer called for the previous question, which, being seconded, the main question was ordered to be put by the house.

Mr. Campbell offered the following provisos to the first section, which were declared out of order by the president, the main question having been ordered:

Provided, That the same shall not go into effect until the year one thousand nine hundred, and that the State shall accept the proposition of the government of the United States made to the Slave States on that basis ;

Provided further, That all legislation hereafter had on the subject of slavery, shall look to the amelioration of the condition of the slaves, with a view to their final and complete emancipation on the first day of January, in the year 1900 as *offered* by the government of the United States, through the president, and which offer (the basis of 1900,) we, the people of Louisiana, in convention assembled, do now accept.

On the motion to adopt the first section, the yeas and nays were ordered resulting as follows:

YEAS— Messrs. Ariail, Austin, Bailey, Barrett, Bell, Bonzano, Brott, Burke, Cazabat, Cook J. K., Cook T., Crozat, Cutler, Davies, Duane, Dupaty, Edwards, Ennis, Fish, Flagg, Flood, Foley, Fosdick, Fuller, Goldman, Gorlinski, Healy, Harnan, Hart, Henderson, Hills, Hire, Howes, Maas, Mann, Millspaugh, Murphy E., Newell, Normand, O'Conner, Ong, Payne J., Pintado, Purcell J., Purcell S., Schroeder, Shnurr, Shaw, Smith, Spellicy, Stocker, Stumpf, Stiner, Stauffer, Taliaferro, Terry, Thorpe, Thomas, Wells and Wilson—60.

NAYS— Messrs. Abell, Bofill, Buckley, Campbell, Collin, Dufresne, Duke, Gastinel, Heard, Knobloch, Maurer, Mayer, Mendiverri, Montamat, Murphy M. W., Seymour, Sullivan and Waters—18.

Consequently the first section was adopted.

Mr. Montamat moved to adjourn, upon which motion the yeas and nays were ordered, resulting:

YEAS—Messrs. Abell, Buckley, Barrett, Bofill, Campbell, Collin, Cook J. K., Crozat, Dufresne, Duke, Flagg, Fuller, Gastinel, Hart, Heard, Knobloch, Maas, Maurer, Mayer, Mendiverri, Millspaugh, Montamat, Murphy M. W., Ong, Seymour, Stumpf, Sullivan, Waters, and Wilson—29.

NAYS—Messrs. Ariail, Austin, Bailey, Bell, Bonzano, Brott, Burke, Cazabat, Cook T., Cutler, Davies, Duane, Dupaty, Edwards, Ennis, Fish, Flood, Foley, Fosdick, Goldman, Gorlinski, Healy, Harnan, Henderson, Hills, Hire, Howes, Mann, Murphy E., Newell, Normand, O'Conner, Payne J., Pintado, Purcell J., Purcell S., Schroeder, Schnurr, Shaw, Smith, Spellicy, Stocker, Stiner, Stauffer, Taliaferro, Terry, Thorpe, Thomas and Wells—49.

The second section being read, on a motion to adopt the same the yeas and nays were ordered, with the following result:

YEAS—Messrs. Ariail, Austin, Bailey, Barrett, Bell, Bonzano, Brott, Burke, Collin, Cazabat, Cook J. K., Cook T., Crozat, Cutler, Davies, Duane, Dupaty, Edwards, Ennis, Fish, Flagg, Flood, Foley, Fosdick, Fuller, Goldman, Gorlinski, Healy, Harnan, Hart, Henderson, Hills, Hire, Howes, Maas, Mann, Millspaugh, Murphy E., Murphy M. W., Newell, Normand, O'Conner, Ong, Payne J., Pintado, Purcell J., Purcell S., Schroeder, Schnurr, Shaw, Smith, Spellicy, Stocker, Stumpf, Stiner, Stauffer, Taliaferro, Terry, Thorpe, Thomas, Wells, Wilson—62.

NAYS— Messrs. Abell, Bofill, Buckley, Campbell, Dufresne, Duke, Gastinel, Heard, Knobloch, Maurer, Mayer, Mendiverri, Montamat, Seymour, Sullivan, Waters—16.

Consequently, the second section was adopted.

The Convention then adjourned until 12 o'clock to-morrow.

Minutes adopted.

JOHN E. NEELIS,
Secretary.

TUESDAY, May 10th, 1864.

The Convention met pursuant to adjournment, and after prayer by the Rev. Mr. Strong, the roll was called and the following members answered to their names:

Messrs. Abell, Ariail, Austin, Barrett, Baum, Beauvais, Bell, Bennie, Bofill, Bonzano, Burke, Collin, Cazabat, Cook J. K., Crozat, Decker, Duane, Dufresne, Duke, Edwards, Ennis, Fish, Flagg, Flood, Fosdick, Gastinel, Geier, Goldman, Gorlinski, Healy, Harnan, Hart, Heard, Hills, Hire, Kavanagh, Knobloch, Maas, Mann, Mayer, Mendiverri, Millspaugh, Murphy M. W., Newell, Normand, O'Conner, Ong, Orr, Payne J., Poynot, Pursell S., Schroeder, Stauffer, Schnurr, Seymour, Spellicy, Stumpf, Stiner, Sullivan, Taliaferro, Terry, Thomas, Wells and Wilson—64.

There being no quorum present, the sergeant-at-arms was ordered to bring in absent members.

After some delay, Messrs. Bailey, Beauvais, Buckley, Cook T., Davies, Dupaty, Foley, Henderson, Morris, Murphy, Montamat, Maurer, Purcell J., Stocker and Thorpe, having taken their seats and answered to their names, the president declared a quorum present.

The minutes of yesterday were read and, previous to their adoption, Mr. Campbell asked a suspension of the rules, in order that his provisos offered to first section of the majority report of the Committee on Emancipation, might be read.

The House having refused to suspend the rules, the minutes were adopted.

On motion of Mr. Hills, the names of the members who did not vote on the question of the rejection of the minority report of the Committee on Emancipation, were called, with a view to their voting on that

AND AMENDMENT OF THE CONSTITUTION OF LOUISIANA. 71

question, when Mr. Ong voted yea, and Mr. Schnurr voted nay.

Mr. Hills also asked that the roll of members who were absent and did not vote on the adoption of the first and second sections of the majority report of the Committee on Emancipation, be read.

The president put the question on the adoption of the first section, and the secretary called the roll, with the following result:

Messrs. Baum, Beauvais, Geier, Kavanagh, Morris, Orr, Poynot and Wenck—8 voted yea.

Messrs. Balch and Decker, voted nay.

The president then put the question on the adoption of the second section of the majority report of the Committee on Emancipation, in order that said members should record their votes thereon, when the secretary called the roll, and the following members voted yea:

Messrs. Baum, Beauvais, Geier, Kavanagh, Morris, Orr, Poynot, Wenck—8.

Messrs. Balch and Decker voted nay.

Mr. Gorlinski, chairman of the Committee on Internal Improvements, submitted a written report.

Mr. Campbell, also of the Committee on Internal Improvements, submitted a minority report.

On motion of Mr. Hills, the reports were received and ordered to be printed, and taken up in their regular order.

Mr. Stocker, chairman of Special Committee on Absent Members, stated that the members whose names had been referred to the committee were all present excepting one, and that the committee were not yet prepared to report regarding him.

Mr. Stumpf called up his resolution of yesterday, which was read.

Mr. Hire moved to refer it to the Committee on Emancipation, but that committee being declared an improper one, for the question, no action was taken on the motion.

Mr. Cazabat offered the following resolution as a substitute for that of Mr. Stumpf.

Resolved, That a committee of five be appointed by the president of this Convention, to draw appropriate resolutions expressing and recommending to the President and Congress of the United States the justice and equity of making such appropriations as may be deemed proper and right for a fair compensation to loyal citizens of Louisiana for the loss of their property upon such terms, conditions and proof as may be required.

Mr. Abell moved to amend Mr. Cazabat's substitute by adding a proviso, restraining the effect of the emancipation clause in the constitution until compensation shall have been made for the slaves affected thereby.

Which amendment was declared not in order, for the reason that it required an impossibility.

The substitute offered by Mr. Cazabat was then taken up and adopted.

The resolution offered by Mr. S. Pursell on yesterday, was then taken up, and, on motion of Mr. Stauffer, was referred to a special committee of five.

Mr. Thorpe offered the following:

Resolved, That the chairman of the Committee on Enrollment be permitted to add the words, "and debates," to the resolution calling for the printing of 200 copies of the journals.

A motion to suspend the rules for the purpose of taking up the resolution, was lost.

Mr. Abell gave notice that he would offer amendments to the several remaining articles of the report of the Committee on Emancipation.

The report of the Committee on Emancipation being unfinished business, was next taken up.

Mr. Abell offered the following proviso to section 3d:

Provided always, That the Legislature shall never pass any act authorizing free negroes to vote, or to immigrate into this State under any pretence whatever.

Mr. Foley moved a division of the proviso. Carried.

The first division, "*Providing always*, That the Legislature shall never pass any act authorizing free negroes to vote," was stated to the Convention. A motion to lay it on the table was lost upon the following vote:

YEAS—Messrs. Ariail, Austin, Bennie, Bonzano, Collin, Cazabat, Cook J. K., Davies, Dupaty, Ennis, Flagg, Flood, Fosdick, Goldman, Gorlinski, Hills, Hire, Maas, Newell, Pintado, Schroeder, Shaw, Stauffer, Taliaferro, Thorpe and Wells—26.

NAYS—Messrs. Abell, Bailey, Barrett,

Baum, Beauvais, Bell, Bofill, Buckley, Burke, Cook T., Crozat, Decker, Duane, Dufresne, Duke, Edwards, Fish, Foley, Gastinel, Geier, Gruneberg, Healy, Harnan, Hart, Heard, Henderson, Kavanagh, Knobloch, Mann, Maurer, Mayer, Mendiverri, Millspaugh, Montamat, Morris, Murphy E., Murphy M. W., Normand, O'Conner, Ong, Orr, Payne J., Poynot, Purcell J., Pursell S., Schnurr, Seymour, Spellicy, Stocker, Stumpf, Stiner, Sullivan, Terry, Thomas, Wenck and Wilson—55.

The question then recurred upon the adoption of the first clause of the proviso, when the vote was taken with the following result:

YEAS—Messrs. Abell, Ariail, Bailey, Barrett, Baum, Bennie, Beauvais, Bell, Bofili, Bonzano, Brott, Buckley, Burke, Cutler, Campbell, Cook J. K., Cook T., Crozat, Davies, Decker, Duane, Dufresne, Duke, Edwards, Ennis, Fish, Flood, Foley, Fuller, Gastinel, Geier, Gruneberg, Healy, Harnan, Hart, Heard, Henderson, Kugler, Kavanagh, Knobloch, Maas, Mann, Maurer, Mayer, Mendiverri, Millspaugh, Montamat, Morris, Murphy E., Murphy M. W., Newell, Normand, O'Conner, Ong, Orr. Payne J., Poynot, Purcell J., Pursell S., Schroeder, Schnurr, Seymour, Spellicy, Stocker, Stumpf, Stiner, Stauffer, Sullivan, Taliaferro, Terry, Thomas, Wenck, Waters, Wells and Wilson—68.

NAYS—Messrs. Austin, Bennie, Collin, Cazabat, Dupaty, Flagg, Fosdick, Goldman, Gorlinski, Hills, Hire, Pintado, Shaw, Smith, Thorpe—15.

Consequently, the first clause of the proviso was adopted.

Mr. Duane moved to lay the second clause of the proviso on the table, upon which motion the yeas and nays were called, and the vote taken as follows:

YEAS—Messrs. Ariail, Bailey, Bennie, Bonzano, Brott, Burke, Collin, Cazabat, Davies, Duane, Dupaty, Edwards, Ennis, Fish, Flagg, Flood, Fosdick, Geier, Goldman, Gorlinski, Hart, Henderson, Hills, Hire, Maas, Mann, Morris, Murphy E., Normand, Payne J., Pintado, Poynot, Pursell S., Shaw, Smith, Spellicy, Stiner, Stauffer, Terry, Thorpe—40.

NAYS—Messrs. Abell, Austin, Baum, Barrett, Beauvais, Bell, Bofill, Buckley, Cook J. K., Cook T., Crozat, Decker, Dufresne, Duke, Foley, Gastinel, Harnan, Healy, Heard, Kavanagh, Knobloch, Maurer, Mayer, Mendiverri, Millspaugh, Montamat, Murphy M. W., O'Conner, Ong, Orr, Purcell J., Schnurr, Seymour, Stocker, Stumpf, Sullivan, Thomas, Waters, Wenck, Wilson—40.

There being a tie vote, the president voted in the negative, consequently the motion to lay on the table was lost.

Pending discussion on the adoption of the second clause of the proviso, the Convention adjourned until 12 o'clock to-morrow. Adopted.

JOHN E. NEELIS,
Secretary.

WEDNESDAY, May 11th, 1864.

The Convention met at 12 o'clock M., and the proceedings were opened with prayer by the Rev. Mr. Andrews.

The roll was called and the following members answered to their names:

Messrs. Abell, Ariail, Austin, Beauvais, Bell. Bennie, Bofill, Bonzano, Bromley, Buckley, Burke, Campbell, Collin, Cook J. K. Cook T., Davies, Decker, Duane, Dufresne, Duke, Edwards, Flagg, Flood, Fosdick, Gastinel, Goldman, Geier, Gorlinski, Gruneberg, Healy, Hart, Heard, Henderson, Hills, Hire, Howes, Kavanagh, Kugler, Maas, Mann, Maurer, Mayer, Millspaugh, Murphy M. W., Newell, Normand, O'Conner, Payne J., Pintado, Pursell S., Schnurr, Seymour, Shaw, Smith, Spellicy. Stumpf, Stiner, Stauffer, Taliaferro, Terry, Waters and Wenck—62.

There not being a quorum present the sergeant-at-arms was directed to procure the attendance of absent members.

Messrs. Barrett, Baum, Fish, Foley, Fuller, Mendiverri, Montamat, Orr, Poynot, Purcell J., Schroeder, Stocker, Sullivan, Thorpe, Thomas and Wells—16, having taken their seats, the president announced that a quorum was present.

The minutes of yesterday were read and their adoption suspended for the purpose of allowing several gentlemen to record their votes, as follows:

On the adoption of first clause of Mr. Abell's proviso to the 3d section of the majority report of the Committee on Emancipation. Messrs. Campbell, Bennie, Cutler, Fuller, Paine J. T. and Waters, voted yea. Mr. Kugler voted nay.

On the second clause of the same proviso. Messs. Paine J. T. and Campbell voted yea, and Mr. Gruneberg voted nay.

On the adoption of the first and second article of the majority report of the Committee on Emancipation, Mr. Kugler voted yea.

Mr. Heard rose to a question of privilege

AND AMENDMENT OF THE CONSTITUTION OF LOUISIANA. 73

and read an article from the morning's Era, containing some strictures against the members who voted against the majority report of the Committee on Emancipation, against which he protested and read some remarks of his own expressive of his opinion that the Convention should be dictated to by no one.

On the committee, under Mr. Cazabat's resolution relative to compensation to loyal persons for loss of property, the president appointed Messrs. Cazabat, Wells, Fosdick, Abell and Taliaferro.

Mr. Thorpe called up his resolution of yesterday allowing him to amend his former resolution relative to the publication of two thousand copies of the journals in French and English, by adding the words " and debates."

Mr. Abell moved to amend the resolution by inserting "five thousand," instead of two thousand.

Mr. Edwards moved to lay the amendment on the table. Lost.

Mr. Abell's amendment was then adopted.

The question then recurred upon the adoption of the resolution as amended, which was carried and the resolution adopted.

The report of the Committee on Emancipation being unfinished business, was taken up.

Mr. Stauffer moved to strike out entirely the 3d section with the amendments thereto.

Messrs. Bonzano and Thomas moved to amend Mr. Stauffer's motion by adding 4th and 5th sections, which amendments were accepted.

Mr. Stocker called Mr. Stauffer to order, as he thought it was a motion to strike out something not before the House, the pending question being on the adoption of the second clause of Mr. Abell's proviso to the 3d section:

The president decided that Mr. Stauffer was in order.

Mr. Abell moved to lay the motion to strike out on the table, upon which the yeas and nays were ordered, resulting as follows :

YEAS—Messrs. Abell, Barrett, Bofill, Buckley, Campbell, Crozat, Decker, Dufresne, Duke, Edwards. Gastinel, Gruneberg, Heard, Kugler, Mann, Maurer, Mayer, Mendiverri, Montamat, Murphy M. W., Normand, Payne J., Stocker, Stumpf, Sullivan—25.

NAYS—Messrs. Ariail, Austin, Bailey, Beauvais, Bell, Bennie, Bonzano, Bromley, Burke, Collin, Cook J. K., Cook T., Cutler, Davies, Duane, Dupaty, Flood, Foley, Fosdick, Fuller, Geier, Goldman, Gorlinski, Healy, Harnan, Hart, Henderson, Hills, Hire, Howes, Maas, Millspaugh, Murphy E., Newell, O'Conner, Orr, Paine J. T., Pintado, Poynot, Purcell J., Pursell S., Schroeder, Schnurr, Shaw, Smith Spellicy, Stiner, Stauffer, Taliaferro, Terry, Thorpe, Thomas, Wenck, Wells, Wilson—55

The previous question was then called for by Mr. Austin, and, upon a division was carried, and the main question was then put :

Shall the 3d, 4th and 5th articles of the report of the Committee on Emancipation be stricken out?

The yeas and nays being ordered, the vote was as follows :

YEAS—Messrs. Ariail, Austin, Bailey, Beauvais, Bell, Bennie, Bonzano, Bromley, Burke, Collin, Cook J. K., Cook T., Cutler, Davies, Duane, Dupaty, Fish, Flood, Foley, Fosdick, Fuller, Geier, Goldman, Gorlinski, Healy, Harnan, Hart, Henderson, Hills, Hire, Howes, Maas, Mann, Millspaugh, Morris, Murphy E., Newell, O'Conner, Orr, Payne J., Paine J. T., Pintado, Poynot, Purcell J., Schroeder, Schnurr, Shaw, Smith, Spellicy, Stocker, Stumpf, Stiner, Stauffer, Taliaferro, Terry, Thorpe, Thomas, Wenck, Wells, Wilson—60.

NAYS—Messrs. Abell, Barrett, Bofill, Buckley, Crozat, Decker, Dufresne, Duke, Edwards, Flagg, Gastinel, Gruneberg, Heard, Kugler, Maurer, Mayer. Mendiverri, Montamat, Morris, Murphy M. W., Normand, Ong, Pursell S., Sullivan—24.

Consequently the motion was carried, and the second reading completed.

The special order of the day, viz: the report of the Committee on Assault of Members, being next in order, was, on motion of Mr. Thorpe, laid over until Monday, 16th instant.

Mr. Bonzano moved to suspend the rules in order to take up the report of the Committee on Emancipation, on its third reading.

On a division, there being no quorum voting, a call of the House was ordered, and 85 members answered to their names.

Mr. Campbell moved to recommit the whole matter relative to emancipation to a select committee of —— members, to be chosen by the House.

74   JOURNAL OF THE CONVENTION FOR THE REVISION

The president declared Mr. Campbell out of order.

Messrs. Thorpe and Henderson renewed Mr. Bonzano's motion to suspend the rules for the purpose of putting the report of the Committee on Emancipation on its third reading, upon which motion the yeas and nays were ordered, and the following vote was taken :

YEAS—Messrs. Ariail, Austin, Bailey, Barrett, Beauvais, Bell, Bennie, Bofill, Bonzano, Bromley, Burke, Collin, Cook J. K., Cook T. Crozat. Cutler, Davies, Duane, Dupaty, Edwards, Fish, Flagg, Flood, Foley, Fosdick, Fuller, Gastinel, Geier, Goldman, Gorlinski, Harnan, Hart, Healy, Henderson, Hills, Hire, Howes, Kugler, Maas, Mann, Mayer, Millspaugh, Montamat, Morris, Murphy E., Murphy M. W.. Newell, Normand, O'Conner, Orr, Payne J.. Paine J. T., Pintado, Poynot, Purcell J., Pursell S., Schroeder, Schnurr, Shaw, Smith, Spellicy, Stocker, Stumpf, Stiner, Stauffer, Taliaferro, Terry, Thorpe, Thomas, Wenck, Wells, Wilson—72.

NAYS—Messrs. Abell, Buckley, Campbell, Decker, Dufresne, Duke, Gruneberg, Heard, Maurer, Mendiverri, Ong, Sullivan—12.

The rules being suspended the report was then taken up and read by the secretary.

Messrs. Abell and Campbell offered amendments to the report, but were declared out of order.

The previous question was called for by Mr. Bonzano and ordered.

The main question was then put. Shall the report of the Committee on Emancipation be adopted, viz : ?

Section 1. *Slavery and Involuntary Servitude*, except as a punishment for crime, whereof the party shall have been duly convicted, are hereby forever ABOLISHED AND PROHIBITED throughout the State.

Sec. 2. The Legislature shall make no law recognizing the RIGHT OF PROPERTY IN MAN.

The vote was as follows :

YEAS—Messrs. Ariail, Austin, Barrett, Beauvais, Bofill, Bell, Bennie, Bonzano, Bromley, Burke, Collin, Cook J. K., Cook T., Crozat, Cutler, Davies, Duane, Dupaty, Edwards, Fish, Flagg, Flood, Foley, Fosdick, Fuller, Geier, Goldman, Gorlinski, Healy, Harnan, Hart, Henderson, Hills, Hire, Howes, Kugler, Maas, Mann, Millspaugh, Montamat, Morris, Murphy E., Murphy M. W., Newell, Normand, O'Conner, Ong, Orr, Payne J., Paine J. T., Pintado. Poynot, Purcell J.. Pursell S.. Schroeder, Schnurr, Sullivan, Shaw. Smith. Spellicy, Stocker, Stumpf, Stiner, Stauffer, Taliaferro, Terry, Thorpe, Thomas, Wenck, Wells, Wilson. and Mr. President—72.

NAYS—Messrs. Abell, Buckley, Campbell, Decker, Dufresne, Duke, Gastinel, Gruneberg, Heard, Maurer. Mayer. Mendiverri. Waters—13.

On motion of Mr. Thomas the Convention adjourned until 12 o'clock to-morrow.

Approved.

JOHN E. NEELIS,
Secretary.

THURSDAY, May 12th, 1864.

The Convention met pursuant to adjournment, and, after prayer by the Rev. Mr. Andrews, the roll was called and the following members answered to their names :

Messrs. Ariail, Bennie, Bonzano, Bofill, Burke, Collin, Crozat, Decker, Dufresne, Duke, Edwards, Ennis, Gorlinski, Heard, Howes, Kugler, Millspaugh, Murphy M. W.. Newell, Normand, O'Conner, Pintado. Pursell S., Shaw, Spellicy, Stumpf, Stiner, Sullivan, Taliaferro. Thorpe, Thomas, Wells and Wilson—33.

After some delay the following members entered the hall and took their seats :

Messrs. Abell, Austin, Bailey, Barrett. Bell, Bromley, Beauvais, Buckley, Campbell, Cazabat. Cook J. K., Cook T., Cutler, Fish, Flagg, Flood, Foley, Fosdick, Gastinel, Geier Goldman, Gruneberg, Healy, Harnan, Hart, Hills, Hire, Maas, Mann, Maurer. Mayer, Mendiverri, Montamat, Morris, Murphy E., Poynot, Purcell J.. Schroeder, Schnurr, Smith. Stauffer. Waters and Wenck—43.

The president announced that there was a quorum. The minutes of yesterday were read, and, previous to there adoption, Messrs. Bofill and Sullivan were allowed to change their vote from nay to yea, on the adoption of the majority report of the Committee on Emancipation.

The minutes were accordingly amended and adopted.

The following gentlemen having been absent at the time the vote was taken on the adoption of the 1st and 2d sections of the majority report of the Committee on Emancipation, were to-day called upon to record their votes, thereon, viz : Messrs. Cazabat and Ennis, both of whom voted yes.

Mr. Bennie was called upon to record his

vote on the motion to reject the minority report of the Committee on Emancipation. He voted yes.

Mr. Wilson moved to adjourn until Monday next. Lost.

Mr. Abell asked to be excused from serving on the committee appointed under Mr. Cazabat's resolution relative to correspondence with the authorities of the government at Washington for reasons which he stated to the Convention. On motion of Mr. Bonzano, Mr. Abell was excused, and the President then appointed Mr. Ariail on said committee.

Mr. Heard, chairman of the Committee on Preamble, submitted a report on the substitute (for preamble) offered by Mr. Cazabat.

On motion of Mr. Hills, the report was accepted and the committee discharged.

Mr. Thorpe, chairman of the Committee on Enrollment, reported as correctly enrolled.

1. An ordinance to abolish slavery and involuntary servitude.
2. A resolution relative to printing five thousand copies of the journal and debates.

Mr. Thomas called attention to the omission of the words "in the year of our Lord," and "sitting," in the ordinance abolishing slavery, and moved to refer it back to the Committee on Enrollment, which motion was carried.

The resolution as enrolled was received, and on motion of Mr. Bell, the president was requested to affix his signature thereto.

The president appointed on the committee raised by Mr. Pursell's resolution relative to city currency, Messrs. Pursell, Fosdick, Stauffer, Bonzano, and Brott.

The president laid before the Convention a communication from Dr. A. P. Dostie, state auditor, containing a statement showing the receipts and expenditures of the treasury during the administration of Brig. Gen. G. F. Shepley, late military governor of the State.

Mr. Austin moved to refer the matter to a select committee of five, to be appointed by the president. Carried.

The president appointed on said committee, Messrs. Austin, Thomas, Fish, Wells and Beauvais.

On motion of Mr. Mendiverri, one thousand (1000) copies were ordered to be printed.

Mr. Hills wished to know if the reports of the Committees on Preamble and Distribution of Powers had been finally adopted.

Upon a reference to the minutes, it was ascertained that those reports had only passed their second reading, consequently they came up for a third reading.

The report of the Committee on Preamble was then read, with a view to its final adoption, the rules having been suspended on motion of Mr. Mann for that purpose.

Mr. Cutler thought the words "and we recommend its adoption," unnecessary.

The president replied that it was a part of the report and not of the preamble.

Mr. Henderson moved the previous question, which being ordered, the main question was put. The yeas and nays were ordered, with the following result:

YEAS—Messrs. Abell, Ariail, Austin, Barrett, Bailey, Beauvais, Bell, Bennie, Bofill. Bonzano, Bromley, Buckley, Burke, Campbell, Cazabat, Collin, Cook J. K., Cook T., Crozat, Cutler, Decker, Dufresne, Duke, Dupaty, Edwards, Ennis, Fish, Flagg, Flood, Foley, Fosdick, Gastinel, Geier, Goldman. Gorlinski, Gruneberg, Harnan, Hart, Healy. Heard, Henderson, Hills, Hire, Howes, Kugler, Maas, Mann, Maurer, Mayer, Mendiverri, Millspaugh, Montamat, Morris, Murphy E., Murphy M. W., Newell, Normand, O'Conner, Pintado, Poynot, Purcell J., Pursell S., Schroeder. Schnurr, Shaw, Smith, Spellicy, Stocker, Stumpf, Stiner, Stauffer, Sullivan. Taliaferro, Thorpe, Thomas, Waters, Wells, Wenck. Wilson—79.

NAYS—None.

The report of the Committee on the Distribution of Powers, was then taken up and passed its second reading.

On motion of Mr. Henderson the rules were suspended, and the report put upon its third reading.

Mr. Hills moved that it be adopted and enrolled as title 1st and art. 1, and 2 of the Constitution.

The question was then put on the final adoption of the report, and carried by the following vote:

Yeas—Messrs. Abell, Ariail, Austin, Barrett, Beauvais, Bell, Bennie, Bofill, Bonzano, Bromley, Buckley, Burke, Campbell, Collin, Cazabat, Cook J. K., Cook T., Crozat, Cutler, Decker, Dufresne, Duke, Dupaty, Edwards, Ennis, Flagg, Flood, Foley, Fosdick, Gastinel, Geier, Goldman, Gorlinski, Gruneberg, Harnan, Hart, Heard, Henderson, Hills, Hire, Howes, Kugler, Maas, Mann, Maurer, Mayer, Mendiverri, Millspaugh, Montamat, Morris, Murphy E., Murphy M. W., Newell, Normand, O'Connor, Pintado, Poynot, Purcell J., Purcell S., Schroeder, Schnurr, Shaw, Smith, Spellicy, Stocker, Stumpf, Stiner, Stauffer, Sullivan, Taliaferro, Thorpe, Thomas, Waters, Wenck, Wells and Wilson—76.

On motion of Mr. Hills, the numbering and arrangement of the different parts of the Constitution were ordered to be postponed until the whole shall have been adopted.

On motion of Mr. Abell, the report of the Committee on Legislative Department was fixed for its second reading on Tuesday, May 17th, at 1 o'clock P. M.

The Convention then adjourned until Tuesday next, May 17th, at 12 o'clock M. Approved.

JOHN E. NEELIS,
Secretary.

TUESDAY, May 17th, 1864.

The Convention met at 12 o'clock M., pursuant to adjournment.

The roll was called and the following members answered to their names:

Messrs. Abell, Arlall, Balch, Barrett, Beauvais, Bell, Bennie, Bofill, Bonzano, Burke, Cook T., Crozat, Davis, Duane, Dufresne, Edwards, Ennis, Fish, Flagg, Flood, Fosdick, Geier, Goldman, Gorlinski, Hart, Henderson, Hills, Howes, Kugler, Maas, Mann, Mayer, Millspaugh, Montague, Murphy M. W., Newell, Normand, Pintado, Purcell J., Pursell S., Schroeder, Seymour, Shaw, Smith, Spellicy, Stumpf, Stiner, Taliaferro, Terry, Thorpe, Wenck, Wells, Wilson, and Mr. President—54. No quorum.

The sergeant-at-arms was directed to procure the attendance of absent members.

The following gentlemen having taken their seats, viz: Messrs. Austin, Bailey, Baum, Bromley, Buckley, Campbell, Cazabat, Cook J. K., Cutler, Dupaty, Fuller, Healy, Howell, Maurer, Mendiverri, Montamat, Morris, O'Conner, Ong, Orr, Poynot, Stocker, Stauffer, Sullivan and Thomas, 25 members, the president announced a quorum present.

The minutes of Thursday, 12th inst., were read and approved.

Messrs. Montague, Seymour and Howell, having been absent at the time the vote was taken on the reports of the Committee on Emancipation, desired to record their votes thereon.

On the motion to reject the minority report each of them voted "yes."

On the adoption of the majority report as passed, each of them voted "yes."

Mr. John Purcell offered the following resolution:

Resolved, That all bills of the official printer of this Convention, be audited and approved by the Committee on Printing, the Committee on Finance, and the Committee on Expenses, in accordance with the rates fixed by the Convention, before payment, and that all bills so audited and approved be paid upon the warrant of the president upon the treasurer of the State out of any moneys not otherwise appropriated.

The rules were suspended and the resolution adopted.

Mr. Henderson offered the following preamble and resolutions:

Whereas, It has been the invariable custom of every Legislature of the State to make liberal appropriations from the general fund for the support and relief of all incorporated charitable institutions, and in respect to which she is second to no State in the Union, whether numbers, variety or extent of the field of charitable labor is considered; *and, whereas,* the Legislature of 1860 did make appropriations as follows under that head, to-wit:

For the Orphans' Home, in New Orleans,	$1500
For the St. Mary's Catholic Orphan Boys' Asylum in New Orleans,	4000
For the Female Orphan Asylum, Camp Street,	4000
For the House of the Good Shepherd,	250
For the Jewish Widows' and Orphans' Asylum,	500
For the St. Joseph Catholic Orphan Asylum,	1500
For the St. Elizabeth House of Industry,	1000
For the Society for the relief of the Orphan Boys, Fourth District,	1000
For the Institution for Indigent Colored Boys, Third District,	1000
For the Ladies of Providence, Third District,	750
For St. Anna's Asylum for Destitute Widows and Children,	1500
For the Children's Home of the Protestant Episcopal Church,	500
For the Catholic Institute of Destitute Orphans,	750

AND AMENDMENT OF THE CONSTITUTION OF LOUISIANA. 77

For the Catholic Benevolent Association, Baton Rouge,.......... 250
For the Female Orphan Asylum, Baton Rouge,................ 500
For the St. Vincent Orphan Asylum, Donaldsonville,.............. 500
For the Milne Asylum, New Orleans, 500

Total,................... $20,000

And, whereas, In consequence of the calamities, growing out of the rebellious war now prevailing, which has not only dried up to a great extent the sources of private benevolence and diminished their revenues to almost nothing, but has been the means of greatly increasing their burthens by the addition it has made to the list of orphans, indigent widows, and the destitute of all classes who stand in the need of charity, so that the worthy, patient and self-sacrificing sisters and managers of these heavenly endowed institutions are reduced to the greatest distress to provide food and raiment for the thousands of helpless beings under their charge; and were it not for the bounty of the Federal Government, through its officers of this department, in donating them daily army rations for their support, many of them wohld be compelled to close their doors; be it therefore

Resolved, That the sum of $20,000 be and is hereby appropriated from the general fund for the support and relief of the charitable institutions as named in the foregoing schedule, to be divided according to the amounts therein stated, and to be paid in the usual manner, by warrants from the auditor on the treasurer, in favor of the managers and authorized agents of said institutions.

Laid over until to-morrow.

Mr. Foley presented the following:

Whereas, Several members of the Louisiana Constitutional Convention have been elected as delegates to Baltimore; *and, whereas,* it is vitally important to the interests of Louisiana that the Convention should complete its work without adjournment, therefore

Be it resolved, That the members of this Convention, who are elected to the Baltimore Convention, and who choose to go there, shall resign their seats in this Convention immediately, and the governor be requested to issue his proclamation for an election to fill the vacancies in the different Parishes and Representative Districts so vacated.

Laid over.

Mr. Thomas moved the adoption of the report of the Committee on Printing, which motion was carried and the report adopted.

Mr. Montamat, submitted the following report of the Committee of Finance which was then adopted.

REPORT OF THE FINANCE COMMITTEE OF THE CONSTITUTIONAL CONVENTION OF THE FUNDS FOR THE PAYMENT OF PER DIEM OF MEMBERS AND SALARIES OF OFFICERS.

May 9, 1864, paid warrant No. 27. $2,930 00
" 9,   "   "   "   " 28.   405 00
" 10, "   "   "   " 29.   696 00
" 10, "   "   "   " 30. 3,500 00
" 14, "   "   "   " 31. 2,520 00
" 14, "   "   "   " 32. 1,275 00
" 15, "   "   "   " 34. 1,420 00

$12,764 00
May 17—Balance on hand this day..............·....$55,485 40

$68,231 40

REPORT ON THE FUNDS FOR CONTINGENT EXPENSES.

May 15, 1864, paid warrant No. 33 to Mr. DeCoursey, as per voucher No. 4.......$ 1,747 37
May 17, 1864, balance on hand to date................... 9,585 48

$11,332 85

The order of the day was then taken up-viz: the report of the Committee on Legislative Department, and was read section by section.

On the adoption of the first article, the yeas and nays were called with the following result:

YEAS—Messrs. Abell, Ariail, Austin, Bailey, Barrett, Beauvais, Bell, Bennie, Bofill, Bonzano, Bromley, Buckley, Burke, Campbell, Cazabat, Cook J. K., Cook T., Crozat, Cutler, Davies, Decker, Duane, Dufresne, Edwards, Ennis, Fish, Flood, Foley, Fosdick, Fuller, Gastinel, Geier, Goldman, Healy, Hart Henderson, Hills, Hire, Howell, Howes, Kugler, Maas, Maurer, Mayer, Mendiverri, Millspaugh, Montamat, Montague, Morris, Murphy M. W., Newell, Normand, O'Conner, Ong, Orr, Payne J., Paine J. T., Pintado, Poynot, Purcell J., Pursell S., Schroeder, Seymour, Shaw, Smith, Spellicy, Stocker, Stumpf, Stiner, Stauffer, Sullivan, Taliaferro, Terry, Thorpe, Thomas, Wenck, Wells, Wilson—78.

NAYS—None.

The second article was then taken up.

Mr. Howell moved to suspend the rules, requesting the yeas and nays to be taken, but the House refused to suspend the rules, and the second article was then adopted by the following vote:

YEAS—Messrs. Abell, Ariail, Austin, Balch, Bailey, Barrett, Beauvais, Bell, Bennie, Bofill, Bonzano, Bromley, Buckley, Burke, Campbell, Cazabat, Cook J. K., Cook T., Cutler, Davies, Decker, Duane, Dufresne, Edwards, Ennis, Fish, Flagg, Flood, Foley, Fosdick, Fuller, Gastinel, Geier, Goldman, Healy, Hart, Hills, Hire, Howell, Howes, Kugler, Maas, Mann, Maurer, Mayer, Mendiverri, Millspaugh, Montamat, Montague, Morris, Newell, Normand, O'Conner, Ong, Orr, Payne J., Pintado, Poynot, Purcell J., Pursell S., Schroeder, Seymour, Shaw, Smith, Spellicy, Stocker, Stumpf, Stiner, Stauffer, Taliaferro, Terry, Thorpe, Thomas, Wenck, Wells, Wilson—76.

NAYS—None.

Article third was then taken up and read.

Mr. Montamat moved to strike out the word "first" in the third line, and insert the word "third."

Mr. Montague moved to amend by striking out " first Monday in January " in the third line, inserting "first Monday in December," which was lost on a division--ayes 23; nays 51.

A division was then called upon Mr. Montamat's amendment—ayes 22; nays 51. Lost.

Mr. Stocker moved to strike out the words "unless a different day be appointed by law" in the fourth line, which motion was laid on the table.

Mr. Morris moved to amend the first line, by inserting after the word "on" the words "Tuesday after." Laid on the table.

The question then recurred on the adoption of the third article as reported, and the yeas and nays were called with the following result :

YEAS—Messrs. Ariail, Austin, Bailey, Bell, Bennie, Bofill, Bonzano, Bromley, Buckley, Burke, Campbell, Cazabat, Cook J. K., Cook T., Crozat, Cutler, Davies, Decker, Duane, Dufresne, Edwards, Ennis, Fish, Flagg, Flood, Foley, Fosdick, Gastinel, Geier, Gorlinski, Goldman, Hart, Healy, Henderson, Hills, Hire, Howell, Howes, Kugler, Maas, Mann, Mayer, Mendiverri, Millspaugh, Montague, Morris, Murphy M. W., Newell, Normand, O'Conner, Ong, Orr, Payne J., Paine J. T., Pintado, Poynot, Schroeder, Seymour, Shaw, Smith, Spellicy, Stocker, Stumpf, Stiner, Stauffer, Taliaferro, Terry, Thorpe, Thomas, Wenck, Wells, Wilson—72.

NAYS— Messrs. Abell, Barrett, Maurer, Montamat, Purcell J., Pursell S.—6.

Mr. Abell offered the following amendment to art. 6 :

Every qualified elector who shall have attained twenty-four years of age shall be eligible to a seat as representative in the General Assembly, and every qualified elector who shall have attained twenty-eight years of age shall be eligible to a seat in the Senate ; provided, that no person shall be a representative or senator unless he be, at the time of his election, a duly qualified voter of the Representative or Senatorial District from which he is elected.

Laid on the table.

On the adoption of the 4th article, as reported, the following vote was taken :

YEAS—Messrs. Ariail, Austin, Bailey, Barrett, Bell, Bennie, Bofill, Bonzano, Bromley, Buckley, Burke, Cazabat, Cook J. K., Cook T., Crozat, Cutler, Davies, Decker, Duane, Dufresne, Dupaty, Edwards, Ennis, Fish, Flagg, Flood, Foley, Fosdick, Geier, Goldman, Gorlinski, Hart, Healy, Henderson, Hills, Hire, Howell, Howes, Knobloch, Kugler, Maas, Mann, Maurer, Mayer, Mendiverri, Millspaugh, Montague, Morris, Newell, Normand, Ong, Orr, Payne J., Pintado, Poynot, Purcell J., Pursell S., Schroeder, Seymour, Shaw, Smith, Spellicy, Stiner, Stocker, Stumpf, Stauffer, Taliaferro, Terry, Thorpe, Thomas, Wenck, Wells, Wilson--72.

NAYS—Messrs. Abell, Campbell, Gastinel, Montamat, Murphy M. W., O'Conner, Sullivan--7.

Article 5th was adopted upon the following vote :

YEAS—Messrs. Abell, Ariail, Austin, Bailey, Barrett, Beauvais, Bell, Bennie, Bofill, Bonzano, Bromley, Buckley, Burke, Campbell, Cazabat, Cook J. K., Cook T., Crozat, Cutler, Davies, Decker, Duane, Dufresne, Dupaty, Edwards, Ennis, Fish, Flagg, Flood, Foley, Fosdick, Fuller, Gastinel, Geier, Gorlinski, Goldman, Gruneberg, Hart, Henderson, Hills, Howell, Howes, Knobloch, Kugler, Maas, Mann, Maurer, Mayer, Mendiverri, Millspaugh, Montamat, Montague, Morris, Murphy M. W., Newell, Normand, O'Conner, Ong, Orr, Payne J., Pintado, Poynot, Purcell J., Pursell S., Schroeder, Seymour, Shaw, Smith, Spellicy, Stocker, Stumpf, Stiner, Stauffer, Sullivan, Taliaferro, Terry, Thorpe, Thomas, Wells, Wilson—80.

NAYS—None.

Article 6th was then taken up and read.

Mr. Abell moved to amend by striking out the words " qualified electors," in the third line, and inserting the words " total population," which amendment was laid on the table.

Mr. Abell then moved to amend by striking out the words " number of electors," in the fifth line, and inserting the words "total population." Laid on the table.

AND AMENDMENT OF THE CONSTITUTION OF LOUISIANA.   79

Mr. Abell also offered the same amendment to the eighth line. Lost.

Mr. Abell moved to strike out all after the word "district," in the sixteenth line to the close of the eighteenth line, as superfluous. Lost.

Mr. Abell also moved to amend by striking out the words "qualified electors," in the twenty-first line, and inserting "total population," which motion was laid on the table.

Mr. Abell also moved to strike out the word "the," in the twenty-third line, and insert "its," which, on motion of Mr. Hills, was laid on the table.

Mr. Abell also moved to strike out in the twenty-fourth line the words "number of electors," and insert the word "population," which motion was also laid on the table.

Mr. Abell also moved to strike out the figure "3" opposite the words "fifth district," fixing the number of representatives for that district, and insert the figure "5," whereupon a discussion arose relative to the proper apportionment and basis of representation, pending which, on motion of Messrs. Hills and S. Pursell, the secretary was directed to procure the returns of the late elections in this State, in order that the same might be laid before the Convention on to-morrow.

Mr. Howell moved to adjourn until 7½ o'clock this evening. Lost.

The Convention then adjourned until 12 o'clock to-morrow.

Adopted.

JOHN E. NEELIS,
Secretary.

WEDNESDAY, May 18, 1864.

The Convention met pursuant to adjournment. The roll was called, and the following gentlemen answered to their names :

Messrs. Abell, Ariail, Balch, Barrett, Baum, Bell, Bennie, Bofill, Bonzano, Burke, Campbell, Duane, Dufrense, Dupaty, Edwards, Ennis, Fish, Flood, Foley, Fosdick, Geier, Goldman, Gruneberg, Gaidry, Henderson, Howell, Howes, Kavanagh, Mass, Mann, Mayer, Montague, Murphy M. W., Newell, Normand, O'Conner, Pintado, Pursell S., Schroeder, Schnurr, Shaw, Smith, Spellicy, Stumpf, Stiner, Stauffer, Taliaferro, Terry, Waters, Wells, Wilson and Mr. President—52.

There being no quorum present, the sergeant-at-arms was directed to bring in absent members.

After some delay, the following gentlemen having entered and taken their seats, viz: Messrs. Austin, Bromley, Buckley, Cook J. K., Crozat, Decker, Flagg, Fuller, Gastinel, Healy, Hart, Hills, Hire, Knobloch, Kugler, Mendiverri, Millspaugh, Montamat Morris, Orr, Paine J. T., Poynot, Purcell J., Stocker, Sullivan, Thorpe and Thomas—27, the president announced that there was a quorum present.

The minutes of yesterday were read, corrected and adopted.

Mr. Hills offered the following :

Whereas, The absence of a few members of this Convention at the first roll-call, seriously interrupts and retards its business, frequently delaying the commencement of the session for a whole hour after the time fixed for meeting ; therefore

Resolved, That any member, who is absent without leave or satisfactory excuse, at the 12 o'clock roll-call shall forfeit his per diem allowance for every day of such absence.

Mr. Foley moved to suspend the rules to take up Mr. Hills's resolution, which being refused, the resolution was laid over.

Mr. Wilson offered the following :

Whereas, The Convention has now performed the heaviest part of the labor for which it was called together ; therefore be it

Resolved, That it do adjourn *sine die* on the first day of June ; and that evening sessions be held daily (Sundays excepted) to the date of adjournment.

Mr. S. Pursell offered the following :

Resolved, That this Convention meet at 11 o'clock A. M., instead of 12.

Mr. Bonzano presented the following :

Whereas, The public interest requires that this Convention should not be interrupted in its business without sufficient cause ;

Resolved, That no motion for an adjournment for a longer time than twenty-four hours shall be put to question unless it be seconded by a majority of the members present, and if so seconded the yeas and shall be called.

Judge Howell proffered the following :

Resolved, That the secretary be instructed to collect and collate all motions and resolutions heretofore adopted, as bearing upon the mode of conducting the business, or amending the rules and regulations of this Convention, and report to-morrow.

Mr. Cazabat moved to suspend the rules in order to take up Mr. Howell's resolution, which motion being lost, the resolution was laid over.

There being no report from committees, the unfinished business was taken up.

Mr. Henderson called up his resolution of yesterday, which was read by the secretary.

Mr. Campbell offered the following amendment:

Provided, A like sum of $20.000 be and is hereby appropriated for the relief of the destitute widows and orphans of the soldiers in the First and Second Louisiana Infantry, First and Second Louisiana Cavalry, and First and Second New Orleans Volunteers.

On motion of Mr. Henderson Mr. Campbell's amendment was laid on the table.

Mr. Montamat moved to lay Mr. Henderson's resolution on the table, whereupon the yeas and nays were called, with the following result:

YEAS—Messrs. Abell, Austin, Baum, Beauvais, Bennie, Bromley, Brott, Burke, Campbell, Cazabat, Decker. Dupaty, Edwards, Ennis, Flagg, Gruneberg, Gaidry, Hills, Hire, Howell, Knobloch, Kugler, Maas, Mann, Mayer, Mendiverri, Millspaugh, Montamat, Montague, Morris, Newell, Normand, Paine J. T., Pintado, Pursell S., Seymour, Stauffer, Thomas—38.

NAYS—Messrs. Balch, Barrett, Bell, Bofill, Bonzano, Buckley, Cook J. K., Cook T., Crozat, Duane, Dufresne, Fish, Flood, Foley, Fosdick, Fuller, Gastinel, Geier, Goldman, Gorlinski, Healy, Harnan, Hart, Henderson, Howes, Kavanagh, Murphy E., Murphy M. W., O'Conner, Orr, Poynot. Purcell J., Schroeder, Schnurr, Shaw, Smith, Spellicy, Stocker, Stumpf, Stiner. Stauffer, Sullivan, Taliaferro,Terry,Thorpe,Waters,Wilson—47.

Consequently the Convention refused to lay the resolution on the table.

Mr. Hills offered a substitute for the resolution, which was ruled out of order.

Mr. Bonzano offered the following amendment, to be included :

Children's Home, Moreau street, 54 children, $500.

Mr. Thorpe offered the following amendment:

St. Vincent's Orphan Asylum, corner of Race and Magazine streets, $500.

Both of which amendments were accepted.

Mr. Montamat moved to further amend by adding the words :

To the Firemen's Charitable Association, $5000.

The yeas and nays were ordered upon the question of the adoption of Mr. Montamat's amendment, resulting as follows :

YEAS—Messrs. Abell, Austin, Balch, Baum, Beauvais, Bell, Bofill, Bromley, Brott, Buckley, Campbell, Cook T., Crozat, Ennis, Fish, Flagg, Foley, Fuller, Geier, Goldman, Gruneberg, Knobloch, Mayer, Mendiverri, Montamat, Montague, Morris, Murphy M. W., O'Conner, Orr, Purcell J., Seymour, Shaw, Spellicy, Stocker, Stumpf, Stauffer, Sullivan, Taliaferro, Terry, Thomas, Waters, Wilson—43.

NAYS—Messrs. Ariail, Barrett, Bennie, Bonzano, Burke, Cook J. K., Cutler, Decker, Duane, Dufresne, Edwards, Flood, Fosdick, Gastinel, Gorlinski, Gaidry, Healy, Harnan, Hart, Henderson, Hills, Hire, Howell, Howes, Kavanagh, Kugler, Maas, Mann, Millspaugh, Murphy E., Newell, Normand, Paine J. T., Pintado, Poynot, Pursell S., Schroeder, Schnurr, Smith, Stiner, Thorpe, Wells—42.

Consequently the amendment was adopted.

Mr. Campbell asked to be excused from voting on Mr. Montamat's amendment, which request was refused by the Convention.

Mr. Campbell offered the following amendment :

Provided, The destitute widows and orphans of the soldiers who have lost their lives in battle, be included.

Which amendment was rejected.

On the adoption of the original resolution, as amended, the yeas and nays were called, and being ordered, Messrs. Barrett, Bell, Bofill, Bonzano, Buckley, Cook T., Crozat, Fish, Flagg, Flood, Foley, Fosdick, Fuller, Geier, Gruneberg, Healy, Harnan, Hart, Henderson, Kavanagh, Montamat, Murphy M. W., O'Conner, Orr, Purcell J., Schroeder, Schnurr, Shaw, Spellicy,Stocker, Stumpf, Stiner, Sullivan, Taliaferro, Terry, Thorpe, Waters, Wilson—38 voted yea.

NAYS—Messrs. Abell, Ariail, Austin, Baum, Beauvais, Bennie, Bromley, Burke, Campbell, Cazabat, Cook J. K., Cutler, Decker, Duane, Dufresne, Dupaty, Edwards, Ennis, Flagg, Fosdick, Fuller, Gastinel, Goldman, Gorlinski, Gaidry, Hills, Hire, Howell, Howes, Knobloch, Kugler, Maas, Mann, Mayer, Mendiverri. Millspaugh, Montague, Morris, Murphy E., Newell, Normand, Ong, Paine J. T., Pintado, Poynot, Pursell S., Seymour, Smith, Stauffer, Thomas, Wells—51.

Consequently the resolution as amended was rejected.

Mr. Foley called up his resolution of yesterday, relative to members of this Convention who are delegates to the Baltimore Convention.

AND AMENDMENT OF THE CONSTITUTION OF LOUISIANA. 81

On the motion to lay the resolution on the table, a rising vote was taken, when the president decided the motion carried.

Mr. Stiner moved a re-consideration of the foregoing vote, which was ordered by the Convention, and on the motion to lay the resolution on the table the yeas and nays were ordered, and being taken resulted as follows:

YEAS — Messrs. Austin, Barrett, Baum, Beauvais, Bennie, Bofill, Bromley, Burke, Cook J. K., Cutler, Decker, Duane, Dufresne, Dupaty, Edwards, Ennis, Fish, Flagg, Fuller, Gastinel, Gaidry, Geier, Goldman, Hart, Hire, Howell, Kavanagh, Kugler, Maas, Mann, Mendiverri, Millspaugh, Montamat, Montague, Morris, Newell, Ong, Orr, Paine J. T., Pintado, Purcell J., Purcell S., Seymour, Shaw, Spellicy, Stauffer, Sullivan, Taliaferro, Terry, Thomas, Waters, Wells, Wilson—53.

NAYS—Messrs. Abell, Ariail, Bell, Bromley, Buckley, Campbell, Cazabat, Cook T., Flood, Foley, Fosdick, Gorlinski, Gruneberg, Harnan, Healy, Hills, Howes, Knobloch, Mayer, Murphy E., Murphy M. W., Normand, O'Conner, Schroeder, Schnurr, Smith, Stocker, Stumpf, Stiner, Thorpe—30.

ORDER OF THE DAY.

The Convention then resumed the consideration of the report of the Committee on Legislative Department.

Mr. S. Pursell moved to strike out of the eighty-sixth and eighty-seventh lines the words "and able to read and write."

On this motion the yeas and nays were ordered.

YEAS—Messrs. Abell, Ariail, Austin, Barrett, Balch, Beauvais, Bell, Bennie, Bofill, Bonzano, Bromley, Burke, Cazabat, Cook J. K., Cook T., Crozat, Cutler, Decker, Duane, Dupaty, Edwards, Ennis, Fish, Flood, Foley, Fuller, Gastinel, Gaidry, Geier, Gorlinski, Gruneberg, Harnan, Hart, Healy, Henderson, Howell, Howes, Knobloch, Kugler, Maas, Mann, Mayer, Millspaugh, Montamat, Montague, Morris, Murphy E., Murphy M. W., Newell, Normand, O'Conner, Ong, Orr, Pintado, Purcell J., Pursell S., Schroeder, Schnurr, Smith, Spellicy, Stocker, Stumpf, Stiner, Stauffer, Sullivan, Taliaferro, Terry, Thomas, Waters, Wilson—71.

NAYS—Messrs. Flagg, Fosdick, Goldman, Hills, Hire, Seymour, Shaw, Thorpe, Wells —9.

Consequently the motion prevailed.

Mr. Montamat moved to adjourn, on which motion the yeas and nays were ordered.

YEAS—Messrs. Abell, Balch, Burke, Cook J. K., Dufresne, Dupaty, Gruneberg, Knobloch, Montamat, Murphy M. W., O'Conner, Stumpf, Sullivan, Waters—14.

NAYS— Messrs. Ariail, Austin, Barrett, Beauvais, Bell, Bennie, Bofill, Bonzano, Bromley, Cazabat, Cook T., Crozat, Cutler, Decker, Duane, Edwards, Ennis, Fish, Flagg, Flood, Foley, Fosdick, Fuller, Gaidry, Gastinel, Geier, Goldman, Gorlinski, Harnan, Hart, Healy, Henderson, Hills, Hire, Howell, Howes, Kugler, Maas, Mann, Maurer, Mayer, Montague, Morris, Murphy E., Newell, Normand, Ong, Orr, Pintado, Purcell J., Pursell S., Schroeder, Schnurr, Seymour, Shaw, Smith, Spellicy, Stocker, Stiner, Stauffer, Taliaferro, Terry, Thorpe, Thomas, Wells, Wilson—66.

Consequently the Convention refused to adjourn.

Mr. Thomas moved to amend the report by striking out, in the apportionment of representatives, as follows, viz:

First District—Strike out five and insert three.

Second District—Strike out eight and insert five.

Third District—Strike out six and insert seven.

Fifth District—Strike out three and insert four.

Sixth District—Strike out three and insert two.

Eighth District—Strike out two and insert three.

Tenth District—Strike out seven and insert eight.

Which amendments were accepted by the committee.

Pending discussion on the foregoing amendments, the Convention adjourned.

Approved.

JOHN E. NEELIS,
Secretary.

THURSDAY, May 19, 1864.

The president called the Convention to order at 12 o'clock M., and, after prayer by the Rev. Mr. Strong, the roll was called and the following members answered to their names:

Messrs. Abell, Ariail, Austin, Balch, Bailey, Baum, Bell, Bofill, Bonzano, Bromley, Burke, Campbell, Crozat, Davies, Decker, Duane, Dufresne, Edwards, Ennis, Fish, Flood, Foley, Fosdick, Geier, Gruneberg, Gaidry, Healy, Hart, Henderson, Hire, Howell, Howes, Kavanagh, Knobloch, Maas, Mann, Maurer, Mayer, Millspaugh, Montague, Murphy M. W., Newell, Normand, O'Conner, Orr, Payne J., Pintado, Poynot,

Purcell J., Pursell S., Schroeder, Schnurr, Smith, Stumpf, Stiner, Stauffer, Taliaferro, Terry, Waters, Wells,Wilson, and Mr. President—62 members present.

There being no quorum present the sergeant-at-arms was directed to procure the attendance of absent members.

The following members having entered the hall and taken their seats, viz : Cook J. K., Cook T., Cutler, Dupaty, Flagg, Gastinel, Gorlinski, Harnan, Hills, Mendiverri, Seymour, Shaw, Thorpe and Thomas—14, the president declared a quorum present.

The minutes of yesterday were read, corrected and adopted.

Mr. Henderson moved to reconsider the vote by which his resolution of yesterday relative to charitable institutions was lost, but Mr. Henderson having voted with the minority on that resolution, the president informed him that he could not move the reconsideration, whereupon Mr. Gorlinski renewed the motion.

A motion to lay Mr. Gorlinski's motion on the table being lost, the question recurred upon the reconsideration, and upon a division resulted : ayes 40, nays 29 ; consequently the resolution was reconsidered.

On motion of Mr. Cutler the resolution was referred to a select committee of five, to be appointed by the president.

Mr. Austin offered the following resolution :

Resolved, That two-thirds of all the members of this Convention, as ascertained from the rolls of those elected and qualified, shall hereafter constitute a quorum of this body.

Mr. Campbell offered the following :

Whereas, The misfortunes of war has thrown in upon us, many Union refugees, from different parts of our State and the neighboring States, who are now in a destitute condition and want and require immediate relief ; *and whereas*, this Convention does sympathize with those who have had to leave their homes on account of their Union sentiments ; therefore

Resolved, That the sum of ——— dollars be and is hereby authorized to be placed at the disposal of the governor to relieve the distressed refugees in our city.

On motion of Mr. Hills the resolution was referred to the Select Committee on Charity.

Mr. Austin, chairman of the Select Committee on Auditor's Report, reported progress.

There being no other reports from committees, the unfinished business of yesterday came next in order.

Mr. Hills called up his resolution of yesterday, relative to dilatory members.

A motion to lay on the table was lost by the following vote :

YEAS—Messrs. Abell, Austin, Bailey. Buckley, Campbell, Cutler, Dufresne, Dupaty, Flagg, Gruneberg, Gaidry, Henderson. Hire, Kavanagh, Knobloch, Maurer, Mendiverri, Montamat, Paine J. T., Pursell S., Schnurr, Waters—22.

NAYS—Messrs. Balch, Baum, Bell, Bofill, Bonzano, Bromley, Burke, Cook J. K., Cook T., Crozat, Davies, Decker, Duane, Edwards, Ennis, Flood, Foley, Fosdick, Gastinel, Geier, Goldman, Gorlinski, Healy, Harnan, Hart, Hills, Howell, Howes Maas, Mann, Mayer, Millspaugh, Morris, Murphy M. W., Newell, Normand, O'Conner, Orr, Payne J., Pintado, Poynot, Purcell J., Schroeder, Seymour, Shaw, Smith, Stumpf, Stiner, Stauffer, Sullivan, Taliaferro, Terry, Thorpe, Thomas, Wells, Wilson—56.

Mr. Hills moved the previous question, which, being lost, the question recurred upon the adoption of the resolution.

Mr. Montamat moved to amend by inserting the word "not," so as to make the resolution read "shall not forfeit." Lost.

On the adoption of the resolution, the yeas and nays were called, resulting :

YEAS—Messrs. Austin, Balch, Barrett, Bofill, Bonzano, Burke, Crozat, Davies, Duane, Ennis, Flood, Foley, Fosdick, Geier, Goldman, Gorlinski, Harnan, Hart, Hills, Howell, Kavanagh, Knobloch, Maas, Mann, Millspaugh, Montague, Newell, Normand, O'Conner, Orr, Payne J., Pintado. Purcell J., Schroeder, Shaw, Smith, Stumpf. Stiner, Stauffer, Taliaferro, Terry, Wells, Wilson—43.

NAYS—Messrs. Abell, Bailey, Baum, Bell, Bromley, Buckley, Campbell, Cook J. K., Cook T., Cutler, Decker, Dufresne, Dupaty, Edwards, Flagg, Gastinel, Gruneberg, Gaidry, Henderson, Hire, Howes, Kavanagh, Knobloch, Maurer, Mayer, Mendiverri, Montamat, Murphy M. W., Ong, Paine J., T., Poynot, Pursell S., Schnurr, Seymour. Sullivan, Thorpe, Thomas, Waters—38.

Mr. Wilson called up his resolution relative to adjourning *sine die* on 1st day of June next.

Mr. Sullivan moved to lay the resolution on the table, which motion was carried.

Mr. S. Pursell's resolution, relative to meeting at 10 o'clock A. M., was taken up. read, and laid on the table.

AND AMENDMENT OF THE CONSTITUTION OF LOUISIANA.

Mr. Bonzano's resolution providing that no adjournment for a longer period than twenty-four hours shall be made, unless such motion to adjourn shall have been seconded by a majority of the Convention and requiring the yeas and nays thereon, was taken up.

A motion to lay on the table was made and lost, and the resolution was adopted by a rising vote of 38 yeas to 29 nays.

The order of the day was then taken up, to-wit: The report of the Committee on Legislative Department.

Mr. S. Pursell moved to strike out the 88th, 89th, 90th, and 91st lines of article 6.

Mr. Goldman moved to lay the motion on the table. Lost.

On the adoption of the motion to strike out, the yeas and nays were ordered, resulting as follows:

YEAS—Messrs. Abell, Balch, Bailey, Barrett, Baum, Bell, Bofill, Buckley, Burke, Campbell, Cook J. K., Cook T., Crozat, Cutler, Decker, Duane, Dufresne, Edwards, Flagg, Flood, Foley, Gastinel, Geier, Gruneberg, Healy, Harnan, Hart, Kavanagh, Knobloch, Mann, Maurer, Mayer, Mendiverri, Millspaugh, Montamat, Murphy M. W., Newell, O'Conner, Ong, Orr, Payne J., Purcell J., Pursell S., Schroeder, Seymour, Smith, Stumpf, Sullivan, Taliaferro, Terry, Thomas, Waters, Wilson—53.

NAYS—Messrs. Austin, Bonzano, Bromley, Davies, Dupaty, Ennis, Fosdick, Goldman, Henderson, Hills, Hire, Howell, Maas, Montague, Normand, Paine J. T., Pintado, Schnurr, Shaw, Stiner, Stauffer, Thorpe, Wells—23.

Mr. Smith moved to strike out of article 6 the word one, opposite the words "Parish of St. Mary," and insert two, which motion was lost.

Mr. Balch moved to strike out "one" opposite the words "Parish of Iberville" and insert "two." Lost.

Mr. Bromley moved to re-commit that portion of article 6 of the report, between the 33d and 80th lines, inclusive. Lost.

Mr. Shaw moved to amend the 16th line of article 6, by inserting after the word "informality" the words "omission or error," which amendment was accepted by the committee.

Mr. Mann moved to amend by striking out of the 11th line the word "seventy" and insert "seventy-five," and in the 11th and 12th lines to strike out entirely the words "the third in the year one thousand eight hundred and seventy-six."

Mr. Terry's motion, allowing parties not citizens to vote in consideration of military and other services, was lost.

Mr. Henderson moved to amend lines 3d, 5th, 8th, 15th, 21st and 24th of article 6, by striking out the word "electors" and inserting "total white population," which amendments were lost.

Mr. Flagg moved to amend line 33 by striking out the word "Algiers" and inserting the words "Orleans, right bank." Carried.

Mr. Bromley moved to amend line 33 by striking out "two" and inserting "three" opposite the word "Lafourche," and strike out "three" and insert "two" opposite the word "Claiborne."

Mr. Bell moved to amend article 6, line 33, by striking out the word "three" and insert "four" opposite the word "First District." Lost.

Mr. Montamat called for the previous question, which being carried, the main question was put and article 6, as amended, was adopted.

Articles 7, 8, 9, 10 and 11, were each read and adopted.

Article 12th was then read. Mr. Stocker moved to strike out in the 5th line, the words "At the discretion of the Legislature." Lost.

The article was then adopted as reported.

The remainder of the report was then read section by section and adopted as read.

The Convention then adjourned until 12 o'clock M. to-morrow.

Adopted.

JOHN E. NEELIS,
Secretary.

FRIDAY, May 20th, 1864.

The Convention was called to order by the president, pursuant to adjournment, and the roll being called the following members answered to their names:

Messrs. Abell, Ariail, Austin, Balch, Bailey, Barrett, Baum, Beauvais, Bell, Bofill, Bonzano, Bromley, Buckley, Burke, Campbell, Collin, Cook J. K., Cook T., Crozat,

JOURNAL OF THE CONVENTION FOR THE REVISION

Cutler, Davies, Duane, Dufresne, Dupaty, Edwards, Ennis, Fish, Flagg, Flood, Foley, Fosdick, Fuller, Gastinel, Geier, Goldman, Gorlinski, Gruneberg, Gaidry, Healy, Hart, Henderson, Hills, Howell, Howes, Kavanagh, Knobloch, Kugler, Maas, Mann, Maurer, Mayer, Mendiverri, Millspaugh, Montamat, Montague, Morris, Murphy E., Murphy M. W., Newell, Normand, O'Conner, Ong, Orr, Payne J., Paine J. T., Pintado, Poynot, Purcell J., Pursell S., Schroeder, Schnurr, Seymour, Shaw, Smith, Spellicy, Stocker, Stumpf, Stiner, Stauffer, Sullivan, Taliaferro, Terry, Thomas, Waters, Wenck, Wells, Wilson, and Mr. President—88.

A quorum being present the proceedings were opened with prayer by the Rev. Mr. Gregg.

The journal of yesterday was read, corrected and approved.

On motion of Mr. Abell, Mr. Duke, of Ascension, was excused for non-attendance in consequence of illness in his family.

Mr. Bofill moved a re-consideration of the vote by which Mr. Hills's resolution, relative to absent members, was yesterday adopted.

Mr. Stauffer moved to lay the motion of Mr. Bofill on the table, on which motion the yeas and nays were demanded, and being ordered resulted as follows:

YEAS—Messrs. Ariail, Bonzano, Bromley, Duane, Edwards, Ennis, Foley, Fosdick, Fuller, Goldman, Gorlinski, Harnan, Hart, Hills, Howell, Kugler, Maas, Mann, Millspaugh, Montague, Morris, Murphy M. W., Newell, Normand, O'Conner, Orr, Payne J., Paine J. T., Pintado, Poynot, Schroeder, Schnurr, Shaw, Spellicy, Stiner, Stauffer, Taliaferro, Terry, Wells—39.

NAYS—Messrs. Abell, Austin, Balch, Bailey, Barrett, Baum, Beauvais, Bell, Bofill, Buckley, Burke, Campbell, Collin, Cook J. K., Cook T., Crozat, Cutler, Davies, Decker, Dufresne, Dupaty, Fish, Flagg, Flood. Gastinel, Geier, Gruneberg, Gaidry, Healy, Henderson, Hire, Howes, Kavanagh, Knobloch, Maurer, Mayer, Mendiverri, Montamat, Murphy E., Ong, Purcell J., Pursell S., Seymour, Smith, Stocker, Stumpf, Sullivan, Thomas, Waters, Wenck, Wilson —51.

Consequently the Convention refused to table the motion to re-consider, and on the reconsideration Mr. Hills's motion, was tabled.

Mr. Austin called up his resolution of yesterday relative to quorum, and on motion, it was tabled.

ORDER OF THE DAY.

Third reading of report of Committee on Legislative Department was taken up, and finally passed as it had been amended on its second reading.

SECOND READING.

The Convention then took up the report of the Committee on Executive Department on its second reading.

The first section of the report was adopted without amendment.

The second section being read, Mr. Sullivan moved to strike out in the second line the words "twenty-eight" and insert in lieu thereof the word "thirty," and strike out "four" in the fourth line and insert "ten," so that the section will read as follows:

ART. —. No person shall be eligible to the office of governor or lieutenant governor who shall not have attained the age of thirty years, and been a citizen and resident within the State for the space of ten years next preceding his election.

On the motion to lay the amendments on the table. The yeas and nays were called and resulted as follows:

YEAS—Messrs. Ariail, Bonzano, Bromley, Collin, Cazabat, Duane, Dupaty, Ennis, Fish, Flood, Foley, Fosdick. Geier, Goldman, Gorlinski, Gaidry, Hills, Hire, Maas, Morris, Murphy E., Payne J., Paine J. T., Pintado, Purcell J., Pursell S., Schroeder, Schnurr. Shaw, Smith, Stiner, Stauffer, Wenck—33.

NAYS—Messrs Abell, Austin, Balch, Bailey, Barrett, Baum, Beauvais, Bell, Bofill, Buckley, Burke, Campbell. Cook J. K., Cook T., Crozat, Cutler, Decker, Dufresne, Edwards, Flagg, Fuller, Gastinel, Gruneberg, Harnan, Hart, Howell, Howes, Kavanagh, Knobloch, Kugler, Mann, Maurer, Mayer, Millspaugh, Montamat. Montague, Murphy M. W., Newell, Normand, O'Conner, Ong, Orr, Poynot, Seymour, Spellicy, Stocker, Stumpf, Sullivan, Taliaferro, Thomas, Waters, Wells, Wilson,—53.

Consequently the motion to lay the amendments on the table was lost.

On the adoption of the section as amended the yeas and nays were called for, with the following result:

YEAS—Messrs. Abell, Ariail, Austin, Bailey, Balch, Barrett, Baum, Bofill, Buckley, Burke, Campbell. Cazabat, Cook T., Crozat, Cutler, Decker. Dufresne, Edwards, Flagg, Fuller, Gastinel, Gaidry, Geier, Gruneberg, Harnan, Hart, Howes, Kavanagh, Knobloch, Kugler, Mann, Maurer, Mayer, Millspaugh, Montamat, Montague, Murphy M. W., Newell, Normand, O'Conner, Ong, Orr, Seymour, Spellicy, Stocker, Stumpf, Stauffer, Sullivan, Taliaferro, Waters, Wells, Wilson—52.

NAYS—Messrs. Beauvais, Bell, Bonzano, Bromley, Collin, Duane, Dupaty, Ennis, Fish, Flood, Foley, Fosdick, Goldman, Gorlinski, Hills, Hire, Howell. Maas, Morris, Payne J., Paine J.T., Pintado, Poynot, Purcell J., Pursell S., Schroeder, Schnurr, Shaw, Smith, Stiner, Thomas, Wenck—32.

The amendment was adopted, and the section adopted as amended.

The third section being read, Mr. Mann moved to strike out the word "fourth" in the second line and insert "second," so that the section, as amended, will read as follows:

Art. —. The governor shall enter on the discharge of his duties on the second Monday of January next ensuing his election, and shall continue in office until the Monday next succeeding the day that his successor shall be declared duly elected, and shall have taken the oath or affirmation required by the constitution.

The section was then adopted as amended.

On motion of Mr. Sullivan, the fourth section was stricken out.

The fifth section was read. Mr. Wells moved to amend by adding after the word "Congress," in the first line, "minister of any religious denomination," so that the section will read as follows: "No member of Congress, minister of any religious denomination, or any person holding office under the United States government, shall be eligible to the office of governor or lieutenant governor."

The amendment was adopted, and the section adopted as amended.

Mr. Abell moved a reconsideration of the vote striking out the fourth section.

Mr. Bofill moved to table the motion to reconsider. The motion to table was put, and on a rising vote—43 voted yea and 29 voted nay.

No quorum voting, a call of the House being demanded, 87 members answered to their names.

The yeas and nays were then demanded on Mr. Bofill's motion, with the following result:

YEAS—Messrs. Austin, Bailey, Beauvais, Bofill, Burke, Cazabat, Collin, Cook T., Crozat, Cutler, Davies, Duane, Dupaty, Edwards, Ennis, Fish, Flagg, Fuller, Gaidry, Geier, Henderson, Hire, Howes, Kugler, Montamat, Morris, Ong, Payne J., Pursell S., Schroeder, Seymour, Smith, Stocker, Stauffer, Sullivan, Terry, Thomas, Waters, Wenck, Wells—40.

NAYS—Messrs. Abell, Ariail, Baum, Barrett, Bell, Buckley, Campbell, Cook J. K., Decker, Dufresne, Edwards, Flood, Foley, Fosdick, Gastinel, Goldman, Gorlinski, Gruneberg, Harnan, Hart, Healy, Hills, Howell, Kavanagh, Knobloch, Maas, Mann, Maurer, Mayer, Montague, Murphy M. W., Newell, Normand, O'Conner, Orr, Paine J. T., Pintado, Poynot, Purcell J., Schnurr, Shaw, Spellicy, Stumpf, Stiner, Taliaferro, Wilson—46.

The motion to table was therefore lost.

On the original motion to reconsider a rising vote was taken, when 20 members voted yea and 52 voted nay. The motion to reconsider was therefore lost.

The 6th, 7th and 8th sections were adopted without amendments.

The 9th section being read, Mr. Beauvais offered a substitute, which was tabled, and the section adopted without amendment, as was also the 10th section.

Mr. Thomas proposed the following substitute for the 11th section:

The governor shall receive for his services a compensation of ten thousand dollars per annum, payable quarterly, on his own warrant.

On motion of Mr. Smith, the substitute was amended by inserting "eight" instead of "ten thousand," and the substitute adopted as amended.

The 12th section was read, and, on motion of Mr. Stauffer, the words "army and navy" were stricken out and the word "militia" inserted in lieu thereof. The section was adopted as amended.

Sections 13, 14, 15, 16, 17, 18, 19, 20 and 21 were adopted without amendments.

On motion of Mr. Davies, the 22d section was adopted by inserting the word "four" in lieu of "two," and the section adopted as amended.

The secretary read the next section.

Sec. 25. The free white men of the State shall be armed and disciplined for its defence: but those who belong to religious societies whose tenets forbid them to carry arms, shall not be compelled to do so, but shall pay an equivalant for personal services.

Mr. Stauffer's motion to strike out and insert "all able-bodied citizens of the State shall be immediately armed and disciplined for the defence of the State, and those refusing to do so, shall be sent across the United States lines into the so-called Confederacy," was laid on the table.

Mr. Thomas's motion to strike out the word "free" was lost.

Mr. Orr's amendment, "All free white males between the ages of 18 and 45 shall be armed and disciplined for the defence of the State;" and to strike out the remainder of the article was laid on the table, by a rising vote of ayes 33, nays 30, whereupon Mr. Stauffer asked to have every man's vote on the question, and the roll was called, resulting as follows:

YEAS—Messrs. Abell, Ariail, Balch, Barrett, Beauvais, Bofill, Buckley, Burke, Cazabat, Crozat, Decker, Duane, Dufresne, Edwards, Ennis, Flagg, Foley, Fosdick, Fuller, Gorlinski, Gruneberg, Harnan, Hart, Hire, Howell, Howes, Kavanagh, Knobloch, Mann, Maurer, Montamat, Murphy M. W., Newell, Normand, O'Conner, Poynot, Schnurr, Seymour, Shaw, Smith, Spellicy, Stocker, Stauffer, Sullivan, Taliferro, Terry, Waters, Wenck, Wells, Wilson—59.

NAYS—Messrs. Baum, Bell, Bonzano, Campbell, Cook J. K., Cook T., Cutler, Davies, Fish, Flood, Goldman, Gaidry, Healy, Henderson, Hills, Kugler, Maas, Mayer, Morris, Ong, Orr, Payne J., Pintado, Pursell S., Schroeder, Stumpf, Stiner, Thomas—28.

The amendment was tabled.

Mr. Smith moved to strike out the word "white," first line of section 25.

A motion to lay the amendment on the table was lost by a rising vote of 30 ayes, 40 nays. The amendment was adopted. Upon putting the section before the Convention as amended, it was lost by a rising vote of yeas 40; nays 30.

The section was the adopted in its original form.

Mr. Sullivan moved to adjourn. Upon motion the yeas and nays were ordered, which resulted as follows:

YEAS—Messrs. Abell, Austin, Balch, Bailey, Barrett, Baum, Bofill, Buckley, Campbell, Cook J. K., Cook T., Crozat, Duane, Dufresne, Dupaty, Flagg. Flood, Foley, Gorlinski, Gruneberg, Gaidry, Healy, Hart, Hills, Howes, Kavanagh, Kugler, Maurer, Mayer, Murphy E., O'Conner, Orr, Poynot, Pursell S., Schnurr, Smith, Spellicy, Stocker, Sullivan, Terry,—39.

NAYS—Messrs. Ariail, Beauvais, Bell, Bonzano, Buckley, Cazabat, Cutler, Davies, Decker, Edwards, Ennis, Goldman, Harnan, Henderson, Hire, Howell, Kugler, Maas, Mann, Montague, Morris, Murphy M. W., Newell, Normand, Orr, Payne J., Paine J. T., Pintado, Pursell S., Schroeder, Seymour, Stocker, Stumpf, Stiner, Stauffer, Taliaferro, Thomas, Waters, Wenck, Wells, Wilson—41.

The motion to adjourn was therefore lost.

The 25th section was then adopted as originally reported.

Section 26 was adopted without amendment.

Mr. Bell moved to suspend the rules to put the report on its third reading, which was lost, and the report was ordered to be engrossed for its third reading on to-morrow.

The president announced that he had appointed as the "Special Committee" on Charitable resolutions, the following members: Messrs. Henderson, chairman; Hills, Bonzano, Shaw and Thorpe.

The Convention then adjourned.

Adopted.

JOHN E. NEELIS,
Secretary.

SATURDAY, May 21, 1864.

The Convention met pursuant to adjournment, and was called to order by the president.

The roll was called, and the following members answered to their names, viz:

Messrs. Abell, Ariail, Austin, Bailey, Baum, Bell, Bonzano, Bromley, Burke, Collin, Cook J. K., Cook T., Crozat, Cutler, Davies, Decker, Dufresne, Dupaty, Edwards. Ennis, Fish, Flagg, Flood, Foley, Fosdick. Gastinel, Gaidry, Geier, Gorlinski, Gruneberg, Harnan, Hart, Henderson, Hills, Howell, Howes, Knobloch, Kugler, Maas, Mann. Maurer, Mendiverri, Millspaugh, Montague. Murphy M. W., Normand, O'Conner. Orr. Paine J. T., Pintado, Poynot, Purcell J., Pursell S., Schroeder, Schnurr, Seymour, Spellicy, Stumpf, Stiner, Stauffer, Taliaferro. Terry, Wilson and Mr. President—64.

There being no quorum present, the sergeant-at-arms was directed to procure the attendance of absent members, and after some delay the following gentlemen entered the hall and answered to their names: Messrs. Barrett, Beauvais, Duane, Smith, Waters, Murphy E., Bofill, Buckley, Healy. Fosdick, Goldman, Montamat—12.

AND AMENDMENT OF THE CONSTITUTION OF LOUISIANA. 87

The minutes of yesterday's proceedings were read, amended and adopted.

There being no reports of committees submitted, the order of the day—to-wit: the third reading of the report of the Committee on Executive Department—was taken up and read by the secretary.

Mr. Cutler offered the following riders: 1st. In art. 9, omitting the words, "while he acts as president of the Senate," so that the article shall read:

Art. 9. The lieutenant governor shall receive for his services a salary of five thousand dollars per annum, to be paid quarterly." The remainder of the article, as reported, to be stricken out.

And also in art. 22, regarding the tenure of office of the treasurer, strike out "two years" and insert "four years;" and after the word "treasurer," insert the words, "and auditor of public accounts."

And also in art. 23, as reported, after the word "State," in the first line, strike out "and;" after second word "State," insert "auditor of public accounts."

After the word "State," in second line, same article, insert, " auditor shall receive a salary of five thousand dollars; the state treasurer shall receive a salary of five thousand dollars, and the secretary of state shall receive a salary of five thousand dollars."

All of which riders were accepted, and the report, as amended, was adopted.

The report of the Committee on the Judiciary was next taken up on its second reading.

Mr. Abell moved to defer the second reading of the report of the judiciary department until next Monday, which was, on motion of Mr. Stauffer, laid on the table by a rising vote of 36 yeas to 26 nays.

Mr. Montamat moved to adjourn, and the yeas and nays being ordered thereon, resulted as follows:

YEAS—Messrs. Abell, Bell, Burke, Collin, Cook T., Decker, Dufresne, Dupaty, Flagg, Foley, Fosdick, Gastinel, Gaidry, Gruneberg, Hart, Healy, Henderson, Knobloch, Mayer, Montamat, Purcell J., Schroeder, Seymour, Smith, Stocker, Stiner, Sullivan, Waters, Wilson—29.

NAYS—Messrs. Ariail, Austin, Bailey, Barrett, Baum, Beauvais, Bofill, Bonzano, Bromley, Collin, Cook J. K., Crozat, Cutler, Davies, Duane, Ennis, Fish, Flood, Fuller, Geier, Harnan, Hills, Howell, Kugler, Maas, Mann, Mendiverri, Millspaugh, Montague, Morris, Murphy E., Murphy M. W., Newell, Normand, Orr, Paine J. T., Pintado, Poynot, Pursell S., Schnurr, Spellicy, Stumpf, Stauffer, Taliaferro, Terry, Thorpe, Thomas, Wenck, Wilson—49.

The report was then read and taken up section by section, and the first and second articles were adopted as reported, without opposition.

At this juncture, Mr. Abell insisted that there had been offered substitutes for the report which had not been acted upon, and moved that they be read; but, upon motion of Mr. Foley, the Convention adjourned until Monday, 23d instant.

Adopted.

JOHN E. NEELIS,
Secretary.

MONDAY, May 23, 1864.

The president called the Convention to order at 12 o'clock M., and the roll being called the following members answered to their names:

Messrs. Ariail, Austin, Balch, Bailey, Barrett, Baum, Beauvais, Bell, Bromley, Buckley, Burke, Campbell, Collin, Crozat, Davies, Duane, Duke, Edwards, Ennis, Flood, Gaidry, Geier, Goldman, Haley, Henderson, Hills, Howell, Kavanagh, Kugler, Maas, Mendiverri, Morris, Murphy M. W., Newell, Normand, Payne J., Pintado, Purcell J., Pursell S., Schroeder, Schnurr, Seymour, Shaw, Smith, Spellicy, Stumpf, Stiner, Stauffer, Taliaferro, Terry, Thomas, Waters, Wenck, and Mr. President—54.

There being no quorum, the sergeant-at-arms was directed to bring in absent members; and the following members having entered the hall and taken their seats, viz: Messrs. Abell, Bofill, Cazabat, Dufresne, Fish, Flagg, Foley, Fuller, Gastinel, Gruneberg, Hart, Howes, Knobloch, Maurer, Mayer, O'Conner, Ong, Poynot, Stocker, Orr, Thorpe and Wilson, (22,) the president announced a quorum present. The two assistant secretaries being absent, the president requested Messrs. Winfree and Russ to act as secretaries *pro tem.* The president called Mr. Hills to the chair, the minutes were read, and no objection being made, they were declared approved.

The Committees on Schedule and Ordinance reported progress.

The Committee on Finance submitted the following reports:

REPORT OF THE FINANCE COMMITTEE.

May 17—Balance on hand as per
report No. 5 .... $55,485 40
May 17—Paid warrant
No. 35 .... $1,040 00
May 18—Paid warrant
No. 36 ....   644 00
May 19—Paid warrant
No. 38 ....   520 00
May 21—Paid warrant
No. 39 .... 1,240 00
May 21—Paid warrant
No. 40 .... 1,130 00
May 21—Paid warrant
No. 41 ....   860 00
May 21—Paid warrant
No. 42 ....   411 00
May 21—Paid warrant
No. 43 ....   108 00
May 21—Paid warrant
No. 44 ....   470 00
May 21—Paid warrant
No. 46 .... 1,876 00— 8,299 00
                                   ─────────
                                   $47,186 40
May 23—Balance on hand to date of the funds appropriated for the payment of per diem of members and salaries of officers, forty-seven thousand one hundred and eighty-six dollars and forty cents.

REPORT OF THE FINANCE COMMITTEE OF THE FUNDS APPROPRIATED FOR CONTINGENT EXPENSES.

May 17—Balance on hand as per
report No. 5 .... $9,585 48
May 20—Paid M. DeCoursey, warrant No. 15 ....   826 00
                                   ─────────
                                   $8,759 48
May 23—Balance on hand this day, eight thousand seven hundred and fifty-nine dollars and forty-eight cents.
May 18—The sum of fifteen thousand dollars was paid to W. R. Fish for printing and advertising, on warrant No. 37, out of the funds not otherwise appropriated by the Convention, as appears per voucher No. 5, on file.

Mr. Henderson, on behalf of the Special Committee on Charitable Institutions, submitted a report recommending an appropriation of twenty-one thousand dollars, as follows:

For the Orphans' Home, in New Orleans .... $ 1,500 00
For the St. Mary's Catholic Asylum 4,000 00
For the Female Asylum, Camp street 4,000 00
For the House of the Good Shepherd 250 00
For the Jewish Widows' and Orphans' Home 500 00
For the St. Joseph's Catholic Orphan Asylum 1,500 00
For the Elizabeth House of Industry 1,000 00
For the Society for the Relief of the Orphan Boys, Fourth District 1,000 00
For the Institution for Indigent Colored Boys, Third District   1,000 00
For the Ladies of Providence, Third District 750 00
For the St. Anna's Asylum for Destitute Widows and Children 1,500 00
For the Childrens' Home, of the Protestant Episcopal Church   500 00
For the Catholic Institute of Destitute Orphans 750 00
For the Catholic Benevolent Association, Baton Rouge 250 00
For the Female Orphan Asylum, Baton Rouge 500 00
For the St. Vincent's Orphan Asylum, Donaldsonville 500 00
For the Milne Asylum, New Orleans 500 00
For the St. Vincent's Orphan Asylum 500 00
For the Moreau Street Orphan Asylum 500 00
                                   ─────────
                                   $21,000 00

On motion, the foregoing report was taken up for action.

Mr. Sullivan moved to amend by adding, "To the Firemens' Charitable Association, $3000."

Mr. Montamat amended the amendment by increasing the amount to $5000, which was accepted by Mr. Sullivan.

Mr. Davies moved to lay the amendment on the table, on which motion the yeas and nays were demanded and taken, as follows:

YEAS—Messrs. Burke, Campbell, Collin. Cazabat, Davies, Duane, Dupaty, Edwards, Ennis, Flagg, Flood, Foley, Fuller, Gaidry, Goldman, Gruneberg, Harnan, Hart, Henderson, Hills, Howell, Knobloch, Kugler, Maas, Mann, Murphy E., Murphy M. W., Newell, Normand, Ong, Pintado, Poynot, Schroeder, Schnurr, Smith, Stauffer, Thorpe, Wells—38.

NAYS—Messrs. Abell, Ariail, Austin, Barrett, Balch, Bailey, Bell, Bofill, Bromley, Buckley, Cook J. K., Crozat, Decker, Duke. Dufresne, Gastinel, Geier, Healy, Howes. Maurer, Mayer, Mendiverri, Morris, Montamat, Orr, Payne J., Purcell J., Pursell S., Seymour, Shaw, Spellicy, Stumpf, Stiner, Sullivan, Terry, Waters, Wenck, Wilson —38.

AND AMENDMENT OF THE CONSTITUTION OF LOUISIANA.

The chairman (Mr. Hills) declared that as a majority did not vote in favor of the motion, it was lost.

Mr. Henderson moved to lay the whole subject on the table, on which motion the yeas and nays were demanded and taken, as follows:

YEAS—Messrs. Abell, Ariail, Austin, Balch, Bromley, Burke, Collin, Cook T., Crozat, Cutler, Davies, Decker, Edwards, Ennis, Flagg, Flood, Fuller, Goldman, Hart, Harnan, Henderson, Hills, Howell, Knobloch, Kugler, Maas, Mann, Mendiverri, Morris, Newell, Normand, Ong, Pintado, Poynot, Pursell S., Schroeder, Schnurr, Seymour, Smith, Stauffer, Wenck—41.

NAYS—Messrs. Barrett, Beauvais, Bell, Bofill, Buckley, Campbell, Cook J. K., Dufresne, Duane, Dupaty, Duke, Foley, Gastinel, Geier, Gorlinski, Gruneberg, Healy, Howes, Maurer, Mayer, Montamat, Murphy E., Murphy M. W., O'Conner, Orr, Payne J., Purcell J., Shaw, Spellicy, Stocker, Stumpf, Stiner, Sullivan, Terry, Thorpe, Waters, Wilson—37.

Consequently the motion prevailed, and the whole subject was laid on the table.

ORDER OF THE DAY.

The Convention then took up the order of the day, being the report of the Committee on the Judiciary.

On motion of Mr. Howell, the vote of Saturday, by which the 1st and 2d sections were adopted, was reconsidered, and the 1st section having been read, was, on motion, adopted.

The 2d section was read, together with the following amendment of Mr. Abell:

It shall have a general superintending control over all inferior and other courts of law; shall have power to issue writs of errors and supersedeas, certiorari, habeas corpus and quo warranto and other remedial writs, and to hear and determine the same.

Mr. Pursell moved to lay the amendment on the table, which, on a division of the House, was negatived by a vote of 28 yeas to 33 nays.

On the motion to adopt the amendment the yeas and nays were demanded and taken, as follows:

YEAS—Messrs. Abell, Balch, Bailey, Bell, Bofill, Buckley, Burke, Campbell, Collin, Cook T., Decker, Duane, Dufresne, Dupaty, Duke, Ennis, Flood, Gaidry, Gruneberg, Knobloch, Maurer, Mayer, Mendiverri, Montamat, Murphy E., Murphy M. W., Normand, Ong, Orr, Schroeder, Schnurr, Smith, Stiner, Stocker, Stumpf, Terry, Waters—37.

NAYS—Messrs. Ariail, Austin, Barrett, Beauvais, Bromley, Cook J. K., Crozat, Cutler, Edwards, Fuller, Gastinel, Geier, Goldman, Harnan, Hart, Henderson, Hire, Howell, Kugler, Maas, Mann, Morris, Newell, Payne J., Poynot, Purcell J., Pursell S., Seymour, Shaw, Spellicy, Stauffer, Sullivan, Wilson—33.

No quorum voting, on a motion to adjourn the yeas and nays were demanded and taken, as follows:

YEAS—Messrs. Abell, Austin, Balch, Bailey, Bofill, Buckley, Burke, Campbell, Cook J. K., Cook T., Crozat, Cutler, Decker, Duke, Duane, Dufresne, Edwards, Flood, Fuller, Gastinel, Goldman, Gruneberg, Hart, Knobloch, Maas, Maurer, Mayer, Mendiverri, Montamat, Murphy E., Murphy M. W., O'Conner, Ong, Orr, Poynot, Schnurr, Seymour, Smith, Spellicy, Stocker, Stumpf, Sullivan, Waters—43.

NAYS—Messrs. Ariail, Barrett, Beauvais, Bell, Bromley, Collin, Dupaty, Ennis, Geier, Gaidry, Henderson, Hire, Howell, Kugler, Mann, Morris, Newell, Normand, Payne J., Purcell J., Pursell S., Schroeder, Stauffer, Stiner, Terry, Thorpe, Thomas, Wenck, Wells, Wilson—30.

Consequently the chairman (Mr. Shaw) declared that the Convention stands adjourned until 12 o'clock M. to-morrow.

Adopted.

JOHN E. NEELIS,
Secretary.

TUESDAY, May 24, 1864.

The Convention met and was called to order by the president at 12 o'clock M.

The roll being called, the following members answered to their names:

Messrs. Abell, Ariail, Austin, Bailey, Barrett, Beauvais, Bell, Bofill, Bromley, Burke, Campbell, Cazabat, Collin, Cook T., Cook J. K., Davies, Decker, Dufresne, Duke, Edwards, Ennis, Fish, Flagg, Flood, Foley, Fosdick, Geier. Goldman, Gorlinski, Gruneberg, Healy, Heard, Henderson, Hills, Hire, Howell, Knobloch, Maas, Mann, Montamat, Morris, Murphy M. W., Newell, Normand, O'Conner, Payne J., Pintado, Poynot, Pursell S., Shaw, Smith, Spellicy, Stumpf, Stiner, Terry, Wenck, Wells, and Mr. President—58.

There being no quorum, the sergeant-at-arms was directed to bring in absent members, and after some delay the following members entered the hall and took their seats:

Messrs. Baum, Cutler, Duane, Dupaty, Fuller, Gastinel, Gaidry, Harnan, Hart, Howes, Kugler, Mayer, Mendiverri, Murphy

E., Schroeder, Stocker, Stauffer, Sullivan, Thorpe, Waters, Wilson—21.

The president announced a quorum.

When the minutes were read, Mr. Abell asked to have the words "no quorum voting" stricken out, as being incorrect, and appealed to the president for a decision.

The president stated that he was not in the chair when the vote was taken on yesterday, but he would submit the question to the decision of the Convention.

The minutes were declared correct by a rising vote of 43 yeas to 18 nays, and were adopted without alteration.

RESOLUTIONS.

Mr. Montamat presented the following:

Resolved, That Major Gen. N. P. Banks and staff be respectfully invited to visit this Convention, and that a committee of five members be appointed by the chair to wait on Gen. Banks and communicate this resolution to him.

On motion of Mr. Montamat the rules were suspended and the resolution was unanimously adopted, and the president appointed on the committee under this resolution, Messrs. Montamat, Shaw, Cutler, Howell and Heard.

Mr. Hills offered the following:

Whereas, The absence of a few members at the 12 o'clock roll-call results in a great delay of business, therefore,

Resolved, That the members of the Convention who do not answer to their names within fifteen minutes after 12 o'clock M., shall forfeit their per diem allowance for every day of such absence.

Mr. Montamat offered the following:

Resolved, That the office of assistant secretary, occupied by Mr. T. H. Murphy, be declared vacant.

Resolved, further, That the scretary be authorized to appoint a suitable person to fill said vacancy during the balance of the session.

Mr. Terry presented the following:

Resolved, That the sum of one hundred dollars is hereby allowed out of any funds in the State treasury, not otherwise appropriated, to defray the expenses necessary for the enrollment on parchment, framing, etc., of the act of emancipation, in English and French, adopted by this Convention on the 11th day of May, 1864.

Mr. Thorpe offered the following:

Resolved, That the official printer be requested to publish every morning, in the "True Delta," as full a report of the previous day's proceedings of the Convention as possible, including the votes on the call for yeas and nays, and so much of the debates as will give to members of the House a clear idea of each day's proceedings.

The foregoing resolutions were ordered to lie over until to-morrow, the Convention refusing to suspend the rules in order to consider them.

Mr. Stocker offered the following, which lays over until to-morrow:

Resolved, That the sum of twenty-two thousand five hundred dollars be, and the same is hereby, appropriated out of any money now in the treasury, not otherwise appropriated, for charitable purposes.

Be it further Resolved, That a committee of five be appointed by the chair to carry the above resolution into effect.

Mr. Henderson informed the Convention that Mr. Hamilton, one of the assistant secretaries, being unwell, and asks leave of absence for a few days. On motion of Mr. Henderson, Mr. Hamilton was granted leave of absence.

Mr. Henderson moved to reconsider the vote of yesterday, by which the report of the Special Committee on Charitable Appropriations was tabled.

Mr. Hills moved to lay the motion to reconsider on the table. Carried.

The Committee on Schedule reported progress.

Mr. Austin, on behalf of the Committee on the Report of the Auditor, stated that one of the members of the committee was absent, and another (Mr. Wells) will be absent in a day or two, and asked that the president appoint two others, which was ordered, and the president appointed Mr. Cutler in place of Mr. Thomas, and Mr. Heard in place of Mr. Wells.

The president laid before the Convention a communication from the secretary of state, relative to a portion of the State library, which, on motion of Mr. Hills, was referred to a special committee of three, upon which the president appointed Messrs. Hills, Howell and Campbell.

ORDER OF THE DAY.

The second reading of the report of the Committee on the Judiciary was then called for, and being taken up, the 2d section was

AND AMENDMENT OF THE CONSTITUTION OF LOUISIANA. 91

read; also, the amendments of Mr. Abell and Mr. Henderson.

It being determined to take up Mr. Abell's amendment first, the president decided it must be acted on *de novo.*

Mr. Cazabat moved to amend by striking out the words "error and."

Mr. Cutler moved to lay the amendment, and the amendment to the amendment, on the table, upon which motion the yeas and nays were demanded, and being taken, resulted as follows:

YEAS—Messrs. Ariail, Austin, Bailey, Barrett, Beauvais, Burke, Cazabat, Cook J. K., Crozat, Cutler, Davies, Edwards, Fish, Fuller, Geier, Goldman, Hart, Henderson, Heard, Howell, Howes, Kugler, Maas, Mann, Morris, Newell, Normand, Ong, Orr, Payne J., Pintado, Poynot, Purcell J., Pursell S., Schroeder, Shaw, Stumpf, Stauffer, Thorpe, Wenck, Wells—41.

NAYS—Messrs. Abell, Bell, Bofill, Bromley, Campbell, Collin, Cook T., Decker, Dufresne, Duane, Duke, Dupaty, Ennis, Flood, Foley, Fosdick, Gastinel, Gaidry, Gorlinski, Gruneberg, Harnan, Healy, Hills, Knobloch, Mayer, Montamat, Murphy E., Murphy M. W., O'Conner, Smith, Stocker, Stiner, Sullivan, Terry, Waters, Wilson—36.

The amendments were therefore laid on the table.

Mr. Henderson's amendment being next in order, was taken up and read.

Mr. Pursell moved to lay the amendment on the table, upon which motion the yeas and nays were demanded, and being taken, resulted as follows:

YEAS—Messrs. Ariail, Bailey, Barrett, Beauvais, Bromley, Campbell, Cazabat, Cook J. K., Crozat, Edwards, Fuller, Gaidry, Hart, Harnan, Heard, Howell, Howes, Knobloch, Kugler, Mann, Mayer, Morris, Newell, Normand, Payne J., Pintado, Poynot, Purcell S., Shaw, Stumpf, Terry, Thorpe, Wells—33.

NAYS—Messrs. Abell, Austin, Bell, Bofill, Burke, Collin, Cook T., Cutler, Davies, Decker, Duane, Duke, Dupaty, Ennis, Fish, Flagg, Flood, Foley, Fosdick, Gastinel, Geier, Goldman, Gorlinski, Gruneberg, Henderson, Healy, Hills, Maas, Montamat, Murphy E., Murphy M. W., O'Conner, Ong, Purcell J., Schroeder, Stocker, Stauffer, Stiner, Sullivan, Wenck, Wilson—41.

The motion was therefore declared lost.

A call of the House was demanded, and being taken, 70 members answered to their names. There being no quorum, on motion, the Convention adjourned.

Adopted.

JOHN E. NEELIS, *Secretary.*

WEDNESDAY, May 25, 1864.

The president called the Convention to order at 12 o'clock M., and the roll being called the following members answered to their names:

Messrs. Abell, Ariail, Barrett, Beauvais, Bell, Bofill, Bromley, Buckley, Burke, Cazabat, Campbell, Collin, Cook J. K., Cook T., Crozat, Davies, Decker, Duane, Dufresne, Dupaty, Duke, Edwards, Ennis, Fish, Flagg, Flood, Foley, Fosdick, Fuller, Gastinel, Gaidry, Geier, Goldman, Gorlinski, Gruneberg, Harnan, Heard, Henderson, Hills, Hire, Howell, Knobloch, Kugler, Maas, Mann, Maurer, Mayer, Mendiverri, Montamat, Morris, Murphy M. W., Newell, Normand, O'Conner, Payne J., Pintado, Poynot, Purcell S., Shaw, Schnurr, Smith, Spellicy, Stumpf, Stiner, Stauffer, Sullivan, Terry, Thorpe, Wenck, Wells, Wilson and Mr. President—72.

No quorum being present, the sergeant-at-arms was directed to bring in absent members.

After some delay the following members appeared and took their seats:

Messrs. Baum, Hart, Healy, Kavanagh, Murphy E., Purcell J.—6.

A quorum was announced by the president, and the journal of yesterday was read and approved.

The president laid before the Convention a bill of the city of New Orleans against the State of Louisiana. amounting to $6139 13, expenses paid for fitting up Liberty Hall for the use of the Convention, which was referred to the Committee on Contingent Expenses.

Mr. Hills called up his resolution of yesterday, relative to absent members.

A motion of Mr. Waters to table the resolution failed.

Mr. Stocker moved to amend by adding the words, "without a good excuse," to come in after the word "absence." This amendment was accepted.

On the adoption of the resolution the yeas and nays were taken, with the following result:

YEAS—Messrs. Ariail, Austin, Barrett, Bell, Bromley, Burke, Cazabat, Collin, Cook T., Davies, Duane, Dufresne, Ennis, Fish, Flood, Foley, Fosdick, Geier, Goldman, Gorlinski, Harnan. Healy, Hills, Howell, Kugler, Maas, Mann, Mayer, Montamat, Morris, Newell, Normand, Pintado, Purcell J., Schroeder, Shaw, Smith, Stocker, Stumpf, Stiner, Stauffer, Terry, Thorpe, Wells. Wilson—45.

NAYS—Messrs. Abell, Bailey, Beauvais, Bofill. Buckley, Campbell, Cook J. K., Crozat, Decker, Dupaty, Duke, Edwards, Flagg, Fuller, Gastinel, Gaidry, Gruneberg, Hart, Heard, Henderson, Hire. Howes. Kavanagh, Knobloch. Maurer, Mendiverri, Murphy E., Murphy M. W., O'Conner, Ong, Orr, Payne J., Poynot, Pursell S.. Schnurr, Seymour, Spellicy, Sullivan, Waters—39.

The resolution was therefore adopted.

Mr. Terry called up his resolution of yesterday, appropriating one hundred dollars to pay for enrolling, framing, etc., of the ordinance of emancipation; and, on motion of Mr. Wilson, it was referred to the Committee on Contingent Expenses.

JOURNAL OF THE CONVENTION FOR THE REVISION

Mr. Stocker called up his resolution appropriating $22,500 for charitable purposes.

Mr. Smith moved to lay the resolution on the table, which motion prevailed by a rising vote of 47 yeas to 27 nays. But as there was no quorum voting,

Mr. Stocker moved a call of the House, which was ordered, and 84 members found to be present.

Mr. Stocker insisting on every member voting, the vote was taken by yeas and nays, with the following result :

YEAS—Messrs. Abell, Ariail, Austin, Bailey, Baum, Beauvais, Bofill, Bromley, Burke, Cazabat, Collin, Crozat, Davies, Decker, Dupaty, Duane, Duke, Edwards, Ennis, Flagg, Fosdick, Fuller, Goldman, Henderson, Hills, Hire, Howell, Howes, Knobloch, Kugler, Maas, Maurer, Mayer, Mendiveren, Morris, Montamat, Murphy M. W., Newell, Normand, Ong, Orr, Payne J., Pintado, Poynot, Seymour, Shaw, Smith, Spellicy, Stauffer, Sullivan, Waters, Wenck, Wells—53.

NAYS—Messrs. Barrett, Bell, Buckley, Campbell, Cook J. K., Cook T., Dufresne, Fish, Flood, Foley, Gastinel, Gaidry, Geier, Gorlinski, Gruneberg, Harnan, Hart, Healy, Heard, Kavanagh, Mann, Murphy E., Ong, Orr, Payne J., Purcell J., Pursell S., Schnurr, Schroeder, Stocker, Stumpf, Stiner, Terry, Thorpe, Wilson—33.

The resolution was therefore tabled.

ORDER OF THE DAY.

The Convention resumed the consideration of the report of the Committee on Judiciary.

The 2d article was read, together with Mr. Henderson's amendment, when, with the consent of the Convention, Mr. Henderson withdrew his original amendment and offered a substitute.

Mr. Pursell moved to lay the substitute on the table. Lost by a rising vote of 32 yeas to 14 nays.

On the motion to adopt Mr. Henderson's substitute, the yeas and nays were taken, with the following result :

YEAS—Messrs. Abell, Bailey, Buckley, Collin, Cook T., Decker, Duane. Dufresne, Dupaty, Duke, Ennis, Fish, Flagg, Flood, Foley, Fosdick, Gaidry, Gorlinski, Gruneberg, Henderson, Hills, Kavanagh, Maurer, Maas, Mendiverri, Murphy M. W., Murphy E., O'Conner, Orr, Schroeder, Seymour, Smith, Stumpf, Stiner, Stauffer, Sullivan, Terry, Thorpe, Waters—39.

NAYS—Messrs. Ariail, Austin, Baum, Barrett, Beauvais, Bell, Bofill, Bromley, Burke, Campbell, Cazabat, Cook J. K., Crozat, Davies, Edwards, Fuller, Geier, Goldman, Harnan, Hart, Healy, Heard, Hire, Howell, Howes, Knobloch, Kugler, Mann, Mayer, Montamat, Morris, Newell, Normand, Ong, Payne J., Pintado, Poynot, Purcell J., Pursell S., Schnurr, Shaw, Spellicy, Stocker, Wenck, Wells, Wilson—47.

The substitute was therefore not adopted.

Art. 2d was then adopted as originally reported by the committee.

Art. 3d was read, and Mr. Sullivan offered a substitute.

Mr. Cazabat moved to lay the substitute on the table. Lost.

Pending the discussion on the 3d article and Mr. Sullivan's substitute, the Convention adjourned.

Adopted.

JOHN E. NEELIS, *Secretary.*

THURSDAY, May 26, 1864.

The president called the Convention to order at 12 o'clock M.

Prayer was offered by the Rev. Mr.Gilbert.

The roll being called, the following members answered to their names :.

Messrs. Abell, Ariail, Austin, Bailey, Barrett, Baum, Beauvais, Bell, Bennie, Bofill, Bromley, Buckley, Burke, Campbell, Collin, Cook J. K., Cook T., Crozat, Cutler, Davies, Duane, Dufresne, Duke, Dupaty, Edwards, Ennis, Fish, Flagg, Flood, Foley, Fosdick, Fuller, Gaidry, Geier, Goldman, Gorlinski, Gruneberg, Harnan, Hart, Healy, Heard, Henderson, Hills, Hire. Howell, Howes, Kavanagh, Knobloch, Kugler, Maas, Mann, Maurer, Mayer, Mendiverri, Montamat, Murphy E., Murphy M. W., Newell, Normand, O'Conner, Ong, Orr, Payne J., Paine J. T., Pintado, Poynot, Purcell J., Pursell S., Schroeder, Schnurr, Seymour, Shaw, Smith, Spellicy, Stocker, Stumpf, Stiner, Stauffer, Sullivan, Terry, Thorpe, Waters, Wenck, Wells, Wilson and Mr. President—86.

A quorum being present, the journal of yesterday was read and approved.

Mr. Thorpe presented the following resolution, which lies over under the rules :

Resolved, That the pen used by the president of this Convention iin signing the ordinance of emancipation, be presented, along with proper endorsements of its genuineness, to Major Gen. N. P. Banks, commanding the Department of the Gulf.

REPORTS OF COMMITTEES.

The Committee on Schedule reported progress.

The Committee on Finance, no report.

The Committee on Expenses, no report.

The Committee on Compensation, no report.

The Committee on Currency, no report.

The Committee on Auditor reported progress.

Mr. Montamat moved a reconsideration of the vote of yesterday on the adoption of Mr. Hills's resolution relative to members who fail to answer at roll call.

Mr. Hills moved that Mr. Montamat's motion be laid on the table, upon which motion the yeas and nays were demanded, and being taken resulted as follows :

YEAS—Messrs. Ariail, Barrett, Beauvais, Bell, Bromley, Burke. Collin, Cook T., Dufresne, Duane, Edwards, Ennis, Flood, Fosdick, Foley, Geier, Goldman, Gorlinski, Harnan. Hills, Howell, Kugler, Mann. Newell, Normand, Payne J., Purcell J., Pursell S.. Schroeder, Shaw, Smith, Stiner, Stauffer, Terry. Thorpe, Wells, Wilson—36.

NAYS—Messrs. Abell. Bailey, Baum, Bennie. Beauvais, Bofill, Buckley, Campbell, Cook J. K., Crozat, Cutler, Davies, Decker

Duke, Dupaty, Fish, Flagg, Fuller, Gaidry, Gruneberg, Hart, Healy, Heard, Henderson, Hire, Howes, Kavanagh, Knobloch, Maas, Maurer, Mayer, Mendiverri, Montamat, Murphy E., Murphy M. W., O'Conner, Ong, Orr, Paine J. T., Pintado, Poynot, Schnurr, Seymour, Spellicy, Stocker, Stumpf, Sullivan, Waters, Wenck—49.

The motion was therefore lost.

On the motion to reconsider the yeas and nays were demanded, and being taken, resulted as follows :

YEAS — Messrs. Abell, Austin, Bailey, Baum, Beauvais, Bennie, Bofill, Buckley, Campbell, Cook J. K., Crozat, Cutler, Davies, Decker, Duke, Dupaty, Fish, Flagg, Fuller, Gaidry, Gruneberg, Hart, Healy, Heard, Henderson, Hire, Howes, Kavanagh, Knobloch, Maas, Maurer, Mayer, Mendiverri, Montamat, Murphy E., Murphy M. W., Ong, O'Conner, Orr, Paine J. T., Pintado, Poynot, Schnurr, Seymour, Spellicy, Stocker, Sullivan, Waters, Wenck—49.

NAYS—Messrs. Ariail, Barrett, Bell, Bromley, Burke, Collin, Cook T., Duane, Dufresne, Edwards, Ennis, Flood, Foley, Fosdick, Geier, Goldman, Gorlinski, Harnan, Hills, Howell, Kugler, Mann, Newell, Normand, Payne J., Purcell J., Pursell S., Schroeder, Shaw, Smith, Stumpf, Stiner, Stauffer, Terry, Thorpe, Wells, Wilson—37.

The motion to reconsider prevailed, and, on motion of Mr. Montamat, the resolution of Mr. Hills was laid on the table.

ORDER OF THE DAY.

The Convention resumed the consideration of art. 3d of the report of the Judiciary Committee, together with Mr. Sullivan's substitute, which was taken up as the order of the day, being the unfinished business of yesterday.

After an able and protracted discussion, the Convention adjourned.

Adopted.

JOHN E. NEELIS,
Secretary.

FRIDAY, May 27, 1864.

The president called the Convention to order at 12 o'clock M.

The roll was called and the following members answered to their names :

Messrs. Abell, Ariail, Austin, Balch, Bailey, Barrett, Baum, Beauvais, Bell, Bennie, Bofill, Bromley, Brott, Buckley, Burke, Cazabat, Collin, Cook J. K., Cook T., Crozat, Davies, Decker, Duane, Dufresne, Dupaty, Duke, Edwards, Ennis. Fish, Flagg, Flood, Foley, Fuller, Gastinel, Gaidry, Geier, Goldman, Gruneberg, Hart, Healy, Heard, Henderson, Howell, Howes, Knobloch, Maurer, Maas, Mann, Mayer, Mendiverri, Montamat. Morris, Murphy M. W., Newell, Normand, O'Conner, Orr, Payne J., Pintado, Poynot, Purcell J., Pursell S., Schroeder, Schnurr, Seymour, Shaw, Smith, Spellicy, Stocker, Stumpf, Stiner, Sullivan, Terry, Thorpe, Waters, Wells, Wilson, and Mr. President—78.

The journal of yesterday was read and approved.

RESOLUTIONS.

The following resolutions were presented and laid over under the rules.

By Mr. Bell :

Resolved, That the following be adopted as a standing rule of this Convention :

When a question has been once decided by the Convention, it shall not again be brought up for consideration, except by a motion to reconsider, which motion must be made on the same or succeeding day, or by a vote of two-thirds of the members present.

By Mr. Waters :

Be it Resolved, That from and after this date, the police force of the city of New Orleans shall receive from the city treasury the annual pay of one thousand dollars, payable monthly, and shall furnish bond in the sum of one thousand dollars for the faithful performance of their duties while acting in the capacity of policemen.

Mr. Foley moved a suspension of the rules, in order to act on the foregoing resolution. Lost.

REPORTS OF COMMITTEES.

Mr. Cazabat, on behalf of the Special Committee on Compensation to loyal owners for emancipated slaves, stated that the committee will report on Monday.

Mr. Montamat, on behalf of the Special Committee to wait on Gen. Banks and invite him and his staff to visit this Convention, reported that the committee had performed the duty assigned them, and that Gen. Banks would visit the Convention at 1 o'clock P. M. to-day.

No other reports of committees.

Mr. Thorpe called up his resolution of yesterday, relative to presenting to General Banks the pen with which the president of this Convention signed the ordinance of emancipation. The resolution was unanimously adopted.

ORDER OF THE DAY.

The report of the Judiciary Committee was taken up as the order of the day.

On Mr. Hills's motion, the rule limiting members to half an hour in debate, was suspended during the discussion on the subject of the judiciary.

The door-keeper announced Gen. Banks, when all the members rose, and Gen. Banks entered the hall, accompanied by his staff and his excellency, Gov. Hahn. The distinguished visitors were escorted to the president's stand by the committee, when Gen. Banks was welcomed by the president in a short and appropriate address, to which the general replied in a few eloquent and well-timed remarks. Expressing thanks to the president and the Convention, he announced his cordial approval of what the Convention has already done, and his confidence that the work which remains to be completed will be equally well done.

At the conclusion of Gen. Banks's remarks, on motion of Mr. Stocker, the Convention took a recess of twenty minutes.

On reassembling, Mr. Abell obtained a suspension of the rules and offered the following resolution, which was unanimously adopted:

Resolved, That this Convention tenders to Major General Banks its acknowledgments of his eminent public services, first, as a civilian; next, as a soldier; and in both capacities, as a man ready and willing to give up his all for his country.

The discussion on the Judiciary Report was then resumed, pending which the Convention adjourned.

Adopted.

JOHN E. NEELIS,
Secretary.

SATURDAY May 28, 1864.,

The president called the Convention to order at 12 o'clock M., and the roll being called the following members answered to their names:

Messrs. Abell, Ariail, Balch, Bailey, Barrett, Bell, Bofill, Bromley, Buckley, Burke, Campbell, Cazabat, Cook J. K., Crozat, Decker, Duane, Dufresne, Duke, Dupaty, Edwards, Ennis, Flood, Foley, Geier, Goldman, Gorlinski, Harnan, Hart, Healy, Henderson, Heard, Howes, Kavanagh, Maurer, Maas, Mann, Mayer, Montamat, Morris, Murphy M. W., Newell, Normand, O'Conner, Orr, Pintado, Poynot. Pursell S., Schroeder, Schnurr, Shaw, Smith, Spellicy, Stauffer, Stiner, Stumpf, Sullivan, Terry, Waters, Wells, Wilson and Mr. President—61.

There being no quorum, the sergeant-at-arms was directed to bring in absent members.

After some delay the following members appeared and took their seats:

Messrs. Baum, Collin, Fish, Mendiverri, Fosdick, Kugler, Cook T., Seymour, Fuller, Austin, Davies, Howell, Hire, Beauvais, Stocker, Thorpe—16.

A quorum being announced, the journal of yesterday was read and approved.

Mr. Cazabat presented a resolution to the effect that this Convention will adjourn *sine die* on the 6th day of June.

Mr. Montamat moved a suspension of the rules in order to consider the foregoing resolution, but two-thirds not voting in favor of the motion, the resolution was laid over under the rules.

Mr. Pursell, on behalf of the Committee on Contingent Expenses, reported favorably on the bill of the city of New Orleans for fitting up Liberty Hall for the use of the Convention, and accompanied the report with a resolution providing for the payment of said bill.

The same member, on behalf of the same committee, reported unfavorably on the resolution of Mr. Terry, to appropriate one hundred dollars for enrolling on parchment, and framing, etc., of the ordinance of emancipation.

On motion, the report was adopted.

Mr. Austin, on behalf of the Committee on the Report of the Auditor of Public Accounts, stated that the committee will be ready to report on Monday.

Mr. Bell called up his resolution to amend the rules, and on motion the same was laid on the table.

Mr. Waters called up his resolution relative to the city police.

On a motion to table the resolution the yeas and nays were demanded, and being taken resulted as follows:

YEAS—Messrs. Ariail, Balch, Bailey, Beauvais, Collin, Cazabat, Crozat, Davies, Duke, Dufresne, Dupaty, Edwards, Ennis, Fosdick, Heard, Hills, Hire, Howell, Howes, Kugler, Mann, Mayer, Morris, Orr, Pintado, Pursell S., Shaw, Stauffer, Thorpe, Wells—30.

NAYS—Messrs. Abell, Barrett, Bell, Bofill, Buckley, Burke, Campbell, Cook T., Cook J. K., Duane, Fish, Flood, Foley, Fuller, Geier, Goldman, Gorlinski, Harnan, Hart,

AND AMENDMENT OF THE CONSTITUTION OF LOUISIANA. 95

Healy, Henderson, Howes, Maas, Maurer, Mendiverri, Montamat, Murphy M. W., Normand, O'Conner, Poynot, Purcell J., Schroeder, Schnurr, Seymour, Smith, Spellicy, Stocker, Stumpf, Stiner, Sullivan, Terry, Waters, Wenck, Wilson—44.

Mr. Sullivan offered a substitute for Mr. Waters's resolution. The substitute was accepted.

Mr. Cazabat moved to table the substitute, upon which motion the yeas and nays were demanded, and being taken resulted as follows :

YEAS—Messrs. Ariail, Austin, Balch, Bailey, Beauvais, Bromley, Burke, Campbell, Collin, Cazabat, Cutler, Davies, Dufresne, Duke, Dupaty, Edwards, Ennis, Fosdick, Gorlinski, Heard, Hills, Hire, Howell, Kugler, Mann, Mayer, Morris, Orr, Payne J., Paine J. T., Pintado, Purcell S., Shaw, Stumpf, Thorpe, Wells, Wilson—37.

NAYS—Messrs. Abell, Barrett, Bell, Bofill, Buckley, Cook J. K., Cook T., Duane, Fish, Flood, Foley, Fuller, Geier, Goldman. Harnan, Hart, Healy, Henderson, Howes, Maas, Maurer, Mendiverri, Montamat, Murphy M. W., Normand, O'Conner, Poynot, Purcell J., Schroeder, Schnurr, Seymour, Smith, Spellicy, Stocker, Stiner, Stauffer, Sullivan, Terry, Waters, Wenck—40.

Consequently the motion was lost, and on motion of Mr. Abell the substitute was ordered to be printed and made the order of the day for Monday, June 6th.

Mr. Bofill asked a call of the House, which was ordered, when 77 members answered.

The order of the day being the report of the Judiciary Committee, together with Mr. Sullivan's substitute for the 3d article of said report, was then taken up and discussed, pending which the Convention adjourned.

Adopted.

JOHN E. NEELIS,
Secretary.

MONDAY, May 30, 1864.

The Convention met pursuant to adjournment, and after prayer by the Rev. Mr. Horton, the roll was called and the following members answered to their names :

Messrs. Abell, Ariail, Balch, Bailey, Beauvais, Bofill, Bromley, Buckley, Burke, Campbell, Collin, Crozat, Davies, Dufresne, Duke, Edwards, Ennis, Fish, Flagg, Flood, Foley, Fosdick, Gastinel, Geier, Harnan, Hart, Healy, Heard, Hills, Howell, Howes. Kavanagh, Kugler, Maas, Mann, Maurer, Mayer, Montamat, Murphy E., Murphy M. W., Newell, Normand, O'Conner, Ong, Orr, Paine J. T., Pintado, Poynot, Purcell J., Pursell S., Schnurr, Seymour, Shaw, Smith, Spellicy, Stumpf, Stiner, Stauffer, Sullivan, Terry, Thorpe, Waters, Wenck, Wells, Wilson and Mr. President—66.

There being no quorum, the sergeant-at-arms was directed to procure the attendance of absent members.

The following members having entered and taken their seats, viz : Messrs. Barrett, Cazabat, Cook T., Cutler, Duane, Fuller, Henderson, Hire, Morris, Schroeder and Stocker, (11,) the president announced that there was a quorum present.

Mr. Hills offered the following :

Resolved, That members of this Convention who have not leave of absence, and who shall fail to answer to the roll-call within twenty minutes after 12 M., shall forfeit their per diem allowance for every day of such absence, unless able to give a satisfactory excuse to the Convention.

Mr. Stocker moved to suspend the rules in order to take up Mr. Hills's resolution, but the Convention refusing to suspend the rules, the resolution was laid over.

Mr. Montamat offered the following :

Resolved, That a copy of the resolution adopted by this Convention, tendering thanks to Major General N. P. Banks, be sent to him, (the same to be written on parchment.)

Mr. Orr offered the following :

Resolved, That it shall be the duty of the Legislature, at its first session, to fix, by legislative enactments, the compensation to be paid to foremen, mechanics, cartmen and laborers employed on the public works under the government of the State of Louisiana and the city of New Orleans, at not less than the following rates:

Foreman of mechanics..... $4 00 per day.
Foreman of carts.......... 3 00 " "
Foremen of laborers....... 3 00 " "
Mechanics................. 3 00 " "
Laborers.................. 2 00 " "

Mr. Wells, on behalf of the Committe on Compensation of loyal owners of slaves, submitted a written report and memorial, and also reported the following resolutions :

Resolved, That the Committee on the Compensation of loyal citizens for slaves emancipated, be directed to cause the accompanying memorial to be engrossed in duplicate, signed by themselves and attested by the president and secretary of this Convention, and that they also transmit one copy of the same to the Senate and the other to the House of Representatives of the United States.

Resolved, That the committee be instructed to correspond, upon the subject of compensating loyal owners, with such members of Congress of the United States as they may think proper.

Mr. Abell offered the following amendment:

That the payment be made to loyal citizens before the final adoption of this constitution.

The question being put upon the adoption of Mr. Abell's amendment, the same was rejected, and so announced by the president; whereupon Messrs. Abell and Montamat appealed from the decision of the chair to the Convention, which sustained the decision of the chair.

The report of the Committee on Compensation was then adopted, and on motion of Mr. Montamat, two hundred copies was ordered to be printed.

Mr. Abell moved that two hundred copies of his amendment be printed.

A motion to lay on the table being lost, Mr. Abell's motion was then carried.

Mr Montamat, on behalf of the Committee on Finance, submitted the following report of the Finance Committee of the State Convention, of the funds appropriated for the payment of per diem of members and salaries of officers:

May 23—Balance on hand as
    per report No. 6.... $47,186 40
May 4—P a i d warrant No. 47. $1349 00
May 24—P a i d warrant No. 48. 416 00
May 25—P a i d warrant No. 49. 1730 00
May 28—P a i d warrant No. 50. 1630 00
May 28—P a i d warrant No. 51. 2330 00
May 28—P a i d warrant No. 52. 1828 00
May 28—P a i d warrant No. 54. 860 00—$10,143 00

May 30—Balance on hand this day.................$37,043 40
Thirty-seven thousand and forty-three dollars and forty cents.

JOHN P. MONTAMAT,
Chairman pro tem., Finance Committee.
New Orleans, May 30, 1864.

Mr. Montamat, as chairman *pro tem.* of the Committee on Finance, also submitted the following report of the Finance Committee of the State Convention, of the funds appropriated for contingent expenses:

May 23—Balance on hand as per
    report No. 6............$8759 48
May 27—Paid M. DeCoursey for contingent expenses, as per voucher on file, warrant No. 53............ 1830 85
May 30—Balance on hand this day.$6928 63
Six thousand nine hundred and twenty-eight dollars and sixty-three cents.

JOHN P. MONTAMAT,
Chairman pro tem., Finance Committee.
New Orleans, May 20, 1864.

Mr. Cazabat's resolution relative to the final adjournment of the Convention on the 6th day of June, was taken up, and, on motion of Mr. Buckley, was laid on the table.

The report of the Committee on the Judiciary being the special order of the day was then taken up, and after a lengthy discussion, the Convention adjourned until tomorrow at 12 o'clock M.

Adopted.

JOHN E. NEELIS,
Secretary.

TUESDAY, May 31, 1864.

The Convention met pursuant to adjournment, and was called to order by the president.

The proceedings were opened with prayer by the Rev. Mr. Strong.

The roll was called, and the following members answered to their names:

Messrs. Abell, Balch, Bailey, Barrett, Bofill, Bromley, Buckley, Burke, Campbell, Collin, Cook J. K., Crozat, Decker, Duke, Dufresne, Edwards, Ennis, Fish, Flagg, Flood, Foley, Gorlinski, Harnan, Healy, Heard, Hills, Howell, Howes, Kavanagh, Mass, Mann, Mayer, Mendiverri, Montamat, Morris, Murphy M. W., Newell, Normand, O'Conner, Ong, Orr, Payne J., Paine J. T., Pintado, Poynot, Purcell J., Pursell S., Schroeder, Schnurr, Seymour, Shaw, Spellicy, Stumpf, Stiner, Stauffer, Sullivan, Terry, Waters, Wells and Mr. President—60.

There being no quorum present, the sergeant-at-arms was directed to procure the attendance of absent members.

After some delay, Messrs. Beauvais, Bell, Fosdick, Gastinel, Geier, Goldman, Hart, Henderson, Hire, Maurer, Murphy E., Smith, Stocker, Thorpe, Wenck and Wilson entered, took their seats and answered to their names.

AND AMENDMENT OF THE CONSTITUTION OF LOUISIANA. 97

The president then announced a quorum present.

The minutes of yesterday were read and approved.

The president having read the order of business, Mr. Stocker moved that the rules be suspended, to allow Mr. Thorpe to introduce a resolution, which motion was carried and the rules accordingly suspended.

Mr. Thorpe then offered the following:

Resolved, That after this date (May 31st, 1864) the order of the day shall be taken up immediately after the minutes shall have been read by the clerk and accepted by the Convention, and that Saturday of each week shall be appropriated to miscellaneous business.

Mr. Wilson moved a suspension of the rules in order to take up the resolution, which was carried.

The resolution was then read by the secretary, when Mr. Montamat moved to lay it on the table, which motion being lost, the resolution was taken up and adopted by a rising vote of 54 yeas and 18 nays.

Mr. Sullivan demanded a call of the House, when seventy-six members answered to their names.

Mr. Hills called up his resolution of yesterday.

Mr. Montamat offered the following amendment:

That the honorable member of the Second Representative District (Mr. Hills) shall forfeit his per diem for every day he shall fail to answer to his name within fifteen minutes after 12 o'clock M.

On motion of Mr. Sullivan, the resolution and amendment were both laid on the table.

Mr. Orr called up his resolution of yesterday.

Mr. Hills moved to lay it on the table, which motion was carried by a rising vote of 40 yeas to 35 nays.

Mr. Montamat called up his resolution relative to furnishing Major General Banks a copy of the resolution of thanks lately adopted by this Convention.

The resolution was read and unanimously adopted.

The Convention then resumed its action on the report of the Committee on the Judiciary, and the substitute offered therefor, being the special order of the day.

After a lengthy discussion the question was called for, but a call of the House having been demanded by Mr. Sullivan the roll was called, when only seventy-three members answered to their names.

There being no quorum, the sergeant-at-arms was dispatched for absent members.

Mr. Foley moved to adjourn. Lost.

Several members having entered the hall and taken their seats, the roll was again called, when seventy-six members answered to their names, and a quorum was declared to be present.

The question upon the adoption of Mr. Sullivan's amendment was then put, when the yeas and nays being ordered, the following vote was taken:

YEAS—Messrs. Bell, Buckley, Campbell, Collin, Duke, Flood, Gastinel, Goldman, Gruneberg, Harnan, Howes, Maurer, Morris, Murphy M. W., O'Conner, Orr, Poynot, Pursell Sam., Schnurr, Smith, Stocker, Stauffer, Sullivan, Terry, Waters—25.

NAYS—Messrs. Abell, Ariail, Bailey, Barrett, Beauvais, Bofill, Bromley, Brott, Burke, Cazabat, Cook J. K., Cook Terrance, Crozat, Cutler, Decker, Edwards, Ennis, Fish, Flagg, Foley, Fosdick, Fuller, Gorlinski, Healy, Hart, Heard, Henderson, Hills, Hire, Howell, Kavanagh, Maas, Mann, Mendiverri, Montamat, Murphy E., Newell, Normand, Ong, Payne J., Pintado, Purcell J., Schroeder, Seymour, Shaw, Spellicy, Stumpf, Stiner, Thorpe, Wenck, Wells, Wilson—52.

Consequently the amendment was rejected.

The question then recurred upon the adoption of the 3d article of the report.

The yeas and nays were ordered, with the following result:

YEAS—Messrs. Ariail, Bailey, Beauvais, Bofill, Bromley, Brott, Burke, Cazabat, Crozat, Cutler, Ennis, Fish, Flagg, Fuller, Gorlinski, Healy, Heard, Henderson, Hire, Howell, Mann, Newell, Pintado, Seymour, Shaw, Stumpf, Thorpe, Wenck, Wells, Wilson—30.

NAYS—Messrs. Abell, Barrett, Bell, Buckley, Campbell, Collin, Cook J. K., Cook T., Decker, Duke, Edwards, Flood, Foley, Fosdick, Gastinel, Goldman, Gruneberg, Hart, Harnan, Hills, Howes, Kavanagh, Maurer, Maas, Mendiverri, Montamat, Morris, Murphy E., Murphy M. W., Normand, O'Conner, Ong, Orr, Payne J., Poynot, Purcell J., Pursell S., Schroeder, Schnurr, Smith, Spellicy, Stocker, Stiner, Stauffer, Sullivan, Terry, Waters—47.

On motion the Convention then adjourned til to-morrow at 12 o'clock M.
Adopted.
JOHN E. NEELIS,
Secretary.

WEDNESEAY, June 1, 1864.

The Convention met pursuant to adjournment. The roll was called by the secretary, and the following members answered to their names:

Messrs. Ariail, Austin, Balch, Baum, Barrett, Buckley, Burke, Campbell, Cook J. K., Collin, Decker, Dufresne, Duke, Edwards, Flagg, Flood, Fuller, Geier, Goldman, Gorlinski, Gruneberg, Healy, Heard, Hills, Howell, Howes, Mann, Montamat, Newell, Normand, O'Conner, Pintado, Poynot, Pursell S., Schroeder, Schnurr, Shaw, Spellicy, Stumpf, Stiner, Stauffer, Sullivan, Wells and Mr. President—44.

There being no quorum present, the sergeant-at-arms was directed to procure the attendance of absent members.

After some delay the following gentlemen entered and took their seats: Messrs. Abell, Bailey, Beauvais, Bell, Bofill, Brott, Bromley, Crozat, Cutler, Duane, Fish, Foley, Fosdick, Gastinel, Hart, Henderson, Hire, Kavanagh, Maas, Mayer, Mendiverri, Morris, Murphy M. W., Ong, Orr, Purcell J., Smith, Stocker, Terry, Thorpe, Waters, Wenck, Wilson—33.

The president announced that a quorum was present.

The minutes of yesterday were read, amended and adopted.

Mr. Montamat moved a reconsideration of the vote by which article 3d of the report of the Judiciary Committee was rejected on yesterday, which motion was carried and the article reconsidered.

Mr. Montamat then moved to amend by substituting "seven thousand five hundred dollars" instead of "ten thousand dollars," as the salary of the chief justice, and "seven thousand dollars" instead of "nine thousand dollars," as the salary per annum of the associate judges.

Mr. Stiner moved to stike out "seven thousand five hundred dollars" and insert "eight thousand dollars" instead, which motion was laid on the table.

Mr. Thorpe offered to amend by striking out entirely all that part of the article relating to salaries, so as to leave the fixing thereof to the Legislature.

Laid on the table.

Mr. Hills moved to lay Mr. Montamat's amendment on the table, upon which the yeas and nays were ordered with the following result:

YEAS—Messrs. Abell, Balch, Baum, Bailey, Bromley, Brott, Collin, Cook J. K., Davies, Decker, Duane, Dufresne, Duke, Edwards, Flood, Foley, Fosdick, Gorlinski, Healy, Hills, Hire, Howell, Howes, Murphy M. W., Normand, O'Conner, Orr, Poynot, Schroeder, Smith, Spellicy, Stocker, Terry, Thorpe, Wenck, Wilson—36.

NAYS—Messrs. Arial, Austin, Barrett, Beauvais, Bofill, Buckley, Burke, Campbell, Cazabat, Crozat, Cutler, Fish, Flagg, Fuller, Gastinel, Geier, Goldman, Gruneberg, Hart, Heard, Maas, Mann, Mayer, Montamat, Morris, Newell, Ong, Pintado, Purcell J., Pursell S., Schnurr, Seymour, Shaw, Stumpf, Stiner, Stauffer, Sullivan, Waters, Wells—39.

Consequently Mr. Hills's motion was lost.

Soon after a call of the House being ordered the roll was called, and seventy-seven members responded to their names.

Mr. S. Pursell offered to amend by inserting after the word "annually" the words "until otherwise provided by law," which amendment was accepted by Mr. Montamat.

The question was then put upon the adoption of the article as amended and was carried; consequently the article, as amended, was adopted.

Articles 4, 5, 6, 7 and 8 were then adopted without opposition.

When article 9 was read, Mr. Campbell moved to amend by striking out in the 4th line the words "three-fourths" and inserting the word "majority."

Mr. Cazabat moved to lay Mr. Campbell's amendment on the table. Lost.

Mr. Campbell's amendment was then adopted.

Mr. Stocker moved to amend by striking out in the 4th line the words "present in" and inserting the words "elected to," which amendment was carried.

Article 9 was then adopted as amended.

Article 10 was read, when Mr. Cazabat moved to strike out after "salary" the words "which shall not be diminished during their continuance in office," which amendment was laid on the table.

Mr. S. Pursell offered an amendment, in-

AND AMENDMENT OF THE CONSTITUTION OF LOUISIANA.

serting after the word "be," in the 2d line, the words "increased or."

Mr. Henderson moved to lay the amendment on the table. Carried. Consequently Mr. Pursell's amendment was lost.

The amendments were then withdrawn and the article adopted as reported.

Article 11 was then read, together with the substitute offered by Mr. Stauffer and the amendments of Messrs. Montamat and Sullivan.

Mr. Cazabat moved to lay both the substitute and amendments on the table, upon which question the yeas and nays were ordered, with the following result:

YEAS — Messrs. Ariail, Bailey, Baum, Beauvais, Bofill, Burke, Cazabat, Crozat, Cutler, Duane, Fish, Flagg, Fuller, Geier, Heard, Hire, Howell, Mayer, Newell, Normand, Ong, Poynot, Purcell J., Schnurr, Seymour, Stumpf, Thorpe, Waters, Wenck, Wells, Wilson—31.

NAYS—Messrs. Abell, Austin, Balch, Bell, Bromley, Brott, Buckley, Campbell, Collin, Cook J. K., Cook T., Decker, Dufresne, Duke, Edwards, Flood, Foley, Fosdick, Gastinel, Goldman, Gorlinski, Gruneberg, Hart, Henderson, Healy, Hills, Howes, Maas, Mann, Mendiverri, Montamat. Morris, Murphy M. W., O'Conner, Orr, Pintado, Pursell S., Shaw, Smith, Spellicy, Stocker, Stauffer, Stiner, Sullivan, Terry—45.

Consequently the motion to lay on the table was lost.

Mr. Montamat then withdrew his amendment.

The substitute offered by Mr. Stauffer was then taken up.

Mr. Gruneberg moved to strike out the words "the court shall have power to appoint its own clerks," as superfluous, the same being previously provided for, which amendment was accepted by Mr. Stauffer.

On the adoption of Mr. Stauffer's substitute the yeas and nays were ordered, resulting as follows:

YEAS—Messrs. Bell, Buckley, Campbell, Cook T., Decker, Dufresne, Duke, Flagg, Gastinel, Geier, Goldman, Gruneberg, Howes, Mayer, Morris, O'Conner, Orr, Poynot, Sullivan, Schnurr, Smith, Stocker, Stauffer, Terry—24.

NAYS—Messrs. Abell, Ariail, Austin, Barrett, Balch, Bailey, Baum, Beauvais, Bofill, Bromley, Brott, Burke, Cazabat, Cook J. K., Collin, Crozat, Cutler, Duane, Edwards,

Fish, Flood, Foley, Fosdick, Fuller, Gorlinski, Hart, Healy, Heard, Henderson, Hills, Hire, Howell, Maas, Mann, Mendiverri, Montamat, Murphy M. W., Newell, Normand, Ong, Pintado, Purcell J., Pursell S., Shaw, Seymour, Spellicy, Stumpf, Stiner, Thorpe, Waters, Wenck, Wells, Wilson—53.

Consequently the substitute was rejected.

Mr. Sullivan's amendment was then taken up, and the yeas and nays being ordered thereon, resulted as follows:

YEAS—Messrs. Bell, Buckley, Campbell. Collin, Cook J. K., Cook T., Decker, Duke, Flagg, Flood, Geier, Goldman, Gorlinski, Gruneberg, Howes, Mayer, O'Conner, Orr, Poynot, Pursell S., Smith, Spellicy, Stocker, Stauffer, Sullivan, Terry—26.

NAYS—Messrs. Abell, Ariail, Austin, Barrett, Balch, Bailey, Baum, Beauvais, Bofill, Bromley, Brott, Burke, Cazabat, Crozat, Cutler, Duane, Dufresne, Edwards, Fish, Foley, Fosdick, Fuller, Gastinel, Hart, Healy, Heard, Henderson, Hills, Hire, Howell, Maas, Mann, Mendiverri, Montamat, Morris, Murphy M. W., Newell, Normand, Ong, Pintado, Purcell J., Schnurr, Shaw, Stiner, Seymour, Stumpf, Thorpe, Waters, Wenck, Wells, Wilson—51.

Consequently the amendment was rejected.

Mr. Shaw offered an amendment to the article as reported, by striking out all after the word "Senate" and inserting the words, "the judges of the Supreme Court shall hold their offices during the term of six years, and the judges of the inferior courts. for the term of four years."

After a lengthy discussion, Mr. Sullivan moved to adjourn, which was carried on a division of ayes 54, noes 23. Consequently he Convention adjourned until to-morrow at 12 o'clock M.

Adopted.

JOHN E. NEELIS,
Secretary.

THURSDAY, June 2, 1864.

The Convention met pursuant to adjournment.

The roll was called and the following members answered to their names:

Messrs. Ariail, Austin, Balch, Baum, Barrett, Bell, Burke, Campbell, Cazabat, Collin, Cook J. K., Crozat, Decker, Duane, Duke,

Dufresne, Edwards, Flagg, Flood, Foley, Gastinel, Gaidry, Geier, Goldman, Gruneberg, Harnan, Healy, Heard, Henderson, Hills, Howell, Knobloch, Maas, Mann, Maurer, Mayer, Montamat, Morris, Newell, Normand, O'Conner, Payne J., Pintado, Pursell S., Schnurr, Seymour, Shaw, Spellicy, Stauffer, Stumpf, Sullivan, Terry, Wells, Wilson, and Mr. President—55.

There being no quorum present, the sergeant-at-arms was directed to bring in absent members.

After some delay the following members entered the hall and answered to their names:

Messrs. Abell, Bailey, Beauvais, Bofill, Bromley, Fish, Fosdick, Fuller, Gorlinski, Hart, Hire, Howes, Mendiverri, Murphy M. W., Ong, Orr, Paine J. T., Purcell J., Smith, Stocker, Stiner, Waters—22.

The president announced a quorum present.

The minutes of yesterday's proceedings were read and adopted.

Mr. Montamat moved a suspension of the rules in order to introduce a resolution, which motion was carried, and the rules were accordingly suspended.

Mr. Montamat then offered the following:

Resolved, That the office of assistant secretary, now filled by Mr. T. H. Murphy, be and is hereby declared vacant.

Resolved, further, That the secretary be authorized to employ a proper person to fill said vacancy during the balance of the session.

Mr. Cazabat moved to reject the resolution. Lost.

The resolution was adopted.

The secretary thereupon appointed Mr. Philip Winfree to fill the vacancy occasioned by the adoption of said resolution.

The Convention then resumed its action on Mr. Shaw's amendment to art. 11 of the report of the Committee on the Judiciary.

Mr. Hills offered an amendment to Mr. Shaw's amendment, substituting the words "ten years" for the words "six years," as the term of office of the judges of the Supreme Court, and also substituting the words "eight years" for the words "four years," as the term of office of the judges of the inferior courts.

On a motion to lay Mr. Hills's amendment on the table the yeas and nays were ordered, with the following result:

YEAS—Messrs. Bailey, Bell, Buckley, Campbell, Collin, Cook J. K., Cook T., Decker, Flood, Geier, Goldman, Gruneberg, Howell, Knobloch, Maas, Mann, Mayer, Morris, Murphy M. W., O'Conner, Orr. Payne J., Poynot, Purcell J., Pursell S., Schroeder, Schnurr, Shaw, Smith, Stauffer, Sullivan, Terry, Wenck—33.

NAYS—Messrs. Abell, Ariail, Austin, Barrett, Balch, Baum, Beauvais, Bofill, Bromley, Burke, Cazabat, Crozat, Duane, Duke, Dufresne, Edwards, Fish, Flagg, Foley, Fosdick, Fuller, Gaidry, Gorlinski, Harnan, Hart, Healy, Heard, Henderson, Hills, Hire, Howes, Maurer, Mendiverri, Montamat, Normand, Newell, Ong, Paine J. T., Pintado, Seymour, Spellicy, Stocker, Stumpf, Stiner, Thorpe, Waters, Wells, Wilson—48.

Consequently the motion to lay on the table was lost.

After some discussion Mr. Austin moved to adjourn, and the yeas and nays being ordered resulted as follows:

YEAS—Messrs. Abell, Austin, Baum, Bailey, Buckley, Campbell, Cook J. K., Crozat, Decker, Dufresne, Duke, Flagg, Flood, Foley, Gaidry, Goldman, Gruneberg, Hart, Maurer, Mendiverri, Murphy M. W., Newell, Normand, O'Conner, Ong, Orr, Poynot, Purcell J., Schroeder, Spellicy, Stocker, Stumpf, Sullivan, Waters—34.

NAYS—Messrs. Ariail, Barrett, Beauvais, Bell, Bofill, Bromley, Burke, Cazabat, Collin, Cook T., Cutler, Duane, Edwards, Fish, Fosdick, Fuller, Gastinel, Geier, Gorlinski, Harnan, Healy, Heard, Henderson, Hills, Hire, Howell, Howes, Knobloch, Maas, Mann, Mayer, Montamat, Morris, Payne J., Paine J. T., Pintado, Pursell S., Schnurr, Seymour, Shaw, Smith, Stiner, Stauffer, Terry, Thorpe, Wenck, Wells, Wilson—48.

Consequently the Convention refused to adjourn.

The question on the adoption of Mr. Hills's amendment was then put, when the yeas and nays being ordered, the following vote was taken:

YEAS—Messrs. Bromley, Cazabat, Duane, Fish, Foley, Fosdick, Fuller, Goldman, Gorlinski, Harnan, Healy, Henderson, Hills, Hire, Mayer, Normand, Paine J. T., Pintado, Stumpf, Stiner, Thorpe, Waters—22.

NAYS—Messrs. Abell, Ariail, Austin, Bailey, Barrett, Baum, Beauvais, Bell, Bofill, Buckley, Burke, Campbell, Collin, Cook T., Cook J. K., Crozat, Cutler, Decker, Duke,

AND AMENDMENT OF THE CONSTITUTION OF LOUISIANA. 101

Dufresne, Edwards, Flagg, Flood, Gastinel, Gaidry, Geier, Gruneberg, Hart, Heard, Howell, Howes, Knobloch, Maas, Maurer, Mann, Mendiverri, Morris, Murphy M. W., Newell, O'Conner, Ong, Orr, Payne J., Poynot, Purcell J., Pursell S., Schroeder, Seymour, Schnurr, Shaw, Smith, Spellicy, Stauffer, Stocker, Sullivan, Terry, Wenck, Wells, Wilson—59.

Consequently Mr. Hills's amendment was lost.

Mr. Shaw's amendment was then taken up, and on the question of its adoption the yeas and nays were ordered, with the following result:

YEAS—Messrs. Barrett, Baum, Bell, Buckley, Campbell, Cook J. K., Cook T., Decker, Duane, Dufresne, Duke, Fish, Flagg, Flood, Fosdick, Gastinel, Gaidry, Geier, Goldman, Gorlinski, Gruneberg, Harnan, Hart, Hire, Howes, Knobloch, Maas, Maurer, Mayer, Mendiverri, Morris, Murphy M. W., Normand, O'Conner, Ong, Orr, Payne J., Paine J. T., Poynot, Purcell J., Pursell S., Shaw, Schroeder, Schnurr, Seymour, Smith, Stiner, Spellicy, Stocker, Stumpf, Stauffer, Sullivan, Terry—53.

NAYS—Messrs. Abell, Ariail, Austin, Bailey, Beauvais, Bofill, Bromley, Burke, Cazabat, Collin, Crozat, Cutler, Edwards, Foley, Fuller, Healy, Heard, Henderson, Hills, Howell, Mann, Newell, Pintado, Thorpe, Waters, Wenck, Wells, Wilson—28.

Mr. Shaw's amendment was therefore adopted.

On motion the Convention adjourned until Friday, 12 o'clock M.

Adopted.

JOHN E. NEELIS,
Secretary.

FRIDAY, June 3, 1864.

The Convention met at 12 o'clock M. and was called to order by the president. The roll was called and the following members answered to their names:

Messrs. Abell, Ariail, Austin, Barrett, Baum, Bell, Bromley, Burke, Campbell, Collin, Cook T., Crozat, Davies, Decker, Dufresne, Dupaty, Flagg, Flood, Foley, Gaidry, Gastinel, Geier, Gorlinski, Harnan, Healy, Heard, Henderson, Hills, Howell, Kavanagh, Knobloch, Maas, Mann, Mayer, Maurer, Montamat, Morris, Murphy E., Newell, O'Conner, Ong, Payne J., Pintado, Poynot, Purcell J., Pursell S., Schroeder, Schnurr, Shaw, Smith, Spellicy, Stiner, Stauffer, Sullivan, Terry, Waters, Wells, Wilson and Mr. President—59.

There being no quorum the sergeant-at-arms was directed to bring in absent members, and after some delay the following members took their seats and answered to their names, viz:

Messrs. Bailey, Bofill, Cazabat, Cook J. K., Duane, Duke, Edwards, Fish, Fosdick, Hart, Hire, Howes, Murphy M. W., Normand, Seymour, Stocker, Stumpf—17.

The president announced a quorum present.

The minutes of yesterday's proceedings were read, amended and adopted.

Mr. Baum moved to reconsider the vote of yesterday on Mr. Shaw's amendment.

On a motion to lay Mr. Baum's motion on the table the yeas and nays were ordered, resulting as follows:

YEAS — Messrs. Barrett, Bell, Buckley, Campbell, Cook J. K., Cook T., Davies, Dufresne, Dupaty, Flood, Gastinel, Gaidry, Geier, Gorlinski, Harnan, Howes, Henderson, Knobloch, Maurer, Montamat, Morris, Murphy M. W., Normand, O'Conner, Orr, Payne J., Poynot, Pursell S., Schnurr, Spellicy, Smith, Stocker, Stauffer, Sullivan, Terry, Waters—36.

NAYS—Messrs. Abell, Ariail, Austin, Bailey, Baum, Beauvais, Bofill, Bromley, Burke, Collin, Cazabat, Crozat, Cutler, Decker, Duane, Edwards, Fish, Flagg, Foley, Fosdick, Hart, Healy, Heard, Hills, Hire, Howell, Kavanagh, Maas, Mann, Mayer, Murphy E., Newell, Ong, Pintado, Schroeder, Seymour, Shaw, Stumpf, Stiner, Wells, Wilson—41.

Consequently the motion to lay on the table was lost.

The question was then put on Mr. Baum's motion to reconsider the vote on Mr. Shaw's amendment, and the yeas and nays being demanded the following was the result:

YEAS—Messrs. Ariail, Austin, Baum, Bailey, Beauvais, Bofill, Bromley, Burke, Cazabat, Collin, Crozat, Cutler, Duane, Dupaty, Edwards, Fish, Flagg, Foley, Fosdick, Gaidry, Hart, Heard, Henderson, Hills, Hire, Howell, Kavanagh, Knobloch, Maas, Mann, Mayer, Murphy M. W., Newell, Ong, Pintado, Seymour, Shaw, Stumpf, Waters, Wenck, Wells, Wilson—42.

NAYS—Messrs. Abell, Barrett, Bell, Buckley, Campbell, Cook J. K., Cook T., Davies, Decker, Dufresne, Flood, Gastinel, Geier, Gorlinski, Harnan, Healy, Howes, Maurer, Montamat, Morris, Murphy E., Normand, O'Conner, Orr, Payne J., Poynot, Pursell S., Schroeder, Schnurr, Smith, Spellicy, Stiner, Stocker, Stauffer, Sullivan, Terry—36.

Mr. Shaw's amendment was therefore reconsidered.

Mr. Foley moved to reject the amendment.

Mr. Montamat moved to lay Mr. Foley's motion on the table, whereupon Mr. Foley withdrew his motion, when the same was renewed by Mr. Mann.

The yeas and nays were ordered on the motion to reject the amendment, and the following vote was taken:

YEAS—Messrs. Abell, Ariail, Austin, Bailey, Baum, Beauvais, Bell, Bofill, Bromley, Burke, Cazabat, Crozat, Cutler, Davies, Dupaty, Duane, Edwards, Fish, Flagg, Flood, Foley, Fosdick, Fuller, Gaidry, Gorlinski, Hart, Healy, Heard, Henderson, Hills, Hire, Howell, Kavanagh, Knobloch, Maas, Mann, Mayer, Murphy E., Murphy M. W., Newell, Ong, Pintado, Seymour, Stumpf, Stiner, Thorpe, Waters, Wenck, Wells, Wilson—50.

NAYS—Messrs. Barrett, Buckley, Campbell, Collin, Cook J. K., Cook T., Decker, Dufresne, Gastinel, Geier, Harnan, Howes, Maurer, Montamat, Morris, Normand, Orr, O'Conner, Payne J., Poynot, Pursell S., Schroeder, Schnurr, Shaw, Smith, Spellicy, Stocker, Stauffer, Sullivan, Terry—30.

Consequently the amendment was rejected.

Mr. Terry offered the following substitute for article 11 of the report of the Committee on Judiciary Department, viz:

The judges, both of the Supreme and Inferior Courts, and justices of the peace, shall be elected by the qualified voters of the State; provided, that until two years after the present rebellious war is ended in this State, the proof of which shall be a proclamation from the President of the United States to that effect, the said judges and justices of the peace shall be appointed by the governor, by and with the advice and consent of the Senate, and the term of office as herein expressed and for which they shall have been so appointed, shall be stipulated in the commissions of the said judges and justices of the peace.

After that period, the governor shall issue his proclamation ordering an election for judges of the Supreme Court, Inferior Courts and justices of the peace, by the legal voters of the State, in accordance with the enactment contained in this article.

Mr. Wells moved to lay the substitute on the table, and the yeas and nays being demanded thereon the roll was called and the following vote taken:

YEAS—Messrs. Abell, Ariail, Austin, Bailey, Baum, Beauvais, Bofill, Bromley, Burke, Cazabat, Collin, Cook J. K., Cook T., Crozat, Cutler, Davies, Decker, Duane, Dupaty, Dufresne, Edwards, Fish, Foley, Fosdick, Fuller, Gastinel, Gorlinski, Harnan, Hart, Healy, Heard, Henderson, Hills, Hire, Howell, Kavanagh, Maas, Mann, Maurer, Mayer, Murphy E., Murphy M. W., Newell, Normand, Ong, Pintado, Poynot, Schroeder, Schnurr, Shaw, Spellicy, Stiner, Stauffer, Thorpe, Waters, Wenck, Wells, Wilson—58.

NAYS—Messrs. Barrett, Bell, Buckley, Campbell, Flagg, Flood, Gaidry, Geier, Howes, Knobloch, Morris, O'Conner, Orr, Payne J., Pursell S., Seymour, Smith, Stocker, Stumpf, Sullivan, Terry—21.

Consequently Mr. Terry's substitute was laid on the table.

Mr. Montamat moved a recess of ten minutes. Lost.

Mr. Hills then offered the following substitute for article 11:

The judges, both of the Supreme and Inferior Courts, shall be appointed by the governor, by and with the advice and consent of the Senate. The judges of the Supreme Court shall hold their offices for the term of twelve years, and the judges of the Inferior Courts (except justices of the peace) shall hold their offices during the term of ten years; but all appointments of judges, made by the present governor, shall expire with his term of office.

On a motion to lay Mr. Hills's substitute on the table, the yeas and nays were ordered with the following result:

YEAS—Messrs. Abell, Ariail, Barrett, Baum, Beauvais, Bell, Bofill, Bromley, Buckley, Burke, Collin, Cook J. K., Cook T., Crozat, Cutler, Davies, Decker, Duane, Dufresne, Dupaty, Flagg, Flood, Foley, Fuller, Gastinel, Geier, Goldman, Gaidry, Haley, Hart, Heard, Hire, Howell, Howes, Knobloch, Maas, Maurer, Montamat, Morris, Murphy M. W., Mayer, Normand, O'Conner, Orr, Payne J., Pintado, Poynot, Pursell S., Seymour, Smith, Spellicy, Stiner, Stauffer, Sullivan, Terry, Wenck, Wilson—57.

NAYS—Messrs. Austin, Bailey, Campbell, Cazabat, Edwards, Fish, Fosdick, Gorlinski, Harnan, Henderson, Hills, Kavanagh, Murphy E., Newell, Ong, Schroeder, Schnurr, Shaw, Stocker, Stumpf, Thorpe, Waters, Wells—23.

Mr. Hills's substitute was therefore laid on the table.

Mr. Stiner offered the following substitute for article 11:

The judges of the Supreme Court shall be appointed for the term of ——— years, and the judges of the Inferior Courts shall be appointed for the term of ——— years.

When the first appointments are made under this constitution, the chief justice shall be commissioned for ——— years, one of the associate justices for ———

years, one for ——— years, one for ———
years and one for ——— years.

The inferior judges shall be divided by lot into four classes, as nearly equal as can be, and the judges of the first class shall be commissioned for ——— years, those of the second for ——— years, those of the third for ——— years, and those of the fourth for ——— years.

Mr. Montamat offered the following amendment to the substitute:

The judges, both of the Supreme and Inferior Courts, except justices of the peace, shall be appointed by the governor, with the consent of the Senate and House of Representatives in joint session. The judges of the Supreme Court shall hold their offices for a term of eight years, and those of the Inferior Courts, except justices of the peace, for a term of six years.

Both substitute and amendment were laid on the table.

Mr. Smith offered the following substitute for article 11.

The judges of the Supreme and Inferior Courts shall be appointed by the governor during the existence of the present war, and for two years thereafter; at the expiration of that time the judges of the Supreme Court shall be elected by the lower branch of the General Assembly, the judges of the Inferior Courts to be elected by the qualified voters of their respective districts, their term of office to be fixed by the Legislature.

On a motion to lay Mr. Smith's substitute on the table, the yeas and nays were called with the following result:

YEAS—Messrs. Abell, Ariail, Austin, Bailey, Baum, Beauvais, Bofill, Bromley, Burke, Collin, Crozat, Cutler, Davies, Dupaty, Edwards, Fosdick, Fuller, Heard, Hills, Hire, Howell, Kavanagh, Newell, Normand, Ong, Shaw, Thorpe, Waters, Wenck, Wells, Wilson—31.

NAYS—Messrs. Barrett, Bell, Buckley, Campbell, Cazabat, Cook J. K., Cook T., Decker, Duane, Dufresne, Fish, Flagg, Flood, Foley, Gastinel, Geier, Goldman, Gorlinski, Gruneberg, Gaidry, Haley, Harnan, Hart, Henderson, Howes, Knobloch, Maas, Mann, Maurer, Montamat, Morris, Murphy E., Murphy M. W., Mayer, O'Conner, Orr, Payne J., Pintado, Poynot, Purcell J., Pursell S., Schroeder, Schnurr, Seymour, Smith, Spellicy, Stocker, Stumpf, Stiner, Stauffer, Sullivan, Terry—52.

The motion to lay on the table was therefore lost.

Mr. Baum offered the following substitute for Mr. Smith's substitute:

The judges both of the Supreme and Inferior Courts shall be appointed by the governor by and with the advice and consent of the Senate. The judges of the Supreme Court shall hold their offices during a term of ten years and those of the Inferior Courts during a term of seven years. Their terms shall commence with the date of their commission.

Provided, That appointments made during the existence of the present rebellion shall not be construed as within the meaning of this article.

The first appointments and confirmations under this article shall be made during the first session of the Legislature that may be held after the restoration of peace.

Mr. Baum's substitute was laid on the table by the following vote:

YEAS—Messrs. Abell, Ariail, Barrett, Bell, Buckley, Campbell, Cook J. K., Cook T., Decker, Duane, Dufresne, Dupaty, Fish, Flagg, Flood, Gastinel, Geier, Goldman, Gorlinski, Gruneberg, Gaidry, Harnan, Howes, Knobloch, Maurer, Montamat, Morris, Murphy M. W., Mayer, Normand, O'Conner, Orr, Payne, J., Poynot, Purcell J., Pursell S., Seymour, Smith, Stiner, Stauffer, Sullivan, Terry, Waters, Wells and Wilson—45.

NAYS—Austin, Bailey, Baum, Beauvais, Bofill, Bromley, Burke, Collin, Cazabat, Crozat, Cutler, Davies, Edwards, Foley, Fosdick, Fuller, Healy, Hart, Heard, Hills, Hire, Howell, Kavanagh. Maas, Mann, Murphy E., Newell, Ong. Pintado, Schroeder, Schnurr, Shaw, Spellicy, Stoker, Stumpf, Thorpe and Wenck—37.

Mr. Baum moved to strike out all after the first three lines of Mr. Smith's substitute.

Laid on the table.

Mr. Baum then moved to adjourn.

Lost.

Mr. Cazabat offered the following as a substitute for Mr. Smith's substitute:

The judges both of the Supreme and Inferior Courts shall be elected by the qualified voters of their respective districts for the terms to be provided by the Legislature.

But the yeas and nays having been ordered on the adoption of Mr. Smith's substitute previous to Mr. Cazabat's offering his substitute, no action was taken thereon.

The vote was then taken, and Mr. Smith's substitute adopted, as follows:

YEAS—Messrs. Barrett, Baum, Bell, Buckley, Campbell, Cook J. K., Cook T., Decker, Duane, Dufresne, Duke, Fish, Flagg, Flood, Foley, Gastinel, Geier, Goldman, Gorlinski, Gruneberg, Gaidry, Healy, Harnan, Hart,

Howes, Knobloch, Maas, Maurer, Montamat, Morris, Murphy M. W., Mayer, O'Conner, Orr, Payne J., Poynot, Purcell J., Pursell S., Schnurr, Seymour, Smith, Spellicy, Stocker, Stiner, Stauffer, Sullivan and Terry—47.

NAYS—Messrs. Abell, Ariail, Austin, Bailey, Beauvais, Bofill, Bromley, Burke, Colin, Cazabat, Crozat, Cutler, Davies, Dupaty, Edwards, Fosdick, Fuller, Heard, Henderson, Hills, Hire, Howell, Kavanagh, Mann, Murphy E., Newell, Normand, Ong, Pintado, Shaw, Stumpf, Thorpe, Waters, Wenck, Wells and Wilson—36.

On motion of Mr. Hills the Convention then adjourned.

Adopted.

JOHN E. NEELIS,
Secretary.

SATURDAY, June 4th, 1864.

The Convention met pursuant to adjournment. The roll was called and the following members answered to their names:

Messrs. Abell, Ariail, Austin, Balch, Barrett, Baum, Bell, Bofill, Bromley, Buckley, Burke, Campbell, Cook J. K., Crozat, Davies, Decker, Duane, Dufresne, Edwards, Flood, Foley, Geier, Goldman, Gorlinski, Gruneberg, Healy, Hart, Heard, Knobloch, Maas, Mann, Maurer, Mendiverri, Montamat, Murphy E., Murphy M. W., Normand, O'Conner, Orr, Pintado, Poynot, Purcell Jno., Pursell S., Schroeder, Smith, Stumpf, Stiner, Stauffer, Sullivan, Terry, Wenck, Wilson and Mr. President—53.

There being no quorum, the sergeant-at-arms was directed to bring in absent members.

Messrs. Cook T., Dupaty, Flagg, Hills, Hire, Morris, Ong, Schnurr, Seymour, Shaw, Spellicy, Stocker and Waters entered and took their seats.

The president having temporarily vacated the chair, on motion of Mr. Waters, the secretary was called to the chair, and on motion of Mr. Gorlinski, Mr. Hills was chosen to preside as president *pro tem.*

The convention then adjourned until Monday next at 12 M.

Adopted.

JOHN E. NEELIS,
Secretary.

MONDAY, June, 6, 1864.

The Convention met and was called to order, pursuant to adjournment, Hon. E. H. Durell, president, in the chair, and the following members present, viz:

Messrs. Abell, Ariail, Balch, Baum, Bell, Bromley, Brott, Burke, Campbell, Cook T., Cook J. K., Crozat, Davies, Edwards, Ennis, Flagg, Foley, Fuller, Geier, Goldman, Gorlinski, Gruneberg, Gaidry, Hart, Heard, Henderson, Howell, Kavanagh, Knobloch, Maas, Maurer, Murphy E., Murphy M. W., Mayer, Newell, Normand, O'Conner, Pintado, Poynot, Pursell S., Schroeder, Schnurr, Smith, Spellicy, Stumpf, Stiner, Stauffer, Waters, Wilson—50.

There being no quorum, the sergeant-at-arms was directed to bring in absent members.

After some delay, the following members appeared and took their seats: Messrs. Austin, Bailey, Barrett, Bofill, Dufresne, Dupaty, Fish, Flood, Fosdick, Gastinel, Harnan, Hills, Hire, Howes, Kugler, Mann, Montamat, Morris, Orr, Paine J. T., Purcell J., Seymour, Shaw, Stocker, Sullivan, Terry and Thorpe—27.

The president announced a quorum present.

The minutes of Friday and Saturday were read and approved.

Mr. Montamat on behalf of the Committee Finance submitted the followng report:

REPORT OF THE FINANCE COMMITTEE OF THE FUNDS APPROPRIATED FOR THE PAYMENT OF PER DIEM OF MEMBERS, MILEAGE AND SALARIES OF OFFICERS.

1864.
May 30, Balance on hand as per
    Report No. 7........$37,043 40
May 30, Paid warrant
    No. 55.....$ 654 00
May 31, Paid warrant
    No. 56..... 385 00
June 1, Paid warrant
    No. 57..... 952 00
June 4, Paid warrant
    No. 58..... 2230 00
June 4, Paid warrant
    No. 59..... 1412 00
June 4, Paid warrant
    No. 60..... 1450 00
June 4, Paid warrant
    No. 62..... 1080 00
    ————— $8,163 00

June 6, 1864, balance on hand
this day............$28,880 40

Twenty-eight thousand eight hundred and eighty dollars and forty cents.

JOHN P. MONTAMAT,
Chairman, *pro tem.*, Finance Committee

REPORT OF THE FINANCE COMMITTEE OF THE FUNDS APPROPRIATED FOR CONTINGENT EXPENSES.
1864.
May 30, Balance on hand as per
　　　　per Report No. 7.....$6,928 63
June 3, Paid Warrant No. 61.... 2,276 10

June 6, Balance on hand this day $4,652 53
Four thousand six hundred and fifty-two dollars and fifty-three cents.
　　　　　　JOHN P. MONTAMAT,
　　Chairman, *pro tem.*, Finance Committee.

Mr. Sullivan called up his resolution, which had been made the speciel order for to-day.

The president having decided that under the resolution heretofore adopted, in the following words, viz:

"*Resolved*, That after this date, May 31st, 1864, the order of the day shall be taken up immediately after the minutes have been read by the clerk and accepted by the Convention, and that Saturday of each week shall be appropriated to miscellaneous business,"
the report of the Judiciary Committee took precedence of Mr. Sullivan's resolution, which he decided was of a miscellaneous character, and could only be called up on Saturday.

Mr. Abell appealed from the decision of the president, on the ground that Mr. Sullivan's resolution had been made the order of the day for this day, previous to the adoption of the resolution upon which the president's decision was based.

The yeas and nays being taken on the appeal, resulted as follows: Messrs. Ariail, Austin, Barrett, Bromley, Burke, Campbell, Crozat, Davies, Dupaty, Edwards, Ennis, Fish, Flagg, Fosdick, Fuller, Gaidry, Goldman, Gruneberg, Heard, Hills, Hire, Howell, Knobloch, Kugler, Mann, Morris, Newell, Paine J. T., Pintado, Pursell S., Schroeder, Seymour, Shaw, Stumpf, Stauffer, Thorpe and Wilson, (37,) voted in favor of sustaining the decision of the president; and Messrs. Abell, Balch, Bailey, Baum, Bell, Bofill, Buckley, Cook J. K., Cook T., Dufresne, Flood, Foley, Gastinel, Gorlinski, Harnan, Hart, Henderson, Howes, Kavanagh, Maas, Maurer, Mayer, Montamat, Murphy M.W., Normand, O'Conner, Orr, Poynot, Purcell J., Schnurr, Smith, Spellicy, Stiner, Stocker, Sullivan, Terry and Waters, (37,) voted against the decision.

There being no quorum voting, Mr. Henderson moved a call of the House, when 76 members was found to be present.

Mr. Cutler having entered after the vote was taken, was, on motion of Mr. Sullivan, allowed to vote, which he did in favor of the appeal, whereupon the president declared that his decision was not sustained, and directed the secretary to read Mr. Sullivan's resolution, which is in the following words:

The city of New Oleans shall maintain a Police force, which shall be uniformed with distinction of grade, to consist of permanent resident citizens, of good character, to be selected by the mayor of the city, to hold office during good behavior, and removable only by a Police Commission, composed of five citizens, viz: one to be selected from each district of the city, the mayor to be president of the Board, the Commission to be appointed by the governor of the State, a majority of whom shall remove for delinquencies. Members of the Police, when removed, shall not again be eligible to any position on the Police for a term of one year.

The chief of police shall give a penal bond in the sum of ten thousand dollars; lieutenants of police, each five thousand dollars; sergeants, clerks and corporals, each three thousand dollars, and privates one thousand dollars each, with good and solvent security as the law directs for the faithful performance of their duty whilst acting in the capacity of Policemen.
The chief of police to receive per
　month................. ....$275
The ileutenants　"　　　"　　..... 150
The sergeants　　"　　　"　　..... 100
The clerks　　　"　　　"　　..... 100
The corporals　　"　　　"　　..... 90
The privates (day and night)　..... 80
which pay shall not be reduced.

Mr. Foley moved to strike out the number "275" and insert "200" as the salary per month of the chief of police.

Mr. Orr proposed the following proviso as an amendment to the resolution, viz:

Provided, That the compensation of all foremen, mechanics, cartmen and laborers employed on public works under the governments of the State of Louisiana, city of New Orleans, and Police Juries of the various loyal parishes of the State, shall also be increased to not less than the following rates, viz:
All foremen not less than $3 50 per day.
All mechanics not less than $3 00 per day

All cartmen not less than $3 00 per day. All laborers not less than $2 00 per day.

Mr. S. Pursell moved to lay the the whole matter, including the resolution and amendments, on the table.

Mr. Abell raised the point of order, that a motion had heretofore been made to lay the resolution on the table and was lost, whereupon Mr. Pursell's motion was changed, to lay the amendments on the table, on which motion the yeas and nays were taken with the following result:

YEAS—Messrs. Abell, Bailey, Barrett, Baum, Bofill, Cutler, Gruneberg, Kavanagh and Normand—9.

NAYS—Messrs. Ariail, Austin, Balch, Bell, Bromley, Buckley, Burke, Campbell, Cook J. K., Cook T., Crozat, Davies, Dufresne, Dupaty, Edwards, Ennis, Fish, Flagg, Flood, Foley, Fosdick, Fuller, Gastinel, Goldman, Gorlinski, Gaidry, Harnan, Hart, Heard, Henderson, Hills, Hire, Howell, Howes, Knobloch, Kugler, Maas, Mann, Maurer, Montamat, Morris, Murphy M. W., Mayer, Newell, O'Conner, Orr, Paine J. T., Pintado, Poynot, Purcell J., Pursell S., Schroeder, Schnurr, Seymour, Shaw, Smith, Spellicy, Stocker, Stumpf, Stiner, Stauffer, Sullivan, Terry, Thorpe, Waters, Wilson—66.

Consequently the motion to lay on the table was lost.

Messrs. Austin, Burke and Henderson first voted in the affirmative and subsequently changed their votes to the negative.

The question then recurred on the adoption of Mr. Orr's proviso, when the yeas and nays were called with the following result:

YEAS—Messrs. Abell, Ariail, Austin, Balch, Barrett, Baum, Beauvais, Bell, Bennie, Bromley, Buckley, Burke, Campbell, Cook J. K., Cook T., Crozat, Cutler, Davies, Dufresne, Dupaty, Edwards, Ennis, Fish, Flagg, Flood, Foley, Fosdick, Fuller, Gastinel, Goldman, Gorlinski, Gaidry, Healy, Harnan, Hart, Henderson, Hills, Hire, Howes, Knobloch, Kugler, Maas, Mann, Maurer, Montamat, Morris, Murphy M. W., Mayer, Normand, O'Conner, Orr, Poynot, Purcell J., Pursell S., Schroeder, Schnurr, Seymour, Shaw, Smith, Spellicy, Stocker, Stumpf,. Stiner, Sullivan, Terry, Thorpe, Waters—67.

NAYS—Messrs. Bailey, Bofill, Cazabat, Gruneberg, Heard, Howell, Kavanagh, Newell, Paine J. T., Pintado—10.

Consequently Mr. Orr's proviso was adopted.

Mr. Abell first voted in the negative, and afterwards changed his vote to the affirmative.

Mr. Foley's amendment was then adopted.

On the adoption of Mr. Sullivan's resolution as amended, the yeas and nays were ordered, and being taken, resulted as follows:

AYES—Messrs. Abell, Barrett, Baum, Beauvais, Bell, Bofill, Buckley, Cook J. K., Cook T., Cutler, Dufresne, Fish, Flood, Foley, Fuller, Gastinel, Gorlinski, Gruneberg, Healy, Harnan, Hart, Henderson, Hire, Howes, Kavanagh, Kugler, Maas, Maurer, Montamat, Murphy M. W., Normand, O'Conner, Orr, Poynot, Purcell J., Pursell S., Schroeder, Schnurr, Smith, Spellicy, Stocker, Stumpf, Stiner, Sullivan, Terry, Waters —46.

NAYS—Messrs. Ariail, Austin, Balch, Bailey, Bennie, Bromley, Burke, Campbell, Cazabat, Crozat, Davies, Dupaty, Edwards, Ennis, Flagg, Fosdick, Goldman, Gaidry, Heard, Hills, Howell, Knobloch, Mann, Morris, Mayer, Newell, Paine J. T., Pintado, Seymour, Shaw, Thorpe—31.

Consequently the resolution as amended was adopted.

Messrs. Hire and S. Pursell first voted in the negative and subsequently changed their votes to the affirmative.

On motion of Mr. Smith the Convention then adjourned.

Adopted,

JOHN E. NEELIS,
Secretary.

TUESDAY, June 7, 1864.

Pursuant to adjournment the Convention met, and was called to order at 12 o'clock M. The roll was called, and the following members answered to their names:

Messrs. Abell, Bell, Bennie, Burke, Buckley, Cook J. K., Cook T., Crozat, Edwards, Ennis, Fish, Flagg, Foley, Geier, Gorlinski, Healy, Heard, Henderson, Knobloch, Mann, Mayer, Montamat, Morris, Normand, O'Conner, Pintado, Poynot, Pursell S., Spellicy, Shaw, Stumpf, Stiner, Stauffer, Sullivan and Mr. President—35.

After some delay the following members answered to their names:

Messrs. Austin, Bailey, Barrett, Baum, Beauvais, Bofill, Bromley, Campbell, Collin, Cutler, Davies, Flood, Fosdick, Fuller, Gastinel, Gaidry, Gruneberg, Harnan, Hart, Hills, Hire, Howell, Howes, Kugler, Maas, Maurer, Mendiverri, Murphy M.W., Murphy E., Newell, Ong, Orr, Purcell J., Schroeder

AND AMENDMENT OF THE CONSTITUTION OF LOUISIANA. 107

Seymour, Smith, Stocker, Terry, Thorpe, Waters, Wenck, Wilson—42.

A quorum was then announced as being present.

The minutes of yesterday's proceedings were read and adopted.

Mr. S. Pursell moved to reconsider the vote by which Mr. Sullivan's resolution was adopted on yesterday.

Mr. Bofill moved to lay Mr. Pursell's motion on the table, which motion was carried by the following vote :

YEAS—Messrs. Abell, Bailey, Baum, Bell, Beauvais, Bofill, Buckley, Cook J. K., Cook T., Cutler, Fish, Flagg, Flood, Foley, Gastinel, Geier, Gorlinski, Gruneberg, Harnan, Hart, Healy, Henderson, Howes, Maurer, Maas, Mendiverri, Montamat, Murphy M.W., Murphy E., O'Conner, Orr, Poynot, Smith, Schroeder, Seymour, Spellicy, Stocker, Stiner, Stumpf, Sullivan, Terry, Waters—42.

NAYS—Messrs. Austin, Balch, Bennie, Bromley, Burke, Campbell, Collin, Crozat, Davies, Ennis, Fosdick, Gaidry, Heard, Hire, Hills, Howell, Knobloch, Kugler, Mayer, Mann, Morris, Newell, Normand, Ong, Pintado, Pursell S., Shaw, Stauffer, Thorpe, Wenck, Wilson—31.

Mr. Baum moved a reconsideration of the vote adopting Mr. Smith's substitute for art. 11 of the report of the Committee on the Judiciary.

This motion was ruled out of order by the president, as being too late.

Mr. Cutler appealed from the decision of the chair, when the decision was sustained by a rising vote of 37 ayes to 35 nays.

A call of the House being ordered, 76 members answered to their names.

The order of the day was then taken up, and art. 12 of the report of the Committee on the Judiciary was read, as follows :

Art. 12. The clerks of the inferior courts shall be appointed by the judges thereof, and they shall hold their offices during good behavior, subject to removal by the judges respectively, with the right of appeal in all such cases to the Supreme Court.

The following substitutes and amendments were also read, viz :

Mr. Sullivan's substitute for art. 12.

The clerks in the inferior courts in this State shall be elected for the term of four years, and should a vacancy occur subsequent to an election, it shall be filled by the judge of the court in which the vacancy exists, and the person so appointed shall hold his office until the next general election.

Mr. Montamat offered the following amendment to the substitute, which was accepted by Mr. Sullivan, viz :

Art. 12. The clerks of the inferior courts shall be appointed by the governor during the existing war, and two years thereafter ; then, to be elected by the qualified voters for a term of four years.

On a motion to lay Mr. Montamat's amendment on the table the yeas and nays were called, with the following result :

YEAS — Messrs. Baum, Beauvais, Burke, Campbell, Collin, Foley, Fosdick, Gastinel, Gorlinski, Gruneberg, Hart, Hills, Howell, Howes, Knobloch, Kugler, Mann, Maurer, Morris, Normand, Orr, Pintado, Poynot, Pursell S., Schroeder, Stauffer, Waters, Wenck, Wilson—29.

NAYS—Messrs. Abell, Austin, Balch, Barrett, Bailey, Bell, Bennie, Bofill, Bromley, Buckley, Cook J. K., Cook T., Crozat, Cutler, Davies, Edwards, Ennis, Fish, Flagg, Flood, Gaidry, Geier, Harnan, Healy, Heard, Henderson, Hire, Maas, Mayer, Mendiverri, Montamat, Murphy E., Murphy M. W., Newell, O'Conner, Ong, Seymour, Shaw, Smith, Spellicy, Stocker, Stumpf, Stiner, Sullivan, Terry, Thorpe—46.

Consequently the motion to lay on the table was lost.

On the motion to adopt Mr. Sullivan's substitute as amended, the ayes and nays were called with the following result :

YEAS—Messrs. Abell, Balch, Barrett, Bell, Bennie, Bofill, Buckley, Burke, Cook T., Crozat, Edwards, Ennis, Fish, Flagg, Flood, Geier, Gaidry, Healy, Harnan, Henderson, Maas, Mendiverri, Montamat, Murphy E., Murphy M. W., Normand, O'Conner, Seymour, Shaw, Smith, Stocker, Stumpf, Stiner, Stauffer, Sullivan, Terry, Thorpe—37.

NAYS—Messrs. Austin, Bailey, Baum, Beauvais, Bromley, Campbell, Collin, Cook J. K., Cutler, Davies, Foley, Fosdick, Gastinel, Gorlinski, Gruneberg, Hart, Heard, Hills, Hire, Howell, Howes, Knobloch, Kugler, Mann, Maurer, Morris, Mayer, Newell, Ong, Orr, Pintado, Poynot, Pursell S., Schroeder, Spellicy, Waters, Wenck, Wilson—38.

Consequently Mr. Sullivan's substitute was lost.

Mr. Stauffer then called for the reading of his substitute for Art. 12, which is in the following words :

Clerks of the inferior courts in this State shall be elected for the term of four years, and should a vacancy occur subsequent to an election it shall be filled by the Judge of the Court in which such vacancy exists.

and the person so appointed shall hold his office until the next general election.

Mr. Terry moved to strike out the word "four" in the second line of the subsitute and insert the word "two." Laid on the table.

Mr. Stauffer's substitute was then adopted by the following vote:

YEAS—Messrs. Abell, Balch, Bailey, Barrett, Baum, Bell, Bofill, Buckley, Campbell, Collin, Cook J. K., Cook T., Davies, Ennis, Fish, Flagg, Flood, Gastinel, Geier, Gorlinski, Gruneberg, Healy, Harnan, Hart, Henderson, Howes, Knobloch, Maas, Maurer, Mendiverri, Montamat, Morris, Murphy E., Mayer, Orr, Poynot, Pursell S., Shaw, Smith, Spellicy, Stocker, Stiner, Stauffer, Sullivan, Terry, Thorpe, Waters—47.

NAYS—Messrs. Austin, Beauvais, Bennie, Bromley, Burke, Crozat, Cutler, Edwards, Foley, Fosdick, Gaidry, Heard, Hills, Hire, Howell, Kugler, Mann, Murphy M. W., Newell, Normand, Ong, Pintado, Schroeder, Seymour, Stumpf, Wenck, Wilson—27.

Art. 13 was read and adopted as reported.

Art. 14 was read, together with the following substitute offered by Mr. Sullivan:

Art. 14. The jurisdiction of justices of the peace shall be limited in civil cases to cases where the matter in dispute does not exceed two hundred dollars exclusive of interest, subject to appeal in such cases as shall be provided for by law. They shall be elected by the qualified electors of each parish, district or ward, for the term of two years, in such manner, and shall have such criminal jurisdiction as shall be provided by law.

Mr. Flood offered an amendment to Mr. Sullivan's substitute, providing that all differences and disputes under twenty-five dollars, shall be finally settled by arbitration. Laid on the table.

Mr. Stiner offered an amendment to Mr. Sullivan's substitute, making the offices of justice of the peace appointive until two years after the present war, which amendment was laid on the table.

Mr. Flagg offered an amendment providing that justices of the peace shall be appointed by the governor, and shall hold their offices until two years after the proclamation of peace, after which time they shall be elected by the people, and further providing that their jurisdiction shall not exceed one hundred dollars.

Mr. Flagg's amendment was laid on the table by a rising vote of 45 ayes, 17 nays.

Mr. S. Pursell moved to amend Mr. Sullivan's substitute by striking out, in the fifth line, the word "two," and inserting the word "four," making the term of office four years.

A motion to lay Mr. Pursell's amendment on the table was lost, on a division, ayes 26, nays 47.

Mr. Pursell's amendment was then adopted.

The question was then put on the adoption of Mr. Sullivan's substitute as amended, when the same was adopted.

Art. 15 was then read, together with the following substitute, offered by Mr. Sullivan:

There shall be an attorney general, who shall be elected by the qualified voters of the State, and the district attorneys by the qualified voters of each district, on the day of the election of governor of the State. They shall hold their offices for a term of four years.

Mr. Terry moved to amend by inserting between the words "State and" the words "who shall receive a salary of five thousand dollars," which amendment was accepted by Mr. Sullivan.

On the question of the adoption of Mr. Sullivan's substitute, as amended, a division was ordered, resulting ayes 32, nays 40. The substitute was therefore lost.

Mr. Montamat moved to reconsider the vote by which Mr. Sullivan's substitute was rejected, which being carried, he then moved to strike out "five thousand dollars" and insert "four thousand dollars" as the salary of the attorney general.

Lost on a division of ayes 30, nays 39.

Mr. Sullivan's substitute as amended was then adopted on a division, ayes 42, nays 31.

Art. 16 was then read, together with the following substitute offered by Mr. Sullivan:

A sheriff and a coroner shall be elected in each parish by the qualified voters thereof, who shall hold their office for the term of two years, unless removed. The Legislature shall have the power to increase the number of sheriffs in any parish. Should a vacancy occur in either of these offices subsequent to an election, it shall be filled by the governor; and the person so appointed shall continue in office until his successor shall be elected and qualified.

The Legislature may determine the mode

of filling vacancies in the offices of the inferior judges, attorney general, district attorneys, and all other officers not otherwise provided for in this constitution.

Mr. Henderson moved to amend by striking out "two years" in the second line, and inserting "four years."

Laid on the table.

Mr. Montamat moved to amend by making the term of office of the coroner one year, and of the sheriff two years.

Laid on the table.

Mr. Sullivan's substitute was then adopted.

The report of the committee on the Judiciary as amended was then adopted as a whole.

On motion the Convention adjourned. Adopted.

JOHN E. NEELIS,
Secretary.

WEDNESDAY, June 8, 1864.

The Convention met and was called to order pursuant to adjournment, Hon. E. H. Durell, president, in the chair. Fifty members answered to their names at first roll call.

After some delay, twenty-eight other members appeared and answered to their names, when a quorum was announced. Absent—the following members:

Messrs. Balch, Baum, Bonzano, Brott, Cazabat, Decker, Duane, Duke, Flagg, Fuller, Goldman, Kavanagh, Lobdell, Millspaugh, Montague, Payne J., Paine J. T., Taliaferro and Thomas—19.

The journal of yesterday was read and approved.

Mr. Heard asked for a suspension of the rules, in order to allow him to present the following resolution:

Resolved, That from and after to-day every member who fails to answer to his name at roll-call, or within fifteen minutes thereafter, shall forfeit his per diem, unless he be absent by leave, or can furnish some legitimate excuse for his absence.

The reading of the resolution being called for, the secretary was directed to read it for the information of the Convention, which being done, Mr. Foley moved a suspension of the rules, in order to act upon the resolution; but objection being made, and two thirds of the members not voting in favor of the motion, the rules were not suspended.

Mr. Bofill moved a reconsideration of the vote of yesterday, adopting as a whole the report of the Committee on the Judiciary, as it had been amended by the Convention.

Mr. Smith moved to lay the motion to reconsider on the table, upon which motion the yeas and nays were demanded, and being taken, resulted as follows:

YEAS—Messrs. Austin, Buckley, Burke, Cook J. K., Flood, Harnan, Henderson, Howes, Maurer, Morris, Murphy M. W., Orr, Poynot, Purcell J., Pursell S., Schroeder, Schnurr, Smith, Spellicy, Stocker, Stauffer, Sullivan, Terry, Waters—24.

NAYS—Messrs. Abell, Ariail, Bailey, Barrett, Beauvais, Bell, Bennie, Bofill, Bromley, Campbell, Collin, Cook T., Crozat, Cutler, Davies, Dufresne, Dupaty, Edwards, Ennis, Fish, Foley, Fosdick, Gastinel, Geier, Gorlinski, Gruneberg, Gaidry, Healy, Hart, Heard, Hills, Hire, Howell, Knobloch, Kugler, Maas, Mann, Montamat, Mendiverri, Murphy E., Mayer, Newell, Normand, O'Conner, Ong, Pintado, Seymour, Shaw, Stumpf, Stiner, Thorpe, Wenck, Wells, Wilson—54.

Consequently the motion was lost.

The question recurring on the motion to reconsider, the yeas and nays were demanded, and being taken, resulted as follows:

YEAS—Messrs. Abell, Ariail, Bailey, Barrett, Beauvais, Bennie, Bofill, Bromley, Burke, Campbell, Collin, Cook T., Crozat, Cutler, Davies, Dufresne, Dupaty, Edwards, Ennis, Fish, Foley, Fosdick, Gastinel, Gorlinski, Gaidry, Hart, Heard, Hills, Hire, Howell, Knobloch, Kugler, Maas, Mann, Mendiverri, Murphy E., Mayer, Newell, Normand, O'Conner, Ong, Pintado, Schroeder, Seymour, Shaw, Stumpf, Stiner, Thorpe, Waters, Wenck, Wells and Wilson—52.

NAYS—Messrs. Austin, Bell, Buckley, Cook J. K., Flood, Geier, Gruneberg, Healy, Harnan, Henderson, Howes, Maurer, Montamat, Morris, Murphy M. W., Orr, Poynot, Purcell J., Pursell S., Schnurr, Smith, Spellicy, Stauffer, Stocker, Sullivan, Terry—26.

Consequently the motion prevailed, and the vote was reconsidered.

On motion of Mr. Wilson, the whole report, with amendments, was recommitted to a special committee of nine members. The president appointed Messrs. Wilson, Bofill, Cutler, Abell, Poynot, Smith, Buckley, Purcell J., and Murphy M. W., to compose said committee.

The report of the Committee on Impeachment, being next in order, was taken up and read.

When, on motion of Mr. Foley, the Convention adjourned until 12 o'clock M., on Monday, the 13th inst.

Approved.

JOHN E. NEELIS,
Secretary.

MONDAY, June 13, 1864.

The Convention met and was called to order pursuant to adjournment, Hon. E. H. Durell, president, in the chair, and the following members present:

Messrs. Abell, Austin, Barrett, Bofill, Campbell, Collin, Cook J. K., Crozat, Dufresne, Edwards, Ennis, Fish, Flood, Foley, Fosdick, Fuller, Gastinel, Geier, Gorlinski, Healy, Heard, Henderson, Hire, Howell, Howes, Maas, Maurer, Mayer, Mendiverri, Montamat, Morris, Newell, Normand, O'Conner, Payne J., Pintado, Poynot, Seymour, Smith, Spellicy, Stocker, Stumpf, Stiner, Stauffer, Sullivan, Terry, Wells and Wilson—48.

After some delay the following members appeared and answered to their names, when a quorum was announced as being present:

Messrs. Bailey, Baum, Bell, Bromley, Buckley, Cook T., Cutler, Davies, Duane, Dupaty, Flagg, Harnan, Hart, Hills, Kavanagh, Kugler, Mann, Murphy M. W., Paine J. T., Purcell J., Pursell S., Schroeder, Schnurr, Shaw, Thorpe, Waters and Wenck —27.

The journal of the last session was read and approved.

The special committee, to which had been recommitted the report of the Judiciary Committee, submitted the following report:

REPORT OF THE SPECIAL JUDICIARY COMMITTEE.

The Special Judiciary Committee respectfully submit the following report:

Article I. The Judiciary power shall be vested in a supreme court, in such inferior courts as the Legislature may, from time to time, order and establish, and in justices of the peace.

Art. II. The jurisdiction of the supreme court shall extend to all cases where the matter in dispute exceeds three hundred dollars, exclusive of interest; to all cases in which the constitutionality or legality of any tax, toll or impost whatsoever, or of any fine, forfeiture, or penalty imposed by a municipal corporation shall be in contestation; and to all criminal cases on questions of law alone, whenever the offence charged is punishable with death, or imprisonment at hard labor, or when a fine exceeding three hundred dollars is actually imposed. It shall also exercise a general superintending control over all inferior and other courts of law, and shall have the power to issue the writs necessary for that purpose. The Legislature shall have power to restrict the jurisdiction of the supreme court in civil cases to questions of law only.

Art. III. The supreme court shall be composed of one chief justice and four associate justices, a majority of whom shall constitute a quorum. The chief justice shall receive a salary of $7500 and each of the associate justices a salary of $7000 annually, until otherwise provided by law. The court shall appoint its own clerks.

Art. IV. The supreme court shall hold its sessions in New Orleans from the first Monday in the month of November to the end of the month of June inclusive. The Legislature shall have power to fix the sessions elsewhere during the rest of the year; until otherwise provided, the sessions shall be held as heretofore.

Art. V. The supreme court, and each of the judges thereof, shall have power to issue writs of *habeas corpus* at the instance of all persons in actual custody under process, in all cases in which they may have appellate jurisdiction.

Art. VI. No judgment shall be rendered by the supreme court without the concurrence of a majority of the judges comprising the court. Whenever the majority cannot agree, in consequence of the recusation of any member or members of the court, the judges not recused shall have power to call upon any judge or judges of the inferior courts, whose duty it shall be, when so called upon, to sit in the place of the judge or judges so recused and to aid in determining the case.

Art. VII. All judges, by virtue of their office, shall be conservators of the peace throughout the State. The style of all process shall be, "the State of Louisiana." All prosecutions shall be carried on in the name and by the authority of the "State of Louisiana," and conclude against the peace and dignity of the same.

Art. VIII. The judges of all courts within the State shall, as often as it may be possible so to do, in every definitive judgment, refer to the particular law in virtue of which such judgment may be rendered, and in all cases adduce the reasons on which their judgment is founded.

Art. IX. The judges of all courts shall be liable to impeachment; but for any reasonable cause, which shall not be sufficient ground for impeachment, the governor shall remove any of them on the address of a majority of the members elected to each

House of the General Assembly. In every such case the cause or causes for which such removal may be required shall be stated in full in the address and inserted in the journal of each House.

Art. X. The salaries of the judges of the supreme and inferior courts shall not be changed during their term of office.

Art. XI. The judges both of the supreme and inferior courts and justices of the peace shall be appointed by the governor, by and with the advice and consent of the Senate. The judges of the supreme court to hold office for the term of six years, the judges of the inferior courts for four, justice of the peace for two—after which term the judges of the supreme, inferior and justices courts shall be elected by the legally qualified voters. Appointments in every instance to date from the ratification of this constitution by the people. The Legislature to fix the day for election.

Art. XII. The clerks of the inferior courts shall be appointed by the governor, for the same term as the judges, but, on the commission of any crime, may be moved, with the power of an appeal to the supreme court. After the service of this term they shall be elected by the legally qualified voters for the same term as the judges.

Art. XIII. The Legislature shall have power to vest in clerks of courts authority to grant such orders and do such acts as may be deemed necessary for the administration of justice ; but in all such cases the powers thus granted shall be specified and determined.

Art. XIV. Justices of the peace shall have jurisdiction in civil cases, the sum not to exceed one hundred dollars, exclusive of interest. They shall receive a salary of $2500 in the city, and the Legislature shall fix the salaries in the country parishes. Returns shall be made by them quarterly to the auditor of public accounts under oath, and all fees received over the above salary must be faithfully returned to said auditor.

Art. XV. There shall be an attorney general for the State. He shall be appointed by the governor, by and with the advice and consent of the Senate, and shall hold his office for the term of four years, after which term he shall be elected by the legal voters. He shall receive a salary of $5000.

Art. XVI. There shall be as many district attorneys appointed by the governor, by and with the advice and consent of the Senate, as may be hereafter found necessary, their term of office to be two years from the date of the ratification of this constitution. The Legislature to fix their salaries, and declare office elective after first term.

Art. XVII. A coroner shall be appointed by the governor, by and with the advice and consent of the Senate, for two years. After which term he shall be elected. The General Assembly to fix his salary at its first session.

Art. XVIII. The governor shall appoint, by and with the advice and consent of the Senate, sheriffs for the several parishes of the State. They shall hold office for two years. The Legislature shall have the power to increase the number of the sheriffs in any of the parishes whenever it may be deemed necessary. They shall be all elected after the first term, which dates, as in every other case, in this report, from the ratification of this constitution by the legally qualified voters of this State.

Art. XIX. Grand and petit jurors shall be paid the sum of three dollars and a half per day for each day of service during term.

(Signed) J. H. WILSON, Chairman.
CHARLES SMITH,
JNO. PURCELL,
O. H. POYNOT,
M. W. MURPHY,
JOHN BUCKLEY, JR.

Mr. Hills moved a suspension of the rules in order to put the report on its second reading.

Mr. Sullivan moved to lay Mr. Hills's motion on the table. Lost.

The question recurring on Mr. Hills's motion, and two-thirds not voting in its favor, the rules were not suspended.

Mr. Sullivan moved that the report be printed and made the order of the day for Monday next.

Mr. Hills amended the motion by making the report the order of the day for to-morrow. The amendment was adopted, and the motion prevailed as amended.

Mr. Thorpe asked for a suspension of the rules in order to allow him to introduce a resolution, which was read for information; but two-thirds not voting in favor of the motion to suspend the rules, the request was not granted.

The Committee on Finance submitted the following :

REPORT OF THE FINANCE COMMITTEE OF THE STATE CONVENTION OF THE FUNDS APPROPRIATED FOR THE PAYMENT OF PER DIEM AND SALARIES AND MILEAGE.

1864.
June 6, Balance on hand as per
   Report No. 8........$28,888 40
June 6, Paid warrant
   No. 63.....$1390 00
June 7. Paid warrant
   No. 64..... 84 00

June 11, Paid warrant
 No. 66..... 4180 00
June 11, Paid warrant
 No. 67..... 2520 00
June 13, Paid warrant
 No. 68..... 2139 00
—————$10,313 00

June 13, 1864, balance on hand
 this day............$18,567 40
Eighteen thousand five hundred and sixty-seven dollars and forty cents.

June 8, 1864, the sum of six thousand one hundred and thirty-nine dollars and thirteen cents ($6,139 13) was paid per warrant No. 65, to the city of New Orleans, (out of the funds appropriated for that special purpose.)

Respectfully submitted,
JOHN P. MONTAMAT,
Chairman *pro tem.* Finance Committee.

REPORT OF THE FINANCE COMMITTEE OF THE STATE CONVENTION OF THE FUNDS APPROPRIATED FOR CONTINGENT EXPENSES.

No warrant having been drawn since the last report No. 8, the balance on hand still remains, viz :.................$4,652 53

Respectfully submitted,
JOHN P. MONTAMAT,
Chairman *pro tem.* Finance Committe.

The report of the Committee on Impeachment being next in order, was taken up and read by the secretary.

A call of the House was demanded, and being taken 67 members answered to their names.

On motion, the Convention adjourned until 12 o'clock M. to-morrow.

Approved.
JOHN E. NEELIS,
Secretary.

TUESDAY, June 14, 1864.

The Convention met and was called to order pursuant to adjournment, Hon. E. H. Durell, president, in the chair, and the following members present:

Messrs. Abell, Austin, Balch, Bell, Bromley, Buckley, Burke, Campbell, Collin, Cazabat, Cook J. K., Cook T., Crozat, Davies, Decker, Dufresne, Duke, Ennis, Fish, Flagg, Flood, Foley, Fosdick, Geier, Gorlinski, Harnan, Howes, Maas, Mann, Maurer, Mayer, Murphy E., Murphy M. W., Newell, Normand, Payne J., Purcell J., Pursell S., Schroeder, Smith, Stocker, Stumpf, Stiner, Stauffer, Terry, Waters, Wilson—48.

After considerable delay, the following members appeared and answered to their names: Messrs. Bailey, Barrett, Beauvais, Bofill, Cutler, Dupaty, Fuller, Gastinel, Gaidry, Healy, Hart, Hills, Hire, Howell, Kugler, Mendiverri, Montamat, O'Conner, Ong, Orr, Paine J. T., Pintado, Seymour, Shaw, Sullivan, Thorpe, Wenck, Wells—28.

Absent — Messrs. Ariail, Baum, Bennie, Bonzano, Brott, Duane, Edwards, Goldman, Gruneberg, Heard, Henderson, Kavanagh, Knobloch, Lobdell, Millspaugh, Montague, Morris, Poynot, Schnurr, Spellicy, Taliaferro, Thomas—22.

A quorum being present, on motion of Mr. Montamat, the reading of the minutes was dispensed with.

Mr. Terry asked for a suspension of the rules, in order to present the following resolution :

Resolved, That from and after the 14th day of June all members absent fifteen minutes after the first roll-call, without a good and sufficient excuse, shall forfeit their *per diem.*

The resolution having been read for information, the rules were suspended and the same was taken up for action.

Mr. Mann offered the following substitute :

Whereas, Members of this Convention, elected by the people for the purpose of amending and revising the constitution of the State of Louisiana, have absented themselves without permission, or giving any reason therefor ; therefore, be it

Resolved, That from and after this date each and every member of this body, who shall not have been granted leave of absence for cause that is satisfactory to this Convention, who are not present to answer to his or their name, at 12 o'clock roll-call, they shall not be allowed their *per diem*, for each and every day that they are delinquent ; and the secretary is hereby required to furnish to the chairman of the Finance Committee the names of delinquents, that the deductions from their *per diem* may be made, for each and every day of such delinquency.

The substitute was accepted, and on motion the same was adopted.

Mr. Abell asked leave of absence for Mr. Heard. The request was not granted.

ORDER OF THE DAY.

The president declared the report of the special Committee on the Judiciary as the order of the day, on its second reading, and called Mr. Abell to the chair.

The report having been read by the secretary, Mr. Stocker offered the following substitute:

MR. STOCKER'S SUBSTITUTE TO THE REPORT OF THE SPECIAL JUDICIARY COMMITTEE.

Article I. The judiciary power shall be vested in a supreme court, in such inferior courts as the Legislature may, from time to time, order and establish, and in justices of the peace.

Art. II. The supreme court, except in cases hereafter provided, shall have appellate jurisdiction only; which jurisdiction shall extend to all cases when the matter in dispute shall exceed three hundred dollars; to all cases in which the constitutionality or legality of any tax, toll or impost whatsoever, or of any fine, forfeiture or penalty imposed by a municipal corporation, shall be in contestation; and to all criminal cases on questions of law alone whenever the offence charged is punishable with death or imprisonment at hard labor, or when a fine exceeding three hundred dollars is actually imposed.

Art. III. The supreme court shall be composed of one chief justice and four associate justices, a majority of whom shall constitute a quorum. The court shall appoint its own clerks.

Art. IV. The supreme court shall hold its sessions in New Orleans from the first Monday of the month of November to the end of the month of June inclusive. The Legislature shall have power to fix the sessions elsewhere during the rest of the year: until otherwise provided, the sessions shall be held as heretofore.

Art. V. The supreme court and each of the judges thereof shall have power to issue writs of *habeas corpus*, at the instance of all persons in actual custody under process, in all cases in which they may have appellate jurisdiction.

Art. VI. No judgment shall be rendered by the supreme court without the concurrence of a majority of the judges comprising the court. Whenever the majority cannot agree, in consequence of the recusation of any member or members of the court, the judges not recused shall have power to call upon any judge or judges of the inferior courts, whose duty it shall be, when so called upon, to sit in the place of the judge or judges recused, and to aid in determining the case.

Art. VII. All judges, by virtue of their office, shall be conservators of the peace throughout the State. The style of all process shall be "the State of Louisiana." All prosecutions shall be carried on in the name and by the authority of the State of Louisiana, and conclude against the peace and dignity of the same.

Art. VIII. The judges of all courts within the State shall, as often as it may be possible so to do, in every definitive judgment refer to the particular law in virtue of which such judgment may be rendered, and in all cases adduce the reasons on which their judgment is founded.

Art. IX. The judges of all courts shall be liable to impeachment; but for any reasonable cause, which shall not be sufficient ground for impeachment, the governor shall remove any of them, on the address of a majority of the members elected to each House of the General Assembly. In every such case the cause or causes for which such removal may be required shall be stated at length in the address, and inserted in the journal of each House.

Art. X. The judges both of the supreme and inferior courts shall, at stated times, receive a salary which shall be fixed by the Legislature; and they are prohibited from receiving any fees of office or other compensation than their salaries for any civil duties performed by them.

Art. XI. The chief justice of the supreme court shall be elected by the qualified voters of the State, and the associate judges of the supreme court, together with the judges of the inferior courts, shall be elected by the qualified voters of their several districts, as determined by the Legislature, and they shall hold their several offices during such term or terms as shall be fixed by the Legislature.

Art. XII. The clerks of the inferior courts shall be elected by the qualified voters of their several districts, and shall hold their offices during such term or terms as shall be fixed by the Legislature, subject to removal by the judges respectively, with the right of appeal in all such cases to the supreme court.

Art. XIII. The Legislature shall have power to vest in clerks of courts authority to grant such orders and do such acts as may be deemed necessary for the furtherance of the administration of justice, and in all cases the powers thus granted shall be specified and determined.

Art. XIV. The jurisdiction of justices of the peace shall not exceed, in civil cases, the sum of one hundred dollars, exclusive of interest, subject to appeal in such cases as shall be provided for by law. They shall be elected by the qualified voters of their several districts, and shall hold their offices during such term or terms as shall be fixed by the Legislature. They shall have such criminal jurisdiction as shall be provided by law.

Art. XV. There shall be an attorney general for the State, and as many district attorneys as may be hereafter found necessary. The attorney general shall be elected by the qualified voters of the State; the district attorneys shall be elected by the qualified voters of their several districts. The attorney general and district attorneys shall severally hold their offices during such term or terms, and shall severally receive such salaries as shall be determined by the Legislature.

Art. XVI. A sheriff and coroner shall be elected for each parish by the qualified voters of the same ; and they shall severally hold their offices for such term or terms, and shall receive such remuneration for their services as the Legislature may determine.

Mr. Smith moved to reject the substitute, but subsequently withdrew his motion.

A motion to adjourn was lost.

Mr. Foley moved that the substitute be taken up section by section, upon which motion Mr. Hills called the previous question, which was seconded.

The President resumed the chair, when sections one and two of the substitute were severally read and adopted.

Section three having been read, Mr. Montamat moved to adjourn, upon which motion the yeas and nays were demanded, and being taken, resulted as follows :

YEAS—Messrs. Balch, Bailey, Barrett, Beauvais, Burke, Cook J. K., Cook T., Crozat, Decker, Duke, Gruneberg, Gaidry, Healy, Harnan, Knobloch, Maas, Mendiverri, Montamat, Murphy E., Murphy M. W., Orr, O'Conner. Ong, Payne J., Schroeder, Seymour, Sullivan, and Waters—28.

NAYS—Messrs. Abell, Austin, Bell, Bofill, Bromley, Campbell, Collin, Cazabat, Cutler, Davies, Dufresne, Dupaty, Ennis, Fish, Flagg, Flood, Foley, Fosdick, Fuller, Gastinel, Geier, Gorlinski, Hart, Henderson, Hills, Hire, Howell, Howes, Kugler, Mann, Maurer, Mayer, Newell, Normand, Paine J. T., Pintado, Purcell J., Pursell S., Shaw, Smith, Stocker, Stumpf, Stiner, Stauffer Terry, Thorpe, Wells and Wilson—48.

Consequently the Convention refused to adjourn.

The question recurring on the third article, Mr. Howell offered the following amendment :

The chief justice shall receive a salary of $7500, and each of the associate justices a salary of $7000, annually, until otherwise provided by law.

A *viva voce* vote having been taken, the amendment was declared lost.

On motion the Convention adjourned until 12 o'clock M., to-morrow.

Approved.

JOHN E. NEELIS,
Secretary.

WEDNESDAY, June 15, 1864.

The Convention met and was called to order pursuant to adjournment.

Present, Hon. E. H. Durell, president, in the chair, and the following members :

Messrs. Abell, Austin, Bailey, Barrett, Baum, Beauvais, Bell, Bofill, Bromley, Buckley, Burke, Campbell, Collin, Cazabat, Cook J. K., Cook T., Crozat, Cutler, Davies, Decker, Duane, Dufresne, Duke, Ennis, Fish, Flagg, Flood, Foley, Fosdick, Fuller, Gastinel, Geier, Gorlinski, Gruneberg, Gaidry, Healy, Harnan, Hart, Henderson, Hills, Hire, Howell, Howes, Kavanagh, Knobloch, Kugler, Maas, Mann, Maurer, Mayer, Mendiverri, Montamat, Morris, Murphy E., Murphy M. W., Newell, Normand, O'Conner, Ong, Orr, Payne J., Paine J. T., Pintado, Purcell J., Pursell S., Schroeder, Schnurr, Seymour, Shaw, Smith, Spellicy, Stocker, Stumpf, Stiner, Stauffer, Sullivan, Terry, Thorpe, Waters, Wenck, Wells and Wilson—83.

Absent : Messrs. Ariail, Balch, Bennie, Bonzano, Brott, Edwards, Goldman, Heard, Lobdell, Millspaugh, Montague, Poynot, Taliaferro and Thomas—15.

On motion of Mr. Spellicy, Mr. Poynot's absence was excused on account of sickness.

The journal of yesterday was read and approved.

The president laid before the Convention the following communication from Mr. Goldman :

NEW ORLEANS, June 7, 1864.
To the president and members of the Constitutional Convention.

GENTLEMEN — The undersigned hereby tenders his resignation as a member of the "Louisiana State Convention." Having come into that honorable body with the intention to assist in accomplishing the work of statesmen, and not that of municipal politicians, I consider this course consistent and even incumbent upon me after yesterday's action in passing the police bill.

I have the honor to remain respectfully yours, etc.,

EDMUND GOLDMAN.

On motion, Mr. Goldman's resignation was accepted, by a rising vote of 40 yeas to 32 nays.

Mr. Gruneberg presented the following, which was ordered to lay over under the rules :

Resolved, That the sergeant-at-arms, or his assistants, be sent instanter to summon before this Convention all the members ab-

AND AMENDMENT OF THE CONSTITUTION OF LOUISIANA. 115

sent, whether residing inside or outside of New Orleans, and compel their attendance.

And resolved, That the traveling or other expenses incurred by the sergeant-at-arms, or his assistants, for the purposes aforesaid, shall be collected from the members so in default.

ORDER OF THE DAY.

The Convention resumed the consideration of Mr. Stocker's substitute for the report of the Special Committee on the Judiciary. The third article of said substitute being under consideration,

On the suggestion of Mr. Hills that the amendment of Mr. Howell to the third article of the substitute had been rejected through a misunderstanding, a second vote was taken thereon, when the same was adopted, by a rising vote of ayes 54, nays 12.

The third article was then adopted as amended.

Articles 4, 5, 6, 7, 8 and 9 were severally read and adopted.

Article 10 being read, on motion of Mr. Howell it was amended by striking out the words "fixed by the Legislature," and inserting in lieu thereof the words, "not be diminished during their continuance in office."

The section was then adopted as amended.

Article 11 was read, when Mr. Bofill offered the following substitute:

The judges of the Supreme Court shall be appointed by the governor, by and with the advice and consent of the Senate, for a term of eight years. The judges of the inferior courts for a term of six years.

Mr. Stauffer moved to lay the substitute on the table, whereupon the yeas and nays were called, with the following result:

YEAS — Messrs. Bell, Buckley, Campbell, Collin, Cook J. K., Cook T., Decker, Duke, Dupaty, Flagg, Flood, Geier, Gorlinski, Gruneberg, Gaidry, Harnan, Howes, Knobloch, Maas, Mayer, Morris, O'Conner, Orr, Purcell J., Purcell S., Schnurr, Smith, Spellicy, Stocker, Stiner, Stauffer, Sullivan, Terry—33.

NAYS—Messrs. Abell, Austin, Bailey, Barrett, Baum, Beauvais, Bofill, Bromley, Burke, Cazabat, Crozat, Cutler, Davies, Dufresne, Duane, Ennis, Fish, Foley, Fosdick, Fuller, Gastinel, Healy, Hart, Henderson, Hills, Hire, Howell, Kavanagh, Kugler, Mann, Maurer, Mendiverri, Montamat, Murphy E., Murphy M. W., Newell, Normand, Ong, Payne J., Paine J. T., Pintado, Schroeder, Seymour, Shaw, Stumpf, Thorpe, Waters, Wenck, Wells, Wilson—50.

Consequently the motion to lay on the table was lost.

Mr. Ong moved to amend the substitute by striking out the word "eight" and inserting the word "nine," and also by striking out the word "six" and inserting the word "seven" in lieu thereof, which amendment was laid on the table.

Mr. Smith offered the following substitute:

Art. 11. The judges, both of the supreme and inferior courts, shall be appointed by the governor. The judges of the supreme court to hold office for the term of six years, the judges of the inferior courts for four years, after which term the judges of the supreme and inferior courts shall be elected by the legally qualified voters. Appointments in every instance to date from the ratification of this constitution by the people.

On motion, Mr. Smith's substitute was laid on the table.

On the question of the adoption of Mr. Bofill's substitute, the yeas and nays were ordered, with the following result:

YEAS—Messrs. Abell, Austin, Bailey, Baum, Beauvais, Bofill, Bromley, Burke, Cazabat, Crozat, Cutler, Davies, Duane, Dufresne, Ennis, Fish, Foley, Fosdick, Fuller, Gastinel, Healy, Hart, Henderson, Hills, Hire, Howell, Kavanagh, Kugler, Mann, Maurer, Mendiverri, Montamat, Murphy E., Murphy M. W., Newell, Normand, Ong, Payne J., Paine J. T., Pintado, Schroeder, Seymour, Shaw, Spellicy, Stumpf, Thorpe, Waters, Wenck, Wells and Wilson—50.

NAYS—Messrs. Barrett, Bell, Buckley, Campbell, Collin, Cook J. K., Cook T., Decker, Duke, Dupaty, Flagg, Flood, Geier, Gorlinski, Gruneberg, Gaidry, Harnan, Howes, Knobloch, Maas, Mayer, Morris, O'Conner, Orr, Purcell J., Purcell S., Schnurr, Smith, Stocker, Stiner, Stauffer, Sullivan and Terry—33.

Consequently Mr. Bofill's substitute was adopted.

Mr. Montamat offered an amendment providing that clerks of the inferior courts shall be appointed for the same term as the respective judges, but for any crime may be removed by the Supreme Court.

Laid on the table.

Mr. Smith moved to strike out of Mr. Stocker's substitute for article 12 the words "and shall hold their offices during such term or terms as shall be fixed by the Legislature."

Laid on the table.

On the adoption of article 12 of Mr. Stocker's substitute, a division was called, resulting—ayes 29, noes 50.

Mr. Fosdick moved to reconsider the vote on the substitute for article 12. Carried.

Mr. Hills moved to strike out the words, "by the judges respectively," and insert the words, "by the Legislature." Lost.

Mr. S. Pursell moved to strike out all after the words "Legislature," in the third line.

Mr. Hills moved to amend by striking out all after the word "offices," in the second line, and insert the words, "during a term of four years," which amendment was adopted. The substitute for article 12 was then adopted as amended.

Article 13 of the substitute was then adopted, and article 14 was taken up.

Mr. Sullivan moved to strike out the words "one hundred" and substitute therefor the words "two hundred."

Laid on the table.

Mr. Smith moved to strike out "one hundred" and insert "seventy-five" in lieu thereof.

Laid on the table.

Mr. Thorpe offered the following substitute to article 14:

The jurisdiction of justices of the peace shall not exceed in civil cases the sum of one hundred dollars, exclusive of interest, subject to appeal in such cases as shall be provided for by law. They shall hold their offices during such term or terms as shall be fixed by the Legislature. They shall have such criminal jurisdiction as shall be provided by law. Returns shall be made by them, under oath, quarterly to the auditor of public accounts; and all fees received over the fixed salary must be faithfully returned to said auditor. A failure to make such returns as herein provided shall be cause of removal. They shall be appointed by the governor, by and with the advice and consent of the Senate.

On Mr. Sullivan's motion to lay Mr. Thorpe's substitute on the table, a division was called for, resulting—ayes 43, noes 32; consequently the substitute was laid on the table.

Mr. Hills moved to amend by striking out of the 4th line the words "be elected by the qualified voters," and inserting the words "be appointed by the governor, by and with the advice and consent of the Senate." Lost.

Mr. Terry called for the previous question. Lost.

Mr. Montamat moved to amend by making the term of office of justices of the peace two years, upon which a division was called resulting—ayes 41, noes 32; consequently the amendment was adopted.

Article 14 as amended was then adopted, and article 15 of the substitute was taken up.

Mr. Bell offered the following substitute:

There shall be an attorney general for the State and as many district attorneys as may hereafter be found necessary.

The attorney general shall be elected every four years, by the qualified voters of the State. He shall receive a salary of $5000 per annum, payable on his own warrant quarterly.

The district attorneys shall be elected by the qualified voters of their respective districts, for a term of four years. They shall receive such salaries as shall be provided by the Legislature.

A motion to lay on the table being lost, Mr. Bell's substitute was adopted on a rising vote—ayes 58, noes 22.

Article 16, of Mr. Stocker's substitute, being read, Mr. Sullivan offered the following substitute:

A sheriff and a coroner shall be elected in each parish by the qualified voters thereof, who shall hold their offices for the term of two years, unless sooner removed.

The Legislature shall have the power to increase the number of sheriffs in any parish. Should a vacancy occur in either of these offices subseqnent to an election, it shall be filled by the governor, and the person so appointed shall continue in office until his successor shall be elected and qualified.

A motion to lay on the table being lost, Mr. Stocker moved to strike out the words "unless sooner removed." Carried.

The substitute was then adopted.

Mr. S. Pursell offered the following as an additional article:

Art. 17. The governor shall fill, by appointment, all offices whose election are provided for in this title, who shall hold their various positions for the same terms as if elected, dating from the time of the ratification of this constitution, except in the parish of Orleans, in which elections shall be ordered by the first Legislature held under this constitution.

On motion of Mr. Montamat, the additional article was laid on the table.

The substitute, as amended, was then adopted, as a whole, by the following vote:

YEAS—Abell, Austin, Bailey, Baum, Beauvais, Bofill, Bromley, Burke, Cazabat, Cook J. K., Crozat, Cutler, Davis, Decker, Duane, Dufresne, Ennis, Fish, Flagg, Foley, Fosdick, Fuller, Gastinel, Gorlinski, Gruneberg, Gaidry, Healy, Harnan, Hart, Henderson, Hills, Hire, Howell, Kavanagh, Kugler, Maas, Mann, Maurer, Mendiverri, Montamat, Morris, Murphy E., Murphy M. W., Newell, O'Conner, Ong, Payne J., Paine J. T., Pintado, Purcell J., Schroeder, Schnurr, Shaw, Spellicy, Stumpf, Stiner, Thorpe, waters Wenck, Wilson—60

NAYS—Barrett, Bell, Buckley, Campbell, Collin, Cook T., Duke, Dupaty, Flood, Geier, Howes, Knobloch, Mayer, Normand, Orr, Pursell S., Seymour, Smith, Stocker, Stauffer, Sullivan, Terry, Wilson—23.

On motion of Mr. Stocker, the rules were suspended and the substitute as amended taken up on a third reading.

Mr. Henderson offered the following rider:

Art. 2. The supreme court, except in cases otherwise provided in this constitution, shall have appellate jurisdiction only, which jurisdiction shall extend to all cases when the matter in dispute shall exceed three hundred dollars exclusive of interest; to all cases in which the constitutionality or legality of any tax, toll or impost whatsoever, or of any fine, forfeiture or penalty imposed by a municipal corporation shall be in contestation, and to all criminal cases, both as to law and fact, with such exceptions and under such regulations as the Legislature shall make.

Mr. Montamat moved to lay on the table. Carried.

The yeas and nays were ordered on the adoption of Mr. Stocker's substitute, as amended on its third reading, resulting as follows:

YEAS—Messrs. Abell, Austin, Baum, Bailey, Beauvais, Bofill, Bromley, Burke, Cazabat, Cook J. K., Crozat, Cutler, Davies, Dufresne, Duane, Ennis, Fish, Flagg, Foley, Fosdick, Fuller, Gastinel, Gaidry, Gorlinski, Gruneberg, Healy, Harnan, Hart, Hills, Hire, Howell, Kavanagh, Kugler, Maurer, Maas, Mann, Mendiverri, Montamat, Morris, Murphy E., Murphy M. W., Newell, Normand, O'Conner, Ong, Payne J., Paine J. T., Pintado, Purcell J., Schroeder, Schnurr, Shaw, Stumpf, Stiner, Thorpe, Waters, Wells, Wenck—58.

NAYS— Messrs. Barrett, Bell, Buckley, Campbell, Collin, Cook T., Decker, Duke, Dupaty, Flood, Geier, Henderson, Howes, Knobloch, Mayer, Orr, Pursell S., Seymour, Smith, Spellicy, Stocker, Stauffer, Sullivan, Terry, Wilson—25.

Mr. Bofill moved a reconsideration of the vote by which the substitute was adopted on its third reading, which being lost, the Convention adjourned.

Approved.

JOHN E. NEELIS,
Secretary.

THURSDAY, June 16, 1864.

The Convention was called to order pursuant to adjournment. Present, Hon. E. H. Durell, president, in the chair, and the following members:

Messrs. Abell, Austin, Balch, Bailey, Barrett, Baum, Beauvais, Bell, Bofill, Bromley, Buckley, Burke, Campbell, Collin, Cazabat, Cook J. K., Cook T., Crozat, Cutler, Davies, Decker, Duane, Dufresne, Dupaty, Ennis, Fish, Flagg, Flood, Foley, Fosdick, Fuller, Gastinel, Geier, Gorlinski, Gruneberg, Gaidry, Healy, Harnan, Hart, Henderson, Hills, Hire, Howell, Howes, Kavanagh, Knobloch, Kugler, Maas, Mann, Maurer, Mayer, Mendiverri, Montamat, Morris, Murphy E., Murphy M. W., Normand, O'Conner, Ong, Orr, Payne J., Paine J. T., Pintado, Purcell J., Pursell S., Schroeder, Schnurr, Seymour, Shaw, Smith, Spellicy, Stocker, Stumpf, Stiner, Stauffer, Sullivan, Terry, Thorpe, Waters, Wenck, Wells, Wilson—83.

Absent—Messrs. Ariail, Bennie, Bonzano, Brott, Duke (excused,) Edwards (excused,) Heard, Lobdell, Millspaugh, Montague, Newell, Poynot (excused,) Taliaferro and Thomas—14.

On motion of Mr. Smith, Mr. Balch was excused for his absence on yesterday.

On motion of Mr. Knobloch, Mr. Duke was excused for non-attendance.

On motion of Mr. Wells, Mr. Edwards was excused for non-attendance.

The journal of yesterday was read and approved.

On motion, Mr. Henderson was allowed to change his vote on the the third reading of the judiciary bill, from "no" to "yes."

ORDER OF THE DAY.

The report of the Committee on Impeachment, being the order of the day, was taken up on its second reading.

The first section was read and adopted.

The second section was read, when Mr. Harnan moved to amend by striking out the words "two-thirds" and inserting the word "majority." Lost.

On motion of Mr. Hills, the second line was amended by inserting after the word "treasurer" the words "auditor of public accounts."

On motion of Mr. Foley, lines eight and nine were amended by striking out the words "two-thirds present," and inserting the words "a majority elected."

The second section was then adopted as amended.

The third section was read and adopted.

The fourth section was read, when, on motion of Mr. Wilson, the word "such" was substituted for the word "each," in the third line, and the section was then adopted as amended.

The fifth section was read and adopted.

The report was then adopted as a whole on its second reading.

On motion of Mr. Hills, the rules were suspended for the purpose of putting the report on its third reading.

On the adoption of the report on its third reading, the yeas and nays were ordered, with the following result:

YEAS—Messrs. Abell, Austin, Balch, Bailey, Barrett, Baum, Beauvais, Bell, Bofill, Bromley, Buckley, Burke, Campbell, Collin, Cazabat, Cook J. K., Cook T., Crozat, Cutler, Davies, Decker, Duane, Dufresne, Ennis, Fish, Flagg, Flood, Foley, Fosdick, Fuller, Gastinel, Gaidry, Geier, Gorlinski, Gruneberg, Healy, Harnan, Hart, Hills, Hire, Howell, Howes, Kavanagh, Knobloch, Kugler, Maas, Mann, Maurer, Mayer, Mendiverri, Montamat, Morris, Murphy E., Murphy M. W., Normand, O'Conner, Ong, Orr, Payne J., Paine J. T., Pintado, Pursell S., Schroeder, Schnurr, Seymour, Shaw, Smith, Spellicy, Stocker, Stumpf, Stiner, Stauffer, Sullivan, Terry, Thorpe, Wilson—76.

NAYS—Messrs. Dupaty, Henderson, Waters, Wenck, Wells—5.

Consequently the report passed its third reading.

Mr. Thorpe moved a reconsideration of the vote just taken, which motion was laid on the table.

The report of the Committee on General Provisions was next taken up and read.

Mr. Sullivan being in the chair, Mr. Cutler moved the following:

Article 1. Slavery and involuntary servitude are forever abolished and prohibited throughout this State, and the Legislature shall make no laws recognizing the right of property in man.

The president having taken the chair, decided the proposition out of order, inasmuch as the report of the Committee on Emancipation, containing a like provision, had passed its third reading, and become a part of the constitution, it cannot be inserted in another report, where it might be rejected.

Mr. Cutler appealed from the decision of the chair, but subsequently withdrew his appeal, as well as the original proposition.

Articles 1 and 2 were read and adopted.

Article 3 being read, Mr. Stauffer moved to strike out all after the word "treason," in the second line, which motion was lost.

Mr. Hills moved to strike out, in the second and third lines, the words "or forfeiture," which was tabled, on a rising vote of 43 ayes, 23 noes.

Articles 3, 4 and 5 were then adopted, without amendment.

Article 6 being read, Mr. Montamat moved to amend by inserting a proviso that "no negro be allowed to vote."

The president ruled that the question of the qualification of voters had been disposed of under the title of "Legislative Department," and could not again be brought up.

Mr. Montamat appealed from the decision of the chair, whereupon the ayes and nays were called, resulting as follows:

YEAS—Messrs. Austin, Bailey, Baum, Beauvais, Bell, Bromley, Burke, Collin, Cazabat, Cook J. K., Cook T., Crozat, Cutler, Davies, Duane, Dupaty, Ennis, Fish, Flagg, Flood, Foley, Fosdick, Fuller, Geier, Gorlinski, Gruneberg, Gaidry, Healy, Harnan, Hart, Henderson, Hills, Hire, Howell, Howes, Kavanagh, Knobloch, Kugler, Mann, Mayer, Murphy E., Normand, Ong, Payne J., Paine J. T., Pintado, Purcell J., Pursell S., Schroeder, Schnurr, Seymour, Smith, Spellicy, Stocker, Stumpf, Stiner, Stauffer, Terry, Thorpe, Wenck—60.

NAYS — Messrs. Abell, Balch, Bofill, Buckley, Campbell, Decker, Dufresne, Gastinel, Maas, Maurer, Mendiverri, Montamat, Murphy M. W., Orr, Sullivan, Waters, Wilson—17.

Consequently the decision of the chair was sustained.

The president here stated to the Conven-

AND AMENDMENT OF THE CONSTITUTION OF LOUISIANA. 119

tion that the rules require a two-thirds vote to over-rule a decision of the chair, but that he had heretofore waived this rule in deference to the Convention.

Mr. Sullivan offered the following :

No negro shall be allowed to practice law or physic in this State, nor shall they be taught or instructed in the art or mystery of any trade or profession, under such penalties as may be fixed by the Legislature.

Laid on the table by a rising vote of 48 ayes to 20 nays.

Article 6 was then adopted as reported.

Article 7 being read, Mr. Hills moved to amend by adding : "No negro shall be allowed to draw money from the State treasury."

A motion to lay the amendment on the table being lost, the Convention adjourned, on a rising vote of ayes 35. nays 34.

Approved.

JOHN E. NEELIS,
Secretar .

FRIDAY, June 17, 1864.

Pursuant to adjournment, the Convention met at 12 o'clock M., Hon. E. H. Durell, president, in the chair.

The roll was called and the following members found to be present :

Messrs. Abell, Austin, Balch, Bailey, Barrett, Baum, Beauvais, Bell, Bofill, Bromley, Buckley, Burke, Campbell, Collin, Cazabat, Cook J. K., Cook T., Crozat, Cutler, Davies, Decker, Duane, Dufresne, Duke, Dupaty, Ennis, Fish, Flagg, Flood, Foley, Fosdick, Fuller, Gastinel, Geier, Gorlinski, Gruneberg, Gaidry, Healy, Harnan, Hart, Henderson, Hills, Hire, Howell, Howes, Kavanagh, Knobloch, Kugler, Maas, Mann. Maurer, Mayer, Mendiverri, Montamat, Morris, Murphy E., Murphy M.W., Newell, Normand, O'Conner, Ong, Orr, Payne J., Paine J. T., Pintado, Purcell J., Pursell S., Schroeder, Schnurr, Seymour, Shaw, Smith, Spellicy, Stocker, Stumpf, Stiner, Stauffer, Sullivan, Terry, Thorpe, Waters, Wenck, Wells, Wilson—85.

Absent : Messrs. Ariail, Bennie, Bonzano, Brott, Edwards, (excused) Heard, Lobdell, Millspaugh, Montague, Poynot, (excused) Taliaferro and Thomas—12.

The minutes of yesterday were read and adopted.

The report of the Committee on General Provisions being the order of the day, was taken up.

Articles 7 and 8 were read and adopted.

Article 9 was read, together with the following substitute, offered by Mr. Samuel Pursell, viz :

Art. 9. All civil officers for the State at large shall be voters of and reside within the State, and all district or parish officers shall be voters of and reside within their respective parish or district, and shall keep their offices at such places therein as may be required by law.

The question being put on Mr. Pursell's substitute, the same was adopted.

Upon article 10 being read, Mr. Smith moved to amend by striking out the words "and inferior courts," in the second line, which being lost, a rising vote was taken on the adoption of the article as reported, resulting in ayes 22 noes 35. Consequently the article was rejected.

Article 11 was then taken up and read.

Mr. Smith moved to amend by striking out, in the last line, the words "*viva voce*" and inserting "yeas and nays."

Mr. Samuel Pursell, with the consent of Mr. Smith, moved a reconsideration of the vote just taken on article 10. which being carried, Mr. Abell moved a reference of the article to a special committee of three. Laid on the table.

Mr. Wilson moved to amend by striking out the words "two-thirds" and inserting the words "a majority," and also by striking out after "members," in the third line, the word "of" and inserting in lieu thereof the words "elected to," which motion having prevailed, article 10 was then adopted as amended.

The question then recurred on the adoption of Mr. Smith's amendment to article 11, striking out the words "*viva voce*," and substituting therefor the words "yeas and nays," which being carried, article 11 was adopted as amended.

Article 12 was read and adopted as reported.

Article 13 being read, Mr. Stauffer moved to strike out in the second line the words " or be employed in the public works," and also all the article after the word " State " in the third line, which being carried, the article was adopted as amended.

Article 14 was adopted as reported.

Article 15 was then read, when Mr. Howell moved to strike out in the first line the word "that," and further to amend by inserting after the word "laws" in the first line, the words " of this State," and after the word "by" in the second line, the words, " the Legislature or by its," which amendments having prevailed, the article was adopted as amended.

Article 16 was adopted as reported.

Article 17 was read.

Mr. Howell moved to strike out the entire article, and substitute therefor article 104 of the constitution of 1852, which motion prevailed and the substitue was adopted.

Articles 18 and 19 were read and adopted as reported.

Article 20 being read, Mr. Campbell moved to amend by adding, after the word "made" in the last line, the following words: " And no attorney shall give evidence in any case or suit, in which he or they may be employed," which amendment having been accepted by the Convention, the article as amended was adopted.

Article 21 being taken up and read, Mr. Cutler moved to reject the entire article, which being lost, the article was adopted as reported.

Article 22 was read, when Mr. Sullivan moved to strike out all after the words "subjects," in the second line, and insert " but the writer shall take the consequences of its abuse and malignity," which being laid on the table, the article was adopted or reported.

Upon article 23 being taken up, Mr. Terry offered the following amendment:

No monopoly shall be created by the Legislature, by the grant to joint stock companies or to individuals of exclusive rights to build and operate canals, railroads, plank or other roads in this State or through any portion thereof; neither shall exclusive rights for any kind of manufacture be granted.

Mr. Smith offered the following amendment:

The Legislature shall have no power to grant aid to companies or associations of individuals formed for any purpose.

On motion of Mr. Montamat, Mr. Smith's amendment was laid on the table.

Mr. Terry's amendment was then taken up, and, on motion of Mr. Baum, was laid on the table by a rising vote of ayes 42, noes 34.

Mr. Howell moved to amend by inserting betweeen the words "shall" and "have" the word "not," and between the words "individuals" and "formed" the words "except to such as are."

Mr. Howell's amendment was amended, on motion of Mr. Campbell, by inserting, "and shall be," so as to make the article read : "The Legislature shall not have power to grant aid to companies or associations of individuals, except to such as are and shall be formed," etc.

Mr. Cazabat offered a substitute for the article in the following words : " The Legislature shall have no power to grant exclusive privileges or monopolies of any kind to individuals, companies or corporations whatsoever, except for charitable purposes," which was laid on the table by a rising vote of ayes 44, noes 15.

The amendments of Mr. Howell, as amended by Mr. Campbell, were accepted, and the article adopted as amended.

Articles 24, 25 and 26 were severally read, and adopted as reported.

Article 27 was then read, together with Mr. Stiner's amendment, prohibiting the licensing of gambling houses.

Mr. Howell, on behalf of the committee, accepted Mr. Stiner's amendment.

Mr. Montamat moved, as a substitute for the article and the amendment, "lottery and gambling houses shall be licensed by the Legislature."

Mr. Stocker offered the following as a substitute for the whole :

The Legislature may grant licenses to gambling houses in this State, provided the tax shall not be less than ten thousand dollars per annum on each house so licensed.

Mr. Montamat withdrew his substitute, and offered the following additional proviso to Mr. Stocker's substitute :

Provided, That duly licensed gambling houses shall have the right to sell lottery tickets.

The proviso was accepted by Mr. Stocker.

Mr. Cutler offered the following as a substitute for the article, substitutes and amendments :

The Legislature shall have the power to license the selling of lottery tickets and

AND AMENDMENT OF THE CONSTITUTION OF LOUISIANA.   121

the keeping of gambling houses; said houses in all cases shall be on the first floor and kept with open doors; but in all cases not less than ten thousand dollars per annum shall be levied as a license or tax on each vendor of lottery tickets and on each gambling house, and five hundred dollars on each tombola.

Mr. Harnan offered the following, which was laid on table:

No lottery shall be authorized by this State, but every tombola shall be allowed by paying to the State, for each and every tombola, the sum of five hundred dollars; the same to be divided *pro rata* to each inmate which are beholding to receive charity in the orphan asylums within this State.

Mr. Howes moved to amend Mr. Cutler's substitute by adding: "a large sign shall be placed over the door, with the words gambling house painted thereon." The amendment was tabled.

Mr. Hills moved to lay the original article and all the substitutes and amendments thereto on the table, which was lost.

The question then recurred upon the adoption of Mr. Cutler's substitute, whereupon the yeas and nays were called, with the following result:

YEAS—Messrs. Abell, Bailey, Barrett, Baum, Beauvais, Bell, Bofill, Buckley, Burke, Cook J. K., Cook T., Crozat, Cutler, Davies, Decker, Dufresne, Duke, Ennis, Fish, Flood, Foley, Gastinel, Geier, Gruneberg, Gaidry, Healy, Harnan, Hart, Henderson, Howes, Knobloch, Kugler, Maas, Maurer, Mayer, Mendiverri, Montamat, Murphy E., Murphy M. W., Newell, O'Conner, Ong, Orr, Purcell J., Purcell S., Schroeder, Schnurr, Seymour, Spellicy, Stocker, Stumpf, Stauffer, Sullivan, Terry, Thorpe, Waters, Wells—57.

NAYS—Messrs. Austin, Balch, Bromley, Campbell, Collin, Cazabat, Dupaty, Flagg, Fosdick, Gorlinski, Hills, Hire, Howell, Kavanagh, Mann, Morris, Normand, Payne J., Paine J. T., Pintado, Seymour, Smith, Stiner, Wilson—24.

Consequently the substitute was adopted.

Mr. Foley moved to adjourn. The yeas and nays being demanded thereon, were taken with the following result:

YEAS—Messrs. Abell, Austin, Balch, Bailey, Bofill, Buckley, Campbell, Decker, Dufresne, Duke, Ennis, Flagg, Foley, Gastinel, Gruneberg, Gaidry, Healy, Harnan, Hart, Henderson, Kavanagh, Knobloch, Maas, Maurer, Mayer, Mendiverri, Murphy E., Murphy M. W., Newell, Normand, O'Conner, Orr, Pintado, Purcell J., Schroeder, Schnurr, Seymour, Shaw, Spellicy, Stumpf, Stiner, Sullivan, Waters and Wells—44.

NAYS—Messrs. Barrett, Baum, Beauvais, Bell, Bromley, Burke, Collin, Cazabat, Cook J. K., Cook T., Crozat, Cutler, Davies, Dupaty, Fish, Flood, Fosdick, Geier, Gorlinski, Hills, Hire, Howell, Kugler, Mann, Montamat, Morris, Ong, Payne J., Paine J. T., Purcell S., Smith, Stocker, Stauffer, Terry, Thorpe and Wilson—36.

Consequently the motion prevailed and the Convention adjourned.

Approved.

JOHN E. NEELIS,
Secretary.

SATURDAY, June 18, 1864.

The Convention met and was called to order pursuant to adjournment, Hon. E. H. Durell, president, in the chair, and the following members present:

Abell, Austin, Balch, Bailey, Barrett, Baum, Beauvais, Bell, Bofill, Bromley, Buckley, Burke, Collin, Cazabat, Cook J. K., Cook T., Crozat, Cutler, Davies, Decker, Duane, Dufresne, Duke, Dupaty, Ennis, Fish, Flagg, Flood, Foley, Fosdick, Fuller, Gastinel, Geier, Gorlinski, Gruneberg, Gaidry, Healy, Harnan, Hart, Henderson, Hills, Hire, Howell, Howes, Knobloch, Kugler, Maas, Mann, Maurer, Mayer, Mendiverri, Montamat, Morris, Murphy E., Murphy M. W., Newell, Normand, O'Conner, Orr, Payne J., Paine J. T., Pintado, Poynot, Purcell J., Purcell S., Schroeder, Schnurr, Seymour, Shaw, Smith, Spellicy, Stocker, Stumpf, Stiner, Stauffer, Sullivan, Terry, Thorpe, Waters, Wenck, Wilson—82.

Absent—Messrs. Ariail, Bennie, Bonzano, Brott, Campbell, Edwards (excused,) Heard, Kavanagh, Lobdell, Millspaugh, Montague, Ong, Taliaferro, Thomas and Wells—15.

The minutes of yesterday were read, amended and adopted.

On motion of Mr. Howell, the vote on article 23 was reconsidered, with a view of amending the same so as to exempt charitable institutions from the prohibitions contained in said article. Further action thereon was then deferred until Monday next.

Mr. Thorpe offered the following:

Resolved, That a committee of five be appointed to wait on Maj. Gen. Canby and Maj. Gen. Sickles, and learn from them when it would be agreeable to them to receive an official visit from the members of the Convention.

The rules were suspended and the resolution adopted; whereupon the president appointed Messrs. Thorpe, Sullivan, Cutler, Terry and Campbell on the committee raised thereby.

Mr. Fosdick offered the following preamble and resolutions:

Whereas, In the opinion of this Convention a large majority of the loyal people of the city of New Orleans are desirous of having the civil government of the city re-established:

Be it therefore Resolved, That his excellency the governor of the State be and he is hereby requested to immediately issue his order of election for mayor, recorders, street commissioner, aldermen and assistant aldermen, in conformity with the city charter.

Resolved, That the secretary of this Convention be and he is hereby instructed to transmit a copy of the foregoing resolution to his excellency the governor.

After some discussion, Mr. Shaw moved to postpone the further consideration of the resolutions until Saturday next.

A motion to adjourn having been made, the yeas and nays were ordered thereon, resulting as follows:

YEAS—Beauvais, Buckley, Burke, Crozat, Davies, Duane, Dufresne, Duke, Ennis, Flagg, Foley, Hire, Maas, Maurer, Murphy E., Murphy M. W., O'Conner, Payne J., Schroeder, Stiner, Wilson—21.

NAYS—Messrs. Abell, Austin, Balch, Bailey, Barrett, Baum, Bell, Bromley, Bofill, Collin, Cazabat, Cook T., Cook J. K., Cutler, Dupaty, Fish, Flood, Fosdick, Gastinel, Geier, Gorlinski, Gruneberg, Gaidry, Harnan, Hills, Howes, Knobloch, Kugler, Mann, Mayer, Montamat, Morris, Newell, Normand, Orr, Paine J. T., Pintado, Poynot, Purcell J., Pursell S., Schnurr, Seymour, Shaw, Smith, Spellicy, Stocker, Sullivan, Stumpf, Stauffer, Terry, Thorpe, Waters—52.

Consequently the Convention refused to adjourn.

Mr. Davies offered the following amendment:

Resolved, That the governor of the State be requested to order that elections be held in every incorporated city and town within the Union lines for all city and town officers; said elections to be held on the same day as the elections of officers for the city of New Orleans.

Mr. Shaw called for the question on his motion to postpone the further consideration of the subject until Saturday, 25th inst., which being put, was carried, and the Convention then adjourned.

Approved.

JOHN E. NEELIS,
Secretary.

MONDAY, June 20, 1864.

The Convention met, pursuant to adjournment.

Present, the Hon. E. H. Durell, president, and the following members:

Messrs. Abell, Austin, Balch, Bailey, Baum, Beauvais, Bell, Bofill, Bromley, Buckley, Burke, Campbell, Collin, Cazabat, Cook J. K., Cook T., Crozat, Cutler, Davies, Duane, Dufresne, Duke, Dupaty, Ennis, Fish, Flagg, Flood, Foley, Fosdick, Fuller, Gastinel, Geier, Gorlinski, Gruneberg, Gaidry, Healy, Harnan, Hart, Henderson, Hills, Hire, Howell, Howes, Kavanagh, Knobloch, Kugler, Maas, Mann, Maurer, Mayer, Mendiverri, Montamat, Murphy M. W., Murphy E., Newell, Normand, O'Conner, Orr, Payne J., Paine J. T., Poynot, Purcell J., Pursell S., Schroeder, Schnurr, Seymour, Shaw, Smith, Spellicy, Stocker, Stumpf, Stiner, Stauffer, Sullivan, Terry, Thorpe, Waters, Wenck, Wells and Wilson—81.

Absent—Messrs. Ariail, Barrett, Bennie, Bonzano, Brott, Decker, Edwards, (excused,) Heard, Lobdell, Millspaugh, Montague, Morris, Ong, Taliaferro, Thomas and Pintado, (excused.)

The minutes of Saturday's proceedings were read and adopted.

Mr. Terry asked for a suspension of the rules for the purpose of presenting a memorial, signed by a large number of citizens, relative to the hours for laborers to be employed on public works.

The rules being suspended, the memorial was received, and on motion of Mr. Montamat, was referred to a select committee of seven—consisting of the following members, viz: Messrs. Terry, Geier, Stiner, O'Conner, Balch, Burke and Orr.

Mr. Fosdick moved a suspension of the rules for the purpose of taking up his resolution of Saturday last, relative to the election of officers for the city government of New Orleans.

A motion to lay on the table being lost, the yeas and nays were ordered on the motion to suspend the rules—resulting as follows:

YEAS—Messrs. Abell, Austin, Balch, Bailey, Baum, Bell, Bofill, Buckley, Campbell, Cook J. K., Cook T., Dufresne, Duke, Flagg, Flood, Fosdick, Gastinel, Geier, Gorlinski, Gruneberg, Harnan, Hart, Hills, Howes,

Knobloch, Maas, Maurer, Mayer, Montamat, Murphy E., O'Conner, Orr, Poynot, Purcell J., Smith, Sullivan, Thorpe, Waters, Wilson—39.

NAYS—Messrs. Beauvais, Bromley, Burke, Collin, Crozat, Cutler, Davies, Duane, Dupaty, Ennis, Fish, Foley, Fuller, Gaidry, Healy, Henderson, Hire, Howell, Kugler, Mann, Murphy M. W., Newell, Normand, Payne J., Paine J. T., Pursell S., Schroeder, Schnurr, Seymour, Shaw, Stocker, Stumpf, Stiner, Stauffer, Terry, Wells—36.

Consequently, the motion to suspend the rules was lost.

Mr. Montamat then moved a suspension of the rules, for the purpose of submitting a report of the Finance Committee, which being carried, he submitted the following:

REPORT OF THE FINANCE COMMITTEE, UP TO JUNE 18.

1864.

June 18—Amount paid out, as per warrants up to date, for per diem of members, mileage and salaries of officers	$94,485 60
June 18—Balance on hand to date	5,514 40
	$100,000 00
June 18—Amount paid out for contingent expenses, as per vouchers and warrants	$18,027 97
June 18—Balance on hand, to date	6,972 03
	$25,000 00

June 18—Amount paid out for printing and advertising, as per vouchers and warrants, $48,218 32. This sum was paid out of funds not otherwise appropriated, with the exception of seven thousand dollars, which was paid from the funds appropriated for contingent expenses, and is to be refunded to that account.

June 8—The sum of six thousand one hundred and thirty-nine dollars and thirteen cents, ($6,139 13,) was paid to J. S. Walton, treasurer of the city of New Orleans, for fitting up Liberty Hall.

Your committee respectfully report that it is necessary that an appropriation be made for the payment of members, officers and employés of this Convention, for the balance of the term; wherefore, your committee beg leave to recommend the following resolution:

Resolved, That the sum of twenty thousand dollars be and the same is hereby appropriated out of the general funds of the State treasury, not otherwise appropriated, for the payment of *per diem* and salaries of members and officers.

JOHN T. MONTAMAT,
Acting Chairman Finance Committee,
L. P. NORMAND,
JOHN SULLIVAN,
MARTIN SCHNURR.

New Orleans, June 18, 1864.

The report was received and the accompanying resolution adopted.

On motion of Mr. Hire, Mr. Pintado was excused, on account of sickness.

ORDER OF THE DAY—REPORT OF THE COMMITTEE ON GENERAL PROVISIONS.

Mr. Howell moved to amend article 23, by adding the words: "Provided, this article shall not apply to charitable associations."

Mr. Cazabat moved to strike out all after the word "improvement," in the third line, and add the words "and for charitable purposes." Lost.

Mr. Howell's amendment was then accepted by the Convention, and article 23 was adopted as amended.

Article 28 being taken up and read, Mr. Smith moved to amend by adding the words, "nor shall any minor be emancipated." Lost.

Mr. Wilson moved to amend by inserting the word "not" between the words "be" and "granted." Lost.

Mr. Fosdick offered the following substitute:

The Legislature may enact general laws regulating the adoption of children, emancipation of minors, changing of names, and the granting of divorces, but no special laws shall be enacted relating to particular or individual cases.

Mr. Foley moved to strike out the words, "changing of names," which motion being laid on the table. Mr. Fosdick's sustitute was adopted.

Articles 29, 30 and 31 were respectively read and adopted as reported.

When article 32 was taken up and read, Mr. Howell, on behalf of the committee, reported the following substitute:

Art. 32. Corporations shall not be created in this State by special laws except for political or municipal purposes, but the Legislature shall provide by general laws for the organization of all other corporations, except corporations with banking or discounting privileges, the creation, renewal or extension of which is hereby prohibited.

The substitute was adopted as reported.

Article 33 was read, when Mr. Smith moved to amend by inserting the word "not" after shall in the first line, which motion was laid on the table and the article adopted.

Article 34 was read. Mr. Cazabat moved to amend by striking out the works "except that of justice of the peace," which motion was lost, and the article was then adopted.

For article 35 Mr. Samuel Pursell offered the following substitute, which was read and adopted :

Art. 35. Taxation shall be equal and uniform throughout the State. All property shall be taxed in proportion to its value, to be ascertained as directed by law. The General Assembly shall have power to exempt from taxation property actually used for church, school or charitable purposes. The General Assembly shall levy an income tax upon all persons pursuing any occupation, trade or calling, and all such persons shall obtain a license, as provided by law. All tax on income shall be pro rata on the amount of income or business done.

For article 36 Mr. Sullivan offered a substitute relative to city police.

On a motion to lay on the table the yeas and nays were ordered, resulting as follows:

YEAS—Messrs. Austin, Bromley, Burke, Campbell, Collin, Cazabat, Cutler, Davies, Duke, Dupaty, Ennis, Flagg, Fosdick, Gorlinski, Gaidry, Henderson, Hire, Howell, Knobloch, Kugler, Mann, Mayer, Newell, Payne J., Paine J. T., Purcell J., Pursell S., Schnurr, Seymour, Stauffer, Thorpe. Wenck, Wells, Wilson—34.

NAYS—Messrs. Abell, Balch, Beauvais, Bailey, Bell, Bofill, Buckley, Cook J. K., Cook T., Crozat, Dufresne, Flood, Foley, Fuller, Gastinel, Geier, Gruneberg, Harnan, Hart, Hills, Howes, Maas, Maurer, Montamat, Murphy E., Murphy M. W., Normand, O'Conner, Orr, Poynot, Schroeder, Smith, Stocker, Stumpf. Stiner, Sullivan. Terry, Waters—38.

Consequently the motion to lay on the table was lost.

Mr. Cutler moved a reference of the whole matter to a committee of three, which motion was carried ; whereupon the president appointed on said committee Messrs. Cutler, Abell and Sullivan.

Articles 37, 38, 39 and 40 were severally read and adopted.

Mr. Howell offered the following additional articles to the report, viz. :

Art. 41. No liability, either State, parochial or municipal, shall exist for any debts contracted for, or in the interest of the rebellion against the authority of the United States government.

Art. 42. The seat of government shall be and remain at New Orleans, and shall not be removed without the consent of two-thirds of both Houses of the General Assembly.

Art. 43. The Legislature may determine the mode of filling vacancies in all offices for which provision is not made in this constitution.

Article 41 was read and adopted.

Article 42 was taken up and read.

Mr. Abell moved to amend by striking out the words "two-thirds" and substituting the words "a majority," which amendment was accepted by Mr. Howell.

Mr. Samuel Pursell offered the following substitute :

Art. 42. The seat of government shall be at the city of New Orleans. The General Assembly shall have power to dispose of the present capitol property in Baton Rouge and provide, by purchase or otherwise, suitable lands and buildings for a State capitol in New Orleans.

Laid on the table.

Mr. Cazabat moved to amend by striking out the words "New Orleans" and substituting "parish of Jefferson." Laid on the table.

Mr. Stauffer called for the reading of his substitute, viz :

No debt created by or under the so-called Confederate States, or under tho sanction of any usurping power, shall be recognized or paid.

Mr. Stauffer's substitute was laid on the table, when the question recurred on the adoption of Mr. Howell's additional article 42, upon which a division was called for, resulting ayes 44, nays 13.

Article 42 was therefore adopted as amended.

Article 43 was read and adopted.

Mr. Thorpe, as chairman of the committee appointed to wait upon Maj. Gen. Canby and Maj. Gen. Sickles. submitted the following report :

The committee would respectfully report that they waited upon Maj. Gen. Canby and Maj. Gen. Sickles and represented the desire of the Convention to pay them a ceremonious visit.

The distinguished soldiers replied, in substance, that they felt deeply grateful for the compliment paid them by the members of the Louisiana Free State Convention, and instead of receiving a formal visit from the members of the Convention, that they would take an early opportunity of paying their personal respects to the honorable members of this Convention.

The report was received and unanimously adopted.

Mr. Wilson, with leave of the Convention, offered the following resolution, which was unanimously adopted, viz:

Resolved, That the president of this Convention be instructed to invite Maj. Gen. Canby and Maj. Gen. Sickles to visit this Convention.

The Convention then adjourned until to-morrow at 12 o'clock M.

Approved.

JOHN E. NEELIS,
Secretary.

TUESDAY, June 21, 1864.

The Convention was called to order pursuant to adjournment.

Present, Hon. E. H. Durell, president, and the following members:

Messrs. Abell, Austin, Balch, Bailey, Barrett, Baum, Beauvais, Bell, Bofill, Bromley, Buckley, Burke, Campbell, Cazabat, Collin, Cook J. K., Cook T., Crozat, Cutler, Davies, Decker, Dufresne, Duke, Dupaty, Edwards, Ennis, Fish. Flagg, Flood, Foley, Fosdick, Fuller, Gastinel, Geier, Gorlinski, Gruneberg, Gaidry, Healy, Harnan, Hart, Henderson, Hills, Hire, Howell, Howes, Kavanagh, Knobloch, Kugler, Maas, Mann, Maurer, Mayer, Mendiverri, Montamat, Morris, Murphy E., Murphy M. W., Newell, Normand, O'Conner, Orr, Payne J., Paine J. T., Poynot, Purcell J., Pursell S., Schroeder, Schnurr, Seymour, Spellicy, Smith, Stocker, Stumpf, Stiner, Stauffer, Sullivan, Terry, Thorpe, Waters, Wenck, Wells, Wilson—83.

Absent—Messrs. Ariail, Bonzano. Brott, Duane, Heard, Lobdell, Millspaugh, Montague, Ong, (excused) Pintado, (excused) Talliaferro and Thomas.

The minutes of yesterday were read and approved.

On motion of Mr. Cutler, Mr. Ong was excused for his absence on account of sickness.

Mr. Fosdick moved a suspension of the rules to take up his resolution relative to city government.

A motion to lay on the table having been lost, the yeas and nays were ordered on the motion to suspend, resulting as follows:

YEAS — Messrs. Abell, Balch, Bailey, Baum, Bell, Bofill, Buckley, Campbell, Cook J. K., Cutler, Decker, Dufresne, Duke, Flagg, Flood, Fosdick, Gastinel, Gorlinski, Gruneberg, Healey, Hills, Knobloch, Maas, Maurer, Mendiverri, Murphy E., Newell, O'Conner, Orr, Poynot, Smith, Stauffer, Sullivan, Thorpe, Waters, Wenck, Wells, Wilson—38.

NAYS—Beauvais, Bromley, Burke, Collin, Cazabat. Crozat, Davies. Dupaty, Edwards, Ennis, Fish, Foley, Fuller, Geier, Gaidry, Harnan, Hart, Henderson, Hire, Howell, Howes, Kavanagh, Kugler, Mann, Mayer, Montamat, Morris, Murphy M. W., Normand, Payne J., Paine J. T., Purcell J., Pursell S., Schroeder, Schnurr, Seymour, Shaw, Spellicy, Stocker, Stumpf, Stiner, Terry—42.

Consequently the motion was lost.

Mr. Terry, as chairman of the select committee on the memorial of certain working men, submitted the following report:

Mr. President, your committee on memorial, after careful deliberation, respectfully present the following report:

Believing that our mechanics, artizans of every grade, and laboring men are the most afflicted portion of our race; working for the most part under the most depressing circumstances, they live and have their being at a great disadvantage. Unless capricious fortune seems to smile especially upon their efforts, laboring people, in the present social disorder, are most likely to be kept down in the cesspool of poverty, simply by the antagonism between labor and capital. It is unspeakably difficult for a laboring man to earn enough to meet the current expenses of his family and at the same time avoid debt and dishonesty. If he does this in our city, he must forego every species of comforting luxury and all cultivated amusements. His disadvantages are very numerous. If he be a mechanic, there are, probably, certain months in each year when his services are not required. But his house-rent and family expenses go on just the same as when his labor is in demand. The wealthy man can pay cash for his dry goods and groceries and can purchase them at wholesale prices, which gives him the advantage. But the poor man must buy in small quantities, must pay high interest for credit, and so lives at a perpetual loss. When he goes to the market he pays the butchers and stall-keepers fifty per cent. more than the original cost of the articles. When he goes to the grocer, he must defray the accumulated and combined profits upon tea, sugar, soap, molasses, etc.; first, of the producer; second, of the wholesale merchant; third, of the retailer. Here is a mass of profits which the consumer must pay, and he must work hard and live very economically to do it. Again, when he wants muslin, cloth, and calico for his family, he must pay sufficient *over and above* the actual cost and value of these fabrics originally, to support the manufacturer, the various second-handers and wholesale go-betweens, and lastly the retailer of whom the goods are purchased. Your committee believe this is *all wrong*, and the laboring classes—who produce all the wealth there is in the State—are the constant and only real sufferers under this system. To illustrate the injustice of this system, the manufacturer, the wholesale merchant, and the flourishing retailer, can live in $50,000 houses, environed with all the comforts and privileges thereof, the poor hard-working man and woman, with a large family of children to feed, clothe and educate, are compelled to occupy uncomfortable rooms for which they pay a high rent and toil perpetually on, ofttimes without the least glimmering of a hope that their circumstances will ever improve. Your committee, knowing full well that all the multitudinous complications of the mercantile world must be supported, desire to show that between the producer and the consumer there now exist in all kinds of industry, numerous intermediates; these produce nothing, they add nothing valuable to the State, they serve as speculative go-betweens. But they must all be fed, clothed and enriched, and the mechanic and laboring classes must do it all. These must support all non-producers; not by direct taxation, but in this way: producers support non-producers by paying higher prices for everything they purchase, and by paying rents to landlords, who, out of it, pay the taxes. This popular speculating, this fashionable subsisting upon the labor of the mechanics and workingmen, is becoming well-nigh intolerable. The homage that capital requires of labor is beginning to be insupportable and detestable. Some efficient plan must soon be instituted to relieve the poor man from his manifold, oppressive disadvantages; to give him a fair and equal chance to enjoy his existence; to emancipate him from the mountainous interests and antagonisms that now oppress and keep him in bondage to poverty—therefore your committee, after carefully examining into the facts of your honorable petitioners, (though their request being a subject more appropriate for a legislative body) are in favor of granting their humble request, in order to enable your petitioners to devote a part of their time to domestic scenes and the cultivation of the mind, respectfully submit the following article to be inserted in report of General Provisions:

Article —. Nine hours shall constitute a day's labor for all mechanics, artisans and laboring men employed on public works of the State and city.

J. RANDALL TERRY, Chairman,
GEORGE GEIER,
BENJAMIN H. ORR.
YOUNG BURKE,
P. K. O'CONNER,
J. A. STINER.

The report of the committee was received and ordered to be spread upon the minutes.

Mr. Schroeder offered a memorial, and additional articles to the report of the Committee on General Provisions, but previous to their being read, Mr. Montamat rose to a point of order, and objected to the reading of the memorial without a suspension of the rules, which point was sustained by the chair, and the order of the day was then taken up.

Mr. Cutler, as chairman of the select committee on article 36 of the report of the Committee on General Provisions, submitted the following report:

REPORT OF SPECIAL COMMITTEE ON ARTICLE NO. 36 OF THE REPORT OF THE COMMITTEE ON GENERAL PROVISIONS.

The citizens of the city of New Orleans shall have the right of appointing the several public officers necessary for the administration of the police of said city, pursuant to the mode of elections which shall be prescribed by the Legislature.

Provided that the mayor and recorders shall be ineligible to a seat in the General Assembly, and the mayor and recorders shall be commissioned by the governor as justices of the peace, and the Legislature may vest in them such criminal jurisdiction as may be necessary for the punishment of minor offences, and as the police and good order of said city may require.

And that the city of New Orleans shall maintain a police force which shall be uniformed with distinction of grade, to consist of permanent citizens of the State of Louisiana, to be selected by the mayor of the city, and to hold office during good behavior, and removable only by a police commission composed of five citizens, viz: one to be selected from each district of the city, and the mayor, who shall be president of the board. The commission to be appointed by the governor of the State for the term of two years, at a salary of not less than one thousand dollars each per annum; a majority of whom shall remove for delinquencies. Members of the police when removed shall not again be eligible to any position on the police for a term of one year.

Interfering or meddling in elections in any manner will be a sufficient cause for instant dismissal from the police by the board.

The chief of police shall give a penal bond in the sum of ten thousand dollars; lieutenants of police, five thousand dollars; sergeants and clerks, each three thousand dollars; coporals, two thousand dollars, and privates one thousand dollars, with good and solvent security, as the law directs, for the faithful performance of their duties.

The various officers shall receive a salary of not less than the following rates:

The chief of police.......$250 per month.
" lieutenants of police.. 150 " "
" sergeants of police... 100 " "
" clerks of police....... 100 " "
" corporals of police.... 90 " "
" privates (day and night each)................ 80 " "

The Legislature may establish the price and pay of foremen, mechanics, laborers and others employed on the public works of the State or parochial or city governments.

R. KING CUTLER, Chairman.
JOHN SULLIVAN.
E. ABELL.

After some discussion on the report, the previous question was called for, and lost on the following vote:

YEAS—Messrs. Abell, Austin, Bailey, Baum, Bofill, Bromley, Burke, Collin, Crozat, Cutler, Duke, Dupaty, Fish, Flagg, Fuller, Gaidry, Hart, Henderson, Kavanagh, Purcell J., Schnurr, Seymour, Thorpe, Wilson—24.

NAYS—Messrs. Bell, Buckley, Campbell, Cazabat, Cook J. K., Cook T., Davies, Deeker, Dufresne, Edwards, Ennis, Flood, Foley, Fosdick, Gastinel, Geier, Gorlinski, Healy, Harnan, Hills, Hire, Howell, Howes, Knobloch, Kugler, Maas, Mann, Maurer, Mayer, Montamat, Morris, Murphy E., Murphy M. W., Newell, Normand, O'Conner, Orr, Payne J., Paine J. T., Poynot, Pursell S., Schroeder, Shaw, Smith, Spellicy, Stocker, Stumpf, Stiner, Stauffer, Sullivan. Terry, Waters, Wenck, Wells—54.

Mr. Orr offered the following proviso, as an amendment to the report:

Provided, That the compensation to be paid to all foremen, mechanics, cartmen and laborers employed on the public works under the government of the State of Louisiana, city of New Orleans and the police juries of the various parishes of the State, shall not be less than as follows, viz: Foremen, $3 50 cents per day; mechanics, $3 00 per day; cartmen, $3 00 per day; laborers, $2 00.

Mr. Cazabat offered the following amendment:

Provided, That laborers working on public works shall not be required to work more than nine hours per day, and will receive one hundred dollars per month; and provided also, that the salaries of the police will be one hundred and twenty dollars per month for corporals and clerks, and one hundred dollars per month for (night and day) privates.

Mr. Davies offered the following amendment:

That no person shall be eligible to serve on the police of this city who has not been a resident thereof at least two years previous to his appointment; and that preference shall be given in all cases to heads of families to serve as policemen.

After a lengthy discussion, the president having decided that Mr. Cutler, chairman of the select committee on the article under consideration, who had obtained the floor and claimed the right to close the debate, was entitled to that privilege, and that no further discussion from other members could be heard, Mr. Stauffer appealed from the decision, but previous to the question being put, a call of the ayes and noes was demanded—and there being no quorum present, the Convention adjourned until 12 o'clock M. to-morrow.

Approved.

JOHN E. NEELIS,
Secretary.

WEDNESDAY, June 22, 1864.

The Convention met pursuant to adjournment, and was called to order by the president.

The roll was called and the following members answered to their names:

Messrs. Abell, Austin, Balch, Bailey, Barrett, Baum, Beauvais, Bell, Bofill, Bromley, Buckley, Burke, Campbell, Collin, Cook J. K., Cook T., Crozat, Cutler, Davies, Decker, Duane, Dufresne, Duke. Dupaty, Edwards, Ennis, Fish, Flagg, Flood, Foley, Fosdick, Fuller, Gastinel, Geier, Gorlinski, Gruneberg, Gaidry, Healy, Harnan, Hart, Henderson, Hills, Hire, Howell, Howes, Kavanagh, Knobloch, Kugler, Maas, Mann,

Maurer, Mayer, Mendiverri, Montamat, Morris, Murphy E., Murphy M. W., Newell, Normand, O'Conner, Orr, Payne J., Paine J. T., Pintado, Poynot, Purcell J., Pursell S., Schroeder, Schnurr, Seymour, Shaw, Smith, Spellicy, Stocker, Stumpf, Stiner, Stauffer, Sullivan, Terry, Thorpe, Waters, Wenck, Wells, Wilson—85.

Absent—Messrs. Ariail, Bennie, Bonzano, Brott, Cazabat, Heard, Lobdell, Millspaugh, Montague, Ong, (excused,) Taliaferro and Thomas.

The minutes of yesterday were read and adopted.

The order of the day, being the report of the special committee on article 36 of the report of the Committee on General Provisions, was taken up.

Mr. Davies's amendment of yesterday was read. Mr. Howes moved to amend by striking out the word "two" and inserting "five," making the time of residence required five years.

Mr. Austin moved to lay the motion on the table, which being lost, the amendment was adopted.

The question then recurring upon the adoption of Mr. Davies's amendment, a division was demanded, resulting ayes 32, noes 18, consequently the amendment was adopted.

Mr. Orr moved a reconsideration of the vote just taken, when the yeas and nays being ordered thereon, resulted as follows:

YEAS—Messrs. Balch, Barrett, Buckley, Bell, Cook J. K., Cook T., Decker, Duane, Dufresne, Edwards, Ennis, Flagg, Fish, Flood, Foley, Fosdick, Geier, Gorlinski, Gaidry, Healy, Hart, Hills, Hire, Maas, Mann, Mayer, Maurer, Montamat, Morris, Murphy E., Newell, Normand, O'Conner, Orr, Payne J., Poynot, Pursell S., Schroeder, Seymour, Shaw, Smith, Spellicy, Stocker, Stauffer, Terry, Thorpe, Waters, Wenck—48.

NAYS—Messrs. Abell, Austin, Beauvais, Bailey, Baum, Bofill, Bromley, Burke, Collin, Campbell, Crozat, Cutler, Davies, Duke, Dupaty, Gastinel, Gruneberg, Harnan, Henderson, Howell, Howes, Kavanagh, Knobloch, Kugler, Mendiverri, Murphy M. W., Paine J. T., Purcell J., Schnurr, Stumpf, Stiner, Sullivan, Wells, Wilson—34.

The vote was therefore reconsidered.

Mr. Foley moved to amend by adding, after the word "resident," the words "and shall be a citizen of the United States."

Mr. Stauffer moved to lay Mr. Foley's motion on the table. Lost.

Mr. Wells moved to lay the whole subject, including all amendments, on the table. Lost.

Mr. Thorpe moved to amend by adding the words "and no one shall be appointed on the police who shall have been mustered into the rebel army."

On a motion to lay Mr. Thorpe's amendment on the table, the yeas and nays were ordered with the following result:

YEAS—Messrs. Abell, Austin, Balch, Barrett, Baum, Bell, Bofill, Buckley, Cook T., Cutler, Decker, Duane, Dufresne, Edwards, Fish, Foley, Fosdick, Fuller, Gastinel, Geier, Gruneberg, Healy, Hart, Henderson, Howell, Kavanagh, Knobloch, Kugler, Mann, Mayer, Mendiverri, Montamat, Murphy E., Murphy M. W., Normand, O'Conner, Orr, Poynot, Purcell J., Schroeder, Schnurr, Seymour, Shaw, Spellicy, Stocker, Stumpf, Stiner, Sullivan, Waters, Wilson—50.

NAYS—Messrs. Bailey, Beauvais, Bromley, Burke, Campbell, Collin, Cook J. K., Crozat, Davies, Duke, Dupaty, Ennis, Flagg, Flood, Gorlinski, Gaidry, Harnan, Hills, Howes, Maurer, Morris, Newell, Payne J., Paine J. T., Pursell S., Smith, Stauffer, Terry, Thorpe, Wenck, Wells—31.

The amendment was therefore laid on the table.

The several amendments proposed by Messrs. Davies, Foley and Cazabat, were all laid on the table.

Mr. Orr's amendment was taken up and read.

A motion to lay on the table having been made, the yeas and nays were taken thereon, as follows:

YEAS—Messrs. Abell, Austin, Balch, Bailey, Beauvais, Bofill, Bromley, Burke, Campbell, Crozat, Cutler, Duke, Edwards, Gruneberg, Gaidry, Henderson, Howell, Kavanagh, Mayer, Mendiverri, Murphy M. W., Newell, Shaw, Wenck, Wells, Wilson—26.

NAYS—Messrs. Barrett, Baum, Bell, Buckley, Collin, Cook J. K., Cook T., Davies, Decker, Duane, Dufresne, Dupaty, Ennis, Fish, Flagg, Flood, Foley, Fosdick, Fuller, Gastinel, Geier, Gorlinski, Healy, Harnan, Hart, Hills, Hire, Howes, Knobloch, Kugler, Maas, Mann, Maurer, Montamat, Morris, Murphy E., Normand, O'Conner, Orr, Payne J., Paine J. T., Poynot, Purcell J., Pursell S., Schroeder, Schnurr, Seymour, Smith, Spellicy, Stocker, Stumpf, Stiner, Stauffer, Sullivan, Terry, Waters—56.

Consequently the motion to lay on the table was lost.

The question was then put upon the adoption of Mr. Orr's amendment, and the yeas and nays being ordered, resulted as follows:

YEAS — Messrs. Abell, Balch, Barrett, Baum, Bell, Bromley, Buckley, Collin, Cook J. K., Cook T., Davies, Decker, Duane, Dufresne, Duke, Dupaty, Ennis, Fish, Flagg, Flood, Foley, Fosdick, Fuller, Gastinel, Geier, Gorlinski, Gaidry, Healy, Harnan, Hart, Henderson, Hills, Hire, Howes, Knobloch, Kugler, Maas, Mann, Maurer, Montamat, Morris, Murphy E., Murphy M. W., Normand, O'Conner, Orr, Payne J., Poynot, Purcell J., Pursell S., Schroeder, Schnurr, Seymour, Smith, Spellicy, Stocker, Stumpf, Stiner, Stauffer, Sullivan, Terry, Waters—62.

NAYS—Messrs. Austin, Bailey, Beauvais, Bofill, Burke, Campbell, Crozat, Cutler, Edwards, Gruneberg, Howell, Kavanagh, Mayer, Mendiverri, Newell, Paine J. T., Shaw, Wenck, Wells, Wilson—20.

Consequently the amendment was adopted.

On the adoption of the report of the special committee as amended, the yeas and nays were ordered, resulting as follows:

YEAS—Messrs. Abell, Balch, Barrett, Bell, Baum, Buckley, Cook J. K., Cook T., Crozat, Decker, Duane, Dufresne, Fish, Flood, Foley, Fuller, Gastinel, Geier, Gorlinski, Healy, Harnan, Hart, Henderson, Hills, Hire, Howes, Kavanagh, Kugler, Maurer, Maas, Mendiverri, Montamat, Murphy E., Murphy M. W., Normand, O'Conner, Orr, Poynot, Purcell J., Schroeder, Schnurr, Smith, Spellicy, Stocker, Stumpf, Stiner, Sullivan, Terry, Waters—50.

NAYS—Messrs. Bailey, Beauvais, Burke, Campbell, Collin, Cutler, Davies, Duke, Dupaty, Ennis, Flagg, Fosdick, Gruneberg, Gaidry, Howell, Knobloch, Mann, Mayer, Morris, Newell, Payne J., Paine J. T., Pursell S., Seymour, Shaw, Stauffer, Wenck, Wells, Wilson—31.

The report was therefore adopted as amended.

Mr. Hills moved to suspend the rules to take up the report of the Committee on General Provisions for its third reading, which motion being lost, the report was ordered to be engrossed for its third reading on to-morrow.

The report of the Committee on Internal Improvements, as also the minority report presented by Mr. Campbell, being next in order, were taken up and read.

Mr. Terry offered a substitute for the whole.

Mr. Smith moved to amend so as to make the State engineer appointive by the governor for the first three years, and afterwards to be elected by the people; and also to strike out the clause relative to his salary, so as to leave the fixing of the same to the Legislature.

Mr. ——— called for a division of the question on the amendments, which was ordered, and, on motion of Mr. Wilson, the first amendment was laid on the table.

Pending discussion on the second division of the amendment, the door-keeper announced Major Genls. Canby and Sickles, who were conducted to the platform by Mr. Thorpe, where they were duly received and welcomed by the Convention.

After a recess of ten minutes, a call of the House was had, and there being no quorum, the Convention adjourned.

Approved.

JOHN E. NEELIS,
Secretary.

THURSDAY, June 23, 1864.

The Convention met pursuant to adjournment.

Present—the Hon. E. H. Durell, president, in the chair, and the following members:

Messrs. Abell, Austin, Balch, Bailey, Barrett, Baum, Beauvais, Bell, Bofill, Bromley, Buckley, Burke, Collin, Cook J. K., Cook T., Crozat, Cutler, Davies, Decker, Duane, Dufresne, Duke, Dupaty, Edwards, Ennis, Fish, Flagg, Flood, Foley, Fosdick, Gastinel, Geier, Gorlinski, Gruneberg, Gaidry, Healy, Harnan, Hart, Henderson, Hills, Hire, Howell, Howes, Kavanagh, Knobloch, Kugler, Maas, Mann, Maurer, Mayer, Mendiverri, Montamat, Morris, Murphy E., Murphy M. W., Newell, Normand, O'Conner, Orr, Payne J., Paine J. T., Pintado, Poynot, Purcell J., Pursell S., Schroeder, Schnurr, Seymour, Shaw, Smith, Spellicy, Stocker, Stumpf, Stiner, Stauffer, Sullivan, Terry, Thorpe, Waters, Wenck, Wells, Wilson—83.

Absent—Messrs. Ariail, Bennie, Bonzano, Brott, Campbell, (excused,) Cazabat, Fuller, Heard, Lobdell, Millspaugh, Montague, Ong, (excused,) Taliaferro and Thomas.

On motion of Mr. Abell, Mr. Campbell was excused for absence.

The minutes of yesterday were read and adopted.

Mr. S. Pursell moved a reconsideration of the vote of yesterday, on the adoption of the report of the Committee on General Pro-

visions, as amended on its second reading.
Mr. Orr moved to lay the motion on the table, which being lost, the motion to reconsider was put and carried, on a rising vote of ayes 54, nays none.

Mr. Pursell then offered the following additional article:

Art. —. No profession, occupation, business or calling, requiring a license from any authority within this State, shall be carried on, exercised or followed by any other than citizens of the United States, or those having made legal declaration of becoming citizens.

Mr. Harnan moved to lay the article on the table, which being lost, a lengthy discussion ensued, after which the article was rejected by the following vote, taken on a motion to adopt:

YEAS—Messrs. Bofill, Bromley, Burke, Cook J. K., Decker, Ennis, Flagg, Flood, Geier, Gaidry, Kugler, Maas, O'Conner, Paine J. T., Poynot, Pursell S., Schroeder, Smith—18.

NAYS—Messrs. Austin, Balch, Bailey, Barrett, Baum, Beauvais, Bell Buckley, Collin, Cook T., Crozat, Cutler, Davies, Duane, Dufresne, Duke, Dupaty, Edwards, Fish, Foley, Fosdick, Gastinel, Gorlinski, Gruneberg, Healy, Harnan, Hart, Henderson, Hills, Hire, Howell, Howes, Kavanagh, Knobloch, Mann, Maurer, Mayer, Mendiverri, Montamat, Morris, Murphy E., Murphy M. W., Newell, Normand, Orr, Payne J., Pintado, Purcell J., Schnurr, Seymour, Shaw, Spellicy, Stocker, Stumpf, Stinor, Stauffer, Sullivan, Terry, Thorpe, Wenck, Wells, Wilson—62.

Mr. Pursell then offered the following as an additional article:

Art. —. The General Assembly shall provide by law for the establishment of a poor-house in each parish of the State, for the care of the destitute within their respective limits, and to be conducted as shall be provided by law.

On motion of Mr. Harnan, it was laid on the table.

Mr. Gorlinski offered the following additional article:

Art. —. The Legislature shall have power to pass laws extending the right of suffrage to such persons, citizens of the United States, as by military service, by taxation to support the government, or by intellectual fitness, may be deemed entitled thereto.

Mr. Sullivan moved to lay it on the table. Lost.

On the adoption of the article, the yeas and nays were demanded, with the following result:

YEAS—Messrs. Austin, Barrett, Bell, Bromley, Collin, Cook T., Crozat, Cutler, Davies, Duane, Dupaty, Ennis, Fish, Flagg, Flood, Foley, Fosdick, Geier, Gorlinski, Healy, Harnan, Henderson, Hills, Hire, Howell, Howes, Kavanagh, Kugler, Mann, Murphy E., Newell, Normand, O'Connor, Paine J. T., Pintado, Purcell J., Schroeder, Seymour, Shaw, Smith, Spellicy, Stumpf, Stiner, Stauffer, Terry, Thorpe, Wenck, Wells—48.

NAYS—Messrs. Balch, Bailey, Baum, Beauvais, Bofill, Buckley, Burke, Cook J. K., Decker, Dufresne, Duke, Edwards, Gastinel, Gruneberg, Gaidry, Hart, Knobloch, Maas, Maurer, Mayer, Mendiverri, Montamat, Morris, Murphy M. W., Orr, Payne J., Poynot, Pursell S , Schnurr, Stocker, Sullivan, Wilson—32.

The additional article was therefore adopted.

Mr. Terry offered the following additional article:

Nine hours shall constitute a day's labor for all mechanics, artizans and laborers in the public works of the State.

A motion to lay on the table was lost on a rising vote—ayes 33, nays 37.

Mr. Thorpe moved to amend by striking out "nine," and inserting "seven" instead. Lost.

On the question of the adoption of Mr. Terry's additional article, the yeas and nays were ordered, with the following result:

YEAS—Messrs. Bailey, Barrett, Baum, Bell, Buckley, Burke, Collin, Cook J. K., Cook T., Crozat, Davies, Duane, Dufresne, Duke, Dupaty, Ennis, Fish, Flood, Foley, Fosdick, Geier, Gorlinski, Gaidry, Harnan, Healy, Henderson, Hills, Hire, Howes, Knobloch, Maas, Maurer, Montamat, Morris, Murphy E., Murphy M. W., Newell, Normand, O'Conner, Orr, Payne J., Pintado, Poynot, Purcell J., Pursell S., Schroeder, Seymour, Shaw, Smith, Stocker, Stumpf, Stauffer, Stiner, Sullivan, Terry, Thorpe—56.

NAYS—Messrs. Abell, Austin, Balch, Beauvais, Bofill, Bromley, Cutler, Decker, Edwards, Flagg, Gastinel, Gruneberg, Hart, Howell, Kavanagh, Kugler, Mann, Mayer, Mendiverri, Paine J. T., Schnurr, Spellicy, Wenck, Wells, Wilson—25.

The article was therefore adopted.

Mr. Foley offered the following as an additional article:

The Legislature shall pass no laws requiring property qualification for office.

On motion of Mr. Healy, the article was adopted.

AND AMENDMENT OF THE CONSTITUTION OF LOUISIANA. 131

Mr. Bromley offered the following as an additional article:

No member of this Convention shall be eligible to any office under the municipal government of New Orleans during a term of three years from the adoption of the free State constitution.

Laid on the table.

The report of the Committee on General Provisions, as amended, was then adopted as a whole, on a rising vote of ayes 47, noes 24.

Mr. Terry moved to suspend the rules to take up the report on its third reading. Lost.

The Convention then resumed its action on Mr. Terry's substitute for the report of the Committee on Internal Improvements, together with the amendments offered thereto.

Mr. Wilson withdrew his amendment relative to term of office.

Mr. Stocker moved to amend the first article of Mr. Terry's substitute, by striking out all after the word "per annum" down to the word "State."

Mr. Healy moved to lay the amendment on the table, which being lost, the amendment was adopted. A call of the House was demanded, when seventy-six members answered to their names.

Mr. Gastinel moved to strike out the words "six thousand" and substitute "four thousand," making the salary of the chief engineer four thousand dollars.

A motion to lay on the table being lost, the amendment was adopted, on a rising vote of yeas 32, nays 23.

Mr. Stocker offered an amendment leaving the appointment and salary of the chief engineer's assistants to be regulated and provided for by the Legislature. Adopted.

The second article of Mr. Terry's substitute was then taken up.

Mr. Sullivan offered the following amendment:

And that the municipal corporation of the city of New Orleans shall be prohibited from adjudicating, selling by sealed proposals, or in any manner contracting for the working or completing of any public works under their supervision and control. Adopted.

Article 3 was read and adopted.

Article 4 was then taken up, and, with the consent of Mr. Terry, was amended by striking out the word "two-thirds" and substituting the word "majority." The article as amended was then adopted.

A motion to take up the substitute, as amended, for its third reading being lost, the Convention adjourned.

Adopted.

JOHN E. NEELIS,
Secretary.

FRIDAY, June 24, 1864.

The Convention met, pursuant to adjournment. Present, the Hon. E. H. Durell, president, and the following members:

Messrs. Abell, Austin, Balch, Bailey, Barrett, Baum, Beauvais, Bell, Bofill, Bromley, Buckley, Burke, Campbell, Collin, Cazabat, Cook J. K., Cook T., Crozat, Cutler, Davies, Decker, Duane, Dufresne, Duke, Dupaty, Edwards, Ennis, Fish, Flagg, Flood, Foley, Fosdick, Fuller, Gastinel, Geier, Gorlinski, Gruneberg, Gaidry, Healy, Harnan, Hart, Henderson, Hills, Hire, Howell, Howes, Kavanagh, Knobloch, Kugler, Maas, Mann, Maurer, Mayer, Mendiverri, Montamat, Murphy M. W., Newell, Normand, O'Conner, Orr, Payne J., Paine J. T., Pintado, Poynot, Purcell J., Pursell S., Schroeder, Schnurr, Seymour, Shaw, Smith, Spellicy, Stocker, Stumpf, Stiner, Stauffer, Sullivan, Terry, Thorpe, Waters, Wenck, Wells, Wilson—85.

The minutes of yesterday's proceedings were read and adopted.

Mr. Terry asked a suspension of the rules for the purpose of introducing a resolution relative to the celebration of the 4th of July, prox., but upon the question being put the suspension was refused.

Mr. Bell moved to reconsider the vote by which article 1 of the report of the Committee on Internal Improvements was adopted, which motion was subsequently withdrawn.

Mr. Gruneberg presented his report on behalf of the Committee on Schedule, which was partially read, but being signed by but two members of the committee, the same was declared by the president to be no report.

The substitute for the report of the Committee on Internal Improvements was then taken up for its third reading.

Mr. Gorlinski moved to strike out the

word "four" in the twelfth line and insert "five," so as to make the salary of the chief engineer five thousand dollars; and also to strike out all of the second article after the word "State" in the seventh line.

Mr. Gorlinski's rider was rejected, and the report then passed its third reading and was adopted.

The Convention then took a recess of fifteen minutes, at the expiration of which time the roll was called and seventy-seven answered to their names.

The report of the Committee on General Provisions was then taken up on its third reading, and being read the following riders were offered:

Mr. Davies moved to strike out all of article 36, after line 28. Lost.

Mr. S. Pursell offered to strike out all of article 3, after the word "blood," in the second line. Lost.

Mr. Foley moved to amend article 4, by adding the words, "or who have registered themselves enemies of the United States." Lost, on a division, ayes 12, noes 57.

Mr. Cazabat moved to insert the words, "or retroactive," after the words "*ex post facto*," in article 20, and to strike out all after the word "made," in the fourth line of the same article. Adopted.

Mr. Cazabat also offered the following rider, by way of amendment to article 5, viz:

But capital punishment is forever abolished and prohibited in this State.

Mr. Henderson moved to amend Mr. Cazabat's rider, by adding the words, "unless the jury shall determine otherwise."

Mr. Cazabat accepted this amendment, and the rider, as amended, was lost, on a rising vote of ayes 20, noes 50.

Mr. S. Pursell offered the following amendment to article 44:

Provided the conditions herein contained shall only apply to white persons.

A call of the House was ordered, and seventy-nine members found to be present. After a short discussion, the Convention adjourned.

Approved.

JOHN E. NEELIS,
Secretary.

SATURDAY, June 25, 1864.

The Convention met pursuant to adjournment. The roll was called and the following members answered to their names:

Messrs. Abell, Austin, Balch, Bailey, Barrett, Beauvais, Bell, Bofill, Bromley, Buckley, Burke, Campbell, Cazabat, Collin, Cook J. K., Cook T., Crozat, Cutler, Davies, Decker, Duane. Dufresne, Duke, Dupaty, Edwards, Ennis, Fish. Flagg, Flood, Foley, Fosdick, Fuller, Gastinel, Geier, Gorlinski, Gruneberg, Gaidry, Healy, Harnan, Hart, Henderson, Hills, Hire, Howell, Howes, Kavanagh, Knobloch, Kugler, Maas, Mann, Maurer, Mayer, Mendiverri, Montamat, Morris, Murphy E., Murphy M. W., Newell, Normand, O'Conner, Orr, Payne J., Pintado, Poynot, Purcell J., Pursell S., Shaw, Schroeder, Schnurr, Seymour, Spellicy, Smith, Stocker, Stumpf, Stiner, Sullivan, Terry, Thorpe, Waters, Wenck, Wells, Wilson—83.

On motion, Mr. Stauffer was excused for non-attendance.

The minutes of yesterday were read and adopted.

Mr. Sullivan offered the following:

Resolved, That the sum of twenty-four thousand two hundred and fifty dollars be, and is hereby, appropriated out of the State treasury, to be distributed to the following charitable institutions of the city and State, as follows:

For the Orphans' Home, New Orleans	$1,500
For the St. Mary's Catholic Asylum	4,000
For the Female Asylum, Camp street	4,000
For the House of the Good Shepherd	500
For the Jewish Widows' and Orphans' Home	500
For the St. Joseph Catholic Orphan Asylum	1,500
For the Firemen's Charitable Association, benefit of its widows and orphans	3,000
For the Elizabeth House of Industry	1,000
For the Society for the Relief of Orphan Boys, Fourth District	1,000
For the Institution for Indigent Colored Boys, Third District	1,000
For the Ladies of Providence, Third District	750
For the St. Ann's Asylum for Destitute Widows and Children	1,500
For the Childrens' Home of the Protestant Episcopal Church	500
For the Catholic Institute for Destitute Orphans	750
For the Catholic Benevolent Association of Baton Rouge	250

For the Female Orphan Asylum, Baton Rouge	500
For the Milne Asylum, New Orleans	500
For the St. Vincent's Orphan Asylum	500
For the Moreau Street Orphan Asylum	500
For the St. Vincent Orphan Asylum, Donaldsonville	500
	$24,250

On a motion to lay on the table, the yeas and nays were ordered, with the following result:

YEAS—Messrs. Abell, Balch, Campbell, Collin, Cutler, Davies, Decker, Dufresne, Dupaty, Edwards, Ennis, Flagg, Gruneberg, Gaidry, Howell, Kugler, Mann, Maurer, Mendiverri, Newell, Normand, Pintado, Seymour, Wenck, Wells—25.

NAYS—Messrs. Austin, Bailey, Barrett, Beauvais, Bell, Bofill, Bromley, Buckley, Burke, Cazabat, Cook J. K., Cook T., Crozat, Duane, Duke, Fish, Flood, Foley, Fosdick, Fuller, Gastinel, Geier, Gorlinski, Hart, Henderson, Hills, Hire, Howes, Knobloch, Maas, Mayer, Montamat, Morris, Murphy E., Murphy M. W., O'Conner, Payne J., Poynot, Purcell J., Pursell S., Schroeder, Schnurr, Shaw, Smith, Spellicy, Stocker, Stumpf, Stiner, Sullivan, Terry, Thorpe, Waters, Wilson—53.

Mr. Foley moved to strike out the appropriation for the Firemen's Charitable Association.

On a motion to lay on the table the yeas and nays were taken as follows:

YEAS—Messrs. Abell, 'Barrett, Beauvais, Bell, Bofill, Buckley, Burke, Collin, Cook J. K., Cook T., Crozat, Cutler, Decker, Duane, Dufresne, Dupaty, Fish, Fuller, Gastinel, Geier, Gruneberg, Gaidry, Henderson, Hire, Howes, Kugler, Maas, Maurer, Mayer, Mendiverri, Montamat. O'Conner, Payne P., Pintado, Poynot, Purcell J., Pursell S., Schroeder, Schnurr, Seymour, Shaw, Spellicy, Stocker, Stumpf, Stiner, Sullivan, Terry, Waters, Wenck, Wilson—50.

NAYS — Messrs. Austin, Balch, Bailey, Bromley, Campbell, Cazabat, Davies, Duke, Edwards, Ennis, Flagg, Flood, Foley, Fosdick, Gorlinski, Harnan, Hart, Hills, Howell, Knobloch, Mann, Morris, Murphy E., Murphy M. W., Newell, Normand, Smith, Thorpe, Wells—29.

Consequently, Mr. Foley's motion was laid on the table.

Mr. Gorlinski offered the following substitute:

Resolved, That the sum of twenty-five thousand dollars be and is hereby appropriated out of the general fund for different charitable institutions and other purposes, to be expended under direction of a board of almoners, consisting of five citizens, to be appointed by the governor.

Laid on the table.

Mr. Davies moved to amend by appropriating $25,000 for the relief of all widows and orphans in this city, whose husbands and fathers have lost their lives in fighting to uphold the government of the United States.

Laid on the table.

Mr. Beauvais moved to amend by including the convent of the "Sacred Heart," in the Parish of St. James, for the sum of five hundred dollars, which amendment was accepted by Mr. Sullivan.

Mr. S. Pursell moved to amend by including the Female Asylum in the parish of Jefferson, for one thousand dollars.

Accepted.

Mr. Burke moved to amend by including the widows and orphans in the parish of St. John the Baptist, who are in a destitute condition, for the sum of one thousand dollars, which amendment was accepted.

Mr. Cazabat offered to amend as follows:

Provided, That all of said appropriations for charitable purposes be paid from the last amount of twenty thousand dollars already appropriated for the per diem pay of the members of this Convention.

And, provided also, That the following be included, to-wit:

For the relief of destitute Union refugees from Louisiana	$3,000
Orphans' Asylum in Jefferson parish	2,000
Pioneers' Fire Co. No. 1, city of Jefferson	1,000
St. Vincent's Asylum, Donaldsonville	1,000
Orphans and widows of Union soldiers from Louisiana, who lost their lives in the United States service	1,000

Which amendment was laid on the table.

On the adoption of Mr. Sullivan's resolution as amended, the yeas and nays were ordered, with the following result:

YEAS—Messrs. Austin, Barrett, Beauvais, Bell, Bofill, Buckley, Burke, Cook T., Crozat, Duane, Fish, Flood, Fuller, Gastinel, Geier, Gorlinski, Harnan, Hart, Henderson, Hills, Hire, Howes, Murphy E., Murphy M. W., O'Conner, Orr, Purcell J., Pursell S., Schroeder, Shaw, Stocker, Stiner, Sullivan, Terry, Waters, Wilson—36.

NAYS — Messrs. Abell, Balch, Bailey,

Bromley, Campbell, Collin, Cazabat, Cook J. K., Cutler, Davies, Decker, Dufresne, Duke, Dupaty, Edwards, Ennis, Flagg, Foley, Fosdick, Gruneberg, Gaidry, Howell, Knobloch, Kugler, Maas, Mann, Maurer, Mayer, Mendiverri, Montamat, Morris, Newell, Normand, Payne J., Pintado, Poynot, Schnurr, Seymour, Smith, Spellicy, Stumpf, Thorpe, Wenck, Wells—44.

Consequently the resolution was lost.

Mr. Terry offered the following:

Resolved, That the sum of one thousand dollars be and is hereby appropriated out of the State funds, not otherwise appropriated, for the celebration of the 4th of July, and that a committee of five be appointed to consult with the city authorities regarding its proper expenditure.

Laid on the table.

Mr. Abell offered the following:

Resolved, That the sum of one hundred dollars be allowed to each of the reverend clergymen who have officiated in this Convention.

Laid on the table.

Mr. Austin, chairman of the special committee on the auditor's report, submitted the following report:

To the president and members of the State Constitutional Convention of Louisiana:

Your committee to whom was referred the report of the Auditor of Public Accounts, beg leave to make the following report, to-wit:

Under all the surrounding circumstances, we find no serious objection to the manner and form in which the State auditor has seen proper to present his report. As to the Confederate notes, we look upon them as trash, and lost to the State.

Your committee are of opinion that we should not interfere with the military powers, and therefore, are unanimous in saying that, inasmuch, as the late auditor of public accounts, the Hon. S. H. Torrey, has issued warrants only by authority of the military governor, Gen. Shepley, he is not only excusable, but justifiable. As to the Hon. R. K. Howell and the Hon. A. M. Buchanan, your committee are of opinion that they have drawn their salary according to the constitution and the laws of the State of Louisiana, and that the opinion of our auditor, the Hon. A. P. Dostie, "That rebellion had terminated the existence of the Supreme Court," is unfounded and contrary to the prevailing opinion of all loyal citizens of Louisiana, "*that the State has never been out of the Union.*"

As to the Hon. Charles A. Peabody, your committee are of opinion that he never was Chief Justice of the State of Louisiana, for the irresistible reasons that neither the military authorities, nor the civil powers in this State, ever created a supreme court since the arrival of the honorable gentleman in this State, nor was he eligible to a seat on the bench of the one created previous to his arrival, because he was not, and is not, a citizen of the State of Louisiana. And, further, because he was, and is a judge created by the president of the United States, to preside over a court created by the same authority, "the United States Provisional court for the State of Louisiana." That as judge of said court, he has been receiving a salary from the United States government; and therefore, he has received the sum of $3541 66 from the treasury of the State of Louisiana, as salary, under the pretence of being chief justice of the State, without any authority, and in open violation of the constitution and laws of the State of Louisiana.

Under these circumstances, your committee recommend that in consequence of these illegal acts of the said Charles A. Peabody, in obtaining said sum from the State as aforesaid, that the attorney general of the State be requested to institute such legal proceedings as may be necessary to recover said sum, with interest, damages and costs. Your committee further recommend, that inasmuch as the necessity for said U. S. Provisional Court has long since ceased to exist, and that the same is but a stumbling block in the way of the administration of justice, and to the loyalty of the good people of Louisiana, that the commanding general of this department, Maj. Gen. N. P. Banks, and his excellency, M. Hahn, governor of the State of Louisiana, be requested to petition the president of the United States to withdraw the commission from, and recall the said Charles A. Peabody, and thereby put an end to the further existence of said court.

As to Mr. Serpas, sheriff of the parish of St. Bernard, your committee are of opinion that as the Confederate notes in his possession were received for taxes collected by him during Confederate rule, he should be exonerated from all blame and released from all responsibility on handing over the same to the treasurer of the State.

O. W. AUSTIN, Chairman.
W. R. FISH,
R. BEAUVAIS,
R. KING CUTLER.

On motion of Mr. Terry, the report was ordered to be printed and made the order of the day for Saturday next.

Mr. Schroeder submitted the following memorial and resolution:

To the Constitutional Convention of Louisiana:

The memorial of the undersigned respect-

AND AMENDMENT OF THE CONSTITUTION OF LOUISIANA. 135

fully begs leave to call your honorable body's attention to the defects in the law relative to births and deaths, and the necessity of amending the same, as the law as it now stands is defective. By the acts of 1855, page 41, relative to births and deaths, it will be seen that in case of a birth or death, the declaration of the party declaring the same, in the parish of Orleans, (persons residing in the country parishes are not required to record either,) is not supported by an affidavit, thus leaving the door open to fraud; as, for example: suppose a man is married to a woman who possesses in her own right property, both real and personal, and that their marriage is barren of issue; and suppose the wife has relations in the ascending or collateral line, who are non-residents of the State, and who are ignorant of her circumstances, and, may be, of her existence, and, for argument's sake, say the latter; and suppose, too, this man, unknown to his wife, to go, under the provision of the law referred to, and declare before the recorder that a child had been born to him by his wife; and suppose his wife to die intestate, and in total ignorance of such a declaration, what would be the consequence? The husband would, with the assistance and connivance of others, proceed in his right as the natural tutor of his minor (fictitious) child, to get the administration and possession of his deceased wife's estate, and by fictitious claims swallow up the movable property, together, probably, that of the realty, thus defrauding the legal heirs. This, however, is but one way of committing a fraud to the prejudice of the wife's legal heir, for the wife herself could connive at the proceedings of her husband, for the purpose of cutting off her ascending heirs if she so desired. What may be said of births may be said of deaths, for instance: a person of the next of kin to an heir of an estate in Europe, residing in this country, to whom such inheritance is unknown, may declare here, before the recorder of births and deaths, the death of the heir, and get a certificate from him to that effect, and have the same certified to by the proper consul, go to Europe, and by the production of such proof obtain, as next of kin, the property bequeathed to or inherited by the heir represented as dead.

These are a few of the defects of the law of 1855. There are others: It will be seen that in the parish of Orleans only is it compulsory for persons to record births and deaths. It is not so in the country. Why is this? If fraud can be practiced in this parish, what a greater latitude there is for its practice in the country parishes.

We, your memorialists, therefore, pray that your honorable body will give this matter your consideration, and devise such means as will prevent the abuses to which, by the villainy of man, the law of 1855 is subject. CHARLES F. WARNEY,
JOHN SMITH,
and others.

Resolved, That the Legislature shall, at its first session after the adoption of this constitution, provide in each parish an officer for the registration of births, marriages and deaths throughout the State, whose duty shall be to keep for the purpose suitable books, and cause to be entered therein a registry of each birth, marriage and death, giving the name of each parent and the sex of every child born within their parish as above provided; and they shall further enact a law providing for punishment, by suitable fine, all parents of children, born as above stated, who do not report within a reasonable time, to the register above named, the birth and sex of each child so borne; and, also, it shall be the duty of each register above named to keep a registry of the death and marriage of all persons, giving their sex, age and name, with sufficient proof of the same.

The memorial was accepted.

Mr. Hills offered the following:

Resolved, That a committee of five be appointed to report on Saturday next what appropriations are necessary for the various charitable institutions of this State.

Adopted.

The president appointed on the committee raised by said resolution, Messrs. Hills, Howell, Smith, Stocker and Sullivan.

Mr. Wells offered the following:

Whereas, There are many truly loyal ladies teaching the youth of our country and filling the various positions in our public schools with honor to themselves and the community generally, and who are dependent upon their daily labor for the support of themselves and their families:

Therefore be it resolved, That the proper authorities be notified to raise their salaries twenty-five per cent. on the original sum.

On a motion to lay on the table the yeas and nays were demanded with the following result:

YEAS — Messrs. Bell, Duke, Edwards, Hills, Howell, Knobloch, Mayer, Murphy M. W., Normand, Payne J., Schnurr, Smith, Sullivan, Wenck—14.

NAYS—Abell, Austin, Barrett, Beauvais, Bofill, Bromley, Buckley, Burke, Campbell, Colin, Cazabat, Cook J. K., Cook T., Crozat, Cutler, Davies, Duane, Dufresne, Dupaty, Ennis, Fish, Flagg, Flood, Foley, Fosdick, Fuller, Gastinel, Geier, Gorlinski, Gruneberg, Gaidry, Harnan, Hart, Henderson, Hire, Howes, Maas, Mann, Maurer, Mendiverri, Montamat, Morris, Murphy E., Newell, O'Conner, Orr, Pintado, Poynot, Purcell J., Pursell S., Schroeder, Seymour, Shaw, Spellicy, Stocker, Stumpf, Stiner, Terry, Wells, Wilson—60.

The motion to lay on the table was therefore lost.

Mr. Howes moved to amend by adding the words "if compatible with the public interest." Lost.

Mr. Wells's resolution was then adopted.

Mr. Beauvais offered the following :

Resolved, That this Convention will adjourn, *sine die*, on the 2d day of July, prox.

Laid on the table.

Mr. Fosdick's resolution, relative to election of officers of the city government of New Orleans, together with Mr. Davies's amendment thereto, were taken up.

On motion of Mr. Foley, the amendment was laid on the table.

Mr. Bofill moved to lay the original resolution on the table. Lost.

Mr. Stocker moved to postpone the resolution indefinitely, but subsequently withdrew his motion, after a lengthy discussion.

Mr. Cutler offered the following :

Resolved, That the subject of calling a city election be referred to a committee of five, to be appointed by the chair, with instructions to examine whether any practical difficulties exist in the way of, or against putting in force the provisions of the charter of the city, and what provisions, if any, may be required to be passed on the subject by this Convention.

On the question on the adoption of the resolution, the yeas and nays were ordered, and the vote resulted as follows :

YEAS—Messrs. Austin, Barrett, Bell, Bofill, Bromley, Burke, Campbell, Collin, Cazabat, Crozat, Cutler, Davies, Duane, Dupaty, Edwards, Ennis, Flagg, Flood, Foley, Fuller, Geier, Gruneberg, Gaidry, Healy, Harnan, Hart, Henderson, Hire, Howes, Mann, Mayer, Mendiverri, Montamat, Morris, Murphy M. W., Newell, Normand, Payne J., Pintado, Purcell J., Schroeder, Schnurr, Seymour, Shaw, Smith, Spellicy, Stocker, Stumpf, Stiner, Sullivan, Terry, Wenck, Wilson—53.

NAYS—Messrs. Abell, Balch, Bailey, Buckley, Cook J. K., Cook T., Dufresne, Duke, Fish, Fosdick, Gastinel, Gorlinski, Hills, Knobloch, O'Conner, Orr, Poynot, Pursell S., Thorpe, Waters, Wells, Durell—22.

Mr. Howell being in the chair, the president voted.

The resolution was therefore adopted.
The Convention then adjourned.
Approved.

JOHN E. NEELIS,
Secretary.

MONDAY, June 27, 1864.

The Convention met pursuant to adjournment. Present, the Hon. E. H. Durell, president, and the following members :

Messrs. Abell, Austin, Balch, Bailey, Barrett, Baum, Beauvais, Bell, Bofill, Bromley, Buckley, Burke, Campbell, Collin, Cazabat, Cook J. K., Cook T., Crozat, Cutler, Davies, Duane, Dufresne, Duke, Dupaty, Edwards, Fish, Flagg, Flood, Foley, Fosdick, Fuller, Gastinel, Gaidry, Geier, Gorlinski, Gruneberg, Healy, Harnan, Hart, Henderson, Hills, Hire, Howell, Hawes, Maas, Mann, Maurer, Mayer, Mendiverri, Montamat, Morris, Murphy E., Murphy M. W., Newell, Normand, O'Conner, Ong, Orr, Payne J., Paine J. T., Pintado, Poynot, Purcell J., Schroeder, Schnurr, Seymour, Shaw, Smith, Spellicy, Stocker, Stumpf, Stiner, Sullivan, Taliaferro, Terry, Thorpe, Waters, Wells, Wilson---80.

On motion, the following gentlemen were excused for non-attendance, viz : Messrs. Knobloch, Baum, Kugler, Ennis, S. Pursell and Orr.

The minutes of Saturday's proceedings were read and adopted.

The president appointed on the committee raised by Mr. Cutler's resolution of Saturday last, relative to the election of officers of the city government, Messrs. Cutler, Fosdick, Hills, Orr and Henderson.

The third reading of the report of the Committee on General Provisions being the order of the day, was next taken up.

Mr. Hills moved the previous question, which being carried, the question was put and the report adopted on its third reading.

The report of the Committee on Public Education being next in order, was taken up on its second reading and read section by section, together with the substitutes and amendments offered thereto.

Mr. S. Pursell's substitute was laid on the table.

Mr. Bonzano's amendment to article 3, and his substitutes for articles 5 and 7, were severally taken up and laid on the table.

On the suggestion of Mr. Hills, the report was then taken up and considered section by section, and the several substitutes and amendments, taken up in their regular order, as the sections to which they applied came up.

Article 1 was then taken up and read.

Mr. Seymour moved to strike out of the first line the word "two" and insert "four," which being accepted, the article was adopted as amended.

Art. 2 was read, as also Mr. Sullivan's substitute therefor.

On a motion to lay Mr. Sullivan's substitute on the table, the yeas and nays were taken, as follows :

YEAS—Messrs. Abell, Austin, Bell, Bromley, Burke, Collin, Cazabat, Cook J. K., Cook T., Davies, Duane, Dupaty, Fish, Flagg, Flood, Foley, Fosdick, Gorlinski, Gaidry, Healy, Henderson, Hills, Hire, Howell, Mann, Maurer, Murphy E., Newell, Normand, O'Conner, Paine J. T., Pintado, Poynot, Purcell J., Schnurr, Seymour, Shaw, Smith, Spellicy, Stumpf, Stiner, Taliaferro, Wells, Wilson—44.

NAYS—Messrs. Balch, Bailey, Barrett, Baum, Beauvais, Bofill, Buckley, Campbell, Crozat, Cutler, Dufresne, Duke, Edwards, Fuller, Gastinel, Geier, Gruneberg, Hart, Howes, Maas, Mayer, Mendiverri, Montamat, Morris, Murphy M. W., Ong, Orr, Payne J., Stocker, Sullivan, Terry, Thorpe, Waters—33.

The substitute was therefore laid on the table.

The question then recurred upon the adoption of article 2, when the yeas and nays being demanded, the following vote was taken :

YEAS — Messrs. Austin, Barrett, Bell, Bromley, Burke, Collin, Cazabat, Cook T., Davies, Duane, Dupaty, Fish, Flagg, Flood, Foley, Fosdick, Gorlinski, Gaidry, Healy, Harnan, Henderson, Hills, Hire, Howell, Howes, Mann, Maurer, Murphy E., Murphy M. W., Newell, Normand, O'Conner, Ong, Payne J., Paine J. T., Pintado, Poynot, Purcell J., Seymour, Shaw, Smith, Spellicy, Stumpf, Stiner, Taliaferro, Terry, Thorpe, Wells, Wilson—49.

NAYS — Messrs. Abell, Balch, Bailey, Baum, Beauvais, Bofill, Buckley, Campbell, Cook J. K., Crozat, Cutler, Dufresne, Duke, Edwards, Fuller, Gastinel, Geier, Gruneberg, Hart, Maas, Mayer, Mendiverri, Montamat, Morris, Orr, Schnurr, Stocker, Sullivan, Waters—29.

Article 2 was therefore adopted.

Article 3 was next taken up and read.

Mr. Montamat moved to lay the article on the table, upon which the yeas and nays were demanded, and the following vote taken :

YEAS—Messrs. Baum, Beauvais, Bofill, Bromley, Cazabat, Cutler, Davies, Duke, Dupaty, Edwards, Fish, Gaidry, Hire, Howell, Mann, Mayer, Montamat, Newell, Normand, Ong, Payne J., Paine J. T., Pintado, Shaw, Smith, Stumpf, Taliaferro—27.

NAYS—Messrs. Abell, Austin, Balch, Bailey, Barrett, Bell, Buckley, Burke, Campbell, Collin, Cook J. K., Cook T., Crozat, Duane, Dufresne, Flagg, Flood, Foley, Fosdick, Fuller, Gastinel, Geier, Gorlinski, Gruneberg, Healy, Harnan, Hart, Henderson, Hills, Howes, Maas, Maurer, Mendiverri, Morris, Murphy E., Murphy M. W., O'Conner, Orr, Poynot, Purcell J., Schnurr, Seymour, Spellicy, Stocker, Stiner, Sullivan, Terry, Thorpe, Waters, Wells, Wilson—51.

The motion to lay on the table was therefore lost.

Mr. Foley moved to amend, by adding in line 7 the words, "provided such schools shall be loyal."

Mr. Thorpe offered the following substitute for the article :

That the schools of the parish of Orleans under the immediate charge of the Roman Catholics receive from the State treasury such sums of money for the support of education as will be fairly equal to the appropriation made for the public school system adopted by the State.

On motion of Mr. Foley, the substitute was laid on the table, by the following vote :

YEAS—Messrs. Bailey, Baum, Bofill, Bromley, Burke, Campbell, Collin, Cazabat, Cook J. K., Cutler, Duke, Dupaty, Edwards, Fish, Flagg, Foley, Gastinel, Geier, Gaidry, Hart, Hire, Howell, Maas, Mann, Maurer, Mayer, Montamat, Morris, Newell, Normand, Ong, Payne J., Paine J. T., Pintado, Poynot, Purcell J., Seymour, Shaw, Smith, Spellicy, Stumpf, Taliaferro, and Wells—43.

NAYS — Messrs. Abell, Austin, Balch, Barrett, Beauvais, Bell, Buckley, Cook T., Crozat, Davies, Duane, Dufresne, Flood, Fosdick, Fuller, Gorlinski, Gruneberg, Healy, Harnan, Henderson, Hills, Howes, Mendiverri, Murphy E., Murphy M. W., O'Conner, Orr, Schnurr, Stocker, Stiner, Sullivan, Terry, Thorpe, Waters, Wilson—35.

Mr. Cazabat offered the following substitute :

No appropriation whatever shall be made by the General Assembly for the support of private schools, but encouragement may be granted to public schools throughout the State.

There having been a question raised as to the correctness of the vote on the substitute offered by Mr. Thorpe, as announced by the president, the vote, as taken by the secretary, was called out by the president, and found to be correct.

On a motion to lay Mr. Cazabat's substitute on the table, the following vote was taken:

YEAS—Messrs. Abell, Austin, Balch, Barrett, Bell, Buckley, Burke, Cook T., Cutler, Duane, Dufresne, Flagg, Flood, Foley, Fosdick, Fuller, Gorlinski, Gruneberg, Healy, Harnan, Henderson, Hills, Howes, Maurer, Mayer, Mendiverri, Murphy E., Murphy M. W., O'Conner, Orr, Purcell J., Schnurr, Spellicy, Stiner, Sullivan, Terry, Waters, Wells, Wilson---39.

NAYS—Messrs. Bailey, Baum, Beauvais, Bofill, Bromley, Campbell, Collin, Cazabat, Cook J. K., Crozat, Davies, Duke, Dupaty, Edwards, Fish, Gastinel, Geier, Gaidry, Hart, Hire, Howell, Maas, Mann, Montamat, Morris, Newell, Normand, Ong, Paine J. T., Payne J., Pintado, Poynot, Seymour, Shaw, Smith, Stocker, Stumpf, Taliaferro, Thorpe ---39.

There being a tie, the president cast his vote in the negative.

The motion to lay on the table was therefore lost.

Mr. Cazabat having stricken out of his substitute the words, "but encouragement may be granted to public schools throughout the State," the substitute was laid on the table.

Article 3 was then rejected, by the following vote:

YEAS---Messrs. Abell, Austin, Balch, Barrett, Bell, Buckley, Cook T., Duane, Dufresne, Flagg, Flood, Fosdick, Gorlinski, Gruneberg, Healy, Harnan, Henderson, Hills, Howes, Maurer, Mayer, Morris, Murphy E., Murphy M. W., O'Conner, Orr, Purcell J., Stocker, Stiner, Sullivan, Terry, Thorpe, Waters, and Wilson----34.

NAYS---Messrs. Bailey, Baum, Beauvais, Bofill, Bromley, Burke, Campbell, Collin, Cazabat, Cook J. K., Crozat, Cutler, Davies, Duke, Dupaty, Edwards, Fish, Foley, Fuller, Gastinel, Geier, Gaidry, Hart, Hire, Howell, Maas, Mann, Mendiverri, Montamat, Newell, Normand, Ong, Payne J., Paine J. T., Pintado, Poyont, Schnurr, Seymour, Shaw, Smith, Spellicy, Stumpf, Taliaferro, and Wells---44.

Mr. Foley moved a reconsideration, which motion was laid on the table.

A motion to adjourn was made and lost.

Article 4 was then taken up.

Mr. Hills offered a substitute, as follows:

Art. 4. The general exercises in the common schools shall be conducted in the English language.

Mr. Cazabat moved to amend by inserting the words "and French," so that the article would read, "the English and French languages." Lost.

Mr. Montamat moved to amend by adding the words, "the English language shall be taught in the public schools of this State."

A motion to lay both substitute and amendment on the table being lost, the question on the adoption of the amendment offered by Mr. Montamat was put and lost on a division---ayes 31, noes 36.

Mr. Hills's substitute was then adopted.

Art. 5 was taken up.

Mr. Gorlinski moved to strike out all after the word organization. Lost.

Mr. Howell offered to substitute article 139 of the constitution of 1852. Lost.

Mr. Smith moved to amend by striking out the word "New Orleans." Laid on the table.

Mr. Montamat moved to strike out the whole article. Tabled.

The article was then adopted by a rising vote—yeas 43, nays 23.

On motion of Mr. Sullivan, a call of the House was ordered, when 78 members answered to their names.

Art. 6 was taken up and read, when Mr Cazabat moved to insert "public" between the words "of and schools." Adopted.

Mr. Harnan moved to strike out the whole article. Lost.

The article was then adopted, as amended.

On the question of adopting the report as amended as a whole, the following vote was taken:

YEAS---Messrs. Austin, Barrett, Bell, Bromley, Burke, Cazabat, Collin, Cook J. K., Davies, Fish, Flagg, Flood, Fosdick, Fuller, Geier, Gorlinski, Gaidry, Hills, Hire, Howell, Mann, Morris, Murphy E., Normand, Payne J., Paine J. T., Pintado, Poynot, Seymour, Shaw, Smith, Spellicy, Stumpf, Thorpe, Wells, Wilson---36.

NAYS---Messrs. Abell, Balch, Baum, Bailey, Beauvais, Bofill, Buckley, Campbell, Cook T., Crozat, Cutler, Duane, Dufresne Duke, Edwards, Foley, Gastinel, Gruneberg'

Healy, Harnan, Hart, Henderson, Howes, Maas, Maurer, Mayer, Mendiverri, Montamat, Murphy M. W., Newell, O'Conner, Ong, Orr, Purcell J., Schnurr, Stocker, Stiner, Sullivan, Taliaferro, Terry- Waters—41.

The report, as amended, was therefore rejected.

Mr. Montamat, on behalf of the Committee on Finance, submitted the following report:

REPORT OF THE FINANCE COMMITTEE OF THE CONSTITUTIONAL CONVENTION OF THE FUNDS FOR PER DIEM OF MEMBERS, MILEAGE, AND SALARIES OF OFFICERS.

1864.
June 18—Balance cash on hand
  this day,................. $5,514 40
June 21—Appropriation made. 20,000 00

      Total balance,........$25,514 40
June 25—Paid warrant No. 78..... $2,030 00
June 25—Paid pay
  roll No. 2....... 2,170 00
June 25—Paid pay
  roll No. 3....... 2,110 00
June 25—Paid warrant No. 79.... 2,141 00— $8,451 00

June 27—Bal. on hand this day... $17,063 40
Seventeen thousand sixty-three dollars and forty cents.

FUNDS FOR CONTINGENT EXPENSES.
June 18, Balance on hand as per
  last report...........$6,972 53
" 24, Paid warrant No. 80.... 1,660 25

". 27, Balance on hand....... $5,311 78
Five thousand three hundred and eleven dollars and seventy-eight cents.

Respectfully submitted,
  JOHN P. MONTAMAT,
Acting Chairman Finance Committee.

The Convention then adjourned until to-morrow at 12 M.
Approved.
  JOHN E. NEELIS,
    Secretary.

TUESDAY, June 28, 1864.

The Convention met pursuant to adjournment. Present, the Hon. E. H. Durell, president, and the following members:

Messrs. Abell, Austin, Balch, Bailey, Barrett, Baum, Beauvais, Bell, Bofill, Bromley, Buckley, Burke, Campbell. Collin, Cazabat, Cook J. K., Cook T., Crozat, Davies, Decker, Duane, Dufresne, Duke, Dupaty, Edwards, Fish, Flagg, Flood, Foley, Fosdick, Fuller, Gastinel, Geier, Gorlinski, Gruneberg, Gaidry, Healy, Harnan, Hart, Henderson, Hills, Hire, Howell, Howes, Maas, Mann, Maurer, Mayer, Mendiverri, Montamat, Morris, Murphy E., Murphy M. W., Newell, Normand O'Conner, Ong, Payne J., Paine J. T., Pintado, P●ynot, Purcell J., Pursell S., Schroeder, Schnurr, Seymour, Shaw, Smith, Spellicy, Stocker, Stumpf, Stiner, Sullivan, Taliaferro, Terry, Thorpe, Waters, Wenck, Wells, Wilson—81.

The minutes of Monday's proceedings were read and adopted.

On motion of Mr. Campbell, Mr. Stauffer was excused for non-attendance, on account of sickness.

Mr. Cazabat moved a suspension of the rules for the purpose of introducing a resolution relative to adjournment *sine die*.

Lost.

Mr. Beauvais moved a reconsideration of the vote rejecting the report of the Committee on Education ; which motion being carried, he then moved to refer the report to a select committee of five, to report on to-morrow. Adopted.

The president appointed on said committee Messrs. Beauvais, Howell, Wells, Sullivan and Campbell.

The report of the Committee on the mode of Revising the Constitution was then taken up on its third reading.

Mr. Montamat offered as a rider article 141 of the constitution of 1852, which reads as follows :

"Art. 141. Any amendment or amendments to this constitution may be proposed in the Senate or House of Representatives, and if the same shall be agreed to by two-thirds of the members elected to each House, such proposed amendment or amendments shall be entered on their journals, with the yeas and nays taken thereon, and the secretary of state shall cause the same to be published three months before the next general election for representatives of the State Legislature in at least one newspaper in French and English, in every parish in the State in which a newspaper shall be published, and such proposed amendment or amendments shall be submitted to the people at said election ; and if a majority of the voters at said election shall approve and ratify such amendment or amendments the same shall become a part of the constitution.

" If more than one amendment be submitted at a time, they shall be submitted in such manner and form that the people may vote for or against each amendment separately."

On motion of Mr. Cazabat, the rider was rejected by a rising vote—ayes 44, noes 18.

Mr. Smith moved to strike out the words "two-thirds," and insert "a majority."

On motion of Mr. Montamat, Mr. Smith's rider was rejected by a rising vote—ayes 33, noes 31.

The report was then adopted.

On motion of Mr. Shaw, a recess of half an hour was taken, at the expiration of which time the president called the Convention to order, and the roll being called, only sixty-seven members answered to their names.

The sergeant-at-arms was sent for absent members.

After some delay, Mr. Harnan moved to adjourn, when the yeas and nays were ordered, with the following result:

YEAS—Messrs. Abell, Balch, Bailey, Bofill, Buckley, Burke, Campbell, Cook J. K., Crozat, Decker, Dufresne, Duke, Fosdick, Fuller, Gastinel, Gruneberg, Harnan, Hart, Hills, Hire, Maas, Maurer, Mayer, Montamat, Murphy M. W., O'Conner, Payne J., Pintado, Poynot, Schroeder, Schnurr, Seymour, Shaw, Spellicy, Stumpf, Stiner, Sullivan, Waters—38.

NAYS—Messrs. Austin, Barrett, Beauvais, Bell, Bromley, Cazabat, Cook T., Davies, Edwards, Fish, Flagg, Flood, Foley, Geier, Gorlinski, Gaidry, Henderson, Howes, Howell, Mann, Morris, Murphy E., Newell, Normand, Ong, Purcell J., Pursell S., Smith, Stocker, Taliaferro, Terry, Thorpe, Wenck, Wells, Wilson—35.

Consequently the motion prevailed, and the president declared the Convention adjourned until to-morrow at 12 o'clock M.

Approved.

JOHN E. NEELIS,
Secretary.

WEDNESDAY, June 29, 1864.

The Convention met and was called to order, pursuant to adjournment.

Present, Hon. E. H. Durell, president, in the chair, and the following members:

Messrs. Austin, Balch, Barrett, Baum, Bell, Beauvais, Bofill, Buckley, Burke, Campbell, Cazabat, Collin, Cook J. K., Cook T., Crozat, Davies, Decker, Duane, Dufresne, Dupaty, Duke, Edwards, Fish, Flagg, Flood, Foley, Fosdick, Fuller, Gastinel, Geier, Gorlinski, Gruneberg, Gaidry, Healy, Harnan, Hart, Henderson, Hills, Hire, Howell, Howes, Kavanagh, Maas, Mann, Maurer, Mayer, Mendiverri, Montamat, Morris, Murphy E., Murphy M. W., Newell, Normand, O'Conner, Orr, Payne J., Paine J. T., Pintado, Poynot, Purcell J., Pursell S., Schroeder, Schnurr, Shaw, Smith, Stocker, Stumpf, Stiner, Sullivan, Taliaferro, Terry, Thorpe, Waters, Wells, Wilson—76.

Absent, the following members:

Messrs. Abell, (excused,) Ariail, Bennie, Bonzano, Bromley, Brott, Cutler, Ennis, (excused,) Heard, Knobloch, (excused,) Kugler, (excused,) Lobdell, Millspaugh, Montague, Ong, Seymour, (excused,) Stauffer, (excused,) Thomas and Wenck.

On motion, Messrs. Abell and Seymour were excused, as also Mr. Spellicy.

The journal of yesterday was read and approved.

Mr. Fosdick moved a suspension of the rules, in order to correct an error in the report of the Committee on Legislative Department.

Mr. Howell, on behalf of the Special Committee on Public Education, submitted a majority report.

Messrs. Beauvais and Sullivan each submitted a minority report on behalf of the Committee on Public Education.

Mr. Flagg, on behalf of the Committee on Schedule, submitted a majority report.

Mr. Gruneberg, on behalf of the same committee, submitted a minority report.

Mr. Shaw, chairman of the Committee on Ordinance, submitted a report.

Upon Mr. Gruneberg's minority report of the Committee on Schedule being taken up, Mr. Wilson moved to lay it on the table without its being read, but the motion was declared out of order.

Mr. Shaw moved to suspend the rules in order to amend the report of the Committee on Legislative Department; which being carried,

Mr. Stocker offered the following amendment to the third article of the report of the Committee on Legislative Department, to wit, by adding:

There shall also be a session of the General Assembly in the city of New Orleans on the first Monday of October, 1864; and it shall be the duty of the governor, as soon as practicable, after the acceptance of this constitution, to cause a special election to be held for members of the General Assembly in all the parishes where the same may be held with safety to the electors, and in other parishes or districts he shall cause elections to be held as soon as it may become practicable, to fill the vacancies for such parishes or districts in the General Assembly.

The term of office of the first General Assembly shall expire as though its members had been elected on the first Monday of November, 1863.

Mr. Stocker's amendment was adopted by a rising vote—yeas 46, nays 20.

Mr. Hills, with leave of the Convention, presented the following resignation of Mr. Bailey:

To the president and members of the Constitutional Convention:

GENTLEMEN—My objections to the ―― article of the report on general provisions, relative to the extension of the elective franchise to all persons, without distinction of race or color, under certain specified conditions, being such that I could not conscientiously sign the constitution of which that article was made a part by the vote taken on yesterday, I hereby most respectfully tender my resignation as a member of your honorable body.

Respectfully, A. BAILEY.
New Orleans, June 29th.

The resignation was accepted by a rising vote—ayes 54, noes 14.

Mr. Howell moved to suspend the rules, for the purpose of taking up the majority and minority reports of the Committee on Education. Lost.

A motion to suspend the rules, for the purpose of taking up the reports of the Committee on Schedule, was lost.

Mr. Foley then moved to suspend the rules, for the purpose of taking up the report of the Committee on Ordinance. Lost.

Mr. Beauvais moved to reconsider the vote refusing to suspend the rules to take up the reports of the Committee on Education. Lost.

The Convention then adjourned until tomorrow at 12 o'clock M.

Approved.

JOHN E. NEELIS,
Secretary.

THURSDAY, June 30, 1864.

The Convention met pursuant to adjournment. Present, the Hon. E. H. Durell, president, and the following members:

Messrs. Abell, Austin, Balch, Barrett, Baum, Beauvais, Bell, Bennie, Bofill, Burke, Buckley, Campbell, Collin, Cazabat, Cook J. K., Cook T., Crozat, Cutler, Davies, Duke, Decker, Duane, Dufresne, Dupaty, Edwards, Ennis, Fish, Flagg, Flood, Foley, Fosdick, Fuller, Gastinel, Geier, Gorlinski, Gaidry, Gruneberg, Healy, Harnan, Hart, Heard, Henderson, Hills, Howell, Howes, Knobloch, Kavanagh, Maas, Mann, Mendiverri, Maurer, Mayer, Montamat, Morris, Murphy E., Murphy M. W., Normand, O'Conner, Ong, Orr, Payne J., Paine J. T., Pintado, Poynot, Purcell J., Pursell S., Schroeder, Schnurr, Seymour, Shaw, Smith, Spellicy, Stocker, Stumpf, Stiner, Stauffer, Sullivan, Taliaferro, Terry, Thorpe, Waters, Wenck, Wells, Wilson—86.

Absent—Messrs. Ariail, Bonzano, Brott, Lobdell, Millspaugh, Montague and Thomas.

Mr. Kugler was excused.

The minutes of yesterday's proceedings were read and approved.

On motion of Mr. Montamat, Mr. Heard was excused for his late absence, he having been engaged in the discharge of his official duties as district judge in the parish of East Baton Rouge.

On motion of Mr. Wells, Messrs. Newell and Normand were excused.

The majority and minority reports of the Special Committee on Education being the order of the day, were taken up.

Mr. Sullivan's minority report was read.

Mr. Howell moved to amend article 1, by striking out the word "two" in the second line, and inserting "four." Adopted.

Mr. Terry moved to amend the same article, by striking out in the third and fourth lines the words, "such compensation as the Legislature may direct," and inserting the words, "a salary of four thousand dollars per annum."

On motion of Mr. Montamat, Mr. Terry's amendment was laid on the table.

Mr. S. Pursell offered the following substitute:

Art. ――. There shall be elected a superintendent of public education, who shall hold his office for the term of four years. His duties shall be prescribed and compensation fixed by the General Assembly.

Mr. Montamat moved to lay the substitute on the table. Carried.

Article 1 was then adopted as amended.

Article 2 was then taken up and read.

Mr. Davies moved its rejection.

Mr. Henderson offered the following amendment:

Provided, No religious or sectarian principles shall be taught in the public schools of this State.

Mr. Smith moved to strike out after the word "appropriated" in the eighth line.

Mr. Austin offered the following amendment, to be added to the article:

Provided, That the Legislature shall make no special appropriations for the support of such associations, after their recognition as public schools.

The question then recurred on Mr. Davies's motion to reject, when the yeas and nays were ordered, and the following vote taken thereon:

YEAS—Messrs. Abell, Austin, Balch, Baum, Beauvais, Bofill, Buckley, Campbell, Collin, Crozat, Cutler, Davies, Decker, Dufresne, Duke, Dupaty, Edwards, Ennis, Flagg, Flood, Gastinel, Gruneberg, Gaidry, Hart, Howell, Kavanagh, Knobloch, Maas, Maurer, Mayer, Mendiverri, Morris, Normand, Ong, Payne J., Pintado, Poynot, Pursell S., Schroeder, Schnurr, Shaw, Stumpf, Stauffer, Taliaferro, Wenck, Wells—46.

NAYS—Messrs. Barrett, Bell, Bennie, Burke, Cook J. K., Cook T., Duane, Fish, Foley, Fosdick, Fuller, Gorlinski, Healy, Harnan, Heard, Henderson, Hills, Howes, Mann, Murphy E., Murphy M. W., O'Conner, Orr, Paine J. T., Purcell J., Smith, Spellicy, Stocker, Stiner, Sullivan, Terry, Thorpe, Waters, Wilson—34.

Article 2 of Mr. Sullivan's substitute was therefore rejected.

Article 3 was then taken up and adopted.

Article 4 was read.

Mr. Smith moved to strike out the words "New Orleans," and insert instead the words "such place as may be fixed by the Legislature;" upon which motion no action was taken.

Mr. Stauffer offered the following substitute:

Art. 3. A university, composed of a law department, a medical department and a collegiate department, combining therewith the State seminary of learning, shall be established and maintained.

Mr. Sullivan moved to lay the substitute on the table, upon which motion a rising vote was taken—ayes 37, noes 37, and there being a tie, the President voted in the affirmative.

Mr. Stauffer's substitute was therefore tabled, and article 4 of Mr. Sullivan's substitute again taken up.

Mr. Gorlinski moved to strike out all after the word "organization" in the fourth line.

A motion to lay on the table was lost on a rising vote—ayes 32, noes 33.

Mr. Cutler moved to amend Mr. Gorlinski's motion, by adding, after the word "organization," the words "and maintenance," which amendment was accepted by Mr. Gorlinski, and his motion as amended was adopted.

Article 4 was then adopted as amended.

Articles 5 and 6 were severally read and adopted.

On motion of Mr. Waters, the Convention then adjourned, on a rising vote—ayes 43, noes 33.

Approved.

JOHN E. NEELIS,
Secretary.

FRIDAY, July 1, 1864.

The President called the Convention to order at 12 o'clock M. The secretary called the roll and the following members answered to their names:

Messrs. Abell, Austin, Balch, Barrett, Baum, Beauvais, Bell, Bennie, Buckley. Burke, Campbell, Collin, Cazabat, Cook J. K., Cook T., Crozat, Cutler, Davies. Decker, Duane, Dufresne, Duke, Dupaty, Edwards, Ennis, Fish, Flagg, Flood, Foley, Fosdick, Fuller, Gastinel, Geier, Gorlinski, Gruneberg, Gaidry, Hart, Heard Healy, Harnan, Henderson, Hills, Hire, Howell, Howes, Kavanagh, Knobloch, Maas, Mann, Maurer, Mayer, Mendiverri, Montamat, Morris, Murphy E., Murphy M. W., Newell, Normand, O'Conner, Ong, Orr, Payne J., Paine J. T., Pintado, Poynot, Purcell J., Pursell S., Schroeder, Schnurr, Shaw, Seymour, Smith, Spellicy, Stocker, Stumpf, Stiner, Stauffer, Sullivan, Taliaferro, Terry, Thorpe, Waters, Wenck, Wells, Wilson—86.

Absent, ten members.

The minutes of yesterday were read and adopted.

On motion of Mr. Crozat, Mr. Bofill was excused.

The reports of the special Committee on Education being the order of the day, were taken up.

Article 1 of Mr. Beauvais's minority report was read.

Mr. Sullivan offered the following amendment:

Insert the word "white" between the words "all" and "children;" and add the words "and private schools of every denomination, numbering over two hundred scholars, shall be considered public schools."

Mr. Smith moved to strike out the word "white" in Mr. Sullivan's amendment; upon a motion to table Mr. Smiths motion the yeas and nays were ordered, with the following result:

YEAS—Messrs. Abell, Balch, Baum, Barrett, Buckley, Campbell, Collin, Cook J. K., Crozat, Decker, Dufresne, Duke, Edwards, Gastinel, Geier, Gruneberg, Hart, Heard, Kavanagh, Knobloch, Maas, Maurer, Mayer, Mendiverri, Montamat, Morris, Murphy M.W., O'Conner, Poynot, Purcell J., Pursell S., Stocker, Sullivan, Waters, Wenck—35.

NAYS—Messrs. Austin, Beauvais, Bennie, Bell, Burke, Cazabat, Cook T., Davies, Duane, Dupaty, Ennis, Fish, Flagg, Flood, Foley, Fosdick, Gaidry, Gorlinski, Healy, Harnan, Henderson, Hills, Hire, Howell, Howes, Mann, Murphy E., Newell, Normand, Payne J., Paine J. T., Pintado, Schroeder, Schnurr, Seymour, Shaw, Smith, Spellicy, Stumpf, Stiner, Stauffer, Taliaferro, Terry, Wells, Wilson—45.

Motion to lay on the table was therefore lost.

On the question on the adoption of the motion to strike out, the yeas and nays were ordered, with the following result:

YEAS—Messrs. Austin, Bell, Bennie, Burke, Collin, Cazabat, Cook T., Davies, Duane, Dupaty, Ennis, Flagg, Flood, Foley, Fosdick, Gorlinski, Henderson, Hills, Hire, Howell, Howes, Mann, Murphy E., Newell, Normand, Payne J., Paine J. T., Pintado, Schroeder, Shaw, Smith, Stumpf, Stiner. Stauffer, Taliaferro, Terry, Wenck, Wells, Wilson—39.

NAYS—Messrs. Abell, Balch, Barrett, Baum, Beauvais, Buckley, Campbell, Cook J. K., Crozat, Cutler, Decker, Dufresne, Duke, Edwards, Fish, Gastinel, Geier, Gruneberg, Gaidry, Healy, Harnan, Hart, Heard, Kavanagh, Knobloch, Maas, Maurer, Mayer, Mendiverri, Montamat, Morris, Murphy M. W., O'Conner, Poynot, Purcell J., Pursell S., Schnurr, Seymour, Stocker, Sullivan, Waters—41.

The motion to strike out was therefore lost.

Mr. Henderson offered the following amendment:

Provided, That no religious, nor any religious sectarian doctrine, shall be taught in the public schools.

Mr. Montamat offered the following substitute:

Art. 3. The General Assembly shall establish free public schools throughout the State, for white children only, and shall provide for their support by general taxation, on property or otherwise; and all moneys so raised or provided shall be distributed in proportion to the number of children between such ages as shall be fixed by the General Assembly.

On motion of Mr. Duane, the substitute was laid on the table by the following vote:

YEAS—Messrs. Austin, Bell, Bennie, Burke, Collin, Cazabat, Cook T., Duane, Dupaty, Ennis, Fish, Flagg, Flood, Foley, Fosdick, Gorlinski, Gaidry, Healy, Harnan, Henderson, Hills, Hire, Howell, Howes, Mann, Murphy E., Newell, Normand, Payne J., Paine J. T., Pintado, Poynot, Schroeder, Shaw, Smith, Spellicy, Stumpf, Stiner, Taliaferro, Terry, Wenck, Wells, Wilson—43.

NAYS—Messrs. Abell, Balch, Barrett, Baum, Beauvais, Buckley, Campbell, Cook J. K., Crozat, Cutler, Davies, Decker, Dufresne, Duke, Edwards, Gastinel, Geier, Gruneberg, Hart, Heard, Kavanagh, Knobloch, Maas, Maurer, Mayer, Mendiverri, Montamat, Morris, Murphy M. W., O'Conner, Purcell J., Pursell S., Schnurr, Seymour, Stocker, Stauffer, Sullivan, Waters—38.

Mr. Terry offered the following substitute:

Art. 1. The Legislature shall establish free public schools throughout this State, and provide for their support by taxation on property or otherwise, of white persons, and all moneys so raised shall be distributed to each parish in proportion to the number of white children between certain fixed ages.

Public schools shall also be organized throughout the State for colored children, and all colored persons shall be taxed for their support.

Mr. Terry's substitute was adopted, without opposition.

The majority and minority reports of the Committee on Schedule were taken up on a second reading.

Mr. Gruneberg's minority report was read, and, on motion of Mr. Hills, was laid on the table.

The majority report was then read, when Mr. Gruneberg moved to lay it on the table. Lost.

Article 1 was read and adopted.

Article 2 was read, when Mr. Henderson offered the following amendment, which was laid on the table:

Provided, That all persons now on a charge of a criminal offence, or hereafter to be on such charge, any time before the adoption of this constitution by the people, shall be bailable by sufficient securities, before and after conviction, as soon as this Convention, by the signature of its members, shall prepare said constitution for adoption as aforesaid.

Provided, That no bail shall be allowed in capital cases, where the proof is evident, or presumption great.

Article 2 was then adopted.

Articles 3 and 4 were severally read and adopted.

Mr. Howell then offered the following additional articles :

Art. 5. Appointments to office by the executive, under this constitution, shall be made by the governor to be elected under its authority.

Art. 6. The term of service of all officers chosen by the people, at the first election under this constitution, shall terminate as though the election had been holden on the first Monday of November, 1863, and they had entered on the discharge of their duties at the time designated therein. The first class of senators, designated in article —, shall hold their seats until the day of the closing of the general elections in November, 1865, and the second class until the general elections in November, 1867.

Mr. Howell's additional articles being severally read and laid on the table, the report was then adopted as a whole, on its second reading.

The report of the Committee on Ordinance was then taken up on its second reading.

Articles 1 and 2 were severally read and adopted.

Article 3 being read, Mr. Thorpe offered the following substitute :

The officers of the State elected on the 22d of February, 1864, shall hold their offices until the 2d Monday of January, 1866, and the election of their successors shall take place on the first Monday in November, 1865, unless otherwise provided by law.

Laid on the table.

Mr. Baum offered the following substitute :

The officers of the State elected on the 22d of February, 1864, shall hold their offices for the respective terms assigned to said officers in this constitution ; but the said terms shall expire as though their installation into office had taken place on the second Monday in January, 1864.

Laid on the table.

The previous question called for by Mr. Montamat was lost.

Mr. Fosdick offered the following substitute :

ORDINANCE.

Should this constitution be accepted by the people, it shall also be the duty of the governor forthwith to issue his proclamation directing the several officers of the State authorized by law to hold elections, or, in default thereof, such officers as he shall designate, to hold an election at the places designated by law the same day on which the election for members of the General Assembly is ordered by article 3, of the report of the Committee on Legislative Department, for governor, lieutenant governor, secretary of state, attorney general, treasurer, auditor, and all officers elected by the people under this constitution ; said election to be conducted and the returns thereof made as provided in the second preceding article.

The governor and lieutenant-governor shall be installed in office during the first week of the session of the General Assembly as ordered in the legislative department of this constitution, and all other officers so elected shall be immediately commissioned by said governor, and hold their offices as provided for in this constitution.

On motion of Mr. Smith, Mr. Fosdick's substitute was laid on the table.

Mr. Shaw moved to strike out in the fifth line the words "officers of the State," and insert "for governor, lieutenant governor, secretary of state, auditor of public accounts, treasurer, attorney general, and superintendent of public education." Adopted.

Article 3, as amended, was then adopted by the following vote :

YEAS—Messrs. Abell, Austin, Balch, Barrett, Baum, Beauvais, Bell, Bennie, Buckley, Cazabat, Collin, Cook J. K., Cook T., Crozat, Cutler, Davies, Decker, Dufresne, Duane, Edwards, Ennis, Fish, Flagg, Flood, Foley, Fuller, Geier, Gorlinski, Gaidry, Healy, Harnan, Hart, Heard, Henderson, Hire, Howes, Maas, Maurer, Mendiverri, Montamat, Murphy E., Murphy M. W., Newell, Normand, O'Conner, Payne J., Pintado, Poynot, Purcell J., Pursell S., Schroeder, Schnurr, Seymour, Shaw, Smith, Spellicy, Stocker, Stumpf, Stiner, Stauffer, Sullivan, Taliaferro, Terry, Thorpe, Wenck, Wells—66.

NAYS—Messrs. Burke, Campbell, Duke, Dupaty, Fosdick, Gastinel, Gruneberg, Hills, Howell, Knobloch, Mann, Mayer, Morris, Paine J. T., Waters—15.

Article 4 was then taken up and read.

AND AMENDMENT OF THE CONSTITUTION OF LOUISIANA.   145

Mr. Campbell moved to amend by including the word "German."

Mr. Healy moved to strike out the word "French."

Mr. Shaw moved to amend by inserting after the word "in," in the second line, the words "two newspapers, and in one newspaper published in the German language, the papers to be selected by the president of the Convention."

Mr. Healy's motion was then taken up and laid on the table.

Mr. Austin moved to adjourn. Lost by the following vote:

YEAS—Messrs. Austin, Balch, Burke, Collin, Duke, Dupaty, Edwards, Fosdick, Gorlinski, Healy, Harnan, Kavanagh, Normand, Purcell J., Terry, Waters, Wells—17.

NAYS—Messrs. Abell, Barrett, Baum, Beauvais, Bell, Bennie, Buckley, Campbell, Cazabat, Cook J. K., Cook T., Crozat, Cutler, Davies, Decker, Duane, Dufresne, Ennis, Fish, Flagg, Flood, Foley, Gastinel, Geier, Gruneberg, Gaidry, Hart, Heard, Henderson, Hills, Hire, Howell, Howes, Knobloch, Maas, Mann, Maurer, Mayer, Mendiverri, Montamat, Morris, Murphy E., Murphy M. W., Newell, O'Conner, Ong, Payne J., Paine J. T., Pintado, Poynot, Pursell S., Schroeder, Schnurr, Seymour, Shaw, Smith, Spellicy, Stocker, Stumpf, Stiner, Stauffer, Sullivan, Taliaferro, Thorpe, Wenck, Wilson—66.

Mr. Montamat offered the following substitute:

This constitution shall be published in English in the Era, and the official paper of this Convention, and in French in the New Orleans Bee.

Laid on the table by a rising vote—ayes 42, noes 27.

Mr. Shaw's amendment was then adopted.

Article 4, as amended, was then adopted.

Mr. Howell offered the following additional article:

Art. 5. At the election for the adoption or rejection of this constitution there shall be had at each poll an additional ballot-box, in which shall be deposited the vote of each qualified voter, on which shall be written: "The ordinance of emancipation accepted," or "The ordinance of emancipation rejected;" and if said ordinance be adopted, it shall be a part of the constitution of the State, and be inserted as the first and second articles of the General Provisions.

On motion to lay the additional article on the table, the yeas and nays were ordered, with the following result:

YEAS—Messrs. Abell, Barrett, Bennie, Bell, Burke, Collin, Cazabat, Cook J. K., Cook T., Davies, Decker, Duane, Edwards, Ennis, Flagg, Flood, Foley, Geier, Gaidry, Gorlinski, Healy, Harnan, Henderson, Hire, Hills, Howes, Maas, Maurer, Morris, Murphy E., Murphy M. W., Newell, Normand, O'Conner, Paine J. T., Payne J., Pintado, Poynot, Purcell J., Pursell S., Schroeder, Schnurr, Shaw, Smith, Spellicy, Stocker, Stumpf, Stiner, Stauffer, Taliaferro, Terry, Thorpe, Wells—53.

NAYS—Messrs. Austin, Balch, Beauvais, Baum, Buckley, Campbell, Crozat, Cutler, Dufresne, Duke, Fish, Fosdick, Gastinel, Gruneberg, Hart, Heard, Howell, Kavanagh, Knobloch, Mann, Mayer, Mendiverri, Montamat, Ong, Seymour, Sullivan, Wilson, Waters, Wenck—29.

Mr. Howell's article was therefore laid on the table.

The report, as amended, was then adopted on its second reading as a whole.

The Convention then adjourned.

Approved.

JOHN F. NEELIS,
  Secretary.

SATURDAY, July 2, 1864.

The Convention met pursuant to adjournment. Present, the Hon. E. H. Durell, president, and the following members:

Messrs. Abell, Austin, Balch, Barrett, Baum, Beauvais, Bell, Bennie, Bofill, Buckley, Burke, Campbell, Collin, Cazabat, Cook J. K., Cook T., Crozat, Cutler, Davies, Decker, Duane, Dufresne, Duke, Dupaty, Edwards, Ennis, Fish, Flagg, Flood, Foley, Fosdick, Gastinel, Geier, Gorlinski, Gruneberg, Gaidry, Healy, Harnan, Hart, Heard, Henderson, Hills, Hire, Howell, Howes, Kavanagh, Knobloch, Maas, Mann, Maurer, Mayer, Mendiverri, Montamat, Morris, Murphy E., Murphy M. W., Newell, Normand, O'Conner, Ong, Orr, Payne J., Paine J. T., Pintado, Poynot, Purcell J., Pursell S., Schroeder, Schnurr, Seymour, Shaw, Smith, Spellicy, Stocker, Stumpf, Stiner, Stauffer, Sullivan, Taliaferro, Terry, Thorpe, Waters, Wenck, Wells, Wilson—86.

The minutes of yesterday were read and adopted.

On motion of Mr. Wells, Mr. Gaidry was excused.

Mr. Orr was excused for his absence on yesterday.

Mr. Montamat presented the following

petition, and offered the accompanying resolution:

To the honorable president and members of the Constitutional Convention:

GENTLEMEN---The undersigned residents of suburb Trémé, in the Second District of the city of New Orleans, most respectfully petition your honorable body to pass an ordinance making it the duty of the city authorities to cause to be constructed, as soon as possible, on Galvez street, across Canal Carondelet, a bridge exactly similar to the one built across said Canal Carondelet, on Broad street. The advantages to result by its construction will be immense to the large number of persons residing in that part of the city, enabling them to supply their families at the Trémé Market, the improvement asked by your petitioners shortening the present distance almost one mile, and opening also a direct communication with the First and Third Districts.

The whole is most respectfully submitted to your honorable body, and your petitioners will ever pray.

New Orleans, June 28, 1864.

John Murphy,
John Fisher,
John Siegenthaler,
Antonie Ramusat,
Nicholaris Frietsch,
Karl Steitz,
J. Neuhauser,
F. Aufenkolk,
Peter Leind,
S. Joseph,
Ph. Shindler,
E. Hacker,
Peter Freibert,
George Woerney,
P. Kerwann,
S. Kaller,
Fr. Robert,
O. Noack,
Adam Spies,
Mrs. E. H. Behan,
Cassimer Glade,
J. W. Bailey,
John Henneberg,
Henry Leebis,
Hte. Demoreulle,
Ernest Demoreulle,
J. Demoruelle,
D. Barker,
Pat. Killea,
Larins McDonell,
Felix M. Jacobs,
Joseph Fisher,
William Rourke,
Garret Kirwan,
Francis Cullen,
James Cullen,
P. Deverges,
James Lilly,
Chas. Lawson,
John P. Montamat,
George Merz,
George Eikz,
Michael Sehally,
Adam Kurtmann,
B. Camet,
T. Kiphaut,
Joseph Gros,
M. Bourlett,
M. Fritz,
L. Latto,
Klotot,
Pour,
George P. Lombard,
D. Laborde,
K. Burkert,
John Schonhardt,
P. W. Sheridan,
C. Murphy,
J. Rolling,
H. Rolling,
Ch. Rolling,
S. Oswald,
Thomas Killea,
P. Grant,
Morris Hiccey,
F. A. Siener,
Joney Poley,
Mike Byrne,
Dan. Byrne,
James Dunn,
P. Mofit,
John Cavanagh,
Jary Murphy,
J. Warner,
Laurence Rinney,
S. Roman,
A. Garrer,
Conrad Brand,
Ph. Hoffman,
F. Graeser,
John McVittie,
Ruston Newlove,
Henry Gallew,
Joseph Upulte,
Heinriez Scheulte,
Pinna Clemant,
Hugh Doherty,
Thaddeus Oberyefell,
A. Beaise,
J. Baldwin,
Valentine Rothany,
S. Shmizer,
Jos. Muller,
Burgard Torer,
Daniel Sheply,
Chas. J. Lester,
Wm. Graham,
Frank Goulemus,
Wm. C. Harrison,
John Koepfer,
James Woulfe,
Freedolin Hesty,
John Foley,
Jeremiah Ryan,
William Myhar,
Henry Steward,
C. Winketsmann,
Paul,
John Funk,
Peter Funk,
M. Christoffel,
M. Halbritter,
J. Relin,
M. Conway,
Henry Jollissaint,
N. Chenal,
Dennis Murphy,
D. Constantine,
A. Herbee,
W. Graff,
Wolf Shreber,
Conrad Graff,
S. Lacost,
Murtz Coners,
Barney Kelley,
John Coner,
James Butler,
Mrs. Filsgerlid,
Ed. Blust,
A. Schamber,
G. Doll,
Patrick Burke,
Raynal Auguste,
Edward Moran,
L. C. Preston,
James Fallon,
Alexander Lea,
John T. Ives,
John Fisher,
John Buckley, Jr.,
Jas. A. Mourton,
Vor. Hébert, Jr.,
M. O'Donnell,
Louis Brevier,
Conrad Murlsnur,
Ge Bilher-Barb,
B. Lanaberi,
Jacob Eichhorn,
J. B. Henry,
Abrusir Storck,
John Orth,
Joseph Henry,
Louis Koch,
T. F. Kavanagh,
Ernest J. Wonoli,
Henry Boeylin.

Resolved, That the Legislature shall, at its first session, pass an act making it the duty of the city authorities of the city of New Orleans to build, as soon as possible, on Galvez street, across Canal Carondelet, a bridge exactly similar to the one built across said Canal Carondelet on Broad street.

On motion of Mr. Wells, the petition and resolution were laid on the table by a rising vote—ayes 46, noes 23.

Mr. Hills, chairman of the special committee on charitable institutions, submitted the following report:

To the President and members of the Constitutional Convention of Louisiana:

GENTLEMEN—The undersigned members of your committee on public charities respectfully report:

That in view of the wide-spread destitution and suffering in this community, and the inadequacy of means in the hands of our various charitable institutions, they are of opinion that relief should be afforded by this body, and they therefore recommend the adoption of the following:

Resolved, That the sum of thirty-five thousand dollars be, and the same is hereby, appropriated from the State treasury for purposes of charity, the same to be distributed by a board of almoners to be appointed by the Governor, and to consist of five citizens, three of whom shall constitute a quorum for business. The Governor o the State shall be ex-officio president of the board, and the money shall be drawn on his warrant, countersigned by the secretary of the board.

All of which is respectfully submitted.
ALFRED C. HILLS, Chairman.
JOHN SULLIVAN,
W. T. STOCKER,
CHARLES SMITH.

Mr. Beauvais moved to lay on the table, upon which motion the yeas and nays were ordered, with the following result:

YEAS — Messrs. Burke, Collin, Cazabat, Davies, Decker, Duke, Dupaty, Ennis, Flagg, Howell, Knobloch, Normand, Paine J. T., Wenck, Wells—15.

NAYS — Messrs. Abell, Austin, Barrett, Baum, Beauvais, Bell, Bennie, Bofill, Buckley, Cook J. K., Cook T., Cutler, Duane, Dufresne, Edwards, Fish, Flood, Foley, Fosdick, Gastinel, Geier, Gorlinski, Gruneberg, Healy, Harnan, Hart, Heard, Henderson, Hills, Hire, Howes, Kavanagh, Maas, Mann, Maurer, Mayer, Mendiverri, Montamat, Morris, Murphy E., Murphy M. W., Newell, O'Conner, Orr, Payne J., Poynot, Purcell J., Pursell S., Schroeder, Schnurr, Shaw, Smith, Spellicy, Stumpf, Stiner, Stauffer, Sullivan, Taliaferro, Terry, Thorpe, Waters, Wilson—62.

The motion to lay on the table was therefore lost.

Mr. Cazabat offered the following amendment:

Provided, This appropriation for charitable purposes will apply to the relief of destitute Union refugees from Louisiana, and the widows and orphans of Union soldiers who have lost their lives in the service of the United States army.

Laid on the table.

Mr. Smith moved the adoption of the report and resolution, upon which the yeas and nays were ordered, resulting as follows:

YEAS — Messrs. Abell, Austin, Barrett, Baum, Beauvais, Bell, Bennie, Bofill, Buckley, Cook J. K., Cook T., Crozat, Cutler, Decker, Duane, Dufresne, Edwards, Fish, Flood, Foley, Fosdick. Gastinel, Geier, Gorlinski, Gruneberg, Healy, Harnan, Hart, Heard, Henderson, Hills, Hire, Howes, Kavanagh, Maas, Mann, Maurer, Mayer, Montamat, Morris, Murphy E., Murphy M. W.. O'Conner, Orr, Payne J., Poynot, Purcell J., Pursell S., Schroeder, Schnurr, Seymour, Shaw, Smith, Spellicy, Stocker, Stumpf, Stiner, Stauffer, Sullivan, Terry, Thorpe, Waters, Wilson—63.

NAYS — Messrs. Burke, Collin, Cazabat, Davies, Duke, Dupaty, Ennis, Flagg, Howell, Knobloch, Newell, Normand, Paine J. T., Pintado, Taliaferro, Wells—16.

The report and resolution were then adopted.

Mr. Austin called up the report of the special committee on the report of the auditor of public accounts.

Mr. Hills moved that the reading be dispensed with and the whole matter laid on the table. Lost.

The report was then read.

Messrs. Harnan and Thorpe moved to lay it on the table, which motion was lost on a division—ayes 15, noes 45.

Mr. Abell moved to postpone the matter until this day two weeks hence.

Mr. Terry moved to lay Mr. Abell's motion on the table, upon which a division was called for, resulting—ayes 32, noes 32. There being a tie, the president voted in the negative, and the motion to lay on the table was therefore lost.

A rising vote was then taken on Mr. Abell's motion to postpone, resulting— yeas 33, nays 39. The motion was therefore lost.

The report was then adopted by the following vote:

YEAS—Messrs. Austin, Barrett, Baum, Beauvais, Bennie, Bofill, Burke, Collin, Cazabat, Crozat, Cutler, Decker, Duane, Duke, Dupaty, Ennis, Fish, Flagg, Foley, Gastinel, Geier, Healy, Hart, Heard, Hire, Howes, Kavanagh, Knobloch, Mann, Maurer, Mendiverri, Morris, Newell, Normand, O'Conner, Orr, Payne J., Paine J. T., Pintado, Purcell J., Pursell S., Schroeder, Schnurr, Seymour, Shaw, Spellicy, Stocker, Stumpf, Stiner, Stauffer, Taliaferro, Terry, Thorpe, Wenck, and Wells—55.

NAYS — Messrs. Abell, Bell, Buckley, Cook J. K., Cook T., Dufresne, Flood, Fosdick, Gorlinski, Gruneberg, Harnan, Henderson, Hills, Maas, Mayer, Montamat, Murphy E., Murphy M. W., Poynot, Sullivan, Waters, and Wilson—22.

Mr. Hills moved to adjourn until Tuesday, 5th inst., at 12 o'clock, M. Lost on a division—ayes 28, nays 44.

Mr. Burke moved to adjourn until the

11th inst., at 12 o'clock, M. Lost on a division—ayes 35, noes 49.

The Convention then adjourned until Wednesday next, 6th inst., at 12 o'clock, M. Approved.

JOHN E. NEELIS,
Secretary.

WEDNESDAY, July 6, 1864.

The Convention met pursuant to adjournment, and the president being absent, on motion of Mr. Beauvais, Mr. Hills was called to the chair.

The secretary called the roll, and the following members answered to their names:

Messrs. Austin, Balch, Barrett, Baum, Beauvais, Bell, Bofill, Bromley, Buckley, Burke, Campbell, Collin, Cook J. K., Cook T., Crozat, Cutler, Davies, Duane. Dufresne, Edwards, Ennis, Flood, Foley, Geier, Gorlinski, Gruneberg, Gaidry, Healy, Harnan, Hart, Heard, Hills, Howes, Kavanagh, Knobloch, Maas, Mann, Maurer, Mayer, Mendiverri, Montamat, Morris, Murphy E., Murphy M. W., Newell, Normand, O'Conner, Payne J., Paine J. T., Pintado, Poynot, Purcell J., Pursell S., Schroeder, Schnurr, Shaw, Smith, Spellicy, Stocker, Stumpf, Stiner, Stauffer, Sullivan, Taliaferro, Terry, Wells, Wilson—67.

There being no quorum, the sergeant-at-arms was dispatched for absent members.

On motion of Mr. Shaw, a recess of fifteen minutes was taken, at the expiration of which the roll was again called, and the following members answered to their names:

Messrs. Austin, Balch, Barrett, Baum, Beauvais, Bell, Bofill, Bromley, Buckley, Burke, Campbell, Collin, Cook J. K., Cook T., Crozat, Cutler, Davies, Duane, Dufresne, Edwards, Ennis, Flood, Foley, Fosdick, Fuller, Gastinel, Geier, Gorlinski, Gruneberg, Gaidry, Healy, Harnan, Hart, Heard, Hills, Hire, Howell, Howes, Kavanagh, Knobloch, Maas, Mann, Maurer, Mayer, Mendiverri, Montamat, Morris, Murphy E., Murphy M. W., Newell, Normand, O'Conner, Payne J., Paine J. T., Pintado, Poynot, Purcell J., Pursell S., Schroeder, Schnurr, Shaw, Smith, Spellicy, Stocker, Stumpf, Stiner, Stauffer, Sullivan, Taliaferro, Terry, Wells, Wilson—72.

Absent—Mr. President and Messrs. Abell, Ariail, Bennie, Bonzano, Brott, Cazabat, Decker, Duke, Dupaty, Fish, Flagg, Henderson, Lobdell, Millspaugh, Montague, Ong, Orr, Seymour, Thorpe, Waters, Thomas and Wenck—23.

No quorum.

Mr. Balch moved to adjourn. Lost on a division—yeas 25, nays 33.

After some delay, there still being no quorum, on motion of Mr. Smith, the Convention adjourned until 12 o'clock, M., tomorrow. Approved.

JOHN E. NEELIS,
Secretary.

THURSDAY, July 7, 1864.

The Convention met, pursuant to adjournment. Present, the Hon. E. H. Durell, president, and the following members:

Messrs. Abell, Austin, Balch, Barrett, Baum, Beauvais, Bell, Bennie, Bofill, Bromley, Buckley, Burke, Campbell, Collin, Cazabat, Cook J. K., Cook T., Crozat, Cutler, Davies, Decker, Duane, Dufresne, Edwards, Ennis, Fish, Flagg, Flood, Foley, Fosdick, Fuller, Gastinel, Geier, Gorlinski, Gruneberg, Gaidry, Healy, Harnan, Hart, Heard, Henderson, Hills, Hire, Howell, Howes, Kavanagh, Knobloch, Kugler, Maas, Mann, Maurer, Mendiverri, Montamat, Morris, Murphy E., Murphy M. W., Newell, Normand, O'Conner, Ong, Orr, Paine J. T., Pintado, Poynot, Purcell J., Pursell S., Schroeder, Schnurr, Seymour, Shaw, Smith, Spellicy, Stocker, Stumpf, Stiner, Stauffer, Sullivan, Taliaferro, Terry, Thorpe, Waters, Wenck, Wells, Wilson—84.

The minutes of Saturday's and Wednesday's proceedings were read and adopted.

Mr. Shaw moved that a Committee on Form and Arrangement be appointed by the chair, to consist of five members, with instructions to re-arrange and number the articles, correct mistakes, and make a printed report to the Convention; which motion having been carried, the president appointed on said committee Messrs. Shaw, Thorpe, Henderson, Cazabat and Smith. On motion of Mr. Thorpe, the President was added to said committee.

Mr. Smith offered the following resolution, which was laid over:

Whereas, during the present rebellion individuals, as well as corporations and parishes, have issued a worthless paper currency, and forced its circulation on the poorer and only loyal classes of the community, therefore be it

Resolved, That a special committee of five be appointed to take into consideration the propriety of forming an article or articles to prevent the recurrence of the same in future, and to hold the property of what

AND AMENDMENT OF THE CONSTITUTION OF LOUISIANA. 149

ever character, whether belonging to husband or wife, parishes or corporations for the redemption of the same, and that the committee be also instructed to submit to this Convention, for its approval or rejection, the draft of a petition to be sent to the Congress of the United States, asking them to empower the parishes of the State of Louisiana to apply the proceeds of sales of property of disloyal citizens for the purpose of redeeming the paper currency issued by them.

Mr. Abell moved a reconsideration of the vote of Friday last, on Mr. Howell's additional article, relative to submitting the emancipation ordinance to a vote of the people.

Mr. Montamat, on behalf of the Committee on Finance, submitted the following:

REPORT OF THE FINANCE COMMITTEE OF THE CONSTITUTIONAL CONVENTION OF THE FUNDS FOR THE PAYMENT PER DIEM OF MEMBERS, SALARIES OF OFFICERS AND EMPLOYEES.

1864.
June 25---Balance on hand in
  the State treasury........ $19,074 10
July 2---Paid warrant No. 81..... $2,030 00
July 2---Paid warrant No. 81..... 2,170 00
July 2---Paid warrant No. 81..... 2,860 00
July 2---Paid warrant No. 82..... 1,981 00
July 2---Paid warrant No. 83..... 1,199 82--- $10,240 82

July 6---Balance on hand....... $8,806 28
To which must be added the sum of......................... 1,199 82
paid for salaries of employés, which properly belongs to expense account.
The sum of $2328 08, being the balance on hand of the appropriation for contingent expenses, was paid out, that account fell short $1199 82, which was drawn from the appropriation for per diem and salaries, as stated above.
Real balance................ $10,006 10

Mr. Montamat also submitted the following recommendation, on be behalf of said committee:

The Convention being on the eve of adjourning, your committee respectfully recommend that a compensation be given to the following officers of this body:

J. E. Neelis, secretary, $500; L. O. Mau-

reau, warrant clerk and clerk of finance committee, $250.
  Respectfully submitted,
    JOHN P. MONTAMAT,
  Acting Chairman Finance Committee.
    JOHN SULLIVAN,
    L. P. NORMAND.

Mr. S. Pursell submitted the following report of the Committee on Contingent Expenses:

To the honorable the president and members of the Constitutional Convention:

GENTLEMEN—Your Committee on Contingent Expenses, have the honor to report the exhaustion of the amount of twenty-five thousand dollars, formerly appropriated, and ask for a further appropriation of five thousand dollars, and offer the following resolution:

Resolved, That the sum of five thousand dollars be and the same is hereby appropriated out of the general funds of the State for the purpose of paying the contingent expenses of this Convention.
    S. PURSELL, Chairman,
    JOHN PAYNE,
    JOHN A. NEWELL,
    JAMES DUANE,
    ROBT. B. BELL.

The rules were suspended and the resolution adopted.

Mr. Stauffer rose to a question of privilege, and said that he was informed that Mr. Knobloch had not voted on the emancipation ordinance, whereupon the secretary was directed to report to the Convention on to-morrow the names of such members as have not recorded their votes on that question.

Mr. Austin offered the following resolution:

Resolved, That the members of this Convention, who went to Baltimore as delegates, be entitled to their per diem pay.

Laid over.

Mr. Abell called for the reading of Mr. Howell's additional article, offered on Friday last, on his motion to reconsider, which being read, Mr. Smith moved to lay the motion to reconsider on the table, which was carried by a rising vote—ayes 46, noes 27.

The Convention then resumed its action on the second reading of the minority report of the Special Committee on Education, presented by Mr. Sullivan.

The report, as heretofore amended, was read, when Mr. Terry offered the following substitute for article 2:

Art. 2. The Legislature shall establish free public schools throughout the State for the education of white children, and shall provide for their support by taxation laid upon property of white persons; and all moneys so raised shall be distributed to each parish in proportion to the number of white children contained therein, between such ages as shall be fixed by law.

The Legislature shall also establish free public schools throughout the State, for the education of colored children, and shall provide for their support by taxation laid upon property of colored persons; and all moneys so raised shall be distributed to each parish in proportion to the number of colored children contained therein, between such ages as shall be fixed by law.

Mr. Henderson offered the following substitute for Mr. Terry's, viz:

Art. 2. The Legislature shall levy a special tax on the property of white persons owning property in the State, for the purpose of public schools for the education of white children, and money so arising shall not be otherwise appropriated.

The Legislature shall levy a special tax on colored persons in the State and their property, for the purpose of public schools for the education of colored children, and money so arising shall not be otherwise appropriated.

Mr. Davies offered as a substitute, the first article of the majority report of the committee. Rejected.

The question was then put on the adoption of Mr. Henderson's substitute, and a division being called for, the substitute was adopted by the following vote: yeas 50, nays 19.

Mr. Hills offered the following additional article:

All asylums for orphans, containing over two hundred scholars, shall be considered public schools of the State.

On a motion to lay on the table, the yeas and nays were ordered and the following vote taken:

YEAS—Messrs. Baum, Beauvais, Burke, Campbell, Collin, Cazabat, Cook J. K., Davies, Decker, Edwards, Ennis, Flagg, Flood, Gastinel, Geier, Gaidry, Hart, Heard, Hire, Howell, Kavanagh, Kugler, Maas, Mann, Mendiverri, Morris, Newell, Normand, Ong, Paine J. T., Pintado, Purcell S., Schroeder, Seymour, Shaw, Stumpf, Taliaferro, Wenck, Wells—39.

NAYS—Messrs. Abell, Austin, Balch, Barrett, Bell. Bennie, Bofill, Bromley, Buckley, Cook T., Crozat, Duane, Dufresne, Fish, Foley, Fosdick, Fuller, Gorlinski, Gruneberg, Healy, Harnan, Henderson, Hills, Howes, Knobloch, Maurer, Montamat, Murphy M. W., O'Conner, Orr, Poynot, Purcell J., Schnurr, Smith, Spellicy, Stocker, Stiner, Stauffer, Sullivan, Terry, Thorpe, Waters, Wilson—43.

The motion to lay on the table was therefore lost.

A call for the previous question was made and lost.

Mr. Cazabat offered the following substitute for Mr. Hills' article, to-wit:

No appropriation shall be made by the Legislature for the support of any private school or institution of learning whatever, but the highest encouragement shall be granted to public shools throughout the State.

A motion to lay on the table was lost on a rising vote—yeas 36, nays 53.

A motion to adjourn was made, and the yeas and nays ordered thereon, resulting as follows:

YEAS—Messrs. Buckley, Burke, Edwards, Waters—4.

NAYS—Messrs. Abell, Austin, Barrett, Bell, Bennie, Bofill, Campbell, Collin, Cazabat, Cook T., Crozat, Cutler, Davies, Decker, Duane, Dufresne, Ennis, Fish, Flagg, Flood, Foley, Fosdick, Fuller, Gastinel, Geier, Gorlinski, Gruneberg, Gaidry, Healy, Harnan, Hart, Heard, Henderson, Hills, Hire, Howell, Howes, Knobloch, Kugler, Maas, Mann, Maurer, Montamat, Morris, Murphy M. W., Newell, Normand, O'Conner, Ong, Orr, Paine J. T., Pintado, Poynot, Purcell J., Pursell S., Schroeder, Schnurr, Shaw, Smith, Spellicy, Stocker, Stumpf, Stiner, Stauffer, Sullivan, Taliaferro, Terry, Wenck, Wells, Wilson—71.

The motion to adjourn was therefore lost.

Mr. Cazabat's substitute was then adopted by the following vote:

YEAS—Messrs. Austin, Bennie, Bofill, Bromley, Burke. Campbell, Collin, Cazabat, Cook J. K., Davies, Decker, Edwards, Ennis, Fish, Flagg, Flood, Gastinel, Gaidry, Hart, Heard, Hire, Howell, Kugler, Maas, Mann, Maurer, Montamat, Morris, Newell, Normand, Ong, Paine J. T., Pintado, Poynot, Pursell S., Schroeder, Shaw, Smith, Spellicy, Stumpf, Stauffer, Taliaferro, Wenck, Wells, Wilson—45.

NAYS—Messrs. Abell, Barrett, Bell, Buckley, Cook T., Crozat, Cutler, Duane, Dufresne, Foley, Fosdick, Fuller, Geier, Gorlinski, Gruneberg, Healy, Harnan, Henderson, Hills, Howes, Knobloch, Murphy M. W., O'Conner, Orr. Purcell J., Schnurr, Stocker, Stiner, Sullivan, Terry, Thorpe, Waters—32.

AND AMENDMENT OF THE CONSTITUTION OF LOUISIANA. 151

The report as amended was then adopted as a whole on its second reading by the following vote :

YEAS—Messrs. Austin. Barrett. Bell, Bennie, Bromley, Burke, Campbell, Cazabat, Cook J. K., Crozat, Davies, Edwards, Ennis. Fish, Flagg, Flood, Gastinel, Geier, Gorlinski, Hart, Henderson, Hills, Hire, Howell, Kugler, Maas, Mann, Maurer, Montamat. Morris, Newell, Normand, Ong. Paine J. T., Pursell S., Schroeber, Schnurr, Smith, Stumpf, Stauffer, Taliaferro, Wenck, Wells, Wilson—44.

NAYS—Messrs. Abell, Bofill, Buckley, Collin, Cook T., Cutler, Decker, Duane, Dufresne, Foley, Fosdick, Fuller, Gruneberg, Gaidry, Healy, Harnan, Heard, Howes, Knobloch, Murphy M. W., O'Conner, Orr, Pintado, Purcell J., Shaw, Spellicy, Stocker, Stiner, Sullivan, Terry, Thorpe, Waters—32.

The Convention then adjourned until to-morrow at 12 o'clock M.

Approved.

JOHN E. NEELIS,
Secretary.

FRIDAY, July 8, 1864.

The Convention met, pursuant to adjournment, and was called to order by the president.

The secretary called the roll, and the following members answered to their names :

Messrs. Abell, Austin, Balch, Barrett, Baum, Beauvais, Bell, Bennie, Bofill, Bromley, Buckley, Burke, Campbell, Collin, Cazabat, Cook J. K., Cook T., Crozat, Cutler, Davies, Decker, Duane, Dufresne, Edwards, Ennis, Fish, Flagg, Flood, Foley, Fosdick, Fuller, Gastinel, Geier, Gorlinski, Gruneberg, Gaidry, Healy, Harnan, Hart, Heard, Henderson, Hills, Hire, Howell, Howes. Kavanagh, Knobloch, Kugler, Maas, Mann, Maurer, Mendiverri, Mortamat. Morris, Murphy E., Murphy M. W., Newell, Normand, O'Conner, Orr, Payne J., Paine J. T., Pintado, Poynot, Purcell J., Pursell S., Schroeder, Schnurr. Seymour, Shaw, Smith, Spellicy, Stocker, Stumpf, Stiner, Stauffer, Sullivan, Taliaferro, Terry, Thorpe, Waters, Wenck, Wells, Wilson, and Mr. President—84.

The minutes of yesterday's proceedings were read and adopted.

Mr. Davies offered the following resolution :

Be it resolved, That the Legislature of this State, during its next session, be instructed to order the authorities of this city to cause a bridge to be constructed on Claiborne street, across the new canal, belonging to the Canal and Banking Company.

Laid over.

Mr. Montamat offered the following :

An ordinance authorizing the city corporation of New Orleans to build a bridge over the Canal Carondelet, opposite Galvez street, similar to the one now at Broad street.

Be it ordained, That the city corporation of New Orleans be and is hereby authorized to build a bridge over the Canal Carondelet, opposite Galvez street, (similar to the one now built at the foot of Broad street,) in such manner as not to prevent the free ingress and egress of vessels; this ordinance to take effect from and after its passage.

Laid over.

The report of the special committee on education was taken up on its third reading.

Mr. Sullivan offered the following rider to article 2 :

Provided, That all institutions, of every denomination, comprising the mixed character of charity and asylums for orphans which educate children, shall be considered public schools of the State, and shall receive their pro rata of the school fund.

Mr. Stauffer moved to lay the rider on the table, upon which question the yeas and nays were ordered, resulting as follows :

YEAS—Messrs. Baum, Beauvais, Bennie, Bofill, Bromley, Burke, Campbell, Collin, Cook J. K., Davies, Edwards, Ennis, Flagg, Flood, Gastinel, Geier, Gaidry. Hart, Hire, Howell, Kugler, Maas, Morris, Newell, Normand, Payne J., Paine J. T., Pintado, Pursell S., Schroeder, Seymour, Shaw, Smith, Stumpf, Stauffer, Taliaferro, Wenck. Wells, Wilson—39.

NAYS—Messrs. Abell, Austin, Balch, Barrett, Bell, Buckley, Cook T., Crozat, Decker, Duane, Dufresne, Fish, Foley, Fosdick, Fuller, Gorlinski, Gruneberg, Healy, Harnan, Heard, Henderson, Hills, Howes, Kavanagh, Knobloch, Mann, Maurer, Montamat, Murphy E., Murphy M. W., Orr, Poynot, Purcell J., Schnurr, Spellicy, Stiner, Sullivan, Terry, Thorpe, Waters—40.

The motion to lay on the table was therefore lost.

On motion to adopt the rider, the yeas and nays were ordered, and the rider was rejected by the following vote :

YEAS—Messrs. Abell, Austin, Balch, Barrett, Beauvais, Bell, Buckley, Cook T., Decker, Duane, Dufresne, Fish, Foley, Fosdick, Fuller, Gorlinski, Healy, Harnan. Heard, Henderson, Hills, Howes, Kavanagh, Knobloch, Murphy E., Murphy M. W.,

Orr, Purcell J., Schnurr, Spellicy, Stocker, Stiner, Sullivan, Terry, Thorpe, Waters—36.

NAYS—Baum, Bennie, Bofill, Bromley, Burke, Campbell, Collin, Cook J. K., Crozat, Davies, Edwards, Ennis, Flagg, Flood, Gastinel, Geier, Gruneberg, Gaidry, Hart, Hire, Howell, Kugler, Maas, Mann, Maurer, Mendiverri, Montamat, Morris, Newell, Normand, Payne J., Paine J. T., Pintado, Poynot, Pursell S., Schroeder, Shaw, Smith, Stumpf, Stauffer. Taliaferro, Wenck, Wells, Wilson—44.

Mr. Smith moved the adoption of the report on its third reading, whereupon the yeas and nays were ordered, and the following vote taken:

YEAS—Messrs. Austin, Barrett, Beauvais, Bell, Bennie, Bromley, Burke, Campbell, Collin, Cook J. K., Davies, Edwards, Ennis, Fish, Flagg, Flood, Gastinel, Geier, Gaidry, Hart, Henderson, Hills, Hire, Howell, Knobloch, Kugler, Maas, Mann, Mendiverri, Morris, Murphy E., Newell, Normand, Payne J., Paine J. T., Pintado, Poynot, Purcell J., Pursell S., Schroeder, Schnurr, Seymour, Smith, Stumpf, Stiner, Stauffer, Taliaferro, Wenck, Wells, Wilson —50.

NAYS—Abell, Balch, Baum, Bofill, Buckley, Cook, T., Crozat, Decker, Duane, Dufresne, Foley, Fosdick, Fuller, Gorlinski, Gruneberg, Healy, Harnan, Heard, Howes, Kavanagh, Maurer, Montamat, Murphy M. W., O'Conner, Orr, Shaw, Spellicy, Stocker, Sullivan, Terry, Thorpe, Waters—32.

The motion was therefore carried and the report adopted on its third reading.

The report of the Committee on Schedule was then taken up on its third reading.

Mr. Henderson offered the following as a rider:

Common carriers, in all cases of contracts and quasi-contracts, offences and quasi-offences, where by law there are parties, may be liable in vindictive damages where, under the American and English jurisprudence regulating common carriers, such damages are legitimate and proper.

On a motion to adopt the rider the following vote was taken:

YEAS—Messrs. Balch, Bell, Bennie, Buckley, Campbell, Cook J. K., Cook T., Crozat, Duane, Flood, Foley, Gorlinski, Healy, Harnan, Henderson, Hills, Hire, Howes, Kavanagh, Murphy E., Murphy M. W., O'Conner, Orr, Paine J. T., Poynot, Smith, Stocker, Stiner, Terry, Thorpe, Wilson—31.

NAYS—Messrs. Abell, Austin, Barrett, Baum, Beauvais, Bofill, Bromley, Burke, Collin, Cutler, Davies, Decker, Dufresne, Edwards, Ennis, Fish, Flagg, Fuller, Gastinel, Geier, Gruneberg, Gaidry, Hart, Heard, Howell, Knobloch, Kugler, Maas, Mann, Maurer, Mendiverri, Montamat, Morris, Newell, Normand, Payne J., Pintado, Purcell J., Pursell S., Schroeder, Schnurr, Seymour, Shaw, Spellicy, Stumpf, Stauffer, Sullivan, Taliaferro, Waters, Wenck, Wells —51.

Mr. Henderson's rider was therefore rejected.

The report was then adopted on its third reading.

The report of the Committee on Ordinance was then taken up on its third reading.

Mr. Shaw offered a rider, striking out in the fifth line of the first article, the word "third," and substituting the word "first," and in the sixth line striking out "July" and substituting "September," and also in the first line of the second article striking out the word "first" and inserting "third," and in the second line of same article, striking out the word "August" and inserting "September;" and further, inserting after the word "office" in the eighth line of the third article, the words "and shall hold their offices for the terms prescribed in this constitution, counting from the second Monday of January next, preceding their entering into office, in case they do not enter into office on that date," and inserting after the word "constitution," in the twelfth line of the same article, the words "and if not sooner held, the election of their successors shall take place on the first Monday of November, 1867, in all parishes where the same can be held, the officers elected on that date to enter into office on the second Monday of January, 1868;" and further, inserting in the first line of the fourth article, after the word "in," the words "three papers to be selected by the president of the Convention, whereof two shall publish the same in English and French, and one in German;" and also inserting in the third line of the same article, after the word "adjournment," the words "of the Convention " striking out in the same line the word "third," and inserting "first," and in the fourth line striking out the word "July" and inserting "September."

Mr. Shaw's rider was accepted by the Convention; and the report was then adopted on its third reading.

AND AMENDMENT OF THE CONSTITUTION OF LOUISIANA. 153

The Convention then adjourned until 12 o'clock M., to-morrow.
Approved.
JOHN E. NEELIS,
Secretary.

SATURDAY, July 9, 1864.

The Convention met pursuant to adjournment.
Present the Hon. E. H. Durell, president, and the following members:]
Messrs. Abell, Austin, Balch, Barrett, Bell, Bennie, Buckley, Burke, Collin, Cook J. K., Crozat, Decker, Duane, Dufresne, Edwards, Ennis, Fish, Flood, Foley, Fosdick, Fuller, Gastinel, Geier, Gorlinski, Gruneberg, Healy, Harnan, Hart, Heard, Henderson, Hills, Hire, Howell, Howes, Knobloch, Kugler, Mann, Maurer, Mayer, Montamat, Murphy M. W., Newell, Normand, O'Conner, Pintado, Poynot, Pursell S., Schroeder, Schnurr, Seymour, Shaw, Smith, Spellicy, Stocker, Stumpf, Stiner, Stauffer, Sullivan, Taliaferro, Terry, Waters, Wenck, Wells, Wilson—65.

After some delay a quorum being present the Convention adjourned until Thursday, 14th inst., at 12 o'clock M.
[Approved.]
JOHN E. NEELIS,
Secretary.

THURSDAY, July 14, 1864.

The Convention met, pursuant to adjournment. Present, the Hon. E. H. Durell, president, and the following members:
Messrs. Abell, Austin, Balch, Barrett, Baum, Beauvais, Bell, Bennie, Buckley, Burke, Campbell, Collin, Cazabat, Cook J. K., Cook T., Crozat, Cutler, Davies, Decker, Duane, Dufresne, Dupaty, Edwards, Ennis, Fish, Flagg, Flood, Foley, Fosdick, Fuller, Gastinel, Geier, Gorlinski, Gruneberg, Healy, Harnan, Hart, Heard, Henderson, Hills, Hire, Howell, Howes, Kavanagh, Knobloch, Kugler, Maas, Mann, Maurer, Mayer, Mendiverri, Montamat, Morris, Murphy E., Murphy M. W., Newell, Normand, O'Conner, Ong, Orr, Payne J., Pintado, Poynot, Purcell J., Pursell S., Schroeder, Schnurr, Seymour, Shaw, Smith, Spellicy, Stocker, Stumpf, Stiner, Sullivan, Taliaferro, Terry, Thorpe, Thomas, Waters, Wenck, Wells, Wilson—83.

The minutes of Friday and Saturday's proceedings were read and adopted.

On motion of Mr. Abell, Mr. Stauffer was excused on account of illness.

Mr. Hills, chairman of the Special Committee on the State Library, submitted a verbal report and asked that the committee be discharged from further consideration of the subject. He also offered the following resolution:

Resolved, That the thanks of this Convention be and are hereby tendered to Maj. Gen. Banks and to Michael Hahn, governor of the State, for their willingness to bring from Baton Rouge to this city various volumes belonging to the State Library, as set forth in the communication of the secretary of state and of the state librarian.

The report and resolution were adopted, and the committee discharged.

Mr. Bell offered the following resolution:

Whereas, There exists an indebtedness resulting from the inauguration on the 4th of March, 1864, of the first free State officers of Louisiana, and other expenses incurred for the furtherance of free State government in Louisiana, amounting to about $10,000;

Therefore be it resolved, That the sum of ten thousand dollars, be and is hereby appropriated for the payment of the same, which may be approved by a committee of seven, consisting of state auditor, state treasurer, secretary of state, and four members of this Convention, to be appointed by the president.

Mr. Henderson offered the following as a substitute, which was accepted by Mr. Bell:

Whereas, A debt of ten thousand dollars has been created in the formation of the free State of Louisiana;

Therefore it is resolved, That said sum be paid out of the treasury of the State, upon the warrant of the governor of said State.

The resolution was put upon its passage, and the yeas and nays having been ordered, the following vote was taken:

YEAS—Austin, Barrett, Beauvais, Bell, Buckley, Burke, Collin, Cook T., Cook J. K., Crozat, Cutler, Davies, Duane, Edwards, Ennis, Fish. Flagg, Flood, Foley, Fuller, Gastinel, Geier, Gorlinski, Healy, Harnan. Hart, Henderson, Hire, Howes, Mann, Maurer, Mendiverri, Murphy E., Newell, Normand, O'Conner, Ong. Orr, Pintado, Poynot, Pursell S., Schroeder, Schnurr, Seymour, Shaw, Smith, Spellicy, Stocker, Stumpf, Stiner, Taliaferro, Terry, Thorpe, Thomas, Waters, Wenck, Wells, Wilson—58.

NAYS—Messrs. Abell, Balch, Decker, Dufresne, Heard, Howell, Kugler, Maas, Mayer, Montamat, Morris, Murphy M. W., Payne J., Sullivan—14.

There being no quorum voting, a call of the House was ordered, when only seventy-five members responded to their names.

The sergeant-at-arms was sent for absent members. Some of the absent members having taken their seats, the vote was again taken upon the adoption of Mr. Henderson's substitute, resulting as follows:

YEAS—Messrs. Austin, Barrett, Beauvais, Bell, Buckley, Burke, Collin, Cook J. K., Cook T., Crozat, Cutler, Davies, Duane, Dupaty, Edwards, Ennis, Fish, Flagg, Flood, Foley, Fuller, Gastinel, Geier, Gorlinski, Healy, Harnan, Hart, Henderson, Hire, Howes, Mann, Maurer, Mendiverri, Murphy E., Murphy M. W., Newell, Normand, O'Conner, Ong, Orr, Pintado, Poynot, Purcell J., Pursell S., Schroeder, Schnurr, Seymour, Shaw, Smith, Spellicy, Stocker, Stumpf, Stiner, Taliaferro, Terry, Thorpe, Thomas, Waters, Wells, Wilson—60.

NAYS—Messrs. Abell, Balch, Decker, Dufresne, Heard, Howell, Kugler, Maas, Mayer, Montamat, Morris, Payne J., Sullivan, Wenck—14.

Mr. Henderson's substitute was therefore adopted.

Mr. Hills was excused from voting on the foregoing question.

Mr. Montamat submitted the following report as chairman of the Finance Committee:

REPORT OF THE FINANCE COMMITTEE.

Amount paid for per diem of members from 2d to July 9th, 1864.......................$7,800 00
Amount for salaries of officers... 1,981 00
Amount for contingent expenses. 2,411 25

$12,192 25

Balance on hand $1,124 03 belonging to contingent expense account.

Your committee recommend that they be authorized to draw from the general funds out of the treasury of the State the amount necessary for the payment of members, officers, employés and contingent expenses, until the end of the session.

Respectfully submitted,
JOHN T. MONTAMAT,
Acting Chairman Finance Committee.
New Orleans, July 8, 1864.

On motion the report and recommendation were adopted.

Mr. Thorpe offered the following resolution:

Resolved, That all decisions of the courts of the State that declare slavery exists in the State, are contrary to the fundamental laws of the State, and is a contempt of the emancipation ordinance passed by this Convention.

Mr. Sullivan moved to lay the resolution on the table, upon which question the yeas and nays were ordered with the following result:

YEAS — Messrs. Abell, Balch, Barrett, Beauvais, Buckley, Crozat, Cutler, Decker, Dufresne, Edwards, Fish, Fuller, Gastinel, Geier, Gruneberg, Healy, Heard, Howell, Knobloch, Maas, Mayer, Mendiverri, Montamat, Morris, Murphy M. W., Newell, Normand, Ong, Purcell J., Schnurr, Seymour, Stumpf, Sullivan, Thomas, Waters, Wenck, Wells, Wilson—38.

NAYS—Messrs. Austin, Bell, Bennie, Burke, Collin, Cook J. K., Cook T., Davies, Duane, Dupaty, Ennis, Flagg, Flood, Foley, Gorlinski, Harnan, Hart, Henderson, Hills, Hire, Howes, Kugler, Mann, Maurer, Murphy E., O'Conner, Orr, Payne J., Pintado, Poynot, Pursell S., Schroeder, Shaw, Smith, Spellicy, Stocker, Stiner, Taliaferro, Terry, Thorpe—40.

The motion to lay on the table was therefore lost.

After a lengthy discussion the Convention adjourned until 12 M. to-morrow.

Approved.
JOHN E. NEELIS,
Secretary.

FRIDAY, July 15, 1864.

The Convention met pursuant to adjournment. Present, the Hon. E. H. Durell, and the following members:

Messrs. Abell, Austin, Balch, Barrett, Baum, Beauvais, Bell, Bennie, Bofill, Buckley, Burke, Campbell, Collin, Cazabat, Cook J. K., Cook T., Crozat, Cutler, Davies, Decker, Duane, Dufresne, Dupaty, Edwards, Ennis, Fish, Flagg, Flood, Foley, Fuller, Gastinel, Geier, Gorlinski, Gruneberg, Gaidry, Healy, Harnan, Hart, Heard, Henderson, Hills, Hire, Howell, Howes, Kavanagh, Knobloch, Kugler, Maas, Mann, Maurer, Mayer, Mendiverri, Montamat, Morris, Murphy E., Murphy M. W., Newell, Normand, O'Conner, Payne J., Paine J. T., Pintado, Poynot, Purcell J., Pursell S., Shroeder, Schnurr, Shaw, Smith, Spellicy, Stocker, Stumpf, Stiner, Sullivan, Taliaferro, Terry, Thorpe, Thomas, Waters, Wenck, Wells, Wilsom—83.

The minutes of yesterday's proceedings were read and adopted.

On motion of Mr. Flagg, Mr. Seymour was excused for non-attendance.

Mr. Montamat, chairman of the Finance Committee, offered the following resolution, which was adopted, viz:

Resolved, That the Finance Committee be, and is hereby authorized, to draw from the treasury of the State, (from all moneys not otherwise appropriated,) any amount necessary for the payment of members, officers, employés, and contingent expenses of this Convention.

Mr. Smith offered the following resolution:

Resolved, That in view that this Convention has adopted an article separating taxation, for the benefit of education, under two distinct heads—one for the education of the white and the other for the education of the colored children—it becomes necessary, in order to avoid difficulty in the future, that it should also define what degree of blood constitutes a colored person.

Mr. Montamat moved to lay the resolution on the table. Lost on a rising vote—ayes 30, nays 33.

The resolution was then put upon its passage and lost by a rising vote of ayes 23, nays 47.

Mr. Montamat called up the following ordinance:

An ordinance authorizing the city corporation of New Orleans to build a bridge over the Canal Carondelet, opposite Galvez street, similar to the one now at Broad street.

Be it ordained, That the city corporation of New Orleans be, and is hereby authorized to build a bridge over the Canal Carondelet, opposite Galvez street, (similar to the one now built at the foot of Broad street) in such manner as not to prevent the free ingress and egress of vessels ; this ordinance to take effect from and after its passage.

On a motion to lay on the table, a division was called for, resulting—yeas 32, nays 19.

The ordinance was therefore laid on the table.

Mr. Smith called up the following preamble and resolution :

Whereas, during the present rebellion, individuals as well as corporations and parishes have issued a worthless paper currency and forced its circulation on the poorer and only loyal class of the community ;

Therefore be it Resolved, That a special committee of five be appointed to take into consideration the propriety of framing an article or articles to prevent the recurrence of the same in future, and to hold the property, of whatever character, whether belonging to husband or wife, parishes or corporations, for the redemption of the same, and that the committee be also instructed to submit to this Convention, for its approval or rejection the draft of a petition to be sent to the Congress of the United States, asking them to empower the parishes of the State of Louisiana to apply the proceeds of sales of property of disloyal citizens for the purpose of redeeming the paper currency issued by them.

A motion to lay on the table being lost, the resolution was adopted by the following rising vote : ayes 39, nays 22.

There being an objection raised that no quorum voted, a call of the House was had, when seventy-eight members answered to their names, whereupon the President declared the resolution adopted.

The Convention then resumed its action on Mr. Thorpe's resolution of yesterday.

After a lengthy discussion, the resolution was put upon its passage and adopted by the following vote :

YEAS—Messrs. Austin, Barrett, Baum, Beauvais, Bell, Bennie, Bofill, Burke, Collin, Cazabat, Cook J. K., Cook T., Crozat, Davies, Duane, Dupaty, Ennis, Fish, Flagg, Flood, Foley, Fuller, Geier, Gorlinski, Gaidry, Healy, Harnan, Hart, Henderson, Hills, Hire, Howes, Kavanagh, Kugler, Maas, Mann, Maurer, Murphy E., Murphy M. W., Newell, Normand, O'Conner, Payne J., Paine J. T., Pintado, Poynot, Pursell S., Schroeder, Schnurr, Smith, Spellicy, Stocker, Stiner, Taliaferro, Terry, Thorpe, Thomas, Wenck—58.

NAYS—Abell, Balch, Buckley, Campbell, Cutler, Decker, Dufresne, Edwards, Gastinel, Gruneberg, Heard, Howell, Knobloch, Mayer, Mendiverri, Montamat, Morris, Sullivan, Waters, Wells, Wilson—21.

The Convention then adjourned until 12 o'clock M., to-morrow.

Approved.

JOHN E. NEELIS,
Secretary.

SATURDAY, July 16, 1864.

The Convention met pursuant to adjournment. Present, the Hon. E. H. Durell, president, and the following members:

Messrs. Abell, Austin, Barrett, Baum, Beauvais, Bell, Bennie, Buckley, Burke, Campbell, Collin, Cook J. K., Cook T., Crozat, Cutler, Davies, Decker, Duane, Dufresne, Dupaty, Edwards, Ennis, Fish, Flagg, Flood, Foley, Fuller, Gastinel, Geier, Gorlinski, Gruneberg, Gaidry, Healy, Harnan, Hart, Heard, Henderson, Hills, Hire, Howell, Howes, Kavanagh, Knobloch, Kugler, Maas, Mann, Maurer, Mayer, Montamat, Morris, Murphy M. W., Newell, Normand, O'Conner, Orr, Payne John, Pintado, Poynot, Purcell John, Pursell S., Schroeder, Schnurr, Seymour, Shaw, Smith, Spellicy, Stocker, Stumpf, Stiner, Sullivan.

Taliaferro, Terry, Thorpe, Thomas, Waters, Wenck, Wells, Wilson—79.

The minutes of yesterday's proceedings were read and adopted.

The president announced that he had appointed on the special committee, raised by Mr. Smith's resolution of yesterday relative to worthless currency, the following members, viz: Messrs. Smith, O'Conner, Balch, T. Cook and Poynot.

The president then laid before the Convention the resignation of Mr. J. T. Paine, which reads as follows:

NEW ORLEANS, July 16, 1864.

To the Secretary State Convention,

SIR: I hereby resign my seat in the State Constitutional Convention.

It seems to me that the session is being uselessly prolonged at a great expense to the public. I do not countenance the proceedings. Having received an appointment under the government, I wish to attend to my proper duties.

Respectfully,
I am your obedient servant,
J. T. PAINE.

Mr. Thorpe moved that Mr. J. T. Paine be expelled for the indignity offered the Convention in the language and address of his resignation.

Mr. Hills moved as a substitute for Mr. Thorpe's motion, that the sergeant-at-arms be sent for Mr. Paine, and that he be brought before the Convention. Lost.

The question having recurred upon the adoption of Mr. Thorpe's motion, that gentleman, with the consent of his second, (Mr. Stocker,) withdrew his motion, when the same was immediately renewed by Mr. Harnan.

Mr. Wilson then offered the following as a substitute:

Resolved, That J. T. Paine, of East Feliciana, is an unfit person to receive any employment from the government, on account of the disrespect offered to this Convention.

The substitute was lost on the following vote on the question of its adoption:

YEAS — Messrs. Austin, Burke, Collin, Cook T., Davies, Dupaty, Ennis, Flagg, Flood, Foley, Gorlinski, Gaidry, Harnan, Newell, Normand, Schroeder, Seymour, Smith, Taliaferro, Thorpe, Thomas, Wells, Wilson—23.

NAYS—Messrs. Abell, Barrett, Beauvais, Bell, Bennie, Buckley, Cook J. K., Crozat, Cutler, Duane, Dufresne, Edwards, Fish, Fuller, Gastinel, Geier, Gruneberg, Healy, Hart, Heard, Henderson, Hills, Hire, Howell, Howes, Knobloch, Kugler, Maas, Mann, Maurer, Mayer, Montamat, Morris, Murphy M. W., O'Conner, Orr, Pintado, Poynot, Purcell J., Pursell S., Schnurr, Shaw, Spellicy, Stocker, Stumpf, Stiner, Sullivan, Terry, Waters, Wenck—50.

The question was about to be put on the adoption of Mr. Harnan's motion to expel, when Mr. Henderson raised a point of order to the effect that Mr. Harnan's motion was out of order, since no charges had been preferred, and, under parliamentary law and the rules governing this Convention, Mr. Paine had a right to be heard, which point of order was sustained by the President, who refused to entertain the motion.

Mr. Sullivan was called to the chair.

Mr. Terry offered the following resolution:

" Resolved, That the sum of one hundred dollars be appropriated out of the general fund of the State, not otherwise appropriated, to each of the clergy who have officiated during the session of the convention.

Previous to any action on Mr. Terry's resolution, a motion to adjourn was made and carried, whereupon the chair declared the Convention adjourned until 12 o'clock, M., on Monday, 18th inst.

Approved.

JOHN E. NEELIS,
Secretary.

MONDAY, July 18, 1864

The Convention met pursuant to adjournment. Present, the Hon. E. H. Durell, President, and the following members:

Messrs. Abell, Austin, Balch, Barrett, Baum, Beauvais, Bell, Bennie, Buckley, Burke, Campbell, Collin, Cazabat, Cook J. K. Cook T., Cutler, Davies, Decker, Duane, Dufresne, Dupaty, Edwards, Ennis, Fish, Flagg, Flood, Foley, Fosdick, Fuller, Gastinel, Geier, Gorlinski, Gruneberg, Healy, Harnan, Hart, Heard, Henderson, Hills, Hire, Howell, Howes, Kavanagh, Knobloch, Kugler, Maas, Mann, Maurer, Mayer, Mendiverri, Montamat, Morris, Murphy E., Murphy M. W., Newell, Normand, O'Conner, Ong, Orr, Payne J., Pintado, Poynot, Purcell J., Pursell S., Schroeder, Schnurr, Seymour, Shaw, Smith, Spellicy, Stocker, Stumpf, Stiner, Stauffer, Sullivan, Taliaferro, Terry, Thorpe, Thomas, Waters, Wenck, Wells, Wilson—84.

Messrs. Crozat and Bofill were excused.

The minutes of yesterday's proceedings were read and adopted.

Mr. Montamat was called to the chair. The president took the floor and made a personal explanation relative to his remarks of Friday last, on the decision of Hon. W. W. Handlin, late judge of the Third District Court of New Orleans, on the emancipation question.

Mr. Abell rose to a question of privilege, and stated that he had received a communication of an extraordinary character, and believing it to be a breach of privilege, he wished to lay it before the Convention, and for that purpose asked that it might be read by the secretary, which was accordingly done as follows:

[*Confidential.*]

NEW OTLEANS, July 15th, 1864.
E. ABELL, Esq.,

Dear sir: I entertain so strong an aversion to the incorporation into the "organic law" of the words "white," "black" and "color," that I am induced in this confidential note, (accompanied by a proposed "rider") to ask you to consider the propriety of altering the language of certain portions of the new constitution, so as to harmonize with the principle contained in this proposed "rider." Many members of the Convention have had the kindness to say to the governor and myself, that they will do what they can to expunge the obnoxious words from the militia and educational bills, before the question of final adoption, as a whole, comes up.

Very respectfully yours,
A. P. DOSTIE.

Art. —. The Legislature shall provide for the education of all children of the State, between the ages of six and eighteen years, by maintenance of free public schools.

Art. —. A university, composed of a law school, a medical school and a collegiate school, combining therewith the State seminary of learning, shall be established and maintained.

Art. —. All moneys arising from grants, donations, or other sources, for educational purposes, shall be and remain a perpetual fund, the interest of which, at seven per cent. per annum, shall be appropriated exclusively to sai l purposes.

Mr. Thomas offered the following resolution:

Resolved, That the adjutant general shall receive a salary at the rate of three thousand dollars per annum from the time of his entering into office and until otherwise provided by law.

Adopted.

The president laid before the Convention the following explanation from Mr. J. T. Paine:

NEW ORLEANS, LA., July 18th, 1864.

To the president and members of the State Constitutional Convention:

In explanation of my communication of July 10th, I have to say that it was designed to be presented to the Convention *through* the secretary, and not *to* the secretary for action.

In apologizing for the inadvertency, allow me to say that I mean no disrespect to the Convention or any member of it.

I again respectfully tender my resignation as a member of the Convention, and urge that it may be accepted.

Respectfully,
I am your obedient servant,
J. T. PAINE.

On motion to accept Mr. Paine's resignation, a division was had—yeas 17, nays 49. Therefore the resignation was rejected.

Mr. Smith offered the following:

In view of the different degrees of blood in that portion of the population of Louisiana, denominated "colored," comprehending the pure African to those apparently white, it becomes imperative on this Convention that it should define as clearly as possible, the status of a "colored" person.

Therefore be it resolved, That a committee of five, of which the honorable president shall be chairman, be appointed by the chair, to take this matter into consideration, and to report by resolution or otherwise, at the earliest opportunity to this Convention, defining what degree of blood shall constitute a "person of color."

A motion to adopt was lost, therefore the resolution was rejected.

Mr. Balch offered the following:

Resolved, That the sum of five hundred dollars is hereby appropriated to Judge J. N. Carrigan, State Librarian, for services rendered by him in furnishing books and documents to this Convention.

Adopted by a rising vote—yeas 38, nays 22.

Mr. Terry offered the following:

Whereas, It is desirable that the work of this Convention should be completed without unnecessary delay, be it

Resolved, That all motions relating to the adoption of the constitution or any part thereof, shall be put to vote without debate.

Laid on the table.

On motion of Mr. Austin, the following resolution was taken up and passed, viz:

Resolved, That the members of this Convention, who went to Baltimore as delegates, be entitled to their per diem pay.

Mr. Shaw, chairman of the Special Committee on Form and Arrangement, submitted a written report, together with a printed copy of the constitution as reported.

Mr. Abell moved to fix the report of the committee for Thursday next.

A motion to lay on the table being lost, the yeas and nays were demanded on the adoption of Mr. Abell's motion, resulting as follows:

YEAS — Messrs. Abell, Austin, Barrett, Baum, Beauvais, Bell, Buckley, Burke, Collin, Cook J. K., Cutler, Decker, Dufresne, Dupaty, Edwards, Gastinel, Gruneberg, Healy, Harnan, Kavanagh, Knobloch, Maas, Maurer, Mayer, Mendiverri, Montamat, Murphy M. W., Normand, O'Conner, Orr, Pintado, Schroeder, Schnurr, Seymour, Shaw, Stumpf, Sullivan, Thomas, Waters, Wenck —40.

NAYS—Messrs. Balch, Cazabat, Cook T., Davies, Duane, Ennis, Fish, Flagg, Flood, Foley, Fuller, Geier, Gorlinski, Hart, Heard, Henderson, Hills, Hire, Howes, Mann, Morris, Murphy E., Newell, Ong, Payne J., Poynot, Pursell S., Smith, Spellicy, Stocker, Stiner, Stauffer, Taliaferro, Terry, Thorpe, Wells, Wilson—37.

The motion was therefore adopted and the report made the order of the day for next Thursday, 21st inst.

Mr. Bell offered a resolution relative to extra compensation of certain officers of this Convention, which, on motion of Mr. Healy, was laid on the table.

Mr. Austin introduced the following preamble and resolutions:

Whereas, The perpetuity of our national government is now imperiled by a stupendous rebellion against the constitution and laws of our common country, originated, supported and carried on by wicked and designing men, for the purpose of establishing a despotic oligarchy, based upon human slavery, an institution reprobated and abhorred by the civilized world and common humanity:

And whereas, The stability of republican institutions, as well as the liberties of the people, requires that the government of the United States should be preserved intact, and its laws executed throughout the whole domain;

And whereas, The period of election for president and vice-president of the United States is now approaching and near at hand; therefore, be it

Resolved, That owing to the existing rebellion and the present condition of our national affairs, any change in the policy of the executive department of the government will embarrass and delay the vigorous prosecution of the war, and be productive of the most disastrous results.

Be it further resolved, That we recognize in Abraham Lincoln a wise president, true patriot and able statesman, who has been tried in the scales and not found wanting, whose past administration is a credit to himself and an honor to the country, and whose policy for the suppression of the rebellion meets our entire approbation. That we also recognize in Andrew Johnson a wise statesman, endowed with wisdom, patriotism, and integrity, and in every way most worthy of the full confidence of the people; therefore,

Be it further resolved, That we most cordially endorse the action of the National Convention lately held at Baltimore, and will give to the nominees thereof our hearty support, and use every honorable means to secure their election.

Upon the adoption of the foregoing preamble and resolutions, the yeas and nays were ordered and the following vote taken:

YEAS—Messrs. Austin, Barrett, Baum, Beauvais, Bell, Bennie, Burke, Cazabat, Cook, J. K., Cook, T., Davies, Duane. Dupaty, Edwards, Ennis, Fish, Flagg, Flood, Foley, Fuller, Geier, Gorlinski, Healy, Harnan, Henderson, Hills, Hire, Howes, Mann, Montamat, Morris, Murphy E., Murphy M. W., Newell, Normand, O'Conner, Orr, Payne J., Pintado, Poynot, Purcell J., Pursell S., Schroeder, Schnurr, Seymour, Shaw, Smith, Spellicey, Stocker, Stumpf, Stiner, Stauffer, Sullivan, Taliaferro, Terry, Thorpe, Thomas, Wenck, Wells, Wilson—60.

NAYS—Messrs. Abell, Balch, Buckley, Collin, Cutler, Decker, Dufresne, Gastinel, Gruneberg, Hart, Heard, Howell, Kavanagh, Knobloch, Maas, Maurer, Mayer, Mendiverri, Ong, Waters—20.

Mr. Thorpe offered the following:

AN ORDINANCE TO PROVIDE FOR AN ELECTION TO FILL VACANCIES IN THE REPRESENTATION OF THE STATE OF LOUISIANA IN THE XXXVIIITH CONGRESS.

Section 1. *Be it ordained by the people of the State of Louisiana in Convention assembled,* That an election shall be held by the qualified electors of the State of Louisiana on the first Monday of September, 1864, for Representatives in the Congress of the United States of America, to fill the vacancies now existing in the XXXVIIIth Congress, and to serve until the end of the term of the said Congress.

Sec. 2. *Be it further ordained,* That until otherwise directed by law the State shall be divided into five Congressional Districts as follows, and the qualified electors of each District shall choose one representative:

The First Congressional District shall comprise the parishes of St. Bernard and Plaquemines, the right bank of the parish of Orleans, the Ninth, Eighth, Seventh, Sixth, Fifth Representative Districts of the parish of Orleans, and that portion of the Fourth Representative District of the parish of Orleans which is included between St. Louis, Rampart and Canal streets, and the Lake Pontchartrain.

The Second Congressional District shall comprise that portion of the Fourth Representative District of the parish of Orleans, which is included between St. Louis, Rampart and Canal streets and the Mississippi river; the Third, Second and First Representative Districts of the parish of Orleans, and that portion of the Tenth Representative District of the parish of Orleans which is known and designated by existing statutes as the Tenth Ward of the city of New Orleans.

The Third Congressional District shall comprise that part of the Tenth Representative Distict of the parish of Orleans which is known and designated as the Eleventh Ward of the city of New Orleans; and the parishes of Jefferson, Washington, St. Tammany, St. Helena, Livingston, St. Charles, St. John the Baptist, St. James, Ascension, East Baton Rouge, East Feliciana, West Feliciana, Terrebonne and Lafourche.

The Fourth Congressional District shall comprise the parishes of Natchitoches, Sabine, Rapides, Calcasieu, St. Landry, Vermillion, Avoyelles, Point Coupée, Lafayette, St. Martin, West Baton Rouge, Iberville, Assumption and St. Mary.

The Fifth Congressional District shall comprise the parishes of Bossier, Claiborne, Union, Morehouse, Carroll, Bienville, Jackson, Ouachita, Caldwell. Franklin, Madison, Tensas, Concordia, Catahoula, Winn, Caddo and DeSoto.

Sec. 3. *Be it further ordained*, That the several officers of the State, authorized by law to hold elections, or in default thereof, such officers as the governor shall designate or authorize, shall open and hold polls in the several Congressional Districts of the State, to choose representatives as aforesaid. At the conclusion of the said election, the officers and commissioners presiding over the same shall carefully examine and count each ballot as deposited, and shall forthwith make due return thereof to the secretary of state in conformity to the provisions of law and usages in regard to elections.

Sec. 4. *Be it further ordained*, That upon the receipt of said returns, or on the third Monday of September, if the returns be not sooner received, it shall be the duty of the governor, jointly with the secretary of state and the judge of one of the district courts of the State, in the presence of all such persons as may choose to attend, to proceed to ascertain from the said returns, the persons duly elected, a certificate of which shall be entered on record by the secretary of state, and signed by the governor, and a copy thereof, subscribed as aforesaid, shall be delivered to the person so elected, and another copy transmitted to the House of Representatives of the Congress of the United States, directed to the speaker thereof.

Sec. 5. *Be it further ordained*, That this ordinance shall be in force and take effect from and after its passage, and shall have the force and effect of a statute of the State.

Done in Convention, at the city of New Orleans, on the —— day of July, 1864.

Ordered to be printed and made the order of the day for Wednesday next.

On motion of Mr. Abell, the Convention adjourned until Wednesday next, at 12 o'clock M.

Approved.

JOHN E. NEELIS,
Secretary.

WEDNESDAY, July 20, 1864.

The Convention met pursuant to adjournment. Present, the Hon. E. H. Durell, President, and the following members:

Messrs. Abell, Austin, Barrett, Baum, Beauvais, Bell, Bennie, Bofill, Buckley, Burke, Collin, Cazabat, Cook J. K., Cook Terrence, Crozat, Cutler, Decker, Duane, Dufresne, Dupaty, Edwards, Ennis, Fish, Flagg, Flood, Foley, Fuller, Gastinel, Geier, Gorlinski, Gruneberg, Gaidry, Healey, Harnan, Hart, Heard, Henderson, Hills, Hire, Howell, Howes, Kavanagh, Knobloch, Kugler, Maas, Mann, Maurer, Mendiverri, Montamat, Morris, Murphy E., Murphy M. W., Newell, Normand, O'Conner, Ong, Orr, Payne John, Pintado, Poynot, Purcell John, Pursell Sam'l., Shroeder, Schnurr, Seymour, Shaw, Smith, Spellicy, Stocker, Stumpf, Stiner, Stauffer, Sullivan, Taliaferro, Terry, Thorpe, Thomas, Waters, Wenck, Wells, Wilson—82.

The minutes of last Monday's proceedings were read and adopted.

Mr. Smith, chairman of the Special Committee on Worthless Paper Currency, submitted the following report:

NEW ORLEANS, July 18, 1864.

To the honorable president and members of the Constitutional Convention of Louisiana:

GENTLEMEN—The undersigned, a committee appointed by your honorable body for the purpose of taking into consideration the propriety of providing for the redemption of a worthless paper currency, issued and forced upon the poor and only loyal class of the population of Louisiana since the outbreak of the rebellion, by private individuals, as well as by corporations and parochial authorities in the different sections and localities of the State, most respectfully beg leave to report that we have duly weighed the subject matter contained in the resolution submitted to our consideration, and being fully convinced that some action should be taken in the matter by this Convention, beg leave to offer the following article as the result of our deliberations, to be incorporated as one of the ordinances of the constitution:

Art. —. That the property of all individuals, firms and companies, the taxable property situated in all villages, towns, cities and parishes, shall be liable and held responsible for the redemption in current funds of the United States, for all notes issued as a circulating medium during the present rebellion, to the extent of the amount issued by such individual, firm, company, village, town, city or parish respectively, recoverable before any court of competent jurisdiction, in due process of law.

     CHARLES SMITH,
     JOS. H. BALCH,
     O. H. POYNOT,
     TERENCE COOK,
     P. K. O'CONNER.

Mr. Burke moved to reject the report, which motion was carried on a rising vote, ayes 40, nays 20.

Mr. Cazabat moved to suspend the rules for the purpose of adopting the constitution as a whole without further debate. No action taken.

A call of the House was ordered, when eighty members answered to their names.

Mr. Cutler offered the following resolution:

Resolved, That the sum of one thousand dollars be and the same is hereby appropriated out of any moneys in the treasury of the State not otherwise appropriated, for the purpose of paying the secretary of this Convention and his two assistants, for extra services rendered this Convention, and that the same be paid on their own warrants, as follows: To John E. Neelis, secretary, five hundred dollars; to S. G. Hamilton and Philip Winfree, assistant secretaries, two hundred and fifty dollars each.

Mr. Montamat offered the following amendment:

Be it further resolved, That the sum of two hundred and fifty dollars be and is hereby appropriated from the general funds in the State treasury not otherwise appropriated, to L. O. Maureau, warrant clerk, payable on his own warrant, as extra compensation for extra services rendered.

Mr. Cutler having accepted the amendment, the resolution was adopted as amended.

Mr. Henderson moved to reconsider the vote of Monday last, fixing the report of the Committee on Form and Arrangement for Thursday.

A motion to lay on the table was lost by a rising vote of 36 ayes to 42 nays.

The question on the motion to reconsider was then put and lost.

Mr. Thorpe's ordinance providing for an election to fill the vacancies in the representation of the State, in the thirty-eighth Congress of the United States, was then taken up.

Mr. Henderson being temporarily in the chair, motions were made first to lay on the table and second to adopt. Amidst much confusion the temporary president declared the question carried; but many members enquiring what the question was, which the chair declared carried, and he failing to inform the Convention, the president resumed the chair.

Mr. Abell moved to amend the second section, by striking out all after the word Orleans in the seventh line, and inserting in the sixth line the word "and fourth," after the word "fifth," so as to include the whole of the Fourth Representative District of the parish of Orleans.

Laid on the table by a rising vote—yeas 43, nays 32.

After a lengthy discussion, on motion of Mr. Cutler, the question was postponed until Saturday next.

The Convention then adjourned until 12 o'clock M., to-morrow.

Approved.

     JOHN E. NEELIS,
      Secretary.

THURSDAY, July 21, 1864.

The Convention met pursuant to adjournment, and was called to order by the president. The secretary called the roll and the following members answered to their names:

Messrs. Abell, Austin, Barrett, Baum, Beauvais, Bell, Bennie, Bofill, Buckley, Burke, Campbell, Collin, Cazabat, Cook J. K., Cook T., Crozat, Cutler, Davies, Decker, Duane, Dufresne, Dupaty, Edwards, Ennis, Fish, Flagg, Flood, Foley, Fosdick, Fuller, Gastinel, Geier, Gorlinski, Gruneberg, Gaidry, Healy, Harnan, Hart, Heard, Henderson, Hills, Hire, Howell, Howes, Kavanagh, Knobloch, Kugler, Maas, Mann, Maurer, Mayer, Mendiverri, Montamat, Morris, Murphy E., Murphy M W., Newell, Normand, O'Conner, Ong, Orr, Payne J., Pintado, Poynot, Purcell John, Pursell S., Schroeder, Schnurr, Seymour, Shaw, Smith, Spellicy, Stocker, Stumpf, Stiner, Stauffer, Sullivan, Taliaferro, Terry, Thorpe, Thomas, Waters, Wenck, Wells, Wilson—86.

The minutes of yesterday's proceedings were read and adopted.

The order of the day being the report of the Special Committee on Form and Arrangement of the Constitution was taken up, and the reading of the constitution began, with a view to its adoption as a whole. The president suggested that the secretary, in reading the constitution, should pause at the close of each article, when members desiring to offer riders would have opportunity to do so.

Mr. Cazabat moved to adopt the constitution as a whole, without further delay. No action.

The preamble being read, Mr. Henderson offered the following substitute, as a rider:

We, the representatives of the people of the State of Louisiana in Convention assembled, do define the boundaries of said State to be as follows: Beginning at the mouth of the river Sabine, thence by a line to be drawn along the middle of said river, including all its islands, to the thirty-second degree of latitude, thence due north to the northernmost part of the thirty-third degree of north latitude; thence along the said parallel of latitude to the river Mississippi; thence down the said river to the river Iberville and from thence along the middle of said river and Lakes Maurapas and Pontchartrain to the Gulf of Mexico; thence bounded by the said Gulf to the place of beginning including all islands within three leagues of the coast, and do ordain and establish this constitution.

A motion to reject the rider being made, after some discussion, Mr. Hills moved the previous question, which being ordered, the question was put, and Mr. Henderson's rider was rejected.

The secretary then proceeded with the reading of the constitution, and upon reading article seven, Mr. Cutler moved to strike out the words "with safety to the electors," in the eighth line on the second page.

Carried.

Mr. Shaw moved to amend the twelfth article, by striking out the word "four" and substituting the word "five," and also by striking out the word "three" in the third line from the bottom, and substitute therefor the word "four," in the second line from the bottom on page four, thereby giving to the city of New Orleans nine instead of seven senators.

In article 14, Mr. Cutler moved to strike out the word "six" and substitute the word "three," making the parochial residence required of voters three instead of six months.

Mr. Stauffer moved to reject, which motion being lost, on a rising vote of yeas 35, nays 42, Mr. Cutler's rider was then adopted.

Mr. Shaw moved to amend article 22, by striking out "thirty-four," and substituting thirty-six," so as to make the number of senators thirty-six; and in the last line of said article, by striking out seven and substituting nine, so as to make the proviso read "that no parish be entitled to more than nine senators." Adopted.

Mr. Shaw also moved to strike out in the second line of article 23, the words "thirty-four," and substitute the words "thirty-six," so as to make said article correspond with the previous amendments. Carried.

In article 44, Mr. Foley moved to strike out "ten" and insert "five," so as to make the necessary residence in the qualifications for governor five years.

Mr. Flood moved to substitute two years, which being lost, Mr. Foley's amendment was then adopted.

Mr. Henderson moved to amend article 47, by striking out in the fourth line, the word "residue," and inserting the word "remainder," in lieu thereof. Rejected.

In article 67, Mr. Cutler moved to strike out the words "free white men," and substitute therefor the words "all able-bodied men of the State."

Adopted on a rising vote—yeas 51, nays 18.

Mr. Smith offered the following rider:

All able-bodied male residents between the ages of eighteen and forty-five years, (except subjects or citizens of foreign powers who have never voted in the United States nor declared their intention to become citizens,) shall be enrolled in the militia, and subject to military service, according to law.

Laid on the table.

Mr. Cutler moved to strike out all that part of article 67 after the word "defence," in the second line; which motion was adopted on a rising vote of 58 yeas to 11 nays.

When article 79 was read, Mr. Sullivan offered the following as a rider:

And that the judges of the Supreme Court be elected by the people for a term of eight years. Also that the judges of the inferior courts be elected by the people of their several Districts for a term of six years, and that it shall be the duty of the Legislature to fix the time for holding elections for all judges, at a time which shall be different from that fixed for all other elections.

On a motion to adopt, the question was put, and Mr. Sullivan's rider was rejected.

Mr. Henderson offered the following rider to article 106:

All persons shall be bailable, by sufficient sureties, except for capital offences, where the proof is evident or presumption great; and this right of bail shall take place on appeal to the Supreme Court.

On motion the rider was rejected.

Mr. Cazabat moved to strike out the whole of article 116.

Mr. Davies moved to strike out all after the words "gambling houses," in the second line of said article.

Laid on the table.

Mr. Cazabat moved to strike out all of said article after the word "tickets."

On motion of Mr. Sullivan the motion was laid on the table.

Mr. Austin renewed Mr. Cazabat's motion to strike out the whole article.

Laid on the table.

Upon article 117 being read, Mr. Stauffer moved to strike out all after the word "divorces."

Laid on the table.

In article 122, Mr. Smith moved to insert after the word "be" in the second line, the word "not." Lost.

Article 123 was read, and a motion to strike out the words "except that of Justice of the Peace." Lost.

When article 130 was read, Mr. Hills moved to strike out the word "majority" and insert the words "two-thirds," so as to require a two-thirds vote of the General Assembly to remove the seat of government.

On motion of Mr. Wenck, Mr. Hills' amendment was laid on the table by a rising vote—yeas 40; nays 26.

A motion to take a recess of fifteen minutes being lost, the reading of the constitution was resumed.

Mr. Cazabat moved to amend article 133, by adding after the words "following rates" in the last line on page 20. the words "until otherwise provided by law." Lost.

Messrs. Cutler and Cazabat moved to strike out all of said article after the word "duties,"—

After some discussion, Mr. Cutler with the consent of his second, withdrew his motion.

Mr. Sullivan moved to strike out the first, second and third lines of article 134. Laid on the table.

Mr. Terry moved to strike out the word "may" and substitute "shall" in the first line of said article. A motion to lay on the table was made. Upon which motion the yeas and nays were ordered, resulting as follows:

YEAS—Messrs. Abell, Austin, Barrett, Baum, Beauvais, Bennie, Burke, Campbell, Cazabat, Crozat, Cutler, Davies, Decker, Edwards, Ennis, Fish, Flagg, Fuller, Gastinel, Gruneberg. Heard, Henderson, Kavanagh, Knobloch, Kugler, Mann, Mayer, Newell, Normand, Ong, Pintado. Pursell Sam'l., Schnurr, Seymour, Shaw, Stumpf, Stiner, Stauffer, Taliaferro, Wenck, Wells, Wilson—42.

NAYS — Bell, Bofill, Buckley, Collin, Cook J. K., Cook Terrance, Duane, Dufresne, Flood, Foley, Fosdick, Geier, Gorlinski, Gaidry, Healy, Harnan, Hart, Hills, Hire, Howes, Maas, Maurer, Mendiverri, Montamat, Morris, Murphy E., Murphy M. W., O'Conner, Orr, Payne John, Poynot, Schroder, Smith, Spellicy, Stocker, Sullivan, Terry, Thorpe, Thomas, Waters—40.

Mr. Terry's rider was therefore laid on the table.

Mr. Wells moved to strike out the whole of title 9; upon which motion the yeas and nays were ordered, and the following vote was taken:

YEAS—Austin, Beauvais, Bennie, Crozat, Cutler, Decker, Edwards, Fish, Flagg, Fuller, Heard, Kavanagh, Kugler, Mann, Newell, Ong, Pursell S., Seymour, Shaw, Taliaferro, Thorpe, Wenck, Wells, Wilson—24.

NAYS—Abell, Barrett, Baum, Bell, Bofill, Buckley, Burke, Campbell, Collin, Cazabat, Cook J. K., Cook T., Davies, Duane, Dufresne, Duke, Dupaty, Ennis, Flood, Foley, Fosdick, Gastinel, Geier, Gorlinsky, Gruneberg, Gaidry, Healy, Harnan, Hart, Henderson, Hills, Hire, Howes, Knobloch, Maas, Maurer, Mayer, Mendiverri, Montamat, Morris, Murphy E., Murphy M. W., Normand, O'Conner, Orr, Payne J., Pintado, Poynot, Schroeder, Schnurr, Smith, Spellicy, Stocker, Stumpf, Stiner, Stauffer, Sullivan, Terry, Thomas, Waters—60.

Mr. Wells' motion was therefore lost.

The previous question was ordered, and title 9 adopted.

Upon a motion to adjourn, the yeas and nays were ordered, and the following vote taken:

YEAS—Campbell, Collin, Cook J. K., Dufresne, Dupaty, Flagg, Gaidry, Harnan, Knobloch, Mayer, Mendiverri, Murphy M. W., Newell, O'Conner, Orr, Pintado—16.

NAYS—Abell, Austin, Barrett, Baum, Beauvais, Bell, Bennie, Bofill, Buckley, Burke, Cazabat, Cook T., Crozat, Cutler, Davies, Decker, Duane, Edwards, Ennis, Fish, Flood, Foley, Fosdick, Fuller, Gastinel, Geier, Gorlinski, Gruneberg, Healy, Hart, Heard, Henderson, Hills, Hire, Howes, Kavanagh, Kugler, Maas, Mann, Maurer, Montamat, Morris, Murphy E., Normand, Ong, Payne J., Pursell S., Schroeder, Schnurr, Seymour, Shaw, Smith, Spellicy, Stocker, Stumpf, Stiner, Stauffer, Sullivan, Taliaferro, Terry, Thorpe, Thomas, Waters, Wenck, Wells, Wilson—66.

Article 136 was read, when Mr. Hills moved to strike out "four" and insert "five," and also to add, "until otherwise provided by law," so as to make the article read: "His salary shall be five thousand dollars per annum, until otherwise provided by law."

A motion to lay on the table being lost, Mr. Hills' rider was adopted.

Mr. Stauffer moved as a rider to article 137, to strike out all that part of the article following the word "State."

A motion to lay on the table being lost, Mr. Stauffer's rider was adopted.

Mr. Campbell offered the following rider to article 137, viz:

Provided, That the city of New Orleans shall comprise one internal improvement and drainage district, and appropriations made for that purpose shall be paid into the treasury of the city of New Orleans.

Mr. Sullivan moved to lay on the table, which motion was carried on a rising vote, yeas 46, nays 21.

Article 140 was read. Mr. Terry moved to insert after the word "receive," in the third line, the words "a compensation of three thousand five hundred dollars per annum."

Laid on the table.

Mr. Beauvais moved to amend by substituting five thousand dollars as the salary of the superintendent of public education.

Lost.

Mr. Fish moved to insert after the word receive, the words "a salary of four thousand dollars per annum."

A motion to lay on the table being lost, Mr. Fish's rider was then adopted.

On motion of Mr. Hills, the words "such compensation as the Legislature may direct," was stricken out in order to make said article harmonize with the foregoing amendment.

Carried.

The Convention then adjourned until 12 M., to-morrow.

Approved.

JOHN E. NEELIS,
Secretary.

FRIDAY, July 22, 1864.

The Convention met, pursuant to adjournment. Present, the Hon. E. H. Durell, president, and the following members:

Messrs. Abell, Austin, Barrett, Baum, Beauvais, Bell, Bennie, Bofill, Buckley, Burke, Campbell, Collin, Cazabat, Cook J. K., Cook T., Crozat, Cutler, Davies, Decker, Duane, Dufresne, Dupaty, Edwards, Ennis, Fish, Flagg, Flood, Foley, Fosdick,

Fuller, Gastinel, Geier, Gorlinski, Gaidry, Gruneberg, Healy, Harnan, Hart, Heard, Henderson, Hills. Hire, Howes, Kavanagh, Knobloch, Kugler, Maas, Mann, Maurer, Mayer, Mendiverri, Montamat, Morris, Murphy E., Murphy M. W., Newell, Normand, O'Conner, Ong, Orr, Payne J., Poynot, Purcell J., Pursell S., Schroedor, Schnurr, Seymour, Shaw, Smith, Spellicy, Stocker, Stumpf, Stiner, Stauffer, Sullivan, Taliaferro, Terry, Thorpe, Thomas, Waters, Wenck, Wells, Wilson—84.

The minutes of yesterday's proceedings were read and adopted.

The President arose to a question of privilege, and called the attention of the Convention to a scurrilous article published in the newspaper called the New Orleans *Times*, of this date, which he declared to be a libel against himself and this Convention, whereupon Mr. Stauffer offered the following resolution:

Resolved, That the sergeant-at-arms be ordered to take immediate possession of the paper called the New Orleans *Times*, and that the publication of the paper be suspended until its responsible editor, Thomas P. May, Esq., appear before this Convention and purge himself of the *libel* he has published in the issue of this date regarding the proceedings of this Convention of the 21st of July, 1864.

Mr. Hills moved to lay the resolution on the table, whereupon the yeas and nays were ordered, with the following result:

YEAS — Abell. Baum, Bofill, Buckley, Campbell, Cazabat, Decker, Dufresne, Edwards, Ennis, Fish, Fosdick, Gastinel, Gorlinski, Gruneberg, Hart, Heard, Hills, Kavanagh, Knobloch, Mann, Maurer, Morris, Murphy E., Murphy M. W., Ong, Orr, Poynot, Shaw, Stumpf, Sullivan, Waters—32.

NAYS—Austin, Barrett, Beauvais, Bell, Bennie, Burke, Collin, Cook J. K., Cook T., Crozat, Cutler, Davies, Duane, Dupaty, Flagg, Flood, Foley, Fuller, Geier, Healy, Harnan, Henderson, Hire, Howes, Kugler, Maas, Mayer, Montamat, Newell, Normand, O'Conner, Payne J., Pursell S., Schroeder, Schnurr, Seymour, Smith, Spellicy, Stocker, Stiner, Stauffer, Terry, Thorpe, Thomas, Wenck, Wells, Wilson—47.

The motion to lay on the table was therefore lost.

Mr. Cutler offered the following substitute:

Resolved, That Thomas P. May, editor of the New Orleans Times, be brought before this Convention forthwith by the sergeant-at-arms, and that he be required to purge himself of the contempt and libel on this body as published in the issue of July 22, 1864, or that he be otherwise dealt with as the Convention may deem proper and just.

On motion, Mr. Cutler's substitute was adopted.

On motion of Messrs. Cazabat and Smith, the order of the day was taken up and the final reading of the constitution resumed.

Mr. Terry offered the following rider to article 141:

The Legislature shall provide for the education of all children of the State between the ages of six and eighteen years, by maintenance of free public schools by taxation or otherwise.

Mr. Sullivan moved to lay the rider on the table, on which motion the yeas and nays were taken, as follows:

YEAS--Messrs. Abell, Bofill, Buckley, Campbell, Crozat, Decker, Dufresne, Edwards, Fuller, Gastinel, Geier, Gruneberg, Heard, Henderson, Knobloch, Maas, Mayer, Mendiverri, Montamat, Morris, Murphy M. W., Newell, Normand, Ong, Orr, Pursell S., Sullivan, Thomas, Waters—29.

NAYS—Messrs. Austin, Barrett, Baum, Beauvais, Bell, Bennie, Burke, Collin, Cazabat, Cook J. K., Cook T., Cutler, Davies, Duane, Dupaty, Ennis, Fish, Flagg, Flood, Foley, Fosdick, Gorlinski, Healy, Harnan, Hart, Hills, Hire, Howes, Kavanagh, Kugler, Mann, Maurer, Murphy E., O'Conner, Payne J., Poynot, Schroeder, Schnurr, Seymour, Shaw, Smith, Spellicy, Stocker, Stumpf, Stiner, Stauffer, Terry, Thorpe, Wells, Wilson—50.

Consequently the motion to table was lost.

On the motion to adopt the rider it was carried by the following vote, the yeas and nays being ordered and taken:

YEAS---Messrs. Austin, Barrett, Baum, Beauvais, Bell, Bennie, Burke, Collin, Cazabat, Cook T., Crozat, Cutler, Davies, Duane, Dupaty, Ennis, Fish, Flagg, Flood, Foley, Fosdick, Geier, Gorlinski, Healey, Harnan, Henderson, Hills, Hire, Howes, Kavanagh, Mann, Maurer, Murphy E., Newell, Normand, O'Conner, Payne J., Poynot, Purcell J., Schroeder, Shaw, Smith, Spellicy, Stocker, Stumpf, Stiner, Stauffer, Terry, Thorpe, Thomas, Wells, Wilson---53.

NAYS—Messrs. Abell. Bofill, Buckley, Campbell, Decker, Dufresne, Edwards, Fuller, Gastinel, Gruneberg, Hart, Heard, Knobloch, Kugler, Maas, Mayer, Mendiverri, Montamat, Morris, Murphy M. W., Ong, Orr, Pursell S., Schnurr, Seymour, Sullivan, Waters—27.

Mr. Terry's rider was therefore adopted.

AND AMENDMENT OF THE CONSTITUTION OF LOUISIANA. 165

Upon article 143 being read, Mr. Smith moved to strike out the words "in the city of New Orleans, and insert the words "by the Legislature."

Laid on the table.

Mr. Foley moved to strike out the whole of article 146.

Mr. Smith moved to lay that motion on the table, upon which a rising vote was had, resulting in yeas 54, nays 12.

The motion to lay on the table was therefore carried.

In article 147 Mr. Bofill moved to strike out in line third, the words "two-thirds" and insert the words " a majority."

Adopted.

In article 154, Mr. Shaw moved to strike out the words "without hostile molestation or interference." Adopted.

The last reading being at length concluded, the question was put on the adoption of the constitution of the State of Louisiana as a whole, whereupon the yeas and nays were ordered, and the following vote taken :

YEAS—Messrs. Austin, Barrett, Baum, Beauvais, Bell, Bennie, Burke, Collin, Cazabat, Cook J. K., Cook T., Crozat, Cutler, Davies, Duane, Dupaty, Edwards, Ennis, Fish, Flagg, Flood, Foley, Fuller, Geier, Gorlinski, Healy, Harnan, Hart, Heard, Henderson, Hills, Hire, Howes, Kavanagh, Kugler, Mann, Maurer, Montamat, Morris, Murphy E., Murphy M. W., Newell, Normand, O'Conner, Ong, Payne J., Poynot, Purcell J., Pursell S., Shroeder, Schnurr, Seymour, Shaw, Smith, Spellicy, Stocker, Stiner, Stauffer, Taliaferro, Terry, Thorpe, Thomas, Wenck, Wells, Wilson and Mr. President—66.

NAYS — Messrs. Abell, Bofill, Buckley, Decker, Dufresne, Gastinel, Gruneberg, Gaidry, Knobloch, Maas, Mayer, Mendiverri, Orr, Stumpf, Sullivan, Waters—16.

Upon Mr. Mendiverri's name being called by the secretary, that gentleman submitted his reasons for voting as he did, in writing, which reasons were ordered to be published in the debates of this Convention.

Previous to the vote being declared, Mr. Hills moved that the president be requested to cast his vote. Carried.

Mr. Hills also moved that all members who were absent at the time of taking this vote be requested to record their votes.

Mr. Thomas moved to amend by inserting the word "required" instead of "requested," which being accepted, Mr. Hills' motion was adopted.

Mr. Newell presented the following written authorization from Mr. Taliaferro, which was read :

NEW ORLEANS, July 22, 1864.

I hereby authorize John A. Newell, of Rapides, to cast my vote in the affirmative on the adoption of the constitution as a whole.

R. W. TALIAFERRO.

Mr. Newell then requested permission to record the vote of Mr. Taliaferro, which being granted, it was recorded in the affirmative.

The President then declared the foregoing vote, after which he cast his own vote in the affirmative

He then declared the constitution of the State of Louisiana adopted as a whole on its final reading.

Mr. Montamat moved that the Committee on Enrollment be instructed to have the constitution duly enrolled by 12 o'clock M., to-morrow.

Carried.

The president announced that in accordance with the requirements of article 155 of the constitution just adopted, he had selected as the three papers in which the said constitution shall be published, the True Delta and The Era, to publish the same in English and French, and the German Gazette, to publish the same in the German languge.

The Convention then adjourned until 12 o'clock M., to-morrow.

Approved.

JOHN E. NEELIS,
Secretary.

SATURDAY, July 22, 1864.

The Convention met, pursuant to adjournment, and was called to order by the president. After prayer by the Rev. Mr. Strong, the secretary called the roll, and following members answered to their names :

Messrs. Abell, Austin, Balch, Barrett, Baum, Beauvais, Bell, Bennie, Buckley, Burke, Campbell, Collin, Cazabat, Cook J K., Cook T., Cutler, Davies, Decker, Duane, Dufresne, Dupaty, Edwards, Ennis, Fish, Flagg, Flood, Foley, Fosdick, Fuller, Gastinel, Geier, Gorlinski, Gruneberg, Healy,

Harnan, Hart, Heard, Henderson, Hills, Hire, Howes, Kavanagh, Kugler, Maas, Mann, Maurer, Mayer, Mendiverri, Montamat, Morris, Murphy E., Murphy M. W., Newell, Normand, O'Conner, Ong, Orr, Payne J., Pintado, Poynot, Purcell J., Pursell S., Schroeder, Schnurr, Seymour, Shaw, Smith, Spellicy, Stocker, Stumpf, Stiner, Stauffer, Sullivan, Taliaferro, Terry, Thorpe, Thomas, Waters, Wenck, Wells, Wilson—82.

Messrs. Crozat, Bofill and Knobloch were excused for non-attendance.

In obedience to a resolution of yesterday, the sergeant-at-arms presented Thomas P. May, Esq., at the bar of the Convention. The president, having read the resolutions passed on the day previous, asked Mr. May what reply he had to make. Thereupon that gentleman read the following paper:

"I am here with the provost marshal to obey a military order issued by Major Gen. Banks, and not in obedience to a resolution of this Convention. At the proper time, in the proper place, and in pursuance of the forms of law, I will answer to any charge made against me and my paper, the Times."

Mr. Henderson moved that Mr. May's answer be considered an additional contempt.

Mr. Abell moved an indefinite postponement of the whole matter.

Upon a motion to lay Mr. Abell's motion on the table the yeas and nays were ordered and the following vote taken:

YEAS—Messrs. Austin, Barrett, Beauvais, Dell, Bennie, Burke, Collin, Cook T., Cutler, Davies, Duane, Dupaty, Edwards, Ennis, Flagg, Flood, Foley, Fuller, Healy, Harnan, Hart, Henderson, Hire, Howes, Maas, Mann, Murphy E., Newell, Normand, O'Conner, Payne J., Poynot, Pursell S., Schroeder, Schnurr, Seymour, Smith, Spellicy, Stocker, Stumpf, Stiner, Stauffer, Taliaferro, Terry, Thomas, Wells, Wilson—47.

NAYS—Messrs. Abell, Balch, Baum, Buckley, Campbell, Cazabat, Cook J. K., Decker, Dufresne, Fish, Fosdick, Geier, Gorlinski, Gruneberg, Heard, Hills, Maurer, Mayer, Mendiverri, Montamat, Morris, Murphy M. W., Ong, Orr, Pintado, Purcell J., Shaw, Sullivan, Thorpe, Waters, Wenck—31.

Mr. Abell's motion was therefore laid on the table. After some discussion the previous question was ordered, and Mr. Henderson's motion adopted.

At the request of Mr. Abell the president read the following order of Gen. Banks:

HEADQUARTERS DEPARTMENT OF THE GULF, }
New Orleans, 23d July, 1864. }

The provost marshal general is directed, upon receipt of this order, to take such measures as may be necessary to enable Mr. De Coursey, sergeant-at-arms of the Constitutional Convention, to bring before that Convention Thomas P. May, Esq., assistant treasurer of the United States, and proprietor and publisher of the New Orleans Times newspaper, to answer to that body for an infringement of its privileges as a representative assembly of the people of Louisiana.

This order will be executed immediately.
N. P. BANKS,
Maj. Gen. Commanding.
OFFICIAL:
W. W. HOWE,
Major and A. A. A. Gen.

Mr. Thomas offered the following preamble and resolutions:

Whereas, Thos. P. May, Esq., editor and proprietor of the newspaper called the New Orleans Times, published in the city of New Orleans, has, within the past six months published articles in said paper which, in the opinion of this Convention, were disloyal in their sentiments to the government, and many of which were in contempt of this Convention, and

Whereas, In the issue of said paper of the 22d of July, a gross libel was published upon the president and members of this Convention, and upon being brought to the bar thereof has refused to purge himself in any manner of said libel and contempt, therefore be it

Resolved, That Thos. P. May, Esq., for his said contempt, committed upon the president and members of this Convention, in publishing in said newspaper said libel, shall be imprisoned in the Parish Prison of the Parish of Orleans for the space of ten days, unless this Convention sooner adjourns; and that the sergeant-at-arms be directed and authorized to carry this resolution into effect.

Be it further Resolved, That the military authorities of this department be respectfully requested by this Convention to suppress the publication of said newspaper.

Re it further Resolved, That the President of the United States be respectfully requested by this Convention to remove the said Thos. P. May, Esq., from the office of assistant treasurer of the United States in New Orleans that he now holds.

Mr. Terry moved the previous question, upon which the yeas and nays were called and the resolution adopted by the following vote:

YEAS—Messrs. Austin, Barrett, Baum, Beauvais, Bell, Bennie, Burke, Collin, Cook

J. K., Cook T., Cutler, Davies, Duane, Dupaty, Edwards, Ennis, Flagg, Flood, Foley, Fuller, Healey, Hart, Henderson, Hire, Howes, Maas, Maurer, Murphy E., Newell, Normand, O'Conner, Payne J., Poynot, Purcell J., Pursell S., Schnurr, Seymour, Smith, Spellicy, Stocker, Stiner, Stauffer, Taliaferro, Terry, Thorpe, Thomas, Wenck, Wells, Wilson—49.

NAYS—Messrs. Abell, Balch, Buckley, Campbell, Cazabat, Decker, Dufresne, Fish, Fosdick, Gastinel, Geier, Gorlinski, Gruneberg, Harnan, Heard, Hills, Kavanagh, Mann, Mayer, Mendiverri, Montamat, Morris, Murphy M. W., Ong, Orr, Pintado, Schroeder, Shaw, Stumpf, Sullivan, Waters—31.

The president then directed the secretary to furnish the sergeant-at-arms with a copy of the resolution, who was asked to carry it into effect.

Mr. Thorpe's ordinance for redistricting the State into congressional districts was taken up and passed. Mr. Thorpe also offered the following, which was adopted:

Resolved, That until otherwise fixed by the Legislature, the salary of the private secretary of the governor shall be twenty-five hundred dollars per annum, and the salary of the chief clerk of the secretary of state shall be two thousand dollars per annum, payable by the auditor of public accounts, quarterly, on their own warrants, and to take effect from the 4th of March, 1864.

Mr. Thomas offered the following resolution, which was adopted:

Resolved, That all bills, indebtedness and unsettled accounts of this Convention accruing at, or after its adjournment, shall be referred to a special auditing committee, to be composed of five members to be appointed by the president. No bills shall be paid without being examined, audited and approved by a majority of said committee ; and bills so audited and approved shall be paid on the warrant of the president on the treasurer of the State, out of any moneys in the treasury of the State not otherwise appropriated.

The president appointed on the committee, raised by Mr. Thomas's resolution, the following members, viz: Messrs. Thomas, Montamat, Barrett, Crozat and Buckley.

Mr. Wells offered the following:

Resolved, That the reporters of this Convention each receive from the funds in the public treasury not otherwise appropriated, the sum of five hundred dollars, as extra compensation for their arduous labor during this Convention, and for the necessary work to be performed after the adjournment of this body—said sums to be drawn upon their own warrants.

Mr. Montamat offered the following substitute :

Resolved, That the following employees of the Convention shall receive the following compensation, to be paid out of the funds of contingent expenses of this Convention:

Sergeant-at-arms,................$200 00
Chief of Enrolling Clerks,...... 100 00
Enrolling Clerks, (each).......... 100 00
Postmaster,..................... 50 00
Doorkeeper,.................... 100 00
Messengers, (each)............. 25 00
Reporter and assistants, (each).... 200 00

Mr. Stiner offered the following amendment, which was accepted by Mr. Montamat :

Resolved, That the sum of two hundred and fifty dollars, each, be paid to Messrs. Matthew Whilldin and J. N. Russ, reporters, for services rendered to this Convention.

The resolution as amended was then adopted.

Mr. Abell offered the following :

Whereas, During the absence of the official reporter the duty of reading and revising the manuscripts and proofs, the compilation of the debates and other duties of the position, have been performed under the direction of the president, by H. A. Gallup, Esq., assistant reporter, in addition to his duties as such—

Resolved, That for such services so rendered H. A. Gallup receive, in addition to his salary as assistant reporter, the same compensation as is provided for the official reporter for such time as may be found due by the president, to be paid on the warrant of the president out of any money in the treasury not otherwise appropriated.

Adopted by a rising vote of 45 yeas to 15 nays.

Mr. Waters moved that each of the reporters of this Convention receive $500. Carried.

Mr. Thorpe moved that each of the porters receive $100.

Mr. Sullivan moved that the door-keeper and post-master, each, receive $150.

The President remarked that these motions were somewhat out of order, as they were merely verbal and made no provision for the manner in which they should be paid. It would, therefore, be better to present them in proper form, which being assented to, Mr. Waters reduced his to writing, as follows :

Resolved, That the reporters of this Convention receive five hundred dollars each, out of any moneys in the treasury not otherwise appropriated, payable on their own warrant.

Adopted.

Mr. Thorpe, chairman of the Committee on Enrollment, reported that the Constitution, as enrolled, was in his hands, but not having had time to read and compare it, he would reserve until Monday's session, when submit the constitution for signature.

The Convention then adjourned until Monday, 25th inst., at 12 o'clock, M.

Approved,
JOHN E. NEELIS,
Secretary.

MONDAY, July 25, 1864.

The Convention met pursuant to adjournment, and was called to order by the president. The secretary called the roll, and the following members answered to their names:

Messrs. Abell, Austin, Balch, Barrett, Baum, Beauvais, Bell, Bofill, Buckley, Burke, Campbell, Collin, Cazabat, Cook J. K., Cook T., Crozat, Cutler, Davies, Decker, Duane, Dufresne, Duke, Dupaty, Edwards, Ennis, Fish, Flagg, Flood, Foley, Fosdick, Fuller, Gastinel, Geier, Gorlinski, Gruneberg, Healy, Harnan, Hart, Heard, Henderson, Hills, Hire, Howes, Kavanagh, Knobloch, Kugler, Maas, Mann, Maurer, Mendiverri, Montamat, Morris, Murphy E., Murphy M. W., Normand, O'Conner, Orr, Payne J., Pintado, Poynot, Purcell J., Pursell S., Schroeder, Schnurr, Seymour, Shaw, Smith, Spelliey, Stocker, Stumpf, Stiner, Stauffer, Sullivan, Terry, Thorpe, Thomas, Waters, Wenck, Wells, Wilson—80.

The day's proceedings were then opened with prayer by the Rev. Mr. Strong.

The minutes of yesterday's proceedings were read and adopted.

Mr. Cutler offered the following resolution as a substitute for and in lieu of the appropriations and resolutions for extra compensation of officers and others of this Convention, passed on Saturday last, viz:

Resolved, That the following named officers of this Convention, and others, receive as extra compensation the following sums from the treasury of the State, on the warrant of the president, from money not otherwise appropriated :
To Hon. J. N. Carrigan, state librarian $500 00
To each of the reporters......... 500 00
To the sergeant-at-arms 500 00
To each of the deputy sergeants-at-arms 100 00
To the post-master............. 150 00
To the door-keeper.............. 300 00
To the chief enrolling clerk..... 100 00
To each enrolling clerk......... 100 00
To each messenger.............. 50 00
To three porters, each.......... 50 00
To four policemen, each......... 100 00
To J. N. Russ, of the State Gazette, M. Whilldin and T. H. Draper, of the True Delta, (reporters,) each 250 00

The previous question being ordered, the resolution was adopted by the following rising vote: yeas 61, nays 7.

Mr. Fish offered the following preamble and resolutions:

Whereas, A Convention, claiming to act in the name of the State of Louisiana, did, on the 26th day of January, 1861, pass an ordinance entitled "An ordinance to dissolve the union between the State of Louisiana and other States united with her under the compact entitled 'The Constitution of the United States of America,'" therein declaring and ordaining the repeal of "all laws and ordinances by which the State of Louisiana became a member of the Federal Union," and absolving "her citizens from all allegiance to said Government;"

And whereas, Such ordinance of secession was based upon an unfounded assumption of State sovereignty, and a perverted theory of State rights, and brought about in the interest of slavery; therefore, be it

Resolved, That we, the people of Louisiana in Convention assembled, do solemnly denounce the doctrines of "State Rights" and State sovereignty (interpreted as they have been into a justification of secession) as utterly subversive of our form of government, and tending to confusion, anarchy and national destruction.

Resolved, That we hold and maintain that our primary allegiance is due to the government of the United States; that the constitution and laws of the United States are the supreme law of the land, anything in the constitution or laws of any State to the contrary notwithstanding; that no State convention, whether fairly representing the people or not, has any right, power or authority to absolve us from that allegiance, and that, consequently, the act commonly called the "Ordinance of Secession" is, and has always been, null and void.

Resolved, That having legally abolished the institution of slavery in this State, as an evil in itself and a constant source of national disturbance and danger, and desiring for the same reasons to see it legally abolished throughout the country, we are in favor of so amending the constitution of the United States as to secure this object.

Adopted by the following vote:

YEAS—Messrs. Austin, Barrett, Baum, Beauvais, Bell, Bofill, Buckley, Burke, Campbell, Collin, Cazabat, Cook T., Crozat, Cutler, Davies, Duane, Duke, Dupaty, Edwards, Ennis, Fish, Flagg, Flood, Foley, Fosdick, Fuller, Geier, Gorlinski, Healy, Harnan, Hart, Henderson, Hills, Hire, Howes, Kavanagh, Kugler, Mann, Maurer, Montamat, Morris, Murphy E., Normand, O'Conner, Orr, Payne J., Pintado, Poynot, Purcell J., Pursell S., Schroeder, Schnurr, Seymour, Shaw, Smith, Spellicy, Stocker, Stumpf, Stiner, Stauffer, Sullivan, Terry, Thorpe, Thomas, Waters, Wenck, Wells, Wilson—68.

NAYS—Messrs. Abell, Balch, Decker, Dufresne, Gruneberg, Maas, Mendiverri, Murphy M. W.—8.

Mr. Thomas offered the following:

AN ORDINANCE DEFINING THE QUALIFICATIONS OF VOTERS.

SECTION 1. *Be it ordained by the people of the State of Louisiana in Convention assembled*, That until otherwise provided by law, all commissioners, or other officers or persons presiding over elections held in this State, shall require that each voter shall possess the qualifications defined in the constitution as adopted and submitted by this Convention, and shall have declared his allegiance to the United States government according to the provisions of the president's proclamation of December the 8th, 1863.

SEC. 2. *Be it further ordained*, That the executive officers of the State be charged with the execution of this ordinance, and the providing of such details and instructions as may be necessary to carry the same into effect.

SEC. 3. *Be it further ordained*, That this ordinance shall have the force and effect of law from and after its passage until hereafter repealed or modified by the Legislature of the State.

Adopted by a rising vote of yeas 60, nays 9.

Mr. Fosdick offered the following:

Whereas, The adoption of article 36 of the constitution, excluding ministers of every persuasion or calling from a seat in the Legislature of this State is liable to a misconstruction, be it therefore

Resolved, That the adoption of said article was intended solely to separate the holy calling of the ministry from the arena of politics, believing by such a course we are furthering the true interests of the gospel.

Resolved, That the sum of $1000 be paid on the warrant of the president of this Convention out of any moneys in the State treasury not otherwise appropriated, to be by him distributed among the clergy who have officiated by prayer during the session of this Convention.

Mr. Montamat moved to lay the resolution on the table, on which question the yeas and nays were ordered, resulting as follows:

YEAS — Messrs. Collin, Davies, Dupaty, Edwards, Gastinel, Healy, Harnan, Hart, Kugler, Montamat, Murphy M. W., Normand, Schnurr, Seymour, Stocker, Stumpf, Sullivan, Waters, Wenck—19.

NAYS — Messrs. Abell, Austin, Balch, Barrett, Baum, Beauvais, Bell, Bennie, Bofill, Buckley, Burke, Campbell, Cazabat, Cook T., Crozat, Cutler, Decker, Duane, Dufresne, Duke, Ennis, Fish, Flagg, Flood, Foley, Fosdick, Fuller, Geier, Gorlinski, Gruneberg, Henderson, Hills, Hire, Howes, Kavanagh, Maas, Mann, Maurer, Mendiverri, Morris, Murphy E., O'Conner, Orr, Payne J., Pintado, Poynot, Purcell J., Pursell S., Schroeder, Shaw, Smith, Spellicy, Stiner, Stauffer, Terry, Thorpe, Thomas, Wells, Wilson—58.

The motion to lay on the table being lost, Mr. Stauffer offered the following substitute for Mr. Fosdick's resolution:

Resolved, That the thanks of this Convention are due, and hereby tendered, to those ministers of the gospel who have officiated during its sessions.

A motion to lay Mr. Stauffer's substitute on the table was made, and a rising vote being taken, resulted—yeas 29, nays 29, and there being a tie the president cast his vote in the affirmative, therefore Mr. Stauffer's substitute was laid on the table.

Mr. Fosdick's resolution was then adopted on a rising vote—yeas 56, nays 20.

Mr. Shaw offered the following resolution:

Resolved, That such officers and employees of the Convention as may be necessary for the completion of its work shall, after adjournment, be under the direction of the chairman of the Committee of Enrollment and the president of the Convention, and the services of all officers and employees not required by said president or chairman, or either of them, shall have power to discharge any of said officers for want of promptness, or on account of the completion of their work.

Resolved, That after adjournment any of the Standing Committees may perform such duties as may have been assigned them by the rules or resolutions of the Convention, and which may be necessary for winding up and perfecting the work of the Convention, and the president shall require any such duties to be performed by such committees if deemed by him necessary in case of their neglect.

Adopted.

Mr. Cutler offered the following :

Resolved, That the salary of the clerk of the treasurer and the chief clerk of the auditor of public accounts of the State of Louisiana, shall be three thousand dollars per annum, until otherwise provided by law. This resolution to take effect from its passage

Laid on the table.

Mr. Cutler offered the following resolution :

Resolved, That when this Convention adjourns, it shall be at the call of the president, whose duty it shall be to reconvoke the Convention for any cause, or in case the Constitution should not be ratified, for the purpose of taking such measures as may be necessary for the formation of a civil government for the State of Louisiana. He shall also, in that case, call upon the proper officers of the State to cause elections to be held to fill any vacancies that may exist in the Convention, in parishes where the same may be practicable.

Resolved, That in case of the ratification of the Constitution, it shall be in the power of the Legislature of the State, at its first session, to reconvoke the Convention, in like manner, in case it should be deemed expedient or necessary, for the purpose of making amendments or additions to the Constitution that may, in the opinion of the Legislature, require a reassembling of the Convention, or, in case of the occurrence of any emergency, requiring its action.

Resolved, That no per diem of members shall be allowed during the adjournment.

The previous question was ordered and the following vote taken on the adoption of the resolution :

YEAS—Messrs. Austin, Balch, Barrett, Baum, Beauvais, Bell, Burke, Collin, Cazabat, Cook T., Crozat, Cutler, Davies, Duane, Dufresne, Duke, Dupaty, Edwards, Ennis, Fish, Flagg, Flood, Foley, Fuller, Geier, Gorlinski, Gruneberg, Hart, Henderson, Hire, Howes, Kavanagh, Kugler, Maas, Mann, Maurer, Morris, Murphy E., Normand, O'Conner, Orr, Payne J., Pintado, Poynot, Purcell J., Pursell S., Schroeder, Schnurr, Seymour, Shaw, Smith, Spellicy, Stocker, Stumpf, Stiner, Stauffer, Terry, Thorpe, Thomas, Waters, Wells, Wilson—62.

NAYS—Messrs. Abell, Bofill, Buckley, Campbell, Decker, Fosdick, Gastinel, Healy, Hills, Mendiverri, Montamat, Murphy M. W., Sullivan, Wenck—14.

The resolution was therefore adopted.

On motion of Mr. Thorpe, the state librarian was directed to furnish each member with fifty copies each of the Minutes, the Journal of Debates and Constitution, as soon as the same shall have been printed.

Mr. Thorpe, chairman of the Committee on Enrollment, presented the constitution of the State of Louisiana duly enrolled, which was then signed by the President.

The following members signed the Constitution :

Messrs. Austin, Barrett, Baum, Beauvais, Bell, Burke, Collin, Cazabat, Cook T., Crozat, Cutler, Davies, Duane, Dupaty, Edwards, Ennis, Fish, Flagg, Flood, Foley, Fosdick, Fuller, Geier, Gorlinski, Healy, Hart, Henderson, Hills, Hire, Howes, Kavanagh, Kugler, Mann, Maurer, Montamat, Morris, Murphy E., Murphy M. W., Normand, O'Conner, Payne J., Pintado, Poynot, Purcell J., Pursell S., Schroeder, Schnurr, Seymour, Shaw, Smith, Spellicy, Stocker, Stiner, Stauffer, Terry, Thorpe, Thomas, Wenck, Wells, Wilson.

The following members declined to sign the same, viz : Messrs. Abell, Balch, Bofill, Buckley, Campbell, Decker, Dufresne, Duke, Gastinel, Gruneberg, Knobloch, Maas, Mendiverri, Orr, Stumpf, Sullivan and Waters.

The remaining members were absent or did not answer to their names when called.

On declining to sign, Mr. Mendiverri submitted the following reasons therefor : "Under my honest convictions of what is politic, just and right, I cannot sign this constitution."

Mr. Bofill also submitted his reasons for not signing, in writing, which were ordered to be published in the journal of debates.

On motion of Mr. Thorpe, the constitution was ordered to be deposited in the office of the secretary of state, in order that members who were absent to-day, might affix their signatures thereto.

Mr. Shaw being in the chair, Mr. Fosdick offered the following :

Resolved, That the thanks of this Convention are eminently due, and are hereby tendered to the Hon. E. H. Durell, for the courteous, just and dignified manner with which he has presided over our deliberations.

The resolution was unanimously adopted.

The president having resumed the chair, Mr. Shaw informed him of the will of the Convention, and read the resolution which had been adopted with such unanimity, to which the President replied by returning his thanks to the Convention in a most feeling and appropriate manner.

His Excellency Governor Hahn being present was called upon and delivered an able and interesting address to the Convention, after which the proceedings were closed with an appropriate prayer by the Rev. Dr. Newman.

The Convention then adjourned subject to the call of the president, in pursuance of the resolutions this day adopted.

E. H. DURELL,
President Convention.

JOHN E. NEELIS.
Secretary.

CONSTITUTION OF THE STATE OF LOUISIANA.

ADOPTED IN CONVENTION, JULY 23, 1864.

PREAMBLE.

We, the people of the State of Louisiana, do ordain and establish this Constitution.

TITLE I.

EMANCIPATION.

Article 1. Slavery and involuntary servitude, except as a punishment for crime, whereof the party shall have been duly convicted, are hereby forever abolished and prohibited throughout the State.

Art. 2. The Legislature shall make no law recognizing the right of property in man.

TITLE II.

DISTRIBUTION OF POWERS.

Art. 3. The powers of the government of the State of Louisiana shall be divided into three distinct departments, and each of them shall be confined to a separate body of magistracy, to-wit: those which are legislative to one, those which are executive to another, and those which are judicial to another.

Art. 4. No one of these departments, nor any person holding office in one of them, shall exercise power properly belonging to either of the others, except in the instances hereinafter expressly directed or permitted.

TITLE III.

LEGISLATIVE DEPARTMENT.

Art. 5. The legislative power of the State shall be vested in two distinct branches, the one to be styled "the House of Representatives," the other "the Senate," and both "the General Assembly of the State of Louisiana."

Art. 6. The members of the House of Representatives shall continue in service for the term of two years from the day of the closing of the general elections.

Art. 7. Representatives shall be chosen on the first Monday in November every two years, and the election shall be completed in one day. The General Assembly shall meet annually on the first Monday in January, unless a different day be appointed by law, and their sessions shall be held at the seat of government. There shall also be a session of the General Assembly in the city of New Orleans, beginning on the first Monday of October, eighteen hundred and sixty-four; and it shall be the duty of the governor to cause a special election to be held for members of the General Assembly, in all the parishes where the same may be held, on the day of the election for ratification or rejection of this Constitution—to be valid in case of ratification; and in other parishes or districts he shall cause elections to be held as soon as it may become practicable, to fill the vacancies for such parishes or districts in the General Assembly. The term of office of the first General Assembly shall expire as though its members had been elected on the first Monday of November, eighteen hundred and sixty-three.

Art. 8. Every duly qualified elector under this constitution shall be eligible to a seat in the General Assembly: *Provided*, that no person shall be a representative or senator unless he be, at the time of his election, a duly qualified voter of the representative or senatorial district from which he is elected.

Art. 9. Elections for the members of the General Assembly shall be held at the several election precincts established by law.

Art. 10. Representation in the House of Representatives shall be equal and uniform, and shall be regulated and ascertained by the number of qualified electors. Each parish shall have at least one representative. No new parish shall be created with a territory less than six hundred and twenty-five square miles, nor with a number of electors less than the full number entitling it to a representative; nor when the creation of such new parish would leave any other parish without the said extent of territory and number of electors. The first enumeration by the State authorities, under this constitution, shall be made in the year eighteen hundred and sixty-six, the second in the year eighteen hundred and seventy, the third in the year eighteen hundred and seventy-six; after which time the General Assembly shall direct in what manner the

174 CONSTITUTION OF THE STATE OF LOUISIANA.

census shall be taken, so that it be made at least once in every period of ten years for the purpose of ascertaining the total population, and the number of qualified electors in each parish and election district; and in case of informality, omission or error, in the census returns from any district, the the Legislature shall order a new census taken in such parish or election district.

Art. 11. At the first session of the Legislature after the making of each enumeration, the Legislature shall apportion the representation amongst the several parishes and election districts on the basis of qualified electors as aforesaid. A representative number shall be fixed, and each parish and election district shall have as many representatives as the aggregate number of its electors will entitle it to, and an additional representative for any fraction exceeding one-half the representative number. The number of representatives shall not be more than one hundred and twenty, nor less than ninety.

Art. 12. Until an apportionment shall be made, and elections held under the same, in accordance with the first enumeration to be made, as directed in article 10. the representation in the Senate and House of Representatives shall be as follows:

For the parish of Orleans, forty-four representatives, to be elected as follows:

First Representative District	3
Second do.	5
Third do.	7
Fourth do.	3
Fifth do.	4
Sixth do.	?
Seventh do.	3
Eighth do.	3
Ninth do.	4
Tenth do.	8
Orleans, Right Bank	2
For the parish of Livingston	1
do. St. Tammany	1
do. Pointe Coupée	1
do. St. Martin	2
do. Concordia	1
do. Madison	1
do. Franklin	1
do. St. Mary	1
do. Jefferson	3
do. Plaquemines	1
do. St. Bernard	1
do. St. Charles	1
do. St. John the Baptist	1
do. St. James	1
do. Ascension	1
do. Assumption	3
do. Lafourche	3
do. Terrebonne	2
do. Iberville	1
do. West Baton Rouge	1
do. East Baton Rouge	2
do. West Feliciana	1
do. East Feliciana	1
For the Parish of Washington	1
do. St. Helena	1
do. Vermillion	1
do. Lafayette	2
do. St. Landry	4
do. Calcasieu	2
do. Avoyelles	2
do. Rapides	3
do. Natchitoches	2
do. Sabine	1
do. Caddo	2
do. DeSoto	2
do. Ouachita	1
do. Union	2
do. Morehouse	1
do. Jackson	2
do. Caldwell	1
do. Catahoula	2
do. Claiborne	3
do. Bossier	1
do. Bienville	2
do. Carroll	1
do. Tensas	1
do. Winn	2
Total	118

And the State shall be divided into the following senatorial districts: All that portion of the parish of Orleans lying on the left bank of the Mississippi river shall be divided into two senatorial districts; the First and Fourth Districts of the city of New Orleans shall compose one district and shall elect five senators; and the Second and Third Districts of said city shall compose the other district, and shall elect four senators.

The parishes of Plaquemines, St. Bernard and all that part of the parish of Orleans on the right bank of the Mississippi river shall form one district, and shall elect one senator.

The parish of Jefferson shall form one district, and shall elect one senator.

The parishes of St. Charles and Lafourche shall form one district, and shall elect one senator.

The parishes of St. John the Baptist and St. James shall form one district, and shall elect one senator.

The parishes of Ascension, Assumption and Terrebonne shall form one district, and shall elect two senators.

The parish of Iberville shall form one district, and shall elect one senator.

The parish of East Baton Rouge shall form one district, and shall elect one senator.

The parishes of West Baton Rouge, Point Coupée and West Feliciana shall form one district, and shall elect two senators.

The parish of East Feliciana shall form one district, and shall elect one senator.

The parishes of Washington, St. Tammany, St. Helena and Livingston shall form one district, and shall elect one senator.

The parishes of Concordia and Tensas shall form one district, and shall elect one senator.

The parishes of Madison and Carroll shall form one district, and shall elect one senator.

The parishes of Morehouse, Ouachita, Union and Jackson shall form one district, and shall elect two senators.

The parishes of Catahoula, Caldwell and Franklin, shall form one district, and shall elect one senator.

The parishes of Bossier, Bienville, Claiborne and Winn shall form one district, and shall elect two senators.

The parishes of Natchitoches, Sabine, DeSoto and Caddo shall form one district, and shall elect two senators.

The parishes of St. Landry, Lafayette and Calcasieu shall form one district, and shall elect two senators.

The parishes of St. Martin and Vermillion shall form one district, and shall elect one senator.

The parish of St. Mary shall form one district, and shall elect one senator.

The parishes of Rapides and Avoyelles shall form one district, and shall elect two senators.

Art. 13. The House of Representatives shall choose its speaker and other officers.

Art. 14. Every white male who has attained the age of twenty-one years, and who has been a resident of the State twelve months next preceding the election, and the last three months thereof in the parish in which he offers to vote, and who shall be a citizen of the United States, shall have the right of voting.

Art. 15. The Legislature shall have power to pass laws extending suffrage to such other persons, citizens of the United States, as by military service, by taxation to support the government, or by intellectual fitness, may be deemed entitled thereto.

Art. 16. No voter, on removing from one parish to another within the State, shall lose the right of voting in the former until he shall have acquired it in the latter. Electors shall in all cases, except treason, felony or breach of the peace, be privileged from arrest during their attendance at, going to, or returning from elections.

Art. 17. The Legislature shall provide by law that the names and residence of all qualified electors shall be registered in order to entitle them to vote; but the registry shall be free of cost to the elector.

Art. 18. No pauper, no person under interdiction, nor under conviction of any crime punishable with hard labor, shall be entitled to vote at any election in this State.

Art. 19. No person shall be entitled to vote at any election held in this State except in the parish of his residence, and, in cities and towns divided into election precincts, in the election precinct in which he resides.

Art. 20. The members of the Senate shall be chosen for the term of four years. The Senate, when assembled, shall have the power to choose its own officers.

Art. 21. The Legislature, in every year in which they apportion representation in the House of Representatives, shall divide the State into senatorial districts.

Art. 22. No parish shall be divided in the formation of a senatorial district, the parish of Orleans excepted. And whenever a new parish shall be created, it shall be attached to the senatorial district from which most of its territory was taken, or to another contiguous district, at the discretion of the Legislature; but shall not be attached to more than one district. The number of senators shall be thirty-six; and they shall be apportioned among the senatorial districts according to the electoral population contained in the several districts: *Provided*, that no parish be entitled to more than nine senators.

Art. 23. In all apportionments of the Senate, the electoral population of the whole State shall be divided by the number thirty-six, and the result produced by this division shall be the senatorial ratio entitling a senatorial district to a senator. Single or contiguous parishes shall be formed into districts, having a population the nearest possible to the number entitling a district to a senator; and if in the apportionment to make a parish or district fall short of or exceed the ratio, then a district may be formed having not more than two senators, but not otherwise. No new apportionment shall have the effect of abridging the term of service of any senator already elected at the time of making the apportionment. After an enumeration has been made as directed in the 10th article, the Legislature shall not pass any law until an apportionment of representation in both Houses of the General Assembly be made.

Art. 24. At the first session of the General Assembly, after this constitution takes effect, the senators shall be equally divided by lot, into two classes; the seats of the senators of the first class shall be vacated at the expiration of the term of the first House of Representatives; of the second class at the expiration of the term of the second House of Representatives; so that one-half shall be chosen every two years, and a rotation thereby kept up perpetually. In case any district shall have elected two or more senators, said senators shall vacate their seats respectively at the end of the term aforesaid, and lots shall be drawn between them.

Art. 25. The first election for senators shall be held at the same time that the election for representatives is held; and thereafter there shall be elections of senators at the same time with each general election of representatives, to fill the places of those senators whose term of service may have expired.

Art. 26. Not less than a majority of the members of each House of the General Assembly shall form a quorum to do business; but a smaller number may adjourn from day to day, and shall be authorized by law to compel the attendance of absent members.

Art. 27. Each House of the General Assembly shall judge of the qualifications, elections and return of its members; but a contested election shall be determined in such a manner as shall be directed by law.

Art. 28. Each House of the General Assembly may determine the rules of its proceeding, punish a member for disorderly behavior, and, with a concurrence of two-thirds, expel a member; but not a second time for the same offence.

Art. 29. Each House of the General Assembly shall keep and publish weekly a journal of its proceedings; and the yeas and nays of the members on any question shall, at the desire of any two of them, be entered on the journal.

Art. 30. Each House may punish, by imprisonment, any person not a member, for disrespectful and disorderly behavior in its presence, or for obstructing any of its proceedings. Such imprisonment shall not exceed ten days for any one offence.

Art. 31. Neither House, during the sessions of the General Assembly, shall, without the consent of the other, adjourn for more than three days, nor to any other place than that in which they may be sitting.

Art. 32. The members of the General Assembly shall receive from the public treasury a compensation for their services, which shall be eight dollars per day, during their attendance, going to and returning from the sessions of their respective Houses. The compensation may be increased or diminished, by law, but no alteration shall take effect during the period of service of the members of the House of Representatives by whom such alteration shall have been made. No session shall extend to a period beyond sixty days, to date from its commencement, and any legislative action had after the expiration of the said sixty days, shall be null and void. This provision shall not apply to the first Legislature which is to convene after the adoption of this constitution.

Art. 33. The members of the General Assembly shall in all cases, except treason, felony, breach of the peace, be privileged from arrest during their attendance at the sessions of their respective Houses, and going to or returning from the same; and for any speech or debate in either House shall not be questioned in any other place.

Art. 34. No senator or representative shall, during the term for which he was elected, nor for one year thereafter, be appointed to any civil office of profit under this State, which shall have been created, or the emoluments of which shall have been increased during the time such senator or representative was in office, except to such offices as may be filled by the election of the people.

Art. 35. No person, who at any time may have been a collector of taxes, whether State, parish or municipal, or who may have been otherwise entrusted with public money, shall be eligible to the General Assembly, or to any office of profit or trust, under the State government, until he shall have obtained a discharge for the amount of such collections, and for all public moneys with which he may have been entrusted.

Art. 36. No person, while he continues to exercise the functions of a clergyman of any religious denomination whatever, shall be eligible to the General Assembly.

Art. 37. No bill shall have the force of a law until, on three several days, it be read over in each House of the General Assembly, and free discussion allowed thereon; unless in case of urgency, four-fifths of the House, where the bill shall be pending, may deem it expedient to dispense with this rule.

Art. 38. All bills for raising revenue, shall originate in the House of Representatives; but the Senate may propose amendments, as in other bills: *Provided*, they shall not introduce any new matter, under the color of an amendment, which does not relate to raising revenue.

Art. 39. The General Assembly shall regulate, by law, by whom, and in what manner, writs of election shall be issued to fill the vacancies which may happen in either branch thereof.

Art. 40. The Senate shall vote on the confirmation or rejection of the officers, to be appointed by the governor with the advice and consent of the Senate, by yeas and nays; and the names of the senators voting for and against the appointments, respectively, shall be entered on a journal to be kept for that purpose, and made public at the end of each session, or before.

Art. 41. Returns of all elections for members of the General Assembly shall be made to the secretary of state.

Art. 42. In the year in which a regular election for a senator of the United States is to take place, the members of the General Assembly shall meet in the hall of the House of Representatives on the second Monday following the meeting of the Legislature, and proceed to said election.

TITLE IV.

EXECUTIVE DEPARTMENT.

Art. 43. The supreme executive power

of the State shall be vested in a chief magistrate, who shall be styled the governor of the State of Louisiana. He shall hold his office during the term of four years, and, together with the lieutenant governor, chosen for the same term, be elected as follows: The qualified electors for representatives shall vote for governor and lieutenant governor at the time and place of voting for representatives; the returns of every election shall be sealed up and transmitted by the proper returning officer to the secretary of state, who shall deliver them to the speaker of the House of Representatives on the second day of the session of the General Assembly then to be holden. The members of the General Assembly shall meet in the House of Representatives to examine and count the votes. The person having the greatest number of votes for governor shall be declared duly elected; but if two or more persons shall be equal and the highest in the number of votes polled for governor, one of them shall immediately be chosen governor by joint vote of the members of the General Assembly. The person having the greatest number of votes polled for lieutenant governor shall be lieutenant governor; but if two or more persons shall be equal and highest in the number of votes polled for lieutenant governor, one of them shall be immediately chosen lieutenant governor by joint vote of the members of the General Assembly.

Art. 44. No person shall be eligible to the office of governor or lieutenant governor who shall not have attained the age of thirty-five years, and been a citizen and resident within the State for the period of five years next preceding his election.

Art. 45. The governor shall enter on the discharge of his duties on the second Monday of January next ensuing his election, and shall continue in office until the Monday next succeeding the day that his successor shall be declared duly elected, and shall have taken the oath or affirmation required by the constitution.

Art. 46. No member of Congress, minister of any religious denomination, or any person holding office under the United States government, shall be eligible to the office of governor or lieutenant governor.

Art. 47. In case of impeachment of the governor, his removal from office, death, refusal or inability to qualify, resignation or absence from the State, the powers and duties of the office shall devolve upon the lieutenant governor for the residue of the term, or until the governor, absent or impeached, shall return or be acquitted. The Legislature may provide by law for the case of removal, impeachment, death, resignation, disability or refusal to qualify, of both the governor and the lieutenant governor, declaring what officer shall act as governor, and such officer shall act accordingly, until the disability be removed, or for the remainder of the term.

Art. 48. The lieutenant governor or officer discharging the duties of governor, shall, during his administration, receive the same compensation to which the governor would have been entitled had he continued in office.

Art. 49. The lieutenant governor shall, by virtue of his office, be president of the Senate, but shall have only a casting vote therein. Whenever he shall administer the government, or shall be unable to attend as president of the Senate, the senators shall elect one of their own members as president of the Senate for the time being.

Art. 50. The governor shall receive for his services a compensation of eight thousand dollars per annum, payable quarterly, on his own warrant.

Art. 51. The lieutenant governor shall receive for his services a salary of five thousand dollars per annum, to be paid quarterly.

Art. 52. The governor shall have power to grant reprieves for all offences against the State, and, except in cases of impeachment, shall, with the consent of the Senate, have power to grant pardons, remit fines and forfeitures, after conviction. In cases of treason, he may grant reprieves until the end of the next session of the General Assembly, in which the power of pardoning shall be vested.

Art. 53. He shall be commander-in-chief of the militia of this State, except when they shall be called into the service of the United States.

Art. 54. He shall nominate, and, by and with the advice and consent of the Senate, appoint all officers whose offices are established by the constitution, and whose appointments are not herein otherwise provided for: *Provided*, however, that the Legislature shall have a right to prescribe the mode of appointment to all other offices established by law.

Art. 55. The governor shall have power to fill vacancies that may happen during the recess of the Senate, by granting commissions which shall expire at the end of the next session thereof, unless otherwise provided for in this constitution; but no person who has been nominated for office and rejected by the Senate, shall be appointed to the same office during the recess of the Senate.

Art. 56. He may require information, in writing, from the officers in the executive department upon any subject relating to the duties of their respective offices.

Art. 57. He shall, from time to time, give to the General Assembly information respecting the situation of the State, and recommend to their consideration such measures as he may deem expedient.

Art. 58. He may, on extraordinary occasions, convene the General Assembly at the seat of government, or at a different place if that should have become dangerous from an enemy, or from epidemic; and, in case of disagreement between the two Houses as to the time of adjournment, he may adjourn them to such time as he may think proper, not exceeding four months.

Art. 59. He shall take care that the laws are faithfully executed.

Art. 60. Every bill which shall have passed both Houses shall be presented to the governor; if he approves, he shall sign it, if not, he shall return it with his objections to the House in which it originated, which shall enter the objections at large upon its journal, and proceed to consider it; if, after such consideration, two-thirds of all the members elected to that House shall agree to pass the bill, it shall be sent, with the objections, to the other House, by which it shall be likewise considered, and if approved by two-thirds of the members elected to that House, it shall be a law; but in such cases the vote of both Houses shall be determined by yeas and nays, and the names of the members voting for or against the bill shall be entered on the journal of each House respectively. If any bill shall not be returned by the governor within ten days (Sundays excepted) after it shall have been presented to him, it shall be a law in like manner as if he had signed it; unless the General Assembly, by adjournment, prevent its return.

Art. 61. Every order, resolution or vote, to which the concurrence of both Houses may be necessary, except on a question of adjournment, shall be presented to the governor, and before it shall take effect, be approved by him, or, being disapproved, shall be repassed by two-thirds of the members elected to each House of the General Assembly.

Art. 62. There shall be a secretary of state who shall hold his office during the term for which the governor shall have been elected. The records of the State shall be kept and preserved in the office of the secretary; he shall keep a fair register of the official acts and proceedings of the governor, and when necessary shall attest them; he shall, when required, lay the said register, and all papers, minutes and vouchers relative to his office, before either House of the General Assembly, and shall perform such other duties as may be enjoined on him by law.

Art. 63. There shall be a treasurer of the State, and an auditor of public accounts, who shall hold their respective offices during the term of four years.

Art. 64. The secretary of state, treasurer of state and auditor of public accounts shall be elected by the qualified electors of the State; and in case of any vacancy caused by the resignation, death or absence of the secretary, treasurer or auditor, the governor shall order an election to fill said vacancy.

Art. 65. The secretary of state, the treasurer and the auditor shall receive a salary of five thousand dollars per annum each.

Art. 66. All commissions shall be in the name and by the authority of the State of Louisiana, and shall be sealed with the State seal and signed by the governor.

Art. 67. All able-bodied men in the State shall be armed and disciplined for its defence.

Art. 68. The militia of the State shall be organized in such manner as may be hereafter deemed most expedient by the Legislature.

TITLE V.

JUDICIARY DEPARTMENT.

Art. 69. The judiciary power shall be vested in a Supreme Court, in such inferior courts as the Legislature may, from time to time, order and establish, and in justices of the peace.

Art. 70. The Supreme Court, except in cases hereafter provided, shall have appellate jurisdiction only; which jurisdiction shall extend to all cases when the matter in dispute shall exceed three hundred dollars; to all cases in which the constitutionality or legality of any tax, toll or impost whatsoever, or of any fine, forfeiture or penalty imposed by a municipal corporation, shall be in contestation; and to all criminal cases on questions of law alone whenever the offence charged is punishable with death or imprisonment at hard labor, or when a fine exceeding three hundred dollars is actually imposed.

Art. 71. The Supreme Court shall be composed of one chief justice and four associate justices, a majority of whom shall constitute a quorum. The chief justice shall receive a salary of seven thousand five hundred dollars, and each of the associate justices a salary of seven thousand dollars, annually, until otherwise provided by law. The court shall appoint its own clerks.

Art. 72. The Supreme Court shall hold its sessions in New Orleans from the first Monday in the month of November to the end of the month of June, inclusive. The Legislature shall have the power to fix the sessions elsewhere during the rest of the year; until otherwise provided the sessions shall be held as heretofore.

Art. 73. The Supreme Court, and each of the judges thereof, shall have power to issue writs of *habeas corpus*, at the instance of all persons in acutual custody under process, in all cases in which they may have appellate jurisdiction.

Art. 74. No judgment shall be rendered

by the Supreme Court without the concurrence of a majority of the judges comprising the court. Whenever the majority cannot agree, in consequence of the recusation of any member of the court, the judges not recused shall have power to call upon any judge or judges of the inferior courts, whose duty it shall be, when so called upon, to sit in the place of the judge or judges recused, and to aid in determining the case.

Art. 75. All judges, by virtue of their office, shall be conservators of the peace throughout the State. The style of all process shall be "the State of Louisiana." All prosecutions shall be carried on in the name and by the authority of the State of Louisiana, and conclude against the peace and dignity of the same.

Art. 76. The judges of all courts within the State shall, as often as it may be advisable so to do, in every definitive judgment, refer to the particular law in virtue of which such judgment may be rendered, and in all cases adduce the reasons on which their judgment is founded.

Art. 77. The judges of all courts shall be liable to impeachment; but for any reasonble cause, which shall not be sufficient ground for impeachment, the governor shall remove any of them, on the address of a majority of the members elected to each House of the General Assembly. In every such case the cause or causes for which such removal may be required shall be stated at length in the address, and inserted in the journal of each House.

Art. 78. The judges both of the Supreme and inferior courts shall receive a salary which shall not be diminished during their continuance in office; and they are prohibited from receiving any fees of office or other compensation than their salaries for any civil duties performed by them.

Art. 79. The judges of the SupremeCourt shall be appointed by the governor, by and with the advice and consent of the Senate, for a term of eight years; the judges of the inferior courts for a term of six years.

Art. 80. The clerks of the inferior courts shall be elected by the qualified voters of their several districts, and shall hold their offices during a term of four years.

Art. 81. The Legislature shall have power to vest in clerks of courts authority to grant such orders, and do such acts as may be deemed necessary for the furtherance of the administration of justice, and in all cases the powers thus granted shall be specified and determined.

Art. 82. The jurisdiction of justices of the peace shall not exceed, in civil cases, the sum of one hundred dollars, exclusive of interest, subject to appeal in such cases as shall be provided for by law. They shall be elected by the qualified voters of their several districts, and shall hold their office during a term of two years. They shall have such criminal jurisdiction as shall be provided by law.

Art. 83. There shall be an attorney general for the State, and as many district attorneys as the Legislature shall find necessary. The attorney general shall be elected every four years, by the qualified voters of the State. He shall receive a salary of five thousand dollars per annum, payable on his own warrant quarterly. The district attorneys shall be elected by the qualified voters of their respective districts, for a term of four years. They shall receive such salaries as shall be provided by the Legislature.

Art. 84. A sheriff and a coroner shall be elected in each parish by the qualified voters thereof, who shall hold their offices for the term of two years. The Legislature shall have the power to increase the number of sheriffs in any parish. Should a vacancy occur in either of these offices subsequent to an election, it shall be filled by the governor, and the person so appointed shall continue in office until his successor shall be elected and qualified.

TITLE VI.

IMPEACHMENT.

Art. 85. The power of impeachment shall be vested in the House of Representatives.

Art. 86. Impeachments of the governor, lieutenant governor, attorney general, secretary of state, state treasurer, auditor of public accounts, and the judges of the inferior courts, justices of the peace excepted, shall be tried by the Senate; the chief justice of the Supreme Court, or the senior judge thereof, shall preside during the trial of such impeachment. Impeachments of the judges of the Supreme Court shall be tried by the Senate. When sitting as a court of impeachment, the senators shall be upon oath or affirmation, and no person shall be convicted without the concurrence of a majority of the senators elected.

Art. 87. Judgments in case of impeachment shall extend only to removal from office, and disqualification from holding any office of honor, trust or profit under the State; but the convicted parties shall, nevertheless, be subject to indictment, trial and punishment, according to law.

Art. 88. All officers against whom articles of impeachment may be preferred, shall be suspended from the exercise of their functions during the pendency of such impeachment; the appointing power may make a provisional appointment to replace any suspended officer until the decision of the impeachment.

Art. 89. The Legislature shall provide by law for the trial, punishment, and removal from office of all other officers of the State by indictment or otherwise.

CONSTITUTION OF THE STATE OF LOUISIANA.

TITLE VII.
GENERAL PROVISIONS.

Art. 90. Members of the General Assembly and all officers, before they enter upon the duties of their offices, shall take the following oath or affirmation :

"I, (A B) do solemnly swear (or affirm) that I will support the constitution and laws of the United States, and of this State, and that I will faithfully and impartially discharge and perform all the duties incumbent on me as ——, according to the best of my abilities and understanding, so help me God !"

Art. 91. Treason against the State shall consist only in levying war against it, or in adhering to its enemies, giving them aid and comfort. No person shall be convicted of treason, unless on the testimony of two witnesses to the same overt act, or his own confession in open court.

Art. 92. The Legislature shall have power to declare the punishment of treason ; but no attainder of treason shall work corruption of blood or forfeiture, except during the life of the person attainted.

Art. 93. Every person shall be disqualified from holding any office of trust or profit, in this State, and shall be excluded from the right of suffrage, who shall have been convicted of treason, perjury, forgery, bribery or other high crimes or misdemeanors.

Art. 94. All penalties shall be proportioned to the nature of the offence.

Art. 95. The privilege of free suffrage shall be supported by laws regulating elections, and prohibiting, under adequate penalties, all undue influence thereon from power, bribery, tumult, or other improper practice.

Art. 96. No money shall be drawn from the treasury but in pursuance of specific appropriation made by law ; nor shall any appropriation of money be made for a longer term than two years. A regular statement and account of the receipts and expenditures of all public moneys shall be published annually, in such manner as shall be prescribed by law.

Art. 97. It shall be the duty of the General Assembly to pass such laws as may be proper and necessary to decide differences by arbitration.

Art. 98. All civil officers for the State at large shall be voters of, and reside within the State ; and all district or parish officers shall be voters of, and reside within their respective districts or parishes, and shall keep their offices at such places therein as may be required by law.

Art. 99. All civil officers shall be removable by an address of a majority of the members elected to both Houses, except those the removal of whom has been otherwise provided by this constitution.

Art. 100. In all elections by the people, the vote shall be taken by ballot ; and in all elections by the Senate and House of Representatives, jointly or separately, the vote shall be given *viva voce.*

Art. 101. No member of Congress, nor person holding or exercising any office of trust or profit under the United States, or under any foreign power, shall be eligible as a member of the General Assembly, or hold or exercise any office of trust or profit under the State.

Art. 102. None but citizens of the United States shall be appointed to any office of trust or profit in this State.

Art. 103. The laws, public records, and the judicial and legislative written proceedings of the State, shall be promulgated, preserved, and conducted in the language in which the constitution of the United States is written.

Art. 104. No power of suspending the laws of this State shall be exercised, unless by the Legislature or by its authority.

Art. 105. Prosecutions shall be by indictment or information. The accused shall have a speedy public trial, by an impartial jury of the parish in which the offence shall have been committed. He shall not be compelled to give evidence against himself; he shall have the right of being heard, by himself or counsel ; he shall have the right of meeting the witnesses face to face, and shall have compulsory process for obtaining witnesses in his favor. He shall not be twice put in jeopardy for the same offence.

Art. 106. All persons shall be bailable by sufficient sureties, unless for capital offences, where the proof is evident or presumption great ; or, unless after conviction for any offence or crime punishable with death or imprisonment at hard labor. The privilege of the writ of *habeas corpus* shall not be suspended, unless, when in cases of rebellion or invasion, the public safety may require it.

Art. 107. Excessive bail shall not be required ; excessive fines shall not be imposed, nor cruel and unusual punishments inflicted.

Art. 108. The right of the people to be secure in their persons, houses, papers and effects, against unreasonable searches and seizures, shall not be violated ; and no warrants shall issue but upon probable cause, supported by oath or affirmation, and particularly describing the place to be searched and the person or thing to be seized.

Art. 109. No *ex post facto* or retroactive law, nor any law impairing the obligations of contracts, shall be passed, nor vested rights be divested, unless for purposes of public utility, and for adequate compensation previously made.

Art. 110. All courts shall be open ; and

CONSTITUTION OF THE STATE OF LOUISIANA.

every person, for any injury done him, in his lands, goods. person, or reputation, shall have remedy by due course of law, and right and justice administered without denial or unreasonable delay.

Art. 111. The press shall be free; every citizen may freely speak, write and publish his sentiments on all subjects—being responsible for an abuse of this liberty.

Art. 112. The Legislature shall not have power to grant aid to companies or associations of individuals, except to charitable associations, and to such companies or associations as are and shall be formed for the exclusive purpose of making works of internal improvement, wholly or partially within the State, to the extent only of one-fifth of the capital of such companies, by subscription of stock or loan in money or public bonds; but any aid thus granted shall be paid to the company only in the same proportion as the remainder of the capital shall be actually paid in by the stockholders of the company; and, in case of loan, such adequate security shall be required, as to the Legislature may seem proper. No corporation or individual association, receiving the aid of the State as herein provided, shall possess banking or discounting privileges.

Art. 113. No liability shall be contracted by the State as above mentioned, unless the same be authorized by some law for some single object or work, to be distinctly specified therein, which shall be passed by a majority of the members elected to both Houses of the General Assembly; and the aggregate amount of debts and liabilities incurred under this and the preceding article shall never, at any time, exceed eight millions of dollars.

Art. 114. Whenever the Legislature shall contract a debt exceeding in amount the sum of one hundred thousand dollars, unless in case of war, to repel invasion, or suppress insurrection, they shall, in the law creating the debt, provide adequate ways and means for the payment of the current interest and of the principal when the same shall become due. And the said law shall be irrepealable until principal and interest are fully paid and discharged, or unless the repealing law contains some other adequate provision for the payment of the principal and interest of the debt.

Art. 115. The Legislature shall provide by law for all change of venue in civil and criminal cases.

Art. 116. The Legislature shall have the power to license the selling of lottery tickets and the keeping of gambling houses; said houses in all cases shall be on the first floor and kept with open doors; but in all cases not less than ten thousand dollars per annum shall be levied as a license or tax on each vendor of lottery tickets, and on each gambling house, and five hundred dollars on each tombola.

Art. 117. The Legislature may enact general laws regulating the adoption of children, emancipation of minors, changing of names, and the granting of divorces; but no special laws shall be enacted relating to particular or individual cases.

Art. 118. Every law enacted by the Legislature shall embrace but one object, and that shall be expressed in the title.

Art. 119. No law shall be revived or amended by reference to its title; but in such case the act revived, or section amended, shall be re-enacted and published at length.

Art. 120. The Legislature shall never adopt any system or code of laws by general reference to such system or code of laws; but in all cases shall specify the several provisions of the laws it may enact.

Art. 121. Corporations shall not be created in this State by special laws except for political or municipal purposes; but the Legislature shall provide by general law for the organization of all other corporations, except corporations with banking or discounting privileges, the creation, renewal or extension of which is hereby prohibited.

Art. 122. In case of the insolvency of any bank or banking association, the bill holders thereof shall be entitled to preference in payment over all other creditors of such bank or association.

Art. 123. No person shall hold or exercise, at the same time, more than one civil office of trust or profit, except that of justice of the peace.

Art. 124. Taxation shall be equal and uniform throughout the State. All property shall be taxed in proportion to its value, to be ascertained as directed by law. The General Assembly shall have power to exempt from taxation property actually used for church, school or charitable purposes. The General Assembly shall levy an income tax upon all persons pursuing any occupation, trade or calling, and all such persons shall obtain a license, as provided by law. All tax on income shall be pro rata on the amount of income or business done.

Art. 125. The Legislature may provide by law in what case officers shall continue to perform the duties of their offices until their successors shall have been inducted into office.

Art. 126. The Legislature shall have power to extend this constitution and the jurisdiction of this State over any territory acquired by compact, with any State, or with the United States, the same being done by consent of the United States.

Art. 127. None of the lands granted by Congress to the State of Louisiana for aiding in constructing the necessary levees and drains, to reclaim the swamp and overflowed lands of the State, shall be diverted from the purposes for which they were granted.

Art. 128. The Legislature shall pass no law excluding citizens of this State from office for not being conversant with any language except that in which the constitution of the United States is written.

Art. 129. No liability, either State, parochial or municipal, shall exist for any debts contracted for, or in the interest of the rebellion against the United States government.

Art. 130. The seat of government shall be and remain at New Orleans, and shall not be removed without the consent of a majority of both Houses of the General Assembly.

Art. 131. The Legislature may determine the mode of filling vacancies in all offices for which provision is not made in this constitution.

Art. 132. The Legislature shall pass no law requiring a property qualification for office.

TITLE VIII.

CORPORATION OF THE CITY OF NEW ORLEANS.

Art. 133. The citizens of the city of New Orleans shall have the right of appointing the several public officers necessary for the administration of the police of said city, pursuant to the mode of elections which shall be prescribed by the Legislature ; *Provided*, that the mayor and recorders shall be ineligible to a seat in the General Assembly; and the mayor and recorders shall be commissioned by the governor as justices of the peace, and the Legislature may vest in them such criminal jurisdiction as may be necessary for the punishment of minor offences, and as the police and good of said city may require.

The city of New Orleans shall maintain a police which shall be uniformed with distinction of grade, to consist of permanent citizens of the State of Louisiana, to be selected by the mayor of the city, and to hold office during good behavior, and removable only by a police commission composed of five citizens and the mayor, who shall be president of the board. The commission to be appointed by the governor of the State for the term of two years, at a salary of not less than one thousand dollars per annum ; a majority of whom shall remove for delinquencies. Members of the police when removed shall not again be eligible to any position on the police for a term of one year.

Interfering or meddling in elections in any manner will be a sufficient cause for instant dismissal from the police by the board.

The chief of police shall give a penal bond in the sum of ten thousand dollars ; lieutenants of police, five thousand dollars ; sergeants and clerks, each three thousand dollars ; corporals, two thousand dollars : and privates one thousand dollars; with good and solvent security, as the law directs, for the faithful performance of their duties.

The various officers shall receive a salary of not less than the following rates :

The chief of police........$250 per month.
The lieutenants of police.. 150 do. do.
The sergeants of police.... 100 do. do.
The clerks of police...... 100 do. do.
The corporals of police... 90 do. do.
The privates (day and night) each.................. 80 do. do.

TITLE IX.

LABOR ON PUBLIC WORKS.

Art. 134. The Legislature may establish the price and pay of foremen, mechanics, laborers and others employed on the public works of the State or parochial or city governments : *Provided*, That the compensation to be paid all foremen, mechanics, cartmen and laborers employed on the public works, under the government of the State of Louisiana, city of New Orleans, and the police juries of the various parishes of the State, shall not be less than as follows, viz : Foremen, $3 50 per day ; mechanics, $3 00 per day ; cartmen, $3 50 per day ; laborers, $2 00 per day.

Art. 135. Nine hours shall constitute a day's labor for all mechanics, artizans and laborers employed on public works.

TITLE X.

INTERNAL IMPROVEMENTS.

Art. 136. There shall be appointed by the governor a state engineer, skilled in the theory and practice of his profession, who shall hold his office at the seat of government for the term of four years. He shall have the superintendence and direction of all public works in which the State may be interested, except those made by joint stock companies or such as may be under the parochial or city authorities exclusively and not in conflict with the general laws of the State. He shall communicate to the General Assembly, through the governor, annually, his views concerning the same, report upon the condition of the public works in progress, recommend such measures as in his opinion the public interest of the State may require, and shall perform such other duties as may be prescribed by law. His salary shall be five thousand dollars per annum, until otherwise provided by law. The mode of appointment. number and salary of his assistants shall be fixed by law. The state engineer and assistants shall give bonds for the performance of their duties as shall be prescribed by law.

CONSTITUTION OF THE STATE OF LOUISIANA.

Art. 137. The General Assembly may create internal improvement districts, composed of one or more parishes, and may grant a right to the citizens thereof to tax themselves for their improvements. Said internal improvement districts, when created, shall have the right to select commissioners, shall have power to appoint officers, fix their pay and regulate all matters relative to the improvements of their districts, provided such improvements will not conflict with the general laws of the State.

Art. 138. The General Assembly may grant aid to said districts out of the funds arising from the swamp and overflowed lands, granted to the State by the United States for that purpose or otherwise.

Art. 139. The General Assembly shall have the right of abolishing the office of state engineer, by a majority vote of all the members elected to each branch, and of substituting a board of public works in lieu thereof, should they deem it necessary.

TITLE XI.

PUBLIC EDUCATION.

Art. 140. There shall be elected a superintendent of public education, who shall hold his office for the term of four years. His duties shall be prescribed by law, and he shall receive a salary of four thousand dollars per annum until otherwise provided by law: *Provided*, that the General Assembly shall have power by a vote of a majority of the members elected to both Houses, to abolish the said office of superintendent of public education, whenever, in their opinion, said office shall be no longer necessary.

Art. 141. The Legislature shall provide for the education of all children of the State, between the ages of six and eighteen years, by maintenance of free public schools by taxation or otherwise.

Art. 142. The general exercises in the common schools shall be conducted in the English language.

Art. 143. A university shall be established in the city of New Orleans. It shall be composed of four faculties, to-wit: one of law, one of medicine, one of the natural sciences, and one of letters; the Legislature shall provide by law for its organization and maintenance.

Art. 144. the proceeds of all lands heretofore granted by the United States to this State for the use or purpose of the public schools, and of all lands which may hereafter be granted or bequeathed for that purpose, and the proceeds of the estates of deceased persons to which the State may become entitled by law, shall be and remain a perpetual fund on which the State shall pay an annual interest of six per cent., which interest together with the interest of the trust funds, deposited with the State by the United States, under the act of Congress, approved June 23, 1836, and all the rents of the unsold lands shall be appropriated to the purpose of such schools and the appropriation shall remain inviolable.

Art. 145. All moneys arising from the sales which have been, or may hereafter be made of any lands heretofore granted by the United States to this State for the use of a specific seminary of learning, or from any kind of a donation that may hereafter be made for that purpose, shall be and remain a perpetual fund, the interest of which at six per cent. per annum shall be appropriated to the promotion of literature and the arts and sciences, and no law shall ever be made diverting said funds to any other use than to the establishment and improvement of said seminary of learning: and the General Assembly shall have power to raise funds for the organization and support of said seminary of learning in such manner as it may deem proper.

Art. 146. No appropriation shall be made by the Legislature for the support of any private school or institution of learning whatever, but the highest encouragement shall be granted to public schools throughout the State.

TITLE XII.

MODE OF REVISING THE CONSTITUTION.

Art. 147. Any amendment or amendments to this constitution may be proposed in the Senate or House of Representatives, and if the same shall be agreed to by a majority of the members elected to each House, such proposed amendment or amendments shall be entered on their journals, with the yeas and nays taken thereon. Such proposed amendment or amendments shall be submitted to the people at an election to be ordered by said Legislature, and held within ninety days after the adjournment of the same, and after thirty day's publication according to law; and if a majority of the voters at said election shall approve and ratify such amendment or amendments, the same shall become a part of the constitution. If more than one amendment be submitted at a time, they shall be submitted in such manner and form, that the people may vote for or against each amendment separately.

TITLE XIII.

SCHEDULE.

Art. 148. The constitution adopted in 1852 is declared to be superceded by this constitution; and in order to carry the same into effect, it is hereby declared and ordained as follows:

Art. 149. All rights, actions, prosecutions, claims and contracts, as well of individuals as of bodies corporate, and all laws in force at the time of the adoption of this constitution, and not inconsistent therewith, shall continue as if the same had not been adopted.

Art. 150. In order that no inconvenience may result to the public service from the taking effect of this constitution, no officer shall be superceded thereby; but the laws of this State relative to the duties of the several officers, executive, judicial and military, except those made void by military authority, and by the ordinance of emancipation, shall remain in full force, though the same be contrary to this constitution, and the several duties shall be performed by the respective officers of the State, according to the existing laws, until the organization of the government under this constitution, and the entering into office of the new officers to be appointed under said government, and no longer.

Art. 151. The Legislature shall provide for the removal of all causes now pending in the Supreme Court or other courts of the State under the constitution of 1852, to courts created by or under this constitution.

TITLE XIV.

ORDINANCE.

Art. 152. Immediately after the adjournment of the Convention, the governor shall issue his proclamation directing the several officers of this State, authorized by law to hold elections, or in default thereof such officers as he shall designate, to open and hold polls in the several parishes of the State, at the places designated by law, on the first Monday of September, 1864, for the purpose of taking the sense of the good people of this State in regard to the adoption or rejection of this constitution: and it shall be the duty of said officers to receive the suffrages of all qualified voters. Each voter shall express his opinion by depositing in the ballot-box a ticket whereon shall be written "The Constitution accepted," or, "The Constitution rejected." At the conclusion of the said election, the officers and commissioners appointed to preside over the same shall carefully examine and count each ballot as deposited, and shall forthwith make due return thereof to the secretary of state, in conformity to the provisions of law and usages in regard to elections.

Art. 153. Upon the receipt of said returns, or on the third Monday of September, if the returns be not sooner received, it shall be the duty of the governor, the secretary of state, the attorney general and the state treasurer, in the presence of all such persons as may choose to attend, to compare the votes at the said election for the ratification or rejection of this constitution, and if it shall appear at the close. that a majority of all the votes given is for ratifying this constitution, then it shall be the duty of the governor to make proclamation of the fact, and thenceforth this constitution shall be ordained and established as the constitution of the State of Louisiana. But whether this constitution be accepted or rejected it shall be the duty of the governor to cause to be published the result of the polls, showing the number of votes cast in each parish for and against this constitution.

Art. 154. As soon as a general election can be held under this constitution in every parish of the State, the governor shall, by proclamation, or in case of his failure to act, the Legislature shall, by resolution, declare the fact, and order an election to be held on a day fixed in said proclamation or resolution, and within sixty days from the date thereof, for governor, lieutenant governor, secretary of state, auditor, treasurer, attorney general and superintendent of education. The officers so chosen shall, on the fourth Monday after their election, be installed into office; and shall hold their offices for the terms prescribed in this constitution, counting from the second Monday in January next preceding their entering into office in case they do not enter into office on that date. The terms of office of the State officers elected on the 22d day of February, 1864, shall expire on the instalation of their successors as herein provided for; but under no state of circumstances shall their term of office be construed as extending beyond the length of the terms fixed for said offices in this constitution; and, if not sooner held, the election of their successors shall take place on the first Monday of November, 1867, in all parishes where the same can be held, the officers elected on that date to enter into office on the second Monday in January, 1868.

Art. 155. This constitution shall be published in three papers to be selected by the president of the Convention, whereof two shall publish the same in English and French, and one in German, from the period of the adjournment of the Convention until the election for ratification or rejection on the first Monday of September, 1864.

INDEX.

INDEX TO THE OFFICIAL JOURNAL.

	PAGE.
Absent members	29, 52, 54, 57, 79, 82, 84, 90, 91, 92, 95, 97, 109
Address of President Durell	7
Adjournment, resolution relative to	79, 82, 83, 94, 96, 170
Adjutant general, salary of	157
Appeals from the decision of the chair	11, 18
Appointment of Committee on Statue of Washington	38
Assaulted members	8
Assaulted Members, report of Committee on	52, 68, 73
Assistant secretary, resolution relative to	90, 100
Assistant sergeant-at-arms	27
Auditor public accounts, special report of	75
Auditor's report, report of Special Committee on	134, 147
Baltimore Convention, nominations of	158
Bailey A., resignation of	141
Banks Maj. Gen., invitation to	90
" " " pen presented to	92, 93
" " " visit to the Convention	94
" " " resolution of thanks to	94, 95 97
Bill for fitting up Liberty Hall	91, 94
Bills,—indebtedness of Convention	167
Bills of official printer	76
Bridges, etc.,	145, 151, 155
Brott, resignation of as member of committee	35
Canby and Sickles, Maj. Gens. visit from	129
Carrigan Judge, appropriation to	157
Charitable institutions	76, 80, 82, 86, 88, 90, 92, 132, 135, 146
Chief reporter, election of	26
City currency, resolution relative to	68, 71
City officers, election of	122, 125, 136
City police	105, 107, 127, 128
City of New Orleans, bill of	91, 94
Clergy, resolution relative to	134, 156, 169
Clerks of auditor and treasurer, salary of	170
Compensation, report of Committee on	37, 45
" of officers of the Convention	48, 49, 50, 53, 54, 56
" resolution relative to	47
Committee on Credentials, appointment of	4
" " " report of	5
Committee on Rules and Regulations	5, 12, 19, 20, 21
" " " " report of	14
Committees, (standing)	28, 39

INDEX.

	PAGE.
Committee on Federal Relations	32
Committee on Statue of Washington	38
Contingent Expenses, report of Committee on	149
Contingent expenses—money appropriated, ($25,000)	57
Contested seats—Lombard and Decker	6
Congress, ordinance to fill vacancy in	158, 160, 167
Currency, resolution relative to	148, 155, 159
Delegates to Baltimore Convention	77, 80, 157
Delinquent members	112
Distribution of Powers—report, etc	32, 35, 75
Education, report of Committee on	59, 61
" action on report of Committee on	136, 139, 140, 141, 142, 149, 151
Election of members, returns of	3, 4
" returns, parish Iberville	10
" of official printer	12
" of secretary	7, 26
" of chief reporter	26
" of Benjamin H. Orr	57
" of John A. Mayer	61
Emancipation, report of Committee on	53, 63
" vote on	65
" amendment to section VI, minority report	65
" action on minority report	69, 71, 73, 74
Executive Department, action on report of Committee	84, 87
Extra compensation	160, 167, 169
Federal Relations, appointment of Committee on	28
" " report of Committee on	51, 53, 56
" " —resolutions relative thereto	54
" " minority report on	56
Finance Committee, report of	77, 88, 96, 104, 116, 123, 139, 149, 154
" " resolutions relative to	154
Form and Arrangement	148, 158, 161
Gambling houses, etc	59
General Provisions, report of Committee on	40, 56, 63
" " action on report of	118, 119, 123, 129, 132, 136
Goldmann—resignation of	114
Governor's private secretary, salary of	167
" address to the Convention	170
Guerrillas, resolution relative to	67
Hour of meeting—resolution fixing the same	33, 39
Howell—resolution relative to his absence	64
" resignation of	65, 68
Impeachment, report of Committee on	36, 45
" action on	112, 117
Inauguration—expenses relative thereto	153
Industrial Arts, no tax on capital invested in	59
Internal Improvements	129, 131
Judiciary Department, report of Committee on	43
" substitute for nine articles of	53
" second reading of report on	58
" action on report of Committee on	87, 88, 89, 90, 92, 93, 94, 96, 97, 98, 100, 101, 102, 107, 109, 110, 112, 115

INDEX. iii
PAGE.
Ladies invited to visit the Convention..68
Legislative Department, report of Committee on............................62, 77
    "   "   action on report of............................77, 81, 83
Loyal owners of emancipated slaves..................................68, 71, 95, 96
Mechanics and laborers, pay of............................95, 97, 105, 127, 128
Memorial of Prof. A. Vallas...53
    "   "   "   "   report on.....................................57
    "   relative to banking corporations.................................55, 57
    "   "   hours of labor.....................................122, 125
    "   "   births and deaths.................................126, 134
    "   "   bridge on Galvez street........................145, 151, 155
Mode of Revising the Constitution, report of Committee on.............47, 54, 139
Meyer J. A., election of..61
Nomiuations of Baltimore Convention endorsed................................158
Official printer, bills of...76
    "   "   resolution relative to..................................90
Officers and employés, exemption of.......................................62, 63
Order of business, resolution relative to....................................97
Ordinance of secession—resolution relative to same..........................22
    "   of emancipation, "   "   " 90, 91, 94
    "   relative to elections...144, 152
Organization, temporary...3
    "   permanent..6, 7, 8, 9
Orr, election of...57
Preamble, substitute for report of the Committee on.......................54, 75
    "   report of Committee on...................................35, 75, 161
    "   and resolution relative to compensation to slave owners...........25
    "   "   "   "   "   members of foreign birth..........26, 31
    "   "   "   "   "   resignation of Hon. C. Roselius......32
    "   "   "   "   "   money in hands of F. S. G. Committee..64
    "   "   "   "   "   office-holders, not citizens of the U. S...91
    "   "   "   "   "   presidential electors................59
    "   "   "   "   "   reports of committees.........54, 58, 61
    "   "   "   "   "   granting bounty to 1st and 2d La. volunteers..36, 45
    "   "   "   "   "   depredations of guerrillas........52, 67
    "   "   "   "   "   adjournment..........................52
    "   "   "   "   "   ordinance of secession..............168
Printer, election of...12
    "   bills of..76
Petition of H. Copeland..57
Paine J. T., resignation of..156, 157
President, resolution of thanks to..170
Qualifications of state and municipal officers.......................40, 48, 169
Quorum, resolution relative to..29, 82, 84
Resolution of Abell relative to general order number XXXVIII........23, 24, 25
    "   "   "   "   reports of committees.................40, 51
    "   "   "   "   reading of reports (seriatim)............47
    "   "   "   "   reporter.................................167
    "   "   "   "   official reporter........................167
    "   "   "   "   Hon. R. K. Howell.........................64
    "   "   "   "   Maj. Gen. N. P. Banks.....................94
    "   " Austin   "   members of foreign birth..................10
25

INDEX.

					PAGE.
Resolution of Austin relative to quorum...82
" " " " " compensation...47
" " " " " delegates to Baltimore Convention...159
" " " " " endorsing nominees of Baltimore Convention...158
" " Balch " " appropriation to Judge Carrigan...157
" " Bell " " publishing proceedings...10, 93
" " " " " clerks...30
" " " " " thanks to Mayor Hoyt, etc...64
" " " " " inauguration expenses...153
" " Brott " " adjournment *sine die*...67
" " Bromley " " compensation and sessions...61
" " " " " guerrillas...67
" " Cutler " " report of Committee on Judiciary...58
" " " " " secretary of the Convention...160
" " " " " extra compensation...168
" " " " " clerks of auditor and treasurer...170
" " " " " city election...136
" " " " " final adjournment...170
" " Campbell " " vote on emancipation...66
" " " " " committee on assaulted members...67
" " " " " donation to distressed refugees...82
" " Davies " " bridge on Claiborne street...151
" " " " " elections, etc...122
" " Fish " " election in Tenth Representative District...27
" " " " " rescinding ordinance of secession...168
" " Fosdick " " city election...122
" " " " " clergy...169
" " " " " vote of thanks to President Durell...170
" " Foley " " printing reports, etc...47
" " " " " delegates to Baltimore Convention...77
" " Fuller " " notice to be given of amendments proposed...47, 51
" " Gastinel " " printing the journal and debates...30
" " Gorlinski " " organization...10
" " " " " fixing the hour of meeting...38, 30
" " " " " statue of Washington...36, 45
" " Goldmann " " publication of debates in German language...34, 36
" " " " " banking corporations...55
" " Gruneberg " " delinquent members...114
" " Harnan " " assaulted members...8
" " " " " absent members...57
" " Hire " " evening sessions...67
" " Heard " " Committee on Rules...9
" " " " " Absent members...109
" " Hills " " Judge A. A. Atocha...33
" " " " " vote on emancipation...66
" " " " " amendment of rule XXXII...37
" " " " " dispensing with reading of roll call...47
" " " " " absent members...52, 54, 79, 82, 84, 90, 91, 92, 95, 97
" " " " " charitable institutions...135
" " Howell " " { appointment of standing committees relative to the abolition of slavery...12
" " " " " state librarian...27

INDEX. v
PAGE..

Resolution of Howell relative to hour of meeting and order of the day..........33, 38
" " " " " instruction to secretary of the Convention...........79
" " Kavanagh " " pay of police on duty at Convention................50
" " Mendiverri " state auditor...................................33, 39
" " Montamat " " election of delegates............................9
" " " " " invitation to State officers.......................12
" " " " " compensation of members........................23
" " " " " ratification of constitution......................23
" " " " " appropriation of $100,000......................28, 30
" " " " " clerks 29
" " " " " Judge A. A. Atocha.............................30
" " " " " Finance Committee.........................26, 154
" " " " " officers and employés...........................167
" " " " " Maj. Gen. Banks and staff.......................90
" " " " " office of assistant secretary.................90, 100
" " Murphy M. W. " compensation................................28, 53
" " Purcell J. " " bills of official printer.........................76
" " Pursell S. " " clergy.......................................10, 23
" " " " " Hon. C. Roselius................................27
" " " " " article 96 of the constitution....................30
" " " " " persons not citizens of the United States............31
" " " " " meeting at 11 A. M..............................79
" " Smith " " shinplasters................................33, 38
" " " " " paper currency.............................148, 155
" " " " " status of colored persons.......................155
" " Shaw " " officers and employés (retained)..................169
" " Stiner " " unofficial reporters.............................167
" " Stauffer " " Committee on Rules, etc........................9, 11
" " " " " State bonds issued for rebel purposes...............29
" " " " " New Orleans Times.............................164
" " Schroeder " " fixing compensation............................46
" " Stocker " " rules and regulations......................27, 32, 34
" " " " " appropriation for charitable purposes...............90
" " " " " absent members................................29
" " " " " { printing journal in English, French, German and Spanish }..................................31
" " Seymour " " Hon. C. Roselius................................32
" " Sullivan " " officers and employés...........................11
" " " " " statue of Washington........................33, 38
" " " " " members of foreign birth......................26 31
" " " " " exemptions from jury duty.....................62, 63
" " " " " charitable institutions...........................132
" " " " " order of the day...............................105
" " Terry " " ordinance of secession..........................22
" " " " " status of members..............................8, 9
" " " " " qualifications of State and municipal officers...40, 48, 60
" " " " " celebration of 4th of July (1864)................134
" " " " " delinquent members...........................112
" " " " " enrollment on parchment of emancipation ordinance...90
" " " " " clergy......................................156
" " " " " order of business..............................157
" " Thomas " " election of official printer.......................11

INDEX.

					PAGE
Resolution of Thomas relative to salary of adjutant general 157
" " " " " unsettled accounts of the Convention 167
" " " " " Thomas P. May 166
" " Thorpe " " appointment of Committee on Federal Relations 28
" " " " " quorum 29
" " " " " decisions of courts (slavery) 154, 155
" " " " " salary of the governor's private secretary, etc 167
" " " " " printing the journal, etc 65, 90
" " " " " order of the day 97
" " " " " Maj. Gen. Canby and Maj. Gen. Sickles 121
" " Waters " " official reporters 167
" " " " " city police 93
" " Wells " " teachers in the public schools 135
" " " " " official reporters 167
" " " " " adjournment 52
" " " " " compensation to loyal owners 95
" " Wilson " " adjournment *sine die* and evening sessions 79
" " " " " J. T. Paine 156
Schedule, report of Committee on 131, 140, 152
Secession ordinance, preamble and resolution relative to 168
Shinplasters 33, 38
State officers, in relation to 12
State bonds issued for rebel purposes 29
State Library, resolution relative to 90
" " report of Committee on 153
" Librarian, resolution relative to 27
" Auditor 33, 39
Statue of Washington 33, 36, 38, 45
Status of members of the Convention 8, 9
" " colored person, etc 155
Standing Committees 28, 39
Substitutes, resolution relative to 47, 51
" for article 35, General Provisions 46
" for articles 1st and 2d report of Committee on Education 60, 61, 62
Teachers, resolution increasing salary of 135
Times N. O., action relative to 164, 166
Union refugees, resolution relative to 82
Vallas, memorial of 53, 57
Voters, ordinance defining qualification of 169
Warrant Clerk 32
Yeas and nays on tabling Terry's resolution requiring members to exhibit their iron-
clad oaths 9
" on adoption of Terry's resolution 10
" on the adoption of Thomas's resolution to elect printer 11
" on Gastinel's appeal from decision of the chair 11
" on second vote on adoption of Thomas's resolution to elect printer 12
" on Stauffer's appeal from decision of the chair 18
" on the adoption of Montamat's resolution on compensation of members .. 22
" on tabling Abell's preamble and resolution in reference to general
order No. 38 24
" on tabling Sullivan's preamble and resolution as relating to members of foreign birth 26

INDEX.

PAGE.

Yeas and nays on the adoption of Montamat's resolution appropriating $100,000 to pay officers and members...28
" on tabling Montamat's resolution inviting Judge Atocha to a seat within the bar...30
" on tabling Hills' amendment striking out the French language........31
" on adopting Terry's motion to publish proceedings in Irish..........31
" on the adoption of Wenck's motion to reconsider the vote to print in French and English...33
" on tabling Terry's resolution defining the qualification of State and municipal officers...48
" on the adoption of said resolution..................................48
" on tabling Hills' motion to strike out compensation of president.......48
" on the direct vote on Hills' motion to strike out......................49
" on the adoption of the report of the Committee on Compensation......50
" on motion to table Hills' resolution relative to attendance of members..54
" on adopting report of Committee on Federal Relations................56
" on tabling Goldman's resolution relative to banks and banking.......57
" on adoption of Gastinel's motion to print the report of Committee on Printing..59
" on tabling Davies' amendment, striking out that portion of the report of Committee on Education authorizing the Legislature to abolish the office of superintendent of public education....................59
" on the adoption of Terry's resolution relative to persons who are holding State and municipal offices...60
" on adopting Pursell's substitute for article 1st of report of Committee on Education...61
" on suspending the rules to take up the report of Committee on Emancipation...63
" on tabling minority report on emancipation.........................63
" on suspending the rules with a view to adjournment................64
" on Mr. Hills' appeal from decision of the chair......................66
" on rejection of minority report on emancipation....................66
" on suspending the rules with a view to rescinding the acceptance of Howell's resignation...67
" on rescinding the acceptance of Howell's resignation................68
" on adjournment...69
" on tabling Wilson's amendment to emancipation ordinance...........69
" on adjournment...69
" on adoption of 1st section of ordinance of emancipation..............70
" on adjournment...70
" on adoption of 2d section of ordinance of emancipation...............70
" on tabling Abell's proviso to 3d section of ordinance of emancipation..71
" on adoption of 1st clause of Abell's proviso.........................72
" on tabling 2d clause of Abell's proviso..............................72
" on tabling the motion to strike out entirely section 3d...............73
" on striking out the 3d, 4th, and 5th articles of the report of the Committee on Emancipation...73
" on suspending the rules for third reading of the emancipation report....74
" on final vote on adoption of said report............................74
" on the final adoption of the report of Committee on Preamble.........75
" on the final adoption of the report of Committee on Distribution of Powers..75

INDEX.

		PAGE.
Yeas and nays	on the adoption of article 1st of report of Committee on Legislative Department	77
"	on the adoption of article 2d of said report	78
"	on the adoption of article 3d of said report	78
"	on the adoption of article 4 of said report	78
"	on the adoption of article 5 of said report	78
"	on appropriation to Firemen's Charitable Association	80
"	on the adoption of resolution making charitable appropriations	80
"	on tabling Foley's resolution relative to members of Convention who are delegates to the Baltimore Convention	81
"	on striking out the words "and able to read and write as a qualification for voters"	81
"	on adjournment	81
"	on tabling Hills' resolution relative to absent members	82
"	on the adoption of said resolution	82
"	on striking out 88, 89, 90, 91, lines of article 6, of the report of Committee on Legislative Department	83
"	on tabling the motion to reconsider Mr. Hills' resolution relative to dilatory members	84
"	on tabling amendment to 2d section of report of Committee on Executive Department	84
"	on the adoption of 2d section of said report	84
"	on tabling the motion to reconsider the vote striking out the 4th section of said report	85
"	on Mr. Orr's amendment to the 25th section of said report	86
"	on adjournment	86
"	on adjournment	87
"	on tabling appropriation to Firemen's Charitable Association	88
"	on tabling resolution making appropriations to charitable institutions	89
"	on tabling Abell's amendment to 2d section of judiciary report	89
"	on adjournment	89
"	on tabling the amendments to 2d section of said report	91
"	on the adoption of Hills' resolution relative to absent members	91
"	on tabling Stocker's resolution relative to charitable purposes	92
"	on the adoption of Henderson's substitute for 2d article judiciary report	92
"	on tabling the motion to reconsider Hills' resolution relative to absent members	93
"	on the reconsideration of said resolution	93
"	on tabling Waters' resolution relative to city police	94
"	on tabling Sullivan's substitute for said resolution	95
"	on the adoption of Sullivan's substitute for the report of Committee on Judiciary	97
"	on the adoption of 3d article of said report	97
"	on tabling amendment to 3d article of said report	98
"	on tabling the substitute and amendment to 11th article of said report	99
"	on the adoption of Stauffer's substitute for said article	99
"	on the adoption of Sullivan's amendment for same article	99
"	on tabling Hills' amendment for said article	100
"	on the adoption of Hills' amendment to said article	100
"	on adjournment	100
"	on the adoption of Shaw's amendment to article 11th judiciary report	101
"	on tabling the motion to reconsider said vote	101

INDEX. ix

	PAGE.
Yeas and nays on direct vote on reconsideration	101
" on motion to reject Shaw's amendment	102
" on tabling Terry's substitute for article 11, judiciary report	102
" on tabling Hills' substitute for article 11, judiciary report	102
" on tabling Smith's substitute for article 11, judiciary report	103
" on tabling Baum's substitute for Smith's substitute	103
" on the adoption of Smith's substitute	103
" on tabling the amendments to the police bill	106
" on the adoption of Orr's proviso for police bill	106
" on the adoption of police bill as amended	106
" on tabling motion to reconsider the foregoing vote	107
" on tabling Montamat's substitute to article 12, judiciary report	107
" on the adoption of Sullivan's substitute for said article	107
" on the adoption of Stauffer's substitute for said article	108
" on tabling the motion to reconsider the vote on adopting the report of Committee on Judiciary	109
" on the direct vote on motion to reconsider	109
" on adjournment	114
" on tabling Bofill's substitute for artcle 11, report Judiciary Committee	115
" on the adoption of Bofill's substitute article 11	115
" on the adoption of Stocker's substitute	117
" on the adoption of Stocker's substitute as amended on its third reading	117
" on the adoption of report of Committee on Impeachment	118
" on Montamat's appeal from the decision of the chair	118
" on the adoption of Cutler's substitute relative to gambling houses	121
" on adjournment	122
" on tabling Fosdick's motion to take up his resolution relative to election of city officers	122
" on tabling Sullivan's substitute for article 36 of report of Committee on General Provisions	124
" on Fosdick's motion to suspend the rules to take up his resolution relative to election of city officers	125
" on call for the previous question on report of Special Committee article 36 of General Provisions	127
" on reconsideration of the vote on Davies' amendment to article 36 General Provisions	128
" on tabling Thorpe's amendment to article 36 General Provisions	128
" on tabling Orr's amendment to article 36 General Provisions	128
" on adoption of Orr's amendment to General Provisions	129
" on adoption of report of Special Committee as amended	129
" on adoption of additional article authorizing the Legislature to extend the right of suffrage	130
" on adoption of additional article constituting nine hours a day's labor	130
" on tabling Sullivan's charity resolutions	133
" on motion to strike out appropriation to Fireman's Charitable Association	133
" on the adoption of Sullivan's charity resolution	133
" on tabling Wells' resolution for increase of compensation to teachers	135
" on referring the subject of city elections to Special Committee	136
" on tabling Sullivan's substitute for article 2d report of Committee on Education	137

INDEX.

	PAGE.
Yeas and nays on adoption of article 2d of said report...........................137
" on tabling article 3 of said report.................................137
" on tabling Thorpe's substitute for article 3 (Education)..............137
" on tabling Cazabat's substitute for article 3 (Education)..............138
" on rejection of article 3 of said report............................138
" on the adoption of the report of Committee on Education as a whole..138
" on adjournment..140
" on rejection of article 2d of Sullivan's substitute for report of Committee on Education...142
" on tabling motion to strike out white in same report.................142
" on adoption of the motion to strike out............................ 143
" on tabling substitute for article 3d of said report.................. 143
" on adoption of article 3d as amended..............................144
" on adjournment..145
" on tabling Howell's 5th additional article to said report............145
" on adoption of report of Committee on Charitable Institutions........147
" on adoption of report of Special Committee on Auditor's Report.....147
" on tabling Hills' additional article on Education....................150
" on adjournment..150
" on tabling Cazabat's substitute for Hills' additional article...........150
" on the adoption of Cazabat's substitute............................150
" on the adoption of report of Committee on Education as a whole—second reading...151
" on tabling Sullivan's rider to article 2 report of Committee on Education..151
" on adoption of said rider..151
" on adoption of report of Committee on Education—third reading.....152
" on adoption of Henderson's rider to report of Committee on Schedule.152
" on adoption of preamble and resolutions to pay expenses of inauguration..153
" on second vote on same...154
" on tabling resolution relative to decision of courts on slavery........154
" on adoption of said resolution.....................................155
" on adoption of resolution relative to resignation of J. T. Paine......156
" on postponing action on the report of Committee on Form and Arrangement..158
" on adoption of preamble and resolutions endorsing the Baltimore nominations...158
" on tabling Terry's rider to article 134 of constitution................162
" on striking out article 9 of constitution............................163
" on adjournment..163
" on tabling Stauffer's resolution relative to New Orleans Times........164
" on tabling Terry's rider to article 141 of constitution................164
" on adoption of said rider..164
" on final adoption of constitution as a whole........................165
" on tabling motion to postpone action in relation to New Orleans Times..166
" on adoption of preamble and resolutions relative to Thomas P. May, editor of New Orleans Times.....................................166
" on adoption of preamble and resolutions relative to States' rights....169
" on tabling resolution relative to clergy.............................169
" on adoption of resolutions relative to adjournment..................170

JOURNAL

OFFICIEL DES TRAVAUX

DE LA

CONVENTION

REUNIE POUR

REVISER ET AMENDER

LA CONSTITUTION

DE

L'ETAT DE LA LOUISIANE.

PAR AUTORITE.

NOUVELLE ORLEANS:
W. R. FISH, IMPRIMEUR DE LA CONVENTION.
1864.

JOURNAL OFFICIEL DES TRAVAUX

DE LA CONVENTION

REUNIE POUR AMENDER ET REVISER LA CONSTITUTION

DE

L'ETAT DE LA LOUISIANE.

Mercredi, 6 avril 1864.

La Convention s'assemble à la salle de la Liberté, à la Nlle-Orléans, à midi précis, en conséquence du paragraphe XI, de l'ordre général No. 35 du Major-Général N. P. Banks, Commandant général du Département du Golfe, et conçue ainsi qu'il suit :

Paragraphe XI. Les délégués dûment élus à la Convention s'assembleront en la salle de la Liberté, au siége de l'Exécutif, en la ville de la Nlle-Orléans, à midi précis, mercredi le sixième jour d'avril 1864.

A midi et quart, F. B. Thorpe, membre de la Convention, demande l'appel à l'ordre.

J. R. Terry propose Alfred Shaw aux fonctions de président temporaire. Adopté à l'unanimité.

W. R. Fish propose Alfred C. Hills aux fonctions de secrétaire pro tem. Adopté à l'unanimité.

En réponse à la demande unanime de la Convention, le Révérend Dr. Newman offre la prière d'action de grâces.

Lecture est donnée de la communication ci-dessous du Secrétaire d'Etat, S. Wrotnoski.

Etat de la Louisiane,
Bureau du Secrétaire d'Etat.
Conformément à l'ordre général No. 25, en date du 11 Mars dernier, du Major-Général N. P. Banks, commandant le Département du Golfe, ainsi que la proclamation de Son Excellence, Michael Hahn, Gouverneur de cet Etat, en date du 16 du dit mois, convoquant une élection pour le 28 de mars, à l'effet de choisir des délégués à une Convention Constitutionnelle devant s'assembler afin de réviser et d'amender la Constitution de l'Etat de la Louisiane, le soussigné, a, ce jour, examiné les rapports reçus des votes déposés à l'élection du 28 mars dernier, et il en appert que les délégués ci-après nommés ont obtenu dans les paroisses suivantes, le plus grand nombre de votes, comme le portent les rapports reçus jusqu'à ce jour, savoir :

PAROISSE D'ORLEANS.

Premier District Représentatif — Joseph Gorlinski, R. B. Bell, Geo. B. Brott, W. T. Stocker, John Stumpf, J. B. Shroeder, E. Murphy.

Deuxième District Représentatif—Terrance Cook, Joseph H. Wilson, John Henderson, Jr., J. H. Stiner, M. W. Murphy, P. K. O'Conner, Alfred C. Hills, T. B. Thorpe, J. J. Healy, Geo. A. Fosdick, W. H. Hire.

Troisième District Représentatif — John W. Thomas, James Fuller, John Sullivan, J. R. Terry, O. W. Austin, John Foley, George Howes, H. W. Waters, P. Harnan.

Quatrième District Représentatif—Alfred Shaw, R. King Cutler, Judge E. H. Durell, E. J. Wenck, Louis Gastinel.

Cinquième District Représentatif—Edmund Abell, John Buckley, Jr., Xavier Maurer, J. P. Montamat, A. Mendiverri.

Sixième District Représentatif—J. V. Bofill, F. M. Crozat, Dr. M. F. Bonzano, Adolphe Bailey.

Septième District Représentatif — Judge R. K. Howell, J. J. Baum, M. D. Kavanagh, H. Millspaugh.

Huitième District Représentatif — J. A. Spellicy, O. H. Poynot, J. K. Cook.

Neuvième District Représentatif—H. Maas, E. Goldman, Edward Hart.

Dixième District Représentatif—John Purcell, C. W. Stauffer, W. B. Fish, Benj. Campbell, T. Barrett, Geo. W. Geier, R. S. Abbott, James Duane, Edmund Flood, J. L. Davies.

Rive Droite du Mississippi (Alger)—J. H. Flagg, W. H. Seymour.

ASCENSION.
Robert J. Duke, Emile Collin and J. E. Richard ont obtenu chacun 61 voix. Election contestée.

ASSOMPTION.
Joseph Dupaty, James Ennis, E. J. Pintado.

EST BATON ROUGE.
W. D. Mann, P. A. Kugler, H. J. Heard.

OUEST BATON ROUGE.
Sidney A. Lobdell.

CONCORDIA.
Robert W. Taliaferro.

EST FELICIANA.
Jansen T. Paine, Martin Schnurr.

JEFFERSON.
Robert Morris, Samuel Pursell, Christian Roselius, John Paine.

LAFOURCHE.
J. B. Bromley, E. H. Knobloch, C. H. L. Gruneberg.

MADISON.
R. V. Montague,

PLAQUEMINES.
Louis Lombard, Thos. J. Decker. Election contestée. Le vote monte, à ce qu'on suppose, à 246 voix. Non entièrement rapporté.

ST. BERNARD.
Thomas Ong.

ST JACQUES.
R. Beauvais.

ST. JEAN BAPTISTE.
Young Burke.

STE-MARIE.
Charles Smith.

TERREBONNE.
R. W. Bennie, Adolphe Gaidry.

Nombre total des délégués—Orléans....63
Paroisses des campagnes..............27
En somme............90

Nombre total des votes reçus jusqu'au 5 avril 1864, à 2 heures de l'après midi...................... 6184

A ces causes, le soussigné a l'honneur de transmettre aux Honorables MM. le Président et les Membres de la Convention le dit état ainsi que tous les originaux des rapports des paroisses de la Louisiane.

Signé de sa main, à la Nlle-Orléans, le 6e jour d'avril de l'an de grâce mil huit cent soixante-quatre et de l'Indépendance des Etats-Unis d'Amérique le quatre-vingt-huitième.

(Signé) S. WROTNOWSKI,
Secrétaire d'Etat.

Etat de la Louisiane,
Bureau du Secrétaire d'Etat
Nlle-Orléans, 6 avril 1864.

A l'Honorable Président de la Convention de la Louisiane :

MONSIEUR,— Permettez-moi de vous remettre et de laisser à votre disposition les ouvrages suivants :

1o. Réglement et Ordres de la Chambre des Représentants ; 2o. le Guide Législatif, apartenant à la Bibliothèque de l'Etat, et veuillez me croire, Monsieur, votre très-humble servitenr,

[Signé] S. WROTNOWSKI.
Secrétaire d'Etat.

Les livres et rapports ci-dessus accusés, sont reçus en même temps que les dites communications.

Puis à l'appel du rôle fait par le secrétaire, les délégués ci-dessous, au nombre de quatre-vingt-deux, répondent à leurs noms:

Joseph Gorlinski, John Stumpf, R. B. Bell, J. B. Schroeder, Geo F. Brott, E. Murphy, W. T. Stocker, Terrance Cook, Alfred C. Hills, Joseph H. Wilson, T. B. Thorpe, John Henderson, Jr., J. J. Healy, J. H. Stiner, George A. Fosdick, M. W. Murphy W. H. Hire, P. K. O'Conner, John W. Thomas, John Foley, James Fuller, George Howes, John Sullivan, H. W. Waters, J. R. Terry, P. Harnan, O. W. Austin, Alfred Shaw, E. J. Wenck, R. King Cutler, Louis Gastinel, E. H. Durell, Edmund Abel, J. P. Montamat, John Buckley, Jr., A. Mendiverri, Xavier Maurer, J. V. Bofill, Dr. M. E. Bonzano, F. M. Crozat, Adolphe Bailey, R. K. Howell, M. D. Cavanagh, J. J. Baum, H. Millspaugh, J. A. Spellicy, J. K. Cook, O. H. Poynot, H. Maas, Edward Hart, E. Goldman, John Purcell, Geo. W. Geier, C. W. Stauffer, W. R. Fish, James Duane, Benjamin Campbell, Edmund Flood, J. L. Davies, J. T. Barrett, J. H. Flagg, W. H. Seymour, Joseph Dupaty, James Ennis, H, J. Heard, P. A. Kugler, Martin Schnurr, Robert Morris, Sam'l Pursell, Christian Roselius, John Payne, J. B. Bromley, E. H. Knobloch, C. H. L. Gruneberg, Lewis Lombard, Thomas J. Decker, Thomas Ong, R. Beauvais, Young Burke, Chas. Smith, R. W. Bennie, Adolphe Gaidry.

ET L'AMENDEMENT DE LA CONSTITUTION DE LA LOUISIANE.

M. Montamat présente la motion de référer la communication du secrétaire d'Etat, contenant une liste des délégués élus, à un comité de cinq. Adopté.

Le président nomme de ce comité MM. Wm. Thomas, Samuel Pursell, R. W. Bennie, C. H. L. Gruneberg et George F. Brott; et subséquemment, sur l'observation du président, que, par inadvertance, il avait omis de nommer de ce comité M. Montamat, l'auteur de la motion, et qu'il désirerait l'y porter, en qualité de président du dit comité, sous l'approbation de la Convention, résolu que M. Montamat soit ainsi nommé.

Motion de M. Fish à l'effet de nommer un comité de cinq chargé de faire un rapport sur les réglements de la Couvention et sur le nombre d'employés nécessaires à l'expédition des affaires de cette assemblée—mise aux voix et rejetée. Sur la demande du vote nominal, M. Howell demande la division de la question; et sur ce M. Fish retire la dernière partie de sa motion.

Le vote sur la première partie de la motion accuse trente voix pour et quarante et une contre cette motion, qui en conséquence est rejetée.

M. Terry propose que les membres de la Convention procèdent par voie du sort pour décider du siége qu'ils occuperont respectivement.

Sur la demande de M. Stocker cette motion est rejetée.

M. Harnan propose que toute motion ou résolution soit présentée par écrit. Déposé.

Sur motion de M. Thomas, la Convention s'ajourne jusqu'à Jeudi, à midi.

ALFRED C. HILLS,
Secrétaire *pro tem.*

JEUDI, 7 Avril 1864.

La Convention s'assemble à midi, ce jour, jeudi le 7 avril 1864.

M. Shaw est le président *pro tem.*

L'appel du rôle accuse un quorum.

M. le révérend J. Horton fait la prière.

Le procès-verbal de la première séance est lu et approuvé.

M. Montamat, du Comité de vérification des pouvoirs, soumet le rapport suivant :

Aux Honorables le Président et
les Membres de la Convention :

Votre comité de vérification des pouvoirs vous soumet le rapport suivant : Après examen des rapports d'élection dans les paroisses ci-après nommées, il est arrivé à la conclusion que les personnes dont les noms suivent ont été dûment élues :

PAROISSE D'ORLÉANS.

Premier District Représentatif—Joseph Gorlinski, R. B. Bell, Geo. F. Brott, W. T. Stocker, John Stumpf, J. B. Schroeder, E. Murphy.

Deuxième District Représentatif—Terrance Cook, Joseph H. Wilson, John Henderson, jr., J. H. Stiner, M. W. Murphy, P. K. O'Conner, Alfred C. Hills, T. B. Thorpe, J. J. Healy, Geo. A. Fosdick, W. H. Hire.

Troisième District Représentatif—John W. Thomas, James Fuller, John Sullivan, J. R. Terry, O. W. Austin, John Foley, George Howes, H. W. Waters, P. Harnan.

Quatrième District Représentatif—Alfred Shaw, R. King Culter, Judge E. H. Durell, E. J. Wenck, Louis Gastinel.

Cinquième District Représentatif—Edmund Abell, John Buckley, jr., Xavier Maurer, J. P. Montamat, A. Mendiverri.

Sixième District Représentatif—J. V. Bofill, F. M. Crozat, Dr. M. F. Bonzano, Adolph Bailey.

Septième District Représentatif—Judge R. K. Howell, J. J. Baum, M. D. Kavanagh, H. Millspaugh.

Huitième District Représentatif—J. A. Spellicy, O. H. Poynot, J. K. Cook.

Neuvième District Représentatif—H. Maas, E. Goldman, Edward Hart.

Dixième District Représentatif—John Purcell, C. W. Stauffer, W. R. Fish, Ben. Campbell, J. T. Barrett, Geo. W. Geier, B. S. Abbott, James Duane, Edmund Flood, J. L. Davis.

Rive droite du Mississipi (Alger)—J. H. Flagg, W. H. Seymour.

ASSOMPTION.

Joseph Dupaty, James Ennis, E. J. Pintado.

AVOYELLES.

L. P. Normand, H. C. Edwards.

EST-BATON ROUGE.

W. D. Mann, P. A. Kugler, H. J. Heard.

OUEST-BATON ROUGE.

Sidney A. Lobdell.

CONCORDIA.

Robert W. Talliaferro.

EST-FELICIANA.

Jansen T. Paine, Martin Schnurr.

JEFFERSON.

Robert Morris, Samuel Pursell, P. A. Christian Roselius, John Payne.

LAFOURCHE.

J. B. Bromley, E. H. Knobloch, C. H. Gruneberg.

MADISON.

R. V. Montague.

RAPIDES.

M. R. Ariail, A. Cazabat, J. H. Newell, Thos. M. Wells.

ST. BERNARD.

Thos. Ong.

ST. JACQUES.

R. Beauvais.

ST. JEAN BAPTISTE.

Young Burke.

ST. MARIE.

Charles Smith.

TERREBONNE.

B. W. Bennie, Adolphe Gaidry.

Votre comité conclut que dans la paroisse d'Ascension, Robert J. Duke a obtenu le plus grand nombre de votes, et est dûment élu.

Que Emile Collins et J. E. Richard ont tous deux reçu un nombre égal de votes, et qu'en conséquence aucun d'eux n'est élu.

C'est pourquoi votre comité considère qu'il est convenable d'ordonner une nouvelle élection dans cette paroisse, pour un délégué.

Après enquête, votre comité reconnait que le shériff de la paroisse Plaquemines est coupable d'actes de négligence qui rendent l'élection de cette paroisse nulle et non avenue, ainsi :

1o. Il n'a point nommé de députés et n'a point fait ouvrir les polls dans tous les précincts de cette paroisse.

2o. Il n'a fait faire aucun rapport du résultat de l'élection au Fort Jackson.

3. Il n'a fait aucun rapport officiel quelconque de l'élection dans cette paroisse.

Votre comité recommande donc d'ordonner une nouvelle élection dans cette paroisse. Et c'est avec respect qu'il vous soumet le présent rapport.

JOHN MONTAMAT,
Président.

Motion secondée pour l'adoption de ce rapport ; et sur ce MM. Lombard et Decker prennent la parole devant la Convention sur leurs droits respectifs à un siége.

L'amendement de M. Terry pour nommer un comité de cinq afin d'étudier la question des droits respectifs des délégués de Plaquemines, est, sur motion, déposé sur le bureau par un vote de 49 voix contre 16.

Motion de M. Cazabat pour ajourner jusqu'à lundi à midi.

L'appel nominal accuse sept voix pour l'affirmative contre soixante-seize pour la négative.

La question d'adoption du rapport se présentant de nouveau, M. Terry amende sa motion en ces termes :

" Que le rapport du comité de vérification des pouvoirs soit adopté, sans y comprendre tout se qui s'y rapporte aux siéges contestés, soit déposé sur le bureau et que la Chambre passe outre."

Sur motion de M. Stocker, l'amendement est déposé ; puis le raport est adopté.

M. Bell propose de s'occuper de l'organisation permanente de la Convention.

M. Thomas propose comme substitut la nomination d'un comité de cinq, chargé d'aviser au nombre d'employés nécessaires à la Convention, et à leurs attributions. Rejeté

M. Montamat propose que la Convention s'occupe de la nomination d'un président, d'un secrétaire, d'un sergent d'armes, d'un portier et d'un messager. Adopté.

La motion de M. Henderson de nommer au scrutin le président, sur motion de M. Montamat, et après appel, est déposée par un vote de 65 voix contre 24.

M. Abell propose d'admettre MM. Balch et Dufresne comme délégués de la paroisse d'Iberville.

La motion de M. Wilson d'en référer au comité de vérification est perdue et les susdits Balch et Dufresne sont alors, sur motion, reconnus membres de la Convention.

La Chambre passe à l'élection d'un président ; sont candidats MM. R. K. Howell, E. H. Durell, M. F. Bonzano, Christian Roselius, T. B. Thorpe, J. R. Terry et Alfred Shaw ; ces deux derniers retirent leur candidature.

Sur appel nominal il appert que M. Howell obtient 25 voix; E. H. Durell 35; M. F. Bonzano 15 ; Christian Roselius 7 et B. Thorpe 1.

Le résultat étant nul, les noms de MM. Bonzano, Roselius et Thorpe sont retirés, et le second tour de vote donne pour résultat 43 voix à M. E. H. Durell, savoir :

MM. Gorlinski, Bell, Brott, Stumpf, E. Murphy, Cook, M. W. Murphy, Stiner, O'Conner, Thorpe, Healy, Thomas, Fuller, Sullivan, Terry, Waters, Shaw, Bofill, Crozat, Bailey, Howell, Maas, Goldman, Hart, John Purcell, Stauffer, Fish, Campbell, Barrett, Geier, Duane, Davies, Flagg, Seymour, Schnurr, Roselius, Paine, Gaidry, Knobloch, Gruneberg, Smith, Bennie, Gaidry—43.

Et quarante et une pour M. R. K. Howell, savoir :

MM. Stocker, Schroeder, Wilson, Henderson, Fosdick, Austin, Foley, Harnan, Cutler, Durell, Gastinel, Wenck, Abell, Buckley, Maurer, Montamat, Mendiverri, Bonzano, Baum, Millspaugh, Kavanagh, Spellicy, Poynot, Cook, Flood, Dupaty, Ennis, Kugler, Heard, Morris, Samuel Pursell, Ong, Beauvais, Burke, Normand, Edwards, Cazabat. Newell, Balch, Dufresne, Hills—41.

Sur motion de M. Thorpe l'élection de M. Durell est prononcée faite à l'unanimité. Puis MM. Howell, Roselius et Bonzano sont nommés d'un comité chargé d'installer le président élu, et après avoir pris possession de la présidence, M. Durell prononce le discours suivant :

Messieurs de la Convention — Je vous remercie chaudement de l'honneur que vous m'avez conféré en me nommant votre président, et plus chaudement encore de cette preuve de confiance en mes capacités et en mon patriotisme. Lorsque dans le cours de ma présidence, je montrerai de la faiblesse, vous me prêterez votre force, je le sais. Et mon attente de trouver en vous cette aménité qui est la meilleure assistance pour diriger tout corps législatif, ne sera point déçue. Dans ce temps de troubles publics, à l'heure suprême du combat de votre pays pour son existence, vos concitoyens vous ont confié des devoirs égaux à ceux du soldat sur le champ de bataille. C'est à vous qu'il appartient de terminer la tâche que le soldat laisse nécessairement incomplète. Le 26 Janvier 1861, un petit nombre d'hommes ambitieux et méchants, se réunirent en convention, et représentant une minorité de la Louisiane, ils déclarèrent "rompu à jamais, le lien qui attache la Louisiane à l'Union Fédérale ;" et vous, messieurs, les élus du peuple loyal de ce même pays, vous avez été choisis pour défaire l'œuvre de la folie et du crime ; pour rétablir l'Etat dans son ancienne position légitime au sein de l'Union et pour le remettre sous les plis protecteurs de ce drapeau qui, partout, est salué comme le symbole de la liberté et de l'égalité. Vous connaissez le grand drame qui se déroule sous nos yeux et auquel nous participons aussi ; cette connaissance vous fera accepter les idées nouvelles qu'enfante le progrès, les changements que les grandes révolutions dans les maximes et dans les sociétés humaines, rendent nécessaires; et volontiers, vous abandonnerez un passé mort pour un avenir rempli des promesses d'une vie nouvelle. La première et la principale cause de cette rébellion est évidente pour vous tous ; vous avez été appelés à vous réunir, investis des pouvoirs absolus, qui, d'après nos institutions, appartiennent à un corps organique, non seulement afin de rétablir l'Etat dans l'Union, mais encore afin de faire disparaître à jamais, de la Louisiane, cette cause fatale de luttes et de rébellion. Vous accomplirez, je le sais, ces devoirs et d'autres nombreux encore, qui vous incombent, avec courage et fermeté, ne vous occupant que de la prospérité et du bonheur de notre Etat et de notre commune patrie.

Motion de M. Bell de nommer un secrétaire par voie du scrutin, sur motion de M. Montamat est rejetée ; les candidats sont : MM. Neelis, McClellan, Gérard, White, Reynolds, Holland, Derickson et Murphy, et l'appel nominal, donne pour résultat, l'élection de Neelis par 44 voix, tandis que M. Derickson n'obtient que dix voix, M. J. E. Holland 6, M. John McClellan 8, M. White 6, M. Gérard 4, et M. Murphy 2. Sur ce MM. Henderson, et Thorpe sont nommés du comité chargé d'installer M. Neelis comme secrétaire.

La motion d'élire au scrutin un sergent d'armes, est déposée, et les voix prises sur l'élection des candidats suivants : MM. McGuire, C. Baumbach, Thos. K. Flanagan, et DeCoursey, mais sans résultat. Sur ce, M. Flanagan retire sa candidature, et après un appel aussi infructueux que le premier, on procède à un troisième appel qui donne 41 voix pour M. DeCoursey, 36 pour Baumbach, et 1 pour McGuire : ainsi M. DeCoursey est élu ; et M. Brott propose que le comité d'installation du secrétaire soit chargé de la même mission auprès de M. de Coursey. Adopté.

Sur motion, la Convention s'ajourne à vendredi à midi.

ALFRED C. HILLS,
Secrétaire *pro tem.*

VENDREDI, 8 Avril 1864.

A midi et un quart, le Président appelle à l'ordre la Convention, et annonce que M. le révérend Bass offrira la prière.

Sur l'appel nominal du secrétaire, 78 membres ayant répondu, le président déclare qu'il y a quorum et que la séance est ouverte.

M. Hills, le secrétaire *pro tem.*, annonce qu'il est prié de lire le procès-verbal de la séance d'hier, et sur ce, lecture en est ordonnée et faite.

M. Harnan présente le préambule et la résolution qui suivent :

Considérant, que nous sommes instruits, par ce qui paraît être bonne autorité, que déjà, deux membres de cette Convention ont été assaillis, et l'un d'eux, dans l'accomplissement de ses devoirs de conventionnel, en conséquence,

Résolu, Les inculpés susdits seront dénoncés aux autorités compétentes pour être traités comme de droit.

En présentant cette résolution, M. Harnan dit que lui-même et un autre membre ont été violemment assaillis à cause de leurs actes officiels dans cette Convention, et qu'à son avis, la Chambre doit s'occuper de ces faits.

La motion de déposer est perdue, et sur la motion de M. Bell, un comité de trois chargé de procéder à une enquête, après prononcé du président, sur appel nominal, est adoptée par 48 voix contre 30.

Le président nomme de ce comité .MM Rosélius, Wilson, et Morris. Sur motion d'y adjoindre M. Thorpe, M. Thorpe demande à en être dispensé. Adopté.

M J. W. Thomas propose que la Convention s'occupe des affaires non terminées du jour précédent, et complète son organisation par l'élection d'un portier et d'un messager.

M. Cazabat présente un amendement à l'effet de remettre au président la nomination des officiers non encore choisis.

.M Wilson propose pour substitut de laisser au sergent d'armes le droit de choisir ses aides, le portier et le messager y compris.

M. Montamat ayant obtenu la parole, dit, qu'à son avis, toutes ces motions ne sont pas à l'ordre, et il demande que la Convention procède à l'élection d'un portier.

Une autre motion propose de laisser cette nomination au Président.

Déclaré que la nomination d'un portier est à l'ordre, et M. Crozat propose M. A. Martin ; M. Harnan, Mallory ; M. Duane McCarty ; M. Healy, Coyle ; M. Purcell, Bombach ; M. Stauffer, Piersell ; M. Shaw, Frieny ; Dr. Gruneberg, F. X. Martin ; M. Terry, Sullivan ; M. Cook, Miller ; et enfin M. Maurer propose Ernst.

Sur le vote nominal, M. Mallory obtient 3 voix, M. Piersell 4, M. McCarty 4, M. Coyle 15, M. Bombach 29, M. Frieny 3, M. Sullivan 6, M. Miller 1, M. Ernst 1.

En conséquence, d'élection point, faute de majorité.

M. Baum propose que tous les candidats, sauf les trois qui ont obtenu le plus grand nombre de voix, soient retirés. Adopté. Au second tour, M. Bombach obtient 45 voix, M. A. Martin 14 et M. Coyle 22.

M. Montamat propose de déclarer à l'unanimité M. Bombach élu. Adopté.

Pour la nomination d'un messager M. Maurer nomme M. Leclerc, M. Terry nomme M. E. G. Maguire, M. Duane nomme M. Murrphy, jr., M. Gorlinski nomme M. Piotrowski, M. Thomas nomme M. Clark, M. Healy nomme M. Coyle.

Au premier tour, 9 voix pour M. Leclerc, 17 pour M. McDonald, 2 pour M. Mcguire, 3 pour M. Murphy, et aucune pour M. Piotrowski. L'élection n'ayant pas eu lieu, M. Stauffer propose un second tour et que l'on ne vote que pour les deux candidats qui viennent d'obtenir le plus grand nombre de voix au premier tour.

Adopté, et M. Clark obtient 44 voix, contre Coyle 36.

Sur motion de M. Wilson, Clark est déclaré élu à l'unanimité.

M. Heard propose de procéder à l'élection d'un secrétaire-adjoint. Repoussé.

M. Stauffer propose qu'un comité soit nommé par le president afin de faire un rapport sur les règlements qui doivent régir la Convention, ainsi que le surplus d'employés nécessaires au travail de l'assemblée et sur les capacités requises d'eux.

M. Heard, comme substitut, présente la résolution suivante :

"Le président nommera un comité de sept chargé de préparer des règlements pour cette Convention, et que jusqu'à ce que le comité ait fait son rapport, les débats seront dirigés suivant les principes du Manuel de Jefferson, et par les règlements du Sénat et de la Chambre des Représentants de l'Etat de la Louisiane, adoptés en 1856." Déposé.

M. Stauffer retire sa motion afin de permettre à M. Montamat de présenter la sienne.

Résolu : Le Gouverneur est invité à lancer sa proclamation, à l'effet d'ordonner une élection, aussitôt que faire se pourra, d'un délégué de la paroisse Plaquemines et d'un autre pour la paroisse Ascension, qui devront représenter ces paroisses à la Convention. Adopté.

M. Terry offre la résolution suivante :

Tout membre de cette Convention devra justifier des qualités et conditions suivantes : 1o. électeur de cet Etat, d'après les dispositions de la loi, ayant de plus prêté le serment prescrit par la proclamation du Président en date du 8 décembre 1863; présentation au secrétaire, le 9 avril courant, vers l'heure de midi, d'un certificat de prestation du serment d'allégence, ou prestation du dit serment en présence du président de la Convention.

Une motion est faite pour déposer la résolution sur le bureau.

Le vote nominal est demandé et la motion est rejetée.

Ont voté pour la résolution :

Messieurs Gorlinsky, Brott, Stocker, Stumpf, Thomas, Fuller, Sullivan, Austin, Waters, Cutler, Abell, Bailey, Howell, Kavanagh, Spellicy, Poynot, Hart, Flagg, Seymour, Mann, Heard, Roselius, Gaidry, Balch, Dufresne, Bonzano—26.

Ont voté contre :

Messieurs Bell, Schroeder, Murphy E., Cook, Henderson, Wilson, Stiner, Murphy, O'Conner, Hills, Thorpe, Healy, Fosdick, Hire, Terry, Foley, Harnan, Shaw, Buckley, Maurer, Montamat, Mendiverri, Bofill, Crozat. Baum, Millspaugh J. K., Cook, Maas, Goldmann, Stauffer, Fish, Campbell, Barrett, Geier, Duane, Flood, Davies, Dupaty, Ennis, Norman, Edwards, Kugler, Schnurr, Morris, Purcell, Cazabat, Payne, Bromley, Knobloch, Newell, Ong, Smith, Bennie.—53.

M. Thomas propose, comme amendement, que le Président de la Convention administre le "serment blindé" à chacun des membres de cette Convention.

Motion est faite de déposer cet amendement sur le bureau. Cette motion est rejetée.

M. Cazabat propose comme substitut, que tous les membres de la Convention se lèvent à l'instant même, que chacun d'eux lève la main droite, et qu'en présence du Dieu Tout-Puissant et de cette Convention, le Président leur administre à tous en même temps le serment prescrit par la proclamation du Président, du 8 décembre 1863.

Le substitut est rejeté.

Motion est alors faite de déposer l'amendement de M. Thomas sur le bureau. La motion est adoptée, et l'amendement déposé.

Nouvelle motion de déposer la motion originaire de M. Terry. Le dépôt est refusé.

Une nouvelle motion d'ajournement est faite et rejetée.

Un membre propose que le secrétaire prenne note de la date du "serment blindé" de chaque membre, et en donne lecture à l'assemblée. Cette proposition est rejetée.

Nouvelle motion d'ajournement. Rejetée.

La question revenant alors à la résolution originaire, le vote nominal sur cette résolution est demandé et donne le résultat suivant :

Pour la résolution :

MM. Gorlinski, Bell, Stocker, Buckley, Stumpf, Schroeder, Gastinel, E. Murphy, Cook, Wilson, Stiner, Murphy M. W., Abell, O'Conner, Hills, Thorpe, Healy, Fosdick, Hire, Thomas, Austin, Foley, Harnan, Shaw, Cutler, Wenck, Maurer, Terry, Montamat, Mendiverri, Bofill, Crozat, Baum, Kavanagh, Millspaugh, Poynot, Spellicy, Cook, Goldman, Hart, Purcell, Stauffer, Fish, Campbell, Barrett, Geier, Duane, Flood, Davies, Dupaty, Ennis, Normand, Edwards, Mann, Kugler, Schnurr, Morris, Pursell. Paine, Bromley, Gruneberg, Cazabat, Newell, Ong, Beauvais, Burke, Gaidry, Smith, Bennie, Dufresne.

M. Thomas demande à être dispensé de voter. Le président soumet la question à la Convention, et M. Thomas retire sa demande et vote pour la résolution.—Total, 70 voix.

Contre la résolution :

MM. Brott, Henderson, Fuller, Sullivan, Waters, Bonzano, Bailey, Howell, Maas, Flagg—10.

M. Austin présente la résolution suivante :

Résolu, Que chaque membre de cette Convention, étant d'origine étrangère, sera tenu de fournir au président la preuve de sa citoyenneté avant samedi, 9 du courant, à midi.

M. Hills se lève pour une question d'ordre. Il pense que la substance de cette résolution se trouve comprise dans la résolution de M. Terry, qui déjà a été adoptée.

M. Harnan pense qu'il y a erreur et que la motion est rejetée.

M. Hire affirme qu'elle est rejetée.

Le vote est repris, et le dépôt de la résolution est prononcé.

M. Gorlinski offre la résolution suivante :

Résolu, Que cette Convention complète son organisation par l'élection des officiers suivants, savoir : un vice-président, un assistant secrétaire, un maître de poste, un imprimeur et quatre rapporteurs.

Cette résolution est déposée sur le bureau, et M. R. B. Bell offre la résolution suivante :

Resolu, Que les travaux de la Convention soient publiés chaque jour dans les journaux le *True Delta*, l'*Era* et le *Times* de cette ville.

Cette résolution est également déposée sur le bureau.

M. Samuel Purcell offre la résolution suivante :

Résolu, Que le clergé de cette ville et des environs est invité à se concerter et à fournir une liste de ceux de ses membres qui désirent faire fonctions de chapelains à cette Convention, à tour de rôle et chacun pour un jour.

On propose alors de s'ajourner jusqu'au lendemain à midi. Adopté.

JOHN E. NEELIS,
Secrétaire.

SAMEDI, 9 Avril 1864.

La Convention se réunit conformément à l'ajournement, à midi.

L'Hon. E. H. Durell, président.

La prière est dite par le Rév. M. Strong.

Le rôle est ensuite appelé, et les membres suivants répondent à leurs noms :

MM. Abell, Austin, Bailey, Barrett, Baum, Bell, Benniw, Bofill, Bromley, Drott, Buckley, Burke, Balch, Campbell Cook, J. K., Crozat, Davies, Dufresnes, Edwards, Fish, Flagg, Flood, Foley, Fosdick, Fuller, Gastinel, Geier, Goldman, Gruneberg, Gaidry, Healy, Harnan, Hart, Heard, Henderson, Hills, Hire, Howell, Howes, Kavanagh, Kugler, Maas, Mann, Maurer, Millspaugh, Montamat, Montague, Morris, Murphy E, Murphy M. W., Newell, Normand, Ong, Payne, de Jefferson; Payne, de Feliciana, Poynot, Purcell J.,P ursell S., Schroeder, Seymour, Shaw, Smith, Spellicy, Stocker, Stumpf, Stiner, Stauffer, Sullivan, Terry, Thorpe, Thomas, Waters, Wenck, Wilson, et le président—75.

Le nombre des membres étant de soixante-quinze seulement, le président ordonne au sergent d'armes d'amener un membre, afin de faire un *quorum*.

Deux membres entrent en ce moment, et le président annonce qu'il y a *quorum*.

Le procès-verbal de la session précédente est lu et adopté, et le secrétaire procède à la lecture de diverses communications—l'une du secrétaire d'Etat, accompagnant les retours de l'élection dans la paroisse d'Iberville, annonçant l'élection de MM. Balch et Dufresne ; une autre de M. R. S. Abbott, offrant sa démission comme membre de la Convention ; et une troisième de M. Roselius, au même effet.

M. Foley propose que ces démissions soient acceptées.

M. Hills propose comme amendement que la démission de M. Abbott soit acceptée, et que M. Roselius soit invité à déduire les motifs de sa démission.

La motion est mise aux voix et acceptée. Ont voté pour la motion 44 membres, et contre 32.

M. Hills demande la reconsidération de la motion.

Le même membre demande ensuite que l'amendement soit déposé sur le bureau.

La question étant mise aux voix—le président déclare qu'il y a doute sur le résultat du vote et ordonne la division.

Le résulat est comme suit : pour le rejet de l'amendement, 44 membres ; contre, 32. L'amendement est déposé.

M. Balch demande le vote nominal sur la résolution principale.

M. Hills demande que cette résolution soit déposée sur le bureau. Cette motion est rejetée.

Le vote nominal est alors pris sur la résolution, et en voici le résultat : pour la résolution, 47 voix ; contre, 27. La résolution est adoptée.

M. Sullivan offre la résolution suivante :

Résolu, Que nul ne sera éligible à aucun office ou emploi quelconque, à la nomination de cette Convention, s'il n'est votant dûment qualifié de l'Etat et des Etats-Unis; et s'il ne prouve au président de la Convention qu'il s'est conformé aux ordres de la proclamation présidentielle du 8 décembre 1863.

Un membre propose de déposer cette résolution sur le bureau.

Le vote nominal est demandé, et la résolution est déposée sur le bureau par 66 voix contre 13.

M. Thomas propose de retrancher le passage qui s'applique aux messagers.

ET L'AMENDEMENT DE LA CONSTITUTION DE LA LOUISIANE.   11

Motion est faite de déposer la résolution sur le bureau.

Le vote par division est pris, et la motion est adoptée par 66 voix contre 13.

M. Thomas offre la résolution ci-après :

Résolu, Qu'il soit procédé par la Convention à l'élection d'un Imprimeur officiel de la dite Convention ; lequel sera chargé d'imprimer et de publier les travaux de cette Convention, et de faire toutes les autres impressions qui pourront être ordonnées par elle, et sera responsable de l'exécution ponctuelle et satisfaisante du travail.

Une motion pour le rejet de cette résolution est faite et rejetée.

La résolution elle-même est alors mise aux voix et le résultat du vote est comme suit :

Pour la résolution :

MM. Austin, Bailey, Barrett, Baum, Beauvais, Bell, Bennie, Edwards, Fish, Flagg, Foley, Fosdick, Fuller, Geier, Murphy E., Murphy M. W., Newell, Normand, Jno. Payne, Paine T. J., Purcell Jno., Bofill, Bonzano, Bromley, Brott, Buckley, Burke, Balch, Campbell, Cazabat, Cook J. K., T. Cook, Cutler, Duane, Dupaty, Dufresne, Goldman, Gruneberg, Gaidry, Hart, Heard, Henderson, Hills, Hire, Howes, Kavanagh, Knobloch, Kugler, Maurer, Millspaugh, Montague, Seymour, Shaw, Smith, Spellicy, Stocker, Stumpf, Stiner, Stauffer, Sullivan, Terry, Thorpe, Thomas, Waters, Wilson—65.

Contre la résolution :

MM. Flood, Gastinel, Howell, Mann, Montamat, O'Conner, Pursell S., Schroeder, Wenk—10.

Le président déclare que la résolution est adoptée.

M. Gastinel appelle de la décision du président en se fondant sur ce qu'il n'y avait pas de quorum.

La question est soumise à la Convention, et le vote donne le résultat suivant :

Pour ratifier la décision du président :

MM. Abell, Austin, Bailey, Barrett, Baum, Beauvais, Bell, Bennie, Bofill, Bonzano, Bromley, Brott, Buckley, Burke, Balch, Campbell, Cazabat, Cook T., Cutler, Davies, Duane, Dufresne, Edwards, Fish, Flagg, Flood, Fuller, Geier, Gorlinski, Gruneberg, Gaidry, Hart, Heard, Henderson, Hills, Hire, Howes, Kavanagh, Knobloch, Kugler, Mann, Maurer, Millspaugh, Montamat, Murphy E., Murphy M. W., Newell, Normand, O'Conner, Paine J. T., Poynot, Purcell Jno., Pursell S., Schroeder, Schnurr, Seymour, Shaw, Spellicy, Stocker, Stumpf, Sullivan, Stiner, Stauffer, Terry, Thorpe, Thomas, Waters, Wilson—68.

Contre cette ratification :

MM. J. K. Cook, Foley, Fosdick, Howell, Montague, Morris, Smith—7.

Le président annonce que la décision est soutenue ; que s'il y avait *quorum*, on doit considéré que plusieurs membres se sont abstenus de voter.

M. Foley demande l'appel du rôle pour vérifier si en effet il y avait quorum.

Le président soutient que c'est là le moyen convenable de décider la question.

Le rôle est appelé, et il est constaté que 75 membres seulement étaient présents.

Une motion pour l'ajournement à lundi est faite et rejetée.

La Convention suspend la séance pour un quart d'heure.

M. Thomas demande que le sergent d'armes soit envoyé à la recherche des membres absents.

Après un court espace de temps le rôle est de nouveau appelé, et 81 membres se trouvant présents, la résolution est de nouveau mise aux voix et adoptée—deux membres de plus étant entrés pendant l'appel des noms, le vote est de 83.

Ont voté pour la résolution :

MM. Abell, Austin, Bailey, Barrett, Baum, Beauvais, Bennie, Bofill Bonzano, Bromley, Brott, Buckley, Burke, Balch, Campbell, Cazabat, Cook J. K., Cook T., Cutler, Davies, Duane, Dufresne, Edwards, Fish, Flagg, Foley, Fosdick, Fuller, Gastinel, Geier, Goldman, Gorlinski, Gruneberg, Gaidry, Healy, Harnan, Hart, Heard, Henderson, Hills, Hire, Howell, Howes, Kavanagh, Knobloch, Kugler, Maas, Mann, Maurer, Mendiverri, Millspaugh, Montamat, Montague, Morris, Murphy E., Murphy M. W., Newell, Normand, O'Conner, Ong, Payne Jno., Paine J. T., Poynot, Purcell J., Pursell S., Schroeder, Schnurr, Seymour, Shaw, Smith, Spellicy, Stocker, Stumpf, Stinner, Stauffer, Sullivan, Terry, Thorpe, Thomas, Waters, Wenck, Wilson—82.

Contre :

M. Flood—1.

La résolution est adoptée.

Les nominations ayant été déclarées à l'ordre,

M. Thomas désigne M. Fish.

M. Mann désigne M. Hills.

M. Brott désigne M. May.

M. Gorlinski désigne MM. Fish et Hills.

M. Campbell demande le vote au scrutin secret.

Sur motion, cette demande est rejetée.

Le vote nominal est pris et donne le résultat suivant :

Ont voté pour M. Fish les membres ci-après nommés :

MM. Abell, Abbott, Austin, Bailey, Barrett, Baum, Beauvais, Bell, Bennie, Bofill, Bonzano, Buckley, Burke, Campbell, Cazabat, Cook J., K. Cook T., Cutler, Davies, Duane, Edwards, Flagg, Foley, Fuller, Gastinel, Geier, Goldman, Gruneberg, Gaidry. Healy, Hart, Heard, Henderson, Hire, Howes, Kavanagh, Knobloch, Maas, Maurer, Mendiverri, Millspaugh, Montamat, Morris, Murphy E., Murphy M. W., Newell, Normand, O'Conner, Ong, Payne J., Poynot, Purcell J., Pursell S., Schroeder, Seymour, Spellicy, Stocker, Stumpf, Stiner, Stauffer, Sullivan, Terry, Thorpe, Thomas, Waters—65.

Ont voté pour M. Hills :

MM. Dupaty, Harnan, Montague, Dufresne, Howell, J. T. Paine, Flood, Kugler, Schnurr, Fosdick, Mann, Smith—12.

Ont voté pour M. May :

MM. Bromley, Balch, Wilson, Brott, Hills—5.

Ont voté pour MM. Fish et Hills, les membres suivants :

MM. Gorlinski, Wench—2.

M. Hills propose que M. Fish soit déclaré élu imprimeur à l'unanimité.

M. Foley demande si tout le monde s'est conformé à la résolution adoptée hier, requérant tous les membres de la Convention de prouver qu'ils ont prêté le serment exigé par la proclamation présidentielle du 8 décembre 1863. Après un certain temps pris pour la vérification, la liste est lue, et il est annoncé que tous les membres se sont conformés à la résolution, à l'exception de MM. Ariail, Crozat, Ennis, Lobdell, Wenck, Wells et Pintado.

Ces membres n'étaient pas présents, et plusieurs d'entr'eux n'avaient pas encore paru à la Convention depuis son ouverture.

M. Stauffer appelle l'attention de la Convention sur la résolution suivante, déposée sur le bureau le 6 :

Résolu, Qu'un comité de cinq soit nommé pour préparer un projet de réglements pour la Convention, et que ce comité fasse son rapport lundi soir.

La résolution est adoptée.

Le président nomme MM. Stauffer, Thomas, Heard et Bennie, membres de ce comité.

M. Montamat offre la résolution suivante :

Résolu, Que le gouverneur et les officiers d'Etat élus le 22 février dernier, ainsi que le captaine Stephen Hoyt, faisant fonctions de maire de la ville de la Nouvelle-Orléans, sont, par la présente, invités à s'asseoir dans l'enceinte réservée, toutes les fois que la Convention ne siègera pas à huis-clos.

La résolution est mise aux voix et adoptée.

M. Cazabat fait passer une motion tendant à reconsidérer l'action de la Convention en ce qui touche la démission de MM. Roselius et Abbott.

Le président décide que les membres doivent présenter leurs projets de résolutions de leurs places.

Le Colonel Thorpe demande que l'on reconsidère l'action de la Convention en ce qui regarde l'acceptation des démissions de MM. Abbott et Roselius, par le motif qu'il n'y avait pas *quorum* présent quand le vote a été pris.

Le juge Howell offre les résolutions suivantes, et demande qu'elles soient lues par le secrétaire, et mises à l'ordre du jour pour lundi ·

Résolu, Qu'il soit nommé par le président de cette Convention, un comité de —— membres auquel sera référée la la question de l'abolition immédiate et permanente de l'esclavage dans l'Etat de la Louisiane, et qui devra présenter, dans le plus bref délai possible, un projet d'ordonnance ou un chapitre sur cette motion, propre à être incorporés dans la constitution de l'Etat.

2. Qu'il soit nommé par le président un comité de —— membres, chargé de préparer le préambule de la nouvelle constitution et de faire son rapport à ce sujet dans le plus bref délai possible.

3. Qu'il soit nommé par le président un comité de —— membres, devant lequel sera renvoyée la question de la distribution des pouvoirs du gouvernement de l'Etat de la Louisiane, tel qu'elle est établie dans le titre premier de la constitution de l'Etat adoptée en 1852, lequel comité sera chargé de recommander les changements, modifications ou amendements qu'il croira opportuns, et de faire un rapport à ce sujet aussi promptement que faire se pourra.

4. Qu'il soit nommé par le président de

la Convention un comité de —— membres, devant lequel sera renvoyée la question du département législatif, telle qu'elle est exposée dans le titre second de la dite constitution, et qui sera chargé de recommander les changements, modifications et amendements, qu'il croira propres, et de faire son rapport dans le plus bref délai.

5o. Qu'il sera nommé par le président un comité de —— membres, devant qui sera renvoyée la question du département exécutif, telle qu'on la trouve dans le titre troisième de la dite constitution, lequel comité devra proposer tels changements, modifications et amendements, qu'il croira propres, et faire son rapport à ce sujet aussitôt que possible.

6. Qu'il soit nommé par le président un comité de —— membres, devant lequel sera renvoyée la question du département judiciaire, dont les bases sont établies au titre quatrième de la dite constitution, et qui proposera tels changements, modifications et amendements qu'il jugera convenables, et présentera un rapport sur ce sujet dans le plus bref délai possible.

7. Qu'il soit nommé par le président un comité de —— membres, devant lequel sera renvoyée la question de la mise en accusation des officiers public (impeachment), telle qu'on la trouve exposée sous le titre cinq de la dite constitution, et qui devra proposer tels changements, modifications et amendements qu'il croira à propos, et faire son rapport sur ce sujet dans le plus bref délai possible.

8. Qu'il sera nommé par le président un comité de —— membres, devant lequel sera renvoyée la question des dispositions générales, telle qu'elle est développée sous le titre six de la dite constitution, et qui sera chargé de proposer tels changements, modifications et amendements qu'il croira opportuns, et de faire son rapport sur ce sujet le plus promptement possible.

9. Qu'il sera nommé par le président un comité de —— membres, devant lequel sera renvoyée la question des améliorations intérieures, telle qu'elle est exposée sous le titre sept de la dite constitution, et qui sera chargé de suggérer tels changements, modifications et amendements qu'il jugera à propos, et de faire son rapport à ce sujet dans le plus bref délai possible.

10. Qu'il sera nommé par le président un comité de —— membres, devant lequel sera renvoyée la question de l'instruction publique, telle qu'elle est développée sous le titre huit de la dite constitution, et qui sera chargé de proposer tels changements, modifications et amendements qu'il croira opportuns, et de faire son rapport sur ce sujet le plus tôt possible.

11. Qu'il sera nommé par le président un comité de —— membres, devant lequel sera renvoyée la question du mode de révision de la constitution, tel qu'il est développé sous le titre neuf de la dite constitution, et qui sera chargé de suggérer tels changements, modifications et amendements qu'il croira à propos, et de faire son rapport à ce sujet dans le plus bref délai.

12. Qu'il sera nommé par le président un comité de —— membres, devant lequel sera renvoyée la question des dispositions transitoires (schedule), telle qu'elle est exposée sous le titre dix de la dite constitution, et qui sera chargé de suggérer tels changements, modifications et amendements qu'il croira à propos, et de faire son rapport à ce sujet dans le plus bref délai.

13. Qu'il sera nommé par le président un comité de —— membres, devant lequel sera renvoyée la question de la mise en exécution de la constitution (ordinance), telle qu'elle est réglée sous le titre onze de la dite constitution, et qui sera chargé de proposer tels changements, modifications et amendements qu'il croira opportuns, et de faire son rapport à ce sujet le plus promptement possible.

M. Montamat propose l'impression de 300 exemplaires de ces résolutions pour l'usage des membres.—Adopté.

Un membre demande que ces résolutions soient déposées sur le bureau. Cette motion est rejetée.

L'ajournement à lundi, à midi, est proposé et adopté.

JOHN E. NEELIS,
Secrétaire.

———

LUNDI, 11 avril 1864.

A midi le président appelle la Convention à l'ordre, et la séance commence par une prière prononcée par le Rév. M. D'Ossey, membre de la Commission Chrétienne.

A l'appel du rôle, les membres suivants répondent à leurs noms :

MM. Abell, Bailey, Barrett, Beauvais, Bell, Bofil, Bonzano, Bromley, Brott, Buckley, Balch, Burke, Campbell, Crozat, Davies, Dufresne, Edwards, Flagg, Flood, Foley, Fosdick, Geier, Goldman, Gorlinski, Gruneberg, Gaidry, Healy, Harnan, Heard, Henderson, Hills, Howell, Howes, Kavanagh, Knobloch, Kugler, Maas, Mann, Maurer, Millspaugh, Montamat, Montague, Morris, Murphy E., Murphy M. W., Newell, Norman, O'Conner, Ong, Schnurr, Seymour, Shaw, Smith, Spellicy, Stocker, Stumpf, Stiner, Stauffer, Sullivan, Terry, Thomas, Waters, Wenck, Wilson, et M. le président—65.

Il n'y a pas quorum, et le président donne au sergent d'armes l'ordre d'aller à la recherche des membres manquants ; et à l'appel nominal suivant, les membres ci-après dénommés répondent :

MM. Abell, Austin, Bailey, Barrett, Bell, Bofil, Bonzano, Bromley, Brott, Buckley, Burke, Balch, Campbell, Cazabat, Crozat, Davies, Duane, Dupaty, Dufresne, Edwards, Fish, Flagg, Flood, Foley, Fosdick, Fuller, Gastinel, Geier, Goldman, Gorlinski, Gruneberg, Gaidry, Healy, Harnan, Hart, Heard, Henderson, Hills, Hire, Howell, Howes, Kavanagh, Knobloch, Kugler, Maas, Mann, Maurer, Mendiverri, Millspaugh, Montamat, Montague, Morris, Murphy E., Murphy M. W., Newell, Norman, O'Conner, Ong, Poynot, Purcell, J. Shroeder, Schnurr, Seymour, Shaw, Smith, Spellicy, Stocker, Stumpf, Stiner, Stauffer, Sullivan, Terry, Thorpe, Thomas, Waters, Wenck, Wilson et M. le Président—78.

M. Stauffer, président du comité chargé de présenter les règles et réglements pour les séances de la Convention, soumet le rapport suivant :

Reglements de la Convention.

DU PRESIDENT—SES DEVOIRS ET SES DROITS.

I. Le président prendra son siége tous les jours à l'heure pour laquelle la Chambre se sera ajournée le jour précédent, et il appellera de suite les membres à l'ordre. Si une majorité est présente, il fera lire le journal de la séance précédente.

II. Le président maintiendra l'ordre et le décorum. Sur des questions d'ordre, il pourra parler avant les membres, et si son désir est tel, il lui suffira de se lever de son siége. Il décidera les questions d'ordre, mais il suffira de deux membres pour appeler à la Chambre de ses décisions ; et sur l'appel ainsi fait, aucun membre ne pourra parler plus d'une fois sans la permission de la Convention.

III. Le président se lèvera pour mettre une question aux voix, mais il pourra l'expliquer en restant assis.

IV. Les questions devront être mises aux voix distinctement et dans la forme suivante : "Tous ceux qui sont d'opinion que (suivant la question) diront oui," "tousceux qui sont d'une opinion contraire diront non." Si le président reste dans le doute, ou si la division est demandée, la Chambre se divisera, et ceux qui ont voté dans l'affirmative se lèveront d'abord, puis ceux qui se seront prononcés dans le sens négatif. Le président se lèvera alors et fera connaître la décision de la Convention.

V. Le président aura le droit d'examiner et de corriger le journal avant qu'il ne soit lu. Il aura la direction générale des travaux. Il pourra se faire remplacer au fauteuil par tout membre de la Chambre ; mais le remplacement ainsi fait ne s'étendra pas au-delà de l'ajournement.

VI. Toutes les fois que la Convention procèdera à une élection, le président votera ; mais dans les autres cas il ne votera pas, à moins que la Chambre ne soit également divisée, ou à moins que sa voix donnée à la minorité ne produise une division égale, et dans ce dernier cas la question sera perdue.

VII. Tous les comités seront nommés par le président, à moins que la Convention n'en ordonne autrement d'une manière spéciale, et dans ce cas ils seront élus par la Chambre ; et si après un ballot, le nombre requis n'est pas élu par la majorité des votes donnés, la Chambre procèdera à un second ballot, dans lequel la pluralité des voix prévaudra ; et s'il arrive qu'un nombre égal de voix ait été donné à plus de membres qu'il n'en faut pour composer ou compléter un comité, la Chambre procèdera à un autre ballot.

VIII. Tous les actes, toutes les adresses et toutes les résolutions de la Convention seront signés par le président ; et tous les ordres, mandats ou *subpœnas* seront revêtus de sa signature, et devront être contresignés par le secrétaire.

IX. En cas de trouble ou de conduite malséante dans les galeries ou dans le lobby, le président (ou le *chairman* du Comité Général) aura le droit de les faire évacuer.

DE L'ORDRE A SUIVRE DANS LES DEBATS.

X. Lorsqu'un membre sera sur le point de parler dans une discussion, ou de présenter un sujet quelconque à la Convention, il devra se lever de son siége et s'adresser respectueusement au président.

XI. Si un membre, en parlant ou autrement, enfreint les réglements de la Convention, le président devra, et tout autre membre pourra, l'appeler à l'ordre ; et dans ce cas, le membre ainsi appelé devra s'asseoir immédiatement, à moins qu'il n'obtienne permission de s'expliquer ; et la Convention devra, si elle est appelée à le faire, décider la question, mais cela sans débat. Si la décision est en faveur du membre appelé à l'ordre, il pourra continuer si bon lui semble ; mais si la décision est contre lui, et suivant que le cas l'exige, il sera passible de la censure de la Convention.

XII. Lorsque deux ou plusieurs membres se lèveront en même temps, le président désignera celui d'entr'eux qui aura le premier la parole.

XIII. Aucun membre ne parlera plus de deux fois sur le même sujet, et plus d'une heure chaque fois, sans la permission de la Convention ; et il ne pourra prendre la parole plus d'une fois qu'après que tous ceux des membres qui la réclameront auront parlé. Mais l'auteur d'une proposition aura le droit d'ouvrir et de clore le débat. Et si la proposition émane d'un comité, le membre qui aura fait le rapport au nom du comité pourra alors ouvrir et clore le débat de la même manière.

XIV. Tandis que l'on procède à l'appel nominal, ou que l'on compte les voix, aucun membre n'aura le droit de se rendre au bureau du secrétaire.

XV. Nul membre ne pourra voter sur aucune question dont le résultat lui est d'un intérêt direct ou indirect, ni dans aucun cas s'il se trouvait absent de l'enceinte de la Convention lorsque la question a été soulevée. Lorsqu'un membre demandera le droit de voter, le président lui posera la question suivante : *Vous trouviez-vous dans l'enceinte de la Convention lorsque la question a été soulevée ?* Mais lorsque l'appel nominal aura été fait, et qu'un membre demandera la permission de voter, le président lui demandera s'il se trouvait dans l'enceinte de la Chambre *lorsque son nom a été appelé ?*

XVI. Sur une division de la Convention, et lorsque l'on comptera les voix, il ne sera pas tenu compte des membres qui se trouveront hors de l'enceinte.

XVII. Chaque membre présent dans la Convention lorsqu'une question est mise aux voix devra voter, à moins que la Chambre, pour des raisons alléguées, ne le dispense de le faire. Il ne sera permis à aucun membre d'entrer en des explications sur le vote qu'il est sur le point de donner, ou de demander qu'on le dispense de voter, après que le secrétaire, sur l'ordre qu'il aura reçu de la Convention, aura commencé l'appel nominal.

XVIII. Une motion étant faite et secondée, elle devra être énoncée par le président ; ou, si elle est écrite, elle sera remise au président, qui la fera lire à haute voix par le secrétaire avant qu'elle ne soit discutée.

XIX. Chaque proposition doit être mise en écrit, si le président ou tout autre membre le désire.

XX. Nul ne sera admis dans l'enceinte de la Convention, sauf le général commandant le Département du Golfe, le gouverneur de tout État, les chefs des différents départements de cet Etat, le maire de la Nlle-Orléans, et toutes autres personnes que le président ou les membres jugeront convenable d'inviter à prendre place dans la Convention.

XXI. Après qu'une proposition aura été énoncée par le président, ou lue par le secrétaire, elle sera considérée en possession de la Convention, mais, son auteur pourra cependant la retirer, avec le consentement du membre qui l'aura secondée.

XXII. Lorsqu'un sujet quelconque est livré à la discussion, aucune proposition ne sera admissible, excepté les suivantes : 1o. l'ajournement ; 2o. le rejet ; 3o. la question préalable ; 4o. l'ajournement à un jour désigné ; 5o. le renvoi à un comité ; 6o. la proposition d'amender, ou 7o. le renvoi indéfini ; lesquelles diverses propositions auront la priorité dans l'ordre d'après lequel elles sont classées ; et aucune proposition de renvoyer à un jour désigné, de référer à un comité ou de renvoyer indéfiniment, ne pourra, après qu'elle aura été décidée, être admise de nouveau dans la même séance et au même degré où sera arrivé le bill ou la proposition. La motion de biffer d'un bill les mots : "La Convention décrète," aura la priorité sur celle d'amender, et si elle est décidée dans l'affirmative, elle équivaudra au rejet du bill.

XXIII. La question préalable sera posée d'après la formule suivante : "La question principale sera-t-elle maintenant mise aux voix?" Elle ne sera admise qu'autant qu'elle aura été appuyée par la majorité des membres présents, et elle aura pour effet de mettre un terme à tout débat, et d'amener la Chambre à un vote direct : 1o. sur l'amendement pendant et ainsi de suite en rétrogradant jusqu'au premier amendement proposé ; 2o. sur les amendements, rapportés par un comité, s'il en existe aucun, et 3o sur la question principale.

Sur la motion de passer à la question préalable, et avant qu'elle soit secondée, l'appel du rôle de la Convention sera à l'ordre ; mais après qu'elle aura été appuyée par une majorité, l'appel du rôle ne sera à l'ordre qu'autant que la question préalable ait été décidée. La motion de passer à la question préalable ne donnera lieu à aucun débat.

Toutes questions incidentes d'ordre soulevées après que la question préalable aura été demandée, et tant que cette question sera devant la Convention, seront décidées, soit sur appel ou autrement, mais sans débat. Après qu'une motion de passer à la question préalable a été appuyée par la Convention, les questions seront mises aux voix et décidées, dans l'ordre ci-dessus, mais sans débats, soit sur les amendements, soit sur la question principale.

XXIV. Tout membre a le droit de demander la division de la question, lorsque la question sera divisible.

XXV. Aucune motion ou proposition nouvelle sur un sujet différent de celui qui est devant la Convention ne sera admise soit comme amendement, soit en remplacement de la motion ou de la proposition livrée au débat.

XXVI. Lorsqu'une motion a été faite et décidée dans l'affirmative ou la négative, tout membre qui aura voté avec la majorité aura le droit de demander la reconsidération de son vote ; il est entendu que la demande devra en être faite pendant la séance du jour ou à la séance suivante, avant que la Convention ne soit passée à ses ordres du jour.

XXVII. Lorsque la leccture d'une pièce quelconque est demandée, et que l'on y objecte, la Convention décidera si la pièce sera lue ou non.

XXVIII. Si l'ajournement de la Convention, laisse en suspens la question pendante, et si cette question est ravivée le jour suivant, tout membre qui aura parlé deux fois la veille, ne pourra prendre la parole de nouveau sans la permission de la Convention.

XXIX. Lorsque des motions sont faites de référer un sujet à un comité spécial, soit à un comité permanent, la question de renvoi au comité permanent aura la priorité sur l'autre.

DE L'ORDRE DES TRAVAUX DU JOUR.

XXX. Dès que le journal est lu et que les membres ont été appelés par leurs noms, le président demandera s'il y a des pétitions, mémoires ou résolutions à présenter. Les pétitions, mémoires ou résolutions étant présentés, et la Convention en ayant disposé, les rapports des comités permanents d'abord, puis des comités spéciaux, seront demandés ; ensuite viendront les notices de bills et les bills que les membres auront à présenter ; après quoi le président diposera des messages, des communications et des bills qui seront sur son bureau, et procédera alors à appeler les ordres du jour.

XXXI. L'affaire inachevée dont la Convention s'occupait lors de son dernier ajournement, aura la priorité sur les ordres du jour ; et aucune motion, aucune autre affaire ne sera reçue sans la permission spéciale de la Chambre, qu'après qu'on aura disposé de la première. L'ordre du jour sera comme suit :

1. Les affaires inachevées dont s'occupait la Convention lors de son dernier ajournement.

2. Les ordres spéciaux du jour, s'il s'en trouve.

3. Les ordonnances et résolutions, dans leur ordre d'introduction devant la Convention.

XXXII. Les pétitions, mémoires et autres pièces adressés à la Convention seront présentés par le président ou par un membre, de sa place. Le membre qui les présentera fera verbalement un exposé sommaire de leur contenu.

XXXIII. Dix membres, après l'organisation de la Convention, auront autorité pour forcer les membres absents à se rendre à la séance.

XXXIV. Sur les appels de la Convention, et lorsque l'appel nominal aura lieu sur une question quelconque, les noms des membres seront appelés par ordre alphabétique.

XXXV. Toutes les questions relatives à la propriété des affaires seront décidées sans débat.

XXXVI. La motion d'ajournement, et celle fixant le jour auquel la Convention s'ajourne, seront toujours à l'ordre ; excepté lorsque l'appel nominal a lieu, et lorsque la question a été précédemment soulevée et rejetée ; ces motions, et celle du sujet seront décidées sans discusion.

XXXVII. Aucun membre ne s'absentera à moins qu'il n'ait obtenu un congé, ou bien qu'il ne puisse pas assister aux séances pour cause de maladie.

XXXVIII. Le Comité d'Enrôlement pourra faire ses rapports en tous temps.

XXXIX. Tous les officiers nommés ou élus par la Convention ne seront en fonctions que pour le temps qu'il plaira à la Convention.

XL. Toutes les ordonnances soumises à la Convention seront appelées pour être votées d'après leurs numéros d'ordre ; le secrétaire devra numéroter chaque ordonnance suivant son ordre régulier à sa première lecture.

XLI. Aucun réglement permanent ou ordre de cette Convention ne sera rescindé ou changé que sur motion à cet effet, signifiée au moins un jour d'avance. Et nul ordre ne sera suspendu qu'en vertu d'un vote des deux tiers des membres présents et l'ordre des affaires, établi par les réglements de cette Convention, ne sera interverti que sur un vote d'au moins les deux tiers des membres présents.

XLII. Sitôt qu'une résolution aura été adoptée par cette Convention elle sera écrite à la grosse en belle écriture ; et après que le Comité d'Enrôlement l'aura examinée et rapportée, le président et le secrétaire la signeront.

XLIII. Les délibérations de la Convention, lorsqu'elle ne siègera pas en comité général, seront portées sur le journal aussi sommairement que possible, en ayant soin toutefois de rendre un compte exact et fidèle des délibérations.

XLIV. Chaque vote de la Convention sera porté sur le journal et sera accompagné d'un exposé concis de la question ; et un court exposé de chaque pétition.

XLV. Toutes les fois que l'un des secrétaires, le sergent d'armes ou le portier de la Convention manquera de remplir son devoir, le secrétaire devra en informer immédiatement la Convention.

XLVI. Le secrétaire lira le journal tous les jours sur les feuilles sur lesquelles il est écrit ; et après qu'elles auront été ainsi lues et corrigées, ces minutes seront enregistrées dans le journal, et une copie dans les deux langues, sous la signature du secrétaire, sera préparée pour être délivrée à l'imprimeur le lendemain du jour où elle aura été lue, à dix heures.

XLVII. Le secrétaire est responsable de l'exactitude de la rédaction du procès-verbal et de la fidélité et la prompte exécution de tout travail ordonné par la Convention. Il tiendra un journal des bills, écrit de sa main; il endossera toutes les résolutions et tous les documents devant être endossés. Il aura à sa charge tous les bills et documents à la garde de la Convention, et les tiendra en bon ordre.

XLVIII. Le sergent d'armes devra assister aux séances de la Convention; il aura à sa charge la salle de la Convention, celle des chambres des comités et celles des commis, et les tiendra en bon ordre ; et ses devoirs seront de mettre en exécution de temps à autres les ordres de la Convention, ainsi que tous les mandats qui auront été lancés par son autorité, et cela de la manière qui lui sera indiquée par le président.

XLIV. Le secrétaire ou l'assistant secrétaire sera tenu de rester debout pendant la lecture des documents de la Convention.

L. L'assistant secrétaire de la Convention dans le cas d'absence, de résignation ou de mort du secrétaire en chef, prendra la charge de tous les devoirs de l'office jusqu'à ce que son successeur soit nommé. Il sera alors son devoir d'écrire de sa propre main, le journal de la Convention, si toutefois il n'agit pas comme secrétaire.

LI. Le portier devra garder les portes de l'enceinte, annoncer les messages, et remplir tous autres devoirs que le président lui assignera.

LII. Un cinquième des membres présents, seul, aura le droit de demander l'appel nominal sur toute question.

LIII. La présence de soixante-sept membres élus et admis à siéger dans cette Convention, constituera un quorum.

LIV. Cette Convention aura pour officiers un président, un secrétaire, deux secrétaires-adjoints, un sergent d'armes et autant de commis qu'il sera nécessaire; un imprimeur officiel, un rapporteur, un portier, deux messagers, un maître de poste et tous autres employés que cette Convention jugera utile, au fur et à mesure des besoins du service.

LV. Lorsque les présents réglements seront muets ou obscurs sur toute question d'ordre ou d'usage parlementaire, le Manuel de Jefferson ou l'ouvrage de Cushing, sur la loi parlementaire, seront considérés comme faisant autorité.

Le président nommera les Comités Permanents de la Convention, savoir :

1. Un Comité d'Elections, composé de cinq membres.
2. Un Comité sur le Préambule et la Distribution des Pouvoirs, composé de cinq membres.
3. Un Comité sur le Législatif, composé de sept membres.
4. Un Comité sur l'Exécutif, composé de sept membres.
5. Un Comité sur le Judiciaire, composé de sept membres.
6. Un Comité sur les Mises en Accusation des officiers publics (impeachment) composé de trois membres.
7. Un Comité sur les Dispositions Générales, composé de sept membres.
8. Un Comité sur les Améliorations Intérieures, composé de cinq membres.
9. Un Comité sur l'Education Publique, composé de cinq membres.
10. Un Comité sur le Mode de révision de la Constitution, composé de cinq membres.
11. Un Comité sur les Dispositions Transitoires, composé de trois membres.
12. Un Comité sur les Ordonnances, composé de cinq membres.
13. Un Comité d'Enrôlement, composé de cinq membres.
14. Un Comité d'Impressions, composé de trois membres.
15. Un Comité de Finances, composé de trois membres.

[Signé] W. STAUFFER, Président.

M. Montamat propose d'imprimer 300 exemplaires de ce rapport pour l'usage de la Convention et que ce rapport soit à l'ordre du jour pour le 12 à 2 heures.

M. Stauffer propose d'amender en substituant le nombre "200" au nombre "300." L'auteur de la motion acceptant le substitut, la motion est votée et acceptée.

Motion de M. Wilson proposant que le président nomme en remplacement de M. C. Roselius, démissionnaire, un membre du comité d'enquête établi pour faire un rapport sur les voies de fait commises contre deux Conventionnels, sur la demande de M. Harnan. Adoptée, et M. Shaw nommé en conséquence.

Les résolutions présentées à la séance d'hier par M. Howell étant à l'ordre du jour, le président annonce que la Chambre est appelée à s'en occuper.

M. Thomas dit que ces résolutions sont déjà incorporées dans le rapport du Comité des Réglements, il propose en conséquence qu'elles soient renvoyées au 12 courant.

M. Brott propose de substituer "au 12 courant," les mots : "sujet à appel."

L'amendement est accepté par l'auteur de la motion ; et, sur le vote, le président dans l'impossibilité de prononcer, ordonne l'appel nominal, qui a pour résultat de rejeter la motion par 47 voix pour la négative contre 29 pour l'adoption.

M. Mann propose l'adoption des résolutions, mais retire sa motion afin de permettre à M. Howell de remplir lui-même les blancs.

Le substitut proposé par M. Abell est déclaré n'être pas à l'ordre.

Motion de M. Howell proposant de remplir le blanc dans la première résolution par le nombre 5 ; dans la seconde par le nombre 3 ; dans la troisième par le nombre 3 ; dans la quatrième par le nombre 5 ; dans la cinquième par le nombre 7 ; dans la sixième par le nombre 11 ; dans la septième par le nombre 5 ; dans la huitième par le nombre 13 ; dans la neuvième par le nombre 3 ; dans la dixième par le nombre 9 ; dans la onzième par le nombre 5 ; dans la douzième par le nombre 5, et dans la treizième par le nombre 5.

M. Abell annonce qu'il est sur le point de présenter un substitut à toutes les résolutions Howell. Le président décide qu'il n'est pas à l'ordre.

M. Harnan propose d'amender la motion Howell en ce qui concerne le remplissage des blancs, par la suppression du nombre 9 dans la résolution dixième, et l'insertion des mots : "un membre de chaque circonscription électorale de la Paroisse d'Orléans, et un membre de chacune des autres paroisses."

M. Shaw propose de s'occuper des résolutions et de remplir les blancs, au fur et à mesure.

La motion Harnan étant retirée, celle de M. Shaw est adoptée.

M. Stauffer demande que le substitut de M. Abell soit lu.

Le président déclare qu'il n'est pas à l'ordre, non plus que M. Abell qui insistait sur ce point.

Appel de M. Stauffer sur la décision du président ; ce dernier établit que les résolutions Howell sont actuellement à l'ordre quant aux blancs, et que pour le moment, tout substitut n'y est pas.

Sur ce, appel nominal, et la décision du président est approuvée par les 57 voix suivantes :

MM. Austin, Barrett, Bell, Buckely, Burke, Balch, Cazabat, T. Cook, Crozat, Duane, Dupaty, Fish, Flagg, Flood, Foley, Fosdick, Fuller, Gastinel, Geier Gorlinski, Gruneberg, Guidry, Healy, Harnan, Henderson, Hills, Hire, Howell, Howes Kavanagh, Knobloch, Kugler, Mann, Mendiverri, Millspaugh, Montamat, Montague, E. Murphy, M. W. Murphy, Newell, Normand, O'Conner, Payne, de Jefferson ; Poynot, J. Purcell, Schnurr, Shaw, Smith, Spellicy, Stocker, Stumpf, Stiner, Sullivan, Terry, Thorpe, Waters, Wenck, Wilson—57.

Contre, les 18 suivantes :

MM. Bailey, Baum, Beauvais, Bennie, Bonzano, Brott, J. K. Cook, Davies, Dufresne, Goldman, Heard, Maas, Maurer, Morris, Ong, S. Pursell, Stauffer, Thomas—18.

Motion de procéder à l'élection d'un secrétaire-adjoint.

Un membre demande s'il y a quorum.

Sur l'appel, il appert que les 75 personnes dont les noms suivent sont seules présentes :

MM. Abell, Austin, Bailey, Barrett, Beauvais, Bell, Bofill, Bonzano, Bromley, Brott, Buckley, Burke, Campbell, Cazabat, T. Cook, Crozat, Davies, Duane, Dupaty, Edwards, Fish, Flagg, Flood, Foley, Fosdick, Fuller, Gastinel, Geier, Goldman, Gorlinski, Gruneberg, Guidry, Healy, Harnan, Hart, Heard, Henderson, Hills, Hire, Howell, Howes, Kavanagh, Knobloch, Kugler, Maas, Mann, Maurer, Millspaugh, Montague, Morris, E. Murphy, M. W. Murphy, Newell, Normand, O'Conner, Ong, Payne, J. Purcell, E. Purcell, Schroeder, Schnurr, Seymour, Shaw, Smith, Stocker, Stumpf, Stiner, Stauffer, Sullivan, Terry, Thorpe, Thomas, Waters, Wenck, Willson.

M. Thomas propose d'ajourner au lendemain, à 2 heures.

Le président étant dans l'impossibilité de décider le vote, l'appel nominal donne pour résultat 43 voix affirmatives contre 32 négatives.

La proposition est adoptée.

JOHN E. NEELIS,
Secrétaire.

JEUDI, 12 Avril.

La Convention se réunit conformément à l'ajournement.

A deux heures le président appelle la Convention à l'ordre, et les membres suivants répondent à leurs noms:

MM. Abell, Ariail, Austin, Barrett, Baum, Bell, Bofill, Bonzano, Brott, Buckley, Burke, Campbell, Cazabat, J. K. Cook, T. Cook, Crozat, Davies, Duane, Dufresne, Dupaty, Fish, Flagg, Flood, Foley, Fosdick, Fuller,

Gastinel, Geier, Goldman, Gorlinski, Gruneberg, Guidry, Healy, Hart, Heard, Hills, Hire, Howell, Howes, Knobloch, Kugler, Maas, Mann, Maurer, Mendiverri, Millspaugh, Montamat, Montague, Morris, E. Murphy, M. W. Murphy, O'Conner, Ong, Paine, Poynot, J. Purcell, S. Pursell, Schroeder, Schnurr, Seymour, Shaw, Smith, Spellicy, Stocker, Stumpf, Stiner, Staufer, Sullivan, Terry, Thorpe, Thomas, Waters, Wenck, Wilson et M. le Président—75 membres.

Le quorum faisant faute, le président envoie le sergent d'armes à la recherche d'un membre, qui est amené.

Le procès-verbal de la séance précédente est lu et adopté.

Le président annonce que la question à l'ordre, est le "Réglement de la Convention," et il en ordonne la lecture.

Motion d'en faire lecture par son titre. Adopté.

Motion de M. Hills d'amender le titre "Réglements de la Convention du Peuple de la Louisiane," en y substituant ces mots: "pour amender et réviser la Constitution de la Louisiane" aux mots "du peuple de la Louisiane." Adopté et approuvé tel.

La motion de prendre le rapport section par section est adopté.

La 1re section est prise et adoptée ;
La 2e section est adoptée ;
La 3e section est adoptée :
La 4e section est adoptée :
La 5e section est adoptée ;
La 6e section est adoptée ;
La 7e section est prise en considération.

M. Foley propose de biffer le mot "scrutin" dans la cinquième ligne, et d'y substituer le mot "vote." Adopté tel.

Dans la section VIII, M. Hills propose d'effacer les mots "résolution conjointe" à la première ligne. Adopté tel.

La section IX est adoptée.

La section X est adoptée telle, nonobstant l'amendement proposé par M. Bell d'ajouter les mots "et les membres," lequel est rejeté.

Les sections XI et XII sont adoptées.

A la section XIII M. Foley propose d'insérer le mot "demie" avant le mot "heure,". Adoptée.

La 14e section est adoptée ;
La 15e section est adoptée ;
La 16e section est adoptée ;
La 17e section est adoptée ;
La 18e section est adoptée ;

Section XIX. M. Hills propose de donner à cette section un caractère de nécessité absolue, en substituant au mot "should" le mot "shall," à la première ligne.

Autre amendement proposé à l'effet de substituer le mot "résolution" au mot "motion."

M. Hills accepte l'amendement, et le vote de l'assemblée l'adopte.

M. Goldman propose d'amender par l'adjonction des mots "Avis sera donné au président de l'Intention de l'offrir." Rejeté sur motion à cet effet.

La 20e section est adoptée :
La 21e section est adoptée ;

La section XXII est adoptée, nonobstant l'amendement de M. Thorpe à l'effet de biffer les mots "mais pour s'ajourner" à la seconde ligne, lequel est rejeté.

La 23e section est adoptée.
La 24e section est adoptée.

La motion de biffer les mots "quand faire se pourra" est rejetée par 44 voix contre 9.

Section 25. M. Cazabat propose de l'amender en y insérant le mot "résolution" après le mot "motion" à la première ligne. Sur motion, l'amendement est rejeté.

Section 26. M. Gorlinski propose de l'amender en effaçant les mots "le même jour," à la quatrième ligne. Rejeté.

La motion de M. Goldman d'effacer les mots: "pourvu que cela soit fait le même jour," est rejetée.

La 27e section est adoptée :
La 28e section est adoptée ;

Section 29. La motion de biffer le mot "permanent," à la deuxième ligne, second mot, est adoptée.

La motion d'effacer le mot "et" et d'y substituer le mot "ou," à la deuxième ligne, est adoptée ainsi que la section rédigée telle.

Section 30. M. Cazabat propose de substituer "une heure" à "midi". Rejeté sur la motion de M. Goldman.

M. Hills propose de laisser en blanc l'heure. Motion rejetée.

Motion d'effacer la huitième ligne et les trois derniers mots de la septième ligne, est adoptée ainsi que la section avec cette nouvelle rédaction.

Section 31. Motion d'amender en effaçant sur les lignes 3 et 4 les mots "et nulle motion ou aucune autre affaire, n'aura la priorité sur l'ordre du jour" est adoptée.

La 32e section est adoptée ;
La 33e section est adoptée ;
La 34e section est adoptée ;
La 35e section est adoptée ;
La 36e section est adoptée ;
La 37e section est adoptée.

Section 38. La motion de l'effacer du rapport a été adoptée.

La 39e section est adoptée.

La section 40 est amendée, sur la motion de M. Cazabat, en insérant les mots "leurs emplois" au lieu du pronom.

La 41e section est adoptée ;
La 42e section est adoptée ;
La 43e section est adoptée ;
La 44e section est adoptée ;
La 45e section est adoptée ;

Section 46. M. Wilson propose d'effacer les mots "le secrétaire devra en faire un rapport" et d'y substituer "le président en informera." Adopté.

Section 47. Motion d'amender en biffant les mots "dix heures" à la cinquième ligne. Sur motion cet amendement est rejeté.

Section 48. M. Cazabat propose d'effacer les mots "bills" et "conjoints." Adopté.

M. Wilson demande la reconsidération. Refusé.

La 49e section est adoptée ;
La 50e section est adoptée ;
La 51e section est adoptée ;
La 52e section est adoptée ;

Section 53. M. Montamat propose de biffer les mots "pas moins d'un cinquième" à la première ligne et d'y substituer "deux membres seuls."

La motion de rejeter passe aux voix, et le président, dans l'impossibilité de décider le vote ordonne l'appel nominal, qui donne pour résultat le rejet, par 39 voix contre 33.

M. Montamat propose de substituer aux mots "pas moins d'un cinquième" les mots "tout nombre."

M. Shaw prend la parole pour une question d'ordre.

Le président décide que la motion est à l'ordre ; mais, sur motion, l'amendement est rejeté et la section est adoptée.

Section 54. Motion de rédiger cette section ainsi : "soixante-seize membres formeront un quorum."

Proposition de la rejeter, et appel nominal demandé, duquel il appert que les 23 membres suivants votent en faveur :

MM. Beauvais, Bell, Brott, Burke, J. K. Cook, Terrance Cook, Fish, Flagg, Fuller, Goldman, Guidry, Heard, Henderson, Hire, Maas, M. W. Murphy, O'Conner, J. Purcell, Seymour, Smith, Stauffer, Terry, Wilson —23.

Et les 59 suivants contre, savoir :

MM. Abell, Ariail, Austin, Bailey, Barrett, Baum, Bofill, Bonzano, Buckley, Campbell, Cazabat, Crozat, Davies, Duane, Dupaty, Dufresne, Flood, Foley, Fosdick, Gastinel, Geier, Gorlinski, Gruneberg, Healy, Harnan, Hills, Howell, Howes, Knobloch, Kugler, Mann, Maurer, Mendiverri, Millspaugh, Montamat, Montague, Morris, E. Murphy, Newell, Ong, J. Payne, Poynot, Sam Pursell, Schroeder, Schnurr, Shaw, Spellicy, Stocker, Stumpf, Stiner, Sullivan, Thorpe, Thomas, Waters, Wenck —59.

M. Hills propose d'amender en ajoutant les mots "tout membre qui s'absentera de l'assemblée pendant trois séances consécutives, sans offrir une excuse raisonnable, perdra son siége, et ordre sera donné de procéder à une nouvelle élection afin de pourvoir à son remplacement."

Sur motion, cet amendement est rejeté et la section est adoptée avec la rédaction du premier amendement.

Section 55. M. Montamat propose d'effacer les mots "quatre rapporteurs," à la troisième ligne et d'y insérer à leur place "un rapporteur officiel et trois aides."

M. Cazabat propose d'amender en substituant le mot "deux" au mot "quatre" à la troisième ligne.

M. Shaw propose de rejeter l'amendement. Adopté.

M. Howell propose de substituer les mots "un rapporteur" à ceux de "quatre rapporteurs." Adopté, ainsi que la section avec sa nouvelle rédaction.

Section 56. M. Henderson propose d'efface les mots "ou l'ouvrage de Cushing sur la loi parlementaire," à la deuxième et troisième lignes, et tout ce qui suit cette dernière ligne.

La motion de rejeter l'amendement est repoussée.

L'amendement et la section sont adoptés.

La motion de reconsidérer la section 55 est adoptée.

Une motion d'amender par l'insertion des mots "sergent d'armes" à la seconde ligne, est adoptée ainsi que la section.

Un membre propose de reconsidérer la section 21. Réfusé.

M. Wilson propose d'adopter en totalité le rapport tel qu'amendé. Adopté.

M. Shaw propose de s'occuper des résolutions de M. Howell.

Cette motion est mise à l'ordre du jour. Le président annonce qu'en conséquence la Chambre aura à s'en occuper.

M. Cazabat propose un recès de cinq minutes.

M. Beauvais propose d'ajourner au lendemain à 4 heures de relevée.

La motion d'amender en substituant le mot "midi" à "4 heures" est adoptée, et la Convention s'ajourne.

La minute est adoptée.

JOHN E. NEELIS,
Secrétaire.

MERCREDI, 13 Avril 1864.

A midi et vingt minutes, le président appelle la Convention à l'ordre, et la séance s'ouvre par la prière du Rév. J. G. Bass.

L'appel nominal est fait, et les membres suivants répondent à l'appel de leurs noms :

MM. Abell, Ariail, Austin, Bailey, Barrett, Baum, Beauvais. Bell, Bonzano. Brott, Buckley, Burke, Campbell, Cazabat, Cutler, Davies, Duane, Dupaty, Edwards, Ennis, Fish, Flagg, Flood, Foley, Fosdick, Fuller, Geier, Goldman, Gorlinski, Gruneberg, Guidry, Healy, Harnan, Hart, Head, Henderson, Hills, Hire, Howell, Howes, Kugler, Maas, Mann, Mendiverri, Montamat, Montague, Morris, Murphy E., Newell, Normand, O'Conner, Ong, Payne, Pintado, Purcell, Schnurr, Seymour, Shaw, Smith, Spellicy, Stocker, Stumpf, Stiner, Stauffer, Sullivan, Terry, Thorpe, Thomas, Wilson et M. le président—70.

Le président ordonne au sergent d'armes d'amener les membres absents.

Après environ un quart d'heure d'attente, MM. Murphy, Wenck, Milspaugh, Knobloch, Kavanagh, Mendiverri et Gastinel étant entrés dans la salle, il est constaté qu'il y a un quorum.

Le procès-verbal de la séance précédente est lu et adopté.

Le président annonce que la première chose à l'ordre du jour est la réception des pétitions.

Aucune pétition n'étant présentée, les résolutions viennnent à leur tour.

M. J. Randall Terry présente la résolution suivante :

Attendu, Qu'à une Convention de délégués réunis dans cette salle le 26 janvier 1861, prétendant représenter le peuple de cet Etat, il a été ordonné et déclaré ce qui suit :

Ordonnance à l'effet de dissoudre l'union qui existe entre l'Etat de la Louisiane et les autres Etats, en vertu du pacte intitulé: "La Constitution des Etats-Unis d'Amerique."

Nous, le peuple de l'Etat de la Louisiane, assemblé en Convention, déclarons et ordonnons, et il est par ces présentes déclaré et ordonné :

Que l'ordonnance décrétée par nous en Convention, le 22e jour de novembre de l'année 1811, par laquelle la Constitution des Etat-Unis, ainsi que les amendements faits à la dite Constitution furent adoptés, et aussi toutes les lois et ordonnances en vertu desquelles l'Etat de la Louisiane est devenu membre de l'Union fédérale sont et demeurent rappelées et abrogées, et que l'union qui existe maintenant entre la Louisiane et les autres Etats sous le nom de "Etats-Unis d'Amérique," est par les présentes dissoute.

Nous déclarons et ordonnons de plus, que l'Etat de la Louisiane reprend, par ces présentes, tous droits et pouvoirs autrefois délégués au gouvernement des Etats-Unis d'Amérique ; que ses citoyens sont relevés de toute allégeance au dit gouvernement, et qu'il se remet en possession et dans le plein exercice de tous les droits de souveraineté qui appartiennent à un Etat libre et indépendant.

Nous déclarons et ordonnons de plus, Que tous les droits acquis en vertu de la Constitution des Etats-Unis ou d'actes du Congrès, traités ou toutes lois de cet Etat, qui ne sont pas en contradiction avec cette ordonnance, resteront en force et auront le même effet que si cette ordonnance n'avait point été adoptée.

Nous le peuple de l'Etat de la Louisiane, fidèle à la Constitution du gouvernement des Etats-Unis, faisons savoir, déclarons et ordonnons, que la dite prétendue ordonnance de sécession, passée par des traîtres et déloyaux, sans aucune autorité du peuple et en violation de la constitution fédérale, ensemble avec tous autres actes, ordonnances, et procédures des dits sécessionistes dans la dite Convention, et du soi-disant gouvernement institué en vertu de la dite ordonnance de sécession, soient *entièrement nuls* et non avenus.

Résolu, Que, représentant le peuple de l'Etat de la Louisiane, cette Convention déclare adhérer, et le peuple de l'Etat de la Louisiane adhère à la Constitution des Etats Unis, et que nous soutiendrons et maintiendrons par tous les moyens en notre pouvoir le gouvernement des États-Unis, dans tous les efforts qu'il fera pour supprimer cette injuste et détestable rébellion.

M. Henderson demande le dépôt de la résolution sur le bureau. Cette motion est adoptée par 42 voix contre 21.

M. Montamat présente la résolution qui suit :

Résolu, Que les membres de cette Convention auront droit à une indemnité de huit piastres par jour chacun, pendant toute la durée de leurs services comme membres de la dite Convention, laquelle indemnité leur sera payée sur les fonds du Trésor public.

Résolu en outre, Qu'il soit nommé par le président un comité de cinq membres, chargé de fixer les salaires des différents officiers et employés de cette Convention, ainsi que le chiffre de l'allocation qu'il croira nécessaire pour faire face aux dépenses, et de présenter un rapport sur ce sujet dans le plus bref délai possible.

M. Harnan demande qu'on retranche le passage qui fixe l'indemnité à huit piastres par jour, et qu'on lui substitue ces mots : "les membres ne receveront aucune indemnité pour leurs services."

Sur motion, l'amendement est déposé sur le bureau.

M. Cazabat demande également le dépôt de la résolution principale.

La motion est rejetée.

M. Montamat demande l'adoption de la résolution.

Le vote nominal est demandé, et donne le résultat suivant :

Ont voté pour l'adoption de la résolution: MM. Abell, Austin, Baum, Beauvais, Bell, Buckley, Burke, J. K. Cook, Crozat, Duane, Flagg, Foley, Gastinel, Geier, Gruneberg, Gaidry, Healy, Henderson, Howes, Kavanagh, Knobloch, Mendiverri, Montamat, M. W. Murphy, Normand, O'Conner, Pintado, Poynot, John Purcell, Sam. Pursell, Schroeder, Seymour, Smith, Spellicy, Stocker, Stiner, Sullivan, Terry—39.

Ont voté contre :

MM. Ariail, Barrett, Bonzano, Brott, Campbell, Cazabat, T. Cook, Cutler, Dupaty, Ennis, Fosdick, Goldman, Gorlinski, Harnan, Hart, Heard, Fish, Flood, Hills, Hire, Howell, Kugler, Maas, Mann, Millspaugh, Montague, Morris, E. Murphy, Newell, Ong, John Payne, J. T. Paine, Schnurr, Shaw, Stumpf, Stauffer, Thorpe, Thomas, Waters, Wenck, Wilson—39.

Les voix étant également partagées, le président vote contre la résolution, qui, en conséquence, est rejetée.

M. Montamat présente la résolution suivante:

Résolu, Que la Constitution que va faire la présente Convention n'aura d'effet qu'autant qu'elle aura été ratifiée par la majorité des votants dûment qualifiés de la Louisiane, au scrutin tenu dans la forme établie pour l'élection des officiers de l'Etat. Ceux qui voteront pour la Constitution inscriront sur leur ticket, "Ratification."

Le Gouverneur lancera et publiera une proclamation dans le but de faire connaître au peuple de l'Etat le jour où le vote public aura lieu, et d'ordonner aux shérifs des diverses paroisses de l'Etat de faire prendre ce vote conformément aux lois existantes. Ce vote public aura lieu vingt jours après l'ajournement de la Convention.

Sur motion de M. Wilson, la résolution est déposée sur le bureau.

M. Purcell, de Jefferson, offre la résolution suivante :

Résolu, Que le clergé de la ville et des environs soit invité à se concerter et à fournir une liste de ceux d'entre ses membres qui désirent remplir les fonctions de chapelains de la Convention, à tour de rôle et chacun pour un jour seulement.

Déposé sur le bureau.

M. Abell lit le projet de préambule et les résolutions qui suivent :

Attendu, Que par l'Ordre Général No. 38, daté du Quartier Général du Département du Golfe, 22 Mars 1864, les Etats-Unis, par l'entremise de leur représentant, le Major-Général Banks, n'ont pas craint d'imposer et de percevoir des taxes au préjudice du peuple de cet Etat sans son consentement, et d'en approprier le montant à des intérêts domestiques, ainsi qu'il appert de l'ordre suivant concernant l'instruction publique, publié officiellement dans les termes suivants, savoir :

EDUCATION DES AFFRANCHIS.

QUARTIER GENERAL. DEPARTEMENT
DU GOLFE.
Nouvelle-Orléans 22 mars, 1864.

Ordres Généraux No. 38.

Conformément à l'ordre général No. 23,

ET L'AMENDEMENT DE LA CONSTITUTION DE LA LOUISIANE.

pour l'instruction élémentaire des affranchis de ce Département, d'après lequel on doit leur donner les moyens d'acquérir les éléments des connaissances qui peuvent rendre le travail plus intelligent et en augmenter la valeur, et qui réduit les clauses nécessaires pour cela à un système d'écoles économique et efficace.

Il est ordonné par le présent qu'il soit formé un bureau d'éducation composé de trois personnes, qui auront les devoirs et les pouvoirs suivants :

1. D'établir une ou plusieurs écoles communes dans chacun des districts d'école qui ont été ou qui seront désignés par les maréchaux prévôts de paroisse, d'après l'ordre du maréchal prévôt général.

2. D'acquérir par achat ou autrement les portions de terre que le bureau jugera nécessaires et convenablement situées pour écoles, dans les districts des plantations, et ne devant point avoir moins d'un demi-acre d'étendue ; d'en être eux-mêmes les dépositaires jusqu'à ce que ces écoles aient été établies, époque à laquelle ils auront à transférer au surintendant des écoles publiques ou autres autorités d'Etat compétentes tous les droits et titres dont ils pourront avoir été investis.

3. D'élever sur les dites terres telles maisons d'écoles qu'ils jugeront nécessaires et qui seront proportionnées aux besoins de la population de ce district, quand il n'y aura point de bâtisses propres à être converties en écoles, et en cela comme dans toutes leurs autres charges, ils agiront avec la plus stricte économie.

4. De choisir et d'employer des professeurs convenables pour les dites écoles, et pris, autant qu'il sera possible, parmi les habitants loyaux de la Louisiane, et qu'ils pourront obliger à se présenter au moins pendant une semaine, pour y être instruits de leurs devoirs, à une école normale dirigée par le bureau.

5. D'acheter et de procurer les livres nécessaires, le papier et autres articles à l'usage des écoles, et outre cela, d'acheter et de fournir des livres pour former une bibliothèque bien choisie, etc., pour l'usage des personnes libres qui, dans les différents districts, auront passé l'âge de suivre l'école, ce qui coûtera à chacune d'elles une somme qui n'excèdera point deux piastres et demie, laquelle somme sera comprise dans la taxe générale stipulée ci-après, et qui devra être déduite des gages du travailleur par son patron, lorsque les livres en question auront été fournis.

6. De régler le cours des études, la discipline, les heures d'instruction pour les enfants pendant la semaine et pour les adultes le dimanche, de requérir telle similitude dans les réglements et tels rapports de la part des professeurs qu'ils jugeront nécessaires pour assurer l'uniformité et tout ce qui constitue une bonne organisation.

7. D'avoir en général la même autorité et de remplir les mêmes devoirs que les assesseurs, inspecteurs et commissaires dans les Etats du Nord, pour ce qui concerne l'établissement et la façon de diriger les écoles communales.

Et pour arriver à ces fins, et accomplir les devoirs qui doivent lui incomber, le Bureau aura pleine autorité pour assurer et lever les taxes d'école sur les propriétés foncières et personnelles, y compris les récoltes des plantations dans chaque district d'école sus-mentionné. Les dites taxes levées de cette façon devront être calculées pour faire face aux dépenses que devront causer dans le courant de l'année, l'établissement, les fournitures et l'entretien de ces écoles ainsi organisées dans chacun des districts, et les dites taxes seront collectées des personnes occupant les propriétés assessées.

8. Les taxes ainsi levées dans chaque district seront versées entre les mains du Bureau par le Maréchal Prévôt de paroisse dans les trente jours après que la liste et l'état des taxes auront été remis entre ses mains ; et il fera de suite un rapport au Bureau indiquant s'il y a dans les districts de sa paroisse quelque bâtisse qui puisse servir de maison d'école et il assistera le Bureau de son autorité chaque fois qu'il en sera requis, pour faire exécuter l'esprit de l'ordre. Les taxes, lorsqu'elles seront collectées, seront immédiatement déposées dans la Première Banque Nationale de la Nouvelle-Orléans, sujettes seulement à l'ordre du Bureau entier qui présentera chaque mois au Commandant Général ses comptes détaillés et le raport de ce qu'il aura fait.

9. Dans l'accomplissement de tous ces devoirs, le Bureau coopérera autant que cela sera possible avec le Surintendant des Ecoles Publiques, nouvellement élu.

10. L'année scolaire courante commencera à partir du 1er février 1864, pour finir le 1er février 1865.

11. Les officiers et citoyens suivants sont nommés pour composer ce Bureau et on leur obéira et on les respectera en conséquence.

Le Col. H. N. Frisbie, 22e Corps d'Afrique.

Lieut. E. M. Wheelock, 4e Corps d'Afrique.

Isaac Hubbs, Nlle-Orléans.

Par ordre du Major-Général BANKS,
      RICHARD B. IRVIN.

Attendu, que toute imposition de taxes faite sans le consentement du peuple est inconstitutionnelle et est un outrage fait à ses droits et à ses libertés ; il est

Résolu, 1o.—Que les pouvoirs qu'on prétend avoir et affirmer dans l'ordre qui précède sont attentatoires à l'honneur de l'Etat et aux plus chers droits du peuple ;

2o.—Que toute législation, ou tentative de législation, ainsi que tout amendement ou toute tentative d'amendement de la constitution de la Louisiane, serait une admision partielle du droit que l'on réclame, et un abandon des droits les plus précieux du peuple de la Louisiane ;

3o.—Qu'il est du devoir de cette Convention de s'ajourner jusqu'à ce que tous les pouvoirs qui appartiennent au peuple, et qui sont menacés par l'ordre ci-dessus, lui soient rendus par ses représentants.

4o. — Que cette Convention s'ajourne jusqu'au jour de—1864 afin de pouvoir correspondre avec le général Banks ou avec les autorités du gouvernement général des Etats-Unis, avant de rien faire, et qu'il soit pris jour pour s'assurer de la volonté et du dessein du gouvernement général sur le sujet dont il s'agit ;

5o.—Que les résolutions qui précèdent n'ont pas pour objet de mettre en question le droit du Gouvernement général d'obliger l'Etat de la Louisiane à contribuer, dans une juste proportion, au moyen de taxes ou autrement, aux dépenses de la guerre.

M. Brott demande le rejet de cette résolution.

Le vote nominal est demandé et donne le résultat qui suit :

Ont voté pour le rejet de la résolution :

MM. Ariail, Austin, Bailey, Barrett, Beauvais, Bell, Bonzano, Brott, Burke, Cazabat, J. K. Cook, T. Cook, Crozat, Cutler, Duane, Dupaty, Edwards, Ennis, Fish, Flagg, Flood, Foley, Fosdick, Gastinel, Goier, Gorlinski, Guidry, Harnan, Hart, Heard, Henderson, Hills, Hire, Howell, Howes, Kavanagh, Knobloch, Kugler, Mann, Maurer, Mendiverri, Millspaugh, Montague, Morris, E. Murphy, M. W. Murphy, Newell, Normand, O'Conner, Ong, John Payne, J. T. Paine, Poynot, John Purcell, Sam. Pursell, Schroeder, Schnurr, Seymour, Shaw, Smith, Spellicy, Stocker, Stumpf, Stiner, Stauffer, Sullivan, Terry, Thorpe, Thomas, Waters, Wenck, Wilson—72.

Votent contre le rejet :

MM. Abell, Baum, Buckley, Campbell, Goldman, Gruneberg, Maas, Montamat, Pintado—9.

Le rejet de la résolution est prononcé.

L'heure fixée pour la délibération sur les résolutions de M. Howell, comme étant spécialement à l'ordre du jour étant arrivée, la Convention passe à la discussion de ces résolutions :

M. Hills demande à ce que chacune de ces résolutions soit discutée séparément et à tour de rôle.

La motion est adoptée.

La 1ère section est lue.

M. Abell offre le substitut suivant :

Attendu, Que l'esclavage ayant existé dans ce pays par droit coutumier depuis les premiers temps de sa colonisation, avec la sanction de la constitution et des lois des Etats-Unis, et aussi avec la sanction de la constitution et des lois de cet Etat ; et

Attendu, Que les propriétaires d'esclaves ont acquis ce genre de propriété en vertu du dit droit coutumier, des dites constitution et lois, et sous la protection et garantie de ces mêmes droits coutumiers, constitution et lois ; et

Attendu, Que tout ce qu'il y a de bon et de véritablement grand dans les individus comme dans les Etats doit nécessairement reposer sur la bonne foi et la justice ; il est en conséquence,

Résolu, Que cette Convention ne prendra en considération aucune proposition ayant pour objet " l'abolition de l'esclavage " qu'autant qu'on aura pris les mesures nécessaires pour assurer à tous les légitimes propriétaires d'esclaves une pleine, loyale et équitable indemnité, soit au moyen du travail futur de l'esclave, soit au moyen d'un remboursement pris sur les fonds du trésor de cet Etat ou de celui des Etats-Unis, et pour l'exportation de tous les esclaves émancipés hors du territoire de cet Etat.

Un membre propose le rejet de ce substitut.

La motion est adoptée.

M. Cazabat propose d'amender la résolution en insérant à la seconde ligne les mots " sans condition" au lieu et place du mot "immédiate."

Sur motion, l'amendement de M. Cazabat est rejeté.

Motion est faite de rejeter la proposition originaire.

La motion est rejetée.

M. Cutler propose de remplir le blanc de la 1re section par le mot "cinq". Adopté.

La résolution est ensuite mise aux voix et adoptée.

La reconsidération du vote est demandée et acceptée.

Un membre propose de remplacer le mot "cinq" par le mot "onze." Adopté.

La section ainsi amendée est ensuite mise aux voix et adoptée.

La discussion s'ouvre sur la section 2e.

Un membre propose de remplir le blanc par le mot "sept," et la résolution est adoptée.

La discussion s'ouvre sur la section troisième.

Le mot "sept" est proposé pour remplir le blanc.

Cette section est adoptée, et la section est votée.

On passe à la section 4e.

M. Baum propose de remplir le blanc par le mot "treize."

Un autre membre propose le mot "cinq."

Motion est faite de rejeter la dernière proposition. Cette motion est rejetée.

Motion est faite d'adopter la résolution en remplissant le blanc par le mot "cinq." Cette motion est rejetée.

M. Purcell propose de remplir le blanc avec le nombre "9."

Cette motion l'emporte, et la section avec le mot "neuf" est adoptée.

La discussion s'ouvre sur la section 5e.

M. Abell propose de remplir le blanc par le nombre "7."

La motion est accueillie et la section adoptée.

On passe à la section 6e.

Un membre propose de remplir le blanc par le nombre "7."

Motion est faite pour le rejet de cette proposition.

Cette motion est rejetée.

Sur motion, le blanc est rempli par le mot "sept."

La section est ensuite adoptée.

On passe ensuite à la section 7e.

M. Hills propose de remplir le blanc par le nombre "5."

M. Baum propose de remplir le blanc par le nombre "9."

M. Goldman demande le rejet de cette proposition.

La motion de M. Baum est rejetée.

La motion de M. Hills proposant le nombre "5" l'emporte, et la section est adoptée.

La discussion s'ouvre sur la section 8e.

Le nombre "11" est proposé et adopté pour remplir le blanc, et la section est ensuite adoptée.

On passe à la section 9e.

Le nombre "5" est ensuite proposé et accepté pour semplir le blanc, et la section est ensuite adoptée.

On passe à la section 10e.

Le nombre "7" est proposé et accepté pour remplir le blanc, et la section est adoptée.

La discussion s'ouvre sur la section 11e.

Le nombre "5" est proposé et accepté pour remplir le blanc, et la question est adoptée.

On passe à la section 12e.

Le nombre "7" est proposé et accepté pour remplir le blanc, et la section est adoptée

On passe à la section 13e.

Le nombre "5" est proposé et accepté pour remplir le blanc, et la section est adoptée.

M. Montamat propose l'addition d'une section 14e, ainsi conçue :

Résolu, Que les comités suivants soient nommés par le président, savoir : un comité d'Enrôlement, composé de cinq membres ; un comité de Finances, composé de cinq membres ; un comité des Dépenses Eventuelles, composé de cinq membres, et un comité d'Impressions, composé de trois membres.

La motion est adoptée.

M. Montamat demande l'adoption de l'ensemble des résolutions.

La motion est accueillie, et l'ensemble des résolutions est adopté.

M. Howell demande la reconsidération du vote.

Cette motion est rejetée.

M. Gorlinski offre la résolution qui suit :

Résolu, Que tous applaudissements dans la salle pendant les délibérations sont interdits.

La motion est rejetée.

Motion est faite pour le rejet de cette résolutton.

La résolution est ensuite mise aux voix et rejetée.

M. Sullivan offre la résolution suivante :

Attendu, Que le bruit s'est répandu qu'un grand nombre des membres de cette Convention ne sont pas citoyens des Etats-Unis, mais doivent allégeance à des puissances étrangères ; et

Attendu, Qu'il est du devoir de la Convention de placer les membres au-dessus du soupçon ; il est en conséquence

Résolu, Que les membres de cette Convention, qui sont d'origine étrangère, sont requis de produire au président de cette Convention les preuves de leur naturalisation, d'ici à jeudi prochain, 11 du courant, à midi.

M. Hire propose le rejet de cette résolution.

Cette motion est rejetée.

Motion est faite d'adopter la résolution.

Le vote nominal est pris, et donne le résultat suivant :

Ont voté pour la résolution :

MM. Ariail, Austin, Barrett, Baum, Beauvais, Bell, Bennie, Brott, Buckley, Balch, Campbell, J. K. Cook, T. Cook, Cutler, Duane, Dufresne, Edwards, Flagg, Flood, Foley, Gastinel, Gorlinski, Gaidry, Healy, Harnan, Hart, Heard, Hills, Howes, Kavanagh, Knobloch, Mann, Maurer, Montamat, Montague, M. W. Murphy, Normand, Newell, O'Conner, Ong, John Payne, J. T. Paine, Pintado, Sam. Pursell, Seymour, Smith, Spellicy, Sullivan, Terry, Thomas, Waters—51.

Ont voté contre la résolution :

MM. Bailey, Bonzano, Burke, Crozat, Dupaty, Ennis, Fish, Fosdick, Geier, Goldman, Gruneberg, Henderson, Hire, Howell, Kugler, Maas, Millspaugh, E. Murphy, John Purcell, Schroeder, Shaw, Stocker, Stiner, Stauffer, Thorpe, Wenck, Wilson—27.

La résolution est adoptée.

Une motion pour l'ajournement est faite et rejetée.

M. Bell offre la résolution suivante :

Résolu, Que nous procédions à l'élection de deux assistants secrétaires, d'un maître de poste, d'un rapporteur et d'un messager,

La résolution est adoptée.

La nomination des assistants secrétaires étant à l'ordre, les candidats suivants sont présentés : MM. Murphy, Hamilton, Gannon, Winfrie et Parkhurst.

Au premier vote aucun candidat n'ayant obtenu la majorité de tous les votes, il n'y a pas eu d'élection.

Au second vote M. Murphy ayant obtenu la majorité de tous les votes donnés, est déclaré élu.

MM. Hamilton, Winfrie, Gordon et Kruse sont désignés comme candidats pour la place de second assistant secrétaire.

Au premier vote aucun candidat n'ayant obtenu la majorité de tous les votes donnés, il n'y a pas eu d'élection.

Le second vote donne le même résultat.

Au troisième vote, M. S. J. Hamilton ayant reçu la majorité des votes donnés, est déclaré élu.

M. Henderson propose que les deux assistants secrétaires soient déclarés élus à l'unanimité

La motion est adoptée.

M. Brott présente la résolution suivante :

Résolu, Que l'Adjudant-Général L. Thomas, de l'armée des Etats-Unis, est invité à s'asseoir dans l'nnceinte de la Convention.

La résolution est adoptée.

MM. A. P. Bennett et H. A. Gallup sont désignés comme candidats à la place de rapporteur.

Au premier vote, M. Bennet reçoit 50 voix et M. Gallup 24.

M. Bennet est élu.

M. Terry propose de nommer un sténographe.

La motion est rejetée.

M. Thomas demande que le rapporteur soit autorisé à employer trois assistants.

M. Montamat soutient la proposition en substituant le mot "deux" au mot "trois."

M. Cazabat propose le rejet de l'amendement.

Cette motion est rejetée.

La motion de M. Thomas est adoptée.

Sont désignés comme candidats à l'emploi de maître de poste MM. Toomey, Davies, Miller, Gannon, Gordon, Smith et Kock.

Au premier vote, aucun candidat n'ayant obtenu la majorité des votes donnés, il n'y a pas d'élection.

Au second vote, M. Gannon reçoit 47 votes et M. Kock 30.

M. Gannon ayant obtenu la majorité des votes donnés, est déclaré élu.

M. Brott propose que Charles Benedict soit élu messager par acclamation.

La motion est adoptée.

M. Thomas propose que le sergent d'armes soit autorisé à employer deux assistants.

M. Montamat demande le rejet de cette proposition. Cette motion est rejetée.

La motion de M. Thomas est ensuite mise aux voix et adoptée.

On propose d'ajourner jusqu'à vendredi 15 courant, à midi.

Cette motion est adoptée.

La Convention s'ajourne

Approuvé.

JOHN E. NEELIS,
Secrétaire.

VENDREDI, 15 avril 1864.

Le Président appelle la Convention à l'ordre à midi, et annonce que la séance va s'ouvrir par la prière que va faire le révérend M. Masson, de l'église catholique.

M. Masson dit la prière en français.

Le secrétaire appelle le rôle, et les membres suivants répondent à l'appel de leurs noms :

MM. Abell, Ariail, Austin, Bailey, Barrett, Baum, Beauvais, Bell, Bonzano, Brott, Buckley, Burke, Bennie, Bofill, Bromley, Campbell, Cazabat, Cutler, J. K. Cook, T. Cook, Crozat, Davies, Duane, Dupaty, Edwards, Ennis, Fish, Flagg, Flood, Foley, Fosdick, Fuller, Geier, Goldman, Gorlinski, Gruneberg, Gaidry, Healy, Harnan, Hart, Heard, Henderson, Harris, Hyer, Howell, Howes, Kugler, Mass, Mann, Mendiverri, Montamat, Montague, Morris, E. Murphy, Newell, Normand, O'Conner, Ong, Paine, Pintado, Purcell, Schnurr, Seymour, Shaw, Smith, Spellicy, Stocker, Stumpf, Stiner, Stauffer, Sullivan, Terry, Thorpe, Thomas, Wilson et M. le président—76.

M. Heard se lève pour une question de privilége.

Il demade un congé d'absence pour son collègue, M. Kugler, à raison de la maladie d'un membre de sa famille.

Le congé est accordé.

M. Fish propose la résolution suivante :

Résolu, Que le Gouverneur de l'Etat est invité à lancer une proclamation ordonnant une élection dans le 10e district représentatif, pour remplir la vacance par la nomination d'un délégué à cette Convention.

M. Henderson désire savoir s'il n'y a pas quelqu'autre vacance à remplir, et propose que les démissions de M. Rosélius et M. Abott soient acceptées, et que le gouverneur soit invité à ordonner une élection pour remplir ces vacances.

M. Cazabat demande le rejet de la résolution.

Sa motion est rejetée.

La motion de M. Henderson est ensuite mise aux voix et adoptée.

M. Stocker offre une résolution ordonnant à l'imprimeur de la Convention d'imprimer 300 exemplaires des Constitutions de 1812, 1845 et 1852.

M. Montamat propose d'en imprimer seulement 200.

Cette motion est adoptée.

Le juge Howell offre le sub^{s}ti suivant :

Résolu, Que le Bibliothécaire d'Etat soit invité à fournir à chaque membre un exemplaire des *Statuts Révisés* de Phillips, pour l'usage des membres pendant la durée de la Convention.

Le substitut est adopté.

M. Stocker présente la résolution suivante :

Résolu, Que les réglements sont amendés en ce sens, que désormais il devra s'écouler au moins un jour entre la présentation de toutes ordonnances et résolutions, et toute action de la Convention à leur sujet. Elle pourront seulement être renvoyées à un comité.

Il est décidé que d'après les réglements la résolution doit rester pendant un jour sur le bureau avant qu'elle soit soumise à l'action de la Convention, et M. Stocker donne avis qu'il présentera la résolution le lendemain.

M. Thomas demande que l'imprimeur soit requis de fournir 200 exemplaires des résolutions du Juge Howell pour l'usage de l'Assemblée.

M. Montamat demande que la liste des différents comités soit imprimée en regard.

M. Hills propose d'ordonner à l'imprimeur de mettre les titres des différentes sections en marge.

Les amendements sont adoptées, et la résolution ainsi amendée passe.

M. Purcell offre la résolution suivante :

Résolu, Que en considération des services précédemment rendus par lui à la cause de l'Union, et aussi à raison du fait de son élection spontanée par les citoyens vraiment loyaux de la paroisse où ses longs et loyaux services sont justement appréciés, l'Hon. C. Rosélius est invité à retirer sa démission et à reprendre son siége dans cette Convention.

M. Henderson propose le rejet de cette résolution.

La résolution est rejetée.

M. M. W. Murphy présente la résolution suivante :

Résolu, Qu'il sera payé aux membres de cette Convention et sur les fonds du Trésor, une somme de dix piastres par jour, à titre d'indemnité, pendant toute la durée de leurs services :

Résolu de plus, Que le Président nommera un comité de cinq membres, lequel sera chargé de déterminer le chiffre des salaires à payer aux officiers et employés de cette Convention, ainsi que les frais de déplacement des membres des paroisses de la campagne, et de faire son rapport sur ce sujet le plus promtement possible.

M. Brott demande le vote divisionnel sur les résolutions.

M. Foley demande le dépôt des dites résolutions sur le bureau, sujettes à appel.

Un membre en propose le rejet absolu, mais cette motion n'est pas accueillie, et les résolutions étant mise aux voix, sont adoptées.

Le Col. Thorpe offre la résolution suivante :

Résolu, Qu'il sera nommé par le président un comité de——membres devant lequel seront renvoyées toutes les questions et affaires soumises à cette Convention, qui peuvent avoir trait à nos relations avec le Gouvernement Fédéral. Ce comité portera le nom de "Comité des Relations Fédérales."

M. Brott propose que ce comité soit composé de cinq membres.

L'amendement est accueilli et la résolution adoptée.

M. Montamat présente la résolution suivante :

Résolu, Qu'il soit par ces présentes fait une allocation de cent mille piastres, à prendre sur les fonds du Trésor Public, qui sera employée à payer l'indemnité ou *per diem* et les frais de déplacement dûs aux membres de cette Convention, ainsi que les salaires de ses officiers et employés ; ladite somme sera payée par le Trésorier de l'Etat sur le mandat du président de la Convention.

M. Cazabat demande le rejet de la résolution.

Cette motion est rejetée.

La résolution est mise aux voix, et voici le résultat du vote nominal :

On voté pour l'adoption de la résolution :

Messieurs Abell, Austin, Baum, Beauvais, Bell, Bennie, Bofill, Buckley, J. K. Cook, T. Cook, Crozat, Duane, Dufresne, Foley, Gorlinski, Gaidry, Healy, Heard, Henderson, Howes, Mann, Maurer, Mendiverri, Montamat, Montague, M. W. Murphy, O'Conner, Poynot, S. Pursell, Schroeder, Smith, Spellicy, Stiner, Sullivan, Terry, Waters, Wilson—37.

On voté pour le rejet :

Messieurs Barrett, Bonzano, Bromley, Brott, Burke, Campbell, Cazabat, Davies, Dupaty, Ennis, Fish, Flagg, Flood, Fosdick, Gastinel, Geier, Goldman, Harnan, Hart, Hills, Hire, Howell, Maas, Millspaugh, Morris, E. Murphy, Ong, Jon. Paine, Pintado, J. Purcell, Seymour, Shaw, Stocker, Stumpf, Stauffer, Thorpe Thomas—37.

Les voix étant également partagées, le président vote pour le rejet.

M. Cazabat demande l'appel nominal, attendu que le chiffre des votes est au-dessous du quorum.

Le vote est appelé et 77 membres répondent à leurs noms.

Le vote est recommencé sur l'ordre du président.

Votent pour l'adoption de la résolution :

Messieurs Abell, Austin, Baum, Beauvais, Bell, Bennie, Bofill, Buckley, Burke, J. K. Cook, T. Cook, Crozat, Davies, Duane, Dufresne, Flagg, Foley, Geier, Gorlinski, Gaidry, Healy, Heard, Henderson, Hire, Howes, Maurer, Mendiverri, Millspaugh, Montamat, M. W. Murphy, O'Conner, Poynot, J. Purcell, S. Pursell, Schroeder, Seymour, Smith, Spellicy, Stiner, Sullivan, Terry, Thorpe Montague, Wenck et Wilson—45.

Votent pour le rejet :

Messieurs Ariail, Bailey, Barrett, Bromley, Bonzano, Brott, Campbell, Cazabat, Dupaty, Ennis, Fish, Fosdick, Gastinel, Goldman, Harnan, Hart, Hills, Howell, Maas, Mann, Morris, E. Murphy, Ong, J. Paine, Pintado, Shaw, Stocker, Stumpf, Stauffer, Thomas—30.

En conséquence la résolution est adoptée.

Le sécrétaire donne lecture de la composition des différents comités nommés par le président, en exécution de résolutions précédemment adoptées.

Il sont composés comme suit :

Emancipation.—Bonzano, chairman ; Howell, Abell, Edwards, Goldman, Stocker, Cazabat, Bennie, E. Murphy, J. T. Paine, Schroeder—11.

Préambule.—Heard, chairman ; Montague, Sullivan, T. Cook, O'Conner, Spellicy, Waters—7.

Distribution des Pouvoirs.—Thamas, chairman ; Kugler, Foley, Bofill, Stumpf, Ong, Bromley—7.

Département Législatif.—Fosdick, chairman ; Thorpe, Stauffer, Cazabat, Hire, Knobloch, Schnurr, Taliaferro, Wells—9.

Département de l'Exécutif.—Fish, chairman ; Austin, Gruneberg, Bromley, Crozat, Davies, Mann—7.

Département du Judiciaire.—Howell, chairman ; Heard, Beauvais Fuller, Henderson, Cutler, Seymour—7.

Mise en Accusation des officiers de l'Etat.—Wilson, chairman ; Bailey, Gastinel, Morris, J. T. Paine, Smith—6.

Dispositions Générales.—Mann, chairman; J. K. Cook, Foley, Geier, Maas, Wenck, Buckley—7.
Améliorations Intérieures. — Gorlinski, chairman ; Ariail, Campbell, Flood, Healy—5.
Instruction Publique. — Hills, chairman ; Howes, Lobdell, Burke, Hart, M. W. Murphy, Terry, Wells, Gaidry, Balch, Edward, Maurer—11.
Mode de révision de la Constitution.—Cutler, chairman ; Knobloch, Baum, Stiner, Harnan—5.
Dispositions Transitoires. — Gruneberg, chairman ; Dupaty, Shaw, Dufresne, Ennis, Flagg, Gaidry—7.
Mise à exécution de la Constitution.— Shaw, chairman ; Poynot, Kavanagh, Kugler, Mendiverri—5.
Enrôlement. — Thorpe, chairman ; Brott, Millspaugh, Pintado, Crozat—5.
Finances.—Brott, chairman ; Montamat, Normand, Schnurr, Sullivan—5.
Dépenses.— S. Pursell, chairman ; Bell, Duane, Newell, J. Paine de Jefferson—5.
Impressions.—J. Purcell, chairman ; Fuller, Barret—3.

M. Stauffer présente la résolution suivante, dont il demande la lecture immédiate et le dépôt sur le bureau jusqu'à demain :

Résolu, Qu'il sera nommé par le président un comité de cinq membres chargé de s'informer auprès des officiers d'Etat que cela peut regarder, de la quantité et du montant des bons d'Etat qui ont été émis pour l'armement et équipement de la milice de l'Etat contre l'autorité légitime des Etats-Unis, en violation de la Constitution et des lois de cet Etat, et pour quelle somme il y en a aujourd'hui dehors.

M. Montamat propose la résolution suivante, avec dispense de l'application des réglements.

Résolu, Que le comité d'enrôlement est autorisé à nommer un commis en chef et la quantité de commis enrôleurs qu'il croira nécessaires.

La résolution est adoptée.

M. Hills propose que lorsque la Convention s'ajournera, elle s'ajourne pour demain à 5 heures du soir.

M. Montamat propose une heure de l'après-midi ; M. Stauffer, midi ; et M. Harnan, 7 heures du soir.

Sur motion, tous ces amendements sont rejetés.

L'ajournement proposé par M. Hills est mis aux voix et adopté.

M. Stocker présente la résolution suivante :

Résolu, Qu'il sera nommé par le président un comité de cinq membres, qui sera chargé de s'informer des motifs de l'absence de messieurs Webbs, des Rapides, et Taliaferro de Concordia, et aussi de voir s'il ne serait pas opportun d'ordonner de nouvelles élections pour remplir les vacances.

M. Heard demande d'amender, en ajoutant le nom de M. Lobdell, de Ouest-Baton-Rouge.

M. Cazabat propose le rejet de l'amendement.

Sa motion est rejetée.

L'amendement est accepté, et la résolution adoptée avec l'amendement.

Le président nomme MM. Stocker, Montague, Ariail, Mann et Heard, membres du comité ci-dessus.

M. Gastinel offre la résolution suivante, laquelle est adoptée.

Résolu, Qu'il soit nommé par le président un comité de cinq membres, pris dans le sein de la Convention, lequel comité sera chargé de se rendre auprès du Gouverneur et de lui annoncer que la Convention est organisée et est prête à recevoir toutes communications qu'il peut avoir à lui faire.

Sont nommés membres du comité Messieurs Gastinel, Shaw, Thomas, Goldman, et Bofill.

Le colonel Thorpe offre la résolution suivante :

Résolu, Que la section 54 des réglements de la Convention soit amendée de façon à lire comme suit : *Le quorum* sera des deux tiers des membres élus et admis à cette Convention.

Rejeté.

M. Howell annonce qu'il a été invité par le président à prier les membres de rester après l'ajournement, afin de parfaire l'organisation des comités.

La Convention s'ajourne ensuite jusqu'à demain, à 5 heures du soir.

Adopté.

JOHN E. NEELIS,
Secrétaire.

SAMEDI, le 16 avril, 1864.

Conformément à l'ajournement, la Convention s'assemble.

En l'absence du président, le secrétaire prend le fauteuil et appelle la Convention à l'ordre.

M. Hills propose que M. Howell soit appelé à présider provisoirement.

Adopté à l'unanimité.

M. Howell, en prenant la présidence, présente le Rév. Hopkins, lequel prononce la prière.

A l'appel nominal du rôle, les membres suivants répondent à leurs noms :

MM. Abell, Ariail, Austin, Bailey, Barrett, Baum, Beauvais, Bell, Bofill, Bonzano, Bromley, Brott, Buckley, Burke, Cazabat, J. K. Cook, T. Cook, Crozat, Cutler, Davies, Duane, Dufresne, Edwards, Ennis, Fish, Flagg, Flood, Foley, Fosdick, Fuller, Gastinel, Geier, Goldman, Gorlinski, Gaidry, Healy, Hart, Heard, Henderson, Hills, Hire, Howell, Howes, Kavanagh, Knobloch, Maas, Mann, Maurer, Mendiverri, Millspaugh, Montamat, Montague, Morris, E. Murphy, M. W. Murphy, Newell. Normand, O'Conner, Payne, Pintado, Poynot, J. Purcell, S. Pursell, Schroeder, Schnurr, Seymour, Shaw, Smith, Spellicy, Stocker, Stumpf, Stiner, Sullivan, Terry, Thorpe, Thomas, Wenck, Wilson—78.

Le secrétaire commençant à lire la minute du procès-verbal, M. Montamat propose une dispense de cette lecture.

M. Cazabat propose de rejeter cette motion.

On se prononce contre lui ; mais à l'appel nominal il est décidé que cette lecture aura lieu, comme de fait ; et le procès-verbal est adopté sans correction aucune.

M. Montamat présente la résolution suivante :

Résolu, La somme de $100 sera payée à l'adjoint-secrétaire provisoire, pour services par lui rendus avant l'organisation de la Convention. Adopté à l'unanimité.

Motion de M. Bell autorisant chaque comité à employer autant de commis qu'il le jugera nécessaire.

Référé au comité d'Enrôlement.

M. S. Pursell présente la résolution suivante :

La Convention décrète, L'article quatre-vingt-seize de la constitution de l'État de la Louisiane sera changé et amendé de manière à présenter le texte suivant : Tous les officiers civils de l'Etat en général, devront posséder la qualité d'électeurs de cet Etat et y résider, et tous les officiers de district ou de paroisse devront y avoir le droit de vote et y résider ; ils devront tenir leur bureau en tel endroit désigné par la loi.

Après motion de la référer au comité sur les Dispositions Générales, cette résolution est rejetée.

M. Montamat présente la résolution suivante :

Résolu, L'Honorable A. A. Atocha, juge prévôt du Département du Golfe, est invité à prendre un siége dans l'enceinte de cette Convention.

Sur la motion de M. Goldman de rejeter cette proposition, M. Montamat demande l'appel nominal, dont il appert qu'il y a onze voix en faveur de la motion Goldman et soixante-sept contre elle, savoir :

Votent dans l'affirmative :

Messieurs Bailey, Bonzano, Bromley, Ennis, Flagg, Goldman, Hills, Mann, Millspaugh.

Votent dans la négative :

Messieurs Abell, Ariail, Austin, Barrett, Beauvais, Baum, Bell, Bofill, Brott, Buckley, Burke, Cazabat, J. K. Cook, T. Cook, Crozat, Cutler, Davies, Duane, Dufresne, Edwards, Fish, Flood, Foley, Fosdick, Fuller, Geier, Gastinel, Gorlinski, Gaidry, Healy, Harnan, Hart, Heard, Henderson, Hire, Howell, Howes, Kavanagh, Knobloch, Kugler, Lobdell, Mann, Maurer, Mendiverri, Montamat, Montague, Morris, E. Murphy, M. W. Murphy, Newell, Normand, O'Conner, Payne, de Jefferson, Poynot, J. Purcell, S. Pursell, Schroeder, Schnurr, Seymour, Shaw, Smith, Spellicy, Stocker, Stumpf, Stiner, Stauffer, Sullivan, Terry, Thorpe, Thomas, Waters, Wenck, Wilson.

M. Thorpe propose, pour amendement, d'inviter tous les officiers judiciaires de cette ville à prendre un siége dans l'enceinte de cette Convention.

Accepté, et l'on met définitivement aux voix sa résolution ; après quoi, on demande l'appel nominal, dont il résulte 68 voix affirmatives contre 8 négatives.

La rédaction amendée de cette résolution est adoptée.

M. Brott présente cette résolution :

Résolu, Le procureur-général de l'Etat est invité à faire connaître à cette Convention son opinion, comme jurisconsulte, sur le droit que cette Convention aurait d'exercer des pouvoirs législatifs. et d'allouer des fonds du trésor public.

Sur motion de M. Henderson, cette résolution est rejetée.

M. Gastinel présente la résolution suivante :

Résolu, Le procès-verbal et les débats de la Convention seront imprimés séparément en Anglais et en Français par l'imprimeur officiel ; et chaque conventionnel recevra trois exemplaires de ces procès-verbaux et débats, pour les distribuer parmi leurs constituants, réservant au dit conventionnel le droit de choisir ces exemplaires, en l'une ou l'autre langue.

ET L'AMENDEMENT DE LA CONSTITUTION DE LA LOUISIANE.

M. Hills propose d'amender par la suppression de la langue Française, et sur ce, M. Healy conclut au rejet de l'amendement.

A cet effet, on demande l'appel nominal dont il résulte 60 voix pour le rejet, savoir :

MM. Abell, Austin, Bailey, Baum, Beauvais, Bell, Bofill, Bonzano, Bromley, Brott, Buckley, Cazabat, J. K. Cook, T. Cook, Crozat, Cutler, Dupaty, Edwards, Ennis, Fish, Flagg, Foley, Fosdick, Fuller, Gastinel, Goldman, Gorlinski, Gruneberg, Gaidry, Healy, Hart Heard, Hire, Howes, Maas, Mann, Maurer, Mendiverri, Millspaugh, Montamat, M. W. Murphy, Newell, Normand, Pintado, J. Purcell, Poynot, Schnurr, Seymour, Shaw, Smith, Spellicy, Stocker, Stumpf, Stiner, Sullivan, Terry, Thorpe, Thomas, Wenck—60.

Et 20 voix contre, savoir :

MM. Ariail, Barrett, Burke, Campbell, Davies, Duane, Flood, Geier, Henderson, Hills, Howell, Montague, Morris, E. Murphy, O'Conner, J. Payne, S. Purcell, Schroeder, Stauffer, Wilson—20.

En conséquence, rejet de l'amendement Hills.

Acceptation de l'amendement Goldman, proposant la publication en langue Allemande.

M. Stocker propose le substitut suivant :

Résolu, L'Imprimeur officiel devra, pour l'usage de la Convention, imprimer trois cents exemplaires du procès-verbal dans chacune des langues suivantes : Anglais, Français, Allemand et Espagnol.

Rejeté.

M. Terry propose d'amender le substitut par l'adjonction du mot "Irlandais ;" lequel le président déclare être adopté, et l'appel nominal ayant lieu donne le résultat suivant :

Pour l'affirmative :

Messieurs Campbell, Crozat, Davies, Flagg, Flood, Geier. Healy, Terry et Wenck—9.

Pour la négative :

Messieurs Austin, Bailey, Barrett, Baum, Beauvais, Bell, Bofill, Bonzano, Bromley, Brott, Buckley, Cazabat, J. K. Cook, T. Cook, Cutler, Dufresne, Duane, Dupaty, Edwards, Ennis, Fish, Foley, Fosdick, Fuller, Gastinel, Gorlinski, Gaidry, Hart, Heard, Henderson, Hills, Hire, Howell, Howes, Maas, Mann, Maurer, Mendiverri, Millspaugh, Montague, Morris, E. Murphy, M. W. Murphy, Normand, Newell, O'Conner, J. Payne, Poynot, J. Purcell, S. Pursell, Schroeder, Schnurr, Seymour, Shaw, Smith, Spellicy, Stocker, Stumpf, Stiner, Stauffer, Sullivan, Thorpe, Thomas, Wilson—64.

La motion Terry est donc rejetée.

Motion d'effacer le tout, sauf les langues Anglaise et Française.

M. Cazabat propose de rejeter le substitut. Adopté.

La motion Gastinel est donc proposée et adoptée.

M. Sullivan propose :

Résolu, Les délégués de naissance étrangère, qui n'ont pas encore justifié de leurs lettres de naturalisation, montrant qu'ils sont citoyens des Etats-Unis d'Amérique, conformément à la résolution passée mercredi dernier, auront à le faire immediatement, sinon leurs siéges dans cette Convention seront déclarés vacants.

M. Foley propose d'amender en ces termes :

Ceux qui n'ont pas justifié de cette naturalisation, devront déclarer sous serment qu'ils ont été naturalisés citoyens des Etats-Unis.

M. Healy déclare que certains d'entre ces membres, habitant à la campagne, étaient dans l'impossibilité matérielle de présenter leurs lettres de naturalité, et propose de repousser la proposition tout entière. Adopté.

M. Bell propose que le secrétaire donne lecture des noms des membres, de naissance étrangère, qui ont présenté leurs lettres de naturalité au président, en exécution de la dite résolution ; mais sur les observations de plusieurs membres, cette proposition est rejetée.

Résolution Purcell :

Résolu, Ce qui suit sera adopté comme article faisant partie de la constitution de la Louisiane, savoir : Nul, s'il n'est citoyen des Etats-Unis ou s'il n'a déclaré son intention de le devenir, ne pourra exercer aucune profession, se livrer à aucune occupation lucrative, faire aucun négoce ou suivre aucun métier qui nécessite l'obtention d'une licence, soit des autorités de cet Etat, soit de toutes autres existantes dans son sein.

Motion secondée ; M. Cazabat propose de la rejeter, et M. Thomas de la référer au comité sur les dispositions générales, et tous deux sont secondés.

Le président déclare qu'il considère que ces trois motions ne sont pas à l'ordre, mais qu'il les y mettra, si l'Assemblée le désire. Aucune requête à cet effet n'a été présentée.

Motion nouvelle.

Résolu, Le sergent-d'armes devra procurer à chaque membre et au secrétaire de cette Convention, cinq exemplaires de tels journaux quotidiens qu'ils désigneront. Secondé.

M. Thomas propose de substituer trois à cinq. Secondé et adopté avec l'amendement.

M. Montamat propose que le comité des Finances soit autorisé à nommer un commis aux mandats. Adopté.

M. Seymour présente ce qui suit :

Attendu, Que la résolution adoptée le—courant, requérant les conventionels de justifier de leur prestation de serment d'allégeance, prescrit par la proclamation du président, en date du 8 décembre 1863, ne devait s'appliquer, et devait s'interpréter comme ne s'appliquant qu'aux membres seuls, (s'il en existe) qui, jusqu'à ce jour n'avaient pas prêté le serment d'allégeance aux Etats-Unis, sous l'empire des ordres militaires, dans ce département, en conséquence :

La Convention décrète, La démission de l'Hon. Ch. Roselius n'est pas acceptée, et il sera invité à reprendre sa place comme membre de cette Convention.

La résolution a été rejetée.

M. Fosdick propose l'ajournement jusqu'au 21 de ce mois à midi, en considération des séances des comités. Rejeté.

M. Healy propose l'ajournement à lundi à 3 heures de relevée. Secondé.

M. Cazabat propose à lundi en huit à 5 heures. Secondé.

M. Sullivan propose de rejeter la motion et l'ajournement. Adopté.

M. Hills propose que, lorsque la Convention s'ajournera, elle le fasse jusqu'à samedi à 4 heures du soir, pour les raisons déjà exposées. Rejeté.

M. Terry propose de fixer l'époque de l'ajournement à mercredi à 5 heures du soir. Adopté par un vote de 46 voix contre 26.

Le président nomme du comité permanent des Relations Fédérales, MM. Howell, Brott, Montague et Henderson.

Le président nomme membres du comité de Rétribution des officiers et employés de la Convention, MM. M. W. Murphy, Terry, Mann, Fosdick et Ennis.

M. Stocker appelle la résolution suivante présentée vendredi :

Résolu, Le réglement est amendé de manière, à ce que les ordonnances et résolutions, (à moins qu'elles ne soient référées à quelque comité) ne seront sujettes à l'action de la Convention qu'après l'intervalle d'un jour, depuis leur date d'ordre. Adopté.

M. Thomas, président du comité sur la Distribution des Pouvoirs, rapporte que ce comité a décidé à l'unanimité que la partie de la constitution de 1852, qui traite de la distribution des pouvoirs, n'a pas besoin d'aucun changement, et il soumet ce rapport.

M. Brott propose de référer ce rapport au comité, avec instruction d'incorporer le titre de cette matière dans son rapport. Adopté.

Une motion d'ajournement est adoptée, et le président déclare cette Convention ajournée à mercredi prochain à 5 heures du soir.

La minute est adoptée.

JOHN E. NEELIS,
Secrétaire.

MERCREDI, 20 avril 1864.

La Convention s'assemble conformément à l'ajournement, et est appelée à l'ordre par le président, à 5 heures du soir.

La séance s'ouvre par la prière du Rév. M. Andrews.

L'appel nominal est fait par le secrétaire et les membres suivants répondent à l'appel de leurs noms :

Messieurs Abell, Ariail, Austin, Barrett, Bell, Bofill, Bonzano, Bromley, Burke, Cazabat, J. K. Cook, T. Cook, Crozat, Davies, Dutresne, Duane, Dupaty, Durell, Edwards, Ennis, Foley, Fuller, Gastinel, Geier, Goldman, Gorlinski, Gruneberg, Gaidry, Healy, Harnan, Hart, Heard, Henderson, Hills, Hire, Howell, Howes, Kavanagh, Knobloch, Maas, Mann, Maurer, Mendiverri, Millspaugh, Montague, Morris, E. Murphy, M. W. Murphy, Newell, Normand, O'Conner, Ong, J. Payne, Poynot, J. Purcell, S. Pursell, Schroeder, Schnurr, Seymour, Shaw, Smith, Spellicy, Stocker, Stumpf, Stiner, Stauffer, Sullivan, Terry, Thorpe, Thomas, Waters, Wenck, et Wilson—71.

Le nombre des membres présents étant insuffisant pour former un quorum, le président ordonne au sergent-d'armes d'amener les membres absents.

MM. Balch, Bailey, Baum, Beauvais, Buckley, Brott, Campbell, Fish, Flood et Montamat étant entrés dans la salle et ayant pris leurs sièges, le président annonce qu'il y a quorum.

Le procès-verbal de samedi est lu et amendé puis adopté. M. Foley demande la reconsidération du vote sur la résolution relative à la publication des travaux de cette Convention en anglais et en français. Le président déclare que la motion n'est pas à l'ordre.

Les résolutions étant à l'ordre du jour, M. Howell propose les suivantes :

Résolu, Qu'à l'avenir la Convention se réunira à 11 heures du matin et s'ajournera à 3 heures tous les jours, (les dimanches exceptés,) et que l'ordre du jour sera pris ponctuellement chaque jour à midi.

La résolution est déposée sur le bureau jusqu'au lendemain

M. Smith offre la résolution suivante :

Résolu, Que le comité des Dispositions Générales devra incorporer dans son rapport un ou plusieurs articles obligeant la première Législature qui se réunira en vertu de la nouvelle Constitution, à ordonner aux diverses paroisses ou corporations, ainsi qu'aux particuliers, qui, dans cet Etat, ont émis des mandats à vue, des bons ou des billets appelés *shinplasters*, payables en billets confédérés, d'avoir à prendre les mesures nécessaires pour en opérer le rachat en monnaie courante.

M. Mendiverri propose la résolution suivante :

Résolu, Que l'Auditeur d'Etat présentera à cette Convention, aussitôt que cela sera praticable, un état des recettes et dépenses du trésor de l'Etat, pendant l'administration du général G. F. Shepley, ex-gouverneur militaire de l'Etat, autant du moins qu'il pourra l'établir d'après les livres et archives qui sont en sa possession, avec le détail de chaque item des recettes et dépenses. Ce tableau devra également indiquer s'il a été reçu une balance du dernier trésorier, et, en cas d'affirmative, spécifier le montant et la nature de ces fonds ou valeurs.

M. Wilson demande le rejet de cette résolution. La motion est rejetée, et la résolution est adoptée.

M. Stocker rappelle à la Convention la règle qu'elle a adoptée, sur sa proposition à sa dernière séance, laquelle ordonne que toute résolution doit rester déposée sur le bureau au moins un jour, à moins qu'elle ne soit renvoyée devant un comité spécial.

M. Hills offre la résolution suivante, qui restera sur le bureau jusqu'au lendemain :

Résolu, Que le secrétaire soit requis de retrancher du procès-verbal de la Convention la résolution invitant le juge A. A. Atocha et les officiers judiciaires de cette paroisse à s'asseoir dans l'enceinte réservée de la Convention.

M. Wilson demande le rejet de cette résolution. Il est décidé que M. Wilson n'est pas à l'ordre.

M. Sullivan offre la résolution suivante :

Résolu, Qu'il sera nommé par le président un comité de cinq membres, qui sera chargé de correspondre avec les autorités militaires à Washington, et de leur demander la restitution à l'Etat de la Louisiane, de la statue de Washington par Powers, laquelle a été enlevée de l'édifice du Capitole, à Baton-Rouge, par les troupes des Etats-Unis, lors de l'occupation de cette place par les armées Fédérales, et a été par elles envoyée comme trophée pour orner le Parc Central, dans la ville de New-York, où cette statue se trouve en ce moment.

La résolution est mise aux voix, et le vote se trouvant douteux, le vote nominal est ordonné et donne le résultat suivant :

En faveur de la résolution, 49 voix et contre, 23.

La résolution est adoptée.

M. Wenck offre la résolution suivante, laquelle est secondée.

Je demande la reconsidération du vote adoptant la résolution qui ordonne la publication du procès-verbal des débats de la Convention en anglais et en français, et la distribution de trois exemplaires des dites publications à chaque membre.

M. Montamat demande le rejet de cette proposition.

La motion est mise aux voix et adoptée par 42 voix contre 37.

La question revient à la motion de M. Wenck de reconsidérer le vote.

Votent pour la reconsidération :

MM. Ariail, Barret, Bonzano, Brott, Burke, Campbell, J. K. Cook, Davies, Duane, Ennis, Flood, Fosdick, Geier, Goldman, Gorlinski, Harnan, Heard, Henderson, Hills, Howell, Howes, Kavanagh, Kugler, Lobdell, Maas, Mann, Montague, Morris, Ong. J. Payne, Pintado, S. Pursell, Schroeder, Smith, Spellicy, Stocker, Stumpf, Stiner, Stauffer, Sullivan, Wenck, Wilson--40.

Votent contre la reconsidération :

MM. Abell, Austin, Balch, Bailey, Baum, Beauvais, Bell, Bofil, Buckley, Cazabat, T. Cook, Crozat, Cutler, Dufresne, Dupaty, Durell, Edwards, Fish, Flagg, Foley, Fuller, Gastinel, Gruneberg, Gaidry, Healy, Hart, Hire, Knobloch, Lobdell, Maurer, Mendiverri, Millspaugh, Montamat, E. Murphy, M. W. Murphy, Newell, Normand, O'Conner, Pintado, Poynot, Seymour, Shaw, Terry, Thorpe et Thomas—44.

M. Gorlinski présente la résolution suivante :

Résolu, Qu'à l'avenir la Convention se réunira régulièrement à midi, et tout membre qui, lors de l'appel du rôle, ne répondra pas à l'appel de son nom, sera puni d'une amende de deux piastres, laquelle sera déduite de son *per diem ;* et que tout membre qui s'absentera de son siége pendant une séance entière, perdra son *per diem* par chaque jour d'absence, à moins qu'il n'ait préalablement obtenu de la Convention un congé d'absence, ou qu'il ne soit malade, lui, ou quelque membre de sa famille, auquel cas il devra en fournir la preuve par la production d'un certificat délivré par un médecin diplômé.

Résolu en outre, Que le secrétaire tiendra note des noms des membres qui ne répondront pas à leurs noms au moment de l'appel du rôle, ainsi que des noms de ceux qui se seront absentés tout un jour, et aussi du nombre des jours d'absence, à moins d'absence par congé ; et qu'il en dressera, à la fin de chaque semaine, une liste dont il remettra une copie au Président de la Convention, qui devra faire exécuter rigoureusement les peines portées par la section précédente.

Les résolutions sont secondées.

M. Austin en demande le rejet.

M. Stocker demande que la résolution adoptée la veille sur sa proposition, soit relue à la Convention, pour mémoire.

Lecture est donnée comme suit :

Résolu, Que les réglements sont amendés en ce sens, qu'à l'avenir tous les ordres et résolutions devront rester un jour entier sur le bureau, avant que la Convention puisse rien décider à leur égard. Elles pourront seulement être renvoyées devant un comité.

M. Sullivan demande le rejet de la résolution.

Le président déclare qu'il n'est pas à l'ordre.

M. Montamat donne avis à la Convention qu'il présentera à la prochaine séance une résolution pour amender l'article 52 des Réglements.

M. Gaidry offre la résolution suivante :

Attendu, Que toutes les constitutions antérieures de l'Etat ont décrété que tous les actes judiciaires et législatifs seraient publiés en Anglais et en Français ;

Et attendu, Que plusieurs membres de cette Convention, qui sont de vrais républicains et fidèles à la cause, mais ne sont pas familiers avec la langue anglaise, ont été délégués à cette Convention par des constituants qui, eux-mêmes n'ont pas la connaissance de cette langue ; attendu que ces constituants étaient en droit de choisir leurs délégués à leur convenance, comme faisant partie du *souverain*, et que leur dénier ce droit serait porter atteinte à leurs franchises ;

Il est résolu, Que toutes les résolutions et motions qui seront présentées à cette Convention seront traduites en Français, de manière à ce que les délégués des paroisses de la campagne qui n'entendent pas la langue anglaise, puissent savoir au juste ce sur quoi ils sont appelés à voter.

M. Cazabat annonce que, pour faciliter l'expédition des affaires, il présente la résolution suivante :

Attendu, Que cette Convention s'est réunie dans le but unique de réviser et d'amender la Constitution de la Louisiane, et non à d'autres fins,

Il est résolu, Qu'aucune résolution ayant un autre objet que celui-là ne sera reçue ou écoutée par la Convention.

M. Wenck offre la résolution qui suit :

Résolu, Que la résolution allouant une indemnité de dix piastres par jour à chaque membre de la Convention, est et demeure rappelée.

M. Harnan demande la lecture de la résolution présentée par le juge Howell, et ainsi conçue :

Résolu, Que la résolution adoptée vendredi, 15 avril 1864, en les termes suivants :

Résolu, Qu'il est par les présentes fait allocation d'une somme de cent mille piastres, à prendre sur le fond général, et destinée à payer l'indemnité ou *per diem* les frais de déplacement dûs aux membres de la Convention et le salaire de ses officiers et employés ; laquelle somme sera payée par le trésorier de l'Etat sur le mandat du président de la Convention est, et demeure rappelée.

Il est de plus résolu, Que la résolution adoptée le 15 avril 1864, et ainsi conçue : "Tous les membres de cette Convention auront droit à une indemnité de dix piastres par jour pendant toute la durée de leurs services, laquelle somme leur sera payée sur les fonds du trésor public," est également rappelée.

Il est de plus résolu, Que l'indemnité à payer aux membres de cette Convention pour leurs services, sera la même que celle à laquelle les membres de l'Assemblée Générale avaient droit, en vertu de la constitution de 1852.

Cette proposition est secondée par M. Goldman.

M. Montamat fait remarquer que cette proposition a déjà été rejetée, et le président lui répond que la résolution restera déposée sur le bureau jusqu'au lendemain.

M. Austin parle dans le même sens que M. Montamat, et reçoit la même réponse du président.

M. Goldman présente la résolution suivante :

Résolu, Que la motion originaire ordonnant la publication des travaux de la Convention en Anglais et en Français, est amendée de façon à comprendre l'Allemand dans la même résolution.

Le président déclare que la motion n'est pas à l'ordre.

M. Cazabat demande la reconsidération du vote sur la résolution de M. Sullivan, relative à la statue de Washington. M. Sullivan répond qu'il n'objecte pas à ce que la résolution reste déposée jusqu'au lendemain.

M. Brott offre sa démission de membre du comité d'Enrôlement. Cette démission est acceptée, et le président nomme M. Mendiverri en son lieu et place.

Le président annonce que l'ordre est à la présentation des rapports des comités.

M. Bonzano, président du Comité de l'Emancipation, déclare que ce comité n'a pas encore achevé son travail.

M. Heard, président du comité du Préambule, soumet le rapport suivant :

Aux Honorables Messieurs les Président et Membres de la Convention Constitutionnnelle:

Le comité nommé par le président pour préparer un projet de préambule à la nouvelle constitution que doit faire cette Convention, vous soumet le rapport suivant :

Le comité est d'avis qu'on ne saurait mieux faire que de conserver le préambule des constitutions de 1845 et de 1852, ainsi conçu : "Nous, le peuple de la Louisiane, ordonnons et établissons la présente constitution"—et le comité en propose l'adoption.

Avec respect,
H. J. HEARD, Président.

Le rapport est adopté.

M. Thomas, président du comité de la Distribution des Pouvoirs, soumet le travail suivant :

Votre comité de la Distribution des Pouvoirs soumet respectueusement le rapport ci-après :

Le comité est d'avis qu'il ne faut en aucune façon modifier ou altérer les articles 1er et 2e de la constitution de 1862, ainsi conçus :

Art. 1.—Les pouvoirs du gouvernement de l'Etat de la Louisiane seront divisés en trois départements distincts, et chacun de ces départements sera confié à un corps séparé de magistrats, savoir : à l'un, le département du Législatif, à l'autre le département de l'Exécutif, et au troisième le département du Judiciaire.

Art. 2.—Aucun de ces départements, ni aucun officier attaché à l'un d'eux ne pourra légalement excercer aucune autorité dans aucun des deux autres, excepté dans les cas ci-après expressément ordonné sou permis. Respectueusement soumis,
JOHN W. THOMAS, Président.

Le rapport est adopté.

M. Fosdick, président du comité du Législatif, annonce que le travail du comité est en voie d'achèvement.

M. Fish, président du comité de l'Exécutif, et M. Howell, président du comité Judiciaire, font la même déclaration.

M. Wilson président du comité de la Mise en Accusation des officiers de l'Etat (Impeachment), soumet le rapport de ce comité. Mais M. Hills demande que ce rapport soit renvoyé à ce comité pour être remanié ; cette motion est adoptée.

M. Mann, président du comité des Dispositions Générales, annonce que le travail du comité est en bonne voie. M. Gorlinski, au nom du comité des Améliorations Intérieures, et M. Hills, au nom du comité de l'Instruction Publique, font la même déclaration.

M. Cutler, président du comité du Mode de Révision de la Constitution, annonce que le travail du comité se poursuit. M. Gruneberg, au nom du comité des Dispositions Transitoires (Schedule,) et M. Shaw, au nom du comité de la Mise à Exécution de la Constitution (Ordinance,) font la même déclaration.

M. Thorpe, président du comité d'Enrôlement, annonce que le rapport de ce comité est entre les mains du président.

M. Brott, président du comité des Finances, rapporte que le comité n'a aucuns fonds en mains, et n'a pas eu l'occasion de tirer aucun mandat.

M. S. Pursell, président du comité des Dépenses, et M. J. Purcell, au nom du comité des Impressions, rapporte que le travail du comité se poursuit.

M. Wilson propose de s'ajourner à lundi prochain, à cinq heures du soir, afin que les comités aient le temps de préparer leurs rapports.

La motion est secondée.

M. Crozat propose l'ajournement à midi pour le même jour, et M. Montamat à samedi, à midi. Ces motions sont rejetées.

Sur motion de M. Bell, la Convention s'ajourne jusqu'à jeudi, 21 courant, à midi.

Le procès-verbal est adopté.

JOHN E. NEELIS,
Secrétaire.

JEUDI, le 21 avril 1864.

La Convention se réunit à midi, conformément à l'ajournement, et le président l'appelle à l'ordre.

Prière par le révérend Gilbert.

A l'appel du rôle les membres suivants répondent à leurs noms :

Messieurs Abell, Ariail, Austin, Balch, Bailey, Barrett, Beauvais, Bell, Bofill, Bonzano, Brott, Buckley, Campbell, Cazabat, J. K. Cook, Crozat, Davies, Dufresne, Duane, Edwards, Ennis, Fish, Flagg, Flood, Foley, Fosdick, Geier, Goldman, Gorlinski, Gruneberg, Gaidry, Healy, Harnan, Hart, Heard, Henderson, Hills, Hire, Howell, Howes, Kavanagh, Knobloch, Kugler, Maas, Mann, Maurer, Mendiverri, Millspaugh, Montamat, Montague, Murphy, Newell, Normand, O'Conner, Poynot, S. Pursell, Schroeder, Seymour, Shaw, Smith, Spellicy, Stumpf, Stiner, Stauffer, Sullivan, Terry, Thorpe, Thomas, Wenck et Wells.

Le président déclare la présence du quorum.

Lecture par le secrétaire des minutes de la séance précédente.

Sur motion de M. Stiner, dispense de la lecture des noms des membres.

Cette motion est adoptée.

Les minutes sont adoptées.

M. Goldman prend la parole et dit qu'au moment où il a présenté sa motion, statuant que l'amendement qu'il ordonnait que la publication en langue Allemande était incorporée dans la motion originelle ordonnant la publication en Anglais et en Français. Le président décide que cette dite motion n'était pas à l'ordre, et qu'il désirait maintenant savoir si le président avait le droit de décider qu'une pareille motion n'était pas à l'ordre, quand l'amendement lui-même avait été adopté ; il fait observer qu'il n'avait pas sur le moment entendu la décision du président, car autrement il en aurait fait appel, et, en présence de ces faits, il demande que la Convention lui confère le droit d'appel.

Le président déclare qu'appel aurait dû être formé au monent de la décision.

Sur motion de M. Thomas, demandant congé, à raison de maladie, M. Sullivan propose de l'accorder. Adopté.

M. Golman demande au président si son appel est considéré comme n'étant pas à l'ordre, et la Convention, par son vote, soutient la décision du président.

M. Heard, au nom de M. Schnurr, son collègue, demande congé pour ce dernier, pour cause de maladie d'un membre de sa famille. Accordé.

M. Gorlinski propose ce qui suit :

Attendu, Qu'à l'époque de l'évacution de la ville de Baton-Rouge, après la mémorable bataille du 5 août 1862, le colonel Payne, du 4e Wisconsin, commandant alors le poste de Baton-Rouge, a couronné ses actes d'héroïsme par une mesure qui a assuré à la Convention et à cet Etat l'usage d'une bibliothèque de grande valeur et du grand tableau représentant le général Zacharie Taylor, ainsi que d'autre qui maintenant ornent la salle de nos délibérations, en même temps qu'il a sauvé la statue de Washington, par Hiram Powers, qui actuellement est dit-on, au bureau des Brévets, dans le Capitole National, tous objets d'art qui auraient été perdus par le feu, par lequel le Capitole de l'Etat a été détruit, ou volés, si le colonel Payne n'avait donné l'ordre de les transporter en cette ville, où par commandement du Général Butler ils ont été protégés comme propriétés de l'Etat : en conséquence,

La Convention décrète, Le major-général Butler et le colonel Payne ont droit aux remercîments de la Convention et du peuple de la Louisiane, et il leur sont offerts pour avoir sauvé ces propriétés d'Etat, qui sont d'un grand prix.

Décrète de plus, Le gouverneur est invité à ouvrir une correspondance avec les autorités de Washington à ce sujet, et à prendre les mesures convenables pour faire revenir et recevoir la susdite statue de Washington et aviser à l'usage qu'il pourra en être fait dans cet Etat.

M. Campbell présente la résolution suivante :

Attendu, Que la prime payée par les Etats-Unis aux soldats s'engageant dans l'armée, ne peut être payée aux hommes entrant dans les Premier et Second Régiments de la Nlle-Orléans, que lèvent actuellement les colonels Kilborn et Brown, par la raison que ces régiments s'organisent pour un objet spécial, la défense de la ville ; et à l'effet d'aider à cette dite organisation,

La Convention décrète, La somme de—— piastres est par le présent allouée par l'Etat, à l'effet de payer une prime à chaque homme qui à l'avenir s'engagera dans le Premier et le Second régiments de volontaires de la Nlle-Orléans ; et le Gouverneur est chargé de la mise à exécution du présent décret, au mieux des intérêts de l'Etat.

M. Stocker dit, que dans son opinion, ectte résolution est très-importante, et qu'afin que tous les membres puissent donner leur vote en connaissance de cause, il propose d'en ordonner l'impression et la distribution pour le lendemain.

La motion est secondée, mais perdue en apparence sur le vote *viva voce.*

On demande un appel nominal dont il résulte 36 voix négatives contre 34 affirmatives.

M. Hills présente la résolution suivante :

Il est décrété, L'article XXXII des réglements de cette Convention est amendé de manière à obliger les membres qui présentent des résolutions à les lire de leur place, ou à en donner un aperçu.

M. Stocker propose la suspension des réglements afin d'adopter de suite cette motion.

La motion est secondée.

M. Stauffer dit, qu'à son avis, l'article 32 couvrait cette proposition, mais à l'appel nominal, il a été décidé en faveur de la suspension du réglement par 54 voix contre 5.

La résolution est adoptée à l'unanimité.

Les présidents des comités permanents d'Emancipation, des Pouvoirs Législatifs, du Judiciaire et de l'Exécutif ont déclaré que leurs rapports étaient en voie de progrès.

M. Wilson, président du comité sur la Mise en Accusation des officiers publics (*Impeachment,*) soumet ce qui suit :

Votre comité vous soumet le rapport suivant :

La Chambre des Représentants sera investie du droit de mettre en accusation les officiers publics.

La mise en accusation du Gouverneur, du Lieutenant Gouverneur, de l'Avocat-Général, du Secrétaire d'Etat, du Trésorier d'Etat et des Juges des cours inférieures, sauf les Juges de Paix, appartiendra au Sénat.

Le Grand-Juge de la Cour Suprême ou le doyen de cette cour, présidera au procès de mise en accusation. Le Sénat jugera les juges de la Cour Suprême mis en accusation.

Quant les sénateurs siègeront comme cour de mise en accusation, ils devront prêter le serment ou l'affirmation ; et nul ne sera condamné sans le concours des deux tiers des sénateurs présents.

L'effet des jugements par suite d'une mise en accusation n'entraînera que la perte des fonctions ou la privation de tout office d'honneur, de confiance ou de profit relevant de l'Etat, sans toutefois préjudicier au droit d'accusation publique, de poursuite et condamnation, d'après les lois ordinaires, contre le coupable.

Tout officier contre lequel il y aura mise en accusation, sera suspendu de l'exercice de ses fonctions pendant la durée de l'instance susdite, et l'autorité de la nomination de laquelle ces fonctions relèvent, pourra nommer provisoirement un remplaçant jusqu'à ce que l'action de mise en accusation soit décidée.

La Législature pourvoira par loi spéciale au jugement de tous autres officiers d'Etat mis en accusation, à la peine qui leur sera appliquée et à leur renvoi, par voie d'accusation publique ou autrement.

La motion de M. Foley ordonnant l'impression de deux cents exemplaires de ce projet est rejeté.

MM. Mann, Gorlinski, Hills, Cutler, Gruneberg et Shaw, président des différents comités sur les Dispositions Générales, l'instruction Publique, le Mode de Révision de la Constitution, sur les Dispositions Transitoires et la Mise à Exécution de la Constitution, annoncent que leurs rapports sont en voie d'achèvement.

MM. Brott, S. Pursell et J. Purcell, présidents des comités des Finances, des Dépenses et des Impressions, annoncent qu'ils n'ont pas de rapport à présenter.

M. Thorpe, du comité des Relations Fédérales, annonce qu'il présentera son rapport le lendemain.

M. Gastinel soumet le rapport suivant au nom du comité spécial :

Au nom du comité nommé afin de se rendre auprès de Son Excellence le Gouverneur afin de lui annoncer que l'organisation de la Convention était complète, et de lui demander s'il avait quelque communication à lui faire, je vous soumets le rapport suivant :

Le comité s'est rendu auprès de son Excellence, et en a recueilli en somme pour réponse que son Excellence ne considérait ni convenable ni comme lui appartenant, de transmettre à la Convention aucun message ou de lui faire aucune suggestion ou recommandation ; mais qu'elle se tenait en tout temps à la disposition de la Convention pour lui procurer tous les renseignements ou commodités que l'exécutif serait appelé à fournir.

M. Murphy, président du comité spécial pour déterminer les appointements des officiers et employés de cette Convention, soumet le rapport suivant :

M. le Président—Votre comité nommé pour déterminer le salaire des officiers et employés de la Convention, fait le rapport suivant :

John E. Neelis, secrétaire	$14 par jour.
Thomas W. Murphy, sous-secrétaire	10 ..
S. G. Hamilton	10 ..
Michael DeCourcey, sergent-d'armes	10 ..
Les deux assistants sergents d'armes, chacun	5 ..
Les deux messagers, chacun	5 ..
Le maître de poste	5 ..
Le portier	5 ..
Le rapporteur et deux assistants, chacun	6 ..
Le commis aux mandats (caissier)	6 ..
Les commis enrôleurs	6 ..

Pour ce qui regarde les sommes à payer à l'imprimeur de la Convention, le comité demande qu'il lui soit accordé un délai pour plus amples informations.

W. W. MURPHY, Président.
GEORGE A. FOSDICK,
J. RANDALL TERRY,
W. D. MANN.

Les frais de déplacement de tous les membres des paroisses de la campagne sont fixés à 20 cents par mille pour l'aller et le retour. Le salaire des officiers et employés commencera du jour de leur élection ou nomination.

Sur motion de Messieurs Wilson et Heard, le rapport est renvoyé de nouveau au comité.

M. Stauffer prend la parole pour une question d'ordre, et demande le rapport du comité spécial élu au commencement de la session pour faire une enquête sur l'accusation d'assaut et batterie contre des membres de la Convention.

M. Wilson, comme présidnt du dit comité, annonce que le rapport de ce comité sera présenté incessamment.

Le président annonce que l'ordre du jour est aux résolutions déposées la veille, et invite les membres qui les ont présentées à les appeler suivant leur tour de rôle.

La résolution de M. Howell est lue la première. Elle est ainsi conçue :

Résolu, Qu'à l'avenir la Convention se réunira à 11 heures du matin et s'ajournera à 3 heures de l'après-midi, tous les jours, les dimanches exceptés, et que l'ordre du jour sera pris rigoureusement à midi.

M. Stauffer propose comme amendement 10 heures du matin, pour l'heure de la réunion, et la suppression des mots "3 heures de l'après-midi."

La motion est secondée.

M. Wilson offre comme substitut "de se réunir régulièrement à 5 heures du soir."

La moton est appuyée puis rejetée.

Après une discussion de quelques instants, la résolution est amendée par l'insertion des mots "à midi," et l'heure pour la discussion des questions à l'ordre du jour ayant été fixée à 1 heure de l'après-midi, la résolution est adoptée.

La résolution suivante présentée par M. Cazabat, est lue et rejetée :

Attendu, Que cette Convention s'est réunie dans le seul but de réviser et d'amender la constitution de la Louisiane, et non à d'autres fins ;

Il est résolu, Qu'aucune résolution ou aucune question autre que celles ayant trait à l'objet ci-dessus, ne sera reçue ou écoutée par cette Convention.

Vient ensuite la résolution de M. Sullivan :

Résolu, Qa'il sera nommé par le président un comité de cinq membres, qui sera chargé de correspondre avec les autorités militaires à Washington, et de leur demander la restitution à l'Etat de la Louisiane, de la statue de Washington par Powers, laquelle a été enlevée de l'édifice du Capitole, à Baton-Rouge, par les troupes des Etats-Unis lors de l'occupation de cette place par les armées fédérales, et par elles envoyée au "Patent Office," à Washington, où elle se trouve en ce moment.

M. Gorlinski offre un substitut, mais le président décide qu'il n'est pas à l'ordre.

La résolution est mise aux voix, et le vote divisionnel étant demandé et pris. 53

membres votent en faveur de la dite résolution, et 21 contre.

La résolution est adoptée.

Le président nomme membres de ce comité MM. Sullivan, Stiner, Burke, Ennis et Waters.

La résolution de M. Smith est appelée à son tour. Elle est ainsi conçue :

Résolu, Que le comité des Dispositions Générales soit invité à introduire dans son rapport un ou plusieurs articles obligeant la première Législature qui se réunira, en vertu de la nouvelle constitution, à ordonner, aux diverses paroisses et corporations, ainsi qu'aux particuliers qui, dans cet Etat, ont émis des mandats à vue, des bons ou des billets appelés *shinplasters*, payables en billets confédérés, d'avoir à prendre les mesures nécessaires pour en opérer le rachat en monnaie courante.

M. Cazabat demande le rejet de la résolution. La motion est secondée, puis mise aux voix et rejetée.

M. Cutler demande le renvoi de la résolution devant le comité des Dispositions Générales.

Avant que la question soit mise aux voix, M. Stocker, demande une seconde lecture de la résolution.

La motion de renvoi devant le comité est rejetée.

La résolution est alors mise aux voix, et le vote divisionnel étant pris, 48 membres votent contre son adoption et 13 voix pour.

M. Howell demande que ses résolutions soient mises en délibération. Elles sont ainsi conçues :

Résolu, Que la résolution adoptée le vendredi 15 avril 1864, en les termes suivants : "*Résolu* qu'il est, par les présentes, fait allocation d'une somme de cent mille piastres, à prendre sur le fonds général et destinée à payer l'indemnité ou *per diem* et les frais de déplacement dûs aux membres de la Convention et le salaire de ses officiers et employés, laquelle somme sera payée par le Trésorier de l'Etat sur le mandat du président de la Convention," est et demeure rappelée.

Il est de plus résolu, Que la résolution adoptée le 15 avril 1864, et ainsi conçue : "Tous les membres de la Convention auront droit à une indemninté de dix piastres par jour pendant toute la durée de leurs services, laquelle somme leur sera payée sur les fonds du trésor public," est également rappelée.

Il est de plus résolu, Que l'indemnité à payer aux membres de la Conenvtion pour leurs services sera la même que celle à laquelle les membres de l'Assemblée Générale avaient droit en vertu de la constitution de 1852.

Sur motion de M. Sullivan, ces résolutions sont mises aux voix et rejetées.

M. Gorlinski demande l'ordre du jour pour ses résolutions ainsi conçues :

Résolu, Qu'à l'avenir la Convention se réunira régulièrement à midi, et que tout membre qui, lors de l'appel du rôle, ne répondra pas à l'appel de son nom, sera puni d'une amende de deux piastres, laquelle sera déduite de son *per diem* ; et que tout membre qui s'absentera de son siége pendant une séance entière perdra son *per diem* pour chaque jour d'absence, à moins qu'il n'ait préalablement obtenu de la Convention un congé d'absence, ou qu'il ne soit malade, lui, ou quelque membre de sa famille—auquel cas il devra en fournir la preuve par la production d'un certificat délivré par un médecin diplômé.

Résolu en outre, Que le secrétaire tiendra note des noms des membres qui ne répondront pas à leurs noms au moment de l'appel du rôle, ainsi que des noms de ceux qui se seront absentés tout un jour, et aussi du nombre des jours d'absence, à moins d'absence par congé, et qu'il en dressera, à la fin de chaque semaine, une liste dont il remettra une copie au président de la Convention, qui devra faire exécuter rigoureusement les peines portées par la section précédente.

La résolution est mise aux voix et rejetée.

M. Cazabat appelle l'attention de la Convention sur ce fait que la résolution de M. Mendiverri, ordonnant la production d'un tableau indiquant les recettes et dépenses du trésor de l'Etat sous l'administration du général G. F. Shepley, ex-gouverneur militaire de l'Etat, a été adoptée en violation des réglements, qui ordonnent que toutes les résolutions doivent rester déposées pendant un jour, avant que la Convention puisse prendre aucune décision à leur égard.

Il demande, en conséquence, que le vote par lequel cette résolution a été adoptée, soit reconsidéré.

A une question à lui posée par le président, M. Cazabat ayant répondu qu'il avait voté contre la résolution, le président lui déclare qu'il n'est pas à l'ordre.

Le président dit ensuite qu'il croit que la résolution a été adoptée suivant les règles.

Sur motion de M. Shaw, la Convention s'ajourne à vendredi, 22 avril, à midi. Approuvé.

JOHN E. NEELIS,
Secrétaire.

VENDREDI, 22 avril 1864.

A midi la Convention est appelée à l'ordre par le président. La prière est dite par le Rév. M. Jones, et le secrétaire fait ensuite l'appel du rôle.

Sont présents :

MM. Abell, Ariail, Balch, Barrett, Baum, Bell, Bofill, Bonzano, Buckley, Burke, Campbell, Cazabat, J. K. Cook, Crozat, Cutler, Davies, Dufresne, Duane, Durell, Edwards, Ennis, Fish, Flagg, Flood, Foley, Fosdick, Fuller, Geier, Goldman, Gorlinski, Gruneberg, Gaidry, Healy, Harnan, Hart, Heard, Henderson, Hills, Hire, Howell, Howes, Kavanagh, Knobloch, Kugler, Maas, Mann, Maurer, Mendiverri, Millspaugh, Montamat, Montague, Morris, E. Murphy, M. W. Murphy, Newell, Normand, O'Conner, J. Payne, Poynot, J. Purcell, S. Pursell, Schroeder, Seymour, Shaw, Smith, Spellicy, Stocker, Stumpf, Stiner, Stauffer, Sullivan, Terry, Wenck, Wells, Wilson et M. le président—76.

Un quorum étant présent le procès-verbal de la précédente séance est lu et adopté.

M. Terry propose la résolution suivante, pour être déposée suivant le règlement :

Décrété, Que nul ne sera éligible à aucunes fonctions d'Etat ou municipales, s'il ne possède les qualités requises pour être membre de cette Convention. Et s'il se trouve en ce moment en fonctions un ou plusieurs officiers de ce genre, qui ne possèdent pas les qualités susdites, il sera pourvu de suite à leur remplacement.

M. Gorlinski dépose la résolution suivante :

Décrété, Que la disposition suivante sera insérée dans le règlement de la Convention.

Art. 55. Tout membre de la Convention qui aura présenté un projet de résolution, pourra ensuite proposer un amendement ou un substitut à la résolution primitive, sans qu'il soit pour cela obligé d'en donner avis préalable—sans que pourtant cette clause puisse venir en conflit avec l'article 25 du règlement.

M. Abell présente la résolution suivante :

Décrété, Que le rapport du comité des Amendements soit imprimé et reste ensuite déposé pendant au moins deux jours.

La résolution est secondée, et, l'application des règlements ayant été suspendue, est immédiatement adoptée.

MM. Bonzano et Fosdick, présidents du comité de l'Emancipation et du comité du Département Législatif, déclarent que le travail se poursuit.

M. Fish, président du comité de l'Exécutif, annonce qu'il n'y a pas eu de rapport.

M. Howell, président du comité du Judiciaire, rapporte que le travail s'avance.

A la requête de M. Mann, président du comité des Dispositions Générales, M.— donne lecture du travail suivant :

M. le Président—Votre comité des Dispositions Générales demande à soumettre le rapport qui suit :

Art. 1. Les membres de l'Assemblée Générale et tous les officiers publics, avant d'entrer en fonctions, prêteront le serment suivant :

Je (A B) jure solennellement (ou offirme) que je soutiendrai la constitution et les lois des Etats-Unis et de cet Etat, et que je remplirai avec fidélité et impartialité tous les devoirs qui me seront imposés par mes fonctions de———au mieux de mes capacités et de mon entendement. Dieu me soit en aide !

Art. 2. Le crime de haute trahison consistera uniquement dans le fait de susciter une guerre contre l'Etat, ou de pactiser avec ses ennemis, ou de leur donner aide et assistance. Personne ne pourra être déclaré convaincu du crime de haute trahison que sur la déposition de deux témoins du même fait de trahison ouvert, ou sur sa propre confession à l'audience de la cour.

Art. 3. La Législature aura le pouvoir de déterminer la peine du crime de haute trahison ; mais

Art. 4. Sera incapable d'exercer aucunes fonctions publiques dans l'Etat, honorifiques ou autre ; et sera privée du droit de suffrage toute personne qui aura été convaincue du crime de trahison, de parjure, de faux, de concussion, ou de tous autres crimes et offenses.

Art. 5. Toutes les peines seront proportionnées à la nature de l'offense.

Art. 6. L'exercice du droit de libre suffrage sera protégé par des lois régularisant les élections, et défendant, sous des peines sévères, l'emploi de toute influence illégitime de la part du pouvoir, de toute corruption d'électeurs, tous désordres ou autres menées inconvenantes.

Art. 7. Il ne sera tiré du trésor aucune somme, si ce n'est sur une allocation spécifique faite par la loi : et aucune allocation de fonds ne pourra être faite à l'avance pour plus de deux ans. Un état et compte régulier des recettes et dépenses du trésor sera publié annuellement dans la forme qui sera prescrite par la loi.

Art. 8. L'Assemblée Générale devra faire les lois qu'elle jugera convenables et nécessaires pour régler les affaires litigieuses et soumises à des arbitres.

Art. 9. Tous les officiers civils de l'Etat en général, résideront dans l'Etat, et tous les officiers de district ou de paroisse résideront dans leurs paroisses ou districts respectifs, et tiendront leurs offices à tels endroits qui pourront être requis par la loi.

Art. 10. Tous les officiers civils, à l'exception du gouverneur et des juges de la Cour Suprême et des cours inférieures, pourront être révoqués sur la demande des deux tiers des membres des deux Chambres. Ne sont pas compris dans cet article les officiers à la révocabilité desquels la présente constitution a autrement pourvu.

Art. 11. Dans toutes les élections par le peuple, le vote se fera au scrutin secret, et dans toutes les élections par le Sénat et la Chambre des Représentants, ensemble ou séparément, le vote sera donné de vive voix.

Art. 12. Ne pourront être éligibles à l'Assemblée Générale, ni exercer aucunes fonctions publiques, honorifiques ou autres, dans l'Etat, les membres du Congrès ni aucune personne exerçant des fonctions publiques, honorifiques ou autres, pour le compte du gouvernemeut général des Etats-Unis, ou de l'un de ces Etats, ou d'une puissance étrangère.

Art. 13. Ne pourront être nommés à aucunes fonctions publiques, honorifiques ou autres, ou employés aux travaux publics de l'Etat, quant ils seront exécutés aux frais du trésor, que des citoyens des Etats-Unis, excepté lorsque le salaire sera de moins de neuf cents piastres par an.

Art. 14. Les lois de l'Etat seront promulguées, les livres et archives publics tenus et conservés, et les procédures écrites de la Législature ou des cours de justice conduites en la langue en laquelle est écrite la constitution des Etats-Unis.

Art. 15. Les lois ne pourront être suspendues que par la volonté de la Législature.

Art. 16. Toute poursuite en matière criminelle, sera basée sur un acte d'accusation. L'accusé aura droit à être jugé promptement, et par un juri impartial de la paroisse dans laquelle le crime aura été commis. Il ne sera point obligé à s'accuser lui-même ; il aura droit à être entendu, soit par lui-même, soit par un défenseur. Il aura droit à voir les témoins face à face, et il lui sera fourni les moyens nécessaires pour se procurer des témoins à décharge. Il ne pourra être poursuivi deux fois pour la même offense.

Art. 17. Tout accusé pourra toujours demander à être mis en liberté en fournissant une caution suffisante, excepté en cas d'accusation capitale, lorsque la preuve sera évidente ou la présomption forte ; et le privilége du droit d'*habeas corpus* ne sera point suspendu, excepté lorsque, dans les cas de rébellion ou d'invasion, la raison de salut public peut rendre cette mesure nécessaire.

Art. 18. Il ne pourra être exigé des cautions exagérées, ni imposé des amendes excessives, ni infligé des peines cruelles ou contraires aux usages.

Art. 19. Le droit des particuliers à être protégés dans leurs personnes, dans leurs domiciles, dans leurs papiers et effets, contre toutes les visites domiciliaires ou saisies déraisonnables ne sera point violé et il ne sera accordé aucun ordre de recherche, de saisie ou d'arrestation que sur des causes probables, appuyées d'un serment ou d'une affirmation ; et ces ordres devront décrire avec précision les lieux où doivent s'opérer les recherches, les personnes qui doivent être arrêtées ou les objets qui doivent être saisis.

Art. 20. Il ne sera passé aucune loi ayant un effet rétroactif ou portant atteinte à la validité des contrats, ou aux droits acquis, si ce n'est pour cause d'utilité publique et après indemnité préalable.

Art. 21. Toutes les cours de justice seront tenues ouvertes, et tout particulier qui sera attaqué dans sa personne, dans sa réputation ou dans ses biens, aura droit d'en demander la réparation dans les formes indiquées par la loi, et il lui sera fait droit sans qu'on puisse lui opposer un déni de justice ou des lenteurs déraisonables.

Art. 22. La presse sera libre. Tout citoyen peut parler, écrire et publier ses sentiments sur tous sujets ; il sera seulement responsable de l'abus de cette liberté.

Art. 23. La Législature aura le pouvoir de venir en aide aux compagnies ou associations particulières, formées dans le but exclusif de faire des travaux qui tourneront, en tout ou en partie, à l'avantage de l'Etat, mais seulement jusqu'à concurrence de "un cinquième" du capital entier de ces compagnies, et ce, soit au moyen de souscription d'actions, soit par prêt d'argent, soit par émission de bons publics. Mais toutes avances ainsi accordées ne seront versées à la compagnie que dans la même proportion que le reste du capital sera effectivement versé par les actionnaires de la compagnie ; et, en cas d'emprunt, la compagnie fournira telles garanties que la Législature jugera convenables. Les corporations ou associations individuelles recevant aide et assistance de l'Etat, comme il vient d'être dit, ne pourront posséder aucune obligation de banque ou d'escompte.

Art. 24. L'Etat ne pourra contracter aucune obligation de la nature ci-dssus mentionnée sans y être autorisé par une loi expresse et pour un objet ou un travail qui y sera distinctement spécifié, laquelle loi sera votée par la majorité des membres élus aux deux Chambres de l'Assemblée Générale ; et le montant total des dettes et obligations contractées au nom de l'Etat, en vertu de cet article et du précédent, ne pourront jamais, en aucun temps, excéder huit millions de piastres.

Art. 25. Toutes les fois que la Législature contractera une dette dont le montant excèdera cent mille piastres, à moins que ce ne soit en cas de guerre et pour repousser l'invasion ou supprimer l'insurrection, elle devra, dans la loi qui créera cette dette, pourvoir aux moyens de payer l'intérêt courant et le principal à l'époque de leurs échéances. Et cette loi ne pourra être rappelée jusqu'à ce que la dette principale et ses intérêts aient été acquittés, à moins toutefois que la loi nouvelle qui l'abrogera ne pourvoie par d'autres mesures suffisantes aux moyens de payer la dite dette en principal et intérêts.

Art. 26. La Législature pourvoiera au transfert des affaires civiles et criminelles d'une juridiction à une autre.

Art. 27. Aucune loterie ne sera autorisée dans cet Etat, et la vente et l'achat de tous billets de loterie dans les limites de l'Etat, sera interdite.

Art. 28. Aucun divorce ne pourra être accordé par la Législature.

Art. 29. Toute loi passée par la Législature n'embrassera qu'un seul objet, et cet objet sera imprimé dans son titre.

Art. 30. Aucune loi ne pourra être remise en vigueur ou amendée sur le simple énoncé de son titre ; mais en pareil cas, la loi remise en vigueur ou la section amendée sera ré-édictée, et publiée à nouveau tout au long.

Art. 31. La Législature n'adoptera jamais un système de droit ou un code de loi en indiquant d'une manière générale le dit système ou le dit code. Elle doit dans tous les cas spécifier les diverses dispositions qu'elle veut décréter.

Art. 32. Les corporations possédant le privilége de faire des opérations de banque ou d'escompte peuvent être créées soit par des lois spéciales, soit en vertu de lois générales. Mais aucune corporation ni aucun particulier n'aura le privilége de mettre en circulation des bons ou des billets, à l'exception de ceux qui en ont déjà obtenu l'autorisation par une charte.

Art. 33. Dans le cas où une banque ou une association, faisant les opérations de banque, serait en faillite, les détenteurs de leurs billets auront le droit d'être payés avant les autres créanciers.

Art. 34. Nul n'occupera à la fois plus d'une place civile, salariée ou honorifique, sauf celle de juge de paix.

Art. 35. L'impôt sera égal et uniforme dans tout l'Etat. Tous les biens sur lesquels l'impôt est prélevé, seront taxés en proportion de leur valeur, laquelle sera déterminée de la manière indiquée par la loi. Aucune classe de propriété ne sera grévée d'un impôt plus onéreux qu'une autre classe de propriétés d'égale valeur sur lesquelles sera prélevée une taxe. La Législature aura le droit de percevoir une taxe sur le revenu, et de frapper d'un impôt toute personne exerçant un métier, une industrie ou une profession quelconque.

Art. 36. Les citoyens de la Nouvelle-Orléans ont le droit de nommer les divers officiers publics nécessaires à l'administration et à la police de la ville, conformément au mode d'élection prescrit par la Législature. Néanmoins le maire et les recorders sont inéligibles à l'Assemblée Générale. Le maire et les recorders recevront du gouverneur une commission comme juges de paix, et la Législature pourra leur attribuer telle juridiction criminelle qu'elle jugera nécessaire, pour la répression des crimes et délits secondaires.

Art. 37. La Législature déterminera par la loi dans quel cas les officiers continueront à exercer leurs fonctions jusqu'à ce que leurs successeurs les remplacent régulièrement.

Art. 38. La Législature, moyennant le consentement des Etats-Unis, aura le droit d'étendre l'autorité de cette constitution et la juridiction de cet Etat à tout territoire acquis par un traité avec un autre Etat ou avec les Etats-Unis.

Art. 39. Aucune partie des terres concédées par le Congrès à l'Etat de la Louisiane pour lui faciliter la construction de levées et autres travaux nécessaires au dessèchement des terrains inondés de l'Etat, ne sera appliquée à un autre objet que celui en vue duquel elles ont été concédées.

Art. 40. La Législature ne pourra faire aucune loi à l'effet d'exclure un citoyen de l'Etat d'un emploi public, à raison de ce qu'il ignorait une langue autre que celle dans laquelle est écrite la Constitution des Etats-Unis.

Respectueusement soumis,
W. D. Mann,
Président du Comité.
Ernest Wenck,
John Foley,
J. K. Cook,
John Buckley, Jr.,
Geo. Geier,
H. Maas.

M. Harnan propose que le rapport du comité soit adopté, et que la discussion de la question soit mise à l'ordre spécial du jour pour jeudi prochain.

La motion est secondée et adoptée.

Lecture est ensuite donnée, pour la satisfaction de la Convention, de la résolution de M. Abell, par laquelle il demande le dépôt du rapport.

M. Hills, président du comité de l'Instruction Publique, lit son rapport :

Au Président et aux Membres de la Convention pour la révision et l'amendement de la Constitution de la Louisiane:

Les soussignés, membres du comité de l'Instruction Publique, ont l'honneur de soumettre le rapport suivant :

RAPPORT.

Art. —. Il sera élu un surintendant de l'instruction publique, qui exercera ses fonctions pendant une période de deux années. Ses devoirs seront prescrits par la loi, et il recevra un traitement que fixera la Législature. Néanmoins l'Assemblée Générale, pourra, par un vote de la majorité des membres élus aux deux Chambres, abolir la place de surintendant de l'instruction publique, quand elle jugera que cette place n'est plus nécessaire.

Art. —. L'Assemblée Générale établira des écoles publiques gratuites pour tous les enfants, dans tout l'Etat, et devra pourvoir à leur entretien, au moyen d'une taxe générale sur les propriétés ou autrement. Les sommes ainsi perçues ou obtenues de toute autre façon, seront distribuées entre les différentes paroisses proportionnellement au nombre des enfants qu'elles renfermeront, de l'âge indiqué par l'Assemblée Générale ; mais toutes les écoles pour les enfants de couleur seront distinctes et séparées de celles pour les enfants blancs.

Art. —. En vue de propager l'enseignement et l'étude, l'Assemblée Générale fera une allocation annuelle pour l'encouragement des écoles privées dans l'Etat ; mais l'Assemblée Générale ne pourra être requise de faire aucune allocation en faveur des écoles privées établies dans la paroisse d'Orléans, qui ne compteraient pas deux cents élèves ; et à l'égard des autres paroisses, la Législature déterminera quelles sont les écoles assez considérables pour mériter une allocation de ce genre.

Art. —. La langue Anglaise sera seule enseignée dans les écoles publiques de l'Etat.

Art. —. Il sera créé une Université dans la ville de la Nouvelle-Orléans. Cette Université se composera de quatre facultés, savoir : une faculté de droit, une faculté de médecine, une faculté des sciences naturelles et une faculté des lettres. La Législature pourvoiera par une loi à leur organisation, mais elle ne sera nullement tenue de contribuer à l'établissement ou à l'entretien de la dite Université par allocation.

Art. —. Le produit de toutes les terres concédées jusqu'à ce moment par le Congrès des Etats-Unis à cet Etat pour l'entretien des écoles ; celui de toutes les terres qui pourront dans l'avenir être concédées ou léguées à l'Etat, sans destination expresse, et dont l'Etat pourra plus tard disposer, ainsi que le produit des successions échues à l'Etat, conformément à la loi, resteront en la possession de l'Etat à titre de prêt et formeront une rente perpétuelle dont l'Etat acquittera annuellement l'intérêt à raison de six pour cent. Cet intérêt, joint à celui remis par les Etats-Unis à cet Etat, à titre de dépôt, en vertu d'une loi du Congrès du 23 juin 1836, sera affecté, ainsi que la totalité de la rente des terres non vendues, à l'entretien des écoles publiques, et cette allocation restera inviolable.

Art. —. Le revenu provenant de la vente de toute terre accordée jusqu'à ce moment à cet Etat par le gouvernement fédéral, pour l'entretien d'une maison d'éducation, que la vente ait déjà eu lieu ou qu'elle s'accomplisse plus tard, ainsi que le revenu provenant d'une donation quelconque faite à l'Etat dans le but ci-dessus indiqué, formera un fonds perpétuel dont l'intérêt, à raison de six pour cent par an, sera appliqué à l'entretien d'une institution destinée aux progrès de la littérature, des arts et des sciences. La Législature ne pourra voter aucune loi pour appliquer les fonds ci-dessus mentionés à un autre but que la création et l'amélioration de l'institution susdite, et l'Assemblée Générale aura le pouvoir de lever une somme pour l'organisation et l'entretien de cette même institution, par les voies et moyens qu'elle croira convenables.

ALFRED C. HILLS,
Président du comité.
M. W. MURPHY,
X. MAURER,
RANDALL TERRY,
T. M. WELLS,
GEORGE HOWES.

M. Edward Hart signe ce rapport, se réservant seulement de présenter un amendement à la troisième clause.

M. H. C. Edwards le signe également, mais annonce qu'il est entièrement opposé à la troisième clause dudit rapport.

Je partage l'opinion de M. Edwards.

(Signé) JOHN BURKE.

M. Montamat propose de faire de la discussion du rapport l'ordre spécial du jour pour mardi prochain.

M. Hart, du comité de l'Instruction Publique, donne avis qu'il se propose d'offrir l'amendement suivant :

En vue de propager l'enseignement et

l'étude, l'Assemblée Générale devra voter des allocations annuelles pour l'encouragement de toutes les écoles privées dans toute l'étendue de l'Etat, qui sont ou pourront être incorporées par la Législature.

M. Balch donne avis à la Convention que, bien qu'étant membre du comité, il a été, par suite d'indisposition, dans l'impossibilité d'assister à ses réunions, et demande que la discussion du rapport soit renvoyée à lundi, 30 du courant, attendu qu'il se propose d'en discuter plusieurs clauses. Adopté.

M Stocker dit qu'il croyait s'être levé à temps pour objecter à l'adoption de l'amendement, attendu qu'il pensait que les amendements devaient être présentés en même temps que le rapport ; mais il reconnaît que l'amendement de M. Hart est, en réalité, un rapport de la minorité.

M. Cutler, president du comité du Mode de Révision de la Constitution, annonce que le travail se pousruit.

Aucun rapport n'est présenté au nom du comité des Dispositions Transitoires.

M. Shaw, président du comité de l'Ordonnance (ou mise à exécution de la Constitution), annonce que le travail se poursuit.

Même rapport au nom du comité d'Enrôlement.

Le comité des Finances n'a aucun rapport à faire. Il en est de même du comité des Impressions.

Le comité des Dépenses, par l'organe de son président, M. S. Pursell, annonce que le travail se fait.

Le comité des Relations Fédérales n'a pu s'entendre sur aucun rapport.

M. Howell, comme président du comité du Judiciaire, soumet le rapport suivant :

Au Président et aux Membres de la Convention, réunie pour la révision et l'amendement de la Constitution de l'Etat de la Louisiane :

Le comité du Département Judiciaire a l'honneur de présenter les articles suivants, dont il recommande l'adoption et l'insertion dans la constitution de l'Etat, au chapitre du Judiciaire, savoir :

TITRE IV.

POUVOIR JUDICIAIRE.

Art. 1. Le pouvoir judiciaire est confié à une Cour Suprême, à telles Cours inférieures que la Legislature jugera convenable de créer et aux justices de paix.

Art. 2. La Cour Suprême, sauf les cas ci-après spécifiés, n'aura qu'une juridiction d'appel, laquelle embrassera toutes les affaires où la valeur de l'objet en litige excèdera la somme de trois cents piastres, et toutes celles où la constitutionnalité ou la légalité d'une taxe, d'un péage, d'un impôt quelconque, ou bien d'une amende, d'une confiscation ou d'une pénalité infligée par une corporation municipale sera mise en question. La juridiction de la Cour Suprême comprendra, en matière criminelle, la solution des questions de droit seulement, lorsque le crime imputé entraîne la peine de mort ou les travaux forcés, ou encore lorsque l'amende qui est infligée excède trois cents piastres.

Art. 3. La Cour Suprême se composera d'un juge-président et de quatre juges associés, dont la majorité constituera un quorum. Le juge-président recevra un salaire de dix mille piastres, et chacun des juges-associés un salaire de neuf mille piastres par an, jusqu'à ce qu'il y soit autrement pourvu par la loi. La Cour Suprême nommera ses greffiers.

Art. 4. La Cour Suprême siègera à la Nouvelle-Orléans depuis le premier lundi du mois de novembre jusqu'à la fin du mois de juin inclusivement ; la Législature aura le pouvoir d'indiquer les localités où elle devra siéger pendant le reste de l'année. La Cour Suprême tiendra ses sessions comme par le passé, jusqu'à ce qu'il y soit autrement pourvu.

Art. 5. La Cour Suprême, ainsi que chacun des juges qui la composent, aura le pouvoir, dans les affaires qui sont du ressort de sa juridiction d'appel, de lancer des ordres d'*habeas corpus*, à la requête de toute personne détenue en vertu d'un ordre judiciaire.

Art. 6. Aucun jugement ne pourra être rendu par la Cour Suprême, qu'à la majorité des juges composant cette cour. Et lorsque par suite de la récusation d'un ou plusieurs des membres de la cour, il sera impossible d'obtenir l'accord de la majorité pour une décision, les juges non récusés auront le droit d'appeler un ou plusieurs juges des cours inférieures ; et il sera du devoir du juge ou des juges ainsi appelés, de prendre la place du juge ou des juges récusés et de prendre part à la décision de la cause.

Art. 7. Tous les juges sont, en vertu de leurs fonctions, conservateurs de la paix dans tout l'Etat. Les ordres ou mandats judiciaires seront précédés de ce titre : "l'Etat de la Louisiane." Les poursuites criminelles seront dirigées "au nom et par l'autorité de l'Etat de la Louisiane," et seront terminées par cette formule : "en violation de la paix et de la dignité de l'Etat."

Art. 8. Les juges de toutes les cours de cet Etat, devront, aussi souvent que faire se pourra, dans tout jugement définitif, citer la loi en vertu de laquelle le jugement est rendu ; et dans tous les cas ils devront exposer les motifs sur lesquels est basé leur jugement.

Art. 9. Les juges de toutes les cours peuvent être mis en accusation par voie d'*impeachment*. Lorsque cependant leur faute ne sera pas assez grave pour motiver des poursuites aussi rigoureuses, le gouverneur pourra les destituer purement et simplement à la requête des trois-quarts des membres présens dans chaque Chambre de l'Assemblée Générale. Dans ces cas, la cause qui a provoqué la destitution sera énoncée dans le mémoire de l'Assemblée Générales et insérée au procès-verbal de chacune des Chambres.

Art. 10. Les juges de la Cour Suprême et ceux des cours inférieures recevront, à des époques fixes, un traitement dont le chiffre ne pourra être diminué tant que leur mandat ne sera pas expiré. Il leur est interdit de recevoir des honoraires ou aucune rétribution autre que leur traitement, pour les devoirs qu'ils sont appelés à remplir.

Art. 11. Les juges de la Cour Suprême et ceux des cours inférieures seront nommés par le gouverneur de l'avis et du consentement du Sénat, et ils resteront en fonctions tant qu'ils n'auront pas démérité.

Art. 12. Les greffiers de la Cour Suprême et des cours inférieures seront nommés par les juges de ces mêmes cours, et ils resteront en fonctions tant qu'ils n'auront pas démérité, auquel cas ils pourront être destitués par le juge ou les juges de la cour à laquelle ils appartiendront respectivement, sauf leur droit d'appel à la Cour Suprême, dans tous les cas.

Art. 13. La Législature pourra autoriser les greffiers des cours à lancer tels ordres et à accomplir tels actes qui pourront être jugés nécessaires pour faciliter l'administration de la justice. Néanmoins, les pouvoirs ainsi accordés aux greffiers devront toujours être spécifiés et clairement définis.

Art. 14. La juridiction des juges de paix en matière civile, sera limitée aux réclamations dont le montant n'excèdera pas cent piastres, non compris l'intérêt. Appel pourra être intergeté dans les cas déterminés par la loi. Ils seront nommés par le gouverneur, de l'avis et du consentement du Sénat, et ils resteront en fonctions tant qu'ils n'auront pas démérité. Ils exerceront, en matière criminelle, telle juridiction que la loi déterminera.

Art. 15. Il y aura un avocat-général pour l'Etat et autant d'avocats de district qu'il pourra par la suite être jugé nécessaire. Ils seront nommés par le gouverneur, de l'avis et du consentement du Sénat, et ils resteront en fonctions jusqu'à l'expiration du terme d'office du gouverneur qui les aura nommés. Leurs fonctions seront déterminées par la loi.

Art. 16. Il y aura dans chaque paroisse un shérif et un coroner qui seront nommés par le gouverneur, de l'avis et du consentement du Sénat, et ils resteront en fonctions jusqu'à la fin du terme d'office du gouverneur qui les aura nommés, à moins qu'ils ne soient déplacés plus tôt. La Législature aura le pouvoir d'augmenter le nombre des shérifs dans les paroisses où elle jugera convenable de lé faire.

Respectueusement soumis.
R. K. HOWELL, Président.
H. J. HEARD,
R. KING CUTLER,
JOHN HENDERSON, JR.,
R. BEAUVAIS,
WM. H. SEYMOUR,
JAMES FULLER.

Sur motion de M. Harnan la discussion de ce rapport est mise à l'ordre du jour pour vendredi 29 du courant.

M. Sullivan présente un amendement, mais il lui est répondu qu'attendu qu'il n'est pas membre du comité, il ne pourra le faire que lorsque la discussion sera ouverte.

MM. Montamat et Wilson, en leur qualité de présidents du comité de la Vérification des Pouvoirs et du comité Spécial nommé pour faire une enquête sur l'assaut commis contre deux membres, rapportent que le travail se poursuit.

M. Stocker, comme président du comité Relatif aux Membres Absents, déclare que ce comité a fait les diligences nécessaires pour tâcher de se mettre à même de fournir un rapport, mais que les renseignements qu'il n'a pu recueillir ne sont pas suffisants pour lui permettre d'en produire un.

M. M. W. Murphy, président du comité des Salaires, présente le travail suivant :

M. le Président—

Votre comité nommé pour déterminer le salaire des officiers et des employés de cette Convention, demande qu'il lui soit permis de soumettre le tableau suivant :

Président de la Convention	$20 par jour	
John E. Neelis, secrétaire	15	..
S. G. Hamilton, secrétaire-adjoint	10	..
Thomas H. Murphy, secrétaire-adjoint	10	..
M. DeCourcey, sergent-d'armes	15	..
Deux sergents-d'armes adjoints	6	..
Deux messagers	5	..
Un maître de poste	8	..
Un portier	8	..
1er Rraporteur sténographe	12	..
Trois assistant rapporteurs		

chacun................ 10 par jour.
Un commis aux mandats..... 10   ..
Commis enrôleurs.......... 6   ..

Les frais de dépenses (mileage) de chacun des délégués des paroisses de la campagne, vingt cents par mille, pour l'aller et le retour.

Le salaire des officiers et employés commence à courir du jour de leur élection ou nomination.

Le tout respectueusement soumis,
M. W. MURPHY, Président.
W. D. MNNN,
JAMES ENNIS.

M. Fosdick présente le rapport suivant de la minorité :

Au Président et aux Membres
de la Convention :

Le soussigné, faisant partie du comité nommé pour fixer le salaire des officiers et employés de la Couvention, demande à soumettre son rapport comme représentant la minorité du comité. Suivant ce rapport, les officiers et employés de la Convention recevraient le traitement suivant :

Secrétaire .... $15 par jour.
Secrétaire adjoint, chacun.. 10   ..
Sergents-d'armes............ 10   ..
Deux sergents-d'armes adjoints,
  chacun.................. 6   ..
Deux messagers, chacun..... 3   ..
Un maître de poste......... 5   ..
Un portier................. 5   ..
Un sténographe rapporteur.. 8   ..
Trois sténographes adjoints,
  chacun.................. 8   ..
Un commis aux mandats..... 6   ..
Commis enrôleurs, chacun... 6   ..
Ttraducteurs, chacun....... 8   ..

Le millage de chacun des délégués des paroisses de la campagne, vingt cents par mille, pour l'aller et le retour. Le salaire des officiers et employés commencera à courir du jour de leur élection ou nomination.

Respectueusement soumis,
GEORGE A. FOSDICK.

M. Hills propose de faire de la discussion de ce rapport l'ordre spécial du jour pour samdi, 23 du courant. Secondé

M. Bell se lève pour un point d'ordre, et fait remarquer que les rapports doivent rester déposés pendant deux jours avant leur discussion. Le président lui répond que cette règle ne s'applique qu'aux rapports des comités permanents.

La motion de M. Hills est appuée et adoptée.

La résolution présentée par M. Edwards, à l'effet de faire imprimer 200 exemplaires du rapport sur le judiciaire, est déclaré n'être pas à l'ordre.

Lecture est donnée d'une communication du secrétaire d'Etat, annonçant l'élection de deux nouveaux membres, MM. Duke et Collin, délégués de la paroisse Ascension.

Sur motion de M. Gastinel, cette communication est renvoyée devant le comité de la Vérification des Pouvoirs.

Les affaires non terminées sont maintenant à l'ordre.

Lecture est donné de la résolution présentée par M. Gorlinski.

Attendu, Que l'ors de l'évacuation de Bâton-Rouge, après la bataille à jamais mémorable du 5 août 1862, le colonel Payne, du Quatrième Volontaire du Wisconsin, commandant alors la place de Bâton-Rouge, a couronné ses héroïques exploits de ce même jour par un acte qui a conservé à cette Convention et à l'Etat l'usage d'une bibliothèque publique d'une grande valeur, qu'il a sauvé en même temps le grand portrait en pied du général Zachary Taylor, par Thorpe, et autres peintures, qui maintenant ornent la salle où se réunit cette Convention, et aussi la grande statue de Washington, par Hiram Powers, laqelle est dit-on, en ce moment, dans le bureau dit "Patent Office" dans la capitale des Etats-Unis ; que tous ces objets de prix auraient été ou volés ou détruits par le feu qui a consumé la Maison d'Etat, si le colonel Payne n'avait pas eu la précaution de les envoyer en cette ville, lorsque par ordre du général Butler, ils furent protégés comme étant la propriété de l'Etat ;

Par ces motifs, il est :

Décrété, Que la Convention est le peuple de la Louisiane offrent ici leurs remerciments au major-général B. F. Butler et au colonel Payne, pour avoir sauvé les objets précieux ci-dessus mentionnés, appartenant a l'Etat.

Décrété en outre, Que le gouverneur soit invité à correspondre avec les autorités à Washington, et à prendre les arrangements nécessaires pour obtenir la restitution et le renvoi en Louisiane de la statue de Washington.

La résolution est secondée.

M. Sullivan en propose le rejet. Cette proposition est rejetée.

M Goldman demande le vote nominal. mais sa demande n'est pas appuyée.

Il est ordonné que lecture de la résolution de M. Campbell soit donné par le président. Cette lecture est donnée comme suit :

Attendu, Que la prime ou gratification payée par les Etats-Unis aux soldats qui s'enrôlent dans l'armée, ne peut pas être payée aux hommes qui s'enrôlent dans le 1er et 2e régiments des volontaires de la Nouvelle-Orléans, que lèvent en ce moment les colonels Kilborn et Brown, par la raison que ces deux régiments s'organisent et se lèvent pour un but spécifique, celui de la défense de la ville seulement, et attendu que cette Convention désire aider à la formation de ces régiments ;

Il est décrété, Que la somme de ―――― piastres est, par les présentes, allouée sur le trésor de l'Etat, pour être employée à payer, à titre de gratification ou de prime, à chaque homme qui à partir de ce jour s'enrôlera dans le 1er ou le 2e régiment des volontaires de la Nouvelle-Orléans, et que le gouverneur est autorisé à faire exécuter cette résolution au mieux de son jugement.

M. Montamat propose de renvoyer cette question devant la prochaine Législature.

Sur motion d'un autre membre, la résolution est rejetée.

M. Harnan propose l'ajournement. Refusé.

M. Schroeder offre le projet de résolution ci-après, lequel restera déposé jusqu'à demain :

Décrété, Que la résolution adoptée vendredi 15 avril 1864, et ainsi conçue :

" *Résolu,* Que les membres de la Convention recevront, sur les fonds du trésor public, et à titre d'indemnité, une somme de dix piastres par jour, pendant la durée de leurs services," est et demeure rescindée.

Décrété en outre, Que l'affaire sera renvoyée devant un comité spécial, lequel sera chargé de fixer le chiffre de l'indemnité de service à payer aux membres de cette Convention.

M. Stocker remarque qu'on a déja présenté hier une résolution semblable sur laquelle la Convention s'est prononcée, et il désire savoir s'il est convenable de revenir sans cesse sur ce sujet ; à quoi le président répond que la Convention est maîtresse de passer une résolution un jour et de la rescinder le lendemain ; mais qu'à tout évènement, il est vraisemblable que la Convention répondrait par un refus significatif aux membres qui essaieraient de retarder inutilement l'expédition des affaires.

Sur motion de M. Kavanagh, la Convention s'ajourne jusqu'à samedi, 23 courant, à midi.

Approuvé.

JOHN E. NEELIS,
Secrétaire.

SAMEDI, le 23 avril 1864.

La Convention se réunit à midi, conformément à l'ajournement ; et après la prière offerte par le Rév. Thomas, le secrétaire fait l'appel du rôle auquel répondent les membres suivants :

MM. Abell, Ariail, Austin, Balch, Bailey, Barrett, Beauvais, Bell, Bofill, Buckley. Burke, Campbell, Cazabat, Collin, J. K. Cook, T. Cook, Davies, Duane, Dufresne, Duke, Dupaty, Edwards, Ennis, Fish, Flagg, Flood, Foley, Fosdick, Fuller, Gastinel, Geier, Goldman, Gorlinski, Gruneberg, Gaidry, Healy, Harnan, Hart, Heard, Henderson, Hills, Howes, Kavanagh, Knobloch, Kugler, Mann, Maas, Maurer, Mendiverri, Millspaugh, Montamat, Morris, E. Murphy, M. W. Murphy, Newell, Normand, O'Conner, J. Payne, Pintado, Poynot, J. Purcell, S. Pursell, Schroeder, Seymour, Shaw, Smith, Spellicy, Stumpf, Stiner, Stauffer, Terry, Thomas, Thorpe, Wells, Wilson—78 membres présents, constituant un quorum.

Le secrétaire lit le procès-verbal de la séance précédente.

M. Hills propose :

Dispense de la lecture des résolutions et rapports des comités consignés au procès-verbal, avant que ce procès-verbal n'ait été annoncé et adopté.

M. S. Pursell présente la motion suivante, dans l'espoir qu'on n'en disposera point d'une manière sommaire, mais qu'elle sera l'objet d'une étude sérieuse de la part de la Convention :

Décrète, L'article suivant est offert comme substitut de l'art. 35 dans le rapport du comité sur les Dispositions Générales ; il sera mis à l'ordre du jour et appelé en même temps que le dit rapport :

Art. 35. L'impôt sera égal et uniforme dans tout l'Etat. L'impôt sera réparti sur tous les biens proportionnellement à leur valeur, laquelle sera déterminée de la manière indiquée par la loi.

L'Assemblée Générale pourra exempter d'impôts les biens consacrés à l'usage des églises, des écoles ou d'autres institutions de charité publique.

L'Assemblée Générale imposera le revenu de toute personne de profession, de métier, d'art et d'autre emploi ; et toute susdite personne devra prendre, comme la loi le prescrit, une patente.

Tout impôt sur le revenu sera proportionnel au montant du revenu ou des affaires que le contribuable fait.

Cette motion est déclarée n'être pas à l'ordre.

M. Austin propose que le rapport du comité chargé de déterminer les appointements des officiers et des employés de cette Convention, soit amendé, de manière à ce que les copistes de l'enrôlement soient payés huit piastres par jour, et que les officiers et employés reçoivent leurs appointements à compter du jour de l'ouverture de la Convention.

M. Hills propose une suspension des réglements, afin d'adopter la motion suivante :

Le secrétaire, en faisant la lecture du procès-verbal, se dispensera de lire l'appel du rôle, n'en donnant que les résultats ; les résolutions déposées ; toutes celles qui sont rejetées et tous les rapports imprimés, à moins que la Convention n'en ordonne autrement.

Motion de dispense du réglement à l'effet d'adopter cette résolution immédiatement. Adoptée.

M. Abell propose :

Tout rapport d'un comité permanent sera considéré *seriatim*, c'est-à-dire section par section, et aucune section ne sera adoptée, à moins d'avoir subi trois lectures successives, à trois différents jours.

Motion de M. Fuller :

Tout amendement ou substitut proposé au rapport d'un comité permanent, le sera au moins un jour d'avance.

Motion de M. Foley :

Le secrétaire devra faire imprimer tous les rapports des comités de cette Convention, sous une forme telle que l'on puisse insérer les amendements proposés.

Le secrétaire devra faire imprimer ces rapports immédiatement par l'imprimeur de la Convention.

M. Foley propose une suspension des réglements afin d'adopter cette résolution sur le champ.

Accordé, et la résolution est adoptée à l'unanimité.

APPEL DES RAPPORTS DES COMITÉS PERMANENTS.

Comité d'Emancipation. Pas de rapport.

Les comités sur le Législatif et sur l'Exécutif annoncent que leurs rapports s'achèvent.

M. Cutler, président du comité sur le Mode de Révision de la Constitution, propose le rapport suivant :

M. le Président, MM. les Conventionnels :

Votre comité chargé de s'occuper du Mode de Révision de la Constitution, vous demande la permission de vous soumettre le rapport suivant, et vous en recommande l'adoption en lieu et place de l'art. 141 de la constitution de 1852.

Tout amendement à cette constitution peut être proposé au Sénat ou à la Chambre des Représentants. Si l'amendement est accepté par les deux tiers des membres élus dans chaque Chambre, il sera inséré au procès-verbal avec le vote par oui et par non.

L'amendement proposé sera soumis au suffrage du peuple, au jour désigné à cet effet, par la Législature ; et ce jour sera pris dans les quatre-vingt-dix qui suivront l'ajournement de cette Législature, et après les trente jours de publications voulues par la loi.

Si une majorité des suffrages approuve et ratifie le dit amendement, il formera partie de la constitution.

Si plusieurs amendements sont soumis à la fois au peuple, ils le seront de manière à ce que le peuple puisse donner sa voix en faveur de chacun de ces amendements, ou contre chacun d'eux, séparément.

Avec respect,
R. KING CUTLER, président.
E. A. KNOBLOCH,
JOS. G. BAUM,
J. H. STINER,
PATRICK HARNAN.

La motion de recevoir ce rapport, d'en ordonner l'impression à 200 exemplaires, et de le mettre à l'ordre du jour de mardi le 3 mai, est amendée par M. Hills, proposant mardi prochain, et adoptée telle.

MM. Gruneborg et Shaw, présidents des comités sur les Dispositions Transitoires et sur la Mise à Exécution de la constitution, annoncent que leurs rapports sont en voie d'achèvement.

Ni le comité d'Enrôlement ni le comité de Finances ne présentent de rapport.

M. S. Pursell, du comité des Dépenses, et M. J. Purcell, du comité des Impressions, annoncent que leurs rapports se préparent.

Pas de rapport du comité des Relations Fédérales.

Le comité sur les Voies de Fait sur la personne de certains membres, annonce que son rapport se prépare.

Point de rapport du comité Special ou du comité de Vérification des Pouvoirs.

M. Stocker, du comité sur l'Absence de certains Membres, annonce qu'il n'est pas encore prêt à présenter un rapport satisfaisant.

Le secrétaire donne lecture d'un message

du secrétaire d'Etat, au sujet de M. T. J. Decker, déclaré élu par la paroisse Plaquemines.

Sur motion de M. Hills, référé au comité sur la Vérification des Pouvoirs.

Les affaires non terminées sont maintenant à l'ordre du jour.

M. Terry demande lecture de la proposition suivante :

Nul ne sera éligible à une charge d'Etat ou de municipalité, s'il ne possède les qualités requises de tout électeur pour être membre de cette Convention, et toute personne qui aurait actuellement une charge municipale ou d'Etat, sans posséder les susdites qualités, en sera dépouillée sur le champ.

La motion de rejeter est secondée, puis elle est rejetée par 7 votes contre 37 ; sur ce, demande d'appel nominal, d'où il résulte :

Pour l'affirmative :

Messieurs Ariail, Austin, Cutler, Flagg, Henderson, Maas, Mann, Newell, J. Payne, Seymour, Wells—11.

Pour la négative :

Messieurs Abell, Bailey, Baum, Barrett, Beauvais, Bell, Bofill, Burke, Campbell, Cazabat, J. K. Cook, T. Cook, Crozat, Davies, Dufresne, Duane, Dupaty, Edwards, Flood, Foley, Fosdick, Gastinel, Geier, Gorlinski, Goldman, Gruneberg, Gaidry, Healy, Harnan, Hart, Hills, Hire, Howell, Howes, Kavanagh, Knobloch, Kugler, Maurer, Mendiverri, Millspaugh, Montamat, Montague, Morris, E. Murphy, M. W. Murphy, Normand, O'Conner, Ong, Pintado, Poynot, J. Purcell, S. Pursell, Schroeder, Shaw, Spellicy, Stocker, Stumpf, Stiner, Stauffer, Sullivan, Terry, Thorpe, Thomas, Wenck, Wilson, Collin, Duke—68.

Après une longue discussion, à laquelle plusieurs membres prennent part, on propose l'adoption de la résolution primitive, et sur demande de l'appel nominal, il appert que

18 votent pour l'affirmative :

Messieurs Bailey, Baum, Campbell, Flagg, Flood, Foley, Fosdick, Gastinel, Harnan, Healy, Hills, Howes, E. Murphy, M. W. Murphy, Sullivan, Terry, Thorpe, Wilson—18.

Et 68 pour la négative, savoir :

Messieurs Abell, Ariail, Austin, Barrett, Balch, Beauvais, Bell, Bofill, Buckley, Burke, Cazabat, J. K. Cook, T. Cook, Collin, Crozat, Cutler, Davies, Dufresne, Duane, Dupaty, Duke, Edwards, Ennis, Fish, Fuller, Gaidry, Geier, Goldman, Gorlinski, Gruneberg, Hart, Heard, Henderson, Hire, Howell, Kavanagh, Knobloch, Kugler, Maas, Mann, Maurer, Mendiverri, Millspaugh, Montamat, Montague, Morris, Newell, Normand, O'Conner, Ong, J. Payne, J. T. Pintado, Poynot, J. Purcell, S. Pursell, Schroeder, Seymour, Shaw, Smith, Spellicy, Stocker, Stumpf, Stiner, Stauffer, Thomas, Wenck et Wells—68.

La résolution est donc rejetée.

Une heure de l'après-midi étant arrivée, M. Stocker demande l'ordre du jour.

M. Montamat demande lecture de la résolution de M. Gaidry.

M. Stocker s'en réfère au président afin de savoir si sa motion ne doit pas avoir la préférence sur la précédente.

Le président décide que la résolution de M. Gaidry étant classée au rang des affaires non terminées, elle a droit à la préférence.

A la demande de M. Montamat, lecture de la résolution Gaidry est faite :

Attendu, Que toutes les constitutions jamais faites en cet Etat, ont décrété que toutes les procédures judiciaires et législatives auraient lieu en Anglais et Français ;

Attendu de plus, Que plusieurs membres de cette Convention, qui sont de véritables républicains et foncièrement loyaux, ne sont pas en même temps très-familiers avec la langue anglaise, et ont **été députés à** cette Convention par des constituants qui, eux aussi, ignorent cette dite langue, en vertu du droit qui leur appartient, en leur capacité de peuple souverain, de choisir tels députés qui leur conviennent, et leur dénier ce droit équivaudrait à dépouiller ce peuple de toute franchise et liberté ; en conséquence :

La Convention décrète, Toutes les résolutions et motions présentées à cette Convention seront traduites en langue française, afin que les membres des paroisses qui ne sont pas familiers avec la langue anglaise, soient parfaitement renseignés sur le sujet de leurs délibérations.

Sur motion de M. Henderson, la résolution est rejetée.

ORDRE SPÉCIAL DU JOUR.

Appel du rapport du comité sur les appointements des officiers et employés de la Convention.

M. Hills propose d'effacer du rapport la clause déterminant les appointements du président.

Secondé par M. Goldman.

Amendement de M. Montamat portant

les émoluments du président à quinze dollars par jour.

M. Goldman propose le rejet de cet amendement.

M. Terry propose le dépôt sujet à l'appel.

Cette proposition est rejetée, et la motion est adoptée.

M. Henderson propose de rejeter la motion Hills, et ce dernier demande l'appel nominal, qui donne pour résultat :

Affirmative :

Messieurs Abell, Austin, Barrett, Beauvais, Bell, Burke, Campbell, T. Cook, Crozat, Cutler, Ennis, Fish, Fuller, Geier, Goldman, Heard, Henderson, Kugler, Maas, Maurer, Mendiverri, Montamat, M. W. Murphy, O'Conner, J. Payne, J. Purcell, Shaw, Stocker, Stumpf, Stiner, Sullivan, Terry, Thorpe et Thomas—36.

Négative :

Messieurs Ariail, Bailey, Baum, Balch, Bofill, Buckley, J. K. Cook, Collin, Davies, Duane, Dupaty, Duke, Edwards, Flagg, Flood, Foley, Fosdick, Gastinel, Gorlinski, Gruneberg, Gaidry, Healy, Hart, Harnan, Hills, Howell, Hire, Howes, Kavanagh, Knobloch, Morris, Millspaugh, Montague, E. Murphy, Newell, Normand, Ong, Pintado, Poynot, Schroeder, Seymour, Smith, Spellicy, Stauffer, Wenck, Wells—46.

Cette dite motion est donc rejetée.

Sur la question de supprimer la clause, il y a appel nominal, ainsi que suit :

Affirmative :

Messieurs Ariail, Bailey, Baum, Beauvais, Bofill, Buckley, Burke, Campbell, Cook J. K., Collin, Duane, Dufresne, Duke, Flagg, Fosdick, Foley, Gastinel, Gaidry, Goldman, Gruneberg, Harnan, Hart, Hills, Howell, Howes, Kavanagh, Maas, Maurer, Mendiverri, Millspaugh, E. Morris, Newell, Normand, Ong, Pintado, Poynot, S. Pursell, Seymour, Smith, Stumpf, Stauffer, Sullivan, Wenck, Wells—46.

Messieurs Abell, Austin, Barrett, Bell, Cazabat, T. Cook, Crozat, Cutler, Davies, Dupaty, Edwards, Ennis, Fish, Flood, Fuller, Geier, Gorlinski, Healy, Heard, Henderson, Hire, Knobloch, Kugler, Mann, Montamat, Montague, M. W. Murphy, O'Conner, Spellicy, Stocker, Stiner, Terry, Thorpe, Thomas, Wilson—34.

La motion est rejetée.

TRAITEMENT DU SECRETAIRE.

M. Montague propose de le porter à vingt dollars.

La proposition est secondée.

Motion de rejet par M. Montamat.

Adoptée.

Le rapport est adopté.

SECRETAIRES-ADJOINTS.

L'amendement de M. Stocker portant leur traitement à douze dollars et demi est rejeté.

Le rapport primitif est adopté.

SERGENT D'ARMES.

L'amendement de Fosdick portant dix dollars, est rejeté sur la motion de M. Henderson.

Le rapport primitif est adopté.

AIDE-SERGENT D'ARMES.

L'amendement de M. Healy portant dix piastres par jour, est rejeté sur motion de M. Montamat, par 51 voix contre 26, ainsi que l'amendement de M. Foley, portant huit piastres.

Le rapport primitif est donc adopté.

MESSAGER.

L'amendement de M. Fosdick portant trois piastres, sur motion de M. Henderson est rejeté, ainsi que l'amendement Healy portant six piastres, sur motion de M. Goldman.

Le rapport primitif est adopté.

MAITRE DE POSTE.

Amendement Fosdick portant cinq piastres, rejeté.

Le rapport primitif est adopté.

PORTIER.

Le rapport est adopté.

RAPPORTEUR EN CHEF.

L'amendement de M. Stocker portant quinze piastres par jour est adopté, et le rapport aussi, avec ce dit amendement.

AIDES-RAPPORTEURS.

Le rapport est adopté.

COMMIS AUX MANDATS.

Le rapport est adopté.

Le rapport sur le traitement des copistes et sur les frais de route alloués, est adopté.

M. Stocker propose qu'il soit décrété que le traitement des officiers court du 6 avril. Adopté.

Le rapport, ainsi amendé, est adopté tout entier.

M. Montamat propose d'employer des traducteurs avec traitement de dix piastres par jour.

La proposition est rejetée.

Le rapport, amendé et adopté, se lit ainsi que suit :

John E. Neelis, secrétaire	$15 00
Aides-secrétaires	10 00
Sergent-d'armes	15 00
Aides-sergents-d'armes	6 00
Deux Messagers, chacun	5 00
Maître de poste	8 00
Portier	8 00
Rapporteur en chef	15 00
Trois Aides-rapporteurs, chacun	10 00
Commis aux mandats	10 00
Copistes, chacun	6 00

Sur motion de M. Montague, la Convention s'ajourne à lundi à midi.

Approuvé :

JOHN E. NEELIS,
Secrétaire.

LUNDI, 25 Avril 1864.

La Convention se réunit aujourd'hui à midi, conformément à l'ajournement, sous la présidence de l'Hon. E. H. Durell.

La prière est offerte par le révérend Hopkins.

Le secrétaire fait l'appel nominal, auquel les membres suivants répondent :

Messieurs Abell, Ariail, Austin, Bailey, Barrett, Baum, Bennie, Bofill, Bonzano, Bromley, Burke, Campbell, T. Cook, Crozat, Cutler, Duke, Davies, Dufresne, Duane, Edwards, Ennis, Fish, Flagg, Flood, Foley, Fosdick, Fuller, Gastinel, Geier, Goldman, Gorlinski, Graneberg, Gaidry, Healy, Harnan, Hart, Heard, Henderson, Hills, Howes, Howell, Kavanagh, Knobloch, Kugler, Maas, Mann, Maurer, Millspaugh, Montamat, E. Murphy, M. W. Murphy, Newell, Normand, O'Conner, Ong, J. Payne, Pintado, Poynot, J. Purcell, S. Pursell, Schroeder, Seymour, Shaw, Smith, Spellicy, Stocker, Stumpf, Stiner, Stauffer, Sullivan, Terry, Thorpe, Thomas, Wells, Wilson et M. le Président—78 membres présents.

Le secrétaire lit le procès-verbal, qui, après correction, est adopté.

M. Goldman prend la parole sur une question de privilége, mais le président décide qu'il n'est pas à l'ordre.

Il propose ensuite que la Convention s'ajourne jusqu'à demain, afin d'aller se présenter en corps à l'amiral Farragut, pour le féliciter à l'occasion de l'anniversaire de la prise de la Nlle-Orléans par les troupes fédérales.

Sur motion de M. Montamat, la proposition est rejetée.

Comme il n'y a aucun placet ou mémoire à l'ordre, la Convention s'occupe des résolutions présentées.

M. Crozat demande la reconsidération de son vote sur l'amendement de M. Hills, relatif au traitement du président.

Secondé par M. Montamat.

M. Foley présente un amendement à l'effet de reprendre en considération toute la question, dans le sens d'en supprimer toute la clause du traitement du président.

Secondé.

La motion de M. Goldman à l'effet de rejeter cet amendement est rejetée ; et de l'appel nominal il résulte 63 voix négatives contre 5 affirmatives.

La motion pour la reconsidération est donc présentée et acceptée.

M. Goldman propose de la rejeter. Refusé.

La motion d'adopter le rapport est donc faite, on demande l'appel nominal et il en résulte

44 voix affirmatives :

Messieurs Abell, Austin, Bailey, Barrett, Beauvais, Bell, Bennis, Bofill, Burke, Cazabat, T. Cook, Crozat, Cutler, Davies, Duane, Dupaty, Ennis, Fish, Fuller, Gaidry, Heard, Henderson, Hire, Kugler, Maas, Mann, Maurer, Mendiverri, Montamat, Montague, M. W. Murphy, O'Conner, Payne J., Pintado, J. Purcell, S. Pursell, Shaw, Smith, Stocker, Stiner, Terry, Thorpe, Thomas, Wilson—44.

38 négatives :

Messieurs Ariail, Baum, Bonzano, Bromley, Collin, Campbell, J. K. Cook, Duke, Dufresne, Edwards, Flagg, Flood, Foley, Fosdick, Gastinel, Geier, Goldman, Gorlinski, Gruneberg, Healy, Harnan, Hart, Hills, Howes, Kavanagh, Knobloch, Millspaugh, E. Murphy, Normand, Ong, Poynot, Schroeder, Seymour, Spellicy, Stumpf, Stauffer, Sullivan, Wells—38.

Le rapport est adopté en conséquence de ce vote.

M. Kavanagh présente la résolution suivante :

Les officiers de police en fonctions auprès de cette Assemblée recevront la somme de quatre piastres par jour, en rétribution de leurs services en cette qualité.

M. Foley propose une suspension des règlements, à l'effet d'adopter cette dite résolution.

Accepté.

M. Thomas propose de leur allouer le

même salaire que celui qu'ils recevaient de la ville.

M. Foley propose de rejeter cette proposition.

Adopté.

M. Foley propose alors d'adopter la résolution primitive.

Accepté par un vote de 46 voix contre 27.

Rapports des comités permanents :

Pas de rapport du comité d'Emancipation.

Le comité sur le Législatif annonce que son rapport est en voie de progrès.

M. Fish, du comité sur l'Exécutif, annonce que son comité est d'avis d'adopter le troisième article tel qu'il existe, sans amendement aucun.

M. Foley demande la lecture de l'article.

M. Goldman demande au président l'autorisation de se retirer de l'Assemblée, sous prétexte que ce jour est un jour férié.

Le président l'invite à siéger jusqu'après la lecture du rapport.

M. Fish lit donc l'article en question.

M. J. Purcell propose d'accepter le rapport.

M. Fosdick demande que le comité présente un rapport écrit.

Adopté

Le comité des Améliorations Intérieures, le comité sur les Dispositions Générales et le comité sur les Dispositions Transitoires annoncent que leurs rapports sont à l'étude.

Le comité des Relations Fédérales présente le rapport suivant :

Messieurs les Conventionnels—Le président du comité des Relations Fédérales demande la permission de vous soumettre le rapport suivant :

La Constitution et les lois des Etats-Unis seront la loi suprême du pays, nonobstant toute Constisution ou loi d'Etat y-contraires.

(Signé)   T. B. THORPE,
Président.
JOHN HENDERSON,
R. V. MONTAGUE.

Rapports des comités spéciaux :

M. Montamat, président du comité sur la Vérification des Pouvoirs, présente le rapport suivant :

Messieurs les Conventionnels—Votre comité de Vérification des Pouvoirs ayant examiné les rapports sur les élections de la paroisse Plaquemines, pour l'élection d'un délégué à cette Convention, de cette paroisse. vous annonce respectueusement que M. Tomas J. Decker est bien et dûment élu, et qu'ayant pris qualité, il a droit à siéger dans cette Convention.

(Signé)   JOHN T. MONTAMAT.
Président.

Le Col. T. B. Thorpe, au nom du comité d'Enrôlement, annonce que les personnes suivantes sont dûment nommées :

M. Félix Lambert, commis en chef à l'enrôlement.

MM. Léon Laugrin et Elzéar Cambray, traducteurs.

M. Wilson propose de porter ces noms sur la liste du comité des Rémunérations.

M. Hills propose de les porter à la liste des employés de la Convention.

Adopté.

M. Maurer propose que la question de rémunération soit référée au comité de Finances, et l'amendement de M. Hills, demandant que le référé soit au comité des Rémunérations, est adopté.

Le président du comité des Dépenses annonce que son rapport sera bientôt prêt.

Pas de rapport du comité sur les impressions.

Le comité sur les Voies de Fait envers certains membres, annonce qu'il présentera son rapport à la séance prochaine.

Le comité au sujet de la Statue de Washington ne présente aucun rapport.

AFFAIRES NON TERMINEES.

Elles sont déclarées à l'ordre.

M. Thomas demande la lecture de la résolution présentée par M. Fuller, samedi, et le Secrétaire la lit :

Décrète. Tout amendement ou substitut que l'un des comités permanents proposera devra être notifié à cette assemblée au moins un jour à l'avance.

La motion de M. Foley pour le rejet est secondée et adoptée, et sur demande d'appel nominal, il appert qu'elle est rejetée par un vote de 49 voix contre 26.

Lecture de la résolution de M. Abell :

Lorsqu'il y aura délibération sur un rapport de comité permanent, il sera pris en considération *seriatim*, section par section ; et nulle section ne sera adoptée avant d'avoir subi trois lectures successives à trois différents jours.

ET L'AMENDEMENT DE LA CONSTITUTION DE LA LOUISIANE.

M. Montamat propose l'adoption, secondée et approuvée.

Sur motion de M. Kavanagh, la Convention s'ajourne à demain, à midi.

Approuvé :
          JOHN E. NEELIS.
              Secrétaire.

        MARDI, 26 avril 1864.

Aujourd'hui, à midi, la Convention est appelée à l'ordre par le président, et après la prière offerte par le Rév. Newman, le secrétaire fait l'appel nominal, et les membres suivants répondent à leurs noms :

Messrs. Abell, Ariail, Austin, Balch, Bailey, Barrett, Beauvais, Bell, Bonzano, Bromley, Brott, Buckley, Burke, Cazabat, Cook T., Collin, Crozat, Davies, Decker, Dupaty, Dufresne, Duane, Duke, Edwards, Ennis, Fish, Flagg, Flood, Foley, Fosdick, Gastinel, Gaidry, Geier, Goldman, Gorlinski Gruneberg, Harnan, Hart, Healy, Heard, Henderson, Hills, Hire, Kavanagh, Knobloch, Kugler, Maas, Maurer, Mendiverri, Millspaugh, Montamat, Montague, Murphy E., M. W. Murphy, Newell, Normand, Ong, O'Conner, J. Payne, Pintado, Poynot, Purcell J., S. Pursell, Schroeder, Seymour, Shaw, Smith, Spellicy, Stumpf, Stiner, Staufer. Sullivan, Thomas, Wenck, Wells, Wilson—76 membres présents.

Le secrétaire donne lecture du procès-verbal de la dernière séance, lequel, après amendement, est adopté.

M. Edwards présente la résolution suivante :

Attendu, Que les membres de cette Convention ont appris de source certaine que toutes sortes de déprédations sont journellement commises dans la paroisse des Avoyelles et dans d'autres parties de la Louisiane comprises dans les lignes fédérales, par des guérillas et par des bandes d'hommes non régulièrement organisés ; qu'il n'y a ni sauvegarde ni protection pour la vie et les biens des citoyens loyaux, qui sont chassés de leurs demeures et du sein de leurs familles, à raison de leur dévouement à la cause sacrée de l'Union et de la Liberté, et que ces bandes féroces ne respectent ni le sexe, ni l'âge, ni la condition des personnes, en conséquence :

La Convention décrète, L'adjudant-général de l'Etat devra s'occuper de la déplorable position actuelle, des choses dans la paroisse des Avoyelles, afin de mettre en œuvre les mesures nécessaires à la sauvegarde et à la protection des citoyens loyaux contre les atteintes des guérillas, contre les attaques ou les courses spoliatrices de l'ennemi.

Décrète de plus, Le président de cette Convention nommera un comité de trois membres chargé de conférer à ce sujet avec l'adjudant-général de l'Etat, et de lui fournir tous les renseignements nécessaires à cet égard.

Mr. Cazabat propose une suspension du réglement, afin de mettre cette proposition aux voix. Adopté.

M. Hills en propose le rejet.

Cette dernière proposition est acceptée.

M. Hills propose ce qui suit :

La Convention décrète, Les membres de cette Convention, absents sans congé, qui ne répondront pas au premier appel du rôle par le secrétaire, perdront la moitié de leurs appointements pour chaque jour de leur absence.

La motion de dispenser du réglement, afin de passer cette motion, est rejetée, et la résolution est renvoyée au lendemain.

       RAPPORT DES COMITES.

M. Fish, président du comité sur l'Exécutif, soumet un rapport.

Sur motion de M. Austin, dispense de la lecture de ce rapport est accordée, attendu que la Convention en a pris connaissance à la séance d'hier.

Sur motion de M. Sullivan, le rapport est accepté et mis à l'ordre du jour pour lundi, le 2 de mai 1864.

Mr. Wilson, Président du comité sur les Voies de Fait contre certains membres, soumet le rapport avec les preuves à l'appui.

M. Duane propose la suppression des aveux des accusés. Rejeté.

M. Montamat propose de rejeter le rapport. Sa motion est rejetée.

M. Gastinel propose de remettre l'examen de ce rapport jusqu'à ce que les cours de justice saisies de ces accusations aient prononcé. Rejeté.

M. Hills propose la nomination d'un comité de trois membres chargé de l'examen de cette affaire. Rejeté.

M. Brott propose de renvoyer ce rapport au comité primitif ; cette proposition est acceptée, en y comprenant l'amendement de M. Foley, demandant de porter M. Thorpe comme membre de ce comité.

       ORDRE DU JOUR.

Le rapport du comité sur le Mode de Révision de la Constitution, est appelé et subit sa première lecture.

M. Hills en propose l'adoption.

Le président décide que la motion n'est pas à l'ordre, attendu que, d'après le réglement, ce rapport doit avoir deux autres tours d'ordre.

M. Heard propose la suspension du réglement afin de donner la seconde et la troisième lecture de ce rapport pour en demander l'adoption.

L'appel nominal sur cette question étant demandé, il en résulte 28 voix affirmatives contre 42 négatives, et la motion est rejetée.

M. Montamat propose l'ajournement, mais retire sa proposition pour permettre à M. Wells de présenter la résolution suivante :

Attendu, Qu'il convient qu'un certain délai soit donné à la Convention, suffisant pour qu'elle puisse prendre en considération les questions importantes et difficiles qui lui sont soumises, et afin que les paroisses de la campagne jouissent de plus grandes facilités et d'un laps de temps plus étendu pour envoyer leurs délégués, de manière à ce que l'Etat en général soit plus amplement représenté et mieux entendu ; en conséquence :

La Convention décrète, Cette Convention s'ajournera samedi prochain, le 30, jusqu'au premier juin 1864, à midi, ou jusqu'à tel jour pour lequel il plaira à son président de la convoquer.

La motion d'ajournement de M. Montamat est rejetée, sur l'appel nominal, par 42 voix contre 29.

M. Cazabat propose la suspension du réglement afin de s'occuper de la résolution de M. Wells.

La proposition est rejetée.

M. M. W. Murphy présente la résolution suivante :

Décrète, Le traitement du commis en chef au bureau de l'enrôlement sera de douze piastres par jour ; celui des deux traducteurs employés sera de dix piastres par jour, pour chacun d'eux.

M. S. Pursell annonce qu'il désire présenter cinq substituts aux cinq premiers articles du rapport du comité d'Instruction Publique ; il donne lecture des susdits substituts.

M. Stocker propose de faire imprimer ces substituts pour l'usage de la Convention.

Adopté.

Sur motion de M. Hills, la Convention s'ajourne à demain, à midi.

Journal adopté.

JOHN E. NEELIS,
Secrétaire.

MERCREDI, le 27 Avril 1864.

Le Président appelle la Convention à l'ordre, et après la prière dite par le révérend Deossy, membre de la Commission Chrétienne des Etats-Unis, le secrétaire appelle le rôle et les membres suivants répondent à leurs noms :

MM. Abell, Ariail, Balch, Barrett, Beil, Bofill, Bonzano, Buckley, Burke, Campbell, Cazabat, J. K. Cook, T. Cook, Crozat, Collin, Davies, Dufresne, Decker, Dupaty, Edwards, Ennis, Fish, Flagg, Foley, Fosdick, Geier, Goldman, Gorlinski, Gruneberg, Gaidry, Healy, Harnan, Hart, Heard, Hills, Kavanagh, Kugler, Maas, Maurer, Millspaugh, E. Murphy, M. W. Murphy, Newell, Normand, O'Conner, Ong, J. Payne, Pintado, Poynot, J. Purcell, Seymour, Shaw, Smith, Spellicy, Stumpf, Stiner, Sullivan, Wells, et M. le Président—59.

A raison de l'absence d'un quorum, le président donne au sergent d'armes l'ordre d'aller à la recherche des membres absents.

Messieurs Austin, Bromley, Brott, Gastinel, Hire, Howell, Knobloch, Mendiverri, Montamat, Montague, Morris, S. Pursell, Schroeder, Stocker, Stauffer, Wilson et Beauvais entrant à ce moment, il en résulte que M. le président annonce l'existence du quorum.

Lecture du procès-verbal de la séance précédente, qui après amendement, est adopté.

M. Bonzano présente un mémoire de M. le Docteur Vallas, ancien surintendant et professeur de l'école scientifique de la Louisiane, au sujet de l'instruction publique.

Après lecture du mémiore, M. Bonzano propose qu'il soit référé au comité de l'Instruction publique, et qu'il soit imprimé pour l'usage de la Convention.

La motion est adoptée.

M. Bonzano, en sa qualité de président du comité d'Emancipation, présente un rapport qui est accepté et mis à l'ordre du jour pour mercredi, le 4 mai.

M. Abell, membre de ce même comité, présente le rapport de la minorité.

M. Hills propose de le recevoir et de le mettre à l'ordre spécial du jour pour lundi prochain.

M. Stauffer propose, par voie d'amendement, de le mettre à l'ordre du jour pour mercredi, le 4 mai. Adopté.

M. Sullivan présente des substituts aux neuf articles du rapport du comité judiciaire.

Sur motion de M. Wilson, les dits substituts sont acceptés et l'impression en est ordonnée.

Sur motion de M. Stocker, les substituts sont mis à l'ordre du jour pour vendredi, le 29 courant.

M. Brott, président du comité des Finances, présente un rapport qui est adopté.

Le rapport du comité des Relations Fédérales est appelé et subit sa seconde lecture.

M. Brott demande la permission de présenter le rapport de la minorité, demain. Accordé.

M. Thorpe, président du comité d'Enrôlement, annonce que les résolutions suivantes sont correctement enrôlées. :

"Résolution allouant à M. H. A. Galup, la somme de cent piastres en rémunération de ses services comme secrétaire-adjoint avant l'organisation de cette Convention."

"Résolution requérant le bibliothécaire d'Etat de fournir à chaque membre de la Convention un exemplaire des Statuts Révisés."

"Résolution déterminant la rétribution des conventionnels et nommant en même temps un comité de cinq pour établir les émoluments des officiers et des employés de cette Convention."

"Résolution invitant le Gouverneur à lancer sa proclamation à l'effet de convoquer une élection pour la nomination d'un délégué dans le Dixième District Représentatif."

Sur motion de M. Montamat, le rapport est accepté et le président est invité à signer les résolutions y mentionnées.

M. Samuel Pursell présente le substitut suivant au rapport du comité des Relations Fédérales, savoir :

Les Etats-Unis d'Amérique forment un seul gouvernement: les divers Etats de l'Union en sont les auxiliaires et n'ont que des pouvoirs locaux.

M. Wilson propose de le rejeter. Repoussé.

Sur motion de M. Shaw, le substitut est référé au comité des Relations Fédérales.

M. Cazabat présente un substitut au rapport du comité sur le Préambule.

Sur motion, ce substitut est référé au dit comité.

M. Hills demande appel de la résolution relative à la présence des membres.

M. Montamat propose de la rejeter, et sur ce, appel nominal, ainsi que suit :

Pour l'affirmative :

MM. Austin, Balch, Baum, Beauvais, Bofil, Bromley, Buckley, Burke, Campbell, Crozat, Cutler, Davies, Dufresne, Dupaty, Decker, Edwards, Fish, Gastinel, Gruneberg, Harnan, Heard, Hire, Kavanagh, Knobloch, Kugler, Mendiverri, Montamat, Morris, M. W. Murphy, Newell, Normand O'Conner, Ong, J. Paine, Pintado, J. Purcell, Seymour, Stocker, Sullivan, S. Pursell, Thorpe—41.

Pour la négative :

MM. Abell, Ariail, Barrett, Bell, Bonzano, Brott, Cazabat, J. K. Cook, T. Cook, Collins, Ennis, Foley, Fosdick, Goldman, Gorlinski, Gaidry, Healy, Hart, Hills, Howell, Maas, Maurer, Millspaugh, Montague, E. murphy, Poynot, Schroeder, Shaw, Smith Spellicy, Stumpf, Stiner, Stauffer, Thomas, Wenk, Wilson—31.

La résolution est donc rejetée.

M. M. W. Murphy demande appel de la résolution relative à la rémunération des traducteurs et des copistes.

Sur motion, elle est référée au comité des rémunérations.

ORDRE SPÉCIAL DU JOUR.

Le rapport sur le mode de réviser la constitution subit une seconde lecture.

M. Howell propose d'amender la troisième ligne de l'article, en effaçant les mots "deux tiers," et de leur substituer les mots "trois quarts."

Une motion de rejeter cet amendement est repoussée par 41 voix contre 17.

Une motion de prendre en reconsidération ce même vote, est adoptée.

M. Thorpe présente la résolution suivante :

Le vote final sur la section relative à la révision ou l'amendement de la constitution sera ajourné jusqu'à ce que tous les articles de cette Constitution qui précèdent dans leur ordre la section susdite, aient été adoptés.

Messieurs S. Pursell et Cazabat proposent de dispenser du réglement, afin de procéder à l'adoption de la susdite résolution: mais le président déclare que la question maintenant à l'ordre est au sujet de l'adoption de l'amendement de M. Howell. C'est donc là ce qui est mis aux voix et l'amendement est rejeté.

Dispense du réglement est accordée, la résolution de M. Thorpe est prise et adoptée, et la Convention s'ajourne à demain à mid.

Approuvé :

JOHN E. NEELIS,
Secrétaire.

JEUDI, 28 avril 1864.

Conformément à l'ajournement, la Convention se réunit à midi ; le président l'appelle à l'ordre, et après la prière faite par le Rév. Strong, le secrétaire procède à l'appel du rôle, auquel répondent les membres suivants :

Messieurs Abell, Ariail, Austin, Balch, Bailey, Barrett, Baum, Beauvais, Bell, Bofill, Bonzano, Bromley, Buckley, Brott, Burke, J. K. Cook, T. Cook, Crozat, Cutler, Collin, Davies Dufresne, Duane, Decker, Dupaty, Edwards, Ennis, Fish, Flagg, Flood, Foley, Fosdick, Geier, Goldman, Gorlinski, Gruneberg, Gaidry, Healy, Harnan, Hart, Heard, Hills, Hire, Kavanagh, Knobloch, Kugler, Maas, Maurer, Mendiverri, Millspaugh, Montamat, Montague, M. W. Murphy, Newell, Normand, O'Conner, J. Payne, Pintado, Poynot, J. Purcell, S. Pursell, Seymour, Shaw, Smith, Spellicy, Stumpf, Stiner, Stauffer, Sullivan, Terry, Thomas et Wells.

Seulement 72 membres sont présents; et afin de former un quorum le sergent-d'armes est envoyé à la recherche des absents, et la présence de Messieurs Henderson, Howell, E. Murphy et Stocker survenant alors, complète le nombre requis.

Lecture du procès-verbal d'hier et adoption d'icelui.

M. Goldman présente un mémoire.

Le président l'informe que ce mémoire n'étant signé que par son auteur, il ne pouvait pas, en sa qualité de conventionnel, le présenter lui-même.

M. Goldman présente en conséquence la résolution suivante :

Les associations de banque incorporées en vertu des lois de cet État, sont défendues ; toutes banques qui exercent coment telles, ou l'ont fait jusqu'à présent, som averties d'avoir à cesser ce genre d'affaires.

(Signé) EDMOND GOLDMAN.

Rejetée.

M. Gruneberg présente la résolution suivant :

Attendu, Que la cause principale de convocation de notre Convention constitutionnelle a été dans le but de décider la question d'abolition de l'esclavage dans cet État; *Attendu*, que l'adoption de cette mesure, en quelque forme ou manière possible, nécessitera indubitablement de grandes modifications dans toutes les parties de la loi organique de l'Etat; *Attendu*, qu'à ces causes, cette Convention ne peut ou ne doit décider en dernier ressort sur aucun des rapports des comités permanents sur les amendements à la constitution, avant que l'émancipation n'ait été mise aux voix ; *Attendu de plus*, que la question d'émancipation, étant la plus importante de toutes, elle exige les profrondes et longues délibérations de cette Assemblée ; en conséquence :

La Convention décrète, La Convention s'occupera d'abord des rapports de tous les comités permanents sur les amendements à la constitution, leurs substituts et sous amendements (le rapport sur l'émancipation excepté,) et ces rapports ne subiront que leur seconde lecture, et alors viendra le rapport sur l'émancipation, lequel pasera par les formalités voulues y compris le vote final : après quoi, viendront les rapports des comités permanents, qui subiront leur troisième lecture et le vote final.

Décrète de plus, La Convention ne s'ajournera que de jour en jour, jusqu'à ce que les rapports des comités permanents sur les amendements à la constitution, (celui sur l'émancipation excepté,) aient subi leur seconde lecture. Déposé.

RAPPORTS DES COMITES PERMANENTS.

Le rapporteur du comité sur la Législatif annonce que son rapport progresse.

Le comité sur l'Exécutif ne présente pas de rapport, non plus que ceux des Améliorations Intérieures, des Dispositions Transitoires et de la Mise à Exécution de la Constitution.

M. Millspaugh, au nom de M. Thorpe, président du comité d'Enrôlement, annonce comme correctement enrôlées les résolutions suivantes :

1. Résolution invitant le gouverneur à lancer sa proclamation pour l'élection de délégués dans les paroisses Plaquemines et Ascension.

2. Résolution relative à la statue de Washington.

3. Résolution relative à la Rémunération des Membres.

4. Résolution relative à l'Auditeur des Comptes Publics, à l'effet de fournir un état des dépenses de l'administration de son Excellence Geo. F. Shepley, dernièrement gouverneur militaire.

Sur motion de M. Bell, le rapport et accepté et le président est invité à signer ces dites résolutions.

M. Balch demande lecture de la résolution relative à la proclamation du gouverneur.

Sur motion de M. Stiner, il y a dispense de cette lecture.

Le comité relatif aux Voies de Fait contre les membres, annonce que son rapport progresse.

M. Sullivan, président du comité relatif à la statue de Washington, annonce que le comité a commencé à correspondre avec le ministre de la guerre au sujet de cette statue.

Accepté.

M. M. W. Murphy présente le suivant :

M. le Président et MM. les membres de la Convention :

Le comité institué à l'effet de déterminer la rémunération des officiers et employés de cette Convention, vous soumet le rapport suivant sur les affaires non-terminées :

La rétribution du commis en chef de l'enrôlement sera de dix piastres par jour ; celle de deux traducteurs sera de dix piastres par jour pour chacun d'eux, à compter du 6 avril 1864.

(Signé)   M. W. MURPHY, président.
                J. R. TERRY,
                JAMES ENNIS,
                GEO. A. FOSDICK.

Sur motion de M. Foley, le rapport est adopté.

M. Brott, président du comité des Finances dit, que dans son opinion, l'allocation de $100,000 faite par la Convention, ne devait servir qu'au paiement du millage et du *per diem* des membres, et des employés de la Convention ; c'est pourquoi M. Brott désire que le comité des Dépenses présente son rapport, avant que celui des Finances ne fasse aucun autre rapport.

Le rapport du comité n'est pas prêt.

M. Stocker dit que d'après ses souvenirs, la susdite somme de $100,000 avait été allouée pour couvrir les dépenses casuelles.

La résolution à ce sujet est lue.

Motion de M. Brott, demandant que le comité des Dépenses soit chargé de dresser un état estimatif d'icelles et de préparer un bill à cet égard.

M. Purcell, président du comité des Dépenses, explique que ce comité s'est contenté d'approuver les comptes.

M. Brott dit que sa motion est secondée par M. Beauvais.

Le président déclare qu'elle doit être déposée pendant un jour.

ORDRE SPECIAL DU JOUR.

Rapport du comité sur les Dispositions Générales ; lecture en est donnée, et sur motion de M. Cutler, la seconde et la troisième lecture sont différées jusqu'à ce que les rapports des autres comités aient été examinés.

Lecture du rapport du comité sur les Relations Fédérales.

M. Brott présente le rapport de la minorité.

M. Balch propose de rejeter ce rapport, et M. Foley demande l'appel nominal.

Sur motion de M. Bell, ce rapport est adopté ; mais, sur l'observation de M. Hills qu'il y avait eu demande d'appel nominal, le président ordonne de le faire, et il en résulte :

Pour l'affirmative :

Messieurs Abell, Balch, Davies, Henderson—4 voix.

Pour la négative :

MM. Ariail, Austin, Bailey, Barrett, Bell, Beauvais, Bofill, Bonzano, Brott, Bromley, Burke, Campbell, T. Cook, J. K. Cook, Crozat, Cutler, Collin, Decker, Dufresne, Duane, Dupaty, Ennis, Fish, Flagg, Flood, Foley, Fosdick, Gastinel, Gaidry, Geier, Goldman, Gorlinski, Harnan, Hart, Healy, Heard, Hills, Hire, Kavanagh, Knobloch, Kugler, Maas, Maurer, Mendiverri, Millspaugh, Montague, E. Murphy, M. W. Murphy, Newell, Normand, O'Conner, J. Payne, Pintado, Poynot, J. Purcell, S. Pursell, Schroeder, Shaw, Smith, Spellicy, Seymour, Stumpf, Stine, Stauffer, Sullivan, Terry, Thorpe, Thomas, Wells, Wilson—70 voix.

En conséquence, la motion Balch est repoussée.

M. Wilson propose que les deux rapports, celui de la majorité et celui de la minorité, du comité des Relations Fédérales, soient mis à l'ordre du jour pour mardi le 3 mai 1864. Adopté.

Sur motion de M. Austin, l'impression du rapport de la minorité est ordonnée.

M. Balch demande l'ajournement indéfini. Rejeté.

M. Stauffer prend la parole sur une question de privilége, et demande qu'ordre soit donné au sergent-d'armes de faire sortir le membre d'Iberville et que la Convention lui inflige la censure.

M. Stocker demande le rejet, et l'appel nominal montre 25 voix affirmatives contre 48 négatives.

Sur appel nominal, afin de s'assurer de la présence d'un quorum, 76 membres répondent à leurs noms.

A la suggestion de M. Hills, M. Stauffer déduit ses raisons pour présenter la résolution et la retire.

M. Balch explique ses raisons pour sa proposition d'ajournement indéfini.

Lecture est faite du substitut de M. Purcell, au rapport des Relations Fédérales, présenté hier.

M. Hills propose de différer d'agir sur ce rapport jusqu'à ce que celui de minorité soit présenté. Adopté.

M. Hills, du comité de l'Instruction Publique, soumet un rapport sur le mémoire de M. A. Vallas.

Sur motion de M. Wilson, l'impression et la mise à l'ordre pour le jour où on s'occupera du dit mémoire, sont ordonnées.

Sur motion, la Convention s'ajourne à vendredi à midi, le 29 courant.

JOHN E. NEELIS,
  Secrétaire.

VENDREDI, 29 Avril 1864.

Le président appelle la Convention à l'ordre à midi. La prière est dite par le Rév. M. Gilbert, et le secrétaire fait l'appel nominal.

Sont présents :

Messrs. Abell, Ariail, Austin, Balch, Bailey, Barrett, Baum, Beauvais, Bell, Bofill, Bonzano, Bromley, Buckley, Burke, Cazabat, Cook J. K., Cook T., Crozat, Collin, Davies, Dufresne, Decker, Dupaty, Edwards, Ennis, Fish, Flagg, Flood, Fosdick, Fuller, Geier, Goldman, Gorlinski, Gruneberg, Gaidry, Healy, Harnan, Hart, Heard, Henderson, Hills, Howell, Kavanagh, Knobloch, Kugler, Maas, Maurer, Mendiverri, Millspaugh, Montamat, Montague, Morris, Murphy E., Murphy M. W., Newell, Normand, O'Conner, Ong, Payne J., Pintado, Poynot, Purcell J., Pursell S., Schroeder, Schnurr, Seymour, Shaw, Smith, Spellicy, Stocker, Stumpf, Stiner, Stauffer, Sullivan, Terry, Thorpe, Thomas, Waters, Wenck, Wells and Wilson—81 membres présents.

Le procès-verbal de la séance de la veille est lu et approuvé.

M. Harnan présente une résolution relative aux membres absents, et aux moyens de prévenir de semblables absences.

M. Montamat demande que l'application du réglement soit suspendue en ce qui regarde cette résolution. La motion est adoptée.

M. Montamat demande ensuite le rejet de la résolution. Le vote divisionnel est demandé. Le rejet est prononcé par 37 voix contre 26.

M. Bell demande à présenter une pétition. Accordé.

Il présente alors une pétition de M. Henry Copeland, demandant une indemnité de services pour avoir rempli les fonctions de sergent-d'armes provisoire pendant les six premières séances de la Convention.

Sur motion de M. Wilson, la pétition est renvoyée devant le comité des Salaires des Officiers et Employés.

M. S. Pursell, président du comité des Dépenses, offre une résolution à l'effet d'allouer vingt-cinq mille piastres pour dépenses éventuelles de cette Convention.

L'application du réglement est suspendue, et la résolution est adoptée.

Le secrétaire donne lecture d'une communication du secrétaire d'Etat, relative à l'élection de Benjamin H. Orr, comme délégué du Dixième District représentatif, et d'un protêt contre la dite élection par T. F. McGuire.

M. Hills demande que le tout soit renvoyé devant le comité de la Vérification des Pouvoirs.

M. Goldman demande qu'on passe à la discussion de sa résolution de la veille, relative aux banques et aux opérations de banque.

Un membre demande le rejet de cette résolution ; sur quoi le vote nominal est demandé et pris.

Ont voté pour le rejet pur et simple :
Messieurs Abell, Austin, Bailey, Barrett, Baum, Beauvais, Bell, Bofill, Bromley, Buckley, Burke, Cook T., Crozat, Dufresne, Edwards, Fish, Flagg, Flood, Fuller, Geier, Healy, Harnan, Henderson, Hire, Kavanagh, Maas, Mendiverri, Montamat, Murphy E., Murphy M W., Howell, Harnan, Poynot, Shaw, Stocker, Spellicy, Stumpf, Terry, Wilson—39.

Votent contre le rejet :
Messieurs Ariail, Bonzano, Cazabat, Cook J. K., Collin, Davies, Duane, Decker, Ennis, Foley, Fosdick, Goldman, Gorlinski, Gruneberg, Gaidry, Hart, Heard, Hills, Howell, Knobloch, Kugler, Maurer, Millspaugh, Montague, Morris, O'Conner, Ong, Payne J., Pintado, Purcell J., Pursell S., Schroeder, Seymour, Smith, Stiner, Stauffer, Sullivan, Thorpe, Thomas, Waters, Wenck, Wells—42.

La motion de rejet n'est pas adoptée.

M. Thomas demande le renvoi de la résolution au comité des Dispositions Générales.

M. Stauffer propose d'amender la motion de M. Thomas en renvoyant la résolution à un comité de cinq, que nommera le président, et qui s'appellera comité des Banques et des Opérations de Banque. Cet amendement est rejeté.

M. Campbell demande qu'on en renvoie la discussion à un jour déterminé. Rejeté.

M. Stocker demande que cette discussion soit mise à l'ordre spécial du jour pour le premier janvier 1865.

M. Davies demande le rejet de cette motion.

Le vote divisionnel est ordonné, et la motion est rejetée par 55 voix contre 10.

M. Hills renouvelle sa motion de renvoyer la résolution devant le comité des Dispositions Générales.

La question est soumise à la Convention, et la motion est adoptée.

M. Foley propose que le nom de M. Howell soit ajouté aux noms des membres du comité des Dispositions Générales, à raison de la maladie du président de ce comité. Cette proposition est déposée provisoirement.

Lecture est donnée de la résolution présentée la veille par M. Gruneberg, à l'effet d'ajourner toute décision et toute action sur le rapport du comité d'Emancipation, jusqu'à ce que les rapports de tous les autres comités permanents aient subi leur seconde lecture. Sur motion de M. Thomas, l'impression de la résolution est ordonnée, et la discussion en est mise à l'ordre du jour pour lundi prochain, 2 mai.

L'ordre spécial du jour est, maintenant, la seconde lecture du rapport du comité du Judiciaire, ensemble avec les amendements de MM. Henderson et Sullivan.

M. Cazabat propose l'ajournement. Rejeté.

M. Stauffer offre un substitut pour les articles 11 et 12. L'impression en est ordonnée.

M. Montamat offre un amendement aux sections 11 et 12. L'impression en est ordonnée.

Motion est faite de fixer la discussion du rapport et des amendements à vendredi prochain, 6 mai 1864. Rejeté.

La troisième lecture est ensuite fixée au vendredi, 6 mai.

M. Cutler demande que les rapports des comités soient discutés dans leur ordre régulier, suivant la classification de la constitution de 1852, et présente une résolution à cet effet.

Motion est faite de reconsidérer le vote fixant à vendredi, 6 mai, la troisième lecture. Cette motion est adoptée.

M. Henderson demande la suspension du réglement afin que le rapport, les amendements et les substituts soient discutés dès à présent.

M. Cutler dit que sa résolution mettrait fin à tous débats ; et, pour favoriser la discussion, il retire sa résolution.

M. S. Pursell demande qu'on discute les amendements de M. Sullivan.

M. Shaw demande qu'on discute le rapport section par section. Adopté.

M. Wilson propose d'ajourner les débats jusqu'à lundi prochain, 2 mai.

Motion est faite de rejeter cette proposition.

La question est mise aux voix. 47 membres votent contre le rejet, et 25 pour le rejet.

La question retourne à la proposition de M. Wilson, d'ajourner le débat jusqu'à lundi prochain.

Le vote divisionnel est ordonné.

Votent pour la proposition 31 membres ; contre, 51.

La proposition est rejetée.

M. Cutler offre alors la résolution suivante :

Résolu, Que la troisième lecture du rapport du comité du Judiciaire, et de tous les amendements et substituts, sera renvoyée jusqu'à ce que la Convention ait statué sur tous les rapports qui, suivant l'ordre des matières adopté par la constitution de 1852, sont les premiers en rang.

Adopté.

M. Stauffer propose d'adopter le premier article du rapport. Adopté.

M. Abell présente un substitut au second article. Reçu et lu.

M. Henderson présente également un substitut au même article. Reçu et lu.

Sur motion de M. Sullivan, la Convention s'ajourne.

Procès-verbal adopté.

JOHN E. NEELIS,
Secrétaire.

SAMEDI, le 30 avril 1864.

Le président appelle la Convention à l'ordre à midi.

Après la prière dite par le Rév. Gilbert, le secrétaire fait l'appel du rôle.

Sont présents :

Messieurs Abell, Austin, Bailey, Barrett, Baum, Beauvais, Bell, Bofill, Brott, Buckley, Burke, Collin, Cazabat, Cook J. K., Cook T., Crozat, Davies, Decker, Dufresne, Edwards, Ennis, Fish, Flagg, Flood, Foley, Geier, Goldman, Gorlinski, Gruneberg, Gaidry, Healy, Harnan, Hart, Heard, Henderson, Hills, Hire, Kavanagh, Knobloch, Kugler, Maas, Mann, Maurer, Mendiverri, Millspaugh, Montamat Montague. E. Murphy, M. W. Murphy, Newell, Normand, O'Conner, Pintado, Poynot, J. Purcell, Schroeder, Schnurr, Seymour, Shaw, Smith, Stumpf, Stiner, Stauffer, Sullivan, Terry, Thomas, Waters, Wilson, Wells—69 membres.

Le nombre de membres n'étant pas suffisant pour former un quorum, le président donne ordre au sergent d'armes d'aller à la recherche des absents.

L'entrée de MM. Bromley, Campbell, Cutler, Duane, Howell et Wenck complète le nombre nécessaire.

Le président annonce que la Convention est en quorum.

Lecture du procès-verbal d'hier, lequel est approuvé.

M. Thomas présente un préambule et des résolutions concernant les électeurs présidentiels.

Après dispense du réglement, les résolutions sont adoptées.

Le président nomme membres du comité chargé, en vertu des dites résolutions, de faire un rapport pour proposer la manière de choisir sept électeurs dans cet Etat, pour nommer le président et le vice-président des Etats-Unis à la prochaine élection :

MM. Thomas, président, Cazabat; S. Pursell, Fish et Heard.

M. Campbell présente l'amendement suivant.

Art. —. L'Assemblée Générale n'imposera aucune taxe, soit municipale, soit d'Etat, sur le capital actuellement employé dans les industries suivantes : toutes manufactures de drap, de cuir et aussi de souliers; pourvu que ces manufactures de souliers emploient au moins vingt ouvriers.

L'Assemblée Générale pourra cependant exempter d'impôt telles autres industries qu'elle jugera convenable : et cette exemption durera dix ans à compter de son établissement.

Mr. Stiner propose :

Art. —. Nulle maison de jeu dans cet Etat ne recevra de licence.

Sur motion de M. Hills, les deux propositions précédentes sont référées au comité sur les dispositions générales.

M. Gorlinski annonce, au nom du comité des Améliorations Intérieures, qu'il présentera son rapport lundi.

M. Millspaugh annonce que la résolution allouant $25,000 pour les dépenses casuelles de la Convention est correctement enrôlée.

M. J. Purcell, au nom du comité des Impressions, présente un rapport écrit.

M. Gastinel propose d'imprimer le rapport et de le mettre à l'ordre du jour de vendredi prochain, le 5 mai.

L'appel nominal est fait sur cette question et il en résulte :

60 voix affirmatives, savoir :

Messieurs Ariail, Austin, Bailey, Barrett, Beauvais, Bonzano, Bromley, Burke-Campbell, T. Cook, Cutler, Davies, Dufresne, Edwards, Ennis, Flagg, Foley, Fosdick, Gastinel, Gaidry, Geier, Goldman, Gorlinski, Gruneberg, Harnan, Hart, Heard, Henderson, Hills, Hire, Howell, Knobloch, Kugler, Maas, Mann, Maurer, Millspaugh, Montague, Morris, E. Murphy, M. W. Murphy, Newell,

ET L'AMENDEMENT DE LA CONSTITUTION DE LA LOUISIANE.

Normand, O'Conner, Ong, Pintado, Purcell J., Pursell S., Schroeder, Schnurr, Seymour, Smith, Stumpf, Stiner, Stauffer, Sullivan, Terry, Thorpe, Waters, Wenck—60.

16 voix négatives, savoir :

Messieurs Abell, Baum, Bell, Bofill, Buckley, Collin, J. K. Cook, Crozat, Decker, Duane, Flood, Montamat, Poynot, Stocker, Thomas, Wilson—16.

En conséquence la motion est adoptée.

M. Wilson, membre du comité des Voies de Fait, annonce qu'il présentera son rap-rapport jeudi prochain.

Les autres comités ont annoncé que leurs rapports étaient en voie de progrès.

M. Foley appelle à l'ordre sa résolution relative à la nomination de M. Howell, comme membre du comité des Dispositions Générales. Adopté.

Sur motion de M. Abell, la discussion sur le rapport du comité Judiciaire, ainsi que sur les amendements y-relatifs, est renvoyée jusqu'à ce que ce que les rapports des comités qui précèdent le Judiciaire aient subi l'action de la Convention.

Le rapport du comité de l'Instruction Publique est à l'ordre du jour ; en conséquence lecture en est ordonnée, ainsi que des substituts Purcell et Hart.

Messieurs Sullivan, Stauffer, Davies, Gruneberg et Bonzano présentent des amendements à différentes sections du rapport, mais sur motion de M. Heard, le rapport est discuté section par section, et les amendements sont retirés afin d'être présentés à la section dont ils traitent.

Après lecture de l'article 1 du rapport, M. Davies présente un amendement à l'effet de supprimer toute la clause abolissant les fonctions de surintendant de l'instruction publique.

Sur motion de rejet, il y a appel nominal, et il en résulte 41 voix affirmatives contre 39 négatives, savoir :

Dans l'affirmative :

Messieurs Baum, Austin, Balch, Barrett, Baum, Bell, Buckley, Campbell, Cazabat, J. K. Cook, T. Cook, Cutler, Decker, Duane, Dufresne, Edwards. Fosdick, Gorlinski, Harnan, Hart, Healy, Heard, Henderson, Hills, Howell, Maurer, Montamat, Montague, M. W. Murphy, Newell, Normand, O'Conner, Ong, Poynot, Smith, Spellicy, Sullivan, Terry, Thorpe, Wells, Wilson—41.

Dans la négative :

Messieurs Bailey, Beauvais, Bofill, Bonzano, Bromley, Burke, Crozat, Davies, Ennis, Fish. Flagg, Flood. Foley, Gastinel, Gaidry, Geier, Goldman, Gruneberg, Hire, Knobloch, Kugler, Maas, Mann, Mendiverri, Millspaugh, Morris, E. Murphy, J. Purcell. S. Pursell, Schroeder, Schnurr, Seymour, Stocker, Stumpf, Stiner, Stauffer, Thomas, Waters, Wenck—39.

M. Purcell présente le substitut suivant :

Il sera élu un surintendant de l'instruction publique ; il restera en fonctions pendant quatre années. L'Assemblée Générale déterminera la nature de ses devoirs et le traitement attaché à ses fonctions.

Sur la motion d'adopter le substitut, il y a appel nominal, savoir :

Dans l'affirmative :

Messieurs Abell, Bailey, Barrett, Beauvais, Bell, Bromley, Burke, Campbell, Collin, Cutler, Davies, Duane, Ennis, Flagg, Foley, Gastinel, Gaidry, Geier, Goldman, Healy, Hire, Knobloch, Maas, Mann, Maurer, Mendiverri, Millspaugh, Morris, Murphy E., Normand, Ong, Pursell S., Schroeder, Shaw, Spellicy, Stocker. Stumpf, Stiner, Stauffer, Terry, Thorpe, Thomas. Wenck—43.

Dans la négative :

Messieurs Ariail. Austin, Buckley. Cazabat. Cook J. K., Cook T., Decker, Dufresne, Dupaty, Flood, Fosdick, Gorlinski. Gruneberg, Harnan, Hart, Heard, Henderson, Hills, Howell, Kugler, Montamat, Montague, Murphy M. W., Newell, O'Conner, Pintado, Poynot, Schnurr. Sullivan, Waters, Wilson—31.

Le vote n'indiquant pas un quorum, on procède à un appel nominal, et il en résulte que le nombre de membres présents n'est pas suffisant, et en conséquencce, sur motion, la Convention s'ajourne à lundi prochain, à midi.

JOHN E. NEELIS,
Secrétaire.

Lundi, le 2 mai 1864.

La Convention se réunit à midi, et à l'appel du rôle répondent les membres suivants :

Messieurs Abell, Ariail, Austin, Barrett, Bell, Bofill, Bonzano, Bromley, Brott, Burke, Campbell, J. K. Cook, Crozat, Davies, Dufresne, Duane, Duke, Edwards, Ennis, Fish, Flagg, Flood. Foley, Fosdick, Gastinel, Geier, Gorlinski, Gaidry, Healy, Harnan, Hart, Heard, Henderson, Hills, Hire, Kavanagh, Kugler, Maas, Mann, Millspaugh, Montamat, Montague, M. W. Murphy, Normand, O'Conner, Ong, Payne J., Pintado, Poynot, J. Purcell, S. Pursell, Schroeder,

Schnurr, Seymour, Smith, Spellicy, Stocker, Stumpf, Stiner. Stauffer, Sullivan, Terry, Thomas, Waters, Wells et Wilson— 66 membres présents.

Le nombre n'étant pas suffisant pour un quorum, le sergent-d'armes reçoit l'ordre d'aller à la recherche des absents.

L'entrée de MM. Cutler, Baum, Mendiverri, Buckley, Collin, Cook, Thorpe, Beauvais, Wenck et Cazabat complète le nombre de membres présents pour un quorum.

Le procès-verbal, après lecture, est approuvé.

M. Terry propose la résolution suivante :

Attendu, Que plusieurs personnes qui ne jouissent point de la qualité de citoyen de cet Etat, ou qui n'en n'ont pas rempli les conditions, telles que la prestation du serment prescrit par la proclamation du 8 décembre 1863, occupent des offices, soit de municipalité soit d'Etat.

En conséquence :

La Convention décrète, Toute personne qui occupe des offices, soit de municipalité, soit d'Etat, sans jouir de la qualité de citoyen de l'Etat ou sans avoir prêté le serment prescrit par la proclamation du président, en date du 8 decembre 1863, doit, dans l'opinion de cette Convention, être destituée immédiatement par qui de droit. Le gouverneur de l'Etat et le maire de cette ville, sont invités à tenir la main à l'exécution de la présente résolution.

Après dispense de règlement, une motion de rejet est repoussée.

La question d'adopter cette résolution se présentant de nouveau, il y a appel nominal, ainsi que suit :

Affirmative :

Messieurs Baily, Bell, Bofill, Bonzano, Bromley, Campbell, Cazabat, J. K. Cook, T. Cook, Crozat, Collin, Duke, Davies, Duane, Durfresne, Ennis, Fish, Flagg, Flood, Foley, Geier, Gorlinski, Gaidry, Healy, Harnan, Hart, Henderson, Hills, Hire, Kavanagh, Maas, Millspaugh, E. Murphy, Newell, Normand, O'Conner, J. Payne, Poynot, J. Purceil, S. Pursell, Schroeder, Seymour, Shaw, Smith, Spellicy, Stocker, Stumpf, Stiner, Stauffer, Sullivan, Terry, Thorpe, Waters, Wenck, Wells et Wilson —56.

Négative :

Messieurs Abell, Austin, Barrett, Baum, Beauvais, Brott, Buckley, Burke, Cutler, Fuller, Gastinel, Heard, Kugler, Mann, Mendiverri, Montamat, Montague, M. W. Murphy, Ong, Schnurr and Thomas— 21.

En conséquence la résolution est adoptée.

La demande de reconsidération de ce vote faite par M. Henderson est refusée.

M. Bromley présente les résolutions suivantes :

La Convention décrète, A l'avenir, les séances de cette Convention ne dureront pas moins de quatre heures.

La Convention décrète. La rétribution quoitidienne des conventionnels cessera d'être payée à dater du quarantième jour après l'organisation de cette Convention.

Après dispense du règlement, sur motinode M. Montamat, les résolutions précédentes sont rejetées.

M. Montamat, au nom du comité de la Vérification des Pouvoirs, annonce que M. T. F McGuire demande la permission de retirer sa protestation contre l'élection de M. Orr. Accordé ; et sur ce, M. Montamat présente le rapport suivant :

M. le Président et MM. les membres de la Convention :

Messieurs -Votre comité de la Vérification des Pouvoirs, après interrogatoire de tous les témoins présenté par M. T. F. McGuire, contestant l'élection de M. Orr, comme délégué du 10e District Représentatif, demande la permission de vous annoncer que M. Orr a été dûment élu délégué pour représenter le 10e District Représentatif de la ville de la Nouvelle-Orléans ; qu'il possède toutes les qualités requises et qu'il a droit à un siège dans cette Convention.

John P. Montamat,
Président.

Après acceptation de ce rapport, M. Orr prend possession de son siège.

M. Henderson demande et obtient un congé, pour M. Montague.

Le président porte à la connaissance de la Convention une missive du secrétaire d'Etat, renfermant les rapports concernant la dernière élection tenue dans la paroisse Jefferson, pour pourvoir au remplacement de M. C. Roselius, démissionnaire.

Référé au comité de Vérification.

Les résolutions suivantes étant à l'ordre du jour sont appelées :

Attendu, Que la Convention constitutionnelle a été convoquée principalement dans le but de s'occuper de la question d'abolition de l'esclavage en Louisiane ; *Attendu,* que l'adoption de cette mesure, de quelque manière et sous quelque forme que ce soit, nécessitera de grandes modifications dans toutes les parties de la loi organique de l'Etat ; *Attendu,* que pour ces diverses raisons, cette Convention ne peut et ne devrait en venir à une solution définitive des rapports d'aucun des comités permanents sur les amendements à la constitution, avant le vote de la question d'émancipation ; *Et Attendu de plus,* que les points que soulève la question d'émancipation sont les plus importants de tous, et exigent de cette Assemblée une longue et profonde disscusion ; en conséquence, cette Convention prendra d'abord en considération les rapports de tous les comités permanents sur les amendements à la constitution, y compris les sous-amendements et substituts, à l'exception du Rapport du comité d'Emancipation, et ne les poussera que jusqu'à leur seconde lecture, et alors s'occupera du Rapport sur l'Emancipation et le discutera en plein, jusqu'à clôture parfaite de toute action à son sujet ; après quoi tous les autres rapports des comités permanents subiront leur troisième lecture et leur vote final ; de plus, cette Convention ne s'ajournera que de jour à jour, sans intervalle, jusqu'à ce que tous les rapports des comités permanents, à l'exception de celui du comité d'Emancipation, aient subi en tous points leur seconde lecture.

Sur motion de M. Wilson, la proposition ci-dessus est adoptée.

La Convention reprend en considération les affaires non-terminées qui l'ont occupée samedi passé, savoir : la seconde lecture du rapport du comité de l'Instruction Publique.

M. Purcell propose l'adoption du substitut suivant au premier article de ce rapport :

Un surintendant de l'Instruction Publique sera élu ; il restera en fonctions pendant quatre années ; l'Assemblée Générale déterminera ses devoirs et le traitement attaché à ses fonctions.

L'appel nominal, sur cette question d'adoption, donne pour résultat :

Affirmative :

Messieurs Abell, Bailey, Barrett, Beauvais, Bell, Bennie, Bonzano, Bromley, Brott, Buckley, Burke, Campbell, Collin, Crozat, Cutler, Davies, Duane, Dufresne, Duke, Ennis, Fish, Flagg, Flood, Foley, Fuller, Gastinel, Gaidry, Geier, Gruneberg, Heard, Hire, Kugler, Maas, Mann, Mendiverri, Millspaugh, Montague, E. Murphy, Normand, Ong, Orr, J. Payne, Pintado, J. Purcell S. Pursell, Schroeder, Seymour, Shaw, Stocker, Stumpf, Stiner, Stauffer, Terry, Thomas, Wenck—55.

Négative :

Messieurs Ariail, Austin, Cazabat, J. K. Cook, T. Cook, Edwards, Gorlinski, Harnan, Hart, Healy, Hills, M. W. Murphy, Newell, O'Conner, Poynot, Schnurr, Spellicy, Sullivan, Thorpe, Waters, Wells, Wilson—22.

Le substitut est donc adopté.

M. Sullivan propose le substitut suivant à la seconde section du rapport, savoir :

L'Assemblée Générale établira des écoles publiques gratuites partout l'Etat, ouvertes aux enfants libres de race blanche ; elle pourvoira à leurs dépenses par le mode de contribution générale ou par tout autre ; et les fonds seront répartis entre les différentes paroisses, proportionnellement au nombre d'enfants de race blanche compris dans certaines limites d'âge que prescrira l'Assemblée Générale.

La motion de rejet est refusée ; sur ce s'élève une longue discussion, au milieu de laquelle la Convention s'ajourne.

JOHN E. NEELIS,
Secrétaire.

MARDI, 3 mai 1864.

La Convention est appelée à l'ordre par le président, à midi. La prière est dite par le Rév. M. Horton, et le rôle est appelé par le secrétaire.

Sont présents :

Messieurs Abell, Barrett, Bennie, Bofill, Bonzano, Bromley, Buckley, Burke, Collin, J. K. Cook, Crozat, Davies, Decker, Duane, Dufresne, Duke, Edwards, Ennis, Foley, Fosdick, Fuller, Geier, Goldman, Healy, Heard, Henderson, Hills, Howes, Kavanagh, Maas, Mann, Hillspaugh, M. W. Murphy, Newell, Normand, O'Conner, J. Payne, T. J. Paine, Pintado, Poynot, S. Pursell, Schroeder, Schnurr, Stumpf, Terry, Thomas, Wells, Wilson et M. le President—50 membres.

Attendu qu'il n'y a pas quorum, le sergent-d'armes est requis d'amener les membres absents.

Messieurs Ariail, Balch, Baum, Beauvais, Bell, Campbell, T. Cook, Dupaty, Fish, Flagg, Gastinel, Gaidry, Harnan, Hart, Hire, Kugler, Mendiverri, Montamat, E. Murphy, Ong, Orr, Smith, Stiner, Stauffer, Sullivan, Thorpe et Waters, ayant pris leurs siéges, le président déclare qu'il y a quorum.

Le procès-verbal de la séance précédente est lu et adopté.

M. Sullivan offre la résolution suivante, qui reste déposée conformément au réglement :

Résolu, Que les greffiers, officiers et employés de cette Convention sont dispensés, pendant la durée des travaux de la Convention, de faire partie du juri dans les diverses cours de cette paroisse.

M. Montamat offre la résolution suivante :
Résolu, Que la résolution adoptée par la Convention, et fixant à midi l'heure de ses réunions, est et demeure rappelée.

Résolu en outre, Qu'à l'avenir la Convention se réunira à 11 heures du matin.

M. Fosdick propose de suspendre l'application du réglement à propos de cette résolution. Rejeté.

M. Fosdick, président du comité du Législatif, soumet un rapport écrit.

M. Hills propose que le rapport soit accepté, et mis à l'ordre du jour pour mardi de la semaine prochaine.

M. Stauffer demande que le rapport soit déposé, pour prendre son tour régulier, ce qui est accepté, et la résolution de M. Hills ainsi amendée, est adoptée.

M. Montamat, président du comité de la Vérification des Pouvoirs, soumet un rapport favorable au sujet de l'élection de M. John A. Meyer. Ce rapport est adopté, et M. Meyer est, en conséquence, invité à prendre son siége dans la Convention.

M. M. W. Murphy, président du comité des Salaires des Officiers et Employés de la Convention, rapporte que M. Copeland demande à retirer sa pétition, précèdemment renvoyée devant ce comité.

Le rapport est accueilli, et la demande faite par M. Copeland lui est octroyée.

Il est passé à une seconde lecture du rapport du comité de l'Instruction Publique, comme faisant partie des affaires non-terminées, et ce rapport donne lieu à de longs débats.

M. Hire propose que la Convention s'ajourne à 6 heures, ce soir ; mais la motion est rejetée, et la Convention s'ajourne à demain à midi.

Procès-verbal adopté.

JOHN E. NEELIS,
Secrétaire.

MERCREDI, le 4 mai 1864.

La Convention est appelée à l'ordre par le président.

Le Rév. Andrews dit la prière.

A l'appel du rôle les membres suivants répondent à leurs noms :

Messrs. Abell, Ariail, Austin, Balch, Barrett, Bell, Bennie, Bofill, Bonzano, Bromley, Buckley, Burke, Campbell, Collin, Cook J. K., Cook T., Crozat, Davies, Decker, Duane, Dufresne, Duke, Dupaty, Edwards, Ennis, Flood, Fosdick, Geier, Goldman, Gorlinski, Gruneberg, Gaidry, Healy, Hart, Heard, Henderson, Hills, Hire, Howes, Knobloch, Kugler, Maas, Mann, Maurer, Mayer, Millspaugh, Montamat, Murphy M. W., Newell, Normand, Ong, Orr, Payne J., Pintado, Poynot, Purcell J., Pursell S., Schroeder, Schnurr, Seymour, Shaw, Smith, Spellicy, Stumpf, Stiner, Stauffer, Sullivan, Terry, Thorpe, Waters, Wells, Wilson—72.

L'entrée de MM. Fish, Flagg, Foley, Montamat et E. Murphy complète le nombre suffisant pour un quorum.

Après lecture, le procès-verbal des délibérations d'hier est approuvé.

M. Stauffer présente les résolutions suivantes :

La Convention décrète, Les articles suivants seront imprimés et inclus dans la motion à l'effet d'amender le rapport du comité des Dispositions Générales.

Art. —. Toute personne qui actuellement occupe, ou à l'avenir occupera des fonctions civiles ou militaires sous l'autorité des Etats soi-disant Confédérés ou sous l'autorité de toute organisation opposée et hostile aux Etats-Unis, ne sera éligible à aucune fonction d'honneur, de confiance ou de profit, dans cet Etat.

Art. —. Ne sera reconnue ou payée aucune dette créée par les Etats soi-disant Confédérés ou par tout pouvoir usurpateur.

Déposé.

APPEL DES RAPPORTS DES COMITES.

M. Shaw, du comité sur la Mise à Exécution de la constitution, annonce que son rapport s'achève.

M. Wilson annonce qu'il présentera demain son rapport sur les voies de fait sur la personne des conventionnels.

Aucun autre rapport ne se présentant, M. Sullivan demande la discussion de sa résolution de la veille, à l'effet d'exempter les officiers et employés de cette Convention de service comme jurés pendant la session de cette Convention. Adopté.

M. Bonzano demande la discussion du Rapport sur l'Emancipation. Déclaré n'être pas à l'ordre.

M. Thorpe demande dispense du réglement afin de passer à l'ordre du jour, c'est-à-dire au Rapport sur l'Emancipation.

ET L'AMENDEMENT DE LA CONSTITUTION DE LA LOUISIANE.

Sur cette motion, l'appel nominal donne pour résultat 54 voix affirmatives contre 26 négatives, ainsi que suit :

Dans l'affirmativee :

Messieurs Austin, Bell, Bennie, Bonzano, Bromley, Brott, Buckley, Burke, Collin, Cook J. K., Cook. T., Davies, Duane, Duke, Edwards, Ennis, Fish, Flagg, Flood, Foley, Fosdick, Gastinel, Geire, Goldman, Gorlinski, Gaidry, Healy, Hart, Henderson, Hills, Hire, Howes, Kugler, Maas, Mann. Millspaugh, Murphy E., Newell, Normand, Pintado, Poynot, Purcell J., Pursell S., Schroeder, Schnurr, Shaw, Smith, Spellicy, Stiner, Stauffer, Terry, Thorpe, Thomas, Wilson—54.

Dans la négative :

Messieurs Abell, Balch, Bailey, Barrett, Bofill, Campbell, Crozat, Decker, Dufresne, Dupaty, Gruneberg, Heard, Knobloch, Maurer, Mayer, Mendiverri, Montamat, Murphy M. W., O'Conner, Ong, Orr, Seymour, Stumpf, Sullivan, Waters, Wells—26.

Sur quoi, le président déclare dispense du réglement, et la discussion sur le Rapport touchant l'Emancipation commence.

M. Abell demande que cette discussion soit mise à l'ordre du jour pour lundi prochain.

Rejeté.

M. Hills propose de terminer définitivement la discussion sur la question d'Emancipation, avant de passer à toute autre question. Accepté.

M. Bonzano demande la lecture du rapport, sur quoi M. Montamat demande la lecture du rapport de la minorité, en vertu du réglement qui lui assure la préférence.

Le secrétaire en donne lecture.

M. Foley propose de rejeter ce rapport, sur quoi l'appel nominal donne le résultat suivant :

Affirmative, 35 voix, savoir :

Messieurs Bell, Bennie, Bromley, Burke, Collin, Cook J. K., Davies, Duane, Dupaty, Fish, Flagg, Flood, Foley, Fosdick, Geier, Goldman, Gorlinski, Gaidry, Healy, Hills, Hire, Knobloch, Maas, Morris, Newell, Normand, Pintado, Pursell S., Schroeder, Schnurr, Shaw, Smith, Stauffer, Terry, Thorpe—35.

Dans la négative :

Messieurs Abell, Balch, Bailey, Barrett, Beauvais, Bofill, Bonzano, Brott, Buckley, Campbell, Cazabat, Cook T., Crozat, Cutler, Decker, Dufresne, Duke, Edwards, Ennis, Gastinel, Heard, Henderson, Howes, Kugler, Maurer, Mayer, Mendiverri, Mills, paugh, Montamat, Murphy E., Murphy M. W., O'Conner, Ong, Orr, Purcell J., Poynot, Seymour, Spellicy, Stocker, Stumpf, Stiner, Sullivan, Thomas, Waters, Wenck, Wells and Wilson—47.

M. Henderson propose de rejeter le rapport de la minorité.

M. Bonzano propose de renvoyer la question à lundi.

M. le président déclare qu'il doit y avoir dispense du réglement avant que cette question puisse être posée.

M. Stocker propose, en conséquence, la dispense du réglement à cet effet.

L'appel étant fait, faute de quorum prétendu, il en résulte 44 voix négatives contre 41 voix affirmatives, savoir :

Dans l'affirmative :

Messieurs Abell, Austin, Balch, Bailey, Barrett, Bell, Bofill, Bonzano, Buckley, Campbell, Cook T., Crozat, Decker, Dufresne, Duke, Edwards, Fosdick, Gastinel, Healy, Heard, Maurer, Mendiverri, Millspaugh, Montamat, Murphy M. W., Murphy E., Normand, O'Conner, Ong, Orr, Poynot, Schroeder, Seymour, Spellicy, Smith, Stocker, Stumpf, Stiner, Sullivan, Waters, Wenck—41.

Dans la négative :

Messieurs Ariail, Beauvais, Bennie, Bromley, Brott, Burke, Collin, Cazabat, Cook J. K., Cutler, Davies, Duane, Ennis, Fish, Flagg, Flood, Foley, Geier, Goldman, Gorlinski, Gaidry, Hart, Henderson, Hills, Hire, Howes, Kavanagh, Knobloch, Kugler, Maas, Mann, Mayer, Morris, Newell, Pintado, Purcell J., Pursell S., Schnurr, Shaw, Stauffer, Terry, Thorpe, Wells, Wilson—44.

La motion de dispense est rejetée.

Après une longue discussion, la motion d'ajourner est rejetée.

M. Hills ayant parlé le dernier, le président le rappelle à l'ordre à cause de l'expiration du délai accordé à chaque orateur ; et sur motion d'étendre ce délai, M. Hills remercie l'Assemblée de sa courtoisie, et annonce qu'il ne saurait continuer aujourd'hui la discussion.

Sur motion de M. Austin, la Convention s'ajourne jusqu'à demain à midi.

JOHN E. NEELIS,
Secrétaire.

JEUDI, 5 mai, 1864.

A midi, le président appelle la Convention à l'ordre.

Le rôle est appelé. Sont présents :

MM. Abell, Ariail, Austin, Bailey, Barrett, Baum, Beauvais, Bell, Bofill, Bonzano, Bromley, Buckley, Burke, Campbell, J. K. Cook, T. Cook, Crozat, Davies, Decker, Duane, Dufresne, Duke, Edwards, Ennis, Fish, Flagg, Flood, Foley, Fosdick, Gastinel, Goldman, Geier, Gorlinski, Gruneberg, Gaidry, Healy, Hart, Heard, Hills, Howes, Kavanagh, Kugler, Knobloch, Maas, Mann, Maurer Mayer, Mendiverri, Millspaugh, Montamat, E. murphy, M. W, Murphy, Newell, Normand, O'Conner, Orr, J. Payne, Pintado, Poynot, J. Purcell, S. Pursell, Schroeder, Schnurr, Seymour, Shaw, Smith, Spellicy, Stumpf, Stiner, Stocker, Stauffer, Sullivan, Terry, Thorpe, Waters, Wells, Wilson—77.

Le journal de la veille est lu et approuvé.

Pas de rapport des comités.

M. Terry offre le préambule et la résolution qui suivent :

Attendu, Que dans le cours de l'année dernière, des dons considérables en argent ont été faits à cet Etat, pour être employés à aider à la formation d'un gouvernement d'Etat libre en Louisiane, et qu'il est temps aujourd'hui que cet argent soit employé selon l'intention patriotique des donateurs; *Et attendu*, que cette Convention est informée que les sommes dont il s'agit sont entre les mains du soi-disant "comité Général pour la formation d'un Etat libre," du quel Thos. J. Durand est le président, James Graham le secrétaire, et Edward Heath le trésorier;

Il est résolu, Que l'Auditeur et le Trésorier de l'Etat sont invités à faire connaître à cette Assemblée si les dites sommes ont été versées au Trésor de l'Etat, pour être employées selon les vues des souscripteurs ; et que dans le cas contraire, les dits auditeur et trésorier sont autorisés à réclamer de Messieurs Thomas J. Durand, James Graham et Edward Heath, et des officiers du comité plus haut mentionné, la remise des dites sommes, ou une note exacte de l'emploi qu'ils en ont pu faire ; et que les dits auditeur et trésorier sont invités à faire telles enquêtes et investigations qu'ils jugeront nécessaires, et en feront leur rapport à la Convention.

Déposé pendant un jour, suivant le réglement.

M. Bell offre la résolution suivante :

Résolu, Que la Convention offre ses remerciements au Capitaine Stephen Hoyt, de l'armée des Etats-Unis, faisant les fonctions de Maire de la ville, et à G. W. R. Bailey, Voyer de la ville, pour l'attention qu'ils ont eue de préparer cette salle pour la Convention, et qu'elle leur offre en même temps ses félicitations pour l'habileté et le goût dont ils ont fait preuve.

M. Stauffer demande la discussion de la résolution de la veille, laquelle, sur motion de M. Hills, est renvoyée devant le comité des Dispositions Générales.

M. Abell offre la résolution suivante :

Résolu, Que le sergent d'armes est requis de s'assurer des motifs de l'absence de l'Hon. R. K. Howell, du Septième District représentatif.

M. Hills propose d'amender cette résolution de façon à ce qu'elle s'applique à tous les membres absents.

Le réglement est suspendu, et la résolution passe ainsi amendée.

M. Campbell offre la résolution suivante :

Résolu, Qu'il ne sera pris aucun vote sur la question d'émancipation, tant que tous les membres de la Convention ne seront pas présents.

Cette résolution est déposée pour un jour, suivant le réglement. On passe aux affaires non terminées.

M. Brott offre un amendement à la section 6e du rapport de la minorité du comité d'émancipation.

M. Sullivan propose l'ajournement. Rejeté.

M. Abell prend alors la parole et termine son argumentation en concluant à l'adoption du rapport de la minorité.

M. Cazabat lui succède, et demande à exprimer ses vues sur le sujet, se réservant le privilége de reprendre son argumentation plus tard.

M. Cazabat ayant parlé pendant le temps accordé par les réglements, la Convention s'ajourne.

Procès-verbal adopté.

JOHN E. NEELIS,
Secrétaire.

VENDREDI, 6 mai 1864.

La Convention est appelée à l'ordre par le président, conformément à l'ajournement.

La prière est dite par le Rév. M. Strong, et il est procédé à l'appel nominal.

Sont présents :

Messieurs Ariail, Balch, Bailey, Beauvais, Bofil, Bromley, Burke, Campbell, Collin, J. K. Cook, T. Cook, Crozat, Decker, Dufresne, Duke, Dupaty, Edwards, Ennis, Fish, Flagg, Flood, Geier, Goldman, Gorlinski, Gruneberg, Gaidry, Healy, Hart, Heard, Henderson, Hills, Hire,

Howes, Kavanagh, Kugler, Maas, Mann, Maurer, Mayer, Millspaugh, Montamat, Normand, Orr, Pintado, Poynot, Schroeder, Schnurr, Seymour, Shaw, Smith, Spellicy, Stumpf, Stiner, Stauffer, Sullivan, Taliaferro, Terry, Thorpe, Waters, Wells, Wilson et M. le Président—63.

Attendu qu'il n'y a pas de quorum, le sergent-d'armes est requis d'amener les membres absents.

MM. Austin, Bell, Bonzano, Davies, Foley, Fosdick, Fuller, Harnan, Knobloch, Morris, J. Payne, J. T. Payne, J. Purcell, S. Pursell et Stocker ayant pris leurs sièges, le président annonce qu'il y a quorum.

Le journal de la veille est lu et approuvé.

M. Thorpe, comme président du comité d'Enrôlement, rapporte la résolution suivante :

Résolu, Que l'imprimeur de la Convention est requis d'imprimer deux mille exemplaires du journal, moitié de ce nombre en langue française, et l'autre moitié en langue anglaise.

M. Wilson propose de porter, par amendement, le nombre des exemplaires à deux mille dans chaque langue.

Non décidé.

M. Montamat propose de porter le nombre à trois mille.

L'amendement de M. Montamat est mis aux voix et rejeté.

La résolution est ensuite adoptée, telle qu'elle a été présentée par le comité.

Pas de rapports de comités.

M. Wilson, président du comité nommé pour faire une enquête et un rapport sur l'assaut commis contre deux membres de la Convention, rapporte que par suite d'un malentendu causé par la résolution présentée par M. Henderson, le comité n'est pas en état de produire son rapport en ce moment.

Le président communique à la Convention la démission de M. Howell, laquelle est lue par le secrétaire.

M. Henderson propose d'accepter cette démission ; il propose en outre que le gouverneur soit dûment informé de la vacance de son siège.

Sur cette motion, le vote divisionnel est demandé.

Pour la motion, 55 voix ; contre, 22

M. Campbell appelle la discussion de la résolution de la veille, tendant à ce qu'il ne soit pris aucun vote sur la question d'émancipation que lorsque tous les membres seront présents.

M. Foley demande demande le rejet de cette résolution.

Sur cette motion, le vote divisionnel est demandé.

Pour la motion, 45 voix ; contre, 23.

M. Foley demande la reconsidération du vote sur l'acceptation de la démission de M. Howell.

M. Henderson demande le rejet de cette motion. La motion est rejetée.

L'affaire non terminée de la veille (le Rapport du comité d'Emancipation,) est appelée, et la discussion reprise.

M. Abell prend la parole, et une demi-heure s'étant écoulée, le président l'appelle à l'ordre.

M. Hills se lève pour un point d'ordre, et constate que la Convention, par son vote de la veille, a accordé à M. Abell le droit de parler librement.

Le président s'étant prononcé pour la négative, M. Hills en appelle à la Convention, et, sur cette question, le vote nominal est ordonné.

Votent dans le sens de M. le président :

MM. Burke, Bell, Collin, Cazabat, Crozat, Cutler, Davies, Ennis, Fish, Flagg, Flood, Foley, Goldman, Gorlinski, Gaidry, Heard, Henderson, Hire, Mann, Morris, Newell, J. Payne, J. Purcell, S. Pursell, Shaw, Schroeder, Schnurr, Stauffer, Thorpe et Wilson—30.

Dans le sens de M. Hills :

MM. Abell, Bailey, Barrett, Beauvais, Bofill, Bonzano, Bromley, Buckley, Campbell, J. K. Cook, T. Cook, Decker, Dufresne, Dupaty, Edwards, Fosdick, Fuller, Gastinel, Geier, Healy, Harnan, Hart, Hills, Kavanagh, Knobloch, Maas, Maurer, Mayer, Mendiverri, Millspaugh, Montamat, Normand, Orr, J. T. Paine, Pintado, Poynot, Seymour, Smith, Spellicy, Stocker, Stumpf, Stiner, Sullivan, Taliaferro, Terry, Thomas et Wells—47.

En conséquence, la décision du président est renversée, et M. Abell continue son argumentation.

Le discours de M. Abell terminé, M. Hills présente la résolution suivante :

Résolu, Que tous les votes sur la question d'émancipation seront pris nominalement, et que le sergent-d'armes sera envoyé à la recherche des membres absents, lesquels seront requis de faire enregistrer leurs votes.

L'appel du rôle étant demandé, 76 membres se trouvent présents, ce qui constitue un quorum.

Une motion d'ajournement est faite et rejetée sur un vote divisionnel, par 47 voix contre 20.

M. Hills demande la suspension du réglement pour l'examen de sa résolution.

M. Henderson objecte et demande la stricte observation de l'article du réglement qui veut un vote des deux tiers pour suspendre le réglement.

Le vote divisionnel est demandé sur la question de suspension, et cette suspension est accordée par 61 voix contre 2.

Revient alors la question de l'adoption de la résolution de M. Hills, et le vote divisionnel étant demandé et ordonné, la résolution est adoptée par 66 voix contre 1.

Le président annonce alors qu'on va voter sur la motion de rejeter le rapport de la minorité du comité d'Emancipation.

Ce vote est recueilli et donne le résultat suivant :

Votent pour le rejet du rapport :

MM. Ariail, Austin, Bailey, Barrett, Baum, Brott, Beauvais, Bell, Bonzano, Bromley, Burke, Cazabat, Collin, J. K. Cook, T. Cook, Crozat, Cutler, Davies, Dupaty, Duane, Edwards, Ennis, Fish, Flagg, Flood, Foley, Fosdick, Fuller, Geier, Goldman, Gaidry, Gorlinski, Healy, Hart, Heard, Henderson, Hills, Hire, Harnan, Howes, Kavanagh, Knobloch, Kugler, Maas, Mann, Morris, Millspaugh, E. Murphy, Newell, Normand, Orr, J. Payne, J. T. Paine, Pintado, Poynot, J. Purcell, S. Pursell, Schroeder, Seymour, Shaw, Smith, Spellicy, Stocker, Stiner, Stauffer, Taliaferro, Terry, Thorpe, Thomas, Wells et Wilson—71.

Contre le rejet :

MM. Abell, Balch, Bofill, Buckley, Campbell, Decker, Dufresne, Duke, Gastinel, Gruneberg, Maurer, Mayer, Mendiverri, Montamat, M. W. Murphy, O'Conner, Stumpf, Sullivan, Waters—19.

En conséquence, le rapport de la minorité est rejeté.

Sur motion, la Convention s'ajourne.

Procès-verbal adopté.

JOHN E. NEELIS,
Secrétaire.

SAMEDI, le 7 Mai 1864.

La Convention se réunit à midi et le président l'appelle à l'ordre.

A l'appel du rôle, les membres suivants répondent à leurs noms :

Messieurs Ariail, Austin, Abell, Balch, Bailey, Barett, Baum, Bell, Bofill, Bonzano, Bromley, Brott, Buckley, Burke, Campbell, Collin, J. K. Cook, Crozat, Davies, Decker, Duane, Dufresne, Duke, Dupaty, Edwards, Ennis, Fish, Flagg, Flood, Foley, Fosdick, Geier, Goldman, Gorlinski, Gruneberg, Healy, Harnan, Hart, Heard, Henderson, Hills, Hire, Howes, Kavanagh, Knobloch, Kugler, Maas, Mann, Maurer, Mayer, Mendiverri, Millspaugh, E. Murphy, M. W. Murphy, Newell, Normand, O'Conner, Orr, J. Payne, J. T. Paine, Pintado, J. Purcell, Poynot, S. Pursell, Schroeder, Seymour, Shaw, Smith, Spellicy, Stumpf, Stiner, Stauffer, Sullivan, Taliaferro, Terry, Thomas, Waters, Wells et Wilson—79 membres présents.

On donne lecture du procès-verbal d'hier, et sur motion de M. Abell on en diffère l'adoption, afin de permettre aux membres absents à la dernière séance de voter *nunc pro tune* sur la motion de rejet du rapport de la minorité du comité d'émancipation ; en conséquence MM. Baum, Brott, Collin, Dupaty, Gorlinski, Harnan, E. Murphy et J. T. Paine (huit voix,) ont voté en faveur du rejet ; et MM, Balch, Bofill, Campbell, Dufresne, Gruneberg et Mendiverri (six voix,) contre.

Le procès-verbal est donc amendé, sur la motion de M. Abell, de manière à inclure les noms des membres susdits parmi ceux des votants d'hier ; puis ce procès-verbal est adopté avec ce dit amendement.

Sur la motion de M. Hills, ordre est donné au sergent-d'armes de rechercher les membres absents qui n'ont pas voté sur la question d'émancipation, afin qu'ils viennent enregistrer leurs votes.

M. Henderson propose dispense du réglement, afin de rescinder la résolution acceptant la démission de M. Howell.

M. Hills propose d'amender par une reprise en considération du vote sur la démission de M. Howell.

Sur la question de dispense du réglement, il résulte 49 voix affirmatives, savoir :

Messieurs Ariail, Bailey, Barrett, Baum, Bell, Bonzano, Bromley, Brott, Burke, Collin, J. K. Cook, T. Cook, Crozat, Duane, Duke, Dupaty, Ennis, Flagg, Flood,

ET L'AMENDEMENT DE LA CONSTITUTION DE LA LOUISIANE.

Foley, Fosdick, Gastinel, Geier, Goldman, Gorlinski, Heard, Henderson, Hills, Hire, Howes, Kavanagh, Maas, Mayer, Mendiveri, Millspaugh, Murphy E., Orr, Poynot, Seymour, Shaw, Smith, Spellicy, Stocker, Stumpf, Stiner, Stauffer, Taliaferro, Terry et Wilson—49.

Contre 26 voix négatives, savoir :

Messieurs Abell, Balch, Bofill, Buckley, Campbell, Davies, Decker, Dufresne, Gruneberg, Healy, Harnan, Hart, Knobloch, Mann, Maurer, Montamat, M. W. Murphy, Normand, O'Conner, Jno. Payne, Payne J. T., Pintado, Purcell Jno, Sam. Pursell, Sullivan et Waters—26.

Ainsi les deux tiers ne se trouvant point en faveur de la dispense, cette motion est rejetée.

M. Bromley présente la résolution suivante, laquelle est rejetée, savoir :

Attendu, Que les citoyens de cet Etat habitant les paroisses de la campagne, sont continuellement dans un état d'alarmes et de panique, qui menace d'une cessation entière de tout travail, à cause de l'abandon simultané qu'ils feront des paroisses non protégées dans la campagne, contre les incursions de guerillas ; en conséquence :

La Convention décrète, Un comité de cinq sera nommé, chargé de se mettre en rapport avec le gouverneur et l'adjudant-général de l'Etat, à l'effet de prendre les mesures nécessaires pour organiser la milice et protéger convenablement notre existence, notre liberté et notre recherche du bonheur.

M. Sam. Pursell présente la résolution suivante :

Art. —. L'impôt sera égal et uniforme dans tout l'Etat. Tous les biens seront imposés proportionnellement à leur valeur, laquelle sera déterminée de la manière indiquée par la loi. L'Assemblée Générale pourra exempter d'impôt les biens actuellement consacrés au service des églises, des écoles ou d'institutions charitables. L'Assemblée Générale devra imposer le revenu de toute personne ayant une profession, un emploi, un commerce ou un métier, et toute personne devra obtenir une *licence* de la manière indiquée par la loi.

Tout impôt sur le revenu sera proportionnel à la somme de revenus ou d'affaires faites.

Art. —. Nul, excepté les citoyens des Etats-Unis ou les personnes ayant déclaré formellement leur intention de le devenir, ne pourra exercer la profession, l'emploi, le métier, ou faire le commerce, qui, d'après les lois de cet Etat, nécessite une *licence.*

Art.—L'Assemblée Générale pourvoiera, par une loi, à l'établissement d'une maison de refuge dans chacune des paroisses de cet Etat, affectée à l'entretien des indigents dans ses limites respectives, et ses maisons de refuges seront dirigées conformément aux dispositions prescrites par la loi.

Art.—.Tous les officiers civils de l'Etat en général devront en être résidents et électeurs ; tous les officiers de paroisse ou de District devront être résidents et électeurs respectivement dans leur paroisse ou District ; et ils tiendront leur bureau aux lieux et places désignés par la loi.

Art.—. La ville de la Nouvelle-Orléans sera le siège du gouvernement. L'Assemblée Générale pourra disposer de la propriété du Capitole actuel à Bâton-Rouge, et procurer par acquisition ou autrement, le terrain et les bâtisses nécessaires à un Capitole d'Etat à la Nouvelle-Orléans.

M. Brott propose que cette Convention s'ajourne indéfiniment le 25 courant à 2 heures après-midi.

M. Hire propose ce qui suit :

Résolu, Après lundi prochain, cette Convention aura une séance du soir, commençant à 6 heures P. M., afin de laisser à tous les membres l'occasion et le temps de parler, sans prolonger la session de la Convention pendant un temps inutile.

M. Millspaugh, du comité d'Enrôlement, annonce comme étant correctement enrôlée la résolution relative à la publication de deux milles exemplaires du journal en Anglais et en Français.

M. Wilson, du comité sur les Voies de Fait sur la personne de certains conventionnels, annonce que son rapport s'achève.

M. Campbell propose que ce comité soit maintenant déchargé.

On passe à l'ordre du jour, mais au préalable, M. Abell propose l'ajournement jusqu'à lundi à midi.

Le vote divisionel sur cette question donne pour résultat 51 voix affirmatives et 31 voix négatives ; en conséquence la proposition est acceptée et la Convention s'ajourne.

Approuvé.

JOHN E. NEELIS,
Secrétaire.

LUNDI, 9 mai 1864.

La Convention s'assemble à midi, et est appelée à l'ordre par le président.

L'appel du rôle est fait par le secrétaire.

Sont présents :

Messieurs Abell, Ariail, Bell, Bonzano,

Buckley, Burke, J. K. Cook, Crozat, Dufresne, Duke, Edwards, Ennis, Fish, Flagg, Geier, Goldman, Gruneberg, Healy, Hart, Heard, Henderson, Hills, Howes, Maas, Mann, Mayer, Millspaugh, M. W. Murphy, Newell, Normand, O'Conner, Ong, Pintado, S. Pursell, Schroeder, Schnurr, Seymour Shaw, Spellicy, Stocker, Stumpf, Stiner, Terry, Thorpe, Waters, Wenck, Wells, Wilson et M. le President—49 membres présents.

Attendu qu'il n'y a pas quorum le président ordonne au sergent-d'armes d'amener les membres absents.

Au bout de quelques instants les membres dont les noms suivent viennent prendre leurs siéges, savoir :

Messieurs Austin, Bailey, Barrett, Bofill, Brott, Campbell, Collin, T. Cook, Davies, Dupaty, Flood, Foley, Fosdick, Fuller, Gastinel, Gorlinski, Harnan, Hire, Maurer, Mendiverri, Montamat, E. Murphy, J. Payne, J. Purcell, Smith, Stauffer, Taliaferro et Thomas—28 membres.

Le président annonce qu'il a quorum.

Le procès-verbal de la veill, est lu et adopté.

RESOLUTIONS.

M. S. Pursell présente la résolution qui suit :

Attendu, Que les billets émis par la ville de la Nouvelle-Orléans étant, à l'exception des billets des Etats-Unis, la seul monnaie courante, parmi celle en circulation dans cette Etat, qui ait droit à la pleine confiance du peuple ; *Et attendu*, que des hommes méchants et mal intentionnés, traitres à leur pays, et sans reconnaissance pour la généreuse magnanimité qui leur permet de vivre paisiblement à l'abri et sous la protection d'un bon gouvernement, ont recours à toutes sortes de moyens pour déprécier les dits billets de la ville de la Novelle-Orléans. Il est en conséquence

Résolu, Que tout établissement ou toute personne qui refusera de recevoir les dits billets de ville, soit en dépôt, soit en paiement, est indigne de la confiance du peuple, et appelle la surveillance des autorités à qui appartient la connaissance de ces matières ;

Résolu, Que cette Convention recommande instamment et exprime le désir que les chefs de départements, soit civils, soit militaires, ayant autorité et pouvoir pour ce faire, suppriment toutes les banques autorisées à fonctionner, qui manqueraient à leurs devoirs en refusant de se conformer aux exigences des temps.

Déposé sur le bureau conformément au règlement.

Sur motion de M. Stocker, l'impression en est ordonnée.

M. S. Pursell offre la résolution suivante :

Attendu, Qu'il est entré dans le plan d'installation de la salle de réunion de la Convention de disposer des siéges pour le public, et qu'une portion de ces siéges a été spécialement réservée pour les dames ; mais, attendu, que ces faits n'ont pas été portés à la connaissance du public. Par ces motifs, il est

Résolu, Que les dames sont, par les présentes, invitées à assister aux séances de la Convention.

Le règlement est suspendu, et la résolution est adoptée.

M. Stumpf présente à son tour la résolution suivante :

Attendu, Que l'objet de cette guerre faite par les Etats-Unis contre les soi-disant Etats Confédérés, est avant tout de maintenir l'Union, d'assurer l'exécution des lois et de soutenir la constitution de ces mêmes Etats-Unis, ainsi que tous les actes du Congrès passés en vertu de la dite constitution ;

Et attendu, qu'en conformant notre conduite à ces vues, nous ne devons pas oublier ces citoyens vraiment loyaux dont, tous les intérêts et toute la fortune reposent uniquement sur cette espèce de propriété que la guerre vient de détruire ou de rendre sans valeur en tant que propriété. Par ces motifs, il est

Résolu, Que tous les citoyens vraiment loyaux de la Louisiane, qui, à l'heure qu'il est, ont prêté le serment d'amnistie prescrit par la proclamation présidentielle du 8 décembre 1863, recevront du Gouvernement des Etats Unis une indemnité raisonnable pour chacun des esclaves assessés en leurs noms, comme propriété, pour l'année 1863.

Déposé selon le règlement.

M. Thorpe, au nom du comité d'enquête sur l'assaut commis contre certains membres, soumet un rapport écrit, lequel est reçu et mis à l'ordre du jour pour mercredi prochain, 11 du courant.

M. Henderson évoque sa résolution tendant à rescinder l'action de l'Assemblée au sujet de l'acceptation de la démission de M. Howell.

Sur l'adoption de la résolution, le vote est pris par *"assis et levés"*; 34 voix pour l'adoption et 40 pour le rejet. Mais attendu qu'il n'y a pas quorum de votants, le vote nominal est ordonné, lequel se traduit comme suit :

ET L'AMENDEMENT DE LA CONSTITUTION DE LA LOUISIANE. 71

Votent pour l'adoption :

Messieurs Ariail, Bailey, Barrett, Bonzano, Brott, Campbell, Cazabat, J. K. Cook, T. Cook, Cutler, Davies, Duane, Dufresne, Duke, Ennis, Fosdick, Fuller, Gastinel, Goldman, Gorlinski, Harnan, Heard, Henderson, Hills, Hire, Howes, Knobloch, Maas, Mann, Mendiverri, Millspaugh, E. Murphy, Normand, Ong, J. Payne, Seymour, Spellicy, Stocker, Stumpf, Stiner, Taliaferro, Thorpe, Waters, Wells et Wilson—45.

Pour le rejet :

Messieurs Abell, Bell, Bofill, Buckley, Burke, Collin, Crozat, Dupaty, Edwards, Flagg, Flood, Geier, Gruneberg, Healy, Hart, Maurer, Montamat, M. W. Murphy, Mayer, Newell, O'Conner, Pintado, J. Purcell, S. Pursell, Schroeder, Schnurr, Stauffer, Sullivan et Terry—29.

En conséquence, la résolution de M. Henderson est adoptée, et le président annonce le fait à l'Assemblée.

M. Montamat constate qu'il n'y a pas eu quorum de votants, et propose l'ajournement, sur quoi le vote divisionnel est demandé et pris.

Pour l'ajournement, 34 voix,—contre, 38.

Attendu qu'il n'y a pas quorum de votants, l'appel du rôle est ordonné, et 75 membres sont trouvés présents, ce qui ne constitue pas encore un quorum.

M. Montamat renouvelle alors sa proposition d'ajournement, et le vote nominal est ordonné sur cette proposition.

Votent pour l'ajournement :

Messieurs Abell, Ariail, Bailey, Bofill, Brott, Buckley, Burke, Collin, Cook J. K., Dufresne, Duke, Dupaty, Flagg, Fuller, Gastinel, Geier, Gruneberg, Harnan, Hart, Heard, Henderson, Howes, Knobloch, Maas, Maurer, Mayer, Mendiverri, Montamat, M. W. Murphy, O'Conner, J. Purcell, Schnurr, Seymour, Spellicy, Sullivan et Waters—36.

Votent contre l'ajournement :

Messieurs Barrett, Bell, Bonzano, Cazabat, T. Cook, Crozat, Cutler, Davies, Duane, Edwards, Ennis, Flood, Fosdick, Goldman, Gorlinski, Healy, Hills, Hire, Mann, Millspaugh, E. Murphy, Newell, Normand, Ong, J. Payne, Pintado, S. Pursell, Schroeder, Shaw, Smith, Stocker, Stumpf, Stiner, Stauffer, Taliaferro, Terry, Thorpe, Wells et Wilson—39.

En conséquence l'ajournement est refusé.

La Convention reprend ses délibérations sur le rapport de la majorité du comité d'émancipation, lequel est lu et ensuite mis en discussion section par section.

M. Wilson propose d'amender la première section en ajoutant à la troisième ligne les mots "et que les propriétaires loyaux recevront une indemnité."

M. Goldman s'oppose à cet amendement et en demande le rejet.

Sur cette demande de rejet le vote nominal est ordonné.

Votent pour le rejet de l'amendement :

Messieurs Ariail, Austin, Bailey, Bonzano, Burke, Collin, Cazabat, J. K. Cook, Cutler, Davies, Duane, Dupaty, Edwards, Ennis, Fish, Flagg, Flood, Foley, Fosdick, Goldman, Gorlinski, Healy, Harnan, Hills, Hire, Howes, Maas, Mann, Millspaugh, Murphy E., Newell, Normand, J. Payne, Pintado, S. Pursell, Schroeder, Schnurr, Shaw, Smith, Spellicy, Stauffer, Taliaferro, Terry, Thorpe, Wells—45.

Votent pour l'adoption de l'amendement :

Messieurs Abell, Barrett, Bell, Bofill, Brott, Buckley, T. Cook, Crozat, Dufresne, Duke, Fuller, Gruneberg, Hart, Heard, Henderson, Knobloch, Maurer, Mayer, Mendiverri, Montamat, M. W. Murphy, O'Conner, Ong, Seymour, Stocker, Stumpf, Stiner, Sullivan, Waters, Wilson—30.

En conséquence, l'amendement est rejeté.

M. Montamat propose l'ajournement, sur quoi le vote nominal est ordonné.

Votent pour l'ajournement :

Messieurs Abell, Bofill, Buckley, Burke, Collin, J. K. Cook, Crozat, Duane, Dufresne, Duke, Dupaty, Fuller, Heard, Henderson, Knobloch, Maas, Maurer, Mayer, Mendiverri, Montamat, M. W. Muryhy, O'Conner, Ong, Schnurr, Seymour, Stocker, Stumpf, Sullivan, Waters—29.

Votent contre l'ajournement :

Messieurs Ariail, Austin, Bailey, Barrett, Bell, Bonzano, Brott, Cazabat, Cook T., Cutler, Davies, Ennis, Flagg, Flood, Foley, Fosdick, Goldman, Gorlinski, Healy, Harnan, Hart, Hills, Hire, Howes, Mann, Millspaugh, E. Murphy, Newell, Normand, J. Payne, Pintado, S. Pursell, Schroeder, Shaw, Smith, Spellicy, Stiner, Stauffer, Taliaferro, Terry, Thorpe, Wells et Wilson—43.

L'ajournement est refusé.

Les membres ne se trouvant plus en nombre suffisant pour former un quorum, ordre est donné de fermer les portes, et le sergent-d'armes est envoyé à la recherche des membres absents.

Après quelques instants, le rôle est appelé, et 78 membres sont trouvés présents.

Le président annonce qu'il y a quorum.

M. Stauffer demande la question préalable ; sa demande est secondée, et la question principale est posée devant l'Assemblée.

M. Campbell offre le *proviso* suivant à la première section, savoir :

Il est entendu, Que la présente section n'aura effet qu'à partir de l'année mil neuf cent, et que l'Etat acceptera la proposition faite par le gouvernement des Etats-Unis aux Etats à esclaves, sur cette base ;

Il est entendu en outre, Que toute législation qui pourra intervenir au sujet de l'esclavage ne devra pas perdre de vue l'amélioration de la condition des esclaves, en vue de leur finale et complète émancipation pour le 1er janvier de l'an 1900, suivant l'offre faite par le gouvernement des Etats-Unis, par l'organe du président, offre que nous, le peuple de la Louisiane, réuni en Convention, acceptons aujourd'hui.

Sur motion d'adopter la première section, le vote nominal est pris.

Votent pour l'adoption :

Messieurs Ariail, Austin, Bailey, Barrett, Bell, Bonzano, Brott, Burke, Cazabat, J. K. Cook, T. Cook, Crozat, Cutler, Davies, Duane, Dupaty, Edwards, Ennis, Fish, Flagg, Flood, Foley, Fosdick, Fuller, Goldman, Gorlinski, Healy, Harnan, Hart, Henderson, Hills, Hire, Howes, Maas, Mann, Millspaugh, E. Murphy, Newell, Normand, O'Conner, Ong, J. Payne, Pintado, J. Purcell, S. Purcell, Schroeder, Shnurr, Shaw, Smith, Spellicy, Stocker, Stumpf, Stiner, Stauffer, Taliaferro, Terry, Thorpe, Thomas, Wells et Wilson—60.

Votent pour le rejet :

Messieurs Abell, Bofill, Buckley, Collin, Campbell, Dufresne, Duke, Gastinel, Heard, Knobloch, Maurer, Mayer, Mendiverri, Montamat, Murphy M. W., Seymour, Sullivan et Waters—18.

En conséquence, la première section est adoptée.

M. Montamat propose l'ajournement, sur quoi le vote nominal est demandé et ordonné.

Votent pour l'ajournement :

Messieurs Abell, Buckley, Barrett, Bofill, Campbell, Collin, J. K. Cook, Crozat, Dufresne, Duke, Flagg, Fuller, Gastinel, Hart, Heard, Knobloch, Maas, Maurer, Mayer, Mendiverri, Millspaugh, Montamat, Murphy M. W., Ong, Seymour, Stumpf, Sullivan, Waters, et Wilson—29.

Votent contre l'ajournement :

Messieurs Ariail, Austin, Bailey, Bell, Bonzano, Brott, Burke, Cazabat, T. Cook, Cutler, Davies, Duane, Dupaty, Edwards, Ennis, Fish, Flood, Foley, Fosdick, Goldman, Gorlinski, Healy, Harnan, Henderson, Hills, Hire, Howes, Mann, E. Murphy, Newell, Normand, O'Conner, J. Payne, Pintado, J. Purcell, S. Pursell, Schroeder, Schnurr, Shaw, Smith, Spellicy, Stocker, Stiner, Stauffer, Taliaferro, Terry, Thorpe, Thomas et Wells—49.

Lecture est donnée de la seconde section, et le vote nominal est pris sur motion de son adoption.

Votent pour l'adoption :

Messieurs Ariail, Austin, Bailey, Barrett, Bell, Bonzano, Brott, Burke, Collin, Cazabat, J. K. Cook, T. Cook, Crozat, Cutler, Davies, Duane, Dupaty, Edwards, Ennis, Fish, Flagg, Flood, Foley, Fosdick, Fuller, Goldman, Gorlinski, Healy, Harnan, Hart, Henderson, Hills, Hire, Howes, Maas, Mann, Millspaugh, E. Murphy, M. W. Murphy, Newell, Normand, O'Conner, Ong, Payne J., Pintado, J. Purcell, S. Pursell, Schroeder, Schnurr, Shaw, Smith, Spellicy, Stocker, Stumpf, Stiner, Stauffer, Taliaferro, Terry, Thorpe, Thomas, Wells, Wilson—62.

Votent contre l'adoption :

Messieurs Abell, Bofill, Buckley, Campbell, Dufresne, Duke, Gastinel, Heard, Knobloch, Maurer, Mayer, Mendiverri, Montamat, Seymour, Sullivan, Waters—16.

En conséquence, la seconde section est adoptée.

La Convention s'ajourne à demain à 11 heures.

Procès-verbal adopté.

JOHN E. NEELIS,
Secrétaire.

MARDI, le 10 mai 1864.

Conformément à l'ajournement la Convention se réunit, et après la prière dite par le Rév. Strong, on procède à l'appel nominal :

Membres présents :

Messieurs Abell, Ariail, Austin, Barrett, Baum, Beauvais, Bell, Bennie, Bofill, Bonzano, Burke, Collin, Cazabat, J. K. Cook, Crozat, Decker, Duane, Dufresne, Duke, Edwards, Ennis, Fish, Flagg, Flood, Fosdick, Gastinel, Geier, Goldman, Gorlinski, Healy, Harnan, Hart, Heard, Hills, Hire, Kavanagh, Knobloch, Maas, Mann, Mayer, Mendiverri, Millspaugh, M. W. Murphy, Newell, Normand, O'Conner, Ong, Orr, J. Payne, Poynot, S. Pursell, Schroeder, Stauffer, Schnurr, Seymour, Spellicy, Stumpf, Stiner, Sullivan, Taliaferro, Terry, Thomas, Wells et Wilson—64.

Le sergent-d'armes reçoit l'ordre d'aller à la recherche d'autres membres, afin de compléter le nombre requis pour faire un quorum ; et l'entrée de MM. Bailey, Beauvais, Buckley, Cook, Davies, Dupaty, Foley, Henderson, Morris, Murphy, Montamat, Maurer, J. Purcell, Stocker et Thorpe formant le nombre requis, le président déclare l'existence du quorum.

Après lecture, le procès-verbal d'hier est adopté.

A la demande de M. Hills, appel est fait des noms des membres qui n'ont pas voté au sujet du rapport de la minorité du comité d'Emancipation.

Sur ce, M. Ong vote en faveur du rejet de ce rapport, et M. Schnurr contre.

M. Hills propose l'appel des noms des membres absents au vote sur la 1e et la 2e section du rapport de la majorité du comité d'Emancipation :

Sur la 1e section, MM. Baum, Beauvais, Geier, Kavanagh, Morris, Orr, Poynot et Wenck, votent en faveur de son adoption ;

Et MM. Balch et Decker contre.

Même vote sur la 2e section de ce rapport.

M. Gorlinski, président du comité des Améliorations Intérieures, présente le rapport écrit de la majorité, et M. Campbell présente celui de la minorité.

Sur motion de M. Hills, il est ordonné d'imprimer ces deux rapports sujets à être appelés à leur tour.

M. Stocker, du comité relatif aux Membres absents, déclare qu'il n'a pu constater l'absence que d'un seul membre, et qu'il n'est pas prêt à présenter son rapport à son égard.

Sur la demande de M. Stumpf, lecture est faite de sa résolution présentée hier.

M. Hills propose de la référer au comité d'Emancipation, mais la Convention décidant qu'elle n'est pas du ressort de ce comité, on ne donne pas suite à la motion Hills.

M. Cazabat présente, comme substitut à la résolution Stumpf, ce qui suit :

Le président de cette Convention nommera un comité de cinq membres, à l'effet de rédiger des résolutions pour représenter et recommander au président et au Congrès des Etats-Unis, les raisons de droit et d'équité qui militent pour accorder une indemnité équitable aux citoyens loyaux de la Louisiane, en compensation de la perte de leurs biens, à telles conditions que l'on jugera devoir imposer.

M. Abell propose de substituer à la motion de M. Cazabat, une résolution ayant pour effet de déclarer inopérative la clause d'émancipation, aussi longtemps qu'il n'y aura point d'indemnité décrétée pour les esclaves émancipés en vertu de cette clause.

L'amendement Abell est déclaré n'être pas à l'ordre.

Le substitut de M. Cazabat est adopté.

La résolution présentée hier par M. S. Pursell est, sur motion de M. Stauffer, référée à un comité de cinq.

M. Thorpe présente la résolution suivante :

Que le président du comité d'Enrôlement pourra ajouter le mot "débats" à la résolution demandant l'impression de deux cents exemplaires du journal.

La proposition de suspendre le réglement, afin de passer aux voix cette dite résolution, est rejetée.

M. Abell donne avis qu'il présentera des amendements aux sections du bill d'émancipation qui suivent les deux premières.

Sur ce, le rapport du comité d'Emancipation étant à l'ordre du jour, M. Abell présente, comme substitut à la section 3 :

Bien entendu, Que la Législature n'adoptera jamais aucun acte permettant au nègre affranchi de voter ou d'immigrer dans cet Etat, sous quelque prétexte que ce soit.

M. Foley propose un vote divisionnel. Adopté.

La demande préalable de rejet de mise aux voix de la première partie de cette résolution concernant le droit de vote de l'affranchi, est repoussée, ainsi que suit :

Affirmative :

Messieurs Ariail, Austin, Bennie, Bonzano, Collin, Cazabat, J. K. Cook, Davies, Dupaty, Ennis, Flagg, Flood, Fosdick, Goldman, Gorlinski, Hills, Hire, Maas, Newell, Pintado, Schroeder, Shaw, Stauffer, Taliaferro, Thorpe et Wells—26 voix.

Négative :

Messieurs Abell, Bailey, Barrett, Baum, Beauvais, Bell, Bofill, Buckley, Burke, T. Cook, Crozat, Decker, Duane, Dufresne, Duke, Edwards, Fish, Foley, Gastinel, Gruneberg, Geier, Healy, Harnan, Hart, Heard, Henderson, Kavanagh, Knobloch, Mann, Maurer, Mayer, Mendiverri, Millspaugh,

Montamat, Morris, E. Murphy, M. W. Murphy, Normand, O'Conner, Ong, Orr, J. Payne, Poynot, J. Purcell, S. Pursell, Seymour, Schnurr, Spellicy, Stocker, Stumpf, Stiner, Sullivan, Terry, Thomas, Wenck et Wilson—55 voix.

Sur la question d'adopter cette première partie de la résolution, l'appel nominal donne le résultat suivant :

Affirmative :

Messieurs Ariail, Bailey, Bennie, Bonzano, Brott, Burke, Collin, Cazabat, Davies, Duane, Dupaty, Edwards, Ennis, Fish, Flagg, Flood, Fosdick, Geier, Goldman, Gorlinski, Hart, Henderson, Hills, Hire, Maas, Mann, Morris, E. Murphy, Normand, J. Payne, Pintado, Poynot, S. Pursell, Shaw, Smith, Spellicy, Stiner, Stauffer, Terry, Thorpe—40 voix.

Négative :

Messieurs Abell, Austin, Baum, Barrett, Beauvais, Bell, Bofill, Buckley, J. K. Cook, T. Cook, Crozat, Decker. Dufresne, Duke, Foley, Gastinel, Harnan, Healy, Kavanagh, Heard, Knobloch, Maurer, Mayer, Mendiverri, Montamat, Millspaugh, M.W. Murphy, O'Conner, Ong, Orr, J. Purcell, Schnurr, Seymour, Stocker, Stumpf, Sullivan, Thomas, Waters, Wenck et Wilson—40.

Le nombre de voix étant égal (40) de part et d'autre, le président donne le vote prépondérant en faveur du rejet, et cette proposition est donc repoussée.

Au milieu de la discussion au sujet de l'adoption de la seconde partie de cette résolution, la Convention s'ajourne à demain à midi.

Approuvé.

JOHN E. NEELIS,
Secrétaire.

MERCERDI, le 11 mai 1864.

La Convention se réunit à midi et la séance s'ouvre par la prière dite par le Rév. Andrews.

Sont présents à l'appel du rôle :

Messieurs Abell, Ariail, Austin, Beauvais, Bell, Bennis, Bofill, Bonzano, Bromley, Buckley, Burke, Campbell, Collin, J. K. Cook, T. Cook, Davies, Decker, Duane, Dufresne, Duke, Edwards, Flagg, Flood, Fosdick, Gastinel, Goldman, Geier, Gorlinski, Gruneberg, Healey, Hart, Heard, Henderson, Hills, Hire, Howes, Kavanagh, Kugler, Maas, Mann, Maurer, Mayer, Millspaugh, M. W. Murphy, Newell, Normand, O'Conner, J. Payne, Pintado, S. Pursell, Schnurr, Seymour, Shaw, Smith, Spellicy, Stumpf, Stiner, Stauffer, Taliaferro, Terry, Waters et Wenck—62.

Le sergent-d'armes reçoit l'ordre d'amener d'autre membres absents, et l'entrée de Messieurs Barret, Baum, Fish, Foley, Fuller, Mendiverri, Montamat, Orr, Poynot, J. Purcell, Schroeder, Stocker, Sullivan, Thorpe, Thomas et Wells—16, constitue un quorum, ainsi que le président en donne avis.

Lecture du procès-verbal d'hier est faite, et avant de l'approuver, certains membres sont autorisés à enregistrer leur vote sur la première clause du substitut Abell à la 3ème section du rapport de la majorité du comité d'Emancipation ; en conséquence, Messieurs Campbell, Bennie, Cutler, Fuller, Paine et Waters votent pour l'affirmative et M. Kugler pour la négative.

A l'égard de la seconde partie du dit substitut, Messieurs Paine et Campbell votent pour l'affirmative et M. Gruneberg pour la négative.

En ce qui concerne l'adoption de la première et de la seconde section du rapport de la majorité du comité d'Emancipation, M. Kugler vote en faveur.

M. Heard prend la paroles pour une question de privilége, et donne lecture d'un article de l'*Era* dans son édition du matin, contenant des attaques contre les membres qui ont voté contrairement au rapport de la majorité du comité d'Emancipation.

M. Heard proteste contre cette censure du journal, et lit quelques remarques expriment son opinion que la Convention ne doit être le but des attaques de nulle personne.

Le président nomme MM. Cazabat, Wells, Fosdick, Abell et Taliaferro, membres du comité d'Indemnités à accorder aux citoyens loyaux dépouillés de leurs biens.

M. Thorpe demande la mise à l'ordre de sa résolution d'hier, lui permettant d'amender sa résolution primitive au sujet de la publication de deux mille exemplaires des journaux en Anglais et en Français, en y insérant et "les débats."

M. Abell propose d'amender en substituant les mots "cinq mille" à "deux mille."

M. Edwards propose de rejeter l'amendement. Refusé.

Alors l'amendement de M. Abell est adopté.

ET L'AMENDEMENT DE LA CONSTITUTION DE LA LOUISIANE.

La question se représente au sujet de l'adoption de la résolution avec son amendement. Adopté, ainsi que la résolution.

Le rapport du comité d'Emancipation, étant au nombre des affaires non-terminées, est appelé.

M. Stauffer propose de retrancher entièrement la troisième section.

MM. Bonzano et Thomas proposent d'amender la proposition de M. Stauffer en y ajoutant les sections quatre et cinq. Cet amendement est adopté

M. Stocker appelle M. Stauffer à l'ordre, en se fondant sur ce que dans son opinion, la motion de ce dernier propose la suppression d'un article sur lequel, la Chambre, n'est pas appelée à délibérer, en ce moment, attendu, que la question actuelle concerne l'adoption du substitut Abell, à la troisième section du rapport.

Le président décide que M. Stauffer est à l'ordre.

M. Abell propose de rejeter la motion de suppression ; et, sur ce. l'appel nominal donne le résulta suivant :

Affirmative :

Messieurs Abell, Barrett, Bofill, Buckley, Campbell, Crozat, Decker, Dufresne, Duke, Edwards. Gastinel, Gruneberg, Heard, Kugler, Mann, Maurer, Mayer, Mendiverri, Montamat, M. W. Murphy, Normand, J. Payne, Stocker, Stumpf, Sullivan—25.

Négative :

Messieurs Ariail, Austin, Bailey, Beauvais, Bell, Bennie, Bonzano, Bromley, Burke, Collin, J. K .Cook, T. Cook, Cutler, Davies, Duane, Dupaty, Flood, Foley, Fosdick, Fuller, Geier, Goldman, Gorlinski, Healy, Harnan, Hart, Henderson, Hills, Hire, Howes, Maas, Millspaugh, E. Murphy, Newell, O'Conner, Orr, J. T. Paine, Pintado, Poynot, J. Purcell, S. Pursell, Schroeder, Schnurr, Shaw, Smith Spellicy, Stiner, Stauffer, Taliaferro, Terry, Thorpe, Thomas, Wenck, Wells, Wilson—55

La question préalable est demandée par W. Austin, et sur vote divisionnel est acceptée, et la question principale est posée en ces term s :

Les articles 3, 4 et 5 du rapport du comité d'Emancipation seront-ils supprimés ?

L'appel nominal donne le résultat suivant :

Affirmative :

Messieurs Ariail, Austin, Bailey, Beauvais, Bell, Bennie, Bonzano, Bromley, Burke, Collin, J. K. Cook, T. Cook, Cutler, Davies, Duane, Dupaty, Fish, Flood, Foley, Fosdick, Fuller, Geier, Goldman, Gorlinski, Healy, Harnan, Hart, Henderson, Hills, Hire, Howes, Maas, Mann, Millspaugh, Morris, E. Murphy, Newell, O'Conner, Orr, J. Payne, J. T. Paine, Pintado, Poynot, J. Purcell, Schroeder, Schnurr, Shaw, Smith, Spellicy, Stocker, Stumpf, Stiner, Stauffer, Taliaferro, Terry, Thorpe, Tomas, Wenck, Wells, Wilson—60.

Négative :

Messieurs Abell, Barrett, Bofill, Buckely, Crozat, Decker, Dufresne, Duke, Edwards, Flagg, Gastinel, Gruneberg, Heard, Kugler, Maurer, Mayer, Mendiverri, Montamat, M.W. Murphy, Normand, Ong, S. Pursell, Sullivan—23.

La motion est donc adoptée et la seconde lecture terminée.

Le rapport spécial du comité sur les Voies de Fait, étant ensuite à l'ordre, sur motion de M. Thorpe, il est remis au 16 courant.

M. Bonzano propose la dispense du réglement, afin de faire subir au rapport du comité d'Emancipation sa troisième lecture.

Sur le vote divisionnel, le quorum n'étant pas apparent, on procède à l'appel nominal, lequel accuse la présence de 85 membres.

M. Campbell propose de referer toute la question d'Emancipation à un comité composé de——membres, que la Chambre désignera elle-même.

Le président déclare que cette motion n'est pas à l'ordre.

MM. Thorpe et Henderson renouvellent la proposition de M. Bonzano, à l'effet d'accorder la dispense du réglement, dans le but de faire subir au rapport du comité d'Emancipation sa troisième lecture ; sur quoi, on demande l'appel nominal, et il donne pour résultat :

Affirmative :

Messieurs Ariail, Austin, Bailey, Barrett, Beauvais, Bell, Bennie, Bofill, Bonzano, Bromley, Burke, Collin, J. K. Cook, T. Cook, Crozat, Cutler, Davies, Duane, Dupaty, Edwards, Fish, Flagg, Flood, Fosdick, Fuller, Gastinel. Geier, Goldman, Gorlinski, Harnan, Hart, Healy, Henderson, Hills, Hire, Howes, Kugler, Maas, Mann, Mayer, Millspaugh, Montamat, Morris, E. Murphy, M. W. Murphy, Newell, Normand, O'Conner, Orr, J. Payne, J. T. Paine, Pintado,

Poynot, J. Pusell, S. Pursell, Schroeder, Schnurr, Shaw, Smith, Spellicy, Stocker, Stumpf, Stiner, Stauffer, Taliafero, Terry, Thorpe, Thomas, Wenck, Wells, Wilson—72.

Négative :

Messieurs Abell, Buckley, Campbell, Decker, Dufresne, Duke, Gruneberg, Heard, Maurer, Mendiverri, Ong, Sullivan —12

La dispense du réglement étant accordée, le secrétaire donne lecture du rapport.

MM. Abell et Campbell proposent des amendements à ce rapport, mais le président les déclare n'être pas à l'ordre.

Sur demande de M. Bonzano, on passe à la question préalable, et la Chambre est appellée à voter sur ce qui suit :

Section 1. L'esclavage et la servitude involontaire, excepté dans le cas de punition pour un crime dont l'accusé aura été reconnu coupable, sont abolis à tout jamais et défendus dans cet Etat.

Section 2. La Législature ne fera point de loi reconnaissant le droit de propriété sur l'homme.

Et le vote suivant est donné.

Affirmative.

Messieurs Ariail, Austin, Barrett, Beauvais, Bofill, Bell, Bennie, Bonzano, Bromley, Burke, Collin, J. K. Cook, T. Cook, Crozat, Culter, Davies, Duane, Dupaty, Edwards, Fish, Flagg, Flood, Foley Fosdick, Fuller, Geier, Goldman, Gorlinski, Healy, Harnan, Hart, Henderson, Hills, Hire, Howes, Kugler, Maas, Mann, Millspaugh, Montamat, Morris, E. Murphy, M. W. Murphy, Newell, Normand, O'Conner, Ong, Orr, J. Payne, J. T. Paine, Pintado, Poynot, J. Purcell, S. Pursell, Schroeder, Schnurr, Sullivan, Spellicy, Shaw, Smith, Stocker, Stumpf, Stiner, Stauffer, Taliaferro, Terry, Thorpe, Thomas, Wenck, Wells, Wilson et M. le président—72.

Négative :

Messieurs Abell, Buckley, Campbell, Decker, Dufresne, Duke, Gastinel, Gruneberg, Heard, Maurer, Mayer, Mendiverri, Waters—13

Sur motion de M. Thomas la Convention s'ajourne à demain à midi.

Approuvé.

JOHN E. NEELIS,
Secrétaire.

JEUDI, 12 mai 1864.

La Convention se réunit conformément à l'ajournement, et la prière est dite par le Rév. M. Andrews.

Le vote est ensuite appelé.

• Sont présents :

Messieurs Ariail, Bennie, Bonzano, Bofill, Burke, Collin, Crozat, Decker, Dufresne. Duke, Edwards, Ennis, Gorlinski, Heard, Howes, Kugler, Millspaugh, M. W. Murphy, Newell, Normand, O'Conner, Pintado, S. Pursell, Shaw, Spellicy, Stumpf, Stiner, Sullivan, Taliaferro, Thorpe, Thomas, Wells et Wilson—33.

Puis, quelques instants après, entrent les membres suivants :

Messieurs Abell, Austin, Bailey, Barrett, Bell, Bromley, Beauvais, Buckley, Campbell, Cazabat, J. K. Cook, T. Cook, Cutler, Fish, Flagg, Flood, Foley, Fosdick, Gastinel, Geier Goldman, Gruneberg, Healy, Harnan, Hart, Hills, Hire, Maas, Mann, Maurer, Mayer, Mendiverri, Montamat, Morris, Murphy E., Poynot, J. Purcell, Schroeder, Schnurr, Smith, Stauffer, Waters et Wenck—43.

Le président annonce qu'il y a quorum.

Le journal de la veille est lu, et avant son adoption MM. Bofill et Sullivan, qui avaient voté pour le rejet du rapport de la majorité du comité d'émancipation, sont autorisés à changer leurs votes de manière à voter pour l'adoption.

Le procès-verbal est amendé en conséquence et ensuite adopté.

Les membres suivants, qui se trouvaient absents au moment du vote sur les deux premières sections du rapport de la majorité du comité d'Emancipation, sont invités à faire enregistrer leurs votes à ce sujet.

Messieurs Cazabat et Ennis se prononcent pour l'adoption.

M. Bennie est invité à donner son vote sur la motion du rejet du rapport de la minorité de ce même comité et vote pour le rejet.

M. Wilson propose d'ajourner jusqu'à lundi prochain. Rejeté.

M. Abell demande à être dispensé de faire partie du comité nommé sur l'adoption de la résolution de M. Cazabat, pour correspondre avec les autorités du Gouvernement de Washington, et expose à la Convention les motifs de sa demande.

Sur motion de M. Bonzano, M. Abell est dispensé de faire partie de ce comité, et le président désigne M. Ariail pour remplir la vacance.

M. Heard, président du comité du Préambule, soumet un rapport sur le substitut présenté à ce sujet par M. Cazabat.

Sur motion de M. Hills, le rapport est accepté et le comité est déchargé.

M. Thorpe, président du comité d'Enrôlement, rapporte comme étant correctement enrôlées :

1o. L'ordonnance à l'effet d'abolir l'esclavage et toute servitude involontaire.

2o. La résolution relative à l'impression de cinq mille exemplaires du Journal et des Débats.

M. Thomas appelle l'attention de la Convention sur l'omission des mots "dans l'année de Notre Seigneur" et du mot "siégeant," dans l'ordonnance à l'effet d'abolir l'esclavage, et propose de la retourner au comité d'Enrôlement.

La motion est acceptée.

Quant à la résolution, elle est acceptée telle quelle et enrôlée, et le président est prié d'y apposer sa signature.

Le président désigne pour composer le comité chargé de faire son rapport sur la résolution de M. Purcell, relative aux billets de circulation émis par la ville, Messieurs Purcell, Fosdick, Sauffer, Bonzano, et Brott.

Le président soumet à la Convention une communication de l'Hon. A. P. Dostie, Auditeur d'Etat, renfermant un état des recettes et dépenses du Trésor pendant l'administration du Brig. Gén. G. F. Shepley, ex-gouverneur militaire de l'Etat.

M. Austin propose de renvoyer l'affaire devant un comité spécial de cinq membres, à la nomination du Président.

Le président désigne pour composer ce comité, MM. Austin, Thomas, Fish, Wells et Beauvais.

Sur motion de M. Mendiverri, on ordonne l'impression de mille exemplaires.

M. Hills demande si les rapports du comité sur le Préambule et sur la Division des Pouvoirs avaient été définitivement adoptés.

En consultant le procès-verbal, on s'assure que ces rapports n'avaient subi que leur seconde lecture : il leur restait donc à subir la troisième lecture.

Le rapport du comité sur le Préambule est donc lu, après dispense du réglement, sur motion de M. Mann.

M. Cutler est d'opinion que les mots "et nous en recommandons l'adoption" sont inutiles.

Le président répond qu'ils font partie du rapport et non du préambule.

M. Henderson demande la question préalable.

Accepté, et l'appel nominal donne le résultat suivant :

Dans l'affirmative :

MM. Ariail, Abell, Bailey, Barrett, Beauvais, Bell, Bennie, Bofill, Bonzano, Bromley, Buckley, Burke, Campbell, Collin, Cazabat, J. K. Cook, T. Cook, Crozat, Cutler, Decker, Dufresne, Duke, Dupaty, Edwards, Ennis, Fish, Flagg, Flood, Foley, Fosdick, Gastinel, Geier, Goldman, Gorlinski, Gruneberg, Healy, Harnan, Hart, Heard, Henderson, Hills, Hire, Howes, Kugler, Maas, Mann, Maurer, Mayer, Mendiverri, Millspaugh, Montamat, Morris, E. Murphy, M. W. Murphy, Newell, Normand, O'Conner, Pintado, Poynot, J. Purcell, S. Pursell, Schroeder, Schnurr, Shaw, Smith, Spellicy, Stocker, Stumpf, Stiner, Stauffer, Sullivan, Taliaferro, Thorpe, Thomas, Waters, Wenck, Wells, et Wilson—79.

Le rapport du comité sur la Distribution des Pouvoirs est alors appelé et subit sa seconde lecture.

Sur motion de M. Henderson, il y a dispense du réglement, et le rapport subit sa troisième lecture.

M. Hills propose de l'adopter, et l'enrôlement du dit rapport sous la désignation de titre 1, articles 1 et 2 de la constitution.

La Convention vote sur l'adoption et l'accepte par une majorité de 76 voix, savoir :

Messieurs Abell, Ariail, Balch, Barrett, Baum, Bell, Bofill, Bonzano, Buckley, Burke, Campbell, Cazabat, J. K. Cook, Crozat, Cutler, Davies, Dufresne, Duane, Durell, Edwards, Ennis, Fish, Flagg, Flood, Foley, Fosdick, Fuller, Geier, Goldman, Gorlinski, Gruneber, Gaidry, Healy, Harnan, Hart, Heard, Henderson, Hills, Hire, Howell, Howes, Kavanagh, Knobloch, Kugler, Maas, Mann, Maurer, Mendiverri, Millspaugh, Montamat, Montague, Morris, E. Murphy, M. W. Murphy, Newell, Normand, O'Conner, J. Payne, Poynot, J. Purcell, S. Pursell, Schroeder, Seymour, Shaw, Smith, Spellicy, Stocker, Stumpf, Stiner, Stauffer, Sullivan, Terry, Wenck, Wells et Wilson.

Sur motion de M. Hills, la distribution et le numérotage des différentes parties de la constitution sont renvoyés jusqu'à ce que toutes les parties de la constitution aient été adoptées.

Sur motion de M. Abell, le rapport du comité sur le Département concernant le Législatif devra subir sa seconde lecture mardi, le 17 mai, à 1 heure P. M.

Puis la Convention s'ajourne à mardi prochain, le 17 à midi.

Approuvé.

JOHN E. NEELIS,
Secrétaire.

MARDI, le 17 mai 1864.

La Convention se réunit à 11 heures conformément à l'ajournement. Le rôle est appelé.

Sont présents :

Messieurs Abell, Ariail, Balch, Barrett, Beauvais, Bell, Bennie, Bofill, Bonzano, Burke, T. Cook, Crozat, Davies, Duane, Dufresne, Edwards, Ennis, Fish, Flagg, Flood, Fosdick, Geier, Goldman, Gorlinski, Hart, Henderson, Hills, Howes, Kugler, Maas, Mann, Mayer, Millspaugh, Montague, M. W. Murphy Newell, Normand, Pintado, J. Purcell, S. Pursell, Schroeder, Seymour, Shaw, Smith, Spellicy, Stumpf, Stiner, Taliaferro, Terry, Thorpe, Wenck, Wells, Wilson et M. le Président—54.

Pas de quorum.

Le sergent-d'armes est envoyé à la recherche des membres absents.

Messieurs Austin, Bailey, Baum, Bromley, Buckley, Campbell, Cazabat, J. K. Cook, Cutler, Dupaty, Fuller, Healy, Howell, Maurer, Mendiverri, Montamat, Morris, O'Conner, Ong, Orr, Poynot, Stocker, Stauffer, Sullivan et Thomas—25 membres étant ensuite entrés dans la salle, le président annonce qu'il y a un quorum.

Le procès-verbal de jeudi, 12, est lu et approuvé.

MM. Montague, Seymour et Howell s'étant trouvé absents au moment du vote sur les rapports du comité d'Emancipation, demandent à déposer leurs votes.

Sur la motion de rejeter le rapport de la minorité, chacun d'eux vote affirmativement.

Sur la motion d'adoption, du rapport de la majorité, tel qu'il a été, ils votent également pour l'affimative.

M. John Purcell offre la résolution suivante :

Résolu, Que tous les bills de l'imprimeur officiel de la Convention soient examinés et approuvés par le comité des Impressions, par le comité des Finances et par le comité des Dépenses, en prenant pour base les prix fixés par la Convention, avant qu'ils soient payés, et que tous les bills ainsi vérifiés et approuvés seront payés sur le mandat du président par le trésorier de l'Etat sur tous fonds non autrement appropriés.

Le réglement est suspendu et la résolution est adoptée.

M. Henderson présente le préambule et la résolution qui suivent :

Attendu, Que toutes les Législatures de l'Etat ont été dans l'habitude invariable de faire des allocations libérales sur le fonds général pour venir en aide à toutes les institutions charitables incorporées, et que sous le rapport soit du nombre, soit de la variété ou de l'étendue de ces sortes d'institutions, la Louisiane ne le cède à aucun autre Etat de l'Union ; *et attendu*, que la Législature de 1860 a fait les allocations suivantes, savoir :

Pour l'Asile des orphelins de la Nouvelle-Orléans	$1500.
Pour l'Asile des Orphelins catholiques de St. Marie, à la N.-O	4000
Pour la Maison du Bon Pasteur	250
Pour l'Asile des veuves juives et orphelins juifs	500
Pour l'Asile des Orphelins catholiques de St. Joseph	1500
Pour la Maison de Ste. Elizabeth (House of Industry)	1000
Pour la Société de Secours des orphelins mâles du quatrième District	1000
Pour l'Institution des enfants de couleur indigents du 3e District	1000
Pour les dames de la Providence du 3e District	750
Pour l'Asile des veuves et enfants pauvres, dit Asile St. Anne	1500
Pour l'Asile des enfants de l'Eglise Potestante Episcopale	500
Pour l'Institut catholique des Orphelins indigents	750
Pour la Société catholique de Bienfaisance à Bâton-Rouge	250
Pour l'Asile des Orphelins à Bâton-Rouge	500
Pour l'Asile des Orphelins de St. Vincent	500
Pour l'Asile "Milne," à la Nouvelle-Orléans	500
Total	$20,000

Et attendu, Que par suite des calamités qui sont la conséquence de la guerre actuelle, laquelle non-seulement a tari les sources de la charité privée et réduit jusqu'à néant les revenus des institutions charitables, mais encore a servi à augmenter considérablement leurs charges par le nombre des nouveaux orphelins, de nouvelles veuves et de nouveaux indigents que cette guerre a créés, de telle façon que les dignes sœurs et directrices de ces divines institutions sont réduites à la plus grande détresse et à l'impossibilité absolue de fournir aux premiers besoins des milliers d'êtres abandonnés qui sont tombés à leur charge ; *Et attendu*, que sans les soins bienveillants du gouvernement Fédéral et des officiers militaires de ce département, qui ont eu l'attention de faire distribuer à ces mêmes institutions des rations quotidiennes de l'armée, un grand nombre d'entr'elles se seraient vues forcées de fermer leurs portes, il est en conséquence,

Résolu, Que la somme de $20,000 est et demeure allouée et appropriée sur le fonds général du trésor pour être employé à venir en aide aux institutions charitables dénommées dans le tableau qui procède, et pour être distribuée entr'elles dans les proportions indiquées au dit tableau, et être payée, comme il est d'usage, par mandats de l'auditeur sur le trésorier, aux directeurs, directrices ou agents autorisés des dites institutions.

Déposé conformément au réglement jusqu'à demain.

M. Foley présente la résolution suivante:

Attendu, Que plusieurs membres de la Convention constitutionnelle de la Louisiane ont été élus délégués à la Convention de Baltimore ; *Et attendu*, Qu'il est d'une importance vitale pour les intérêts de la Louisiane que la Convention termine son œuvre sans ajournement ;

La Convention décrète, Que ceux des membres de cette Convention qui ont été élus à la Convention de Baltimore et qui ont dessein de s'y rendre, devront résigner sans délai leurs fonctions de membres de cette Convention ; et que le gouverneur est invité à pourvoir à de nouvelles élections pour remplir les vacances dans les différentes paroisses et les divers districts représentatifs.

Déposé.

. Thomas propose l'adoption du rapport du comité des Impressions. Cette motion est appuyée, et le rapport est adopté.

M. Montamat soumet le rapport suivant au nom du comité des Finances, lequel rapport est adopté.

RAPPORT DU COMITE DES FINANCES de la Convention constitutionnelle au sujet du fonds destiné au paiement de l'indemnité de service des membres et du salaire des officiers.

Mai 9, 1864, payé mandat No. 27	$2,930 00
" 9, " " " 28	405 00
" 10, " " " 29	696 00
" 10, " " " 30	3,500 00
" 14, " " " 31	2,520 00
" 14, " " " 32	1,275 00
" 15, " " " 34	1,420 00

$12,764 00

Mai 17—Balance en mains ce jour................$55,485 40

$68,231 40

RAPPORT CONCERNANT LE FONDS DES DEPENSES CONTINGENTES.

Mai 15, 1864, payé mandat No. 33 à M. DeCoursey, suivant document No. 4........$ 1,747 37
Mai 17, 1864, balance en mains à ce jour............... 9,585 48

$11,332 85

L'ordre du jour se trouve maintenant être : le rapport du comité du Législatif, lequel est lu section par section.

Sur l'adoption du premier article, le vote nominal est demandé et ordonné.

Votent pour l'adoption :

Messieurs Abell, Ariail, Austin, Bailey, Barrett, Beauvais, Bell, Bennie, Bonzano, Bofill, Bromley, Buckley, Burke, Campbell, Cazabat, J. K. Cook, T. Cook, Crozat, Cutler, Davies, Decker, Duane, Dufresne, Edwards, Ennis, Fish, Flood, Foley, Fosdick, Fuller, Gastinel, Geier, Goldman, Healy, Hart, Henderson, Hills, Howell, Hire, Howes, Kugler, Maas, Maurer, Mayer, Mendiverri, Millspaugh, Montamat, Montague, Morris, M. W. Murphy, Normand, Newell, O'Conner, Ong, Orr, J. Payne, J. T. Paine, Pintado, Poynot, J. Purcell, S. Pursell, Schroeder, Seymour, Shaw, Smith, Spellicy, Stocker, Stumpf, Stiner, Stauffer, Sullivan, Taliaferro, Terry, Thorpe, Thomas, Wenck, Wells, Wilson—78.

Contre : 0.

On passe à l'article deux.

M. Howell demande la suspension du réglement, qui exige le vote nominal ; mais la Chambre s'y refuse, et l'adoption du dit article est votée comme suit :

Pour l'adoption :

Messieurs Abell, Ariail, Austin, Balch, Bailey, Barrett, Beauvais, Bell, Bennie, Bofill, Bonzano, Bromley, Buckley, Burke, Campbell, Cazabat, J. K. Cook, T. Cook, Cutler, Davies, Decker, Duane, Dufresne, Edwards, Ennis, Fish, Flagg, Flood, Foley, Fosdick, Fuller, Gastinel, Geier, Goldman, Healy, Hart, Hills, Hire, Howell, Howes, Kugler, Maas, Mann, Maurer, Mendiverri, Mayer, Millspaugh, Montamat, Montague,

Morris, Newell, Normand, O'Conner, Ong, Orr, J. Payne, Pintado, Poynot, J. Purcell, S. Purcell, Schroeder, Seymour, Shaw, Smith, Spellicy, Stocker, Stumpf, Stiner, Stauffer, Taliaferro, Terry, Thomas, Thorpe, Wells, Wenck, Wilson—76.

Contre : 0.

Lecture est donnée de l'article trois.

M. Montamat propose de retrancher le mot "premier" à la troisième ligne, et de le remplacer par le mot "troisième."

M. Montague demande qu'on retranche les mots "premier lundi de janvier" à la troisième ligne, et qu'on les remplace par les mots "premier lundi de décembre." Cette motion est rejetée sur un vote divisionnel, par 51 voix contre 23.

Le vote divisionnel est ensuite pris sur l'amendement de M. Montamat, et cet amendement est à son tour rejeté par 51 voix contre 22.

M. Stocker propose de supprimer, à la quatrième ligne, les mots : "à moins qu'un autre jour ne soit désigné par la loi." Cette motion est rejetée.

M. Morris propose d'amender la première ligne en insérant les mots : "le mardi qui suivra." Rejeté.

La question retourne alors à l'adoption du troisième article, tel qu'il est au rapport, et le vote nominal est ordonné.

Votent pour l'adoption :

Messieurs Ariail, Austin, Bailey, Bell, Bennie, Bofill, Bonzano, Bromley, Buckley, Burke, Campbell, Cazabat, J. K. Cook, T. Cook, Crozat, Cutler, Davies, Decker, Duane, Dufresne, Edwards, Ennis, Flagg, Fish, Flood, Foley, Fosdick, Gastinel, Geier, Gorlinski, Goldman, Hart, Healy, Henderson, Hills, Hire, Howell, Howes, Kugler, Maas, Mann, Mayer, Mendiverri, Millspaugh, Montague, Morris, M. W. Murphy, Newell, Normand, O'Conner, Ong, Orr, J. Payne, J. T. Paine, Pintado, Poynot, Schroeder, Seymour, Shaw, Smith, Spellicy, Stocker, Stumpf, Stiner, Stauffer, Taliaferro, Terry, Thorpe, Thomas, Wenck, Wells, Wilson—72.

Votent contre :

Messieurs Abell, Barrett, Maurer, Montamat, J. Purcell, S. Purcell.

M. Abell offre l'amendement suivant à l'article 6 :

Tout électeur qualifié qui aura atteint l'âge de vingt-quatre ans sera éligible aux fonctions de représentant à l'Assemblée Générale, et tout électeur qualifié, qui aura atteint l'âge de vingt-huit ans pourra être élu membre du Sénat ; mais nul ne sera représentant ou sénateur, qu'à la condition qu'il sera, au moment de son élection, votant dûment qualifié du District Représentatif ou sénatorial dans lequel il aura été élu.

Rejeté.

L'adoption du 4me article, tel qu'il est au rapport, est alors mise aux voix.

Votent pour l'adoption :

Messieurs Ariail, Austin, Bailey, Barrett, Bell, Bennnie, Bofil, Bonzano, Bromley, Buckley, Burke, Cazabat, J. K. Cook, T. Cook, Crozat, Cutler, Davies, Decker, Duane, Dufresne, Dupaty, Edwards, Ennis, Fish, Flagg, Flood, Foley, Fosdick, Geier, Goldman, Gorlinski, Hart, Healy, Henderson, Hills, Hire, Howell, Howes, Knobloch, Kugler, Maas, Mann, Maurer, Mayer, Mendiverri, Millspaugh, Montague, Morris, Newell, Normand, Ong, Orr, J. Paine, Pintado, Poynot, J. Purcell, S. Pursell, Schroeder, Seymour, Shaw, Smith, Spellicy, Stiner, Stocker, Stumpf, Stauffer, Taliaferro, Terry, Thorpe, Thomas, Wenck, Wells, Wilson—72.

Votent contre :

Messieurs Abell, Campbell, Gastinel, Montamat, M. W. Murphy, O'Conner, Sullivan, —7.

L'article 5 est ensuite adopté par le vote suivant :

Pour l'adoption :

Messieurs Abell, Ariail, Austin, Bailey, Barrett, Beauvais, Bell, Bennie, Bofill, Bonzano, Bromley, Buckley, Burke, Campbell, Cazabat, J. K. Cook, T. Cook, Crozat, Cutler, Davies, Decker, Duane, Dufresne, Dupaty, Edwards, Ennis, Fish, Flagg, Flood, Foley, Fosdick, Fuller, Gastinel, Geier, Gorlinski, Goldman, Gruneberg, Hart, Henderson, Hills, Howell, Howes, Knobloch, Kugler, Maas, Mann, Maurer, Mayer, Mendiverri, Millspaugh, Montamat, Montague, Morris, M. W. Murphy, Newell, Normand, O'Conner, Ong, Orr, J. Payne, Pintado, Poynot, J. Purcell, S. Pursell, Schroeder, Seymour, Shaw, Smith, Spellicy, Stocker, Stumpf, Stiner, Stauffer, Sullivan, Taliaferro, Terry, Thorpe, Thomas, Wells et Wilson—80.

Il n'y a pas de votes contre l'adoption.

Lecture est donnée de l'article 6.

M. Abell propose de retrancher les mots "les électeurs qualifiés," à la troisième ligne, et d'insérer les mots "la population totale."

Rejeté.

M. Abell propose alors de retrancher les mots "nombre des électeurs," à la 5me li-

gne, et de les remplacer par les mots "population totale."
Rejeté.

M. Abell offre le même amendement pour la huitième ligne.
Rejeté.

M. Abell propose de retrancher tout ce qui suit le mot "district," à la 16me ligne, jusqu'à la fin de la 18me ligne, comme étant superflu.
Rejeté.

M. Abell propose également de retrancher les mots "électeurs qualifiés" à la vingt-unième ligne et de les remplacer par les mots "population totale."
Rejeté.

M. Abell propose aussi de retrancher les mots "l'article défini," à la 23me ligne, et de les remplacer par le pronom possessif.
Sur motion de M. Hills, cette proposition est rejetée.

M. Abell propose de retrancher à la 24e ligne les mots "nombre des électeurs," et de les remplacer par les mots "population."
Rejeté.

Enfin M. Abell propose de retrancher le chiffre "3," en face des mots "Cinquième District," fixant le nombre des représentants pour ce District, et de le remplacer par le chiffre "5," sur quoi une discussion s'élève au sujet de la base de la répresentation, pendant laquelle, sur motion de MM. Hills et S. Purcell, le secrétaire est invité à se procurer les retours des dernières élections de l'Etat, de façon à pouvoir les produire à la Convention, demain.

M. Howell propose, d'ajourner jusqu'à sept heures et demie du soir. Rejeté.

La Convention s'ajourne ensuite à demain, à midi.

Procès-verbal adopté.

JOHN E. NEELIS,
Secrétaire.

MERCREDI, le 18 Mai 1864.

La Convention se réunit conformément à l'ajournement.

A l'appel nominal les membres suivants répondent :

Messieurs Abell, Ariail, Balch, Barrett, Baum, Bell, Bennie, Bofill, Bonzano, Burke Campbell, Duane, Dufresne, Dupaty, Edwards, Ennis, Fish, Flood, Foley, Fosdick, Geier, Goldman, Gruneberg, Gaidry, Henderson, Howell, Howes, Kavanagh, Maas, Mann, Mayer, Montague, M. W. Murphy, Newell, Normand, O'Conner, Pintado, S. Purcell, Schroeder, Schnurr, Shaw, Smith, Spellicy, Stumpf, Stiner, Stauffer, Taliaferro, Terry, Waters, Wells, Wilson et M. le Président—52 membres.

Le sergent-d'armes reçoit l'ordre d'aller à la recherche de membres afin de compléter le quorum.

Messieurs Austin, Bromley, Buckley, J. K. Cook, Crozat, Decker, Flagg, Fuller, Gastinel, Healy, Hart, Hills. Hire, Knobloch, Kugler, Mendiverri, Millspaugh, Montamat, Morris, Orr, J. T. Paine, Poynot, J. Purcell, Stocker, Sullivan, Thorpe et Thomas—27 membres—étant entrés, le président déclare qu'il y a quorum.

Après lecture et correction, le procès-verbal de la dernière séance est adopté.

M. Hills propose ce qui suit :

Attendu, Que l'absence d'un petit nombre de membres à l'appel du rôle de présence interrompt sérieusement et retarde les délibérations de la Convention, pour une heure entière quelquefois ; en conséquence,

Il est décrété, Que tout membre absent sans congé ou qui ne pourra excuser son absence d'une manière satisfaisante à l'appel de midi, perdra sa rétribution quotidienne chaque jour d'absence.

M. Foley propose la dispense du réglement, afin de s'occuper de cette susdite résolution. Refusé.

M. Wilson propose ce qui suit :

Considérant, Que la Convention a maintenant accompli la partie principale de la tâche pour laquelle on l'avait convoquée ;

Il est décrété, Qu'elle s'ajournera le premier juin et qu'elle siégera tous les jours jusqu'à cette époque, excepté les dimanches.

M. S. Pursell présente ce qui suit :

Considérant, Que l'intérêt du public exige que les travaux de cette Convention ne soient pas interrompus sans cause suffisante ;

Il est décrété, Qu'aucune motion d'ajournement pour plus de 24 heures ne sera mise aux voix, à moins que cette dite motion ne soit secondée par la majorité des membres présents ; et, dans ce cas, on procèdera à l'appel nominal.

M. Howell propose que le secrétaire soit chargé de réunir et de collationner toutes les motions et résolutions jusqu'ici adoptées, en ce qui concerne la conduite des travaux de cette Chambre ou bien celles qui amendent le réglement, et qu'il en fasse un rapport le lendemain.

M. Cazabat propose la dispeuse du réglement afin de s'occuper de cette susdite motion. Refusé.

On passe aux affaires non terminées. A la demande de M. Henderson, le secrétaire donne lecture de sa résolution par lui présentée hier.

M. Campbell propose l'amendement suivant :

Pourvu qu'une semblable somme de $20,000 soit allouée à l'effet de prêter aide et assistance aux indigents parmi les veuves et orphelins des soldats des régiments Louisianais connus comme le 1er et le 2e d'infanterie, le 1er et le 2e de cavalerie, et le 1er et le 2e des Volontaires de la Nlle-Orléans.

Sur motion de M. Henderson, ce dit amendement est rejeté.

Sur la proposition de M. Montamat de rejeter la résolution présentée par M. Henderson, il y a appel nominal, ainsi que suit :

Affirmative :

Messieurs Abell, Austin, Baum, Beauvais, Bennie, Bromley, Brott, Burke, Campbell, Cazabat, Decker, Dupaty, Edwards, Ennis, Flagg, Gruneberg, Gaidry, Hills, Hire, Howell, Knobloch, Kugler, Maas, Mann, Mayer, Mendiverri, Millspaugh, Montamat, Montague, Morris, Newell, Normand, J. T. Paine, Pintado, S. Pursell, Seymour, Stauffer, Thomas—39.

Dans la négative :

Messieurs Balch, Barrett, Bell, Bofill, Bonzano, Buckley, J. K. Cook, T. Cook, Crozat, Duane, Dufresne, Fish, Flood, Foley, Fosdick, Fuller, Gastinel, Geier, Goldman, Gorlinski, Healy, Harnan, Hart, Henderson, Howes, Kavanagh, E. Murphy, M. W. Murphy, O'Conner, Orr, Poynot, J. Purcell, Schroeder, Schnurr, Shaw, Smith, Spellicy, Stocker, Stumpf, Stiner, Stauffer, Sullivan, Taliaferro, Terry, Thorpe, Waters, Wilson—46.

La proposition de M. Montamat est donc repoussée.

Et le substitut proposé par M. Hills est déclaré n'être pas à l'ordre.

M. Bonzano propose de porter au rapport l'allocation suivante : Pour l'Asile des Enfants de la rue Moreau, comptant 54 enfants, $500.

M. Thorpe propose pour l'Asile des Orphelins St-Vincent, à l'angle des rues Race et Magazine, $500.

Ces deux amendements sont acceptés.

M. Montamat propose d'allouer à l'Association de Bienfaisance des Pompiers la somme de $500 ; sur quoi, il y a appel nominal, duquel il résulte :

Affirmative :

Messieurs Abell, Austin, Balch, Baum, Beauvais, Bell, Bofill, Bromley, Brott, Buckley, Campbell, T. Cook, Crozat, Ennis, Fish, Flagg, Foley, Fuller, Geier, Goldman, Gruneberg, Knobloch, Mayer, Mendiverri, Montamat, Montague, Morris, M. W. Murphy, O'Conner, Orr, J. Purcell, Seymour, Shaw, Spellicy, Stocker, Stumpf, Stauffer, Sullivan, Taliaferro, Terry, Thomas, Waters, Wilson—43.

Négative :

Messieurs Ariail, Barret, Bennie, Bonzano, Burke, J. K. Cook, Cutler, Decker, Duane, Dufresne, Edwards, Flood, Fosdick, Gastinel, Gorlinski, Gaidry, Healy, Harnan, Hart, Henderson, Hills, Hire, Howell, Howes, Kavanagh, Kugler, Maas, Mann, Millspaugh, E. Murphy, Newell, Normand, J. T. Paine, Pintado, Poynot, S. Pursell, Schroeder, Schnurr, Smith, Stiner, Thorpe, Wells—42.

L'amendement est donc adopté.

M. Campbell demande à être dispensé de voter sur l'amendement ci-dessus. Refusé.

M. Campbell propose ce qui suit :

Pourvu que les veuves et les orphelins, dans l'indigence, des soldats morts au champ d'honneur, y soient compris.

Cet amendement est rejeté.

Sur l'acceptation de la résolution primitive avec l'amendement, l'appel nominal donne le résultat suivant :

Affirmative :

Messieurs Barrett, Bell, Bofill, Bonzano, Buckley, T. Cook, Crozat, Fish, Flagg, Flood, Foley, Fosdick, Fuller, Geier, Gruneberg, Healy, Harnan, Hart, Henderson, Kavanagh, Montamat, M. W. Murphy, O'Conner, Orr, J. Purcell, Schroeder, Schnurr, Spellicy, Stocker, Stumpf, Stiner, Sullivan, Taliaferro, Terry, Thorpe, Waters, Wilson—35.

Négative :

Messieurs Abell, Ariail, Austin, Baum, Beauvais, Bennie, Bromley, Burke, Campbell, Cazabat, J. K. Cook, Cutler, Decker, Duane, Dufresne, Dupaty, Edwards, Ennis, Flagg, Fosdick, Fuller, Gastinel, Goldman, Gorlinski, Gaidry, Hills, Hire, Howell, Howes, Knobloch, Kugler, Lobdell, Maas, Mann, Mayer, Mendiverri, Millspaugh, Montague, Morris, E. Murphy, Newell, Normand, Ong, J. T. Paine, Pintado, Poynot, S. Pursell, Seymour, Smith, Stauffer, Thomas et Wells—51 voix.

La résolution et l'amendement sont donc rejetés.

ET L'AMENDEMENT DE LA CONSTITUTION DE LA LOUISIANE. 83

M. Foley appelle sa résolution présentée hier relativement aux délégués à la Convention de Baltimore, membres de cette Assemblée.

Sur la motion de rejet de cette résolution, le président la déclare acceptée par le vote; cependant M. Stiner demande la reprise en considération de ce dit vote, ce qui est accordé, et sur la question de rejet l'appel nominal donne :

Affirmative :

Messieurs Austin, Barrett, Baum, Beauvais, Bennie, Bofill, Bromley, Burke, J. K. Cook, Cutler, Decker, Duane, Dufresne, Duke, Dupaty, Edwards, Ennis, Fish, Flagg, Fuller, Gastinel, Gaidry, Geier, Goldman, Hart, Hire, Howell, Kavanagh, Kugler, Maas, Mann, Mendiverri, Millspaugh, Montamat, Montague, Morris, Newell, Ong, Orr, J. T. Paine, Pintado, J. Purcell, S. Pursell, Seymour, Shaw, Spellicy, Stauffer, Sullivan, Taliaferro, Terry, Thomas, Waters, Wells, Wilson—54.

Négative :

Messieurs Abell, Ariail, Bell, Buckley, Campbell, Cazabat, T. Cook, Flood, Foley, Fosdick, Gorlinski, Gruneberg, Harnan, Healey, Hills, Howes, Knobloch, Mayer, E. Murphy, M. W., Murphy, Normand, O'Conner, Schroeder, Schnurr, Simth, Stumpf, Stiner, Stocker, Thorpe—29.

ORDRE DU JOUR.

La Convention passe au rapport sur le Législatif.

M. Pursell propose de supprimer sur les lignes 86 et 87 les mots "sachant lire et écrire."

L'appel nominal à cet égard donne pour résultat :

Affirmative :

Messieurs Abell, Ariail, Austin, Barrett, Balch, Beauvais, Bell, Bennie, Bofill, Bonzano, Bromley, Burke, Cazabat, J. K. Cook, T. Cook, Crozat, Culter, Decker, Duane, Dupaty, Edwards, Ennis, Fish, Flood, Foley, Fuller, Gastinel, Gaidry, Geier, Gorlinski, Gruneberg, Harnan, Hart, Healy, Henderson, Howell, Howes, Knobloch, Kugler, Maas, Mann, Mayer, Millspaugh, Montamat, Montague, Morris, E. Murphy, W. M. Murphy, Newell, Normand, O'Conner, Ong, Orr, Pintado, J. Purcell, S. Pursell, Schroeder, Schnurr, Smith, Spellicy, Stocker, Stumpf, Stiner, Stauffer, Sullivan, Taliaferro, Terry, Thomas, Waters, Wilson—71.

Négative :

Messieurs Flagg, Fosdick, Goldman Hills, Hire, Seymour, Shaw, Thorpe, Wells —9 voix.

La motion est donc acceptée.

M. Montamat demande l'ajournement ; on le refuse par le vote suivant :

Affirmative :

Messieurs Abell, Balch, Burke, J. K. Cook, Dufresne, Dupaty, Gruneberg, Knobloch, Montamat, M. W Murphy, O'Conner, Stumpf, Sullivan, Waters—14 voix.

Négative :

Messieurs Ariail, Austin, Barrett, Beauvais, Bell, Bennie, Bofill, Bonzano, Bromley, Cazabat, T. Cook, Crozat, Cutler, Decker, Duane, Edwards, Ennis, Fish, Food, Flagg, Foley, Fosdick, Fuller, Gaidry, Gastinel, Geier, Goldman, Gorlinski, Harnan, Hart, Healy, Henderson, Hills, Hire, Howell, Howes, Kugler, Maas, Mann, Maurer, Mayer, Montague, Morris, E. Murphy, Newell, Normand, Ong, Orr, Pintado, J. Purcell, S. Pursell, Schroeder, Schnurr, Seymour, Shaw, Stiner, Spellicy, Stocker, Stiner, Stauffer, Taliaferro, Terry, Thorpe, Thomas, Wells, Wilson—66.

M. Thomas propose de modifier le rapport en substituant dans la répatition représentative, pour le premier District, "trois à cinq ;" pour le second, "cinq à huit ;" pour le troisième District, "sept à six ;" pour le cinquième, "quatre à trois ;" pour le sixième, "deux à trois ;" pour le huitième, "trois à deux ;" pour le dixième, "huit à sept."

. Le comité accepte ces amendements, et la Convention s'ajourne pendant la discussion qu'ils soulèvent.

Approuvé.

JOHN E. NEELIS,
Secrétaire.

JEUDI, le 19 mai 1864.

Le président appelle la Convention à l'ordre, et après la prière du Rév. Strong, on procède à l'appel nominal, duquel il appert que les 62 membres suivants sont présents :

Messieurs Abell, Ariail, Austin, Balch, Bailey, Baum, Bell, Bofill, Bonzano, Bromley, Burke, Campbell, Crozat, Davies, Decker, Duane, Dufresne, Edwards, Ennis, Fish, Flood, Foley, Fosdick, Geier, Gruneberg, Gaidry, Healy, Hart, Henderson, Hire, Howell, Howes, Kavanagh, Knobloch, Maas, Mann, Maurer, Mayer, Millspaugh, Montague, M. W. Murphy, Newell, Normand, O'Conner, Orr, J. Payne, Pintado, Poynot, J. Purcell, S. Pursell, Schroeder,

Schnurr, Smith, Stumpf, Stiner. Stauffer, Taliaferro, Terry, Waters, Wells, Wilson et M. le président.

En l'absence d'un quorum, le président donne au sergent d'armes l'ordre d'aller à la recherche d'autres membres.

MM. J. K. Cook, T. Cook, Cutler, Dupaty, Flagg, Gastinel, Gorlinski, Harnan, Hills, Mendiverri, Seymour, Shaw, Thorpe et Thomas (14) se présentant, le quorum existe.

Le procès-verbal d'hier est lu, corrigé et approuvé.

M. Henderson propose de prendre en considération nouvelle le vote sur sa résolution d'hier, concernant les institutions de charité, par suite duquel cette dite résolution a été repoussée.

Le président déclarant qu'il n'a pas le droit d'en demander la reconsidération, M. Gorlinski renouvelle la motion.

La motion de rejeter la proposition Gorlinski étant refusée, la question de reconsidération reparaît, et elle est adoptée par 40 voix contre 29.

Sur la proposition de M. Cutler, elle est référée à un comité de cinq, à la nomination du président.

M. Austin présente la résolution suivante: Les deux tiers des membres de cette Convention, à compter d'après le rôle, formeront désormais le quorum.

M. Campbell présente une résolution à l'effet de venir en aide aux réfugiés politiques, par suite de notre guerre civile.

Sur motion de M. Hills, cette résolution est référée au comité d'Assistance Publique.

M. Austin, président du comité chargé de l'examen du rapport de l'Auditeur, annonce que son rapport est en voie d'achèvement.

M. Hills demande la mise à l'ordre du jour de sa résolution concernant les membres retardataires.

La motion de rejet est repoussée par le vote suivant :

Affirmative :

Messieurs Abell, Austin, Bailey, Buckley, Campbell, Cutler, Dufresne, Dupaty, Flagg, Gruneberg, Gaidry, Henderson, Hire, Kavanagh, Knobloch, Maurer, Mendiverri, Montamat, J. T. Paine, S. Pursell, Schnurr, Waters—22.

Négative :

Messieurs Balch, Baum, Bell, Bofill, Bonzano, Bromley, Burke, J. K. Cook, T. Cook, Crozat, Davies, Decker, Duane, Edwards, Ennis, Flood, Foley, Fosdick, Gastinel, Geier, Goldman, Gorlinski, Healy, Harnan, Hart, Hills, Howell, Howes, Maas, Mann, Mayer, Millspaugh, Morris, M. W. Murphy, Newell, Normand, O'Conner, Orr, J. Payne, Poynot, Pintado, J. Purcell, Schroeder, Seymour, Shaw, Smith, Stumpf, Stiner, Stauffer, Sullivan, Taliaferro, Terry, Thorpe, Thomas, Wells, Wilson—56.

M. Hills propose la question préalable, laquelle étant repoussée, la question se présente de nouveau sur l'adoption de la résolution.

M. Montamat propose d'amender par l'insertion d'une négative, de manière à ce que le sens soit "ne perdra point." Rejeté.

Sur l'adoption de la résolution on donne le vote suivant :

Affirmative :

Messieurs Austin, Balch, Barrett, Bofill, Bonzano, Burke, Crozat, Davies, Duane, Ennis, Flood, Foley, Fosdick, Geier, Goldman, Gorlinski, Harnan, Hart, Hills, Howell, Kavanagh, Knobloch, Maas, Mann, Millspaugh, Montague, Newell, Normand, O'Conner, Orr, J. Payne, Pintado, J. Purcell. Schroeder, Shaw, Stumpf, Smith, Stiner, Stauffer, Taliaferro, Terry, Wells, Wilson—43.

Négative :

Messieurs Abell, Bailey, Baum, Bell, Bromley, Buckley, Campbell, J. K. Cook, T. Cook, Cutler, Decker, Dufresne, Dupaty, Edwards, Flagg, Gastinel, Gruneberg, Gaidry, Henderson, Hire, Howes, Kavanagh, Knobloch, Maurer, Mayor, Mendiverri, Montamat, M. W. Murphy, Ong, J. Paine, Poynot, S. Pursell, Schnurr, Seymour, Sullivan, Thorpe, Thomas, Waters—38.

M. Wilson appelle sa résolution concernant l'ajournement *sine die* à partir du 1er juin.

M. Sullivan propose le rejet. Adopté.

La motion de M. S. Pursell ordonnant réunion à 10 heures du matin est également rejetée.

M. Bonzano propose qu'il n'y ait point d'ajournement pour plus de 24 heures, à moins que la majorité ne seconde la motion d'ajournement.

Sur appel nominal, adopté par 38 voix contre 29.

RAPPORT DU COMITÉ SUR LE LEGISLATIF.

M. S. Pursell propose le rejet des lignes 88, 89, 90 et 91 de l'article 6.

ET LA'MENDEMENT DE LA CONSTITUTION DE LA LOUISIANE. 85

Rejet de la motion Goldman à l'effet de repousser l'amendement.

Sur motion de retrancher les susdites lignes, l'appel nominal donne pour résultat :

Affirmative :

Messieurs Abell, Balch, Bailey, Barrett, Baum, Bell, Bofill, Buckley, Burke, Campbell, J. K. Cook, T. Cook, Crozat, Cutler, Decker, Duane, Dufresne, Edwards, Flagg, Flood, Foley, Gastinel, Geier, Gruneberg, Healy, Harnan, Hart, Kavanagh, Knobloch, Mann, Maurer, Mayer, Mendiverri, Millspaugh, Montamat, M. W. Murphy, Newell, O'Conner, Ong, Orr, J. Payne, J. Purcell, S. Pursell, Schroeder, Seymour, Smith, Stumpf, Sullivan, Taliaferro, Terry, Thomas, Waters et Wilson—53.

Négative :

Messieurs Austin, Bonzano, Bromley, Davies, Dupaty, Ennis, Fosdick, Goldman, Henderson, Hills, Hire, Howell, Maas, Montague, Normand, J. T. Paine, Pintado, Shaw, Schnurr, Stiner, Stauffer, Thorpe et Wells —23.

M. Smith propose de retrancher de l'article 6 le mot "un," en regard des mots "paroisse de Ste-Marie," et d'y substituer le mot "deux."

Rejeté.

M. Balch propose de retrancher le mot "un" en regard des mots "paroisse d'Iberville," et d'y substituer le mot "deux."

Rejeté.

M. Bromley propose la reconsidération de l'article 6 du rapport, de la ligne 33 à la ligne 80, inclusivement.

Rejeté.

M. Mann propose de substituer au mot "soixante-dix," à la ligne 11, le mot "soixante-quinze."

La motion de M. Terry, permettant à des personnes ne jouissant pas de la qualité de citoyen, de voter en récompense de certains services rendus, est rejetée.

M. Flagg propose d'amender la ligne 33 substituant "Orléans, rive droite," au mot "Alger."

Accepté.

M. Bromley propose de substituer à la ligne 33, "trois" à "deux," en regard du mot "Lafourche," ainsi que de substituer "deux" à "trois" en regard du mot "Claiborne."

M. Bell propose d'amender l'article six, ligne 33, en substituant au mot "trois" le mot "quatre," en regard des mots "premier District."

Rejeté.

M. Montamat demande la question préalable, et, sur son adoption, la question principale au sujet de l'article 6 est mise aux voix, et cet article est adopté tel que l'amendement le demande.

Sur lecture, les articles 7, 8, 9, 10 et 11 sont adoptés.

A l'article 12, M. Stocker propose de supprimer à la ligne 5 les mots "sous le bon plaisir de la Législature."

Rejeté.

L'article est adopté suivant sa teneur primitive.

Le reste du rapport, après lecture de chaque section, est adopté.

La Convention s'ajourne au lendemain à midi.

Procès-verbal adopté.

JOHN E. NEELIS,
Secrétaire.

VENDREDI, le 20 mai 1864.

Conformément à l'ajournement, le président appelle la Convention à l'ordre.

Membres présents :

Messieurs Abell, Ariail, Austin, Balch, Bailey, Barrett, Baum, Beauvais, Bell, Bofill, Bonzano, Bromley, Buckley, Burke, Campbell, Collin, J. K. Cook, T. Cook, Crozat, Cutler, Davies, Dufresne, Duane, Dupaty, Edwards, Ennis, Fish, Flagg, Flood, Foley, Fosdick, Fuller, Gastinel, Geier, Goldman, Gorlinski, Gruneberg, Gaidry, Healy, Hart, Henderson, Hills, Howell, Howes, Kavanagh, Knobloch, Kugler, Maas, Mann, Maurer, Mayer, Mendiverri, Millspaugh, Montamat, Montague, Morris, E. Murphy, M. W. Murphy, Newell, Normand, O'Conner, Ong, J. Payne, Pintado, Poynot, J. Purcell, S. Pursell, Schroeder, Schnurr, Seymour, Shaw, Smith, Spellicy, Stocker, Stumpf, Stiner, Stauffer, Sullivan, Terry, Taliaferro, Thomas, Waters, Wenck, Wells, Wilson et M. le Président—88.

Après la prière dite par le Rév. Gregg, lecture est faite du procès-verbal de la dernière séance, lequel est corrigé et approuvé.

Sur motion de M. Abell, on excuse l'absence de M. Duke, de l'Ascension, occasionnée par la maladie d'un membre de sa famille.

M. Bofill propose de reconsidérer le vote

par lequel la motion de M. Hills concernant l'absence des membres a été adoptée.

M. Stauffer propose le rejet de la motion de M. Bofill ; sur quoi on demande l'appel nominal, lequel donne pour résultat 39 voix affirmatives contre 51 négatives.

Par conséquent, la Convention refuse le rejet.

M. Austin appelle sa motion relative au quorum : elle est rejetée.

ORDRE DU JOUR.

La troisième lecture du Rapport du comité sur le Législatif a lieu, et le dit rapport est adopté tel qu'il avait été amendé lors de sa seconde lecture.

La Convention s'occupe du Rapport du comité sur l'Exécutif, alors à sa seconde lecture.

La première section du rapport est adoptée sans amendement.

A la lecture de la seconde section, M. Sullivan propose d'en retrancher les mots "vingt-huit," et de les remplacer par "trente," ainsi que de substituer "dix" au mot "quatre," à la quatrième ligne, de manière à présenter le texte suivant :

Art. —. Nul ne sera éligible aux fonctions de gouverneur ou de lieutenant-gouverneur s'il n'est âgé de trente ans, et s'il n'a résidé dans l'Etat pendant dix années consécutives avant son élection.

Sur la motion de rejet des amendements, l'appel nominal donne le résultat suivant :

Affirmative :

Messieurs Ariail, Bonzano, Bromley, Collin, Cazabat, Duane, Dupaty, Ennis, Fish, Flood, Foley, Fosdick, Geier, Goldman, Gorlinski, Gaidry, Hills, Hire, Maas, Morris, E. Murphy, J. Payne, J. T. Paine, Pintado, J. Purcell, S. Pursell, Schroeder, Schnurr, Shaw, Smith, Stiner, Stauffer, Wenck—33.

Négative :

Messieurs Abell, Austin, Balch, Bailey, Barrett, Baum, Beauvais, Bell, Bennie, Bofill, Burke, Campbell, J. K. Cook, Crozat, T. Cook, Cutler, Decker, Dufresne, Edwards, Flagg, Fuller, Gastinel, Gruneberg, Harnan, Hart, Howell, Howes, Kavanagh, Knobloch, Kugler, Mann, Maurer, Mayer, Millspaugh, Montamat, Montague, M. W. Murphy, Newell, Normand, O'Conner, Ong, Orr, Poynot, Seymour, Spellicy, Stocker, Stumpf, Sullivan, Taliaferro, Thomas, Waters, Wells, Wilson, Buckley et M. le Président—53 membres.

La motion du rejet des amendements est donc repoussée, et la section amendée passe aux voix, ainsi que suit :

Affirmative :

MM. Abell, Ariail, Austin, Bailey, Balch, Barrett, Baum, Bofill, Buckley, Burke, Campbell, Cazabat, T. Cook, J. K. Cook, Crozat, Cutler, Decker, Dufresne, Edwards, Flagg, Fuller, Gastinel, Gaidry, Geier, Gruneberg, Harnan, Hart, Howes, Kavanagh, Knobloch, Kugler, Mann, Maurer, Mayer, Millspaugh, Montamat, Montague, M. W. Murphy, Newell, Normand, O'Conner, Ong, Orr, Seymour, Spellicy, Stocker, Stumpf, Stauffer, Sullivan, Taliaferro, Waters, Wells, Wilson—52.

Négative :

MM. Beauvais, Bell, Bonzano, Bromley, Brott, Collin, Duane, Dupaty, Ennis, Fish, Flood, Foley, Fosdick, Goldman, Gorlinski, Hills, Hire, Howell, Maas, Morris, J. Payne, J. T. Paine, Pintado, Poynot, J. Purcell, S. Pursell, Schroeder, Schnurr, Shaw, Smith, Stiner, Thorpe, Thomas, Wenck—34.

La section et l'amendement sont adoptés.

A la lecture de la 3e section, M. Mann propose de retrancher le mot "quatrième" à la seconde ligne, et d'y substituer le mot "deuxième," afin de lui donner la teneur suivante :

Art. —. Le gouverneur entrera dans l'exercice de ses fonctions le deuxième lundi de janvier, immédiatement après son élection, et y demeurera jusqu'au lundi immédiatement après le jour où son successeur aura été déclaré dûment élu et aura prêté le serment ou l'affirmation requise par la constitution.

Cette section est amendée et adoptée telle.

Sur motion on supprime la 4e section.

M. Wells propose d'amender la 5e section par l'adjonction du mot "Congrès," à la 1re ligne, et "ministre de toute secte religieuse," afin de lui donner la teneur suivante :

Aucun membre du Congrès ou ministre de toute secte religieuse, ou personne acceptant une charge sous l'autorité des Etats-Unis, ne sera éligible aux fonctions de gouverneur et de lieutenant-gouverneur.

L'amendement et la section sont adoptés.

M. Abell demande la reconsidération du vote rejetant la quatrième section.

M. Bofill propose le rejet de la demande

en considération, et le vote étant douteux, on a recours à l'appel nominal, qui donne le résultat suivant :

Affirmative :

MM. Austin, Bailey, Beauvais, Bofill, Burke, Cazabat, Collin, T. Cook, Crozat, Cutler, Davies, Duane, Dupaty, Edwards, Ennis, Fish, Flagg, Fuller, Gaidry, Geier, Henderson, Hire, Howes, Kugler, Montamat, Morris, Ong, J. Payne, S. Pursell, Schroeder, Seymour, Smith, Stocker, Stauffer, Sullivan, Terry, Thomas, Waters, Wenck, Wells—39.

Négative :

MM. Abell, Ariail, Baum, Barrett, Bell, Buckley, Campbell, J. K. Cook, Decker, Dufresne, Edwards, Flood, Foley, Fosdick, Gastinel, Goldman, Gorlinski, Gruneberg, Harnan, Hart, Healy, Hills, Howell, Kavanagh, Knobloch, Maas, Mann, Maurer, Mayer, Montague, M. W. Murphy, Newell, Normand, O'Conner, Orr, J. T. Paine, Pintado, Poynot, J. Purcell, Schnurr, Shaw, Spellicy, Stumpf, Stiner, Taliaferro, Wilson —46.

La susdite motion est donc rejetée.

Les sections 6, 7 et 8 sont adoptées sans amendement.

A la lecture de la section 9, M. Beauvais présente un substitut, lequel est rejeté.

La section est adoptée sans amendement ainsi que la dixième.

M. Thomas propose le substitut suivant à la section 11.

Le Gouverneur recevra un traitement de dix mille piastres, payable trimestriellement sur son propre ordre.

Sur motion de M. Smith, on substitue "huit" au mot "dix."

Adopté.

A la section 12, M. Stauffer propose de supprimer les mots "armée et marine" et de les remplacer par "milice."

Adopté tel.

Les sections 13, 14, 15, 16, 17, 18, 19, 20 et 21 sont adoptées sans amendement.

Sur motion de M. Davies, la 22e section est adoptée avec l'insertion du mot "quatre" au lieu de "deux."

Adopté tel.

Le secrétaire donne lecture de la section suivante.

Section 25. Les hommes libres et blancs de l'Etat seront armés et diciplinés pour sa défense ; mais ceux d'entre eux qui appartiendront à des sociétés religieuses dont les principes leur interdisent la profession des armes, ne seront point contraints à un service militaire, mais il paieront une somme équivalente pour jouir de cette immunité.

L'amendement de M. Stauffer, proposant d'armer et discipliner immédiatement tous les citoyens valides de l'Etat pour la défense de l'Etat, et d'envoyer par de là en lignes des Etats-Uniss dans la soi-disant Confédération, ceux qui refuseraient leurs services, est rejetée.

La motion de M. Thomas, de supprimer le mot "libres," est rejetée.

L'amendement de M. Orr : "Tous les hommes libres et blancs âgés de 18 à 45 ans seront armés et diciplinés pour la défense de l'Etat ;" et sa suite, demandant la suppression entière du reste de l'article, est rejeté par un vote de 33 contre 30 voix, sur quoi M. Stauffer demande l'appel nominal duquel il résulte :

Affirmative :

Messieurs Abell, Ariail, Balch, Barrett, Beauvais, Bofill, Buckley, Burke, Cazabat, Crozat, Decker, Duane, Dufresne, Edwards, Ennis, Flagg, Foley, Fosdick, Fuller, Gorlinski, Gruneberg, Harnan, Hart, Hire, Howell, Howes, Kavanagh, Knobloch, Mann, Maurer, Montamat, M. W. Murphy, Newell, Normand, O'Conner, Poynot, Schnurr, Seymour, Shaw, Smith, Spellicy, Stocker, Stauffer, Sullivan, Taliaferro, Terry, Waters, Wells, Wilson—49.

Négative :

Messieurs Baum, Bell, Bonzano, Campbell, J. K., Cook, T. Cook, Cutler, Davies, Fish, Flood, Goldman, Gaidry, Healy, Henderson, Hills, Kugler, Maas, Mayer, Morris, Ong, Orr, J. Payne, Pintado, S. Pursell, Schroeder, Stumpf, Stiner, Thomas —26.

M. Smith, propose de supprimer le mot "blancs" à la première ligne. Accepté.

Mais au vote de la section amendée, elle est rejetée par 40 voix contre 30. Puis la section est adoptée dans sa teneur primitive.

M. Sullivan demande l'ajournement et l'appel nominal le refuse par 41 voix contre 39, savoir :

Affirmative :

Messieurs Abell, Austin, Balch, Bailey, Barrett, Baum, Bofill, Buckley, Campbell, J. K. Cook, T. Cook, Crozat, Duane, Dufresne, Dupaty, Flagg, Flood, Foley, Gorlinski, Gaidry, Gruneberg, Healy, Hart, Hills, Howes, Kavanagh, Kugler, Maurer,

Mayer, E. Murphy, O'Conner, Orr, Poynot, S. Pursell, Schnurr, Smith, Spellicy, Stocker, Sullivan, Terry—39.

Négative :

Messieurs Ariail, Beauvais, Bell, Bonzano, Bruckley, Cazabat, Cutler, Davies, Decker, Edwards, Ennis, Goldman, Harnan, Henderson, Hire, Howell, Maas, Mann, Montamat, Morris, M. W. Murphy, Newell, Normand, Orr, J. Payne, J. T. Paine, Pintado, S. Pursell, Schroeder, Seymour, Stocker, Stumpf, Stiner, Stauffer, Thomas, Waters, Wenck, Wells, Wilson—41.

La section 26 est adoptée sans amendement.

M. Bell propose la dispense du réglement à sa troisième lecture. Rejeté.

Le président annonce qu'il a nommé du comité spécial au sujet des Institutions Charitables, MM. Henderson, président, Hills, Bonzano, Shaw et Thorpe.

La Convention s'ajourne.

Approuvé.

JOHN E. NEELIS,
Secrétaire.

SAMEDI, le 21 Mai 1864.

Conformément à l'ajournement, la Convention se réunit.

64 membres sont présents, savoir :

MM. Abell, Ariail, Austin, Bailey, Baum, Bell, Bonzano, Bromley, Burke, Collin, J. K. Cook, T. Cook, Crozat, Cutler, Davies, Decker, Dufresne, Dupaty, Edwards, Ennis, Fish, Flagg, Flood, Foley, Fosdick, Gastinel, Gaidry, Geier, Gorlinski, Gruneberg, Harnan, Hart, Henderson, Hills, Howell, Howes, Knobloch, Kugler, Maas, Mann, Maurer, Mendiverri, Millspaugh, Montague, M. W. Murphy, Normand, O'Conner, Orr, J. T. Paine, Pintado, Poynot, J. Pursell, S. Pursell, Schroeder, Seymour, Schnurr, Spellicy, Stumpf, Stiner, Stauffer, Taliaferro, Terry, Wilson et M. le Président—64.

En l'absence d'un quorum, le sergent-d'armes se met à la recherche d'autres membres. L'entrée de MM. Barrett, Beauvais, Duane, Smith, Waters, E. Murphy, Bofill, Buckley, Healy, Fosdick, Goldman et Montamat complète le nombre.

Lecture est faite du procès-verbal d'hier, lequel est approuvé.

On passe à la troisième lecture du Rapport du comité sur l'Exécutif.

M. Cutler propose de retrancher ce qui suit : "tandis qu'il agit comme président du Sénat," de sorte que l'article 9 présente le texte suivant :

Le lieutenant-gouverneur recevra un traitement annuel de cinq mille piastres, payable par trimestre.

Le reste de l'article au rapport est supprimé, ainsi que le remplacement à l'article 22, au sujet de la durée des fonctions du trésorier, du mot "deux" par "quatre annnées," et l'insertion après "trésorier" des mots "l'auditeur des comptes publics."

Après le mot "Etat" à l'article 23, à la première ligne, supprimer "et;" insérer après le second mot "Etat," auditeur des comptes publics. Après le mot "Etat," à la seconde ligne, au même article, insérer "l'auditeur recevra un traitement de dix mille piastres ; le trésorier d'Etat et le secrétaire d'Etat recevront chacun un traitement de cinq mille piastres."

Tous les changements ci-dessus proposés sont adoptés, ainsi que le rapport avec ses amendements.

On passe au rapport du comité du judiciaire. M. Abell propose de remettre la seconde lecture à lundi. Sur la proposition de M. Stauffer, 36 voix contre 26 rejettent cette motion.

M. Montamat propose l'ajournement, sur quoi l'appel nominal, ainsi que suit :

Affirmative ; 29 voix, savoir :

Messieurs Abell, Bell, Burke, Collin, T. Cook, Decker, Dufresne, Dupaty, Flagg, Foley, Fosdick. Gastinel, Gaidry, Gruneberg, Hart, Healy, Henderson, Knobloch, Mayer, Montamat, J. Purcell, Schroeder, Seymour, Smith, Stocker, Stiner, Sullivan, Waters, Wilson—29.

Négative :

Messieurs Ariail, Austin, Bailey, Barrett, Baum, Beauvais, Bofill, Bonzano, Bromley, J. K. Cook, Crozat, Cutler, Davies, Duane, Ennis, Fish, Flood, Fuller, Geier, Harnan, Hills, Howell, Kugler, Maas, Mann, Mendiverri, Millspaugh, Montague, Morris, E. Murphy, M. W. Murphy, Newell, Normand, Orr, J. T. Paine, Pintado, Poynot, S. Pursell, Schnurr, Spellicy, Stumpf, Stauffer, Taliaferro, Terry, Thorpe, Thomas, Wenck, Wilson—49.

Lecture du rapport, section par section ; le premier et le second article sont, à l'unanimité, adoptés, dans les termes du rapport.

M. Abell interrompt la question, en prétendant que différents substituts ont été offerts pour le rapport, et que la Convention ne s'en étant pas encore occupé, il en demande la lecture.

Mais sur la motion de M. Foley, la Convention s'ajourne.

Approuvé.

JOHN E. NEELIS,
Secrétaire.

LUNDI, le 23 mai 1864.

Le président appelle la Convention à l'ordre à midi, et les membres suivants répondent à l'appel du rôle :

MM. Ariail, Austin, Balch, Bailey, Barrett, Baum, Beauvais, Bell, Brombley, Buckley, Burke, Campbell, Collin, Crozat, Davies, Duane, Duke, Edwards, Ennis, Flood, Gaidry, Geier, Goldman, Healy, Henderson, Hills, Howell, Kavanagh, Kugler, Maas, Mendiverri, Morris, M. W. Murphy, Newell, Normand, J. Payne, Pintado, J. Purcell, S. Pursell, Schroeder, Schnurr, Seymour, Shaw, Smith, Spellicy, Stumpf, Stiner, Stauffer, Taliaferro, Terry, Thomas, Waters, Wenck et M. le président —54.

Le nombre de membres n'étant pas suffisant pour former un quorum, le président donne l'ordre au sergent d'armes d'aller à la recherche des absents.

L'entrée de MM. Abell, Bofill, Cazabat, Dufresne, Fish, Flagg, Foley, Fuller, Gastinel, Gruneberg, Hart, Howes, Knobloch, Maurer, Mayer, O'Conner, Ong, Poynot, Stocker, Orr, Thorpe et Wilson (22 membres) complétant le nombre requis, le président annonce l'existence du quorum, et il invite MM. Winfree et Russ à remplir par intérim les fonctions des deux secrétaires-adjoints non présents.

M. Hills est invité à présider la séance.

Après lecture, le procès-verbal est approuvé.

Le comité sur les Dispositions transitoires et sur la Mise à Exécution, annonce que son rapport est en voie de progrès.

Le comité des Finances présente les rapports suivants :

RAPPORT DU COMITE DES FINANCES.

17 mai—En caisse d'après le mandat No. 5	$55,485 40	
17 mai—Payé le mandat No. 35	$1,040 00	
18 mai—Payé le mandat No. 36	644 00	
19 mai—Payé le mandat No. 38	520 00	
21 mai—Payé le mandat No. 39	1,240 00	
21 mai—Payé le mandat No. 40	1,130 00	
21 mai—Payé le mandat No. 41	860 00	
21 mai—Payé le mandat No. 42	411 00	
21 mai—Payé le mandat No. 43	108 00	
21 mai—Payé le mandat No. 44	470 00	
21 mai—Payé le mandat No. 46	1,876 00	8,299 00
		$47,186 40

23 mai—Balance en caisse à cette date des fonds alloués pour le paiement du *per diem* des membres et de la rémunération des employés de la Convention, quarante-sept mille cent quatre-vingt-six piastres et quarante cents.

RAPPORT DU COMITE DES FINANCES SUR LES FONDS DES DEPENSES CASUELLES.

17 mai—Balance en caisse d'après le rapport No. 5	$9,585 48	
21 mai—Payé à DeCoursey, le mandat No. 45	826 00	
	$8,759,48	

23 mai—Balance en caisse ce jour, huit mille sept cent cinquante-neuf piastres et quarante-huit cents.

18 mai—Payé la somme de quinze mille piastres à W. R. Fish, pour impressions et annonces, sur le mandat No. 37, des fonds non autrement alloués par la Convention, comme il appert de la pièce justificative No. 5, enregistrée.

M. Henderson, au nom du comité spécial sur les Institutions d'assistance publique, présente un rapport recommandant une allocation de vingt-et-une mille piastres, distribuable ainsi que suit, savoir :

Pour l'Asile des Orphelins, Nlle-Orléans	$ 1,500 00
Pour l'Asile Catholique de Ste-Marie	4,000 00
Pour l'Asile des Femmes, rue du Camp	4,000 00
Pour la Maison du Bon Pasteur	250 00
Pour l'Asile des Veuves et Orphelins Israélites	500 00
Pour l'Asile Catholique de St-Joseph	1,500 00
Pour la Maison de Travail Ste-Elizabeth	1,000 00
Pour la Société d'Assistance aux Orphelins, 4e District	1,000 00

Pour l'Institution des Garçons

de Couleur Indigents, dans le 3e District............	1,000 00
Pour les Dames de la Providence, 3e District...........	750 00
Pour l'Asile Ste-Anne pour les Veuves et Orphelins dans l'indigence..............	1,500 00
Pour l'Asile des Enfants de l'Eglise Episcopale Protestante.....................	500 00
Pour l'Asile Catholique des Orphelins Indigents.........	750 00
Pour l'Association Catholique de Bienfaisance, à Baton-Rouge...................	250 00
Pour l'Asile des Orphelines à Baton-Rouge...........	500 00
Pour l'Asile St-Vincent des Orphelins, à Donaldsonville..	500 00
Pour l'Asile Milne, à la Nlle-Orléans	500 00
Pour l'Asile St-Vincent des Orphelins.................	500 00
Pour l'Asile des Orphelins dans la rue Moreau...........	500 00
	$21,000 00

Sur motion, ce rapport est à l'ordre du jour.

M. Sullivan propose d'y ajouter une allocation de $3000, au profit de l'Association de Bienfaisance des Pompiers.

M. Montamat propose de porter l'allocation à $5000.

M. Sullivan y consent.

M. Davies demande le rejet de ce sous-amendement, et de l'appel nominal il résulte:

Affirmative :

Messieurs Burke, Campbell, Collin, Cazabat, Davies. Duane, Dupaty, Edwards, Ennis, Fiagg, Flood, Foley Fuller, Gaidry, Goldman, Gruneberg, Harnan, Hart Henderson, Hills, Howell, Knobloch, Kugler, Maas, Mann, E. Murphy, M. W Murphy, Newell, Normand, Ong, Pintado, Poynot, Schroeder, Schnurr, Smith, Stauffer, Thorpe, Wells—38 voix.

Négative :

Messieurs Abell, Ariail, Austin, Barrett, Balch, Bailey, Bell, Bofill, Bromley, Buckley, J. K., Cook Crozat, Decker, Duke, Dufresne, Gastinel, Geier, Healy, Howes, Maurer, Mayer, Mendiverri, Morris, Montamat, Orr, J. Payne, J. Purcell, S. Pursell, Seymour, Shaw, Spellicy. Stumpf, Stiner, Sullivan, Terry, Waters, Wenck, Wilson—38 voix.

Le président par intérim déclare qu'une majorité n'ayant pas voté en faveur de la motion, elle est rejetée.

M. Henderson propose de rejeter, toute la question en entier ; sur quoi, l'appel nominal donne le résultat suivant :

Affirmative:

Messieurs Abell, Ariail, Austin, Balch, Bromley, Burke, Collin, T. Cook, Crozat, Cutler, Davies, Decker, Edwards, Ennis, Flagg, Flood, Fuller, Goldman, Hart, Harnan, Henderson, Hills, Howell, Knobloch, Kugler, Maas, Mann, Mendiverri, Morris, Newell, Normand, Ong, Pintado, Poynot, S. Pursell, Schroeder, Schnurr, Seymour, Smith, Stauffer, Wenck—41 voix.

Négative :

Messieurs Barrett, Beauvais, Bell, Bofill, Buckley, Campbell, J. K. Cook, Dufresne,, Duane, Dupaty, Duke, Foley, Gastinel, Geier. Gorlinski, Gruneberg, Healy, Howes, Maurer, Mayer, Montamat, E. Murphy, M. W. Murphy, O'Conner, Orr, J. Payne, J. Purcell, Shaw, Spellicy, Stocker, Stumpf-Stiner, Sullivan, Terry, Thorpe, Waters, Wilson—37 voix.

La question en entier, est donc rejetée.

ORDRE DU JOUR.

On s'occupe du Rapport du comité sur le Judiciaire.

Sur motion de M. Howell, le vote de samedi dernier, en vertu duquel les sections 1 et 2 furent adoptées, est repris en considération ; et, après lecture, la première section est adoptée.

Lecture est donnée de la deuxième section, avec l'amendement de M. Abell, savoir :

Elle aura un droit de contrôle général sur tous les tribunaux inférieurs ou supérieurs ; elle pourra lancer des *writs* d'erreur, de *supersedeas*, de *certiorari*, d'*habeas corpus*, de *quo-warranto* et autres *writs* de secours et protection ; en évoquer l'audition et prononcer souverainement en ces causes.

M. Pursell propose de rejeter l'amendement.

Rufusé par 33 voix contre 28.

Sur la question d'adopter, l'amendement, l'appel nominal donne le résultat suivant :

Affirmative :

Messieurs Abell, Balch, Bailey, Bell, Bofill, Buckley, Burke, Campbell, Collin, T. Cook, Decker, Duane, Dufresne, Dupaty, Duke, Ennis, Flood, Gaidry, Gruneberg, Knobloch, Maurer, Mayer, Mendiverri, Montamat, E. Murphy, M. W. Murphy, Normand, Ong, Orr, Schroeder, Schnurr, Smith, Stiner, Stocker, Stumpf, Terry, Waters—37 voix.

Négative :

ET L'AMENDEMENT DE LA CONSTITUTION DE LA LOUISIANE.

MM. Ariail, Austin, Barrett, Beauvais, Bromley, J. K. Cook, Crozat, Cutler, Edwards, Fuller, Gastinel, Geier, Goldman, Harnan, Hart, Henderson, Hire, Howell, Kugler, Maas, Mann, Morris, J. Newell, J. Payne, Poynot, J. Purcell, S. Pursell, Seymour, Shaw, Spellicy, Stauffer, Sullivan, Wilson—33.

Dans l'absence d'un quorum, une motion d'ajournement est portée, et de l'appel nominal il résulte ce qui suit :

Affirmative :
MM. Abell, Austin, Balch, Bailey, Bofill, Buckley, Burke, Campbell, J. K, Cook, T. Cook, Crozat, Cutler, Decker, Duke, Duane, Dufresne, Edwards, Flood, Fuller, Gastinel, Goldman, Gruneberg, Hart, Knobloch, Maas, Maurer, Mayer, Mendiverri, Montamat, E. Murphy, M. W. Murphy, O'Conner, Ong, Orr, Poynot, Schnurr, Seymour, Smith, Spellicy, Stocker, Stumpf, Sullivan, Waters—43 voix.

Négative :
MM. Ariail, Barrett, Beauvais, Bell, Bromley, Collin, Dupaty, Ennis, Geier, Gaidry, Henderson, Hire, Howell, Kugler, Mann, Morris, Newell, Normand, J. Payne, J. Purcell, S. Pursell, Schroeder, Stauffer, Stiner, Terry, Thorpe, Thomas, Wenck, Wells, Wilson—30 voix.

En conséquence, le président par intérim déclare que la Convention est bien dûment ajournée au lendemain à midi.

Approuvé.
JOHN E. NEELIS, Secrétaire.

MARDI, le 24 mai 1864.
La Convention se réunit à midi.
L'appel du rôle indique la présence de 58 membres, savoir :

MM. Abell, Ariail, Austin, Bailey, Barrett, Beauvais, Bell, Bofill, Bromley, Burke, Campbell, Cazabat, Collin, J. K. Cook, T. Cook, Davies, Decker, Dufresne, Duke, Edwards, Ennis, Fish, Flagg, Flood, Fcley, Fosdick, Geier, Goldman, Gorlinski, Gruneberg, Healy, Heard, Henderson, Hills, Hire, Howell, Knobloch, Maas, Mann, Montamat, Morris, M. W. Murphy, Newell, Normand, O'Conner, J. Payne, Pintado, Poynot, S. Pursell, Shaw, Smith, Spellicy, Stumpf, Stiner, Terry, Wenck, Wells et M. le président—58.

Le nombre pour le quorum manquant, le sergent-d'armes reçoit l'ordre d'aller à la recherche des absents : et les membres suivants étant entrés, le président annonce que .e quorum existe : ces membres sont MM. Baum, Cutler, Duane, Dupaty, Fuller, Gastinel, Gaidry, Harnan, Hart, Howes, Kugler, Mayer, Mendiverri, E. Murphy, Schroeder, Stocker, Sullivan, Thorpe, Waters, Wilson --21.

A la lecture du procès-verbal, M. Abell propose de le corriger en biffant les mots "pas de quorum de votants." Le président remet la décision à l'Assemblée, laquelle refuse la correction proposée, déclarant que le procès-verbal est exact, par un vote de 43 voix contre 18.

M. Montamat propose ce qui suit :
Le major général N. P. Banks et son état-major seront respectueusement invités à se présenter à la Convention ; un comité de cinq, nommé par le président, se rendra auprès du Gén. Banks, afin de lui faire part de la présente résolution.

Sur motion de M. Montamat. on se dispense du réglement. et cette résolution est adoptée à l'unanimité.

Le président désigne comme membres de ce comité MM. Montamat. Shaw. Cutler, Howell et Heard.

M. Hills propose ce qui suit :
Attendu, Que l'absence de quelques membres à l'appel du rôle d'entrée à midi, cause un grand retard dans les travaux de la Convention ;
Il est résolu, Que les membres qui manqueront de répondre à leurs noms dans les quinze minutes suivant l'heure de midi, perdront leur rétribution quotidienne pour chaque jour d'absence.

M. Montamat demande :
Que la place de secrétaire-adjoint, actuellement occupée par M. F. H. Murphy, soit déclarée vacante, et que le secrétaire soit autorisé à y nommer une personne capable pour en remplir les devoirs pendant le reste de cette session.

M. Terry propose:
Une somme de cent piastres sera payée de tous fonds au trésor non autrement alloués, à l'effet de payer les frais d'enrôlement de l'acte d'émancipation, sur parchemin, en langues anglaise et française, adoptée en cette Convention le 11 mai 1864.

Par M. Thorpe :
Résolution—L'imprimeur officiel de cette Convention est invité à publier tous les matins, dans le *True Delta*, un rapport aussi complet que possible des travaux de la séance de la veille. y comprenant un tableau des votes sur les appels, et une portion suffisante des débats, pour donner une idée claire des travaux quotidiens.

Il est décidé que cette résolution sera déposée jusqu'à nouvel ordre, la Convention refusant dispense du réglement.

Résolution présentée par M. Stocker. déposée jusqu'au lendemain :

Résolu. Que la somme de $22,500 00 est allouée de tous fonds au trésor, non autrement affectés, pour objets de charité.

Résolu. Qu'un comité de cinq sera chargé de la distribution de cette dite somme.

M. Henderson annonce que M. Hamilton, l'un des secrétaires, étant indisposé, demande un congé de quelques jours.

Sur la proposition de M. Henderson, ce congé est accordé.

M. Henderson demande la reprise en considération du vote à la séance d'hier, par lequel la résolution relative aux objets de bienfaisance a été repoussée.

M. Hills propose le rejet de cette présente motion. Accepté.

Le comité sur les Dispositions Transitoires annonce que son rapport progresse.

M. Austin, au nom du comité chargé de s'occuper du rapport de l'auditeur, annonce que l'un des membres est absent, et qu'un autre le sera sous peu ; en conséquence, il propose leur remplacement.

Le président nomme M. Cutler et M. Heard en lieu et place de M. Thomas et de M. Wells.

Le président soumet à la Convention un rapport du secrétaire d'Etat relatif à une partie de la Bibliothèque d'Etat.

Sur motion de M. Hills, cette affaire est référée à un comité de trois, et le président nomme MM. Hills, Howell et Campbell.

ORDRE DU JOUR.

La seconde lecture du rapport sur le Judiciaire a lieu, en commençant par la seconde section, et les amendements de MM. Abell et Henderson.

Sur la décision de s'occuper d'abord de l'amendement Abell, le président déclare que la question est ouverte de nouveau.

M. Cazabat propose de biffer les mots "erreur et."

M. Cutler propose le rejet de l'amendement et du sous-amendement, sur quoi l'appel nominal ainsi que suit :

Affirmative :

Messieurs Ariail, Austin, Bailey, Barrett, Beauvais, Burke, Cazabat, J. K. Cook, Crozat, Cutler, Davies, Edwards, Fish, Fuller, Geier, Goldman, Hart, Henderson, Heard, Howell, Howes, Kugler, Maas, Mann, Morris, Newell, Normand, Ong, Orr, J. Payne, Pintado, J. Purcell, S. Pursell, Poynot, Schroeder, Shaw, Stumpf, Stauffer, Thorpe, Wenck, Wells—41.

Négative :

MM. Abell, Bell, Bofill, Bromley, Campbell, Collin, T. Cook, Decker, Dufresne, Duane, Duke, Dupaty, Ennis, Flood, Foley, Fosdick, Gastinel, Gaidry, Gorlinski, Gruneberg, Harnan, Healy, Hills, Knobloch, Mayer, Montamat, E. Murphy, M. W. Murphy, O'Conner, Smith, Stocker, Stiner, Sullivan, Terry, Waters, Wilson—36.

L'amendement est donc rejeté.

L'amendement de Henderson venant en suite, M. Pursell en propose le rejet, sur l'appel nominal, lequel donne pour résultat :

Affirmative :

MM. Ariail, Bailey, Barrett, Beauvais, Bromley, Campbell, Cazabat, J. K. Cook, Crozat, Edwards, Fuller, Gaidry, Hart, Harnan, Heard, Howell, Howes, Knobloch, Kugler, Mann, Mayer, Morris, Normand, Newell, J. Payne, Pintado, Poynot, S. Pursell, Shaw, Stumpf, Terry, Thorpe, Wells—33.

Négative :

MM. Abell, Austin, Bell, Bofill, Burke, Collin, T. Cook, Cutler, Davies, Decker, Duane, Duke, Dupaty, Ennis, Fish, Flagg, Flood, Foley, Fosdick, Gastinel, Geier, Goldman, Gorlinski, Gruneberg, Henderson, Healy, Hills, Maas, Montamat, E. Murphy, M. W. Murphy, O'Conner, Ong, J. Purcell, Schroeder, Stocker, Stauffer, Stiner, Sullivan, Wenck, Wilson—41.

La motion est donc repoussée.

On demande l'appel du rôle, et 70 membres seulement répondant à leurs noms, la Convention s'ajourne faute de quorum.

JOHN E. NEELIS, Secrétaire.

MERCREDI, le 25 mai 1864.

La séance s'ouvre à midi, et l'appel nominal donne pour résultat :

MM. Abell, Ariail, Barrett, Beauvais, Bell, Bofill, Bromley, Buckley, Burke, Cazabat, Campbell, Collin, J. K. Cook, T. Cook, Crozat, Davies, Decker, Duane, Dufresne, Dupaty, Duke, Edwards, Ennis, Fish, Flagg, Flood, Foley, Fosdick, Fuller, Gastinel, Gaidry, Geier, Goldman, Gorlinski, Gruneberg, Harnan, Heard, Henderson, Hills, Hire, Howell, Knobloch, Kugler, Maas, Eann, Maurer, Mayer, Mendiverri, Montamat, Morris, M. W. Murphy, Newell, Normand, O'Conner, J. Payne, Pintado, Poynot, S. Pursell, Shaw, Schnurr, Smith, Spelley, Stumpf, Stiner, Stauffer, Sullivan, Terry, Thorpe, Wenck, Wells, Wilson, et M. le president—72.

L'entrée subséquente de MM. Baum, Hart, Healy, Kavanagh, E. Murphy, J. Purcell complète le nombre pour un quorum.

Après lecture, le journal de la dernière séance est approuvé.

Le président soumet à la Convention un compte porté par la ville de la Nouvelle-

ET L'AMENDEMENT DE LA CONSTITUTION DE LA LOUISIANE.

Orléans contre l'Etat de la Louisiane, s'élevant à $6,139, 13 pour frais de préparatifs, afin de rendre la salle de la Liberté propre à l'usage de la Convention.

M. Hills demande sa résolution concernant les membres absents.

La motion de rejet par M. Waters est repoussée.

M. Stoker, propose d'ajouter après absence, les mots, "sans excuse satisfaisante." Accepté.

Sur l'adoption définitive, l'appel nominal donne pour résultat :

Affirmative :

MM. Ariail, Austin, Barrett, Bell, Bromley, Burke, Cazabat, Collin, T. Cook, Davies, Duane, Dufresne, Ennis, Fish, Flood, Foley, Fosdick, Geier, Golman, Gorlinski, Harnan, Healy, Hills, Howell, Kugler, Maas, Mann, Mayer, Montamat, Morris, Newell, Normand, Pintado, J. Purcell, Schroeder, Shaw, Smith, Stocker, Stumpf, Stiner, Stauffer, Terry, Thorpe, Wells, Wilson—45.

Négative :

MM. Abell, Bailey, Beauvais, Bofill, Buckley, Campbell, J. K. Cook, Crozat, Decker, Dupaty Duke, Edwards, Flagg, Fuller, Gastinel, Gaidry, Gruneberg, Hart, Heard, Henderson, Hire, Howes, Kavanagh, Knobloch, Maurer Mendiverri, E. Murphy, M. W. Murphy, O'Conner, Ong, Orr, J. Payne, Poynot, S. Purcell, Schnurr, Seymour, Spellicy, Sullivan, Waters—39.

La résolution est donc adoptée.

M. Foley demande sa résolution relative à l'allocation de $100 pour l'enrôlement du décret d'émancipation du 11 mai 1864.

Sur motion de M. Wilson. on en réfère au comité des Dépenses Casuelles.

M. Stocker demande sa résolution pour l'allocation des $22,500 pour objets de bienfaisance.

M. Smith propose le rejet : accepté par un vote par assis et levé de 47 membres contre 27.

Comme il n'y point de quorum, M. Stocker demande un appel général, insistant sur un vote obligatoire. Accordé, et il en résulte :

Affirmative :

MM. Abell, Ariail, Austin, Bailey, Baum, Beauvais, Bofill, Bromley, Burke, Cazabat, Collin, Crozat, Davies, Decker, Dupaty, Duane, Duke, Edwards, Ennis, Flagg, Fuller, Fosdick, Goldman, Henderson, Hills, Hire, Howell, Howes, Knoblock, Kugler, Maas, Maurer, Mayer, Mendiverri, Montamat, Morris, M. W. Murphy, Newell, Normand, Ong. Orr, J. Payne, Pintado, Poynot, Seymour, Shaw, Smith, Spellicy, Stauffer, Sullivan, Waters, Wenck, Wells—53.

Néative :

MM. Barrett, Bell, Buckley, Campbell, J. K. Cook, T. Cook, Dufresne, Fish, Flood, Foley, Gastinel, Gaidry, Geier, Gorlinski, Gruneberg, Harnan, Hart, Healey, Heard, Kavanagh, Mann, E. Murphy, O'Conner, J. Purcell, S. Pursell, Schnurr, Schroeder, Stocker, Stumpf, Stiner, Terry, Thorpe, Wilson—33.

La résolution est donc rejetée.

ORDRE DU JOUR.

La question est l'examen du rapport sur le Judiciaire.

Lecture de la seconde section et de l'amendement de M. Henderson ; sur ce, avec la permission de la Convention. M. Henderson retire son amendement et présente un susbtitut.

M. Pursell demande le rejet du susbtitut ; cette demande est repoussée par un vote par assis et levé de 44 membres contre 32.

Sur la question d'adopter le substitut de M. Henderson, l'appel nominal donne :

Affirmative :

MM. Abell, Bailey, Buckley, Collin, T. Cook, Decker, Duane, Dufresne, Dupaty Duke, Ennis, Fish, Flagg, Flood, Foley, Fosdick, Gairdy, Gorlinski, Gruneberg, Henderson, Hills, Kavanagh, Maurer, Maan, Mendiverri, M. W. Murphy, E. Murphy, O'Conner, Orr, Schroeder, Seymour, Smith, Stumpf, Stiner, Stauffer, Sullivan, Terry, Thorpe, Waters—39.

Négative:

MM. Ariail, Austin, Baum, Barrett, Beauvais, Bell, Bofill, Bromley, Burke, Campbell, Cazabat, J. K. Cook, Crozat, Davies, Edwards, Fuller, Gastinel, Geier, Goldman, Harnan, Hart, Healy, Heard, Hire, Howell, Howes, Knobloch, Kugler, Mann, Mayer, Montamat, Morris, Newell, Normand, Ong, J. Payne, Pintado, Poynot, J. Purcell, S. Purcell, Schnurr, Shaw, Spellicy, Stocker, Wenck, Wells et Wilson—47.

L'article 2 est donc adopté tel que le comité l'avait rédigé.

Lecture de l'article 3, et M. Sullivan présente un substitut.

M. Cazabat en propose le rejet. Refusé.

Durant la discussion au sujet de l'article 3, la Convention s'ajourne.

Approuvé.

JOHN E. NEELIS,
Secrétaire.

JEUDI, le 26 mai 1864.

La séance s'ouvre à midi. La prière est dite par le Rév. Gilbert.

L'appel du rôle montre la présence de MM. Abell, Ariail, Austin, Bailey, Barrett, Baum, Beauvais, Bell, Bennie, Bofill, Bromley, Buckley, Burke, Campbell, Collin, J. K. Cook, T. Cook, Crozat, Cutler, Davies, Duane, Dufresne, Duke, Dupaty, Edwards, Ennis, Fish, Flagg, Flood, Foley, Fosdick, Fuller, Gaidry, Geier, Gorlinski, Goldman, Gruneberg, Hrrnan, Hart, Healy, Heard, Henderson, Hills, Hire, Howell, Howes, Kavanagh, Knobloch, Kugler, Maas, Mann, Maurer, Mayer, Mendiverri, Montamat, E. Murphy, M. W. Murphy, Newell, Normand, O'Conner, Ong, Orr, J. Payne, J. T. Paine, Pintado, Poynot, J. Purcell, S. Pursell, Schroeder, Schnurr, Seymour, Shaw, Smith, Spellicy, Stocker, Stumpf, Stiner, Stauffer, Sullivan, Terry, Thorpe, Waters, Wenck, Wells, et Wilson et M. le président—86.

Il y a quorum.

Lecture et adoption du procès-verbal de la dernière séance.

M. Thorpe présente la résolution suivante, qui est déposée, sujette aux réglements.

"La plume dont le président de cette Convention s'est servi pour apposer sa signature à l'ordonnance d'émancipation, sera présentée au Major-Général Banks, accompagné d'un certificat constatant son identité."

RAPPORT DES COMITES.

Le comité sur les Dispositions Transitoires annonce que son rapport progresse ; celui des Finances n'en présente point, non plus que ceux sur les Dépenses, sur les Rétributions et sur la Circulation.

Le comité sur le rapport de l'Auditeur annonce que son rapport progresse.

M. Montamat propose la reprise en considération de la résolution de M. Hills, adoptée hier, concernant les membres absents à l'appel du rôle d'ouverture.

M. Hills propose le rejet de la motion de M. Montamat ; et sur ce appel nominal, lequel donne le résultat suivant :

Affirmative :

MM. Ariail, Barrett, Beauvais, Bell, Bromley, Burke, Collin, T. Cook, Dufresne, Duane, Edwards, Ennis, Flood, Fosdick, Foley, Geier, Goldman, Gorlinski, Harnan, Hills, Howell, Kugler, Mann, Newell, Normand, J. Payne, J. Purcell, S. Pursell, Schroeder, Shaw, Smith, Stiner, Stauffer, Terry, Thorpe, Wells, Wilson—36.

Négative :

MM. Abell, Bailey, Baum, Bennie, Beauvais, Bofill, Buckley, Campbell, J. K. Cook, Crozat, Cutler, Davies, Decker, Duke, Dupaty, Fish, Flagg, Fuller, Gaidry, Gruneberg, Hart, Healy, Heard, Henderson, Hire, Howes, Kavanagh, Knobloch, Maas, Maurer, Mayer, Mendiverri, Montamat, E. Murphy, M. W. Murphy, O'Conner, Ong, Orr, J. T. Paine, Pintado, Poynot, Schnurr, Seymour, Spellicy, Stocker, Stumpf, Sullivan, Waters, Wenck—49.

La motion est donc rejetée.

Sur la reconsidération, l'appel donne pour résulat, savoir :

Affirmative :

MM. Abell, Austin, Bailey, Baum, Beauvais, Bennie, Bofill, Buckley, Campbell, J. K. Cook, Crozat, Cutler, Davies, Decker, Duane, Dupaty, Fish, Flagg, Fuller, Gaidry, Gruneberg, Hart, Healey, Heard, Henderson, Hire, Howes, Kavanagh, Knobloch, Mars, Maurer, Mayer, Mendiverri, Montamat, E. Murphy, M. W. Murphy, Ong, O'Conner, Orr, J. T. Paine, Pintado, Poynot, Schnurr, Seymour, Spellicy, Stocker, Sullivan, Waters, Wenck—49.

Négative :

MM. Ariail, Barrett, Bell, Bromley, Burke, Collin, T. Cook, Duane, Dufresne, Edwards, Ennis, Flood, Foley, Fosdick, Geier, Goldman, Gorlinski, Harnan, Hills, Howell, Kugler, Mann, Newell, Normand, J. Payne, J. Purcell, S. Pursell, Schroeder, Shaw, Smith, Stumpf, Stiner, Stauffer, Terry, Thorpe, Wells, Wilson—37.

La motion de prise en considération prévaut, et la motion Hills est repoussée.

ORDRE DU JOUR.

On reprend l'examen de la section 3 du judiciaire et du substitut de M. Sullivan.

Après une longue et habile discussion, la Convention s'ajourne.

Approuvé :

JOHN E. NEELIS,
Secrétaire.

VENDREDI, le 27 mai 1864.

Le président appelle la Convention à l'ordre, et les membres suivants répondent à l'appel du rôle :

Messieurs Abell, Ariail, Austin, Balch, Bailey, Barrett, Baum, Beauvais, Bell, Bennie, Bofill, Bromley, Brott, Buckley, Burke, Cazabat, Collin, J. K. Cook, T. Cook, Crozat, Davies, Decker, Duane, Dufresne, Dupaty. Duke, Edwards, Ennis, Fish, Flagg. Flood, Foley. Fuller, Gastinel, Gaidry, Geier, Goldman, Gruneberg, Hart, Healy, Heard, Henderson, Howell,

Howes, Knobloch, Maurer, Maas, Mann, Mayer, Mendiverri, Montamat, Morris, M. W. Murphy, Newell, Normand, O'Conner, Orr, J. Payne, Pintado, Poynot, J. Purcell, S. Pursell, Schroeder, Schnurr, Seymour, Shaw, Smith, Spellicy, Stocker, Stumpf, Stiner, Sullivan, Terry, Thorpe, Waters, Wells, Wilson et le président—78.

Le journal d'hier est lu et approuvé.

RESOLUTIONS.

Les résolutious suivantes sont présentées et déposées pour attendre leur tour d'ordre, conformément au réglement.

Par M. Bell :

Résolu, Que ce qui suit fera désormais partie du réglement de cette Convention : Lorsqu'une question aura été une fois décidée par la Convention, elle ne pourra plus lui être soumise de nouveau, à moins que ce ne soit sous forme de motion de reconsidération ; et cette motion devra être faite le jour même ou le jour suivant, et appuyée par un vote des deux tiers des membres présents.

Par M. Waters :

Résolu, A partir de ce jour, les membres de la police de la Nouvelle-Orléans recevront du Trésor de l'Etat un salaire annuel de mille piastres chacun, payable mensuellement, par douzième ; et ils fourniront leur obligation ou (*bond*) de la somme de mille piastres, pour garantie de l'accomplissement fidèle de leurs devoirs pendant l'exercice de leurs fonctions.

M. Foley demande la suspension du réglement pour statuer sur la résolution ci-dessus.

Rejeté.

RAPPORT DES COMITES.

M. Cazabat, au nom du comité spécial des Indemnités à payer aux propriétaires loyaux d'esclaves émancipés, déclare que le comité fera son rapport lundi.

M. Montamat, au nom du comite spécial chargé d'aller trouver le Gén. Banks, et de l'inviter, lui et son état-major, à faire visite à la Convention, rapporte que le comité s'est acquitté de son devoir, et que le Gén. Banks se rendra au sein de la Convention aujourd'hui, à 1 heure de l'après-midi.

Il n'est pas présenté d'autres rapports.

M. Thorpe demande l'ordre du jour pour sa résolution de la veille, par laquelle il propose que le président de cette Convention présente au Général Banks la plume avec laquelle il a signé l'ordonnance d'émancipation. La résolution est unanimement adoptée.

ORDRE DU JOUR.

Le rapport du comité Judiciaire est à l'ordre du jour.

Sur motion de M. Hills, l'article du réglement qui limite à une demi-heure le temps pendant lequel les membres peuvent parler sur une question, est suspendu pendant la durée de la discussion de la question du Judiciaire.

Le portier annonce le Gén. Banks. Tous les membres se lèvent, et le Gén. Banks entre dans la salle, accompagné de son état-major et de son Excellence le Gouverneur Hahn. Ces visiteurs de distinction sont escortés par le comité jusqu'à l'estrade où siège le président.

Le président lui souhaite la bienvenue dans une allocution courte et de circonstance, à laquelle le Gén. Banks répond par quelques mots éloquents et bien sentis. Après avoir exprimé ses remerciements à la Convention et à son président, il déclare qu'il approuve cordialement tout ce que la Convention a déjà fait, et qu'il a la confiance que ce qui lui reste à faire sera accompli par elle avec la même sagesse.

Le Gén. Banks ayant terminé ses remarques, la Convention, sur motion de M. Stocker, suspend la séance pendant vingt minutes.

A la reprise de la séance, M. Abell obtient la suspension du réglement et offre la résolution suivante, qui est unanimement adoptée :

Résolu, Que cette Convention offre au général Banks l'expression de sa reconnaissance à raison des services qu'il a rendus au pays, d'abord comme citoyen, et en second lieu comme soldat ; s'étant montré, dans les deux cas, prêt à tous les sacrifices pour le salut de la nation.

La discussion sur le rapport du comité Judiciaire est ensuite reprise ; et pendant cette discussion la Convention s'ajourne.

Procès-verbal adopté.

JOHN E. NEELIS,
Secrétaire.

SAMEDI, le 28 mai 1864.

Le président appelle la Convention à l'ordre. A l'appel du rôle sont présents :

MM. Abell, Ariail, Balch, Baley, Barrett, Bell, Bofill, Bromley, Buckley, Burke, Campbell, Cazabat, J. K. Cook, Crozat, Decker, Duane, Dufresne, Duke, Dupaty,

Edwards, Ennis, Flood, Foley, Geier, Goldman, Gorlinski, Harnan, Hart, Healy, Henderson, Heard, Howes, Kavanagh, Maurer, Maas, Mann, Mayer, Montamat, Morris, W. M. Murphy, Newell, Normand, O'Conner, Orr, Pintado, Poynot, S. Pursell, Schroeder, Schnurr, Shaw, Smith, Spellicy, Stauffer, Stiner, Stumpf, Sullivan, Terry, Waters, Wells, Wilson et M. le président.

Le quorum faisant faute, le sergent-d'armes reçoit l'ordre de rechercher les absents.

L'entrée de MM. Baum, Collin, Fish, Mendiverri, Fosdick, Kugler, T. Cook, Séymour, Fuller, Austin, Davies, Howel, l Hire, Beauvais, Stocker, Thorpe, au nombre de 16, constitue un quorum. Après lecture le procès-verbal est approuvé.

M. Cazabat propose l'ajournement indéfini de la Convention pour le 6 juin.

M. Montamat propose la dispense du réglement afin de prendre en considération la susdite résolution, mais l'appui des deux tiers faisant faute la résolution est remise conformément au réglement.

M. Pursell, au nom du comité des Dépenses Casuelles, présente un rapport favorable au projet d'allocation pour indemniser la ville de la Nuovelle-Orléans, des dépenses par elle faites pour rendre la salle de la Liberté propre à la réception de la Convention.

Il présente ensuite un rapport contraire à l'allocation demandée par M. Terry pour l'enrôlement du décret d'Emancipation.

Sur motion, le rapport est adopté.

M. Austin annonce que son comité pourra présenter son rapport concernant le rapport de l'auditeur d'Etat, lundi prochain.

M. Bell demande que sa motion à l'effet d'amender le réglement soit à l'ordre, mais la Chambre le refuse.

M. Waters appelle sa motion relative à la police urbaine.

La proposition de rejeter cette motion est repoussée par le vote suivant :

Affirmative :

MM. Ariail, Balch, Bailey, Beauvais, Collin, Cazabat, Crozat, Davies, Duke, Dufresne, Dupaty, Edwards, Ennis, Fosdick, Heard, Hills, Hire, Howell, Howes, Kugler, Mann, Mayer, Morris, Orr, Pintado, S. Pursell, Shaw, Stauffer, Thorpe, Wells—30.

Négative :

MM. Abell, Barrett, Bell, Bofill, Buckley, Burke, Campbell, T. Cook, J. K. Cook, Duane, Fish, Flood, Foley, Fuller, Geier, Goldman, Gorlinski, Harnan, Hart, Healy, Henderson, Howes, Maas, Maurer, Mendiverri, Montamat, M. W. Murphy, Normand, O'Conner, Poynot, J. Purcell, Schroeder, Schnurr, Seymour, Smith, Spellicy, Stocker, Stumpf, Stiner, Sullivan, Terry, Waters, Wenck, Wilson—44.

M. Sullivan propose un substitut à la résolution de M. Waters, lequel est adopté.

Sur la proposition de M. Cazabat de rejeter le substitut, l'appel nominal donne :

Affirmative :

MM. Ariail, Austin, Balch, Bailey, Beauvais, Bromley, Burke, Campbell, Collin, Cazabat, Cutler, Davies, Dufresne, Duke, Dupaty, Edwards, Ennis, Fosdick, Gorlinski, Heard, Hills, Hire, Howell, Kugler, Mann, Mayer, Morris, Orr, J. Payne, J. T. Paine, Pintado, S. Pursell, Shaw, Stumpf, Thorpe, Wells, Wilson—37.

Négative :

MM. Abell, Barrett, Bell, Bofill, Buckley, J. K. Cook, T. Cook, Duane, Fish, Flood, Foley, Fuller, Geier, Goldman, Harnan, Hart, Healy, Henderson, Howes, Maas, Maurer, Mendiverri, Montamat, M. W. Murphy, Normand, O'Conner, Poynot, J. Purcell, Schroeder, Schnurr, Seymour, Smith, Spellicy, Stocker, Stiner, Stauffer, Sullivan, Terry, Waters, Wenck—40.

La motion est donc rejetée, et sur demande de M. Abell on ordonne l'impression de ce substitut et sa mise à l'ordre du jour pour le 6 juin.

M. Bofill demande l'appel du rôle ; il en résulte la présence de 77 membres constatée.

Au milieu de la discussion du rapport sur le Judiciaire, au sujet du substitut de M. Sullivan pour la 3e section, la Convention s'ajourne.

JOHN E. NEELIS,
Secrétaire.

LUNDI, le 30 mai 1864.

La Convention se réunit, et après la prière du Rév. Horton, l'appel nominal accuse la présence des 66 membres suivants :

MM. Abell, Ariail, Balch, Bailey, Beauvais, Bofill, Buckley, Bromley, Burke, Collin, Campbell, Crozat, Davies, Dufresne, Duke, Edwards, Ennis, Fish, Flagg, Flood, Foley, Fosdick, Gastinel, Geier, Harnan, Hart, Heard, Healy, Hills, Howell, Howes, Kavanagh, Kugler, Maas, Mann, Maurer, Mayer, Montamat, E. Murphy, M. W. Murphy, Newell, Normand, O'Conner, Ong,

Orr, J. T. Paine, Pintado, Poynot, J. Purcell, S. Pursell, Schnurr, Seymour, Shaw, Smith, Spellicy, Stumpf, Stiner, Stauffer, Sullivan, Terry, Thorpe, Waters, Wenck, Wells, Wilson et M. le Président—66,

Nombre insuffisant, que complète l'entrée de MM. Barrett, Cazabat, T. Cook, Cutler, Duane, Fuller, Henderson, Hire, Morris, Schroeder et Stocker (11).

M. Hills présente ce qui suit:

Tout membre de la Convention, qui, n'ayant point de congé, manquera de répondre à l'appel d'ouverture dans les vingt minutes qui suivront midi, perdra sa rétribution quotidienne chaque jour d'absence, à moins qu'il ne puisse justifier son absence.

M. Stocker propose la dispense du réglement, afin de s'occuper de ce susdit projet. Refusé.

Par M. Montamat:

Résolu, Qu'un exemplaire de la résolution adoptée par cette Convention, à l'effet de congratuler le général Banks, lui soit envoyée inscrite sur parchemin.

Par M. Orr:

Résolu, La Législature, en sa première session, devra déterminer par une loi le salaire alloué aux chefs d'atelier, artisans, charretiers et manœuvres employés aux travaux publics par l'Etat de la Louisiane et par la ville de la Nouvelle-Orléans; ce salaire ne sera pas inférieur au taux ci-dessous:

Conducteurs d'artisans.... $4 00 par jour.
Conducteurs de charretiers. 3 00   do
Conducteurs de manœuvres. 3 00   do
Artisans................. 3 00   do
Manœuvres............... 2 00   do

M. Wells, au nom du comité pour l'indemnité à payer aux propriétaires loyaux pour leurs esclaves, présente dans son rapport la résolution suivante:

Résolu, Le comité pour l'indemnité à accorder aux propriétaires loyaux pour leurs esclaves émancipés, fera écrire à la grosse le mémoire ci-joint, par duplicata, portant la signature de ses membres et l'attestation du président et du secrétaire de cette Convention: il en fera parvenir un exemplaire au Sénat et l'autre à la Chambre des Représentants des Etats-Unis.

Résolu de plus, Ce dit comité devra correspondre au sujet de l'indemnité, avec tels membres du Congrès des Etats-Unis qu'il jugera nécessaire.

M. Abell présente l'amendement suivant-
Paiement en sera fait aux citoyens loyaux avant que la présente constitution n'ait été adoptée.

Cet amendement est rejeté, d'après l'avis du président.

MM. Abell et Montamat en appellent à la Convention, laquelle se prononce pour l'avis du président.

Adoption du rappoet du comité d'indemnité, et à la demande de M. Montamat on en ordonne l'impression à 200 exemplaires.

M. Abell demande l'impression de 200 exemplaires de son amendement. Refusé.

M. Montamat, au nom du comité des Finances, présente le rapport suivant au sujet des fonds alloués au paiement du *per diem* des conventionnels et des employés.

Mai 23—A caisse, d'après le rapport No. 6. $47,186 40
Mai 4—Payé ordre No. 47..............$1349 00
Mai 24—Payé ordre No. 48.............. 416 00
Mai 25—Payé ordre No. 49.............. 1730 00
Mai 28—Payé ordre No. 50.............. 1630 00
Mai 28—Payé ordre No. 51.............. 2330 00
Mai 28—Payé ordre No. 52.............. 1828 00
Mai 28—Payé ordre No. 54.............. 860 00 $10,143 00
Mai 30 — Balance en caisse ce jour....... $37,043 40
Nlle-Orléans, le 30 mai 1864.

J. P. MONTAMAT,
Président par intérim.

M. Montamat, en sa qualité de président par intérim du comité des Finances présente aussi le rapport suivant au sujet des fonds alloués aux dépenses casuelles:

Mai 23 —En caisse d'après rapport No. 6.............. $8759 48
Mai 27—Payé de Courcey, d'après ordre No. 53.......... 1830 85
Mai 30— Balance en caisse ce jour..................... $6928 63
Nouvelle-Orléans, le 30 mai 1864.

J. P. MONTAMAT,
Président par intérim.

La résolution de M. Cazabat relative à l'ajournement définitif, au 6 juin, sur motion de M. Buckley, est rejetée.

Le rapport sur le Judiciaire étant à l'ordre spécial du jour, la discussion s'engage à ce sujet, et la Convention s'ajourne au lendemain à midi.

JOHN F. NEELIS, Secrétaire.

MARDI, le 31 mai 1864.

La Convention se réunit : elle est appelée à l'ordre par le président.

Le Rév. Strong dit la prière.

A l'appel nominal, les membres suivants répondent à leurs noms :

Messieurs Abell, Balch, Bailey, Barrett, Bofill, Bromley, Buckley, Burke, Campbell, Collin, J. K. Cook, Crozat, Decker, Duke, Dufresne, Edwards, Ennis, Fish, Flagg, Flood, Foley, Gorlinski, Harnan, Healy, Heard, Hills, Howell, Howes, Kavanagh, Maas, Mann, Mayer, Mendiverri, Montamat, Morris, M. W. Murphy, Newell, Normand, O'Conner, Ong, Orr, J. Payne, J. T. Paine, Pintado, Poynot, J. Purcell, S. Purcell, Schroeder, Schnurr, Seymour, Shaw, Spellicy, Stumpf, Stiner, Stauffer, Sullivan, Terry, Waters, Wells et M. le président—60.

Le quorum manquant, le sergent-d'armes reçoit l'ordre de rechercher les absents, et l'entrée de Messieurs Beauvais, Bell, Fosdick, Gastinel, Geier, Goldman, Hart, Henderson, Hire, Maurer, E. Murphy, Smith, Stocker, Thorpe, Wenck et Wilson, complète le nombre requis.

Après lecture, le procès-verbal de la dernière séance est adopté.

Le président ayant désigné l'ordre des travaux, M. Stocker demande la suspension du réglement, afin de permettre à M. Thorpe de présenter une résolution. Adopté.

Résolution de M. Thorpe.

A dater du 31 mai 1864, l'ordre du jour occupera les délibérations immédiatement après la lecture du procès-verbal et son adoption, et toutes les affaires diverses seront remises au samedi de chaque semaine.

M. Wilson demande la suspension du réglement, afin de s'occuper de cette résolution. Accepté.

Le secrétaire en donne lecture et M. Montamat en propose le rejet ; mais cette proposition est repoussée et la résolution est adoptée par un vote de 54 contre 18.

M. Sullivan demande l'appel et 76 membres répondent à leurs noms.

M. Hills appelle sa résolution d'hier, et M. Montamat présente l'amendement suivant :

L'honorable Hills, représentant le second district représentatif, perdra son *per diem* chaque jour qu'il manquera de répondre à l'appel de son nom dans les quinze minutes qui suivront l'heure de midi.

Sur motion de M. Sullivan, la résolution et l'amendement sont rejetés.

M. Orr appelle sa résolution d'hier.

M. Hills propose de la rejeter : cette proposition est acceptée par 40 voix contre 35.

M. Montamat appel sa résolution relative à la présentation au Gen. Banks d'un exemplaire de la résolution de congratulation dernièrement adoptée par cette Convention.

Lecture en est donnée et elle est adoptée à l'unanimité.

La Convention s'occupe alors du rapport sur le Judiciaire et du substitut proposé ; cette question étant à l'ordre spécial du jour.

Après une longue discussion, on demande la question préalable. M. Sullivan ayant proposé l'appel nominal, le secrétaire y procède et 73 membres répondent à leurs noms.

Le quorum manquant, le sergent-d'armes est envoyé à la recherche des absents.

M. Foley propose l'ajournement. Refusé.

Plusieurs membres entrant, on fait un nouvel appel du rôle, et 76 membres répondant à leurs noms, le président déclare que le quorum existe.

On porte alors la question sur l'adoption de l'amendement de M. Sullivan, et l'appel nominal à ce sujet donne le résultat suivant :

Affirmative :

MM. Bell, Buckley, Campbell, Collin, Duke, Foley, Gastinel, Goldman, Gruneberg, Harnan, Howes, Maurer, Morris, M. W. Murphy, O'Conner, Orr, Poynot, S. Purcell, Schnurr, Smith, Stocker, Stauffer, Sullivan, Terry, Waters—25.

Négative :

MM. Abell, Ariail, Bailey, Barrett, Bauvais, Bofill, Bromley, Brott, Burke, Cazabat, J. K. Cook, T. Cook, Crozat, Cutler, Decker, Edwards, Ennis, Fish, Flagg, Foley, Fosdick, Fuller, Gorlinski, Healy, Hart, Heard, Henderson, Hills, Hire, Howell, Kavanagh, Maas, Mann, Mendiverri, Montamat, E. Murphy, Newell, Normand, Ong, J. Payne, Pintado, J. Purcell, Seymour, Shaw, Spellicy, Stumpf, Smith, Schroeder, Thorpe Wenck, Wells, Wilson—52.

L'amendement est donc rejeté.

La question se présente de nouveau sur l'adoption de l'article 3 du Rapport, et à cet effet, il y a appel, ainsi que suit :

ET L'AMENDEMENT DE LA CONSTITUTION DE LA LOUISIANE. 99

Affirmative :

MM. Ariail, Bailey, Beauvais, Bofill, Bromley, Brott, Burke, Cazabat, Crozat, Cutler, Ennis, Fish, Flagg, Fuller, Gorlinski, Healy, Heard, Henderson, Hire, Howell, Mann, Newell, Pintado, Seymour, Shaw, Stumpf, Thorpe, Wenck, Wells, Wilson—30.

Négative :

MM. Abell, Barrett, Bell, Buckley, Campbell, Collin, J. K. Cook, T. Cook, Decker, Duke, Edwards, Flood, Foley, Fosdiek, Gastinel, Goldman, Gruneberg, Hart, Harnan, Hills, Howes, Kavanagh, Maurer, Maas, Mendiverri, Montamat, Morris, E. Murphy, M. W. Murphy, Normand, O'Conner, Ong, Orr, J. Payne, Poynot, J. Purcell, S. Pursell, Schroeder, Schnurr, Smith, Spellicy, Stocker, Stiner, Stauffer, Sullivan, Terry, Waters—47.

Sur motion, la Convention s'ajourne aut lendemain à midi.

Approuvé.

JOHN E. NEELIS,
Secrétaire.

MERCREDI, le 1er juin 1864.

Conformément à l'ajournement, la Convention se réunit.

A l'appel du rôle répondent :

MM. Ariail, Austin, Balch, Baum, Barrett, Buckley, Burke, Campbell, J. K. Cook, Collin, Decker, Dufresne, Duke, Edwards, Flagg, Flood, Fuller, Geier, Goldman, Gorlinski, Gruneberg, Healy, Heard, Hills, Howell, Howes, Mann, Montamat, Newell, Normand, O'Conner, Pintado, Poynot, S. Pursell, Schroeder, Schnurr, Shaw, Spellicy, Stumpf, Stiner, Stauffer, Sullivan, Wells et M. le président—44.

Le quorum faisant faute, le sergent d'armes est envoyé à la recherche des absents; et l'entrée de MM. Abell, Bailey, Beauvais, Bell, Bofill, Brott, Bromley, Crozat, Cutler, Duane, Fish, Foley, Fosdick, Gastinel, Hart, Henderson, Hire, Kavanagh, Maas, Mayer, Mendiverri, Morris, M. W. Murphy, Ong, Orr, J. Purcell, Smith, Stocker, Terry, Thorpe, Waters, Wenck, Wilson,—33 constitue le quorum.

Après lecture, le procès-verbal de la dernière séance est amendé et approuvé.

M. Montamat propose la reprise en considération du vote en vertu duquel, à la dernière séance, l'article 3 du rapport sur le judiciaire a été rejeté. Adopté et la reprise en considération s'en suit.

M. Montamat propose d'amender en substituant "$7500" à "$10,000" pour le traitement du grand juge, et "$7000" à "$9000" pour celui de juges-adjoints.

M. Stiner propose de biffer "$7500" et d'y substituer "$8000." Rejeté.

M. Thorpe propose de supprimer toute cette partie de la clause se rapportant aux appointements, afin d'en laisser la fixation à la Législature. Refusé.

M. Hills propose le rejet de la motion de M. Montamat, sur quoi, il y a appel nominal, ainsi que suit :

Affirmative :

MM. Abell, Balch, Baum, Bailey, Bromley, Brott, Collin, J. K. Cook, Davies, Decker, Duane, Dufresne, Duke, Edwards, Flood, Foley, Fosdick, Gorlinski, Healy, Hills, Hire, Howell, Howes M. W. Murphy, Normand, O'Conner, Orr, Poynot, Schroeder, Smith, Spellicy, Stocker, Terry, Thorpe, Wenck, Wilson—36

Négative :

MM. Ariail, Austin, Barrett, Beauvais, Bofill, Buckley, Burke, Campbell, Cazabat, Crozat, Cutler, Fish, Flagg, Fuller, Gastinel, Geier, Goldman, Gruneberg, Hart, Heard, Maas, Mann, Mayer, Montamat, Morris, Newell, Ong, Pintado, J. Purcell, S. Pursell, Schnurr, Seymour, Shaw, Stumpf, Stiner, Stauffer, Sullivan, Waters, Wells—39.

En conséquence, la motion de M. Hills est repoussée.

L'appel général du rôle ayant lieu de suite après, il se trouve 77 membres présents.

M. S. Pursell propose d'insérer après le mot "annuellement" les mots "jusqu'à ce qu'une loi en est ordonné autrement."

M. Montamat accepte cet amendement.

La question est alors posée sur l'adoption de l'article ainsi qu'amendé. Adopté.

Les articles 4, 5, 6, 7 et 8 sont adoptés sans opposition.

A la lecture de l'article 9, M. Campbell propose de substituer aux mots "trois quarts" à la 4e ligne le mot "majorité."

M. Cazabat propose de rejeter cet amendement. Refusé.

L'amendement est ensuite adopté.

M. Stocker propose de substituer au mot "présents" le mot "élus." Adopté ainsi que ledit article 9.

A la lecture de l'article 10, M. Cazabat propose de supprimer après le mot "appointements" les mots "lesquels ne seront diminués pendant la durée de leurs fonctions." Rejeté.

M. S. Pursell propose d'insérer à la seconde ligne les mots "augmentés ou."

Sur la proposition de M. Henderson, cet amendement est rejeté.

Alors les amendements sont retirés et l'article est adopté selon la teneur du rapport.

Art. II. Lecture en est donnée, ainsi que des substituts et des amendements présentés respectueusement par MM. Stauffer, Montamat et Sullivan.

M. Cazabat propose de rejeter le substitut et les deux amendements; sur quoi, l'appel nominal donne pour résultat :

Affirmative :

MM. Ariail, Bailey, Baum, Beauvais, Bofill, B.rke, Cazabat, Crozat, Cutler, Duane, Fish, Flagg, Fuller, Geier, Heard, Hire, Howell, Mayer, Newell, Normand, Ong, Poynot, J. Purcell, Schnurr, Seymour, Stumpf, Thorpe, Waters, Wenck, Wells, Wilson—31.

Négative :

MM. Abell, Austin, Balch, Bell, Bromley, Brott, Buckley, Campbell, Collin, J. K. Cook, T. Cook, Decker, Dufresne, Duke, Edwards, Flood, Foley, Fosdick, Gastinel, Goldman, Gorlinski, Gruneberg, Hart, Henderson, Healy, Hills, Howes, Maas, Mann, Mendiverri, Montamat, Morris, W. M, Murphy, O'Conner, Orr, Pintado, S. Pursell, Shaw, Smith, Spellicy, Stocker, Stauffer, Stiner, Sullivan, Terry—45.

La motion de rejet est donc repoussée.

M. Montamat retire son amendement, et le substitut de M. Stauffer est à l'ordre.

M. Gruneberg propose de supprimer "les cours auront le droit de nommer leurs greffiers." Ceci étant prévu par le substitut lui-même.

Accepté.

Sur l'adoption du substitut, on passe aux voix, savoir :

Affirmative :

MM. Bell, Buckley, Campbell, T. Cook, Decker, Dufresne, Duke, Flagg, Gastinel, Geier, Goldman, Gruneberg, Howes, Mayer, Morris, O'Conner, Orr, Poynot, Sullivan, Schnurr, Smith, Stocker, Stauffer, Terry—24.

Négative :

MM. Abell, Ariail, Austin, Barrett, Balch, Bailey, Baum, Beauvais, Bofill, Bromley, Brott, Burke, Cazabat, J. K. Cook, Collin, Crozat, Cutler, Duane, Edwards, Fish, Flood, Foley, Fosdick, Fuller, Gorlinski,

Hart, Healy, Heard, Henderson, Hills, Hire, Howell, Mass, Mann, Mendiverri, Montamat, M. W. Murphy, Newell, Normand, Ong, Pintado, J. Purcell, S. Pursell, Shaw, Seymour, Spellicy, Stumpf, Stiner, Thorpe, Waters, Wenck, Wells, Wilson—53.

Le substitut est donc rejeté.

On passe à l'amendement Sullivan, savoir :

Affirmative :

MM. Bell, Buckley, Campbell, Collin, J. K. Cook, T. Cook, Decker, Duke, Flagg, Flood, Geier, Goldman, Gorlinski, Gruneberg, Howes, Mayer, O'Conner, Orr, Poynot, S. Pursell, Smith, Spellicy, Stocker, Stauffer, Sullivan, Terry—26.

Négative :

MM. Abell, Ariail, Austin, Barrett, Balch, Bailey, Baum, Beauvais, Bofill, Bromley, Brott, Burke, Cazabat, Crozat, Cutler, Duane, Dufresne, Edwards, Fish, Foley, Fosdick, Fuller, Gastinel, Hart, Healy, Heard, Henderson, Hills, Hire, Howell, Maas, Mann, Mendiverri, Montamat, Morris, M. W. Murphy, Newell, Normand, Ong, Pintado, J. Purcell, Schnurr, Shaw, Stiner, Seymour, Stumpf, Thorpe, Waters, Wenck, Wells, Wilson—51.

L'amendement est donc rejeté.

M. Shaw propose un amendement à l'article, ainsi qu'il est rédigé dans le rapport, à l'effet de supprimer tout ce qui suit le mot "Sénat," et d'y ajouter "les juges de la cour suprême exerceront leurs fonctions pendant six années, et les juges des cours inférieures pendant quatre années."

Après une longue discussion, M. Sullivan propose l'ajournement, lequel est accordé par 54 voix contre 23, jusqu'au lendemain à midi.

Approuvé.

JOHN E. NEELY, Secrétaire.

JEUDI, le 2 juin 1864.

La Convention se réunit conformément à l'ajournement. A l'appel du rôle répondent :

MM. Ariail, Austin, Balch, Baum, Barrett, Bell. Burke, Campbell, Cazabat, Collin, J. K. Cook, Crozat, Decker, Duane, Duke, Dufresne, Edwards, Flagg, Flood, Foley, Gastinel, Gaidry, Geier, Goldman, Gruneberg, Harnan, Healy, Heard, Henderson, Hills, Howell, Knobloch, Maas, Mann, Maurer, Mayer, Montamat, Morris, Newell. Normand, O'Conner, J. Payne, Pintado, S. Pursell, Schnurr, Seymour, Shaw, Spellicy, Stauffer, Stumpf, Sullivan, Terry, Wells, Wilson et M. le Président—55.

ET L'AMENDEMENT DE LA CONSTITUTION DE LA LOUISIANE.

Le sergent-d'armes est envoyé à la recherche des absents; et l'entrée de MM. Abell, Bailey, Beauvais, Bofill, Bromley, Fish, Fosdick, Fuller, Gorlinski, Hart, Hire, Howes, Mendiverri, M. W. Murphy, Ong, Orr, J. T. Payne, J. Purcell, Smith, Stocker, Stiner, Waters—22, complète le nombre nécessaire pour le quorum.

Après lecture le procès-verbal de la dernière séance est approuvé.

M. Montamat demande la dispense du réglement afin de présenter la résolution suivante. Adopté, et lecture en est donnée en ces termes :

Résolu, Que la place de secrétaire-adjoint maintenant remplie par M. T. H. Murphy, est déclaré vacante.

De plus, Autorisation est donnée au secrétaire d'employer une personne capable pour exercer les fonctions de cette place jusqu'à la fin de la session.

M. Cazabat propose de rejeter la résolution. Refusé. Puis après, la résolution est adoptée.

Le secrétaire nomme en conséquence M. Philippe Winfree, à ces fonctions.

La Convention s'occupe de l'amendement Shaw à l'art. 11 du comité Judiciaire.

M. Hills propose un sous-amendement à l'amendement Shaw, à l'effet de substituer aux mots "dix ans," les mots "six années," comme terme de la durée des fonctions des juges de la Cour Suprême ; et le mot "huit" à "quatre" pour celui des juges des cours de District.

Sur motion de rejeter la proposition de M. Hlls, l'appel nominal donne :

Affirmative :

MM. Bailey, Bell, Buckley, Campbell, Collin, J. K. Cook, T. Cook, Decker, Flood, Geier, Goldman, Gruneberg, Howell, Knobloch, Maas, Mann, Mayer, Morris, M. W. Murphy, O'Conner, Orr, J. Payne, Poynot, J. Purcell, S. Pursell, Schroeder, Schnurr, Shaw, Smith, Stauffer, Sullivan, Terry, Wenck—33.

Négative :

MM. Abell, Ariail, Austin, Barrett, Balch, Baum, Beauvais, Bofill, Bromley, Burke, Cazabat, Crozat, Duane, Duke, Dufresne, Edwards, Fish, Flagg, Foley, Fosdick, Fuller, Gaidry, Gorlinski, Harnan, Hart, Healy, Heard, Henderson, Hills, Hire, Howes, Maurer, Mendiverri, Montamat, Normand, Newell, Ong, J. T. Payne, Pintado, Seymour, Spellicy, Stocker, Stumpf, Stiner, Thorpe, Waters, Wells, Wilson—48.

La motion de rejet est donc repoussée.

Sur la demande d'ajournement par M. Austin, le vote donne :

Affirmative :

MM. Abell, Austin Baum, Bailey, Buckley, Campbell, J. K. Cook, Crozat, Decker, Dufresne, Duke, Flagg, Flood, Foley, Gaidry, Goldman, Gruneberg, Hart, Maurer, Mendiverri, M. W. Murphy, Newell, Normand, O'Conner, Ong, Orr, Poynot, J. Purcell, Schroeder, Spellicy, Stocker, Stumpf, Sullivan, Waters—34.

Négative :

MM. Ariail, Barrett, Beauvais, Bell, Bofill, Bromley, Burke, Cazabat, Collin, T. Cook, Cutler, Duane, Edwards, Fish, Fosdick, Fuller, Gastinel, Geier, Gorlinski, Harnan, Healy, Heard, Henderson, Hills, Hire, Howell, Howes, Knobloch, Maas, Mann, Mayer, Montamat, Morris, J. Payne, J. T. Paine, Pintado, S. Pursell, Schnurr, Seymour, Shaw, Smith, Stiner, Stauffer, Terry, Thorpe, Wenck, Wells, Wilson—48.

L'ajournement est donc refusé.

Sur la question d'adoption de l'amendement Hills, il résulte du vote :

Affirmative :

MM. Bromley, Cazabat, Duane Fish, Foley, Fosdick, Fuller, Goldman, Gorlinski, Harnan, Healy, Henderson, Hills, Hire, Mayer, Normand J. T. Paine, Pintado, Stumpf, Stiner, Thorpe, Waters—22.

Négative :

MM. Abell, Ariail, Austin, Bailey Barrett, Baum, Beauvais, Bell, Bofill, Buckley, Burke, Campbell, Collin, T. Cook, J. K. Cook, Crozat, Cutler, Decker, Duke, Dufresne, Edwards, Flagg, Flood, Foley, Gastinel, Gaidry, Geier, Gruneberg, Hart, Heard, Howell, Howes, Knobloch, Maas, Maurer, Mann, Mendiverri, Morris, M. W. Murphy, Newell, O'Conner, Ong, Orr, J. Payne, Poynot, J. Purcell, S. Pursell, Schroeder, Seymour, Schnurr, Shaw, Smith, Spellicy, Stauffer, Stocker, Sullivan, Terry, Wenck, Wells, Wilson—59.

Cet amendement est donc rejeté.

Puis l'amendement Shaw est adopté par la majorité suivante.

Affirmative :

MM. Barrett, Baum, Bell, Buckley, Campbell, J. K. Cook, T. Cook, Decker, Duane, Dufresne, Duke, Fish, Flagg, Flood, Fosdick, Gastinel, Gaidry, Geier, Goldman, Gorlinski, Gruneberg, Harnan, Hart, Hire, Howes, Knobloch, Mass, Maurer, Mayer, Mendiverri, Morris, M. W. Murphy, Normand, O'Conner, Ong, Orr, J. Payne, J. T. Paine, Poynot, J. Purcell, S. Pursell, Shaw, Schroeder, Schnurr, Seymour, Smith, Stiner, Spellicy, Stocker. Stumpf. Stauffer, Sullivan, Terry—53.

Négative :

MM. Abell, Ariail, Austin, Bailey, Beauvais, Bofill, Bromley, Burke, Cazabat, Collin, Crozat, Cutler, Edwards, Foley, Fuller, Healy. Heard, Henderson, Hills, Howell, Mann, Newell, Pintado, Thorpe, Waters, Wenck, Wells, Wilson—28.

La Convention s'ajourne à vendredi à midi.

Approuvé.

JOHN E. NEELIS,
Secrétaire.

MERCREDI, le 3 juin 1864.

La Convention se réunit à midi, et à l'appel du rôle les membres suivants répondent :

MM. Abell, Ariail, Austin, Barrett, Baum, Bell, Bromley, Burke, Campbell, Collin, T. Cook, Crozat, Davies, Decker, Dufresne, Dupaty, Flagg, Flood, Foley, Gaidry, Gastinel, Geier, Gorlinski, Harnan, Healy, Heard, Henderson, Hills, Howell, Kavanagh, Knobloch, Maas, Mann, Mayer, Maurer, Montamat, Morris, Murphy E., Newell, O'Conner, Ong, J. Payne, Pintado, Poynot, J. Purcell, S. Pursell, Schroeder, Schnurr, Shaw, Smith, Spellicy, Stiner, Stauffer, Sullivan, Terry, Waters, Wells, Wilson et M. le le Président—59.

Le quorum faisant défaut, le sergent d'armes reçoit l'ordre d'aller à la recherche des absents, et l'entrée de MM. Bailey, Bofill, Cazabat, J. K. Cook, Duane, Duke, Edwards, Fish, Fosdick, Hart, Hire, Howes, M. W. Murphy, Normand, Seymour, Stocker, Stumpf—17,complète le nombre nécessaire.

Après lecture et amendement, le procès-verbal de la dernière séance est adopté.

M. Baum propose la reprise en considération du vote sur l'amendement de M. Shaw, à la dernière séance.

Sur motion de rejeter cette proposition, le vote donne :

Affirmative :

MM. Barrett, Bell, Buckley, Campbell, J. K. Cook, T. Cook, Davies, Dufresne, Dupaty, Flood, Gastinel, Gaidry, Geier, Gorlinski, Harnan, Howes, Henderson, Knobloch, Maurer, Montamat, Morris, M. W. Murphy, Normand, O'Conner, Orr, J. Payne, Poynot, S. Pursell, Schnurr, Spellicy, Smith, Stocker, Stauffer. Sullivan, Terry, Waters—36.

Négative :

MM. Abell, Ariail, Austin, Bailey, Baum, Beauvais. Bofill, Bromley, Burke, Collin. Cazabat, Crozat, Cutler, Decker, Duane, Edwards, Fish, Flagg, Foley, Fosdick, Hart, Healy, Heard, Hills, Hire, Howell, Kavanagh, Maas, Mann, Mayer, E. Murphy, Newell, Ong, Pintado, Schroeder, Seymour, Shaw, Stumpf, Stiner, Wells et Wilson—41.

La motion de rejet est donc repoussée.

La question de reprise en considération est donc posée au vote, et il en résulte :

Affirmative :

MM. Ariail, Austin, Baum, Bailey, Beauvais, Bofill, Bromley, Burke, Cazabat, Collin, Crozat, Cutler, Duane, Dupaty, Edwards, Fish, Flagg, Foley, Fosdick, Gaidry, Hart, Heard, Henderson, Hills, Hire, Howell, Kavanagh, Knoblock, Maas, Mann, Mayer, M. W. Murphy, Newell, Ong, Pintado, Seymour, Shaw, Stumpf, Waters, Wenck, Wells et Wilson—42.

Négative :

MM. Abell, Barrett, Bell, Buckley, Campbell, J. K Cook, T. Cook, Davies, Decker, Dufresne, Flood, Gastinel, Geier, Gorlinski, Harnan, Healey, Howes, Maurer, Montamat, Morris, E. Murphy, Normand, O'Conner, Orr, J. Payne, Poynot, S. Pursell, Schroeder, Schnurr, Smith, Spellicy, Stiner, Stocker, Stauffer, Sullivan et Terry —36.

L'amendement Shaw est donc repris en considération.

M. Foley en propose le rejet.

M. Montamat propose le rejet de la proposition de M. Foley ; et ce dernier la retirant, M. Mann présente de nouveau cette même motion.

Sur cette question de rejet de l'amendement, l'appel nominal donne pour résultat :

Affirmative :

Messieurs Abell, Ariail, Austin, Bailey, Baum, Beauvais, Bell, Bofill, Bromley. Burke, Cazabat, Crozat, Cutler, Davies, Dupaty, Duane, Edwards, Fish, Flagg, Flood. Foley, Fosdick, Fuller, Gaidry, Gorlinski, Hart, Healy, Heard, Henderson, Hills, Hire, Howell, Kavanagh, Knobloch, Maas, Mann, Mayer, E. Murphy, M. W. Murphy, Newell, Ong, Pintado, Seymour, Stumpf, Stiner, Thorpe, Waters, Wenck, Wells, Wilson—50.

Négative :

Messieurs Barrett, Buckley, Campbell, Collin, J. K. Cook, T. Cook, Decker, Dufresne, Gastinel, Geier, Harnan, Howes, Maurer, Montamat, Morris, Normand, Orr, O'Conner, J. Payne, Poynot, S. Pursell, Schroeder, Schnurr, Shaw, Smith, Spellicy, Stocker, Stauffer, Sullivan, Terry—30.

M. Terry présente le substitut suivant

ET L'AMENDEMENT DE LA CONSTITUTION DE LA LOUISIANE.   103

pour l'article 11 du rapport sur le Judiciaire :

Les juges de la Cour Suprême, des cours inférieures et des tribunaux de paix, seront tous élus par les électeurs ayant qualité en cet Etat ; Il est cependant entendu que pendant la durée de cette guerre, et même pendant deux années après sa cessation, dûment annoncée par la proclamation du President des Etats-Unis, lesdits juges seront nommés par le gouverneur, de l'avis et du consentement du Sénat, et la durée de leurs fonctions, ainsi que la présente loi le porte, sera désignée dans leurs commissions respectives.

Après cette époque, le gouverneur lancera sa proclamation, ordonnant une élection aux fonctions judiciaires, conformément aux provisions-du présent article.

Sur la proposition de M. Wells de rejeter ce substitut, il y a appel nominal, ainsi que suit :

Affirmative :

MM. Abell, Ariail, Austin, Bailey, Baum, Beauvais, Bofill, Bromley, Burke, Cazabat, Collin, J. K. Cook, T. Cook, Crozat, Cutler, Davies, Decker, Duane, Dupaty, Dufresne, Edwards, Fish, Foley, Fosdick, Fuller, Gastinel, Gorlinski, Harnan, Hart, Healy, Heard, Henderson, Hills, Hire, Howell, Kavanagh, Maas, Mann, Maurer, Mayer, E. Murphy, M. W. Murphy, Newell, Normand, Ong, Pintado, Poynot, Schroeder, Schnurr, Shaw, Spellicy, Stiner. Stauffer, Thorpe. Waters. Wenck. Wells et Wilson —58.

Négative :

MM. Barrett, Bell, Buckley, Campbell, Flagg, Flood, Gaidry, Geier, Howes, Knobloch, Morris, O'Conner, Orr, J. Payne, S. Pursell, Seymour, Smith, Stocker, Stumpf, Sullivan, Terry—21.

M. Montamat demande un recès de dix minutes. Refusé.

M. Hills propose l'amendement suivant à l'article 11 :

Les juges de la Cour Suprême, des cours inférieures et des tribunaux de paix seront nommés par le gouverneur, de l'avis et du consentement du Sénat. Les juges de la Cour Suprême occuperont leurs fonctions pendant douze années ; et les' juges des cours de district, (les juges de paix exceptés) occuperont leurs fonctions pendant dix ans ; mais toutes nominations aux places de juges faites par le gouverneur actuel, cesseront d'avoir effet à l'expiration de ses fonctions.

Sur motion de rejeter la susdite proposition, il y a appel nominal, asnsi que suit :

Affirmative :

MM. Abell, Ariail, Barret, Baum, Beauvais, Bell, Bofil, Bromley, Buckley, Burke, Collin, J. K. Cook, T. Cook, Crozat, Cutler, Davies, Decker, Duane, Dufresne, Dupaty, Flagg, Flood, Foley, Fuller, Gastinel, Geier, Goldman, Gaidry, Healy, Hart. Heard, Hire, Howell, Howes. Knobloch, Maas, Maurer Montamat, Morris, M. W. Murphy, Mayer, Normand, O'Conner, Orr, J. Payne, Pintado, Poynot, S. Pursell, Seymour, Smith, Spellicy, Stiner. Stauffer, Sullivan, Terry. Wenck. Wilson — 57.

Négative :

MM. Austin, Bailey, Campbell, Cazabat, Edwards, Fish, Fosdick, Gorlinski. Harnan, Henderson, Hills, Kavanagh, E. Murphy, Newell, Ong, Schroeder, Schnurr. Shaw, Stocker, Stumpf, Thorpe. Waters. Wells—23.

Ce substitut est donc rejeté.

M. Stiner offre le substitut suivant :

Les juges de la cour Suprême seront nommés pour le terme de———; les juges de la cour inférieure pour le terme de———.

Aux premières nominations faites en vertu de la présente constitution, le grand juge sera nommé pour le terme de———; le premier des juges-adjoints pour le terme de ———; le second pour le terme de———; le troisième pour le terme de———et le quatrième pour le terme de———.

M. Montamat présente le substitut suivant :

Tous les juges, excepté les juges de paix, seront nommés par le gouverneur, de l'avis et du consentement du Sénat et de la Chambre des Représentants, réunis en Assemblée conjointe ; les juges de la Cour Suprême siégeront pendant huit ans, et les juges inférieurs, excepté les juges de paix, pendant six années.

Le tout est rejeté.

M. Smith propose le substitut suivant :

Les juges des Cours Suprême et inférieures seront nommés par le gouverneur pendant la durée de la présente rébellion. et continueront en fonctions deux ans après sa fin : à cette époque les juges de la Cour Suprême seront alors élus par la Chambre basse de l'Assemblée Générale, et les juges des cours inférieures seront élus par le vote électoral de leur district respectif, laissant à la Législature le droit de déterminer le terme de leurs fonctions.

Sur motion de rejeter le substitut de M. Smith, il y a appel nominal ainsi que suit :

Affirmative :

Messieurs Abell, Ariail, Austin, Bailey, Baum, Beauvais, Bofill, Bromley, Burke. Colin, Crozat, Cutler, Davies, Dupaty, Edwards, Fosdick, Fuller, Heard, Hills, Hire, Howell, Kavanagh, Newell. Nor mand, Ong, Shaw, Thorpe, Waters, Wenck, Wells, Wilson—31.

Négative :

Messieurs Barrett, Bell, Buckley, Campbell, Cazabat, J. K. Cook, T. Cook, Decker, Duane, Dufresne, Fish, Flagg, Flood, Foley, Gastinel, Geier, Goldman, Gorlinski, Gruneberg, Gaidry, Haley, Harnan, Hart, Henderson, Howes, Knobloch, Maas, Mann, Maurer, Montamat, Morris, E. Murphy, M. W. Murphy, Mayer, O'Conner, Orr, J. Payne, Pintado, Poynot, J. Purcell, S. Pursell, Schroeder, Schnurr, Seymour, Smith, Spellicy, Stocker, Stumpf, Stiner, Stauffer, Sullivan, Terry—52.

M. Baum présente le substitut suivant à celui de M. Smith :

Les juges des cours inférieures seront nommés par le gouvereur de l'avis et du consentement du Sénat. Les juges de la Cour Suprême resteront en fonctions pendant dix années, et les juges des cours inférieures pendant sept années. Leurs fonctions commenceront du jour de la date de leur commission.

Il est bien entendu que les nominations faites pendant la durée de cette rébellion ne seront point considérées comme faites sous l'empire de la présente loi.

Les premières nominations et confirmations seront faites pendant la première session de la Législature, après le rétablissement de la paix.

Le substitut de M. Baum est rejeté par le vote suivant :

Affirmative :

Messieurs Abell, Ariail, Barrett, Bell, Buckley, Campbell, J. K. Cook, T. Cook, Decker, Duane. Dufresne, Dupaty, Fish, Flagg, Flood, Gastinel, Geier, Goldman, Gorlinski, Gruneberg, Gaidry, Harnan, Howes, Knobloch, Maurer, Montamat, Morris, M. W. Murphy, Mayer, Normand, O'Conner, Orr, J. Payne, Poynot, J. Purcell, S. Pursell, Seymour, Smith, Stiner, Stauffer, Sullivan, Terry. Waters. Wells et Wilson—45.

Négative :

MM. Austin, Bailey, Baum, Beauvais, Bofill, Bromley, Burke, Collin, Cazabat, Crozat, Cutler, Davies, Edwards, Foley, Fosdick, Fuller, Healy, Hart, Heard, Hills, Hire, Howell, Kavanagh, Maas, Mann, E. Murphy, Newell, Ong, Pintado, Schroeder, Schnurr, Shaw, Spellicy, Stocker, Stumpf, Thorpe, et Wenck—37.

M. Baum propose de rejeter les trois première lignes du substitut de M. Smith. Refusé.

M. Baum propose l'ajournement. Refusé.

M. Cazabat propose le substitut suivant :

Les juges des Cours Suprême et inférieures seront élus par le vote électoral de leur district respectif, pour un temps que la Législature déterminera.

L'appel nominal ayant été ordonné avant la présentation de ce substitut de M. Cazabat, la Convention ne le prend pas en considération, et l'on passe au vote sur le substitut de M. Smith ; il en résulte :

Affirmative :

MM. Barrett, Baum, Bell, Buckley, Campbell, J. K. Cook, T. Cook, Decker, Duane, Dufresne, Duke, Fish, Flagg, Flood, Foley, Gastinel, Geier, Goldman, Gorlinski, Gruneberg, Gaidry, Healy, Harnan, Hart, Howes, Knobloch, Maas, Maurer, Montamat, Morris, M. W. Murphy, Mayer, O'Conner, Orr, J. Payne, Poynot, J. Purcell, S. Pursell, Schnurr, Seymour, Smith, Spellicy, Stocker, Stiner, Stauffer, Sullivan and Terry—47.

Négative :

MM. Abell, Ariail, Austin, Bailey, Beauvais, Bofill, Bromley, Burke, Collin, Cazabat, Crozat, Cutler, Davies, Dupaty, Edwards, Fosdick, Fuller, Heard, Henderson, Hills, Hire, Howells, Kavanagh, Mann, E. Murphy, Newell, Normand, Ong, Pintado, Shaw, Stumpf, Thorpe Waters. Wenck, Wells et Wilson—36.

Sur motion de M. Hills. la Convention s'ajourne.

Approuvé.

JOHN E. NEELIS,
Secrétaire.

SAMEDI, le 4 juin 1864.

La Convention se réunit conformément à l'ajournement.

A l'appel du rôle, les membres suivants répondent :

MM. Abell. Ariail, Austin, Balch, Barrett, Baum, Bell, Bofill, Bromley. Buckley, Burke, Campbell, J. K. Cook, Crozat, Davies, Decker. Duane, Dufresne. Edwards, Flood, Foley, Geier, Goldman, Gorlinski, Gruneberg, Healy, Hart, Heard, Knobloch, Maas, Mann, Maurer, Mendiverri, Montamat, E. Murphy, M. W. Murphy, Normand, O'Conner, Orr, Pintado, Poynot, J. Purcell, S. Pursell, Schroeder. Stumpf. Stauffer Sullivan, Terry, Wenck, Wilson et M. le Président—53.

Le quorum faisant défaut, le sergent-d'armes se met à la recherche des absents.

Puis entrent les membres suivants :

MM. T. Cook, Dupaty, Flagg, Hills, Hire, Morris, Ong, Schnurr, Seymour, Shaw, Spellicy, et Waters.

Le président s'étant absenté temporairement, M. Waters propose d'appeler au fauteuil le serétaire; mais M. Hills, sur motion de M. Gorlinski, est choisi comme président intérimaire.

Puis la Convention s'ajourne, faute de quorum, à lundi à midi.

Approuvé.

JOHN E. NEELIS,
Secrétaire.

LUNDI, le 6 juin 1864.

La Convention se réunit conformément à l'ajournement. A l'appel du rôle répondent les membres suivants :

MM. Abell, Ariail, Balch, Baum, Bell, Bromley, Brott, Burke, Campbell, T. Cook, J. K. Cook, Crozat, Davies, Edwards, Ennis, Flagg, Foley, Fuller, Geier, Goldman, Gorlinski, Gruneberg, Gaidry, Hart, Heard, Henderson, Howell, Kavanagh, Knobloch, Maas, Maurer, E. Murphy, M. W. Murphy, Mayer, Newell, Normand, O'Conner, Pintado, Poynot, S. Purcell, Schroeder, Smith, Schnurr, Spellicy, Stumpf, Stiner, Stauffer, Waters, Wilson—50.

Le quorum faisant défaut, le sergent d'armes reçoit l'ordre de rechercher les membres absents, et les membres suivants : MM. Austin, Bailey, Barrett, Bofill, Dufresne, Dupaty, Fish, Flood, Fosdick, Gastinel, Harnan, Hills, Hire, Howes, Kugler, Mann, Montamat, Morris, Orr, J. T. Paine, J. Purcell, Seymour, Shaw, Stocker, Sullivan, Terry et Thorpe (27) se présentent, le président déclare l'existence du quorum.

Après lecture et amendement, les procès-verbaux des séances de vendredi et samedi sont adoptés.

M. Montamat présente le rapport suivant du comité des Finances :

SUR LES FONDS ALLOUÉS AU PAIEMENT DES MEMBRES ET DES EMPLOYÉS.

1864		
Mai 30—En caisse, d'après le rapport No. 7.		$37,043 40
Mai 30—Payé ordre No. 35	$ 654 00	
Mai 31—Payé ordre No. 56	385 00	
Juin 1—Payé ordre No. 57	952 00	
Juin 4—Payé ordre No. 58	2230 00	
Juin 4—Payé ordre No. 59	1412 00	
Juin 4—Payé ordre No. 60	1450 00	
Juin 6—Payé ordre No. 62	1080 00	$8,163 00

Juin 6 — Balance en caisse ce jour....... $28,880 40

J. P. MONTAMAT,
Président.

RAPPORT SUR LES FONDS DES DÉPENSES CASUELLES.

1864	
Mai 30 —En caisse d'après le rapport No. 7	$6,928 63
Juin 3—Payé l'ordre No. 81	2,276 10
Juin 6 — Balance en caisse ce jour	$4,652 53

J. P. MONTAMAT,
Président.

M. Sullivan appelle la résolution fixée pour ce jour.

Le président déclare qu'en vertu de la résolution du 31 mai 1864, immédiatement après la lecture du procès-verbal, on doit s'occuper de l'ordre du jour, et que par conséquent la préférence appartient au rapport sur le Judiciaire, et la résolution de M. Sullivan est renvoyée à samedi.

M. Abell appelle de la décision du président, en se fondant sur ce que cette résolution Sullivan avait été mise à l'ordre du jour de cette séance, avant que la résolution du 31 mai n'eût été adoptée. Sur quoi, l'appel nominal donne pour résultat :

En faveur du président :

MM. Ariail, Austin, Barrett, Bromley, Burke, Campbell, Crozat, Davies, Dupaty, Edwards, Ennis, Fish, Flagg, Fosdick, Fuller, Gaidry, Goldman, Gruneberg, Heard, Hills, Hire, Howell, Knobloch, Kugler, Mann, Morris, Newell, J. T. Paine, Pintado, S. Purcell, Schroeder, Seymour, Shaw, Stumpf, Stauffer, Thorpe, Wilson—37.

Contre le président :

MM. Abell, Balch, Bailey, Baum, Bell, Bofill, Buckley, J. K. Cook, T. Cook, Dufresne, Flood, Foley, Gastinel, Gorlinski, Harnan, Hart, Henderson, Howes, Kavanagh, Maas, Maurer, Mayer, Montamat, M. W. Murphy, Normand, O'Conner, Orr, Poynot, J. Purcell, Schnurr, Smith, Spellicy, Stiner, Stocker, Sullivan, Terry et Waters—37.

Le vote n'indiquant pas la présence d'un quorum, M. Henderson demande l'appel du rôle, auquel 76 membres répondent.

M. Cutler entrant en ce moment obtient la permission de voter, et il se déclare contre la décision du président, et M. Durell annonce que la proposition Sullivan est par conséquent à l'ordre.

Lecture en est donnée ainsi que suit :

La ville de la Nlle-Orléans entretiendra un corps de police, portant uniforme et insignes des divers grades ; ses membres seront des citoyens résidents, de bonnes mœurs, choisis par le Maire, et nommés à vie, destituables seulement pour démérite, par le jugement de la majorité de la commission de police, composée de cinq citoyens, pris un à un dans chacun des districts de la ville, sous la présidence du Maire et nommés par le Gouverneur. Les officiers de police, après avoir été destitués, ne pourront être nommés qu'après un an de suspension.

Le chef de police fournira un cautionnement de dix mille dollars, les lieutenants en fourniront un de cinq mille respectivement; les sergents, greffiers et caporaux de trois mille chacun, pour garantie du fidèle accomplissement de leurs devoirs, et ils recevront les appointements suivants :

Le chef de police	$275 00	par mois.
Les lieutenants	150 00	..
Les sergents	100 00	..
Les greffiers	100 00	..
Les caporaux	90 00	..
Les simples gardes (de nuit et de jour)	80 00	..

Ces appointements ne seront point réductibles.

M. Foley propose de substituer $200 à $275 pour les appointements mensuels du chef de police.

M. Orr propose le supplément suivant au susdit décret :

Bien entendu, Que les conducteurs des travaux, les artisans, les charretiers et les manœuvres employés aux travaux publics par l'autorité de l'Etat, de la ville ou des juris de police des paroisses loyales recevront un salaire porté à un taux non inférieur à celui du tarif suivant, savoir :

Les conducteurs	$3 50	par jour.
Les artisans	3 00	..
Charretiers	3 00	..
Les manœuvres	2 00	..

M. S. Pursell propose de rejeter le tout, et M. Abell fait un appel à l'ordre, se fondant sur ce que déjà une motion de rejet avait été faite mais inutilement ; sur quoi M. Pursell restreint sa proposition à une demande de rejet du supplément.

L'appel nominal donne le résultat suivant :

Affirmative :

MM. Abell, Bailey, Barrett, Baum, Bofill, Cutler, Gruneberg, Kavanagh et Normand—9.

Négative :

MM. Ariail, Austin, Balch, Bell, Bromley, Buckley, Burke, Campbell, J. K Cook, T. Cook, Crozat, Davies, Dufresne, Dupaty, Edwards, Ennis, Fish, Flagg, Flood, Foley, Fosdick, Fuller, Gastinel, Goldman, Gorlinski, Gaidry, Harnan, Hart, Heard, Henderson, Hills, Hire, Howell, Howes, Knobloch, Kugler, Maas, Mann, Maurer, Montamat, Morris, M. W. Murphy, Mayer, Newell, O'Conner, Orr, J. T. Paine, Pintado, Poynot, J. Purcell, S. Pursell, Schroeder, Schnurr, Seymour, Shaw, Smith, Spellicy, Stocker, Stumpf, Stiner, Stauffer, Sullivan, Terry, Thorpe, Waters, Wilson—66.

La motion de rejet est donc repoussée.

M. Austin, Burke, et Hendrson ayant d'abord voté dans l'affirmative, se prononcent ensuite pour la négative.

La question se représente au sujet de l'adoption du suplément présenté par M. Orr, et l'appel nominal accuse :

Affirmative :

MM. Abell, Ariail, Austin, Balch, Barrett, Baum, Beauvais, Bell, Bennie, Bromley, Buckley, Burke, Campbell, J. K. Cook, T. Cook, Crozat, Cutler, Davies, Dufresne, Dupaty, Edwards, Ennis, Fish, Flagg, Flood, Foley, Fosdick, Fuller, Gastinel, Goldman, Golinski, Gaidry, Healy, Harnan, Hart, Henderson, Hills, Hire, Howes, Knobloch, Kugler, Maas, Mann, Maurer, Montamat, Morris, M. W. Murphy, Mayer, Normand, O'Conner, Orr, Poynot, J. Purcell, S. Pursell, Schroeder, Schnurr, Seymour, Shaw, Smith, Spellicy, Stoker, Stiner, Sullivan, Stumpf, Terry, Thorpe, Waters—67.

Négative :

MM. Bailey, Bofill, Cazabat, Gruneberg, Heard, Howell, Kavanagh, Newell, J. Paine, Pintado—10.

Le Supplément est donc adopté ; puis on adopte l'amendement Foley.

Sur la motion d'adopter la proposition Sullivan, y compris le supplément, il y a appel nominal ainsi que sui :

Affirmative :

MM. Abell, Barrett, Baum, Beauvais, Bell, Bofill, Buckley. J. K. Cook, T. Cook, Cutler, Dufresne, Fish, Flood, Foley, Fuller, Gastinel, Gorlinski, Gruneberg, Healy, Harnan, Hart, Henderson, Hire, Howes, Kugler, Kavanagh, Maas, Maurer, Montamat, M. W. Murphy, Normand, O'Conner, Orr, Poynot, J. Purcell, S. Pursell, Schroeder, Schnurr, Smith, Spellicy, Stocker, Stumpf, Stiner, Sullivan, Terry, Waters—46.

Négative :

MM. Ariail, Austin, Balch, Bailey, Bennie, Bromley, Burke, Campbell, Crozat, Cazabat,

Davies, Dupaty, Edwards, Ennis, Flagg, Fosdick, Goldman, Gaidry, Heard, Hills, Howell, Knobloch, Mann, Morris, Mayer, Newell, J. T. Paine, Pintado, Seymour, Shaw, Thorpe—31.

Cette résolution est donc adoptée.

MM. Hire et S. Pursell, ayant d'abord voté pour la négative, se prononcent pour l'affirmative.

Sur motion de M. Smith, la Convention s'ajourne.

Approuvé.

JOHN E. NEELIS,
Secrétaire.

MARDI, le 7 Juin 1864.

Conformément à l'ajournement, la Convention se réunit et est appelée à l'ordre à midi. L'appel nominal est fait.

Sont présents :

MM. Abell, Bell, Bennie, Burke, Buckley, J. K. Cook, T. Cook, Crozat, Edwards, Ennis, Fish, Flagg, Foley, Geier, Gorlinski, Healy, Heard, Henderson, Knobloch, Mann, Mayer, Montamat, Morris, Normand, O'-Conner, Pintado, Poynot, S. Pursell, Spellicy, Shaw, Stumpf, Stiner, Stauffer, Sullivan et M. le Président—35.

Quelques moments après entrent dans la salle MM. Austin, Bailey, Barrett, Baum, Beauvais, Bofill, Bromley, Campbell, Collin, Cutler, Davies, Flood, Fosdick, Fuller, Gastinel, Gaidry, Gruneberg, Harnan, Hart, Hills, Hire, Howell, Howes, Kugler, Maas, Maurer, Mendiverri, M. W. Murphy, E. Murphy, Newell, Ong, Orr, J. Purcell, Schroeder, Seymour, Smith, Stocker, Terry, Thorpe, Waters, Wenck, Wilson—42.

Le président annonce qu'il y a quorum.

Le procès-verbal de la veille est lu et approuvé.

M. S. Pursell demande la reconsidération du vote d'hier, par lequel la résolution de M. Sullivan a été adoptée.

M. Bofill demande le rejet de cette motion.

Mais la motion de M. Pursell est adoptée par le vote suivant :

Ont voté pour l'adoption de la motion :

MM. Abell, Bailey, Baum, Bell, Beauvais, Bofill, Bromley, J. K. Cook, T. Cook, Cutler, Fish, Flagg, Flood, Foley, Gastinel, Geier, Gorlinski, Gruneberg, Harnan, Hart, Healy, Henderson, Howes, Maurer, Maas, Mendiverri, Montamat, M. W. Murphy, E. Murphy, O'Conner, Orr, Poynot, Smith, Schroeder, Seymour, Spellicy, Stiner. Stocker, Stumpf, Sullivan, Terry et Waters—42.

Pour le rejet :

MM. Austin, Balch, Bennie, Bromley, Burke, Campbell, Collin, Crozat, Davies, Ennis, Fosdick, Gaidry, Heard, Hire, Hills, Howell, Knobloch, Kugler, Mayer, Mann, Morris, Newell, Normand, Ong, Pintado, S. Pursell, Shaw, Stauffer, Thorpe, Wenck, Wilson—31.

M. Baum demande la reconsidération du vote adoptant le substitut de M. Smith à l'article 11 du rapport du comité du Judiciaire.

Le président déclare que la motion n'est pas à l'ordre, comme venant trop tard.

M. Cutler appelle de la décision du président, mais cette décision est soutenue par un vote par assis et levé de 37 voix contre 35.

L'appel nominal étant ordonné, 76 membres répondent à leurs noms.

On prend en mains l'ordre du jour, et lecture est donnée de l'article 12 du rapport du comité du Judiciaire, comme suit :

Art. 12. Les greffiers des Cours inférieures seront nommés par les juges de ces cours, et resteront en fonctions tant qu'ils n'auront pas démérité, mais ils pourront être destitués par les juges de leurs Cours respectives, sauf leur droit d'en appeler, dans tous les cas, à la Cour Suprême.

Il est aussi donné lecture des amendements et substituts suivants, savoir :

M. Sullivan offre le substitut suivant à l'art. 12 :

Les greffiers des Cours inférieures de l'Etat seront nommés à l'élection pour un terme de quatre ans; et dans le cas où une vacance viendrait à survenir après l'élection, le juge de la Cour où cette vacance aura lieu pourvoira au remplacement du titulaire, et la personne qu'il aura choisie pour remplir la vacance restera en fonctions jusqu'à la plus prochaine élection générale.

M. Montamat offre l'amendement suivant au substitut, avec l'assentiment de M. Sullivan, savoir :

Art. 12. Les greffiers des Cours inférieures seront nommés par le Gouverneur tant que la guerre durera, et pendant les deux années qui suivront ; mais à dater de cette époque ils seront nommés par les électeurs dûment qualifiés, pour un terme de quatre ans.

Sur motion de rejeter l'amendement de

M. Montamat, le vote nominal est pris et se traduit comme suit :

Affirmative :

MM. Baum, Beauvais, Burke, Campbell, Collin, Foley, Fosdick, Gastinel, Gorlinski, Gruneberg, Hart, Hills, Howell, Howes, Knoblock, Kugler, Mann, Maurer, Morris, Normand, Orr, Pintado, Poynot, S. Pursell, Schroeder, Stauffer, Waters, Wenck, Wilson —29.

Négative :

MM. Abell, Austin, Balch, Barrett, Bailey, Bell, Bennie, Bofill, Bromley, Buckley, J. K. Cook, T. Cook, Crozat, Cutler, Davies, Edwards, Ennis, Fish, Flagg, Flood, Gaidry, Geier, Harnan, Healy, Heard, Henderson, Hire, Maas, Mayer, Mendiverri, Montamat, E. Murphy, M. W. Murphy, Newell, O'Conner, Ong, Seymour, Shaw, Smith, Spellicy, Stocker, Stumpf, Stiner, Sullivan, Terry, Thorpe—46.

La motion de rejet est repoussée.

Sur motion d'adopter le substitut de M. Sullivan ainsi amendé, le vote nominal est également pris, et en voici le résultat :

Affirmative :

MM. Abell, Balch, Barrett, Bell, Bennie, Bofill, Buckley, Burke, T. Cook, Crozat, Edwards, Ennis, Fish, Flagg, Flood, Geier, Gaidry, Healy, Harnan, Henderson, Maas, Mendiverri, Montamat, E. Murphy, M. W. Murphy, Normand, O'Conner, Seymour, Shaw, Smith, Stocker, Stumpf, Stiner, Stauffer, Sullivan, Terry, Thorpe—37.

Négative :

MM. Austin, Bailey, Baum, Beauvais, Bromley, Campbell, Collin, J. K. Cook, Cutler, Davies, Foley, Fosdick, Gastinel, Gorlinski, Gruneberg, Hart, Heard, Hills, Hire, Howell, Howes, Knobloch, Kugler, Mann, Maurer, Morris, Mayer, Newell, Ong, Orr, Pintado, Poynot, S. Pursell, Schroeder, Spellicy, Waters, Wenck, Wilson—38.

En conséquence, le substitut de M. Sullivan est rejeté.

M. Stauffer demande alors qu'il soit donné lecture de son substitut à l'article 12, ainsi conçu :

Les greffiers des cours inférieures seront élus pour le terme de quatre ans; et dans le cas où il surviendrait une vacance après l'élection, il sera pourvu à cette vacance par le juge de la cour où cette vacance sera survenue, et la personne ainsi nommée pour remplir la vacance restera en fonction jusqu'à la plus prochaine élection générale.

M. Terry demande qu'on substitue le mot "deux" au mot "quatre" à la seconde ligne du substitut. Rejeté.

La résolution de M. Stauffer est ensuite adoptée par le vote suivant :

Pour l'adoption :

MM. Abell, Balch, Bailey, Barrett, Baum, Bell, Bofill, Buckley, Campbell, Collin, J. K. Cook, T. Cook, Davies, Ennis, Fish. Flagg, Flood, Gastinel, Geier, Gorlinski, Gruneberg, Healy, Harnan. Hart. Henderson, Howes, Knobloch, Maas, Maurer, Mendiverri, Montamat, Morris, E. Murphy, Mayer, Orr, Poynot, S. Pursell, Shaw, Smith, Spellicy, Stocker, Stiner, Stauffer, Sullivan, Terry, Thorpe, Waters—47.

Pour le rejet :

MM. Austin, Beauvais, Bennie, Bromley, Duke, Crozat, Cutler, Edwards, Foley, Fosdick, Gaidry, Heard, Hills, Hire, Howell, Kugler, Mann, M. W. Murphy, Newell, Normand, Ong, Pintado, Schroeder, Seymour, Stumpf, Wenck, Wilson—27.

L'article 13 est lu et adopté tel qu'il est au rapport.

Il est donné lecture de l'art. 14, ainsi que du substitut de M. Sullivan, ainsi conçu :

Art. 14. La juridiction des juges de paix sera limitée, en matière civile, aux cas où l'object en litige n'excède pas deux cents piastres, non compris l'intérêt, sauf le droit d'appel dans les cas prévus par la loi. Ils seront nommés par les électeur dûment qualifiés de chaque paroisse, district ou arrondissement, pour un terme de deux années, dans les formes et de la manière prescrites par la loi, et ils auront également en matière criminelle telle juridiction que la loi indiquera.

M. Flood présente un amendement à la résolution de M. Sullivan, tendant à ce que toutes les contestations au-dessous de vingt-cinq piastres soient réglées par arbitrage et sans appel. Rejeté.

M. Stiner offre un amendement au substitut de M. Sullivan, à l'effet de rendre les juges de paix électifs jusqu'à l'expiration des deux années qui suivront la fin de la présente guerre. Rejeté.

M. Flagg offre un amendement disposant que les juges de paix seront nommés par le Gouverneur et resteront en fonctions jusqu'à l'expiration de la deuxième année qui suivra la proclamation de la paix, époque à laquelle ils seront élus par le peuple, et de plus, que leur juridiction ne s'étendra pas au-delà de cent piastres.

L'amendement de M. Flagg est rejeté par un vote par assis et levés, de 45 voix contre 17.

M. S. Pursell propose d'amender le substitut de M. Sullivan, par la substitution du mot "quatre" au mot "deux", à la cinquième ligne, à propos de la durée des fonctions.

Motion est faite de rejeter l'amendement. Cette motion est rejetée sur un vote divisionnel par 47 voix contre 26.

L'amendement de M. Pursell est ensuite adopté.

Le substitut de M. Sullivan, tel qu'il a été amendé, est ensuite mis aux voix et adopté.

Il est donné lecture de l'article 15, en même temps que du substitut suivant offert par M. Sullivan :

"Il y aura un Avocat-Général qui sera nommé par les électeurs qualifiés de l'Etat. Les Avocats de District seront également nommés par les électeurs qualifiés de chaque district, le jour de l'élection du Gouverneur de l'Etat. Ils resteront en fonctions pendant quatre ans."

M. Ferry propose d'insérer dans l'article les mots suivants :

"Ils recevront un traitement de cinq mille piastres chacun."

Cet amendement est accepté par M. Sullivan.

Sur la question d'adoption du substitut de M. Sullivan, tel qu'il est amendé, le vote divisionnel est ordonné, et le substitut est rejeté par 40 voix contre 32.

M. Montamat demande la reconsidération du vote. Cette reconsidération est accordée. Il propose alors d'amender le substitut en fixant à quatre mille piastres au lieu de cinq mille le traitement de l'Avocat-Général.

Rejeté sur un vote divisionnel par 39 voix contre 30.

Le subsitut de M. Sullivan, tel qu'il est amendé, est ensuite adopte sur un vote divisionnel par 42 voix contre 31.

Lecture est ensuite donnée de l'article 16, ainsi que du substitut suivant offert par M. Sullivan :

Il y aura dans chaque paroisse un shérif et un coroner qui seront nommés par les électeurs dûment qualifiés de ces paroisses, et qui resteront en fonctions pendant deux ans, à moins de destitution. La Législature aura le pouvoir d'augmenter le nombre des shérifs dans telle paroisse qu'elle jugera à propos. S'il survient une vacance dans l'une de ces deux places, postérieurement à l'élection, il y sera pourvu par le Gouverneur ; et la personne ainsi nommée en remplacement conservera ses fonctions jusqu'à ce que son successeur ait été élu et qualifié.

La Législature peut déterminer le mode suivant. lequel il sera pourvu, en cas de vacance, au remplacement des Juges Inférieurs, de l'Avocat-Général et de tous les autres officiers dans les cas non prévus par cette Constitution.

M. Henderson propose d'amender en substituant les mots "quatre ans" aux mots "deux ans," à la seconde ligne.

Rejeté.

M. Montamat propose d'amender en réduisant le terme d'office à un an pour le coroner et à deux ans pour le shérif.

Rejeté.

Le substitut de M. Sullivan est ensuite adopté.

Le rapport du comité du judiciaire, tel qu'il a été amendé, est ensuite adopté dans son ensemble.

Sur motion, la Convention s'ajourne.

Approuvé.

JOHN E. NEELIS,
Secrétaire.

MERCREDI, 8 juin 1864.

La Convention se réunit et le président l'appelle à l'ordre conformément à l'ajournement.

Cinquante membres répondent au premier appel du rôle.

Quelques instants après, vingt-huit membres entrent et constituent le nombre requis pour un quorum.

Membres absents :

MM. Balch, Baum, Bonzano, Brott, Cazabat, Decker, Duane, Duke, Flagg, Fuller, Goldman, Kavanagh, Lobdell, Millspaugh, Montague, J. Payne. J. T. Paine, Taliaferro et Thomas—19.

Après lecture, le procès-verbal de la dernière séance est approuvé.

M. Heard demande la suspension du réglement afin de présenter la résolution suivante :

Résolu, Qu'à dater de ce jour, tout membre qui ne répondra point à l'appel de son nom au rôle d'ouverture ou dans les quinze minutes subséquentes, sera privé du paiement de son *per diem*, à moins qu'il ne soit absent par congé ou qu'il ne puisse justifier de son absence d'une manière satisfaisante.

La lecture de cette résolution étant demandée, le secrétaire est invité à la lire ; après quoi, M. Foley propose la suspension du réglement, afin d'agir sur cette motion. Mais sur objection, et le vote à ce sujet n'étant pas des deux tiers, il n'y a pas de suspension du réglement.

M. Bofil propose la reprise en considération du vote d'hier, par lequel la loi sur le judiciaire est adoptée conformément au rapport du comité.

M. Smith propose le rejet de cette motion et l'appel nominal donne pour résultat :

Affirmative :

MM. Austin, Buckley, Burke, J. K. Cook, Flood, Harnan, Henderson, Howes, Maurer, Morris, M. W. Murphy, Orr, Poynot, J. Purcell, S. Pursell, Schroeder, Schnurr, Smith, Spellicy, Stocker, Stauffer, Sullivan, Terry, Waters—24.

Négative :

MM. Abell, Ariail, Bailey, Barrett, Beauvais, Bell, Bennie, Bofil, Bromley, Campbell, Collin, T. Cook, Crozat, Cutler, Davies, Dufresne, Dupaty, Edwards, Ennis, Fish, Foley, Fosdick, Gastinel, Geier, Gorlinski, Gruneberg, Gaidry, Healy, Hart, Heard, Hills, Hire, Howell, Knobloch, Kugler, Maas, Mann, Montamat, Mendiverri, E. Murphy, Mayer, Newell, Normand, O'Conner, Ong, Pintado, Seymour, Shaw, Stumpf, Stiner, Thorpe, Wenck, Wells, Wilson—54.

La motion est donc repoussée.

La question se présentant de nouveau sur la reprise en considération, l'appel nominal donne le résultat suivant :

Affirmative :

MM. Abell, Ariail, Bailey, Barrett, Beauvais, Bennie, Bofill, Bromley, Burke, Campbell, Collin, T. Cook, Crozat, Cutler, Davies, Dufresne, Dupaty, Edwards, Ennis, Fish, Foley, Fosdick, Gastinel, Gorlinski, Gaidry, Hart, Heard, Hills, Hire, Howell, Knobloch, Kugler, Maas, Mann, Mendiverri, E. Murphy, Mayer, Newell, Normand, O'Conner, Ong, Pintado, Schroeder, Seymour, Shaw, Stumpf, Stiner, Thorpe, Waters, Wenck, Wells, Wilson—52.

Négative :

MM. Austin, Bell, Buckley, J. K. Cook, Flood, Geier, Gruneberg, Healy, Harnan, Henderson, Howes, Maurer, Montamat, Morris, M. W. Murphy, Orr, Poynot, S. Purcell, S. Pursell, Schnurr, Smith, Spellicy, Stauffer, Sullivan, Terry—26.

La motion l'emporte donc et la reprise en considération a lieu.

Sur motion de M. Wilson, le rapport tout entier est renvoyé, y compris les amendements, à l'examen d'un comité spécial composé de neuf membres.

Le président nomme de ce comité MM. Wilson, Bofill, Cutler, Abell, Poynot, Smith, Buckley, Purcell et M. W. Murphy.

Le rapport sur la mise en accusation étant à l'ordre du jour, le secrétaire en donne lecture.

Puis, sur la motion de M. Foley, la Convention s'ajourne à lundi à midi, le 13 juin 1864.

Approuvé.

JOHN E. NEELIS,
Secrétaire.

LUNDI, le 13 juin 1864.

La Convention se réunit sous la présidence de M. E. H. Durell, conformément à l'ajournement.

Membres présents :

MM. Abell, Austin, Barrett, Bofill, Campbell, Collin, J. K. Cook, Crozat, Dufresne, Edwards, Ennis, Fish, Flood, Foley, Fosdick, Fuller, Gastinel, Geier, Gorlinski, Healy, Heard, Henderson, Hire, Howell, Howes, Maurer, Maas, Mayer, Mendiverri, Montamat, Morris, Newell, Normand, O'Conner, J. Payne, Pintado, Poynot, Seymour, Smith, Spellicy, Stocker, Stumpf, Stiner, Stauffer, Sullivan, Terry, Wells et Wilson—48.

Après un certain laps de temps, l'entrée de MM. Bailey, Baum, Bell, Bromley, Buckley, T. Cook, Cutler, Davies, Duane, Dupaty, Flagg, Harnan, Hart, Hills, Kavanagh, Kugler, Mann, M. W. Murphy, J. T. Paine, J. Purcell, S. Pursell, Schroeder, Schnurr, Shaw, Thorpe, Waters et Wenck complète le nombre requis pour un quorum.

Après lecture, le procès-verbal de la dernière séance est approuvé.

Le comité spécial sur le Judiciaire, auquel on avait référé le rapport primitif sur cette question, présente le rapport suivant :

Art. I. Le pouvoir judiciaire sera confié à la Cour Suprême, et telles autres cours inférieures que la Législature jugera devoir établir et aux tribunaux de paix.

Art. II. La juridiction de la Cour Suprême couvrira toute affaire où la somme en litige dépassera trois cents dollars, non compris les intérêts ; toute affaire où la constitutionalité ou la légalité d'une taxe, d'un impôt ou contribution quelconque, d'une amende, peine ou forfaiture imposées par une municipalité seront en litige, et aussi toute affaire criminelle, sur la question de droit seulement, lorsque l'offense alléguée sera punissable de mort ou des travaux forcés. Elle exercera aussi un contrôle supérieur sur toutes les cours inférieures, et elle pourra émettre les mandats nécessaires à l'exercice de ce contrôle.

La Législature pourra, par une loi, restreindre la juridiction de la Cour Suprême, en matière civile, aux questions de loi seulement.

Art. III. La Cour Suprême se composera d'un juge-président et de quatre adjoints, la majorité desquels formera un quorum.

Le juge-président recevra un traitement de $7,500, et chacun des adjoints de $7,000, par an, jusqu'à ce qu'il en ait été différemment disposé par une loi. Cette cour nommera ses greffiers et commis.

Art. IV. La Cour Suprême tiendra ses audiences à la Nlle-Orléans du premier lundi de novembre à la fin du mois de juin inclusivement. La Législature pourra assigner le lieu des audiences dans les autres parties de l'Etat ; et jusqu'à ce qu'il en ait été disposé autrement, la cour siègera aux lieux et places jusqu'à ce jour déterminés.

Art. V. La Cour Suprême et chacun des juges la composant, pourra émettre des mandats d'*habeas corpus*, à l'instance de toute personne détenue actuellement en vertu de procédures judiciaires, dans toute affaire où l'appel lui est dévolu.

Art. VI. La Cour Suprême ne rendra point de jugement sans la participation d'une majorité des juges qui la composent. Et lorsqu'il n'y aura point majorité en raison de la récusation de quelques membres de cette cour, les juges non récusés pourront s'adjoindre quelque juge des cours inférieures dont le devoir sera de siéger en lieu et place du juge récusé, et de concourir à la confection de l'arrêt de la Cour.

Art. VII. Tous les juges seront, en vertu de leur charge, conservateurs de la paix publique dans tout l'Etat. Le style de toute procédure sera "Etat de la Louisiane." Toute poursuite se fera au nom et par l'autorité de l'Etat de la Louisiane et concluera contre la paix et la dignité dudit Etat.

Art. VIII. Les uges de toutes les cours de l'Etat devront, quand faire se pourra, dans tout jugement définitif, référer à la loi en vertu de laquelle ledit jugement a été rendu, et dans tous les cas, donner les motifs de leur jugement.

Art. IX. Les juges de toutes les cours seront passibles de la mise en accusation : mais, pour toute cause fondée qui n'entraînera point la mise en accusation, le Gouverneur, sur la requête d'une majorité des membres élus à chacune des chambres de l'Assemblée Générale, pourra destituer tout juge ; et en pareille circonstance, les causes de la requête en destitution seront établies en plein dans la requête et consignées au procès-verbal de chaque Chambre.

Art. X. Le traitement des juges des Cours suprêmes et inférieures ne subira point de changements pendant la durée de leurs fonctions.

Art. XI. Les juges de la cour suprême, des cours inférieures et des tribunaux de paix, seront nommés par le Gouverneur, de l'avis et du consentement du Sénat, Les juges de la Cour Suprême resteront en fonctions pendant six années ; les juges des cours inférieures pendant quatre années, et les juges de paix pendant deux années : après ce terme, toutes les charges de juge seront données par l'élection des votants dûment qualifiés. Les nominations dans tous les cas compteront du jour de la ratification de la présente Constitution par le peuple. La Législature devra fixer le jour de l'élection.

Art. XII. Les greffiers des cours inférieures seront à la nomination du Gouverneur, pour le même temps que les juges, mais, quand ils seront coupables de tout crime ils pourront être destitués, le droit d'appel à la Cour Suprême leur étant réservé. Après l'expiration du terme de leurs fonctions, ils seront élus par le peuple pour le même terme que les juges.

Art. XIII. La Législature pourra donner aux greffiers le pouvoir d'accorder tels ordres et de faire tels actes qu'elle jugera nécessaires à l'administration de la justice : mais, dans ces circonstances, la nature et l'étendue des pouvoirs accordés seront définis et déterminés.

Art. XIV. Les juges de paix auront juridiction en toute matière civile, dont le montant ne dépassera point cent piastres, non compris les intérêts. Ils recevront un traitement de $2,500 à la Nouvelle-Orléans et la Législature fixera le traitement des juges de paix de la campagne. Tous les trimestres, ils présenteront à l'Auditeur des Comptes Publics, un tableau assermenté des taxes par eux perçues, et le surplus des $2.500 de leur traitement devra être fidèlement compté à l'Auditeur.

Art. XV. Il y aura un Procureur-Général pour l'Etat. Il sera nommé par le Gouverneur de l'avis et du consentement du Sénat, et il demeurera en fonctions pendant quatre ans ; après ce terme, il sera élu par les votants dûment qualifiés. Il recevra un traitement de $5,000.

Art. XVI. Il y aura autant d'avocats de district, nommés par le gouverneur, de l'avis et du consentement du Sénat, que l'on jugera nécessaires ; ils resteront en fonctions pendant deux années à compter de la ratification de cette constitution. La Législature déterminera leurs appointements et décrétera l'élection à ses charges, à l'expiration du premier terme.

Art. XVII. Le gouverneur, de l'avis et du consentement du Sénat, nommera les coroners, pour le terme de deux années. Après ce terme, ils seront élus par le suffrage du peuple, et l'Assemblée Générale fixera leurs traitements.

Art. XVIII. Le gouverneur nommera, de l'avis et du consentement du Sénat, les shérifs des différentes paroisses. Ils resteront en fonctions pendant deux années. La Législature aura le pouvoir d'augmenter le nombre des shérifs dans toute paroisse, quand elle le jugera nécessaire. Ils seront tous élus après le premier terme, lequel date du jour de la ratification de la présente constitution, par le peuple de l'Etat.

Art. XIX. Les membres des grands et petits juris recevront une rétribution de $3 50 par jour de service pendant le terme de la cour.

(Signé)   J. H. WILSON, Président.
CHARLES SMITH,
O. H. POYNOT,
M. W. MURPHY,
JOHN BUCKLEY Jr.

M. Hills demande la suspension du réglement, afin de passer à la seconde lecture du susdit rapport.

M. Sullivan propose le rejet de la proposition Hills. Refusé.

La question se présentant de nouveau sur la motion Hills, et le vote n'étant pas des deux tiers, la suspension du réglement est refusée.

M. Sullivan demande l'impression de ce rapport et sa mise à l'ordre du jour de lundi prochain.

M. Hills amende cette motion par sa demande de la mise à l'ordre du jour de demain.

La motion et l'amendement sont adoptés.

M. Thorpe demande la suspension du réglement à l'effet d'introduire une résolution dont on donne lecture ; mais le vote des deux tiers faisant faute, sa demande est repoussée.

Le comité des Finances présente le rapport suivant sur les fonds alloués au paiement des *per diem*, etc.

1864.
Juin 6— Balance en
   caisse d'après le rap-
   port No. 8.......... $28,888 40
Juin 6—Payé l'ordre
   No. 63............$1390 00
Juin 11—Payé l'ordre
   No. 64............   84 00
Juin 11—Payé l'ordre
   No. 66............ 4180 00
Juin 11—Payé l'ordre
   No. 67............ 2520 00
Juin 13—Payé l'ordre
   No. 68............ 2139 00 $10,313 00

Juin 13—Balance en
   caisse ce jour...............$18,567 00

Le 8 juin 1864, la somme de $6139 13 cents a été payée d'après l'ordre No. 65 à la ville de la Nouvelle-Orléans, sur les fonds spécialement affectés à cet effet.

Avec respect,
JOHN P. MONTAMAT,
Président par intérim du comité.

RAPPORT DU COMITÉ DES FINANCES SUR LES FONDS DES DÉPENSES CASUELLES DE LA CONVENTION.

Aucun ordre n'ayant été tiré depuis le rapport No. 8, les fonds en caisse demeurent être de la même somme, savoir : $4,652 53.

J. P. MONTAMAT,
Président.

Le secrétaire donne lecture du rapport sur la Mise en Accusation, qui se trouve être à l'ordre du jour.

On fait l'appel du rôle, il n'y a que 67 membres présents, et sur motion, la Convention s'ajourne à demain à midi.

Approuvé.
JOHN E. NEELIS,
Secrétaire.

MARDI, le 14 juin 1864.

La Convention se réunit et conformément à l'ajournement, le président E. H. Durell l'appel à l'ordre.

Membres présents :

MM. Abell, Austin, Balch, Bell, Bailey, Buckley, Burke, Campbell, Collin, Cazabat, J. K. Cook, T. Cook, Crozat, Davies, Decker, Dufresne, Duke, Ennis, Fish, Flagg, Flood, Foley, Fosdick, Geier, Gorlinski, Harnan, Howes, Maas, Mann, Maurer, Mayer, E. Murphy, M. W. Murphy, Newell, Normand, J. Payne, J. Purcell, S. Pursell, Schroeder, Smith, Stocker, Stumpf, Stiner, Stauffer, Terry, Waters, Wilson—48.

Et après un laps de temps assez long, entrent : MM. Bailey, Barrett, Beauvais, Bennie, Cutler, Dupaty, Fuller, Gastinel, Gaidry, Healy, Hart, Hills, Hire, Howell, Kugler, Mendiverri, Montamat, O'Conner,

Ong, Orr, J. T. Paine, Pintado, Seymour, Shaw, Sullivan, Thorpe, Wenck, Wells—28.

Absents : MM. Ariail, Baum, Bennie, Bonzano, Brott, Duane, Edwards, Goldman, Gruneberg, Heard, Henderson, Kavanagh, Knobloch, Lobdell, Millspaugh, Montague, Morris, Poynot, Schnurr, Spellicy, Taliaferro,Thomas, au nombre de 22, constituant le quorum.

Sur motion de M. Montamat on dispense de la lecture du procès-verbal.

M. Terry demande la suspension du réglement afin de présenter la résolution suivante :

Résolu, Qu'à dater du 14 juin tous les membres absents quinze minutes après le premier appel du rôle, sans bonne et valable excuse, perdront leur rétribution.

Après lecture, la suspension du réglement est accordée.

M. Mann présente le substitut suivant :

Attendu, Que des membres de cette Convention se sont absentés sans permission ou sans expliquer leur absence par aucun motif, en conséquence :

Résolu, Qu'à compter d'aujourd'hui, tout membre qui n'aura point obtenu de congé pour bonne cause, et qui sera absent à l'appel du rôle de midi, ne recevra point de *per diem* pour chaque jour d'absence, et le secrétaire est chargé de fournir au président du comité des Finances, une liste des absences afin détablir les réductions nécessaires pour le *per diem*.

Le substitut est accepté, et sur motion il est adopté.

M. Abell demande un congé pour M. Heard. Refusé.

ORDRE DU JOUR.

Le président annonce que le rapport du comité Spécial sur le Judiciaire est à l'ordre du jour, pour sa seconde lecture. Lecture en étant donnée, M. Stocker présente le substitut suivant :

Art. I. Le pouvoir judiciaire sera confié à la Cour Suprême, et telles autres cours inférieures que la Législature jugera devoir établir et aux tribunaux de paix.

Art. II. La Cour Suprême, excepté dans les cas ci-après prévus, aura une juridiction de cour d'appel seulement. La juridiction de la Cour Suprême couvrira toute affaire où la somme en litige dépassera trois cents dollars, non compris les intérêts ; toute affaire où la constitutionalité ou la légalité d'une taxe, d'un impôt ou contribution quelconque, d'une amende, peine ou forfaiture imposées par une municipalité seront en litige, et aussi toute affaire criminelle, sur la question de droit seulement, lorsque l'offense alléguée sera punissable de mort ou des travaux forcés, ou lorsque l'amende actuellement imposée dépassera $300.

Art. III. La Cour Suprême se composera d'un juge-président et de qurtre adjoints, la majorité desquels formera un quorum. Cette cour nommera ses greffiers.

Art. IV. La Cour Suprême tiendra ses audiences à la Nlle-Orléans du premier lundi de novembre à la fin du mois de juin inclusivement. La Législature pourra assigner le lieu des audiences dans les autres parties de l'Etat ; et jusqu'à ce qu'il en ait été disposé autrement, la cour siègera aux lieux et places jusqu'à ce jour déterminés.

Art. V. La Cour Suprême et chacun des juges la composant, pourra émettre des mandats d'*habeas corpus*, à l'instance de toute personne détenue actuellement en vertu de procédures judiciaires, dans toute affaire où l'appel lui est dévolu.

Art. VI. La Cour Suprême ne rendra point de jugement sans la participation d'une majorité des juges qui la composent. Et lorsqu'il n'y aura point majorité en raison de la récusation de quelques membres de cette cour, les juges non récusés pourront s'adjoindre quelque juge des cours inférieures, dont le devoir sera de siéger en lieu et place du juge récusé, et de concourir à la confection de l'arrêt de la cour.

Art. VII. Tous les juges seront, en vertu de leur charge, conservateurs de la paix publique dans tout l'Etat. Le style de toute procédure sera "Etat de la Louisiane." Toute poursuite se fera au nom de l'autorité de l'Etat de la Louisiane et conclura contre la paix et la dignité dudit Etat.

Art. VIII. Les juges de toutes les cours de l'Etat devront, quand faire se pourra, dans tout jugement définitif, référer à la loi en vertu de laquelle ledit jugement a été rendu, et dans tous les cas, donner les motifs de leur jugement.

Art. IX. Les juges de toutes les cours seront passibles de la mise en accusation ; mais, pour toute cause fondée qui n'entrainera point la mise en accusation, le Gouverneur, sur la requête d'une majorité des membres élus à chacune des chambres de l'Assemblée Générale, pourra destituer tout juge ; et en pareille circonstance, les causes de la requête en destitution seront établies en plein dans la requête et consignées au procès-verbal de chaque Chambre.

Art. X. Les juges de la Cour Suprême et des Cours inférieures recevront à des époques déterminées le traitement que la Législature leur assignera.

Il leur est défendu de recevoir aucun honoraire ou émolument autre que leur traitement pour tout devoir civil rempli par eux.

Art. XI. Le juge-président de la Cour Suprême sera élu par les électeurs dûment qualifiés de l'Etat et les juges adjoints de cette Cour, ainsi que les juges des Cours inférieures seront élus par le peuple de leurs districts, de la manière déterminée par la Législature, et ils occuperont leur charge pendant le temps désigné par la Legislature.

Art. XII. Les greffiers des Cours inférieures seront élus par les électeurs dûment qualifiés de leurs districts, et ils resteront en fonctions pendant le temps déterminé par la Législature : ils pourront être destitués par les juges, tout en leur réservant leur droit d'appel.

Art. XIV. La juridiction des juges de paix ne dépassera point cent piastres, en matière civile, non compris les intérêts : il y aura droit d'appel en la manière prescrite par la loi. Ils seront élus par les électeurs dûment qualifiés de leurs districts, et ils resteront en fonctions pendant le temps désigné par la Législature. Ils auront telle juridiction criminelle qui leur sera accordée par la loi.

Art. XV. Il y aura un procureur-général pour l'Etat et autant d'avocats de district qu'il sera nécessaire. Le procureur-général sera élu par les électeurs dûment qualifiés de l'Etat; les avocats de district le seront par les électeurs de leurs districts. Le procureur-général et les avocats de district resteront en fonctions pendant tel temps, et recevront tel traitement que la Législature déterminera.

Art. XVI. Un shérif et un coroner seront élus dans chaque paroisse par les électeurs y résidant ; et ils resteront en fonctions pendant tel temps, et ils recevront telle rétribution que la Législature déterminera.

Mr. Smith demande le rejet du substitut, et plus tard il retire sa demande.

Motion d'ajourner repoussée.

M. Foley demande que le substitut soit pris section par section, et à ce sujet M. Hills demande la question préalable. Secondé.

Le président reprend le fauteuil ; et les sections 1ère et 2e sont lues et adoptées.

Après lecture de la 3e section, M. Montamat demande l'ajournement ; sur quoi appel nominal, ainsi que suit :

Affirmative :

MM. Balch, Bailey, Barrett, Beauvais, Burke, J. K. Cook, T. Cook, Crozat, Decker, Duke, Gruneberg, Gaidry, Healy, Harnan, Knobloch, Maas, Mendiverri, Montamat, E. Murphy, M. W. Murphy, Orr, O'Conner, Ong, J. Payne, Schroeder, Seymour, Sullivan et Waters—28.

Négative :

MM. Abell, Austin, Bell, Bofill, Bromley, Campbell, Collin, Cazabat, Cutler, Davies, Dufresne, Dupaty, Ennis, Fish, Flagg, Flood, Foley, Fosdick, Fuller, Gastinel, Geier, Gorlinski, Hart, Henderson, Hills, Hire, Howell, Howes, Kugler, Mann, Maurer, Mayer, Newell, Normand, J. T. Paine, Pintado, J. Purcell, S. Purcell, Shaw, Smith, Stocker, Stumpf, Stiner, Stauffer, Terry, Thorpe, Wells, Wilson—48.

La motion est donc rejetée.

La question se présentant de nouveau sur la troisième section, M. Howell présente l'amendement suivant :

Le juge-président recevra $7500 d'appointements, et chacun des juges-adjoints $7000 par an, jusqu'à ce que la loi en ait disposé autrement.

L'amendement est mis aux voix et rejeté.

Sur motion, la Convention s'ajourne à demain, à midi.

Approuvé.

JOHN E. NEELIS,
Secrétaire.

MERCREDI, le 15 juin 1864.

La Convention se réunit et le président l'appelle à l'ordre, conformément à l'ajournement.

Membres présents :

MM. Abell, Austin, Bailey, Barrett, Baum, Beauvais, Bell, Bofill, Bromley, Buckley, Burke, Campbell, Collin, Cazabat, J. K. Cook, T. Cook, Crozat, Cutler, Davies, Decker, Duane, Dufresne, Duke, Ennis, Fish, Flagg, Flood, Foley, Fosdick, Fuller, Gastinel, Geier, Gorlinski, Gruneberg, Gaidry, Healy, Harnan, Hart, Henderson, Hills, Hire, Howell, Howes, Kavanagh, Knobloch, Kugler, Maas, Mann, Maurer, Mayer, Mendiverri, Montamat, Morris, E. Murphy, M. W. Murphy, Newell, Normand, O'Conner, Ong, Orr, J. Payne, J. T. Paine, Pintado, J. Purcell, S. Purcell, Schroeder, Schnurr, Seymour, Shaw, Smith, Spellicy, Stocker, Stumpf, Stiner, Stauffer, Sullivan, Terry, Thorpe, Waters, Wenck, Wells, Wilson et E. H. Durell, président—83.

Membres absents :

MM. Ariail, Balch, Bonnie, Bonzano, Brott, Edwards, Goldman, Heard, Lobdell, Millspaugh, Montague, Poynot, Taliaferro et Thomas—15.

M. Spellicy explique que M. Poynot est absent pour cause de maladie, et sur motion il est excusé.

Après lecture, le procès-verbal de la dernière séance est approuvé.

ET L'AMENDEMENT DE LA CONSTITUTION DE LA LOUISIANE.

Le président présente à la Convention la lettre suivante de M. Goldman.

NOUVELLE-ORLEANS, le 7 juin 1864.

A Messieurs le Président et les Membres de la Convention :

Messieurs,

Le soussigné, par la présente, vous remet sa démission comme membre de la Convention de l'Etat de la Louisiane, Etant entré dans cette Assemblée dans le but d'aider à faire l'œuvre d'homme d'Etat, et non celle d'intriguants politiques dans leur municipalité, après la conduite tenue à l'occasion de l'adoption de la loi sur la police, à la séance d'hier, je considère que je me dois, et que c'est pour moi un devoir impératif de donner ma démission.

J'ai l'honneur d'être votre très humble et très obéissant serviteur,

EDMOND GOLDMAN.

Sur motion, la démission de M. Goldman est adoptée par un vote par levé et assis, de 40 contre 32.

M. Gruneberg présente la résolution suivante, laquelle est déposée, sujette à l'appel, conformément au réglement :

Résolu, Que le sergent d'armes ou ses aides devront immédiatement aller sommer de comparaître, pardevant cette Convention tous les membres absents, qu'ils résident à la Nouvelle-Orléans ou en dehors, et ils devront les forcer à s'y présenter.

Résolu de plus, Que les frais de voyage ou autres, encourus par le sergent d'armes ou ses aides, dans le but précité, seront payés par les membres pris en défaut.

ORDRE DU JOUR.

La Convention reprend en considération le substitut de M. Stocker, au rapport du comité spécial sur le Judiciaire. L'article 3 est actuellement l'objet de ses délibérations.

Sur l'observation faite par M. Hills, que l'amendement présenté par M. Howell, au troisième article du substitut, a été repoussé à cause d'un malentendu, on met aux voix cet amendement une seconde fois, et il est adopté par 54 voix contre 12.

Le troisième article est donc adopté tel qu'amendé.

Les articles 4, 5, 6, 7, 8 et 9 sont adoptés, après lecture.

On lit l'article 10, et sur motion de M. Howell, il est amendé par la suppression des mots "déterminé par la Législature" et l'insertion en leur lieu et place des suivants : "ne sera pas diminué pendant la durée de leurs fonctions."

La section est acceptée avec cet amendement.

On donne lecture de l'article 11, et M. Bofill présente le substitut suivant :

Les juges de la Cour Suprême seront nommés par le gouverneur, de l'avis et du consentement du Sénat, pour la durée de huit ans. Les juges des cours inférieures le seront pour six ans.

M. Stauffer propose le rejet du substitut; sur quoi appel nominal ainsi que suit :

Affirmative :

MM. Bell, Buckley, Campbell, Collin, J. K. Cook, T. Cook, Decker, Duke, Dupaty, Flagg, Flood, Geier, Gorlinski, Gruneberg, Gaidry, Harnan, Howes, Knobloch, Maas, Mayer, Morris, O'Conner, Orr, J. Purcell, S. Pursell, Schnurr, Smith, Spellicy, Stocker, Stiner, Stauffer, Sullivan, Terry—33.

Négative :

MM. Abell, Austin, Bailey, Barrett, Baum, Beauvais, Bofill, Bromley, Burke, Cazabat, Crozat, Cutler, Davies, Dufresne, Duane, Ennis, Fish, Foley, Fosdick, Fuller, Gastinel, Healy, Hart, Henderson, Hills, Hire, Howell, Kavanagh, Kugler, Mann, Maurer, Mendiverri, Montamat, E. Murphy, M. W. Murphy, Newell, Normand, Ong, J. Payne, J. T. Paine, Pintado, Schroeder, Seymour, Shaw, Stumpf, Thorpe, Waters, Wenck, Wells, Wilson—50.

La motion de rejet est donc repoussée.

M. Ong propose d'amender le substitut par la suppression du mot "huit" et par l'insertion du mot "neuf;" ainsi que par la suppression du mot "six" et l'insertion du mot "sept."

Cet amendement est rejeté.

M. Smith propose le substitut suivant :

Art. 11. Les juges de la Cour Suprême et des cours inférieures seront nommés par le gouverneur. Les juges de la Cour Suprême resteront en fonctions huit ans, et ceux des cours inférieures six ; et après ce terme, ils seront élus par les électeurs dûment qualifiés. Et les nominations compteront du jour de la ratification de la constitution par le peuple.

Sur motion, le substitut de M. Smith est rejeté.

Sur la question d'adopter le substitut Bofill, l'appel nominal donne pour résultat :

Affirmative :

MM. Abell, Austin, Bailey, Baum, Beauvais, Bofill, Bromley, Burke, Cazabat, Crozat, Cutler, Davies, Duane, Dufresne,

Ennis, Fish, Foley, Fosdick, Fuller, Gastinel, Healy, Hart, Henderson. Hills, Hire, Howell, Kavanagh, Kugler, Mann, Maurer, Mendiverri, Montamat, E. Murphy, M. W. Murphy, Newell, Normand, Ong, J. Payne, J. T. Paine, Pintado, Schroeder, Seymour, Shaw, Spellicy, Stumpf, Thorpe, Waters, Wenck, Wells. Wilson—50.

Négative :
MM. Barrett, Bell, Buckley, Campbell, Collin, J. K. Cook, T. Cook, Decker, Duke, Dupaty, Flagg, Flood, Geier, Gorlinski, Gruneberg, Gaidry, Harnan, Howes, Knobloch, Maas, Mayer, Morris, O'Conner, Orr, J. Purcell, S. Pursell, Schnurr, Smith, Stocker, Stiner, Stauffer, Sullivan, Terry—33.

Le substitut Bofill est donc adopté.

M. Montamat présente un amendement déclarant que les greffiers des cours inférieures seront nommés pour le même terme que celui de leurs juges respectifs, et que la Cour Suprême pourra, pour crime ou délit, les destituer.

Rejeté.

M. Smith propose de supprimer du substitut de M. Stocker, à l'article 12, les mots : "et ils conserveront leur charge pendant tout le temps que la Législature déterminera."

Rejeté.

Sur l'adoption de l'aticle 12 du substitut Stocker, on demande un vote divisionnel, lequel donne pour résultat 29 voix arffimatives contre 50.

M. Fosdick propose la reprise en considération du vote sur le substitut à l'article 12. Adopté.

M. Hills propose de supprimer les mots "par les juges respectivement" et d'écrire en leur lieu et place "par la Législature."

Rejeté.

M. S. Pursell propose de supprimer tout ce qui suit les mots "charges" à la seconde ligne. et d'y substituer les mots "pendant quatre années." Cet amendement est adopté.

Le substitut à l'article 12 est donc adopté tel qu'amendé.

L'article 13 du substitut est alors adopté et l'on passe à l'article 14.

M. Sullivan propose de supprimer le mot "cent", et de le remplacer par les mots "deux cents."

M. Thorpe présente le substitut suivant à l'article 14 :

La juridiction des juges de paix n'excèdera point. en matière civile, la somme de cent piastres, les intérêts non compris, réservant aux parties le droit d'appel dans tous les cas prévus par la loi. Ils resteront en fonctions pendant le temps que la Législature déterminera. Ils auront telle juridiction criminelle que la loi leur assignera. Ils devront présenter à l'auditeur des comptes publics à la fin de chaque trimestre, un compte assermenté, et le montant des taxes perçues aude-là de leurs appointements, sera fidèlement rapporté à l'auditeur. Le juge manquant de présenter le susdit compte sera passible de destitution. Ils seront nommés par le gouverneur, de l'avis et du consentement du Sénat.

Sur motion de M. Sullivan, de rejeter le substitut Thorpe, il y a vote divisionnel, dont le résultat est 43 voix affirmatives contre 32. Le substitut est donc rejeté.

M. Hills propose de supprimer à la quatrième ligne les mots "élus par électeurs ayant les qualités voulues," et de les remplacer par les mots "nommés par le gouverneur, de l'avis et du consentement du Sénat."

Rejeté.

M. Montamat propose d'amender en fixant à deux ans la durée des fonctions des juges de paix ; sur quoi, il y a division dont le résultat est : affirmative 41, et négative 32. L'amendement est donc adopté.

L'art. 14 est donc adopté tel qu'amendé, et l'on passe à l'article 15 du substitut.

M. Bell présente comme substitut, l'article suivant :

Il y aura un procureur-général pour l'Etat et autant d'avocats de district que l'on jugera nécessaire.

Le procureur-général sera élu tous les quatre ans par les électeurs de l'Etat ayant les qualités requises. Il recevra un traitement de $5000 par an, payable à son propre ordre, tous les trois mois.

Les avocats de district seront élus par les électeurs de leurs districts respectifs, ayant qualité pour le terme de quatre ans. Ils recevront tels émoluments que la Législature déterminera.

La motion de rejet étant repoussée, ce substitut est adopté par 58 voix contre 22.

Art. 16. Après lecture du substitut de M. Stocker, M. Sullivan propose le substitut suivant :

Les électeurs ayant qualité, dans chacune des paroisses, éliront un shérif et un coroner ; ces fonctionnaires resteront en place pendant deux ans, à moins qu'ils ne soient destitués avant l'expiration de ce temps.

La Législature pourra augmenter le nombre des shérifs dans toute paroisse. Si une vacance avait lieu dans quelqu'une de ces charges après l'élection, le gouverneur ferait la nomination, et ce nouvel officier restera en fonctions jusqu'à ce qu'il soit remplacé par un successeur dûment élu et qualifié.

La motion de rejet est repoussée, et M. Stocker propose de supprimer "à moins qu'ils ne soient destitués avant l'expiration de ce terme."

Adopté.

Le substitut est donc adopté.

M. S. Pursell présente un article additionnel ainsi conçu :

Art. 17. Le gouverneur nommera tous les fonctionnaires qui, par la présente loi, doivent être élus, et ils resteront en place le même laps de temps que celui pour lequel ils devaient être élus, à compter de l'époque de la ratification de leur nomination par la Législature. La paroisse d'Orléans sera exceptée de cette disposition ci-dessus, et la première Législature tenue sous l'empire de cette constitution ordonnera des élections pour cette paroisse.

Sur motion de M. Montamat, l'article additionnel est rejeté.

Le substitut est alors adopté tel qu'il est amendé, par le vote suivant :

Affirmative :

MM. Abell, Austin, Bailey, Baum, Beauvais, Bofill, Bromley, Burke, Cazabat, J. K. Cook, Crozat, Cutler, Davies, Decker, Duane, Dufresne, Ennis, Fish, Flagg, Foley, Fosdick, Fuller, Gastinel, Gorlinski, Gruneberg, Gaidry, Healy, Harnan, Henderson, Hart, Hills, Hire, Howell, Kavanagh, Kugler, Maas, Mann, Maurer, Mendiverri, Montamat, Morris, E. Murphy, M. W. Murphy, Newell, O'Conner, Ong, J. Payne, J. T. Paine, Pintado, J. Purcell, Schroeder, Schnurr, Shaw, Spellicy, Stumpf, Stiner, Thorpe, Waters, Wenck, Wells—60.

Négative :

MM. Barrett, Bell, Buckley, Campbell, Collin, T. Cook, Duke, Dupaty, Flood, Geier, Howes, Knobloch, Mayer, Normand, Orr, S. Pursell, Seymour, Smith, Stocker, Stauffer, Sullivan, Terry, Wilson—23.

Sur motion de M. Stocker, le réglement est suspendu, et le substitut avec ses amendements, subit sa troisième lecture.

M. Henderson présente un bill déterminant la juridiction de la Cour Suprême, et, sur motion de M. Montamat, ce bill est rejeté.

Sur l'adoption du substitut de M. Stocker, avec ses amendements, après la troisième lecture, il y a appel nominal, ainsi que suit :

Affirmative :

MM. Abell, Austin, Baum, Bailey, Beauvais, Bofill, Bromley, Burke, Cazabat, J. K. Cook, Crozat, Cutler, Davies, Dufresne, Duane, Ennis, Fish, Flagg, Foley, Fosdick, Fuller, Gastinel, Gaidry, Gorlinski, Gruneberg, Healy, Harnan, Hart, Hills, Hire, Howell, Kavanagh, Kugler, Maurer, Maas, Mann, Mendiverri, Montamat, Morris, E. Murphy, M. W. Murphy, Newell, Normand, O'Conner, Ong, J. Payne, J. T. Paine, Pintado, J. Purcell, Schroeder, Schnurr, Shaw, Stumpf, Stiner, Thorpe, Waters, Wells, Wenck—58.

Négative :

MM. Barrett, Bell, Buckley, Campbell, Collin, T. Cook, Decker, Duke, Dupaty, Flood, Geier, Henderson, Howes, Knobloch, Mayer, Orr, S. Pursell, Seymour, Spellicy, Smith, Stocker, Stauffer, Sullivan, Terry, Wilson—25.

M. Bofill demande la reprise en considération du vote par lequel le substitut a été adopté à sa troisième lecture. Cette demande est repoussée, et la Convention s'ajourne.

Approuvé.

JOHN E. NEELIS,
Secrétaire.

JEUDI, le 16 juin 1864.

La Convention est appelée à l'ordre, conformément à l'ajournement.

Membres présents :

MM. Abell, Austin, Balch, Bailey, Barrett, Baum, Beauvais, Bell, Bofill, Bromley, Buckley, Burke, Campbell, Collin, Cazabat, J. K. Cook, T. Cook, Crozat, Cutler, Davies, Decker, Duane, Dufresne, Dupaty, Ennis, Fish, Flagg, Flood, Foley, Fosdick, Fuller, Gastinel, Geier, Gorlinski, Gruneberg, Gaidry, Healy, Harnan, Hart, Henderson, Hills, Hire, Howell, Howes, Kavanagh, Kuobloch, Kugler, Maas, Mann, Maurer, Mayer, Mendiverri, Montamat, Morris, E. Murphy, M. W. Murphy, Normand, O'Conner, Ong, Orr, J. Payne, J. T. Paine, Pintado, J. Purcell, S. Pursell, Schroeder, Schnurr, Seymour, Shaw, Smith, Spellicy, Stocker, Stumpf, Stiner, Stauffer, Sullivan, Terry, Thorpe, Waters, Wenck, Wells, Wilson, et M. le Président—83.

Membres absents :

MM. Ariail, Bennie, Bonzano, Brott, Duke (excusé,) Edwards (excusé,) Heard, Lobdell, Millspaugh, Montague, Newell,

Poynot, (excusé,) Taliaferro et Thomas—14.

Sur motion de M. Smith, on excuse l'absence de M. Balch à la séance d'hier.

Sur motion de M. Knobloch, l'absence de M. Duke est excusée.

Sur motion de M. Wells, l'absence de M. Edwards est excusée.

Le procès-verbal de la dernière séance est approuvé, après lecture.

Sur motion, M. Henderson obtient l'autorisation de changer son vote sur le bill du Judiciaire à sa troisième lecture, de la négative à l'affirmative.

ORDRE DU JOUR.

Le rapport du comité sur la Mise en Accusation étant à l'ordre du jour, il subit sa seconde lecture.

Après lecture, la seconde section est adoptée.

Sur lecture de la seconde section, M. Harnan propose d'amender par la suppression des mots "deux tiers." et d'y substituer le mot "majorité."

Rejeté.

Sur motion de M. Hills, on amende la seconde ligne, en y insérant après le mot "trésorier" les mots "auditeur des comptes publics."

Sur motion de M. Foley, on amende les lignes huit et neuf, par la suppression des mots "deux tiers présents," et l'insertion en leur lieu et place des mots "majorité élue."

La seconde section est donc adoptée, conformément à l'amendement.

Après lecture, la troisième section est adoptée.

Lecture est donnée de la quatrième section, et sur motion de M. Wilson, on substitue le mot "tel" au mot "chacun," à la troisième ligne.

La section est alors adoptée, conformément à l'amendement.

Après lecture, la cinquième section est adoptée.

Le rapport tout entier est adopté à sa seconde lecture.

Sur motion de M. Hills, on dispense du règlement afin de faire subir à ce rapport sa troisième lecture.

Sur la question d'adoption du dit rapport, il y a appel nominal ainsi que suit:

Affirmative :

MM. Abell, Austin, Balch, Bailey, Barrett, Baum, Beauvais, Bell, Bofill, Bromley, Buckley, Burke, Campbell, Collin, Cazabat, J. K. Cook, T. Cook, Crozat, Cutler, Davies, Decker, Duane, Dufresne, Ennis, Fish, Flagg, Flood, Foley, Foskick, Fuller, Gastinel, Gaidry, Geier, Gorlinski, Gruneberg, Healy, Harnan, Hart, Hills, Hire, Howell, Howes, Kavanagh, Knobloch, Kugler, Maas, Mann, Maurer, Mayer, Mendiverri, Montamat, Morris, E. Murphy, M. W. Murphy, Normand, O'Conner, Ong, Orr, J. Payne, J. T. Paine, Pintado, S. Pursell, Schroeder, Schnurr, Seymour, Shaw, Smith, Spellicy, Stocker, Stumpf, Stiner, Stauffer, Sullivan, Terry, Thorpe, Wilson—76.

Négative :

MM. Dupaty, Henderson, Waters, Wenck, Wells—5.

Le rapport subit donc sa troisième lecture.

M. Thorpe demande la reprise en considération du vote donné sur la motion que l'on vient de rejeter.

On s'occupe du rapport sur les Dispositions Générales.

M. Sullivan préside.

M. Cutler propose ce qui suit :

Art. 1. L'esclavage et la servitude involontaires sont à tout jamais abolis et prohibés dans cet Etat, et la Législature ne fera aucune loi reconnaissant le droit de propriété sur l'homme.

M. Durell, le président, reprenant son fauteuil, déclare que cette proposition n'est pas à l'ordre, attendu que le rapport du comité sur l'Emancipation, contenant une semblable proposition après avoir subi sa troisième lecture, a été adopté et forme partie intégrante de la constitution, de sorte qu'il est impossible de la représenter de nouveau.

M. Cutler fait appel de cette décision, mais il finit par retirer son appel et sa proposition.

Après lecture, les articles 1 et 2 sont adoptés.

Après lecture de l'article 3, M. Stauffer propose la suppression, à la seconde ligne, du mot "trahison."

Rejeté.

M. Hills propose la suppression, aux seconde et troisième lignes, du mot "forfaiture." Rejeté par 43 voix contre 23.

Après lecture, les articles 3, 4 et 5 sont adoptés.

ET L'AMENDEMENT DE LA CONSTITUTION DE LA LOUISIANE.

Après lecture de l'article 6, M. Montamat propose l'amendement suivant :
"Aucun nègre n'aura le droit de vote."

Le président déclare que l'on a déjà déterminé les qualités requises des électeurs dans le rapport sur le Législatif, et qu'ainsi on ne devrait plus s'en occuper.

M. Montamat fait appel de la décision du président, et le vote donne le résultat suivant :

Affirmative :
MM. Austin, Bailey, Baum, Beauvais, Bell, Bromley, Burke, Collin, Cazabat, J. K. Cook, T. Cook, Crozat, Cutler, Davies, Duane, Dupaty, Ennis, Fish, Flagg, Flood, Foley, Fosdick, Fuller, Geier, Gorlinski, Gruneberg, Gaidry, Healy, Harnan, Hart, Henderson, Hills, Hire, Howell, Howes, Kavanagh, Knobloch, Kugler, Mann, Mayer, E. Murphy, Normand, Ong, J. Payne, J. T. Paine, Pintado, J. Purcell, S. Pursell, Schroeder, Schnurr, Seymour, Smith, Spellicy, Stocker, Stumpf, Stiner, Stauffer, Terry, Thorpe, Wenck—60.

Négative :
MM. Abell, Balch, Bofill, Buckley, Campbell, Decker, Dufresne, Gastinel, Maurer, Maas, Mendiverri, Montamat, M. W. Murphy, Orr, Sullivan, Waters, Wilson—17.

La décision du président est donc maintenue.

Le président fait à cette occasion observer que d'après le réglement il faut un vote des deux tiers pour renverser la décision du président, mais jusqu'à ce jour, par déférence pour la Convention, il n'a point usé du bénéfice de cet article du réglement.

M. Sullivan propose ce qui suit :

Les nègres n'auront pas le droit d'exercer le droit ou la médecine dans cet Etat, et on ne leur enseignera non plus l'art ou les mystères d'aucun métier ou profession, à moins d'être passible de telles peines que la Législature prescrira.

Rejeté par un vote de 48 voix contre 20.
Après lecture, l'article 6 est adopté.
Lecture étant donnée de l'article 7, M. Hills propose de l'amender par l'adjonction des mots "aucun nègre n'aura le droit de toucher des fonds du trésor de l'Etat."

La motion de rejet de cet amendement étant repoussée, la Convention s'ajourne par un vote de 35 voix contre 34.
Approuvé.

JOHN E. NEELIS,
Secrétaire.

VENDREDI, le 17 juin 1864.

La Convention se réunit à midi, conformément à l'ajournement. L'hon. E. H. Durell, président, au fauteuil.

L'appel se fait, et les membres suivants répondent à leurs noms.

Membres présents :
MM. Abell, Austin, Balch, Bailey, Barrett, Baum, Beauvais, Bell, Bofill, Bromley, Buckley, Burke, Campbell, Collin, Cazabat, J. K. Cook, T. Cook, Crozat, Cutler, Davies, Decker, Duane, Dufresne, Duke, Dupaty, Ennis, Fish, Flagg, Flood, Foley, Fosdick, Fuller, Gastinel, Geier, Gorlinski, Gruneberg, Gaidry, Healy, Harnan, Hart, Henderson, Hills, Hire, Howell, Howes, Kavanagh, Knobloch, Kugler, Maas, Mann, Maurer, Mayer, Mendiverri, Montamat, Morris, E. Murphy, M. W. Murphy, Newell, Normand, O'Conner, Ong, Orr, J. Payne, J. T. Paine, Pintado, J. Purcell, S. Pursell, Schroeder, Schnurr, Seymour, Shaw, Smith, Spellicy, Stocker, Stumpf, Stiner, Stauffer, Sullivan, Terry, Thorpe, Waters, Wenck, Wells, Wilson—85.

Absents : MM. Ariail, Bennie, Bonzano, Brott, Edwards (excusé), Heard, Lobdell, Millspaugh, Montague, Poynot (excusé), Taliaferro et Thomas—12.

Les minutes de la journée d'hier sont lues et adoptées.

Le rapport du comité sur les Mesures Générales étant à l'ordre du jour, est pris en considération.

Les articles 7 et 8 sont lus et adoptés.

Lecture est faite de l'art. 9, ensemble avec le substitut suivant, présenté par M. S. Pursell, savoir :

Art. 9. Tous les officiers de l'Etat en entier et tous les votants devront résider dans l'Etat, et tous les officiers des districts et paroisses devront résider dans leurs districts et paroisses respectifs, et devront tenir leurs bureaux dans les lieux requis par la loi.

La question sur le substitut de M. Purcell étant posée, est adoptée.

Sur la lecture de l'art. 10, M. Smith propose l'amendement suivant : retrancher les mots "et les Cours inférieures" dans la seconde ligne. L'amendement est rejeté ; un vote par assis et levé a lieu sur l'adoption de l'article comme il a été présenté, le résultat donne oui 22, non 35. Conséquemment l'article est rejeté.

M. Samuel Pursell, avec l'assentiment de M. Smith, demande la reconsidération du vote qui vient de passer sur l'art. 10, sur l'acceptation.

M. Abell propose de référer l'article à un comité spécial composé de trois membres.

Dépôt sur le bureau.

M. Wilson offre un amendement pour retrancher les mots "deux tiers," et en insérant les mots "à la majorité," et aussi en retranchant après "membres," dans la troisième ligne, le mot "des" et en insérant à la place les mots "élus par."

Cette motion ayant été acceptée l'art. 10 a été adopté suivant les amendements.

L'art. 12 est lu et adopté, comme il a été dit.

L'article 13, après lecture, M. Stauffer propose de retrancher dans la deuxième ligne les mots "ou employés dans les travaux publics," et aussi tout l'article après le mot "Etat," dans la troisième ligne.

La motion est adoptée, et l'article passe suivant l'amendement.

L'art. 14 est adopté comme il est dit.

L'article 15 est lu ; alors M. Howell propose de retrancher de la première ligne le mot "que," et d'amender en insérant après le mot "lois," dans la première ligne, les mots "de cet Etat," et après le mot "par," dans la deuxième ligne, les mots "la Législature ou par, etc." L'amendement ayant prévalu, l'article est adopté ainsi qu'il a été amendé.

L'article 16 est lu et adopté.

Lecture est faite de l'article 17.

M. Howell propose la suppression entière de l'article, et d'y substituer l'article 104 de la constitution de 1852.

La motion est acceptée et le substitut adopté.

Les articles 18 et 19 sont lus et adoptés comme il a été dit.

Après la lecture de l'article 20, M. Campbell propose d'amender, en ajoutant, après le mot "faire" dans la dernière ligne, les mots suivants : "et aucun avocat ne pourra donner évidence dans aucun cas, dans aucune affaire, où lui ou eux pourraient être employés." Cet amendement ayant été accepté par la Convention, l'article ainsi amendé passe.

Après lecture de l'article 21, M. Cutler propose le rejet de l'article en entier.

La proposition est rejetée et l'article adopté comme il a été dit :

Après lecture de l'article 22, M. Sullivan propose de tout retrancher après le mot "sujet," dans la seconde ligne, et d'insérer, "mais l'écrivain acceptera les conséquences de sa malice et de sa méchanceté."

La proposition de M. Sullivan ayant été déposée sur le bureau, l'article est adopté comme il a été reporté.

Sur la mise aux débats de l'article 23, M. Terry offre l'amendement suivant :

Aucun monopole ne sera créé par la Législature dans le but d'accorder à des compagnies ou particuliers des droits exclusifs de construire et établir des canaux, chemins de fer, chemins planchéiés ou toute autre voie dans l'Etat ou dans toute partie du dit Etat, ni aucuns droits exclusifs ne sera accordé à aucune manufacture de quelque nature qu'elle soit.

M. Smith offre l'amendement suivant :

La Législature ne pourra prêter aide à aucunes compagnies ou associations d'individus établis pour une exploitation quelconque.

Sur motion de M. Montamat, cet amendement est déposé sur le bureau.

L'amendement de M. Terry est alors pris en considération, et sur motion de M. Baum, il est déposé sur la table sur un vote par assis et levé de 42 oui et 34 non.

M. Howell fait la motion d'amender en insérant entre le mot "aura" les mots "n'aura pas," et entre les mots "individus" et "établis" les mots "excepté celles déjà en opération."

L'amendement de M. Howell est, sur motion de M. Campbell, amendé en insérant "seront," de manière à ce que la résolution soit ainsi conçue :

La Législature n'aura pas le pouvoir de prêter aide à aucune compagnie ou association d'individus, excepté à celles qui sont et pourront être établies.

M. Cazabat offre un substitut dans les mots suivants :

La Législature n'aura pas le pouvoir d'accorder des monopoles ou priviléges exclusifs de quelque nature que ce soit à des individus, compagnies ou corporations quelconques, excepté dans un but charitable.

Ce substitut est déposé sur la table, sur un vote par assis et levé de 44 oui contre 15 non.

Les amendements de M. Howell ainsi

amendés par M. Campbell, sont acceptés et l'article est adopté avec les amendements.

Articles 24, 25 et 26, sont lus séparément et adoptés tels qu'ils sont rapportés.

Article 27 est lu avec l'amendement de M. Stiner prohibant les maisons de jeu.

M. Howell, de la part du comité, accepte l'amendement proposé par M. Stiner.

M. Montamat offre comme substitut pour l'article et l'amendement, "les loteries et maisons de jeu seront licenciées par la Législature."

M. Stocker offre ce qui suit comme substitut sur l'ensemble :

La Législature pourra accorder des licenses aux maisons de jeu dans l'Etat, pourvu que la taxe ne sera pas moins de dix mille piastres par an, et pour chaque maison de jeu.

M. Montamat retire son substitut et offre la clause additionnelle suivante au substitut de M. Stocker :

Pourvu que les maisons de jeu légalement licenciées auront le droit de vendre des billets de loterie.

La clause est acceptée par M. Stocker.

M. Cutler offre comme substitut à l'article, aux amendements et substituts, ce qui suit :

La Législature aura le pouvoir d'accorder des licences aux maisons de jeu et de vendre des billets de loterie. Les dites maisons de jeu seront dans tous les cas tenues au rez-de-chaussée et les portes ouvertes, mais dans aucun cas, non moins de dix mille piastres ne seront exigées comme paiement de la dite licence sur chaque vendeur de billets de loterie et sur chaque maison de jeu, et cinq cents piastres sur chaque tombola.

M. Harnan offre la résolution suivante, qui est déposée sur le bureau :

Aucune loterie ne sera autorisée dans cet Etat, mais chaque tombola sera permise en payant à l'Etat, pour chaque tombola, la somme de cinq cents dollars ; cette somme devra être divisée au *pro rata*, pour le bénéfice des divers établissements d'orphelins, dans les limites de l'Etat.

M. Howes propose d'amender le substitut de M. Cutler en ajoutant : "une large enseigne sera placée au-dessus de la porte, avec les mots Maison de Jeu, peints dessus."

L'amendement est déposé sur le bureau.

M. Hills propose de déposer sur le bureau l'article principal, les substituts ainsi que les amendements.

La proposition est rejetée.

La question revient à l'adoption du substitut de M. Cutler.

L'appel se fait par oui et non, et donne le résultat suivant :

Affirmative :

MM. Abell, Bailey, Barrett, Baum, Beauvais, Bell, Bofill, Buckley, Burke, J. K. Cook, T. Cook, Crozat, Cutler, Davies, Dufresne, Ennis, Fish, Flood, Foley, Gastinel, Geir, Gruneberg, Gaidry, Healy, Harnan, Hart, Henderson, Howes, Knobloch, Kugler, Maurer, Mendiverri, Montamat, E. Murphy, M. W. Murphy, Newell, O'Conner, Ong, J. Purcell, S. Pursell, Schroeder, Schnurr, Seymour, Spellicy, Stocker, Stumpf, Stauffer, Sullivan, Terry, Thorpe, Waters, Wells, Decker, Duke, Mayer, Orr—57.

Négative :

MM. Austin, Balch, Bromley, Campbell, Collin, Cazabat, Dupaty, Flagg, Fosdick, Golinski, Hills, Hire, Howells Kavanagh, Mann, Morris, Normand, J. Payne, J. T. Paine, Pintado, Seymour, Smith, Stiner, Wilson—24.

En conséquence le substitut est adopté.

M. Foley propose l'ajournement ; le oui et non ayant été demandé, donne le résultat suivant :

Affirmative :

MM. Abell, Austin, Balch, Bailey, Bofill, Buckley, Campbell, Dufresne, Decker, Duke, Ennis, Flagg, Foley, Gastinel, Gruneberg, Gaidry, Healy, Harnan, Hart, Henderson, Kavanagh, Knobloch, Mayer, Maas, Maurer, Mendiverri, E. Murphy, M. W. Murphy, Newell, Normand, O'Conner, Orr, Pintado, J. Purcell, Schroeder, Schnurr, Seymour, Shaw, Spellicy, Stumpf, Stiner, Sullivan, Wells Waters—44.

Négative :

MM. Barrett, Baum, Beauvais, Bell, Bromley, Burke, Cazabat, J. K. Cook, T. Cook, Collin, Crozat, Cutler, Davies, Dupaty, Fish, Fosdick, Geier, Gorlinski, Hills, Flood, Hire, Howell, Kugler, Mann, Montamat, Morris, Ong, J. Payne, J. T. Paine, S. Pursell, Smith, Stocker, Stauffer, Terry, Thorpe, Wilson—36.

En conséquence la motion prévaut, et la Convention s'ajourne.

Approuvé.

John E. Neelis,
Secrétaire.

SAMEDI, le 18 juin 1864.

La Convention se réunit à midi, conformément à l'ajournement.

L'honorable E. H. Durell, président, au fauteuil.

L'appel se fait, et les membres suivants répondent à leurs noms.

Membres présents :
MM. Abell, Austin, Balch, Bailey, Barrett, Baum, Beauvais, Bell, Bofill, Bromley, Buckley, Burke, Cazabat, Collin, Decker, Duke, Dufresne, Duane, Dupaty, Ennis, Fish, Flagg, Flood, Foley, Fosdick, Fuller, Gastinel, Geier, Gorlinski, Gruneberg, Gaidry, Healy, Harnan, Hart, Henderson, Hills, Hire, Howell, Howes, Knobloch, Kugler, Maas, Mann, Maurer, Mayer, Mendiverri, Montamat, Morris, E. Murphy, M. W. Murphy, Newell, Normand, O'Conner, Orr, J. Payne, J. T. Paine, Pintado, Poynot, J. Purcell, S. Pursell, Schroeder, Schnurr, Seymour, Shaw, Smith, Spellicy, Stocker, Stumpf, Stiner, Stauffer, Sullivan, Terry, Thorpe, Waters, Wenck et Wilson—82.

Membres absents :
MM. Ariail, Bennie, Bonzano, Brott, Campbell, Edwards (excusé), Heard, Kavanagh, Lobdell, Millspaugh, Montague, Ong, Taliaferro, Thomas et Wells—15.

Les minutes d'hier sont lues et adoptées
Sur motion de M. Howell, le vote sur l'article 23 est reconsidéré, dans le but d'amender le paragraphe relatif à l'exemption des institutions charitables, et de la prohibition contenue dans ledit article.

La discussion a été renvoyée à lundi prochain.

M. Thorpe propose ce qui suit :
Résolu, Qu'un comité de cinq membres se présente devant les Majors-Généraux Canby et Sickles, dans le but de savoir s'il leur serait agréable de recevoir une visite officielle des membres de la Convention.

Les réglements sont suspendus, et la résolution adoptée.

Le président nomme MM. Thorpe, Sullivan, Cutler, Terry et Campbell, comme faisant partie du comité.

M. Fosdick présente les préambules et résolutions suivantes :
Attendu, Que dans l'opinion de la Convention, une grande majorité du peuple loyal de la ville de la Nouvelle-Orléans, désire voir le rétablissement du pouvoir civil ;

Résolu, Que son Excellence le Gouverneur de l'Etat soit requis de donner immédiatement les ordres nécessaires pour l'élection de maire, recorders, commissaires des rues, aldermens et assistants-aldermens, en conformité avec la charte de la ville ;

Résolu, Que le secrétaire de cette Convention soit, et est par les présentes, notifié de transmettre une copie de ces résolutions à son Excellence le Gouverneur.

Après quelques discussions, M. Shaw fait la motion de suspendre la considération des résolutions jusqu'à samedi prochain.

Motion d'ajourner étant faite, on ordonne l'appel nominal qui donne le résultat suivant :

Pour l'ajournement :
MM. Beauvais, Buckley, Burke, Crozat, Dufresne, Duke, Davies, Duane, Ennis, Foley, Hire, Maas, Maurer, E. Murphy, M. W. Murphy, O'Conner, J. Payne, Schroeder, Stiner, Wilson.—21.

Contre l'ajournement :
MM. Abell, Austin, Balch, Bailey, Barrett, Baum, Bell, Bromley, Bofill, Collin, Cazabat, T. Cook, J. K. Cook, Cutler, Dupaty, Fish, Flood, Fosdick, Gastinel, Geier, Gorlinski, Gruneberg, Gaidry, Harnan, Hills, Howes, Knobloch, Kugler, Mann, Mayer, Montamat, Morris, Newell, Normand, Orr, J. T. Payne, Pintado, Poynot, J. Purcell, S. Pursell, Schnurr, Seymour, Shaw, Smith, Spellicy, Stocker, Sullivan, Stauffer, Stumpf, Terry, Thorpe et Waters. 52.

En conséquence de ce vote, la Convention refuse d'ajourner.

M. Davies offre l'amendement suivant :
Résolu, Le gouverneur de l'Etat est requis d'ordonner que des élections soient tenues dans chaque ville incorporée en dedans des lignes de l'Union, pour tous officiers municipaux. Les dites élections seront tenues le même jour que celles de la Nouvelle-Orléans, pour la nomination de ses officiers.

M. Shaw demande la question sur la motion faite par lui de renvoyer la considération de la résolution présentée par M. Fosdick à samedi, 25 du courant, laquelle étant passée est adoptée, et la Convention s'ajourne.

Approuvé.

JOHN E. NEELIS,
Secrétaire.

LUNDI, 20 juin 1864.

La Convention se réunit conformément à l'ajournement.

Sont présents l'honorable E. H. Durell, président, et les membres suivants :
MM. Abell, Austin, Balch, Bailey, Baum, Beauvais, Bell, Bofill, Bromley, Buckley, Burke, Campbell, Cazabat, J. K. Cook,

ET L'AMENDEMENT DE LA CONSTITUTION DE LA LOUISIANE.

T. Cook, Crozat, Cutler, Davies, Dufresne, Duane, Dupaty, Ennis, Fish, Flagg, Flood, Foley, Fosdick, Fuller, Gastinel, Geier, Gorlinski, Gruneberg, Gaidry, Healy, Harnan, Hart, Henderson, Hills, Hire, Howell, Howes, Kavanagh, Knobloch, Kugler, Maas, Mann, Maurer, Mendiverri, Montamat, E. Murphy, M. W. Murphy, Newell, Normand, O'Conner, John Payne, J. T. Paine, Poynot, J. Purcell, S. Purcell, Schroeder, Schnurr, Seymour, Shaw, Smith, Spellicy, Stocker, Stumpf, Stiner, Stauffer, Sullivan, Terry, Thorpe, Waters, Wenck, Wells, Wilson, Collin, Duke, Mayer, Orr.

Absents—MM. Ariail, Barrett, Bennie, Bonzano, Brott, Decker, Edwards, (excusé) Heard, Lobdell, Millspaugh, Montague, Morris, Ong, Taliaferro, Thomas et Pintado (excusé.)

Les minutes de samedi sont lues et adoptées.

M. Terry demande la suspension des réglements, afin de présenter un mémoire signé par un grand nombre de citoyens au sujet des heures de travail à imposer aux manœuvres employés dans les travaux publics. Les réglements sont suspendus. Le mémoire est reçu, et sur motion de M. Montamat, il est référé à un comité choisi, composé de 7 membres, à savoir : MM. Terry, Geier, Stiner, O'Conner, Balch, Burke et Orr.

M. Fosdick demande la suspension des réglements, afin de mettre aux débats sa résolution de samedi, relative à l'élection des officiers pour le gouvernement de la ville de la Nouvelle-Orléans.

Motion est faite de la déposer sur la table, mais elle est repoussée. L'appel nominal est ordonné sur la motion de suspendre les réglements, et donne le résultat suivant:

Pour l'affirmative :

MM. Abell, Austin, Balch, Bailey, Baum, Bell, Bofill, Buckley, Campbell, T. Cook, J. K. Cook, Dufresne, Duke, Flagg, Flood, Fosdick, Gastinel, Geier, Gorlinski, Gruneberg, Harnan, Hart, Hills, Howes, Knobloch, Maas, Maurer, Mayer, Montamat, E. Murphy, O'Conner, Orr, Poynot, J. Purcell W. Smith, Sullivan, Thorpe, Waters, Wilson–39.

Pour la négative :

MM. Beauvais, Bromley, Burke, Collin, Cutler, Davies, Duane, Dupaty, Ennis, Fish, Foley, Fuller, Gaidry, Healy, Henderson, Hire, Howell, Kugler, Mann, W.M. Murphy, Newell, Normand, J. Payne, J. T. Paine, Purcell T. S., Schroeder, Schnurr, Seymour, Shaw, Stocker, Stumpf, Stiner, Stauffer, Terry, Wells.—36.

En conséquence, la motion de suspendre les réglements est rejetée.

M. Montamat demande la suspension des réglements, afin de soumettre le rapport du Comité des Finances. Cette demande est accordée, et il présente le rapport suivant :

RAPPORT DU COMITE DES FINANCES JUSQU'AU 18 JUIN INCLUSIVEMENT.

1864.

Juin 18—Montant payé jusqu'à ce jour, sur mandats, pour le paiement des membres, millage et salaire des officiers, etc.	$ 94,485	60
Juin 18—Balance en caisse, ce jour.	5,514	40
	$100,000	00
Juin 18—Montant payé pour dépenses contingentes (avec les preuves et mandats à l'appui).	18,027	97
Juin 18—Balance en caisse, ce jour.	6,972	03
	25,000	00

Juin 18—Montant payé pour impressions et publications (avec les preuves à l'appui), $48,218 32. Cette somme a été payée des fonds, non autrement affectés, à l'exception d'une somme de $7,000 00, qui a été payée des fonds alloués pour les dépenses contingentes et qui doit leur être remboursée.

Juin 8—La somme de six mille cent trente neuf dollars et treize cents ($6,139 13), a été payée à M. J. S. Walton, trésorier de la ville, pour l'ameublement et la mise en état du Temple de la Liberté, pour recevoir la Convention.

Votre comité représente respectueusement qu'il est nécessaire qu'une allocation soit votée pour le paiement des membres et officiers de cette Convention ; en conséquence, il vous soumet la résolution suivante :

Résolu, La somme de vingt mille piastres est, par le présent, allouée des fonds généraux du Trésor d'Etat, non autrement affectés, à l'effet de solder le *per diem* des conventionnels et la rétribution des employés.

(Signé) J. P. MONTAMAT,
Président *pro tem.*
L. P. NORMAND,
JOHN SULLIVAN,
MARTIN SCHNURR.

Nouvelle-Orléans, le 18 juin 1864.

Le rapport est reçu, et la résolution qui l'accompagne est adoptée.

Sur la motion de M. Hire, M. Pintado est excusé pour motif de maladie.

ORDRE DU JOUR—RAPPORT DU COMITÉ SUR LES DISPOSITIONS GÉNÉRALES.

M. Howell propose d'amender l'art. 23 en ajoutant le mot "pourvu." Cet article ne s'applique pas aux associations charitables.

M. Cazabat propose de tout retrancher après le mot "amélioration," dans la troisième ligne, et y ajoutant les mots "et dans un but charitable."

Rejeté.

L'amendement de M. Howell est alors accepté par la Convention, et l'art. 23 accepté d'après l'amendement.

Après lecture de l'art. 28. M. Smith propose un amendement, en ajoutant les mots : " ni aucun mineur ne sera émancipé."

Rejeté.

M. Wilson propose un amendement en insérant le mot "non" entre les mots "soit" et "accordé."

Rejeté.

M. Fosdick offre le substitut suivant :

La Législature peut faire des lois générales pour la régularisation de l'adoption des enfants, l'émancipation des mineurs, les changements de noms et accorder les divorces ; mais aucunes lois spéciales ne seront émises concernant ou un cas particulier ou individuel.

M. Foley propose de retrancher les mots "changement de noms."

Cette motion ayant été déposée sur le bureau, le substitut de M. Fosdick est adopté.

Les articles 29, 30 et 31 sont lus et adoptés, comme il a été rapporté.

Après lecture de l'art. 32, M. Howell, au nom du comité, présente le substitut suivant :

Art. 32. Les lois spéciales de l'Etat ne pourront créer des corporations, excepté dans un but politique ou municipal, mais la Législature pourvoira par des lois générales à l'organisation de toutes ses corporations, excepté toutes celles qui ont rapport aux maisons de banque et d'escompte dont l'existence est pour toujours prohibée.

Après lecture de l'article 33, M. Smith propose un amendement en insérant le mot "non," après "sera" dans la première ligne. Cette motion est déposée sur le bureau, et l'article adopté.

Art. 34. Après lecture, M. Cazabat propose un amendement en retranchant les mots "excepté ceux de la justice de paix."

Cette motion est rejetée et l'article adopté.

Pour l'article 35, M. S. Pursell offre le substitut suivant, il est lu et adopté :

Art. 35. Les taxes seront égales et uniformes dans tout l'Etat. Chaque propriété sera taxée d'après sa valeur, comme il sera décidé d'après la loi. L'Assemblée Générale aura le pouvoir d'exempter des taxes toutes propriétés à l'usage des églises, écoles ou institutions charitables.

L'Assemblée Générale lèvera une taxe sur les revenus de toutes les personnes poursuivant une occupation quelle qu'elle soit, marchands, ou autres, et toutes ces personnes devront obtenir une licence, ainsi que la loi le prescrit.

Toutes les taxes sur les revenus seront faites au *prorata* d'un montant des revenus ou des affaires faites.

Sur l'article 36, M. Sullivan présente un substitut relatif à la police de ville.

Sur la motion du dépôt sur le bureau, l'appel par oui et par non a lieu, et donne le résultat suivant :

Affirmative :

MM. Austin, Bromley, Burke, Campbell, Collin, Cazabat, Cutler, Davies, Duke, Dupaty, Ennis, Flagg, Fosdick, Gorlinski, Gaidry, Henderson, Hire, Howell, Knobloch, Kugler, Mann, Mayer, Newell, J. Payne, J. T. Paine, J. Purcell, S. Pursell, Schnurr, Seymour, Stauffer, Thorpe, Wenck, Wells.

Négative :

MM. Abell, Balch, Beauvais, Bell, Bennie, Bofill, Buckley, J. K. Cook, T. Cook, Crozat, Dufresne, Flood, Foley, Fuller, Gastluel, Geler, Gruneberg, Harnan, Hart, Hills, Howes, Maas, Maurer, Montamat, E. Murphy, M. W. Murphy, Normand, O'Conner, Orr. Poynot, Schroeder, Smith, Stocker, Stumpf, Stiner, Sullivan, Terry, Waters.

En conséquence, la motion du dépôt sur le bureau est rejetée.

M. Cutler propose de référer toute l'affaire à un comité de trois. Cette motion passe ; alors le président nomme pour faire partie de ce comité MM. Cutler, Abell et Sullivan.

Les articles 37, 38, 39 et 40 sont adoptés après lecture.

M. Howell présente les articles additionnels suivants :

Art. 41. Il n'existera, dans l'Etat, les paroisses ou les municipalités aucune responsabilité pour dettes contractées pour ou dans l'intérêt de la rébellion, contre l'autorité du gouvernement des Etats-Unis.

ET L'AMENDEMENT DE LA CONSTITUTION DE LA LOUISIANE.

Art. 42. Le siége du gouvernement sera et restera à la Nouvelle-Orléans, et ne pourra être changé que par l'assentiment des deux tiers des deux Chambres de l'Assemblée Générale.

Art. 43. La Législature pourra déterminer la méthode de remplir les vacances dans les divers emplois, pour obvier aux lacunes qui pourraient exister dans la Constitution.

L'article 44 est lu et adopté.

Lecture de l'article 42 est donnée.

M. Abell propose un amendement en retranchant les mots "deux tiers" et y substituant "à la majorité."

Cet amendement est accepté par M. Howell.

M. S. Pursell offre le substitut suivant :

Art. 42. Le siége du gouvernement sera dans la ville de la Nouvelle-Orléans. L'Assemblée Générale aura le droit de disposer de la propriété du Capitole de Bâton-Rouge, et de procurer, soit par achat soit autrement, des terres et bâtiments convenables pour un Capitole d'Etat à la Nouvelle-Orléans.

Dépôt sur le bureau.

M. Cazabat propose d'amender en retranchant les mots "Nouvelle-Orléans," et en substituant "paroisse de Jefferson."

Déposé sur le bureau.

M. Stauffer demande la lecture de son substitut :

Nulle dette créée par ou sous les soi-disant Etats-Confédérés, ou sous la sanction d'un pouvoir usurpé, ne sera ni reconnue ni payée.

Le substitut de M. Stauffer est déposé sur le bureau ; alors la question revient sur l'adoption de l'article additionnel de M. Howell (art. 42.) Une divison a lieu, et donne pour résultat oui 44, non 13.

En conséquence, l'article 42 est adopté ainsi qu'il a été amendé.

L'article 43 est adopté après lecture.

M. Thorpe, comme président du comité nommé pour se présenter chez les majors-généraux Canby et Sickles, soumet le rapport suivant :

Le comité soumet respectueusement qu'il s'est présenté chez les majors-généraux Canby et Sickles, leur témoignant le désir de la Convention de leur faire une visite de cérémonie. Ces officiers distingués répondirent en substance, qu'ils étaient très flattés de la démarche faite par les membres de la Convention pour l'Etat libre de la Louisiane, mais que loin de recevoir une visite officielle des membres de la Convention, ils désiraient saisir la première opportunité de présenter leurs respects aux honorables membres de la Convention.

Le rapport reçu est adopté à l'unanimité.

M. Wilson, avec permission de la Convention, présente la résolution suivante qui est adoptée à l'unanimité :

Résolu, Que le président de cette Convention soit autorisé à inviter les majors-généraux Canby et Sickles à visiter la Convention.

La Convention alors s'ajourne à demain à midi.

Approuvé.

JOHN E. NEELIS,
Secrétaire.

MARDI, le 21 juin 1864.

La Convention se réunit conformément à l'ajournement.

Sont présents l'Hon. E. H. Durell, président, et les membres suivants :

Présents 83.

MM. Abell, Austin, Balch, Bailey, Barrett, Baum, Beauvais, Bell, Bennie, Bofill, Bromley, Buckley. Burke, Collin, Campbell, Cazabat, J. K. Cook, T. Cook, Crozat, Cutler, Davies, Decker, Duke, Dufresne, Dupaty, Durell, Edwards, Ennis, Fish, Flagg, Flood, Foley, Fosdick, Fuller, Gastinel, Geier, Goldman, Gorlinski, Gruneberg, Gaidry, Healy, Harnan, Hart, Henderson, Hills, Hire, Howell, Howes, Kavanagh, Knobloch, Kugler, Mayer, Maas, Mann, Maurer, Mendiverri, Montamat, Morris, E. Murphy, M. W. Murphy, Newell, Normand, Orr, O'Conner, [excusé,] J. Payne, J. T. Paine, [excusé,] Poynot, J. Purcell. S. Pursell, Schroeder, Schnurr, Seymour, Shaw, Smith, Spellicy, Stocker, Stumpf, Stiner, Stauffer, Sullivan, Terry, Thorpe, Waters, Wenck, Wells, Wilson.

Absents, 12.

MM. Ariail, Bonzano, Brott, Duane, Heard, Lobdell, Millspaugh, Montague, Ong, [excusé] Pintado, [excusé] Taliaferro et Thomas.

Les minutes d'hier sont lues et adoptées.

Sur la motion de M. Cutler, M. Ong est excusé, pour cause de maladie.

M. Fosdick propose la suspension des réglements pour prendre la résolution relative au gouvernement de la ville.

La motion du dépôt sur le bureau ayant été rejetée, l'appel par oui et non sur la motion de suspension, donne le résultat suivant :

Oui 38.

MM. Abell, Balch, Bailey, Baum, Bell, Bofill, Buckley, Campbell, J. K. Cook, Cutler, Decker, Dufresne, Duke, Flagg, Flood, Fosdick, Gastinel, Gorlinski, Gruneberg, Healy, Hills, Knobloch, Maas, Maurer, Mendiverri, E. Murphy, Newell, O'Conner, Orr, Poynot, Smith, Stauffer, Sullivan, Waters, Wenck, Wells, Wilson.

Non 42.

MM. Beauvais, Bromley, Burke, Crozat, Cazabat, Collin, Davies, Dupaty, Edwards, Ennis, Fish, Foley, Fuller, Geier, Gaidry, Harnan, Hart, Henderson, Hire, Howell, Howes, Kavanagh, Kugler, Mayer, Mann, Montamat, Morris, M. W. Murphy, Normand, J. Payne, J. T. Paine, J. Purcell, S. Pursell, Schroeder, Schnurr, Seymour, Shaw, Spellicy, Stocker, Stumpf, Stiner, Terry.

En conséquence, la motion est rejetée.

M. Terry, comme président du comité choisi pour l'examen d'un mémoire présenté par de certains ouvriers. soumet le rapport suivant :

M. le président—Votre comité sur les mémoires, après mûre délibération, vous soumet respectueusement le rapport suivant :

Croyant que nos mécaniciens, ou artisans de toute espèce et nos manœuvres sont la partie la plus affligée de notre race ; travaillant presque toujours sous des circonstances les plus déplorables, leurs moyens d'existence ne s'acquièrent qu'au prix des plus grands sacrifices, à moins que la fortune capricieuse ne vienne sourire à leurs efforts. La classe ouvrière, dans l'état de désordre qui existe, doit nécessairement rester dans la plus abjecte pauvreté, simplement par suite de l'antagonisme existant entre le travail et le capital. Il est pour ainsi dire de toute impossibilité à un ouvrier de gagner assez pour couvrir les dépenses de sa famille, et en même temps éviter les dettes et le déshonneur. S'il y réussit dans notre ville, il doit renoncer à toute espèce de luxe et à tous délassements. Les désavantages sont très nombreux. S'il est mécanicien, il se trouve probablement certains mois de chaque année où ses services ne sont pas requis ; mais son loyer et les dépenses de sa famille sont toujours tout comme si son labeur était incessant. Le riche peut payer comptant ses marhandises et provisions ; il peut les acheter au prix du gros ce qui lui est un avantage. Le pauvre achète en petite quantité ; il paie un intérêt onéreux pour avoir du crédit et il vit ainsi en éprouvant des pertes continuelles. Va-t-il au marché, il faut qu'il paie aux bouchers et autres marchands 50 pour cent de plus que le prix d'achat des articles. Va-t-il à la grocerie, il doit défrayer les gains accumulés sur le thé, le sucre, le savon et la mélasse ; et d'abord quant au producteur, puis quant au marchand en gros, enfin quant au détaillant. Voici une masse de profits que le consommateur doit payer, et il lui faut travailler dur et vivre très économiquement pour y arriver. De plus, s'il a besoin de mousseline, de drap ou d'indienne pour sa famille, il lui faut payer au-delà du prix ordinaire et de la valeur de ces marchandises, dédommager le manufacturier et les nombreux marchands intermédiaires jusqu'au, et y compris le dernier détaillant de qui les marchandises sont achetées. Votre comité désapprouve tout ceci, et les classes ouvrières dont découle toute la richesse de l'Etat sont les seules et uniques qui aient à en souffrir. Pour démontrer l'injustice de ce système le manufacturier, le marchand en gros et l'heureux détaillant, peuvent se permettre de vivre dans de riches résidences, entourés de toutes les jouissances du luxe, tandis que le pauvre ouvrier, sa femme et ses nombreux enfants sont forcés de vivre dans des chambres incommodes, dont le loyer est très cher, et de travailler perpétuellement, sans avoir, hélas ! de temps à autre, le moindre rayon d'espoir que leur condition puisse s'améliorer. Votre comité appréciant complètement les complications nombreuses que le monde commercial entraîne après lui, désire établir, qu'entre le producteur et le consommateur, il existe aujourd'hui de nombreux intermédiaires dans tous les genres d'industries. Ces intermédiaires ne produisent rien ; ils n'ajoutent rien à la prospérité de l'Etat ; ce ne sont que des agents inutiles. Mais, il faut qu'ils vivent, qu'ils soient vêtus et enrichis aux dépens des classes ouvrières et industrielles. Ces classes, l'objet de notre sollicitude, doivent donc enrichir tous les non producteurs, non pas par la taxation directe, mais de la manière suivante :

Les producteurs soutiennent les non producteurs en payant des prix élevés pour tout ce qu'ils achètent, et en payant des loyers aux propriétaires, qui, de ce produit, peuvent satisfaire les taxes. Cette manière populaire de spéculer, ce système élégant de s'engraisser du travail des ouvriers et des hommes de profession, devient de jour en jour intolérable. L'hommage que le capital exige du labeur commence à devenir détestable. Il faut que l'on songe bientôt à trouver quelque moyen pour dégager le pauvre des désavantages sous lesquels il se trouve placé ; qu'on lui accorde une chance égale de jouir de la vie ; qu'on le dégage té après mûr examen des faits soumis par vos pétitionnaires, quoique leur demande soit plutôt du ressort d'un corps législatif, admet et approuve leur humble requête, afin de permettre que ces mêmes pétitionnaires puissent consacrer une partie de leur temps chaque jour, à la jouissance de leurs devoirs domestiques et à la culture de leur esprit.

Le comité soumet respectueusement l'article suivant pour qu'il soit inséré dans le rapport des mesures générales.

Art.—. Le travail de tous artisans et ouvriers employés aux travaux publics de l'Etat et de la ville sera de neuf heures de durée.

 (Signé) Randall Terry,
      Président.
   George Geier,
   Benjamin H. Orr,
   Young Burke,
   P. K. O'Conner,
   J. A. Stiner.

M. Schroeder présente un mémoire et des articles additionnels sur le rapport du comité pour ses mesures générales, mais avant lecture, M. Montamat élève un point de droit, et objecte à la lecture du mémoire sans la suspension des réglements; le président abonde dans ce sens, et l'ordre du jour est pris en considération.

M. Cutler, comme président du comité choisi sur l'article 36 du rapport du comité sur les Mesures Générales, soumet le rapport suivant :

Rapport du Comité Spécial sur l'article 36 du Rapport du Comité pour les Mesures Générales.

Les citoyens de la ville de la Nouvelle-Orléans auront le droit de nommer les divers officiers publics nécessaires à l'administration de la police de la dite ville, suivant le mode d'élections qui sera prescrit par la Législature.

Pourvu, Que le maire et les recorders ne soient pas éligibles pour siéger à l'Assemblée-Générale, et que le maire et le recorder soient commissionnés par le gouverneur comme juges de paix, et la Législature pourra leur attribuer une certaine juridiction criminelle nécessaire pour la punition de légères offenses, ainsi que le nécessitera la police et le bon ordre de la ville.

Et que la ville de la Nouvelle-Orléans maintiendra une force de police qui portera l'uniforme, avec distinction de grades, consistant de citoyens résidant dans l'Etat de la Louisiane, choisis par le maire de la ville ; qu'ils continueront leurs fonctions aussi longtemps que leur conduite sera bonne ; qu'ils ne pourront être destitués que par une commission composée de cinq citoyens, savoir : un choisi dans chaque district de la ville, et le maire comme président. La commission devra être nommée par le gouverneur de l'Etat, pour le terme de deux années, à un salaire qui ne sera pas moins de $1000 par année ; une majorité de la dite commission pourra destituer pour cause de délits. Lorsqu'un membre de la police aura été destitué, il ne pourra plus être éligible avant un terme d'une année. Intervenir en aucune manière dans les élections sera une cause suffisante pour immédiate destitution.

Le chef de police fournira un cautionnement de $10,000 ; les lieutenants de police, $5,000 ; les sergents et commis, chacun, $3,000 ; les caporaux, $2,000 et les simples officiers, $1,000. avec de bonnes et solvables sécurités, ainsi que la loi l'exige, pour l'accomplissement fidèle de leurs devoirs.

Ces divers officiers recevront un salaire qui ne sera pas moins de :

Le chef de police.........$250 par mois.
Les lieutenants de police... 150 ..
Les sergents.............. 100 ..
Les commis............... 100 ..
Les caporaux.............. 90 ..
Les officiers du jour et de la
 nuit.................. 80 ..

La Législature établira le prix et la solde des contre-maîtres, manœuvres et autres employés dans les travaux publics du gouvernement de l'Etat, des paroisses et de la ville.

   R. King Cutler,
      Président.
   John Sullivan,
   E. Abell.

Après une discussion sur le rapport, la question première est mise à l'ordre du jour et rejetée par le vote suivant :

Affirmative :

MM. Abell, Austin, Bailey, Baum, Bofill, Bromley, Burke, Crozat, Cutler, Collin, Duke, Dupaty, Fish, Flagg, Fuller, Gaidry, Hart, Henderson, Kavanagh, J. Purcell, Schnurr, Seymour, Thorpe, Wilson—24.

Dans la négative :

MM. Bell, Buckley, Campbell, Cazabat, J. K. Cook, T. Cook, Davies, Dufresne, Decker, Edwards, Ennis, Flood, Foley, Fosdick, Gastinel, Geier, Gorlinski, Healy, Harnan, Hills, Hire, Howell, Howes, Knobloch, Kugler, Maas, Mann, Maurer, Montamat, Morris, Mayer, E. Murphy. M. W. Murphy, Newell. Normand, O'Conner, Orr, J. Payne, J. T. Paine, Poynot, J. Purcell, Schroeder, Shaw, Smith, Spellicy, Stocker, Stumpf, Stiner, Stauffer, Sullivan, Terry, Waters, Wenck, Wells—54.

M. Orr présente le proviso suivant comme un amendement au rapport :

Pourvu, Que la compensation à payer aux contre-maîtres, ouvriers, charretiers et manœuvres employés dans les travaux publics sous le gouvernement de l'Etat de la Louisiane, la ville de la Nouvelle-Orléans, et les juris de police des diverses paroisses de l'Etat ne soient pas moins de, savoir :

Contre-maîtres............$3 50 par jour.
Artisans.................. 3 00   do.
Charretiers............... 3 00   do.
Manœuvres................. 2 00   do.

M. Cazabat présente l'amendement suivant :

Pourvu, Que les manœuvres employés aux travaux publics ne travailleront pas plus de neuf heures par jour et recevront cent dollars par mois ; et pourvu aussi que les salaires de la police seront de cent vingt dollars pour les caporaux et commis, et de cent dollars par mois pour les officiers de la nuit et du jour.

M. Davies présente l'amendement suivant :

Que personne ne pourra servir dans la police de la ville, à moins d'une résidence de deux ans avant la nomination ; et que dans tous les cas la préférence sera donnée aux chefs de famille.

Après une longue discussion, le président décide que M. Cutler, président du comité choisi sur l'article en considération, ayant obtenu la parole et réclamant le droit de clore les débats, pouvait jouir du privilége, et qu'une plus longue discussion par d'autres membres ne pouvait avoir lieu.

M. Stauffer fait appel de cette décision ; mais avant que la question ne soit posée, un appel par oui et non a lieu.

Le quorum voulu n'étant pas présent, la Convention s'ajourne à demain, à midi.

Approuvé.

JOHN E. NEELIS,
Secrétaire.

MERCERDI, le 22 juin 1864.

La Convention se réunit conformément à l'ajournement, et est appelée à l'ordre par le président.

A l'appel du rôle les membres suivants répondent à leurs noms :

MM. Abell, Austin, Balch, Bailey Barrett, Baum, Beauvais, Bell, Bofill, Bromley, Burke, Buckley, Campbell, Collin, J. K. Cook, T. Cook, Crozat, Cutler, Davies, Dufresne, Duane, Dupaty, Edwards, Ennis, Fish, Flagg, Flood, Foley, Fosdick, Fuller. Gastinel, Geier, Gorlinski, Gruneberg, Gaidry, Healy, Hlls, Harnan, Hart, Henderson, Hills, Hire, Howes, Howes, Kavanagh, Knobloch, Kugler, Maas, Mann, Maurer, Mendiverri, Montamat, Morris, E. Murphy, M. W. Murphy, Newell, Normand, O'Conner, J. Payne, J. T. Paine, Pintado, Poynot, J. Purcell, S. Pursell, Schroeder, Schnurr, Seymour, Stocker, Shaw, Stumpf, Smith, Spellicy, Stauffer Sullivan, Terry, Thorpe, Waters, Wenck, Wells, Wilson, Duke, Mayer, Orr — 85 membres.

Absents : MM Ariail, Bennie, Bonzano, Brott, Cazabat, Heard, Lobdell, Millspaugh, Montague, Ong (excusé,) Taliaferro et Thomas.

Les minutes d'hier sont lues et adoptées.

Le rapport du comité Spécial sur l'article 36 du rapport du comité des Dispositions Générales étant à l'ordre du jour, il est mis aux débats.

L'amendement proposé hier par M. Davies est lu.

M. Howes fait la motion d'amender en effaçant le mot "deux" et en insérant le mot "cinq," de manière à ce que la résidence requise soit de cinq ans.

M. Austin propose de déposer cette motion sur la table. Sa proposition est repoussée et l'amendement adopté.

La question revient alors sur l'adoption de l'amendment de M. Davies. On demande la division qui donne le résultat suivant : affirmative, 32 négative 18; en conséquence l'amendement est adopté.

M. Orr fait la motion de reconsidérer le vote qui vient d'être donné. L'appel nominal est ordonné et donne le résultat suivant.

Affirmative :

MM. Balch, Barrett, Buckley, J. K. Cook, Duane, Edwards, Ennis, Flagg, Flood, Foley, Fosdick, Geier, Gorlinski, Gaidry, Healy, Hart, Hills, Hire, Maas, Mann, Maurer, Montamat, Morris, E. Murphy, Newell, Normand, O'Conner, J. Payne, Poynot, S. Purcell, Schroeder, Seymour, Shaw, Smith, Spellicy, Stocker, Stauffer, Terry, Thorpe, Waters, Wenck, Decker, Dufresne, Mayer, Orr, Bell, Fish—48.

Négative :

MM. Abell, Austin, Bailey, Beauvais, Baum, Bofill, Bromley, Burke, Collin, Campbell, Crozat, Cutlér, Davies, Duke, Dupaty, Gastinel, Gruneberg, Harnan, Henderson, Howell, Howes, Kavanagh, Knobloch, Kugler, Mendiverri, M. W. Murphy, J. T. Paine, J. Purcell, Schnurr, Stumpf, Stiner, Sullivan, Wells, Wilson—34.

En conséquence, on reconsidère le vote.

M. Foley fait la motion d'amender en ajoutant après le mot "résident," les mots et "sera citoyen des Etats-Unis."

M. Stauffer propose que la motion de M.

ET L'AMENDEMENT DE LA CONSTITUTION DE LA LOUISIANE.

Foley soit déposée sur la table. Cette proposition est repoussée.

M. Wells fait la motion de déposer le rapport du comité sur l'Art. 36, ainsi que tous les amendements offerts.

Sa motion est rejetée.

M. Thorpe fait la motion d'amender en ajoutant les mots "aucune personne ayant servi dans l'armée rebelle ne pourra faire partie de la police."

Sur la motion faite de déposer l'amendement offert par M. Thorpe, l'appel nominal est demandé et donne le résultat suivant :

Affirmative :

MM. Abell, Austin, Balch, Barret, Baum, Bell, Bofill, Buckley, T. Cook, Cutler, Dufresne, Duane, Edwards, Fish, Foley, Fosdick, Fuller, Gastinel, Geier, Gruneberg, Hart, Healy, Henderson, Howell, Kavanagh, Knobloch, Kugler, Mann, Mendiverri, Montamat. E. Murphy, M. W. Murphy, Normand, O'Conner, Poynot, J. Purcell, Schroeder, Schnurr, Seymour, Shaw, Spellicy, Stocker, Stumpf, Stiner, Sullivan, Waters, Wilson, Decker, Mayer, Orr—50.

Contre :

MM. Bailey, Beauvais, Bromley, Burke, Campbell, Collin, J. K· Cook, Crozat, Davies, Duke, Dupaty, Ennis, Flagg, Flood, Gorlinski, Gaidry, Harnan, Hill, Howes, Maurer, Morris, Newell, J. Payne, J. T. Paine, S. Pursell, Smith, Stauffer, Terry, Thorpe, Wenck, Wells—31.

En conséquence, l'amendement est déposé sur le bureau.

Les divers amendements proposés par MM. Davies, Foley et Cazabat, sont également déposés sur la table.

L'amendement de M. Orr, est ensuite lu. Motion de le déposer est faite. On demande l'appel nominal qui donne le résultat suivant :

Oui :

MM. Abell, Austin, Balch, Bailey, Beauvais, Bofill, Bromley, Burke, Campbell, Crozat, Cutler, Duke, Edwards, Gruneberg, Gaidry, Henderson, Howell, Kavanagh, Mayer, Mendiverri, M. W. Murphy, Newell, Shaw, Wenck, Wells, Wilson—21.

Non :

MM. Barrett, Baum, Bell, Buckley, Collin, J. K. Cook, T. Cook, Davies, Decker, Duane, Dufresne, Dupaty, Ennis, Fish, Flagg, Flood, Foley, Fosdick, Fuller, Gastinel, Geier, Gorlinski, Healy, Harnan, Hart, Hills, Hire, Howes, Knobloch, Kugler, Maas, Mann, Maurer, Montamat, Morris, E. Murphy, Normand, O'Conner, Orr, J. Payne, J. T. Payne, Poynot, J. Purcell, S. Pursell. Schroeder, Seymour, Smith, Spellicy, Schnurr, Stocker, Stumpf, Stiner, Stauffer, Sullivan, Terry, Waters—56.

En conséquence, la motion est rejetée.

La question est posée sur l'adoption de l'amendement de M. Orr. L'appel nominal est demandé et donne le résultat suivant :

Oui :

MM. Abell, Balch, Barrett, Baum, Bell. Bromley, Buckley, J. K. Cook, T. Cook, Davies, Dufresne, Duane, Dupaty, Ennis, Fish, Flagg, Flood, Foley, Fosdick, Fuller, Gastinel, Geier, Gorlinski, Gaidry, Healy, Harnan, Hart, Henderson, Hills, Hire, Howes, Knobloch, Kugler, Maas, Mann, Maurer, Montamat, Morris, E. Murphy, M. W. Murphy, Normand, O'Conner, J Payne, Poynot, J. Purcell, Schroeder, Schnurr, Seymour, Smith, Spellicy, Stocker, Stumpf, Stiner, Stauffer, Sullivan, Terry, Waters, Collin, Decker. Duke, Orr. S. Pursell—62.

Non :

MM. Austin, Bailey, Beauvais, Bofill, Burke, Campbell, Crozat, Cutler, Edwards, Gruneberg, Howell, Kavanagh, Mayer, Mendiverri, Newell, J. T. Paine, Shaw, Wenck, Wells et Wilson—20.

L'amendement est donc adopté.

Sur l'adoption du rapport du comité Spécial tel qu'il est amendé, l'appel nominal est ordonné et il en résulte que les membres suivants

Ont voté dans l'affirmative :

MM. Abell, Balch, Barrett, Bell, Buckley, J. K. Cook, T. Cook, Crozat, Dufresne, Duane, Fish, Flood, Foley, Fuller, Gastinel, Geier, Gorlinski, Healy, Harnan, Hart, Henderson, Hills, Hire, Howes, Kavanagh, Kugler, Maas. Maurer, Mendiverri, Montamat, E. Murphy, M. W. Murphy, Normand. O'Conner, Poynot, J. Purcell, Schroeder, Schnurr, Smith, Spellicy, Stocker, Stumpf, Stiner. Sullivan, Terry, Waters. Decker, Orr et Baum—50.

Ont voté dans la négative :

MM. Bailey, Beauvais, Burke, Campbell, Collin, Cutler, Davies, Duke, Dupaty, Ennis, Flagg, Fosdick, Gruneberg, Gaidry, Howell, Knobloch, Mann, Mayer, Morris, Newell, J. Payne, J. T. Paine, S. Pursell, Seymour, Shaw, Stauffer, Wenck, Wells et Wilson—31.

En conséquence, le rapport est adopté tel qu'amendé.

M. Hills demande la suspension des réglements afin de prendre le rapport du, comité sur les Dispositions Générales à sa troisième lecture. Cette demande est refusée. On ordonne qu'il soit grossoyé pour subir sa troisième lecture demain.

Le rapport du comité sur les Améliorations Intérieures, ainsi que le rapport de la minorité du dit comité, présenté par M. Campbell, étant à l'ordre, est lu.

M. Terry offre un substitut pour le tout.

M. Smith fait la motion d'amender de manière à ce que l'ingénieur de l'Etat soit nommé par le gouverneur pour les trois premières années, et après cette période qu'il soit élu par le peuple ; et aussi de retrancher la clause qui a trait à ses salaires, de manière à ce que la Législature fixe elle-même ses émoluments.

M. —— demande la division de la question sur les amendements, laquelle est ordonnée, et sur motion de M. Wilson le premier amendement est déposé sur la table.

Pendant la discussion de l'amendement, le portier annonce l'arrivée des Majors-Généraux Canby et Sickles, qui sont conduits sur la plateforme par M. Thorpe, où ils sont reçus et félicités par la Convention.

Après un recès de dix minutes, l'appel est fait, et le nombre des membres n'étant pas suffisant pour former un quorum la Convention s'ajourne.

Approuvé.

JOHN E. NEELIS.

JEUDI, le 23 juin 1864.

La Convention se réunit conformément à l'ajournement.

Présents : l'Hon. E. H. Durell, président occupe le fauteuil, et les membres suivants répondent à leurs noms :

MM. Abell, Austin, Balch, Bailey, Barrett, Baum, Beauvais, Buckley, Burke, J. K. Cook, T. Cook, Crozat, Cutler, Collin, Davies, Dufresne, Duane, Dupaty, Decker, Duke, Edwards, Ennis, Fish, Flagg, Flood, Foley, Fosdick, Gastinel, Geier, Gorlinski, Gruneberg, Gaidry, Healy, Harnan, Hart, Henderson, Hills, Hire, Howell, Howes, Kavanagh, Knobloch, Kugler, Maas, Mann, Maurer, Mendiverri, Montamat, Morris, E. Murphy, M. W. Murphy, Mayer, Newell, Normand, O'Conner, Orr, J. Payne, J. T. Paine, Pintado, Poynot, J. Purcell, S. Pursell, Schroder, Schnurr, Seymour, Shaw, Smith, Spellicy, Stocker, Stumpf, Stiner, Stauffer, Sullivan, Terry, Waters, Wenck, Wells, Wilson—83 membres.

Absents :

MM. Ariail, Bennie, Bonzano, Brott, Campbell (excusé,) Cazabat, Fuller, Heard, Lobdell, Millspaugh, Ong (excusé,) Taliaferro, Thomas.

Sur la motion de M. Abell, l'absence de M. Campbell est excusée.

Les minutes d'hier sont lues et adoptées.

M. Pursell fait la motion de reconsidérer le vote donné hier sur le rapport du comité sur les Dispositions Générales, ainsi qu'il a été amendé à sa deuxième lecture.

M. Orr propose que cette motion soit déposée sur la table : sa proposition est rejetée. La motion de reconsidérer est mise aux voix et adoptée sur un vote par assis et levé de 54 oui contre 0 non.

M. S. Pursell offre alors l'article additionnel suivant :

Art.— Toutes professions, occupations ou affaires quelconques, requérant une license des autorités de l'Etat, ne pourront être ni exercées ni poursuivies par aucuns individus à moins qu'ils ne soient citoyens des Etats-Unis, ou n'ayant fait leurs déclarations pour le devenir.

M. Harnan fait la motion de déposer cet article sur la table. Cette motion est repoussée après de longs débats, puis le dit article est rejeté par le vote suivant :

Pour l'adoption :

MM. Bofill, Bromley, Burke, J. K. Cook, Decker, Ennis, Flagg, Flood, Geier, Gaidry, Kugler, Maas, O'Conner, J. T. Paine, Poynot, S. Pursell, Schroeder et Smith—18.

Contre l'adoption :

MM. Austin, Balch, Bailey, Barrett, Baum, Beauvais, Bell, Buckley, Collin, T. Cook, Crozat, Cutler, Davies, Duane, Dufresne, Duke, Dupaty, Edwards, Fish, Foley, Fosdick, Gastinel, Gorlinski, Gruneberg, Healy, Harnan, Hart, Henderson, Hills, Hire, Howell, Howes, Kavanagh, Knobloch, Mann, Maurer, Mayer, Mendiverri, Montamat, Morris, E. Murphy, M. W. Murphy, Newell, Normand, Orr, J. Payne, Pintado, J. Purcell, Schnurr, Seymour, Shaw, Spellicy, Stocker, Stumpf, Stiner, Stauffer, Sullivan, Terry, Thorpe, Wenck, Wells et Wilson—62.

M. S. Pursell offre alors comme article additionnel ce qui suit :

Art.—L'assemblée générale pourvoira par une loi à l'établissement d'une maison des pauvres dans chacune des paroisses de l'Etat, pour l'entretien des indigents, dans leurs limites respectives et qui seront dirigées d'après la loi.

Sur motion de M. Harnan, il est déposé sur la table.

M. Gorlinski offre l'article additionnel suivant :

Art—La Législature aura le droit de faire telles lois accordant le droit de suffrage à telles personnes, citoyennes des Etats-Unis, soit par leurs services militaires, soit par les taxes payées par elles pour le soutien du gouvernement des Etats-Unis, ou par leurs capacités intellectuelles seront jugées dignes de l'obtenir.

M. Sullivan propose qu'il soit déposé sur la table.

Sur l'adoption du dit article, on demande l'appel nominal qui donne le résultat suivant :

Oui :

MM. Austin, Barrett, Bell, Bromley, T. Cook, Crozat, Cutler, Davies, Duane, Dupaty, Ennis, Fish, Flagg, Flood, Foley, Fosdick, Geier, Gorlinski, Healy, Harnan, Henderson, Hills, Hire, Howell, Howes, Kavanagh, Kugler, Mann, E. Murphy, Newell, Normand, O'Conner, J. T. Paine, Pintado, J. Purcell, Schroeder, Seymour, Shaw, Smith, Spellicy, Stumpf, Stiner, Stauffer, Terry, Thorpe, Wenck, Wells, Collin —48.

Non :

MM. Balch, Bailey, Baum, Beauvais, Bofill, Buckley, Burke, J. K. Cook, Decker, Dufresne, Duke, Edwards, Gastinel, Gruneberg, Gaidry, Hart, Knobloch, Maas, Maurer, Mayer, Mendiverri, Montamat, Morris, M. W. Murphy, Orr, J. Payne, Poynot, S. Pursell, Schnurr, Stocker, Sullivan, Wilson —32.

L'article additionnel est adopté.

M. Terry offre l'article additionel suivant :

Neuf heures constitueront une journée de travail pour tous artisans, ouvriers et manœuvres dans le service des Travaux Publics de l'Etat.

Motion est faite de le déposer sur la table, mais est repoussée par un vote par assis et levé : oui, 33; non, 37.

M. Thorpe propose qu'on l'amende en effaçant "neuf" et insérant "sept."

Rejeté.

Sur la question de l'adoption de l'article additionnel présenté par M. Terry, l'appel nominal est demandé et donne le résultat suivant :

Affirmative :

MM. Bailey, Barrett, Baum, Bell, Buckley, Burke, J. K. Cook, T. Cook Crozat, Davies, Dufresne, Duane, Dupaty, Ennis, Fish, Flood, Foley, Fosdick, Geier, Gorlinski, Gaidry, Healy, Harnan, Henderson, Hills, Hire, Howes, Knobloch, Maas, Maurer, Morris, E. Murphy, M. W. Murphy, Newell, Normand, O'Conner, J. Payne, Pintado, Poynot, J. Purcell, S. Pursell, Schroeder, Seymour, Shaw, Smith, Stocker, Stumpf, Stauffer, Stiner, Sullivan, Terry, Thorpe, Collin, Duke, Orr—56.

Négative :

MM. Abell, Austin, Balch, Beauvais, Bofill, Bromley, Cutler, Decker, Edwards, Flagg, Gastinel, Gruneberg, Hart, Howell, Kavanagh, Kugler, Mann, Mayer, Mendiverri, J. T. Paine, Schnurr, Spellicy, Wenck, Wells et Wilson—25.

En conséquence, l'article est adopté.

M. Foley offre l'article additionnel suivant :

La Législature ne passera aucune loi requérant des titres de propriétés d'aucune personne ayant un emploi pubic ou qui pourrait en obtenir.

Sur la motion de M. Healy l'article est adopté.

M. Bromley, offre l'article additionnel suivant :

Aucun membre de cette Convention ne sera éligible à un emploi sous le gouvernement municipal de la Nouvelle-Orléans, avant un espace de trois années après l'adoption de cette constitution.

Déposé sur la table.

Le rapport du comité sur les Dispositions Générales, tel qu'amendé, est alors adopté par un vote par assis et levé de 47 pour et 24 contre.

M. Terry fait la motion de suspendre les réglements, afin de prendre le rapport à sa troisième lecture, mais elle est repoussée.

La Convention reprend alors le substitut au rapport du comité sur les Améliorations Intérieures, offert par M. Terry, ensemble avec tous les amendements proposés.

M. Wilson retire son amendement relatif au terme d'office.

M. Stocker fait la motion d'amender le premier article du substitut de M. Terry, en effaçant tout après le mot "par an" jusqu'au mot "Etat."

M. Healy fait la motion de déposer l'amendement sur la table ; mais cette motion étant repoussée, l'amendement est adopté.

L'appel du rôle est demandé, et il est

constaté que 76 membres ont répondu à leurs noms.

M. Gastinel fait la motion d'effacer les mots "six mille" et substituer "quatre mille," portant ainsi le salaire de l'Ingénieur en chef à quatre mille dollars.

Motion est faite de déposer sur la table, et est repoussée.

L'amendement est adopté par un vote d'assis et levé de 32 oui contre 23 non.

M. Stocker offre un amendement laissant à la Législature le pouvoir de déterminer la nomination et fixer les salaires des assistants de l'ingénieur en chef, lequel est adopté.

Le second article du substitut de M. Terry est pris aux débats.

M. Sullivan offre l'amendement qui suit:

"Et que la corporation municipale de la Nouvelle-Orléans ne pourra ni adjuger, ni vendre par soumissions cachetées, ni contracter pour la complétion des travaux publics qui sont sous son contrôle."

Adopté.

L'article 3 est lu et adopté.

L'article 4 est pris ensuite, et avec la permission de M. Terry il est amendé en effaçant les mots "deux tiers" et substituant le mot "majorité," et est adopté avec les amendements.

Motion de prendre le substitut tel qu'il est amendé à sa troisième lecture est faite et repoussée, et la Convention s'ajourne.

La minute est adoptée.

JOHN E. NEELIS,
Secrétaire.

VENDREDI, le 24 juin 1864.

La Convention se réunit conformément à l'ajournement.

Présents, l'Hon. E. H. Durell, président, et les membres suivants:

MM. Abell, Austin, Balch, Bailey, Barrett, Baum, Beauvais, Bell, Bofill, Bromley, Buckley, Burke, Collin, Campbell, Cazabat, J. K. Cook, T. Cook, Crozat, Cutler, Davies, Decker, Dufresne, Duane, Dupaty, Edwards, Ennis, Fish, Flagg, Flood, Foley, Fosdick, Fuller, Gastinel, Geier, Gorlinski, Gruneberg, Gaidry, Healy, Harnan, Hart, Henderson, Hills, Hire, Howell, Howes, Kavanagh, Knobloch, Kugler, Mayer, Maas, Mann, Maurer, Mendiverri, Montamat, M. W. Murphy, Newell, Normand, Orr, O'Conner, J. Payne, J. T. Paine, Pintado, Poynot, J. Purcell, S. Pursell, Schroeder, Schnurr, Seymour, Shaw, Smith, Spellicy, Stocker, Stumpf, Stiner, Stauffer, Sullivan, Terry, Thorpe, Waters, Wenck, Wells, Wilson.

Les minutes d'hier sont lues et adoptées.

M. Terry demande une suspension des réglements dans le but d'introduire une résolution relative à la célébration du 4 juillet prochain; mais sur la question posée, la suspension est refusée.

M. Bell propose de reconsidérer le vote par lequel l'article 1er du rapport du comité pour les améliorations intérieures a été adopté. Cette motion est retirée.

M. Gruneberg présente un rapport sur le comité des Cédules, qui n'ayant été lu qu'en partie et n'étant signé que par deux membres du comité fut déclaré non avenu par le président. Le substitut pour le rapport du comité sur les améliorations intérieures est pris en considération et passe à sa troisième lecture.

M. Gorlinski propose de retrancher le mot "quatre" dans la 12me ligne et d'y insérer "cinq," de manière à porter le salaire du chef ingénieur à cinq mille dollars, et de retrancher le tout dans le 2me article, après le mot "Etat," dans la 7e ligne.

La clause additionnelle à la troisième lecture de M. Gorlinski est rejetée, et le rapport subit sa troisième lecture et est adopté.

La Convention prend alors un repos de quinze minutes, et à l'expiration de ce temps l'appel a lieu et 77 membres y répondent.

Le rapport du comité sur les Mesures Générales est pris en considération pour sa troisième lecture; après quoi, les clauses additionnelles suivantes sont proposées:

M. Davies propose de retrancher tout l'art. 36 après la ligne 28.

Rejeté.

M. S. Pursell propose de retrancher le tout de l'art. 3, après le mot "sang," dans la deuxième ligne.

Rejeté.

M. Foley propose d'amender l'art. 4, en ajoutant les mots: "ou qui se sont fait enregistrer ennemis des Etats-Unis."

Rejeté par un vote divisionnel de 12 oui contre 57 non.

M. Cazabat propose d'insérer les mots "ou rétroactif" après les mots "*ex post facto*" dans l'art. 20, et de retrancher le tout après le mot "faire" dans la quatrième ligne du même article.
Adopté.

M. Cazabat présente aussi la clause additionnelle suivante à la troisième lecture, par voie d'amendement à l'art. 5, savoir : "Mais la peine capitale est pour toujours abolie et prohibée dans cet Etat."

M. Henderson propose d'amender la clause additionnelle de M. Cazabat, en ajoutant les mots "à moins qu'il n'en soit décidé autrement par le juri."

M. Cazabat accepte cet amendement, et la clause additionnelle, comme elle a été amendée, est rejetée, par suite d'un vote par assis et levés : oui 20, non 50.

M. S. Pursell présente l'amendement suivant à l'art. 44 :

Pourvu, Que les conditions contenues ci-dessus ne s'appliqueront qu'aux personnes blanches.

L'appel des membres a lieu, et 79 noms y répondent.

Après une courte discussion, la Convention s'ajourne.

Approuvé.

JOHN E. NEELIS,
Secrétaire.

SAMEDI, le 25 juin 1864.

La Convention se réunit à midi, conformément à l'ajournement, et suivant l'appel, les membres dont les noms suivent y répondent :

MM. Abell, Austin, Balch, Bailey, Barrett, Beauvais, Bell, Bofill, Bromley, Buckley, Burke, Campbell, Cazabat, J. K. Cook, T. Cook, Crozat, Cutler, Davies, Dufresne, Duane, Dupaty, Edwards, Ennis, Fish, Flagg, Flood, Foley, Fosdick, Fuller, Gastinel, Geier, Gorlinski, Gruneberg, Gaidry, Healy, Harnan, Hart, Henderson, Hills, Hire, Howell, Howes, Kananagh, Knobloch, Kugler, Maas, Mann, Maurer, Mendiverri, Montamat, Montague, Morris, E. Murphy, M. W. Murphy, Mayer, Newell, Normand, O'Conner, Orr, J. Payne, Pintado, Poynot, J. Purcell, S. Pursell, Schroeder, Schnurr, Seymour, Shaw, Smith, Spellicy, Stocker, Stumpf, Stiner, Sullivan, Terry, Thorpe, Waters, Wenck, Wells, Wilson, Collin, Decker, Duke.

D'après motion faite, M. Stauffer est excusé pour absence.

Les minutes de la séance d'hier sont lues et adoptées.

M. Sullivan offre la résolution suivante :

Résolu, Que les sommes de $24,250 seront et sont appropriées des fonds du trésor de l'Etat, pour être distribuées aux institutions charitables suivantes de la ville et de l'Etat, comme suit :

Pour l'Asile des Orphelins...	$1,500 00
Pour l'Asile Catholique de Ste-Marie.................	4,000 00
Pour l'Asile des femmes rue du Camp.................	4,000 00
Pour l'Asile du Bon Pasteur..	500 00
Pour l'Asile de veuves juives et orphelins.................	500 00
Pour l'Asile catholique des Orphelins de St-Vincent.......	1,500 00
Pour l'Association Charitable, au bénéfice des veuves et orphelins des pompiers.......	3,000 00
Pour l'Asile de l'Industrie de Ste-Elizabeth..............	1,000 00
Pour la société des secours aux garçons orphelins du 4e dist.	1,000 00
Pour l'institution des garçons de couleur indigents du 3e district.................	1,000 00
Pour les dames de la Providence, 3e district.............	750 00
Pour l'Asile de Ste-Anne, en faveur des veuves et des enfants dans la détresse.......	1,500 00
Pour l'Asile des enfants de l'église épiscopale protestante..	500 00
Pour l'institution catholique des orphelins dans la détresse...	750 00
Pour l'association catholique bienfaisante de Bâton-Rouge..	250 00
Pour l'asile des orphelins, Bâton-Rouge...............	500 00
Pour l'asile de Milne, N-Orleans.	500 00
Pour l'asile des orphelins de St-Vincent.................	500 00
Pour l'asile des orphelins de la rue Moreau...............	500 00
Pour l'asile des orphelins de St Vincent à Donaldsonville....	500 00
Total.................	$24,250 00

Sur la motion du dépôt sur le bureau, l'appel par oui et non a lieu, et donne le résultat suivant :

Affirmative :

MM. Abell, Balch, Campbell, Collin, Cutler, Davies, Decker, Dufresne, Dupaty, Edwards, Ennis, Flagg, Gruneberg, Gaidry, Howell, Kugler, Mann, Maurer, Mendiverri, Newell, Normand, Pintado, Seymour, Wenck, Wells—25.

Négative :

MM. Austin, Bailey, Barrett, Beauvais, Bell, Bofill, Bromley, Burke, Buckley,

Cazabat, J. K. Cook, T. Cook, Crozat, Duane, Duke, Fish, Flood, Foley, Fosdick, Fuller, Gastinel, Geier, Gorlinski, Hart, Henderson, Hills, Howes, Hire, Knobloch, Maas, Montamat, Morris, E. Murphy, M. W. Murphy, Mayer, O'Conner, J. Paine, Poynot, J. Purcell, S. Pursell, Schroeder, Schnurr, Shaw, Smith, Spellicy, Stocker, Stumpf, Stiner, Sullivan, Terry, Thorpe, Waters, Wilson—53.

M. Foley propose de retrancher l'allocation pour l'association charitable des pompiers.

Sur la motion du dépôt sur le bureau, l'appel par oui et non a lieu et donne le résultat suivant :

MM. Abell, Barrett, Beauvais, Bell, Bofill, Buckley, Burke, J. K. Cook, T. Cook, Crozat, Cutler, Collin, Dufresne, Duane, Dupaty, Decker, Fish, Fuller, Gastinel, Geier, Gruneberg, Gaidry, Henderson, Hire, Howes, Maas, Kugler, Maurer, Mendiverri, Montamat, Mayer, O'Conner, J. Payne, Pintado, Poynot, J. Purcell, S. Pursell, Schroeder, Schnurr, Seymour, Shaw. Spellicy, Stocker, Stumpf, Stiner, Terry. Sullivan, Waters, Wenck, Wilson—30.

Négative :

MM. Austin, Balch, Bailey, Bromley, Campbell, Cazabat, Davies, Duke, Edwards, Ennis, Flagg, Flood, Foley, Fosdick, Gorlinski, Harnan, Hart, Hills. Howell. Knobloch, Mann, Morris, E. Murphy, M. W. Murphy, Newell, Normand, Smith, Thorpe, Wells—29.

En conséquence, la motion de M. Foley est déposée sur le bureau.

M. Gorlinski présente le substitut suivant :

Résolu, Qu'une somme de 25,000 piastres soit, et est appropriée des fonds généraux pour les diverses institutions charitables et autres ; cette somme devant être distribuée sous la direction d'un comité d'Aumôniers, consitant de cinq citoyens nommés par le gouverneur.

Dépôt sur le bureau.

M. Davies propose d'amender en appropriant les 25,000 piastres pour le secours à donner aux veuves et aux orphelins de la ville, dont les maris et les pères auraient perdu la vie au service du gouvernement des Etat-Unis.

Dépôt sur le bureau.

M. Beauvais propose d'amender en y comprenant le Couvent du Sacré-Cœur, dans la paroisse de St-Jacques. pour la somme de 500 piastres. Cet amendement est accepté par M. Sullivan.

M. S. Pursell propose d'amender en comprenant l'asile des femmes dans la paroisse de Jefferson, pour une somme de 1000 piastres.

Accepté.

M. Burke propose d'amender en comprenant les veuves et les orphelins de la paroisse de St-Jean-Baptiste, (qui sont dans une destitution complète,) pour une somme de 1000 piastres. Cet amendement est accepté.

M. Cazabat propose d'amender comme suit :

Pourvu, Que toutes lesdites donations dans un but charitable, soient payées des derniers $20,000 déjà alloués pour le paiement journalier des membres de la Convention ; et, pourvu aussi que les amendements suivants y soient introduits, savoir :

Pour le secours des réfugiés de l'Union, dans le besoin, dans l'Etat de la Louisiane	$3,000 00
Pour l'Asile des Orphelins dans la paroisse de Jefferson	2,000 00
Pour la compagnie No. 1, des Pompiers de la ville de Jefferson	1,000 00
Pour l'Asile des Orphelins de Donaldsonville	1,000 00
Pour le secours des veuves et des orphelins des soldats de l'Union, qui ont perdu la vie au service des Etats-Unis	1,000 00

Cet amendement est déposé sur le bureau.

Sur l'adoption de la résolution de M. Sullivan, comme elle a été amendée, l'appel par oui et par non a lieu et donne le résultat suivant :

Affirmative :

MM. Austin, Barrett, Beauvais, Bell, Bofill, Buckley, Burke, T. Cook, Crozat, Duane, Fish, Flood, Fuller, Gastinel, Geier, Gorlinski, Harnan, Hart, Henderson, Hills, Hire, Howes, E. Murphy, M. W. Murphy, O'Conner, Orr, J. Purcell, S. Pursell, Schroeder, Shaw, Stocker, Stiner, Sullivan, Terry, Waters, Wilson—36.

Négative :

MM. Abell, Balch, Bailey, Bromley, Campbell, Collin, Cazabat. J. K. Cook, Cutler, Davies, Dufresne, Decker, Duke, Dupaty, Edwards, Ennis, Flagg, Foley, Fosdick, Gruneberg, Gaidry, Howell, Knobloch, Kugler, Mayer, Maas. Mann, Maurer, Mendiverri, Montamat, Morris. Newell, Normand, J. Payne, Pintado, Poynot, Schnurr, Seymour, Smith, Spellicy, Stumpf, Thorpe, Wenck, Wells—44.

En conséquence la résolution est rejetée.

M. Terry propose ce qui suit :

Résolu, Qu'une somme de mille dollars soit et est appropriée des fonds de l'Etat, pour la célébration du 4 juillet, et qu'un comité composé de cinq membres soit nommé pour se concerter avec les autorités de la ville, relativement à cette dépense.

Dépôt sur le bureau.

M. Abell propose ce qui suit :

Résolu, Qu'une somme de cent dollars soit allouée à chaque ecclésiastique ayant officié dans cette Convention.

Déposé sur le bureau.

M. Austin, président du comité spécial sur le Rapport de l'Auditeur, soumet le rapport suivant :

A M. le Président et aux Membres de la Convention de l'Etat constitutionnel de la Louisiane :

Votre comité, auquel fut référé le rapport de l'auditeur des comptes publics, a l'honneur de soumettre le rapport suivant, savoir :

Eu égard à toutes les circonstances environnantes, nous ne trouvons nulle objection sérieuse sur la manière et la forme dont l'auditeur d'Etat a cru convenable de présenter son rapport. Quant aux billets confédérés, nous les considérons sans valeur et perdus pour l'Etat.

Votre comité est d'opinion que nous ne devrions pas intervenir avec les pouvoirs militaires ; et, en conséquence, il est unanime à dire que, d'autant que le dernier auditeur des comptes publics, l'hon. S. H. Torrey, n'a émis des certificats que par autorité du gouverneur militaire, le général Shepley, il est non-seulement excusable mais justifiable. Quant à l'Hon. R. K. Howell et à l'Hon. A. M. Buchanan, votre comité pense qu'ils ont prélevé leur salaire d'après la constitution et les lois de l'Etat de la Louisiane, et que l'opinion de notre auditeur, l'Hon. A. P. Dostie, "que la rébellion avait achevé l'existence de la Cour Suprême," est erronée et contraire à l'opinion dominante de tous les citoyens loyaux de la Louisiane, qui tiennent " *que l'Etat n'est jamais sorti de l'Union.*"

Quant à l'Hon. C. A. Peabody, votre comité est d'opinion qu'il n'a jamais été président de la Cour Suprême de l'Etat de la Louisiane, par la raison irréfutable que ni les autorités militaires ni les pouvoirs civils de cet Etat n'ont jamais créé une Cour Suprême depuis l'arrivée de l'Hon. Peabody dans cet Etat, et même n'était-il pas éligible à un siége dans la Cour créée antérieurement à son arrivée, parce qu'il n'était pas et qu'il n'est pas même encore citoyen de l'Etat de la Louisiane ; et de plus, parce qu'il a été créé juge par le président des Etats-Unis pour présider une Cour créée par la même autorité : "La Cour provisoire des Etats-Unis pour l'Etat de la Louisiane." Que comme juge de la dite cour il a reçu un salaire du gouvernement des Etats-Unis ; et, en conséquence, il a reçu aussi la somme de $3541 66 du trésor de l'Etat de la Louisiane, comme salaire, sous le prétexte d'être le président de la Cour Suprême de l'Etat, sans nulle autorité et en violation directe de la constitution et des lois de l'Etat de la Louisiane.

Dans ces circonstances votre comité recommande que par rapport à ces actes illégaux dudit C. A. Peabody, en obtenant comme il a été dit ci-dessus, ladite somme de l'Etat, l'avocat-général de cet Etat soit requis d'intenter telles procédures légales qu'il croira nécessaires pour recouvrir ladite somme avec frais, dommages et intérêts.

Votre comité recommande en outre que d'autant que la nécessité de maintenir la cour provisoire des Etats-Unis ayant cessé d'exister depuis longtemps, et que cette cour ne peut servir qu'à faire trébucher l'administration de la justice ainsi que la loyauté du bon peuple de la Louisiane, le commandant-général de ce département, le major-général Banks, et son Excellence M. Hahn, gouverneur de l'Etat de la Louisiane, soient requis de pétitioner au président des Etats-Unis pour qu'il rappelle, ledit Ch. A. Peabody, lui retirant sa commission et mettant ainsi une fin à l'existence suprême de ladite cour.

Quant à M. Serpas, shérif de la paroisse de St.-Bernard, votre comité est d'opinion que comme les billets confédérés qu'il porte furent reçus pour taxes collectées par lui sous le régime confédéré, il devait être exonéré de tout blâme et déchargé de toute responsabilité en versant lesdits billets chez le trésorier de l'Etat.

O. W. AUSTIN,
Président du Comité.
W. R. FISH,
R. BEAUVAIS,
R. KING CUTLER.

Sur la motion de M. Terry, il fut ordonné que le rapport soit imprimé et mis à l'ordre du jour pour samedi prochain.

M. Schroeder soumet le mémoire et la résolution suivants :

A la Convention constitutionnelle de la Louisiane :

Le mémoire que les soussignés soumettent respectueusement appelle l'attention de votre honorable corps au vice de la loi relative aux naissances et décès, et à la nécessité de l'amender, attendu que cette loi est défectueuse.

On peut voir par les Actes de 1855, page 41, relativement aux naissances et décès, que dans le cas d'une naissance ou d'un décès, la partie en faisant la déclaration dans la paroisse d'Orléans, (les personnes résidant dans les paroisses de la campagne n'étant pas requises d'en fournir l'enregistrement) n'est pas tenu de faire un affidavit, laissant ainsi une voie ouverte à la fraude. Par exemple, supposons qu'un homme épouse une femme qui possède en propre des propriétés foncières et personnelles, et qu'il ne survienne pas d'enfants de ce mariage ; supposez que la femme ait des parents dans la ligne ascendante ou collatérale qui ne résident pas dans l'Etat, qui ignorent sa position et peut-être même qu'elle existe. Supposons cette dernière hypothèse ; supposons aussi que cet homme inconnu de sa femme ira sous les dispositions de la loi invoquer et déclarer devant le recorder que sa femme lui a donné un enfant ; supposez ensuite que la femme meure sans tester; et dans l'ignorance d'une telle déclaration, quelles en seront les conséquences ? Le mari agira de connivence avec d'autres personnes dans son droit comme tuteur naturel de son enfant mineur, (chose factice) et il obtiendra l'administration ainsi que la possession des propriétés de sa femme décédée ; et par des réclamations imaginaires il s'imposera de toutes les espèces de propriétés, au préjudice des héritiers légitimes. Ce n'est toutefois ici qu'une seule manière de commettre la fraude au préjudice de l'héritier légal de sa femme, car la femme elle-même pourrait seconder les démarches de son mari, à l'effet de priver de sa succession les héritiers directs, si tel était son bon plaisir. Ce que l'on peut dire des naissances peut être appliqué aux décès ; par exemple, le plus proche parent de l'héritier d'une succession en Europe, résidant dans ce pays, et à qui cet héritage est inconnu, peut déclarer pardevant le recorder des naissances et des décès la mort de l'héritier, et obtenir à cet effet du magistrat un certificat, lequel, après avoir été certifié par le consul de sa nation, lui servirait en Europe de preuve comme le plus proche héritier, pour obtenir la propriété léguée ou dont devait hériter l'héritier donné comme mort, sont quelques-uns des vices de la loi de 1855. Il y en a même d'autres: on peut voir que dans la seule paroisse d'Orléans, il est obligatoire pour les personnes de faire enregistrer les naissances et les décès. Il n'en est pas ainsi dans les campagnes. Pourquoi cela ? Si l'on peut impunément se livrer à la fraude dans cette paroisse, avec quelle plus grande latitude ne pourrait-on pas s'y livrer dans les paroisses rurales ?

En conséquence, nous prions votre honorable Corps d'accorder à ce mémoire toute votre considération, et d'aviser par des moyens quelconques, à prévenir les abus auxquels la loi de 1855 est sujette par suite de la dépravation de l'homme.

CHARLES F. WARNEY,
JOHN SMITH
et autres.

Résolu, Que la Législature, dans sa 1ère session après l'adoption de cette constitution, nommera dans chaque paroisse de l'Etat un officier préposé à l'enregistrement des naissances, mariages et décès; il sera de son devoir de tenir à cet effet des livres convenables et d'y faire l'enregistrement de chaque naissance, mariage ou décès, donnant le nom du père et de la mère, le sexe de chaque enfant né dans les limites de leur paroisse respective comme il est prévu ci-dessus ; en outre elle passera une loi pourvoyant à punir par une amende proportionnée, tous parents d'enfants nés comme il est établi ci-dessus, et qui ne déclareront pas dans un délai raisonnable, au bureau d'enregistrement, la naissance et le sexe de chaque enfant; il sera aussi du devoir de chaque officier préposé de tenir un registre du décès et mariage de toutes personnes avec la déclaration du sexe, de l'âge et du nom, fournissant des preuves à l'appui.

Le mémoire est accepté.

M. Hills propose ce qui suit :

Résolu, Qu'un comité de cinq membres soit nommé pour faire un rapport samedi prochain sur les besoins nécessaires aux diverses institutions charitables de l'Etat.

Adopté.

En conséquence de cette résolution, le président nomme un comité composé de MM. Hills, Howell, Smith, Stocker et Sullivan.

M. Wells propose :

Attendu, Qu'il se trouve beaucoup de dames d'une loyauté éprouvée, préposées à l'instruction de notre jeunesse, et remplissant leurs devoirs dans nos écoles publiques avec honneur pour elles-mêmes et pour la communauté en général, et qui comptent sur leurs travaux journaliers pour leur entretien et celui de leurs familles.

Qu'il soit résolu, Que les autorités compétentes augmentent leurs appointements de 25 pour cent.

Sur la motion du dépôt sur le bureau, l'appel par oui et non a lieu, et donne le résultat suivant :

Affirmative :

MM. Bell, Duke, Edwards, Hills, Howell, Knobloch, Mayer, M. W. Murphy, Normand, J. Payne, Schnurr, Smith, Sullivan, Wenck, —14.

Négative :

MM. Abell, Austin, Barrett, Beauvais, Bofill, Bromley, Buckley, Burke, Campbell, Cazabat, J. K. Cook, T. Cook, Crozat, Cutler, Collin, Davies, Dufresne, Duane, Dupaty. Ennis, Fish, Flagg, Flood, Foley, Fosdick, Fuller, Gastinel, Geier, Gorlinski, Gruneberg, Gaidry, Harnan, Henderson, Hart, Hire, Howes, Maas, Mann, Maurer, Mendiverri, Montamat, E. Murphy, Newell, O'Conner, Orr, Pintado, Poynot, S. Pursell, J. Purcell, Schroeder, Seymour, Shaw, Spellicy, Stocker, Stumpf, Stiner, Terry Wells, Wilson—60.

La motion du dépôt sur le bureau est en conséquence rejetée.

M. Howes propose d'amender en ajoutant les mots : "si cela est compatible avec l'intérêt public."

Rejeté.

La résolution de M. Wells est alors adoptée.

M. Beauvais propose d'ajourner la Convention *sine die* le 2 juillet prochain.

Dépôt sur le bureau.

La résolution de M. Fosdick, relative à l'élection des officiers pour le gouvernement de la ville de la Nouvellle-Orléans, ensemble avec l'amendement de M. Davies, sont alors pris en considération.

Sur la motion de M. Foley, l'amendement est déposé sur le bureau.

M. Bofill propose de déposer sur le bureau la résolution première.

Rejeté.

M. Stocker propose d'ajourner indéfiniment la résolution, mais après une longue discussion, il finit par retirer sa motion.

M. Cutler propose ce qui suit :

Résolu, Que le sujet de faire une élection dans la ville, soit référé à un comité de cinq membres, nommé par le président, avec les instructions nécessaires pour examiner la question de savoir s'il y a des difficultés à mettre en pratique la constitution de la ville, et dans cette hypothèse, comment il serait possible à la Convention d'y remédier.

Sur la question d'adoption de la résolution, l'appel par oui et par non est ordonné, et donne le résultat qui suit :

Affirmative :

MM. Austin, Barrett, Bell, Bofill, Bromley, Burke, Campbell, Cazabat, Crozat, Cutler, Collin, Davies, Dufresne, Duane, Edwards, Ennis, Flagg, Flood, Foley, Fuller, Geier, Gruneberg, Gaidry, Healy, Harnan, Hart, Hire, Howes, Mann, Mendiverri, Montamat, Morris, E. Murphy, Mayer, Newell, Normand, J. Payne, Pintado, J. Purcell, Schroeder, Schnurr, Seymour, Shaw, Smith, Spellicy, Stocker, Stumpf, Stiner, Sullivan, Terry, Wenck, Wilson—53.

Négative :

MM. Abell, Balch, Bailey, Buckley, T. Cook, Duke, Fish, Fosdick, Gastinel, Gorlinski, Hills, Knobloch, O'Conner, Orr, Poynot, S. Pursell, Thorpe, Waters, Wells, Durell—21.

M. Howell étant au fauteuil, le président vote.

La résolution est alors adoptée, et la Convention s'ajourne.

Approuvé.

JOHN E. NEELIS,
Secrétaire.

LUNDI, le 27 juin 1864.

La Convention se réunit conformément à l'ajournement, et est appelée à l'ordre par le président.

A l'appel du rôle les membres suivants répondent à leurs noms :

MM. Abell, Ariail, Austin, Balch, Bailey, Barrett, Baum, Beauvais, Bell, Bofill, Bromley, Buckley, Burke, Collin, Campbell, Cazabat, J. K. Cook, T. Cook, Crozat, Cutler, Decker, Davies, Dufresne, Duane, Dupaty, Edwards, Ennis, Fish, Flagg, Flood, Foley, Fosdick, Fuller, Gastinel, Geier, Gorlinski, Gruneberg, Gaidry, Healy, Harnan, Hart, Henderson, Hills, Hire, Howell, Howes, Kavanagh, Knobloch, Kugler, Maas, Mann, Maurer, Mayer, Mendiverri, Montamat, M. W. Murphy, Newell, Normand, O'Conner, Orr, J. Payne, J. T. Paine, Pintado, Poynot, J. Purcell, S. Pursell, Schroeder, Schnurr, Seymour, Shaw, Smith, Spellicy, Stocker, Stumpf, Stiner, Stauffer, Sullivan, Terry, Thorpe, Waters, Wenck, Wells et Wilson.

Sur motion, les membres suivants sont excusés pour non-attendance, savoir : MM. Knobloch, Baum, Kugler, Ennis, S. Pursell et Orr.

Les minutes de samedi sont lues et adoptées.

Le président nomme MM. Cutler, Fosdick, Hills, Orr et Henderson, membres du comité pour rapporter sur la résolution de M. Cutler de samedi dernier, relative à l'élection des officiers pour le gouvernement de la ville.

La troisième lecture du rapport du comité sur les Mesures Générales étant à l'ordre du jour, est pris en considération.

M. Hills propose la question première, laquelle étant acceptée, est mise aux voix et le rapport adopté après sa troisième lecture.

Le rapport du comité sur l'Education Publique étant le premier à l'ordre du jour, est pris en considération pour sa deuxième lecture et lu section par section, avec les substituts et les amendements ajoutés.

Le substitut de M. S. Pursell est déposé sur le bureau.

L'amendement de M. Bonzano sur l'art. 3, et ses substituts sur les articles 5 et 7, après lecture, sont déposés sur le bureau.

Sur la proposition de M. Hills, le rapport est pris en considération section par section, et les divers substituts et amendements, pris dans l'ordre régulier suivant les sections auxquels ils appartiennent.

Lecture de l'article 1er.

M. Seymour propose de retrancher de la première ligne le mot "deux," et d'y insérer "quatre."

Accepté.

L'article est adopté comme il a été amendé.

Lecture de l'article 2, ainsi que du substitut de M. Sullivan qui y a rapport.

Sur motion de déposer sur le bureau le substitut de M. Sullivan, l'appel par oui et non a lieu et donne le résultat suivant :

Affirmative :

MM. Abell, Austin, Bell, Bromley, Burke, Cazabat, J. K. Cook, T. Cook, Collin, Davies, Duane, Dupaty, Fish, Flagg, Foley, Flood, Fosdick, Gorlinski, Gaidry, Healy, Henderson, Hills, Hire, Howell, Mann, Maurer, E. Murphy, Newell, Normand, O'Conner, J. T. Paine, Pintado, Poynot, J. Purcell, Schnurr, Seymour, Shaw, Smith, Spellicy, Stumpf, Stiner, Taliaferro, Wells, Wilson—44.

Négative :

MM. Balch, Bailey, Barrett, Baum, Beauvais, Bofill, Buckley, Campbell, Crozat, Cutler, Duke, Dufresne, Edwards, Fuller, Gastinel, Geier, Gruneberg, Hart, Howes, Mayer, Maas, Mendiverri, Montamat, Morris, M. W. Murphy, Orr, Ong, J. Payne, Stocker, Sullivan, Terry, Thorpe, Waters—33.

En conséquence, le substitut est déposé sur le bureau.

La question revient alors sur l'adoption de l'article 2. L'appel par oui et par non ayant été demandé, donne le résultat qui suit :

Affirmative :

MM. Austin, Barrett, Bell, Bromley, Burke, Collin, Cazabat, T. Cook, Davies, Duane, Dupaty, Fish, Flagg, Flood, Foley, Fosdick, Gorlinski, Gaidry, Healy, Harnan, Henderson, Hills, Hire, Howell, Howes, Mann, Maurer, E. Murphy, M. W. Murphy, Newell, Normand, O'Conner, Ong, J. Payne, J. T. Paine, Pintado, Poynot, J. Purcell, Seymour, Shaw, Smith, Spellicy, Stumpf, Stiner, Taliaferro, Terry, Thorpe, Wells, Wilson—49.

Négative :

MM. Abell, Balch, Bailey, Baum, Beauvais, Bofill, Buckley, Campbell, J. K. Cook, Crozat, Cutler, Dufresne, Duke, Edwards, Fuller, Gastinel, Geier, Gruneberg, Hart, Maas, Mayer, Mendiverri, Montamat, Morris, Orr, Schnurr, Stocker, Sullivan, Waters—29.

En conséquence l'article 2 est adopté.

L'article 3 est ensuite pris en considération et lu.

M. Montamat propose de déposer l'article sur le bureau.

L'appel par oui et par non est demandé et donne le résultat suivant :

Affirmative :

MM. Baum, Beauvais, Bofill, Bromley, Cazabat, Cutler, Davies, Duke, Dupaty, Edwards, Fish, Gaidry, Hire, Howell, Mann, Mayer, Montamat, Newell, Normand, Ong, J. Payne, J. T. Paine, Pintado, Shaw, Smith, Stumpf, Taliaferro—27.

Négative :

MM. Abell, Austin, Balch, Bailey, Barrett, Bell, Buckley, Burke, Campbell, J. K. Cook, T. Cook, Crozat, Collin, Dufresne, Duane, Flagg, Flood, Foley, Fosdick, Fuller, Gastinel, Geier, Gorlinski, Gruneberg, Healy, Harnan, Hart, Henderson, Hills, Howes, Maas, Maurer, Mendiverri, Morris, E. Murphy, M. W. Murphy, O'Conner, Poynot, J. Purcell, Schnurr, Seymour, Spellicy, Stocker, Stiner, Sullivan, Terry, Thorpe, Waters, Wells, Wilson—51.

La motion du dépôt sur le bureau est en conséquence rejetée.

M. Foley propose d'amender, en ajoutant dans la 7ème ligne, les mots "pourvu que ces écoles soient loyales."

M. Thorpe propose le substitut suivant pour l'article :

Que les écoles de la paroisse de la Nouvelle-Orléans sous la charge immédiate des Catholiques Romains, reçoivent du trésor de l'Etat, une somme égale à celle appropriée par le système existant pour les écoles publiques adoptées par l'Etat.

Sur la motion de M. Foley, le substitut est déposé sur le bureau, par suite du vote suivant :

ET L'AMENDEMENT DE LA CONSTITUTION DE LA LOUISIANE.

Affirmative :

MM. Bailey, Baum, Bofill, Bromley, Burke, Campbell, Cazabat, J. K. Cook, Cutler, Collin, Dupaty, Duke, Edwards, Fish, Flagg, Foley, Gastinel, Geier, Gaidry, Hart, Hire, Howell, Maas, Mann, Maurer, Montamat, Morris, Mayer, Newell, Normand, Ong, J. Payne, J. T. Paine, Pintado, Poynot, J. Purcell, Seymour, Shaw, Smith, Spellicy, Stumpf, Taliaferro, Wells—43.

Négative :

MM. Abell, Austin, Balch, Barrett, Beauvais, Bell, Buckley, T. Cook, Crozat, Davies, Dufresne, Duane, Flood, Fosdick, Fuller, Gorlinski, Gruneberg, Healy, Harnan, Henderson, Hills, Howes, Mendiverri, E. Murphy, M. W. Murphy, O'Conner, Orr, Schnurr, Stocker, Stiner, Sullivan, Terry, Thorpe, Waters et Wilson—35.

M. Cazabat offre le substitut suivant :

Aucune appropriation quelle qu'elle soit ne pourra être faite par l'Assemblée Générale pour le support des écoles particulières, mais des encouragements pourront être donnés aux écoles publiques dans tout l'Etat.

Une question de droit ayant eu lieu au sujet du vote sur le substitut présenté par M. Thorpe, comme il avait été annoncé par le président, le vote pris par le secrétaire est de nouveau appelé par le président, et trouvé parfaitement correct.

Sur la motion de déposer sur le bureau le substitut de M. Cazabat, le vote suivant est rendu :

Affirmative :

MM. Abell, Austin, Balch, Barrett, Bell, Buckley, Burke, T. Cook, Cutler, Duane, Dufresne, Flagg, Flood, Foley, Fosdick, Fuller, Gorlinski, Gruneberg, Healy, Harnan, Henderson, Hills, Howes, Maurer, Mayer, Mendiverri, E. Murphy, M. W. Murphy, O'Conner, Orr, J. Purcell, Schnurr, Spellicy, Stiner, Sullivan, Terry, Waters, Wells, Wilson—39.

Négative :

MM. Bailey, Baum, Beauvais, Bofill, Bromley, Campbell, Collin, Cazabat, J. K. Cook, Crozat, Davies, Duke, Dupaty, Edwards, Fish, Gastinel, Geier, Gaidry, Hart, Hire, Howell, Maas, Mann, Montamat, Morris, Newell, Normand, Ong, J. Payne, J. T. Paine, J. Payne, Pintado, Poynot, Seymour, Shaw, Smith, Stocker, Stumpf, Taliaferro, Thorpe —39.

Le vote étant partagé, le président, donne sa voix pour la négative.

La motion du dépôt sur le bureau est conséquemment rejetée.

M. Cazabat ayant retranché de son substitut les mots "mais des encouragements seront donnés aux écoles publiques dans tout l'Etat," le substitut est déposé sur le bureau.

L'article 3 est alors rejeté, par le vote suivant :

Affirmative :

MM. Abell, Austin, Balch, Barrett, Bell, Buckley, T. Cook, Dufresne, Duane, Flagg, Flood, Fosdick, Gorlinski, Gruneberg, Healy, Harnan, Henderson, Hills, Howes, Maurer, Morris, E. Murphy, M. W. Murphy, Mayer, O'Conner, Orr, J. Purcell, Stocker, Stiner, Sullivan, Terry, Thorpe, Waters, Wilson—34.

Négative :

MM. Bailey, Baum, Beauvais, Bofill, Bromley, Burke, Campbell, Cazabat, J. K. Cook, Crozat, Cutler, Collin, Davies, Dupaty, Duke, Edwards, Fish, Foley, Fuller, Gastinel, Geier, Gaidry, Hart, Hire, Howell, Maas, Mann, Mendiverri, Montamat, Newell, Normand, Ong, J. Payne, J. T. Paine, Pintado, Poynot, Schnurr, Seymour, Shaw, Smith, Spellicy, Stumpf, Taliaferro, Wells—44.

M. Foley propose une reconsidération ; cette motion est déposée sur le bureau.

Une motion d'ajournement a lieu, mais elle est rejetée.

L'article 4 est pris en considération.

M. Hills présente le substitut suivant :

Art. 4. Les études journalières dans les écoles publiques auront lieu dans la langue anglaise.

M. Cazabat propose d'amender en insérant les mots "et en Français," de sorte que l'article dira : "en Anglais et en Français."

Rejeté.

M. Montamat propose d'amender en ajoutant les mots "la langue anglaise sera enseignée dans les écoles publiques de l'Etat."

Une motion de déposer sur le bureau, et le substitut et l'amendement étant rejeté la question de l'adoption de l'amendement présenté par M. Montamat est posée, et donne par suite d'une division le résultat qui suit : oui 31, non 36.

Le substitut de M. Hills est alors adopté.

L'article 5 est pris en considération.

M. Gorlinski propose de retrancher le tout après le mot "organisation."

Rejeté.

M. Howell propose de substituer l'article 139 de la constitution de 1852.

Rejeté.

M. Smith propose d'amender en retranchant le mot "Nouvelle-Orléans."

Dépôt sur le bureau.

M. Montamat propose de retrancher tout l'article.

Dépôt sur le bureau.

L'article est alors adopté par suite d'un vote par assis et levé : oui 43, non 23.

Sur la motion de M. Sullivan, l'appel des membres présents a lieu et 78 membres répondent à leurs noms.

L'article 6 est alors pris en considération, et après lecture M. Cazabat propose d'insérer "publiques" entre les mots "et les écoles."

Adopté.

M. Harnan propose de retrancher tout l'article.

Rejeté.

L'article est alors adopté, suivant amendement.

Sur la question d'adopter le rapport dans son ensemble et suivant amendement, le vote suivant a été pris :

Affirmative:
MM. Austin, Barrett, Bell, Bromley, Burke, Cazabat, Collin, J. K. Cook, Davies, Fish, Flagg, Flood, Fosdick, Fuller, Geier, Gorlinski, Gaidry, Hills, Hire, Howell, Mann, Morris, E. Murphy, Normand, J. Payne, J. T. Paine, Pintado, Poynot, Seymour, Shaw, Smith, Spellicy, Stumpf, Thorpe, Wells, Wilson—36.

Négative :
MM. Abell, Balch, Bailey, Baum, Beauvais, Bofill, Buckley, Campbell, T. Cook, Crozat, Cutler, Dufresne, Duane, Edwards, Foley, Gastinel, Gruneberg, Healy, Harnan, Hart, Henderson, Howes, Maas, Maurer, Mendiverri, Montamat, M. W. Murphy, Mayer, Newell, O'Conner, Orr, Ong, J. Purcell, Schnurr, Stocker, Stiner, Sullivan, Taliaferro, Terry, Waters, Duke—41.

Le rapport, ainsi qu'il a été amendé, est par conséquent rejeté.

M. Montamat, président du comité des Finances, soumet le rapport suivant :

Rapport du comité des Finances de la Convention constitutionnelle, sur les fonds alloués chaque jour aux membres, frais de route, et le salaire des officiers:

1864.
Juin 18—Balance en
 mains ce jour..... $ 5,514 40
Juin 21—Reçu...... 20,000 00

Balance en mains.... $25,514 40

Juin 25—Payé par
 bill No 78........ $2,030 00
Juin 25—Payé par la
 liste No. 2........ 2,170 00
Juin 25—Payé par la
 liste No. 3........ 2,110 00
Juin 25—Payé par
 bill No. 79........ 2,141 00—$8,451 00

Juin 27—Balance en
 mains ce jour..... $17,063 40
(Dix-sept mille soixante-trois piastres et quarante cents.)

FONDS POUR DEPENSES CASUELLES.

Juin 18—Balance en
 mains suivant le
 dernier rapport.... $6,972 53
Juin 24—Payé le bill
 No. 80.......... 1,660 25

Juin 27—Balance en
 mains........... $5,311 78

Soumis respectueusement,
JOHN P. MONTAMAT,
Agissant en qualité de président du comité des Finances.

La Convention s'ajourne alors à demain a midi.

Approuvé.
JOHN E. NEELIS,
Secrétaire.

MARDI, le 28 juin 1864.

La Convention se réunit conformément à l'ajournement.

L'honorable E. H. Durell, président, occupe le fauteuil et les membres suivants répondent à leurs noms :

MM. Abell, Austin, Balch, Bailey, Barrett, Baum, Beauvais, Bell, Bromley, Buckley, Bofill, Burke, Campbell, Cazabat, J. K. Cook, T. Cook, Crozat, Collin, Decker, Duke, Davies, Dufresne, Duane, Dupaty, Edwards, Fish, Flagg, Flood, Foley, Fosdick, Fuller, Gastinel, Geier, Gorlinski, Gruneberg, Gaidry, Healy, Harnan, Hart, Henderson, Hills, Hire, Howell, Howes, Kavanagh, Knobloch, Kugler, Maas, Mann, Maurer, Mendiverri, Montamat, Morris, E. Murphy, M. W. Murphy, Mayer, Newell, Normand, O'Conner, Ong, J. Payne, J. T. Paine, Pintado, Poynot, J. Purcell, S. Pursell, Schroeder, Schnurr, Seymour, Shaw, Smith, Spellicy, Stocker, Stumpf, Stiner, Sullivan, Taliaferro, Terry, Thorpe, Waters, Wenck, Wells, Wilson—80 membres.

Les minutes de lundi sont lues et adoptées.

M. Campbell fait la motion d'excuser M. Stauffer pour cause de maladie.

M. Cazabat fait la motion de suspendre

les règlements, afin d'introduire une résolution relative à l'ajournement *sine die.*
Cette motion est repoussée.

M. Beauvais fait la motion de reconsidérer le vote rejetant le rapport du comité sur l'Education. Cette motion étant adoptée, il propose alors que le rapport soit référé à un comité spécial de cinq membres, lequel comité fera son rapport demain.
Adopté.

Le président nomme de ce comité, MM. Beauvais, Howell, Wells, Sullivan et Campbell.

Le rapport du comité sur le Mode de Révision de la Constitution, est pris alors à sa troisième lecture.

M. Montamat offre comme clause additionelle à sa 3e lecture, l'article 141 de la constitution de 1852, laquelle est conçue en ces termes :

Art. 141. Tout amendement à cette constitution peut être proposé au Sénat ou à la Chambre des Représentant. Si l'amendement est accepté par les deux tiers des membres élus dans chaque Chambre il sera inséré au procès-verbal avec le vote par oui et par non, et le secrétaire d'Etat le fera publier trois mois avant l'élection des membres de l'Assemblée Générale de l'Etat dans au moins une gazette en français et en anglais, dans chaque paroisse de l'Etat dans laquelle on publiera une gazette, et ledit amendement ou amendements seront soumis aux suffrages du peuple à ladite élection des représentants, et si une majorité des votants approuve et ratifie cet amendement ou amendements ils feront dès lors partie de la constitution.

Si plusieurs amendements sont proposés en même temps, ils seront soumis au peuple de manière à ce que les électeurs puissent voter pour ou contre séparém nt.

Sur motion de M. Cazabat, la clause additionnelle (Rider) est rejetée par 44 oui et 18 non.

M. Smith fait la motion d'effacer les mots "deux tiers" et insérer le mot "majorité."

Sur motion de M. Montamat, le "rider" de M. Smith est rejeté par un vote par assis et levé : oui, 33; non, 31.

Le rapport est alors adopté.

Sur motion de M. Shaw, la Convention prend un recès d'une demi-heure, à l'expiration de laquelle le président appelle la Convention à l'ordre; et l'appel nominal étant fait, soixante-sept membres seulement répondent à leurs noms.

Le sergent-d'armes est envoyé à la recherche des membres absents. Après un certain laps de temps M. Harnan fait la motion d'ajourner. L'appel nominal a lieu et donne le résultat suivant :

Affirmative :

MM. Abell, Balch, Bofill, Buckley, Burke, Campbell, J. K. Cook, Crozat, Dufresne, Decker, Duke, Fosdick, Fuller, Gastinel, Gruneberg, Harnan, Hart, Hills, Hire, Maas, Mayer, Maurer, Montamat, M. W. Murphy, E. Murphy, O'Conner, John Payne, Pintado, Poynot, Schroeder, Schnurr, Seymour, Shaw, Spellicy, Stumpf, Stiner, Sullivan, Waters —38.

Négative :

MM. Austin, Barrett, Beauvais, Bell, Bromley, Cazabat, T. Cook, Davies, Edwards, Fish, Flagg, Flood, Foley, Geier, Gorlinski, Gaidry, Henderson, Howes, Howell, Mann, Morris, E. Murphy, Newell, Normand, Ong, J. Purcell, S. Pursell, Smith, Stocker, Taliaferro, Terry, Thorpe, Wenck, Wells, Wilson—35.

En conséquence, la motion prévaut et le président déclare la Convention ajournée à demain à midi.

Approuvé.

JOHN E. NEELIS,
Secrétaire.

MERCREDI, le 29 juin 1864.

La Convention se réunit conformément à l'ajournement, et est appelée à l'ordre par le président.

A l'appel du rôle, les membres suivants répondent à leurs noms :

MM. Austin, Balch, Barrett, Beauvais, Baum, Bell, Bofill, Buckley, Burke, Collin, Campbell, Cazabat, J. K. Cook, T. Cook, Crozat, Davies, Dufresne, Duane, Decker, Duke, Dupaty, Edwards, Flagg, Fish, Flood, Foley, Fosdick, Fuller, Geier, Gastinel, Gorlinski, Gruneberg, Gaidry, Healy, Harnan, Hart, Henderson, Hills, Hire, Howell, Howes, Kavanagh, Maas, Mann, Maurer, Mendiverri, Montamat, Morris, Mayer, E. Murphy, M. W. Murphy, Newell, Normand, O'Conner, Orr, J. Payne, J. T. Paine, Pintado, Poynot, J. Purcell, S. Pursell, Schroeder, Schnurr, Shaw, Smith, Stocker, Stumpf, Stiner, Sullivan, Taliaferro, Terry, Thorpe, Waters, Wells, Wilson.

Absents :

MM. Abell (excusé), Ariail, Bonzano, Bennie, Bromley, Brott, Cutler, Ennis (excusés), Heard, Knobloch (excusés), Kugler (excusé), Lobdell, Millspaugh, Montague,

Ong, Seymour (excusés), Stauffer (excusé), Thomas et Wenck.

D'après motion, MM. Abell et Seymour sont excusés, ainsi que M. Spellicy.

Le journal d'hier est lu et adopté.

M. Fosdick propose la suspension des réglements, à l'effet de corriger une erreur dans le rapport du comité sur le Département Législatif.

M. Howell, de la part du comité spécial sur l'Education Publique, soumet un rapport de la majorité.

MM. Beauvais et Sullivan soumettent un rapport de la minorité, de la part du comité sur l'Education Publique.

M. Flagg, pour le comité des Cédules, soumet un rapport de la majorité.

M. Gruneberg, de la part du même comité, soumet le rapport de la minorité.

M. Shaw, président du comité d'Ordonnance, soumet son rapport.

Sur la prise en considération du rapport de M. Gruneberg, pour la minorité du comité des Cédules, M. Wilson propose le dépôt sur le bureau, sans lecture.

La motion est rejetée.

M. Shaw propose de suspendre les réglements, à l'effet d'amender le rapport du comité pour le Département Législatif, savoir, en ajoutant:

Il y aura aussi une session de l'Assemblée Générale dans la ville de la Nouvelle-Orléans, le 1er lundi du mois d'octobre 1864, et il sera du devoir du gouverneur, aussitôt que possible, après l'acceptation de la constitution, d'ordonner une élection de membres pour l'Assemblée Générale, dans toutes les paroisses où il y aura sécurité pour les électeurs, et dans toutes les autres paroisses ou districts. L'élection devra se faire lorsqu'il y aura possibilité pour remplir les vacances de ces mêmes paroisses ou districts, dans l'Assemblée Générale.

L'expiration de la première Assemblée Générale aura lieu, comme si les membres avaient été élus, le 1er lundi de novembre 1863.

L'amendement de M. Stocker est adopté par un vote assis et levé, donnant. oui, 46 ; non, 20.

M. Hills, avec permission de la Convention, présente la résignation suivante de M. Bailey :

A MM. le Président et Membres
    de la Convention constitutionnelle :

Messieurs—Mon objection sur l'Art.—— du rapport sur les mesures générales, relative à l'extension de la liberté du vote pour toutes personnes, sans distinction de race ou de couleur, sous certaines conditions spécifiées, est telle que je ne puis consciencieusement signer la constitution dans laquelle se trouve compris l'article qui a fait le sujet de votre vote d'hier. En conséquence je vous prie très respectueusement de vouloir bien accepter ma résignation comme membre de votre honorable corps.

Respectueusement, &c.,
A. BAILEY.

Nouvelle-Orléans, le 29 juin 1864.

Un vote par assis et levé donne comme résultat oui, 54, non, 14.

La résignation est acceptée.

M. Howell propose de suspendre les réglements pour la prise en considération des rapports de la majorité et de la minorité des comités sur l'Education Publique.

Rejeté.

La motion de suspendre les réglements pour prendre en considération la majorité et la minorité des rapports du comité sur les Cédules, est rejetée.

M. Foley propose de suspendre les réglements, à l'effet de prendre en considération le rapport du comité sur les Ordonnances.

Rejeté.

M. Beauvais propose de reconsidérer le vote refusant de suspendre les réglements pour la prise en considération des rapports des comités sur l'Education.

Rejeté.

La Convention s'ajourne alors, à demain à midi.

Approuvé   JOHN E. NEELIS.
                      Secrétaire.

JEUDI, le 30 juin 1864.

La Convention se réunit conformément à l'ajournement.

L'honorable E. H. Durell, président, au fauteuil.

A l'appel du rôle, les membres suivants répondent à leurs noms :

MM. Abell, Austin, Balch, Barrett, Baum, Beauvais, Bell, Bennie, Bofill, Buckley, Burke, Campbell, Cazabat, Collin, J. K. Cook, T. Cook, Crozat, Cutler, Davies, Duane, Dufresne, Duke, Dupaty, Decker, Edwards, Ennis, Fish, Flagg, Flood, Foley, Fosdick, Fuller, Gastinel, Geier, Gorlinski, Gruneberg, Gaidry, Healy, Harnan, Hart, Heard, Henderson, Hills, Howell, Howes, Kavanagh, Knobloch, Mayer, Maas, Mann, Maurer, Mendiverri, Montamat, Morris, E.

après le mot "organisation" dans la quatrième ligne.

Une motion de déposer est faite et repoussée par un vote par assis et levé, de 32 oui et 33 non.

M. Cutler fait la motion d'amender la motion de M. Gorlinski, en ajoutant après le mot "organisation" les mots "et maintien," laquelle est acceptée par M. Gorlinski, et sa motion ainsi amendée est adoptée.

L'article 4 est adopté tel qu'il a été amendé.

Les articles 5 et 6 sont lus séparément et adoptés.

Sur motion de M. Waters, la Convention s'ajourne par un vote assis et levé de 43 oui et 33 non.

Approuvé,
JOHN E. NEELIS.
Secrétaire.

VENDREDI, le 1er juillet 1864.

La Convention se réunit conformément à l'ajournement. Le secrétaire fait appel du rôle, et les membres suivants répondent à leurs nosm :

MM. Abell, Austin, Balch, Barrett, Baum, Beauvais, Bell, Bennie, Buckley, Burke, Campbell, Cazabat, J. K. Cook, T. Cook, Crozat, Cutler, Collin, Davies, Dufresne, Duane, Decker, Duke, Ennis, Fish, Flagg, Flood, Foley, Fosdick, Fuller, Gastinel, Geier, Gorlinski, Gruneberg, Gaidry, Healy, Harnan, Hart, Henderson, Hills, Hire, Howell, Howes, Kavanagh, Knobloch, Maas, Mann, Maurer, Mendiverri, Montamat, Morris, E. Murphy, M. W. Murphy, Mayer, O'Conner, Orr, Newell, Normand, Ong, J. Payne, J. T. Paine, Pintado, Poynot, J. Purcell, S. Purcell, Schroeder, Schnurr, Seymour, Shaw, Smith, Spellicy, Stocker, Stumpf, Stiner, Stauffer, Sullivan, Taliaferro, Terry, Thorpe, Waters, Wenck, Wells, Wilson.

Absents, onze membres.

Les minutes d'hier sont lues et adoptées.

Sur la motion de M. Crozat, M. Bofill est excusé.

Le rapport du comité spécial sur l'Education étant à l'ordre du jour, est pris en considération.

Le rapport de la minorité de M. Beauvais sur l'article 1er est lu.

M. Sullivan propose l'amendement suivant :

Insérer le mot "blanc" entre les mots "tous" et "enfants" et ajouter les mots "et toutes les écoles particulières de toutes les dénominations, dont le chiffre sera de plus de 200 élèves, seront considérées comme écoles publiques."

M. Smith propose de retrancher le mot "blanc" dans l'amendement de M. Sullivan; sur cette question l'appel par oui et non a lieu, et donne le résultat suivant :

Affirmative :

MM. Abell, Balch, Barrett, Baum, Buckley, Campbell, J. K. Cook, Crozat, Collin, Dufresne, Decker, Duke, Edwards, Gastinel, Geier, Gruneberg, Hart, Heard, Kavanagh, Knobloch, Maurer, Mendiverri, Montamat, Morris, M. W. Murphy, Mayer, Maas, O'Conner, Poynot, J. Purcell, S. Purcell, Stocker, Sullivan, Waters, Wenck—35.

Négative :

MM. Austin, Beauvais, Bell, Bennie, Burke, Cazabat, T. Cook, Davies, Duane, Dupaty, Ennis, Fish, Flagg, Foley, Flood, Fosdick, Gorlinski, Gaidry, Healy, Harnan, Henderson, Hills, Hire, Howell, Howes, Mann, E. Murphy, Newell, Normand, J. Payne, J. T. Paine, Pintado, Schroeder, Schnurr, Seymour, Shaw, Smith, Spellicy, Stumpf, Stiner, Stauffer, Taliaferro, Terry, Wells, Wilson—45.

La motion du dépôt sur le bureau, est en conséquence rejetée. Sur la question d'adopter la motion de retrancher, l'appel par oui et non, donne le résultat suivant :

Affirmative :

MM. Austin, Bell, Bennie, Burke, Cazabat, T. Cook, Collin, Davies, Duane, Dupaty, Ennis, Flagg, Flood, Foley, Fosdick, Gorlinski, Henderson, Hills, Hire, Howell, Howes, Mann, E. Murphy, Newell, Normand, J. Payne, J. T. Paine, Pintado, Schroeder, Shaw, Smith, Stumpf, Stiner, Stauffer, Taliaferro, Terry, Wenck, Wells, Wilson—39.

Négative :

MM. Abell, Balch, Barrett, Beauvais, Baum, Buckley, Campbell, J. K. Cook, Crozat, Cutler, Dufresne, Decker, Duke, Edwards, Fish, Gastinel, Geier, Gruneberg, Gaidry, Healy, Harnan, Hart, Heard, Kavanagh, Knobloch, Maas, Maurer, Mendiverri, Montamat, Morris, M. W. Murphy, Mayer, O'Conner, Poynot, J. Purcell, S. Purcell, Schnurr, Seymour, Stocker, Sullivan, Waters—41.

La motion de retrancher est en conséquence rejetée.

M. Henderson propose l'amendement suivant :

Pourvu, Qu'aucune religion, ni aucune doctrine de secte religieuse, ne sera enseignée dans les écoles publiques.

Murphy, M. W. Murphy, Normand, Orr, O'Conner, Ong, J. Payne, J. T. Paine, Pintado, Poynot, J. Purcell, S. Pursell, Shaw, Schroeder, Schnurr, Seymour, Spellicy, Smith, Stocker, Stumpf, Stiner, Stauffer, Sullivan, Taliaferro, Terry, Thorpe. Waters, Wenck, Wells, Wilson—86.

Absents :
MM. Ariail, Bonzano, Brott, Lobdell, Millspaugh, Montague et Thomas ; MM Newell et Kugler sont excusés.

Les minutes d'hier sont lues et adoptées.

Sur motion de M. Montamat, l'absence de M. Heard est excusée, étant engagé à remplir ses fonctions comme juge de district dans la paroisse d'Est Bâton-Rouge.

Sur motion de M. Wells, messieurs Normand et Newell sont également excusés.

Les rapports de la majorité et de la minorité du comité spécial sur l'Education étant à l'ordre du jour ils sont mis aux débats.

Le rapport de la minorité présenté par M. Sullivan est lu.

M. Howell fait la motion d'amender l'article 1, en effaçant le mot "deux" dans la econde ligne et insérant le mot "quatre."

Adopté.

M. Terry fait la motion d'amender le dit article en effaçant à la troisième et quatrième lignes les mots "telles compensations que la Législature pourrait fixer," et insérant les mots "un salaire de quatre mille piastres par an."

Sur motion de M. Montamat, l'amendement de M. Terry est déposé sur la table.

M. S. Pursell offre le substitut suivant :

Art.—Il sera élu un Surintendant de l'Education Publique, qui restera en fonctions pendant quatre ans. Ses devoirs seront prescrits et ses appointements fixés par l'Assemblée Générale.

M. Montamat fait la motion de le déposer sur la table.

Adopté.

L'article 1 est alors adopté tel qu'il est amendé.

L'article 2 est lu.

M. Davies propose qu'il soit rejeté.

M. Henderson offre l'amendement suivant :

Pourvu qu'aucuns principes religieux ne soient enseignés dans les Ecoles Publiques de l'Etat.

M. Smith fait la motion d'effacer après le mot "approprié" dans la huitième ligne.

M. Austin offre l'amendement suivant pour être ajouté audit article :

Pourvu, Que la Législature ne fasse aucune allocation spéciale pour le maintien et support de telles associations, après qu'elles auront été reconnues comme écoles publiques.

La question revient alors sur la motion de rejet de M. Davies, l'appel nominal est demandé et donne le résultat suivant :

Affirmative :

MM. Abell, Austin, Balch, Baum, Beauvais, Bofill, Buckley, Campbell, Crozat, Cutler, Collin, Davies, Dufresne, Dupaty, Decker, Duke, Edwards, Ennis, Flood, Gastinel, Gruneberg, Gaidry, Hart, Howell, Kavanagh, Knobloch, Maas, Maurer, Mendiverri, Mayer, Morris, Normand, Ong, J. Payne, Pintado, Poynot, S. Pursell, Schnurr, Schroeder, Shaw, Stumpf, Stauffer, Taliaferro, Wenck, Wells—46.

Négative :

MM. Barrett, Bell, Bennie. Burke, J. K. Cook, T. Cook, Duane, Fish, Foley, Fosdick, Fuller, Gorlinski, Healy, Harnan, Heard, Henderson, Hills, Howes, Mann, E. Murphy, M. W. Murphy, O'Conner, Orr, J. T. Paine, J. Purcell, Smith, Spellicy, Stocker, Stiner, Sullivan, Terry, Thorpe. Waters et Wilson—34.

L'article 2 du substitut de M. Sullivan est en conséquence rejeté.

L'article 3 est adopté.

L'article 4 est lu.

M. Smith propose d'effacer les mots "Nouvelle-Orléans," et insérer à leurs places les mots "tels lieux qui pourront être fixés par la Législature."

Aucune décision n'est prise sur ce sujet.

M. Stauffer offre le substitut suivant :

Art 3. Une université sera établie et maintenue, composé de trois départements, à savoir : département des lois, département médical et département du collège. comprenant ainsi le Séminaire d'Instruction de l'Etat.

M. Sullivan fait la motion de déposer le substitut sur la table.

Un vote par assis et levé est pris sur cette motion et donne comme résultat 37 oui et 37 non.

Les voix étant également partagées, le président vote dans l'affirmative.

Le substitut de M. Stauffer est en conséquence déposé sur la table, et l'article 4 du substitut de M. Sullivan est pris de nouveau.

M. Gorlinski propose de tout effacer

ET L'AMENDEMENT DE LA CONSTITUTION DE LA LOUISIANE.

M. Montamat offre le substitut suivant :

Art. 3.—L'Assemblée Générale établira des écoles publiques dans tout l'Etat, pour les enfants blancs seulement, et pourvoira au maintien de ces écoles, par une taxe générale sur les propriétés ou de toute autre manière, et l'argent ainsi prélevé sera distribué en proportion du nombre des enfants de tels ou tels âges, ainsi qu'il sera fixé par l'Assemblée Générale.

Sur la motion de M. Duane, le substitut a été déposé sur le bureau par suite du vote suivant :

Affirmative :

MM. Austin, Bell, Bennie, Burke, Cazabat, T. Cook, Collin, Duane, Ennis, Fish, Flood, Foley, Fosdick, Flagg, Gorlinski, Gaidry, Healy, Harnan, Henderson, Hills, Hire, Howell, Howes, Mann, E. Murphy, Newell, Normand, J. Payne, J. T. Paine, Piutado, Poynot, Schroeder, Shaw, Smith, Spellicy, Stumpf, Stiner, Taliaferro, Terry, Wenck, Wells, Wilson—42.

Négative :

MM. Abell, Balch, Barrett, Baum, Beauvais, Buckley, Campbell, J. K. Cook, Crozat, Cutler, Davies, Dufresne, Decker, Duke, Edwards, Gastinel, Geier, Gruneberg, Hart, Heard, Kavanagh, Knobloch, Maas, Maurer, Mendiverri, Montamat, Morris, Mayer, M. W. Murphy, O'Conner, J. Purcell, S. Pursell, Schnurr, Seymour, Stocker, Stauffer, Sullivan, Waters—38.

M. Terry offre le substitut suivant :

Art. 1.—La Législature pourvoira à l'établissement d'écoles publiques dans tout l'Etat, et ces écoles seront supportées par des taxes sur les propriétés ou autrement, imposées sur les personnes blanches ; l'argent qui en proviendra sera distribué dans chaque paroisse en proportion du nombre des enfants blancs de tels ou tels âges.

Des écoles publiques seront aussi organisées dans tout l'Etat pour les enfants de couleur, et toutes les personnes de couleur seront taxées pour leur support.

Le substitut de M. Terry est adopté sans opposition.

Le rapport de la majorité et de la minorité du comité sur les Cédules est alors pris en considération pour la deuxième lecture.

Le rapport de la minorité de M. Gruneberg est lu, et sur motion de M. Hills, le dépôt sur le bureau a lieu.

Le rapport de la majorité est alors lu, M. Gruneberg en propose le dépôt sur le bureau.

Rejeté.

L'article 1er est lu et adopté.

L'article 2 est lu.

M. Henderson propose l'amendement suivant, lequel est déposé sur le bureau :

Pourvu, Que toutes les personnes qui seraient maintenant chargées d'une offense criminelle ou qui pourraient l'être avant l'adoption de la constitution par le peuple, seront mises en liberté en fournissant des sécurités solvables, avant et après la conviction, aussitôt que cette Convention, par la signature de ses membres, aura préparé la constitution pour son adoption comme il a été dit ci-dessus.

Pourvu, Qu'aucune mise en liberté sous caution n'ait lieu dans un cas capital, lorsque la preuve est évidente ou la présomption grande.

L'article 2 est alors adopté.

Les articles 3 et 4 sont lus séparément et adoptés.

M. Howell présente alors les articles additionnels suivants :

Art. 5. Les nominations aux emplois par le Pouvoir Exécutif sous la constitution, seront faites par le gouverneur et les élections d'après son autorité.

Art. 6. Le terme de service pour tous les officiers choisis par le peuple à la première élection sous cette constitution, se terminera comme si l'élection avait eu lieu le premier lundi de novembre 1863, et comme si leurs devoirs avaient commencé à cette époque. La première classe des sénateurs désignée dans l'article——, siègera jusqu'au jour de la clôture des élections générales en novembre 1865, et la deuxième classe jusqu'au jour des élections générales en novembre 1867.

Les articles additionnels de M. Howell sont lus séparément et déposés sur le bureau. Le rapport est alors adopté dans son ensemble, d'après la deuxième lecture.

Le rapport du comité sur les Ordonnances est alors pris en mains pour la deuxième lecture.

Les articles 1er et 2e sont lus séparément et adoptés.

Après lecture de l'article 3, M. Thorpe présente le substitut suivant :

Les officiers de l'Etat élus le 22 février 1864, maintiendront leurs sièges jusqu'au 2e lundi de janvier 1866, et l'élection de leurs successeurs aura lieu le 1er lundi de novembre 1865, à moins qu'il n'en soit autrement décidé par la loi.

Dépôt sur le bureau.

M. Baum présente le substitut suivant :

Les officiers de l'Etat élus le 22 février 1864, garderont leurs offices pour les termes assignés aux dits officiers dans cette constitution, mais ce terme expirera comme si leur installation avait eu lieu le 2e lundi de janvier 1864.

La question première demandée par M Montamat est rejetée.

M. Fosdick présente le substitut suivant :

Dans le cas où cette constitution serait acceptée par le peuple, il sera du devoir du gouverneur de publier immédiatement une proclamation ordonnant aux divers officiers de l'Etat, autorisés par la loi, de tenir une élection (ou à défaut de ceux-ci, tous autres qu'il désignera), aux lieux désignés par la loi, le même jour où l'élection pour les membres de l'Assemblée Générale, a été ordonnée par l'article 3 du rapport du comité du Département Législatif, pour les nominations du gouverneur, lieutenant-gouverneur, le secrétaire d'Etat, l'avocat-général, le trésorier, l'auditeur, et tous les officiers élus par le peuple sous cette constitution ; ladite élection dirigée et les rapports faits comme il a été pourvu dans le 2e article précédent. Le gouverneur et le lieutenant-gouverneur prendront possession de leurs offices pendant la première semaine de la session de l'Assemblée-Générale, ainsi qu'il a été ordonné par le département législatif de cette constitution et tous les autres officiers ainsi élus, seront immédiatement commissionnés par le gouverneur, et tiendront leurs offices comme il a été pourvu dans cette constitution.

Sur la motion de M. Smith, le substitut de M. Fosdick est rejeté.

M. Shaw propose de retrancher dans la 5e ligne les mots "les officiers de l'Etat" et d'insérer "pour gouverneur, lieutenant-gouverneur, le secrétaire d'Etat, l'auditeur des comptes publics, le trésorier, l'avocat-général et le surintendant des écoles publiques."

Adopté.

L'article 3, ainsi amendé, est alors adopté par le vote suivant :

Affirmative :

MM. Abell, Austin, Balch, Barrett, Baum, Beauvais, Bell, Bennie, Buckley, Collin, Cazabat, J. K. Cook, T. Cook, Crozat, Cutler, Davies, Decker, Dufresne, Duane, Edwards, Ennis, Fish, Flagg, Flood, Foley, Fuller, Geier, Gorlinski, Gaidry, Healy, Harnan, Hart, Heard, Henderson, Hire, Howes, Maas, Maurer, Mendiverri, Montamat, E. Murphy, M. W. Murphy, Newell, Normand, O'Conner, J. Payne, Pintado, Poynot, J. Purcell, S. Pursell, Schroeder, Schnurr, Seymour, Shaw, Smith, Spellicy, Stocker, Stiner, Stumpf, Stauffer, Sullivan, Terry, Taliaferro, Thorpe, Wenck, Wells—66.

Négative :

MM. Burke, Campbell, Duke, Dupaty, Fosdick, Gastinel, Gruneberg, Hills, Howell, Knobloch, Mann, Mayer, Morris, J. T. Paine, Waters—15.

L'article 4 est alors pris en mains et lu.

M. Campbell propose d'amender en ajoutant le mot "allemand."

M. Healy propose de retrancher le mot "français"

M. Shaw propose d'amender en insérant après le mot "dans" dans la deuxième ligne, les mots "deux journaux, et dans un journal publié dans la langue allemande, les journaux choisis par le président de la Convention."

La motion de M. Foley est alors prise en mains et le dépôt en est fait sur le bureau.

La motion d'ajourner, par M. Austin, est rejetée par le vote suivant :

Oui :

MM. Austin, Balch, Burke, Collin, Duke, Dupaty, Edwards, Fosdick, Gorlinski, Healy, Harnan, Kavanagh, Normand, J. Purcell, Terry, Waters, Wells—17.

Non:

MM. Abell, Barrett, Baum, Beauvais, Bell, Bennie, Buckley, Campbell, Cazabat, J. K. Cook, T. Cook, Crozat, Cutler, Davies, Dufresne, Duane, Decker, Ennis, Fish, Flagg, Flood, Foley, Gastinel, Geier, Gruneberg, Gaidry, Hart, Heard, Henderson, Hills, Hire, Howell, Howes, Knobloch, Maas, Mann, Maurer, Mendiverri, Montamat, Morris, E. Murphy, M. W. Murphy, Mayer, Newell, O'Conner, Ong, J. Payne, J. T. Paine, Pintado, Poynot, S. Pursell, Schroeder, Schnurr, Seymour, Shaw, Smith, Spollicy, Stocker, Stumpf, Stiner, Stauffer, Sullivan, Taliaferro, Thorpe, Wenck, Wilson —66.

M. Montamat offre le substitut suivant :

Cette constitution sera publiée en anglais dans l'*Era* et dans le journal officiel de cette Convention ; et en français dans l'*Abeille* de la Nouvelle-Orléans.

Dépôt sur le bureau par un vote par assis et levé donnant pour résultat : oui 42, non 27.

L'amendement de M. Shaw est alors adopté.

M. Howell présente l'article additionnel suivant :

Art. 5. A l'élection pour l'adoption ou le rejet de cette constitution. il y aura dans chaque bureau d'élection une boîte de ballot additionnelle, dans laquelle sera déposé le vote de chaque votant, et sur laquelle sera écrit : "L'Ordonnance d'Emancipation acceptée" ou "L'Ordonnance d'Emancipation rejetée," et si ladite ordonnance est adoptée, elle fera partie de la constitution de l'Etat, et sera insérée comme le 1er et le 2e article des Mesures Générales.

Sur motion du dépôt sur le bureau de l'article additionnel, le oui et non est demandé et donne le résultat suivant :

Affirmative :

MM. Abell, Burke, Barrett, Bell, Bennie, Cazabat, J. K. Cook, T. Cook, Collin, Decker, Davies, Duane, Edwards, Ennis, Flagg, Flood, Foley, Geier, Gorlinski, Gaidry, Healy, Harnan, Henderson, Hills, Hire, Howes, Maurer, Maas, Morris, E. Murphy, M. W. Murphy, Newell, Normand, O'Conner, J. Payne, J. T. Paine, Pintado, Poynot, J. Purcell, S. Pursell, Schroeder, Schnurr, Shaw, Smith, Spellicy, Stocker, Stumpf, Stiner, Stauffer, Taliaferro, Terry, Thorpe, Wells—53.

Négative :

MM. Austin, Balch, Beauvais, Baum, Buckley, Campbell, Crozat, Cutler, Dufresne, Duke, Fish, Fosdick, Gastinel, Gruneberg, Hart, Heard, Howell, Kavanagh, Knobloch, Mann, Mayer, Mendiverri, Montamat, Ong, Seymour, Sullivan, Wilson, Waters, Wenck—29.

L'article de M. Howell est conséqemment déposé sur le bureau.

Le rapport ainsi amendé est alors adopté dans son ensemble après sa 2e lecture.

La Convention s'ajourne.

Approuvé.

JOHN E. NEELIS,
Secretairé.

SAMEDI, le 2 juillet 1864.

La Convention se réunit conformément à l'ajournement.

Sont présents : l'Hon. E. H. Durell. président, et les membres dont les noms suivent:

MM. Abell, Austin, Balch, Barrett, Baum, Beauvais, Bell, Bennie, Bofill, Buckley, Burke, Campbell, Cazabat, J. K. Cook, T. Cook, Crozat, Cutler, Collin, Davies, Dufresne, Decker, Duke, Duane, Dupaty, Edwards, Ennis, Fish, Flagg, Flood, Foley, Fosdick, Gastinel, Geier, Gorlinski, Gruneberg, Gaidry, Healy, Harnan, Hart, Heard, Henderson, Hills, Hire, Howell, Howes, Kavanagh, Knobloch, Maas, Mann, Maurer, Mendiverri, Montamat, Morris, E. Murphy, M. W. Murphy, Mayer, Newell, Normand, O'Conner, Orr, Ong, J. Payne, J. T. Paine, Pintado, Poynot, J. Purcell, S. Pursell, Schroeder, Schnurr, Seymour, Shaw, Smith, Spellicy, Stocker, Stumpf, Stiner, Stauffer, Sullivan, Taliaferro, Terry, Thorpe, Waters, Wenck, Wells, Wilson.

Les minutes d'hier sont lues et adoptées.

Sur la motion de M. Wells, M. Gaidry est excusé.

M. Orr est excusé pour son absence d'hier.

M. Montamat présente la pétition suivante, et l'accompagne de la résolution suivante :

*A MM. le Président et Membres
de la Convention constitutionnelle :*

Messieurs—Les soussignés résidant dans le faubourg Trémé, second district de la ville de la Nouvelle-Orléans, prient votre honorable corps de passer une ordonnance obligeant les autorités de la ville à faire construire aussitôt que possible, dans la rue Galvez, sur le canal Carondelet, un pont exactement semblable à celui qui existe déjà sur ledit canal, dans la rue Broad. Les avantages devant résulter de cette construction seront immenses pour le grand nombre de personnes qui résident dans cette partie de la ville, en leur facilitant les moyens de suppléer aux besoins de leurs familles au marché Trémé, — l'amélioration que demande vos pétitionnaires abrégeant la distance de près d'un mille, et ouvrant aussi une communication directe avec le premier et le troisième districts.

Le tout est soumis respectueusement à votre honorable corps.

Nouvelle-Orléans, le 28 juin 1864.

John Murphy,	Ruston Newlove,
John Fisher,	Henry Gallew,
John Siegenthaler,	Joseph Upulte,
Antonie Ramusat,	Heinriez Scheu tse,
Nicholaris Frietsch,	Pinna Clément'
Karl Steitz,	Hugh Doherty,
J. Neuhauser,	Ths. Oberyefell,
F. Aufenkolk,	A. Beaise,
Peter Leind,	J. Baldwin,
S. Joseph,	Valentine Rothany,
Ph. Schindler,	S. Shmizer,
E. Hacker,	Jos. Muller,
Peter Freibert,	Burgard Torer,
George Woerney,	Daniel Sheply,
P. Kerwann,	Chas. J. Lester,
S. Kaller,	Wm. Graham,
Fr. Robert,	F. Goulemus,
O. Noack,	Wm. C. Harrison,
Adam Spies,	John Koepfer,
Mme E. H. Behan.	James Woulfe,
Cassimer Glade,	Freedolin Hesty,
J. W. Bailey,	John Foley,
John Henneberg,	Jeremiah Ryan,
Herry Leebis,	William Myhar,
Hte. Demoreulle,	Henry Stward,
Ernest Demoreulle,	C. Winketsmann,
J.‡Demoreulle,	Paul,
D. Barker,	John Funk,
Pat. Killea,	Peter Funk,

Larins McDonell,
Felix M. Jacobs,
Joseph Fisher,
William Rouke,
Garret Kirwan,
Francis Cullen,
James Cullen,
P. Deverges,
James Lilly,
Caarles Lawson,
Ph. Hoffmann,
E. Graeser,
John McWittie,
T. Kiphaut,
Joseph Gros,
M. Bourlett,
M. Fritz,
L. Latto,
Klofot,
Pour,
G. P. Lombard,
D. Laborde,
K. Burkert,
John Schondardt,
P. W. Sheridan,
C. Murphy,
J. Rolling,
H. Rolling,
Ch. Rolling,
S. Oswald,
Ths. Killea,
P. Grant,
Morris Hiccey,
F. A. Siener,
John Poley,
Mike Byrne,
Dane Byrne,
James Dunn,
P. Mofit,
John Cavanagh,
Tary Murphy,
J. Warner,
Laurence Rinney,
S. Roman,
A. Garrer,
Conrad Brand,
D. Constantine,
A. Herbee,
W. Graff,

M. Christotfell,
M. Halbritter,
J. Relin,
M. Conway,
Henry Jollissaint,
N. Chenal,
Dennis Murphy,
John P. Montamat,
George Merz,
George Eikz,
Michael Schally,
Adam Kurtmann,
B. Camet,
Wolf Shreber,
Conrad Graff,
S. Lacost,
Murtz Coners,
Barney Kelley,
John Coner,
James Butler,
Mrs Filsgerliol,
Ed. Blust,
A. Schamber,
G. Doll,
Patrick Burke,
Raynol Auguste,
Edward Moran,
L. C. Preston,
James Fallon,
Alexander Lea,
John T. Ives,
John Fisher,
John Buckley, Jr.,
Jas. A. Mourton,
Vor. Hébert, Jr.,
M. O'Donnell,
Louis Brevier,
Conrad Murlsnur,
Ge. Bilher-Barb,
B. Lanabere,
Jacob Eichhorn,
J. B. Henry,
Abrusir Storck,
John Orth,
Joseph Henry,
Louis Koch,
T. F. Kavanagh,
Ernest J. Wenck,
Henry Boeylin.

Résolu, Que la Législature dans sa première session passera un acte, par lequel les autorités de la ville de la Nouvelle-Orléans s'engageront à faire bâtir, aussitôt que possible, dans la rue Galvez, sur le Canal Carondelet, un pont exactement semblable à celui qui existe sur le dit canal dans la rue Broad.

Sur la motion de M. Wells, la pétition et la résolution sont déposées sur le bureau par suite d'un vote par assis et levé, donnant pour résultat : oui, 46, non, 23.

M. Hills, président du comité spécial sur les Institutions Charitables, soumet le rapport suivant :

A M. le Président et à MM. les Membres de la Convention constitutionnelle de la Louisiane:

Messieurs—Les membres soussignés de votre comité sur les institutions charitables vous soumettent respectueusement le rapport suivant :

Que, en vue de la destitution immense qui existe dans cette communauté, et du manque complet de ressources pour subvenir aux besoins des diverses institutions charitables, ils sont d'opinion que des secours doivent être alloués par votre honorable corps, et en conséquence recommande l'adoption de ce qui suit :

Résolu, Qu'une somme de 35.000 dollars sera, et est appropriée par le trésor de l'Etat pour des mesures charitables ; cette somme sera distribuée par un comité d'Aumôniers ; nommé par le gouverneur, et composé de cinq citoyens dont trois constitueront le quorum pour transiger les affaires. Le gouverneur de l'Etat sera président *ex-officio* du comité, les sommes seront prélevées par ses ordres, contresignés par le secrétaire du comité.

Le tout respectueusement soumis,
ALFRED C. HILLS, président.
JOHN SULLIVAN,
W. T. STOCKER,
CHARLES SMITH.

M. Beauvais demande le dépôt sur le bureau.

Sur cette motion, l'appel par oui et non a lieu, et donne le résultat suivant :

Affirmative :

MM. Burke, Collin, Cazabat, Davies, Decker, Duke, Dupaty, Ennis, Flagg, Howell, Knobloch, Normand, J. T. Paine, Wenck, Wells—15.

Négative :

MM. Abell, Austin, Barrett, Baum, Beauvais, Bell, Bennie, Bofill, Buckley, J. K. Cook, T. Cook, Cutler, Dufresne, Duane, Edwards, Fish, Flood, Foley, Fosdick, Gastinel, Geier, Gorlinski, Gruneberg, Healy, Harnan, Hart, Heard, Henderson, Hills, Hire, Howes, Kavanagh, Maas, Mann, Maurer, Mendiverri, Montamat, Morris, Mayer, E. Murphy, M. W. Murphy, Newell, O'Conner, Orr, J. Payne, Poynot, J. Purcell, S. Pursell, Schroeder, Schnurr, Shaw, Smith, Spellicy, Stumpf, Stiner, Stauffer, Sullivan, Taliaferro, Terry, Thorpe, Waters, Wilson—62.

En conséquence, la motion du dépôt sur le bureau est rejetée.

M. Cazabat offre l'amendement suivant :

Pourvu, Que cette appropriation dans un but charitable s'applique aux réfugiés malheureux de l'Union dans la Louisiane, et aux veuves et orphelins des soldats de

ET L'AMENDEMENT DE LA CONSTITUTION DE LA LOUISIANE.

l'Union qui ont perdu la vie au service de l'armée des Etats-Unis.

Dépôt sur le bureau.

M. Smith propose l'adoption du rapport et de la résolution ; l'appel du oui et non a lieu et donne le résultat suivant :

Affirmative :

MM. Abell, Austin, Barrett, Baum, Beauvais, Bell, Bennie, Bofill, Buckley, J. K. Cook, T. Cook, Crozat, Cutler. Decker, Dufresne, Duane, Edwards, Fish, Flood, Fosdick, Gastinel, Geier, Gorlinski, Gruneberg, Healy, Harnan, Hart, Heard, Hills, Henderson, Hire, Howes, Kavanagh, Maas, Mann, Maurer, Mayer, Montamat, Morris, E. Murphy, M. W. Murphy, O'Conner, J. Payne, Poynot, J. Purcell, S. Pursell, Schroeder, Schnurr, Seymour, Shaw, Smith, Spellicy, Stocker, Stumpf, Stiner, Stauffer, Sullivan, Terry, Thorpe, Waters et Wilson—62.

Négative :

MM. Burke, Collin, Cazabat, Davies, Duke, Dupaty, Ennis, Flagg, Howell, Knobloch, Newell, Normand, J. T. Paine, Pintado, Taliaferro, Wells—16.

Le rapport et la résolution sont alors adoptés.

M. Austin demande le rapport du comité Spécial sur le résultat des comptes de l'auditeur public.

M. Hills propose d'en retrancher la lecture et de déposer le tout sur le bureau.

Rejeté.

Lecture est donnée du rapport.

MM. Harnan et Thorpe proposent le dépôt sur le bureau.

Cette motion est rejetée par une division : oui 15, non 45.

M. Abell propose d'ajourner l'affaire d'aujourd'hui en quinze jours.

M. Terry propose le dépôt sur le bureau de la motion de M. Abell.

Une division a lieu et donne pour résultat : oui 32, non 32.

Le vote étant partagé, le président vote pour la négative.

En conséquence, la motion du dépôt sur le bureau est rejetée.

Un vote par assis et levé a lieu sur la motion de M. Abell, résultat . oui, 33 ; non, 39.

La motion est rejetée.

Le rapport est alors adopté par le vote suivant :

Affirmative :

MM. Austin, Barrett, Baum, Beauvais, Bennie, Bofill, Burke, Cazabat, Collin, Crozat, Cutler, Decker, Duke, Duane, Dupaty, Ennis, Fish, Flagg, Foley, Gastinel, Geier, Healy, Hart, Heard, Hire, Howes, Kavanagh, Knobloch, Mann, Mendiverri, Maurer, Morris, Newell, Normand, Orr, O'Conner, J. Payne, J. T. Paine, Pintado, J. Purcell, S. Pursell, Schroeder, Schnurr, Shaw, Spellicy, Stocker, Seymour, Stiner, Stumpf,, Stauffer, Taliaferro, Terry, Thorpe, Wenck, Wells—55.

Négative :

MM. Abell, Bell, Buckley, J. K. Cook, T. Cook, Dufresne, Flood, Fosdick, Gorlinski, Gruneberg, Harnan, Henderson, Hills, Maas, Mayer, Montamat, E. Murphy, M. W. Murphy, Poynot, Sullivan, Waters et Wilson—22.

M. Hills propose d'ajourner à mardi, 5 courant, à midi.

Rejeté par une division donnant pour résultat : oui 28, non 44.

M. Burke propose l'ajournement jusqu'au 11 à midi.

Rejeté sur un vote divisionnel : oui, 35 ; non, 49.

La Convention s'ajourne alors au mercredi suivant, 6 du courant, à midi.

Approuvé.

JOHN E. NEELIS,
Secrétaire.

MERCREDI. le 6 juillet 1864.

La Convention se réunit conformément à l'ajournement ; et en l'absence du président, sur la motion de M. Beauvais, M. Hills est appelé au fauteuil.

Le secrétaire fait l'appel du rôle. Les membres suivants répondent à leurs noms :

MM. Austin, Balch, Barrett, Baum, Beauvais, Bell, Bofill, Bromley, Buckley, Burke, Campbell, Collin, J. K. Cook, T. Cook, Crozat, Cutler, Davies, Dufresne, Duane, Edwards, Ennis, Flood, Foley, Geier, Gorlinski, Gruneberg, Gaidry, Healy, Harnan, Hart, Heard, Hills, Howes, Kavanagh, Knobloch, Maas, Mayer, Mann, Maurer, Mendiverri, Montamat, Morris, E. Murphy, M. W. Murphy, Newell, Normand, O'Conner, J. Payne, J. T. Paine, Pintado, Poynot, J. Purcell, S. Pursell, Schroeder, Schnurr, Shaw, Smith, Spellicy, Stocker, Stumpf, Stiner, Stauffer, Sullivan, Taliaferro, Terry, Wells, Wilson.

Le quorum n'étant pas présent, le sergent-d'armes est envoyé à la recherche des membres absents.

Sur la motion de M. Shaw une suspension

de quinze minutes a lieu ; à l'expiration l'appel se fait à nouveau et donne le résultat suivant :

MM. Austin, Balch, Barrett, Baum, Beauvais, Bell, Bofill, Bromley, Buckley, Burke, Campbell, Collin, J. K. Cook, T. Cook, Crozat, Cutler, Davies, Dufresne, Duane, Edwards, Ennis, Flood, Foley, Fosdick, Fuller, Gastinel, Geier, Gorlinski, Gruneberg, Gaidry, Healy, Harnan, Hart, Heard, Hills, Hire, Howell, Howes, Kavanagh, Knobloch, Maas, Mann, Maurer, Mendiverri, Montamat, Morris, E. Murphy, M. W. Murphy, Mayer, Newell, Normand, O'Conner, J. Payne, J. T. Paine, Pintado, Poynot, J. Purcell, S. Pursell, Schroeder, Schnurr, Shaw, Smith, Spellicy, Stocker, Stumpf, Stiner, Stauffer, Sullivan, Taliaferro, Terry, Wells, Wilson—72.

Absents : M. le président et MM. Abell, Ariail, Bennie, Bonzano, Brott, Cazabat, Decker, Duke, Dupaty, Fish, Flagg, Henderson, Lobdell, Millspaugh, Montague, Ong, Orr, Seymour, Thorpe, Waters, Thomas et Wenck—23.

Il n'y a pas de quorum.

M. Balch propose d'ajourner.

Rejeté par suite d'une division—oui 25, non 33.

Après un délai, le quorum n'ayant pu être formé, sur la motion de M. Smith, la Convention s'ajourne à demain, à midi.

Approuvé.

JOHN E. NEELIS.

JEUDI, le 7 juillet 1864.

La Convention se réunit conformément à l'ajournement.

L'honorable E. H. Durell, président, au fauteuil.

A l'appel du rôle, les membres dont les noms suivent répondent à leurs noms :

MM. Abell, Austin, Balch, Barrett, Baum, Beauvais, Bell, Bennie, Bofill, Bromley, Buckley, Burke, Campbell, Collin, Cazabat, J. K. Cook, T. Cook, Crozat, Cutler, Decker, Davies, Dufresne, Duane, Edwards, Ennis, Fish, Flagg, Flood, Foley, Fosdick, Fuller, Gastinel, Geier, Gorlinski, Gruneberg, Gaidry, Healy, Harnan, Hart, Heard, Henderson, Hills, Hire, Howell, Howes, Kavanagh, Kugler, Knobloch, Maas, Mann, Maurer, Mendiverri, Montamat, Morris, E. Murphy, M. W. Murphy, Newell, Normand, O'Conner, Ong, Orr, J. T. Paine, Pintado, Poynot, J. Purcell, S. Pursell, Schroeder, Schnurr, Seymour, Shaw, Spelicy, Smith, Stocker, Stumpf, Stiner, Stauffer, Sullivan, Taliaferro, Terry, Thorpe, Waters, Wenck, Wells, Wilson—84.

Les minutes de samedi et mercredi sont lues et adoptées.

M. Shaw propose qu'un comité pour les formes et arrangements soit nommé par le président, consistant de cinq membres, avec instructions de classer et numéroter les articles, corriger les erreurs, et d'en faire un rapport imprimé à la Convention.

Cette motion est acceptée.

Le président appointe pour le dit comité MM. Shaw, Thorpe, Henderson, Cazabat et Smith.

Sur la motion de M. Thorpe, M. le président fait partie du dit comité.

M. Smith présente la résolution suivante qui est déposée sur le bureau :

Attendu, Que pendant la présente rébellion des individus, ainsi que diverses corporations des paroisses, ont émis du papier-monnaie de nulle valeur et ont obligé la classe pauvre et loyale de cette communauté à le recevoir dans la circulation, il est

Résolu, Qu'un comité composé de cinq personnes soit nommé pour prendre en considération la nécessité de former un ou des articles pour prévenir le retour de semblables abus, et de s'emparer des propriétés de n'importe quelle nature appartenant soit au mari, soit à la femme, soit aux paroisses ou aux corporations pour la rédemption des dits billets, et que le comité soit aussi autorisé à soumettre à la Convention, pour être approuvé ou rejeté, un projet de pétition à envoyer au Congrès des Etats-Unis, demandant les pouvoirs nécessaires pour obliger les paroisses de l'Etat de la Louisiane à appliquer le produit de la vente des propriétés des citoyens déloyaux à retirer de la circulation le dit papier.

M. Abell propose la reconsidération du vote de vendredi dernier, sur l'article additionnel de M. Howell, concernant la soumission au vote du peuple de l'ordonnance d'Emancipation.

M. Montamat, pour le comité des Finances, soumet le rapport suivant :

Rapport du comité des Finances de la Convention constitutionnelle sur les fonds servant au paiement journalier des membres, salaire des officiers et employés:

1864.

Juin 25—Balance en mains du trésorier de l'Etat.......... $19,074 10
Juillet 2 — Payé le bill No. 81........$2,030 00
Juillet 2 — Payé le bill No. 81........ 2,170 00
Juillet 2 — Payé le bill No. 81........ 2,860 00

ET L'AMENDEMENT DE LA CONSTITUTION DE LA LOUISIANE.

Juillet 2 — Payé le
bill No. 82........ 1,981 00
Juillet 2 — Payé le
bill No. 83....... 1,199 82—$10,240 82

Juillet 5—Balance en
mains $8,806 28
A laquelle somme il
est bon d'ajouter 1,199 82
payée pour le salaire des employés, ce qui proprement appartient au compte de dépenses.

La somme de $2,328 08 étant la balance en mains pour les dépenses càsuelles, a été dépensée, en conséquence ce compte reste à découvert de la somme de $1,199 82, laquelle somme a été employée comme il est dit ci-dessus.

Balance nette en mains, $10,006 10.

M. Montamat soumet la recommandation suivante au nom dudit comité:

La Convention étant sur le point de s'ajourner, votre comité vous recommande respectueusement qu'une compensation soit donnée aux officiers de votre honorable corps dont les noms suivent :
M. J. E. Neelis, $500 00 ; L. O. Moreau, caissier et secrétaire du comité des Finances, $250 00.
Soumis respectuesement.
JOHN P. MONTAMAT,
Président du comité des Finances.
JOHN SULLIVAN.
L P. NORMAND.

M. S. Pursell soumet le rapport suivant du comité sur les Dépenses Casuelles:

A l'honorable Président et MM. les Membres de la Convention constitutionnelle de la Louisiane :

MESSIEURS—Votre comité sur les Dépenses Casuelles, a l'honneur de vous faire connaître que la somme de $25,000, qui avait été votée pour le contingent est épuisée. Il demande une somme en plus de $5,000, et offre la résolution suivante :

Résolu, Qu'une somme de $5,000 sera et est appropriée des fonds généraux de l'Etat, pour subvenir aux dépenses casuelles de cette Convention.
S. PURSELL, président.
JOHN PAYNE,
JOHN A. NEWELL,
JAMES DUANE,
ROBT. B. BELL.

Les réglements sont suspendus et la résolution adoptée.

M. Stauffer se lève sur une question de privilége, et dit qu'il a appris que M. Knobloch n'avait pas voté sur l'ordonnance d'Emancipation, en conséquence, le secrétaire reçoit l'ordre de faire demain un rapport à la Convention des membres qui n'ont pas voté sur cette question.

M. Austin offre la résolution suivante :

Résolu, Que les membres de cette Convention ayant été envoyés à la Convention de Baltimore soient autorisés à recevoir leur *per diem.*

Dépôt sur le bureau.

M. Abell demande la lecture de l'article additionnel de M. Howell, offerte vendredi dernier, sur la motion de reconsidérer, après la lecture.

M. Smith propose le dépôt sur le bureau de reconsidérer la motion.

Adopté par un vote par assis et levé, oui 46, non 27.

La Convention alors résume la deuxième lecture du rapport de la minorité du comité spécial sur l'Education, présenté par M. Sullivan. Le rapport ainsi qu'il a été amendé est lu ; alors M. Terry offre le substitut suivant à l'article 2:

Art. 2. La Législature établira des Ecoles Publiques dans tout l'Etat pour l'éducation des enfants blancs et pourvoira au soutien des dites écoles par une taxe levée sur les propriétés des personnes blanches ; et le montant qui en proviendra sera distribué dans chaque paroisse en proportion des enfants blancs qui y sont, et suivant l'âge ainsi qu'il sera fixé par la loi.

La Législature pourvoira aussi a l'établissement d'écoles publiques dans tout l'Etat, pour l'éducation des enfants de couleur, et pourvoira au soutien des dites écoles par une taxe levée sur les propriétés des personnes de couleur ; et le montant en sera distribué dans chaque paroisse en proportion du nombre d'enfants de couleur, et suivant l'âge ainsi qu'il sera fixé par la loi.

M. Henderson présente le substitut suivant pour celui de M. Terry, savoir :

Art. 2. La Législature prélevera une taxe sur les propriétés des personnes blanches possédant des propriétés dans l'Etat pour subvenir à l'éducation des enfants blancs dans les écoles publiques, et l'argent qui proviendra de cette source, ne pourra avoir une autre destination.

La Législature lèvera une taxe spéciale sur les personnes de couleur dans l'Etat et sur leurs propriétés, à l'effet de subvenir à l'éducation des enfants de couleur dans les écoles publiques. L'argent provenant de cette source, ne pourra être autrement employé.

M. Davies offre comme substitut le premier article du rapport du comité sur la majorité.

Rejeté.

La question est alors mise aux voix pour l'doption du substitut de M. Henderson.

Sur la demande d'une divivion, le substitut est adopté par le vote suivant : oui 50 non 19.

M. Hills offre l'article additionnel suivant :

Tous les établissements sous le nom d'Asile pour orphelins, qui entretiendront plus de 200 élèves, seront considérés comme écoles publiques de l'Etat.

Sur la motion du dépôt sur le bureau, l'appel par oui et non a lieu, et donne le résultat suivant :

Affirmative:

MM. Baum, Beauvais, Burke, Campbell, Collin, Cazabat, J. K. Cook, Decker, Davies, Edwards, Ennis. Flagg, Flood, Gastinel, Geier, Gaidry, Hart, Heard, Hire, Howell, Kavanagh, Kugler, Maas, Mann, Mendiverri, Morris, Newell, Normand, Ong, J. T. Paine, Pintado, S. Pursell, Schroeder, Seymour, Shaw, Stumpf, Taliaferro, Wenck, Wells—39.

Négative :

MM. Abell, Austin, Balch, Barrett, Bell, Bennie, Bofill, Bromley, Buckley, T. Cook, Crozat, Dufresne, Duane, Fish, Foley, Fosdick, Fuller, Gorlinski, Gruneberg, Healy, Harnan, Henderson, Hills, Howes, Knobloch, Maurer, Montamat, M. W. Murphy, O'Conner, Poynot, J. Purcell, Schnurr, Smith, Spellicy, Stocker, Stiner, Stauffer, Orr, Sullivan, Terry, Thorpe, Waters, Wilson—43.

La motion du dépôt sur le bureau est en conséquence rejetée.

M. Cazabat présente le substitut suivant sur l'article de M. Hills, savoir :

Aucune appropriation ne pourra être faite par la Législature pour le support de n'importe quelle école on institution particulières. mais les plus grands encouragements seront donnés aux écoles publiques dans tout l'Etat.

La motion du dépôt sur le bureau est rejetée par un vote par assis et levé, donnant oui 36, non 53.

La motion d'ajourner est faite, et sur l'appel le résultat suivant est donné :

Affirmative :

MM. Buckley, Burke, Edwards, Waters —4.

Négative :

MM. Abell, Austin, Barrett, Bell, Bennie, Bofill, Campbell, Cazabat, J. K. Cook, T. Cook, Crozat, Cutler, Collin, Davies, Dufresne, Duane, Decker, Ennis, Fish, Flagg, Fosdick, Fuller, Gastinel, Geier, Gorlinski, Gruneberg, Gaidry, Healy, Harnan, Hart, Heard, Henderson, Hills, Hire, Howell. Howes, Knobloch, Kugler, Maas, Mann, Mendiverri, Montamat, Morris, M. W. Murphy, Newell, Normand, O'Conner, Ong, Orr, J. T. Paine, Pintado, Poynot, J. Purcell, S. Pursell, Schroeder, Schnurr, Shaw, Smith, Spellicy, Taliaferro, Terry, Wenck, Wells, Wilson—71.

La motion d'ajourner est par conséquent rejetée.

Le substitut de M. Cazabat, est alors adopté par le vote suivant :

Affirmative :

MM. Austin, Bennie, Bofill, Bromley, Burke, Campbell, Cazabat, J. K. Cook, Collin, Davies, Decker, Edwards, Ennis, Fish. Flagg, Flood, Gastinel, Gaidry, Hart, Hire. Heard, Howell, Kugler. Maas, Mann, Maurer, Montamat, Morris, Newell, Normand, Ong, J. T. Paine, Pintado, Poynot, S. Purcell, Schroeder, Shaw, Smith, Spellicy, Stumpf, Stauffer, Taliaferro, Wenck, Wells. Wilson—41.

Négative :

MM. Abell, Barrett, Buckley, T. Cook, Crozat, Cutler, Dufresne, Duane, Foley, Fosdick. Fuller, Geier, Gorlinski, Gruneberg, Gaidry, Healy, Harnan, Henderson, Hills. Howes, Knobloch, M. W. Murphy, O'Conner, Orr, J. Purcell, Schnurr, Stocker, Stiner, Sullivan, Terry, Thorpe, Waters—32.

Le rapport, ainsi qu'il a été amendé, est alors adopté dans son ensemble, à sa seconde lecture par le vote suivant :

Affirmative :

MM. Austin, Barrett, Bell, Bennie, Bromley. Burke, Campbell, Cazabat, J. K. Cook, Davies, Edwards, Ennis, Fish, Flagg, Flood, Gastinel, Geier, Gorlinski, Hart, Henderson, Hills, Hire, Howell, Kugler, Maas, Mann, Maurer, Montamat, Morris, Newell, Normand, Ong, J. T. Paine, S. Purcell, Schroeder, Schnurr, Smith, Stumpf. Stauffer, Taliaferro, Wenck, Wells, Wilson —44.

Négative:

MM. Abell, Bofill, Buckley, T. Cook, Collin, Cutler, Dufresne, Duane, Decker, Foley, Fosdick, Fuller, Gruneberg, Guidry, Healy, Harnan, Heard, Howes, Knobloch, M. W. Murphy, O'Conner, Orr, Pintado, J. Purcell, Shaw, Spellicy, Stocker, Stiner, Sullivan, Terry, Thorpe, Waters—32.

La Convention s'ajourne alors à demain à midi.

Approuvé

JOHN E. NEELIS,
Secrétaire.

ET L'AMENDEMENT DE LA CONSTITUTION DE LA LOUISIANE.   153

VENDREDI, le 8 juillet 1864.

La Convention se réunit conformément à l'ajournement.

L'honorable E. H. Durell, président, au fauteuil.

A l'appel du rôle, les membres suivants répondent à leurs noms :

MM. Abell, Austin, Balch, Barrett, Baum, Beauvais, Bell, Bennie, Bofill, Bromley, Buckley, Burke, Collin, Campbell, Cazabat, J. K. Cook, T. Cook, Crozat, Cutler, Davies, Dufresne, Duane, Decker, Edwards, Ennis, Fish, Flagg, Flood, Foley, Fosdick, Fuller, Gastinel, Geier, Gorlinski, Gruneberg, Gaidry, Healy, Harnan, Hart, Heard, Henderson, Hills, Hire, Howell, Howes, Kavanagh, Knobloch, Kugler, Maas, Mann, Maurer, Mendiverri, Montamat, Morris, E. Murphy, M. W. Murphy, Newell, Normand, O'Conner, Orr, J. Payne, J. T. Paine, Pintado, Poynot, J. Purcell, S. Pursell, Schroeder, Schnurr, Seymour, Shaw, Smith, Spellicy, Stocker, Stumpf, Stiner, Stauffer, Sullivan, Taliaferro, Terry, Thorpe, Waters, Wenck, Wells, Wilson—84.

Les minutes d'hier sont lues et adoptées.

M. Davies présente la résolution suivante :

Qu'il soit résolu, Que la Législature de l'Etat, dans sa première session, reçoive les instructions nécessaires des autorités de la ville pour la construction d'un pont dans la rue Claiborne, sur le nouveau canal, appartenant au *Canal and Banking Company*.

Dépôt sur le bureau.

M. Montamat présente la résolution suivante :

Une ordonnance autorisant la Corporation de la ville de la Nouvelle-Orléans à bâtir un pont sur le canal Carondelet, en face la rue Galvez, semblable à celui qui existe dans la rue Broad :

Qu'il soit ordonné, Que la Corporation de la ville de la Nouvelle-Orléans soit et est autorisée à bâtir un pont sur le canal Carondelet, opposé à la rue Galvez, semblable à celui qui existe déjà au bas de la rue Broad, de manière à ne pas porter obstacle à la montée ou la descente des vaisseaux ; cette ordonnance devant avoir force de loi de suite après son acceptation.

Dépôt sur le bureau.

Le rapport du comité spécial sur l'éducation est pris en mains pour la troisième lecture.

M. Sullivan présente le proviso suivant à l'article 2 :

Pourvu, Que toutes les institutions, quelle que soit la dénomination, comprenant le caractère mixte de charité et d'asile, servant à l'éducation des orphelins, soient considérées comme écoles publiques de l'Etat, et reçoivent leurs fonds au prorata.

Mr. Stauffer propose le dépôt sur le bureau du proviso—sur quoi la question du oui et non est ordonnée et donne le résultat suivant :

Affirmative:

MM. Baum, Beauvais, Bennie, Bofill, Bromley, Burke, Campbell, J. K. Cook, Collin, Davies, Edwards, Ennis, Flagg, Flood, Gastinel, Geier, Gaidry, Hart, Hire, Howell, Kugler, Maas, Morris, Newell, Normand, J. Payne, J. T. Paine, Pintado, S. Pursell, Schroeder, Seymour, Shaw, Smith, Stumpf, Stauffer, Taliaferro, Wenck, Wells, Wilson—39.

Négative :

MM. Abell, Austin, Balch, Barrett, Bell, Buckley, T. Cook, Crozat, Dufresne, Decker, Duane, Fish, Foley, Fuller, Fosdick, Gorlinski, Gruneberg, Healy, Harnan, Heard, Henderson, Hills, Howes, Kavanagh, Knobloch, Mann, Maurer, Montamat, E. Murphy, M. W. Murphy, Orr, Poynot, J. Purcell, Schnurr, Spellicy, Stiner, Sullivan, Terry, Thorpe, Waters—40.

La motion du dépôt sur le bureau est alors rejetée.

Sur la motion de l'adoption du proviso, l'appel par oui et non a lieu et le proviso rejeté par le vote suivant :

Affirmative :

MM. Abell, Austin, Balch, Barrett, Beauvais, Bell Buckley, T. Cook, Dufresne, Duane, Decker, Fish, Foley, Fosdick, Fuller, Gorlinski, Healy, Harnan, Heard, Henderson, Hills, Howes, Kavanagh, Knobolch, E. Murphy, M. W. Murphy, Orr, J. Purcell, Schnurr, Spellicy, Stocker Stiner, Sullivan. Terry, Thorpe, Waters—36.

Négative :

MM. Baum, Bennie, Bofill, Bromley. Burke, Campbell, J. K. Cook, Crozat, Collin, Davies, Edwards, Ennis, Flagg, Flood, Gastinel, Geier, Gruneberg, Gaidry, Hart, Hire, Howell, Kugler, Maas, Mann, Mendiverri, Montamat, Morris, Newell, Normand, J. Payne, J. T. Paine, Piutado, Poynot, S. Pursell, Schroeder, Shaw, Smith, Stumpf, Stauffer, Taliaferro, Wenck, Wells. Wilson—44.

M. Smith propose l'adoption du rapport, après la troisième lecture, l'appel par oui et non est ordonné et donne le résultat suivant :

Affirmative :

MM. Austin, Barrett, Beauvais, Bell, Bennie, Bromley, Burke, Campbell, Collin, J. K. Cook, Davies, Edwards, Ennis, Fish

Flagg, Flood, Gastinel, Geier, Gaidry, Hart, Henderson. Hills, Hire, Howell, Knobloch, Kugler, Maas, Mann, Mendiverri, Morris, E. Murphy, Newell, Normand, J. Payne. J. T. Paine, Pintado, Poynot, J. Purcell, S. Pursell, Schroeder, Schnurr, Seymour, Smith, Stumpf, Stiner, Stauffer, Taliaferro, Wenck, Wells, Wilson—50.

Négative :

MM. Abell, Balch, Baum, Bofill, Buckley, T. Cook, Crozat, Dufresne, Duane, Decker, Foley, Fosdick, Fuller, Gorlinski, Gruneberg, Healy, Harnan, Heard, Howes, Kavanagh, Maurer, Montamat, M. W. Murphy, O'Conner, Orr, Shaw, Spellicy, Stocker, Sullivan, Terry, Thorpe, Waters—32.

La motion passe, en conséquence, et le rapport est adopté après sa troisième lecture.

Le rapport du comité sur les Cédules est alors pris en considération pour la troisième lecture.

M. Henderson présente le proviso suivant :

Les voituriers par terre et par eau, dans tous les cas de contrats et quasi-contrats, offenses ou quasi-offenses, lorsque d'après la loi ils sont parties intéressées, peuvent être sujets à des dommages et intérêts, d'après la jurisprudence anglaise et américaine qui concerne les voituriers par terre et par eau, de semblables dommages sont légitimes et justes.

Sur la motion d'adopter le proviso, le vote suivant a lieu :

Affirmative :

MM. Balch, Bell, Bennie, Buckley, Campbell, J. K. Cook, T. Cook, Crozat, Duane, Flood, Foley, Gorlinski, Healy, Harnan, Henderson, Hills, Hire, Howes, Kavanagh, E. Murphy, M. W. Murphy, O'Conner, Orr, J. T. Paine, Poynot, Smith, Stocker, Stiner, Terry, Thorpe, Wilson—31.

Négative :

MM. Abell, Austin, Barrett, Baum, Beauvais, Bofill, Bromley, Burke, Cutler, Collin, Davies, Dufresne, Decker, Edwards, Ennis, Fish, Flagg, Fuller, Gastinel, Geier, Gruneberg, Gaidry, Hart, Heard, Howell, Knobloch, Kugler, Maas, Mann, Maurer, Mendiverri, Montamat, Morris, Newell, Normand, J. Payne, Pintado, J. Purcell, S. Pursell, Schroeder. Schnurr, Seymour, Shaw, Spellicy, Stumpf, Stauffer, Sullivan, Taliaferro, Waters, Wenck, Wells—51.

En conséquence, le proviso de M. Henderson est rejeté.

Le rapport est alors adopté après sa 3e lecture.

Le rapport du comité d'Ordonnance est alors pris en considération pour la 3e lecture.

M. Shaw propose comme proviso, de retrancher dans la 5e ligne du 1er article le mot "trois" et d'y substituer le mot "premier" ; et dans la 6e ligne, de retrancher "juillet" et y substituer "septembre." Aussi, dans la 1re ligne du 2e article, retrancher le mot "premier" et y insérer "trois,' et dans la 2e ligne du même article, retrancher le mot "août" et y insérer "septembre"; de plus, insérer après le mot "office" dans la 8e ligne du 3e article, les mots "et retiendront leurs offices pour le terme fixé par la constitution, à partir du second lundi de janvier prochain, dans le cas où ils n'entreraient pas en fonctions à cette époque," et insérer après le mot "constitution", dans la 12e ligne du même article, les mots "et s'ils n'entrent pas en fonctions avant, l'élection de leurs successeurs aura lieu le 1er lundi de novembre 1867; dans toutes les paroisses où l'élection pourra se faire les officiers élus à cette époque entreront en fonctions le 2e lundi de janvier 1868," et de plus, insérer dans la 1re ligne du 4e article, après le mot "en," les mots "trois journaux choisis par le président de la Convention, à savoir : deux publiés en anglais et en français et un en allemand," et insérer aussi dans la 3e ligne du même article, après le mot "ajournement" les mots "de la Convention," retrancher de la même ligne le mot "trois" et insérer "premier" et dans la 4e ligne, retrancher le mot "juillet" et insérer "septembre."

Le proviso de M. Shaw est accepté par la Convention, et le rapport adopté après sa' 3e lecture.

La Convention s'ajourne alors à demain lundi.

Approuvé.

JOHN E. NEELIS, Secrétaire.

SAMEDI, le 9 juillet 1864.

La Convention se réunit conformément à l'ajournement.

Présents l'hon. E. H. Durell, président, et les membres suivants :

MM. Abell, Austin, Balch, Barrett, Bell Bennie, Buckley, Burke, Collin, J. K. Cook Crozat, Decker, Dufresne, Duane, Edwards Ennis, Fish, Flood, Foley, Fosdick, Fuller,

Gastinel, Geier, Gorlinski, Gruneberg, Healy, Harnan, Hart, Heard, Henderson, Hills, Howell, Howes, Knobloch, Kugler, Mayer, Mann, Maurer, Montamat, M. W. Murphy, Newell. Normand, O'Conner, Pintado, Poynot, S. Pursell, Schroeder, Schnurr, Seymour, Shaw, Smith, Spellicy, Stocker, Stumpf, Stiner, Stauffer, Sullivan, Taliaferro, Terry, Waters, Wenck, Wells, Wilson —63.

Après un délai le quorum étant présent, la Convention s'ajourne à jeudi prochain, 14 du courant, à midi.

Approuvé.

JOHN E. NEELIS,
Secrétaire.

JEUDI, le 14 juillet 1864.

La Convention se réunit conformément à l'ajournement.

L'honorable E. H. Durell, président, au fauteuil.

A l'appel du rôle, les membres suivants répondent à leurs noms :

MM. Abell, Austin, Balch, Barrett, Baum, Beauvais, Bell, Bennie, Buckley, Burke, Collin, Campbell, Cazabat, J. K. Cook, T. Cook, Crozat, Cutler, Decker, Davies, Dufresne, Duane, Dupaty, Edwards, Ennis, Fish, Flagg, Flood, Foley, Fosdick, Fuller, Gastinel, Geier, Gorlinski, Gruneberg, Healy, Harnan, Hart, Heard, Henderson, Hills, Hire, Howell, Howes, Kavanagh, Knobloch, Kugler, Mayer, Maas, Mann, Maurer, Mendiverri, Montamat, Morris, E. Murphy, M. W. Murphy, Newell, Normand, Orr, O'Conner, Ong, J. Payne, Pintado, Poynot, J. Purcell, S. Pursell, Schroeder, Schnurr, Seymour, Shaw, Smith, Spellicy, Stocker, Stumpf, Stiner, Stauffer, Sullivan, Taliaferro, Terry, Thorpe, Thomas, Waters, Wenck, Wells, Wilson.

Les minutes de vendredi et de samedi sont lues et adoptées.

Sur la motion de M. Bell, M. Stauffer est excusé pour cause de maladie.

M. Hills, président du comité spécial pour la Librairie de l'Etat, soumet un rapport verbal et demande que le comité soit déchargé de ses devoirs en ce qui concerne cette charge ; il offre également la résolution suivante :

Résolu, Que les remerciments de cette Convention soient et sont ici offerts au général Banks et au gouverneur de l'Etat, Michael Hahn, pour les soins et la bonne volonté qu'ils ont mis à expédier de Bâton-Rouge en cette ville les divers volumes appartenant à la librairie de l'Etat, ainsi qu'il est dit par la communication du secrétaire de l'Etat, ainsi que par le gardien de la librairie.

Le rapport et la résolution sont adoptés et le comité est déchargé.

M. Bell offre la résolution suivante :

Attendu, Qu'il existe une dette résultant de l'inauguration du 4 mars 1864, pour la première élection libre des officiers de l'Etat de la Louisiane et autres dépenses encourues pour le même motif, montant à une somme de $10,000;

Qu'il soit en conséquence résolu, Qu'une somme de $10,000 soit et est appropriée pour l'amortissement de la dite dette, approuvé par un comité de sept membres composé de l'auditeur de l'Etat, du trésorier et du secrétaire de l'Etat, enfin de quatre membres de cette Convention nommés par le président.

M. Henderson offre le substitut suivant qui est accepté par M. Bell :

Attendu, Qu'une dette de $10,000 a été contractée pour la formation de l'Etat libre de la Louisiane ;

Qu'il soit résolu, Que la dite somme soit payée du trésor de l'Etat, sur le warrant du gouverneur du dit Etat.

La résolution est mise aux voix, et sur l'appel par oui et non, le vote suivant est rendu :

Affirmative :

MM. Austin, Barrett, Beauvais, Bell, Buckley, Burke, Collin, J. K. Cook, T. Cook, Crozat, Cutler, Davies, Duane, Edwards, Ennis, Fish, Flagg, Flood, Foley, Fuller, Gastinel, Geier, Gorlinski, Healy, Harnan, Hart, Henderson, Hire, Howes, Mann, Maurer, Mendiverri, E. Murphy, Newell, Normand, Orr, O'Conner, Ong, Pintado, Poynot, S. Pursell, Schroeder, Schnurr, Seymour, Shaw, Smith, Spellicy, Stocker, Stumpf, Stiner, Taliaferro, Terry, Thorpe, Thomas, Waters, Wenck, Wells, Wilson—58.

Négative :

MM. Abell, Balch, Decker, Dufresne, Heard, Howell, Kugler, Maas, Mayer, Montamat, Morris, M. W. Murphy, J. Payne, Sullivan—14.

Par suite du manque de quorum pour voter, l'ordre pour l'appel nominal est donné ; 75 membres seulement y répondent.

Le sergent-d'armes est envoyé à la recherche des membres absents ; quelques-uns ayant repris leurs siéges, le vote sur l'adoption du substitut de M. Henderson a lieu de nouveau et donne le résultat suivant :

Affirmative :

MM. Austin, Barrett, Beauvais, Bell, Buckley, Burke, J. K. Cook, T. Cook, Crozat, Collin,

Culter, Davies, Duane, Dupaty, Edwards, Ennis, Fish, Flagg. Flood, Foley, Fuller, Gastinel, Geier, Gorlinski, Healy. Harnan, Hart, Henderson, Hire. Howes, Mann, Maurer, Mendiverri, E. Murphy. M. W. Murphy, Newell, Normand, O'Conner, Ong, Orr, Pintado, Poynot, J. Purcell, S. Pursell, Schroeder, Schnurr, Seymour, Shaw, Smith, Spellicy, Stocker, Stumpf, Stiner, Taliaferro, Terry, Thorpe. Thomas, Waters, Wells, Wilson—60.

Négative :

MM. Abell, Balch, Decker, Dufresne, Heard, Howell, Kugler, Maas, Mayer, Montamat, Morris, J. Payne, Sullivan. Wenck—14.

Le substitut de M. Henderson est alors adopté.

M. Hills est excusé de voter sur la question précédente.

M. Montamat, président du comité des Finances, soumet le rapport suivant :

RAPPORT DU COMITE DES FINANCES.

Montant de la paie journalière
des membres du 2 au 3 juillet 1864.................. $7,800 00
Payé pour le salaire des officiers..................... 1,981 00
Montant des dépenses diverses   2,411 25
                                              _____
                                              $12,192 25
Balance en mains................ $1,123 03
qui appartiennent au compte des dépenses diverses.

Votre comité recommande qu'il soit autorisé à tirer sur les fonds généraux du trésor de l'Etat la somme nécessaire aux paiements des membres, officiers, employés et dépenses diverses, jusqu'à la fin de la session.

Soumis respectueusement,
JOHN P. MONTAMAT,
Assitant en qualité de président du comité des Finances.
Nouvelle-Orléans, le 8 juillet 1864.

Sur motion faite, le rapport et la recommendation sont adoptés.

M. Thorpe offre la résolution suivante :

Résolu, Que toutes les décisions des cours de l'Etat qui déclarent que l'esclavage existe toujours dans la Louisiane, sont contraires aux lois fondamentales de l'Etat, et en contradiction avec l'ordonnance d'Emancipation passée par cette Convention.

M. Sullivan propose le dépôt de la résolution sur le bureau.

Sur cette question, l'appel par oui et non a lieu et donne le résultat suivant :

Affirmative :

MM. Abell, Balch, Barrett, Beauvais, Buckley, Crozat, Cutler, Dufresne, Decker, Edwards, Fish, Fuller, Gastinel, Geier, Gruneberg, Healy, Heard, Howell, Knobloch, Maas, Mendiverri, Montamat, Morris, Mayer, M. W. Murphy, Newell, Normand, Ong, J. Purcell, Schnurr, Seymour. Stumpf. Sullivan, Thomas, Waters, Wenck. Wells, Wilson—38.

Négative :

MM. Austin, Bell, Burke, Bennie, J.K.Cook. T. Cook, Collin, Davies, Duane, Dupaty, Ennis, Flagg, Flood, Foley, Gorlinski, Harnan, Hart, Henderson, Hills, Hire, Howes, Kugler, Mann, Maurer, E. Murphy, Orr. O'Conner, J. Payne, Pintado, Poynot, S. Pursell, Schroeder, Shaw, Smith, Spellicy, Stocker, Stiner, Taliaferro, Terry, Thorpe—40.

La motion du dépôt sur le bureau et alors rejetée.

Après une longue discussion la Convention s'ajourne à demain à midi.

Approuvé.

JOHN E. NEELIS,
Secrétaire.

VENDREDI, le 15 juillet 1864.

La Convention se réunit conformément à l'ajournement.

Présents l'honorable E. H. Durell, président, et les membres suivants :

MM. Abell, Austin, Balch, Barrett, Baum, Beauvais, Bell, Bennie, Bofill, Buckley, Burke, Collin, Campbell, Cazabat, J. K. Cook. T. Cook, Crozat, Cutler, Decker, Davies, Dufresne, Duane, Dupaty, Edwards, Ennis, Fish, Flagg. Flood, Foley, Fuller. Gastinel, Geier, Gorlinski, Gruneberg, Gaidry, Healy, Harnan, Hart, Heard, Henderson, Hills, Hire, Howell, Howes, Kavanagh, Knobloch, Kugler, Mayer, Maas, Mann, Maurer, Mendiverri, Montamat, Morris, E. Murphy, M. W. Murphy, Newell, Normand, O'Conner, J. Payne, J. T. Paine, Pintado, Poynot, J. Purcell, S. Pursell, Schroeder, Schnurr, Shaw, Smith, Spellicy, Stocker, Stumpf, Stiner, Sullivan, Taliaferro, Terry, Thorpe, Thomas, Waters, Wenck, Wells, Wilson—82.

Les minutes d'hier sont lues et adoptées.

Sur motion de M. Flagg, l'absence de M. Seymour est excusée.

M. Montamat, président du comité des Finances, présente la résolution suivante, qui est adoptée, savoir :

Résolu, Que le comité des Finances soit et est autorisé à tirer sur le trésor de l'Etat le montant des sommes nécessaires pour le paiement des membres, officiers, employés et les dépenses diverses de cette Convention.

M. Smith présente la résolution suivante :

Résolu, Que cette Convention ayant adopté un article séparant les taxes pour le bénéfice de l'éducation sous deux formes différentes, l'une pour l'éducation des enfants blancs et l'autre pour l'éducation des enfants de couleur, il devient indispensable dans le but d'éviter des difficultés à l'avenir, de définir d'une manière claire et précise le degré de sang qui constitue une personne de couleur.

M. Montamat propose le dépôt de la résolution sur le bureau.

Rejeté par un vote par assis et et levé : oui, 30 ; non, 33.

La résolution est alors prise en considération par un vote d'assis et levé donnant 23 oui et 47 non.

La dite résolution est rejetée.

M. Montamat présente l'ordonnance suivante :

Une ordonnance autorisant la Corporation de la ville de la Nouvelle-Orléans à bâtir un pont sur le canal Carondelet, en face la rue Galvez, semblable à celui qui existe à présent dans la rue Broad :

Qu'il soit ordonné, Que la Corporation de la ville de la Nouvelle-Orléans est autorisée à bâtir un pont sur le canal Carondelet, opposé la rue Galvez, semblable à celui qui existe en bas de la rue Broad, de manière à ne pas entraver la navigation, cette ordonnance devant avoir force de loi aussitôt après son acceptation.

Sur motion du dépôt sur le bureau, une division a lieu et donne pour résultat 32 oui et 19 non.

L'ordonnance est en conséquence déposée sur le bureau.

M. Smith présente le préambule et la résolution suivante :

Attendu, Que pendant la présente rébellion des individus et corporations ainsi que des paroisses ont émis du papier sans nulle valeur, et en ont forcé l'aceptation par la classe pauvre et loyale de la communauté ;

Qu'il soit résolu, Qu'un comité spécial de cinq membres soit nommé pour prendre en considération la nécessité de faire un ou des articles, pour prévenir à l'avenir le retour de semblables abus, de s'emparer des propriétés de n'importe quelle qualification, appartenant soit aux maris, soit à la femme, soit aux paroisses, soit aux corporations, pour retirer de la circulation le dit papier ; et que le comité soit autorisé a soumettre à cette Convention, pour être approuvé ou rejeté, un modèle de pétition à envoyer au Congrès des Etats-Unis, demandant les pouvoirs nécessaires pour les paroisses de l'Etat de la Louisiane, d'appliquer le produit de la vente des propriétés des citoyens déloyaux, à retirer de la circulation ledit papier.

La motion du dépôt sur le bureau ayant été rejetée, la résolution est adoptée par un vote par assis et levé : oui 39, non 22.

Sur l'objection faite qu'il n'y avait pas de quorum pour voter, l'appel a lieu et 78 membres répondant à leurs noms, le président déclare la résolution adoptée.

La Convention alors résume son travail, sur la résolution de M. Thorpe.

Après une longue discussion, la résolution est mise aux voix et adoptée par le vote suivant :

Affirmative :

MM. Austin, Barrett, Baum, Beauvais, Burke, Bell, Bennie, Bofill, Cazabat, J. K. Cook, T. Cook, Crozat, Collin, Davies, Duane, Dupaty, Ennis, Fish, Flagg, Flood, Foley, Fuller, Geier, Gorlinski, Gaidry, Healy, Harnan, Hart, Howes, Henderson, Hills, Hire, Kavanagh, Kugler, Maas, Mann, Maurer, E. Murphy, M. W. Murphy, Newell, Normand, O'Conner, J. Payne, Pintado, Poynot, S. Pursell. J. T. Paine, Schroeder, Schnurr, Smith, Spellicy, Stocker, Stiner, Taliaferro, Terry, Thorpe, Wenck—58.

Négative :

MM. Abell, Balch, Buckley, Campbell, Cutler, Decker, Dufresne, Edwards, Gastinel, Gruneberg, Heard, Howell, Knobloch, Mayer, Mendiverri, Montamat, Morris, Sullivan, Waters, Wells, Wilson—21.

La Convention s'ajourne alors à demain à midi.

Approuvé.

     John E. Neelis,
      Secrétaire.

Samedi, le 16 juillet 1864.

La Convention se réunit conformément à l'ajournement.

Présents l'honorable E. H. Durell, président, et les membres suivants :

MM. Abell, Austin, Barrett, Baum, Beauvais, Bell, Bennie, Buckley, Burke, Collin, Campbell, J. K. Cook, T. Cook, Crozat, Cutler, Decker, Davies, Dufresne, Duane, Dupaty, Edwards, Ennis, Fish, Flagg, Flood, Foley, Fuller, Gastinel, Geier, Gorlinski, Gruneberg, Gaidry, Healy, Harnan, Hart, Heard, Henderson, Hills, Hire, Howell, Howes, Kavanagh, Knobloch, Kugler, Mayer, Maas, Mann, Maurer, Montamat, Morris, M. W. Murphy, Newell, Normand, Orr, O'Conner, J. Payne, Pintado, Poynot,

J. Purcell, Schroeder, Schnurr, Seymour, Shaw, Smith, Spellicy, Stocker, Stumpf, Stiner, Sullivan, Taliaferro, Terry, Thorpe, Thomas Waters, Wenck, Wells, Wilson.

Les minutes d'hier sont lues et adoptées.

Le président annonce qu'il a nommé un comité spécial, par suite de la résolution de M. Smith, concernant l'émission de papier de nulle valeur. Ce comité est composé de MM. Smith, O'Conner, Balch, T. Cook et Poynot.

Le président fait part alors à la Convention de la résignation de M. J. T. Paine qui est conçue ainsi :

Nlle-Orleans, le 16 juillet 1864.

Au secrétaire de la Convention de l'Etat :

Monsieur—Je vous offre ma résignation comme membre de la Convention constitutionnelle de l'Etat.

Il me semble que la session se prolonge inutilement et à grands frais pour le public : je n'approuve en aucune façon une semblable manière de faire. Ayant reçu un emploi du gouvernement, je désire remplir mes fonctions avec exactitude.

Je suis respectueusement votre humble serviteur.   J. T. Paine.

M. Thorpe propose l'expulsion de M. J. T. Paine, en raison de l'insulte qu'il offre à la Convention par suite de la teneur de sa résignation.

M. Hills propose comme substitut à la motion de M. Thorpe, que le sergent-d'armes soit envoyé à la recherche de M. Paine, et qu'il soit traduit à la barre de la Convention.

Rejeté.

La question étant revenue sur l'adoption de la motion de M. Thorpe, ce membre, avec l'assentiment de M. Stocker, qui avait secondé la motion, la retire.

La même motion est immédiatement après renouvelée par M. Harnan.

M. Wilson présente alors la résolution suivante comme substitut :

Résolu, Que J. T. Paine, membre pour la paroisse de Féliciana, n'est pas une personne convenable pour remplir un emploi du gouvernement, et ce, en raison du manque de respect dont il a fait preuve vis-à-vis de la Convention.

Le substitut a été rejeté sur la motion d'adoption, par suite du vote suivant :

Négative :

MM. Abell, Barrett, Beauvais, Bell, Bennie, Buckley, J. K. Cook, Crozat, Cutler, Duane, Dufresne, Edwards, Fish, Fuller, Gastinel, Geier, Gruneberg, Healy, Hart, Heard, Henderson, Hills, Hire, Howell, Howes, Knobloch, Kugler, Mayer, Maas, Mann, Maurer, Montamat, Morris, M. W. Murphy, Orr, O'Conner, Pintado, Poynot, J. Purcell, S. Pursell, Schnurr, Shaw, Spellicy, Stocker, Stumpf, Stiner, Sullivan, Terry, Waters, Wenck—50.

Affirmative :

MM. Austin, Burke, Collin, T. Cook, Davies, Dupaty, Ennis, Flagg, Flood, Foley, Gorlinski, Gaidry, Harnan, Newell, Normand, Schroeder, Seymour, Smith, Taliaferro, Thorpe, Thomas, Wells, Wilson—23.

La question de l'adoption de la motion de M. Harnan était sur le point d'être mise aux voix lorsque M. Henderson a présenté un point de droit prouvant que la motion de M. Henderson n'était pas à l'ordre, attendu qu'aucune charge n'avait été faite d'abord, et que d'après les lois parlementaires et les réglements de cette Convention, M. Paine avait le droit d'être entendu.

M. le président approuve le point de droit de M. Henderson et refuse de recevoir sa motion.

M. Terry présente la résolution suivante :

Résolu, Qu'une somme de $100 soit appropriée des fonds généraux de l'Etat pour chaque chapelain qui a officié à la Convention pendant la session.

Avant que la résolution de M. Terry n'ait été résolue, la motion d'ajourner avait été faite et acceptée. En conséquence, le président déclare que la Chambre s'ajourne à lundi, 18 courant, à midi.

Approuvé.

John E. Neelis,
Secrétaire.

Lundi, le 18 juillet 1864.

La Convention se réunit conformément à l'ajournement.

Présents, l'Hon. E. H. Durell, président, et les membres suivants :

MM. Abell, Austin, Balch, Barrett, Baum, Beauvais, Bell, Bennie, Buckley, Burke, Collin, Campbell, Cazabat, J. K. Cook, T. Cook, Cutler Decker, Davies, Dufresne, Duane, Dupaty, Edwards, Ennis, Fish, Flagg, Flood, Foley, Fosdick, Fuller, Gastinel, Geier, Gorlinski, Gruneberg, Healy, Harnan, Hart, Heard, Henderson, Hills, Hire, Howell, Howes, Kavanagh, Knobloch, Kugler, Maas, Mann, Maurer, Mendiverri, Mayer, Montamat, Morris, E. Murphy, M. W. Murphy, Newell, Normand, O'Conner, Ong, Orr, J. Payne, Pintado, Poynot,

J. Purcell, S. Pursell, Schroeder, Schnurr, Seymour, Shaw, Smith, Spellicy, Stocker, Stumpf, Stiner, Stauffer, Sullivan, Taliaferro, Terry, Thorpe, Thomas, Waters, Wenck, Wells et Wilson.

MM. Crozat et Bofill sont excusés.

Les minutes d'hier sont lues et adoptées.

M. Montamat est appelé au fauteuil.

Le président présente une explication personnelle relative aux remarques qu'il a faites vendredi dernier, sur la décision de l'honorable W. W. Handlin, ex-juge de la Cour du Troisième District de la Nouvelle-Orléans, sur la question de l'émancipation.

M. Abell se lève pour une question de privilége, et observe qu'il a reçu une communication d'un caractère extraordinaire, la supposant une violation du droit reconnu ; il désire la déposer devant la Convention. A cet effet, il demande que lecture en soit faite par le secrétaire, ce qui a lieu ainsi qu'il suit :

[Confidentiel.]
Nlle-Orléans, 15 juillet 1864.
E. ABELL, Esq.

Cher Monsieur—Je professe une aversion si profonde pour l'incorporation dans la Loi Organique des mots "blanc," "noir" et de "couleur," que je vous prie dans cette, note confidentielle (accompagnée de mon proviso,) de vouloir bien prendre en considération la nécessité de changer le langage de certaines portions de la nouvelle constitution, de manière à le faire agréer avec le principe contenu dans le proviso que je propose. Beaucoup de membres de la Convention ont eu la bonté de dire au gouverneur et à moi-même qu'ils feraient tout au monde pour rayer ces mots des bills de la milice et de l'éducation, avant que la question finale d'adoption, dans son ensemble, vous soit présentée.

Je suis respectueusement, etc.,
A. P. DOSTIE.

ART. —. La Législature pourvoira à l'éducation de tous les enfants de l'Etat, depuis l'âge de six à dix-huit ans, au moyen d'écoles publiques gratuites.

ART. —. Une université composée d'une école de droit, une école de médecine et un collége, combinant avec cela les diverses branches d'instruction dans l'Etat, sera établie et maintenue.

ART. —. Toutes les sommes provenant de donations ou autres sources, dans un but d'éducation, seront et resteront comme fonds perpétuel, portant intérêt à 7 pour 100 par an. Ces sommes seront appropriées exclusivement dans le but susdit.

M. Thomas offre la résolution suivante :

Résolu, Que l'adjudant-général recevra un salaire de $3000 par an, à partir du jour de son entrée en fonctions et jusqu'à ce qu'il en soit autrement ordonné.

Adopté.

Le président présente à la Convention les explications suivantes de M. J. T. Paine :

Nouvelle-Orléans, le 18 juillet 1864.

Au Président et aux Membres de la Convention, réunie pour la révision et l'amendement de la Constitution de l'Etat de la Louisiane:

Comme rectification à ma communication du 10 juillet, j'ai l'honneur de vous faire connaître que mon intention était d'adresser ma résignation à la Convention par l'intermédiaire du secrétaire ; loin de moi la pensée de la lui avoir adressée personnellement.

Je vous prie de vouloir bien accepter mes excuses et de croire que je n'ai pas voulu manquer de respect à la Convention ni à aucun de ses membres.

De nouveau et respectueusement je vous offre ma résignation comme membre de la Convention, en vous priant de vouloir bien l'accepter.

Respectueusement
Votre très-humble serviteur,
J. T. PAINE.

Sur la motion d'accepter la résignation de M. Paine, une division a lieu, donnant comme résultat : oui 17, non 49.

En conséquence la résignation est rejetée.

M. Smith présente la résolution suivante:

En vue des différents degrés de couleur dans cette portion de la population de la Louisiane, sous la dénomination de "gens de couleur," comprenant l'Africain pur sang et ceux comparativement blancs, il devient indispensable pour cette Convention de définir d'une manière claire et précise ce qui constitue une personne de couleur ; en conséquence :

Il est résolu, Qu'un comité de cinq soit appointé par le président, lui-même dirigeant le comité pour prendre cette affaire en considération, en faire un rapport à la Convention à la première opportunité et définissant quel degré de sang constituera une "personne de couleur."

La motion d'adoption est refusée ; par conséquent, la résolution est rejetée.

M. Balch présente ce qui suit :

Résolu, Qu'une somme de cinq cents dollars est allouée au juge J. H. Carrigan, gardien de la Librairie de l'Etat, pour les services qu'il a rendus à la Convention, en fournissant des livres et des documents.

Adopté par un vote assis et levé, oui 38, non 22.

M. Terry offre ce qui suit :

Attendu, Qu'il est à désirer que les travaux de cette Convention soient complétés sans aucun délai :

Qu'il soit résolu, Que toutes les motions relatives à l'adoption de la Constitution, ou aucune partie, soient mises aux voix sans débats.

Dépôt sur le bureau.

Sur la motion de M. Austin, la résolution suivante est prise en considération et passe, savoir :

Résolu, Que les membres de cette Convention, qui sont allés comme délégués à Baltimore, reçoivent leur *per diem pay*.

M. Shaw, président du comité spécial sur la forme et l'arrangement, soumet un rapport écrit, ainsi qu'une copie imprimée de la Constitution, comme il a été rapporté.

M. Abell propose de fixer jeudi prochain, pour le rapport du comité.

La motion du dépôt sur le bureau ayant été rejetée, l'appel par oui et non est demandé sur l'adoption de la motion de M. Abell, résultant comme suit :

Affirmative :

MM. Abell, Austin, Barrett, Baum, Beauvais, Bell, Buckley, Burke, J. K. Cook, Cutler, Collin, Dufresne, Dupaty, Decker, Edwards, Gastinel, Gruneberg, Healy, Harnan, Kavanagh, Knobloch, Maas, Maurer, Mendiverri, Montamat, M. W. Murphy, Mayer, Normand, O'Conner, Orr, Pintado, Schroeder, Schnurr, Seymour, Shaw, Stumpf, Sullivan, Thomas, Waters, Wenck—40.

Négative :

MM. Balch, Cazabat, T. Cook, Davies, Duane, Ennis, Fish, Flagg, Flood, Foley, Fuller, Geier, Gorlinski, Hart, Heard, Henderson, Hills, Hire, Howes, Mann, Morris, E. Murphy, Newell, Ong, J. Payne, Poynot, S. Pursell, Smith, Spellicy, Stocker, Stiner, Stauffer, Taliaferro, Terry, Thorpe, Wells, Wilson—37.

La motion est en conséquence adoptée et le rapport est mis à l'ordre du jour pour jeudi prochain, 21 courant.

M. Bell présente une résolution relative à une extra compensation pour de certains officiers de cette Convention. Sur la motion de M. Healy, le dépôt en est fait sur le bureau.

M. Austin présente le préambule et les résolutions qui suivent :

Attendu, Que la perpétuité de notre gouvernement national est en grand danger par suite de l'étonnante rébellion contre la constitution et les lois de la patrie commune, prenant son origine et dirigée par quelques hommes vicieux, dans le but avoué d'établir une oligarchie despotique, basée sur l'esclavage, institution réprouvée et détestée par le monde civilisé et l'humanité commune :

Et attendu, Que la stabilité des institutions républicaines aussi bien que les libertés du peuple, requièrent que le gouvernement des Etats-Unis reste intact et que ses lois soient respectées sur toute la surface de ses possessions ;

Et attendu, Que la période pour l'élection d'un président et un vice-président des Etats-Unis approche ;

En conséquence, qu'il soit résolu, Qu'attendu l'existence de la rébellion et la condition présente de nos affaires nationales, aucun changement dans la politique du département exécutif du gouvernement ne pourrait que retarder et embarrasser la poursuite vigoureuse de la guerre et produire les résultats les plus désastreux ;

Qu'il soit de plus résolu, Que nous reconnaissons dans Abraham Lincoln un sage président, un vrai patriote et un excellent homme d'Etat, qui est sorti pur de l'étamine, un homme enfin auquel la dernière administration fait le plus grand crédit, aussi bien qu'elle fait honneur au pays, un homme qui a notre entière approbation quant à sa politique pour la suppression de la rébellion. Que nous reconnaissons aussi dans Andrew Johnson un excellent homme d'Etat, pourvu de sagesse, de patriotisme et d'intégrité ; enfin sous tous les rapports digne de la confiance du peuple ; en conséquence,

Qu'il soit de plus résolu, Que nous endossons cordialement l'action de la Convention Nationale qui a siégée dernièrement à Baltimore ; que nous donnons tout notre support aux délégués, et que nous emploierons tous les moyens honorables pour obtenir leur élection.

Sur l'adoption du préambule et des résolutions ci-dessus, le vote par oui et non a lieu et donne le résultat suivant :

Affirmative :

MM. Austin, Barrett, Baum, Beauvais, Bell, Bennie, Burke, Cazabat, J. K. Cook, T. Cook, Davies, Duane, Dupaty, Edwards, Ennis, Fish, Flagg, Flood, Foley, Fuller, Geier, Gorlinski, Healy, Harnan, Henderson, Hills, Hire, Howes, Mann, Montamat, Morris, E. Murphy, M. W. Murphy, Newell, Normand, Orr, O'Conner, J. Payne, Pintado, Poynot, J. Purcell, S. Pursell, Schroeder, Schnurr, Seymour, Shaw, Smith, Spellicy, Stocker, Stumpf, Stiner, Stauffer, Sullivan,

Taliaferro, Terry, Thorpe, Thomas, Wenck, Wells, Wilson—60.

Négative:

MM. Abell, Balch, Buckley, Collin. Cutler, Decker, Dufresne, Gastinel, Gruneberg, Hart, Heard, Howell, Kavanagh, Knobloch, Maas, Maurer, Mayer, Mendiverri, Ong, Waters—20.

M. Thorpe présente ce qui suit:

Une ordonnance pour pourvoir à une élection pour remplir les vacances dans la représentation de l'Etat de la Louisiane au 38e Congrès.

Section 1re. *Qu'il soit ordonné par le peuple de l'Etat de la Louisiane en Convention assemblé,* Qu'une élection soit tenue par les électeurs qualifiés de l'Etat de la Louisiane le premier lundi de semptembre 1864, à l'effet d'envoyer des représentants au Congrès des Etats-Unis d'Amérique pour remplir les vacances qui existent dans le 38e Congrès, et y remplir leurs fonctions jusqu'à la fin du terme du dit Congrès.

Sect. 2. *Qu'il soit de plus ordonné,* Que jusqu'à ce qu'il en soit autrement fixé par la loi, l'Etat sera divisé en cinq Districts comme suit, et les électeurs qualifiés de chaque District choisiront un représentant:

Le Premier District Congressionnel comprendra les paroisses de St-Bernard et Plaquemines, la rive droite de la paroisse d'Orléans, le 9e, 8e, 7e, 6e et 5e Districts représentatifs de la paroisse d'Orléans, et la partie du 4e District représentatif de la paroisse d'Orléans compris entre les rues St-Louis, Remparts et Canal, et le lac Pontchartrain.

Le Deuxième District Congressionnel comprendra la partie du 4e District représentatif de la paroisse d'Orléans, qui est inclus entre les rues St-Louis, Remparts et Canal et la rivière Mississipi; les 3e, 2e et 1er Districts représentatifs de la paroisse d'Orléans, et la partie du 10e District représentatif de la paroisse d'Orléans, connue et désignée sous le nom de 10e Ward de la ville de la Nouvelle-Orléans.

Le Troisième District Congressionnel comprendra la partie du 10e District représentatif de la paroisse d'Orléans, connue et désignée sous le nom de 11e Ward de la ville de la Nouvelle-Orléans ; et les paroisses de Jefferson, Washington, St-Tammany, St-Héléne, Livingston, St-Charles, St-Jean-Baptiste, St-Jacques, Ascension, Est-Bâton-Rouge, Est-Féliciana, Ouest-Féliciana, Terrebonne et Lafourche.

Le Quatrième District Congressionnel comprendra les paroisses de Natchitoches, Sabine, Rapides, Calcasieu, St-Landry, Vermillion, Avoyelles, Pointe-Coupée, Lafayette, St-Martin, Ouest-Bâton-Rouge, Iberville, Assomption et Ste-Marie.

Le Cinquième District Congressionnel comprendra les paroisses de Bossier, Claiborne, Union, Morehouse, Carroll, Bienville, Jackson, Ouachita, Caldwell, Franklin, Madison, Tensas, Concordia, Catahoula, Winn, Caddo et De Soto.

Sect. 3. *Qu'il soit de plus ordonné,* Que les divers officiers de l'Etat, autorisés par la loi pour tenir les élections, ou à défaut de ceux-ci, tels officiers que le gouverneur désignera ou autorisera, ouvriront et tiendront des *polls* dans les divers Districts Congressionnels de l'Etat, à l'effet de nommer des représentants comme il est dit plus haut. A la conclusion de la dite élection, les officiers et les délégués qui y auront présidés feront le dépouillement du scrutin avec la plus minutieuse exactitude, et en enverront le résultat au secrétaire de l'Etat en conformité avec les lois en usage en ce qui concerne les élections.

Sect. 4. *Qu'il soit de plus ordonné,* Qu'à la réception des dits retours, ou le troisième lundi de septembre, si les retours ne sont pas reçus plus tôt, il sera du devoir du gouverneur, conjointement avec le secrétaire de l'Etat. et le juge de l'une des cours de district de l'Etat, en présence de n'importe qui jugera convenable d'y assister, de s'assurer de la validité de l'élection de la personne ; un certificat de la dite élection sera entré sur les registres par le secrétaire de l'Etat et signé par le gouverneur ; une copie en sera délivrée à la personne élue, et une autre copie envoyée à la Chambre des représentants du Congrès des Etats-Unis adressée au *speaker.*

Sect. 5. *Qu'il soit de plus ordonné,* Que telle ordonnance aura de force de loi et sera en vigueur après son adoption, suivant les réglements de l'Etat.

Fait à la Convention, dans la ville de la Nouvelle-Orléans, le —— jour de juillet 1864.

L'ordre pour l'impression est donné, et la mise à l'ordre du jour fixée pour mercredi prochain.

Sur la motion de M. Abell, la Convention s'ajourne à mercredi prochain, à midi.

Approuvé.

JOHN E. NEELIS,
Secrétaire.

MERCREDI. le 20 juillet 1864.

La Convention se réunit conformément à l'ajournement.

Sont présents : L'Hon. E. H. Durell, président, et les membres suivants :

MM. Abell, Austin, Barrett, Baum, Beauvais, Bell, Bennie, Botill, Buckley, Burke, Collin, Cazabat, J. K. Cook, T. Cook, Crozat, Cutler, Decker, Duane, Dufresne, Dupaty, Edwards, Ennis, Fish, Flagg, Flood, Foley, Fuller, Gastinel, Geier, Gorlinski, Gruneberg, Gaidry, Healy, Harnan, Hart, Heard,

Henderson, Hills, Hire, Howell, Howes, Kavanagh, Knobloch, Kugler, Maas, Mann, Maurer, Mendiverri, Montamat, Morris, E. Murphy, M. W. Murphy, Newell, Normand, Orr, O'Conner, Ong, J. Payne, Pintado, Poynot, J. Purcell, S. Pursell, Schroeder, Schnurr, Seymour, Shaw, Smith, Spellicy, Stocker, Stumpf, Stiner, Stauffer, Sullivan, Taliaferro, Terry, Thorpe, Thomas, Waters, Wenck, Wells, Wilson.

Les minutes de lundi dernier sont lues et adoptées.

M. Smith, président du comité spécial sur le Papier de non Valeur, soumet le rapport suivant :

Nouvelle-Orléans, le 18 juillet 1864.
A *l'honorable Président et MM. les Membres de la Convention constitutionnelle de la Louisiane :*

Messieurs—Les soussignés, comité nommé par votre honorable corps, à l'effet de prendre en considération la justice de retirer de la circulation le papier de non valeur mis en circulation depuis le commencement de la rébellion, et imposé à la population pauvre et loyale de la Louisiane, par des individus, aussi bien que par des corporations et les autorités de paroisses dans différentes sections et localités de l'Etat, avons l'honneur de vous faire connaître respectueusement, qu'après avoir pesé avec soin les causes qui avaient été soumises à votre considération, nous sommes d'avis que cette Convention doit intervenir, d'une manière ou d'autre ; en conséquence, nous offrons, comme résultat de nos délibérations, l'article suivant, pour être incorporé comme l'une des ordonnances de la constitution :

Art. — . Que les propriétés de tous individus, maisons de commerce, ayant des propriétés sujettes aux taxes, situées dans les villages, villes et paroisses, seront sujets et rendus responsables pour la rédemption en argent ayant cours des Etats-Unis, pour tout le papier mis en circulation, comme médium, pendant la présente rébellion, et ce pour le montant mis en circulation par individus, maisons de commerce, village, ville ou paroisse, respectivement ; les dites sommes à recouvrer devant n'importe quelle cour de justice ayant juridiction, et d'après la loi.

CHARLES SMITH,
JOS. H. BALCH,
O. H. POYNOT,
TERRENCE COOK,
C. K. O'CONNER.

M. Burke propose le rejet du rapport.

Cette motion est acceptée par un vote assis et levé ; oui 40, non 20.

M. Cazabat propose de suspendre les réglements à l'effet d'adopter la constitution dans son ensemble et son débat.

La proposition n'est pas prise en considération.

L'appel des membres a lieu et 80 répondent à leurs noms.

M. Cutler présente la résolution suivante :

Résolu, Qu'une somme de 1000 dollars soit, et est appropriée des fonds du trésor de l'Etat à l'effet de payer pour extra services le secrétaire de la Convention et ses deux assistants, cette somme payée d'après leurs propres reçus et comme suit : à John E. Neelis, secrétaire, 500 dollars ; à S. G. Hamilton et Philip Winfree, assistants-secrétaires, 250 dollars à chaque.

M. Montamat présente l'amendement suivant :

Qu'il soit de plus résolu, Qu'une somme de 250 dollars soit, et est appropriée des fonds généraux du trésor de l'Etat, à L. O. Maureau, trésorier de la Convention, payable sur son propre reçu, pour extra services rendus.

M. Cutler ayant accepté l'amendement, la résolution est adoptée ainsi qu'elle a été amendée.

M. Henderson propose de reconsidérer le vote de lundi dernier, fixant le rapport du comité sur la forme et l'arrangement pour jeudi.

La motion du dépôt sur le bureau est rejetée par suite d'un vote par assis et levé, donnant 42 oui contre 36 non.

La question sur la motion de reconsidérer est alors posée et rejetée.

L'ordonnance de M. Thorpe, pour pourvoir à une élection pour remplir les vacances dans la représentation de l'Etat, pour le XXXVIIIe Congrès des Etats-Unis, est alors prise en considération.

M. Henderson étant temporairement au fauteuil, les motions sont faites d'abord du dépôt sur le bureau, puis pour l'adoption. Au milieu d'une grande confusion, le président temporaire déclare que la question est passée ; mais sur la demande de beaucoup de membres, quelle était celle des deux questions qui était passée, M. Henderson ne peut en informer la Convention, alors le président reprend son siège.

M. Abell propose d'amender la seconde section, en retranchant le tout après le mot "Orléans" dans la septième ligne, et insérant dans la sixième ligne le mot "et quatre" après le mot "cinq," de manière à introduire tout le Quatrième District représentatif de la paroisse d'Orléans.

Dépôt sur le bureau par un vote par assis et levé : oui 43, non 32.

Après une longue discussion, et sur motion de M. Cutler, la question est ajournée jusqu'à samedi prochain.

La Convention s'ajourne alors à demain à midi.

Approuvé.

JOHN E. NEELIS,
Secrétaire.

JEUDI, le 21 juillet 1864.

La Convention se réunit conformément à l'ajournement.

Présents l'honorable E. H. Durell, président, et les membres suivants :

MM. Abell, Austin, Barrett, Baum, Beauvais, Bell, Bennie, Bofill, Buckley, Burke, Campbell, Cazabat, Collin, J. K. Cook, T. Cook, Crozat, Cutler, Decker, Davies, Dufresne, Duane, Dupaty, Edwards, Ennis, Fish, Flagg, Flood, Foley, Fosdick, Fuller, Gastinel, Geier, Gorlinski, Gruneberg, Gaidry, Healy, Harnan, Hart, Heard, Henderson, Hills, Hire, Howell, Howes, Kavanagh, Knobloch, Kugler, Mayer, Maas, Mann, Maurer, Mendiverri, Montamat, Morris, E. Murphy, M. W. Murphy, Newell, Normand, O'Conner, Ong, Orr, J. Payne, Pintado, Poynot, J. Purcell, S. Pursell, Schroeder, Schnurr, Seymour, Shaw, Smith, Spellicy, Stocker, Stumpf, Stiner, Stauffer, Sullivan, Taliaferro, Terry, Thorpe, Thomas, Waters, Wenck, Wells, Wilson—86.

Les minutes d'hier sont lues et adoptées.

Le rapport du comité spécial sur la Forme et l'Arrangement de la constitution étant à l'ordre du jour, est pris en considération; la lecture de la constitution commence, avec l'intention de l'adopter dans son ensemble Le président propose que le secrétaire, en lisant la constitution, pose à la fin de chaque article, pour faciliter aux membres qui le désireraient, l'occasion de présenter sans proviso.

M. Cazabat propose d'adopter la constitution dans son ensemble sans autre délai.

Cette demande n'a pas d'effet.

Après lecture du préambule, M. Henderson propose le substitut suivant, comme proviso :

Nous, les Représentants du peuple de l'Etat de la Louisiane, en Convention assemblés, définissons les limites dudit Etat ainsi qu'il suit : Commençant à l'embouchure de la rivière Sabine, de là par une ligne tirée au milieu de ladite rivière y compris toutes les îles jusqu'au 32e degré de latitude, de là du nord à sa partie la plus nord du 33e degré de latitude nord ; puis le long dudit parrallèle de latitude à la rivière Mississipi ; de là, du bas de ladite rivière à la rivière Iberville, et de là du milieu de ladite rivière, et des lacs Maurepas et Pontchartrain jusqu'au Golfe du Mexique, puis borné par ledit golfe, à la place où il commence, y compris toutes les îles dans un rayon de trois lieues de la côte; et nous ordonnons et établissons cette constitution

Après discussion, motion est faite de rejeter le proviso. M. Hills propose la question précédente ; elle est mise aux voix, et le proviso de M. Henderson est rejeté.

Le secrétaire procède alors à la lecture de la constitution, à la lecture de l'article 7, et M. Cutler propose de retrancher les mots "avec sécurité pour les électeurs," dans la 8me ligne de la seconde page.

Approuvé.

M. Shaw propose d'amender le 12me article en retranchant le mot "quatre," et y substituant le mot "cinq," et aussi retranchant le mot "trois" dans la 3me ligne du bas, et y substituer le mot "quatre" dans la seconde ligne du bas de la page quatre, donnant par là à la ville de la Nouvelle-Orléans neuf Sénateurs au lieu de sept.

Dans l'Art. 14, M. Cutler propose de retrancher le mot "six" et y substituer le mot "trois," rendant obligatoire pour les votants la résidence dans les paroisses trois mois au lieu de six.

M. Stauffer propose le rejet, et cette motion n'étant pas adoptée par suite d'un vote par assis et levé; oui 35, non 42, le proviso de M. Cutler est adopté.

M. Shaw propose d'amender l'article 22, en retranchant "trente-quatre" et y substituant "trente-six;" et dans la dernière ligne du même article, en retranchant "sept" et y substituant "neuf," de manière à ce que le proviso soit ainsi compris: "que nulle paroisse n'aura droit à plus de neuf sénateurs."

Adopté.

M. Shaw propose aussi de retrancher dans la seconde ligne de l'article 23, les mots

"trente-quatre," et y substituer les mots "trente-six," de manière à ce que l'article corresponde avec l'amendement précédent.
Adopté.

Dans l'article 44, M. Foley propose de retrancher "dix" et d'insérer "cinq," de manière à rendre obligatoire la résidence de cinq ans pour la qualification de gouverneur.

M. Flood propose de substituer deux ans. Cette motion est rejetée, et l'amendement de M. Foley est alors adopté.

M. Henderson propose d'amender l'article 47, en retranchant de la quatrième ligne le mot "résidence," et y insérant le mot "reste."

Rejeté.

Dans l'article 67, M. Cutler propose de retrancher les mots "homme blanc libre," et les remplacer par les mots "tous les hommes disponibles de l'Etat."

Adopté par un vote d'assis et levé ; oui 51, non 18.

M. Smith propose le proviso suivant :

Tous les hommes disponibles résidents de l'âge de 18 à 45, (excepté les sujets ou citoyens des pouvoirs étrangers qui n'ont jamais voté dans les Etats-Unis ou qui n'ont pas déclaré leur intention de devenir citoyens,) seront enrôlés dans la milice, et sujets au service militaire d'après la loi.

Dépôt sur le bureau.

M. Cutler propose de retrancher toute la partie de l'article 67 après le mot "défense" dans la seconde ligne.

Cette motion est adoptée par un vote d'assis et levé ; oui 58, non 11.

A la lecture de l'article 79, M. Sullivan propose le proviso suivant :

Et que les juges des Cours Suprêmes soient élus par le peuple pour un terme de huit ans—également que les juges des cours inférieures soient élus par le peuple de leurs divers districts pour un terme de six ans, et qu'il sera du devoir de la Législature de fixer le temps pour l'élection de tous les juges, à une époque différente de celle fixée pour toutes les autres élections.

Sur la motion d'adoption, le proviso de M. Sullivan est rejeté.

M. Henderson propose le proviso suivant pour l'Art. 106 :

Toutes personnes pourront être mises sous caution en fournissant des sécurités solvables, excepté pour offense capitale, lorsque la preuve est évidente ou la présomption grande ; et le droit de caution aura lieu par un appel à la Cour Suprême.

Sur motion, le proviso est rejeté.

M. Cazabat propose de retrancher tout l'article 116.

M. Davies propose de tout retrancher après les mots "maisons de jeu," dans la seconde ligne du dit article.

Dépôt sur le bureau.

M. Cazabat propose de retrancher tout le dit article après le mot "billets."

Sur motion de M. Sullivan, le dépôt sur le bureau est ordonné.

M. Austin renouvelle la motion de M. Cazabat de retrancher tout l'article.

Dépôt sur le bureau.

Sur lecture de l'art. 117, M. Stauffer propose de retrancher le tout après le mot "divorces."

Dépôt sur le bureau.

Dans l'article 122, M. Smith propose d'insérer après le mot "soit" dans la seconde ligne, le mot "no."

Rejeté.

L'article 123 est lu, et motion faite de retrancher les mots "excepté celle de juge de paix."

Rejeté.

A la lecture de l'art. 130, M. Hills propose de retrancher le mot "majorité" et insérer les mots "deux tiers," de manière à ce que les deux tiers des votes de l'Assemblée Générale soient nécessaires pour changer le siége du gouvernement.

Sur motion de M. Wenck, l'amendement de M. Hills est déposé sur le bureau par un vote d'assis et levé : oui 40, non 26.

La motion de prendre un repos de quinze minutes ayant été rejetée, la lecture de la constitution est résumée.

M. Cazabat propose d'amender l'article 133, en ajoutant après les mots " les prix suivants," dans la dernière ligne de la page 20, les mots "jusqu'à ce qu'il soit autrement pourvu par la loi."

Rejeté.

MM. Cutler et Cazabat proposent de retrancher tout le dit article après le mot "droits."

Après discussion, M. Cutler, avec le consentement de son second, retire sa motion.

M. Sullivan propose de retrancher la 1ère, 2e et 3e lignes de l'article 134.

ET L'AMENDEMENT DE LA CONSTITUTION DE LA LOUISIANE. 165

Dépôt sur le bureau.

M. Terry propose de retrancher le mot "pourra" et y substituer "sera," dans la 1ère ligne du dit article.

Sur motion du dépôt sur le bureau, l'appel par oui et non a lieu et donne le résultat suivant :

Affirmative :

MM. Abell, Austin, Barrett, Baum, Beauvais, Bennie, Burke, Campbell, Cazabat, Crozat, Cutler, Decker, Davies, Edwards, Ennis, Fish, Flagg, Fuller, Gastinel, Gruneberg, Heard, Henderson, Kavanagh, Knobloch, Kugler, Mayer, Mann, Normand, Newell, Ong, Pintado, S. Pursell, Schnurr, Seymour, Shaw, Stumpf, Stiner, Stauffer, Taliaferro, Wenck, Wells, Wilson—42.

Négative :

MM. Bell, Bofill, Buckley, J. K. Cook, T. Cook, Dufresne, Duane, Flood, Foley, Fosdick, Geier, Gorlinski, Gaidry, Healy, Harnan, Hart, Hills, Hire, Howes, Maurer, Maas, Mendiverri, Montamat, Morris, E. Murphy, M. W. Murphy, Orr, O'Conner, J. Payne, Poynot, Schroeder, Smith, Spellicy, Stocker, Sullivan, Terry, Thorpe, Thomas, Waters, Collin—40.

Le proviso de M. Terry est, en conséquence, déposé sur le bureau.

M. Wells propose de retrancher tout le titre IX.

Sur cette motion, l'appel nominal est ordonné et donne le résultat suivant :

Affirmative :

MM. Austin, Beauvais, Bennie, Crozat, Cutler, Decker, Edwards, Fish, Flagg, Fuller, Heard, Kavanagh, Kugler, Mann, Newell, Ong, S. Pursell, Seymour, Shaw, Taliaferro, Thorpe, Wenck, Wells, Wilson—24.

Négative :

MM. Abell, Barrett, Baum, Bell, Bofill, Buckley, Burke, Campbell, Cazabat, J. K. Cook, T. Cook, Collin, Duke, Davies, Dufresne, Duane, Dupaty, Ennis, Flood, Foley, Fosdick, Gastinel, Geier, Gorlinski, Gruneberg, Gaidry, Healy, Harnan, Hart, Henderson, Hills, Hire, Howes, Knobloch, Mayer, Maas, Maurer, Mendiverri, Montamat, Morris, E. Murphy, M. W. Murphy, Normand, Orr, O'Conner, J. Payne, Pintado, Poynot, Schroeder, Schnurr, Smith, Spellicy, Stocker, Stumpf, Stiner, Stauffer, Sullivan, Terry, Thomas, Waters—60.

En conséquence, la motion de M. Wells est rejetée. La question précédente est ordonnée et le titre IX adopté.

Sur motion d'ajourner, l'appel a lieu et donne le vote suivant :

Affirmative :

MM. Campbell, Collin, J, K. Cook, Dufresne, Dupaty, Flagg, Gaidry, Harnan, Knobloch, Mayer, Mendiverri, M. W. Murphy, Newell, O'Conner, Orr, Pintado—16.

Négative :

MM. Abell, Austin, Barrett, Baum, Beauvais, Bell, Bennie, Bofill, Buckley, Burke, Cazabat, T. Cook, Crozat, Cutler, Decker, Davies, Duane, Edwards, Ennis, Fish, Flood, Fosdick, Fuller, Gastinel, Geier, Gorlinski, Gruneberg, Healy, Hart, Heard, Henderson, Hills, Hire, Howes, Kavanagh, Kugler, Maas, Mann, Maurer, Montamat, Morris, E. Murphy, Normand, Ong, J. Payne, S. Pursell, Schroeder, Schnurr, Seymour, Shaw, Smith, Spellicy, Stocker, Stumpf, Stiner, Stauffer, Sullivan, Taliaferro, Terry, Thorpe, Thomas, Waters, Wenck, Wells, Wilson—66.

L'article 136 est lu. M. Hills propose d'effacer "quatre" et d'insérer "cinq" à la place, et aussi d'ajouter ces mots : "A moins qu'il n'en soit autrement pourvu par la loi," afin de rendre l'article ainsi conçu : "son salaire sera de cinq mille piastres par an, à moins qu'il n'en soit autrement ordonné par la loi."

Motion du dépôt sur la table étant faite sans succès, le proviso de M. Hills est adopté.

M. Stauffer propose, comme proviso à l'article 137, d'effacer toute cette partie de l'article qui suit le mot "Etat."

Motion du dépôt sur la table étant faite sans succès, le proviso de M. Stauffer est adopté.

M. Campbell offre alors la modification suivante à l'article 137, savoir :

Pourvu, Que la ville de la Nouvelle-Orléans comprenne une amélioration intérieure et un district de dessèchement, et que les appropriations faites à cet effet soient tirées du trésor de la ville de la Nouvelle-Orléans.

M. Sullivan propose le dépôt sur le bureau.

La motion est adoptée par un vote de 46 oui et 21 non.

L'article 140 est lu.

M. Terry propose d'insérer, après le mot "recevoir," dans la troisième ligne, les mots "une compensation de trois mille cinq cents dollars par an."

Dépôt sur le bureau.

M. Beauvais propose d'amender en y substituant 5,000 dollars pour le salaire du surintendant de l'éducation publique.

Rejeté.

M. Fish propose d'insérer après le mot "recevoir," les mots "un salaire de 4,000 dollars par année."

La motion du dépôt est rejetée et le proviso de M. Fish est adopté.

Sur motion de M. Hills, les mots "telle compensation que la Législature pourra fixer" sont effacés, afin que l'article soit en harmonie avec l'amendement qui précède.

Adopté.

La Convention s'ajourne alors à demain à midi.

Approuvé.

JOHN E. NEELIS,
Secrétaire.

VENDREDI, le 22 juillet 1864.

La Convention se réunit conformément à l'ajournement.

Présents, l'Hon. E. H. Durell, président, et les membres suivants :

MM. Abell, Austin, Barrett, Baum, Beauvais, Bell, Bennie, Bofill, Buckley, Burke, Campbell, Cazabat, J. K. Cook, T. Cook, Crozat, Cutler, Collin, Davies, Dufresne, Duane, Dupaty, Decker, Edwards, Ennis, Fish, Flagg, Flood, Foley, Fosdick, Fuller, Gastinel, Geier, Gorlinski, Gruneberg, Gaidry, Healy, Harnan, Hart, Heard, Henderson, Hills, Hire, Howes, Kavanagh, Knobloch, Kugler, Maas, Mann, Maurer, Mendiverri, Montamat, Morris, E. Murphy, M. W. Murphy, Mayer, Newell, Normand, O'Conner, Ong, Orr, J. Payne, Poynot, J. Purcell, S. Pursell, Schroeder, Schnurr, Seymour, Shaw, Smith, Spellicy, Stocker, Stumpf, Stiner, Stauffer, Sullivan, Taliaferro, Terry, Thorpe, Thomas, Waters, Wenck, Wells, Wilson.

Les minutes d'hier sont lues et adoptées.

Le président se lève pour une question de privilége ; appelle l'attention de la Convention sur un sale article de ce jour, publié dans un journal nommé le *Times* de la Nouvelle-Orléans, lequel article M. le président le déclare diffamation, et contre lui et contre la Convention; sur quoi M. Stauffer offre la résolution suivante :

Résolu, Que le sergent-d'armes reçoive l'ordre de prendre immédiatement possession du journal nommé le *Times* de la Nouvelle-Orléans, et que la publication de ce journal soit suspendue jusqu'à ce que son éditeur responsable, Thomas P. May, Esq., paraisse devant la Convention, et se disculpe de la diffamation publiée dans son journal de ce jour en ce qui regarde les travaux de la Convention du 21 juillet 1864.

M. Hills propose le dépôt sur le bureau de la résolution. L'appel par oui et non a lieu et donne le résultat suivant :

Affirmative :

MM. Abell, Baum, Bofill, Buckley, Campbell, Cazabat, Dufresne, Decker, Edwards, Ennis, Fish, Fosdick, Gastinel, Gorlinski, Gruneberg, Hart, Heard, Hills, Kavanagh, Knobloch, Mann, Maurer. Morris, E. Murphy, M. W. Murphy, Ong, Orr, Poynot, Shaw, Stumpf, Sullivan, Waters—32.

Nénative :

MM. Austin, Barrett, Beauvais Bell, Bennie, Burke, J. K. Cook, T. Cook, Crozat, Cutler, Collin, Davies, Duane, Dupaty, Flagg, Flood, Foley, Fuller, Geier, Healy, Harnan, Henderson, Hire, Howes, Kugler, Maas, Montamat, Mayer, Newell, Normand, O'Conner, J. Payne, S. Purcell, Schroeder, Schnurr, Smith, Spellicy, Stocker, Stiner, Stauffer, Terry, Thorpe, Thomas, Wenck, Wells, Wilson—47.

La motion du dépôt sur le bureau est en conséquence rejetée.

M. Cutler offre le substitut suivant :

Résolu, Que Thomas May, éditeur du *Times* de la Nouvelle-Orléans, soit amené immédiatement devant cette Convention par le sergent-d'armes et qu'il soit contraint à se disculper de la diffamation dont il s'est rendu coupable envers ce corps, ainsi prouvé par son numéro du 22 juillet 1864, ou alors qu'il soit disposé de lui de telle manière que cette Convention jugera convenable.

D'après motion, le substitut de M. Cutler est adopté.

Sur la motion de MM. Cazabat et Smith, l'ordre du jour est pris en considération et la lecture de la constitution continuée.

M. Terry présente le proviso suivant à l'article 141 :

La Législature pourvoira à l'éducation de tous les enfants de l'Etat de l'âge de six à dix-huit ans, en soutenant des écoles publiques gratis au moyen de taxes ou autrement.

M. Sullivan propose le dépôt du proviso sur le bureau.

Sur cette motion, l'appel par oui et non donne le résultat qui suit :

Affirmative :

MM. Abell, Bofill, Buckley, Campbell, Crozat, Decker, Dufresne, Edwards, Fuller,

Gastinel, Geier, Gruneberg, Heard, Henderson, Knobloch, Mayer, Maas, Mendiverri, Montamat, Morris, M. W. Murphy, Newell, Normand, Orr, Ong, S. Pursell, Sullivan, Thomas, Waters—29.

Négative :

MM. Austin, Barrett, Baum, Beauvais, Bell, Bennie, Burke, Collin, Cazabat, J. K. Cook, T. Cook, Cutler, Davies, Duane, Du, paty, Ennis, Fish, Flagg, Flood, Foley, Fosdick, Gorlinski, Healy, Harnan, Hart, Hills, Hire, Howes, Kavanagh, Kugler, Mann, Maurer, E. Murphy, O'Conner, J. Payne, Poynot, Schroeder, Schnurr, Seymour, Shaw, Smith, Spellicy, Stocker, Stumpf, Stiner, Stauffer, Terry, Thorpe, Wells et Wilson—50.

En conséquence, la motion du dépôt est perdue.

Sur motion d'adopter le proviso, le vote qui suit par l'appel de oui et non donne pour résultat l'adoption du dit proviso :

Affirmative :

MM. Austin, Barrett, Baum, Beauvais, Bell, Bennie, Burke, Collin, Cazabat, 'J. K. Cook, T. Cook, Crozat, Cutler, Davies, Duane, Dupaty, Ennis, Fish, Flagg, Flood, Foley, Fosdick, Geier, Gorlinski, Healy, Harnan, Henderson, Hills, Hire, Howes, Kavanagh, Mann, Maurer, E. Murphy, Newell, Normand, O'Conner, J. Payne, Poynot, J. Purcell, Schroeder, Shaw, Smith, Spellicy, Stocker, Stumpf, Stiner, Stauffer, Terry, Thorpe, Thomas, Wells et Wilson —53.

Négative :

MM. Abell, Bofill, Buckley, Campbell, Decker, Dufresne, Edwards, Fuller, Gastinel, Gruneberg, Hart, Heard, Knobloch, Kugler, Mayer, Maas, Mendiverri, Montamat, Morris, M. W. Murphy, Orr, Ong, S. Pursell, Schnurr, Seymour, Sullivan et Waters—27.

Le proviso de M. Terry est en conséquence adopté.

A la lecture de l'article 143, M. Smith propose de retrancher les mots "dans la ville de la Nouvelle-Orléans" et d'insérer les mots "par la Législature."

Dépôt sur le bureau.

M. Foley propose de retrancher tout l'article 146.

M. Smith demande le dépôt sur la table de la motion résultant par un vote d'assis et levé : Oui 54, non 12.

La motion du dépôt sur la table est adoptée.

Dans l'article 147, M. Bofill propose de retrancher dans la troisième ligne les mots

"deux tiers" et d'y insérer les mots "à la majorité."

Adopté.

Dans l'article 154, M. Shaw propose de retrancher les mots " sans molestation hostile ni interférence."

Adopté.

La dernière lecture étant enfin terminée, la question est mise aux voix pour l'adoption de la constitution de l'Etat de la Louisiane dans son ensemble; l'appel nominal est ordonné et le vote suivant en est le résultat :

Affirmative :

MM. Austin, Barrett, Baum, Beauvais, Bell, Bennie, Burke, Cazabat, J. K. Cook, T. Cook, Collin, Crozat, Cutler, Davies, Duane, Dupaty, Edwards, Ennis, Fish, Flagg, Flood, Foley, Fuller, Geier, Gorlinski, Healy, Harnan, Hart, Heard, Henderson, Hills, Hire, Howes, Kavanagh, Kugler, Mann, Maurer, Montamat, Morris, E. Murphy, M. W. Murphy, Newell, Normand. O'Conner, Ong, J. Payne, Poynot, J. Purcell, S. Pursell, Shroeder, Schnurr, Seymour, Shaw, Smith, Spellicy, Stocker, Stiner, Stauffer, Taliaferro, Terry, Thorpe, Thomas, Wenck, Wells, Wilson et M. le président.—66.

Négative :

MM. Abell, Bofill, Buckley, Decker, Dufresne, Gastinel, Gruneberg, Gaidry, Knobloch, Maas, Mayer, Mendiverri, Orr, Stumpf, Sullivan, Waters—16.

A l'appel du nom de M. Mendiverri par le secrétaire, ce membre soumet ses raisons par écrit, pour voter comme il le fait, lesquelles raisons devront être publiées dans les débats de cette Convention avant que le vote ne soit déclaré. M. Hills propose que le président soit requis de voter.

Adopté.

M. Hills demande également que tous les membres qui étaient absents au moment du vote soient requis de se faire connaître.

La motion de M. Hills est adoptée.

M. Newell présente l'autorisation suivante, écrite par M. Taliaferro, qui est lue :

NOUVELLE-ORLEANS, le 22 juillet, 1864.

Par la présente j'autorise John A. Newell, de la paroisse des Rapides, à voter pour moi dans l'affirmative pour l'adoption de la constitution dans son ensemble.

R. W. TALIAFERRO.

M. Newell demande alors la permission de recorder le vote de M. Taliaferro, ce qui lui est accordé : le vote est pour l'affirmative.

Le président alors déclare le vote précédent, et donne lui-même son vote pour l'affirmative.

Il déclare ensuite la constitution de l'Etat de la Louisiane adoptée dans son ensemble après sa dernière lecture.

M. Montamat propose que le Comité d'Enrôlement reçoive les instructions nécessaires pour faire préparer la constitution pour demain à midi.

Adopté.

Le président annonce que, d'après les réglements de l'article 155, de la constitution qui vient d'être adoptée, il a choisi trois journaux dans lesquels la constitution sera publiée : Le *True Delta* et l'*Era*, qui publieront dans la langue anglaise et la langue française ; et *La Gazette Allemande* qui publiera la dite constitution en Allemand.

La Convention s'ajourne alors à demain à midi.

Approuvé.

JOHN E. NEELIS,
Secrétaire.

SAMEDI, 22 juillet 1864.

La Convention se réunit conformément à l'ajournement, et est appelée à l'ordre par le président.

La prière est faite par le Révérend Strong.

Le secrétaire fait l'appel du rôle et les membres suivants répondent à leurs noms :

MM. Abell, Austin, Balch, Barrett, Baum, Beauvais, Bennie, Bell, Buckley, Burke, Campbell, Collin, Cazabat, T. Cook, J. K. Cook, Cutler, Davies, Decker, Duane, Dufresne, Dupaty, Edwards, Ennis, Fish, Flagg, Flood, Foley, Fosdick, Fuller, Gastinel, Geier, Gorlinski, Gruneberg, Healy, Harnan, Hart, Heard, Henderson, Hills, Hire, Howes, Kavanagh, Kugler, Maas, Mann, Maurer, Mayer, Mendiverri, Montamat, Morris, E. Murphy, M. W. Murphy, Newell, Normand, O'Conner, Ong, Orr, J. Payne, Pintado, Poynot, J. Purcell, S. Pursell, Schroeder, Schnurr, Seymour, Shaw, Smith, Spellicy, Stocker, Stumpf, Stiner, Stauffer, Sullivan, Taliaferro, Terry, Thorpe, Thomas, Waters, Wenck, Wells, Wilson—82.

MM. Crozat, Bofill et Knobloch sont excusés de leur absence.

Conformément à une résolution adoptée hier, le sergent-d'armes présente M. Thomas P. May à la barre de la Convention.

Le président, ayant fait la lecture des résolutions adoptées hier, demande à M. May ce qu'il a à répondre; sur quoi ce monsieur lit le papier suivant :

"Je suis ici avec le prévôt-maréchal pour obéir à un ordre militaire lancé par le Général Banks, et non pour obéir à l'ordre de cette Convention. En temps et lieu, et conformément aux lois, je répondrai à toutes accusations portées contre moi et ma gazette le *Times*."

M. Henderson fait la motion de considérer la réponse de M. May, comme une insulte additionnelle.

M. Abell fait la motion de déposer le tou sur la table indéfiniment.

Sur la motion de M. Abell, l'appel nominal est demandé et donne le résultat suivant:

Affirmative :

MM. Austin, Barrett, Beauvais, Bell, Bennie, Burke, Collin, T. Cook, Cutler, Davies, Duane, Dupaty, Edwards, Ennis, Flagg, Flood, Foley, Fuller, Healy Harnan, Hart, Henderson, Hire, Howes, Maas. Mann, E. Murphy, Newell, Normand, O'Conner, J. Payne, Poynot, S. Pursell, Schroeder, Schnurr, Seymour, Smith, Spellicy, Stocker, Stumpf, Stiner, Stauffer, Taliaferro, Terry, Thomas, Wells, Wilson—47.

Négative :

MM. Abell, Balch, Baum, Buckley, Campbell, Cazabat, J. K. Cook, Decker, Dufresne, Fish, Fosdick, Geier, Gorlinski, Gruneberg, Heard, Hills, Maurer, Mayer, Mendiverri, Montamat, Morris, M. W. Murphy, Ong, Orr, Pintado, J. Purcell, Shaw, Sullivan, Thorpe, Waters, Wenck—31.

En conséquence, la motion de M. Abell est déposée sur la table. Après quelques discussions, la question originale est prise et la motion de M. Henderson adoptée.

A la requête de M. Abell, le président lit l'ordre suivant du Gén. Banks :

QUARTIER GÉNÉRAL,
DÉPARTEMENT DU GOLFE,
Nouvelle-Orléans, 23 juillet 1864.

Le prévôt-maréchal général est requis, à la réception de cet ordre, de prendre les mesures qu'il croira nécessaires, dans le but d'aider M. De Coursey, sergent-d'armes de la Convention constitutionnelle, à mener devant cette Convention M. Thomas P. May, assistant-trésorier des Etats-Unis,et propriétaire et éditeur de la gazette Le *Times* de la Nouvelle-Orléans, pour répondre à l'accusation portée contre lui, pour infraction aux priviléges de cette Assemblée représentative du peuple de la Louisiane.

Cet ordre sera exécuté immédiatement.

N. P. BANKS,
Major Général commandant.

Officiel : W. W. HOWE,
Major et A. A. A. Général.

M. Thomas offre le préambule et les résolutions qui suivent :

Attendu, Que Thomas P. May, éditeur et propriétaire de la gazette nommée *Le Times*, publiée en la ville de la Nouvelle-Orléans, a, durant les derniers six mois, publié dans la dite gazette des articles qui, dans l'opinion de cette Convention, étaient déloyaux dans leurs sentiments au gouvernement, et plusieurs d'entr'eux hostiles à cette Convention ; et

Attendu, Que dans l'émission de cette gazette, le 22 juillet, un honteux libelle contre le président et les membres de cette Convention a été publié, et qu'ayant été traduit à la barre de cette Convention, il a refusé de s'excuser en aucune façon du dit libelle et mépris de cette Convention.

Résolu, Thomas P. May, pour son mépris du président et des membres de cette Convention, en publiant dans sa gazette le dit libelle, sera emprisonné dans la Prison de Paroisse de la paroisse d'Orléans durant l'espace de dix jours, à moins que la Convention ne s'ajourne plus tôt et que le sergent-d'armes soit requis et autorisé à mettre cette résolution à exécution.

Résolu de plus, Les autorités militaires de ce département sont respectueusement invitées par cette Convention à supprimer la publication de la dite gazette ;

Résolu de plus, Le président des Etats-Unis est respectueusement sollicité par cette Convention de démettre de ses fonctions d'assistant-trésorier des Etats-Unis à la Nouvelle-Orléans le dit Thomas P. May, fonctions qu'il occupe en ce moment.

M. Terry fait la motion de prendre la question originale ; elle est mise aux voix et adoptée par le vote suivant :

Affirmative :

MM. Austin, Barrett, Baum. Beauvais, Bell, Bennie, Burke, Collin, J. K. Cook, T. Cook, Cutler, Davies, Duane, Dupaty, Edwards, Ennis, Flagg, Flood, Foley, Fuller, Healy, Hart, Henderson, Hire, Howes, Maas, Maurer, E. Murphy, Newell, Normand, O'Conner, J. Payne, Poynot, J. Purcell. S. Pursell, Schnurr, Seymour, Smith, Spellicy, Stocker, Stiner, Stauffer, Taliaferro, Terry, Thorpe, Thomas, Wenck, Wells et Wilson—49.

Négative :

MM. Abell, Balch, Buckley, Campbell, Cazabat, Decker, Dufresne, Fish, Fosdick, Gastinel, Geier, Gorlinski, Gruneberg, Har-

nan, Heard, Hills, Kavanagh, Mann, Mayer, Mendiverri, Montamat, Morris, M. W. Murphy, Ong, Orr, Pintado, Schroeder, Shaw. Stumpf, Sullivan et Waters—31.

Le président invite alors le secrétaire à fournir au sergent-d'armes une copie de la résolution afin de la mettre à exécution.

L'ordonnance offerte par M. Thorpe ayant pour but de rediviser l'Etat en Districts Congressionels est pris et adopté.

M. Thorpe offre aussi la résolution suivante qui est adoptée :

Résolu, Jusqu'à ce qu'il en soit autrement ordonné par la Législature, le salaire du secrétaire privé du gouverneur sera de deux mille cinq cents piastres par an, et le salaire du commis en chef du secrétaire d'Etat sera de deux mille piastres par an, payables par l'auditeur des Comptes Publics, sur leur propre warrant, trimestriellement. Cette résolution prendra son effet du 4 mars 1864.

M. Thomas offre la résolution suivante, qui est adoptée :

Résolu, Que tous comptes, dettes et réclamations contre cette Convention contractés pendant et après son ajournement, seront soumis à un comité spécial chargé d'auditer les dits comptes, dettes et réclamations. Ce comité se composera de cinq membres nommés par le président. Aucuns comptes ne seront payés avant d'avoir été examinés, audités et approuvés par une majorité de ce dit comité, et les comptes ainsi audités et approuvés, seront payés sur le mandat du président par le trésorier de l'Etat, de tous fonds du trésor de l'Etat non autrement affectés.

Le président nomme de ce comité MM. Thomas, Montamat, Barrett, Crozat et Buckley.

M. Wells offre la résolution suivante :

Résolu, Que les rapporteurs de cette Convention recevront chacun des fonds du trésor public non autrement affectés, la somme de cinq cents piastres comme extra compensation pour leurs travaux pénibles et difficiles pendant la durée de cette Convention, et pour achever l'ouvrage après l'ajournement de cette Assemblée. Les dites sommes seront payées sur leurs propres mandats.

M. Montamat offre le subtitut suivant :

Résolu, Les employés suivants de cette Convention, recevront les gratifications suivantes, qui seront payées de tous fonds des dépenses contingentes de cette Convention :

Sergent-d'armes.................$200 00
Commis en chef des enrôlements.. 100 00
Commis aux enrôlements, (chacun) 100 00

Maître de poste............... 50 00
Portier........................ 100 00
Messagers, (chacun)............ 25 00
Rapporteurs et assistants, (chacun) 200 00

M. Stiner offre l'amendement suivant, lequel est accepté par M. Montamat :

Résolu, La somme de deux cent cinquante dollars, sera payée à chacune des personnes suivantes : MM. Mathew Whilldin et J. A. Russ, rapporteurs, pour services rendus à cette Convention.

La résolution ainsi amendée est adoptée.

M. Abell offre ce qui suit :

Attendu, Que durant l'absence du rapporteur officiel, la lecture et la révision des manuscrits et des épreuves, la complication des débats et autres devoirs de la place, ont été remplis et exécutés sous la direction du président, par M. H. A. Gallup, assistant-rapporteur, en outre de ses devoirs comme tel ;

Résolu, Pour les services par lui rendus; M. H. A. Gallup recevra en sus de ses salaires comme assistant-rapporteur, la même compensation que reçoit le rapporteur officiel, et ce, pour le temps que le président jugera juste et équitable ; la dite somme sera payée sur le mandat du président de tous fonds du trésor non autrement affectés.

Adopté par un vote par assis et levé de 45 oui, contre 15 non.

M. Waters fait la motion que chaque rapporteur de cette Convention reçoive $500. Adopté.

M. Thorpe propose que chacun des portiers reçoivent cent dollars.

M. Sullivan propose que le portier et le maître de poste reçoivent chacun cent cinquante dollars.

Le président remarque que ces motions ne sont pas présentées d'une manière convenable, attendu qu'elles sont faites verbalement, et qu'aucune disposition n'est prise relative à leur paiement. Il serait, en conséquence, préférable de les présenter dans les formes légales.

La Convention y donnant son adhésion, M. Waters offre sa motion par écrit, laquelle est ainsi conçue :

Résolu, Les rapporteurs de cette Convention recevront cinq cent dollars chacun, de tous les fonds du trésor, non autrement affectés, payables sur leurs propres mandats. Adopté.

M. Thorpe, président du comité des Enrôlements, rapporte que la constitution enrôlée est entre ses mains, mais que n'ayant pas eu le temps de la lire et de la comparer, il se réserve jusqu'à lundi pour la soumettre alors à la Convention et recevoir les signatures.

La Convention alors s'ajourne à lundi le 25 juillet à midi.

Approuvé.

JONH E. NEELIS,
Secrétaire.

LUNDI, le 25 juillet 1864.

La Convention se réunit conformément à l'ajournement.

La prière d'ouverture est dite par le Révérend Strong.

Le rôle est appelé et les membres suivants répondent à leurs noms :

MM. Abell, Austin, Balch, Barrett, Baum, Beauvais, Bell, Bofill, Buckley, Burke, Campbell, Collin, Cazabat, J. K. Cook, T. Cook, Crozat, Cutler, Davies, Decker, Duane, Dufresne, Duke, Dupaty, Edwards, Ennis, Fish, Flagg, Flood, Foley, Fosdick, Fuller, Gastinel, Geier, Gorlinski, Gruneberg, Healy, Harnan, Hart, Heard, Henderson, Hills, Hire, Howes, Kavanagh, Knobloch, Kugler, Maas, Mann, Maurer, Mendiverri, Montamat, Morris, E. Murphy, M. W. Murphy, Normand, O'Conner, Orr, J. Payne, Pintado, Poynot, J. Purcell, S. Pursell, Schroeder, Schnurr, Seymour, Shaw, Smith, Spellicy, Stocker, Stumpf, Stiner, Stauffer, Sullivan, Terry, Thorpe, Thomas, Waters, Wenck, Wells, Wilson—80.

Les minutes d'hier sont lues et adoptées.

M. Cutler propose la résolution suivante comme substitut aux appropriations et résolutions pour extra compensation aux officiers et autres de cette Convention, passées samedi dernier, savoir :

Résolu, Que les officiers dont les noms suivent, et autres appartenant à cette Convention, recevront, comme extra compensation du trésorier de l'Etat à titre de compensation extra, (sur le warrant du président), des fonds qui ne sont pas autrement appropriés, savoir :

A l'honorable T. N. Carrigan, gardien de la Librairie d'Etat...... $500 00
A chacun des rapporteurs........ 500 00
Au sergent-d'armes............. 500 00
A chacun des assistants sergents-d'armes......................... 100 00
Au maître de poste............. 150 00
Au portier 300 00
Au chef du bureau d'enrôlement.. 100 00
A chacun des commis d'enrôlement 100 00
A chaque messager............. 50 00

A trois portiers, chaque.......... 50 00
A quatre officiers de police, chaque 100 00
A MM. T. W. Russ, de la *Gazette de l'Etat*, Whildin et Q. H. Draper, du *True Delta*, rapporteurs, chaque................................ 250 00

La question précédente ayant été ordonnée, la résolution est adoptée par le vote suivant par assis et levé : oui 61, non 7.

M. Fish offre le préambule et les résolutions suivantes :

Attendu, Qu'une Convention, réclamant le droit d'agir au nom de l'Etat de la Louisiane, a, le 26me jour du mois de janvier 1861, passé une ordonnance nommée "Ordonnance pour dissoudre l'Union existant entre l'Etat de la Louisiane, et les autres Etats mis avec elle sous le titre de "La Constitution des Etats-Unis d'Amérique," par lequel elle déclare et ordonne le rappel de "toutes les lois et ordonnances par lesquelles l'Etat de la Louisiane devient membre de l'Union fédérale," et déchargeant tous les citoyens de tous leurs devoirs envers ledit gouvernement ;

Et attendu, Qu'une semblable ordonnance de sécession était basée sur une fausse assomption de la souveraineté de l'Etat, une théorie pervertie des droits de l'Etat, et produite seulement dans l'intérêt de l'esclavage ; en conséquence,

Qu'il soit résolu, Que nous, le peuple de la Louisiane en Convention assemblé, dénonçons solennellement les doctrines des "droits de l'Etat" et de la souveraineté de l'Etat, (interprétés comme ils l'ont été en justification de la sécession) comme entièrement subversives à notre forme de gouvernement, et tendant à la confusion, à l'anarchie et à la destruction nationale.

Résolu, Que nous soutenons et maintenons que notre première allégeance est due au gouvernement des Etats-Unis ; que la constitution et les lois des Etats-Unis sont la loi suprême du pays, qu'il n'y a rien dans la constitution ou les lois de l'Etat qui y soit contraire ; qu'aucune Convention d'Etat, représentant avec sincérité le peuple ou non, n'a aucun droit, pouvoir ou autorité de nous absoudre de cette allégeance, et que, en conséquence, l'acte communément nommé "l'Ordonnance de sécession" est, et a toujours été nulle et vide de sens.

Résolu, Qu'ayant légalement aboli l'institution de l'esclavage dans cet Etat comme un mal et une source constante de troubles et de danger pour la nation, et désirant pour les mêmes raisons de la voir légalement abolie dans tout le pays, nous sommes en faveur d'amender la constitution des Etats-Unis de manière à obtenir le résultat.

Adopté par le vote suivant :

Affirmative :

MM. Austin, Barrett, Beauvais, Baum, Bell, Bofill, Buckley, Burke, Campbell, Collin, Cazabat. T. Cook, Crozat, Cutler, Davies, Duane, Duke, Dupaty, Edwards, Ennis, Fish, Flagg, Flood, Foley, Fosdick, Fuller, Geier, Gorlinski, Healy, Harnan, Hart, Henderson, Hills, Hire, Howes, Kavanagh, Kugler, Mann, Maurer, Montamat, Morris, E. Murphy, Normand, O'Conner, Orr, J. Payne, Pintado, Poynot, J. Purcell, S. Pursell, Schroeder, Schnurr, Seymour, Shaw, Smith, Spellicy, Stocker, Stumpf, Stiner, Stauffer, Sullivan, Terry, Thorpe, Thomas, Waters, Wenck, Wells, Wilson—68.

Négative :

MM. Abell, Balch, Decker, Dufresne, Gruneberg, Maas, Mendiverri, M. W. Murphy—8.

M. Thomas présente ce qui suit :

UNE ORDONNANCE DEFINISSANT LA QUALIFICATION DES VOTANTS.

Section 1re. *Qu'il soit ordonné par le peuple de l'Etat de la Louisiane en Convention assemblé*, Que jusqu'à ce qu'il en soit autrement pourvu par la loi, tous les commissionnaires ou autres officiers ou personnes présidant aux élections tenues dans cet Etat, devront exiger que chaque votant possède les qualifications définies dans la constitution ainsi qu'elle a été adoptée par cette Convention, et qu'il aura déclaré son allégeance au gouvernement des Etats-Unis, d'après la proclamation du président du 8 décembre 1863.

Sect. 2. *Qu'il soit de plus ordonné*, Que le pouvoir exécutif de l'Etat soit chargé de l'exécution de cette ordonnance, et de pourvoir aux institutions et aux détails nécessaires à l'effet d'obtenir le but voulu.

Sect. 3. *Qu'il soit de plus ordonné*, Que cette ordonnance aura force de loi de suite après son passage, et jusqu'à ce qu'elle soit ou révoquée ou modifiée par la Législature de l'Etat.

Adopté par un vote d'assis et levé ; oui 60, non 9.

M. Fosdick présente ce qui suit :

Attendu, Que l'adoption de l'article 36 de la constitution qui exclut tous les ministres de n'importe qu'elle religion de siéger à la Législature de cet Etat est sujet à misconstruction, qu'il soit

Résolu, Que l'adoption du dit article n'a d'autre but que de séparer et sauvegarder de l'arène politique le caractère sacré du ministre, et par conséquent protéger les véritables intérêts de l'Evangile.

Résolu, Qu'une somme de 1000 dollars soit payée sur le warrant du président de cette Convention, de l'argent du trésor de l'Etat, non autrement approprié, pour être distribuée parmi les ministres qui ont officié pendant la session de cette Convention.

M. Montamat propose que la résolution soit déposée sur la table ; le oui et non est ordonné, avec le résultat suivant :

Affirmative :

MM. Collin, Davies, Dupaty, Edwards, Gastinel, Healy, Harnan, Hart, Kugler, Montamat, M. W. Murphy, Normand, Schnurr, Seymour, Stocker. Stumpf, Sullivan, Waters, Wenck—19.]

Négative :

MM. Abell, Austin, Balch, Barrett, Baum, Beauvais, Bell, Bennie, Bofill, Buckley, Burke, Campbell, Cazabat, T. Cook, Crozat, Cutler, Decker, Duane, Dufresne, Duke, Ennis, Fish, Flagg, Flood, Foley, Fosdick, Fuller, Geier, Gorlinski, Gruneberg, Henderson, Hills, Hire, Howes, Kavanagh, Maas, Mann, Maurer, Mendiverri, Morris, E. Murphy, O'Conner, Orr, J. Payne, Pintado, Poynot, J. Purcell, S. Pursell, Schroeder, Shaw, Smith, Spellicy, Stiner, Stauffer, Terry, Thorpe, Wells, Wilson—58.

La motion du dépôt sur le bureau ayant été rejetée, M. Stauffer présente le substitut suivant, à la résolution de M. Fosdick :

Résolu, Que les remercîments de cette Convention sont acquis, et offerts aux ministres de l'Evangile qui ont officié pendant la session.

Motion est faite de déposer sur la table le substitut de M. Stauffer, et un vote par assis et levé ayant lieu donne comme résultat : oui 29, non 29. Les voix étant également partagées, le président vote pour l'affirmative, en conséquence le substitut de M. Stauffer est déposé sur le bureau.

Déposé sur le bureau.

La résolution de M. Fosdick est alors adoptée par un vote par assis et levé : oui 56, non 20.

M. Shaw offre la résolution suivante :

Résolu, Que les officiers et les employés de la Convention qui seront nécessaires pour terminer les travaux après l'ajournement, soient placés sous la direction du président du Comité d'Enrôlement et du président de la Convention, que le dit président et le président du Comité d'Enrôlement auront le droit de renvoyer tous officiers ou employés par suite du manque d'exactitude ou pour la non-complétion de leurs travaux.

Résolu, Qu'après l'ajournement, les comités restants auront à continuer les devoirs qui leur sont assignés par les réglements ou les résolutions de cette Convention, et qui seraient nécessaires pour terminer les travaux de la dite Convention, et le président, en cas de négligence, aura le droit de requérir des dits comités l'exécution de leurs devoirs.

Adoptée.

M. Cutler propose ce qui suit :

Résolu, Que le salaire du commis du trésor et celui du commis principal de l'auditeur des comptes publics de l'Etat de la Louisiane, sera de trois milles dollars par année, jusqu'à ce qu'il en soit autrement pourvu par la loi ; cette résolution devant prendre effet immédiatement après son passage.

Déposé sur la table.

M. Cutler offre la résolution suivante :

Résolu, Que lorsque cette Convention s'ajournera, il sera facultatif au président de la reconvoquer pour n'importe quelle cause, ou dans le cas où la constitution ne serait pas ratifiée, dans le but de prendre les mesures nécessaires à la formation d'un gouvernement civil pour l'Etat de la Louisiane. Il devra aussi, dans ce cas, faire appel aux propres officiers de l'Etat à l'effet de faire une élection pour remplir les vacances qui pourraient exister dans la Convention, dans les paroisses où il y aura possibilité de le faire.

Résolu, Que dans le cas où la constitution serait ratifiée, la Législature de l'Etat aura le droit à la première session, de reconvoquer, la Convention de la même manière, dans le cas où elle le jugerait nécessaire, à l'effet de faire des amendements ou des additions à la constitution que, dans l'opinion de la Législature, elle croirait nécessaire, ou encore dans le cas où son action immédiate serait requis par suite d'urgence.

Résolu, Que pendant l'ajournement les membres ne recevront pas leur *per diem*.

La question précédente est ordonnée, et le vote suivant pris sur l'adoption de la résolution.

Pour l'adoption :

MM. Austin, Balch, Barrett, Baum, Beauvais, Bell, Burke, Collin, Cazabat, T. Cook, Crozat, Cutler, Davies, Duane, Dufresne, Duke, Dupaty, Edwards, Ennis, Fish, Flagg, Flood, Foley, Fuller, Geier, Gorlinski, Gruneberg, Hart, Henderson, Hire, Howes, Kavanagh, Kugler, Maas, Mann, Maurer, Morris, E. Murphy, Normand, O'Conner, Orr, J. Payne, Pintado, Poynot, J. Purcell, S. Pursell, Schroeder, Schnurr, Seymour, Shaw, Smith, Spellicy, Stocker, Stumpf, Stiner, Stauffer, Terry, Thorpe, Thomas, Waters, Wells et Wilson—62.

Contre l'adoption :

MM. Abell, Bofill, Buckley, Campbell, Decker, Fosdick, Gastinel, Healy, Hills,

Mendiverri, Montamat, M. W. Murphy, Sullivan, Wenck—14.

En conséquence la résolution est adoptée.

Sur la motion de M. Thorpe, le libraire de l'Etat reçoit les ordres de fournir à chaque membre cinquante copies des minutes, du journal des débats et de la constitution, aussitôt que les travaux seront imprimés.

M. Thorpe, président du comité d'Enrôlement, présente la constitution de l'Etat de la Louisiane dûment enrôlée, laquelle est signée par le président.

Les membres suivants signent la constitution :

MM. Austin, Barrett, Baum, Beauvais, Bell, Burke, Collin, Cazabat, T. Cook, Crozat, Cutler, Davies, Duane, Dupaty, Edwards, Ennis, Fish, Flagg Flood, Foley, Fosdick, Fuller, Geier, Gorlinski, Healy, Hart, Henderson, Hills, Hire, Howes, Kavanagh, Kugler, Mann, Maurer, Montamat, Morris, E. Murphy, M. W. Murphy, Normand, O'Conner, J. Payne, Pintado, Poynot, J. Purcell, S. Pursell, Schroeder, Schnurr, Seymour, Shaw, Smith, Spellicy, Stocker, Stiner, Stauffer, Terry, Thorpe, Thomas, Wenck, Wells, Wilson.

Les membres dont les noms suivent refusent de signer, savoir :

MM. Abell, Balch, Bofill, Buckley, Campbell, Decker, Dufresne, Duke, Gastinel, Gruneberg, Knobloch, Maas, Mendiverri, Orr, Stumpf, Sullivan et Waters.

Le reste des membres étaient absents ou n'ont pas répondu à leurs noms.

En déclarant qu'il refuse de signer, M. Mendiverri donne les raisons suivantes : D'après mes convictions honnêtes de ce qui est politique, juste et légal, je ne puis signer cette constitution.

M. Bofill soumet aussi par écrit les raisons pour lesquelles il refuse de signer la constitution ; l'ordre est donné pour la publication dans le journal des débats.

Sur la motion de M. Thorpe, l'ordre est donné de déposer la constitution dans le bureau du secrétaire de l'Etat, afin que les membres qui sont absents aujourd'hui puissent la signer un autre jour.

M. Shaw étant au fauteuil, M. Fosdick propose ce qui suit :

Résolu, Que les remercîments de cette Convention sont légitimement dûs et sont offerts à l'Hon. E. H. Durell, pour la manière juste et digne avec laquelle il a présidé à nos délibérations.

La résolution est adoptée à l'unanimité.

Le président ayant repris le fauteuil, M. Shaw lui fait connaître le vœu de la Convention, et donne lecture de la résolution adoptée avec une telle unanimité.

Le président remercie la Convention par peu de paroles dignes et appropriées à la circonstance.

Son Excellence le gouverneur Hahn étant présent fait un discours éloquent à la Convention ; après quoi les travaux se terminent par une prière du Rév. Dr. Newman, appropriée à la circonstance.

La Convention s'ajourne alors sujette à l'appel du président, en conformité aux résolutions adoptées ce jour.

E. H. DURELL,
Président de la Convention.

JOHN E. NEELIS,
Secrétaire.

CONSTITUTION DE L'ETAT DE LA LOUISIANE.

ADOPTEE EN CONVENTION, LE 23 JUILLET, 1864.

PREAMBULE.

Nous, le peuple de l'Etat de la Louisiane, ordonnons et établissons cette Constitution.

TITRE I.
EMANCIPATION.

ART. 1. L'esclavage et la servitude involontaire, excepté dans le cas de punition pour un crime dont l'accusé aura été reconnu coupable, sont abolis à tout jamais et défendus dans cet Etat.

ART. 2. La Législature ne fera point de loi reconnaissant le droit de propriété sur l'homme.

TITRE II.
DISTRIBUTION DES POUVOIRS.

ART. 3. Les pouvoirs du Gouvernement de l'Etat de la Louisiane seront répartis en trois départements distincts, et chacun d'eux sera confié à un corps de magistrature séparé, savoir : le Législatif à l'un d'eux, l'Exécutif à un autre, et le Judiciaire au troisième.

ART. 4. Aucun de ces départements, ni aucune personne occupant une charge dans l'un de ces offices, ne pourra exercer de pouvoir en dehors de son département, excepté dans les cas spécifiés plus loin.

TITRE III.
DÉPARTEMENT LEGISLATIF.

ART. 5. Le Pouvoir Législatif de l'Etat est confié à deux Chambres distinctes qui s'appelleront l'une : "Chambre des Représentants," l'autre "Sénat," et qui réunies, porteront ce titre : "Assemblée Générale de l'Etat de la Louisiane."

ART. 6. Les membres de la Chambre des Représentants exerceront leurs fonctions pendant une période de deux années, à partir de la clôture des élections générales.

ART. 7. L'élecction des Représentants aura lieu tous les deux ans, le premier lundi de novembre, et elle ne durera qu'un jour. L'Assemblée Générale se réunira annuellement, le premier lundi de janvier, à moins que cette époque ne soit changé par la loi. La session des Chambres aura di d'otobre 1864, sitôt que faire se pourra ; après l'adoption de la présente constitution, le Gouverneur devra ordonner une élection spéciale pour les membres de l'Assemblée Générale dans toutes les paroisses, dans lesquelles cette élection pourra avoir lieu ; dans les autres paroisses ou districts, il fera faire des élections aussitôt qu'il sera possible, afin de remplir les vacances pour les paroisses ou districts non-représentés à l'Assemblée Générale. Les membres de cet'e première Assemblée Générale conserveront leurs mandats pendant la même durée de temps que s'ils avaient été élus le premier lundi de novembre 1863.

ART. 8. Tout électeur reconnu comme tel par cette constitution, est éligible à l'Assemblée Générale. Nul ne sera Représentant ou Sénateur si à l'époque de son élection, il n'est électeur, soit du District Représentatif. soit du District Sénatorial qui l'a nommé.

ART. 9. L'élection des membres de l'Assemblée Générale sera tenue dans les diverses circonscriptions électorales établies par la loi.

ART. 10. La représentation de la Chambre des Représentants sera égale et uniforme. Elle sera réglée sur la base du nombre d'électeurs dûment qualifiés. Chaque paroisse aura au moins un Représentant. Aucune nouvelle paroisse ne sera créée avec un territoire moindre de six cent vingt-cinq milles carrés, ni avec une population inférieure au chiffre qui lui donnerait droit à un Représentant ; il ne sera point non plus créé de nouvelles paroisses quand par là, une autre paroisse doit être privée de l'étendue du territoire et du chiffre de population exigé comme ci-dessus. Le premier dénombrement que feront exécuter les autorités de l'Etat, en vertu de cette constitution, aura lieu en mil huit cent soixante-six. le second en mil huit cent soixante-dix, et le troisième en mil huit cent soixante-seize, et après cette dernière année, l'Assemblée Générale indiquera de quelle manière doit être opéré le recensement. pourvu qu'il ait lieu une fois au moins tous les dix ans, afin de constater la lieu au siége du gouvernement. Il y aura une session de l'Assemblée Générale en la ville de Nouvelle-Orléans, le premier lundi, population totale de chaque paroisse et de chaque district électoral, et dans le cas d'informalité, d'omission ou d'erreur du recensement dans quelque paroisse ou district, la Législature ordonnera un recensement dans tel district ou paroisse.

ART. 11. A la première session régulière des Chambres qui suivra chaque dénombrement, la Législature répartira la représentation entre les différentes paroisses et les divers districts électoraux, en prenant pour base le nombre d'électeurs dûment qualifiés. Un diviseur sera déterminé, et chaque paroisse et district électoral aura le nombre de Représentants auquel lui donnera droit son nombre d'électeurs, et en outre un Représentant pour toute fraction qui excèdera la moitié du diviseur. Le nombre des Représentants ne dépassera pas cent vingt, et ne sera pas moindre de quatre-vingt dix.

ART. 12. Jusqu'à ce qu'un dénombrement ait été fait et que des élections aient eu lieu sous son empire, conformément au premier dénombremrnt qui sera fait, comil est prescrit dans l'article 10, la représentation au Sénat et à la Chambre des Représentants sera ainsi que suit :

Pour la paroisse d'Orléans, quarante-quatre Représentants qui seront élus de la manière suivante, savoir :

Premier District		3
Second	do	5
Troisième	do	7
Quatrième	do	3
Cinquième	do	4
Sixième	do	2
Septième	do	3
Huitième	do	3
Neuvième	do	4
Dixième	do	8
Paroisse d'Orléans, (rive droite)		2
do.	Livingston	1
do.	St-Tammany	1
do.	Pointe-Coupée	1
do.	St-Martin	2
do.	Concordia	1
do.	Madison	1
do.	Franklin	1
do.	Ste-Marie	1
do.	Jefferson	3
do.	Plaquemines	1
do.	St-Bernard	1
do.	St Charles	1
do.	St-Jean-Baptiste	1
do.	St-Jacques	1
do.	Ascension	1
do.	Assomption	2
do.	Lafourche	2
do.	Terrebonne	2
do.	Iberville	1
do	Ouest-Bâton-Rouge	1
do.	Est-Bâton-Rouge	2
do.	Ouest-Féliciana	1
do.	Est-Féliciana	1
do.	Ste-Hélène	1
do.	Washington	1
do.	Vermillion	1
do.	Lafayette	2
do.	St-Landry	4
do.	Calcasieu	2
do.	Avoyelles	2
do.	Rapides	3
do.	Natchitoches	2
do.	Sabine	1
do.	Caddo	2
do.	De Soto	2
do.	Ouachita	1
do.	Union	2
do.	Morehouse	1
do.	Jackson	2
do.	Caldwell	1
do.	Catahoula	2
do.	Claiborne	3
do.	Bossier	1
do.	Bienville	2
do.	Carroll	1
do.	Tensas	1
no.	Winn	2
	Total	118

Et l'Etat sera divisé en Districts Sénatoriaux, ainsi que suit : Toute cette portion de la paroisse d'Orléans située sur la rive gauche du Mississipi, sera divisée en deux Districts Sénatoriaux ; les Premier et Quatrième Districts de la ville de la Nouvelle-Orléans formeront un district électoral et éliront cinq Sénateurs ; et les Deuxième et Troisième Districts en formeront un aussi et éliront quatre Sénateurs.

Les paroisses de Plaquemines, de St-Bernard, et toute cette partie de la paroisse d'Orléans sur la rive droite du Mississippi, formeront un district et éliront un Sénateur.

La paroisse de Jefferson formera un district et élira un Sénateur.

Les paroisses de St-Charles et Lafourche formeront un district et éliront un Sénateur.

Les paroisses de St-Jean Baptiste et de St-Jacques formeront un district et éliront un Sénateur.

Les paroisses Ascension, Assomption et Terrebonne formeront un district et éliront deux Sénateurs.

La paroisse d'Iberville formera un district et élira un Sénateur.

La paroisse Est-Baton-Rouge formera un district, et élira un Sénateur.

Les paroisses Ouest-Baton-Rouge, Pointe-Coupée et Ouest-Féliciana formeront un district et éliront deux Sénateurs.

La paroisse Est-Féliciana formera un district et élira un Sénateur.

Les paroisses Washington, St-Tammany, Ste-Hélène et Livingston formeront un district et éliront un Sénateur.

CONSTITUTION DE L'ETAT DE LA LOUISIANE.

Les paroisses de Concordia et de Tensas formeront un district et éliront un Sénateur.

Les paroisses de Madison et de Carroll formeront un district et éliront un Sénateur.

Les paroisses de Morehouse, Ouachita, Union et de Jackson formeront un district, et éliront deux Sénateurs.

Les paroisses de Catahoula, Caldwell et de Franklin formeront un district, et éliront un Sénateur.

Les paroisses de Bossier, Bienville, Claiborne et de Winn formeront un district, et éliront deux Sénateurs.

Les paroisses Natchitoches, Sabine, De Soto et de Caddo formeront un district, et éliront deux Sénateurs.

Les paroisses St-Landry, Lafayette et Calcasieu formeront un district, et éliront deux Sénateurs.

Les paroisses St-Martin et Vermillion formeront un district, et éliront un Sénateur.

La paroisse Ste-Marie formera un district, et élira un Sénateur.

Les paroisses Rapides et Avoyelles formeront un district, et éliront deux Sénateurs.

ART. 13. La Chambre des Représentants nommera son Orateur et ses autres officiers.

ART. 14. Aura le droit de voter tout homme libre et blanc qui a atteint l'âge de vingt-et-un ans, qui a résidé dans l'Etat durant les douze mois qui ont précédé immédiatement l'élection, et les trois derniers dans la paroisse où il se présente pour voter, et qui sera citoyen des Etats-Unis.

ART. 15. La Législature aura le pouvoir de passer des lois étendant le droit de sufrage à telles autres personnes, citoyens des Etats-Unis, qui l'auront mérité, soit par leurs services militaires, leur appui pécuniaire prêté au gouvernement, ou par leurs capacités intellectuelles.

ART. 16. L'électeur qui se sera transporté d'une paroisse dans une autre ne perdra pas le droit qu'il avait de voter dans la première, avant de l'avoir acquis dans la seconde. Les électeurs ne pourront jamais, sauf les cas de trahison, de crime, ou de violation de l'ordre public, être arrêtés lorsqu'ils assistent à une élection, qu'ils se rendent au lieu où elle est tenue ou qu'ils en reviennent.

ART. 17. La Législature ordonnera par une loi spéciale que les noms et les domiciles de tous les électeurs soient enregistrés afin qu'ils aient le droit de voter ; l'enregistrement ne devra rien coûter à l'électeur.

ART. 18. Les mendiants, les interdits et les personnes convaincues d'un crime quelconque, entraînant la peine des travaux forcés, ne peuvent voter à aucune élection dans cet Etat.

ART. 19. Nul ne peut voter, à une élection quelconque, en dehors de la paroisse de sa résidence ; et, dans les villes et villages divisés en circonscriptions électorales, en dehors de la circonscription électorale de sa résidence.

ART. 20. Les membres du Sénat seront nommés pour une période de quatre ans. Le Sénat, une fois réuni, aura le pouvoir de désigner ses officiers.

ART. 21. Chaque fois que la Législature répartira la représentation à la Chambre des Représentants, elle divisera l'Etat en Districts Sénatoriaux.

ART. 22. Aucune paroisse, la paroisse d'Orléans exceptée, ne pourra être divisée pour la formation d'un District Sénatorial. Quand une nouvelle paroisse sera créée, elle sera annexée au District Sénatorial d'où provient la plus grande partie de son territoire, ou à un District contigu, au choix de la Législature ; mais elle ne pourra jamais être annexée à plus d'un district. Le nombre des sénateurs sera de trente-six, et ils seront répartis entre les différents Districts Sénatoriaux selon la population électorale que renferme chaque district. Néanmoins aucune paroisse n'aura plus de neuf sénateurs.

ART. 23. Dans toute répartition sénatoriale, la population électorale de tout l'Etat sera divisée par le nombre trente-six. Le résultat obtenu par ce moyen deviendra le diviseur sénatorial, lequel donnera à un District Sénatorial droit à un sénateur. Les districts seront formés soit de simples paroisses, soit de paroisses contiguës, ayant une population qui devra se rapprocher le plus possible du diviseur représentant un sénateur ; si, dans la répartition, une paroisse ou un district manque ou excède le diviseur, il sera permis alors, mais seulement dans ce cas, de former un district qui n'aura pas plus de deux sénateurs. Une fois un sénateur élu, la durée de ses fonctions ne pourra jamais être réduite par suite d'une répartition nouvelle. Lorsque le dénombrement de la population aura été accompli conformément à l'article 10, la Législature ne pourra voter aucune loi avant d'avoir réparti la représentation dans les deux Chambres de l'Assemblée Générale.

ART. 24. A la première session de l'Assemblée Générale qui suivra la mise en vigueur de cette constitution, les Sénateurs seront divisés au sort et par égales parties en deux classes : le mandat des Sénateurs de la première classe expirera à la fin de la seconde année, et celui des Sénateurs de la seconde classe à la fin de la quatrième année, de sorte que la moitié du Sénat sera renouvelée tous les deux ans, et qu'une succession régulière sera maintenue. Quand un district élira deux Sénateurs ou plus, ils tireront entre eux au sort et leur mandat respectif expirera selon la classe qui leur est échue, à la fin de la seconde et de la quatrième année.

ART. 25. La première élection des Sénateurs aura lieu en même temps que l'élection générale des Représentants ; et après cette première élection, les élections de Sénateurs auront lieu en même temps que l'élection générale des Représentants, pour remplacer ceux des Sénateurs dont les mandats seront expirés.

ART. 26. Chaque Chambre de l'Assemblée Générale devra être en quorum pour procéder à ses travaux : une majorité des membres de chaque Chambre constituera le quorum. S'il n'y a qu'une minorité présente, elle pourra s'ajourner de jour en jour, et sera autorisée par la loi à contraindre les absents à se rendre aux séances.

ART. 27. Chaque Chambre de l'Assemblée Générale jugera si les conditions requises pour l'élection de ses membres ont été remplies. La loi déterminera la manière de procéder, toutes les fois que la validité d'une élection sera contestée.

ART. 28. Chaque Chambre de l'Assemblée Générale aura la faculté d'adopter un réglement de punir les membres qui violeront l'ordre, et même, à la majorité des deux tiers, d'en ordonner l'expulsion. Cependant la même faute ne devra jamais être frappée d'un double châtiment.

ART. 29. Chacune des Chambres de l'Assemblée Générale tiendra et publiera hebdomadairement un procès-verbal de ses travaux, et les oui et les non de leurs membres sur chaque question, seront, à la requête de deux d'entre eux, inscrits au procès-verbal susdit.

ART. 30. Chaque Chambre aura la faculté d'ordonner l'emprisonnement de toute personne ne faisant point partie de la dite Chambre qui violera l'ordre, ou bien qui cherchera à entraver ses délibérations. La durée de cet emprisonnement ne dépassera pas dix jours pour une seule et même faute.

ART. 31. Aucune Chambre ne pourra, pendant la session de l'Assemblée Générale, s'ajourner sans le consentement de l'autre pour plus de trois jours, ni changer sans ce même concours, le lieu de ses séances.

ART. 32. Les membres de l'Assemblée Générale recevront du trésor public une rémunération pour leurs services, laquelle sera de huit piastres par jour pendant la durée de la session, y inclus le temps qu'ils mettront pour se rendre au lieu du siége de la Législature, comme pour s'en retourner. La rémunération pourra être augmentée ou réduite par la loi, mais aucun changement n'aura lieu à cet égard pendant la durée du mandat des membres de la Chambre des Représentants qui auront décrété l'augmentation ou la diminution de traitement. La durée des sessions législatives sera bornée à une période de soixante jours, à partir de l'ouverture des Chambres ; toute mesure votée après cette période sera nulle et de nul effet. Cette disposition ne s'applique pas à la première Législature qui se réunira après l'adoption de cette constitution.

ART. 33. Les membres de l'Assemblée Générale ne pourront jamais, sauf dans le cas de trahison, de crime ou de violation de l'ordre public, être arrêtés pendant qu'ils sont en route soit pour se rendre au lieu des sessions, soit pour en revenir. On ne pourra pas, en dehors de la Législature, leur demander compte des discours qu'ils auront prononcés dans l'une ou l'autre Chambre.

ART. 34. Les Sénateurs et Représentants ne peuvent, pendant la durée de leur mandat, être élus ou nommés à aucune fonction civile salariée dépendant de l'Etat, laquelle aurait été créée ou dont la rémunération aurait été augmentée pendant l'exercice de leurs fonctions. Ils sont néanmoins éligibles aux places soumises à l'élection populaire.

ART. 35. Aucune personne chargée à une époque quelconque, de la perception des taxes, soit pour l'Etat, soit pour une paroisse ou une municipalité, ou à qui les deniers publics auront été, d'une façon ou d'une autre, confiés, ne sera éligible à l'Assemblée Générale, à une place salariée ou à un poste honorifique dépendant de l'Etat, si elle n'a préalablement obtenu une quittance pour le montant des taxes qu'elle aura perçues ou pour les fonds publics qui lui auraient été confiés.

ART. 36. Aucune personne engagée dans l'exercice des fonctions de ministre de toute dénomination religieuse ne sera éligible à l'Assemblée Générale.

ART. 37. Aucun bill ne deviendra loi avant d'avoir été lu à trois jours différents dans chaque Chambre de l'Assemblée Générale et d'avoir été librement discuté. Cependant, en cas d'urgence, la Chambre où le bill est pris en considération peut, à la majorité des quatre-cinquièmes des membres, écarter le réglement si elle le juge à propos.

ART. 38. La Chambre des Représentants aura seule le droit de proposer les bills dont l'objet est la perception du revenu ; mais le Sénat aura la faculté de proposer des amendements comme pour les bills ordinaires, pourvu que sous prétexte de modification il n'introduise aucune nouvelle disposition étrangère à la perception du revenu.

ART. 39. L'Assemblée Générale indiquera par une loi la source d'où émaneront les ordres d'élection pour pourvoir aux vacances qui surviendront dans l'une et l'autre Chambre, ainsi que la manière dont ces ordres seront donnés.

ART. 40. Le Sénat statuera par oui et par

non sur la confirmation ou le rejet des officiers que le Gouverneur doit nommer avec le concours du Sénat.

Les noms des Sénateurs qui voteront pour ou contre une nomination quelconque, seront inscrits dans un journal tenu à cet effet et qui sera publié à la fin de chaque session ou même avant cette époque.

Art. 41. Les bulletins d'election des membres de l'Assemblée Générale seront transmis au Secrétaire d'Etat.

Art. 42. L'année où l'élection régulière d'un Sénateur au Congrès des Etats-Unis doit avoir lieu, les membres de l'Assemblée Générale se réuniront dans l'enceinte de la Chambre des Représentants, le second lundi qui suivra l'ouverture de la session législative et procéderont à l'élection susdite.

TITRE IV.
DÉPARTEMENT EXÉCUTIF.

Art. 43. Le pouvoir Suprême de l'Exécutif de l'Etat sera confié à un Chef Magistrat, qui sera désigné sous le nom de Gouverneur de l'Etat de la Louisiane. Il conservera son office pendant quatre années, et, ainsi que le Lieutenant-Gouverneur, nommé pour le même laps de temps, ils seront élus de la manière suivante : Les électeurs qualifiés pour nommer les Représentants voteront pour le Gouverneur et le Lieutenant-Gouverneur à l'heure et au lieu où ils voteront pour les représentants : les retours de chaque élection seront cachetés et transmis, par la voie de l'officier légal, au Secrétaire d'Etat, qui les délivrera à son tour à l'Orateur de la Chambre des Représentants le second jour de la session de l'Assemblée Générale qui sera réunie ensuite. Les membres de l'Assemblée Générale s'assembleront dans la Chambre des Représentants à l'effet d'examiner et de compter les votes. La personne ayant obtenu le plus grand nombre de voix pour l'office de Gouverneur sera déclarée dûment élue ; mais si deux ou plusieurs personnes obtiennent le même nombre de voix,—et le plus grand nombre des votes donnés,—pour l'office de Gouverneur, l'une d'elles sera immédiatement choisie par un vote-conjoint des membres de l'Assemblée Générale. La personne ayant obtenu le plus grand nombre de voix pour Lieutenant-Gouverneur sera déclarée élue Lieutenant-Gouverneur ; mais si deux ou plusieurs personnes obtiennent le même nombre de voix,—et le plus grand nombre des votes donnés,—pour l'office de Lieutenant-Gouverneur, l'une d'elles sera immédiatement choisie par un vote conjoint des membres de l'Assemblée Générale.

Art. 44. Nul ne sera éligible à l'emploi de Gouverneur ou Lieutenant-Gouverneur s'il n'est âgé de trente-cinq ans, et s'il n'est citoyen et résident de cet Etat depuis cinq années consécutives avant son élection.

Art. 45. Le gouverneur entrera en fonctions le second lundi de janvier suivant son élection, et restera en fonctions jusqu'au lundi suivant le jour où son successeur aura été déclaré dûment élu, et après qu'il aura pris le serment ou l'affirmation requis par la constitution.

Art. 46. Aucun membre du Congrès ou ministre d'une religion quelconque, ou aucune personne remplissant un emploi sous le Gouvernement des Etats-Unis, ne sera éligible aux fonctions de Gouverneur ou de Lieutenant-Gouverneur.

Art. 47. En cas de mise en accusation du Gouverneur, ou de sa destitution, de sa mort, de son refus ou de son inhabilité à agir, de sa résignation ou de son absence de l'Etat, les pouvoirs et les devoirs de ses fonctions seront dévolus au Lieutenant-Gouverneur pour la balance du temps à courir, ou jusqu'à ce que le Gouverneur, absent ou mis en accusation, revienne ou soit acquitté. La Législature pourvoira d'après la loi aux cas de destitution, mise en accusation, mort, résignation incapacité, ou refus d'agir, du Gouverneur et Lieutenant-Gouverneur, déclarant quel officier devra exercer les fonctions de Gouverneur, lequel officier agira en conséquence, jusqu'à ce qu'il soit destitué pour son incapacité, ou pour le reste du temps à courir.

Art. 48. Le Lieutenant-Gouverneur ou l'officier remplissant les fonctions de Gouverneur, recevra, pendant son administration, la même rétribution à laquelle le Gouverneur aurait eu droit s'il avait continué ses fonctions.

Art. 49. Le Lieutenant-Gouverneur, en vertu de son office, sera le Président du Sénat, mais il n'aura droit qu'à un seul vote. Soit qu'il prenne l'administration du Gouvernement d'Etat, soit que, par toute autre cause, il ne puisse remplir les fonctions de Président du Sénat, les Sénateurs devront élire un de leurs propres membres comme Président du Sénat pour le temps présent.

Art. 50. Le Gouverneur recevra, pour ses services, un traitement de huit mille piastres par an, payable par trimestre, sur son propre mandat.

Art. 51. Le Lieutenant-Gouverneur recevra, pour ses services, un traitement de cinq mille piastres par an, payable par trimestre.

Art. 52. Le Gouverneur aura le pouvoir d'accorder des sursis pour toutes offenses commises contre l'Etat, et, excepté dans les cas de mise en accusation, il aura, avec le consentement du Sénat, le pouvoir d'accorder des pardons, remettre des amendes et des forfeitures, après conviction de culpabilité. Dans des cas de trahison, il pourra accorder des sursis jusqu'à la fin de la session suivante de l'Assemblée Générale, laquelle sera investie du pouvoir de pardonner.

Art. 53. Il sera le commandant en-chef des milices de cet Etat, à moins qu'elles ne soient appelées au service des Etats-Unis.

Art. 54. Il nommera, et avec l'avis et d'après le consentement du Sénat, désignera tous les officiers dont les offices sont établis par la Constitution, et dont les nominations non pas été autrement pourvues dans la présente : Pourvu, toutefois, que la Législature aura le droit de prescrire le mode de nomination de tous les autres offices établis par la loi.

Art. 55. Le Gouverneur aura le pouvoir de remplir les vacances qui surviendront pendant le recès du Sénat, en accordant des commissions qui expireront à la fin de la session suivante, à moins qu'il n'en soit autrement pourvu dans cette Constitution ; mais aucune personne qui a été nommée à un emploi et rejetée par le Sénat, ne sera nommée au même emploi pendant le recès du Sénat.

Art. 56. Il peut requérir des informations, par écrit, des différents officiers du Département Exécutif, sur n'importe quel sujet ayant rapport aux devoirs de leurs offices respectifs.

Art. 57. Il devra communiquer à l'Assemblée Générale, de temps à autre, des renseignements sur la situation de l'Etat, et recommander à sa considération telles mesures qu'il jugera nécessaires.

Art. 58. Il pourra, dans des cas extraordinaires, convoquer l'Assemblée Générale au siége du gouvernement, ou à une autre place, si celle-ci est devenue dangereuse soit par la présence de l'ennemi, soit par épidémie ; et, en cas de désaccord entre les deux Chambres en ce qui concernera l'époque de l'ajournement, il pourra les ajourner au temps qu'il jugera convenable de le faire, sans toutefois que cela ne soit au-delà de quatre mois.

Art. 59. Il veillera à ce que les lois soient scrupuleusement exécutées.

Art. 60. Chaque bill qui aura passé aux deux Chambres sera présenté au Gouverneur ; si il l'approuve, il le signera ; dans le cas contraire, il le renverra, avec ses objections, à la Chambre dans laquelle il aura pris origine, qui les inscrira au long sur son journal, et les prendra en considération ; si, après considération, les deux tiers de tous les membres élus à cette Chambre adoptent le bill, il sera envoyé, avec les objections, à l'autre Chambre, par laquelle il sera de même pris en considération, et si il est approuvé par les deux tiers de tous les membres élus à cette Chambre, il deviendra loi ; mais dans de tels cas le vote des deux Chambres sera déterminé par les oui et les non, et les noms des membres votant pour ou contre e bill seront enregistrés sur le journal respectif de chaque Chambre. Si un bill quelconque n'est pas renvoyé par le Gouverneur dans l'espace de dix jours, (excepté les dimanches,) après qu'il lui aura été présenté, il deviendra loi de la même manière que s'il l'avait signé, à moins que l'Assemblée Générale,par son ajournement, n'en prévienne son retour.

Art. 61. Chaque ordre, résolution, ou vote auquel le concours des deux Chambres peut être nécessaire, excepté sur la question d'ajournement, sera présenté au Gouverneur, et approuvé par lui avant qu'il ne prenne force de loi ; ou, s'il est désapprouvé, il passera de nouveau par le vote des deux tiers des membres élus à chaque Chambre de l'Assemblée Générale.

Art. 62. Il sera nommé un Secétaire d'Etat qui conservera ses fonctions pour la durée du temps pour lequel le Gouverneur aura été élu. Les archives de l'Etat seront tenues et préservées dans le bureau du Secrétaire ; il tiendra un registre en règle des actes officiels et des ordres du Gouverneur, et devra les attester quand il sera nécessaire ; il devra, lorsqu'il en sera requis, déposer le dit registre et tous les papiers, procès-verbaux et souches relatifs à son office, devant l'une des Chambres de l'Assemblée Générale, et remplir tels autres devoirs qui peuvent lui incomber par la loi.

Art. 63. Il sera nommé un Trésorier d'Etat et un Auditeur des Comptes Publics, qui resteront en fonctions pendant quatre années.

Art. 64. Le Secrétaire d'Etat, le Trésorier d'Etat et l'Auditeur des Comptes Publics, seront élus par les électeurs qualifiés de l'Etat ; et au cas d'une vacance causée soit par la mort, la résignation ou l'absence du Secrétaire, Trésorier ou Auditeur, le Gouvernenr devra ordonner une élection pour remplir la dite vacance.

Art. 65. Le Secrétaire d'Etat, le Trésorier et l'Auditeur recevront chacun un traitement de cinq mille piastres par an.

Art. 66. Toutes les commissions seront délivrées au nom et par l'autorité de l'Etat de la Louisiane, et devront porter le sceau de l'Etat et être signées par le Gouverneur.

Art. 67. Tous les hommes valides de cet Etat seront armés et disciplinés pour sa défense.

Art. 68. La milice de l'Etat sera organisée de telle manière que la Législature jugera convenable de le faire.

TITRE V.

DÉPARTEMENT JUDICIAIRE.

Art. 69. Le pouvoir Judiciaire sera confié à la Cour Suprême et telles autres Cours Inférieures que la Législature jugera devoir établir et aux tribunaux de paix.

Art. 70. La Cour Suprême, excepté dans les cas ci-après prévus, aura une juridiction de Cour d'Appel seulement ; laquelle Cour couvrira toute affaire où la somme en litige dépassera trois cents piastres : toute affaire où la constitutionalité ou la légalité d'une taxe, d'un impôt ou contribution quelconque, d'une amende, peine ou forfaiture imposée par une municipalité seront en litige; et aussi toute affaire criminelle, sur la question de droit seulement, lorsque l'offense alléguée sera punissable de mort ou des travaux forcés, ou lorsque l'amende actuellement imposée dépassera trois cents piastres.

Art. 71. La Cour Suprême se composera d'un juge-président et de quatre juges-adjoints, la majorité desquels formera un quorum. Le juge-président recevra un traitement annuel de sept mille cinq cents piastres, et chacun des juges-adjoints un traitement annuel de sept mille piastres, jusqu'à ce qu'il en soit autrement pourvu par la loi. Cette Cour nommera ses greffiers.

Art. 72. La Cour Suprême tiendra les audiences à la Nouvelle-Orléans du premier lundi de novembre à la fin du mois de juin inclusivement. La Législature pourra assigner le lieu des audiences dans les autres parties de l'Etat pour le reste de l'année ; et jusqu'à ce qu'il en ait été disposé autrement, la Cour siègera aux lieux et places jusqu'à ce jour déterminés.

Art. 73. La Cour Suprême, et chacun des Juges la composant, pourra émettre des mandats *d'habeas corpus*, à l'instance de toute personne détenue actuellement en vertu de procédures judiciaires, dans toute affaire où l'appel lui est dévolu.

Art. 74. La Cour Suprême ne rendra point de jugement sans la participation d'une majorité des juges qui la composent. Et lorsqu'il n'y aura point majorité en raison de la récusation de quelques membres de cette Cour, les juges non récusés pourront s'adjoindre quelque Juge des cours inférieures, dont le devoir sera de siéger en lieu et place du juge récusé, et de concourir à la confection de l'arrêt de la Cour.

Art. 75. Tous les juges seront, en vertu de leur charge, conservateurs de la paix publique dans tout l'Etat. Le style de toute procédure sera "Etat de la Louisiane." Toute poursuite se fera au nom et par l'autorité de l'Etat de la Louisiane et concluera contre la paix et la dignité dudit Etat.

Art. 76. Les juges de toutes les cours de l'Etat devront, quand faire se pourra, dans tout jugement définitif, référer à la loi en vertu de laquelle ledit jugement a été rendu et dans tous les cas, donner les motifs de leur jugement.

Art. 77. Les juges de toutes les cours seront passibles de la mise en accusation ; mais, pour toute cause fondée qui n'entraînera point la mise en accusation, le Gouverneur, sur la requête d'une majorité des membres élus à chacune des Chambres de l'Assemblée Générale, pourra destituer tout juge ; et en pareille circonstance, les causes de la requête en destitution seront établies en plein dans la requête et consignées au procès-verbal de chaque Chambre.

Art. 78. Les juges de la Cour Suprême et des Cours Inférieures recevront un traitement qui ne pourra être diminué pendant qu'ils resteront en fonctions; et il leur est défendu de recevoir aucun honoraire ou émolument, autre que leur traitement pour tout devoir civil rempli par eux.

Art. 79. Les Juges de la Cour Suprême seront nommés par le Gouverneur avec l'avis et le consentement du Sénat, pour un terme de huit années ; les Juges des Cours Inférieures pour un terme de six années.

Art. 80. Les Greffiers des Cours Inférieures seront élus par les électeurs dûment qualifiés de leurs districts, et ils resteront en fonctions pendant le terme de quatre années.

Art. 81. La Législature aura le pouvoir de conférer aux greffiers des cours, l'autorité d'accorder tels ordres et de faire tels actes, qui pourront sembler nécessaires à la bonne administration de la justice ; et dans tous les cas les pouvoirs ainsi accordés devront être spécifiés et déterminés.

Art. 82. La juridiction des juges de paix ne dépassera point cent piastres, en matière civile, non compris les intérêts : il y aura droit d'appel en la manière prescrite par la loi. Ils seront élus par les électeurs dûment qualifiés de leurs districts, et ils resteront en fonctions pendant le terme de deux années. Ils auront telle juridiction criminelle qui leur sera accordée par la loi.

Art. 83. Il y aura un Procureur Général pour l'Etat, et autant d'Avocats de District que la Législature le jugera nécessaire. Le Procureur Général sera élu tous les quatre ans par les électeurs dûment qualifiés de l'Etat. Il recevra un traitement de cinq mille piastres par an, payable trimestriellement sur son propre mandat. Les Avocats de District seront élus par les électeurs dûment qualifiés de leurs districts respectifs, pour un terme de quatre années. Ils recevront tel traitement que la Législature déterminera.

Art. 84. Il y aura dans chaque paroisse un Shérif et un Coroner qui seront nommés par les électeurs dûment qualifiés de ces paroisses, et qui resteront en fonctions pendant deux ans. La Législature aura le pouvoir d'augmenter le nombre des Shérifs dans telle paroisse qu'elle jugera à propos. S'il survient une vacance dans l'une de ces deux places, postérieurement à l'élection, il y sera pourvu par le Gouverneur ; et la personne ainsi nommée en remplacement conservera ses fonctions jusqu'à ce que son successeur ait été élu et qualifié.

TITRE VI.
MISE EN ACCUSATION.

ART. 85. La Chambre des Représentants sera investie du droit de mettre en accusation les officiers publics.

ART. 86. La mise en accusation du Gouverneur, du Lieutenant-Gouverneur, de l'Avocat-Général, du Secrétaire d'Etat, du Trésorier d'Etat et des Juges des cours inférieures, sauf les Juges de Paix, appartiendra au Sénat. Le Grand-Juge de la Cour Suprême ou le doyen de cette cour, présidera au procès de mise en accusation. Le Sénat jugera les juges de la Cour Suprême mis en accusation. Quand les Sénateurs siégeront comme cour de mise en accusation, ils devront prêter le serment ou l'affirmation ; et nul ne sera condamné sans le concours des deux tiers des sénateurs présents.

ART. 87. L'effet des jugements par suite d'une mise en accusation n'entraînera que la perte des fonctions ou la privation de tout office d'honneur, de confiance ou de profit relevant de l'Etat, sans toutefois préjudicier au droit d'accusation publique, de poursuite et condamnation, d'après les lois ordinaires, contre le coupable.

ART. 88. Tout officier contre lequel il y aura mise en accusation sera suspendu de l'exercice de ses fonctions pendant la durée de l'instance susdite, et l'autorité de la nomination de laquelle ces fonctions relèvent, pourra nommer provisoirement un remplaçant jusqu'à ce que l'action de mise en accusation soit décidée.

ART. 89. La Législature pourvoira par la loi au jugement de tous autres officiers d'Etat mis en accusation, à la peine qui leur sera appliquée et à leur renvoi, par voie d'accusation ou autrement.

TITRE VII.
DISPOSITIONS GÉNÉRALES.

ART. 90. Les membres de l'Assemblée Générale et tous les officiers publics, avant d'entrer en fonctions, prêteront le serment suivant :

Je (A B) jure solennellement (ou affirme) que je soutiendrai la constitution et les lois des Etats-Unis et de cet Etat, et que je remplirai avec fidélité et impartialité tous les devoirs qui me seront imposés par mes fonctions de——au mieux de mes capacités et de mon entendement. Dieu me soit en aide!

ART. 91. Le crime de haute trahison consistera uniquement dans le fait de susciter une guerre contre l'Etat, ou de pactiser avec ses ennemis, ou de leur donner aide et assistance. Personne ne pourra être déclaré convaincu du crime de haute trahison que sur la déposition de deux témoins du même fait de trahison ouvert, ou sur sa propre confession à l'audience de la cour.

ART. 92. La Législature aura le pouvoir de déterminer la peine du crime de haute trahison ; mais aucune conviction de trahison n'entraînera l'infamie ou la forfaiture des droits civils et politiques, qu'excepté pendant la vie de la personne convaincue de ce crime.

ART. 93. Sera incapable d'exercer aucunes fonctions publiques dans l'Etat, honorifiques ou autres, et sera privée du droit de suffrage toute personne qui aura été convaincue du crime de trahison, de parjure, de faux, de concussion, ou de tous autres crimes et offenses.

ART. 94. Toutes les peines seront proportionnées à la nature de l'offense.

ART. 95. L'exercice du droit de libre suffrage sera protégé par des lois régularisant les élections, et défendant, sous des peines sévères, l'emploi de toute influence illégitime de la part du pouvoir, de toute corruption d'électeurs, tous désordres ou autres menées inconvenantes.

ART. 96. Il ne sera tiré du trésor aucune somme, si ce n'est sur une allocation spécifique faite par la loi : et aucune allocation de fonds ne pourra être faite à l'avance pour plus de deux ans. Un état et compte régulier des recettes et dépenses du trésor sera publié annuellement dans la forme qui sera prescrite par la loi.

ART. 97. L'Assemblée Générale devra faire les lois qu'elle jugera convenables et nécessaires pour régler les affaires litigieuses soumises à des arbitres.

ART. 98. Tous les officiers civils de l'Etat en général voteront et résideront dans l'Etat, et tous les officiers de district ou de paroisses voteront et résideront dans leurs paroisses ou districts respectifs, et tiendront leurs offices à tels endroits qui pourront être requis par la loi.

ART. 99. Tous les officiers civils pourront être révoqués de leurs fonctions, sur la demande de la majorité des membres élus dans les deux Chambres. Ne sont pas compris dans cet article les officiers à la révocabilité desquels la présente constitution a autrement pourvu.

ART. 100. Dans toutes les élections par le peuple, le vote se fera au scrutin secret, et dans toutes les élections par le Sénat et la Chambre des Représentants, ensemble ou séparément, le vote sera donné de vive voix.

ART. 101. Ne pourront être éligibles à l'Assemblée Générale, ni exercer aucunes fonctions publiques, honorifiques ou autres, dans l'Etat, les membres du Congrès ni aucune personne exerçant des fonctions publiques, honorifiques ou autres, pour le compte du gouvernement général des Etats-Unis, ou d'une puissance étrangère.

ART. 102. Ne pourront être nommés à aucunes fonctions publiques, honorifiques ou de profit, dans cet Etat, que des citoyens des Etats-Unis.

Art. 103. Les lois de Etat seront promulguées, les livres et archives publics tenus et conservés, et les procédures écrites de la Législature ou des cours de justice conduites en la langue en laquelle est écrite la constitution des Etats-Unis.

Art. 104. Les lois ne pourront être suspendues que par la volonté de la Législature.

Art. 105. Toute poursuite en matière criminelle, sera basée sur un acte d'accusation. L'accusé aura droit à être jugé promptement, et par un juri impartial de la paroisse dans laquelle le crime aura été commis. Il ne sera point obligé à s'accuser lui-même ; il aura droit à être entendu, soit par lui-même, soit par un défenseur. Il aura droit à voir les témoins face à face, et il lui sera fourni les moyens nécessaires pour se procurer des témoins à décharge. Il ne pourra être poursuivi deux fois pour la même offense.

Art. 106. Tout accusé pourra toujours demander à être mis en liberté en fournissant une caution suffisante, excepté en cas d'accusation capitale, lorsque la preuve sera évidente ou la présomption forte, ou à moins de conviction pour un crime ou une offense entraînant la peine de mort ou les travaux forcés. Le privilége du droit d'habeas corpus ne sera point suspendu, excepté lorsque, dans les cas de rébellion ou d'invasion, la raison de salut public peut rendre cette mesure nécessaire.

Art. 107. Il ne pourra être exigé des cautions exagérées, ni imposé des amendes excessives, ni infligé des peines cruelles ou contraires aux usages.

Art. 108. Le droit des particuliers à être protégés dans leurs personnes, dans leurs domiciles, dans leurs papiers et effets, contre toutes les visites domiciliaires ou saisies déraisonnables ne sera point violé ; et il ne sera accordé aucun ordre de recherche, de saisie ou d'arrestation que sur des causes probables, appuyées d'un serment ou d'une affirmation ; et ces ordres devront décrire avec précision les lieux où doivent s'opérer les recherches, les personnes qui doivent être arrêtées ou les objets qui doivent être saisis.

Art. 109. Il ne sera passé aucune loi ayant un effet rétroactif ou portant atteinte à la validité des contrats, ou aux droits acquis, si ce n'est pour cause d'utilité publique et après indemnité préalable.

Art. 110. Toutes les cours de justice seront tenues ouvertes, et tout particulier qui sera attaqué dans sa personne, dans sa réputation ou dans ses biens, aura droit d'en demander la réparation dans les formes indiquées par la loi, et il lui sera fait droit sans qu'on puisse lui opposer un déni de justice ou des lenteurs déraisonnables.

Art. 111. La presse sera libre. Tout citoyens peut parler, écrire et publier ses sentiments sur tous sujets ; il sera seulement responsable de l'abus de cette liberté.

Art. 112. La Législature n'aura pas le pouvoir de venir en aide aux compagnies ou associations particulières, excepté aux institutions charitables et à telles compagnies ou associations particulières formées dans le but exclusif de faire des travaux qui tourneront, en tout ou en partie, à l'avantage de l'Etat, mais seulement jusqu'à concurrence de "un cinquième" du capital entier de ces compagnies, et ce, soit au moyen de souscription d'actions, soit par prêt d'argent, soit par émission de bons publics. Mais toutes avances ainsi accordées ne seront versées à la compagnie que dans la même proportion que le reste du capital sera effectivement versé par les actionnaires de la compagnie : et, en cas d'emprunt, la compagnie fournira telles garanties que la Législature jugera convenables. Les corporations ou associations individuelles recevant aide et assistance de l'Etat, comme il vient d'être dit, ne pourront posséder aucune obligation de banque ou d'escompte.

Art. 113. L'Etat ne pourra contracter aucune obligation de la nature ci-dessus mentionnée sans y être autorisé par une loi expresse et pour un objet ou un travail qui y sera distinctement spécifié, laquelle loi sera votée par la majorité des membres élus aux deux Chambres de l'Assemblée Générale ; et le montant total des dettes et obligations contractées au nom de l'Etat, en vertu de cet article et du précédent, ne pourront jamais, en aucun temps, excéder huit millions de piastres.

Art. 114. Toutes les fois que la Législature contractera une dette dont le montant excèdera cent mille piastres, à moins que ce ne soit en cas de guerre et pour repousser l'invasion ou supprimer l'insurrection, elle devra, dans la loi qui créera cette dette, pourvoir aux moyens de payer l'interêt courant et le principal à l'époque de leurs échéances. Et cette loi ne pourra être rappelée jusqu'à ce que la dette principale et ses intérêts aient été acquittés, à moins toutefois que la loi nouvelle qui l'abrogera ne pourvoie par d'autres mesures suffisantes aux moyens de payer la dite dette en principal et intérêts.

Art. 115. La Législature pourvoira au transfert des affaires civiles et criminelles d'une juridiction à une autre.

Art. 116. La Législature aura le pouvoir d'accorder des licences aux maisons de jeu et de vendre des billets de loterie. Lesdites maisons de jeu seront dans tous les cas tenues au rez-de-chaussée et les portes ouvertes; mais dans aucun cas, non moins de dix mille piastres ne seront exigées comme paiement de ladite licence sur chaque vendeur de billets de loterie et sur chaque maison de jeu, et cinq cents piastres sur chaque tombola.

ART. 117. La Législature peut faire des lois générales pour la régularisation de l'adoption des enfants, l'émancipation des mineurs, les changements de noms et accorder les divorces ; mais aucues lois spéciales ne seront émises concernant ou un cas particulier ou individuel.

ART. 118. Toute loi passée par la Législature n'embrassera qu'un seul objet, et cet objet sera imprimé dans son titre.

ART. 119. Aucune loi ne pourra être remise en vigueur ou amendée sur le simple énoncé de son titre ; mais en pareil cas, la loi remise en vigueur ou la section amendée sera ré-édictée, et publiée à nouveau tout au long.

ART. 120. La Législature n'adoptera jamais un système de droit ou un code de loi en indiquant d'une manière générale ledit système ou ledit code. Elle doit, dans tous les cas, spécifier les diverses dispositions qu'elle veut décréter.

ART. 121. Les lois spéciales de l'Etat ne pourront créer des corporations, excepté dans un but politique ou municipal, mais la Législature pourvoira par des lois générales à l'organisation de toutes ces corporations, excepté toutes celles qui ont rapport aux maisons de banque et d'escompte dont l'existence est, par le présent, prohibée.

ART. 122. Dans le cas ou une banque ou une association, faisant les opérations de banque, serait en faillite, les détenteurs de leurs billets auront le droit d'être payés avant les autres créanciers.

ART. 123. Nul n'occupera à la fois plus d'une place civile, salariée ou honorifique, sauf celle du juge de paix.

ART. 124. Les taxes seront égales et uniformes dans tout l'Etat. Chaque propriété sera taxée d'après sa valeur, comme il sera décidé d'après la loi. L'Assemblée Générale aura le pouvoir d'exempter des taxes toutes propriétés à l'usage des églises, écoles ou institutions charitables. L'Assemblée Générale lèvera une taxe sur les revenus de toutes les personnes poursuivant une occupation quelle qu'elle soit, marchands ou autres, et toutes ces personnes devront obtenir une licence, ainsi que la loi le prescrit. Toutes les taxes sur les revenus seront faites au *pro rata* d'un montant des revenus ou des affaires faites.

ART. 125. La Législature déterminera par la loi dans quel cas les officiers continueront à exercer leurs fonctions jusqu'à ce que leurs successeurs les remplacent régulièrement.

ART. 126. La Législature, moyennant le consentement des Etats-Unis, aura le droit d'étendre l'autorité de cette constitution et la juridiction de cet Etat à tout territoire acquis par un traité avec un autre Etat ou avec les Etats-Unis.

ART. 127. Aucune partie des terres concédées par le Congrès à l'Etat de la Louisiane pour lui faciliter la construction de levées et autres travaux nécessaires au dessèchement des terrains inondés de l'Etat, ne sera appliquée à un autre objet que celui en vue duquel elles ont été concédées.

ART. 128. La Législature ne pourra faire aucune loi à l'effet d'exclure un citoyen de l'Etat d'un emploi public, à raison de ce qu'il ignorait une langue autre que celle dans laquelle est écrite la Constitution des Etats-Unis.

ART. 129. Il n'existera, dans l'Etat, les paroisses ou les municipalités, aucune responsabilité pour dettes contractées pour ou dans l'intérêt de la rébellion, contre l'autorité du gouvernement des Etats-Unis.

ART. 130. Le siége du gouvernement sera et restera à la Nouvelle-Orléans, et ne pourra être changé que par l'assentiment des deux tiers des deux Chambres de l'Assemblée Générale.

ART. 131. La Législature pourra déterminer la méthode de remplir les vacances dans les divers emplois, pour obvier aux lacunes qui pourraient exister dans la Constitution.

ART. 132. La Législature ne passera aucune loi requérant des titres de propriétés d'aucune personne ayant un emploi public ou qui pourrait en obtenir.

TITRE VIII.

CORPORATION DE LA VILLE DE LA NOUVELLE-ORLEANS.

ART. 133. Les citoyens de la ville de la Nouvelle-Orléans auront le droit de nommer les divers officiers publics nécessaires à l'administration de la police de la dite ville, suivant le mode d'élection qui sera prescrit par la Législature ; pourvu, que le maire et les recorders ne soient pas éligibles pour siéger à l'Assemblée Générale, et que e maire et le recorder soient commissionnés par le Gouverneur comme juges de paix et la Législature pourra leur attribuer une certaine juridiction criminelle nécessaire pour la punition de légères offenses, ainsi que le nécessitera la police et le bon ordre de la ville.

La ville de la Nouvelle-Orléans maintiendra une force de police qui portera l'uniforme, avec distinction de grades, consistant de citoyens résidant dans l'Etat de la Louisiane, choisis par le Maire de la ville ; qu'ils continueront leurs fonctions aussi longtemps que leur conduite sera bonne; qu'ils ne pourront être destitués que par une commission de police composée de cinq citoyens et le Maire, qui sera le président de cette commission. La commission devra être nommé par le Gouverneur de l'Etat pour le terme de deux années, à un salaire qui ne sera pas moins de $1000 par année ; une majorité de la dite comission pourra destituer pour cause de délits. Lorsqu'un membre de la police aura été destitué, il ne pourra plus être éligible avant un terme d'une année.

Intervenir en aucune manière dans les élections sera une cause suffisante pour immédiate destitution.

Le chef de police fournira un cautionnement de $10,000 ; les lieutenants de police, $5000 ; les sergents et commis, chacun, $3000 ; les caporaux, $2000 ; et les simples officiers $1000, avec de bonnes et solvables sécurités, ainsi que la loi l'exige, pour l'accomplissement fidèle de leurs devoirs.

Ces divers officiers recevront un traitement qui ne sera pas moins de :

Le Chef de Police	$250	par mois.
Les Lieutenants de Police	150	do.
Les Sergents	100	do.
Les Commis	100	do.
Les Caporaux	90	do.
Les officiers du jour et de la nuit	80	do.

TITRE IX.
TRAVAUX PUBLICS.

ART. 134. La Législature établira le prix et la solde des contre-maîtres, manœuvres et autres employés dans les travaux publics du Gouvernement de l'Etat, des paroisses et de la ville.

Pourvu, Que la compensation à payer aux contre-maîtres, ouvriers, charretiers et manœuvres employés dans les travaux publics sous le Gouvernement de l'Etat de la Louisiane, la ville de la Nouvelle-Orléans, et les juris de police des diverses paroisses de l'Etat ne soient pas moins de, savoir :

Contre-maîtres	$3 50	par jour.
Artisans	3 00	do.
Charretiers	3 00	do.
Manœuvres	2 00	do.

ART. 135. Neuf heures constitueront une journée de travail pour les ouvriers, artisans et manœuvres employés aux travaux publics.

TITRE X.
AMELIORATIONS INTERIEURES.

ART. 136. Le Gouverneur nommera un Ingénieur d'Etat, ayant des connaissances approfondies, théoriques et pratiques, de sa profession, et qui tiendra son office pendant la durée de quatre années au siége du Gouvernement. Il aura la surintendance et la direction générale de tous les travaux publics dans lesquels l'Etat pourra être intéressé, excepté ceux entrepris par des compagnies d'actionnaires ou par les autorités de la ville ou des paroisses exclusivement, sans pour cela venir en conflit avec les lois générales de l'Etat. Il communiquera annuellement à l'Assemblée Générale, par la voie du Gouverneur, ses vues au sujet de son emploi ; il fera son rapport sur la condition des travaux publics en voie d'exécution, recommandera telles mesures qu'il croira convenables dans l'intérêt public de l'Etat, et remplira tous autres devoirs qui pourront lui êtrs imposés par la loi. Il recevra un traitement de cinq mille piastres par an, jusqu'à ce qu'il en soit autrement ordonné par la loi. Le mode de nomination, le nombre et le traitement de ses assistants seront dertermiminés par la loi. L'Ingénieur d'Etat et ses assistants devront fournir de bonnes et solvables sécurités comme garantie de la fidèle exécution de leurs devoirs, ainsi qu'il est prescrit par la loi.

ART. 137. L'Assemblée Générale aura le pouvoir de créer des Améliorations Intérieures dans les Districts, composés de une ou plusieurs Paroisses, et accordera aux citoyens y résidant le droit d'imposer des taxes eux-mêmes pour subvenir à ces améliorations. Lorsque les Améliorations Intérieures de Districts auront été décrétées, les districts auront le droit de choisir leurs commissaires, de nommer leurs officiers, de fixer leurs traitements, et de régulariser toutes mesures relatives aux améliorations de leurs districts ; pourvu que les dites améliorations ne viennent pas en conflit avec les lois générales de l'Etat.

ART. 138. L'Assemblée Générale pourra venir en aide aux dits Districts, en leur accordant des fonds provenant des marécages et des terrains inondés cédés à cette fin ou autrement à cet Etat par le Gouvernement des Etats-Unis.

ART. 139. L'Assemblée Générale aura le droit de supprimer l'emploi d'Ingénieur d'Etat, par la majorité du vote de tous les membres élus dans chacune des Chambres, et de substituer en son lieu et place, un Comité des Travaux Publics, si cette mesure est jugée nécessaire.

TITRE XI.
EDUCATION PUBLIQUE.

ART. 140. Il sera élu un surintendant de l'instruction publique, qui exercera ses fonctions pendant une période de deux années. Ses devoirs seront prescrits par la loi, et il recevra un traitement de cinq mille piastres par an, jusqu'à ce qu'il en soit autrement ordonné par la loi. Néanmoins l'Assemblée Générale pourra, par un vote de la majorité des membres élus anx deux Chambres, abolir la place de surintendant de l'instruction publique, quand elle jugera que cette place n'est plus nécessaire.

ART. 141. La Législature pourvoira, soit au moyen de taxes ou autrement, à l'entretien des écoles publiques, pour l'intruction de tous les enfants de l'Etat entre les âges de six et dix-huit ans.

ART. 142. La langue Anglaise sera seule enseignée dans les écoles publiques de l'Etat.

ART. 143. Il sera créé une Universié

dans la ville de la Nouvelle-Orléans. Cette Université se composera de quatre facultés, savoir : une faculté de droit, une faculté de médecine, une faculté des sciences naturelles et une faculté des lettres. La Législature pourvoiera par une loi à leur organisation et à leur maintien.

ART. 144. Le produit de toutes les terres concédées jusqu'à ce moment par le Congrès des Etats-Unis à cet Etat pour l'entretien des écoles ; celui de toutes les terres qui pourront dans l'avenir être concédées ou léguées à l'Etat, ainsi que le produit des sucessions échues à l'Etat, conformément à la loi, resteront en la possession de l'Etat et formeront une rente perpétuelle dont l'Etat acquittera annuellement l'intérêt à raison de six pour cent. Cet intérêt, joint à celui remis par les Etats-Unis à cet Etat, à titre de dépôt, en vertu d'une loi du Congrès du 23 juin 1836, sera affecté, ainsi que la totalité de la rente des terres non vendues, à l'entretien des écoles publiques, et cette allocation restera inviolable.

ART. 145. Le revenu provenant de la vente de toute terre accordée jusqu'à ce moment à cet Etat par le gouvernement fédéral, pour l'entretien d'une maison d'éducation, que la vente ait déjà en lieu ou qu'elle s'accomplisse plus tard, ainsi que le revenu provenant d'une donation quelconque faite à l'Etat dans le but ci-dessus indiqué, formera un fonds perpétuel dont l'intérêt, à raison de six pour cent par an, sera apliqué à l'entretien d'une institution destinée aux progrès de la littérature, des arts et des sciences. La Législature ne pourra voter aucune loi pour appliquer les fonds ci-dessus mentionnés à un autre but que la création et l'amélioration de l'institution susdite, et l'Assemblée Générale aura le pouvoir de lever une somme pour l'organisation et l'entretien de cette même institution, par les voies et moyens qu'elle croira convenables.

ART. 146. Aucune appropriation ne sera faite par la Législature pour l'entretien d'une école ou d'une maison d'éducation particulière quelconque, mais les plus grands encouragements devront être accordés aux écoles publiques dans tout l'Etat.

TITRE VII.

MODE DE REVISION DE LA CONSTITUTION.

ART. 147. Tout amendement à cette Constitution peut être proposé au Sénat ou à la Chambre des Représentants. Si l'amendement est accepté par la majorité des membres élus dans chaque Chambre, il sera inséré au procès-verbal avec le vote par oui et par non. L'amendement proposé sera soumis au suffrage du peuple à une élection qui sera ordonnée par la Législature, et qui devra être tenue dans les quatre-vingt-dix jours qui suivront son ajournement, et après les trente jours de publication requis par la loi ; et si une majorité des suffrages approuve et ratifie le dit amendement, il formera partie de la Constitution.

Si plusieurs amendements sont soumis à la fois au peuple, ils le seront de manière à ce que le peuple puisse donner sa voix en faveur de chacun de ces amendements, ou contre chacun d'eux, séparément.

TITRE XIII.

DISPOSITIONS TRANSITOIRES.

ART. 148. La Constitution adoptée en 1852 est déclarée être remplacée par cette Constitution, et afin qu'elle prenne force de loi, il est, par les présentes, déclaré et ordonné ce qui suit :

ART. 149. Tous les droits, actions légales, poursuites, réclamations et contrats, soit individuels, soit collectifs, et toutes les lois en vigueur au moment de l'adoption de cette Constitution, et qui ne sont pas incompatibles avec celle-ci, demeureront telles qu'elles étaient auparavant la promulgation de cette Constitution.

ART. 150. Afin qu'il ne résulte aucun inconvénient dans la marche du service public par l'effet de cette Constitution, aucun officier public ne sera remplacé en vertu de cette Constitution ; mais les lois de cet Etat, relatives aux devoirs des différents officiers des Départements de l'Exécutif, du Judiciaire et du Militaire—excepté celles rendues nulles par l'autorité militaire et par l'Ordonnance d'Emancipation — seront maintenues dans toute leur force, lors même qu'elles seraient en contradiction directe avec cette Constitution; et les différents devoirs seront remplis par les officiers respectifs de l'Etat d'après les lois existantes, seulement jusqu'à l'organisation du Gouvernement sous cette Constitution et l'entrée en fonctions des nouveaux officiers nommés par ledit Gouvernement.

ART. 151. La Législature pourvoira au transfert de toutes les affaires actuellement pendantes dans la Cour Suprême ou dans les autres Cours de l'Etat sous la Constitution de 1852, aux Cours créées en vertu de cette Constitution.

TITRE IV.

ORDONNANCE.

ART. 152. Imméeiatement après l'ajournement de la Convention, le Gouverneur lancera sa proclamation enjoignant aux divers officiers légaux de cet Etat de tenir des élections; ou, à défaut de ceux-ci, tels officiers qu'il désignera dans les différentes paroisses de l'Etat, aux lieux désignés par la loi le premier lundi de Septembre 1864, afin de soumettre à la volonté du peuple de cet Etat l'adoption ou le rejet de cette Constitution. Il sera du devoir des officiers ainsi nommés de recevoir les votes de tous les électeurs dûment qualifiés. Chaque votant déposera dans la boîte du vote un bulletin sur lequel sera écrit: "Ratification de la Constitution," ou : "Rejet de la Constitution." A la clôture de ladite élection, les officiers et commissaires nommés à cet effet devront examiner soigneusement et compter les bulletins tels qu'ils auront été déposés dans chaque boîte par les votants ; et ils en feront le retour légal au Secrétaire d'Etat, d'après les dispositions de la loi et les usages établis concernant les élections.

Art. 153. Quand les retours d'élection auront été reçus—ou le troisième Lundi de Septembre si les retours ne sont pas reçus plus tôt—il sera du devoir du Gouverneur du Secrétaire d'Etat, du Procureur-Général et du Trésorier d'Etat, et en présence des personnes qui auront été désignées pour assister au dépouillement, de comparer le nombre des votes de la dite élection pour la ratification ou le rejet de cette Constitution ; et si, une fois l'opération terminée, il ressort qu'une majorité des votes est en faveur de la ratification de cette Constitution, il sera du devoir du Gouverneur de lancer une proclamation faisant connaître le fait à tous ; et dès lors, cette Constitution deviendra la Constitution de l'Etat de la Louisiane. Mais quoiqu'il advienne, que cette Constitution soit ratifiée ou rejetée, il sera du devoir du Gouverneur d'ordonner la publication du résultat des élections, démontrant le nombre de votes donnés dans chaque paroisse pour ou contre cette Constitution.

Art. 154. Aussitôt qu'une élection générale pourra être tenue dans chaque paroisse de l'Etat sous l'empire de cette Constitution, le Gouverneur devra lancer une proclamation faisant connaître le fait; ou, à son défaut d'agir, la Législature ordonnera par résolution une élection au jour fixé dans la proclamation ou la résolution, dans les soixante jours qui suivront la promulgation de l'ordre, pour les emplois de Gouverneur, Lieutenant-Gouverneur, Secrétaire d'Etat, Trésorier, Procureur-Général et Surintendant des Ecoles Publiques. Les candidats ainsi élus entreront en fonctions le quatrième Lundi suivant leur élection, et conserveront leurs offices pendant la période de temps prescrite par cette Constitution, à compter du second Lundi de Janvier suivant antérieurement à leur entrée en fonctions, au cas où ils n'entreraient pas en fonctions à cette époque. La durée des fonctions des officiers d'Etat élus le 22 février 1864, expirera à l'installation de leurs successeurs, comme il vient d'être pourvu ci-dessus ; mais, dans aucun cas, leur terme d'office ne pourra s'étendre au-delà des limites fixées dans cette Constitution ; et, au cas où l'élection de leurs successeurs ne serait pas devancée, elle devra avoir lieu le premier Lundi de Novembre 1867, dans toutes les paroisses où faire se pourra, et les officiers élus à cette date entreront en fonctions le second second Lundi de Janvier 1868.

Art. 158. Cette Constitution sera publiée dans trois journaux choisis par le Président de cette Convention, dont deux devront la publier en Anglais et en Français, et un autre en Allemand, à partir d l'ajournement de la Convention jusqu'à l'élection qui sera tenue pour la ratification ou le rejet, le premier Lundi de Septembre 1864.

E. H. DURELL, President.
John E. Neelis, Secretary.

INDEX DU JOURNAL OFFICIEL.

PAGE.

Adresse du président Durell..7
Appels de la décision du président...11, 18
Appointement du comité relatif à la statue de Washington........................39
Assistant sergent-d'armes...26
Appropriation au Juge Carrigan..159, 160
Appointement du comité de la Vérification des Pouvoirs...........................5
Action sur le Rapport du comité sur l'Instruction..........145, 151, 152, 153, 157, 159
Amendement de la section 6 sur le rapport d'Emancipation de la minorité..........63
Action d'émancipation sur le rapport de la minorité...................67, 69, 71, 73
Action sur le rapport du comité du Département Exécutif....................86, 87
Arts industriels exempts de taxes...60
Appointement du comité sur les Relations Fédérales................................28
Action sur le rapport des Dispositions Générales..........119, 120, 121, 130, 133, 138
Adresse du Gouverneur à la Convention..173
Action sur la Mise en Accusation...113, 118
Action sur le rapport du comité du Département Judiciaire { 88, 89, 90, 92, 93, 94, 96, 97, 98, 100, 101, 102, 107, 109, 110, 112, 115, 117.
Action sur le rapport du Département Législatif......................78, 82, 84
Auditeur d'Etat..33, 39
Action relative au "New Orleans Times"...172
Améliorations intérieures...130, 132
Bill pour frais de décoration dans la Salle de la Liberté.........................92, 95
Bills,—dette de la Convention..168
Bills de l'Imprimeur officiel..77
Bill de la police de la Nouvelle-Orléans..106
Bills de l'Imprimeur officiel..76
Bills de l'imprimeur..77
Bons d'Etat rebelles...29
Compensation des officiers de la Convention.................48, 49, 50, 53, 54, 56
Comité des Réglements Généraux.................................5, 12, 19, 20, 21
Comités permanents...28, 39
Comité des Relations Fédérales..28
Comité de la Statue de Washington..38
Comités Permanents..28
Commis aux Mandats...170
Délégués à la Convention de Baltimore.....................................78, 81, 159
Dames invitées à visiter la Convention...70
Dépenses relatives à l'Inauguration...154
Election de l'Imprimeur officiel...11, 13
Election du secrétaire...7, 26

INDEX.

	PAGE.
Election du rapporteur en chef.	26
Election de Benjamin H. Orr.	62
Election de John A. Mayer.	66
Election des officiers de la ville	123, 126, 137
Election du rapporteur en chef.	26
Election de J. A. Mayer.	66
Extra compensation.	161, 168, 170
Election de Orr.	62
Election de l'imprimeur.	12
Exemption des officiers et employés.	62, 63
Forme et arrangement.	149, 159, 162
Invitation au Major-Général Banks	91
Institutions charitables.	148
Membres absents.	29, 40, 52, 54, 57, 80, 83, 85, 91, 92, 93, 96, 98
Membres assaillis.	8
Monnaie appropriée ($25,000) pour les dépenses contingentes.	57
Membres délinquents.	113
Maisons de jeu.	121
Mémoire du Prof. A. Vallas.	53
Mémoire relatif aux corporations de banque.	55, 57
" " aux heures de travail.	126, 127
" " aux naissances et décès.	127, 134, 135
" " au pont de la rue Galvez.	153, 157
Mémoire de Vallas.	53, 57
Nomination de la Convention de Baltimore.	158
Nomination à la Convention de Baltimore endossée.	160
Ordonnance pour remplir une vacance au Congrès.	160, 162, 169
Ordonnance relative aux élections.	146, 154
Organisation temporaire.	3
Organisation permanente.	6, 7, 8, 9
Ordonnance définissant la qualification des votants.	9, 171
Oui et non sur le dépôt de la résolution Terry, requérant les membres d'exhiber leur serment blindé.	9
" Sur l'adoption de la résolution Terry.	10
" Sur l'adoption de la résolution Thomas pour l'élection e'un imprimeur.	11
" Sur l'appel de Gastinel contre la décision du président.	11
" Sur le second vote sur l'adoption de la résolution Thomas, pour l'élection d'un imprimeur.	12
" Sur l'appel de Stauffer contre la décision du président.	18
" Sur l'adoption de la résolution Montamat, relative à la compensation des membres.	22
" Sur le dépôt du préambule et de la résolution d'Abell, en regard à l'ordre général No. 38.	24
" Sur le dépôt du préambule et de la résolution Sullivan, concernant les membres de naissance étrangère.	25
" Sur l'adoption de la résolution Montamat appropriant $100,000 pour payer les officiers et les membres.	28
" Sur le dépôt sur la résolution Montamat invitant le juge Atocha à siéger dans l'enceinte de la Convention.	30
" Sur le dépôt de l'amendement de Hills, retranchant la langue française.	31
"Sur l'adoption de la motion Terry de publier les débats en langue irlandaise.	31

INDEX. iii
PAGE.
Oui et non sur l'adoption de la motion Wenck de reconsidérer le vote d'impressions en
" Anglais et Français..33
" sur le dépôt de la résolution Terry définissant la qualification des officiers
d'Etat et municipaux...49
" sur l'adoption de la dite résolution..................................49
" sur le dépôt de la motion Hills retranchant la compensation du président..50
" sur le vote direct de la motion Hills de retrancher.....................50
" sur l'adoption du rapport du comité des Compensations..................51
" sur la motion de déposer la résolution de Hills relative à la présence des
membres..55
" sur l'adoption du rapport du comité des Relations Fédérales............57
" sur le dépôt de la résolution Goldmann relative aux banques............59
" sur l'adoption de la motion Gastinel d'imprimer le rapport du comité des Impressions..60, 61
" sur le dépôt de l'amendement Davies, retranchant cette portion du rapport du
comité d'Education autorisant la Législature d'abolir l'office de Surintendant de l'Instruction Publique.......................................61
" sur l'adoption de la résolution Terry relative aux personnes qui occupent un
emploi d'Etat ou municipal...62
" sur l'adoption du substitut Pursell pour l'article 1er du rapport du comité de
l'Instruction Publique..63
" sur la suspension des réglements pour prendre en mains le rapport du comité
d'Emancipation...65
" sur le dépôt du rapport de la minorité sur l'Emancipation...............65
" sur la suspension des réglements dans le but d'ajourner................66
" sur l'appel de M. Hills contre la décision du président.................67
" sur le rejet du rapport de la minorité sur l'Emancipation...............68
" sur la suspension des réglements dans le but de rescinder l'acceptation de la
résignation de M. Howell...68, 69
" sur la rescission de l'acceptation de la résignation de M. Howell.........71
" snr l'ajournement...71
" sur le dépôt de l'amendement Wilson à l'Ordonnance d'Emancipation.....71
" sur l'ajournement...71
" sur l'adoption de la 1ère section de l'Ordonnance d'Emancipation........72
" sur l'ajournement..72, 73
" sur l'adoption de la 2e section de l'Ordonnance d'Emancipation..........73
" sur le dépôt du proviso Abell à la troisième section de l'Ordonnance d'Emancipation..75
" sur l'adoption de la 1ère clause du proviso Abell......................75
" sur le dépôt de la 2e clause du proviso Abell..........................76
" sur le dépôt de la motion pour retrancher la section 3 en entier.........77
" sur la suppression des articles 3, 4 et 5 du rapport du comité d'Emancipation..77
" sur la suspension des réglements pour la troisième lecture du rapport d'Emancipation..76
" sur le vote final sur l'adoption du dit rapport........................76
" sur l'adoption finale du rapport du comité du Préambule................77
" sur l'adoption finale du rapport du comité de la Distribution des Pouvoirs.77
" sur l'adoption de l'art. 1er du rapport...............................79
" du comité du Département Législatif...................................79
" sur l'adoption de l'art. 2 du dit rapport.........................79, 80
" sur l'adoption de l'art. 3 du dit rapport.............................80
" sur l'adoption de l'art. 4 du dit rapport.............................80
" sur l'adoption de l'art. 5 du dit rapport.............................80

	PAGE

Oui et non sur une appropriation à l'Association charitable des Pompiers............82
" sur l'adoption d'une résolution faisant des appropriations charitables......82
" sur le dépôt de la résolution Foley relative aux membres de la Convention délégués à la Convention de Baltimore........................83
" sur la suppression des mots : " et capable de lire et écrire pour être votant qualifié"............................83
" sur l'ajournement................................83
" sur le dépôt de la résolution Hills, relative aux membres absents..........84
" sur l'adoption de la dite résolution......................84
" sur la suppression des lignes 88, 89, 90. 91 de l'article 6 du rapport du comité du Département Législatif......................85
" sur le dépôt de l'amendement à la 2e section du rapport du comité du Département Exécutif....................86
" sur l'adoption de la 2e section du dit rapport......................86
" sur le dépôt de la motion de reconsidérer le vote retranchant la 4e section du dit rapport..............................87
" sur l'amendement de M. Orr à la 25e section du dit rapport............87
" sur l'ajournement................................87
" sur l'ajournement................................88
" sur le dépôt de l'appropriation à l'Association charitable des Pompiers...90
" sur le dépôt de la résolution faisant des appropriations aux institutions charitables............................90
" sur le dépôt de l'amendement Abell à la deuxième section du rapport judiciaire................................86
" sur l'ajournement................................88
" sur le dépôt des amendements à la 2e section du dit rapport............87
" sur l'adoption de la résolution Hills relative aux membres absents........93
" sur le dépôt de la résolution Stocker relative aux appropriations charitables,..........................93
" sur l'adoption du substitut Henderson pour le deuxième article du rapport judiciaire............................93
" sur le dépôt de la motion de reconsidérer la résolution Hills relative aux membres absents............................94
" sur la reconsidération de la dite résolution....................94
" sur le dépôt de la résolulion Waters relative à la police de la ville......96
" sur le dépôt du substitut Sullivan pour la dite résolution............96
" sur l'adoption du substitut Sullivan pour le rapport du comité sur le judiciaire................................99
" sur l'adoption du 3e article du dit rapport......................99
" sur le dépôt du substitut et de l'amendement au onzième article du dit rapport................................100
" sur l'adoption du substitut Stauffer pour le dit article..................100
" sur l'adoption de l'amendement Sullivan pour le même article..........100
" sur le dépôt de l'amendement Hills pour le dit article..................101
" sur l'ajournement................................101
" sur l'adoption de l'amendement Shaw à l'article 11 du rapport judiciaire............................101, 102
" sur le dépôt de la motion de reconsidérer le dit vote..................102
" sur le vote direct de la reconsidération....................102
" sur la motion de rejeter l'amendement de Shaw....................102
" sur le dépôt du substitut Terry pour l'article 11 du rapport judiciaire....102
" sur le dépôt du substitut Hills pour l'article 11 du rapport judiciaire....103
" sur le dépôt du substitut Smith pour l'article 11 du rapport judiciaire.103, 104
" sur le dépôt du substitut Baum pour le substitut Smith..................104

INDEX. v

PAGE.

Oui et non sur l'adoption du substitut Smith..................................104
" sur le dépôt des amendements au bill de la police....................106
" sur l'adoption du proviso Orr pour le bill de la police............ 106
" sur l'adoption du bill de la police ainsi amendé 106, 107
" sur le dépôt de la motion de reconsidérer le vote précédent............107
" sur le dépôt du substitut Montamat à l'article 12 du rapport judiciaire...108
" sur l'adoption du substitut Sullivan pour ledit article..................108
" sur l'adoption du substitut Stauffer pour ledit article..................108
" sur le dépôt de la motion de reconsidérer le vote sur l'adoption du rapport du comité sur le judiciaire....................................110
" sur le vote direct sur la motion de reconsidérer.......................110
" sur l'ajournement...114
" sur le dépôt du substitut Bofill, pour l'article 11 du rapport du comité judiciaire...115
" sur l'adoption de l'article 11 du substitut Bofill..................115, 116
" sur l'adoption du substitut Stocker...................................116
" sur l'adoption du substitut Stocker ainsi amendé à sa troisième lecture...117
" sur l'adoption du rapport du comité de la Mise en Accusation...........118
" sur l'appel Montamat contre la décision du président.......... 119
" sur l'adoption du substitut Cutler relatif aux maisons de jeu............121
" sur l'ajournement...121
" sur le dépôt de la motion Fosdick pour prendre en mains la résolution relative à l'élection des officiers de la ville................ 123
" sur le dépôt du substitut Sullivan pour l'article 36 du rapport du comité des Dispositions Générales....... 124
" sur la motion Fosdick de suspendre les réglements pour prendre en mains la résolution relative à l'élection des officiers de la ville..............126
" sur l'appel pour la question précédente sur le rapport du comité spécial, article 36 des Dispositions Générales................................127
" sur la reconsidération du vote sur l'amendement Davies à l'article 36 des Dispositions Générales...128
" sur le dépôt de l'amendement Thorpe à l'article 36 des Dispositions Générales...129
" sur le dépôt de l'amendement Orr à l'article 36 des Dispositions Générales..................... 129
" sur l'adoption de l'amendement Orr aux Dispositions Générales.........129
" sur l'adoption du rapport du comité special ainsi amendé..............129
" sur l'adoption de l'article additionnel autorisant la Législature à étendre le droit de suffrage...131
" sur l'adoption de l'article additionnel fixant la journée de travail à neuf heures... 131
" sur le dépôt des résolutions charitables de Sullivan...............133, 134
" sur la motion de retrancher l'appropriation de l'Association Charitable des Pompiers..134
" sur l'adoption de la résolution charitable de Sullivan..................134
" sur le dépôt de la résolution Wells, augmentant le salaire des professeurs 136, 137
" référant le sujet des élections de la ville à un comité spécial 137
" sur le dépôt du substitut Sullivan pour l'article 2 du rapport du comité d'Education...138
" sur l'adoption de l'article 2 du dit rapport............................138
" sur le dépôt de l'article 3 du dit rapport..............................138

INDEX.

	PAGE.

Oui et non sur le dépôt du substitut Thorpe pour l'article 3 (Education)............139
" sur le dépôt du substitut Cazabat pour l'article 3 (Education)...........139
" sur le rejet de l'article 3 du dit rapport..............................139
" sur l'adoption du rapport du comité de l'Education dans son entier......140
" sur l'ajournement...141
" sur le rejet de l'article 2 du substitut Sullivan, pour le rapport du comité d'Education...143
" sur le dépôt de la motion de retrancher le mot "blancs" dans le même rapport...144
" sur l'adoption de la motion de retrancher.............................144
" sur le dépôt du substitut pour l'article 3 du dit rapport................145
" sur l'adoption de l'article 3 ainsi amendé............................146
" sur l'ajournement..146
" sur le dépôt de l'article 5 additionnel de M. Howell au dit rapport......147
" sur l'adoption du rapport du comité sur les Institutions charitables......147
" sur l'adoption du rapport du comité spécial sur le rapport de l'Auditeur...148
" sur le dépôt de l'article additionnel de M. Hills sur l'Education..........149
" sur l'ajournement..149
" sur le dépôt du substitut Cazabat.....................................149
" pour l'article additionnel de Hills....................................152
" sur l'adoption du substitut Cazabat...................................152
" sur l'adoption du rapport du comité de l'éducation dans son entier—2me lecture...152
" sur le dépôt du *rider* Sullivan à l'article 2 du rapport du comité d'Education...153
" sur l'adoption du dit *rider*...153
" sur l'adoption du rapport du comité d'Education—3me lecture......153, 154
" sur l'adoption du *rider* Henderson..................................154
" sur le rapport du comité des Cédules................................154
" sur l'adoption du préambule et des résolutions pour payer les dépenses d'inauguration...155
" sur le second vote du même article.............................155, 156
" sur le dépôt de la résolution relative à la décision des cours sur l'esclavage...156
" sur l'adoption de ladite résolution..................................157
" sur l'adoption de la résolution relative à la résignation de J. T. Paine...158
" sur l'ajournement de l'action du rapport du comité sur la Forme et l'Arrangement...160
" sur l'adoption du préambule et des résolutions endossant les nominations de Baltimore...160, 161
" sur la suppression de l'article 9 de la constitution....................165
" sur le dépôt de la résolution Stauffer relative au "New Orleans Times"...166
" sur le dépôt du *rider* Terry à l'article 141 de la constitution.......166, 167
" sur l'adoption du dit *rider*..167
" sur l'adoption finale de la constitution dans son entier................167
" sur le dépôt de la motion d'ajourner toute action relative au "New Orleans Times"...168
" sur l'adoption du préambule et des résolutions relatives à Thomas P. May, éditeur du "New Orleans Times"...............................169

INDEX. vii

	PAGE.
Oui et non sur le dépôt du *rider* Terry à l'article 134 de la Constiution	156
" sur l'adoption du préambule et des résolutions relatives aux droits des Etats	171
" sur le dépôt de la résolution relative au clergé	172
" sur l'adoption des résolutions relatives à l'ajournement	172
Plume présentée au Maj.-Gén. Banks	94
Ponts, etc	147, 153, 157
Police de la ville	107, 109, 129, 130
Propriétaires loyaux des esclaves émancipés	69, 73, 97, 98
Préambule et résolution relative à la compensation des propriétaires d'esclaves	25
" " " " aux membres de naissance étrangère	26, 31
" " " " à la résignation de l'Hon. C. Roselius	32
," " " " à l'argent entre les mains du comité de F. S. G.	64, 65
" " " " aux employés non citoyens des Etats-Unis	93
" " " " aux électeurs présidentiels	60
" " " " aux rapports des comités	54, 59, 62
", " " " accordant une prime aux volontaires des 1er et 2e régiments de la Louisiane	46, 47 82
" " " " aux déprédations des guerillas	52, 68
" · " " " à l'ajournement	52
" " " " à l'ordonnance de sécession	171
Pétition de H. Copeland	57
Préambule et résolution relatif à l'ordonnance de sécession	171
Qualification des officiers d'Etat et municipaux	40, 48, 171
Résolution relative à l'ajournement	80, 83, 84, 95, 97, 172
Rapport du comité sur les voies de fait	52, 69, 74
Résolution relative à l'assistant-secrétaire	91, 101
Rapport spécial de l'Auditeur des comptes publics	76
Rapport du comité spécial sur le rapport de l'Auditeur	135
Résignation de A. Bailey	143
Résolution de remerciements au Maj.-Gén. Banks	95, 96, 98
Résignation de M. Brott, comme membre d'un comité	35
Résolution relative au clergé	10, 22
Rapport du comité sur les compensations	34
Résolution relative aux compensations	37, 45
Rapport du comité de la Vérification des Pouvoirs	5, 62
Rapport du comité sur les réglements	5, 12, 19, 20, 21
" " sur les dépenses contingentes	45, 46, 57, 58, 151
Résolution relative à la monnaie courante de la ville	69, 72
Rapport du comité sur la Distribution des Pouvoirs	35
" " sur l'Instruction Publique	43
Retours de l'élection des membres	3, 4
Retours d'élections de la paroisse Iberville	10
Rapport du comité sur l'Emancipation	53, 64
" " sur les Relations Fédérales	52
Résolution relative au comité des Relations Fédérales	54
Rapport de la minorité sur les Relations Fédérales	52
Rapport du comité des Finances	79, 89, 90, 97, 105, 112, 123, 140, 150, 151, 156
Résolution relative au comité des Finances	156, 157
Rapport du comité des Dispositions Générales	40, 41, 42, 57
Résignation de Goldman	115
Résolution relative aux guérillas	68

INDEX.

| | PAGE. |

Résolution fixant l'heure des réunions.................................33, 39
Résolution relative à l'absence de M. Howell....................................65
Résignation de M. Howell..66, 69
Rapport du comité de la Mise en Accusation 37
" " du Département Judiciaire..........44, 45, 100, 111, 112, 113, 114
Rapport du comité du Département Législatif.............................84, 85
Rapport sur le mémoire du Prof. A. Vallas......................................53
Rapport du comité sur le Mode de Révision de la Constitution..............48, 55, 141
Résolution relative à l'imprimeur officiel..91
" " à l'ordre des affaires..98
" " à l'ordonnance de sécession..............................22
" " à l'ordonnance d'émancipation..................91, 92, 95
Rapport du comité sur le Préambule...35
Résignation de J. T. Paine..158
Résolution de remerciements au président....................................173
" relative au quorum...29, 84, 86
Résolution de Abell relative à l'ordre général No. 38.................22, 23, 24
" " " aux rapports des comités......................40, 51
" " " à la lecture des rapports (*seriatim*)............48, 52
" " " au rapporteur..................................170
" " " au rapporteur officiel..........................170
" " " à l'Hon. R. K. Howell............................65
" " " au Maj.-Gén. N. P. Banks........................95
" Austin " aux membres de naissance étrangère.............71
" " ," au quorum......................................32
" " " aux compensations..............................47
" " " aux délégués de la Convention de Baltimore.......151
" " " à l'endossement des membres élus de la convention
                     de Baltimore........................160
" Balch " à une appropriation au juge Carrigan........159, 160
" Bell " à la publication des débats........................95
" " " aux greffiers....................................30
" " " aux remerciements adressés au maire Hoyt, etc.....66
" " " aux dépenses d'inauguration....................155
" Brott " à l'ajournement *sine die*........................68
" Bromley " aux compensations et aux sessions..................52
" " " aux guérillas....................................69
" Cutler " au rapport du comité sur le Judiciaire..............60
" " " au secrétaire de la Convention..................162
" " " à une extra compensation..............162, 170, 171
" " " aux greffiers de l'auditeur et du trésorier..........172
" " " aux élections de ville............................137
" " " à l'ajournement final............................172
" Campbell " au vote sur l'Emancipation......................72
" " " au comité sur les Voies de Fait..................99
" " " aux secours à accorder aux réfugiés unionistes dans
                     la détresse.........................85
" Davies " au pont de la rue Claiborne.....................155
" " " aux élections, etc................................133
" Fish " à l'élection dans le Dixième District Représenta-
                     tif................................27
" " " à la rescission de l'Ordonnance de Sécession......171

INDEX.

			PAGE
Résolution de Fosdick	relative	aux élections de ville	122
"	"	" au clergé	173
"	"	" au vote de remerciements au président Durell	172
"	Foley	" aux rapports imprimés, etc	47
"	"	" aux délégués à la Convention de Baltimore	79
"	Fuller	" à l'avis donné des amendements proposés	52
"	Gastinel	" à l'impression du journal et des débats	30
"	Gorlinski	" à l'organisation	10, 40
"	"	" à l'heure des réunions	34, 39
"	"	" à la statue de Washington	36, 37, 46
"	Goldman	" à la publication des débats en langue allemande	34, 36
"	"	" aux corporations de banques	56
"	Gruneberg	" aux membres délinquents	115
"	Harnan	" aux voies de fait	3
"	"	" aux membres absents	58
"	Hire	" aux sessions du soir	69
"	Heard	" au comité sur les réglements	9
"	"	" aux membres absents	109, 110
"	Hills	" au juge A. A. Atocha	33
"	"	" au vote d'émancipation	68, 69
"	"	" à l'amendement de l'art. 32 du réglement	37
"	"	" à la dispense de lire l'appel du rôle	48
"	"	" aux membres absents	81, 91, 97
"	"	" aux institutions charitables	136
"	Howell	" à la nomination des comités permanents relatifs à l'abolition de l'esclavage	12
"	"	" au bibliothécaire d'Etat	27
"	"	" à l'heure des réunions et à l'ordre du jour	33, 38
"	"	" aux instructions du secrétaire de la Convention	80
"	Kavanagh	" au salaire de la police employée à la Convention	50
"	Mendiverri	" à l'Auditeur d'Etat	33
"	Montamat	" à l'élection des délégués	9
"	"	" à l'invitation aux officiers d'Etat	12
"	"	" à la compensation à accorder aux membres	23
"	"	" à la ratification de la constitution	22
"	"	" à l'appropriation des $100,000	28
"	"	" aux greffiers	29
"	"	" au Juge A. A. Atocha	30
"	"	" au comité des Finances	26, 158
"	"	" aux officiers et employés	169, 170
"	"	" au major-général Banks et à son état-major	91, 97
"	"	" à l'office de l'assistant-secrétaire	91, 101
"	M. W. Murphy	" aux compensations	27, 38, 54
"	J. Purcell	" aux bills de l'imprimeur officiel	78
"	S. Pursell	" au clergé	10, 23
"	"	" à l'Hon. C. Roselius	27
"	"	" à l'article 96 de la Constitution	30
"	"	" aux personnes qui ne sont pas citoyens des Etats-Unis	31
"	"	" fixant l'heure des réunions à 11 A. M	81
"	Smith	" relative aux shinplasters	33, 39
"	"	" à la monnaie courante	150, 157
"	"	" au status des personnes de couleur	157, 159
"	Shaw	" aux officiers et employés retenus	172
"	Stiner	" aux rapporteurs non officiels	170
"	Stauffer	" au comité des réglements, etc	14, 15, 16, 17
"	"	" aux bons d'Etat émis pour des desseins rebelles	29
"	"	" au "New Orleans Times."	166
"	Schroeder	" aux compensations à fixer	27, 32
"	Stocker	" aux réglements	27, 32, 34
"	"	" aux membres absents	29

INDEX.

				PAGE.
Résolution de Stocker	relative	aux appropriations charitables...................92
"	"	"	à l'impression du journal en Anglais, Français, Allemand et Espagnol............................31
"	Seymour	"	à l'Hon. C. Roselius...........................32
"	Sullivan	"	aux officiers et employés.......................10
"	"	"	à la statue de Washington.................33, 38, 57
"	"	"	aux membres de naissance étrangère..............25
"	"	"	aux exemptions des devoirs comme jurés.......63, 64
"	"	"	aux institutions charitables......................133
"	"	"	à l'ordre du jour..............................107
"	Terry	"	à l'Ordonnance de Sécession..................21, 22
"	"	"	au status des membres..........................9
"	"	"	aux qualifications des officiers d'Etat et municipaux................................40, 49, 62
"	"	"	à la célébration du 4 Juillet (1864)...............137
"	"	"	aux membres délinqnents.......................114
"	"	"	à l'encadrement sur parchemin de l'Ordonnance d'Emancipation...................................91
"	"	"	au clergé.....................................158
"	"	"	à l'ordre des affaires...........................160
"	Thomas	"	à l'élection de l'imprimeur officiel................11
"	"	"	au salaire de l'adjudant-général.................159
"	"	"	aux comptes non soldés de la Convention.........169
"	"	"	à Thomas P. May..............................169
"	Thorpe	"	à la nomination du comité......................161
"	"	"	sur les Relations Fédérales.......................28
"	"	"	au quorum...................................29
"	"	"	aux décisions des cours sur l'esclavage............156
"	"	"	au salaire du secrétaire particulier du gouverneur, etc..169
"	"	"	à l'impression du journal, etc................73, 91
"	"	"	à l'ordre du jour...........................55, 98
"	"	"	aux majors-généraux Canby et Sickles........122, 125
"	Waters	"	aux rapporteurs officiels........................170
"	"	"	à la police de la ville...........................95
"	Wells	"	aux professeurs dans les écoles publiques..........136
"	"	"	aux rapporteurs officiels........................169
"	"	"	à l'ajournement...............................
"	"	"	à la compensation à accorder aux propriétaires loyaux......................................97
"	Wilson	"	à l'ajournement *sine die* et aux sessions du soir......81
"	"	"	J. T. Paine..................................158

Rapport du comité des Cédules...............................133, 142, 154
Relatif aux officiers d'Etat..12
Résolution relative à la Librairie d'Etat................................155
Rapport du comité de la Librairie d'Etat................................155
Résolution relative au bibliothécaire d'Etat........................159, 160
    "   " aux substituts.................................47, 51
    " augmentant le salaire des professeurs...........................136
    " relative aux réfugiés unionistes..................................83
Salaire de l'adjudant-général..159
Salaire des greffiers de l'Auditeur et du Trésorier......................172
Siéges contestés,—Lombard et Decker....................................6
Salaire du secrétaire particulier du Gouverneur........................169
Substitut pour neuf articles du Département Judiciaire..................53
Seconde lecture du rapport du Département Judiciaire...................59
Salaire des artisans et manœuvres........................97, 106, 127, 128
Substitut pour le rapport du comité sur le Préambule................54, 76
Shinplasters..33, 39
Statue de Washington...33, 38, 57
Status des membres de la Convention..................................8, 9
Status des personnes de couleur, etc..............................157, 159
Substitut pour l'article 35 des Dispositions Générales....................47
Substitut pour les articles 1er et 2 du rapport du comité d'Education...61, 62, 63
Visite du major-général Banks à la Convention..........................95
Visite des majors-généraux Canby et Sickles............................131
Vote sur le rapport du comité d'Emancipation...........................66

Printed in Dunstable, United Kingdom